INDUSTRIAL ORGANIZATION
IN CONTEXT

INDUSTRIAL ORGANIZATION
IN CONTEXT

STEPHEN MARTIN

DEPARTMENT OF ECONOMICS PURDUE UNIVERSITY

OXFORD
UNIVERSITY PRESS

OXFORD

UNIVERSITY PRESS

Great Clarendon Street, Oxford, OX2 6DP,
United Kingdom

Oxford University Press is a department of the University of Oxford.
It furthers the University's objective of excellence in research, scholarship,
and education by publishing worldwide. Oxford is a registered trade mark of
Oxford University Press in the UK and in certain other countries

Published in the United States of America by Oxford University Press
198 Madison Avenue, New York, NY 10016, United States of America

British Library Cataloguing in Publication Data
Data available

Library of Congress Cataloging in Publication Data
Data available

ISBN 978–0–19–929119–9

Throughout Pareto's presentation of a paper at a seminar in Geneva, the institutional economist Gustav Schmoller muttered from the audience "There are no economic laws." Pareto and Schmoller were not otherwise acquainted, and Pareto was a shabby dresser. Seeing Schmoller on the street the next day, Pareto pretended to be a beggar and went up to him, asking "Please, sir, can you tell me where in Geneva I can find a good restaurant where I can eat for free?" Schmoller replied "My good man, there are no such restaurants, in Geneva or elsewhere, but I can show you where you can have an inexpensive meal." At this, Pareto threw off his cloak and said triumphantly, as he walked away, "So there are economic laws!"

Source: Based on Livingston (1935, p. xviii).

1 Principles of the Book

There are a few general principles that guide the organization of material in this book.

One is that there are economic laws.

Another is that we don't really understand where we are unless we understand how we got here. There is thus rather more economic history and, in some places, history of economic thought, in this book than might be expected.

A third is that markets work, and imperfect markets work imperfectly. Policies that will bring desirable results if applied to perfectly competitive markets may bring quite undesirable results if applied to imperfectly competitive markets.

A fourth is that it is equilibrium conduct, which depends on market structure, that determines market performance and, by feedback relationships, equilibrium market structure. Governments cannot, by legislation, induce firms to depart from value-maximizing behavior. Governments can, by institutional design, alter incentives so that firms' equilibrium conduct changes. Such changes may improve or worsen market performance.

A fifth is that institutions matter; this is one of the lessons of experimental economics. But institutions are not all that matters. It is not the case that books are different from all other industries because they are vehicles of culture, that software is different from all other industries because it is high tech, that aircraft manufacture is different from all other industries because it involves national security, and so on, partridge, pear, tree. Not only are there are economic laws, but there are general economic laws, even though a general economic law may not cover the whole theory of a particular case.[1]

2 Thanks

I thank several cohorts of students at the Copenhagen Business School, the University of Amsterdam and Purdue University, who were the testing ground for early versions of much of the material that appears here. I thank the libraries at Purdue University and particularly its Interlibrary Loan division. I thank Charles J. Parker for clarification of the methodology of Gallo *et al.* (2000), and Tannista Banerjee, Rostislav Bogoslovskiy, and Do-Yeun Park for research assistance. I am grateful for comments received from Bruce T. Allen, Tannista Banerjee, James Brock, Stephen Davies, Bruce Lyons, Hans-Theo Normann, at BiGSEM (University of Bielefeld, Germany), at the Università degli Studi di Lecce, Italy, from anonymous reviewers, and particularly grateful to John T. Scott for careful comments on Chapters 14, 15, and 25. I thank Torsten Schmidt for providing me with material related to Auspitz and Lieben (1889). I thank Victor J. Tremblay and Carol Horton Tremblay for providing data from Tremblay and Tremblay (2005), and Mary Raetz for providing supplemental data associated with the 2008 *Global Market Data Book*. I am uncommonly grateful to the Department of Managerial Economics, Strategy and Innovation at the Katholieke Universiteit Leuven for hosting a visit during the first six months of 2009 that allowed me to complete the book.

This book is dedicated to Linda.

---

[1] As Mill (1869) wrote of Thornton (1870) in response to Thornton's claim to have disproved the Law of Demand and Supply.

CONTENTS

LIST OF FIGURES

Every effort has been made to trace and contact copyright holders prior to going to press but this has not been possible in every case. If notified, the publisher will undertake to rectify any errors or omissions at the earliest opportunity.

INTRODUCTION

One of the uses of history is to free us of a falsely imagined past. The less we know of how ideas actually took root and grew, the more apt we are to accept them unquestioningly ...

Bork (1978, p. 15)

1.1 Origins

The branch of economics known as industrial economics or industrial organization[1] deals with (Stigler, 1988, p. 1733) "the economics of markets and industries and their participants, and public policy toward these entities". It emerged as a distinct branch of microeconomics from the research agenda of a Harvard seminar organized by Edward S. Mason during the 1930s. But the topics that occupy industrial economists today have concerned economists since, and indeed before, political economy itself emerged as a distinct branch of the social sciences with the 1776 publication of Adam Smith's *The Wealth of Nations*.

Interest in many of these topics is driven by their implications for public policy toward business behaviour. Policy questions that remain at the heart of industrial organization were the subject of a widespread academic and popular debate about big business in the United States between 1880 and 1900, a debate that continued at only a slightly less intense level between 1900 and 1920, and in which seven of the first ten presidents of the American Economic Association played active roles.[2] The German economist Robert Liefmann, who had the distinction of being described by Lenin (1917/1964, p. 208) as "an unblushing apologist

---

[1] The terms today are largely synonymous. In historical usage, "industrial organization" indicated a focus on the industry as the unit of analysis; see, for example, Andrews' (1951, p. 153, 1952, p. 74) discussions of Marshall, Bain (1959, p. vii) or Davies and Lyons (1989, p. 1). There have also been times and places in which "industrial organization" would have been taken to include the study of organized labour; see Dorfman's (1949, Volume 4, pp. 267–272) discussion of Seager or Mason (1939, p. 63). "Industrial economics", in contrast, took both firm and industry as objects of study. But there were numerous variations in usage of the two terms, and the distinction, if ever there was one, has faded.

[2] I include in this set Francis A. Walker, John Bates Clark, Henry C. Adams, Arthur T. Hadley, Richard T. Ely, Edwin R. A. Seligman, and Jeremiah W. Jenks. Two others (Tassig and Patten) wrote particularly on tariff policy and among these writings contributed to the literature of what we would now call industrial economics.

of capitalism", wrote on cartels from the end of the nineteenth century onward (Liefmann, 1915, 1922, 1932). Alfred Marshall, the premier economist of his time, and his wife Mary Paley Marshall published *The Economics of Industry* in 1879. Alfred Marshall published *Industry and Trade*, making international comparisons in industrial organization and drawing conclusions for economic development, in 1919. In short, like the bourgeois gentleman who spoke prose without realizing it, economists who studied "railway problems" (Ripley, 1907) or "trust and corporation problems" (Burns, 1937, p. 663) studied industrial economics in everything but name.

1.2 Structure-Conduct-Performance

1.2.1 Models vs. Markets

But the early twentieth-century economists who studied industrial organization had at their disposal analytical tools that seemed to them to be ill-suited to the task. The mainstream price theory of the day was a theory of competitive markets and a theory of monopoly, with a vast wasteland in between. This theory of competitive markets was not the modern model of perfect competition,[3] but its Marshallian predecessor. For a market to be "competitive" in Alfred Marshall's sense required only (Andrews, 1951, p. 141) that it "would be possible for other businesses to produce a commodity with the same technical specifications as the product of any particular firm, and to offer it for sale to that firm's customers". If this condition were met, Marshall argued (Andrews, 1951, pp. 141–142), "the possibility of entry of other producers would ensure that long-run price would be equal to the normal average cost of production".

During the depths of the Great Depression, however, economists were increasingly struck by the disconnect between this theory of competitive markets and the businesses around them. Persistent excess capacity, unemployment, and prices that did not adjust to average costs seemed all too often to be the rule rather than the exception (Mason, 1939).

1.2.2 Pricing Behaviour

Economists thought the need was for a general analytical approach (Burns, 1937, p. 665; emphasis added):

> The primary necessity ... is *some broad framework within which price behavior can be analyzed* in various industries. It must explain the relationship between the organization of production and distribution and the behavior of buyers and of prices.

They wanted to draw on state-of-the-art economic theory (Burns, 1937, p. 669). But they rejected existing mathematical models of imperfectly competitive markets, on the ground that they could not be applied in practice (Mason, 1939, p. 62):[4]

---

[3] Due to Knight (1921), and which we review in Chapter 2.

[4] See similarly Bain (1944, p. 5). Frustration with the state of theory seems periodically to trigger calls by industrial economists for "a return to the data". See Andrews (1951, p. 172, 1952, p. 75) and Coase (1972b, quoted on page 11; 2006).

It would no doubt be extremely convenient if economists knew the shape of individual demand and cost curves and could proceed forthwith, by comparisons of price and marginal cost, to conclusions regarding the existing degree of monopoly power. The extent to which the monopoly theorists, however, refrain from an empirical application of their formulae is rather striking. The alternative, if more pedestrian, route follows the direction of ascertainable facts and makes use only of empirically applicable concepts.

They also rejected the prevailing institutionalist industry-study approach, in which (Burns, 1937, p. 664, emphasis added):[5]

studies of particular industries assumed a conventional pattern. ... The technical processes of production were described. The organization of the industry was discussed in terms of the size and location of plants, the scope of ownership control (the size and extent of integration of firms), the organization of marketing, labor conditions, and the history of mergers in the industry. ... The discussion of wages and possibly profits implied an interest in the functioning of the industry, *but the aspect of its functioning most vital to theorists and purchasers, namely its price policy, received scant attention.*

1.2.3 A General Framework

Instead they looked for a general framework within which the observed institutional detail of many industries could be analysed and compared, not merely described.[6] It was the *structure-conduct-performance (S-C-P) paradigm*, which developed out of Mason's 1930s Harvard seminar, that provided this analytical framework. The S-C-P paradigm was the organizing framework of research in industrial economics, providing the uniformity of approach that Burns and others called for, from the 1930s to the early 1970s. It was the basis of the two successive leading textbooks in the field,[7] and is schematically illustrated in Figure 1.1.

Supply and demand

As described there, the ultimate drivers of market performance are the underlying conditions on the demand and supply sides of the market. These determine market structure, the elements of which are shown in the second box of Figure 1.1.

Market structure

Important elements of market structure describe how nearly a market satisfies the assumptions that define a perfectly competitive market (Section 2.2). In a perfectly competitive market, there are many small buyers and sellers of a standardized product. Among the elements of market structure, it is therefore natural to look at the numbers and size distributions of buyers and sellers.

The many small buyers and sellers of a perfectly competitive market deal in a standardized product. Products are differentiated if consumers regard different varieties of a product as imperfect substitutes. Product differentiation may arise from product characteristics—by design—or from advertising and other types of marketing efforts.

---

[5] Mason (1939, p. 61) specifically rejects the institutionalist approach.

[6] Burns (1937, p. 669). See also Mason (1939, p. 61) and Andrews (1952, p. 75).

[7] These are Bain (1959) and Scherer (1970, 1980), Scherer and Ross (1990). The successor leading textbook, Tirole (1988), child and progenitor of its time, limits its coverage to theoretical industrial organization.

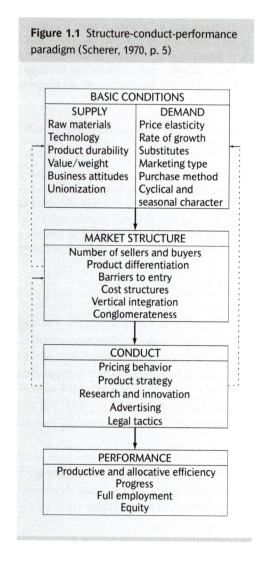

Figure 1.1 Structure-conduct-performance paradigm (Scherer, 1970, p. 5)

The numbers and relative sizes of buyers and sellers and the extent of product differentiation convey information about the nature of rivalry among actual buyers and among actual sellers. There is also free and easy entry into and exit from a perfectly competitive market. Barriers to entry (Section 5.3.1), which might have been better labelled "costs of entry", characterize the investment needed for an enterprise to begin to supply a market. Entry conditions were emphasized particularly by Bain (1956). They convey information about the possibility of rivalry between potential and actual sellers.

Firm conduct

The various elements of market structure feed back to affect basic conditions on the supply side of the market and feed forward to affect firm conduct. "Conduct", the third box in

Figure 1.1, includes pricing behaviour and product strategy, which in part determines the extent of product differentiation (as do advertising and other marketing efforts).

Firm conduct in turn feeds back to influence market structure. Incumbents' advertising and spending on research and development may influence the cost of entry. Incumbents' pricing policies may influence the profit a potential entrant would expect to earn. Firm conduct also feeds back to influence basic conditions on the demand side of the market (for example, advertising may affect the price elasticity of demand). Market structure is thus directly and indirectly (through the conduct-demand conditions link) affected by firm conduct.[8]

Market performance

As conceived in the S-C-P framework, conduct determines the various dimensions of market performance. These include productive efficiency—is production cost as low as technologically possible?—and neoclassical measures of consumer and social welfare (Section 2.3.2). It also determines, among other things, the rate of technological progress.[9]

Industry studies

Coming out of the 1930s and 1940s, early research in the S-C-P tradition took the form of book-length studies of single industries. In 1956, Bain published a comparative study of a small number of industries. Following his lead, industrial economists soon turned to the econometric analysis of cross-section samples of industry data, first of small numbers of industries, and later of large samples covering essentially all manufacturing industries.

Early empirical research in industrial economics emphasized the manufacturing sector. Partly this emphasis was because the manufacturing sector accounted for a much larger part of total economic activity than is now the case. Partly it was because national governments tended then, as they do now, to produce much more data about manufacturing than about other sectors of the economy.

The flavour of the results of these investigations can be seen in Figure 1.2, which shows profitability-seller concentration pairs for 20 industries studied by Bain. Bain measured profitability as profit after taxes as a percentage of stockholders' equity. He measured "fewness of sellers", seller concentration, by the four-firm seller concentration ratio, the sum of the market shares of the four largest firms in the industry. As far as entry conditions were concerned, Bain classified each industry in his sample in one of three groups: low to moderate, substantial, or very high barriers to entry.[10]

The dashed line in Figure 1.2 is the least-squares regression line relating profitability to the concentration ratio. It shows that higher concentration levels and higher profitability tended

---

[8] In the words of Caves (1998, p. 1963) "The core of the SCP taxonomy is the causal relationships starting from the number and size distribution (concentration) of participants in a market and the factors limiting their number or access (entry barriers). Concentration itself is regarded as a consequence of factors limiting the equilibrium number of incumbent firms and/or supplying incumbents with first-mover advantages over subsequent entrants."

[9] Logically, therefore, there should be an arrow indicating a feedback loop from market performance to basic conditions (technology) on the supply side of the market.

[10] The low-to-moderate entry barrier industries in Bain's sample were canned fruit and vegetables, cement, flour, meat packing, rayon, women's and low-priced men's shoes, and tyres and tubes. The substantial-entry-barrier industries were copper, steel, farm machines and tractors, petroleum refining, soap, high-priced men's and specialty shoes, gypsum products, and metal containers. The high-entry-barrier industries were cars, cigarettes, alcohol, typewriters, and fountain pens.

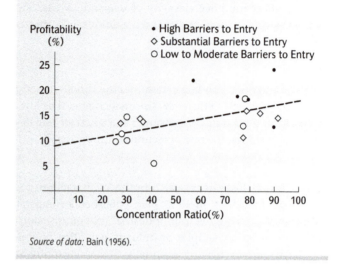

Figure 1.2 Bain Study: Concentration, Entry Conditions, and Profitability, 20 U.S. industries, 1947–1951. Profitability is measured as the after-tax rate of return as a percentage of stockholders' equity. The concentration ratio is the combined market share of the four largest firms

Source of data: Bain (1956).

to go together in Bain's sample. It also appears that profitability tended to be higher in high entry-cost industries than in industries with low, moderate, or substantial entry cost. Bain's results, and many that followed, suggested that on average firms operating in industries that were supplied by few firms, and into which it would be costly for new firms to enter, earned higher rates of return than firms in other types of industries, all else equal.

1.3 The Oligopoly Problem and the First Chicago School

1.3.1 Tacit Collusion

Since the industrial revolution, a central problem for public policy toward business has been that performance in markets supplied by a few large firms often resembles the kind of market performance that results from collusion, whether or not there is reason to think collusion has taken place (Mason, 1949, p. 1277):

> high overhead costs, large cyclical variations in the volume of sales, and immobility of resources are combined in a substantial number of industrial markets. Given these conditions, together with a small number of firms, some economists have contended that such phenomena as price uniformity, price leadership and the relative inflexibility of prices ... are frequently compatible with the independent action of firms all recognizing their interdependence.

The policy question posed by such industries is what, if anything, can be done to obtain good market performance. If it wishes, society can make the decision to fine firms so much if they are caught colluding that profit-maximizing firms will decide, in their own interest, not to collude. But if firms can make independent decisions and reach the same kind of outcome that would result from collusion, the threat of punishment will be ineffective in getting good market performance.

It may well be that the best policy treatment for this type of industry is to do nothing—that the best possible market performance is not very good. Some contend that regulation often begins with the goal of protecting the consumer from the regulated industry and ends up protecting the regulated industry from competition, with the consumer the ultimate loser. Government planning may crash on the shoals of information problems and bureaucracy. Breaking up large, efficient firms for the sake of artificially maintaining a larger number of smaller and less efficient firms would impose unnecessarily high production costs on society. If regulation, government ownership, and limits on firm size are the only policy options, then perhaps to do nothing is best.

1.3.2 Deconcentration

But some U.S. economists advocated a policy of industrial deconcentration—breaking up large firms—as early as the 1930s. One of these was Henry C. Simons (1934, 1936) of the University of Chicago. Simons distrusted private and public concentrations of economic power, and urged the merits of industrial deconcentration as a way of combating both. He believed that most industries could be supplied by a relatively large number of more or less equally sized firms, without sacrificing productive efficiency. Writing during the Great Depression, he thought that if industries were not so organized, the result would be a political backlash that would lead to widespread public ownership of business, a prospect he did not view as a happy one. Although he would have accepted direct government regulation where there were no alternatives, he expected that regulation would be followed by business lobbying to obtain regulation on favourable terms.[11]

Deconcentration proposals came to the fore in the 1950s and 1960s.[12] An influential book by Kaysen and Turner (1959, pp. 113–114) advanced just such a proposal "on the ground that an increase in numbers and reduction of concentration is the surest and most durable way of reducing market power". They would not, however, have broken up existing firms if doing so would have meant the loss of economies of large-scale production.

A U.S. government advisory panel (White House Task Force on Antitrust Policy, 1969) subsequently recommended adoption of a deconcentration law very much like the one suggested by Kaysen and Turner. A bill proposing such a law, Senate Bill 1167 ("The Hart Bill") was introduced in the United States Senate in 1967.

1.4 The Second Chicago School

1.4.1 *Laissez Faire*

The Hart Deconcentration Bill galvanized a later generation of scholars associated with the University of Chicago. In contrast to the First Chicago School of Henry Simons, the charac-

---

[11] Such behaviour is now referred to as *rent seeking*, the expenditure of private funds to obtain economic profits by dint of government protection from competition. See Section 2.3.6.

[12] For one such proposal, see Stigler (1952).

teristic policy position of the Second Chicago School was to advocate a minimal, *laissez faire* economic role for government.[13]

The *laissez faire* approach (Lange, 1945–1946, pp. 31–32) "maintains that the capitalist economy, provided it is not hampered by government planning, spontaneously operates in such a way that it secures the maximum of public welfare". [14]

1.4.2 Good Approximation

As far as public policy toward private enterprise was concerned, the principal positions of the Second Chicago School of economics were:

(a) industrial economists should use formal economic models, and

(b) the "good approximation" assumption (Reder, 1982): the formal model of perfect competition would in general yield satisfactory predictions, even for industries that were imperfectly competitive.

1.4.3 Efficiency Critique

The Second Chicago School put forward a broad critique of the structure-conduct-performance paradigm, which provided the intellectual underpinnings of the Hart Bill. They argued that the results of empirical research in the S-C-P tradition were invalid. S-C-P researchers, they said, had misinterpreted the consistent finding that profit rates tend to be higher where markets are supplied by a small number of firms and where entry is costly (Figure 1.2). In the Second Chicago School view, far from demonstrating the greater ease of tacit or overt collusion in more concentrated markets, this result reflected a causal link going in the other direction, from firm conduct and market performance to market structure.

This *efficiency critique* is that more efficient firms, which are more profitable because they are more efficient, also tend to grow large. Comparing different industries, industries supplied by a few large firms will have higher profit rates, on average, than industries supplied by many small firms, but this is a sign of differential efficiency, not economic profit.[15] This causal link thus implies that market structure is endogenous—determined by economic forces—an endogeneity which, according to the Second Chicago School, the S-C-P paradigm had ignored.[16]

---

[13] In terms of the influence of its policy views, the Second Chicago School never had as much traction in the European Union as in the United States; see Schmidt and Rittaler (1989), Souty (1997). Nor has the location of the Chicago School always been Chicago, manifestations having been documented at various times at the University of California at Los Angeles and at the University of Rochester; see Colander (2006, Chapter 6).

[14] Director (1964, p. 2) wrote that "Laissez faire has never been more than a slogan in defense of the proposition that every extension of state activity should be examined under a presumption of error." For J. M. Clark (1936, p. 335) "laissez faire really means whatever system and degree of control we have become so accustomed to that we accept it as natural".

[15] The efficiency argument is particularly associated with Demsetz (1973, 1974). For a contemporary critical comment, see Rosenbluth (1976). Subsequent research that controls for efficiency differences finds evidence of market power *and* efficiency effects on profitability. See Section 5.3.3, as well as White (2006, Section III).

[16] The case that the structure-conduct-performance school glossed over the endogeneity of market structure is dubious at best; see the feedback links from firm conduct to market structure and basic conditions in Figure 1.1.

1.4.4 Neoclassical Theory

The Second Chicago School also criticized the deconcentration bill on the ground that its theoretical underpinnings, the S-C-P approach, were inconsistent with formal economic theory (Posner, 1979, p. 929):

> Casual observation of business behavior, colorful characterizations (such as the term "barrier to entry"), eclectic forays into sociology and psychology, descriptive statistics, and verification by plausibility took the place of the careful definitions and parsimonious logical structure of economic theory. The result was that industrial organization regularly advanced propositions that contradicted economic theory.

What is meant here by "economic theory" is the neoclassical theory of perfectly competitive markets.

The Hart deconcentration bill never saw the light of day, and for a period of perhaps 10–12 years from the mid 1970s, the Second Chicago School monopolized the giving of antitrust advice to U.S. courts and policymakers.

One of the two central positions of the Second Chicago School—that the analysis of market behaviour should be based on formal models—is now accepted by mainstream industrial economists. But the good approximation assumption was never accepted by mainstream economists.

Table 1.1 reports a classification of 117 papers on industry organization that were presented at the annual meetings of the American Economic Association between 1951 and 1982 (inclusive). The papers are divided into three groups:

- those consistent with the Chicago good approximation assumption;
- those consistent with the structure-conduct-performance framework;
- those critical of both approaches.

About one-fifth of the papers accepted the Second Chicago School approach. Just over half of the papers are consistent with the structure-conduct-performance approach or its policy implications. Almost 30 per cent rejected both approaches, and called for new ways of thinking about market performance.

For comparison purposes, Kearl *et al.* (1979) report the results of a survey of a stratified random sample of 600 individuals who were members of the American Economic

Table 1.1 Classification of 117 articles from the Papers and Proceedings issues of the American Economic Review, 1951–1982

	1950s	1960s	1970–1982	Total
Chicago	7	9	6	22
Mainstream	24	17	20	61
"Think outside the box"	11	9	14	34

Source: Martin (2007a).

Association in 1974. Statement 12 in their survey is "Antitrust laws should be used vigorously to reduce monopoly power from its current level." This statement is inconsistent with the good approximation assumption—if most industries, most of the time, can be treated as if they are perfectly competitive, there is no need for a vigorous antitrust policy. Kearl *et al.* report that 49 per cent of respondents generally agreed with the statement, 36 per cent agreed with provisions, and 15 per cent generally disagreed.

1.5 Game Theory

While the Second Chicago School was disputing policy primacy with the S-C-P paradigm, mathematical economists were turning their attention to industrial (and other branches of) economics. In the 1930s, the developers of the S-C-P approach rejected contemporary economic theory as inadequate for the analysis of imperfectly competitive markets. By the 1970s, the applications of game theory to economic questions began to live up to the promise of Von Neumann and Morgenstern's 1944 *Theory of Games and Economic Behavior*. Game theory extended neoclassical price theory to environments of incomplete and imperfect information, and provides a natural formal framework for the analysis of strategic behaviour.

1.5.1 Realistic Assumptions

Mainstream industrial economists, having faced criticism for the failure to use formal models, were quick to turn to game theory as an alternative approach. What most economists regard as one of the merits of game theory is that—in contrast to the good approximation assumption—it directs attention toward the realism of a model's assumptions (Fudenberg and Tirole, 1987, p. 176):

> Game theory has had a deep impact on the theory of industrial organization ... The reason it has been embraced by a majority of researchers in the field is that it imposes some discipline on theoretical thinking. It forces economists to specify the strategic variables, their timing, and the information structure faced by firms. As is often the case in economics, the researcher learns as much from constructing the model ... as from solving it because in constructing the model one is led to examine its realism. (Is the timing of entry plausible? Which variables are costly to change in the short run? Can firms observe their rivals' prices, capacities, or technologies in the industry under consideration? Etc.)

The decade stretching roughly from the early 1970s through the early 1980s saw a reformulation of the theory of industrial economics around the methodology of game theory. Although industrial economics has always been, at heart, a fundamentally empirical field, the most prominent research during this period was strictly theoretical. More often than not, these game-theoretic analyses produced results much closer to those of the structure-conduct-performance school than to those of the Second Chicago School.

1.5.2 Models of Strategic Behaviour

Like Pandora, who loosed the ills of the world and found they could not be closed up again, the Second Chicago School invoked formal theory in its contest with the S-C-P paradigm, and found it could not close it up again. One reaction of the Second Chicago School to the rise of formal theoretical models that find a middle ground between the neoclassical models of perfect competition and of monopoly was to reject the use of game-theoretic models (Baxter, 1983, p. 320):

> What concerns me is that the economists have rather lapped the bar and the courts. Quite frankly, I do not want them back in the courts talking about new and not well-understood justifications for intervention, some of which [sound] like the half-baked oligopoly theories of twenty years ago (although they are not).

1.5.3 Empirical Foundations

Early in the period of its policy ascendancy, and despite its long emphasis on the sufficiency of the model of perfect competition as an analytical framework, some Chicago School scholars urged a return to empirical research (Coase, 1972, pp. 70–71):

> [I]t is unlikely that we shall see significant advances in our theory of the organization of industry until we know more about what it is that we must explain. An inspired theoretician might do as well without such empirical work, but my own feeling is that the inspiration is most likely to come through the stimulus provided by the patterns, puzzles, and anomalies revealed by systematic data-gathering ...

This has much in common with the position taken by Mason and his students in the 1930s: the theory we have is not sufficient, let us turn to empirical analysis as a prelude to developing an adequate theory. But the empirical work called for seems like the kind of institutional industry study that early S-C-P researchers criticized in the 1930s (Coase, 1972b, p. 73):

> In my view, what is wanted in industrial organization is a direct approach to the problem. This would concentrate on what activities firms undertake, and would endeavor to discover the characteristics of the groupings of activities within firms. Which activities tend to be associated, and which do not? The answer may well differ for different kinds of firm; for example, for firms of different size, or for those with a different corporate structure, or for firms in different industries.

1.6 There and Back Again: Methodological Synthesis

In the 1930s, industrial economists developed the structure-conduct-performance framework in reaction to an existing descriptive, institutionalist approach. The S-C-P framework was a general analytical framework, but discursive and literary rather than formal and mathematical. For ten or twelve years, the structure-conduct-performance approach was succeeded in U.S. policy circles by the Second Chicago School, which operated on the assumption that most real-world markets, most of the time, could be treated as if they were in long-run, perfectly competitive equilibrium. The structure-conduct-performance school was in its turn succeeded in economics by the game-theoretic approach to analysing imperfectly competitive markets. Early applications of game theory to industrial economics were overwhelmingly theoretical. By the mid 1980s, however, the empirical roots of industrial economics reasserted themselves, producing empirical tests of formal models of imperfectly competitive markets.[17]

---

[17] There is always a certain ambiguity in identifying turning points, but the June 1987 special issue of the *Journal of Industrial Economics* on "The Empirical Renaissance in Industrial Economics" is as good a marker as any of this shift.

It is probably fair to write that most industrial economists now accept the view of Coase (2006, p. 276):[18]

> [P]rogress in understanding the working of the economic system will come from an interplay between theory and empirical work. The theory suggests what empirical work might be fruitful, the subsequent empirical work suggests what modification in the theory or rethinking is needed, which in turn leads to new empirical work. If rightly done, scientific research is a never-ending process, but one that leads to greater understanding at each stage.

This does not mean industrial economists agree on the policy implications of their work. But they increasingly agree on the kinds of arguments that need to be mustered to support *any* policy recommendation: empirical evidence viewed through the lens of consistently formulated, industry-specific, game-theoretic models of imperfectly competitive markets.

1.7 Alternative Approaches

Although it is mainstream industrial organization and the Second Chicago School that have hogged the limelight, there are other approaches that concern themselves with questions of industrial organization. These non-neoclassical approaches have not yet occupied centre stage in industrial economics. They continue to have important influences, however, and we mention two of them here.

1.7.1 Managerial/Behavioural

The behavioural approach to the theory of the firm surfaced around the same time as the structure-conduct-performance paradigm, and was a response to the same root cause, namely the perceived difference between the assumptions of the classical model of perfectly competitive markets and the observed behaviour of real-world firms.

Berle and Means (1932/1991) focused on the separation of ownership and control in large, publicly listed corporations as a determinant of business behaviour. An owner-managed firm might reasonably be assumed to be run in the interests of the owner; could the same assumption be casually extended to a firm with many owners, none controlling, and a small cadre of managers? Hall and Hitch (1939) found that businessmen's descriptions of the procedures they followed to set prices seemed distantly related, if at all, to the "marginal revenue equals marginal cost" equilibrium condition of the profit-maximizing firm of neoclassical economic theory. Both studies suggested that business might not simply maximize profit (or, alternatively, value).

If the separation of ownership and control gives management the freedom not to maximize profit, perhaps managers maximize something else. Baumol (1958; 1959/1967) explored the idea that firms maximize sales. Marris (1968) considered size and alternatively growth maximization. Williamson (1964) considered that managers maximize emoluments—(1964, p. 35): "indirect source[s] of status and prestige", not a payment for the value of managerial product but a "result from the strategic advantage that ... management possesses in the distribution of the returns to monopoly power". Alternatively, a firm may not maximize at all—it may "satisfice", (Simon, 1959, p. 263; see also Cyert and March, 1963): "attaining a

---

[18] See also his Nobel lecture, Coase (1992).

certain level or rate of profit, holding a certain share of the market or a certain level of sales". We consider these issues in Chapter 10.

1.7.2 Schumpeter/Dynamic Market Performance

As we will see in Chapter 14, Joseph Schumpeter (1934b) downplayed static competition, rivalry among producers in existing markets, as a determinant of economic performance. He emphasized instead the importance of technological progress, the result of rivalry to create new products. Schumpeter's work stimulated a large literature on the economics of innovation and, more recently, on public policy toward intellectual property rights. It also contributed to the development of behavioural models of the firm. Nelson and Winter's (1982) book, *An Evolutionary Theory of Economic Change*, is Schumpeterian in that it focuses on innovation and technological change as the fundamental determinants of economic performance. It is behavioural in that it gives up the neoclassical assumption of value maximization and examines the implications of adaptive behaviour.

1.8 Organization of the Book

The first 17 chapters of the book examine the topics shown in Figure 1.3, the final 9 chapters deal with U.S. antitrust and EU competition policy treatment of the associated policy questions.

In Part I, we consider basic models of perfect and imperfectly competitive models of market performance (the topics indicated in the upper-left corner of Figure 1.3.) The models of perfectly competitive and monopoly markets, which we review in Chapter 2, are the standards against which models of imperfectly competitive markets are measured. In Chapter 2 we also introduce the experimental methodology that is increasingly used by industrial economists to test models of various types of markets. We introduce models of imperfectly competitive markets in Chapters 3 and 4, and discuss empirical evidence about such models in Chapter 5.

In a first set of applications of the basic models, in Part II, we turn to types of firm conduct that may arise in imperfectly competitive markets. We consider the economics of collusion in Chapter 6, of dominant-firm behaviour in Chapter 7, and of price discrimination in Chapter 8.

Moving on to the lower left of Figure 1.3, the observation that some markets are supplied by many firms and some by few invites inquiry into the factors that explain differences in supply-side market structure. Here we ask questions like "What determines the number and size distribution of firms supplying a market? What determines a firm's cost of entering a market, or of leaving one? Why do some entrants prosper, and others die? These are topics we deal with in Part III. In Chapters 9 and 10 we examine the determinants of market structure and of firm structure. In Chapter 11 we turn to the economics of mergers, which involves firm structure and has implications for market structure.

Virtually all firms operate within networks of contractual relationships with firms in other markets. Such interfirm contractual relationships are as much the lifeblood of commercial enterprise as the employment of workers and the selling of a final product. The impact of such contracts on market performance is a topic of perennial interest for industrial economists, and one we examine in Chapter 12.

Figure 1.3 Topics in industrial organization

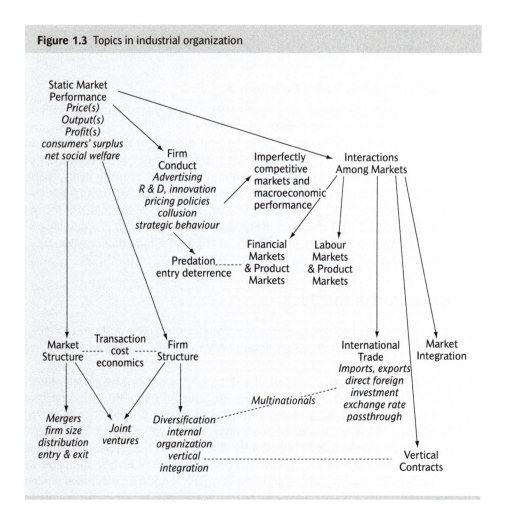

In Part IV we take up a series of specific topics. Advertising and other types of marketing efforts (Chapter 13) inform and persuade consumers, and, over time, shape the nature of demand facing individual firms. Research and development (Chapter 14) lead to the development of new products or production processes, and help determine the rate of technological progress in an industry. There may be a case for public promotion of innovation (Chapter 15). Many international markets are imperfectly competitive. A firm based in one country may export to another country, selling through a foreign distributor. It may open a subsidiary in the export market, becoming a multinational firm. Of course, multinational operation ties into the question of the internal organization of firms. These matters are the subject of Chapter 16.

Extensive trade flows may integrate what were distinct national markets into what is in an economic sense a single or common market. Market integration may occur with or without political integration; it may occur before or after political integration. Market integration is the subject of Chapter 17, and the focus is on market integration in the European Union.

Industrial economists study the topics shown in Figure 1.3 because they are interesting in their own right. But industrial economics has also been heavily involved in the formulation and administration of public policy toward business, and this is the topic of Part V. Chapter 18 lays out the background of U.S. antitrust policy, covering the U.S. economy from the period before the 1890 passage of the Sherman Antitrust Act through the 1914 passage of the Clayton Act and the Federal Trade Commission Act. Chapter 19 deals with the background of European Community competition policy. Chapter 20 deals with public policy toward collusion, Chapter 21 with public policy toward dominant firm behaviour. Chapter 22 examines U.S. and EU merger policy, and Chapter 23 with public policy toward price discrimination. In Chapter 24 we consider public policy toward vertical interfirm relationships contracts, and in Chapter 25 policy issues raised by the overlap of intellectual property policy with antitrust and competition policy. In Chapter 26, we summarize the debate on the role and impact of antitrust and competition policy in market economies.

Elementary economic models are often explained with (mostly two-dimensional) graphs. The level of mathematics involved in working with such graphs includes primarily elementary algebra, analytic geometry, and enough differential calculus to find the slopes of well-behaved curves and then use the results to find minimum or maximum values. In Appendix II ("Just the Math Used in this Book") I explain how mathematics to this level is used in the models of industrial economics presented in the text.[19]

STUDY POINTS

- Structure-conduct-performance paradigm (Section 1.2.1)
- The oligopoly problem (Section 1.3.1)
- The Chicago Schools (Section 1.3.1)
- Hart deconcentration bill (Section 1.3.2)
- *Laissez faire* (Section 1.4.1)
- Game theory (Section 1.5)
- The methodological synthesis (Section 1.6)
- Behavioural and Schumpeterian approaches (Section 1.7.1, Section 1.7.2)

FURTHER READING

I have drawn on Martin (2007, 2008a) for some of the material in this chapter.

For discussions of the development of the field of industrial organization, see Bain (1949a, pp. 129–133), Andrews (1952), Grether (1970), Phillips and Stevenson (1974), David Dale Martin (1976), Hay and Morris (1979, Chapter 1), Schmalensee (1982, 1987, 1988), Kreps and Spence (1985), Davies and Lyons (1989), Bonanno and Brandolini (1990), Corley (1990), Shepherd (1991), and Horowitz (1994). Elzinga (2001) makes the distinction between the First and Second Chicago Schools. Caves (2007) offers

---

[19] Treatments of mathematics that aim to serve the same purpose as the Appendix can be found in the reprinted Fisher (1897) or (downloadable from JSTOR) Crum (1938).

a retrospective on the structure-conduct-performance school. From a perspective of legal scholarship, see Hovenkamp (1991, Chapter 22); from the closely related field of business strategy, see portions of Ghemawat (2002).

The model of monopolistic competition was developed at about the same time as the structure-conduct-performance framework, and in response to many of the same forces. The monopolistic competition literature begins with Chamberlin (1933) and Joan Robinson (1933). See earlier Sraffa (1926) and later (among others) Wolinsky (1986). For discussions, see Schumpeter (1934a), White (1936), Stigler (1949a), Chamberlin (1961), Samuelson (1967), Schneider (1967), Fisher (1989), and Ekelund and Hébert (1990a).

Among the early structure-conduct-performance industry studies are Wallace (1937), Bain (1944), Markham (1952), Kaysen (1956), and Adelman (1959a). Weiss (1971, 1974) surveys cross-section econometric (primarily) industry studies.

For the text of the Hart Deconcentration Bill, see Note (1973) or Goldschmid *et al.* (1974, pp. 444–448). For discussions of the Second Chicago School, see Posner (1979), Reder (1982), Kitch (1983, 1988), Coase (1993), and Van Overtveldt (2007; for present purposes, see particularly the Introduction and Chapter Six). On the intellectual antecedents of the Second Chicago School, see Henry C. Simons (1934, 1936), Breit and Ransom (1971) and de Long (1990). On Simons, see Director (1948).

On *laissez faire*, see Keynes (1972/1926), Lange (1945–1946), and Viner (1960).

The behavioural and managerial literature is reviewed by Mason (1958), Machlup (1967), by Aoki (1983), and by Pierce, Boerner, and Teece (2002). The early behavioural literature more generally is surveyed by Simon (1987). For a discussion of modern behavioral economics, see Camerer and Loewenstein (2003).

BASIC MARKET MODELS

2

[Thales of Miletus] was reproached for his poverty, which was supposed to show that philosophy was of no use. According to the story, he knew by his skill in the stars while it was yet winter that there would be a great harvest of olives in the coming year; so, having a little money, he gave deposits for the use of all the olive-presses in Chios and Miletus, which he hired at a low price because no one bid against him. When the harvest time came, and many wanted them all at once and of a sudden, he let them out at any rate which he pleased, and made a quantity of money. Thus he showed the world that philosophers can easily be rich if they like, but that their ambition is of another sort. He is supposed to have given a striking proof of his wisdom, but ... his device for getting money is of universal application, and is nothing but the creation of a monopoly.

Aristotle, *Politics*.[1]

2.1 Introduction

We begin this chapter with the models of perfect competition and monopoly, which are reference points for the analysis of the kind of imperfectly competitive markets that are most commonly encountered in the real world. We also introduce the experimental approach to testing market models, and examine evidence from experimental tests of the competitive and monopoly models. Finally, we examine measurements of the welfare impact of market power in naturally occurring markets.

2.2 Perfect Competition

Nineteenth-century and early twentieth-century economists worked with what in retrospect seems a rather fuzzy notion of competition. For them, "competition" meant rivalry. One and the same term was used sometimes to mean actual rivalry between active firms

---

[1] Book I, Ch. VII, Jowett edition, 1908; quoted by Mund (1933, p. 3).

and sometimes to mean the impact of potential entrants on the conduct of incumbent firms.

In contrast, the neoclassical model of perfect competition, which comes to us from Frank H. Knight (1921, pp. 76–79, Ch. VI), is antiseptic in its precision. The assumptions of the model are:[2]

(a) there are many small buyers and sellers;

(b) with complete and perfect information about all aspects of the market;

(c) dealing in a standardized product; and

(d) with free and easy entry into and exit from the market, at least in the long run.

Alfred Marshall (1920, p. 348) compared demand and supply to the upper and lower blades of a pair of scissors, together determining price just as the two blades of a scissors together cut a piece of paper. We look in turn at the demand and supply sides of a perfectly competitive market.

2.2.1 Market Demand

Market demand can be represented by an aggregate demand function showing a negative relationship between price p and quantity demanded Q,

$$p = f(Q). \qquad (2.1)$$

Equation (2.1) is said to be written in *inverse form* because it shows the price that corresponds to each quantity demanded, not the quantity that would be demanded at each price. The negative relationship between p and Q means that the slope of the inverse demand function is negative, $f'(Q) < 0$.

The equation of the specific linear inverse demand function shown in Figure 2.1 is:

$$p = 100 - Q, \qquad (2.2)$$

for $0 \leq Q \leq 100$. If equation (2.2) describes the demand side of a market, price must be 90 for consumers to demand 10 units of output, price must be 80 for consumers to demand 20 units of output, and so on.

Price elasticity of demand

One measure the sensitivity of quantity demanded to price is the *price elasticity of demand*, the proportional change in quantity demanded in response to a given proportional change in price:

$$\varepsilon_{Qp} = -\lim_{\Delta p \to 0} \frac{\Delta Q/Q}{\Delta p/p} = \frac{p}{Q}\left(-\frac{dQ}{dp}\right), \qquad (2.3)$$

---

[2] It was once common to make a distinction between "pure" and "perfect" competition, pure competition meaning that economic agents acted as price takers and perfect competition adding the assumption of free and easy entry and exit (Allen, 1966, p. 314; see also Chamberlin, 1933, pp. 6, 25, 28). This distinction has fallen into disuse (Allen, 1949, fn. 7, p. 117, who is cited by Chamberlin, 1957, p. 18).

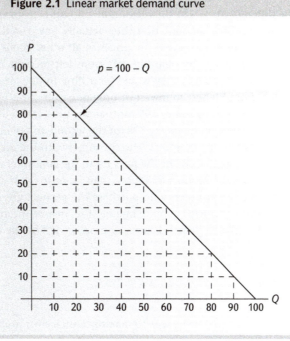

Figure 2.1 Linear market demand curve

where $-dQ/dp$ is the absolute value of the slope of the demand curve. If $\varepsilon_{Qp} = 0$ (as it is for a vertical demand curve), the same quantity is demanded at any price. If $\varepsilon_{Qp} = 1$, a 1 per cent increase in price means a 1 per cent decrease in quantity demanded, and so on.[3]

Marginal revenue

Marginal revenue is the change in total revenue in response to a small change in output,

$$MR = \frac{d(pQ)}{dQ} = p + Q\frac{dp}{dQ} < p. \qquad (2.4)$$

That is, marginal revenue is the revenue received from selling an extra unit of output at price p minus (the first derivative of the inverse demand function, dp/dQ, is negative) the revenue given up on units of output that could have been sold at a slightly higher price.

From equations (2.3) and (2.4), there is a relationship between marginal revenue and the price elasticity of demand, a relationship that will prove useful when we discuss monopoly:

$$MR = p + Q\frac{dp}{dQ} = p\left(1 + \frac{Q}{p}\frac{dp}{dQ}\right) = p\left(1 - \frac{1}{\varepsilon_{Qp}}\right). \qquad (2.5)$$

---

[3] An advantage of measuring the sensitivity of quantity demanded to price in terms of elasticities is that the value of the price elasticity of demand is invariant to the units in which quantity and price are measured. Whether output is measured in pounds or kilograms, the ratio $\Delta Q/Q$ is the same. Whether price is measured in dollars or euros, the ratio $\Delta p/p$ is the same. The value of the price-elasticity of demand at any point on the demand curve, being the ratio of two ratios that are independent of units of measurement, is itself independent of units of measurement.

Consumer surplus

Consumer surplus is the difference between the maximum amount consumers would pay for a given amount of output and the amount that they actually pay. For the linear inverse demand equation (2.2), holding incomes and the prices of all other goods constant, think of consumers as being placed along the quantity axis from left to right in order of their *reservation prices*, the maximum amounts they would be willing to pay for the next unit of output put on the market, from highest to lowest. If only one unit of output is supplied to the market, there is a consumer willing to pay $99 for that one unit. If two units are supplied to the market, there is a consumer willing to pay $98 for the second unit of output. If 60 units of output are sold, price is $40, as in Figure 2.2. The consumer with the highest reservation price values the product $59 more than he or she pays for it, the consumer with the second-highest reservation price values the product $58 more than he or she pays for it, and so on. Adding up the surplus values of consumers who purchase the product gives the amount of *consumer surplus*, the amount of which is approximately the area of the triangle bounded above by the price line, below by the demand curve, and on the left by the vertical axis.

2.2.2 Supply: Single Firm

Price-taking

Taken together, the assumptions that firms seek to maximize their own profit, that there are many small firms, and that there is complete and perfect information *imply* that firms in a perfectly competitive market take price as given.

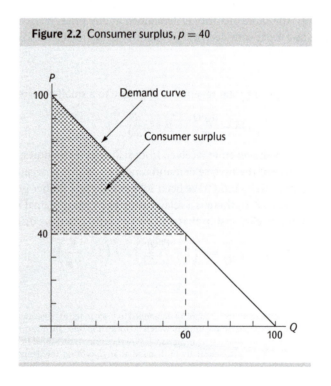

Figure 2.2 Consumer surplus, $p = 40$

The reasoning that leads to the conclusion that firms in a perfectly competitive market must be price takers runs as follows. Firms have complete and perfect knowledge, so they know the market price. Since firms are small in the market, they can sell whatever amount they wish at the market price. To accept anything less than the market price would mean needlessly giving up revenue. Since each firm seeks to maximize its own profit, no firm would be willing to sell for anything less than the market price.

Consumers too have complete and perfect knowledge; they also know the market price. Hence if a firm in a perfectly competitive market tried to sell at a price above the market price, consumers would simply buy the standardized product elsewhere and the firm would sell nothing. Once again, since a firm (by assumption) seeks to maximize its own profit, it would not try to sell at any price above the market price. Thus the only action open to a profit-maximizing firm in a perfectly competitive market is to decide how much to produce to maximize its profit at the market price, which it takes as given.[4]

Cost

Since the firm's profit is the difference between revenue and cost, $\pi = pq - C(q)$, a firm's profit-maximizing output level depends on the way its costs, $C(q)$, vary with its output, q. We divide costs into two categories, variable and fixed. The firm's use of variable inputs changes as the firm's output level changes—hiring more workers as a plant goes from one shift a day to two, for example. The costs of variable inputs are the firm's *variable cost*. The firm's use of fixed inputs does not change as the firm's output level changes—rent on an office building, for example. The costs of the services of fixed inputs are the firm's *fixed cost*.

Variable inputs other than labour are typically consumed in the production process—fuel converted to energy, physical inputs incorporated into the final output. The labour of a worker is at the disposal of the firm during the time period for which the worker is hired. The *cost* of variable inputs is what is paid to purchase them.[5]

Fixed inputs, on the other hand, are typically assets that remain with the firm over time. If a shift ends and a wholly owned factory is closed until the following morning, the factory remains an asset of the firm. Its value is carried on the firm's balance sheet. The economic cost to the firm of using the factory's services to produce its own output is an *opportunity cost*—instead of using the factory for itself, the firm could rent the factory to some other firm in a perfectly competitive rental market for factory services. For this reason, economists speak of the contribution of fixed assets to cost as the *rental cost* of the services of the fixed assets.

The equilibrium rent a firm could obtain by supplying a fixed asset like a factory in a perfectly competitive rental market would include a normal rate of return on investment. If

---

[4] It follows that there is no competition, in the lay sense of rivalry, in a perfectly competitive market (Friedman, 1962/1982, p. 119). Each of the many small firms on the supply side of a perfectly competitive market reacts to the market price; no one of them reacts to any other firm. It follows also that any argument that (1) begins from the observation that firms in a particular market display a high degree of rivalry and (2) reaches the conclusion that *for that reason* the market can be expected to exhibit characteristics that are close to those of the (short- or long-run) equilibrium of a perfectly competitive market, is incorrect.

[5] Hounshell (1984, p. 272, footnote omitted) writes of the care with which the 1920s Ford Motor Company kept track of costs: "Graphs in the Ford Archives ... show the unit cost of materials for the Model T body types plotted on the same page with curves for labor and overhead costs; total factory costs we also plotted with retail sales prices." For discussion of an earlier use of cost analysis in business planning, see the accompanying box.

a firm could invest €100,000 in safe government bonds and earn (say) interest of 8 per cent per year, then in long-run equilibrium, if the firm is to be willing to invest €100,000 in a building and put it on the rental market, the equilibrium rent must offer the firm a return of 8 per cent per year on its investment. And if the rental market is perfectly competitive, the long-run rental rate could not yield any greater return: if it did, since there is free and easy entry and exit, new factories would be built, driving rental rates down. The rental cost of fixed assets thus includes a normal rate of return on investment.[6]

Opportunity cost is a difference between economic and accounting concepts of cost. If the rate of return on investment in a safe asset is 8 per cent, then the *opportunity cost* of investing in some other asset is 8 per cent—the return an investor could earn by putting money in a safe asset. If the accounting rate of return on stockholders' equity for a firm is 7 per cent, and the rate of return on a safe asset is 8 per cent, then the economic rate of return on stockholders' equity in the firm is −1 per cent. Stockholders in such a firm would be losing money compared with the return they might have earned by investing in a safe asset, even though the accounting rate of return is positive.

Unit costs

From fixed cost, variable cost, and their sum, total cost, we derive

- average variable cost (variable cost per unit of output);
- average cost (cost per unit of output); and
- marginal cost (the change in total cost per unit change in output).

Since variable cost is the only portion of total cost that changes as output changes, it is also correct to define marginal cost as the change in variable cost as output changes.

Unit cost curves

We can write the equation of a firm's cost function in general form as:

$$C(q) = F + c(q), \tag{2.6}$$

where fixed cost is F and variable cost is $c(q)$. Average variable cost is $c(q)/q$, and average cost is $[F + c(q)]/q$. Marginal cost is the derivative $dc(q)/dq$.

Figure 2.3 shows conventional ∪-shaped unit cost curves.[7] For a fixed stock of physical capital—fixed factory size, a fixed number of machines—one might expect average cost to be high at either very low or very high output levels. At low output levels, fixed cost per unit will be great. At high output levels, fixed cost per unit of output will be small. But to get high levels of output from a fixed capital stock, large amounts of variable inputs will be needed, making the ratio of fixed to variable inputs inefficiently low. The marginal product of variable inputs will be low, and the cost of the marginal unit of output will be high. Average cost will be low for intermediate output levels, which require enough variable inputs to use fixed inputs efficiently but not so much that congestion sets in.

---

[6] The opportunity cost of investing in a fixed asset also depends on the economic rate of depreciation of the asset, the rate of change of the price of the asset, and on the details of the tax system. Taking these factors explicitly into account complicates the analysis without changing the general nature of the results, and for simplicity we leave them aside here. See Chapter 15, Appendix I for a model of rental cost that includes depreciation and tax rules.

[7] Figure 2.3 is drawn for the cubic cost function $C(q) = 1 + 9q - q^2 + q^3$. See Problem 2–2.

Figure 2.3 Firm cost curves

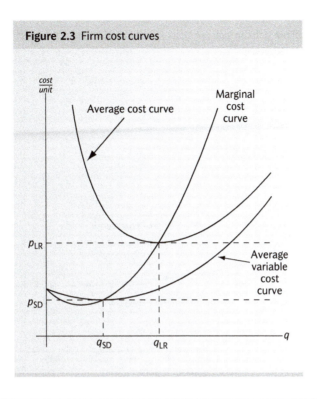

📌 **BOX** **Cost Curves and Firm Decision-Making**

In 1796, Gottfried Härtel acquired control of a Leipzig publishing house. He undertook a detailed analysis of the business, including its extensive operations in the printing of sheet music, for which two technologies were available.

With six to eight hours work, a skilled engraver could prepare a plate from which high-quality sheet music might be printed. Alternatively, a matrix could be typeset with pre-existing type, using techniques that had been improved by the previous owner of the business. Engraving meant higher fixed and variable costs (the surface of the engraved plate needed to be wiped clear of surface ink for each printing) but produced a higher-quality product.

Härtel compiled tables comparing the average cost of the two production processes, from which Scherer (2001) derived the cost curves shown Figure 2.4.

Working backward from the price he expected to be able to charge without attracting entry* and the likely output (300 sheets), Härtel calculated the most he could pay a typesetter, and at the same time cover fixed costs and earn a normal rate of return.

Härtel used this cost information as a basis for negotiations with Ludwig van Beethoven for the right to publish Beethoven's work. Härtel later made comparative cost calculations to decide the kinds of work for which a new production process, lithography, could profitably be substituted for one of the older methods.

---

*This is an example of limit pricing; see Section 7.2.4. (Copyright protection, which would have blocked entry, did not then exist.) *Source:* Scherer (2001).

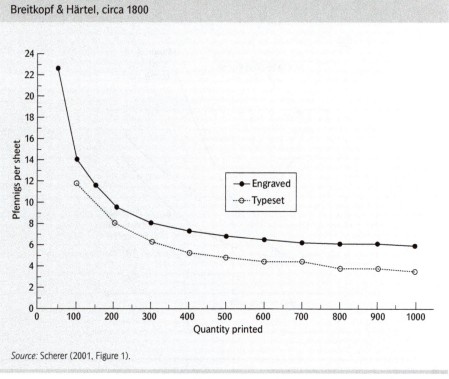

Figure 2.4 Plots of the data on average costs for engraved and typeset sheet music, Breitkopf & Härtel, circa 1800

Source: Scherer (2001, Figure 1).

Marginal cost and average variable cost have the same value at the minimum point on the average variable cost curve. Marginal cost and average cost have the same value at the minimum point on the average cost curve (Viner, 1931). Although these relationships are a matter of economics, they are also a simple property of averages. If the average (say) height of a group of people is calculated, and an additional person who is shorter than the previous average is added to the group, the average height of the larger group will be less than the previous value. If an additional person who is taller than the previous average height is added to the group, the average height of the larger group will be more than the previous value. If an additional person whose height is exactly the previous average height is added to the group, the average height of the larger group will be the same as the previous value. In the same way, if marginal cost is below average cost, average cost is pulled down. If marginal cost is above average cost, average cost is pulled up. If marginal cost equals average cost, average cost is at its minimum value. The same conclusions hold, and by the same argument, for average variable cost.

Many inputs that are fixed in the short run become variable in the long run—over a long enough time horizon, a firm can build a new factory or buy a new machine; it can let existing capital goods wear out or sell them. One might nonetheless appeal to "corporate management" as a factor that must be fixed even in the long run, and if management is a fixed factor, it becomes plausible to think that long-run cost curves too have the ∪-shape of Figure 2.3.

Sunk cost

The cost of investing in a tangible or intangible capital asset is said to be *sunk* if the value of the asset cannot be recovered by resale upon exit from the market. Most investments have an element of sunkenness. A greater percentage of the investment in an asset is likely to be sunk, the narrower the range uses to which the asset can be put. A building designed for use as a bank can be renovated, at some expense, and used for other purposes: investment in a bank building is partially but not completely sunk. Investment in a railroad line is almost entirely sunk—railroad ties might be ripped up and sold for scrap, but this would allow recovery of only a small part of the initial investment.

Sunk costs become important in analyzing dynamic aspects of firm behaviour, including entry and exit decisions. We will see that firms in high-sunk-cost industries have historically tended to form cartels during recessions. Asset specificity is also a factor in determining what activities firms decide to perform internally, rather than relying on independent suppliers.

Firm supply

The short-run output decision of a profit-maximizing firm in a perfectly competitive market involves the relationship between marginal cost, average variable cost, and price. If a price-taking firm produces a quantity that makes its marginal cost less than price, it can increase profit by expanding output. If a price-taking firm produces a quantity that makes its marginal cost greater than price, it can increase profit by reducing output. When the firm produces the quantity that makes its marginal cost equal to price, it maximizes its short-run profit.

This conclusion—that a firm's profit-maximizing output in a perfectly competitive market makes its marginal cost equal to the given market price—holds provided that price is greater than average variable cost. In this case the firm's revenue will pay all its variable costs and some of its fixed cost. But if price is below the minimum value of the firm's average variable cost, its profit-maximizing choice is to shut down (to produce zero output). By shutting down, the firm loses only its fixed cost. By producing any output at all, it loses its fixed cost and some of its variable cost. It follows that *the short-run supply function of a firm in a perfectly competitive industry is the firm's marginal cost function, for prices at or above the minimum value of average variable cost*. For lower prices, the profit-maximizing quantity is zero—the firm shuts down.

2.2.3 Industry Supply and Short-run Equilibrium

In the model of perfect competition, "the short run" is a time period when the number of firms (and plants per firm) supplying the market is fixed. In the short run, the quantity supplied by the industry at any price is the sum of the quantities supplied by the individual firms at that price. The industry supply function is the sum of the supply functions of the firms in the industry.

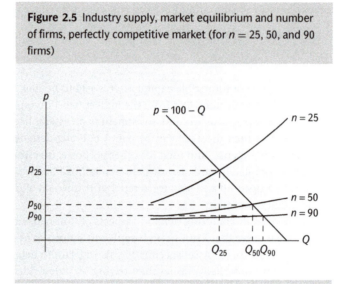

Figure 2.5 Industry supply, market equilibrium and number of firms, perfectly competitive market (for $n = 25$, 50, and 90 firms)

Figure 2.5 shows three short-run industry supply curves, for 25, 50, and 90 firms respectively, if each firm operates one plant and all plants have cost curves of the kind shown in Figure 2.3. The short-run equilibrium price, the price that clears the market, is the price at which the demand curve and the short-run supply curve intersect.

2.2.4 Long-run Perfectly Competitive Equilibrium

In any short-run time period, firms make economic losses (earn less than a normal rate of return on investment) if price is below the minimum value of average cost. Since one of the assumptions about a perfectly competitive industry is that there is free and easy entry into and exit from the market, if price is below the minimum value of average cost some firms will leave the industry, the industry supply curve will shift to the left (a smaller quantity will be offered at any price) and the short-run equilibrium price will increase as the equilibrium point—the intersection of the demand curve and the short-run supply curve—shifts up the demand curve.

In any short-run time period, firms make economic profits (earn more than a normal rate of return on investment) if price is above the minimum value of average cost. Short-run economic profits will attract new firms into the industry, the short-run industry supply curve will shift to the right (a greater quantity will be offered at any price) and the short-run equilibrium price will decrease as the equilibrium point shifts down the demand curve.

The equilibrating process of exit or entry ends—firms earn a normal rate of return on investment and only a normal rate of return on investment—when equilibrium price equals the minimum value of average cost. Since the industry supply curve is constructed by horizontally adding up firms' supply curves, and each firm supplies a quantity that makes its marginal cost equal to price, each firm is maximizing its economic profit. Since price equals the minimum value of average cost, each firm's maximum economic profit is zero; hence there is no incentive for new firms to enter or for incumbent firms to exit.[8]

> In the *long-run equilibrium* of a *perfectly competitive market*, each firm produces an output that makes its marginal cost equal to price (each firm maximizes profit), and price equals average economic cost, which includes a normal rate of return on investment (no incentive for entry or exit).

2.2.5 Rent and Quasi-rent

"Rent" is an elusive concept. One reason is that in scientific work economists use the term "rent" in a technical sense that is only tenuously related to its use in everyday conversation. A second reason is that (as with many other terms), economists use the term "rent" to refer to related but distinct phenomena (differential rent, economic rent, efficiency rent, quasi-rent) without always being precise about just which concept they have in mind. A third reason— most pertinent for the concept of "quasi-rent"—is that the central ideas inherently involve the passage of time. Attempts to develop these ideas using standard static models of firm behaviour necessarily involve a certain imprecision.

Rent

David Ricardo ([1817] 1951, p. 67) defined rent as "that portion of the produce of the earth, which is paid to the landlord for the use of the original and indestructible powers of the soil".

Land is an input that is in fixed supply. Leaving aside exceptions such as the Netherlands and Tokyo Harbour, the amount of land available is given by nature. Other examples of inputs that are in fixed supply are the unique ability of a world-class athlete (also given by nature) or medallions required by law to operate a taxi and issued in limited supply by a local government (the number issued being an outcome of the political process). For an individual producer, rent (of land, of a taxi medallion, as the case may be) is a cost like the cost of any other input. But rent stands in a different relation to competitive equilibrium price than do other types of cost.

To explain, Figure 2.6 shows a stylized market in which there are (potentially) 1000 of each of two types of farms. The first type of farm is able to supply up to 100 quarters of corn, at unit cost c_L per quarter. The unit cost c_L covers the cost of all inputs except land, including a normal rate of return on investment. The average cost curve of a typical low-cost farm is shown in Figure 2.6(a). The farm cannot produce more than 100 quarters of corn at any price; the average cost curve becomes vertical at 100 quarters of output.

The second type of farm can also supply up to 100 quarters of corn, at unit cost $c_H > c_L$ per quarter. This extra cost may be transportation cost, if farms of the second type are farther away from the market than farms of the first type. Alternatively, it may be that farms of the second type cultivate land that is less suited to the growing of corn—less fertile—than do farms of the first type. The unit cost c_H covers the cost of all inputs except land, including

---

[8] The equilibrium number of firms must be an integer. In long-run equilibrium, firms may earn a small economic profit, but not so large that another firm could enter the industry without all firms suffering losses. Since we are dealing with industries for which the equilibrium number of firms is expected to be large, it is safe to treat the equilibrium number of firms as a continuous variable. If the equilibrium number of firms is small, this may not be the case; see Lambson (1987).

Figure 2.6 Differential rent

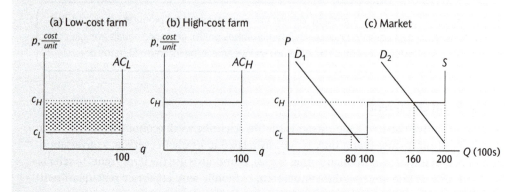

a normal rate of return on investment. The average cost curve of a typical high-cost farm is shown in Figure 2.6(b).

If farms (firms) in this market are price takers, the industry supply curve is as shown in Figure 2.6(c). Up to 100,000 quarters of corn can be supplied, at unit cost c_L, by firms of the first type. An additional 100,000 quarters of corn can be supplied at unit cost c_H, by farms of the second type. The maximum possible quantity supplied in this market is 200,000 quarters of corn.

If the market demand curve is the left-most curve in Figure 2.6(c), D_1, then 80,000 quarters of corn will be supplied at a price c_L per quarter. The long-run competitive equilibrium price just covers the cost of supplying all the inputs needed to produce a quarter of corn, including a normal rate of return on investment. Land—"the original and indestructible powers of the soil"—receives nothing for its services, because for an industry output of 80,000 quarters, land (even high-productivity land) is in excess supply. In the D_1 equilibrium, low-cost land capable of producing 20,000 quarters of corn sits idle. The owners of the land that is in use—whether those owners are owner-farmers or absentee landlords—collect no rent.

If the demand curve shifts outward to D_2, long-run competitive equilibrium output rises to 160,000 quarters of corn, and the competitive equilibrium price rises to c_H. c_H covers all costs of operating a high-cost farm, including a normal rate of return on investment. The income generated by sale of the output of low-cost farms, all of which come into operation when the demand curve is D_2, includes an amount equal to the shaded area in Figure 2.6(a). This amount is $c_H - c_L$ for each quarter of corn grown by a low-cost farm, $100 (c_H - c_L)$ per low-cost farm. It is this income that is an economic rent, an efficiency rent, received by the owner of a low-cost farmland. Whereas the costs of other inputs—costs which enter into c_H—contribute to determining the competitive equilibrium price, rent and rent per unit of output are determined by the competitive price. *Rent is determined by price, not the other way around.*

Quasi-rent

Rent is a payment to an input that exceeds the input's opportunity cost (Buchanan, 1980, p. 3):[9]

---

[9] It seems only fair to note that Buchanan continues "This textbook definition contains ambiguities ... "

Rent is that part of the payment to an owner of resources over and above that which those resources could command in any alternative use. Rent is receipt in excess of opportunity cost. In one sense, it is an allocatively unnecessary payment not required to attract the resources to the particular employment.

For Ricardo, rent is a return received by an input that, like land, is in fixed supply and a gift of nature. A *quasi-rent* is a return above opportunity cost received by a manufactured input, not a gift of nature, that is in fixed supply in the short run.[10]

Quasi-rent includes any short-run return over and above opportunity cost. What, then, is the opportunity cost of a physical asset used by a firm? The answer depends on the extent to which investment in the asset is sunk.

Consider first the case in which an investment in an asset that is *not* sunk. Such an asset can easily be shifted from one market to another. Making allowance for normal wear-and-tear, it can be resold for the original purchase price. In this case, the opportunity cost of investing in the asset in an industry is the normal rate of return on investment. Any return above the normal rate of return on investment is a quasi-rent.

It is also common to define a return above the normal rate of return on investment as economic profit. *A quasi-rent is economic profit.*[11,12] Whether it is useful to have two different names for the same thing is a question we do not pause to consider.

Alternatively, consider a sunk investment. There are degrees of sunkenness. An investment may be completely sunk. A firm deciding whether it is likely to be profitable to enter a new product or geographic market will very likely pay for market studies before it makes a decision. These market studies create an intangible asset, information. The information will be useful to the firm. But if it could be resold at all, it would be for a negligible amount. Such an investment is almost entirely sunk. Investment in tangible assets that are suitable only for highly specific uses—an oil refinery, for example—will also be largely sunk.

Once a completely sunk investment has been made, its opportunity cost is zero. By definition, if an investment is completely sunk, it cannot be liquidated and moved to another market should it fail to earn a normal rate of return on the original investment. Regardless of the expectations investors may have had when they made the decision to make a sunk investment, once the investment is made, *any* positive return is a quasi-rent because the opportunity cost of continuing to use the investment where it is is zero.[13]

---

[10] The distinction between inputs given in fixed supply by nature and manufactured inputs that are in fixed supply over some short run can be unclear. Land may be improved by investments of labour and physical capital—forests may be cleared, deserts may be irrigated. Whatever return is earned by these improvements ought properly to be treated as a quasi-rent rather than an efficiency rent. In practice, the line between the two will be difficult to draw.

[11] Thus in his discussion of Klein and Murphy (1988), Telser (2000, p. 417, emphasis added) writes that they "conjure up the spector of a *quasi rent*, which *is a euphemism for monopoly profit*".

[12] Although quasi-rents are economic profit, not all economic profit is a quasi-rent: see Figure 3.5 and the associated text.

[13] Many firms in deregulated energy industries have complained about the "stranded asset" problem. Stranded assets are highly specific investments that, it is said, were made under regulatory directives with a tacit understanding that investors would be guaranteed at least a normal rate of return. Where technological change makes it feasible to deregulate such an industry and rely instead on market forces for resource allocation, the value of the investments falls. It is the sunk nature of such assets that means investors cannot simply resell them and invest their wealth in other markets.

Between investments that are not sunk at all and investments that are completely sunk are investments that are partially sunk.[14] If a firm does not resell a partially sunk asset and exit its market, the firm may still earn a positive profit, although less than a normal rate of return, until the asset physically depreciates to the point that it can no longer be used. Any return over what could be earned by selling the partially sunk asset at a loss on the original investment and investing the reduced amount that can be recovered elsewhere at a normal rate of return is a quasi-rent.

2.3 Monopoly[15]

2.3.1 Equilibrium

A market is monopolized if it is supplied by one firm *and* the entry of additional firms is impossible. With one difference, the logic behind a monopolist's output decision is the same as the logic behind the output decision of a firm in a perfectly competitive industry. A firm in a perfectly competitive industry is a price taker. If it sells one more unit of output, its revenue changes by the amount received for selling that marginal unit. A monopolist is a price maker. If it sells one more unit of output, the amount it receives for selling that marginal unit increases its total revenue, but price falls, so it collects less revenue per unit sold than it would have if it had not increased sales. Its revenue changes by the amount of marginal revenue, which is less than price (equation (2.4)). Thus, if the monopolist produces an output that makes its marginal cost less than its marginal revenue, the monopolist can increase profit by expanding output. If the monopolist produces an output that makes its marginal cost greater than its marginal revenue, the monopolist can increase profit by reducing output. *If the monopolist produces an output that makes its marginal revenue equal to its marginal cost,*

$$MR = \frac{d(pQ)}{dQ} = p + Q\frac{dp}{dQ} = mc \qquad (2.7)$$

the monopolist maximizes profit. The price at which consumers will just demand this profit-maximizing monopoly output is the monopoly price. Since marginal revenue for any output level is less than price (Figure 2.7), marginal revenue equals marginal cost at a lower output level than price equals marginal cost.[16]

2.3.2 Deadweight Welfare Loss

A monopolist produces a lower output, and charges a higher price, than the long-run equilibrium values of an otherwise identical perfectly competitive industry. The monopolist earns

---

[14] Leaving complications due to physical depreciation aside, if one unit of an asset costs p_A and the asset can be sold for αp_A, with $0 \le \alpha \le 1$, then $(1-\alpha)p_A$ of investment in the asset is sunk. If $\alpha = 0$, investment in the asset is completely sunk. If $\alpha = 1$, none of the investment in the asset is sunk. For positive values of α that are less than one, investment in the asset is partially sunk.

[15] Monopsony, the case of a single buyer facing many small sellers, is the input-market analogue of monopoly. Just as a firm with control over the price consumers pay in the output market may hold price above its perfectly competitive level, so a firm with control over the price input suppliers receive or the wage workers receive may hold input prices or wages below their competitive levels. Applications of the monopsony model and its generalizations to oligopsony include some labour markets and markets for some agricultural products.

[16] What has happened to fixed cost, which determines the shutdown point on the supply curve of a price-taking firm? If fixed cost is so large that monopoly profit is negative, the monopoly is not worth having. The quantity supplied to the market will be zero in a private enterprise system.

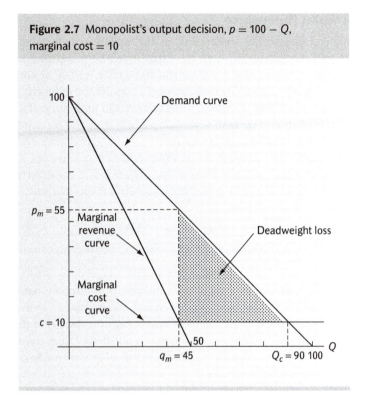

Figure 2.7 Monopolist's output decision, $p = 100 - Q$, marginal cost $= 10$

economic profit, $\pi_m = p_m q_m - C(q_m)$, where q_m is profit-maximizing monopoly output and p_m is the corresponding monopoly price. Consumers who purchase the monopolized product pay more than they would if the industry were perfectly competitive. The extra amount that these consumers pay is economic profit and an income transfer from consumers to producers. Because consumers spend more for the quantity of the monopolized good that they purchase, they have less to spend on other goods. The owners of the firm have more income, to spend as they wish.

Those consumers who would have purchased at the competitive price and do not purchase at the monopoly price lose the surplus value that they would have enjoyed on the output, $Q_c - q_m$, that would have been produced in long-run perfectly competitive equilibrium but is not produced under monopoly. Graphically (Figure 2.7), this lost consumer surplus is the area of the triangle bounded above by the demand curve, below by the marginal cost curve, and on the left by the vertical line at monopoly output. This lost consumer surplus is the *deadweight welfare loss* (DWL) due to the exercise of monopoly power: it is *the reduction in consumer welfare that is not balanced out by an increase in the income of the owners of the firm.*[17]

---

[17] Another result of monopoly output restriction is that consumers do not spend $c(Q_c - q_m)$ in the monopolized industry (where Q_c would be long-run output if the market were perfectly competitive). Instead, they spend this amount in other markets. If other markets are perfectly competitive (and themselves in long-run equilibrium), prices in those other markets are just equal to the average and marginal cost of production. Then there is no gain or loss of consumer surplus in those markets because spending is transferred out of the monopolized market. If

2.3.3 Measuring Market Performance

The characterization of deadweight welfare loss as the welfare cost of monopoly power touches on a deep and contentious issue, an issue that is central to antitrust and competition policy: how should one weight the welfare and changes in welfare of different classes of economic agents in measuring market performance? Consider for simplicity the case of a market in which returns to scale are constant. If the market is in long-run perfectly competitive equilibrium, price equals average cost, economic profit is zero, and consumers enjoy the maximum possible consumer surplus, (say) CS_{max}.

If the industry is supplied by a monopolist, economic profit is positive ($\pi_m > 0$) and consumer surplus is reduced ($CS_m < CS_{max}$). Deadweight welfare loss is the difference between consumer surplus in long-run, perfectly competitive equilibrium and the sum of monopoly profit and monopoly consumer surplus,

$$DWL = CS_{max} - (\pi_m + CS_m). \tag{2.8}$$

The cost *to consumers* of the exercise of market power is the change in consumer surplus,

$$CS_{max} - CS_m. \tag{2.9}$$

Use of deadweight welfare loss as a measure of the cost of monopoly power treats the income gains of the owners of the monopoly firm and lost consumer welfare on a par. Although consumers are worse off by an amount $CS_{max} - CS_m$, the owners of the monopoly are better off by the amount of the economic profit that is transferred from consumers to the firm, π_m, so the loss to consumers *net of the gain to the owners of the firm* is $CS_{max} - CS_m - \pi_m$, and this is the deadweight welfare loss.

Looking at welfare generated rather than welfare lost, if consumer surplus and economic profit are weighted equally, the overall welfare generated in the market is the sum of economic profit and consumer surplus (dropping now, for generality, the subscript m),

$$\pi + CS < CS_{max}. \tag{2.10}$$

Weights

In general, measuring market performance requires making interpersonal welfare comparisons, between the loss of welfare by consumers who pay more for the monopolized product and the increase in income of the owners of the firm. A generalized measure of market performance for a single industry might be written:

$$W = \theta_1 \pi + \theta_2 CS, \tag{2.11}$$

with $0 \leq \theta_1 \leq 1$ and $0 \leq \theta_2 \leq 1$. If $\theta_1 = \theta_2 = 1$, economic profit and consumer surplus are weighted equally in measuring market performance. If $\theta_1 = 0$, $\theta_2 = 1$, market performance is measured by consumer welfare. The question we ask here is, what does economics as a science have to say about the values of the weights θ_1 and θ_2?

The modern literature on this topic begins with Robbins (1932; see also 1938). He emphasized the distinction between positive economics, statements about what is, and normative economics, statements about what ought to be. For Robbins, the positive statements of economics are value neutral, normative statements are not (Robbins, 1982, p. 4):

---

other markets are imperfectly competitive, there will be consumer surplus on some of the spending that is shifted to other markets. In such circumstances, the welfare consequences of output restriction in any one market are ambiguous: lost consumer surplus in a monopolized market may be made up by increases in consumer surplus in other markets. Such *second-best* welfare considerations are taken up by Lipsey and Lancaster (1956–1957).

How desirable it would be if we were able to pronounce as a matter of scientific demonstration that such and such a policy was good or bad. Take, for example, the removal of the protective tariff. Given information about the elasticities of demand and supply of the immediate past, we can certainly make guesses, in price and income terms, about the gains to consumers and the losses to producers of the probable outcome. ... the guesses, such as they are, are on an objective plane. But as soon as we move to the plane of welfare, we introduce elements which are not of that order. ... we are assuming that comparisons between prices and incomes before and after the event can be made a verifiable basis for comparisons between the satisfactions and dissatisfactions of the different persons involved. And that, I would urge, is not warranted by anything which is legitimately assumed by scientific economics.

Hicks-Kaldor compensation principle

Kaldor later advanced the *compensation principle*. If a change in the market reduced one group's welfare and increased the income of other group, the government could always restore the original income distribution by taxing those whose income had gone up and using the receipts to make those whose welfare had gone down as well off as before. If other producers' income was higher even after the taxes, the net effect was positive (Kaldor, 1939, p. 550):

In all cases, therefore, where a certain policy leads to an increase in physical productivity, and thus of aggregate real income, the economist's case for the policy is quite unaffected by the question of the comparability of individual satisfactions; since in all such cases it is possible to make everybody better off than before, or at any rate to make some people better off without making anybody worse off.

Hicks came down on the side of the *compensation principle*, but stood back from the question whether compensation should in fact be made (Hicks, 1939, p. 711):

I do not contend that there is any ground for saying that compensation ought always to be given; whether or not compensation should be given in any particular case is a question of distribution, upon which there cannot be identity of interest, and so there cannot be any generally acceptable principle.

Hicks' view in turn leads to the *potential compensation principle*. Give the welfare losses of one group and the income gains of the other equal weight. If those who gain could be taxed enough to fully compensate those who lose, and those who gain would be better off after paying such taxes, treat the net welfare impact as positive, *whether or not compensation is actually made*.[18] Hicks' purpose in advancing the potential compensation principle was to separate questions of value and questions of distribution:

If measures making for efficiency are to have a fair chance, it is extremely desirable that they should be freed from distributive complications as much as possible.

---

[18] Coleman (1979, 1980) refers to an income redistribution that yields an improvement under the potential compensation standard as *Kaldor-Hicks efficient*. If for a Kaldor-Hicks efficient reallocation, compensation is actually made, the resulting reallocation is Pareto superior, since no agent is made worse off (those who would have lost are compensated) and some are made better off (the gainers). If there is no compensation, a Kaldor-Hicks efficient reallocation is not Pareto-superior to the original allocation, since without compensation some agents (the losers) are made worse off; Coleman (1979, p. 514): " ... a Kaldor-Hicks efficient allocation need neither be Pareto superior nor Pareto optimal though it may be either or both".

Value judgements

But it is Hicks' statement that "here cannot be any generally acceptable principle" on questions of distribution that summarizes the outcome of the extensive debate on this issue. In the words of Chipman and Moore (1978, p. 581):

> After 35 years of technical discussions, we are forced to come back to Robbins' 1932 position. We cannot make policy recommendations except on the basis of value judgments, and these value judgments should be made explicit.

There is no theorem in economics to indicate what the weights in a market performance measure like (2.11) *ought* to be. One often meets the argument that market performance should be measured by an index like (2.11) with $\theta_1 = \theta_2 = 1$ because economics as a science puts forward no reason to treat the welfare of owners of firms and of consumers differently. It is equally correct that economics as a science puts forward no reason to treat the welfare of owners and of consumers identically. Welfare comparisons across groups cannot be made without making value judgements.

Three further points should be made. First, consumer surplus is an index of welfare that is *measured* in (say) euros; economic profit is an income flow that is *measured* in euros. Welfare and income are not the same thing, even if they are measured in the same units.[19]

Second, it is common to speak of profit as going to one group and consumer surplus to another. This need not be the case: some consumers may very well own shares in a firm that charges a price above marginal cost and from which they make some purchases. It is, however, usual to distinguish between income and welfare flows of one and the same person depending on the individual's economic function (as in the familiar circular flow diagram, where the income an individual receives in the labour market is distinguished from the purchases the same individual makes in product markets).

Third, (2.11) is a *partial equilibrium* measure; it refers to a single market. From the point of view of the economy as a whole, defining welfare measures like (2.11) for each market with weights $\theta_1 = 0$, $\theta_2 = 1$ does *not* ignore the welfare of owners of firms that earn economic profit. Such weights measure the welfare of owners of firms in the markets in which they spend their income, not in the markets in which the firms they own generate that income.

2.3.4 Lerner Index of Market Power

Price is equal to marginal cost in the long-run equilibrium of a perfectly competitive industry. Price is greater than marginal cost under monopoly. The *Lerner (1934) index of market power* is the proportional difference between monopoly and competitive prices:

$$\frac{p-c}{p}. \tag{2.12}$$

A monopolist maximizes profit by picking an output that makes marginal revenue equal to marginal cost,

$$MR = c. \tag{2.13}$$

---

[19] In the same way, apples and oranges may be counted or their volume may be measured in (say) bushels. For some purposes, it may be useful to add together the number of bushels of apples and the number of bushels of oranges and report the result as the number of bushels of fruit. Such a calculation does not imply that apples and oranges are perfect substitutes, or that having one more apple compensates for having one less orange.

From equation (2.5), we know that marginal revenue can be expressed in terms of price and the price elasticity of demand, $MR = p\left(1 - \frac{1}{\varepsilon_{Qp}}\right)$. Hence $p\left(1 - \frac{1}{\varepsilon_{Qp}}\right) = c$ for profit-maximizing monopoly output, and the value of the Lerner index for a profit-maximizing monopolist is:

$$\frac{p - c}{p} = \frac{1}{\varepsilon_{Qp}}. \tag{2.14}$$

A monopolist maximizes profit by producing an output that makes the Lerner index of market power equal to the inverse of the price elasticity of demand.

The price elasticity of demand measures the sensitivity of the quantity demanded to price. If the price elasticity of demand is high, a profit-maximizing monopolist will not raise price very much above marginal cost, because to do so would cause the quantity sold to fall so much that profit would fall as well. If the price elasticity of demand is low, the quantity demanded is not very sensitive to price, and a profit-maximizing monopolist will raise price substantially above marginal cost.

2.3.5 Single Supplier with Possible Entry

Just as the word "competition" is often used in the lay sense of "rivalry", so the word "monopoly" is often used to describe a situation in which there is a single active supplier. Figure 2.8 shows the sense in which this usage is misleading.

It shows a market with a demand curve identical to that of Figure 2.7, and supplied by a single firm, but now with another supplier who will put output on the market if price is at least 30. The alternative supplier might be located in another region, in which case the difference between the single local supplier's constant unit cost, 10, and the alternative supplier's constant unit cost could be transportation cost per unit of output shipped into the local market. Or the alternative "supplier" might be one or more small firms, located in the local market, but able to use only a higher-cost technology.[20]

If the product is standardized and consumers have complete and perfect information, then if the single active supplier sets a price above 30, consumers patronize the other firm, and it sells nothing. The single active supplier can sell any amount between zero and 70 units by setting a price just below 30. If it wishes to sell more than 70 units of output, the single active supplier must reduce price below 30 and move down the market demand curve.

Ignoring the small reduction in price below 30 that the single supplier needs to make to undercut the alternative supplier, the single supplier's total revenue function is:

$$TR = \begin{cases} 30q & 0 \leq q \leq 70 \\ (100 - q)\,q & 70 \leq q \leq 100 \end{cases}. \tag{2.15}$$

Its *marginal* revenue function is:

$$MR = \begin{cases} 30 & 0 \leq q \leq 70 \\ 100 - 2q & 70 \leq q \leq 100 \end{cases}. \tag{2.16}$$

---

[20] Judge Learned Hand in the 1916 *Corn Products Refining* decision (234 F. 964 at 975), discussing the situation of a low-cost producer of a product (maltose) facing competition from a higher-cost producer of a perfect substitute, writes "It is quite true that, if for any reason the monopolist of the cheaper material raises the price to that of the dearer, he will at once meet with the competition of the sources of supply so thrown open by his advance. ... his monopoly, where the two commodities compared are indistinguishable in use, is limited by the actual differential in the cost of production between them. Such a monopoly is therefore only a limited one, but within the limits it may be a true one."

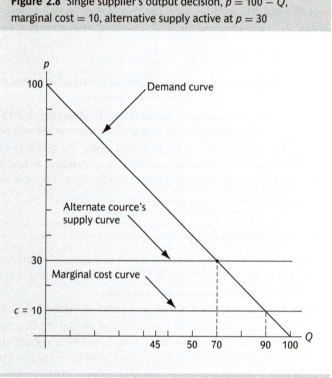

Figure 2.8 Single supplier's output decision, $p = 100 - Q$, marginal cost $= 10$, alternative supply active at $p = 30$

For sales up to 70 units of output, every additional unit of output that the single supplier sells increases its revenue by slightly less than 30, the upper limit on price beyond which it will lose sales to the other supplier. For sales of more than 70 units of output, the single supplier's marginal revenue is negative. The single supplier's profit-maximizing choice is to produce slightly more than 70 units of output, which clear the market at a price slightly less than 30.

What has become of the monopoly profit maximization condition, marginal revenue equals marginal cost? Marginal revenue is discontinuous, 30 for less than 70 units of output and negative for 70 and more units of output. In these circumstances, the profit-maximization condition becomes a pair of inequalities. At the profit-maximizing output, marginal cost is less than the upper value of marginal revenue and greater than the lower value of marginal revenue:

$$30 = MR_-(70) \geq MC = 10 \geq MR_+(70) = -40. \tag{2.17}$$

Here $MR_-(70)$ denotes marginal revenue for a small reduction in sales below 70 units and $MR_+(70)$ denotes marginal revenue for a small increase in sales above 70 units.

The single supplier earns a return:

$$(30 - 10)(70) = 1400. \tag{2.18}$$

The single supplier's marginal cost, 10, includes a normal rate of return on investment. The extra return, 20 per unit sold and 1400 overall, is a quasi-rent and an economic profit. It is more than the zero economic profit that a firm in a perfectly competitive market earns in long-run equilibrium. But it is less than monopoly profit (2025). Simply being the single active supplier in a market does not make a firm a monopolist, if other suppliers have the possibility of coming onto the market.

Whether or not a potential entrant would wish to enter the market if it observes a price greater than 30 depends on what it thinks it would earn in the post-entry market. Whether the single supplier would wish to keep the potential entrant out depends on a comparison between what it thinks it would earn with the entrant out of the market and what it thinks it would earn with the entrant in the market. But there is a ring of plausibility when Kaldor (1950–1951, pp. 20–21) writes that "Under conditions of oligopoly ... we can assume that the prices ruling in an industry are normally set by ... the threat of outside competition, and not by ... the costs of production applicable to 'going concerns'."[21] In such cases, the degree of market power is determined by the price at which entrants will come into the market, not by the inverse of the price elasticity of demand.

> A profit-maximizing monopolist—a single supplier that does not face the threat of entry—maximizes profit by producing an output that makes its marginal cost equal to its marginal revenue. A single supplier that faces the possibility of entry if it should charge the monopoly price either maximizes profit by charging the highest price that will not make entry profitable or else entry occurs and the market becomes an oligopoly.

2.3.6 Rent Seeking and Other Costs of Market Power

Rent seeking

A position of market power may drop like manna from heaven, as in the case of a single car dealership that serves a small town. Such a supplier will not be immune to entry (or, more likely, to the possibility that local consumers may investigate sources of supply in neighboring geographic markets). But it will enjoy at least a modest ability to hold price above marginal cost.

More often, however, a firm that acquires or maintains a position of market power will invest resources to get and keep that position. Such resources may be used to raise the cost of entry; they may be used to advertise;[22] they may be used to lobby the government for protection from the annoying competition of domestic or foreign rivals.[23] Activity devoted to getting and keeping a position of market power is *rent seeking*, and the resources devoted to rent seeking are a social cost of market power.

---

[21] Neufeld gives an example from the early U.S. market for electric power (1987, p. 693, footnote omitted): "[T]he market for artificial lighting was originally served by gas companies, and Edison's initial pricing policies were based not on his production costs but on the cost to his potential customers of gas lighting."

[22] In his study of the credit card market (Section 5.3.3), Ausubel takes note of the lack of price competition in the credit card market, and the diversion of rivalry into non-price competition. This is a form of rent seeking (Ausubel, 1991, p. 75, footnote omitted) "[T]here is a true (and potentially large) deadweight loss when nonprice competition takes the form of advertising. Some banks' reported noninterest expenses increased significantly from 1983 to 1988 even as the intrinsic cost of servicing accounts declined (e.g., Citibank, which advertises on national television); much of the additional expense probably represents marketing, and some fraction of this constitutes social loss."

[23] Under the *Noerr* doctrine (Eastern Railroad Presidents Conference *et al.* v. Noerr Motor Freight Inc., *et al.* 365 U.S. 127), lobbying efforts to persuade the government to adopt policies that restrain trade are not violations of the Sherman Act.

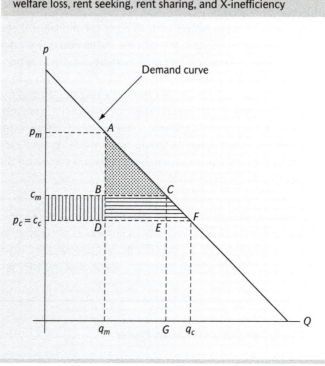

Figure 2.9 Overall welfare impact of market power: deadweight welfare loss, rent seeking, rent sharing, and X-inefficiency

A monopoly supplier of the market illustrated in Figure 2.9,[24] producing with constant marginal and average cost c_m per unit, will generate a deadweight welfare loss equal to the area of the shaded triangle, ABC. Such a firm would collect an economic profit, year after year, in the amount given by the area of the rectangle $p_m ABc_m$. A monopolist or aspiring monopolist would still earn some return (or at least, not lose money) if it spent up to the expected present discounted value of economic profits to obtain the right to enjoy those profits (Tullock, 1967, p. 231). Total spending on rent seeking might be much greater—several firms might compete to get the monopoly; most would have to learn to live with disappointment. If one firm or industry invested in lobbying the government to obtain protection from competition, other economic agents might lobby the government seeking to block the first group.[25] We will use the area $p_m ABc_m$ in Figure 2.9 as an indication of the social cost of rent seeking, while keeping in mind that the actual cost may be much greater.[26]

---

[24] Figure 2.9 is based on Figure 1 of Comanor and Leibenstein (1969).

[25] U.S. steel firms periodically seek protection from the competition of foreign steel producers, and U.S. firms that are major consumers of steel lobby against the granting of such protection.

[26] Posner (1976a) outlines conditions under which, he concludes, rent-seeking expenditures will equal the economic profit $p_m ABc_m$. The conclusion is disputed by Fisher (1985); Fudenberg and Tirole (1987) present examples in which Posner's conclusion does not hold.

Rent sharing

Production cost may exceed competitive levels if the supplier shares some economic profit with the owners of factors of production. Organized labour, for example, may negotiate higher wages and benefits in sectors of the economy where suppliers earn economic profits. If in Figure 2.9 the unit cost of production would be c_c under perfect competition, monopoly means an additional welfare cost in an amount given by the area c_mCFc_c. Part of this social cost is the extra cost of producing the output q_m (c_mBDc_c). A portion of this may be rent sharing, a portion may be X-inefficient waste. Part of the social cost is lost consumer surplus (*BCFD*), lost consumer surplus that is not captured in the shaded area in Figure 2.9.

X-inefficiency

Allocational inefficiency arises if some industries are imperfectly competitive: then overall welfare could be increased by shifting resources from perfectly competitive industries, in which the marginal social benefit and marginal social cost of the incremental unit of output are equal, to imperfectly competitive industries, in which the marginal social benefit of the incremental unit of output exceeds its marginal social cost. There is a welfare loss because resources are misallocated across industries.

Leibenstein (1966) distinguished between allocational inefficiency and the internal-to-the-firm inefficiency that arises if the firm fails to minimize cost. He recognized that inefficiency in this sense is out-of-sync with conventional economic analysis, which simply presumes that firms minimize cost (1966, p. 397). Because the source of welfare losses he analysed fit poorly with neoclassical economics, Leibenstein baptized it "X-inefficiency". Its magnitude was difficult to pin down, but, he argued, might much exceed equally difficult-to-pin-down deadweight welfare loss due to market power. It is likely to have more opportunity to flourish where a supplier is protected from competition (Hand, U.S. *v.* Alcoa, 148 F. 2d 416 at 427):

> Many people believe that possession of unchallenged economic power deadens initiative, discourages thrift and depresses energy; that immunity from competition is a narcotic, and rivalry is a stimulant, to industrial progress; that the spur of constant stress is necessary to counteract an inevitable disposition to let well enough alone.

Overall

Consumers' welfare losses in Figure 2.9 are given by the area p_mAFc_c. The monopolist's profit is given by the area p_mABc_m. If the monopolist's profit and consumer welfare losses are weighted equally, the overall welfare loss due to monopoly power is the difference between consumers' welfare losses and the monopolist's gain, and equals the area c_mBAFc_c.

One element of the social cost of market power is deadweight welfare loss, consumer surplus on output that would be produced in long-run competitive equilibrium but is not produced under monopoly. Market power may also generate social costs due to rent seeking (the expenditure of resources to obtain or maintain market power), rent sharing (payment of more-than-competitive returns to inputs), and X-inefficiency (wasteful organization of production).

2.4 Evidence From Laboratory Markets

2.4.1 Background

Short-run competitive market equilibrium is at the intersection of the market demand curve and the short-run industry supply curve. Long-run competitive market equilibrium is at the intersection of the market demand curve and a particular short-run industry supply curve, the one for which the number of firms has adjusted so that firms earn only a normal rate of return on investment. But we have been studiously vague about how the market gets to the intersection of the demand curve and the pertinent supply curve.

Marshall (1920, pp. 332–334) describes the equilibration of demand and supply in a hypothetical country corn market, with some sellers holding out at first for a price above their marginal cost, some buyers at first offering less than their reservation prices. He expects that "price may be tossed hither and thither like a shuttlecock, as one side or the other gets the better in the 'higgling and bargaining' of the market". He expects also that higgling and bargaining will result in more or less the competitive equilibrium quantity being sold at a closing price near the competitive equilibrium price.

An alternative story about the reaching of market equilibrium, due to Walras ([1926] 1954, p. 242) describes an auctioneer, calling out a tentative price and recording, in virtual time, the quantities firms are willing to supply and consumers to demand at that price. Round after round, the auctioneer adjusts price, upward if there is excess demand, downward if there is excess supply, until the quantity demanded and the quantity supplied are brought to equality. Only when this equality is reached, which occurs at the competitive equilibrium price, does the process of *recontracting* stop and production and exchange take place.

Marshall's "higgling and bargaining" may have more familiar ring than the Walrasian auctioneer. But the higgling and bargaining of Marshall's village corn market has no place in a perfectly competitive market, in which firms and consumers have complete and perfect knowledge and act as price takers.

Arrow (1951) notes that in a market system, all variables, including prices, must be set by some individual agent. Out of equilibrium, he suggests, prices are set by firms, so that perfect competition (1951, p. 41) "can really only prevail at equilibrium".[27]

It is only with the rise of experimental tests of market models that industrial economists have come to grips with the details of the way the equilibration process works, and with the implications that process for market performance. The first known *market* experiment is reported by Chamberlin (1948). He wanted to examine the predictive power of the competitive model in a stylized market in which, realistically, Walrasian recontracting did not occur. Using techniques we discuss in the following section, Chamberlin set up demand and supply sides of a classroom market and allowed student subjects to mill about, offering to buy if on the demand side of the market and offering to sell if on the supply side of the market. As student subjects reached agreement, their deal was recorded and they left the market.

Chamberlin's experimental markets showed prices below, and sales volumes above, the competitive market equilibrium. Chamberlin (1948, pp. 97–98) explained this "excess

---

[27] Arrow also gives up the assumption of complete and perfect information. An interpretation of his analysis, then, is that the model of perfect competition holds only in a run that is long enough for firms and consumers to acquire accurate information.

supply" in terms of trades made at out-of-equilibrium prices. Buyers who would not be willing to pay the competitive equilibrium price might pick up a bargain while milling about on the classroom floor, buying from a seller who did not anticipate that waiting might bring a higher price. Sellers who would lose money from a sale at the competitive equilibrium price might find an unwary buyer who did not anticipate that waiting might bring a lower price. Agreements of either type would push the quantity sold above the competitive equilibrium level.

The absence of recontracting is essential for this result: when two parties make a deal, the agreement is recorded, and they leave the market. Deals are not tentative. There are no later rounds of a virtual auction to reveal the advantages of transacting at a different price.

2.4.2 Experimental Market Demand and Supply

Demand

The nature of the demand side of an experimental market can be determined by assigning *redemption values* to each unit of output that experimental subjects assigned to the demand side of the market are entitled to buy. An example of Smith (1962) is described in Table 2.1.

In this experimental market, one (potential) buyer is given the right to redeem one unit of the good being traded for $3.25 at the end of the period. One buyer is given the right to redeem one unit of the good for $3.00 at the end of the experiment, and so on by 25¢ reductions to the one buyer who is given the right to redeem one unit of the good for $0.75.

If experimental subjects maximize payoffs, the redemption values are nothing other than reservation prices, the highest price the experimental subject will pay for one unit of the product. The redemption values are set by the experimenter. The experimental subject with the highest redemption value will buy nothing at a price above $3.25, will be indifferent between buying and not buying at a price of $3.25, and will enjoy a positive consumer surplus by buying one unit at any price below $3.25. For prices below $3.25, this subject will earn a positive payoff by buying one unit.

The experimental subject with the next-highest redemption value would lose money for a purchase at any price above $3.00, break even on a purchase at a $3.00 price, and earn a positive payoff for a purchase at a price below $3.00. If both these subjects are payoff maximizers, two units of output will be demanded at any price below $3.00 and above $2.75. Continuing the argument in the same way leads to the discontinuous demand curve shown in Figure 2.10.[28]

---

[28] The devil is in the detail, and here we gloss over a host of details. Early market experiments were carried out orally. It is now typical to have market experiments take place over a computer network. Smith (1962) did not actually pay the subjects of his experiments. It is now common to do so. One might nonetheless suspect that if experiments last a long time, or if some subjects know each other outside the laboratory, or if instructions are presented in a way that is not neutral, subjects might deviate from payoff-maximizing behaviour. As the explanation of Table 2.1 should make clear, there are prices at which buyer subjects are indifferent between buying and not buying. In early market experiments, it was common to pay experimental subjects a small commission for each completed trade; this should tip the balance in favour of making a purchase/sale if the payoffs of Tables 2.1 imply indifference.

Davis and Holt (1993, p. 131, fn. 4) suggest that such commissions are now less common in market experiments, since they lack a clear counterpart in naturally-occurring markets. The experimental literature has investigated and generally confirmed the robustness of experimental results reported here to these and other issues. For references, see Davis and Holt (1993), Kagel and Roth (1995).

Table 2.1 Redemption values and implied experimental market demand. Q_d = quantity demanded, TR = total revenue for price at the upper end of the indicated price range, MR = marginal revenue

p	Q_d	TR	MR
$p > 3.25$	0		
$3.25 \geq p > 3.00$	1	3.25	3.25
$3.00 \geq p > 2.75$	2	6.00	2.75
$2.75 \geq p > 2.50$	3	8.25	2.25
$2.50 \geq p > 2.25$	4	10.00	1.75
$2.25 \geq p > 2.00$	5	11.25	1.25
$2.00 \geq p > 1.75$	6	12.00	0.75
$1.75 \geq p > 1.50$	7	12.25	0.25
$1.50 \geq p > 1.25$	8	12.00	−0.25
$1.25 \geq p > 1.00$	9	11.25	−0.75
$1.00 \geq p > 0.75$	10	10.00	−1.25
$0.75 \geq p$	11		

Source: Based on Chart 1, Smith (1962).

Supply

In the same way, the supply side of an experimental market can be set by assigning marginal costs to each unit of output that experimental subjects on the supply side of the market have the right to sell. An example of Smith (1962) is described in Table 2.2. Here no seller is able to supply a unit of output at a cost less than 75¢. For offered prices below 75¢, the quantity offered by payoff-maximizing experimental subjects on the supply side of the laboratory market will be zero. The seller of the lowest marginal cost unit of output is indifferent between selling and not selling at an offered price of 75¢, and will make a positive profit for higher price. For prices greater than 75¢ but less than $1, the quantity supplied should be one unit. At an offered price of $1, there is a supplier who is just indifferent between supplying and not supplying a second unit of output. For prices greater than $1 but less than $1.25, given profit-maximizing supply side behaviour, the quantity supplied will be two units. Continuing in the same way, we obtain the discontinuous competitive market supply curve shown in Figure 2.11.

The competitive equilibrium of this laboratory market is shown in Figure 2.12. In this equilibrium, 6 units will be supplied, and 6 demanded, at a price of $2.00.

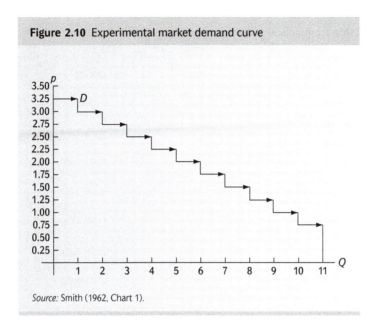

Figure 2.10 Experimental market demand curve

Source: Smith (1962, Chart 1).

2.4.3 Double Auction Competitive Markets

Smith (1962) reports the results of experiments designed as a stylized version of an organized commodity or stock market, which Smith felt would (1962, p. 111) "have the best chance of fulfilling the conditions of an operational theory of supply and demand . . . " Each session of Smith's experiments took place within a class period. He conducted repeated trading periods of five to ten minutes length each. Supply and demand sides of the experimental market were replenished at the start of each trading period. The experiments used the *double auction institution*, which permits buyers to bid prices at which they will buy and sellers to offer prices at which they will sell. In the oral double auction, bids and offers are cried out for the consideration of all participants.

Smith highlights two differences between the double auction institution and Chamberlin's experiments. First, Chamberlin's experiments involved one-on-one bargaining, sequential if need be, until either a deal was concluded or the single experimental session ended. In the double auction mechanism, bids and offers are announced to all participants, giving buyers and sellers information about the entire opposite side of the market. Second, the double auction institution has a sequence of repeated market sessions, allowing buyers and sellers to learn from experience.

Figure 2.13 shows on the left the induced demand and supply curves of Figure 2.11 and on the right, for the first session of five trading periods, the sequence of prices at which trades were made. The treatment changes made by Smith in Chamberlin's experimental design—bids and offers to sell made to all participants and an environment that permits the accumulation of experience—mean a change in results that has proven to be robust to wide variations in experimental design. For many different numbers of buyers and sellers and for alternative shapes of the induced demand and supply curves, experimental transaction

Table 2.2 Marginal cost and implied experimental market supply. Q_s = quantity supplied, MC = marginal cost, TC = total cost

p	Q_s	(MC, TC)
$0.75 > p$	0	$(<0.75, 0)$
$1.00 > p \geq 0.75$	1	$(0.75, 0.75)$
$1.25 > p \geq 1.00$	2	$(1.00, 1.75)$
$1.50 > p \geq 1.25$	3	$(1.25, 3.00)$
$1.75 > p \geq 1.50$	4	$(1.50, 4.50)$
$2.00 > p \geq 1.75$	5	$(1.75, 7.25)$
$2.25 > p \geq 2.00$	6	$(2.00, 9.25)$
$2.50 > p \geq 2.25$	7	$(2.25, 11.50)$
$2.75 > p \geq 2.50$	8	$(2.50, 14.00)$
$3.00 > p \geq 2.75$	9	$(2.75, 16.75)$
$3.25 > p \geq 3.00$	10	$(3.00, 19.75)$
$p \geq 3.25$	11	$(3.25, 23.00)$

Source: Based on Chart 1, Smith (1962).

prices converge promptly to more or less the competitive equilibrium level.[29] Although the standard model of perfectly competitive markets includes no details about the way the market gets to wherever it goes, it does a good job of predicting outcomes in a double auction laboratory market.

2.4.4 Posted-offer Competitive Markets

But the model of perfect competition may perform less well if the market does not use the double auction mechanism. Ketcham *et al.* (1984) report results that are characteristic of the *posted offer* institution, which is designed to resemble the typical retail market. Experimental subjects in a posted-offer market are endowed with supply and demand capabilities in the

---

[29] Joyce (1983) compares the oral double-auction and Chamberlin (meandering about the classroom) institutions, in both cases with and without prices recorded on a blackboard. Joyce does not observe Chamberlin's "excess supply" outcome. In Joyce's experiments, transaction prices converged to the competitive equilibrium for all institutions. Convergence to the competitive price was more rapid, and variance around the competitive price less, the more information was provided to buyers and sellers.

Figure 2.11 Experimental market supply curve

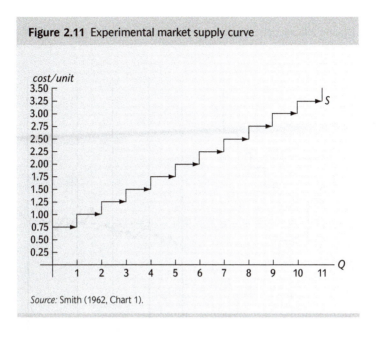

Source: Smith (1962, Chart 1).

Figure 2.12 Competitive equilibrium, experimental market

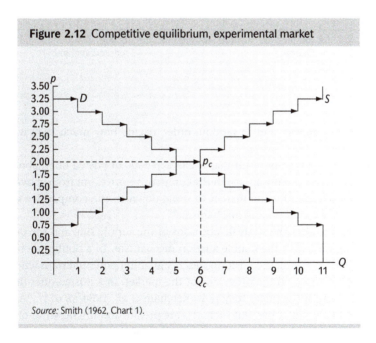

Source: Smith (1962, Chart 1).

general way described in Section 2.4.2. At the start of a period, each experimental subject on the supply side of the market records the price at which he/she will sell and the maximum quantity he/she will sell at that price. These offers, once posted, are fixed for the length of the trading period. After all offers are posted, experimental subjects on the demand side of

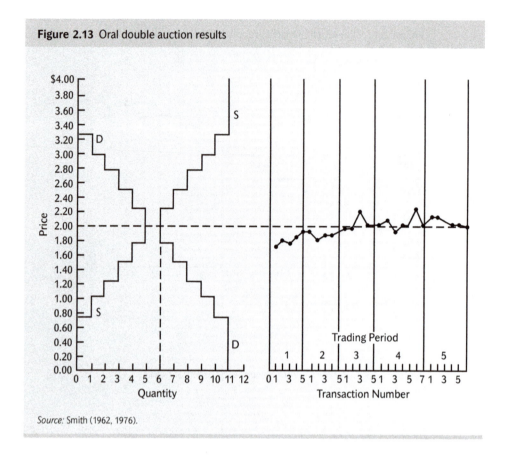

Figure 2.13 Oral double auction results

Source: Smith (1962, 1976).

the market, one after another and in random order, decide how much they will buy and from which suppliers.[30]

Figure 2.14 shows one type of result that is characteristic of posted-offer laboratory markets: transaction prices eventually approach the competitive price, but from above, and more trading periods are required for the market to settle down to the competitive equilibrium than with the double auction trading mechanism.[31]

Posted-offer markets alter the strategic positions of the supply side and the demand side of the market, compared with the double auction mechanism. In a double auction market, buyers and sellers are in symmetric positions, each signalling potential transaction prices to all parties, not just to those on the other side of the market. In a posted-offer market, only sellers signal, by means of the prices they post (Ketcham *et al.*, 1984, p. 611): "A buyer may accept or refuse to accept any offer, but such acts are private and unknown to other buyers. Since only sellers can signal, this favors the possibility of tacit collusion among sellers to coordinate an increase in prices."

---

[30] This brief description omits a wealth of detail, for which the reader may consult Ketcham *et al.* (1984).

[31] For comparison purposes, Ketcham *et al.* report the results of double auction experiments. These results are similar to those described in Figure 2.13: convergence to the competitive equilibrium price after four trading periods.

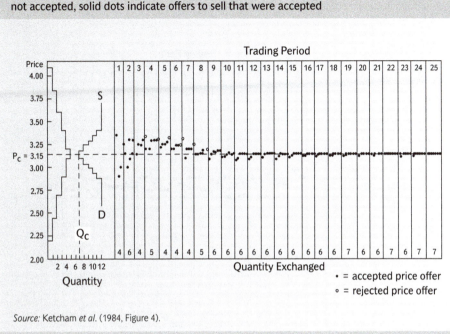

Figure 2.14 Posted offer experimental results. Hollow dots indicate offers to sell that were not accepted, solid dots indicate offers to sell that were accepted

Source: Ketcham *et al.* (1984, Figure 4).

Figure 2.15 shows results of another posted-offer experiment. In contrast to the session described in Figure 2.14, transaction prices in the session shown in Figure 2.15 never settle down to the competitive level. Rather, there are persistent high posted prices (the hollow dots) that seem intended to lure other suppliers to set prices that float above competitive equilibrium.

We will return to the economics of tacit collusion in Chapter 6. The present discussion allows us to draw one of the main lessons of laboratory methods for industrial economics: *institutions matter*. Differences in the details of the way prices are set, the processes by which suppliers interact with other suppliers, buyers interact (or do not interact) with other buyers, and suppliers interact with buyers, lead to fundamental differences in market performance.

2.4.5 Double Auction Monopoly Markets

The demand function of Table 2.1 implies a marginal revenue function.[32] The marginal revenue as each additional unit of output is sold is the change in total revenue (Table 2.1). This change is the revenue generated by sale of an additional unit minus the revenue lost

---

[32] Strictly speaking, since units sold can change only by discrete, integer amounts, we should speak of "incremental revenue" rather than of "marginal revenue".

Figure 2.15 Posted offer experimental results. Hollow dots indicate offers to sell that were not accepted, solid dots indicate offers to sell that were accepted

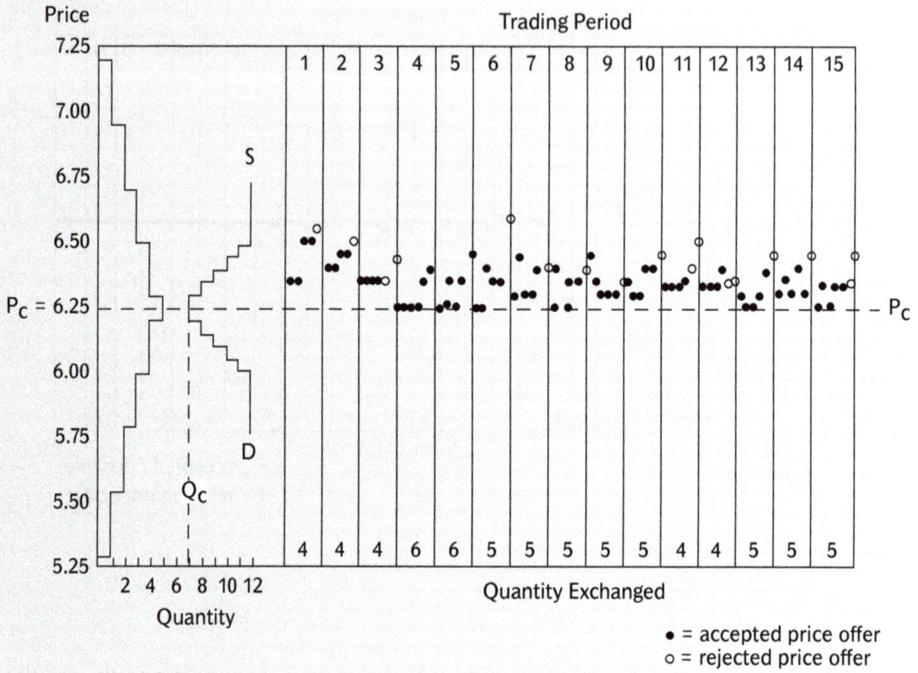

Source: Ketcham et al. (1984, Figure 5).

on units that might have been sold at a higher price. The marginal revenue curve for the demand curve of Figure 2.10 is shown in Figure 2.16.

If the market is served by a single supplier, that supplier's profit-maximizing output makes its marginal revenue equal to its marginal cost. If we reinterpret the marginal cost figures of Table 2.2 as applying to a single firm, profit is maximized for four units of output, sold at a monopoly price of $2.50. The monopoly outcome is depicted in Figure 2.17. This compares with the competitive output of six units and the competitive price of $2.00 (Figure 2.12).

The results of a monopoly double auction experiment reported by Smith (1981a) are shown in Figure 2.18. The supply side of this experiment had one seller able to sell up to 10 units of output, at costs determined by an experimental marginal cost curve. The demand side of the experiment had five buyers, each able to buy up to 2 units of output that could be redeemed for specified values at the end of the experiment. Transaction prices were above or near the monopoly price in the first two trading periods, then fell toward and eventually below the competitive price level. In another experiment reported in the same paper (Smith's Chart 2), transaction prices began above the monopoly level, as in Figure 2.18,

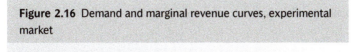

Figure 2.16 Demand and marginal revenue curves, experimental market

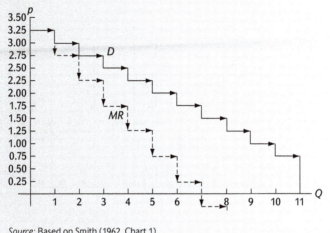

Source: Based on Smith (1962, Chart 1).

Figure 2.17 Monopoly equilibrium, experimental market

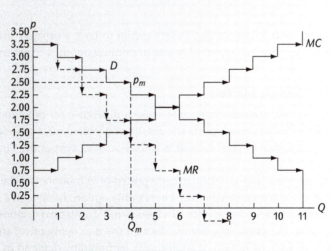

Source: Based on Smith (1962, Chart 1).

and fell toward the competitive price, remaining somewhat above it. In a double auction laboratory environment, five buyers seem to be few enough to invalidate the predictive power of the monopoly model. Smith writes (1981a, p. 90), "the most characteristic feature of these monopoly experiments is the remarkable bargaining resistance of the buyers. In

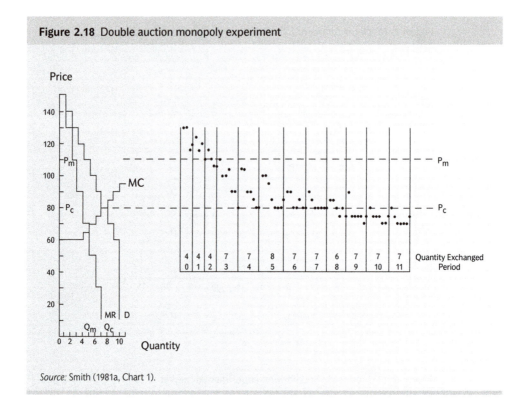

Figure 2.18 Double auction monopoly experiment

Source: Smith (1981a, Chart 1).

double-auction trading with a single seller, buyers appear to have a capacity for tacit collusion against the seller that has not appeared before in nonmonopolistic experiments."

2.4.6 Posted-offer Monopoly Markets

With monopoly supply, institutions once again make a difference for outcomes in experimental markets. Smith (1981a) also reports the results of a posted-offer monopoly experiment with one seller and five buyers, each able to buy at most two units. The results are shown in Figure 2.19.

Among the institutions he studies, Smith expects posted-offer monopoly to be most favorable to the supply side of the market, since the buyer's only option, faced with a high posted price, is not to buy and hope for a lower price in a later round. Smith's expectations are borne out. By the sixth period, the single supplier had located the monopoly price, and afterward stuck to it. Buyers, who had the option of strategically withholding demand in attempts to evoke lower future prices, failed to do so. The monopoly model predicts well for a posted-offer environment.[33]

---

[33] Coursey *et al.* (1984b) report some episodes of demand withholding in posted-offer monopoly experiments where the single supplier was given a declining average cost curve. In such a market, if a buyer withholds an incremental, low-cost, purchase, the buyer costs the supplier its most profitable sales. This creates a powerful incentive for the supplier to hold price down and avoid demand withholding. Coursey *et al.* cite the aircraft industry as a naturally occurring market with characteristics that may match those of their experimental market.

Figure 2.19 Posted offer monopoly experiment

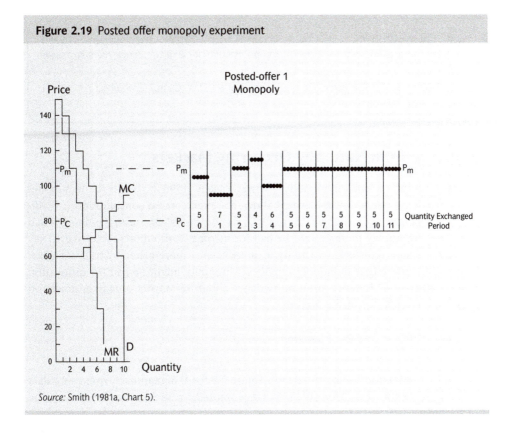

Source: Smith (1981a, Chart 5).

BOX   A Naturally Occurring, Bulletin-Board Market

Very soon after capture people realized that it was both undesirable and unnecessary, in view of the limited size and the equality of supplies, to give away or to accept gifts of cigarettes or food. "Goodwill" developed into trading as a more equitable means of maximising individual satisfaction.

We reached a transit camp in Italy about a fortnight after capture and received 1/4 of a Red Cross food parcel each a week later. At once exchanges ... multiplied in volume. Starting with simple direct barter, such as a non-smoker giving a smoker friend his cigarette issue in exchange for a chocolate ration, more complex exchanges soon became an accepted custom. ...

In this camp we did not visit other bungalows very much and prices varied from place to place; ... By the end of the month, when we reached our permanent camp, there was a lively trade in all commodities and their relative values were well known, and expressed not in terms of one another ... but in terms of cigarettes. The cigarette became the standard of value. In the permanent camp people started by wandering through the bungalows calling their offers—"cheese for seven" (cigarettes)—and the hours after parcel issue were Bedlam. The inconveniences of this system soon led to its replacement by an Exchange and Mart notice board in every bungalow, where under the headings "name", "room number", "wanted" and "offered" sales and wants were advertised. When a deal went through, it was crossed off the board. The public and semi-permanent ❯❯

> ≫ records of transactions led to cigarette prices being well known and thus tending to equality throughout the camp, although there were always opportunities for an astute trader to make a profit from arbitrage.
>
> Source: Radford, R. A. "The economic organization of a P.O.W. Camp", Economica n.s. 12(48), November 1945, pp. 189–201.

2.5 Evidence from Naturally Occurring Markets

"The trouble with the textbook monopolist", writes Vickers (1996, p. 11) "is that it supplies too few widgets. Price per widget is elevated above marginal cost, so consumption is inefficiently low, and a deadweight triangle loss results." He continues "Of course it is about much more than that. Monopoly profits might be bad for income distributional objectives. They might induce wasteful rent-seeking activity. Cost efficiency more generally might slacken because of the quiet life that monopoly provides. Monopoly might be bad for innovation and dynamic efficiency." Here we examine evidence about the impact of market power on performance in naturally occurring markets.

2.5.1 Deadweight Loss and Rent Seeking

Harberger

Harberger (1954) estimates the shaded area in Figure 2.9 for U.S. manufacturing using data on 73 industries for the years 1924–1928. What is wanted for such a measurement is the value of the area:

$$\frac{1}{2}(\Delta p)(-\Delta q),$$ (2.19)

where $-\Delta q > 0$ is output restriction compared with the output that would be demanded if price were c_m and Δp is the corresponding price increase.[34]

Studies of cost and production functions suggest that most firms in most industries produce where returns to scale are constant (Martin, 2004a). Assume this to be the case, so that average cost equals marginal cost. Then the formula (2.19) for the area of the Harberger deadweight welfare loss triangle can be rewritten as:

$$\frac{1}{2}r^2\varepsilon_{qp}p_mq_m,$$ (2.20)

where

$$r = \frac{p_mq_m - c_mq_m}{p_mq_m}$$ (2.21)

is the profit-sales ratio, ε_{qp} is the price elasticity of demand, and p_mq_m is revenue.[35]

Business records allow one to measure revenue and the accounting rate of return on sales. To measure the economic rate of return on sales, r, one must adjust the accounting rate of return on sales to allow for a normal rate of return on investment, the opportunity cost of having firms invest in an industry. Harberger used the average rate of return on capital for

---

[34] Harberger did not consider the possibility that average cost might be higher, the less competitive an industry.

[35] Thus $\frac{1}{2}(\Delta p)(-\Delta q) = \frac{1}{2}(\Delta p)^2\left(-\frac{\Delta q}{\Delta p}\right) = \frac{1}{2}\left(\frac{\Delta p}{p_m}\right)^2\left(-\frac{p_m}{q_m}\frac{\Delta q}{\Delta p}\right)p_mq_m = \frac{1}{2}\left(\frac{p_mq_m-c_mq_m}{p_mq_m}\right)^2\left(-\frac{p_m}{q_m}\frac{\Delta q}{\Delta p}\right)p_mq_m$, and the final expression is (2.20). See Harberger's fn. 2.

the 73 industries in his sample as an estimate of the normal rate of return on investment, and with this, along with accounting values of the industries' capital stocks, he adjusted accounting rates of return on sales to get approximate economic rates of return on sales.

Finally, Harberger made the judgement that the price elasticities of demand for the industries in his sample were relatively low, and assumed that all the elasticities were one. On this basis, Harberger estimated deadweight welfare loss due to market power for the 73 industries in his sample. Then assuming that the level of deadweight welfare loss in these 73 industries was typical of manufacturing as a whole, he reached the result that monopoly deadweight welfare losses were about one-tenth of 1 per cent of U.S. national income.

Cowling and Mueller

Cowling and Mueller (1978) make four observations about Harberger's methodology. The first is that Harberger works with industry profit rates. If some firms in an industry are earning economic profits through the exercise of market power, and others (through bad luck or bad management) are making economic losses, net industry profit will underestimate economic profit. This in turn will result in an underestimate of the area of the deadweight welfare loss triangle.

A second observation is that Harberger's figure for the normal rate of return on investment—the average over all the industries in his sample—will include some return that is due to market power. Harberger's figure for the normal rate of return on investment is therefore too high. When it is used to reduce accounting rates of return and obtain an estimated economic rate of return on sales, the resulting figure will be too small.

A third observation relates to Harberger's use of a unit price elasticity of demand.[36] If firms in an industry manage to maximize industry profit, we have the Lerner index relationship between the price-cost margin and the price elasticity of demand, equation (2.14).[37] In the notation of equation (2.21),

$$\frac{p_m - c_m}{p_m} = \frac{p_m q_m - c_m q_m}{p_m q_m} = r = \frac{1}{\varepsilon_{qp}}. \tag{2.22}$$

Substituting $\varepsilon_{qp} = 1/r$ in (2.20) gives an alternative expression for the size of the deadweight welfare loss welfare triangle,

$$\frac{1}{2}r^2\left(\frac{1}{r}\right)p_m q_m = \frac{1}{2}r p_m q_m$$

$$= \frac{1}{2}\frac{p_m q_m - c_m q_m}{p_m q_m}p_m q_m = \frac{1}{2}\left(p_m q_m - c_m q_m\right) = \frac{1}{2}\pi_m, \tag{2.23}$$

one-half of economic profit.

Cowling and Mueller's final observation is that Harberger does not attempt to measure the cost of rent seeking.

Cowling and Mueller make alternative deadweight welfare loss estimates for the United States and for the United Kingdom, using both Harberger's methodology and their own approach. For their own estimates, they work with firm rather than industry profit rates. Firms making economic losses are treated as earning zero economic profits, so that losses of

---

[36] This assumption is also questioned by Stigler (1956).

[37] This analysis can be generalized, using a conjectural variation approach, to the case of economic profit that falls short of joint profit maximization.

Table 2.3 Alternative estimates of the welfare cost of market power, U.S. and UK. "H" indicates Harberger methodology, "C&M" indicates Cowling and Mueller methodology. U.S. figures: 1963–1969. UK figures: 1968–1969. Both measured as a percentage of corporate output

	U.S.		UK	
	DWL	DWL + rent seeking	DWL	DWL + rent seeking
H	0.40	7.39	0.21	3.05
C&M	3.96	13.14	3.86	7.20

Source: Cowling and Mueller (1978, Table 2, Table 4).

such firms do not offset the economic profits of other firms. As an estimate of the normal rate of return on investment, they use a stock-market figure for the United States, and Bank of England data for the United Kingdom. Both are likely to be less contaminated by monopoly profit than an average of industry profit rates.

Cowling and Mueller treat advertising expenses as expenditures on rent seeking,[38] so that economic profit is the sum of accounting profit and spending on advertising. Including spending on advertising and economic profit, applying (2.23) to the result, and subtracting taxes yields the Cowling and Mueller expression for welfare loss due to the exercise of market power (Littlechild, 1981):

$$\frac{3}{2}\left(\pi_m + p^A A\right) - T. \tag{2.24}$$

The resulting estimates, all made with samples of firm rather than industry data, are shown in Table 2.3. The Harberger-style estimate of deadweight welfare loss alone, using observations on firms, is four times Harberger's result (0.4 as opposed to 0.1). For both the U.S. and the UK, using the Lerner-index formula to evaluate the price-elasticity of demand increases estimated deadweight welfare loss to near 4 per cent of corporate output. Adding in estimated rent seeking expenditures results in a further substantial increase, by a factor of more than three for the U.S. and nearly double for the UK.

Jenny and Weber

When Jenny and Weber (1983) apply the Harberger methodology to French manufacturing industry data for the years 1967–1970, their estimate of deadweight welfare loss due the exercise of market power is one-tenth of 1 per cent of gross domestic product, essentially the same value that Harberger obtained for the United States. In an alternative set of estimates, they identified industries surrounded by high barriers to entry and for those industries used the Lerner index (2.22) to measure the price elasticity of demand. If barriers to entry into

---

[38] Peterson and Connor (1996, p. 241) estimate consumer welfare losses for U.S. food manufacturing industries for 1979–1980 at between "7.4 percent and 8.7 percent of branded food shipments to retail food stores". About 60 per cent of this consumer welfare loss occurred in 15 (p. 243) "heavily advertised, high-value-added [5-digit SIC] consumer products". See also the discussion of credit card advertising in fn. 22.

an industry were low, they assumed incumbents would be in a situation like that depicted in Figure 2.8, maximizing profit under the threat of entry, and setting a price below the unconstrained profit-maximizing level, which implies low price elasticity of demand. For these industries, they retained Harberger's assumption that the price elasticity of demand was one. This approach lead them to estimate welfare loss at 1.26 per cent of gross domestic product.

Resumé

It is likely that Harberger's results underestimate the extent of welfare losses from market power, in particular because of his assumption that the price elasticity of demand equals one. Cowling and Mueller's results probably overestimate the extent of welfare losses from market power, in particular because of their use of the joint-profit-maximization Lerner index. But there are other sources of welfare loss from market power that are not considered by either study.

2.5.2 Rent Sharing

Ng and Seabright (2001) compare the operations of less-regulated U.S. airlines and more-regulated European airlines in the early 1990s. In this industry, restrictions on competition and public ownership seem both to have supported higher wages. Ng and Seabright estimate that if a European airline faced competition from a third airline on an international route, supranormal employee wages would fall 3 per cent, and the airline's costs 2 per cent. They estimated that a 10 percentage point reduction in public ownership would reduce supranormal wages 10 per cent and airline costs 6.5 per cent (in both cases, all else equal). Overall, they (2001, p. 614) "estimate that European Union carriers' costs between 1990–5 were on average some 26 per cent above what they might be under United States conditions, though falling to under 20 per cent towards the end of that period".

Neven *et al.* (2006) examine wages and price-cost margins in the European passenger airline industry for the years 1976–1994, taking into account that wages are determined by bargaining between unions and airlines. Their results suggest that union bargaining pushed fares up around 11 per cent, essentially to the monopoly level, while price–cost margins fell from 47 per cent to 32 per cent. During this period, European air passengers paid monopoly fares, while unions appropriated a large part of monopoly-level profits in the form of higher wages.[39]

2.5.3 Inefficiency

In Section 2.3.6 we introduced the notion that competition in the sense of rivalry improves market performance because it promotes static and dynamic efficiency. We leave the impact of rivalry on innovation for our discussions of Joseph Schumpeter's views on the market structure-technological performance relationship, but here consider evidence on the proposition that product-market rivalry, by stimulating managerial effort, increases the efficiency of operations within firms, so reducing costs, conserving resources, and improving market performance.

---

[39] For other evidence consistent with the view that organized labour is able to share some portion of economic rents, see Blanchflower *et al.* (1996), Fakhfakh and FitzRoy (2002).

Scherer *et al.* (1975, pp. 74–75) report that:

Our interviews provided considerable qualitative evidence [of] pure X-inefficiency … A tour through a European cigarette plant, for example, revealed that the machines were essentially the same as those used in other countries, but that "traditional" machine manning standards were much looser. Executives in several British industries admitted that productivity had hovered at low levels because cartel arrangements fostered complacent attitudes. Sharp improvements were achieved in two cases after competition emerged following cartel dissolutions induced by the Restrictive Trade Practices Act. A well-traveled American paint industry official reported that on his visits to European plants he saw "lots of people hanging around, unneeded," especially in a nation with a history of cartelization among paint makers.

Sakakibara and Porter present evidence on the impact of domestic rivalry on the export performance of Japanese industries. Controlling for differences across industries in other factors expected to affect the share of Japanese firms in world exports, they find that this share is larger, the more unstable are the shares of leading firms in the Japanese market (their index of the intensity of domestic market rivalry). They also find that Japanese firms have a larger share of world exports, the more they spend on research and development (as a fraction of value added), and a smaller share of world exports, the more the Japanese market is protected from foreign competition. These results are that for firms that operate in international markets, intense home-market competition improves performance on the world stage. They are consistent with the hypothesis that home-market rivalry reduces X-inefficiency, improving home-market performance and competitiveness in export markets.

Hay and Liu (1997) directly test the hypothesis that rivalry reduces X-inefficiency. For 19 UK manufacturing industries in the 1970s and 1980s, they estimate the determinants of how nearly firms approach least-cost production. They find that losses in market share and increases in efficiency by a firm's rivals both stimulate a firm to increase its own efficiency.[40]

 BOX   **Franchise Management and Efficiency**

Shelton (1967) compares the profitability of 22 outlets of an anonymous U.S. franchise restaurant chain.

The franchisor rigidly specified every aspect of franchise operations—menu, ingredients, place settings, waitresses' dialogues with customers. The franchisor handled accounting and directly paid an outlet's bills, later to be reimbursed by the franchisee.

Outlets differed in one significant characteristic. The franchisor preferred that outlets be owned and operated by franchisees without prior experience in the restaurant industry, because (p. 1254) "those with prior restaurant experience are likely to think they know so much about the business that they try to install practices other than those specified by the franchisor". But in the normal course of events, franchise owner-operators would occasionally withdraw from the business. ❯❯

---

[40] In similar studies using plant-level data for Australia, Britain, Canada, Japan, Korea, and the United States, Caves and co-researchers find (1992, pp. 11–13) that industry concentration reduces efficiency. Import competition increases efficiency for the U.S. and Britain, reduces it for Canada and Japan. For the U.S., firm diversification reduced efficiency; this confirms an earlier result of Caves and Barton (1992).

>> The franchisor would arrange a successor, but during the transition period, the outlet would be managed by an experienced company employee. Company managers were eligible for bonuses, depending on outlet profitability. The bonuses could reach one-third of the manager's salary, and averaged 15 per cent.

Comparing 22 restaurants where there were one or more changes between franchisee-operator and company manager or between company manager and franchise-owner, the rate of profit as a fraction of sales was higher for franchise operators in all but three cases (p. 1257):

> The profit margins [profit/sales] for [franchisee-operators] averaged 9.5 per cent; the profit margins for [company managers] averaged 1.8 per cent. ... Only two of the 29 observations where [franchisee-operators] were in charge showed losses; in contrast 11 of the 24 cases where [company managers] were running the restaurants showed loss operations.

The greater profitability of franchisee-managed outlets confirms the franchisor's view that more attentive management at the outlet level increases efficiency (p. 1257):

> We don't think there is much change in sales when a restaurant is operated by a franchisee-owner instead of a company manager, but we do think profits go up. This is because franchisee-owners just watch the little things closer; they utilize the cooks and waitresses better; they reduce waste.

Source: Shelton (1967).

2.5.4 Distributional Effects

Economists' primary concern with market power has been its impact on resource allocation. When price rises because of market power raises price, the quantity demanded falls. From the point of view of society as a whole, not enough of the good is produced, and resources are diverted to the production of other goods and services that have a lower value.

Hostility toward great accumulations of wealth, which (correctly or incorrectly) were associated with the trusts, was part of the public debate in the run-up to passage of the Sherman Act. It has also sometimes been a concern of economists (Robinson, 1941, p. 169):

> [I]n some, though not all, cases a monopoly might be more efficient than in a group of competing firms. If that is the case, for any given output fewer resources will be required. But since the monopoly raises the price of the product, some or all of these resources will be more highly rewarded than they would be under competitive conditions. There will thus be a transfer of purchasing power from consumers to the producers of the monopolized goods. Thus society is better off in the sense that these goods have required fewer resources to bring them into existence; it may at the same time be worse off to the extent that purchasing power has been transferred from one group to another group. The practical problems of monopoly are thus very largely concerned with the issue of the better or worse distribution of wealth.

Siegfried *et al.* (1995) summarize and analyse the results of a set of studies matching existing large fortunes in selected industrialized countries with the industries in which those fortunes originated.[41]

---

[41] In addition to the studies cited by Siegfried *et al.* (1995), see Hazledine and Siegfried (1997).

Table 2.4 Proportion of large fortunes generated in competitive and non-competitive manufacturing industries in Australia, Great Britain, and the United States

	Number of manufacturing fortunes	Manufacturing fortunes as a percentage of total fortunes	Percentage of fortunes arising in competitive industries	Percentage of fortunes arising in non-competitive industries
Australia	56.5	21.5	35.4	64.6
Great Britain	43.5	21.8	65.5	34.5
United States	76.5	28.9	37.3	62.7

Source: Siegfried *et al.* (1995, Table III).

Initial lists of wealthy individuals were taken from the popular business press.[42] The industries in which their fortunes had originated were identified. The industries were then classified as "competitive" or "non-competitive" by a panel of (country-specific) economists. An industry was classified as competitive if the panel viewed the industry as being (Siegfried *et al.*, 1995, p. 278) "sufficiently competitive that expected long-run equilibrium economic profits at the margin are negligible". The overall results were that "73 percent of the British fortunes, 67.5 percent of the U.S. fortunes, and 76.6 percent of the Australian fortunes" originated in competitive industries.

Table 2.4 shows the Siegfried *et al.* results for manufacturing industries. It is in the manufacturing sector that market power seems to have been most important in the accumulation of wealth, at least for Australia and the United States.

That so much continuing great wealth has arisen in competitive sectors of these economies is not so paradoxical as might at first appear. As Siegfried *et al.* note (1995, p. 283), "Competitive market theory predicts that *expected* profits *on the margin* will be no larger than opportunity costs (or will equal 'normal profits') when the market *attains equilibrium.*"

Even in a perfectly competitive market, economic profit is zero only in long-run equilibrium. On the way to long-run equilibrium, some firms may earn economic profits. Indeed, it is the lure of such profits that triggers entry.

In short-run equilibrium, some firms may be more efficient than others. Unless and until imitation whittles away at those differences, the more efficient firms will collect an economic profit that is an efficiency rent (Figure 2.6).

Even if expected risk-adjusted profits have been equalized on investments throughout the economy, it is realized profits that influence the distribution of income. The wealth that originates in competitive sectors of the economy may simply be the accumulations of those whose investments, luckily, earned more than expected.

In industrialized countries, stock ownership is now widespread. It may therefore be that contemporary monopoly profit is distributed widely throughout the economy, or at least, more widely than was once the case. Finally, account should be taken of the fact that when

---

[42] *Fortune* magazine, for example, regularly publishes lists of wealthy U.S. citizens.

Siegfried *et al.* study the origin of contemporary great fortunes, their sample includes fortunes of respectable vintage and also fortunes of contemporary origin. The adage "from shirtsleeves to shirtsleeves in three generations"[43] should not be lost sight of. The Siegfried *et al.* results do not speak to the possibility that, for example, the exercise of monopoly power in the late nineteenth-century United States generated great fortunes that were dissipated, perhaps in rent-seeking or rent-preserving expenditures, by the time of World War I or the Great Depression.

SUMMARY

Like all models, the models of perfect competition and monopoly are simplified versions of the reality they purport to describe. In the abstract model of perfect competition, no one economic agent can affect the equilibrium outcome. The decisions of individual price-taking consumers, in the aggregate, determine market demand. The decisions of individual price-taking firms determine market supply. "Market processes" make the quantity demanded equal to the quantity supplied. Freedom of entry and exit ensure that the long-run equilibrium price of a perfectly competitive market is the lowest price that will not cause firms to suffer economic losses and the highest price that will not permit them to enjoy economic profits.

In the abstract model of monopoly, the single supplier of a market into which further entry is impossible determines the equilibrium outcome, given consumer behavior as summarized by the demand curve. The single supplier's choice of quantity supplied determines price, the reduction in consumer welfare, economic profit, and deadweight welfare loss. The choice of quantity supplied depends on the supplier's objective—to maximize profit—and the price elasticity of demand, which measures the sensitivity of quantity demanded to changes in price. The equilibrium degree of monopoly power—the Lerner index—is the inverse of the price elasticity of demand.

A single supplier that faces the possibility of entry can maintain a pseudo-monopoly position by committing to a price below the unit cost of potential entrants. If that is the most profitable option, the equilibrium price is the highest price that will not permit an entrant to come into the market and earn a normal rate of return on investment.

The predictions of the competitive model consistently succeed in predicting outcomes in experimental markets designed to resemble organized real-world markets. The predictive power of the monopoly model in experimental markets, in contrast, depends on the details of institutional design. Double auction monopoly markets often exhibit prices around the competitive level. The results of posted-offer monopoly markets are closer to the predictions of the monopoly model.

The welfare costs of monopoly include deadweight welfare loss, expenditures on rent seeking, rent sharing, and X-inefficiency. Estimates of the size of these welfare costs are necessarily rough, but suggest that they are large enough to merit policy attention. There is little evidence of an enduring impact of income redistribution due to market power on the distribution of wealth.

STUDY POINTS

- perfect competition
  - price elasticity of demand (Section 2.2.1)
  - marginal revenue (Section 2.2.1)

---

[43] Or, if one prefers, "From clogs to clogs in only three generations."

- consumer surplus (Section 2.2.1)

- cost concepts (Section 2.2.2)

- rent and quasi-rent (Section 2.2.5)

- monopoly

   - deadweight welfare loss (Section 2.3.2)

   - measuring market performance (Section 2.3.3)

   - Lerner index of market power (Section 2.3.4)

   - single supplier with possible entry (Section 2.3.5)

- experimental markets

   - imputed demand and supply curves (Section 2.4.2)

   - double auction experimental markets (Section 2.4.3, Section 2.4.5)

   - posted-offer experimental markets (Section 2.4.4, Section 2.4.6)

- market power and market performance in natural markets

   - deadweight welfare loss (Section 2.5.1)

   - X-inefficiency (Section 2.5.3)

   - wealth effects (Section 2.5.4)

   - rent-sharing (Section 2.3.6)

FURTHER READING

Ekelund (1971–1972) documents the efforts of 19th-century U.S. and European railway engineers to esti-mate empirical cost functions.

See Stigler (1957) for a review of the development of the model of perfect competition. On the concept of consumers' surplus, see Hicks (1941), Houghton (1958), Willig (1976), Hausman (1981), Weitzman (1988), and Samuelson (1990).

On rent, see Marshall (1892/1909, Appendix C; 1893), Stigler (1939; 1941, pp. 87–97), Worcester (1946), Dewey (1994), and McChesney (1998). On some aspects of partially sunk costs, see Martin (2002b).

For discussions of interpersonal welfare comparisons, see Robbins (1932, 1938, 1981), Hicks (1939), Chipman and Moore (1978), Coleman (1979), and Martin (2007b, Section 4). Kirkwood (2004, pp. 4–7, pp. 28–36) contrasts the antitrust implications of consumer welfare and net social welfare as measures of market performance.

Berczi (1979) discusses Chamberlin's (1948) experiments. Roth (1995) surveys experimental tests of individual decision-making. For other surveys of experimental economics, see Plott (1982), Davis and Holt (1993, pp. 5–9), Holt (1995), Wellford (2002), and Holt (2006).

On rent seeking, see among others Krueger (1974), Tullock (1967), Posner (1976a), Buchanan (1980), and Fudenberg and Tirole (1987); Ekelund *et al.* (1997) present a case study from medieval Spain. Jenny and Weber (1983, pp. 113–121) and Willner and Ståhl (1992) give clear summaries of the literature that estimates the welfare costs of market power; the latter contains welfare loss estimates for Finnish industries.

See Stigler (1976) for a critique of X-inefficiency, and for surveys Siegfried and Wheeler (1981), and Frantz (1997). Vickers (1995) is a valuable presentation of the conceptual issues.

PROBLEMS

Asterisks indicate advanced problems.

2–1 Find monopoly output, price, deadweight welfare loss, and the Lerner index if the equation of the market inverse demand curve is:

$$p = 100 - Q$$

and marginal cost is 10.

2–2 (a) Graph the average variable, average, and marginal cost curves if the cost function is:

$$C(q) = 1 + 9q.$$

(b) Graph the average variable, average, and marginal cost curves if the cost function is:

$$C(q) = 1 + 9q - q^2 + q^3.$$

2–3* (How to derive a linear demand curve I) Suppose n consumers purchase either 0 or 1 units of a homogeneous product. Let x denote a consumer's (gross) utility from consuming 1 unit of the good. Different consumers have different xs. Assume that the distribution of x is uniform on the interval $0 \leq x \leq \alpha$. (One-tenth of the population has $x \leq \alpha/10$, 1/5 of the population has $x \leq \alpha/5$, and so on.) For simplicity, refer to a consumer who obtains utility x from consuming one unit of the good as "a consumer at x". Then if a consumer at x purchases one unit of the product at price p, that consumer obtains net utility:

$$x - p. \tag{2.25}$$

x is therefore the consumer's reservation price—the highest price the consumer would pay. Consumers who obtain positive or zero net utility buy and consume one unit of the good. Consumers who would obtain negative net utility do not buy the good.

Find the equation of the market demand curve for this product.

2–4* (How to derive a linear demand curve II) Let there be two goods, one sold in amount Q at price p and one sold in amount m at price 1. Preferences are described by the representative consumer welfare function:

$$U(Q, m) = \alpha Q - \frac{1}{2}\beta Q^2 + m, \tag{2.26}$$

which is valid for $Q \geq 0$, $m \geq 0$. The aggregate budget constraint is:

$$Y = pQ + m. \tag{2.27}$$

α and β are positive parameters and Y is aggregate income. Aggregate demand for Q and m is found by maximizing the representative consumer welfare function (2.26) subject to the budget constraint (2.27).

Find the equation of the market demand curve for this product.

OLIGOPOLY I: BASIC MODELS

We few, we happy few, we band of brothers...

Henry V, Act 4, Scene 3

3.1 Introduction

The modern industrial economist's toolbox contains a sometimes bewildering library of models of imperfectly competitive markets. When analysing a particular market, one of these models is selected and adapted for use. In this chapter we introduce basic versions of the models that are the foundation of this library of oligopoly models.

We begin with the original and still most common model of an imperfectly competitive market, the Cournot model of quantity-setting oligopoly, in which firms decide how much to produce and price adjusts to equate quantity demanded with quantity supplied. We then turn to its mirror-image counterpart, the Bertrand model of price-setting oligopoly, in which firms set prices and supply the quantities demanded at those prices. We introduce consumer search models, models of markets in which consumers must make an effort to acquire information about the prices asked and product varieties offered by different suppliers, and models of markets with switching costs, so that it is costly for a consumer to change suppliers. We model markets in which the benefit any one consumer gets from a product depends on how many consumers use the product, and examine a simple model of a platform market, in which firms provide a means for groups on the demand and supply side of a market to interact.

3.2 Cournot Oligopoly

3.2.1 The Basic Model

The seminal model of oligopoly, due to Augustin Cournot ([1838] 1927), has (Machlup, 1967) "a simplicity and elegance that has never been equalled by any later theory". Cournot analysed the smallest possible departure of supply-side market structure from monopoly—two producers (of mineral water drawn from the same underground source) instead of one. Among the assumptions of the model are that each firm knows everything there is to know about the market, in particular market demand and the cost function of the other firm. Each firm knows that the other firm knows as much about the market as it does. Each firm picks how much to produce to maximize its own profit, knowing that the other firm acts in the same way and with the same information. But each firm decides how much to produce without knowing how much the other firm chooses to produce.

Simplifying assumptions of the basic model are that the product is standardized and that the two firms have identical and constant average costs. These are only simplifying assumptions. It is straightforward to generalize the basic Cournot model to allow for differentiated products (Problem 3–2) and cost differences (Section 3.2.4).

Strategic form

For market inverse demand $p = a - bQ$ and constant marginal and average cost c per unit, the *strategic form*[1] of the Cournot duopoly game,

- players: firm 1, firm 2;
- strategy sets: feasible outputs, $0 \leq q_1 \leq q_{max}$, $0 \leq q_2 \leq q_{max}$;
- payoff functions $\pi_i(q_1,q_2) = [a - c - b(q_1 + q_2)]q_i$, $i = 1,2$,

highlights the relationship between choices and payoffs. It identifies the players, the choices open to the players, and the payoffs that result from those choices.

Here, the players are the two firms. Each firm chooses its own output, from a range of possible outputs. In this example, the minimum output is zero. The maximum output, q_{max}, might be taken to be a/b, the output that would make price equal to zero; no profit-maximizing firm would ever produce this much output. Price adjusts so that the quantity consumers demand equals the total quantity supplied. The firms' payoffs are the resulting profits $\pi_1(q_1,q_2)$ and $\pi_2(q_1,q_2)$: each firm's payoff depends on the outputs chosen by both firms, because it is these choices together that determine price.[2]

Static, treated as dynamic

The game-theoretic version of Cournot's model casts it as a one-shot game, a game that is played only once. But economists usually treat the Cournot model as (Shubik, 1968, p. 260) "conversationally dynamic". We write down a game that, in its formal structure, is played once, with simultaneous moves. But it is often easiest to develop the intuition of the game as if it were played over time, with the players were reacting one to another in a sequence of output decisions.[3]

---

[1] An alternative representation, the *extensive form* of a game, includes the information contained in the strategic form and also a game tree that depicts the sequence of moves and the information available to a player when a move is made. For the extensive form of the Cournot duopoly model, see Daughety (1988).

[2] The expressions for payoffs given in the box are valid provided the price implied by the quantities is non-negative. If the total quantity supplied is greater than or equal to a/b (which would not happen in equilibrium), price is zero and each firm's payoff would be $-c$ times its output.

[3] There are parts of Cournot (1838) that are most naturally read as having players make alternating output decisions, out of equilibrium, until the non-cooperative equilibrium output pair is reached. Cournot's work was often, perhaps most often, read in this way before its modern reformulation (Leonard, 1994).

What is meant by "equilibrium"

Cournot began by asking the same questions about his duopoly model that economists ask about the models of perfectly competitive and monopoly markets: in equilibrium, what amounts will the firms produce, and at what price will the product sell?

In the Cournot game, each firm acts independently, and seeks to maximize its own profit. This being so, it makes sense to characterize an equilibrium pair of outputs by the condition that *the quantity each firm produces maximizes its own profit, if the other firm is producing its equilibrium output.* For such an output pair, each firm is making as large a profit as it possibly can, given what the other firm does. Since each firm seeks to maximize its own profit, neither firm would wish to alter its own part of such a pair of outputs.

We begin the task of finding equilibrium outputs by working out the output that will maximize a firm's profit for an arbitrary output level of the other firm. The schedule of all such output pairs is called the firm's *best response function.* We then look for mutually consistent best response outputs of the two firms.

3.2.2 Best-response Functions

We will use a specific example to illustrate the Cournot model. In this example, the market inverse demand equation is:

$$p = 100 - Q = 100 - (q_1 + q_2), \tag{3.1}$$

where q_1 is the output of firm 1 and q_2 is the output of firm 2. The firms have identical cost functions, with constant average and marginal cost, 10 per unit of output:

$$C(q_1) = 10q_1 \qquad C(q_2) = 10q_2. \tag{3.2}$$

If firm 2 produces an output level q_2, the relation between firm 1's output level q_1 and the market-clearing price p is:

$$p = (100 - q_2) - q_1. \tag{3.3}$$

(3.3) is the equation of firm 1's *residual demand function.* It gives the relation between the quantity supplied by firm 1 and price in the part of the market left for firm 1 after firm 2 has disposed of its output. In this leftover part of the market, firm 1 is a monopolist, or at least, it acts as a monopolist, since it takes firm 2's output to be q_2.

The output level that maximizes a monopolist's profit makes its marginal revenue equal to its marginal cost. For a linear demand curve, the marginal revenue curve has the same price-axis intercept as the demand curve (the price-axis intercept of the residual demand curve (3.3) is $100 - q_2$) and a slope that is twice as great in absolute value as the slope of the demand curve. The equation of firm 1's residual marginal revenue function is therefore:

$$MR_1 = (100 - q_2) - 2q_1. \tag{3.4}$$

Firm 1's profit-maximizing output thus satisfies the condition:

$$MR_1 = (100 - q_2) - 2q_1 = 10 = MC. \tag{3.5}$$

This is illustrated in Figure 3.1, which is drawn for $q_2 = 30$.

Solving for q_1, equation (3.5) can be rewritten as:

$$q_1 = \frac{1}{2}(90 - q_2) = 45 - \frac{1}{2}q_2. \tag{3.6}$$

(3.6) is the equation of firm 1's *best response function.* It gives the profit-maximizing output of firm 1 for an arbitrary output of firm 2. For this example, if firm 1's best-response function

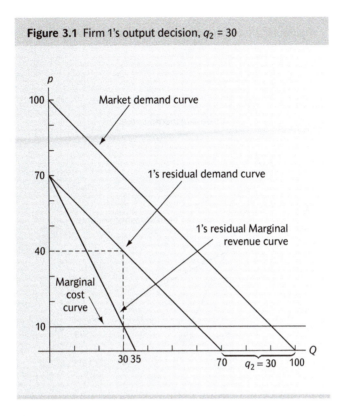

Figure 3.1 Firm 1's output decision, $q_2 = 30$

is drawn on a graph with firm 1's output on the horizontal axis and firm 2's output on the vertical axis, it is a straight line connecting the points $(q_m,0) = (45,0)$ and $(0,Q_c) = (0,90)$ (Figure 3.2).

Going through the same procedure for firm 2, we obtain the equation of firm 2's best-response function. For this example, the equation of firm 2's best-response function is:

$$q_2 = 45 - \frac{1}{2}q_1. \tag{3.7}$$

Firm 2's best-response curve is also graphed in Figure 3.2.

Best-response function

A firm's (quantity) *best-response function* specifies its profit-maximizing output for arbitrary output amounts of other firms.

3.2.3 Cournot Equilibrium

Output levels

When both firms produce their equilibrium output levels, each firm maximizes its own profit, given that the other firm is producing its equilibrium amount. In terms of the best-response curve diagram Figure 3.2, the equilibrium quantities are found at the intersection of the best-response curves.

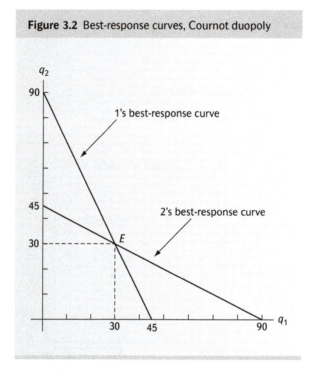

Figure 3.2 Best-response curves, Cournot duopoly

The values of the Cournot equilibrium outputs can be found by solving the equations of the best-response functions, here (3.6) and (3.7). This solution gives the coordinates of the point where the two best-response curves intersect. This example is symmetric, in the sense that the two firms have identical cost functions and identical beliefs each about the other. It follows that the firms will produce identical output levels in equilibrium.[4]

Call the common equilibrium output per firm in this example q_{Cour}. Set $q_1 = q_2 = q_{Cour}$ in (3.6) (the same result would be reached if we made the substitution in (3.7)). This allows us to find the Cournot equilibrium output per firm:

$$2q_{Cour} + q_{Cour} = 3q_{Cour} = 90,$$
$$q_{Cour} = 30. \tag{3.8}$$

Other aspects of Cournot equilibrium

Other characteristics of Cournot equilibrium that are of interest include total output, price, the degree of market power, economic profit, consumer surplus, and deadweight welfare loss. These can all be determined in a straightforward way from the equilibrium outputs.

Adding the quantities produced by the two firms gives total output:

$$Q_{Cour} = 2q_{Cour} = 60. \tag{3.9}$$

---

[4] It is common to use symmetric examples in introductory treatments of the Cournot model. Nothing in the logic of the Cournot model limits its use to cases in which firms are identical.

Cournot equilibrium output is greater than monopoly output (45), but less than long-run competitive equilibrium output (90).

From the equation of the inverse demand curve, the Cournot equilibrium price is:

$$p_{Cour} = 100 - 60 = 40 = 10 + 30. \tag{3.10}$$

This is greater than marginal cost (10), but less than the monopoly price (55).

In Cournot equilibrium, the Lerner index of market power is:

$$\frac{p_{Cour} - c}{p_{Cour}} = \frac{40 - 10}{40} = \frac{3}{4}. \tag{3.11}$$

Profit per firm is:

$$\pi_{Cour} = (p_{Cour} - 10)q_{Cour} = (30)(30) = 900. \tag{3.12}$$

Since there are two firms, total economic profit is twice the profit of a single firm.

The amount of consumer surplus (CS) is given by the area of the triangle bounded above by the demand curve, below by the horizontal line $p_{Cour} = 40$, and on the left by the price axis (see Figure 3.3). This area is:

$$CS = \frac{1}{2}(100 - 40)(60) = \frac{1}{2}(60)^2 = 1800. \tag{3.13}$$

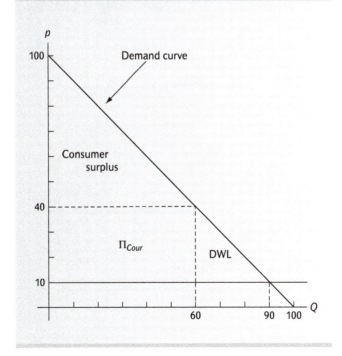

Figure 3.3 Market equilibrium, Cournot duopoly, identical unit costs

The amount of deadweight welfare loss (DWL) is given by the area of the triangle bounded above by the demand curve, below by the marginal and average cost line, and on the left by the vertical line $Q_{Cour} = 60$. This area is:

$$DWL = \frac{1}{2}(40 - 10)(90 - 60) = \frac{1}{2}(30)^2 = 450. \tag{3.14}$$

3.2.4 Cost Differences

It is often useful to think about oligopoly interactions in terms of best response functions. The impact of changes on the market can be worked out by examining how those changes move the best response functions and, therefore, equilibrium.

To illustrate this with the Cournot model, continue to suppose that each firm has constant marginal cost, but change the basic model so that firm 1's marginal cost is c_1 and firm 2's marginal cost is c_2. Going through the steps that lead to (3.6) and (3.7), the equations of the best response functions become:

$$2q_1 + q_2 = 100 - c_1 \tag{3.15}$$

$$q_1 + 2q_2 = 100 - c_2. \tag{3.16}$$

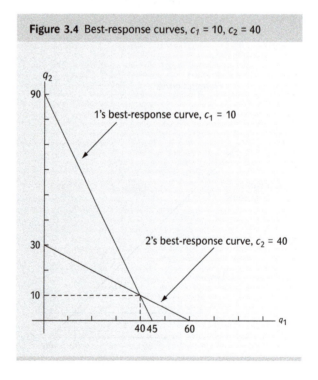

Figure 3.4 Best-response curves, $c_1 = 10$, $c_2 = 40$

The best-response curves for $c_1 = 10$, $c_2 = 40$ are shown in Figure 3.4. Equilibrium output levels are found by solving equations (3.15) and (3.16). The equilibrium outputs are:[5]

$$q_1 = \frac{1}{3}(100 - 2c_1 + c_2) \tag{3.17}$$

and

$$q_2 = \frac{1}{3}(100 + c_1 - 2c_2). \tag{3.18}$$

Each firm produces a larger equilibrium amount, the smaller is its own unit cost and the larger is the unit cost of the other firm. The difference between the equilibrium output levels of the two firms is:

$$q_1 - q_2 = c_2 - c_1. \tag{3.19}$$

If c_1 is less than c_2, then q_1 is greater than q_2, and *vice versa*. In a Cournot duopoly, the firm with lower unit cost produces more, in equilibrium, than the firm with higher unit cost.

Firm-specific Lerner indices

If firms in a Cournot duopoly have different unit costs, the firm with lower cost has a greater degree of market power, as measured by the Lerner index. To see this, rewrite the equation of firm 1's best response function, (3.15), as:

$$100 - q_1 - q_2 = c_1 + q_1. \tag{3.20}$$

But from equation (3.15), the left-hand side of (3.20) is price, p. Thus if firm 1 produces as indicated by its best-response function, which it does in equilibrium,

$$p = c_1 + q_1. \tag{3.21}$$

Then firm 1's Lerner index of market power is:

$$\frac{p - c_1}{p} = \frac{q_1}{p} = \frac{q_1/Q}{p/Q} = \frac{s_1}{\varepsilon_{Qp}}, \tag{3.22}$$

where $s_1 = q_1/Q$ is firm 1's market share and ε_{Qp} is the absolute value of the price elasticity of demand.

Equation (3.22) generalizes the Lerner index of market power from monopoly to Cournot oligopoly with cost differences. In the same way, we find for firm 2:

$$\frac{p - c_2}{p} = \frac{s_2}{\varepsilon_{Qp}}. \tag{3.23}$$

If firm 1 has lower unit cost than firm 2, then in equilibrium it produces more, has a larger market share, and exercises a greater degree of market power than firm 2.

It is equally true that lower cost improves market performance, leading to greater equilibrium output and lower equilibrium price.[6] This is most easily seen by adding equations (3.15) and (3.16), which shows that equilibrium total output is:

$$Q = q_1 + q_2 = \frac{1}{3}[200 - (c_1 + c_2)]. \tag{3.24}$$

Equilibrium output rises as either c_1 or c_2 falls. If output rises as either c_1 or c_2 falls, then equilibrium price and deadweight welfare loss fall as either c_1 or c_2 falls.

---

[5] Expressions (3.17) and (3.18) are valid provided they are non-negative. Firm 2's equilibrium output is zero if firm 2's unit cost is sufficiently greater than 1's average cost; from (3.18), if $c_2 \geq 50 + \frac{1}{2}c_1$. If firm 2's unit cost falls in this range, firm 1 maximizes profit by producing the monopoly output.

[6] This is also true for monopoly.

Industry-average Lerner index

If we multiply equation (3.22) by s_1, multiply equation (3.23) by s_2, and add the results, we get the industry average Lerner index:

$$\frac{p - \widehat{c}}{p} = \frac{s_1^2 + s_2^2}{\varepsilon_{Qp}} = \frac{H}{\varepsilon_{Qp}}. \tag{3.25}$$

In (3.25), $\widehat{c} = s_1 c_1 + s_2 c_2$ is the market-share-weighted average of the unit costs of the two firms. The numerator of the fraction on the right,

$$H = s_1^2 + s_2^2, \tag{3.26}$$

is the Herfindahl or H-index of seller concentration. The H-index is widely used as a summary statistic describing the size distribution of firms on the supply side of a market. We thus obtain the result that in Cournot oligopoly with cost differences, a higher equilibrium industry-average price-cost margin and a higher value of the Herfindahl index go together.

The Herfindahl index

The Herfindahl index is the sum of squares of market shares of all firms in the industry. For n firms, this is:

$$H = s_1^2 + s_2^2 + \ldots + s_n^2. \tag{3.27}$$

Table 3.1 gives examples of four sets of market shares and the corresponding values of the Herfindahl index. If, as in row 1, an industry is supplied by two firms, one with a market share of 75 per cent and the other with a market share of 25 per cent, the value of the H-index is $\left(\frac{3}{4}\right)^2 + \left(\frac{1}{4}\right)^2 = \frac{5}{8}$. The inverse of the H-index is $\frac{8}{5} = 1.6$. If there are two firms and both firms have the same market share (that is, one-half), the value of the H-index is 0.5, and the inverse of the H-index is 2, the number of equally sized firms.

With ten equally sized firms (row 3), the value of the H-index is $1/10$ and $1/H = 10$. In general, if there are n equally-sized firms in an industry, then $H = 1/n$ and $1/H = n$. For this reason, the inverse of the H-index is said to be a *numbers-equivalent* measure of seller concentration.

Thus, if there are three equally sized firms, $H = 1/3$ and $1/H = 3$. If the H-index for any industry is $1/3$, we say as a manner of description that the industry is as concentrated as an industry with three equally sized firms, even though many combinations of market shares will produce an H-index of $1/3$. For example, if there are four firms in an industry, firm 1

Table 3.1 Herfindahl index examples

Industry	Market Shares	H	1/H
1	$s_1 = 75\%, s_2 = 25\%$	0.625	1.6
2	$s_1 = s_2 = 50\%$	0.500	2
3	$s_1 = s_2 = \ldots = s_{10} = 10\%$	0.100	10
4	$s_1 = 91\%, s_2 = \ldots = s_{10} = 1\%$	0.829	1.206

with a market share of 0.4, firms 2 and 3 with identical market shares of 0.2943 each, and firm 4 with a market share of 0.0114, the value of the H-index is $1/3$ and $1/H = 3$. From a numbers-equivalent point of view, we would then say that an industry supplied by four firms with the indicated market shares is as concentrated as an industry supplied by three equally sized firms.

Row 4 of Table 3.1 describes an industry supplied by ten firms, one very much larger than the others. The value of the H-index, 0.829, is close to 1, and $1/H = 1.206$. This allows us to say that the industry is as concentrated as an industry supplied by 1.2 equally sized firms. By this we mean that supply-side concentration is closer to monopoly than to duopoly, even though there are ten active firms in the market.

Welfare

Figure 3.5 illustrates the welfare effects of imperfect competition in a Cournot duopoly with cost differences. Firm 1's unit cost is less than firm 2's unit cost ($c_1 < c_2$). If firms acted as price takers, firm 1 would supply the entire market at a price slightly less than c_2. In Cournot duopoly equilibrium, price is greater than c_2. The higher-cost firm has positive output only because the lower-cost firm does not act as a price taker. Economic profits are $\pi_1 = (p_{Cour} - c_1)q_1$ for firm one and $\pi_2 = (p_{Cour} - c_2)q_2$ for firm 2. A portion $(c_2 - c_1)q_1$ of firm 1's economic profit, shown as the shaded area in Figure 3.5, is an *efficiency quasi-rent* collected by firm 1 on the restricted amount of output that it does produce.

The amounts of economic profit, π_1 and π_2, are income transfers from consumers to producers. Treating the purchasing power lost by consumers and the profit increase of the owners of the firms on equal terms, the net loss of social welfare due to the exercise of market

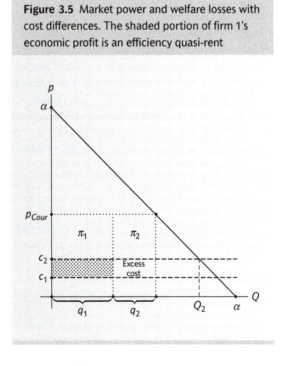

Figure 3.5 Market power and welfare losses with cost differences. The shaded portion of firm 1's economic profit is an efficiency quasi-rent

Table 3.2 Aiginger and Pfaffermayr market power welfare cost estimates. EU15, 1989–1993. *n* indicates number of firms, *H* indicates the Herfindahl index. Estimates assume Cournot conjectures and a rental cost of capital of 9.29 per cent. Welfare figures measured as a percentage of sales

	Pulp and paper mills			Cement		
n, H, 1/H	15	0.11	9.09	17	0.17	5.88
PCM: min, mean, max	3.06	8.95	17.51	6.90	12.95	30.55
DWL		1.85			2.56	
Cost "staircase"		7.93			7.66	
DWL + Cost staircase		9.78			10.22	

Source: Aiginger and Pfaffermayr (1991, Table II, Table III).

power is the deadweight welfare loss from output restriction below Q_2, the amount that would be produced if firms were price takers, *plus* the extra social cost of producing firm 2's output at unit cost c_2 rather than unit cost c_1. This extra amount is $(c_2 - c_1)q_2$.

Aiginger and Pfaffermayr (1991) estimate the welfare consequences of market power in two industries of the 15-member European Union for the years 1989–1993. They work with firm-level data for their two industries, pulp and paper mills and cement, and they allow for cost differences between firms in the same industry. Aiginger and Pfaffermayr's primary results[7] are reported in Table 3.2. The first row shows the number of firms in their sample, the industry Herfindahl index, and the inverse of the Herfindahl index, the "equivalent" number of equally sized firms that would generate the given value of the *H*-index. The second row gives the minimum, weighted average mean (with market shares used as weights), and maximum values of the price-cost margin in their sample. The third and fourth rows give the estimated deadweight welfare loss—lost consumer surplus—and extra production cost incurred due to output restriction and production by less efficient firms.[8] As Aiginger and Pfaffermayr note (1991, p. 256) "the cost staircase is definitely greater than the deadweight welfare loss". This extra production cost is an oligopoly welfare loss due to the exercise of market power.

3.2.5 Conjectural Variations

Thinking about the way best response curves shift if there is a change in the structure of the model is also a way to understand what happens if the Cournot behavioural assumption—

---

[7] They report a number of results obtained under alternative assumptions. They do not estimate welfare losses due to rent seeking.

[8] When there are more than two firms, the area showing extra production cost in a price-quantity diagram assumes the form of a staircase; see Dixit and Stern (1982, Figure 1), Aiginger and Pfaffermayr (1991, Figure 1).

that each firm maximizes its own profit, given the equilibrium output of the other firm—is changed.

To add conjectures about rivals' responses to the static model, suppose that firm 1 expects that for every 1 per cent change in its own output q_1, there will be an α per cent change in q_2:

$$\alpha = \frac{q_1}{q_2}\frac{dq_2}{dq_1}. \tag{3.28}$$

As a proportional rate of change, α is an elasticity.[9]

As we have noted, it is now conventional to treat Cournot's model as a one-shot game. Conjectures—beliefs one firm holds about the way the other will react to what it does—are out of place in a complete information game that is played only once. What basis would firm 1 have for anticipating that firm 1's choice of output level will affect firm 2's choice of output level, since (in a one-shot game) firm 1 knows that neither firm will learn what the other has done until after it has made its own choice? Adding conjectures to a static Cournot model is best thought of as a way of shoehorning behaviour that we think might occur with repeated play into a one-shot framework.

Conjectural marginal revenue

For the inverse demand equation (3.15), firm 1's total revenue is:

$$TR_1 = pq_1 = (100 - q_1 - q_2)\,q_1, \tag{3.29}$$

making its conjectured marginal revenue:

$$MR_1 = 100 - q_1 - q_2 + \left(-1 - \frac{dq_2}{dq_1}\right)q_1 = 100 - 2q_1 - (1+\alpha)\,q_2. \tag{3.30}$$

Conjectural best response

Setting marginal revenue equal to marginal cost gives the equation of firm 1's best-response function in the conjectural variations Cournot model,

$$2q_1 + (1+\alpha)q_2 = 90, \tag{3.31}$$

or

$$q_1 = 45 - \frac{1}{2}(1+\alpha)q_2. \tag{3.32}$$

With Cournot conjectures, $\alpha = 0$ and the slope of the best-response curve is $-1/2$ (as in equation (3.6)).

If $\alpha > 0$, firm 1 expects that if it reduces its quantity supplied, firm 2 will reduce the amount it produces as well. Expecting firm 2 to re-enforce its own actions, for any level of output of firm 2, firm 1 produces less than it would with Cournot conjectures. Firm 1's best-response curve rotates around the q_1-axis intercept toward the origin (that is, in a counterclockwise direction; see Figure 3.6).

If $\alpha < 0$, firm 1 expects that if it reduces its quantity supplied, firm 2 will increase the amount it produces, partially neutralizing the effort to reduce total output. For any output level of firm 2, firm 1 will produce more than it would with Cournot conjectures. With

---

[9] For simplicity, we will assume that firms have identical conjectures. There is nothing inherent in the conjectural approach that requires conjectures to be identical. More generally, we might write α_{12} for the proportional response that firm 1 conjectures by firm 2, and similarly $\alpha_{21} = \frac{q_2}{q_1}\frac{dq_1}{dq_2}$ for the proportional response that firm 2 conjectures by firm 1.

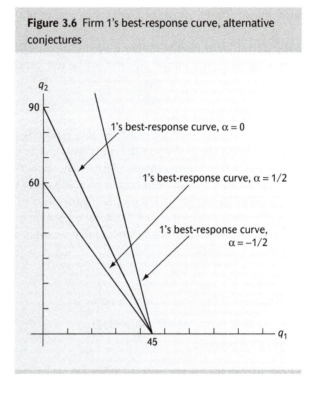

Figure 3.6 Firm 1's best-response curve, alternative conjectures

negative conjectures, firm 1's best response curve rotates around its q_1-axis intercept away from the origin (clockwise).

Conjectural equilibrium

As long as firms have identical conjectures, equilibrium outputs are the same for both firms. Setting $q_1 = q_2 = q_\alpha$ in (3.31) leads to an expression for equilibrium duopoly output per firm with identical conjectures:

$$q_\alpha = \frac{90}{3 + \alpha}. \tag{3.33}$$

Equilibrium outputs are smaller (total output is closer to the monopoly level) for matching conjectures ($\alpha > 0$) and equilibrium outputs are larger (total output is closer to the long-run competitive equilibrium level) for contrarian conjectures ($\alpha < 0$). Matching conjectures move the market toward the kind of outcome associated with collusion; contrarian conjectures move the market toward the kind of outcome associated with perfect competition (Figure 3.7).

If $\alpha = 1$, then (from (3.33)), in equilibrium each duopolist produces half the monopoly output. For this reason, $\alpha = 1$ is sometimes referred to as the case of collusive conjectures.[10] If $\alpha = -1$, then (substituting in equation (3.33)) in equilibrium each firm produces half the

---

[10] This terminology is imprecise in that (as we will see in Chapter 20) if firms make output decisions independently they would not normally be considered to have colluded in a legal sense.

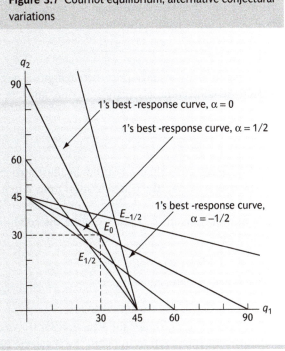

Figure 3.7 Cournot equilibrium, alternative conjectural variations

perfectly competitive output. Total output is what it would be in long-run perfectly competitive equilibrium, even though there are only two firms supplying the market. As we will see in the next section, this is the same result as in the Bertrand model of price-setting duopoly with standardized products. For this reason, $\alpha = -1$ is sometimes referred to as the case of Bertrand conjectures.

Lerner index with conjectures

Finally, another way to write firm 1's conjectured marginal revenue is (Cowling, 1976; Cowling and Waterson, 1976; Clarke and Davies, 1982):

$$MR_1 = p + q_1 \frac{dp}{dQ} \frac{dQ}{dq_1} = p + q_1 \frac{dp}{dQ} \left(1 + \frac{dq_2}{dq_1}\right) = p + p \frac{Q}{p} \frac{dp}{dQ} \frac{q_1 + \alpha q_2}{Q}$$

$$= p \left(1 - \frac{1}{\varepsilon_{QP}} \frac{q_1 + \alpha q_2}{Q}\right) = p \left[1 - \frac{\alpha + (1 - \alpha) s_1}{\varepsilon_{QP}}\right]. \tag{3.34}$$

Here (as before) $s_1 = q_1/Q$ is firm 1's market share and $s_2 = q_2/Q = 1 - s_1$ is firm 2's market share. Then setting marginal revenue equal to marginal cost and rearranging terms slightly gives a further generalization of the Lerner index of market power:

$$\frac{p - c_1}{p} = \frac{\alpha + (1 - \alpha) s_1}{\varepsilon_{QP}}. \tag{3.35}$$

Provided all firms have the same conjecture, (3.35) can be aggregated from the firm to the industry level in the same way that (3.25) was obtained from (3.22). This leads to the industry weighted-average Lerner index with conjectures:

$$\frac{p - \widehat{c}}{p} = \frac{\alpha + (1 - \alpha)H}{\varepsilon_{QP}}.$$ (3.36)

In Cournot equilibrium, the industry-average price–cost margin is larger, the larger the Herfindahl index, the closer the conjectural elasticity α to one, and the smaller the price elasticity of demand.

3.2.6 Many Firms

The general Cournot model—n firms rather than 2—cannot be illustrated graphically. Particularly in the symmetric-firm case, however, the generalization from 2 to n firms is straightforward.

If there are n identical Cournot firms in the industry, write the combined quantity supplied of all firms except firm 1 as:

$$Q_{-1} = q_2 + \cdots + q_n.$$ (3.37)

Then we can write firm 1's residual demand equation as:

$$p = (100 - Q_{-1}) - q_1.$$ (3.38)

This looks very much like firm 1's residual demand equation for the duopoly case, (3.3). The difference between the two equations is that in (3.38) the aggregate output of all other firms, Q_{-1}, appears where the output of firm 2, q_2, appears in equation (3.3).

Proceeding as for duopoly, we can find firm 1's best response equation by setting its marginal revenue equal to its marginal cost:

$$100 - Q_{-1} - 2q_1 = 10,$$ (3.39)

or

$$2q_1 + Q_{-1} = 90.$$ (3.40)

In the symmetric firm case, all firms will produce the same output in equilibrium. Call this common output level q_{Cour}. (3.40) becomes:

$$2q_{Cour} + (n - 1)q_{Cour} = 90,$$ (3.41)

so that

$$q_{Cour} = \frac{90}{n + 1}.$$ (3.42)

If $n = 2$, (3.42) reduces to (3.8). The greater the number of firms, the smaller is equilibrium output per firm.

From the equilibrium output of a single firm, we can work out all the other characteristics of n-firm equilibrium. Here we note two of these, total output and price, which are:

$$Q_{Cour} = \frac{n}{n + 1} 90 = \left(1 - \frac{1}{n + 1}\right) 90$$ (3.43)

and

$$p_{Cour} = 10 + \frac{90}{n + 1}$$ (3.44)

respectively.

If $n = 1$, (3.43) and (3.44) give the monopoly output and price, respectively. As n increases, Cournot equilibrium output increases toward the long-run competitive equilibrium output level, and Cournot equilibrium price falls toward marginal cost. The symmetric Cournot model thus yields the intuitively appealing prediction that market performance will approach that of long-run competitive equilibrium as the number of firms approaches infinity.

3.3 Bertrand Duopoly

Cournot's work was largely ignored in his own lifetime. But in 1883, the French mathematician Bertrand wrote a review of Cournot's 1838 book, criticizing Cournot for assuming that firms picked output levels and that price adjusted so that consumers would willingly demand the total quantity supplied. Since that time, Bertrand's name has been associated with the opposite specification, that in an imperfectly competitive market firms pick prices and sell the quantities demanded at those prices.

3.3.1 Standardized Product

Like Cournot, Bertrand assumed that the outputs of different firms were perfect substitutes. Keeping this and all the other assumptions of the basic Cournot model, firm 1's residual demand curve looks quite different if firms set prices rather than quantities.

Residual demand

This is illustrated in Figure 3.8. If $p_2 = 40$, firm 1 will sell nothing if it sets a price greater than 40, and will supply the entire quantity demanded if it sets a price below 40. There is a discontinuity in firm 1's residual demand curve at $p_1 = 40$, with the quantity demanded jumping from 0 to 60 as p_1 falls from above 40 to below 40.

Firm 1 can sell up to slightly more than 60 units of output at a price slightly below 40. For outputs less than 60 units, firm 1's marginal revenue is slightly less than 40. To sell more than 60 units of output, firm 1 must reduce price and move down the market demand curve. For outputs greater than 60 units, firm 1's marginal revenue curve is the same as the market marginal revenue curve. The horizontal break in firm 1's residual demand curve at a price just less than 40, $p = 40 - \varepsilon$ for some small number ε, means that there is a vertical break in firm 1's marginal revenue curve at an output level slightly greater than $Q = 60$.

For outputs less than 60, firm 1's marginal revenue, $40 - \varepsilon$, is greater than its marginal cost, 10. For outputs greater than 60, firm 1's marginal revenue is less than its marginal cost. To maximize its profit, firm 1 will set a price just a little below 40 and supply the entire quantity demanded at that price. Firm 2 will sell nothing.[11]

This cannot be an equilibrium, however. Firm 2 would have an incentive to undercut firm 1's price slightly, thus recapturing what would be a slightly larger market demand at a slightly lower price. And if firm 2 did this, firm 1 would once again have an incentive to set a price slightly below firm 2's new, lower, price. If either firm sets a price above marginal cost,

---

[11] In Section 2.3.5 we made a similar argument in the case of a single supplier facing the possibility of entry by a higher-cost rival.

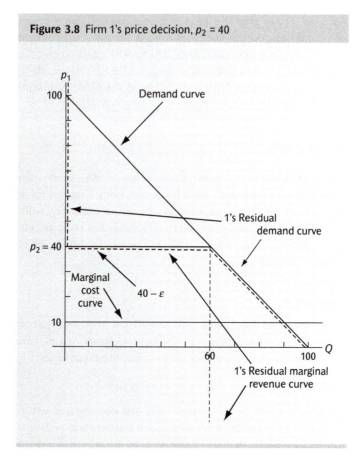

Figure 3.8 Firm 1's price decision, $p_2 = 40$

the other has an incentive to set a lower price. Neither firm would set a price below marginal cost, because that would mean losing money.

The Bertrand paradox

These arguments show that the Bertrand equilibrium price equals marginal cost, $p = 10$. When each firm sets a price equal to marginal cost, each firm is maximizing its own profit, given that the other firm sets a price equal to marginal cost. The Bertrand model there-fore yields the result, sometimes called the *Bertrand Paradox*, that when the product is stan-dardized and firms have identical constant costs, market performance is the same as in the long-run equilibrium of a perfectly competitive market, provided there are at least two firms supplying the market.[12]

---

[12] The Bertrand Paradox depends on the assumption that each firm is able to produce as much or as little as it wishes. If we generalize the model to allow for an upper limit, capacity, on output, the Bertrand Paradox holds if each firm has sufficient capacity to supply the entire quantity demanded at a price equal to its marginal cost. If firms cannot supply the entire quantity demanded at a price equal to marginal cost—if there are capacity constraints—there can be outcomes in a repeated game in which one firm sets a low price and uses all its capacity, while the other sets a higher price in the part of the market that is left over for it (Edgeworth, 1897/1925; Beckmann, 1965; Levitan and Shubik, 1972; Dixon, 1987).

3.3.2 Contestable Markets

A *perfectly contestable market* is (Baumol *et al.*, 1982, p. 5):

> one that is accessible to potential entrants and has the following two properties: First, the potential entrants can, without restriction, serve the same market demands and use the same productive techniques as those available to the incumbent firms. . . . Second, the potential entrants evaluate the profitability of entry at the incumbent firms' pre-entry prices.

The first part of the definition has much in common with Alfred Marshall's notion of a competitive industry (Andrews, 1951, p. 141; Section 1.2.1)—that it "would be possible for other businesses to produce a commodity with the same technical specifications as the product of any particular firm, and to offer it for sale to that firm's customers". The second part of the definition of a perfectly contestable market is that potential entrants are, like the many small firms of the perfectly competitive market, price takers. Large incumbent firms in a contestable market are assumed to believe that when potential entrants decide whether or not to come into a market, the entrants will act as price-taking firms. In a contestable market, incumbents believe that entrants think whatever output they produce will not affect the market price.[13]

The theory of contestable markets shares with the theory of perfect competition the assumption that there is free and easy entry and exit (Baumol, 1982, p. 3): "A contestable market is one into which entry is absolutely free, and exit is absolutely costless. . . . the entrant suffers no disadvantage in terms of production technique or perceived quality relative to the incumbent. . . . " In particular, there are no sunk entry costs.

If the assumptions of perfect contestability hold and there are at least two active firms, then equilibrium price equals marginal cost. The assumptions and the results of the theory of perfectly contestable markets largely overlap with those of the Bertrand model of price-setting oligopoly with standardized products (Knieps and Vogelsang, 1982). As with the Bertrand model, equilibrium price is the same, and equal to marginal cost, if there are 2, 3, 4, . . . suppliers.

Passenger airlines

Early in the development of the theory of contestable markets, the passenger airline industry was put forward as an example of a real-world market that might be approximately contestable. Superficially, this is not implausible: after all, aircraft can be flown into and out of markets, suggesting that the costs of entry and exit are low and that the impact of potential competition on market performance ought to be great.

Empirical evidence, however, suggests that the passenger airline industry is not approximately contestable (see Section 5.3.4). A number of studies show that average airline fares in

---

[13] What Modigliani (1958, p. 217) calls the *Sylos' postulate* is the polar opposite, "that potential entrants behave as though they expected existing firms to adopt the policy most unfavorable to them, namely, the policy of maintaining output while reducing the price (or accepting reductions) to the extent required to enforce such an output policy". Geroski (1995, p. 433) writes that "on the face of it, the evidence suggests that the Sylos Postulate describes a typical response to entry, the obvious alternative hypothesis is that incumbents ignore entrants (at least until they are well established)". "Incumbents ignore entry" would mean entry does not affect incumbents' output rates in quantity-setting markets, and does not affect incumbents' prices in price-setting markets. That incumbents believe entrants expect the latter is assumed for a perfectly contestable market.

a city-pair market rise as the number of airlines serving the city-pair market falls. The theory of contestable markets predicts that if there are two or more airlines serving a city-pair market, fares should equal marginal cost and be unrelated to the number of active airlines. The finding that fares are higher when there are fewer suppliers contradicts the theory of contestable markets.

Part of the explanation for this finding is that although aircraft may fly in and out of markets, they must have landing slots and gate access to pick up and discharge passengers. Investments in slots and gates may be partially sunk, and it may not be possible to acquire them on any terms. Nor does the assumption that incumbents would expect entrants to act as price takers sit well as a description of an industry where computerized fare systems permit fares to be changed at will (Evans and Kessides, 1994).

3.3.3 Differentiated Products

Horizontal vs. vertical product differentiation

Economists conventionally distinguish between two types of product differentiation. Product differentiation is *horizontal* if some consumers prefer one variety, some another, with no universal preference ranking. Horizontal product differentiation may reflect differences in tastes—some consumers prefer apples, others oranges. It may reflect differences in location—consumers may prefer a nearer to a more distant grocery store, and different consumers live closer to different stores. Product differentiation is *vertical* if there is a universally accepted quality ranking of varieties. Passenger airline seat classes are vertically differentiated if all airline passengers agree that a seat in the business class section is a higher-quality product than a seat in the economy section and a seat in first class is a higher-quality product than a seat in business class. Here we consider one of the standard ways of modelling horizontal product differentiation. We discuss vertical product differentiation in Chapter 4.

Bertrand duopoly with horizontal product differentiation

The assumption that the product is standardized is essential for the Bertrand Paradox result that the equilibrium price equals marginal cost if there are at least two firms in the market. To see this, we introduce horizontal product differentiation to the model of price-setting duopoly.

Suppose the two firms produce differentiated brands of mineral water, with the inverse demand equations:

$$p_1 = 100 - (q_1 + \theta q_2), \tag{3.45}$$

$$p_2 = 100 - (\theta q_1 + q_2). \tag{3.46}$$

The product differentiation parameter θ is a number between zero and one that measures the degree of substitutability between the two varieties. For $\theta = 0$, the quantity of variety 2 sold has no influence on the price of variety 1, and *vice versa*. In that case, the two "varieties" are actually completely different products, the quantity demanded of each being unrelated to the quantity supplied of the other. If $\theta = 1$, the two demand equations become identical and reduce to the homogeneous product demand equation (3.1). $\theta = 1$ is the case of "varieties" that are perfect substitutes. For values of θ between zero and one, the closer θ is to one, the greater is the degree of substitutability between the two varieties and the closer are the two varieties to being perfect substitutes.[14]

Strategic form   For linear inverse demands $p_i = a - b\left(q_i + \theta q_j\right)$ (for $i,j = 1,2$ and $i \neq j$) and constant marginal and average cost c per unit, the strategic form of the differentiated-product Bertrand duopoly game is:

- players: firm 1, firm 2;
- strategy sets: feasible outputs, $0 \leq p_1 \leq p_{max}$, $0 \leq p_2 \leq p_{max}$;
- payoff functions $\pi_i\left(p_1,p_2\right) = \left(p_i - c\right)\frac{(1-\theta)a - p_i + \theta p_j}{b(1-\theta^2)}$, $i,j = 1,2$, $i \neq j$.

The players are the two firms. Each firm chooses its own price, from a range of feasible prices, 0 to some very high price.[15] The quantity demanded of each firm depends on the prices set by both firms. Firms produce the quantities demanded, and payoffs are the resulting profits $\pi_1\left(p_1,p_2\right)$ and $\pi_2\left(p_1,p_2\right)$.[16]

Best-response functions   If, for specificity, the product differentiation parameter $\theta = 1/2$, the equations of the inverse demand functions are:

$$p_1 = 100 - \left(q_1 + \frac{1}{2}q_2\right) \qquad p_2 = 100 - \left(\frac{1}{2}q_1 + q_2\right). \qquad (3.47)$$

The equations of the demand functions, obtained by solving the equations (3.47) for quantities as functions of prices, are:

$$q_1 = \frac{2}{3}(100 - 2p_1 + p_2) \qquad q_2 = \frac{2}{3}(100 + p_1 - 2p_2), \qquad (3.48)$$

respectively. In the standardized-product Bertrand model, the quantity demanded of (say) firm 1 is a discontinuous function of firm 1's price: as firm 1's price falls from above to below firm 2's price, the quantity demanded of firm 1 jumps from zero to the entire market demand (Figure 3.8). If varieties are differentiated, the quantity demanded of each firm is a continuous function of the prices of both firms, as with (3.48). If firm 2 reduces its price, some consumers switch from variety 1 to variety 2, but not all, because some consumers have a strong enough preference for variety 1 that they will pay a higher price for it rather than switch to variety 2.

Firm 1's profit as a function of p_1 and p_2 is:

$$\pi_1 = (p_1 - 10)q_1 = \frac{2}{3}(p_1 - 10)(100 - 2p_1 + p_2). \qquad (3.49)$$

---

[14] Varieties are imperfect *substitutes* if each, to some extent, can be used or consumed in place of the other. Products are *complements* if they are (or can be) used or consumed together, as for example rum and Coca-Cola. Negative values of θ in the demand equations (3.45) and (3.46) describe demand for complementary products.

[15] The maximum price, p_{max}, might be taken to be the price at which the quantity demanded equals zero (this is a if the inverse demand equation is $p_1 = a - b\left(q_1 + q_2\right)$). No profit-maximizing firm would ever charge so high a price.

[16] Two restrictions must be satisfied for these payoff functions to be valid. First, the quantities demanded implied by the prices must be non-negative. If the quantity demanded of a firm is zero, its payoff is zero. Second, for the expressions for payoffs to be valid, the two varieties must be imperfect substitutes, with $0 \leq \theta < 1$. As a matter of algebra, θ cannot equal 1 because division by zero is not defined. As a matter of economics, if $\theta = 1$, there is really only one standardized product, not two varieties of a differentiated product. For $\theta = 1$, the total quantity demanded of the two firms is determined once price is given, but the quantity demanded of either firm alone is indeterminate.

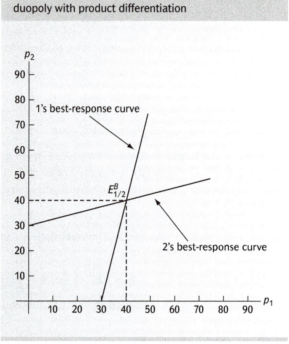

Figure 3.9 Price best-response curves, Bertrand duopoly with product differentiation

The first-order condition to maximize (3.49) with respect to p_1 is:[17]

$$(p_1 - 10)(-2) + (100 - 2p_1 + p_2)(1) \equiv 0. \qquad (3.50)$$

Solving (3.50) for p_1 as a function of p_2 gives the equation of firm 1's price best-response function (Figure 3.9):

$$p_1 = 30 + \frac{1}{4}p_2. \qquad (3.51)$$

When firms set prices, best-response curves slope upward: if firm 2 sets a higher price, some demand is shifted to firm 1, and firm 1's profit-maximizing price is higher than it would be if firm 2 set a lower price, all else equal.

Strategic substitutes, strategic complements   Because firms maximize profit by making choices that make residual marginal revenue equal to marginal cost, the way one firm's choices affect the marginal profitability and marginal revenue of other firms is fundamental to the nature of strategic interactions in imperfectly competitive markets. With linear demand for differentiated products and constant marginal cost, price best-response curves slope upward because if one firm raises its price, it becomes profitable for the other firm to increase its price. Firms' choice variables, prices, are *strategic complements*; increases in one price make profitable an increase in the other price.

---

[17] The second-order condition for a maximum is satisfied.

With linear demand and constant marginal cost, quantity best-response curves slope downward because if one firm produces more output, the marginal profitability of the other firm falls, making it profitable for the other firm to reduce its output. In that case, firms' choice variables, outputs, are *strategic substitutes* (Bulow et al., 1985), an increase in one making profitable a reduction in the other.

Bertrand equilibrium Bertrand equilibrium prices can be found, in general, by solving the system of equations of the firms' price best-response functions. For this example, equilibrium prices can be found by symmetry: the two firms are identical, and in equilibrium they will charge the same price, $p_{1/2}^B$. Setting $p_1 = p_2 = p_{1/2}^B$ in (3.51) and rearranging terms gives:

$$p_{1/2}^B = 40. \tag{3.52}$$

For general values of the product differentiation parameter θ, the equation of firm 1's best-response curve is:

$$p_1 = \frac{1}{2}\left(110 - 100\theta + \theta p_2\right) \tag{3.53}$$

(this corresponds to (3.51), and for $\theta = 1/2$, (3.53) and (3.51) are identical).
  If $\theta = 0$, the two products are independent in demand, and (3.53) reduces to:

$$p_1 = 55, \tag{3.54}$$

which is the monopoly price for a firm that faces no substitute products.
  If $\theta = 1$, the two products are perfect substitutes, and (3.53) reduces to:

$$p_1 = 5 + \frac{1}{2}p_2. \tag{3.55}$$

$\theta = 1$ is the homogeneous-product Bertrand case, and in equilibrium (set $p_1 = p_2 = p_1^B$ in (3.55)) price equals marginal cost:

$$p_1^B = 10. \tag{3.56}$$

With price-setting firms, the greater the degree of product differentiation (the lower is θ), the greater the equilibrium price-cost margin. As long as products are differentiated, equilibrium price-cost margins fall as the number of firms rises (see Problem 3–6).

Welfare What about welfare? With standardized products, sale of one additional unit of output by any firm affects the market in the same way—reduces price by an identical amount, leads to an identical increase in consumer surplus, an identical change in firms' profits, and an identical change in net social welfare (the sum of consumer surplus and firms' profits). With product differentiation, the matter is not so simple. If (say) firm 1 lowers its price, it will increase its own sales (tending to increase consumer welfare) but lower the sales of other firms (tending to reduce consumer welfare and the profits of other firms). The net impact on market performance depends on substitution patterns and on the prices of other firms.[18]

---

[18] The inverse demand equations given in Section 3.3.3 can be derived from an aggregate social welfare function of the form $U(q_1,q_2) = a(q_1 + q_2) - \frac{1}{2}b\left(q_1^2 + 2\theta q_1 q_2 + q_2^2\right)$ (see Problem 3–11). For any pair of outputs (q_1,q_2), subtracting the cost of production $c(q_1 + q_2)$ gives net social welfare; subtracting revenue $(p_1 q_1 + p_2 q_2)$ gives consumer surplus.

3.4 Cournot and Bertrand Compared

The Bertrand equilibrium price for the example of Section 3.3.3 (that is, horizontal product differentiation, with $\theta = 1/2$) is 40, and by substituting $p_{1/2}^B = 40$ in the demand equations (3.48), we find that Bertrand equilibrium outputs are $q_{1/2}^B = 40$.

Working out the Cournot equilibrium values for the same example (horizontal product differentiation, with $\theta = 1/2$; see Problem 3–2) shows that the Cournot equilibrium values are $p_{1/2}^C = 46$, $q_{1/2}^C = 36$. In this example, the equilibrium prices are lower, and quantities supplied higher, if firms pick prices rather than quantities. The result of this example holds generally: in otherwise identical markets, equilibrium prices are lower and outputs higher if firms are price setters than if they are quantity setters. In this sense, market performance is better ("more competitive") if firms set prices than if they set quantities.

The underlying reason that markets in which firms set prices have better market performance than markets in which firms set quantities is illustrated in Figure 3.10.[19] For the example of Section 3.3.3, Figure 3.10 shows firm 1's equilibrium residual demand curves for two cases. In the first case, firm 2 is quantity setter. The equation of firm 1's residual demand curve, from (3.47), and written in inverse form, is:

$$p_1 = \left(100 - \frac{1}{2}q_2\right) - q_1,$$

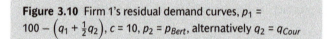

Figure 3.10 Firm 1's residual demand curves, $p_1 = 100 - \left(q_1 + \frac{1}{2}q_2\right)$, $c = 10$, $p_2 = p_{Bert}$, alternatively $q_2 = q_{Cour}$

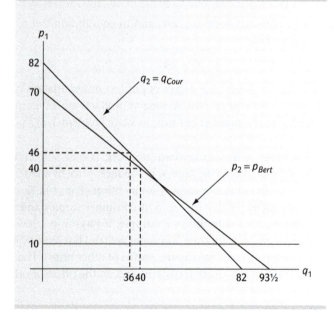

---

[19] To avoid visual clutter, marginal revenue curves are omitted from Figure 3.10. However, the prices and quantities indicated are those that maximize firm 1's payoff for the two alternative cases.

with q_2 set to its Cournot equilibrium value. In the second case, firm 2 is a price setter. The equation of firm 1's residual demand curve, from (3.48), is:

$$q_1 = \frac{2}{3}(100 + p_2) - \frac{4}{3}p_1,$$

with p_2 set to its Bertrand equilibrium value. If firm 2 is a quantity setter, firm 1's equilibrium residual demand curve is relatively steep (slope -1), less inelastic. If firm 2 is a price setter, firm 1's equilibrium residual demand curve is relatively flat, (slope $-3/4$), more elastic.[20] As indicated by the Lerner index of market power, a firm facing a more elastic demand maximizes profit by setting a price closer to marginal cost, all else equal. What drives the result that Bertrand equilibrium prices are closer to marginal cost than are Cournot equilibrium prices in otherwise identical markets is the fact that if competitors set price, a firm faces a more elastic residual demand curve than if competitors set quantities.

3.5 Markets with Consumer Search[21]

3.5.1 Setup

Incomplete consumer information can dramatically affect the results of the model of perfect competition. To see this,[22] keep all but one of the assumptions of the standard model of perfect competition. Let the product be standardized. Suppose there are many firms, with identical cost functions. There are also many consumers. Leaving aside search cost, the net utility of a consumer who purchases one unit of the good from store i at price p_i is the difference between the consumer's reservation price and the price paid:

$$u\left(p_i\right) = \rho - p_i. \tag{3.57}$$

Each consumer will buy one unit of the product if the price is less than or equal to a reservation price ρ, which in this context is the utility obtained by consuming one unit of the product. If the price is greater than ρ, the consumer instead buys an outside good that is traded in a perfectly competitive market.

The single departure we make from the assumptions of the standard model of perfect competition is to suppose that to learn the price charged by a store, a consumer must go to the store, and that it is costly to search stores after the first store that is visited. Firms know what it costs a consumer to search a new store. Consumers know the distribution of prices over stores, but they do not know (in advance of search) the price set by any one store. A consumer remembers the prices set at all stores he or she has visited. Because there are many small firms and many consumers, no one firm can affect consumers' search patterns, and consumers cannot affect firms' price choices.

3.5.2 Equilibrium

Suppose there were a set of prices in which one or more firms had posted a price less than ρ. Could this be an equilibrium—that is, could all firms, including those with prices below ρ,

---

[20] The extreme difference in elasticity occurs if products are standardized; then in Bertrand equilibrium firm 1 faces a demand curve that is flat, infinitely elastic, at a price equal to marginal cost.

[21] We consider search models in more detail in Chapter 13.

[22] Following Stiglitz (1989, pp. 779–782).

be maximizing profit, given consumer behaviour and given the prices set by other firms? With such prices, a low-price store could charge a price that was higher by an amount just below search cost without losing any sales. Since it would cost a consumer already at the store more to search other stores than the amount of the increase in price, consumers in the store would remain and purchase. But then the original set of prices is not an equilibrium: a low-price firm could increase its profit by raising its price.

In equilibrium, all firms set the reservation price ρ, which in this model is the monopoly price. Consumers know the equilibrium distribution of prices—that all firms charge the monopoly price—and in equilibrium each consumer visits one store and purchases one unit of the good.[23] This result, due to Diamond (1971), is known as the *Diamond Paradox*. A seemingly minor change in the assumptions of the perfectly competitive model—the presence of small but positive search costs—upends its predictions.

3.5.3 Extensions

We have seen that the results of the Bertrand model with a standardized product are not robust. With just a small amount of product differentiation, the Bertrand Paradox evaporates. A similar modification of the basic search model changes its results as well.

Anderson and Renault (1999) combine product differentiation with search by introducing consumer uncertainty about product characteristics as well as about price. They write the utility (before allowing for search cost) of consumer l who purchases at store i as:

$$u_{li}(p_i) = \rho\varepsilon_{li} - p_i. \tag{3.58}$$

ε_{li} is a scale factor indicating the way the particular variety of the product offered by store i satisfies consumer l's preferences. Before search, consumer l knows the distribution of ε across stores, but does not know the value of ε_{li} at any one store. Search is necessary not only to learn the price posted at a particular store, but also to learn the precise characteristics of a store's variety. Special cases of their model yield results corresponding to those of the Bertrand and the Diamond models. In the most general version of their model, equilibrium prices rise as search costs rise and equilibrium prices fall as the number of stores rises, so that the Diamond paradox does not hold.

3.5.4 The Incidence of Search in Markets for Perishable Goods

Economists have been wont to use the fish industry for illustrative purposes.[24] Yet when economists study actual fish markets, they find outcomes that differ in significant ways from the predictions of the models fish markets have often been used to illustrate.

A wholesale fish market—in which dealers who have purchased fish at harbour resell to grocers and restaurateurs—would seem to be the prototypical example of a search market.

---

[23] Thus, just as there is no competition (in the sense of rivalry) in the model of perfect competition (Ch. 2, fn. 4), so there is no search, in equilibrium, in this particular search model.

[24] Adam Smith ([1776] 1937, p. 235]) wrote of fisheries as a competitive industry with a rising supply price—to supply an increased demand for fish would require fishing boats to be larger and to go farther out to sea; the average cost of fish would rise with the quantity supplied. Thornton (1870) and John Stuart Mill (1869) debated the workings of dockside fish auctions. Alfred Marshall (1920, p. 477) used the daily fish-market as an example to illustrate competitive equilibrium in the very short run: on a given day, the quantity of fish in the market being predetermined and incapable of storage, it would be sold for what it would bring, and that price would be independent of the cost of production.

Yet the perishable nature of the product leads to outcomes that differ not only from the standard model of perfect competition but also from conventional search models.

During the first week in July, 1987 about 380 buyers and 37 sellers interacted (between 3 a.m. and 8 a.m.) at the Marseille fish market.[25] The wholesale sellers ordered their supplies two days before offering them for resale. Buyers, who themselves purchased for resale, either at grocery stores or restaurants (Kirman and Vriend, 2000, pp. 34–35; not set off as a bullet list in the original):

> shop around, visiting individual sellers. Standing face-to-face with a seller, the buyer tells the seller which type of fish and which quantity he is interested in. The seller then informs him about the price. Prices are not posted. And they are individual in a threefold sense.
>
> - First, each individual seller decides upon his own prices.
> - Second, each seller may have different prices for different buyers.
> - Third, each seller may even ask a different price for a given type and quantity of fish if that is proposed by the same buyer at different times of the day.
>
> A price communicated by an individual seller to an individual buyer for a given transaction is not perceived by other buyers or sellers in the market.

This market seems to come as close to having had "many small buyers" as one could hope for in a real-world market. There were not "many small sellers" of all types of fish,[26] but there were a large number of potential entrants among the 37 active sellers. The customer-specific nature of price information[27] created incentives for customers to search for price information. But the fixed supply of the product on any one day meant that if a customer invested "too much" in search, he/she might return to the vendor who had quoted the best price and find that vendor sold out. The perishable nature of the product placed vendors at risk as well: too high prices would encourage customers to search, leaving unsold fish that could only be thrown away at the end of the day.

One result of these bilateral incentives was the division of buyers into two groups (with occasional movement from one group to the other): loyal buyers who for the most part patronized one seller and searchers, who collected price information from several sellers before making a purchase. Figure 3.11 shows the distribution of buyers by number of sellers patronized. The largest group of buyers purchased from just one seller. The mean and median number of sellers patronized were between three and four; 57 per cent of buyers purchased from three or fewer sellers (Kirman and Vignes, 1991, p. 172).

Standard search models predict wholesale prices at the monopoly level. But the supply and the demand sides of this market both benefited from loyalty. Buyers who were loyal to a particular supplier economized on search costs and ensured themselves of a source of supply. Sellers who "rewarded" loyal customers with less-than-monopoly prices ensured that they would be able to dispose of their stocks by the end of the day. The presence of searchers

---

[25] The Marché d'intérêt national de Saumaty.

[26] See Weisbuch *et al.* (2000, p. 431, Table 2): at this same market over a much longer time period, the market shares of the three largest sellers of cod were 43, 14, and 12 per cent, respectively; for whiting, the corresponding figures were 27, 8, and 8 per cent, and for sole, 15, 14, and 14 per cent.

[27] The private quotation of prices is not idiosyncratic to the Marseille fish market; see Section 5.3.2 and the discussion of the Fulton Fish Market.

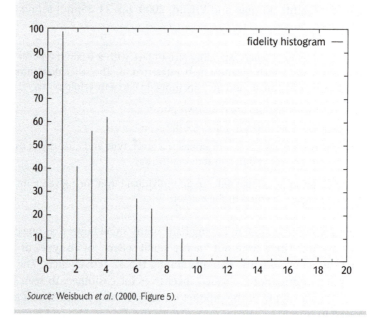

Figure 3.11 Distribution of buyers of cod according to the number of sellers they visit on average during one month in 1990. (Buyers visiting the market more than once per month and in the market for more than six months.)

Source: Weisbuch *et al.* (2000, Figure 5).

served to remind sellers that setting too high a price could cause a loyal buyer to seek supplies elsewhere.

3.6 Switching Costs

Anyone who has changed from using one software package to another functionally equivalent software package will accept the idea that there can be costs of switching from one product to a substitute. Simply knowing how goods are laid out along the aisles of one's regular supermarket makes it easier to shop there than elsewhere.

These kinds of switching costs are inherent in the nature of the product. Other switching costs may be a matter of product design: for someone who has acquired a movie library recorded on HD DVD discs, switching to Blu-ray means giving up the ability to view recordings that have already been paid for. Some kinds of switching costs may be contractual: if a supplier offers customers an annual loyalty rebate that is proportional to total purchases over the year, purchasing from another supplier means giving up some or all of the rebate. Airline frequent-flyer programmes create an incentive for a passenger to concentrate travel on a single line, to avoid deferring or missing entirely the accumulation of sufficient points to qualify for rewards.

One of the lessons of the consumer search literature is that within limits sellers have market power over loyal customers, and that this market power is mitigated if there is a group of customers who search avidly for the best offer. Switching costs create a kind of loyalty, and similarly endow suppliers with some market power over consumers who would have to bear an opportunity or financial cost to change suppliers.

To illustrate this, consider the case of a two-period Cournot duopoly market, with market inverse demand in each period given by the equation:[28]

$$p = 100 - (q_1 + q_2). \tag{3.59}$$

Each firm produces with constant marginal and average cost 10 per unit.

We know from previous discussions that monopoly output in this market is 45, and that Cournot duopoly output per firm is 30. But if each firm sells its Cournot output in the first period and offers repeat customers a "loyalty discount" of 10 in the second period, the second-period equilibrium has each firm producing half the monopoly output.

In first-period Cournot equilibrium, firms charge identical prices. 60 units of output are sold, half by each firm, and reservation prices for these 60 units range linearly from 40 to 100. Assume that in the first period, the firms divide sales for each reservation price. Then in the second period, if each firm confines its sales to its repeat customers, it is in effect a monopoly supplier of the half of market demand made up by those consumers. If, for example, firm 2 sells 30 or fewer units in the second period to its own repeat customers, its demand equation is:

$$q_{22} = \frac{1}{2} \left[100 - (p_{22} - 10) \right], \tag{3.60}$$

since $p_{22} - 10$ is the net price paid by repeat customers in the second period. For second-period sales of 30 units or less, firm 2's inverse demand equation is:

$$p_{22} = 110 - 2q_{22}. \tag{3.61}$$

If firm 2 sells 22.5 units in period 2, its price is 65, its net price after allowing for the loyalty discount is $65 - 10 = 55$, and it earns half the monopoly profit.

Similarly, if firm 1 produces less than 30 units of output in period 2, its inverse demand equation is:

$$p_{12} = 110 - 2q_{12}, \tag{3.62}$$

and its payoff after allowing for the loyalty discount is maximized it produces half the monopoly output, $q_{12} = 22.5$. Thus if firm 2 produces half the monopoly output in the second period, firm 1 maximizes its second-period profit by producing half the monopoly output. By symmetry, the same result holds if firm 1 produces half the monopoly output in the second period, firm 2 also maximizes its profit by producing half the monopoly output.[29]

In this example, contractually-induced switching costs make it possible for duopolists to non-cooperatively exercise more market power in the second period than would otherwise be the case. That is not the entire story, however. In this example, each firm in the second period is able to exercise full monopoly power over its first-period customers. It is valuable, in the second period, to have had more customers in the first period. It follows that in the first period each firm will have an incentive to compete more vigorously than it would

---

[28] This example is due to Klemperer (1987).

[29] Some details of the argument have been omitted. If $p_{12} - 10 > p_{22}$, all of firm 1's first-period customers will buy from 2. If $p_{22} - 10 > p_{12}$, all of firm 2's first-period customers will buy from 1. Hence the inverse demand equation (3.62) and the corresponding payoff function are valid for $p_{22} - d \leq p_{12} \leq p_{22} + d$; for p_{12} outside this range, firm 1's payoff must be computed differently. Examining firm 1's payoff over the complete range does not change the result. See Problem 3–8.

otherwise, to increase sales and the size of its captive second-period market. The net impact of the loyalty-discount scheme on market performance is the (appropriately discounted) sum of the improvement in market performance in the first period and the worsening of market performance in the second period. Whether switching costs are inherent, rooted in product design, or contractual, the market power they support over established customers is an explanation for the intense competition that often occurs when a new product is put before consumers for the first time.

3.7 Network Externalities

3.7.1 Direct, Indirect

A product exhibits *direct* network externalities if the value of the product to any one consumer is greater, the greater the number of consumers who use the product. Every additional telephone that is connected to a telephone network creates the possibility of an additional connection for every existing subscriber; every additional fax machine that is connected to a fax network makes it possible for each machine already in the network to communicate with one additional location.

Network externalities may also be *indirect*. A Blu-ray disc player, in and of itself, yields no utility; it is useful only insofar as there are compatible complementary goods, pre-recorded Blu-ray discs, available for use with the player. The player is a platform that permits consuming the services of pre-recorded discs, and a Blu-ray disc player is more useful, the greater the number of pre-recorded Blu-ray format programs on the market. The larger the number of consumers who use Blu-ray players, the larger the number of Blu-ray discs it will be profitable to put on the market, and the greater the value of Blu-ray disc players to consumers. Thus the issues raised by direct network externalities for market structure and performance can carry over to markets that involve complementary goods—goods that must be used together to yield utility—rather than networks in a literal sense.

3.7.2 Strategic Possibilities

If a market involves indirect network externalities, a firm developing a system good may find it profitable to encourage competitors to come into the market. By ensuring that there are several independent producers of substitute components of a system (CD players; Intel-compatible personal computers), a system innovator can make an effective commitment to potential producers of compatible products (speakers; software, printers) that there will be a market for their goods, increasing the supply of compatible products and thus increasing the value of the innovator's product to consumers.

Compatibility, or the lack of it, raises issues of business strategy and market performance. Suppose that any CD player can be used with any set of speakers and that consumers get utility only from a system composed of a CD player and a set of speakers. Then with m players and n speakers on the market, there are mn potential systems available to consumers. If m is small and n large, manufacturers of CD players could sharply reduce the number of combinations available to consumers by producing only integrated player-speaker sets, or by designing interfaces so that their players would connect only to speakers they produce.[30] Such an integrated system might or might not be more efficient in a technical sense; if it is put on the market, that means the producer expects it to be more profitable than marketing components. Yet the reduction in available product combinations could leave consumers worse off.

3.8 Platform Markets

We have studied models of imperfectly competitive markets with firms on one side of a market and consumers on the other. Yet there are many businesses whose line of work is in the nether region *between* the supply side and the demand side of a market. Newspapers and popular magazines sell news and reading material to subscribers, but also sell the opportunity to deliver messages to potential clients to advertisers. Private television and radio networks do much the same thing, giving away rather than selling their broadcast product. These media enterprises bring together suppliers and consumers of information. Real estate agencies bring together home buyers and home sellers. The producer of a computer operating system provides a platform for transactions between writers and users of software packages. Malls profit by providing a location within which stores and shoppers interact. Firms that supply such *platform markets* intermediate between the demand and supply sides of a market, making it possible for the two sides of a market to interact.[31]

The commercial success of a computer operating system or a video game console depends on bringing together software developers and users. The commercial success of a credit card depends on cultivating a sufficiently large number of individuals who will use the card to make payments and a sufficiently large number of firms that will accept the card as a means of payment. The commercial success of a dating club depends on attracting the right mix of compatible patrons.

Platform markets typically involve uninternalized externalities. A credit card brand is more attractive to stores, the more consumers carry it. But no one consumer takes into account, in deciding to carry a credit card, that the decision to do so makes the credit card brand more attractive to store owners. Nor does a store owner take into account that a decision to accept payment by means of a credit card brand confers a benefit on all consumers who carry that type of credit card.

Firms that supply platform markets internalize these externalities by structuring relative prices to bring both sides into the market. Because profitable operation in a platform market depends on balancing the two sides of the market, intuition based on the way imperfectly competitive one-sided markets work is often misleading when applied to platform markets.

---

[30] In the latter case, an independent firm with sufficient information about the design of the interface might manufacture an adapter that would circumvent the manufacturer's intentions and make it possible to connect the manufacturer's stereo player to speakers produced by other firms.

[31] "Platform markets" are more commonly referrred to as "two-sided markets". Ordover (2007, p. 181) makes a convincing argument that this usage obscures more than it clarifies: "A freshman student in economics or a Nobel prize-winning macroeconomist who has lately stumbled across a journal or two in industrial organization economics may be somewhat perplexed or confused by many references to two-sided markets. Surely, is it not the case that all markets have two sides, namely buyers and sellers? Consequently, to the uninitiated, the concept of a two-sided market offers little, if any, additional analytical insight. Some of that confusion is perhaps dispelled by a more informative description, namely: markets with two-sided platforms."

3.8.1 A Stylized Model of the Market for Credit Cards

Consider, for example, a monopoly supplier of a credit card that may be used to pay for lunch in the immediate neighbourhood of Major Midwestern University (MMU).[32] The credit card firm charges buyers (lunchers) a price p^B and sellers (restaurateurs) a price p^S each time a credit card is used to pay for a meal. It costs the credit card company c to process each transaction.

Quasi-demands

Write *quasi-demand functions* showing the number of buyers willing to pay by credit card and the number of sellers willing to accept payment by credit card as:[33]

$$N^B = D^B\left(p^B\right) \tag{3.63}$$

and

$$N^S = D^S\left(p^S\right), \tag{3.64}$$

respectively. We assume that the quasi-demand functions have negative derivatives: fewer customers will wish to pay by credit card, the larger is p^B; fewer restaurants will wish to accept payment by credit card, the larger is p^S.

In contrast to most markets in which the demand and supply sides interact directly, for platform markets we consider for the possibility that p^B might be negative. A credit card that gives a purchaser a cash rebate, frequent flyer points, or the like is effectively charging a negative price for use of the card. In other types of platform markets, a negative buyer fee may be infeasible. It may nonetheless be a profit-maximizing strategy to simply give the product to one side of the market. An example is local newspapers distributed without charge on subway systems of major cities.

The maximum number of potential credit card transactions is:

$$D^B\left(p^B\right)D^S\left(p^S\right). \tag{3.65}$$

For specificity, we consider a particular lunchtime dining pattern. In search of variety, lunchers who pay by credit card patronize restaurants that accept credit cards one after another, and visit all such restaurants once before patronizing any restaurant a second time. Further, we define a single time period as the number of days required for all lunchers to visit all restaurants once and only once. Then (3.65) gives the actual number of credit card transactions.[34]

Payoff and Lerner indices

Leaving aside fixed cost, the credit card company's profit is its profit per transaction times the number of transactions,

$$\left(p^B + p^S - c\right)D^B\left(p^B\right)D^S\left(p^S\right). \tag{3.66}$$

---

[32] The model that follows is due to Rochet and Tirole (2003). They extend the model to the oligopoly case.

[33] The number of buyers willing to pay for lunch with a credit card will depend on the price of a meal. The equilibrium price for lunch will depend on the extent of product differentiation and on oligopolistic interaction among restaurateurs. It will also depend on the nature of demand from customers who do not wish to pay by credit card. Although we write of "the" price for lunch, different items on a menu will sell for different prices. We ignore all such factors to simplify the discussion and to highlight specific characteristics of platform markets.

[34] This choice of the length of time period is a heuristic device. Qualitatively similar results hold if the actual number of transactions in any time period is proportional to (3.65).

The first-order conditions that characterize the profit-maximizing prices p^B and p^S are:

$$\left(p^B + p^S - c\right) \frac{dD^B\left(p^B\right)}{dp^B} + D^B\left(p^B\right) \equiv 0 \tag{3.67}$$

and

$$\left(p^B + p^S - c\right) \frac{dD^S\left(p^S\right)}{dp^S} + D^S\left(p^S\right) \equiv 0, \tag{3.68}$$

respectively. These can be rewritten as:

$$\frac{p^B - \left(c - p^S\right)}{p^B} = \frac{1}{\varepsilon_B} \tag{3.69}$$

and

$$\frac{p^S - \left(c - p^B\right)}{p^S} = \frac{1}{\varepsilon_S}, \tag{3.70}$$

where ε_B is the price-elasticity of buyers' quasi-demand and ε_S is the price-elasticity of sellers' quasi-demand.[35]

(3.69) and (3.70) are Lerner indices of market power, adapted to allow for the platform nature of the market. An increase in p^B means slightly fewer buyers are willing to carry a credit card. Just how many fewer depends on the elasticity ε_B. For every buyer that does not use a credit card, a transaction does not occur and the firm saves the marginal cost of a transaction, c. But the firm also gives up the fee it would have received from the seller, p^S. In a platform market, the opportunity cost of giving up the marginal buying-side transaction by raising p^B is $c - p^S$, not (as one would expect in a one-sided market) c. Similarly, $c - p^B$ is the opportunity cost of giving up the marginal supply-side transaction by raising p^S.

From (3.69) and (3.70), we obtain a Lerner index that characterizes the optimal total receipts per transaction of the credit card firm, $p^B + p^S$:[36]

$$\frac{p^B + p^S - c}{p^B + p^S} = \frac{1}{\varepsilon_B + \varepsilon_S}. \tag{3.71}$$

The profit-maximizing total price makes the total price-cost margin equal to the inverse of the sum of the quasi-demand elasticities. The total price, $p^B + p^S$, exceeds marginal cost. Either element of total price, p^B or p^S, may be less than marginal cost, if a low price is needed to recruit on one side of the market.

From (3.69) and (3.70), we also obtain a relation between the profit-maximizing fees,

$$\frac{p^B}{p^S} = \frac{\varepsilon_B}{\varepsilon_S}. \tag{3.72}$$

In an imperfectly competitive one-sided market, we expect price and the price-cost margin to be inversely related to the price elasticity of demand. (3.71) tells us that such a relationship

---

[35] That is, $\varepsilon_B = -D^B\left(p^B\right) / \left[p^B \frac{dD^B\left(p^B\right)}{dp^B}\right]$ and $\varepsilon_S = -D^S\left(p^S\right) / \left[p^S \frac{dD^S\left(p^S\right)}{dp^S}\right]$.

[36] Rewrite the first-order conditions as

$$\frac{p^B}{p^B + p^S - c} = \varepsilon_B \text{ and } \frac{p^S}{p^B + p^S - c} = \varepsilon_S.$$

Add these expressions to obtain

$$\frac{p^B + p^S}{p^B + p^S - c} = \varepsilon_B + \varepsilon_S,$$

and invert to reach (3.71).

holds for the total price in a platform market. But (3.72) means that a monopolist of a platform market, having set total price according to (3.71), will charge a relatively lower fee to the side of the market that has the lowest quasi-demand elasticity. The number of transactions is the product $D^B(p^B) D^S(p^S)$ of the number of buyers and the number of sellers in the market. The firm will set a relatively low price for the side of the market that has a low elasticity, to bring the profitable number of transactees on that side into the market. Since the sum of prices, $p^B + p^S$, must satisfy (3.71), a lower price to one side of the market means a higher price for the other. Some transactees on the side of the market getting a higher price will leave the market, reducing $D^B(p^B) D^S(p^S)$, but the increase in the number of transactees on the side of the market getting a lower price will act in the opposite direction, increasing $D^B(p^B) D^S(p^S)$.

SUMMARY

Models of oligopoly with complete and perfect information suggest that fewness of firms (large market shares, large Herfindahl indices) and product differentiation go together with the equilibrium exercise of market power. The theory of contestable markets highlights the importance of potential competition for market performance: the profit-maximizing behaviour of firms in markets with free and easy entry is as effective as non-cooperative rivalry among a large number of incumbents in getting good market performance. The emphasis of the theory of contestable markets on entry conditions is entirely consistent with the structure-conduct-performance paradigm (Baumol, 1982, p. 2; Baumol *et al.*, 1983, p. 494). But the requirements that must be satisfied for potential competition to have an effective impact on market performance are stringent. In addition to these supply-side factors, search models suggest that market performance is likely to be better, the more active are consumers in seeking the best price.

Markets with network externalities may perform well even though supplied by a dominant firm, because the value of a network good to any one user rises, the greater the total number of users. Firms that operate in platform markets set prices to each side to balance quantity demanded and quantity supplied, to the mutual benefit of both sides (and of the firm or firms in the middle). One side or the other may face non-cooperative equilibrium prices that are zero or negative prices.

STUDY POINTS

- Cournot duopoly game (Section 3.2.1)
- Cournot equilibrium (Section 3.2.1)
- Residual demand curve (Section 3.2.2)
- Best-response function (Section 3.2.2)
- Efficiency rent (Section 3.2.4)
- Herfindahl index of seller concentration (Section 3.2.4)
- Conjectural variations (Section 3.2.5)
- Generalized Lerner index of market power (Section 3.2.5)
- Bertrand duopoly game
  - standardized product (Section 3.3.1)
  - differentiated product (Section 3.3.3)

- Search models (Section 3.5), Diamond Paradox (Section 3.5.2)
- Switching costs (Section 3.6)
- Network externalities (Section 3.7.1)
- Platform markets (Section 3.8)

FURTHER READING

On Cournot and his contributions, see Fisher (1898), Moore (1905), Edgeworth (1926), Nichol (1938), Shubik (1987), Daughety (1988, 2007), Vives (1989), Ekelund and Hébert (1990b), and Dimand (1995). Cournot's equilibrium analysis anticipates the modern game-theoretic Nash equilibrium concept (Nash, 1950, 1951). On the relation between the Cournot and Nash equilibrium concepts, see Leonard (1994). For non-technical expositions of the development of game theory, see Poundstone (1992) and Siegfried (2006). For an introduction to game theory, see among many others Gibbons (1992).

On the origins of the Herfindahl index, see Hirschman (1964) (as well as Hirschman (1945), Herfindahl (1950)). On the numbers-equivalent property of the Herfindahl index, see Adelman (1961) and on its properties generally, Kwoka (1985).

For early uses of conjectural variations, see Bowley (1924, p. 38), Frisch (1933, p. 252), and Hicks (1935). More recently, see Dockner (1992) and Cabral (1995), among others, as well as Corts (1999).

For an accessible discussion of the formal assumptions that characterize a perfectly contestable market, see Spence (1983).

The model of horizontal product differentiation introduced in Section 3.3.3 is due to Bowley (1924), and more recently used by Spence (1976), Dixit (1979), Singh and Vives (1984), and Mueller (1986, Chapter 4). See also Martin (2009).

Scitovsky (1950) emphasized the importance of consumer behaviour for market performance. Diamond (1971) triggered the modern literature on markets with imperfect consumer information, for references to which see Stiglitz (1989), Anderson and Renault (1999), and Waterson (2003).

For a survey of the literature on switching costs, see Klemperer (1995). Regarding the literature on network economics, see Economides (1996) and his web site (URL<http://www.stern.nyu.edu/networks/site.html>). Rochet and Tirole (2005) give references to and perspectives on research about platform markets.

On network externalities, see Katz and Shapiro (1985), the symposium on network externalities in the Spring 1994 issue of the *Journal of Economic Perspectives*, Economides (1996), and the October 1996 special issue of the *International Journal of Industrial Organization*. On compatibility, see Matutes and Regibeau (1988), the Symposium on Compatibility in the March 1992 issue of the *Journal of Industrial Economics*, and the 1996 special issue of the *European Journal of Political Economy* on the economics of standardization.

PROBLEMS

Asterisks indicate advanced problems.

3–1 (Cournot duopoly, standardized product) Let the equation of the inverse demand curve for a Cournot duopoly be:

$$p = 195 - Q = 195 - (q_1 + q_2)$$

where q_1 is the output of firm 1 and q_2 is the output of firm 2. The firms have identical cost functions.

$$c(q_i) = 15q_i, i = 1,2.$$

(a) Explain in general terms what firm 1's residual demand curve is. What is the equation of firm 1's residual demand curve for this problem?

(b) Explain in general terms what firm 1's best-response function is. What is the equation of firm 1's best-response function for this problem?

(c) Graph firm 1's best-response function and firm 2's best-response function on the same diagram.

(d) What are the Cournot duopoly equilibrium outputs for this market? What is the Cournot duopoly equilibrium price?

(e) What is economic profit per firm in Cournot duopoly equilibrium?

(f) What is the value of the Lerner index of market power in Cournot duopoly equilibrium for this problem?

(g) What are the amounts of consumers' surplus and deadweight welfare loss in Cournot duopoly equilibrium for this problem?

3–2 (Cournot duopoly, differentiated products) Let the equations of the inverse demand curves for two varieties of a differentiated product be:

$$p_1 = 195 - (q_1 + \theta q_2) \qquad p_2 = 195 - (\theta q_1 + q_2) \qquad (3.73)$$

and suppose both firms operate with constant marginal and average cost 15 per unit. How do the graphs of the best response functions shift as θ varies from 0 to 1? How do equilibrium outputs and prices change?

3–3 (Bertrand differentiated-products duopoly) Let $\theta = \dfrac{1}{2}$ for the inverse demand equations of Problem 3–2:

$$p_1 = 195 - (q_1 + \frac{1}{2}q_2) \qquad p_2 = 195 - (\frac{1}{2}q_1 + q_2). \qquad (3.74)$$

The corresponding demand equations are:

$$q_1 = 130 - \frac{4}{3}p_1 + \frac{2}{3}p_2 \qquad q_2 = 130 + \frac{2}{3}p_1 - \frac{4}{3}p_2. \qquad (3.75)$$

Find equilibrium prices and profits if firms produce with constant marginal and average cost 15 per unit. Compare with the results of Problem 3–2 (for $\theta = \dfrac{1}{2}$).

3–4* For the parameter values of Problem 3–3, suppose firm 1 picks its quantity and firm 2 picks its price. Find non-cooperative equilibrium prices and outputs. Compare with the results of Problem 3–2 (for $\theta = \dfrac{1}{2}$) and Problem 3–3.

3–5 For quantity-setting duopoly with inverse demand curve:

$$p = 100 - (q_1 + q_2) \qquad (3.76)$$

and constant marginal cost 10 per unit, find equilibrium prices and profits if each firm maximizes a weighted average of profit and sales:

$$g_i = (1 - \sigma)\pi_i + \sigma p_i q_i. \qquad (3.77)$$

Illustrate non-cooperative equilibrium on a best-response curve diagram.

3–6 For the price-setting duopoly with product differentiation of Problem 3–3, find equilibrium prices and profits if firm 2 maximizes profit while firm 1 maximizes a weighted average of profit and sales:

$$g_1 = (1 - \sigma)\pi_1 + \sigma p_1 q_1. \tag{3.78}$$

3–7 For a price-setting oligopoly with product differentiation, let the equations of the inverse demand curves be:

$$p_i = 100 - (q_i + \theta Q_{-i}), \tag{3.79}$$

for $i = 1,2,...,n$ and $Q_{-i} = \sum_{j \neq i}^{n} q_j$.
    The equations of the corresponding demand curves are:

$$q_i = \frac{90(1 - \theta) - [1 + (n - 2)\theta](p_i - 10) + \theta \sum_{j \neq i}^{n} (p_j - 10)}{(1 - \theta)[1 + (n - 1)\theta]}. \tag{3.80}$$

If marginal cost is constant at 10 per unit, show that when firms set prices to maximize own profit, equilibrium prices are:

$$p_B = 10 + (1 - \theta)\frac{90}{2 + (n - 3)\theta}, \tag{3.81}$$

so that for all $\theta < 1$, equilibrium prices fall as the number of firms rises.

3–8 (Switching costs) Two quantity-setting firms, each of which produces with constant marginal and average cost c per unit, supply a market that meets for two successive periods. In each period the market demand equation is:

$$p = a - b(q_1 + q_2). \tag{3.82}$$

In the first period, each firm produces its Cournot-equilibrium output. In the second period, each firm offers repeat purchasers a loyalty discount d.
    Show that in second-period equilibrium, each firm produces half the monopoly output.

3–9 (Monopoly platform market) For the model of Section 3.8, let the quasi-demand functions be linear:

$$D^B(p^B) = \alpha^B - \beta^B p^B \text{ and } D^S(p^S) = \alpha^S - \beta^S p^S, \tag{3.83}$$

where α^B, β^B, α^S, and β^S are all positive.
    Find equilibrium prices p^B and p^S and the equilibrium total price, $p^B + p^S$.

3–10* Alter the model of Section 3.2.2 by supposing that the government imposes a tax t on every unit of output sold. How does the tax affect equilibrium outputs, price, consumer surplus, and deadweight welfare loss? What is the upper limit on the value of the tax? What tax level maximizes government tax collections?

3–11* (Representative consumer linear demand, differentiated products; Bowley, 1924, p. 56). Let there be two varieties of a good, variety 1 and variety 2, of which quantities q_1 and q_2 are sold at prices p_1 and p_2, respectively, and a homogeneous good m sold at price 1. Preferences are described by the representative consumer welfare function:

$$U(q_1,q_2,m) = \alpha(q_1 + q_2) - \frac{1}{2}\beta(q_1^2 + 2\theta q_1 q_2 + q_2^2) + m, \tag{3.84}$$

which is valid for $q_1 \geq 0$, $q_2 \geq 0$, $m \geq 0$. The aggregate budget constraint is:

$$Y = p_1 q_1 + p_2 q_2 + m. \tag{3.85a}$$

α and β are positive parameters; θ is a parameter with $0 \leq \theta \leq 1$, and Y is aggregate income. Aggregate demand for q_1 and q_2 and m is found by maximizing the representative consumer welfare function (3.84) subject to the budget constraint (3.85a).

Find the equations of the inverse demand functions for q_1 and q_2.

OLIGOPOLY II: ADDRESS MODELS

I could be bounded in a nutshell, and count myself a king of infinite space.

Hamlet, Act 2, Scene 2

4.1 Introduction

The demand sides of the standard Cournot and Bertrand models make assumptions about *aggregate* demand. An alternative class of models follows the lead of Hotelling (1929) and starts with assumptions about the demands of *individual consumers*. In this second class of models, the properties of aggregate demand are derived from assumptions about individual demand, not assumed to begin with. Aggregate substitutability relationships, whatever they are, are implied by the assumptions made about individual demand. In this type of model, individual consumers are often described as differing in terms of their location in physical space or in their preferences over an abstract space of product characteristics. For this reason, models that begin with assumptions about individual consumers' demands are referred to as spatial, location, or address models. The first such model that we consider is the spatial model of oligopoly with horizontal product differentiation, in the tradition of Hotelling (1929). We then turn to an address model of vertical product differentiation. Although these two types of product differentiation begin with very different stories about consumer preferences, formal analysis reveals that they have significant underlying similarities.

4.2 Spatial Oligopoly

The Cournot and Bertrand oligopoly models, along with the standard models of perfect competition and monopoly, gloss over the fact that markets have a geographic aspect—that a supplier must transport the product to market, or the consumer go to the supplier's retail outlet. In part, this may reflect a judgement that spatial relationships will be important only if transportation cost is a large part of the cost of getting products to consumers, and that for many products, this is not the case. Such a judgement will often be convincing if spatial models are taken literally—one does not expect transportation cost to have an important influence on (say) the market for diamonds.

But in spatial (or address, or location) models "distance" is often interpreted figuratively, in terms of product characteristics. Interpreted literally, a spatial model might picture a consumer who must decide between going to a shopping centre that is five miles away and another that is seven miles away, those being the two closest alternatives. Interpreted figuratively, a spatial model might picture a consumer who must decide between a somewhat larger station wagon that gets 14 miles to the gallon and a somewhat smaller station wagon that gets 18 miles to the gallon, those being the two closest alternatives on the market to the vehicle the consumer would really prefer, which is an intermediate-size station wagon that gets 16 miles to the gallon.

If spatial models are taken figuratively, the neglect of "distance" amounts to the view that the disutility or loss of satisfaction when the best available variety differs from a consumer's first-best choice is small. In view of the finite number of varieties of any particular product that can be produced, and the infinite range of human desire, the argument that "transportation cost" in its figurative interpretation can safely be neglected will be unconvincing for many markets.

We introduce a series of spatial models of horizontal product differentiation. Our first model is of a market in which firms pick location, but not price. Our second model is of a market in which firms pick price, but not location. We then discuss some of the simpler models in which firms pick both location (product characteristics) and price.

4.2.1 The Emperors of Ice Cream

Figure 4.1 shows a one-dimensional spatial market, a beach, of length L. We suppose that it is supplied by two ice-cream vendors, A and B. Consumers are distributed uniformly along the beach,[1] and we may as well assume that there is one consumer per unit distance. There are thus a total of l consumers on the demand side of the beach market for ice cream.

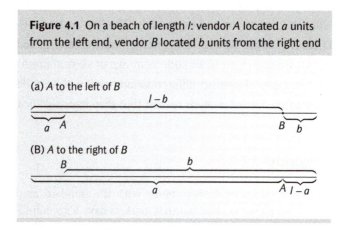

Figure 4.1 On a beach of length l: vendor A located a units from the left end, vendor B located b units from the right end

(a) A to the left of B

$l - b$

a A B b

(B) A to the right of B

B b

a A $l - a$

---

[1] One might expect customers to be clustered around the centre of the beach, the typical location of the lifeguard stand. When the assumption that consumers are uniformly distributed in geographic or product-characteristics space is made, as it often is, it is justified on the ground of simplicity, and we do so here.

We assume that the wholesale price of ice-cream bars (the price paid by the vendors to their suppliers) is constant, and normalize it to be zero. This amounts to measuring retail price as an increase over the wholesale price. The vendors have no variable costs other than what they pay at wholesale to purchase ice-cream bars for resale.

The franchise agreement under which the vendors supply the beach specifies the price that must be charged. This price is sufficiently low that each consumer buys one bar of ice cream. Vanity ensures that no consumer buys more than one bar of ice cream. It is inconvenient to walk to a vendor's location, so each consumer buys from the nearest vendor. If the two vendors locate back-to-back, each supplies half the market.[2]

Equilibrium locations

On these assumptions, the only choice open to a vendor is where to stand on the beach. What are the non-cooperative equilibrium locations of the two vendors? In a configuration like Figure 4.1(a), vendor A sells to the a consumers on its left and to half of the $l - (a + b)$ consumers located between the two vendors. A's sales are:

$$q_A = a + \frac{1}{2}(l - b - a) = \frac{1}{2}(l - b + a). \tag{4.1}$$

Vendor A's best response to a B location like that shown in Figure 4.1(a) is to locate a small distance to the left of B. By so doing, it captures almost all the $l - b$ sales on the left part of the beach. By the same kind of argument, vendor B's best response to an A location like that shown in Figure 4.1(a) is to locate a small distance to the right of A. By so doing, it captures almost all the $l - a$ sales on the right part of the beach. The same sorts of arguments apply if A is located to the right of B, as in Figure 4.1(b). The only equilibrium pair of locations has both vendors back-to-back at the centre of the beach, each supplying half of the market, $l/2$.

Principle of minimum differentiation

This result is consistent with Hotelling's (1929, p. 41) observation of 'an undue tendency for competitors to imitate each other in quality of goods, in location, and in other essential ways' (Hotelling, 1929, p. 54):[3]

> Buyers are confronted everywhere with an excessive sameness. When a new merchant or manufacturer sets up shop he must not produce something exactly like what is already on the market or he will risk a price war of the type discussed by Bertrand ... . But there is an incentive to make the new product very much like the old ... [a] tendency to make only slight deviations in order to have for the new commodity as many buyers of the old as possible, to get ... between one's competitors and a mass of customers.

Boulding (1966) called this tendency the *Principle of Minimum Differentiation.*

In equilibrium, with vendors located at the centre of the beach, consumers travel an average distance one-quarter the length of the beach to reach the nearest ice cream vendor. This outcome is inefficient. Travel distance is minimized if vendors locate at the one-quarter

---

[2] An alternative interpretation of the model (Downs, 1957) is that A and B are political parties, that locations on the line represent the ideological position of the party platform, and that voters, distributed (uniformly or otherwise) along the line according to their own political preferences (left wing, right wing) vote for the political party with a platform that is closest to their own views.

[3] In the political interpretation of fn. 2, the principle of minimum differentiation may be thought to explain the tendency of the platforms of the two major U.S. political parties to resemble each other.

and three-quarters points of the beach. The average distance covered by consumers with this efficient location pattern is one-eighth the length of the beach.[4] The non-cooperative equilibrium location pattern has consumers travel, on average, twice as far as the efficient location pattern.

 BOX   Spatial Duopoly in the Canadian Fur Trade

Canada's fur trade opened up in the seventeenth century, as French and English traders bartered European products, directly and through Indian and European middlemen, for beaver and other fur. Rivalry between the French and the English intensified with the chartering of the Hudson's Bay Company (HBC) in 1670, but the French were excluded from western Canada as an ancillary part of the 1713 Treaty of Utrecht, which settled the War of the Spanish Succession. The Hudson's Bay Company soon faced competition from independent traders, some of whom set up the North West Company in 1787. HBC facilities were initially located where rivers flowed into Hudson Bay, and the Company relied on Indian middlemen to bring furs to trading posts. The North West Company established posts in fur-bearing lands, intercepting the flow of furs to HBC trading posts and making

Figure 4.2 Distribution of competing trading posts in Western Canada, 1810

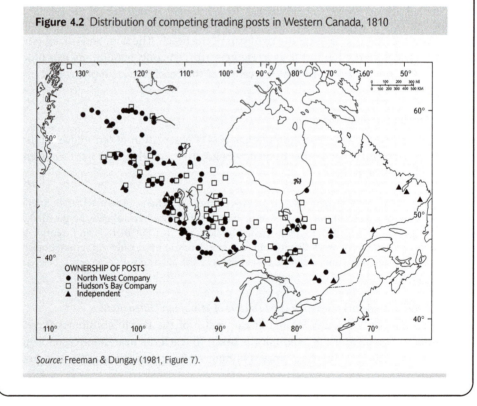

Source: Freeman & Dungay (1981, Figure 7).

---

[4] Since price is set by the franchise contract and the vendors sell the same amounts in either case, they would earn the same amounts at either set of locations.

it unnecessary for trappers to make the long trip to Hudson Bay. The North West personnel took their purchased furs to Montreal and thence to the European market. The Hudson's Bay Company soon established its own posts in the hinterland. As shown in Figure 4.2, by 1810 the trading posts of the two different companies tended very much to cluster, as predicted by the principle of minimum differentiation. The resulting cutthroat competition paved the way for the 1821 merger of the two firms (Freeman and Dungey, 1981, p. 268), "a union which mutual interests, born of near calamitous violence and escalating overhead costs of competitive trade, clearly dictated".

Source: Freeman and Dungey (1981), Spraakman (2002), Roberts (2004).

4.2.2 Main Street

Setup

For a linear market like that of the beach model, which (following custom) we now think of as representing a street rather than a beach, suppose that locations are fixed, as in Figure 4.3, and that each firm sets the price at which it will sell. The street is of length l, and there are l consumers distributed uniformly along the street. Each consumer buys 1 unit of the product from the firm that offers the lowest total price. The total cost of the product to the consumer is the sum of the price paid to the firm at the firm's location (p_A or p_B) plus the cost of transportation from the consumer's location to the location of favoured supplier.

For the moment we assume that transportation cost is a constant t per unit distance. The transportation cost to serve a customer at distance x from firm A and at distance y from firm B is tx if the consumer buys from A and ty if the consumer buys from B. Interpreted literally as transportation cost, the results are the same if we think of the customer as travelling to

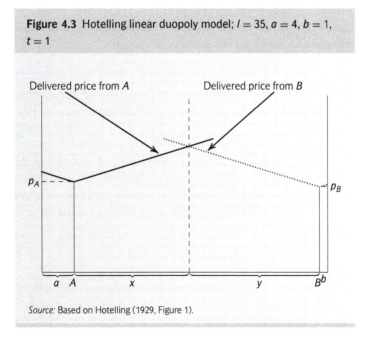

Figure 4.3 Hotelling linear duopoly model; $l = 35$, $a = 4$, $b = 1$, $t = 1$

Source: Based on Hotelling (1929, Figure 1).

and from the plant's location to pick up the product, at cost (say, to buy from A), tx, or if the firm delivers to the customer's location and includes the cost of transportation in the amount paid by the customer ($p_A + tx$). Interpreted figuratively, "transportation cost" corresponds to the utility lost by buying a variety of the product that is not the customer's most-preferred variety.

We assume that marginal production cost is constant. To keep the analysis as simple as possible, we suppose as well that the constant value of marginal cost is zero. This does not affect the nature of the results.

Demand

To analyse pricing decisions, we need to work out the way quantities demanded are related to price. The distance between the locations of the two firms is:

$$l - a - b. \tag{4.2}$$

If firm B sets a price so low that it can undersell firm A at A's location, then all consumers will buy from firm B. Such a price must satisfy the relationship:

$$p_B + t(l - a - b) < p_A. \tag{4.3}$$

If firm B sets a price so high that firm A can undersell firm B at B's location, then all consumers will buy from firm A. Such a price must satisfy the relationship:

$$p_A + t(l - a - b) < p_B. \tag{4.4}$$

Thus we have two parts of firm B's demand equation:

$$q_B(p_A, p_B) = \begin{cases} l & p_B < p_A - t(l - a - b) \\ b + ? & \text{otherwise} \\ 0 & p_A + t(l - a - b) < p_B \end{cases}. \tag{4.5}$$

For very low p_B, firm B supplies the whole market; for very high p_B, firm B makes no sales. What about intermediate values of p_B? For prices in the range:

$$p_A - t(l - a - b) \le p_B \le p_A + t(l - a - b), \tag{4.6}$$

let the distances x from firm A and y from firm B, with $x + y = l - a - b$, indicate the location of the consumer would pay the same total price by buying from either supplier (see Figure 4.3):

$$p_A + tx = p_B + ty. \tag{4.7}$$

Such a consumer would be indifferent between buying from A and buying from B. Consumers to the left of this boundary consumer would pay a lower delivered price to A than to B. Consumers to the right of this consumer would pay a lower delivered price to B than to A.

Substituting $x = l - a - b - y$ in (4.7) and rearranging terms gives the distance on B's left to the border location,

$$y = \frac{1}{2}\left(l - a - b + \frac{p_A - p_B}{t}\right). \tag{4.8}$$

If firm B sets the same price as firm A, then A and B evenly divide sales between their two locations. The lower is firm B's price, the greater is its share of the sales between the locations of the two firms.

For prices in the intermediate range, firm B sells to its hinterland (the interval of length b to the right of B's location) and to consumers on its left out to the boundary location y, so the quantity demanded of firm B is:

$$b + \frac{1}{2}\left(l - a - b + \frac{p_A - p_B}{t}\right) = \frac{1}{2}\left(l - a + b + \frac{p_A - p_B}{t}\right). \tag{4.9}$$

The complete expression for firm B's aggregate demand equation, derived from the demand behaviour of individual consumers, is then:

$$q_B(p_A, p_B) = \begin{cases} l & p_B < p_A - t(l - a - b) \\ \frac{1}{2}\left(l - a + b + \frac{p_A - p_B}{t}\right) & \text{otherwise} \\ 0 & p_A + t(l - a - b) < p_B \end{cases} \tag{4.10}$$

Payoffs

Intuition suggests that firms would not wish to price themselves out of the market (as in the bottom row, when p_B is very large) or allow themselves to be priced out of the market (which firm A would have to do in the top row, when p_B is very low). We will come back to this, and see that intuition can be wrong. But for the moment, let us consider the case in which demand for B's variety is in the intermediate range. Then B's payoff function (recall that we have assumed that average cost is zero) is:

$$\pi_B(p_A, p_B) = \frac{1}{2}p_B\left(l - a + b + \frac{p_A - p_B}{t}\right). \tag{4.11}$$

If we go through the same steps for firm A, we find that its profit function (when the demand for A's variety is in its intermediate range) is:

$$\pi_A(p_A, p_B) = \frac{1}{2}p_A\left(l + a - b + \frac{p_B - p_A}{t}\right). \tag{4.12}$$

Best-response functions

The equation of the first-order condition to maximize $\pi_A(p_A, p_B)$ with respect to p_A is:

$$l + a - b + \frac{p_B - p_A}{t} + p_A\left(-\frac{1}{t}\right) \equiv 0. \tag{4.13}$$

If we solve (4.13) for p_A, it becomes the equation of firm A's price best-response function,

$$p_A = \frac{1}{2}\left[p_B + t(l + a - b)\right]. \tag{4.14}$$

Substituting $l + a - b + (p_B - p_A)/t = p_A/t$ from (4.13) on the right in (4.12), firm A's payoff if it sets price according to its best-response function is:

$$\pi_A = \frac{1}{2t}p_A^2. \tag{4.15}$$

Proceeding in the same way for firm B, we obtain the equation of its best-response function,

$$p_B = \frac{1}{2}\left[p_A + t(l - a + b)\right]. \tag{4.16}$$

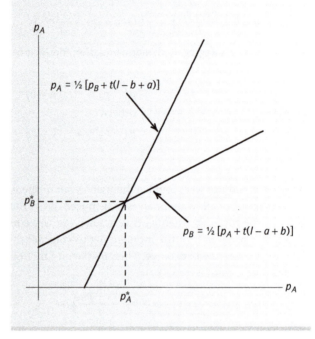

Figure 4.4 Best-response curves, Hotelling linear duopoly model; $l = 35, a = 4, b = 1, t = 1$

The two best-response equations are graphed in Figure 4.4. They slope upward, as in the differentiated-product Bertrand duopoly model (Figure 3.9).[5]

Equilibrium prices and payoffs

Solving the best-response equations gives values for equilibrium prices (these are the coordinates of the intersection of the best-response curves in Figure 4.4):

$$p_A^* = t\left[l + \frac{1}{3}(a - b)\right] \qquad p_B^* = t\left[l + \frac{1}{3}(b - a)\right]. \qquad (4.17)$$

So far, so good. Substituting for p_A in (4.15) and for p_B in the corresponding expression for firm B's profit if it sets price according to its best-response equation gives expressions for the equilibrium profits of the two firms:

$$\pi_A^*(a, b) = \frac{t}{2}\left[l + \frac{1}{3}(a - b)\right]^2 \qquad \pi_B^*(a, b) = \frac{t}{2}\left[l + \frac{1}{3}(b - a)\right]^2. \qquad (4.18)$$

All of this analysis has been carried out treating firms' locations as given, determined by some process that we have not discussed. It is natural to ask how results would change if

---

[5] The best-response curves drawn in Figure 4.4 are valid provided firms price so that neither supplies the entire line. If firm B sets a price so high that firm A supplies the entire market at its monopoly price, firm A's best-response curve is vertical at its monopoly price. Similarly if firm A sets a price so high that firm B supplies the entire market at its monopoly price, firm B's best-response curve is horizontal at its monopoly price. These vertical (firm A) and horizontal (firm B) segments of the best-response curves are not drawn in Figure 4.4.

locations were not given. The answer to this question leads us to consider a different game, a two-stage game. In the first stage, firms simultaneously pick locations. In the second stage, firms pick prices, taking the locations chosen in the first stage as given. In this perspective, it is the second stage of the two-stage game that we have discussed to this point.

Looking at (4.18), it is apparent that π_A^* rises as a rises—as firm A moves toward firm B from firm B's left. Similarly, π_B^* rises as b rises—as firm B moves toward firm A from firm A's right. This suggests—as it did to Hotelling (1929)—that in the equilibrium of the spatial duopoly model, firms will locate back to back and the principle of minimum differentiation will hold, as it does in the beach model.

Whoops

But this conclusion is wrong. We worked out the payoff functions (4.18) on the assumption that firms were on the intermediate range of their demand functions, that neither firm would wish to set so low a price that it would capture the entire market from the other. This is correct if firms are sufficiently far apart. If (say) firm B sets a low enough price to undersell firm A at firm A's location (inequality 4.3), firm B must also take a very low price on sales near its own location.[6] If firms are far apart, then the forgone profit on sales near firm B's plant is so large, relative to the profit gained by capturing sales on the far side of A's plant, that B finds it most profitable to set a relatively high price and share the middle of the line with A.

If firms are sufficiently close together—precisely the case that is of interest if one asks whether the principle of minimum differentiation holds—the situation is different. Then if B undercuts A's price at A's location, B takes a slightly smaller price on sales in its hinterland, but by so doing captures a relatively large number of sales on the far side of A's plant. If A and B are sufficiently close, B finds it most profitable to undercut A's price at A's location and sell to the whole market.

A is in the same situation. The result is that the expressions (4.17) for non-cooperative equilibrium prices, which depend on the two firms sharing the central region of the line, are not valid if the firms are too close to each other. Further, when the two firms are sufficiently close together, it cannot be an equilibrium for either firm to play a *pure strategy* and set *any* specific price with certainty. If it were to do so, it would leave itself open to being undercut by the other firm. To describe equilibrium pricing, the model must be reformulated so that firms play what are called *mixed strategies*. Rather than being pictured as setting some one definite price to maximize profit, firms are modelled as setting any one of a range of prices, each with a different probability, to maximize *expected* profit. If neither firm sets a specific price with certainty, it cannot be undercut with certainty.

d'Aspremont *et al.* (1979) show if firms are located the same distance from their respective ends of the line (if $a = b$), then in equilibrium firms will price to share the centre of the market *if* firms are located in the outer quarters of the line, $a = b \leq 1/4$.[7] In general if firms play mixed pricing strategies, then equilibrium locations are slightly closer to the center of

---

[6] This argument depends on the further assumption that firm B cannot price discriminate: the delivered prices to consumers y and y' from B's location are $p_B + ty$ and $p_B + ty'$, respectively, and the price to each consumer net of transportation cost is identical, p_B. Spatial price discrimination arises in the basing-point system, which we take up in Section 20.3.1.

[7] d'Aspremont *et al.* also give the corresponding restrictions on locations for firms to share the market if locations are not symmetric.

the line than the one-quarter points (Osborne and Pitchik, 1987), not back to back in the centre of the line. The principle of minimum differentiation, despite its intuitive appeal, does not hold in the two-stage version of the basic Hotelling linear market model.

Quadratic transportation cost

Hotelling modelled transportation cost as being proportional to distance: it costs twice as much to travel twice as far. If one takes the model literally, this may be a reasonable approximation (although rivers through a plain or a valley through a mountain range can make it less expensive to ship goods over a longer distance). But if "transportation cost" is a proxy for the utility lost because the most satisfactory variety that is available is not a consumer's ideal variety, it may well be that transportation cost rises more rapidly than "distance". Satisfaction may fall more rapidly, the less the best available variety resembles a consumer's first-best choice.

If transportation cost in the Hotelling model is taken to be proportional to the square of distance, the delivered price of firm A to a consumer at distance x is $p_A + tx^2$. With this modification, the mathematical difficulties of the linear transportation cost model go away: for any location, there is always a pure-strategy equilibrium price. Unfortunately for the result Hotelling thought he had obtained, the principle of minimum differentiation goes away as well. With quadratic transportation cost, firms choose to locate at the end of the line. In equilibrium, with quadratic transportation cost, there is maximum differentiation (see Problem 3–14).

4.2.3 Ringworld

Endpoint effects

In the basic Hotelling model, one factor making it profitable for firms located near an end of the line to move toward the centre is that such a move holds the prospect of capturing some sales that would otherwise go to the rival, but carries little risk of losing sales in the hinterland. Consumers located in a firm's hinterland are a captive market for the firm, unless it sets a price so high that its distant rival can undersell it at its location. While this kind of *endpoint effect* might have an analogue in some spatial markets, for others it may appear more as an artifact of the simplified structure of the linear model.

Similarly, for a linear market with three suppliers (Figure 4.5), there is a fundamental difference between the strategic environment of the centrally located firm and those of its peripheral neighbours. The centrally located firm faces a rival on each side, the peripheral firms face a rival on only the inner part of their markets.

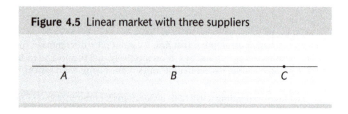

Figure 4.5 Linear market with three suppliers

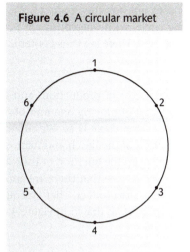

Figure 4.6 A circular market

The linear spatial model is a first step at generalizing economic models to deal with markets that exist in more than one dimension: three if one interprets "space" in a literal sense, many more if one thinks of location models as describing product characteristics and consumers' preferences for those characteristics. The existence *in the model* of a submarket that is shielded from competition because it is on the periphery complicates the analysis by introducing different categories of firms, those on the periphery and those not. It may also lead to results *in the model* that we might think it unlikely to find *in the market* we intend the model to describe. Endpoint effects can be eliminated by what Chamberlin (1953, p. 19) calls "the expedient" of getting rid of the ends, "bending them around and joining them", to obtain a circular market like the one shown in Figure 4.6.[8]

Reservation price

Another characteristic of the basic Hotelling model that contributes to the centralizing tendency when firms are located near the ends of the line is its assumption that the quantity demanded is insensitive to price. In the Hotelling model, each consumer takes one and only one unit of the good from the firm that offers the lowest delivered price, no matter how high that delivered price is. The simplest modification of this approach is to endow each consumer with a *reservation price*, above which the consumer will no longer buy one unit of the product.

Accordingly, for the circle model we change the specification of demand behaviour we used for the linear Hotelling model by adding a reservation price, ρ. We now assume that each consumer buys one unit of the product from the firm that offers the lowest delivered price, provided that price is less than or equal to ρ. If the lowest delivered price to a consumer

---

[8] The other common approach to avoiding endpoint problems is to assume that the line is of infinite length and that firms are located at equal distances along the line.

is greater than ρ, the consumer does not buy the product.[9] We assume that consumers are uniformly distributed around the circle, with one consumer per unit length, and that the circumference of the circular market is l. There are thus l potential consumers in the market.

Other assumptions

We write c for the constant marginal cost of production, and treat transportation cost as being proportional to distance. The cost of moving one unit of the product through an arc-distance x along the circumference of the circle is tx. We suppose that n firms are located on the circle, and retain the assumption of the beach and main-street models that firms can costlessly change location. We will take up the question of the long-run equilibrium number of firms in Chapter 9. Here we simply assume that there are enough firms in the market so that (in equilibrium) all consumers buy the product. Then in equilibrium firms are spaced at equal distances around the circular market, as drawn in Figure 4.6.[10]

Demand equation of a single firm

Since firms are identical, in equilibrium they set identical prices. The first step in analysing firms' pricing decisions is to work out the nature of the demand curve facing one firm, say, firm 1, if all other firms charge an arbitrary but identical price, p_{circ}. The second step is to work out firm 1's profit-maximizing price, given p_{circ}. The third step, since firms are identical, is to set firm 1's profit-maximizing price equal to p_{circ}. Solving for the resulting value of p_{circ} gives the symmetric equilibrium price.

There are three segments to firm 1's demand curve. If firm 1 sets a very high price, it leaves some potential customers on either side unsupplied, but is the only potential supplier of the customers it does serve. If it sets a very low price, it undercuts its immediate neighbours (firms n and 2), captures all sales that might otherwise be shared with them, and competes as an oligopolist with its more distant neighbours (firms $n-1$ and 3). For prices in an intermediate range, all consumers between the locations of firm n and firm 2 are served and firm 1's market is bounded on the left by consumers who buy from firm n and on the right by consumers who buy from firm 2.

Monopoly   The situation of a high-price monopoly supplier is shown in Figure 4.7, in which what is measured on the horizontal axis is the arc-distance along the circumference of the circular market. A consumer located at arc-distance x from the firm who purchases from the single supplier at price p would be willing to pay as much as the reservation price ρ for the product, and actually pays purchase price p plus transportation cost tx. The net utility of such a consumer is the difference between the maximum price that would be paid and the price that is paid,

$$\rho - (p + tx). \tag{4.19}$$

---

[9] A non-purchaser takes his or her purchasing power to another market, a market for an *outside good*. To avoid the need to take the market for the outside good explicitly into account when assessing performance in the circular market, we assume that the market for the outside good is perfectly competitive, so that price in the market for the outside good is (in long-run equilibrium) equal to the marginal cost of producing the outside good.

[10] If firms were not equidistant, a firm located closer to its left-hand rival could always move to the right and gain more sales in that direction, from its right-hand rival, than it would lose on the left. The locational equilibrium is unique up to rotations around the circle that preserve equal spacing.

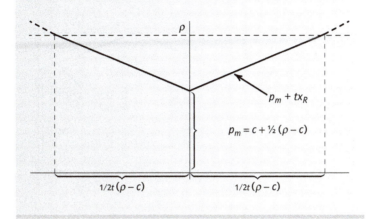

Figure 4.7 Extent of the market, monopoly supplier. Horizontal axis, distance from firm's location; vertical axis, delivered price ($\rho = 11$, $c = t = 1, n = 6, l = 48$)

A consumer will buy 1 unit of the product if net utility is positive. If net utility is zero, the consumer will be indifferent between buying and not buying the product. We suppose that such a consumer buys the product (this makes no difference to the results).

Then, consumers out to an arc-distance at which net utility (4.19) is zero,

$$x = \frac{\rho - p}{t},$$

(4.20)

on either side of the firm's location, each buys 1 unit of the product.[11] Since there is one consumer per unit distance, the equation of the monopolist's demand curve is:

$$q = 2\frac{\rho - p}{t} \text{ or in inverse form } p = \rho - \frac{t}{2}q.$$

(4.21)

The monopolist's payoff as a function of its price is then:

$$\pi = (p - c)\, q = \frac{2}{t}\, (p - c)\, (\rho - p).$$

(4.22)

Setting the derivative of π with respect to p equal to zero and rearranging terms, the price that maximizes the monopolist's payoff is:

$$p_m = c + \frac{1}{2}\, (\rho - c).$$

(4.23)

At this price, the monopolist sells to a distance:

$$x_m = \frac{\rho - p}{t} = \frac{1}{2t}\, (\rho - c)$$

(4.24)

on either side of its location.

---

[11] To avoid dealing with complications that do not occur in equilibrium, we suppose that $x < l/2$: the left- and right-hand sides of the firm's market do not overlap at the bottom of the circle.

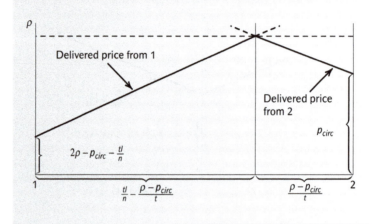

Figure 4.8 Extent of 1's monopoly market on the right, firm 2 and all other firms charging p_{circ}. Horizontal axis, distance from firm's location; vertical axis, delivered price ($\rho = 11, c = t = 1, n = 6, l = 48$)

Oligopoly   Suppose firm 1 sets a price so high that firm 1's immediate neighbours, firms n and 2, lose no sales to firm 1. How high must this price be? Focusing for concreteness on firm 2, if firm 2 is charging price p_{circ} and it loses no sales to firm 1, then firm 2 is selling an arc distance y_L to the left that makes net utility just equal to zero,

$$\rho - p_{circ} - ty_L = 0, \text{ so } y_L = \frac{\rho - p_{circ}}{t} \tag{4.25}$$

(as shown in Figure 4.8).

Since the firms are located at equal distances around the circle, the distance between firm 1 and firm 2 is l/n. Firm 1 can then sell to a distance:

$$x_R = \frac{l}{n} - y_L = \frac{l}{n} - \frac{\rho - p_{circ}}{t} \tag{4.26}$$

to its right without coming into contact with consumers who might buy from firm 2.

For what price would firm 1 sell out to the distance x_R? The price p_1 that makes firm 1's right-side market just equal to x_R satisfies:

$$\frac{\rho - p_1}{t} = x_R = \frac{l}{n} - \frac{\rho - p_{circ}}{t}, \text{ so } p_1 = 2\rho - p_{circ} - \frac{tl}{n}. \tag{4.27}$$

Thus for values of p_1 at least as great as $2\rho - p_{circ} - \frac{tl}{n}$ and below the reservation price,

$$2\rho - p_{circ} - \frac{tl}{n} \le p_1 \le \rho, \tag{4.28}$$

firm 1 is a monopolist, and (4.21) is the equation of its demand/inverse demand function.[12]

---

[12] For prices above (4.27), there is an interval of consumers between firm 1 and firm 2 (and also between firm n and firm 1) who do not buy the product. As noted above, we assume that there are enough firms in the market so that there are no such intervals in equilibrium.

For prices below $2\rho - p_{circ} - \frac{tl}{n}$, all consumers on both sides of firm 1 buy. The share of the circumference on either side of its location that goes to firm 1 depends on its price, p_1, and on the (identical) prices set by its neighbours, p_{circ}. On firm 1's right, there is a location at which consumers face the same delivered price from firm 1 or firm 2,

$$\rho - tx - p_1 = \rho - t\left(\frac{l}{n} - x\right) - p_{circ}. \tag{4.29}$$

Solving (4.29) for x, the clockwise distance of the boundary location from firm 1's location is:

$$x_{12} = \frac{l}{2n} + \frac{p_{circ} - p_1}{2t}. \tag{4.30}$$

The quantity demanded of firm 1 for prices below (4.27) and above a price to be identified momentarily is:

$$q_1 = 2x_{12} = \frac{l}{n} + \frac{p_{circ} - p_1}{t}. \tag{4.31}$$

Solving (4.31) for p_1, the inverse form of the demand equation when p_1 is in the intermediate range is:

$$p_1 = \frac{tl}{n} + p_{circ} - tq_1. \tag{4.32}$$

The equations of the three segments of firm 1's inverse demand function are:

$$p_1 = \begin{cases} \rho - \frac{t}{2}q_1 & 2\rho - p_{circ} - \frac{tl}{n} \leq p_1 \leq \rho \\ \frac{tl}{n} + p_{circ} - tq_1 & p_{circ} - \frac{tl}{n} \leq p_1 \leq 2\rho - p_{circ} - \frac{tl}{n} \\ 2\frac{tl}{n} + p_{circ} - tq_1 & p_1 \leq p_{circ} - \frac{tl}{n} \end{cases}. \tag{4.33}$$

(4.33) is drawn in Figure 4.9.

The first row of (4.33) is (4.21), the monopoly portion of the demand equation. This is the equation of firm 1's inverse demand curve if its price is so high that it is the only potential supplier of the customers it serves (given, that is, that other firms set price p_{circ}). The second row of (4.33) is (4.32), which Salop (1979) calls the "competitive" portion of the

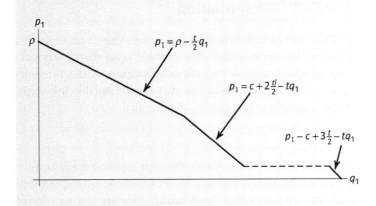

Figure 4.9 Firm 1's equilibrium demand curve, circular market with reservation price ($\rho = 11, c = t = 1, n = 6, l = 48$)

p_1

ρ

$p_1 = \rho - \frac{t}{2}q_1$

$p_1 = c + 2\frac{tl}{2} - tq_1$

$p_1 - c + 3\frac{t}{2} - tq_1$

q_1

firm's demand equation. Here firm 1's sales area is in direct contract with the sales areas of its immediate neighbours.

As firm 1 lowers its price along the second segment of the inverse demand curve, it takes more and more sales from firm 2; the boundary point x_{12} moves in a clockwise direction around the circle market. For very low prices, $p_1 < p_{circ} - \frac{tl}{n}$, firm 1 undersells firm 2 at firm 2's location. For such prices, firm 2 sells nothing, and firm 1's sales jump discontinuously around the circle to a point that marks the boundary of its sales region with the sales of firm 3 (and similarly on the left side of firm 1's market). This is the third row of (4.33). Salop (1979) calls this the "supercompetitive" portion of the firm's demand equation.

Equilibrium prices

We will see in Chapter 9 that in equilibrium, firms will set prices on the second, "competitive", segment of (4.33). What is firm 1's best-response price on this part of its inverse demand curve, if all other firms charge price p_{circ}? Firm 1's profit as a function of its price is:

$$\pi_1 = (p_1 - c)\, q_1 = (p_1 - c)\left(\frac{l}{n} + \frac{p_{circ} - p_1}{t}\right). \tag{4.34}$$

The first-order condition to maximize (4.34) with respect to p_1 is:

$$(p_1 - c)\left(-\frac{1}{t}\right) + \frac{l}{n} + \frac{p_{circ} - p_1}{t} = 0. \tag{4.35}$$

This could be solved for the best-response price, p_1, but we will not do so. Instead, we note that in view of the underlying symmetry of the model, all firms set the same price in equilibrium. Substituting $p_1 = p_{circ}$ into (4.35) and rearranging terms gives the equilibrium price,

$$p_{circ} = c + \frac{tl}{n}. \tag{4.36}$$

The equilibrium price-cost margin is greater, the greater is transportation cost, the greater is the circumference of the circle, and the smaller is the number of firms.

From the first-order condition (4.35), equilibrium profit per firm is:

$$\pi^*_{circ} = \frac{1}{t}\left(p_{circ} - c\right)^2 = t\left(\frac{l}{n}\right)^2. \tag{4.37}$$

Profit per firm is affected by changes in t, l, and n in the same way as is p_{circ}.

4.3 Vertical Product Differentiation

In markets with vertically differentiated products, consumers share a universal quality ranking. This would describe a market in which all consumers agree that a personal computer with more memory is of higher quality than a personal computer with less memory, all else equal, or a market in which all consumers agree that a more durable ink-jet printer is of higher quality than a less durable ink-jet printer, all else equal.

4.3.1 Setup

Varieties of a product will differ in many ways—different car models are larger or smaller, accelerate more or less rapidly, be more or less fuel-efficient. Describing different varieties of a product in terms of differences in a single quality measure is a way of compressing multidimensional product differentiation into one dimension, and this is the approach that

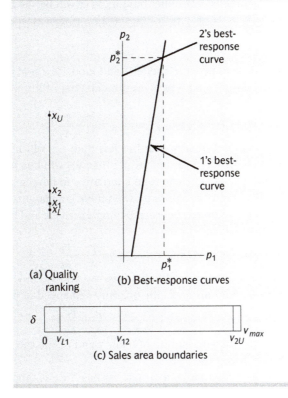

Figure 4.10 Quality differences, best-response curves, and sales area boundaries in a market with two vertically differentiated varieties ($x_L = 1$, $x_1 = 2$, $x_2 = 4$, $x_U = 16$, $p_L = 1$, $p_U = 100$; prices measured as deviations from constant marginal cost)

is taken here. Write, then, x_i for the quality of new car model i. For expositional purposes, we consider a market where there are two types of new cars on the market, model 1 of lower quality and model 2 of higher quality, as shown in Figure 4.10(a):

$$x_1 < x_2. \tag{4.38}$$

The alternative on the low-quality end of the market to buying x_1 is to rely on public transportation or to buy a used car. Write x_L for the quality of the low-quality alternative to buying a new car. Similarly, write x_U for the quality of the high-quality alternative to buying a new car (limousine service, perhaps).

Consumers differ in the importance they attach to quality. Let v denote a consumer's average and marginal utility of quality. We assume that v ranges from 0 to some upper level,

$$0 \leq v \leq v_{max}, \tag{4.39}$$

and that the distribution of v is uniform over this range. There are δv_{max} consumers in all, δ consumers between $v = 0$ and $v = 1$, δ consumers between $v = 1$ and $v = 2$, and so on.

A consumer with marginal utility of quality v who purchases an car of quality x_j at price p_j gets net utility:

$$vx_j - p_j \tag{4.40}$$

from the transaction.[13] If a potential consumer buys a car, it will be the car that yields the largest net utility.

4.3.2 Demand

If we consider the division of sales between model 1 and model 2, there is some consumer with a marginal utility of quality v_{12} who receives the same net utility from buying either model:

$$v_{12}x_1 - p_1 = v_{12}x_2 - p_2, \text{ so } v_{12} = \frac{p_2 - p_1}{x_2 - x_1}. \tag{4.41}$$

Consumers with marginal utility of quality near but less than v_{12} will buy model 1. Consumers with marginal utility of quality near but greater than v_{12} will buy model 2.

On the low end of model 1's market there is an alternative to buying a low-quality new car. If buying a used car has quality x_L and price p_L, then there is a marginal utility of quality v_{1L} that makes a consumer just indifferent between buying a used car and buying the lowest-quality new car that is on the market:

$$v_{1L}x_L - p_L = v_{1L}x_1 - p_1, \text{ so } v_{1L} = \frac{p_1 - p_L}{x_1 - x_L}. \tag{4.42}$$

Consumers with marginal utilities of quality between v_{1L} and v_{12} buy new car model 1. Since there are δ consumers per unit distance, the quantity demanded of model 1 is:

$$q_1 = \delta (v_{12} - v_{1L}) = \delta \left(\frac{p_2 - p_1}{x_2 - x_1} - \frac{p_1 - p_L}{x_1 - x_L} \right). \tag{4.43}$$

The δv_{1L} consumers at the low-marginal-utility-of-quality end of the spectrum drop out of the new car market: they buy used cars.

The upper-end-of-the-market alternative to a new car has price p_U and quality level x_U. There is some marginal utility of quality v_{2U} that makes consumers indifferent between buying the highest-quality new car on the market and dropping out of the upper end of the new car market. v_{2U} satisfies the relationship:

$$v_{2U}x_2 - p_2 = v_{2U}x_U - p_U, \text{ so } v_{2U} = \frac{p_U - p_2}{x_U - x_2}. \tag{4.44}$$

The quantity demanded of model 2 is then:

$$q_2 = \delta (v_{2U} - v_{12}) = \delta \left(\frac{p_U - p_2}{x_U - x_2} - \frac{p_2 - p_1}{x_2 - x_1} \right). \tag{4.45}$$

The $\delta (v_{max} - v_{2U})$ consumers at the high-marginal-utility-of-quality end of the spectrum drop out of the new car market and opt for the high-quality alternative (see Figure 4.10(c)).[14]

---

[13] We assume that the utility the consumer gets from purchasing a new car does not interact with utility from other purchases, and that the consumer has enough income so that it is feasible for the consumer to purchase a new car if that is the consumer's utility-maximizing option.

[14] There is a whole set of restrictions, related to the relative magnitude of the v_{ij}s, that need to be satisfied for this analysis to be valid. Thus, for q_1 to be positive, v_{12} must be greater than v_{L1}. If $v_{L1} < 0$, then no consumers drop out of the new market to buy used cars, and the expression for the quantity demanded of model 1 is slightly different. We ignore the details of all such restrictions here, on the ground that they are either special cases that can be dealt with or that they would not occur in equilibrium, at least under reasonable conditions.

4.3.3 Equilibrium

Having found expressions for the quantities demanded of each firm as functions of the prices set by both firms, we can write down expressions for the firms' profit functions. The tradeoff each firm faces in setting price is that if it raises price, it makes a greater profit on every car it sells, but it loses sales to its neighbours.

Maximizing each firm's payoff with respect to its own price, we find the firms' best-response equations. The best-response equations show each firm's profit-maximizing price as a function of the price of the other firm and the price of its neighbouring outside good (product L for the low-quality model 1, variety U for the high-quality model 2). Best-response functions for a particular example are shown in Figure 4.10(b). By solving the equations of the best-response functions (equivalently, by locating the intersection of the best-response curves), we find the equilibrium prices. Knowing the values of equilibrium prices, we can find market boundaries, quantities sold, and equilibrium profits (see Problem 4–4).

4.3.4 Quality Downshifting

In models of this kind, all equilibrium prices are above marginal cost, and the price-marginal cost gap rises with quality. The prices of the highest-quality new cars are held the most above marginal cost. As a result, some consumers who would buy a high-quality new car model if new cars were priced at marginal cost switch to a lower-quality model. The prices of lower-quality models are also held above marginal cost, although not as much as with high-quality new cars. Again as a result, some consumers who would buy a medium-quality car if all new cars were priced at marginal cost switch to a low-quality car. Some consumers who would buy a low-quality new car if new cars were priced at marginal cost drop out of the market for new cars entirely. There is a general *quality downshifting*, as the excess of price over marginal cost causes most consumers to settle for a lower-quality vehicle than they would select if prices were equal to marginal cost.[15] There is a welfare loss associated with the outcome in which consumers shift down the quality ladder, or drop out of the market entirely.

Bresnahan's (1981) estimates of a vertical product differentiation model for the U.S. car industry suggest (Table 4.1) that welfare losses due to quality downshifting can be substantial. "Producer surplus" is economic profit plus fixed cost. What is labelled "usual" welfare loss is the estimated welfare loss of consumers who would purchase a new car if price were equal to marginal cost, but who in fact drop out of the market. This corresponds to deadweight welfare loss in the case of a homogeneous product market. The total consumer welfare loss includes as well estimated welfare losses due to quality downshifting. Total loss of consumer welfare is much larger than the usual welfare loss, and much larger than producer surplus.[16]

---

[15] In many markets, quality is the result of a producer's decisions about product design. In markets where consumer utility is of the form (1.40), a monopolist supplier of vertically differentiated varieties will lower the quality of all except the highest-quality variety (Mussa and Rosen, 1978). Raising the price of higher-quality varieties makes lower-quality varieties more attractive. Reducing the quality of lower-quality varieties makes them less attractive, inducing some consumers to purchase higher-quality, higher price-cost margin varieties.

[16] The figures in Table 4.1 are statistical estimates. Bresnahan (1981, pp. 220–221) discusses factors affecting the nature of the estimates. Some of these factor affecting the nature of the estimates. Some of these factors tend to make the estimates too large, others too small.

Table 4.1 Estimated welfare consequences of market power, Bresnahan vertical product differentiation automobile study. Sales measured in million dollars, other values in billion dollars

	1977	1978
Unit sales	10.3	10.4
Total revenue	39.9	42.8
Producer surplus	4.11	4.36
Consumer welfare loss: "usual"	0.71	0.82
Total consumer welfare loss	7.23	7.68
Net welfare loss	3.12	3.32

Source: Bresnahan (1981, Table 6).

4.4 Horizontal and Vertical Product Differentiation Compared

At first glance, the horizontal product differentiation and vertical product differentiation ways of conceiving of product variety seem quite different. Beneath the surface, however, demand and supply relationships in the two types of markets have much in common. In each type of market, a firm's profit-maximizing decisions, and the extent of its market, depend in the first instance on the profit-maximizing decisions of its immediate neighbours. In the Hotelling model of horizontal product differentiation, the neighbours are to a firm's immediate left and right. With vertical product differentiation, the neighbours are above and below its quality level. But in both types of markets, oligopolistic interaction is mediated through a chain of immediate substitutes, rather than the universal interactions implied by the representative consumer, aggregate demand approach of the Cournot and Bertrand models.

SUMMARY

The simplest model of horizontal product differentiation yields the intuitively plausible *Principle of Minimum Differentiation*—by moving closer to rivals, in geographic space or in product characteristic space, a firm can capture some sales to consumers who would otherwise be "between" one supplier and another. The end result is that there is no "between" in the model, which matches the common observation of very little "between" in markets—how often does one find more than one petrol station at the same intersection, two bookstores along the same walkway at a mall?

The Principle of Minimum Differentiation generalizes only with difficulty to less simple models, whether of horizontal or vertical product differentiation. Generally, such models support the intuition that firms choose "locations"—literally or figuratively—by trading off the advantage of being close to a large mass of consumers against the disadvantage of being too close to competitors. All firms are drawn to big lumps of potential customers, but distance insulates a firm from competition. In most models, the tradeoff results in some spatial dispersion, some variation in product design, some quality differences—but not so much that most potential sales are left to rivals.

Where products are differentiated by quality, price-cost margins are higher for higher-quality varieties. The result is a welfare loss due to quality downshifting, as buyers respond to equilibrium prices above marginal cost by purchasing lower-quality varieties than they would if price were equal to marginal cost.

STUDY POINTS

- Ice Cream Vendors model (Section 4.2.1)
- Hotelling linear model (Section 4.2.2)
- Circle model (Section 4.2.3)
- Vertical product differentiation (Section 4.3)
  - Quality downshifting (Section 4.3.4)

FURTHER READING

The literature on spatial models is very large, considers many variations on the basic models, and often involves models for which the detail of the mathematics is greater than the complexity of the underlying economic ideas. The earliest known spatial models appear to be those of Launhardt (1885, 1993). Lerner and Singer (1937) and Smithies (1941) offer modifications of Hotelling (1929). On quadratic transportation costs, see d'Aspremont *et al.* (1979). On the circle model, now generally associated with Salop (1979), see Chamberlin (1953), Vickrey (1964, 1999), and Samuelson (1967b). Gupta *et al.* (2004) analyse a circle model in which firms set quantities rather than prices; they give references to other such efforts. Lösch (1944, 1954), Mills and Lav (1964), and Holahan and Schuler (1981) deal with and give further references to two-dimensional location models. The "product characteristics" interpretation of spatial models was pursued by Lancaster (1979). Neven (1986) and Anglin (1992) discuss the relationship between horizontal and vertical models of product differentiation. The term "address models" is used by Archibald *et al.* (1986) and Morris (1997), who survey the literature. Shaked and Sutton (1982) develop a model of vertical product differentiation in which consumers with higher incomes choose higher-quality varieties.

For discussion of the merits and/or demerits of aggregate demand models, with emphasis on macroeconomic applications, see Kirman (1992).

PROBLEMS

Asterisks indicate advanced problems.

4–1 Give the assumptions of the Hotelling linear or "main street" model.

If a linear market is ten kilometres long, there are two suppliers, firm A located two kilometres from the left end of the market and firm B located at the right end of the market, and transportation cost t is 1 per unit distance, what are the equilibrium prices and profits per firm? (Assume marginal and average production cost is zero.) Draw a graph illustrating the equilibrium.

4–2* (Linear duopoly, quadratic transportation cost) Keeping all other assumptions of the Hotelling model unchanged, suppose transportation cost is quadratic. Firm A's delivered price x units from its plant is:

$$p_A + tx^2,$$

and similarly for firm B. Analyse the equilibrium output with locations given, and discuss firms' location incentives if locations are a choice variable.

4–3* (Vertical product differentiation, two varieties) Find equilibrium prices, quantities demanded, and profits in the two-variety model of Section 4.3 if the parameters of the model take the values given in Figure 4.10.

OLIGOPOLY III: EVIDENCE

5

To be sure, facts by themselves are worthless, "a mass of descriptive material waiting for a theory, or a fire" [Coase, 1984, p. 230]. But ... it is worth remembering that theory without evidence is, in the end, just speculation.

Masten (2002, p. 428)

5.1 Introduction

Basic oligopoly models highlight the number of firms, the degree of product differentiation, and potential competition as determinants of market performance. Such models suggest that suggest that fewness of firms (large market shares, large Herfindahl indices) and product differentiation go along with the exercise of market power. The theory of contestable markets emphasizes potential competition as a factor limiting the ability of incumbents to exercise market power, and by this emphasis draws attention to the impact of the condition of entry on market performance. Search models look to the demand side of the market for types of consumer behaviour that make it unprofitable for firms to hold price above marginal cost, and for other types of consumer behaviour that permit firms to do so.

In this chapter we survey evidence from experimental and naturally occurring markets on the predictions of oligopoly models. Laboratory tests compare outcomes with predictions in precisely controlled environments. The match between model and naturally occurring market is inevitably fuzzier. After a preliminary consideration of the concept of barriers to entry into naturally occurring markets, we examine the determinants of entry conditions, focusing on the sunk costs, scale economies, product differentiation, and the investment of financial capital required to operate an efficiently sized plant. These structural characteristics determine the cost of entry. The cost of entry relative to the size of the market determines whether entry is easy or difficult and in turn affects equilibrium market structure and performance. This leads us to consider approaches to the estimation of market size.

We then turn to empirical tests of the determinants of market performance in naturally occurring markets. There are many aspects of "market performance", including the rate of technological progress, competitiveness on international markets, and speed of adjustment to macroeconomic disturbances. In this chapter we review results of the single largest class of empirical studies, those of industry and firm profitability, and later of prices. In addition to reviewing such studies, we look at studies of the extent to which profit endures over time—that is, is not eroded by entry.

5.2 Evidence from Laboratory Markets

5.2.1 Cournot Markets

Holt (1985) reports the results of Cournot duopoly experiments. In these experiments, pairs of subjects selected output levels of a standardized product. Production was costless. Prices were determined by a programmed laboratory inverse demand equation:

$$p = 12 - \frac{1}{2}(q_1 + q_2). \tag{5.1}$$

For this cost and demand structure, Cournot equilibrium outputs are eight units each and joint-profit-maximizing outputs are six units each. The competitive (and also Bertrand) equilibrium total output is 24 units, with price equal to marginal cost, zero.

One session had 12 pairs of students pick outputs for 13 periods. As a follow-up, to investigate the effects of experience, 16 of these students were rematched, and picked outputs in a second session for 9 trading periods.[1]

Figure 5.1 shows the final period outputs for the 12 first-session Cournot pairs (white circles) and the eight second-session Cournot pairs (black circles). The bulk of the final-period outputs are somewhere between the Cournot and monopoly (joint-profit-maximizing) levels. First-session and second-session results are similar; there is no obvious effect of experience. Holt writes that (1985, p. 320) "Regardless of whether the first-market or second-market data are considered, the mean and median (or medians) of the final-period industry outputs are between 14 and 16."

Holt discusses another set of experiments in which 12 subjects took part in a series of single-period markets (with reshuffling of subjects into pairs from period to period). The results were that (1985, pp. 322–323) "[t]he output choices are initially quite diverse, but by period 7 two-thirds of the subjects are choosing outputs of 9. This is followed by a trend toward the symmetric Nash/Cournot outputs of 8, and 7 of the 12 subjects choose 8 in the final period." Thus the Cournot model does well in predicting outcomes of single-period experimental markets.

5.2.2 Bertrand Markets

Huck *et al.* (2000) report the results of experimental tests of the Cournot and Bertrand models in four-supplier markets with horizontal product differentiation. The demand side of the markets was simulated by the computer program written for the experiment.

---

[1] In each session, after the seventh period, the experimenter rolled a die at the start of the period, and the session ended with the first roll of a six. This procedure makes the length of the session unknown in advance, and avoids behaviour that might occur simply because subjects know they are approaching (or in) the final trading period.

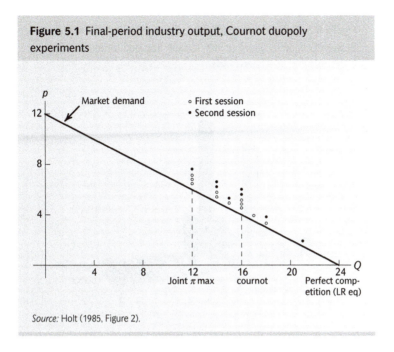

Figure 5.1 Final-period industry output, Cournot duopoly experiments

Source: Holt (1985, Figure 2).

In all experiments, the equation of the inverse demand curve of (for example) supplier 1 was:

$$p_1 = 300 - q_1 - \frac{2}{3}(q_2 + q_3 + q_4). \tag{5.2}$$

With the assumed marginal cost of 2 per unit, the Cournot equilibrium quantity with four suppliers is 74.5. The Bertrand equilibrium price with four suppliers is 39.25, the Bertrand equilibrium quantity 86.9. As expected, equilibrium output is greater if firms set prices than if they set quantities.

Huck *et al.* report an average quantity in the last five (of 40) rounds of 74.20 for the Cournot sessions, an average price in the last five rounds of 41.91 for the Bertrand sessions. As shown in Figure 5.2, outputs in Cournot markets cluster around the Cournot equilibrium prediction, and outputs in the Bertrand markets cluster around the Bertrand equilibrium prediction. On average, the models predict experimental market outcomes very well.

5.2.3 Contestable Markets

Coursey *et al.* (1984a) present the results of experiments that replicate the assumptions of the theory of contestable markets. These include duopoly experiments where each supplier produces with increasing returns to scale (that is, average cost falls as output increases) and there are no sunk entry or exit costs. The experiments support the predictions of the theory of contestable markets (1984a, p. 108): "Four duopoly experiments had price and quantity [outcomes] that converged directly to the competitive predictions. . . . The other two duopoly experiments never achieved the competitive outcomes, although a visual inspection suggests they were tending in that direction."

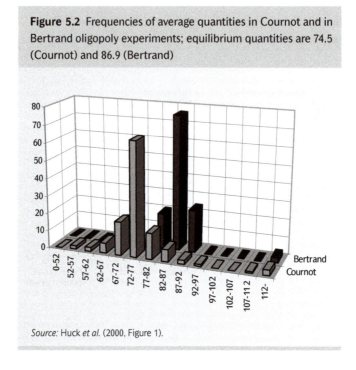

Figure 5.2 Frequencies of average quantities in Cournot and in Bertrand oligopoly experiments; equilibrium quantities are 74.5 (Cournot) and 86.9 (Bertrand)

Source: Huck *et al.* (2000, Figure 1).

Coursey *et al.* (1984b) alter the specification of the first paper to include positive but modest sunk entry costs. They require an experimental seller to purchase a $2 entry permit, valid for five periods, to be allowed to post a price. They find that introducing an entry cost did not stop entry: if it was profitable for experimental subjects to come into the market, taking entry costs into account, entry tended to occur. But sunk costs led to temporary periods of market performance farther from the competitive outcome than would have been predicted in the absence of sunk costs. A range of outcomes was observed, including:

- market performance like that of a perfectly contestable market (that is, one without entry cost);

- price swings: low prices with two sellers in the market, high prices after one seller exits, low prices again after re-entry;

- limit pricing: after exit by one of two suppliers, the remaining supplier keeps price in the competitive range;

- (intermittent) tacit collusion: two suppliers, with episodes of prices held above the competitive level.

Coursey *et al.* (1984b, p. 83) read their results as indicating that market structure matters for market performance, but market structure is not all that matters. Conduct has an independent impact on market performance, and that impact cannot be predicted based on knowledge of market structure alone. Gilbert's (1989, p. 116) assessment is that: "These experiments ... illustrate the limits of potential entry as a constraint on monopoly pricing. In eleven of the twelve cases, high prices are eroded by actual entry, even though entry is inefficient. In these experiments, attempts to extract monopoly profits are followed by the entry of new competition. But prices are controlled by actual entry, not by the threat of potential entry." In the recurring debate over the relative efficacy of actual and potential competition in getting good market performance, these experiments come down rather on the side of actual competition.

5.2.4 Search Markets

Davis and Holt (1996) report the results of experiments designed to test the predictions of consumer search models. Their laboratory markets each involve three buyers (B1, B2, and B3) and three sellers (S1, S2, and S3), with induced demand and supply curves as shown on the right in Figure 5.3. The competitive equilibrium price in the laboratory market is 25 cents, the monopoly price is 55 cents. In all sessions, sellers first set their prices and the maximum amounts they are willing to sell during that trading period. In the posted-offer sessions, buyers were informed of all prices and of remaining quantities for sale. The order in which buyers could make purchases was determined randomly. To visit a store and make a purchase, a buyer had to pay a travel cost of 15 cents. In the otherwise identical search

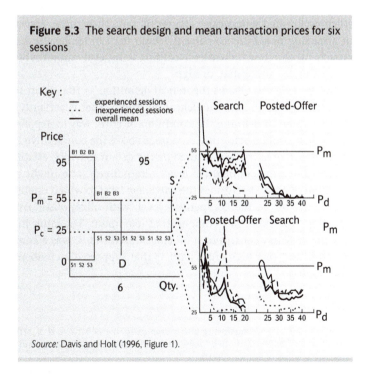

Figure 5.3 The search design and mean transaction prices for six sessions

Source: Davis and Holt (1996, Figure 1).

treatments, a buyer had to pay a 15-cent search cost in order to learn the terms offered at any particular store.

Results are illustrated on the right in Figure 5.3. There is a clear tendency for prices to be closer to the competitive level in the posted offer sessions. Davis and Holt conclude that (1996, p. 145) "The two primary lessons of this research are (1) that the absence of public price information raises prices when shopping is costly, but (2) that the monopoly prices implied by the 'Diamond paradox' are not generally observed."

5.3 Evidence from Naturally Occurring Markets

5.3.1 Barriers to Entry

One might expect to meet the subject of *barriers to entry* into a market as part of a discussion of entry, and so we shall (Chapter 9). But Joe Bain first examined entry conditions as one set of factors explaining interindustry differences in profitability, and it is in that context that we consider them now.

Ability to raise price

A problem in trying to do justice to the literature on entry barriers is not to find a definition of barriers to entry, but to sort through the multitude of definitions that one finds.[2,3] Bain, who titled his seminal 1956 book *Barriers to New Competition*, was in fact sparing in use of the term "barrier to entry". He wrote much more often of the "condition of entry", (1956, p. 3) "the extent to which established sellers can persistently raise their prices above a competitive level without attracting new firms to enter the industry". In applications, Bain used a classification approach, categorizing industries according to his evaluation that the difficulty of entry was low to moderate, substantial, or high.

McAfee *et al.* (2004, p. 462) view Bain's theoretical definition as "flawed in that it builds the consequences of the definition into the definition itself". That is certainly one way to read Bain's work. His purpose in defining the condition of entry was to explain the extent to which established sellers could persistently raise price above the competitive level, and he suggested that the condition of entry be measured by the extent to which established sellers persistently raise price above the competitive level. Alternatively, one might read Bain as saying that the condition of entry determines the *maximum* level to which established sellers can persistently raise price above the competitive level, with oligopolistic rivalry among incumbents determining how close they come to that maximum. The latter interpretation is consistent with some of Bain's conclusions: he emphasized that it was a combination of high seller concentration and very high entry barriers that supported incumbent exercise of market power (1956, p. 201).

---

[2] The list of definitions given in the accompanying box is essentially that of McAfee *et al.* (2004), expanded to include the definitions that they themselves offer. I have omitted the definition of Carlton and Perloff (1994), preferring instead to discuss the views of Carlton (2004).

[3] Perhaps more than any other subject in the field of industrial economics, that of "barriers to entry" brings to mind the quip (usually attributed to George Bernard Shaw) that "If all economists were laid end-to-end, they would not reach a conclusion".

BOX   Barriers to Entry: A Smörgåsbord of Definitions

Bain (1954, p. 215):

The condition of entry is determined by "basic environmental circumstances which influence the ability and disposition of successive additional sellers to enter the industry".

Bain (1956, p. 3):

Let us understand the term "condition of entry" to an industry to mean something equivalent to the "state of potential competition" from possible new sellers. Let us view it moreover as evaluated roughly by the advantages of established sellers in an industry over potential entrant sellers, these advantages being reflected in the extent to which established sellers can persistently raise their prices above a competitive level without attracting new firms to enter the industry.

Stigler (1968b, p. 67):

A barrier to entry may be defined as a cost of producing . . . which must be borne by a firm which seeks to enter an industry but is not borne by firms already in the industry.

Ferguson (1974 p. 10):

A barrier to entry is a factor that makes entry unprofitable while permitting established firms to set prices above marginal cost, and to persistently earn monopoly return.

von Weizsäcker (1980a, p. 400; see also 1980b, p. 13):

[A] barrier to entry is a cost of producing which must be borne by a firm which seeks to enter an industry but is not borne by firms already in the industry and which implies a distortion in the allocation of resources from the social point of view.

Gilbert (1989, p. 478; emphasis in original):

[A] barrier to entry is a rent that is derived from incumbency. It is the additional profit that a firm can earn as a sole consequence of being established in the industry.

McAfee *et al.* (2004, p. 463):

- *Economic barrier to entry*: "a cost that must be incurred by a new entrant and that incumbents do not or have not had to incur".
- *Antitrust barrier to entry*: "a cost that delays entry and thereby reduces social welfare relative to immediate but equally costly entry".
- *Primary barrier to entry*: "a cost that constitutes a barrier to entry on its own".
- *Ancillary barrier to entry*: "a cost that does not constitute a barrier to entry by itself, but reinforces other barriers to entry if they are present". »

> **» Schmalensee (2004, p. 471):**
>
> - *Antitrust barriers to entry:* "conditions that constrain the ability of new entrants into a market to contribute to the achievement of antitrust policy goals".

Sunk entry cost

Stigler's definition of barriers to entry has been influential in characterizing a barrier to entry as a cost, and in its view that barriers arise to the extent that the costs of entrants and incumbents differ. His definition, like those before and after, makes clear that entry is a phenomenon that inherently involves the passage of time. To begin with (pre-entry), there are two sets of firms, those that are in the industry and those that are not. By spending some money, a firm that is not in the industry can become one of the firms that are in the industry. If it does so, action and analysis pass to a post-entry period that is different from the pre-entry period at the very least because there has been a change in the number of active firms, and (an entrant might be expected to anticipate) perhaps also because of a change in conduct as continuing incumbents react to entry. Entry cannot satisfactorily be analysed using a static (timeless) model.

The literature on barriers to entry (and it is not alone in this) often fails to be precise in distinguishing between fixed and sunk costs.[4] One may read Stigler's definition as implying that for a *cost* of entry to constitute a *barrier*, the cost must be sunk. Much of the cost of, say, an oil refinery, is fixed, independent of the rate of throughput, and largely incurred at the time the refinery is built. Suppose (for the sake of discussion) that such an investment is *not* sunk: at any time, if a firm operating an oil refinery wishes to leave the market, it can sell its refinery for what it would cost to build a new refinery of the same capacity. In this case, even though an incumbent oil refiner paid for its plant at the moment it entered the industry, the incumbent "bears the cost" of the refinery, in an opportunity-cost sense, as long as it remains in operation. An entrant must give up $5 billion to build an oil refinery. An incumbent must give up $5 million—the amount for which it could sell the refinery it built in the past—to stay in the industry. Entry costs that are not sunk are borne by entrant and incumbent alike, and are not barriers to entry in Stigler's sense.[5] If entry and operating investments *are* sunk, exit would entail substantial losses, over and above rental costs. Risk-averse potential entrants will require a greater assurance of profitability before coming into

---

[4] Among American economists, the analysis of fixed (overhead) cost came to the fore in connection with rail-roads, in which context it would be natural to assume that fixed costs were, for the most part, also sunk. See, for example, John M. Clark (1923, p. 11): "Large companies, railroad and industrial, failed, were reorganized, and continued in business, often more formidable competitors than before. It became evident that economic law did not insure prices that would yield 'normal' returns on invested capital, because the capital could not get out if it wanted to, and so had to take whatever it could get." Stigler (1963, p. 65) emphasizes that it is not the fixed nature of a cost that makes a barrier to entry, but the extent to which the cost is for use of a durable and specialized asset.

[5] This point is made explicit by von Weizsäcker (1980b, p. 49), who writes that it is only in the presence of sunk cost that the distinction between entrant and incumbent matters. See also Gilbert (1989, p. 109), Kessides (1991, p. 29), and Martin (2002). Spence (1977) emphasizes irreversibility as a characteristic of investments that deter entry, as does von Weizsäcker (1980a, p. 401). See also Schmalensee (2004). McAfee *et al.*'s definition of an economic barrier to entry does not bring out this point.

a market, the greater the extent to which entry involves making sunk investments. In this sense, "barriers to exit are barriers to entry".[6]

Sunk entry cost that distorts welfare

von Weizsäcker (1980a, pp. 399–400; see also 1980b) starts from the proposition that the term "barrier" has a pejorative implication, one that creates a presumption that market performance would be improved if barriers were removed. His suggestion is to extend Stigler's definition by making this welfare implication explicit. von Weizsäcker proposes to evaluate the welfare impact of an entry cost by comparison with the best market performance that could be arranged by an ideal government. If the existence of an entry cost brings market performance closer to this standard, it is not a barrier in von Weizsäcker's sense.

Antitrust barriers to entry

McAfee *et al.* (2004) and Schmalensee (2004) distinguish between economic barriers to entry and antitrust barriers to entry. Schmalensee's definition of antitrust barriers to entry in terms of impact on the relationship between entry and the goals of antitrust policy ties what one classifies as an antitrust barrier to entry to what one views as the goals of antitrust policy, a subject that is itself contentious. Schmalensee specifies that for his discussion he takes the goal of U.S. antitrust policy to be the maximization of consumer welfare.[7]

Barriers to understanding

In Carlton's (2004) view, the concept of barriers to entry is a barrier to understanding. Along the same lines, Fisher (1979, p. 23) writes that "the analysis of barriers to entry is ... the single most misunderstood topic in the analysis of competition and monopoly. ... In large part, this may be due to an unfortunate terminology ... "

The usages that have been proposed for the term "barrier to entry" mix static and dynamic concepts, gloss over the distinction between fixed and sunk cost, glide back and forth between discussions of the impact of entry costs on market structure and the impact of entry costs on market performance, and often fail to make clear whether a potential entrant that remains out of a market expects entry to be unprofitable because of exogenous demand and technology characteristics or because of strategic entry-deterring behaviour on the part of incumbents.[8]

---

[6] Eaton and Lipsey (1980). Much the same point is made by John M. Clark (1923, p. 446).

[7] As we will see, from the last quarter of the twentieth century onward, U.S. antitrust policy has haltingly moved from reliance on the *principle of competition* (which we introduce in Section 20.2.1) to an explicit evaluation of the impact of business practices on market performance (see among other places Section 24.2.2). EC competition policy, with its emphasis on a "more economic approach", is well on the way to reaching a similar position. The implications of von Weizsäcker's reformulation of the concept of entry barriers were important for these shifts. If barriers reduce the impact of potential competition on the conduct of incumbents, and policy relies on the principle of competition to get good market performance, then barriers are bad. If barriers can improve market performance, even though they reduce the impact of potential competition on the conduct of incumbents, an implication is that policy should not rely on competition, alone, to get good market performance. On some level, Schmalensee's definition of antitrust barriers to entry is a direct descendent of von Weizsäcker's work.

[8] Von Weizsäcker (1980b, p. 13) is explicit that he does not model strategic entry deterrence. Sutton, whose work (1991, 1998) we take up in Chapter 9, makes the distinction between exogenous and endogenous sunk entry costs (among which, expenditures on advertising and on research and development) central to his analysis of market structure.

Much clarity could be obtained by leaving the ambiguous notion of barriers to entry behind entirely, and carrying out policy analysis based on models that make explicit assumptions about entry and production costs, demand, and conduct. By and large, these are the kind of models that industrial economists now use for research purposes. But the "barriers to entry" terminology is so deeply entrenched in the industrial economics, antitrust, and competition policy literatures that it seems unlikely ever to fade entirely from the scene.

5.3.2 Determinants of Entry Conditions

The modern literature on entry conditions emphasizes the importance of cost sunkenness as a factor that distinguishes entrant from incumbent. For the classical literature, the condition of entry was determined by the relative size of the cost of entering the market and the profit to be had, once in. The nature of economies of scale in production, the extent of product differentiation, and the size of investment required to operate an efficient-scale plant—so-called absolute capital requirements—were seen as being the major determinants of entry costs. The size of the market was an indicator of the potential for an entrant to earn profit after covering entry costs.

Sunk cost

The extent to which entry costs and the cost of fixed assets are sunk goes to the heart of the relative importance of actual and potential competition in determining market performance. But how important are sunk costs? Much of a firm's investment in intangible assets will be sunk. A firm that invests in new product development or advertising creates intangible assets—brand preference, consumer recognition—that are valuable while its products are on the market. If it exits, it may sell the goodwill that is supported by those assets for a fraction of its worth to a continuing firm, but never for the cost of generating the goodwill in the first place.

Investment in physical assets may also have a large sunk element. This is to be expected for highly specific structures. For example, Tremblay and Tremblay (2005, Table 3.2) report estimates of the value of new and used brewing capacity in the U.S. beer industry at intervals from 1948 to 2002; used capacity, they indicate (2005, p. 51) "is generally valued at about 50 percent of a new plant".

Investment in equipment may also be substantially sunk. Asplund (2000) examined the resale value of used metal-working machinery sold by Swedish firms. He studied changes in capital equipment at ongoing firms (2000, pp. 290): "Assets were not discarded in major divestments, but rather as a matter of day-to-day business operations ... ." Thirty-eight per cent of machine tools for a 1960 sample, and 69 per cent of machine tools for a 1990 sample, were simply scrapped rather than resold, making investment in such assets entirely sunk. He estimated the resale value of a new metal-working machine at about 50 per cent of the purchase price, meaning half the investment in such an asset would be sunk.

Ramey and Shapiro (2001) compare the resale and replacement cost values of aerospace equipment from California plants that were shut down during the downsizing of defence industries that followed the end of the Cold War. They found that used machine tools sold for 40 per cent of replacement cost, a figure close to that obtained by Asplund. The average resale value of all types of equipment in their sample was 28 per cent of replacement cost. They turn to two factors to explain this finding. First, the kind of physical capital they studied is highly industry-specific. Second, resale markets are thin, meaning there are substantial search costs to identify the potential buyers for whom used assets would have the highest value.

Cooper and Haltiwanger (2006) study investment in about 7000 large U.S. manufacturing plants that operated over the period 1972–1988. They estimate the resale value of capital goods at 97.5 per cent of the purchase price of new capital goods (2006, p. 623). They recognize that their estimate of the extent of cost sunkenness is much smaller than those of Ramey and Shapiro (2001). They suggest that the difference in results may reflect the fact that Ramey and Shapiro study replacement values in a declining industry, while their own sample consists of ongoing plants. This would not explain the difference between Cooper and Haltiwanger's results and those of Asplund (2000). In any case, even small amounts of sunk costs are sufficient to substantially reduce the impact of potential competition on market performance (Schwartz and Reynolds, 1983).

Economies of scale

With a ∪-shaped average cost curve, of the kind shown in Figure 2.3, there is a single output level that minimizes average cost. It is natural to say that a plant with such a cost curve that is producing at the average-cost minimizing output level is producing at *minimum efficient scale*. If a technology has a cost curve that is[9] saucer-shaped, falling from low output levels, reaching a minimum, flattening out for a range of outputs, and rising again at some high output level, it is natural to define the smallest output level at which average cost is minimized as the minimum efficient scale output level, as in Figure 5.4.[10]

Bain (1954, pp. 223–224) puts forward two reasons why entry may be difficult if minimum efficient scale output is large relative to industry output. If the output of a minimum efficient scale plant is large in proportion to industry output, incumbent firms would surely notice the arrival of an MES-scale entrant, and might reasonably be expected to try to protect their own market positions.[11] Even if incumbents do not react to entry, if minimum efficient scale output is a large part of industry output, a potential entrant would need to consider the possibility that it might not be profitable to be in the post-entry market, even if pre-entry incumbents are known to be earning economic profits.[12]

The more aggressive a response an entrant expects MES-entry to evoke, and the larger the reduction in price an entrant expects to result from putting its own MES-scale output on the market, the more pre-entry incumbents could expect to be able to raise price without inducing entry. If entry at large scale would be bound to attract attention, an entrant could consider coming into the market with a less-than-MES plant. But then it would have higher

---

[9] In the phrase of Stigler (1958, p. 62).

[10] The left and right segments of the cost curves in Figure 5.4 are drawn for the cost equation $c(q) = 4 + q - \frac{1}{4}q^2 + \frac{1}{16}q^3$.

[11] One of the assumptions of the theory of contestable markets is that entrants evaluate the profitability of entry on the assumption that pre-entry prices will prevail after entry. Thus, one might say that Bain argued, 30 years in advance, that a market in which minimum efficient scale output was a large part of industry output could not be contestable.

[12] Thus, in a discussion of patterns of multinational diversification by U.S. firms, Chandler (1992, p. 89) writes "When the minimum efficient scale of production was very high, as it was in steel, copper and aluminum, building abroad was rare. Such construction would crowd and so bring overcapacity in that market, resulting in the higher costs of operating well below full capacity."

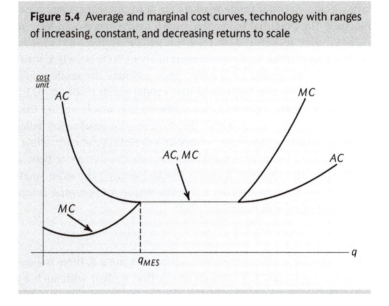

Figure 5.4 Average and marginal cost curves, technology with ranges of increasing, constant, and decreasing returns to scale

average cost, and earn less profit, than larger incumbents. Lower profit would make entry less attractive, all else equal.

Sources of economies of scale

Specialization of tasks

 BOX   **The Division of Labour in Pinmaking**

In 1776, Adam Smith used the production of pins to illustrate the economies of large-scale production, advantages which Smith traced to the productivity increases that accompanied the division of labour:

> ... a workman not educated to this business ... nor acquainted with the use of the machinery employed in it ... could scarce, perhaps, with his utmost industry, make one pin in a day, and certainly could not make twenty. But in the way in which this business is now carried on, ... it is divided into a number of branches ... One man draws out the wire, another straights it, a third cuts it, a fourth points it, a fifth grinds it at the top for receiving the head; to make the head requires two or three distinct operations; to put it on, is a peculiar business, to whiten the pins is another; it is even a trade by itself to put them into the paper; and the important business of making a pin is, in this manner, divided into about eighteen distinct operations, which, in some manufactories, are all performed by distinct hands ... I have seen a small manufactory of this kind where ten men only were employed, and where some of them consequently performed two or three distinct operations. But though they were very poor, and therefore but indifferently accommodated with the necessary machinery, they could, when they exerted themselves, make among them about twelve pounds of pins in a day. There are in a pound upwards of four thousand pins of a middling size. Those ten persons, therefore, could make among them upwards of forty-eight thousand pins in a day.

At the opening of the *Wealth of Nations*, Adam Smith discusses the sources of economies of scale ([1776] 1937, Book I, Chapter I, p. 7):

This great increase of the quantity of work which, in consequence of the division of labour, the same number of people are capable of performing, is owing to three different circumstances; first, to the increase of dexterity in every particular workman; secondly, to the saving of the time which is commonly lost in passing from one species of work to another; and lastly, to the invention of a great number of machines which facilitate and abridge labour, and enable one man to do the work of many.

For Smith, cost per unit of output falls as work becomes more specialized because more specialized tasks are performed more efficiently, because down-time switching from task to task is reduced, and because concentration on narrowly defined tasks facilitates the development of more productive, usually capital-intensive, techniques.

Least common multiple   Smith's remarks on the division of labour are cited by Babbage ([1835] 1963, p. 175), who adds ([1835] 1963, p. 212) the "least common multiple" principle to the list of factors that encourage large scale production and greater productivity. Babbage gives a breakdown of pinmaking in 1830s England into seven processes, requiring the employment of four men, four women, and two children: one man for drawing wire, a woman and a girl for straightening wire, and so on. Efficient expansion of a pinmaking factory using this technology would proceed by teams of ten employees (and the accompanying machinery): to hire just one additional man to draw wire would simply mean producing a quantity of drawn wire that would exceed the capacity of subsequent stages in the production process.[13]

Mechanization   Young (1928, p. 540) emphasizes the mechanization that is made possible by production on a large scale: "The important thing, of course, is that with the division of labour a group of complex processes is transformed into a succession of simpler processes, some of which, at least, lend themselves to the use of machinery." Robinson (1958, p. 19) sees that mechanization may operate in the other direction. After the division of labour into a succession of simple processes, "one large machine can be designed to take over what has hitherto been done by a series ... of operations". Robinson calls this "the integration of processes", and argues that it encourages large-scale enterprise (1958, p. 19): "It is only the large firm that can afford to keep the very expensive machinery of this type running to its full capacity, and the large firm therefore enjoys advantages which are beyond the reach of the self-contained small firm."

> Pratten (1980) documents the later concentration of the UK pinmaking sector:
>
> - early 1800s, 100 or more pin factories, mostly in London, Bristol, and Gloucestershire;
> - 1820: 11 pin factories in Gloucester, employing 1,500 people (one-fifth of the population);

---

[13] Although "fixed coefficient" production processes, in which inputs are efficiently used in technologically-determined proportions, are characteristic of some chemical processes, they are the exception rather than the rule. Most technologies permit some substitutability among inputs. Even allowing for such substitutability, expansion of a "balance of processes" in a cost-minimizing way will favour large-scale production (Robinson, 1958, p. 25).

• 1870: rise of machine manufacture in Birmingham; pins no longer produced in Gloucester;

- 1900: 50 pin manufacturers in Birmingham, others elsewhere;

- 1939: 12 pin manufacturers in the UK; and

- 1980: 2 pin manufacturers in the UK, each operating but one plant, and employing 50 people.

Pratten cites an 1830 estimate indicating that productivity in pin manufacture was 70 per cent above that of Adam Smith's day. Pratten estimates productivity in 1980 as being nearly 100 times greater than in 1830, an increase which Pratten attributes to the substitution of machines for labour.

Factors affecting the cost of entry at the time Pratten wrote were the cost of new pin-making machines (£6,000 in 1977) and the skilled labour required to produce high-quality pins.

Massed reserves In addition, Robinson (1958, p. 26) mentions economies of massed reserves as a factor that promotes the efficiency of large firms, as it does the efficiency of large military units. An Army Division must hold forces in reserve to meet unpredictable battlefield developments; a factory must hold reserve machines, inventory, maintenance personnel to deal with the unpredictable breakdowns. Doubling the size of the Army Division increases the amount of reserves that it is prudent to maintain, but it does not double them. Similarly, doubling the number of machines operated in a plant increases the amount of reserve equipment that it is prudent to hold, but it does not double it.

Surface/volume relationships With some technologies, economies of large scale are rooted in the laws of nature. The cost of building an oil pipeline rises roughly in proportion to its radius, the capacity of a pipeline rises in proportion to the square of its radius. Because of this cross-section/volume relationship, pipeline cost per unit of capacity is lower, the larger is the radius of a pipeline. A similar relationship holds for oil tankers: doubling every dimension of a tanker increases the surface area by a factor of four, the volume by a factor of eight.

Resumé The division of labour, the least common multiple principle, the integration of processes, economies of massed reserves, and surface/volume relationships all promote greater productivity in the large technical unit—the large plant, the large pipeline, the large tanker. The more such factors are present in an industry's technology, the more likely it is that efficient plant size will be large (Robinson, 1958, p. 32):

> Optimum technical units are large in two wholly different types of industry: in those in which the product or the productive machinery is physically very large, as in steel making, the rolling of steel plates and sections, or ship building: and in those in which the final product is highly complex in that it is built up of a great number of small parts, which are conveniently produced under a single roof, as in the case of the manufacture of typewriters, watches, cash registers, or motor cars.

We might today be tempted to substitute "assembly of personal computers" for "manufacture of typewriters", and to add semiconductors and (paradoxically) nanotechnology as sectors where efficient production takes place in large-scale plants.

BOX   Ford: Innovative Organization of Production

At the dawn of the modern motor car era, the specialization of tasks and mechanization combined with the routinization of work to bring the Ford Motor Company to the top of the car industry heap (Raff, 1991, p. 726):

> The thrust of the Ford innovations was to routinize radically all but a handful of the jobs at the plant. Work-force skills that were still crucial for producing autos elsewhere became progressively irrelevant to making cars at Ford, because Ford engineers built those skills into forges, foundries, and (ultimately) single-purpose machine tools that made completely interchangeable parts. Since this development virtually eliminated skilled fitting tasks whose timing was difficult to forecast, the pace of work throughout the factory became amenable to centralized managerial control to an unprecedented degree. The flow of materials through the factory was reorganized so that tasks came to the workers rather than vice versa, further expanding the possibilities for centralized control. Thus even the jobs not directly on the assembly lines came to be driven by the line's rhythms. Accomplishing all this required elaborate investments in physical capital, and the book value of the machines and tools on the Ford shop floor increased more than sevenfold between December 1909 and December 1913.

Popular impression notwithstanding (Raff, 1991, p. 731, fn. omitted):

> . . . the central innovation at Ford was not the conveyor belt. The ideas that made Ford production possible were progressive assembly ("moving the work to the men" . . .) and American System (interchangeable) parts production.

Diseconomies of scale   Large-scale plants typically operate with high levels of fixed costs, and a low level of fixed cost per unit of output at high output levels is one factor behind economies of large-scale production. With a given level of fixed assets, output from a plant can be increased by using more variable inputs. But beyond some point, diminishing returns to the use of the variable factor will set in. In addition, the unit cost of inputs for which there are upward-sloping supply curves—skilled labour, minerals—will rise as the scale of input-using firms increases.[14] For both reasons, above a certain output level, increases in variable cost per unit of output will more than offset the low level of fixed cost per unit of output, and average cost will begin to rise with output as diseconomies of plant scale appear.

Efficient plant size will also be limited by increases in unit transportation cost. As plant scale and output increase, the product will need to be shipped a greater distance from the plant to reach wholesale and retail distributors and the final consumer. Transportation cost per unit of delivered output will rise as the average distance shipped increases, eventually neutralizing lower production costs of a large-scale factory (Jewkes, 1952, p. 248). Thus, Figure 5.5[15] shows an average production cost curve (APC) that declines as output increases: there are persistent economies of scale. ATC_H shows an increasing relation between average

---

[14] It may also happen that the cost per unit of specific inputs increases as industry output increases, even though changes in input use by any one firm have a negligble impact on input cost. This would be an example of an external (to the firm) diseconomy of scale.

[15] Figure 5.5 is inspired by Figure 1 of Scherer (1973).

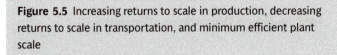

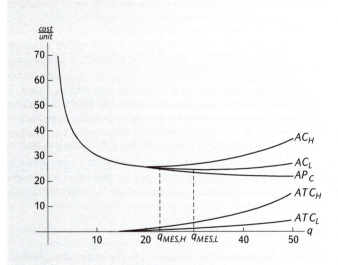

Figure 5.5 Increasing returns to scale in production, decreasing returns to scale in transportation, and minimum efficient plant scale

APC denotes average production cost; ATC_H and ATC_L denote high and low average transportation cost, respectively; $AC_H = APC + ATC_H$; $AC_L = APC + ATC_L$.

transportation cost and output if transportation cost is high; $q_{MES,H}$ is the corresponding minimum efficient plant scale. If transportation cost is lower (ATC_L), minimum efficient scale rises (to $q_{MES,L}$) as the firm can expand output and take greater advantage of declining unit cost in production before it is overwhelmed by increasing unit cost in transportation.[16]

In this context, what is called "transportation cost" in Figure 5.5 can be interpreted as the unit cost of getting the product to the consumer. For some goods, marketing over the internet amounts to a quantum reduction in "transportation cost" in this generalized sense. For such goods, the rise of the internet means a dramatic increase in minimum efficient plant scale, and a corresponding increase in the ability to take advantage of economies of scale in production.

Multiplant operation   Above a certain output level, it will become profitable for a firm that encounters increasing unit cost in a single plant to open a second plant. Multiplant operation can be profitable because it makes the firm's average cost curve a flattened-out version of a U-shaped plant average cost curve (see Section 9.3.3), but not only for that reason.

_____

[16] See Hannah (2008), who finds that at the start of the twentieth century, densely populated Europe, with its highly developed transportation network, accounted for more than half the world's factories employing more than a thousand people, the U.S. under one-fifth. Most U.S. large plants were located in the Northeast, where transportation costs were most like those of Europe.

Scherer *et al.* (1975, Ch. 2) emphasize that economies arising in the way the production of specific products is organized can be as important as economies of plant scale. An apparently suboptimal-scale plant may be one that is dedicated to production of a particular variety of a differentiated product. A larger plant might be more efficient from some points of view, but production of several different varieties of the product in a single plant would mean periodic down time (zero or reduced output) and fixed costs of switching from production of one variety to production of another. By concentrating production of a large-output variety in a single plant, a firm can realize run-length economies by reducing down time from reorganizing production lines.

Economies of scope—associated with producing a range of products—may be a source of economies of scale. For example, Raff (1991) estimates that in 1926 the unit cost of the Ford Model T was $421.99 per vehicle, compared with what would have been a unit cost of $455.24 for General Motor's Chevrolet. But by designing its Pontiac as much as possible to use Chevrolet parts,[17] thus permitting the realization of economies of scale in parts production, General Motors was able to bring the average cost of the Chevrolet down to $427.00, just 1 per cent above the Model T.

Reduced efficiency of large-scale management remains as a factor that may limit firm size. It may, of course, be possible to realize unit cost reductions from the division of managerial labour, as from the division of labour generally. A premise of the modern business school is that management skills can be taught, and particularly as regards day-to-day functional operations of a firm in a mature industry, there seems little reason to doubt it. The pyramid of the corporate organization chart, however, narrows toward the top. If senior executives must process information that reaches them over a hierarchy of many levels from a broad base of activities, perspicacity may suffer, and decreasing returns to scale set in. We return to this topic in Chapter 10.

Measurement of economies of scale

Economists have used three ways to estimate the importance of economies of scale: industry studies, the survivor approach, and statistical estimation of cost or production functions. We leave the fine points of statistical estimation to econometrics textbooks,[18] and defer discussion of the results of some such studies to Section 5.3.4, but here review evidence from these three methodologies on the nature of economies of scale.

Industry studies The *industry study* approach is sometimes described as "engineering estimates", but typically involves more than that. For the twenty industries in his sample, for example, Bain (1956, pp. 48–49):

- reviewed published literature on each industry;
- examined unpublished material, including Ph.D. dissertations, and consulted industry experts; and
- questioned business executives, after which he developed a questionnaire (different for each industry) that became the basis for follow-up interviews.

---

[17] Raff (1991, pp. 741–742) quotes General Motors' president Alfred P. Sloan as referring to the Pontiac as "an Oldsmobile engine and a Chevrolet chassis, to be assembled in Chevrolet plants".

[18] See, for example, Berndt (1991, Chapter 3).

Table 5.1 Industry study estimates of minimum efficient plant scale, U.S. four-digit SIC industries, 1967

Industry	MES as % of 1967 industry shipments or capacity	% increase in unit cost at 50 per cent MES
2823 Cellulosic man-made fibers	11.1	5
3519 Diesel engines	11.1	6.7
2822 Synthetic rubber	7.2	15
2824 Noncellulosic man-made fibers	6.0	10.9
2621 Paper	5.2	11
3612 Transformers	4.9	7.9
3011 Passenger tires	3.8	5
3312 Integrated steel mills with wide strip mill	2.7	10
2092 Soybean mills	2.4	2
3241 Cement	1.6	13
2911 Petroleum refining	1.1	3
2082 Beer	1.0	10
2041 Flour mills	0.7	3
2272 Tufted rugs	0.7	10
2211 Cotton broad woven fabrics	0.2	5

Source: Weiss (1976, Table 7-3).

Following this process, Bain classified industries as having low to moderate, substantial, or high barriers to entry (Figure 1.2). Any such classification, although based on a wide range of data, depends ultimately on the judgement of the investigator.

Table 5.1 shows industry-study estimates of minimum efficient scale, due to Leonard Weiss, for 15 four-digit U.S. SIC industries. For these industries, minimum efficient scale is relatively small (Weiss, 1976, p. 132):

> The overall impression left by these [and other] results is that plants of MES are consistent with quite low concentration in a majority of cases, but MES is 10 percent or more of U.S. output or capacity in the cases of major household appliances, diesel engines, turbogenerators, computers, electric motors, automobiles, and commercial aircraft.

The third column of Table 5.1 shows the relative cost increase of a plant operating at one-half minimum efficient scale. If the cost disadvantage of operating a below-MES plant is small, an entrant might begin production at a low level, implying little downward pressure on price and less likelihood of provoking an aggressive response from incumbents.

In a survey of economies of scale prepared in connection with the European Community's 1992 Single Market programme, Pratten (1988) presents engineering scale economy estimates that suggest both the higher cost of operating at less than minimum efficient scale and the extent to which market integration would permit an increased number of firms without sacrifice of operating efficiency. One minimum efficient scale tractor plant, for example, could have produced essentially all UK output in 1983. An integrated market made up of the 10 EC member states in 1983 would have supported 5 efficient-scale plants. Despite the possible increase in the number of efficient plants, Pratten (1988, p. 2.88) comments that:

> One conclusion is that the economies of scale for production and development costs for complex engineering products such as cars continue to levels of output which represent a substantial fraction of the EC output of the products.

Table 5.2 Engineering estimates of minimum efficient firm scale, 1983, as fraction of UK and of EC output, NACE industies

NACE code	Industry	MES as per cent of		Percentage increase in cost at (fraction) of MES output
		UK output	EC output	
321	Tractors	98	19	6 (1/2)
	Combine Harvester		83	7.7 (1/2)
328	Chain Saws		≈15	–
351	Motor Cars	200	20	15 (1/3)
	Trucks	104	.21	12 (1/3)

Source: Pratten (1988, Table 5.8).

In many industries, market integration on the scale of the European Union has the potential to change equilibrium market structure from a dominant-firm market or small-numbers oligopoly to a large-numbers oligopoly. But a transition to large-numbers oligopoly is not likely to be the most common result.

The survivor approach   The basic idea of the *survivor approach* is disarmingly simple. The results of industries studies must have a subjective element; the accounting cost concepts that are the raw material for statistical analysis differ in many ways from the corresponding economic concepts. Rather than evaluate or estimate minimum efficient scale output, the survivor approach is to let the market do the work (Stigler, 1958, p. 56):

> Classify the firms in an industry by size, and calculate the share of industry output coming from each class over time. If the share of a given class falls, it is relatively inefficient, and in general is more inefficient the more rapidly the share falls.

On this argument, if the share of industry output coming from firms in a certain size class grows over time, then firms of that size class are efficient. The output level of firms in the smallest size class with a share of industry output that grows over time is therefore a survivor measure of the minimum efficient scale output level.

There is an element of tautology in this: "that which is, is best".[19] It is inconsistent with the von Weizsäcker approach of making the analysis of welfare effects an essential element of the characterization of barriers to entry, since firms of a certain size may survive for reasons that reduce welfare (for example, by exercising monopoly or monopsony power, or by strategically deterring the entry of potential entrants as cost-efficient as incumbents). Firms of a certain size class may survive and prosper even through they are inefficient in a unit-cost sense, because even larger firms hold price up, sheltering them under a "price umbrella" (Bain, 1969; Figure 3.5 and the accompanying text).

---

[19] Milton Friedman (1955, p. 237): "If we ask what size firm has minimum costs, and define 'minimum costs' in a sense in which it is in a firm's own interest to achieve it, surely the obvious answer is: firms of existing size."

There is also a "survival of the fittest" flavour to the survivor technique, with respect to which the remarks of Robinson (1958, p. 83) seem to the point:

> If there is a famine, and the fodder of the Indian jungle pastures runs short, the cattle begin to die. The first to die are the cows with the calves at foot, the next the heavy milkers; the survivors are the sterile cows, the yielders of little milk. Because these latter have small drain upon them, they can subsist where others die. And so the system of selection in India selects the cow which gives little milk and has no offspring, and she is doubtless the cow best fitted to survive a famine unaided; but to suggest that she is therefore the most desirable cow from the point of view of the Indian villager would be quite fallacious. The process of the survival of the fittest does not imply that the best survive. It implies only that those survive who do survive; because they survive, we suppose them to have been the fittest to survive.

Application of the survivor technique requires measurement of firm size. Size may be measured in terms of employment, assets, physical output, or value added. No method of measuring size and changes in size over time is free from difficulty.[20]

Changes in technology mean the efficient capital-labour ratio can change over time. But this means that if size is measured by input usage, one result will be obtained if size is measured by employment and another if size is measured by capital. Whichever input is used, what appears to be a change in size over time may in fact be a change in the proportions in which inputs are combined.

Most plants and firms produce several varieties of a differentiated product. The mix of different varieties in total output will change over time. This means that for most industries, it will not be possible to sensibly measure plant or firm size in terms of physical measures of output. If size is measured by value of shipments or value added, changes in the amounts produced of different varieties will show up as differences in size. Further, value of shipments and value added both include economic profits. If, over time, firms of a certain size class are able to reduce output but exercise more market power, the survivor technique could show an increase in their share of industry output, if output is measured in terms of value.

When applied to specific industries, the survivor technique may show that the combined market shares of firms of widely different size classes have grown, or that no size class of firm has suffered a statistically significant decline in market share. In the latter case, the survivor technique would imply that firms of all sizes are efficient, a result that could be correct but might also be thought to reflect a certain lack discriminatory power.

Econometric estimates Modern econometric analyses of market performance yield estimates of both the degree of market power and the extent of economies of scale, and we discuss some such estimates in Section 5.3.4. Here we review the results of Keay (2003), who analysed the nature of returns to scale for four U.S. and Canadian industries (oil refineries, paper mills, steel mills, and textile mills) with a view to assessing the potential impact of the 1989 Canada–U.S. free-trade agreement on market performance. Using data on 44 firms for the years just before the free trade agreement, 1972–1988, he finds that all four of the Canadian industries were producing under conditions of increasing returns to scale and all four of the U.S. industries were producing under conditions of decreasing returns to scale.

---

[20] This discussion follows Jewkes (1952, pp. 237–239).

Free trade would, therefore, permit efficiency gains if the Canadian industries expanded and the U.S. industries contracted.

But his estimates imply that "dramatic" output changes would have been needed to bring the average plant to minimum efficient scale. The average Canadian steel mill or textile mill would have had to double its output to expand to minimum efficient scale. The average U.S. steel mill would have had to reduce its output more than 40 per cent to shrink to minimum efficient scale.[21] Further, Keay's results echoed the common result that long-run average cost curves are very nearly flat (2003, p. 383):

> The Canadian industries tended to have cost curves characterized by very long, slightly down-ward sloping portions, while the U.S. industries tended to have cost curves characterized by very long, slightly upward sloping portions. With such flat long-run average cost curves, the penalty, in terms of forgone average cost savings, associated with production to the left, or right, of minimum efficient scale was small.

Thus, while there were potential gains to formation of a free trade area, for these four industries, contingent on extensive adjustments in market structure, the size of those gains was relatively modest.

Overall   Industry studies, the survivor technique, and econometric estimates complement each other. The results of all three types of studies are generally consistent. For most industries, minimum efficient scale plant output is a small part of industry output, unless a market is very small, and there is a range of outputs, which may extend to a large fraction of industry output, over which average cost is roughly constant.

Product differentiation

Kaldor   Like the literature on barriers to entry, the debate about the impact of product differentiation on market performance has been marked by an almost religious ferocity, a ferocity that has tended to obscure rather than clarify.[22] Many elements of that debate appear in nascent form in an early article by Nicolas Kaldor on the economics of advertising.

Solidifying brand preferences   Kaldor saw advertising as a device producers could use to influence consumer purchasing patterns (1950–1951, p. 18):[23]

> Advertising makes the public "brand-conscious" ; it is not so much a question of making the consumer buy things which he would not have bought otherwise; but of crystallising his routine habits, of making him conscious that keeping to a certain routine in consumption means not only buying the same commodities in a vague sort of way, but sticking to the same brands.

---

[21] The staunchly free-trade George W. Bush administration imposed protectionist tariffs on imported steel between 20 March 2002 and 4 December 2003. The tariffs were ended when it became clear that the World Trade Organization would find that by imposing the tariffs, the United States was in violation of its treaty obligations. Anything remotely approaching a 40 per cent reduction in the output of the average U.S. steel mill would no doubt have evoked a similar "free trade" reaction. See Chapter 16.

[22] Discussing the economics of advertising, Butters (1976, p. 392) writes of an "emotional commitment to conflicting schools of thought".

[23] Modern marketing research confirms Kaldor's view; see Section 13.3.1.

The idea that advertising routinizes consumption patterns anticipates structure-conduct-performance paradigm arguments that advertising creates barriers to entry (Comanor and Wilson, 1967, 1979). If an entrant must accumulate goodwill comparable to that of incumbents, then the mere fact that incumbents advertise will increase entry and operating costs. If the impact of advertising on consumer behaviour is durable and accumulates over time, then for some time after entry, a new firm will have to operate with a lower level of goodwill than incumbents, and spend more than incumbents on advertising as it builds up its stock of goodwill. If incumbents can commit to a price low enough—even though above their own unit cost—that an entrant could not cover its costs, including differentially high advertising costs—incumbents could earn economic profits indefinitely without inducing entry. But evidence is (Section 13.3.1) on balance against the idea that advertising has enduring effects on brand preferences.

Economies of scale in advertising   Further, there will be economies of scale in advertising if the effectiveness of advertising increases more than in proportion to the number of advertising messages that are sent out. There will be economies of scale in advertising if advertising must reach or exceed a threshold level if it is to have any effect at all. If there is a threshold effect, part of the cost of advertising will be a fixed cost, independent of the level of output. Like any fixed cost, so the argument went, a fixed cost of advertising means that advertising cost per unit of output will decline as output rises—economies of scale. There may also be economies of scale in advertising if media rate schedules imply a lower average cost of advertising for large-scale advertisers.

It is possible that advertising persuades consumers to "stick to the same brands", making new brands poorer substitutes for established brands. But it is also possible that advertising is a device an entrant can use to inform consumers that new brand is available, so making the new brand a better substitute for established brands. It seems likely that all advertising has persuasive and informative aspects (Kaldor, p. 3), and that the balance between the two will differ from industry to industry. Whether it is or is not either possible or useful to characterize advertising as informative or persuasive, the ultimate question would now be thought to be the impact of advertising on market performance. That, too, is likely to differ from industry to industry.

If there are economies of scale in advertising, that may tend, like economies of scale in production, to reduce the equilibrium number of firms in the market (Chapter 9). But reasoning by analogy will not do: advertising, like production, generates costs, but advertising also shifts the firm's demand curve (Spence, 1980; Sutton, 1991). Kaldor recognized that advertising would shift demand curves. He expected advertising to increase market concentration because (1950–1951, p. 13) "the larger firms are bound to gain at the expense of the smaller ones . . . if at the start, firms are more or less of equal size, those that forge ahead are bound to increase their lead, as the additional sales enable them to increase their outlay still further".

The distribution chain   Kaldor also highlighted the effect of advertising on the balance of power between manufacturers and wholesale and retail distributors.[24] He described the first

---

[24] Kaldor acknowledges the influence of Hawtrey (1926) on this part of his essay, which has much in common with Alfred D. Chandler's (1977) later discussion of the U.S. experience; see fn. 26.

stage in the rise of mass marketing as one of wholesalers' domination, in which (1950–1951, p. 16) "The manufacturer made things to the orders received from the wholesalers; the retailer selected his own orders from the choice of things offered by the wholesalers, and repeated the orders according to the strength of consumers' demand for the individual products."

By advertising directly to the final consumer—"over the heads" of distributors, manufacturers could create brand preferences that would lead the public to demand their products, dislodging wholesalers from their central position (1950–1951, p. 18):

> Thus the growth of modern advertising is closely linked up with the manufacturers' attempt to obtain control of the marketing and distributive mechanism; and conversely the growth of "manufacturers' domination" was closely linked up with the discovery of the power of advertising.

Kaldor expected manufacturers' domination to be characterized by large-scale production, to which he thought there were efficiency advantages. Not only could large firms profit from economies of scale, but also from run-length economies, and from lower capital costs that would better enable the funding of research and development. But Kaldor also thought (to use a later vocabulary) that if barriers to entry allowed incumbents to earn some economic profit, that profit might simply be competed away in spending on advertising (Kaldor, 1950–1951, p. 21).[25]

Porter   Like Kaldor, Porter (1974) emphasizes the importance of distribution channels for final market performance. It is standard to distinguish between consumer goods and services—those sold to final consumer demand—and producer goods and services—purchased by industry for use as capital goods or as inputs for further production. Product-differentiating activity will most often take the form of advertising, it is usually argued, for consumer good industries.

Within the category of consumer goods, Porter makes a distinction between two types of products (1974, p. 422):

> *Convenience goods*: Goods with relatively small unit price, purchased repeatedly and for which the consumer desires an easily accessible outlet. Probable gains from making price and quality comparisons small relative to consumer's appraisal of search costs.
>   *Shopping goods*: Goods where the consumer compares prices, quality and style; compares several stores; the purchase can be delayed; the purchase is relatively infrequent. Probable gains from making price and quality comparisons large relative to the consumer's appraisal of search costs.

Porter expects these two types of goods to be sold through different types of retail outlets (convenience outlets and non-convenience outlets). For goods sold through convenience outlets, (Porter, 1974, p. 423) manufacturer advertising to cultivate a brand image with final consumers would neutralize retailer bargaining power. Because manufacturers use advertising to invest in the differentiation of goods sold through convenience outlets, spending on

---

[25] Kaldor also discussed a third type of organization, retailers' domination, which he associated with the rise of chain stores and which he expected to have efficiency benefits rooted in less spending on advertising and sales efforts and lower distribution margins. Examples are A&P before Kaldor wrote, and Wal-Mart after.

advertising will be a good measure of product differentiating activity for such products. The retailer is in a much stronger position for goods sold through non-convenience outlets where in-store retailer sales efforts are of paramount importance (Porter, 1974, p. 424). For products sold through non-convenience outlets, spending on advertising will not be a good measure of manufacturers' investments in product differentiation. Manufacturers will instead engage in other types of sales-promoting activity—detail men, employees of the manufacturer who keep tabs on in-store displays, for example—aimed directly at the distributor, not the final consumer.

Resumé   Advertising can raise entry costs if there are economies of scale in advertising and if the effect of advertising is to create a durable intangible asset, brand preference, that an entrant cannot immediately duplicate. But informative advertising may lower entry cost. Advertising is most likely to be effective in increasing product differentiation for consumer goods that are sold through convenience outlets, and for such goods, advertising will increase the bargaining power of manufacturers *vis-à-vis* distributors. For consumer goods that are sold through non-convenience outlets and for producer goods, manufacturer sales efforts are likely to take some form other than advertising.

Absolute capital requirements

Bain (1954, pp. 223–224, 226–227) also identified absolute cost advantages of incumbents over entrants as a source of entry costs. Incumbents might have absolute cost advantages over entrants if incumbents use patented or secret production techniques, or if incumbents control unique high-quality sources of inputs and/or distribution channels. For some technologies, scale economies tied to backward (into input supply) and forward (into distribution) vertical integration simultaneously permit more efficient operation and increase the cost of entry.[26]

Adverse selection   Incumbent firms might enjoy an absolute cost advantage due to adverse selection in financial markets. Adverse selection arises if economic agents on one side of a market have information about their characteristics but cannot communicate that information reliably to economic agents on the other side of the market.[27] Efficient financial markets will make loans at a risk-adjusted interest rate that yields lenders an expected rate of return, allowing for the possibility of default, equal to the normal rate of return on capital. Incumbent firms have established track records that make it possible for financial markets to accurately assess the risk of lending to them. Incumbent firms will generally be able to borrow at interest rates that reflect the risk of their operations, but no more than this. It is otherwise for new or potential firms. They have little in the way of track records. It will be costly, if it is possible at all, for lending firms to precisely estimate the odds that a young firm might default on a loan. The result is that efficient markets for financial capital will adjust

---

[26] Chandler writes of the rise of large business in the United States that (1977, p. 364) "High-volume throughput and stock-turn reduced unit costs. Advertising and the provision of services maintained customer loyalty. Rival firms were rarely able to compete until they had built comparable marketing organizations of their own."

[27] In "The market for lemons" Akerlof (1970) discussed adverse selection in the market for used cars: the price of all used cars will be discounted because buyers cannot unambiguously determine whether or not a particular used car is a lemon, a low-quality vehicle, or not.

the cost of capital upward for all young firms, those that complete and perfect information would reveal as safe risks as well as the others (Stigler, 1967).

Economies of scale in issuing stock   Sullivan (1978, p. 215; 1977, 1982) points out another reason why large firms will be able to borrow at lower cost than small firms. The cost of issuing shares of stock is largely independent of the size of the stock issue. If, when they raise money by the sale of shares of stock, large firms sell larger amounts of stock than small firms, flotation costs per unit of funds raised will be lower for large firms than for small.

Rising industry cost of capital   Both these financial market mechanisms will apply more to entry by a new firm than to entry by diversification of a firm that is established in some other market. If firms in an industry face a rising cost of capital,[28] then entry will increase the cost of borrowing to all firms in an industry. But this means that the cost of capital is lower to incumbents, pre-entry, than it would be to an entrant in the post-entry market (Scott, 1981). Even if a potential entrant, established in another industry, observes incumbents earning economic profits, it will not come into the market if entry would cause too large an increase in the cost of capital.

A higher cost of financial capital will translate into a greater absolute investment needed to set up an efficient-scale firm, all else equal, the larger is minimum efficient plant scale. There is thus an interactive effect of capital requirements and scale economies in determining entry costs.

Evidence   One estimate of the height of the absolute capital requirements barrier to entry appears is an early study by Hall and Weiss (1967). For 341 large U.S. firms for the late 1950s and early 1960s, they found that an increase in the assets of a minimum-efficient-scale plant from $50 million (about the level of the tyre, metal container, and rayon industries) to $500 million (steel) would raise the rate of return on assets from 5.7 per cent to 6.8 per cent, an increase of 19 per cent, all else equal.[29]

Consider this result from the Bainian perspective on entry barriers—that they can be inferred from "the extent to which established sellers can persistently raise their prices above a competitive level without attracting new firms to enter the industry". The difference in the absolute capital requirements to construct minimum efficient scale plant in the steel industry and (say) the tyre industry is $450 million. The estimated difference in profitability for an MES steel plant, compared with an MES tyre plant is $(0.068 - 0.057) \times \$450$ million $= \$4,950,000$. If the steel plants in the sample are earning as much profit as they can without making entry profitable, the sunk entry cost incurred in setting up an efficient-scale steel plant permits *each plant* to earn just under $5 million more economic profit in the steel industry than in the tyre industry. To put this in perspective, Weiss (1971b, p. 148) estimates the cost of a minimum efficient scale integrated steel mill in the mid 1960s at three-quarters of

---

[28] There is evidence that the cost of capital increases as borrowing increases; see Baskin (1987, p. 315), and the references cited therein.

[29] The "all else" that is held equal is differences across industries in seller concentration and the growth rate of industry sales, with annual dummy variables to control for macroeconomic fluctuations. The impact of seller concentration on profitability in their sample is statistically significant (that is, estimated precisely) but small (Hall and Weiss, 1967, p. 326): "A 40-point increase in [the four-firm seller concentration ratio] (from 30 to 70 which includes 77 per cent of our observations) … would increase [the rate of return on assets] by only 0.3 to 0.6 points … ", an increase of between 4 and 9 per cent at the sample mean.

a billion dollars. Against this base, an additional $5 million economic profit is an increase of two-thirds of one percentage point in the rate of return on investment, almost 10 per cent of the 6.8 per cent rate of estimated steel industry return on investment.

These considerations suggest that the efficient operation of financial markets under conditions of imperfect information will place *de novo* entrants at a financial cost disadvantage *vis-à-vis* incumbents. Even established firms in other industries will operate at some cost disadvantage, if their cost of capital rises as they fund greater investment.

The extent of the market

Markets extend over geographic space and over product space. Here we focus on how one might draw the boundaries of a market if the immediate purpose is to analyse the condition of entry. We should be forthright and admit that the economic literature on market definition contains much about which economists ought to be modest. In the words of Joan Robinson (1956, p. 361, footnote omitted; she quotes Davies, 1955, p. 710):

> "A precise and meaningful definition of an industry" is a vain objective. There is no advantage (and much error) in making definitions of words more precise than the subject matter that they refer to. But rough working demarcations of industries are required, for instance, by a group of business-men considering who is eligible to join a trade association or by the compilers of the Census of Production.

Price equality   The starting point for this literature is Cournot, who makes equality of price the defining characteristic of a market ([1838] 1927, p. 51, footnote):

> It is well known that by *market* economists mean, not a certain place where purchases and sales are carried on, but the entire territory of which the parts are so united by the relations of unrestricted commerce that prices there take the same level throughout, with ease and rapidity.

Alfred Marshall, who elsewhere (1920, p. 324) quotes Cournot's definition, takes the same approach (1920, p. 112):

> A perfect market is a district, small or large, in which there are many buyers and many sellers all so keenly on the alert and so well acquainted with one another's affairs that the price of a commodity is always practically the same for the whole of the district.

Marshall takes price differences that are the result of differences in the cost of supply into account (1920, p. 325):

> [T]he more nearly perfect a market is, the stronger is the tendency for the same price to be paid for the same thing at the same time in all parts of the market: but of course if the market is large, allowance must be made for the expense of delivering the goods to different purchasers; each of whom must be supposed to pay in addition to the market price a special charge on account of delivery.

He also (1920, p. 326) remarks on the grading of different qualities of grain in U.S. markets. Allowing for price differences in a market that only reflect differences in the cost of quality is much like allowing for price differences in a market that only reflect differences in transportation cost, and is not inconsistent with treating differently-priced goods as being in the same market.

Market definition and perfect/imperfect competition   Marshall's definition is of a *perfect market*.[30] But almost all real-world markets are imperfectly competitive in some way, and many sufficiently so that those imperfections must be taken into account in analyzing their dimensions.

The price-equality principle for market definition rules out price discrimination (Stigler and Sherwin, 1985, p. 580):

> No volume of physical movement … will insure that two areas are in the same market. Let a substantial amount of the product produced in area A come from B: they are separate markets if price discrimination (the producer in area B is dumping) is causing the price in A to be lower than in B despite the transportation costs.

 BOX   **Price Discrimination at the Fulton Fish Market**

Graddy (1995, 2006) studies market performance at New York's Old Fulton Fish Market, a wholesale market that opened well before dawn five days a week and remained open for five or six hours to supply fish mainly to restaurateurs and retailers. Her analysis of transaction prices for whiting* showed that the roughly 60 per cent of the buyers who were Asian paid on average about 7 per cent less than Causcasian buyers, controlling for differences in time of day of the transaction and in fish quality.

There were six regular suppliers of whiting at the Fulton Fish Market, but another 29 or so dealers who could sell whiting if it became profitable to do so. Even if six is not "many small sellers" (some would argue that it is; see Selten, 1973), 29 is a respectable number of potential entrants. There seems to have been a good real-world approximation to "many small buyers" on the demand side of the market. The product was subject to some physical heterogeneity, but (Graddy, 1995, p. 77) "although a dealer may receive boxes of different quality, these differences are easily detected and quantified and no dealer appears to receive on average a higher quality of whiting than does another dealer". Yet sellers were able to engage in *third-degree price discrimination*: charging a systematically lower price to a group of customers with a higher price elasticity of demand than was charged to other customers.

Persistent third-degree price discrimination was possible because one of the conditions of a perfectly-competitive market—compete and perfect knowledge—was not met (Graddy, 2006, p. 214):

> Why didn't the Asian buyers arbitrage the market, buying low and then reselling to other customers? In all likelihood, it is very unlikely that either white buyers or Asian buyers actually knew this was happening. Prices were quoted discretely for particular customers. White buyers rarely socialized with Asian buyers and hence communication between the two groups was limited.

* She writes (1995, p. 209, fn. 1) "at the time that I was at the market, more transactions took place in whiting than in any other fish" and "whiting do not vary as much in size and quality as other fish".

---

[30] That is, a market in which buyers and sellers act as price takers and there is free and easy entry and exit; see Chapter 2, fn. 2.

But price discrimination—one seller offering physically identical units of a good to different consumers for different prices—is endemic in real-world markets (Chapter 8). If persistent price discrimination is sufficient to place different groups of consumers in different markets, then (see the accompanying box) Asian buyers and Caucasian buyers of whiting at the Old Fulton Fish Market were in different markets, although they passed one by the other and sought to buy the same product from the same suppliers at the same time and place. For most purposes, and certainly for the purpose of examining the condition of entry, this is not a useful way to look at the question of market definition.

Industry versus market   What one would like is a definition of a market that stands on its own, independent of the nature of the competition that goes on within that market. Nightingale offers one (1978, pp. 35–36):

> . . . an "industry" is any grouping of firms which operate similar processes and could produce technically identical products within a given planning horizon. . . . A market, by contrast, is the institution within which a firm attempts to sell his output or buy an input. A firm's behaviour is constrained by other firms selling in that market and by the behaviour of buyers in the market.

Nightingale makes a distinction between an industry, members of which potentially make up the supply side of product markets, and the market, which includes the forces of both demand and supply. This way of conceiving of the term market is consistent with much usage in the literature.

Distance Shipped[31]

Weiss   In an early attempt to characterize the geographic extent of markets in the United States in terms of the distances products were shipped, Weiss (1972, p. 245) took "the geographic market" to be "the set of locations from which plants supply or could profitably supply a given consuming point". He analysed data from the U.S. Census Bureau's 1963 and 1967 *Census of Transportation* to compute (among other statistics) the radius from plant location within which 80 per cent of an industry's products were shipped, which he called R_{80}.[32] A large R_{80} suggests that the commodity is valuable, relative to transportation cost, so it can be profitable to ship the product a long distance.

Weiss recognized, as have others,[33] that distanced-shipped radii are *minimal* estimates of geographic market size. Distance-shipped radii understate the geographic extent of the market if the areas supplied by single sellers interact (as, for example, in circle market of Section 4.2.3) or overlap (as when cross-hauling arises under the basing point pricing system; see Section 2.3.1). More generally, whether or not it is profitable for distant rivals to ship into a region will depend on the extent to which firms located in the region are able to hold

---

[31] For approaches to the problem of geographic market definition in antitrust cases by examining the distances over which producers ship and the distances from which purchasers buy, see Elzinga and Hogarty (1973) and the literature springing therefrom.

[32] Weiss also computed the radius from plant location within which 90 per cent of an industry's products were shipped, the percentage of tonnage of industry output shipped less than 500 miles, and the mean distance shipped. The industry classification scheme used for the Census of Transportation was similar to the Standard Industrial Classification (Weiss, 1972, fn. 7; on the SIC, see Appendix 27). Weiss (1972, p. 248) discusses alternative efforts to make inferences about the geographic extent of U.S. markets by examining the diffusion of production across states or in comparison to the diffusion of population.

[33] Marshall (1920, p. 329); Weiss (1972, fn. 1); Stigler and Sherwin (1985, fn. 2).

Table 5.3 Number of three- or four-digit products in market radius categories and average number of states per market

R_{80} (miles)	Number of Products	Number of Markets in the United States
0–125	13	SMSAs
126–177	2	48
178–217	5	24
218–251	2	16
252–290	1	12
291–356	13	9
357–435	14	6
436–504	17	4
505–617	36	3
618–873	84	2
≥ 874	96	1
Total	283	

Note: U.S. manufacturing industries; continental United States. "SMSA" is an acronym for Standard Metropolitan Statistical Area.
Source: Weiss (1972, Table 4).

price above cost. Unless a market is perfectly competitive, market boundaries and market performance are simultaneously determined.[34]

Table 5.3 summarizes Weiss' results. Row 2, for example, reports that 80 per cent of the shipments of two products[35] were over distances between 126 and 177 miles. This distance shipped implies that there was room for 48 non-overlapping regional shipment areas in the continental United States. For 96 products, 80 per cent of shipments were at least 874 miles, and for these products, the geographic markets (within the continental United States, at least) were national. For 13 products, 80 per cent of shipments were less than 125 miles, and the implied geographic markets were on the scale of a metropolitan area.[36] Weiss saw his findings as showing that most of the products in his sample were sold in regional markets (1972, p. 253): "Manufactured goods seem generally to sell on broad markets, though only a minority are unequivocally national in scope. The more typical markets extend over a half, a third, or a quarter of the country." [37]

---

[34] In one manifestation—market definition for the application of antitrust and competition policy—failure to recognize that market boundaries and market performance are simultaneously determined led to what is known as the *Cellophane* fallacy. The reference is to an antitrust case (U.S. *v.* E.I. du Pont de Nemours & Co. 351 U.S. 377 (1956)) in which other types of flexible packaging materials were judged to be good enough substitutes for cellophane to place them all in the same market. The argument is now made that consumers would not have regarded other flexible wrapping materials as good substitutes for cellophane if cellophane had been priced closer to its marginal cost.

[35] As it happens, the two products were those of industry 2024, Ice Cream and Related Frozen Desserts and industry 3271, Concrete Products.

[36] Until 1983, the term Standard Metropolitan Statistical Area (SMSA) was used by the U.S. Office of Management and Budget to designate an integrated urban economic area with a population of 50 thousand or more. There were 231 SMSAs in 1967 (U.S. Bureau of the Budget, 1967), differing greatly in economic nature (Haro, 1968).

[37] In the same vein, Dunne, Klimek, and Roberts (2005) report that in 1977, over 90 per cent of the products of four U.S. construction industries were shipped less than 100 miles, while between 82 and 95 per cent of shipments of three food industries (milk, baked goods, soft-drink bottling) were shipped less than 200 miles.

Hilberry and Hummels   Hilberry and Hummels (2005) examine the 1997 pattern of shipments from U.S. mining and manufacturing establishments.[38] They are able to identify the origin and destination zip (postal) code for each shipment. The median radius of a five-digit zipcode area was four miles. The average distance between origin and destination zipcode areas in the Hilberry and Hummels sample was 523 miles. But this average reflects a concentration of shipments in plants' immediate areas and a tail of shipments to distant locations. The bulk of output, in value terms, is delivered to customers located in zipcode zones 200 miles or less from a plant's location.

Hilberry and Hummels observe that there are two ways the value of shipments might fall as distance from the plant of origin increases. It could be that the same number of varieties are shipped from an origin zipcode region to all destination zipcode regions, near and far, but that less of each variety is shipped, on average, to distant zipcode regions.

Alternatively, it could be that the value of any one shipment from one zipcode to another is about the same, regardless of distance, but that fewer varieties are shipped from an origin zipcode region to distant destination zipcode regions, all else equal.

Hilberry and Hummels show that it is the second relationship that drives the distance-value of shipments relationship: the greater the distance of alternative sources of supply from a plant's location, the fewer the number of varieties shipped into the plant's zipcode area.

What are the implications for market definition? Begin with the proposition that product differentiation is ubiquitous. It may make sense to think exclusively of "a market" for highly standardized products that are of high value in relation to transportation costs. But leaving aside cases like currency and grain markets, although there is (for example) "a market for laptops," there is also "the market in which Dell laptops compete" and "the market in which Lenovo Thinkpads compete" and "the market in which Apple laptops compete". While these variety-specific markets overlap, they do not coincide. The Hilberry and Hummels' results show that the varieties of distant producers are less likely, all else equal, to be close substitutes in the market for the product of a particular plant. To think of geographic markets as did Weiss, the greater the radial distance from a firm's plant, the fewer the number of varieties that are shipped into its zipcode area. In this sense, the Hilberry and Hummels' results, although suggesting smaller geographic markets than Weiss found, complement his much earlier work.

Parallel price movements   For Stigler and Sherwin (1985, p. 555) "The market is the area within which price is determined: the market is that set of suppliers and demanders whose trading establishes the price of a good", and that gives price a "central role" in drawing the boundaries of a market (1985, p. 561, footnote omitted):[39]

> We are interested in the ability of buyers and sellers to shift between the two or more places: if the price rises in A relative to B, can buyers shift to B or sellers to A? If the prices in the two places have a measure of independence in the short run, but that independence is not large . . . , the two are in one market.

---

[38] In most cases, an "establishment" is a plant or factory. Each plant owned by a multiplant firm is a separate observation in the Commodity Flow Survey database with which Hilberry and Hummels worked.

[39] Harley (1980) applied this methodology to document the integration of world grain markets at the turn of the nineteenth century; see Section 18.3.

Flour milling Applying the price-movement criterion to the U.S. wholesale flour industry, Stigler and Sherwin analyse the regional price indices depicted in Figure 5.6. To the naked eye, the price indices for all three areas seem to move together. Flour milling was an important industry in both Minneapolis, Minnesota and Kansas City, Missouri. The levels of and changes in the two price indices were highly correlated.[40] Major customers bought in both locations. The area within which flour mills located in Minneapolis and the area within which flour mills located in Kansas City overlapped. Stigler and Sherwin concluded that Minneapolis and Kansas City flour millers supplied the same geographic market.

Wholesale flour prices in Minneapolis and in Buffalo, New York moved very closely together, and wholesale flour prices in Kansas City, Missouri and Portland, Oregon moved very closely together.[41] The link between the Buffalo and Portland price indices was less close.[42] Annual price indices, however, move much more closely together than the monthly prices indices. For this specific case, Stigler and Sherwin (1985, p. 564, p. 566) "interpret the

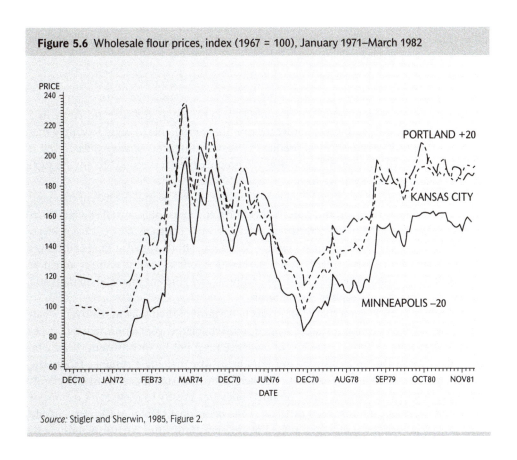

Figure 5.6 Wholesale flour prices, index (1967 = 100), January 1971–March 1982

Source: Stigler and Sherwin, 1985, Figure 2.

---

[40] Correlation coefficients were 0.97 and 0.92, respectively (Stigler and Sherwin, 1985, p. 562).

[41] The correlation coefficient of the logarithms of the Minneapolis, Buffalo prices indices was 0.972; for Kansas City and Portland, 0.975 (Stigler and Sherwin, 1985, Table 1).

[42] The correlation of the logarithm of monthly prices in Buffalo and Portland was 0.928, the correlation of the first-differences of the logarithms of monthly prices 0.807 (Stigler and Sherwin, 1985, Table 1).

lower correlation of price movements in Portland and Buffalo as showing a larger (but not absolutely large) degree of short-run independence of prices."

They acknowledge that there is an element of judgement involved in deciding whether price movements are "close enough" to place different regions (or product varieties) in the same economic market (Stigler and Sherwin, p. 562):[43] "What is the level of correspondence between two price series, either directly or in first differences, that determines that they are in the same market? ... the general answer is that there is no unique criterion: markets can show every level of interdependence from absolute homogeneity to complete independence ... "

Wholesale fuel prices   Another example considered by Stigler and Sherwin is the regional markets for residual fuel oil (1985, p. 576) "which is used as a fuel for merchant ships, is one of the least valuable of the oil products; and because it is a by-product of normal refinery operations, its supply is not easily adapted to local demand". Regional prices indices for residual fuel seem sometimes to move together, other times not.[44] For periods at least as long as one to three years, Stigler and Sherwin conclude, regional sales areas for residual fuel oil were not in the same geographic market.

Resumé

The assessment of entry conditions is a counterfactual exercise. *If* the demand curve in a region shifts outward, will producers in other regions find it profitable to begin to supply that region? *If* the profits of breakfast cereal producers rise, will producers of animal feeds find it profitable to retool their equipment[45] and begin to produce breakfast cereal? To answer such forward-looking questions, what we have is backward-looking evidence.

We can observe the scale at which producers have chosen to operate, the extent to which they have invested in advertising and other sales efforts, their cost of financial capital. What we observe suggests that for most industries, average cost is constant above output levels that are small relative to the size of most markets. Marketing efforts aimed at final consumers require a substantial sunk investment, as do marketing efforts by manufacturers aimed at distributors. Starting a new enterprise is a risky business, and efficient financial markets add a risk premium to the cost of capital of new firms.

Distance-shipped data suggest that most plants make most of their sales in relatively small geographic areas. Price-movement studies suggest somewhat larger geographic markets, especially over longer time periods. These bits of evidence need not be inconsistent. It may be that most plants find themselves supplying sales areas like the single supplier facing the threat of entry of Section 2.3.5: by keeping price below the level that makes most entry profitable, the plants keeps its (geographic or product) sales area mostly to itself. Sales regions of different plants bump up against each other, and the occasional shipment in from outside serves to knit regions that are mostly supplied by different firms into what it is sensible to regard, for long run periods, as a single market.

---

[43] The question and the answer appear in two successive paragraphs.

[44] See their Figure 8.

[45] To the extent that retooling is needed.

5.3.3 Industry Studies (Mostly)

Broad cross-section samples

Joe Bain's seminal (1956) comparison of profitability, seller concentration and entry conditions in a cross-section sample of 20 industries (Figure 1.2) spawned a huge literature. It was the structure-conduct-performance framework that guided the specification of such studies. Neglecting much detail, the hypotheses being tested were that entry barriers due to scale economies, absolute cost advantages, and product differentiation determine the level to which incumbents *can* raise price without inducing entry, while seller concentration has pride of place among factors determining how close incumbents get to the maximum entry-forestalling price.[46] Researchers who contributed to this literature applied progressively more sophisticated econometric techniques to the analysis of progressively larger samples. Most of these samples were constructed from data collected from individual firms by government agencies and aggregated to form industry data. The government agencies collected the greatest variety of information about the manufacturing sector of the economy, with the result that most of the samples analysed by industrial economists were samples of manufacturing industries.

Although the early tillers of this particular field did not do so, conventional oligopoly theory can be made to yield a theoretical rationale for the kind of econometric specification that was common in the cross-section literature (Cowling and Waterson, 1976). Begin with the industry-level Lerner index equation for a Cournot oligopoly when firms have different unit costs, (3.36):

$$\frac{p-c}{p} = \frac{pQ - cQ}{pQ} = \frac{\alpha + (1-\alpha)H}{\varepsilon_{QP}}. \tag{5.3}$$

Here c is a weighted-average value for the average cost of firms in the industry, H is the Herfindahl index of seller concentration, α is the common value of the conjectural variation for all firms in the industry, and ε_{Qp} is the industry price-elasticity of demand.

Multiplying the numerator and denominator of the Lerner index (far left in (5.3)) by industry sales Q converts the Lerner index to the ratio of profit to sales (centre fraction in (5.3)). Now suppose that economic cost cQ has two parts, variable cost and fixed cost:

$$cQ = wL + \rho p^k K. \tag{5.4}$$

wL, which for expositional purposes we can think of as the wages of labour, represents the cost of all variable inputs. $p^k K$ is the amount of industry investment in fixed capital, and ρ is the normal rate of return on investment. Substitute (5.4) into (5.3) and rearrange terms to obtain an expression for the rate of profit over variable cost as a fraction of sales as a function of the Herfindahl index, the industry price elasticity of demand, and the normal rate of return on capital times the capital-sales ratio (*KSR*), investment in fixed capital divided by sales revenue:

$$\frac{pQ - wL}{pQ} = \frac{\alpha + (1-\alpha)H}{\varepsilon_{QP}} + \rho \frac{p^k K}{pQ}. \tag{5.5}$$

Equation (5.5) is a non-cooperative equilibrium relationship, that the industry gross rate of return on sales should be larger as seller concentration (H) is larger, the more firms expect

---

[46] Bain cautioned against (1954, p. 240) "the erroneous belief that there must be a sort of one-to-one correlation between concentration and monopoly pricing tendencies ... "

rivals to match output changes (the closer is α to 1), and the more capital-intensive is the industry's technology (the larger is the capital-sales ratio).[47]

Most structure-conduct-performance studies of profitability or price-cost margins (*PCM*) in cross-section industry samples used a seller concentration ratio (*CR4*) to measure industry concentration, because the Herfindahl index was not available for large numbers of industries. Few studies had direct estimates of the industry price elasticity of demand, so it was typical to assume that the price elasticity of demand was a function of variables that were observable, such as the growth rate of industry sales (*GR*), the advertising-sales ratio (*ASR*, industry spending on advertising divided by sales revenue), and the fraction of industry sales going to final consumer demand (*CDSR*). If available, the import-sales ratio (*IMSR*, the share of industry sales supplied by foreign-based suppliers), would be included on the ground that it affected the price elasticity of demand facing domestic producers. Some measure of entry barriers, most often an estimate of the output of a minimum-efficient-scale plant as a fraction of industry sales (*MES/S*), was typically used to measure differences across industries in the strength of potential competition. Other variables would be added to explain differences in profitability or price-cost margins if they were thought likely to shed light on some particular aspect of structure-conduct-performance relationships.

Equation (5.6) shows characteristic results for this kind of study. It was estimated by Strickland and Weiss (1976, Table 2) for a sample of 408 U.S. four-digit Standard Industrial Classification manufacturing industries. The data are for 1963.[48]

$$PCM = 0.1736 + 0.2326GR + 0.1720\frac{MES}{S} + 1.6256ASR \tag{5.6}$$

$$+ 0.0377CR4 + 0.1165KSR$$

The constant term, 17.36 per cent, is the multidimensional equivalent of the estimated vertical-axis intercept of a straight line. The constant term, 0.1736 (or 17.36 per cent), is what the sample tells the researcher that the price-cost margin would be for an industry with a growth rate of industry sales of zero, with minimum efficient scale zero as a fraction of industry sales, with no advertising, where the largest four firms have a market share of zero, and where the industry has zero investment in fixed capital. But most industry observations will be nowhere near these values of the explanatory variables.

The coefficient of the capital-sales ratio means that the normal rate of return on capital investment for this sample is estimated to be 11.65 per cent. Comparing industries for which sales grew at 10 and 20 per cent per year between 1954 and 1963, price-cost margins in the

---

[47] It was common in the structure-conduct-performance literature to depart from the assumption of non-cooperative behaviour and argue that firms would be more likely to tacitly or overtly collude in more concentrated industries. A simple way to fit this argument into the (5.5) specification is to suppose that α rises with H. If (for simplicity) α is assumed to be proportional to H, $\alpha = \alpha_1 H$, then (5.5) becomes:

$$\frac{pQ - wL}{pQ} = \frac{(1+\alpha_1)H - \alpha_1 H^2}{\varepsilon_{QP}} + \rho\frac{p^k K}{pQ},$$

so that the impact of concentration as measured by the Herfindahl index on the price-cost margin is quadratic. See Neumann and Haid (1985) for models of this kind. See also Clarke and Davies (1982, fn. 4).

[48] I omit discussion of important measurement issues, for which see Strickland and Weiss (1976). They included other explanatory variables in their estimating equation. I have omitted the estimated coefficients of these variables for compactness and because the variables are not directly related to the main structure-performance relationships under discussion here. Of the coefficients reported in equation (5.6), all except those of *CR4* and *MES/S* are statistically significant at the usual level.

higher-growth rate industry are estimated to be $0.2326 \times 0.1 = 0.02326$ or 2.326 percentage points greater, neglecting all other factors. Similarly, comparing two otherwise identical industries, one with minimum efficient scale output 10 per cent of industry sales and one with minimum efficient scale output 25 per cent of industry output, the price-cost margin of the second industry is estimated to be greater by $0.1720 \times (0.25 - 0.10) = 0.0258$ or 2.58 percentage points.

For measurement reasons, spending on advertising is not subtracted from revenue in the price-cost margin on the left in (5.6). It is therefore one minus the estimated coefficient of *ASR* that gives the effect of a change in advertising as a fraction of sales revenue on price-cost margins net of advertising expense. The estimate is that an increase in advertising spending from 10 to 25 per cent of sales revenue would increase price-cost margins, after subtracting spending on advertising, by $0.6256 \times (0.25 - 0.1) = 0.0938$ or 9.38 percentage points. A difference in the combined market share of the largest four firms of 0.4 (say, 0.5 compared with 0.1) means an estimated difference in price-cost margins of $0.0377 \times 0.4 = 0.015$ or 1.5 percentage points.

The coefficients of *MES/S* and *CR4* in equation (5.6) are not estimated precisely. The most likely reason is that differences in the minimum efficient scale fraction of industry output are an important factor explaining differences in the combined market share of the largest four firms, so it is difficult to distinguish the separate influence of *MES/S* and *CR4* on price-cost margins.[49]

The estimated influence of advertising on price-cost margins in (5.6) is large and statistically significant. It was generally a finding in studies of this kind that the impact of advertising on profitability was larger than the influence of seller concentration.

Strickland and Weiss also divided their sample into two subgroups, 102 consumer good industries (at least 50 per cent of industry sales to final consumer demand) and 306 producer good industries (more than 50 per cent of industry sales made to firms in other industries). The estimated impact of seller concentration on price-cost margins is larger and more significant in each subsample than when the two samples are combined. The estimated impact of seller concentration on price-cost margins is larger for consumer good industries than for producer good industries. The growth rate of industry sales has no significant impact on margins in consumer good industries, but is similar to that reported in (5.6) for producer good industries. Differences in *MES/S* have a significant and positive impact on margins in consumer good industries, but no significant impact on margins in producer good industries. Capital intensity has no significant impact on margins for consumer good industries, but for producer good industries the estimated effect is statistically significant and similar in magnitude to the estimate for the combined sample. Advertising intensity has a positive and significant impact on margins in both subsamples. The effect is larger and more significant for producer good industries. One interpretation of this result is that within the producer good industry subsample, industries where advertising is high are more like consumer good industries, all else equal, so that the advertising effect is picking up differences in the demand structure of different producer good industries.

The fact that results of this kind differ when consumer good industries and producer good industries are examined separately suggests that there may be fundamental differences between groups of industries within the manufacturing sector. If one is going to carry out

---

[49] Late in the structure-conduct-performance period, empirical work took explicit account of the fact that seller concentration is an endogenous variable, itself determined by economic forces. The Strickland and Weiss paper was one of the first to do so.

industry studies, therefore, it may make sense to estimate price-cost margin equations like (5.6) for industries or for firms in groups of industries that have similar supply-side technologies, or similar demand-side characteristics. We discuss one such study in Section 5.3.4. But for cross-section samples covering a large number of industries, it may not be possible to get satisfactory data describing the many ways in which industries differ.

Critical concentration ratio

Formal oligopoly models imply that there should be a continuous positive relationship between seller concentration and industry price-cost margins. But some economists looked for a discontinuous relationship between industry-average market power and concentration.

Chamberlin ([1933] 1962 p. 48) reasoned from one of the assumptions of the model of perfect competition, that the supply side of a perfectly competitive market is made up of many firms, each so small that it ignores the impact its actions have on the market. A monopolist will certainly be aware that its actions determine the quantity supplied. Entry by a large rival will transform monopoly to duopoly, but each duopolist will remain aware that its actions affect the total quantity supplied. Taking it for granted that firms in a market system seek to maximize profit, Chamberlin argued, duopolists will be able to approximate the monopoly outcome. They will not need to explicitly collude: an intelligent assessment of the market situation and the expected impact of vigorous rivalry on their bottom lines will lead them to an obvious conclusion. Independent coordination on the mutually advantageous focal point—the monopoly outcome—will continue as long as the number of suppliers is so small that each is conscious of its oligopolistic interdependence with the others. But when the number of suppliers rises above a critical value—when seller concentration falls below a critical level—recognition of oligopolistic interdependence will fade. Below the critical concentration level, firms will act, if not as price takers, at least according to their own best-response functions—every firm for itself, and the devil take the hindmost. There will thus be a discrete shift in the market equilibrium as supplier concentration shifts from above to below the critical concentration level.

But what is the value of the critical concentration level? Figure 1.2 is drawn showing a best-fit regression line with a modest positive slope. But to the naked eye the values shown in Figure 1.2 are at least as consistent with a discontinuous upward shift in profitability when the combined market shares of the four largest firms rise above something like 50 per cent.[50]

---

[50] For the data used to draw Figure 1.2, linear regressions of profitability on entry-condition dummy variables (*S*, substantial; *H*, high) and alternatively continuous (*CR4*) and discrete (*CCR* = 1 for *CR4* ≥ 50, 0 for *CR4* < 50) concentration variables, estimated coefficients are

Constant	S	H	CR4	CCR	R^2
9.770	1.2144	6.0291	0.0407		0.5012
(4.7803)	(0.6636)	(2.6000)	(1.1251)		
10.7083	1.2063	5.2508		3.0208	0.5481
(8.1976)	(0.7109)	(2.3404)		(1.7481)	

Profitability is measured as the after-tax rate of return on stockholders' equity; *t*-statistics are in parentheses. Neither regression suggests that there is any significant difference in the profitability of industries with substantial entry barriers and those with medium or low entry barriers (the omitted entry condition category). Industries with

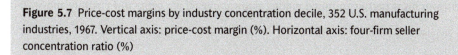

Figure 5.7 Price-cost margins by industry concentration decile, 352 U.S. manufacturing industries, 1967. Vertical axis: price-cost margin (%). Horizontal axis: four-firm seller concentration ratio (%)

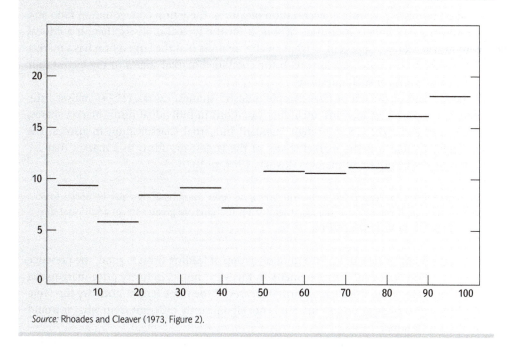

Source: Rhoades and Cleaver (1973, Figure 2).

In an earlier study, Bain (1951) found what appeared to be a discontinuous increase (from 6.9 per cent to 12.1 per cent) in industry profitability when the four-firm seller concentration ratio was 70 per cent or higher. Rhoades and Cleaver (1973) studied a sample of essentially all U.S. manufacturing industries for 1967. The price-cost margin/concentration ratio relationship for 10-percentage-point intervals in their sample is shown in Figure 5.7. There is no obvious relationship between margins and concentration until the four-firm seller concentration ratio reaches 50 per cent (and this is what Rhoades and Cleaver's statistical results show). Above this level, margins rise as concentration rises. White (1976) carries out a sophisticated statistical analysis of the determinants of profitability for a sample of 77 U.S. industries for the years 1963–1965, and finds evidence of a critical four-firm seller concentration ratio around 56 to 58 per cent.

There was thus considerable support in the industry-cross section literature for the idea that supply-side concentration had little impact on profitability or price-cost margins until

high entry barriers are significantly more profitable than other industries, all else equal. Neither concentration variable has a coefficient that is terribly significant in a statistical sense, but the coefficient of CCR is estimated somewhat more precisely than the coefficient of CR4. The coefficient of CCR implies that there is, on average for this sample, a discrete jump in the rate of return on stockholders' equity of 3 percentage points as CR4 rises above 50 per cent. The average rate of return on stockholders' equity for these 20 industries is 14.165 per cent. The critical concentration ratio specification thus seems to perform slightly better than the continuous specification.

the largest four firms had a combined market share above 50 per cent, and possibly above 70 per cent.[51]

Critical market share

Industrial economists' favourite concentration measures, the n-firm concentration ratio and the Herfindahl index, hide a multitude of sins. If for the typical industry there is a critical concentration at $CR4 = 57$ per cent, is what "really" matters that the largest firm has a market share of at least 30 per cent? Working with the combined market shares of the largest four firms, one cannot answer such questions.

Around the end of the era of large-sample industry studies, Kwoka (1979) analysed the determinants of price-cost margins, including variations in individual firms' market shares, for a sample of 314 1972 U.S. four-digit Standard Industrial Classification industries. His evidence suggests that it is the market shares of the largest *two* firms in a market that are critical for the size of price-cost margins (Kwoka, 1979, p. 107):

> If the largest firm is at least 0.26 of the industry, price-cost margins are greater by about four percentage points. If the second share is at least 0.15, margins are greater by an additional five percentage points or so, *ceteris paribus*.

If (from the point of view of firms) a duopoly group of leading firms is good, the presence of a third large firm is a destabilizing element. In Kwoka's sample, industry price-margins *fall* as the market share of the third largest firm increases. If the three largest firms are the same size, the industry-average price-cost margin is not significantly different from what it would be if all firms were small.[52]

Azzam *et al.* (1996) analyse the determinants of the price of Portland cement in 25 regional U.S. markets. Controlling for differences across markets in input costs, age, and capacity of plants, technology use, and other factors, they find a discrete jump in price at a Herfindahl index of 0.32, corresponding to about three equally sized firms. For Portland cement in U.S. regional markets, recognition of oligopolistic interdependence begins as the number of equally sized firms falls from four to three.

Market power and efficiency

Cross-section studies of industry performance were criticized in the 1970s by the Second Chicago School, and fell out of favour. The efficiency critique (Demsetz 1973, 1974) was that the widely observed positive relationship between supply-side concentration and price-cost margins was the result of the lower costs of large, efficient firms, not tacit or overt collusion that raised prices. Demsetz tested the efficiency hypothesis by comparing the concentration-profitability relationship for small and large firms in the same industry. Tacit or overt collusion that succeeded in raising prices, he argued, would raise the profitability of

---

[51] Bradburd and Over (1982) find evidence of two critical concentration ratios, a lower one (46 per cent) at which recognition of oligopolistic interdependence breaks down as concentration falls from high levels, and a higher one (68 per cent) at which recognition of oligopolistic interdependence sets in as concentration rises from low levels.

[52] Kwoka's findings offer a rationale for a merger control policy that is cautious toward mergers that would endow a market with two leading suppliers, or eliminate a third-ranked rival. See the discussion in Section 22.3.5 of European Community policy toward mergers that would create positions of collective dominance.

all firms.[53] If it was lower costs that were responsible for the higher profits of some firms, which grew large because they were more efficient, then only the profitability of large firms would be greater in more concentrated industries.

There are difficulties with this approach. One is the assumption the more efficient, and therefore more profitable firms, will grow at differentially faster rates than less efficient firms. As we will see in Chapter 10, firm growth rates appear to be substantially random. It might also be the case that the reason higher-cost firms are able to survive in a market is because larger firms hold price up, in the process creating a price umbrella under which a fringe of inefficient firms can shelter itself.

Thus if in the market illustrated in Figure 3.5 the more efficient firm, firm 1, were to act as a price taker, it would set a price slightly below the unit cost of the higher-cost firm, firm 2, and supply the entire market at price c_2. The more efficient firm would collect an economic profit-efficiency rent in the amount $(c_2 - c_1) Q(c_2)$, where $Q(c_2)$ is the quantity demanded at price c_2. If instead the more efficient firm acts as a Cournot duopolist, each firm supplies part of the market, the total quantity supplied is less than $Q(c_2)$, and the Cournot equilibrium price is greater than the average cost of the less efficient firm. If firms recognize their oligopolistic interdependence, as one expects in concentrated industries, and if large firms are more profitable in more concentrated industries, a portion of the higher profit enjoyed by more efficient firms is an efficiency rent due to lower cost. But another portion of the higher profit is the result of joint- or single-firm market power.[54]

Clarke *et al.* (1984) tested for the presence of a market-power element in the concentration-profitability relationship. They extended the Cournot conjectural variations model to allow for the possibility of economies of large scale. Based on this model, they estimated a version of the Lerner index along the lines of (3.35) for 29 UK minimum list heading (MLH) industries.[55] By so doing, they obtained estimates of the conjectural variation parameter α for each of the 29 industries. They then found a significant positive relationship between the estimated conjectures and seller concentration,[56]

$$\alpha = 0.170 + 1.682H. \tag{5.7}$$

The estimated conjectures are an index of the degree of tacit collusion. The finding that conjectures rise with market concentration indicates that there is more tacit collusion in more concentrated industries. This does not rule out the possibility that differential efficiency may also contribute to the widely observed positive concentration-profitability relationship. Clarke *et al.* write that their result (1984, p. 448) "suggests to us that, in general, both efficiency and market power effects are at work".

---

[53] Bain (1956, pp. 116–117) explicitly argued that because product differentiation advantages would differ from firm to firm, profit rates would differ from firm to firm as well.

[54] The causal mechanism relied upon by the efficiency critique must involve absolute differences in efficiency of some kind, not merely economies of large scale. If a firm produces in a region of falling average cost, it will set a *lower* price, all else equal, so that it can sell more, produce more, and profit from the lower average cost that comes at higher output levels. Economies of scale, in and of themselves, do not explain a *positive* relationship between firm size or market concentration and price-cost margins. See Martin (1988b).

[55] UK Census of Production MLH industries corresponded to three-digit industries in the U.S. Standard Industrial Classification (Holtermann, 1973, p. 122).

[56] The *t*-statistic for the coefficient of the Herfindahl index is 2.53. They obtain qualitatively similar results if the five-firm seller concentration ratio is used in place of the Herfindahl index.

Martin (1988a) reaches the same conclusion for a sample of 185 U.S. four-digit manu-facturing industries. He estimates typical structure-conduct-performance equations explain-ing the average price-cost margins of the largest four firms, the fifth through eighth firms, and all smaller firms, but adds variables to control for productivity differences among the three groups. Price-cost margins of each group rise with its own productivity, which shows an efficiency element in price-cost margins. But price-cost margins of all three groups (not merely those of four largest firms) are higher if the four-firm concentration ratio is higher, showing a market power element.[57] Martin concludes that the efficiency and market power explanations of differences in industry price-cost margins are complementary, not mutually exclusive.

Consumer behaviour

Search and switching costs   Models of markets with consumer search costs predict that prices will rise with search costs, in the limit (the Diamond Paradox) to the monopoly level, even if there are many small suppliers. In real-world fish markets, the combination of search costs and perishable goods can lead to persistent price dispersion and systematic price discrimi-nation. Empirical tests verify the importance of search and switching costs in determining equilibrium market performance.

Retail petrol   The use of lead additives in petrol to boost engine performance was common from the 1920s. The harmful impact of leaded fuel on the environment was recognized from the 1970s. The use of additives was phased out, and in the United States became illegal for on-road vehicles from 1 January, 1996. In the 1980s, however, leaded and unleaded fuel were both marketed in the United States. The use of leaded fuel is incompatible with the catalytic converters that are standard equipment on new vehicles, making it possible to segment the declining market for leaded fuel and the market for unleaded fuel. Although the wholesale prices of leaded and unleaded petrol were essentially the same, the retail price of unleaded fuel was persistently higher than the retail price of leaded fuel (Borenstein, 1991, p. 354): "In 1987, for instance, wholesale prices of the fuels were nearly equal, but the retail price of unleaded gas averaged five cents greater than the retail price of leaded gasoline." The gap between the two narrowed over time, with the price of leaded fuel rising toward the price of unleaded. Borenstein (1991) considers a number of explanations for the change in relative prices (differences in cost of supplying different types of fuel, different customer characteristics), but concludes that part of the explanation lies in an increase in switching costs. As the use of leaded fuel declined, the number of service stations carrying leaded fuel declined as well, increasing search costs for owners of vehicles able to use leaded fuel. Borenstein's estimates imply that about 25 per cent of the narrowing in the gap between the retail and wholesale prices of unleaded and leaded petrol between 1986 and 1989 for a sample of U.S. Standard Metropolitan Statistical Areas could be explained by the reduction in the number of outlets for leaded fuel (1991, p. 365).

Long-distance telephone service   In 1982, before the rise of cellular telephony transformed the provision of telecommunications services, a settlement agreement[58] in a long-running

---

[57] The higher is the combined market share of the fifth through eight largest firms, the *lower* are the price-cost margins of all three groups. This is consistent with the results of Kwoka (1979).

[58] U.S. *v.* AT & T 552 F. Supp. 131 (1982).

U.S. antitrust case resulted in the break-up of American Telephone and Telegraph Corporation ("Ma Bell"; see Section 7.3.2) into an AT&T, Inc. that was a pale version of its predecessor, charged with the provision of long-distance services, and seven regional Bell operating companies (RBOCs) for the provision of local service. To encourage competition, the competent regulatory agency, the Federal Communications Commission, mandated reductions in access charges, (Knittel, 1997, p. 519, fn. 1) "the per minute charge paid by the long distance carriers to the local Bell's. The fee covers line termination, intercept, local switching, local transport, and common carrier line charges. These charges are set by the FCC to offset the expense incurred by the local telephone companies when long distance calls are routed to the consumer." [59]

Long-distance rates did indeed fall with the entry of new long-distance providers that competed with AT&T. But after an initial decline, the margin of long-distance rates over (reduced) access charges increased. Knittel focuses on the existence of search and switching costs as factors behind the increase (1997, p. 526):

> For search and switching costs to be the cause of market power in the long distance telephone market, long distance rates must be difficult to ascertain and there must be a cost levied on consumers when switching long distance carriers. The long distance market is characterized by an explicit switching cost, namely the fee one must pay to change long distance companies. Search costs exist because of the voluminous nature of long distance rates. The long distance market is unique in its pricing structure. Rates are not set by individual routes, but rather by the mileage of a call. If a consumer wanted to compare or gather price information for every long distance carrier, they would have to do so over every range. To gather this information would obviously take time and resources.

He analyses the determinants of AT&T, MCI, and Sprint long-distance rates over the period 1984–1993. Regarding search costs, Knittel suggests (1997, p. 526, fn. 18) that long-distance rate schedules were sufficiently opaque that not only were consumers at best dimly aware of the rates offered by their supplier's competitors, but they also had scarce understanding of the rates charged by their own suppliers. He finds that the level of rates rises with the standard deviation of long-distance rates, a measure of the complexity of rate schedules.

There were explicit switching costs in this market, fees charged to consumers who switched suppliers. Knittel found that long-distance rates were higher, all else equal, the higher were those fees. He also finds that rates fall as advertising rises, and this for two reasons. By informing customers of alternative rate schedules, advertising lowers search costs. Further, some advertising informed consumers that a company would reimburse a customer for a switching fee paid to a previous supplier, thus making potential consumers aware of lower switching costs.

Knittel's results suggest that search costs and switching costs were important factors supporting the exercise of market power in the marketing of long-distance telephone service to final consumers during the time period he studies.

UK natural gas The 1986 Natural Gas Act introduced a phased deregulation of the UK market for natural gas. The former single supplier and recently privatized British Gas was obliged

[59] The amount of the reduction was large (Knittel, 1997, pp. 522–523): "On the eve of the divestiture, access charges amounted to 17.4 cents per minute, while their [1997] levels [were] 3.6 cents per minute (measured in 1982–1984 dollars)."

to make its pipelines available to competing suppliers. Large industrial customers (1986), smaller users of natural gas (1992), and residential users (1995) were successively permitted to switch suppliers. Giuletti *et al.* (2005) use a 1999 survey to study factors affecting the decision on switching, among users aware that it had become possible to switch. Among their findings are that the probability of switching natural gas supplier, once aware of the possibility, was about 20 per cent. About 12 per cent of the sample could not report the size of their natural gas bill, suggesting they were (2005, p. 960) "less concerned about reducing it". This group was less likely to switch suppliers. Consumers who thought British Gas would *not* match rivals' rates, and therefore expected long-term savings from a switch, were more likely to be influenced to switch by potential savings. Experience with switching suppliers in similar markets (telecommunications, insurance) made it more likely that a user would switch natural gas supplier.

Giuletti *et al.* analyse performance in the market, asking (2005, p. 962) "In 2004, five years after market opening and two years after deregulation, BGas retained 60% of the market. Can the market be considered competitive with so few switchers?" Consumer inertia presents British Gas with a specific version of the usual market power tradeoff: by raising rates, it would induce some users to switch suppliers, but would earn a larger return supplying users who do not switch. The less likely are users to switch, the greater the profit to be earned by raising rates. Giuletti *et al.*'s analysis of their survey data leads them to conclude that (2005, p. 963):

> Until the monthly saving from switching supplier goes beyond £8, the net gain for the incumbent is positive, and thereafter negative, so the incumbent will find it profitable to maintain a price £8 per month above average incremental cost, since even with such a differential, around 55% of customers will remain 'loyal' to the incumbent. In such an equilibrium the majority of customers, who stay with the incumbent, would pay a price around 33% above the competitive level, hardly the hallmark of a strongly competitive market . . .

Users who do switch suppliers pay lower rates and enjoy greater consumer surplus. But the cost to a new supplier of taking on a switching customer was £50 to £60, a fixed cost that Giuletti *et al.* assume would be spread over four years (after which, on average, the user would switch again).

In their best-case scenario, which assumes that British Gas lowers its rates to match those of entrants, there is a modest net improvement in social welfare (firms' profits fall, consumer surplus increases) before taking entrants' cost of switching users into account, and a modest welfare reduction after allowing for such costs. In the worst-case scenario, which assumes that British Gas maximizes profit taking consumer inertia into account, producers' profit rises, even with the cost of switching users, but customers are worse off and the overall (producer and consumer) welfare impact is negative.

Immigrants   Following the collapse of the Soviet Union at the end of the 1980s, a wave of immigration flowed toward Israel. Immigrants accounted for 4 per cent of Israel's population at the end of 1990. Lach (2007) examines the impact of immigrant presence on retail prices for 915 products in 52 Israeli cities. The ratio of immigrants to natives averaged 5.3 per cent, and ranged from zero to 17 per cent. Controlling for other factors, Lach finds that a one-percentage point increase in immigrant presence, relative to natives, reduces retail prices by one-half percentage point. He attributes this result to intensive search by immigrants, who had a low opportunity cost of time as they entered the workforce, and cites survey evidence that in 1991/92 immigrants spent 26 minutes per day shopping, as contrasted with 15 minutes per day for natives. Like the evidence from the British natural gas market, Lach's results confirm the importance of consumer behaviour for market performance.

Human foibles   Elementary models assume that final consumers are rational utility maximizers, members of the species *Homo economicus*. If the demand side of a market is populated by members of a different species, *Homo sapiens*, with all its limitations and idiosyncrasies, there may be opportunities for firms on the supply side of the market to earn persistent economic profits.[60] In such cases, the performance of a market that appears to be competitive in a structural sense may differ significantly from the performance predicted by the model of perfect competition.

Ausubel (1991) puts forward as an example the U.S. bank credit card market, supplied (at the time he studies, the 1980s) by some 4,000 firms and patronized by 75 million consumers. The supply side of the market was unconcentrated—the combined market shares of the ten largest firms was about 40 per cent, and many banks offered credit cards nationwide. Entry was apparently free and easy. Under such conditions, the assumptions of the model of perfect competition are largely met, and that model predicts that credit card interest rates would closely track banks' marginal cost, the major element of which is banks' own cost of funds. Yet (Ausubel, 1991, pp. 63–64):

> [T]he ordinary (pretax) return on equity in banking is on the order of 20 percent per year. Credit card businesses earned annual returns of 60–100 percent or more during the years 1983–1988. Plastic earned strongly positive economic profits: the credit card business earned 3–5 times the ordinary rate of return in the banking industry.

Ausubel's explanation for the sustainability of high economic profit is banks' reaction to the presence of two groups of users of bank credit cards. One group (*Homo economicus*) uses credit cards as a matter of convenience, paying off balances in full at the end of each billing period. This group's demand for credit card services is interest-rate inelastic, since those in the group generally do not make significant interest rate payments on credit card balances. Banks have no incentive to compete for the patronage of this group by lowering rates toward marginal cost, and if they did lower interest rates, the impact on credit card usage would be minimal.

But there is another group of credit card users, those who take out credit cards with every intention of paying balances in full at the end of each billing period but who, afflicted by the slings and arrows of outrageous fortune, fail to do so. Although it is from this group that credit card issuers make much of their living, those in the group are also differentially high credit risks. Banks have a limited incentive to compete for the credit card business of this group, because lower interest rates would attract borrowers who are more likely to default, all else equal.

---

[60] This point is made by Ausubel (1991, p. 75), upon which this section is based. See also Scitovsky's 1951 essay "Ignorance as a source of oligopoly power".

This explanation for credit card profitability is an example of adverse selection: the individuals who are poor credit risks know who they are, but banks do not.[61] It depends on irrational behaviour to the extent that it (Ausubel, 1991, p. 71) "relies on the assumption that there are consumers who do not intend to borrow but continuously do so". Ausubel considers other explanations for bank credit card market power, including search costs and switching costs, but concludes that adverse selection is part of the explanation, and one that is consistent with other features of the market. In particular, since banks refrain from price competition, they compete in other dimensions. One kind of competition—grace periods for repayment, frequent flyer points—makes use of the bank credit card more attractive to users who are good credit risks. It also explains the heavy spending on marketing efforts to attract new credit card users that characterizes this industry.

Resumé Human nature is, of course, what it is. If customers do not wish to search, they cannot be made to do so. But there is evidence that search costs and switching costs worsen performance. Government can take steps to reduce such costs, and also to ensure that businesses do not, in the pursuit of economic profit, take steps to increase them. Straightforward industry-specific measures—mandating transparency in rate schedules or portability of cellphone numbers from one supplier to another, for example—by reducing search costs and switching costs, can increase the share of consumers who decide to search for the best buy. If that share becomes large enough, market performance will improve for all consumers.

5.3.4 Firm-level Evidence

Studies of structure-conduct-performance relationships in large cross-section industry samples of necessity glossed over idiosyncratic industry-specific detail. The policy implications of the results of such studies were the subject of heated dispute. The results themselves were remarkably robust, and they at least had the merit of being general. Studies of structure-conduct-performance relationships among firms in the same industry can take an industry's specific characteristics—major inputs, distribution channels, history of innovation—into account. The results of such studies are, however, specific to their subject industry. In what follows, we discuss the results of studies that exemplify the range of results found with the analysis of firm-level data.

Narrow cross-section samples

Slade (2004) tests alternative explanations for profitability differences among firms in the markets for mining and refining eight non-ferrous metals—aluminum, copper, lead, nickel, tin, zinc, gold, and silver. She emphasizes that although the demand sides of these markets are very different, they involve broadly similar technologies (Slade, 2004, p. 298): "(i) they are homogenous commodities that are sold in world markets, (ii) their technologies exhibit economies of scale, but minimum efficient scales are not usually large relative to market sizes, (iii) they are industrial goods that are not subject to rapid technological change, and (iv) their technologies are capital intensive with similar rates of depreciation across commodities".

---

[61] From another point of view, it is a commitment problem: individuals cannot bind themselves *not* to run up excessive credit card balances. The inability of individuals to commit to future actions makes it unprofitable for banks to lower interest rates.

Slade distinguishes four alternative stories that have been told about the determinants of firm and/or industry profitability:

(1) (Structure-conduct-performance) Differences in industry structure explain differences in profitability; profitability will be greater in concentrated industries into which entry is costly, and such differences are indicative of market power;

(2) (Efficiency) Differences in the market shares of firms explain differences in profitability across firms; more efficient firms will be more profitable, all else equal;

(3) (Financial markets) The rate of return on riskier assets will be higher, to compensate investors who hold such assets for the extra risk they bear;

(4) (Natural resource economics) The rate of return on an exhaustible resource should grow over time at the rate of interest, so that owners of the resource will be willing to spread its extraction over time rather than mine it all at once, sell it, and put the resulting profit in the bank (where they earn a market rate of interest).

Slade's results give comfort to the structure-conduct-performance approach. In her sample, market structure has a significant effect on profitability. Profitability is higher in industries that have higher values of the Herfindahl index. The efficiency explanation is not supported. In Slade's sample (2004, p. 304) "there is no systematic relationship between a firm's market share and its profitability, and, within a market, smaller firms are just as profitable as larger ones". Mining profitability is positively related to risk, as the financial market model suggests, but refining market profitability is not. And there is no evidence that profitability in these natural resource markets rises exponentially over time at the rate of interest.

Scale economies

U.S. census industries Chirinko and Fazzari (1994) estimate firm-specific and industry-average Lerner indexes and returns to scale for firms in 11 four-digit SIC industries[62] over time period 1975–1985. They estimate industry-average Lerner indices that are not significantly different from zero in a statistical sense for four of the 11 industries.[63] For these four industries, estimated returns to scale are constant, in a statistical sense, implying that price equals marginal cost equals average cost, on average. For six of the remaining seven industries, Chirinko, and Fazzari find evidence of increasing returns to scale—if all inputs are increased by 100 per cent, output is estimated to increase by from 126 to 179 per cent. For these six industries, price is significantly above marginal cost: the estimated Lerner index ranges from 0.218 to 0.442. The remaining industry, oil field machinery and equipment, is estimated to have modestly decreasing returns to scale, and a Lerner index 0.07.

---

[62] The industries are 2082 (malt beverages), 2200 (textile mill products), 2300 (apparel and other finished products made from fabrics and similar materials), 2621 (paper mills, except paperboard, building paper, and pulp mills), 2711 (newspapers, publishing and printing), 2834 (pharmaceutical preparations for human and veterinary use), 2844 (cosmetics, perfumes, and other toilet preparations), 3011 (tyres and inner tubes for all types of vehicles), 3312 (steel works, blast furnaces, and rolling mills), 3533 (oil field machinery and equipment), and 3714 (motor vehicle parts and accessories, but not engaged in manufacturing complete motor vehicles).

[63] SIC industries 2300, 2621, 3011, and 3312.

These results give some support to structure-conduct-performance view that in industries where minimum efficient scale is large relative to market size, the equilibrium number of firms will be small enough so that firms recognize oligopolistic interdependence and manage to hold price above marginal cost.

Norwegian manufacturing Klette (1999) estimates price-marginal cost markups[64] and economies of scale over the period 1980–1990 for plants[65] in each of 13 two- to three-digit level Norwegian manufacturing industries. For seven such industries,[66] he estimates small but statistically significant markup ratios, ranging from 1.05 to 1.09.[67] There was no evidence of market power, on average, for the other six industries. He also finds that there are greater differences in markup ratios among plants in the same industry than there are between the average plants in different industries. Although this was not the focus of his study, his data did *not* show that larger plants tended to have higher markups (1999, p. 472). But firms with higher markups had lower productivity, all else equal.

For nine of the industries in Klette's sample, the technology seems to show constant returns to scale. There are moderately decreasing returns to scale for four industries (1999, p. 466).

The fact that (Klette, 1999, p. 451) "[t]he manufacturing sector in Norway is highly exposed to competition in export markets and from imports in domestic markets" may limit the extent to which firms can exercise market power, but does not entirely eliminate their ability to do so. Scale economies are largely absent. There is evidence of efficiency differences between plants in the same industry, but plants with larger price-cost margins are less efficient, in a productivity sense, than plants with smaller price-cost margins, which is evidence of X-inefficiency.

Beef packing Just as a monopolist may profit by holding output prices up, so a monopsonist may profit by holding input prices down. Suppose a monopoly supplier is also the only purchaser of a labour in a one-company town, that one worker is hired to produce each unit of output, and that the firm uses no other inputs. The more units of output the firm produces and sells, the lower the price. Taking its influence on price into account, the firm restricts output compared with price-taking behaviour. In the same way, if there is an upward-sloping supply curve for labour, then the more workers the firm hires, the higher the wage it pays. Taking its impact on wages into account, the firm restricts the number of workers it hires, compared with wage-taking behaviour.

Formally, as shown in Figure 5.8(a), such a firm picks output to maximize:

$$\pi = p(Q)Q - w(Q)Q. \tag{5.8}$$

---

[64] That is, he estimates the ratio p/c, which can easily be transformed into the Lerner index $(p - c)/p$.

[65] Most plants were operated by one-plant firms.

[66] The industries are metals, paper products, wood products, metal products, clothing, furniture, and textiles.

[67] That is, the estimated markups are only slightly above one, but the estimates are very precise, so that the data is sending a clear message that the markup is greater than one.

The firm maximizes profit by picking the output level that makes marginal revenue (the first two terms in the centre of (5.9)) equal to the marginal expense of input (the final two terms in the centre of (5.9)):

$$\frac{d\pi}{dQ} = p + Q\frac{dP}{dQ} - \left(w + \frac{dw}{dQ}Q\right) \equiv 0. \tag{5.9}$$

In Figure 5.8(a), marginal revenue and the marginal expense of input are equal for output level Q^* (in view of the input-output assumptions of this example, Q^* is also the number of workers employed). The monopoly price is p^* and the monopsony wage is w^*. If the firm were to ignore its influence on the wage rate, it would set an output level equating marginal revenue and the wage rate, leading to wage rate $\widehat{w}$.

Morrison Paul (2001a) analyses data for 43 U.S. beef packing plants in 1992–1993 to test for the role of scale economies in the exercise of monopoly (output market) and monopsony (input market) power in the U.S. beefpacking industry in the early 1990s. The kinds of results she obtained are illustrated in Figure 5.8(b). The products in questions are relatively homogeneous (Morrison Paul, 2001b, fn. 23), so the demand curve shown in Figure 5.8(b) should be understood as a residual demand curve facing a single firm, with other firms producing equilibrium outputs. She finds little evidence of monopsony lowering of input prices, which for that reason are left aside in Figure 5.8(b).

Morrison Paul's cost function estimates imply that there are important economies of scale in beefpacking—marginal cost below average cost, average cost falling over the observed range of plant outputs. At the same time, fixed costs are sufficiently large that price is only somewhat above average cost. Firms in the industry hold price substantially above marginal cost but make only modest economic profit. These results suggest that entry by additional large-scale plants would mean losses for all firms.

Figure 5.8 (a) Monopsony Power (D = demand, MR = marginal revenue, w = wage rate, MEI = marginal expense of input); (b) Market Power, Economies of Scale, Low Profit (AC = average cost, AVC = average variable cost, MC = marginal cost)

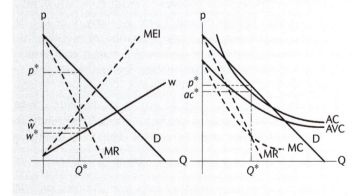

In a companion study (Morrison Paul, 2001b, p. 538), she notes that technical change in the industry had increased minimum efficient plant size and led to a exit by smaller plants. These results are consistent with the structure-conduct-performance view that in markets where minimum efficient plant size is large relative to market size, firms are able to hold price above marginal cost. They are also consistent with the efficiency view that in the absence of strategic entry-deterring behaviour, an industry will be supplied by large firms if it is efficient for firms to operate at large scale.

Financial markets

Cost differences arising in financial markets   In static models of quantity-setting oligopoly, a firm's equilibrium output and profit typically fall as its own costs rise. In static models of price-setting, differentiated product oligopoly, a firm's equilibrium price typically rises, and its profit falls, as its own costs rise. In either type of market, if the cost of borrowing is higher for entrants (to compensate for a higher expected probability of bankruptcy), entrants will have lower equilibrium profits than otherwise identical established firms.

Leveraged buyouts   Chevalier (1995, Section III) compares prices at supermarket chains that had and had not been taken over in leveraged buyouts (LBOs). LBO firms have high debt-equity ratios and will have a higher cost of financial capital if a firm must pay a higher rate of interest, the more it borrows, all else equal. LBO firms will also have a higher cost of financial capital if the debt taken on at the time of the leveraged buyout increases the risk of bankruptcy, raising their risk premium.

Models of price-setting oligopoly predict that firms with higher costs will set higher prices, all else equal, and that is what Chevalier finds. Her results (1995, p. 1110) "clearly suggest that LBO firms are the high priced firms in their cities. On average, the LBO supermarket price level in a city is 2.5 percent higher than the non-LBO supermarket price level".

U.S. banking   Cetorelli and Strahan (2004) provide direct evidence linking financial market structure and product market structure. They look at the impact of U.S. banking deregulation and banking market competition on local product-market structure in two-digit U.S. manufacturing industries between 1977 and 1994. If banks in more concentrated markets are able to raise the price of their product (the loan rate), then the cost of capital will be higher to all firms borrowing from regional suppliers in more concentrated financial markets. The impact might be differentially stronger on small firms, which (a) are likely to have smaller reserves or cash flow to draw on and (b) are less likely to be able to raise funds in other financial markets. Bank deregulation (the relaxation of prohibitions on branch banking across state lines) would certainly increase the potential competition and, over time, perhaps actual competition as well. Cetorelli and Strahan found that regions with lower Herfindahl indices of banking market concentration have product market structures with more firms and smaller average firm size, all else equal. Banking deregulation also increases the weight of small firms in regional product markets. Their results indicate that less competitive financial markets put a higher cost of capital on small than on large firms.

Strategic debt   A firm that finances investment entirely from retained earnings may find that its rate of growth is limited. Borrowing can break a cash constraint, but creates the possibility of bankruptcy. Leaving aside the detail of real-world bankruptcy law, if a firm borrows from a bank or issues bonds and cannot repay the bank or redeem the bonds as agreed, the borrower defaults and the lender becomes the owner of the assets of the firm. Brander and Lewis (1986) point out that debt choice has strategic implications for a firm's product market decisions.

Imagine, for concreteness, that a quantity-setting firm must borrow to finance investment in physical capital before the nature of demand is fully known. Demand is either high (the demand curve far from the origin) or low (demand curve close to the origin). If demand is high, the firm will make enough profit to redeem its bonds and have some economic profit left over for the owners of the firm. If demand is low, the firm cannot redeem its bonds, goes bankrupt, and bondholders assume ownership of the firm's assets.[68]

The *limited liability effect* of corporate debt—the owners of the firm are responsible for its debts only in high-demand states of the world—means that if the firm is managed in the owners' interest, the firm will maximize profit assuming that demand will be high. That would mean planning to produce more than would maximize profit if demand is low, but if demand is low, the owners of the firm don't get anything anyway, because if demand is low, ownership of the assets of the firm is transferred to the lenders.

Quantity-setting firms that borrow to finance investment in fixed capital will commit to producing more, all else equal, because they leave the worst possible outcomes out of the calculation when they maximize expected profits. In duopoly (for example), for any output level of its competitor, a firm will produce more, the more debt it has taken on. That is, its best response curve will shift away from the origin. In quantity-setting duopoly, as a firm's best-response curve shifts away from the origin, its equilibrium output and profit rise, at the expense of its rival. If one firm is able to take on strategic debt, it can improve its profit-market output.

There are several qualifications to this basic story. If in quantity-setting duopoly both firms take on debt, then both expand output, and neither gains a strategic advantage. Showalter (1995) shows that it makes a difference for the strategic debt story whether firms set quantities or prices. In a market with uncertain demand, a price-setting firm that takes on strategic debt commits to a higher price, all else equal, because it leaves low-demand states of the world out of its calculations. Given the upward-sloping best response curves that typically characterize price-setting oligopoly, if one firm takes on debt and commits to higher prices, competitors set higher prices as well. When rivals set higher prices, this increases the profitability of the debt-ridden firm.

It may be that it is cost that is uncertain rather than demand. A price-setting firm with uncertain costs will set lower prices, all else equal, since it leaves high-cost states of the world (when it is more likely to be bankrupt) out of its calculations. But in price-setting oligopoly, if one firm commits to lower prices, other firms will set lower equilibrium prices, reducing the profitability of the debt-ridden firms. Debt does not confer a strategic advantage in price-setting oligopoly if there is cost uncertainty.

Showalter (1999) examines the predictions of the strategic debt literature for 1641 U.S. manufacturing firms using data for periods up to 20 years and ending in 1994. He finds that

---

[68] What we gloss over here, in the interest of simplicity, is that by taking on debt, the firm affects how high demand must be if it is to avoid bankruptcy.

firms in industries subject to demand uncertainty take on more debt, all else equal, and that firms in industries subject to cost fluctuations take on less debt, all else equal. This is what would be expected for price-setting firms in uncertain environments.

Potential competition

Airlines One of the early entries in the literature demonstrating that the passenger airline industry is not perfectly contestable, Call and Keeler (1985), studied fares in 89 U.S. city-pair markets in the immediate post-deregulation period (1977–1981). They find that fares rise as the city-pair market Herfindahl index of supply-side concentration rises, and fall with entry by trunk or non-trunk carriers. If potential competition alone were sufficient to generate good market performance, neither market concentration nor entry would affect fares. Call and Keeler suggest that their results may indicate that incumbents held fares high enough to induce entry, giving up market share and lowering fares when entry actually occurred, or that incumbents lowered price sharply in the face of entry with a view to making entry unprofitable.[69]

Pharmaceuticals Like the U.S. passenger airline industry, the U.S. pharmaceutical industry went through regulatory changes, but in the direction of more rather than less regulation. In 1962 the U.S. Food, Drugs and Cosmetics Act was amended to tighten administrative requirements for bringing a new pharmaceutical to market. Cool *et al.* (1999) study the relative impact of actual and potential competition on the profitability (rate of return on sales) of 22 U.S. drug companies over the period 1963–1982.

During this period, seller concentration was high at the level of therapeutic classes (for example, "cardiovascular drugs" or "pain control medicine"), with four-firm concentration ratios averaging between 44 and 49 per cent and eight-firm concentration ratios averaging between 57 and 68 per cent. The number of drugs introduced increased sharply, but new drug introductions did not, meaning that most new drug products were put on the market to compete with an existing product.

Cool *et al.* examine the influence of a firm's own market share and of a Herfindahl index of rivals' sales concentration on the firm's profitability. They find that a firm's profitability rises with its own market share, and they note that this positive impact may reflect a combination of market power and efficiency effects. The rival Herfindahl index variable is a measure of actual rivalry. Early in their sample period, in the immediate aftermath of regulatory changes, actual rivalry does not appear to have been a significant factor holding down profitability. By the end of the 1970s, however, this had changed, with profitability significantly lower for firms facing fewer and larger actual competitors.

During the period Cool *et al.* study, there was no actual entry into the U.S. pharmaceutical industry. Potential competition thus had to come, if at all, from incumbent firms in other therapeutic classes. As a measure of potential competition, Cool *et al.* start with the

---

[69] A 1999 U.S. Department of Justice antitrust complaint against American Airlines alleged just such behaviour at the Dallas-Fort Worth International Airport, charging that American added flights and cut fares when start-up airlines entered the market, only to reduce the number of flights and raise fares after they exited. The government's claim failed since it did not show that American Airlines had cut fares below its average variable cost. The government's case was *not* dismissed because the government failed to show that American Airlines had behaved in the way claimed, or that the conduct had the effect of driving entrants from the market. See U.S. *v.* AMR Corp. *et al.* 140 F. Supp. 2d 1141 (2001).

correlation coefficient between the shares of a firm's sales in different therapeutic classes and the shares of each rival firm in different therapeutic classes. For any pair of firms, the correlation coefficient ranges from zero (they supply no therapeutic classes in common) to one (they operate in the same therapeutic classes, and in the same proportions). The rationale for interpreting this as a measure of potential competition is that an incumbent firm is most exposed to increased competition from rivals with operations that are most like its own. The potential competition measure for each firm is the weighted sum of the diversification correlation coefficients with all other firms, weights being given by the other firms' sales. Cool *et al.*'s results show that potential rivalry pushes down profitability, but the impact does not change over time (1999, pp. 11–12): "actual rivalry and potential rivalry had about the same effect on firm profitability by the mid-1970s. By 1982, the effect of actual competition had become twice as large as the impact of potential competition."

5.3.5 Price

Weiss (1989) identifies two market structure-price studies reported in Stigler (1964).[70] But the literature did not take off until the late 1970s, around the period that the Second Chicago School efficiency critique called the mainstream interpretation of the robust results of structure-profitability studies into question (Weiss, 1985).

Retail petrol

In retrospect it seems almost a consequence of the tyranny of models that empirical studies of market performance focused on profitability. The models themselves told stories about the way a firm with market power would set output or price. But manipulations of first-order conditions, taking off from Lerner (1934), led to equilibrium expressions for price-cost margins that could easily be transformed into rates of return on sales, or assets, or (a little less easily) stockholders' equity. And so the early literature examined the impact of market structure and firm conduct on profit rates, not on firms' direct decision variables.

When attention did turn to price, many studies using U.S. data were of the retail price of petrol. This is not surprising, given popular interest in the topic and the relative ease with which comprehensive datasets about the market could be put together.

Geithman *et al.* (1981), for example, analyse the impact of seller concentration on the retail price of petrol in 22 U.S. cities over the period 1964–1971.[71] A portion of their results is illustrated in Figure 5.9. The vertical axis in Figure 5.9 shows the average retail price of petrol in cents per gallon. The numbers under the horizontal lines (4, 3, 8, and 7) show the number of cities in each concentration range. The ranges shown are for four-firm seller concentration ratios under 40 per cent, 40 to 50 per cent, and greater than 50 per cent. The horizontal lines show the estimated average petrol prices of different petrol types.[72] The letters "SIG" in the figure indicate that the illustrated impact of supplier concentration on retail price is

---

[70] One study was of advertising rates in 1939, the other of the cost of commercials on AM radio stations. Both are reproduced in Weiss (1989, Ch. 7).

[71] The data set is described, and first analysed, in Marvel (1978).

[72] There were other explanatory variables (in addition to the concentration ratio, that is) in the regressions that produced the results shown in Figure 5.9; see Marvel (1978) for discussion. To draw Figure 5.9, these variables are set at their average values for the sample period (Geithman *et al.*, 1981, p. 348).

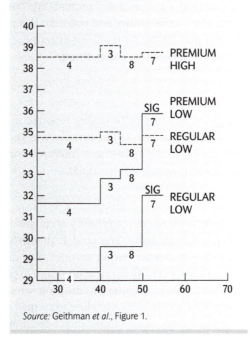

Figure 5.9 Effect of concentration on average, high and low premium and regular gasoline prices for 1964–71 in 22 U.S. cities. Vertical axis: average price in cents per gallon, 1964–1971; horizontal axis, four-firm seller concentration ratio. See text for interpretation

Source: Geithman *et al.*, Figure 1.

statistically significant. The figure suggests the presence of a critical concentration ratio for low-price petrols (Geithman *et al.*, 1981, pp. 348–349):

> Concentration has no important effect on the high prices at all, but it has a clear positive effect on low prices. The sharpest increase in price occurs at a concentration ratio of 50, but there are substantial (though non-significant) increases below that level.

Bread and rolls

Dunne and Roberts (1992) pierce the veil of supplier concentration[73] and directly examine the impact of some basic supply-side conditions on prices charged by 681 U.S. plants that produced either bread or rolls or both in 1977. They had measures of the value of each plant's capital stock, of wages paid at each plant, and of input costs—the price of flour, of electricity, and an average price of a bundle of other inputs. They were able to control for the age of

---

[73] Less picturesquely, but more informatively for those with some econometrics, they carry out a reduced-form analysis.

a plant's equipment, and for differences across plants in the mix of varieties produced. For each plant, they looked at nearby competing suppliers (Dunne and Roberts, 1992, p. 20):

> We do not define specific geographic markets and then attempt to explain price formation within that area as a function of the number of producers in the area. Instead we define service areas for each plant and then attempt to explain the plant's observed price as a function of the number and characteristics of the other plants that could also supply this service area.

Bread being a market for which freshness is important, geographic markets are regional or local. Dunne and Roberts cite the 1977 U.S. Census of Transportation to the effect that 70 of bread was shipped less than 100 miles from the plant, 85 per cent less than 200 miles from the plant. They defined a plant's primary service area as the region not more than 50 miles from the population centre in which the plant is located.

Table 5.4 gives some descriptive statistics of bread prices and costs for plants in their sample. The corresponding statistics for rolls are qualitatively similar. Bread plants range from regional monopolies—13 plants with no rivals in the primary market area—to large numbers oligopoly—471 plants had more than ten rivals in the primary market area.

The pattern of Table 5.4 is striking, with average plant price falling as the number of rivals rises from 0 to 5, and rising thereafter. Average variable cost, with one exception, changes in the same way. Thus it appears that changes in price as the number of regional rivals changes essentially track the way average variable cost changes as the number of regional rivals changes. The statistical analysis confirms the importance of cost for price, to the exclusion of number of rivals, rivals' costs, or market demand characteristics (Dunne and Roberts, 1992, pp. 25–26). This result suggests that the typical bread or roll plant is in a situation much like that of a single supplier facing the possibility of entry (Section 2.3.5): if entry should occur whenever price rises much above average cost, a profit maximizing firm will set a price near potential entrants' average cost, like it or not.

Scientific journals

The internet has sharply reduced the cost of many types of transactions. The rise of electronic publishing and the transition of established research publications to dual-outlet form

Table 5.4 Average bread prices and average variable cost, by number of rival plants in primary service area

Number of rival plants in primary service area	Number of observations	Mean price	Average variable cost
0	13	0.377	0.277
1–2	20	0.331	0.255
3–5	45	0.317	0.247
6–10	75	0.337	0.276
11–20	178	0.341	0.261
21–50	143	0.375	0.312
51–100	90	0.374	0.317
≥ 101	60	0.385	0.323

Note: Average variable cost figures computed for plants that produce bread or rolls or both.
Source: Dunne and Roberts (1992, Table 1).

(print and digital) certainly suggests that this is the case with academic publishing. The work of Dewatripont *et al.* (2007) shows that digital distribution far from eliminates the ability of publishing houses to exercise market power.[74] They relate subscription prices of 2,630 academic journals in 22 academic fields for the year 2003 to journal and publisher characteristics, as well as publisher concentration, by field.

The journal characteristics they studied included (among others) measures of quantity (number of articles published), quality (citations to articles published), and the age of the journal. Publisher characteristics included whether the publisher operated on a for-profit or a not-for-profit basis, and whether the journal was affiliated with a scientific society. The typical market structure seems to be a core of large publishers with a fringe of small rivals.[75]

Dewatripont *et al.* find large price differences across fields, which is to be expected if there is market power, if price elasticities of demand differ, and if consumer arbitrage is impossible. Journal price rises with journal quality, as measured by number of citations. Journal price also rises with publisher concentration. Journals published by for-profit publishers are four times as expensive as journals published by not-for-profit publishers, controlling for journal and field characteristics.

Resumé

There are critiques of the price-study literature (Newmark, 2004), as there were of profitability studies. The consensus is, however, that the price-concentration literature answered the question posed by the Second Chicago School efficiency critique (Koller and Weiss, 1989, pp. 36–37; see also Caves, 2007, p. 3):

> [I]t is clear that concentration does raise price. The basis hypothesis of oligopoly theory has lots of support. Our two-decade digression on concentration and profits and our subsequent 13 years of doubt were unnecessary.

5.3.6 Persistence of Profit

The belief that the market mechanism alone—Adam Smith's *invisible hand*—will be an effective resource allocation mechanism rests on the beliefs that businesses make value-maximizing investment decisions in response to opportunities to make profits or avoid losses, and that such investment decisions tend to make the use of capital equally profitable throughout the economy. The process by which long-run perfectly competitive equilibrium is supposed to be reached is that markets in which incumbents earn a high rate of return attract investment, so reducing the rate of return, while some incumbents exit markets in which the rate of return is low, so increasing the rate of return for those that remain. When

---

[74] The market seems best described as a distinctive type of two-sided market, in which academic researchers provide with and sometimes pay publishing houses to publish the fruits of their labour, which are bundled and sold to libraries to be read by academic researchers. For discussion, see Dewatripont *et al.* (2006). Thus the bread-and-butter of publishing houses, with the increasingly disgruntled assistance of academic librarians, is to provide a platform for the interaction of scholars in their aspect as producers of academic research with scholars in their aspect of consumers of academic research.

[75] In economics, a field of innate importance and particular interest, the largest publisher was Elsevier Science, with a market share of 29 per cent, and the second largest was Blackwell Publishers, with a market share of 21 per cent.

all markets are in long-run perfectly competitive equilibrium, the rate of return on capital is the same in all markets.

Of course, this is the ideal. Markets are continually buffeted by demand shocks and supply shocks. Firms, which buy inputs and sell outputs, are buffeted when they are on the demand sides of their input markets and when they are on the supply sides of their output markets. The most that one might expect of a long-run equilibrium would be that the risk-adjusted expected rate of return be equal for all investment opportunities. Since the long run never arrives, what one might hope to observe is that high rates of return tend to decline, and low rates of return tend to rise, over time, even if new disturbances intervene before equality of rates of return across firms or industries is reached. Persistent differences in firm or industry rates of return on investment are evidence that the invisible hand alone will not lead to optimal resource allocation.

The *persistence-of-profit* literature examines this question directly, analysing changes in firm rates of return over time by looking at the relationship between a firm's current and past rate of return on investment.[76] One of the two most common empirical specifications used to test for convergence estimates a linear relationship between the current rate of return on investment and the same variable lagged one period,[77]

$$\pi(t) = \alpha + \lambda \pi(t-1) + \upsilon(t), \qquad (5.10)$$

where α and λ are parameters to be estimated and υ is a random disturbance term. λ must be less than one in absolute value for the time path of the rate of return implied by (5.10) to be stable.[78]

The estimated values of α and λ provide information about the persistence, or elimination, of profit differences. *If* a firm's profit rate converges to some long-run value π^*, then in the long run $\pi(t) = \pi(t-1) = \pi^*$; substituting in (5.10) and rearranging terms gives

$$\pi^* = \frac{\alpha}{1-\lambda}. \qquad (5.11)$$

as the expected value of the firm's long-run rate of return. If π^* is the same for all firms, profits converge in the long run. If we measure the firm's rate of return on investment as a deviation from the long-run normal rate of return, then if $\alpha = 0$ for all firms, economic rates of return converge to zero in the long run, at which point firms earn only a normal rate of return on investment. $\alpha > 0$ corresponds to persistent economic profit, $\alpha < 0$ to persistent economic losses.

---

[76] Although the persistence-of-profit literature has antecedents, its modern incarnation begins with Mueller (1977), and as a reply to Brozen's (1971a, b) critique that the positive seller concentration-rate of return relationship identified by Bain (1951, 1956) was a disequilibrium phenomenon, one that would be eroded over time by rate-of-return-equilibrating flows of investment.

[77] The other, introduced by Mueller (1977), regresses profit rates on a constant and a polynomial of some order in the inverse of a time trend. For discussion of both specifications, see Mueller (1990, pp. 10–14).

[78] One can reach (5.10) from a formal model in which (a) the firm's current rate of return is reduced by entry, broadly defined to include expansion of incumbents as well as the appearance of new firms, and on its past rate of return, (b) while entry (which cannot be observed directly) is larger, the higher the firm's past rate of return (Geroski, 1990).

Intuitively, we expect λ to be positive. Values λ near one imply that the rate of return converges slowly to the long-run value—profits persist for some time, even if they are eventually eliminated. If λ is near zero, convergence is rapid.[79]

Versions of (5.10) have been estimated for most industrialized countries and a smattering of developing countries. There are country-by-country differences, but the general pattern is clear: relatively rapid convergence eliminates some but not all differences in rates of return (Geroski and Mueller, 1990, p. 196). Seller concentration contributes to persistence in some countries, imports or tariffs in others, and there are indications that product differentiation, based on advertising or research and development, promotes profit persistence (Geroski and Mueller, 1990, pp. 192–193). In most markets and in most countries, the invisible hand works rapidly, but not completely.

Resumé

Stigler (1963a, p. 54) writes that "There is no more important proposition in economic theory then that, under competition, the rate of return on investment tends toward equality in all industries". Stigler himself distinguishes monopolistic and competitive industries, and finds evidence that (1963a, p. 70) unusually profitable monopolistic industries "will be able to preserve their preferential position for considerable periods of time". Epstein (1934, pp. 43–44) earlier found that for a sample of 106 U.S. industries for the decade 1919–1928 "not only do discrepancies exist among the earnings rates of different industries for a period, but the 'high' industries of any given year are also high industries in most succeeding years. While considerable shifting of position takes place, no general tendency towards an 'equality of profit rates' is discernible". The findings of the persistence-of-profit literature are robust: the rate of return on investment does not tend to equality, either across firms within an industry or across industries.

SUMMARY

Experimental tests of the Cournot and Bertrand models suggest that they predict well the outcomes of laboratory markets that are designed to match their assumptions. The theory of contestable markets also predicts well for laboratory markets that match its assumptions. If there are some sunk costs, outcomes may not match those of contestability theory. Firms are more likely to exercise market power in experimental markets if consumers must engage in costly search to acquire information about posted prices.

Early empirical tests of the structure-conduct-performance framework, and somewhat later of formal oligopoly models, for the most part examined the impact of supplier concentration—an index of actual rivalry—and barriers to entry—an indication of the strength of potential competition—on some measure of industry profitability. Entry was expected to be more difficult—more expensive—the greater the sunk investment required to enter an industry, the larger was the output level of an efficient plant relative to market size, the more important advertising and sales efforts in mounting a successful operation, and the larger the financial investment required to set up an efficient plant.

---

[79] Suppose there is a disturbance in period 1, $\pi(1) = \alpha + \upsilon(1)$, and no disturbances thereafter. Then substituting recursively in (5.10) gives $\pi(2) = (1+\lambda)\alpha + \lambda\upsilon(1)$, $\pi(3) = \left(1+\lambda+\lambda^2\right)\alpha + \lambda^2\upsilon(1)$, and so on. If λ is near one, the λ^{t-1} term that multiplies $\upsilon(1)$ in the expression for $\pi(t)$ remains large for some time. If λ is near zero, the λ^{t-1} term quickly goes to zero, and $\pi(t)$ rapidly approaches its long-run value.

The extent of economies of scale depends on advantages of specialization, mechanization, multiplant operation, and technical factors that will be present in some industries and absent in others. One expects that such economies of scale as are present in any one market will eventually be undone by managerial diseconomies of scale. The most common empirical finding is that returns to scale become roughly constant once output rises above some initial region of increasing returns to scale.

Entry costs relating to product differentiation involve not only advertising to final consumers but a complex interaction of marketing efforts at the manufacturing, wholesale, and retail distribution levels. Industry studies generally found that both advertising and seller concentration had positive impacts on profitability, with the impact of advertising larger and more significant than the impact of seller concentration. Several such studies were consistent with the idea that seller concentration increases profitability only if it exceeds some critical level.

There is some evidence that markets for financial capital impose a higher cost of capital on entrants and small incumbents than on large, established, less risky incumbent firms.

Later studies of firm and industry profitability suggest that the seller concentration-profitability relationship combines elements of concentration-market power and concentration-efficiency, and that the mixture of one part and the other differs from industry to industry. Studies of the impact of concentration on price confirm this interpretation. Studies of the persistence of firm profit rates over time suggests that profit rates do not converge to the same level in the long run, either within or across industries. Imperfect competition is a durable characteristic of much of the economic landscape.

STUDY POINTS

- Performance in experimental oligopoly markets (Section 5.2)
- Barriers to entry (Section 5.3.1)
  - Sunk cost
  - Economies of scale: sources; diseconomies; multiplant operation; measurement
  - Product differentiation; convenience goods, shopping goods
  - Absolute capital requirements
- The extent of the market (Section 5.3.2): distance shipped; price convergence
- Market performance (Section 5.3.3)
  - Industry profitability
  - Critical concentration ratio/market share
  - Market power and efficiency
- Search and switching costs (Section 5.3.3)
- Firm performance (Section 5.3.4)
- Market structure and price (Section 5.3.5)

FURTHER READING

On the common failure to distinguish between fixed cost and sunk cost, see Wang and Yang (2001), Colander (2006, Chapter 10). Gilbert (1989) discusses the literature on potential competition (see also the comment by Dick and Lott, 1989). Bateman and Weiss (1975) offer potential competition as one possible explanation for a failure to find much of a concentration-profitability relationship in the pre-Civil War U.S. South.

Huck *et al.* (2004) survey experimental tests of the Cournot model. Cason and Friedman (1999) report experimental results that give some comfort to the predictions of the Diamond search model. For empirical studies investigating the degree of contestability of various markets, see Graham *et al.* (1983), Bailey *et al.* (1985), in addition to Call and Keeler (1985), among others.

For a review of the entry barriers literature, see Geroski (1991, Chapter 5). See Scherer (1973, 1974) for discussions and estimates of the determinants of MES plant scale, and Lyons (1980) for a critical review of approaches to estimating MES output levels. On the survivor technique, see Shepherd (1967), Rees (1973), Burns (1983) and Keeler (1989). For a cautionary note on the idea that "big is better", see Jacquemin and Saez (1976); for a survey of studies of returns to scale, see Martin (2004a) For a discussion of early 19th-century English pinmaking, see Ashton (1925).

Fingleton *et al.* (1999) survey the literature on market definition.

Most cross-section studies of industry profitability were of U.S. manufacturing industries. For studies using United Kingdom data, see for example Shepherd (1972), Hart and Morgan (1977). Weiss (1974) gives references to studies of UK and Japanese samples. For surveys of this literature, see Weiss (1971a, 1974), Datta and Narayanan (1989), and Martin (2001, Chapters 5 and 6). There is a literature debating how one should measure profitability for purposes of economic analysis. An early contribution is Mitchell (1934). More recently, see Fisher and McGowan (1983), Fisher (1987), comments and a reply in the June, 1984 issue of the *American Economic Review* (and for discussion, Martin, 2002a, Section 6.3), and Grout and Zalewsha (2008). Lustgarten (1975) studies the impact of buyer concentration on price-cost margins; Martin (1983) studies the impact of input supplier concentration on price-cost margins. Bradburd (1982), who finds that price-cost margins are larger in producer good industries that supply minor inputs to other industries, also highlights supplier-buyer interaction as a determinant of market performance. Bradburd and Caves (1982) give a refined analysis of the impact of market growth on price-cost margins. White (1976) gives references to the empirical literature on critical concentration levels, and Scott (2006a) surveys the literature on the relationship between seller concentration and price. Maksimovic (2007) surveys the literature on the impact of financial markets on product market performance.

Goeree (2008) finds that limited consumer information in the rapidly evolving personal computer industry permits leading firms to enjoy substantially higher price-cost margins than predicted by models that assume consumers to be fully informed.

The number of contributions to the *persistence-of-profit* literature is large. For references, see Mueller (1986, 1990), the review by Pakes (1987), Schohl (1990), Goddard and Wilson (1999), and Cuaresma and Gschwandtner (2007).

See Bowman (1951) for a survey of the treatment of consumer behaviour in the economics literature. See Greenstein (1993) on federal procurement, Calem and Mester (1995) on credit cards, Elzinga and Mills (1998) on wholesale cigarette distribution, Kiser (2002) on banking, and Israel (2005) on car insurance for empirical studies of search costs and switching costs (in addition to those considered in Section 5.3.3). Waterson's (2003) survey emphasizes the importance of consumer behaviour for market performance.

COLLUSION: ECONOMICS $\quad$ 6

Our competitors are our friends. Our customers are the enemy.
Archer Daniels Midland corporate saying[1]

6.1 Introduction

In imperfectly competitive markets, equilibrium total profit, although positive, typically falls short of the monopoly (maximum) level. It follows that firms supplying imperfectly competitive markets can increase their profit if they are able to raise price and restrict output toward the monopoly levels. The incentives firms face in making decisions about output restriction in imperfectly competitive markets involve intertemporal tradeoffs in a fundamental way. In this chapter, we introduce multi-period models to examine such tradeoffs.

We also analyse the impact of output restriction and of collusion on market performance, and examine practices (basing-point pricing, price leadership, publicity of details of individual transactions) that facilitate output restriction. We review evidence on the kinds of market structure and firm conduct that make it possible for firms to exercise market power.

6.2 Tacit Collusion

There is a tendency to identify output restriction with collusion, but this is imprecise. "The oligopoly problem" is that lower output and higher prices can result from independent behaviour. Whether total output is less than either the perfectly competitive or the non-cooperative equilibrium level is an objective question. If there is a restriction of output, whether that restriction is the result of conduct that constitutes collusion is a legal question.[2] In the legal systems we focus on, the essence of collusion is *agreement*. If output restriction is

---

[1] A companion saying was "We know when we're lying" (Michael D. Andreas, quoted in Eichenwald, 2000, p. 303).

[2] In much the same way, whether one person has killed another is a reasonably objective question. Killing is only murder (a legal concept) if the applicable legal standards are satisfied. In many legal systems, for example, to kill in self-defence is not murder. The common usage of the term "tacit collusion" to refer to conduct that is not collusion is amenable to confusion and regrettable, but well-entrenched. See McGahan (1995, fn. 6) and Borenstein and Shepard (1996, fn. 2) for caveats to the effect that empirical evidence indicating that firms have restricted

the result of independent decisions by independent firms, the firms have not colluded. If output restriction is the result of an agreement among independent firms, firms have colluded. Output restriction need not be the result of collusive conduct, and we begin our discussion with models of equilibrium output restriction that is the result of independent decisions by independent firms.

6.2.1 Trigger Strategy

Tacit or *non-cooperative collusion* involves a tradeoff between current and future profit. Firms can increase their profit if they collectively reduce the total quantity supplied. But the lower is total output, the more profitable it is for any one firm to expand its own sales and seek to profit at the expense of its erstwhile colleagues.

If industry output is less than the non-cooperative equilibrium level, a firm that increases output, hoping to make an extra short-run profit, should anticipate that rivals will eventually realize what it has done, and then increase their own outputs as well. Once they do so, price will fall and all firms will suffer lower profit. It follows that the critical factors affecting whether or not non-cooperative output restriction is a long-run equilibrium for an individual firm are:

- how much extra profit a firm gets by increasing output;
- how much profit it loses when all other firms increase output;
- how quickly rival firms become aware of an output increase; and
- how firms trade off higher profit in the near future against lower profit in the far future.

 BOX   Tacit Collusion Breakdown and a Taxicab Price War

Cassady (1957b) describes an autumn 1947 taxicab price war in suburban Los Angeles, California. Initially, the three firms offering taxi service quoted identical two-part tariffs, 30¢ per flag drop and 30¢ per mile. Then one firm offered a book of tickets good for rides that normally sold for $10 at a price of $9. After unsuccessful attempts to convince the price-cutter to return to the prevailing price, one of the other two firms cut price to a flat rate of 25¢ per ride anywhere in town. The other two firms cut prices to a flat rate of 10¢ per ride. The owner of the 25¢-ride company threatened to cut price to 5¢ per ride, but did not do so. He also paid local high-school students to ride from one end of town to the other in his competitors' taxis. After about three weeks, (and as a result of mediation, the details of which are not reported), the two low-price firms raised their rates back to 30¢ per flag drop and 30¢ per mile. The third company maintained its fare at 25¢ per ride "for several months". In 1949, the suburban city council adopted rate regulations that made price wars a thing of the past. See also Cassady (1957a, 1963).

---

output does not speak to the question whether the way that output restriction has been brought about is or is not collusion.

One way to model the tradeoff between payoffs received at different times is with a *trigger strategy* (Friedman, 1971) in a market where firms repeatedly play a single-period Cournot game. The trigger strategy is that:

- each firm produces its share of the monopoly output in the first period, and produces its share of the monopoly output in each following period if all other firms produced their shares of monopoly output in the previous period;

- if in any period price is different from the monopoly price, all firms produce their Cournot outputs forever after.

Suppose, for example, that a market supplied by two firms that has the linear inverse demand curve:

$$p = 100 - Q \tag{6.1}$$

in every time period and that both firms have constant marginal and average variable cost 10 per unit of output,

$$c(q) = 10q. \tag{6.2}$$

Payoffs

Profit-maximizing monopoly output is 45, and monopoly price 55. Monopoly profit per time period is:

$$\Pi_m = (55 - 10)(45) = 2025. \tag{6.3}$$

If the market is a Cournot duopoly, equilibrium output per firm is 30, Cournot duopoly price is 40, and equilibrium profit per firm per time period is:

$$\pi_{Cournot} = (40 - 10)(30) = 900. \tag{6.4}$$

If each firm produces half the monopoly output, then each firm collects half of the monopoly profit:

$$\pi_m = (55 - 10)(22.5) = 1012.5. \tag{6.5}$$

If firm 2 produces 22.5 units of output, the equation of firm 1's residual demand curve is:

$$p = 100 - 22.5 - q_1 = 77.5 - q_1. \tag{6.6}$$

Picking the output that makes marginal revenue equal to marginal cost along this residual demand curve gives firm 1's one-period profit-maximizing output if firm 2 is producing 22.5 units of output,

$$MR = 77.5 - 2q_1 = 10 \Longrightarrow q_1 = 33.75 > 22.5. \tag{6.7}$$

If firm 2 produces half the monopoly output, firm 1's profit-maximizing output is greater than half the monopoly output. If firm 1 produces as indicated by its best response function, price is less than the monopoly price,

$$p = 100 - 22.5 - 33.75 = 43.75. \tag{6.8}$$

Firm 1's profit is:

$$\pi_{brf} = (43.75 - 10)(33.75) = 1139.0625, \tag{6.9}$$

and this is greater than its profit if both firms restrict output, 1012.5.

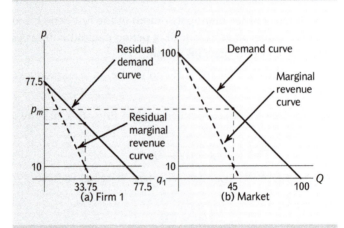

Figure 6.1 Private profit maximization with duopoly output restriction, $p = 100 - Q$, marginal cost $= 10$

Values

But this extra profit is received for only one single period. To work out the consequences of output expansion under a trigger strategy, we move from considering single-period payoffs, profits, to considering present-discounted value. The trigger-strategy equilibrium present-discounted value[3] of a firm is:

$$V_{ts} = \frac{1}{1+r}\pi_m + \frac{1}{(1+r)^2}\pi_m + \ldots = \frac{1}{r}\pi_m, \qquad (6.10)$$

where r is the interest rate used to discount future income and π_m, the firm's share of monopoly profit, is the firm's trigger-strategy payoff in a single period.

If all other firms follow the trigger strategy and if output expansion is detected at the end of the first period it occurs, then after one period of high profit, other firms will revert to producing their one-period Cournot market equilibrium outputs forever. If all other firms produce their one-period Cournot equilibrium outputs, the most profitable option for the defecting firm is to also produce its one-period Cournot equilibrium output—that is how Cournot equilibrium outputs are determined. Thus the present-discounted value of a firm that defects from the trigger strategy, assuming all other firms follow the trigger strategy, is:[4]

$$V_{brf} = \frac{1}{1+r}\pi_{brf} + \frac{1}{(1+r)^2}\pi_{Cournot} + \frac{1}{(1+r)^3}\pi_{Cournot} + \ldots$$

$$= \frac{1}{1+r}\pi_{brf} + \frac{1}{1+r}\frac{1}{r}\pi_{Cournot}. \qquad (6.11)$$

---

[3] On the mechanics of discounting, see Appendix II, Section 8.

[4] What if renegade output expansion is not detected immediately? Then the present discounted value in (6.11) includes more than one appropriately discounted term where the firm's one-period payoff is π_{brf}, and reversion to Cournot payoffs begins sometime after the second post-defection period. You should be able to work out the implied changes in (6.13).

Stability condition

A value-maximizing firm will be willing to follow the trigger strategy if doing so gives it at least as great a value as defecting, that is, if:

$$\frac{1}{r}\pi_m \geq \frac{1}{1+r}\pi_{brf} + \frac{1}{1+r}\frac{1}{r}\pi_{Cournot}. \tag{6.12}$$

Rearranging terms, the trigger strategy stability condition, the condition that must be satisfied in order for output restriction to be a value-maximizing strategy for an individual firm, is:

$$\frac{1}{r} \geq \frac{\pi_{brf} - \pi_m}{\pi_m - \pi_{Cournot}}. \tag{6.13}$$

The numerator of the fraction on the right is positive: in a single period, a firm will earn a greater profit by producing along its best response function than by restricting output, if all other firms restrict output. The denominator of the fraction on the right is also positive: each firm's share of monopoly profit is greater than per-firm Cournot equilibrium profit. Thus the right-hand side of (6.13) is positive. On the left-hand side, as r is smaller, $1/r$ is larger. Thus if the interest rate r that is used to discount future income is sufficiently small, the left-hand side of (6.13) will be greater than the right-hand side. Each firm will then have a greater present-discounted value if it restricts output rather than producing along its one-period best response function.

The smaller the interest rate that is used to discount future income, the more comparable are the dollars the defector receives in the near future and the dollars the defector loses in the distant future. For a small enough interest rate, the discounted lost future profit outweighs the short-run incremental profit from output expansion, and non-cooperative collusion, supported by the trigger strategy, is an equilibrium in the repeated game.

For our numerical duopoly example, the condition (6.13) is $\frac{1}{r} \geq \frac{9}{8}$ or $r \leq \frac{8}{9} = 0.89$ or 89 per cent. This does not seem overly restrictive if, say, the length of the time period is one year.

Non-cooperative collusion

If the present-discounted value of the income to be gained over the long run by restricting output and raising price to increase joint profit is greater than the present-discounted value of the income to be gained by maximizing short-run own profit and accepting lower future profits as rivals also expand output, it will be in the self-interest of each firm, acting independently, to restrict output and raise price.

6.2.2 Uncertainty

There is no uncertainty in the version of the trigger strategy model developed above. This means if price deviates from the trigger strategy equilibrium price, the deviation is an unambiguous signal that some firm has deviated from the trigger strategy.

The link between price and information about rivals' fidelity to output-restricting behaviour is broken if there is uncertainty about the location of the demand curve. For example, Figure 6.2 shows a linear demand curve with a random shock that causes realized demand in any period to be above or below its expected location. Such shocks might be due to changes in consumer tastes, or to changes in other industries (as when an increase

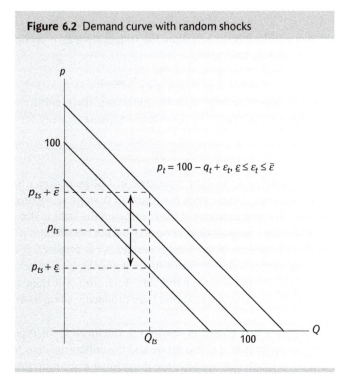

Figure 6.2 Demand curve with random shocks

in the price of petrol causes a reduction in the demand for cars). They might result from the business cycle.

Demand shocks

Assume that the shock has an expected value equal to zero and that value of the shock in every period lies between a lower value, $\underline{\varepsilon} < 0$, and an upper value, $\bar{\varepsilon} > 0$. The expected value of the price-axis intercept of the demand curve is 100. In any period t, the actual value of the price-axis intercept is $100 + \varepsilon_t$, and this can vary between a minimum value of $100 + \underline{\varepsilon}$ and a maximum value of $100 + \bar{\varepsilon}$.

If trigger strategy aggregate output is Q_{ts}, firms know only the expected value of the trigger strategy price. If the realized price is particularly low in one period, that could mean that some firm has defected from the trigger strategy. But it could also mean that there happens to be a large negative disturbance term ε for that period. If demand is subject to random shocks, a low price is not a reliable signal that tacit collusion has broken down.

Extended trigger strategy

Porter (1983a) and Green and Porter (1984) extend the basic trigger strategy model to allow for uncertainty. Their extended version of the trigger strategy has three parts:

- the outputs that are to be produced by each firm;
- a threshold price, a price that is below the expected trigger strategy price, p_{ts} and above the lowest possible realized price, $p_{ts} + \underline{\varepsilon}$ (recall that $\underline{\varepsilon} < 0$);
- a number R of reversion periods.

In this generalized trigger strategy, if the realized price is at or below the threshold price, firms revert to Cournot behaviour for R periods, then once again restrict output.

The generalized trigger strategy may or may not make it an equilibrium to restrict total output to the monopoly level. The closer is output to the monopoly level, the greater is the individual firm's profit from abandoning the trigger strategy. The more uncertain is demand, the lower the threshold price must be to avoid triggering a reversionary period too often. To reduce the temptation to defect when output is highly uncertain, it may be possible to restrict output only part-way toward the monopoly level.

The Green-Porter version of the trigger strategy does not assume that firms, faced with a low price, forever give up the profitable activity of restricting output. It predicts intermittent breakdowns in output restriction, and this is something that seems to be observed in the real world. It predicts that such breakdowns will occur when the realized demand curve is close to the origin.

There is one characteristic that the Green-Porter model shares with the basic trigger strategy model. If the conditions that Green and Porter work out are met, it is a value-maximizing choice for each firm to restrict output under the generalized trigger strategy. If the conditions for the generalized trigger strategy to be an equilibrium are met, no firm ever defects. Output increases when demand is low, but that does not mean non-cooperative collusion has broken down. In the generalized trigger strategy, when firms expand output, they do so as part of equilibrium behaviour, so that all players will understand what the consequences of defection would be. Defection never occurs.

Business Cycles

A business cycle is a pattern of economic activity characterized—at the level of a single market—by a series of demand shocks in the same direction. In a boom, demand is high one period after another; in a slump, demand is low one period after another. The traditional view of the impact on business cycles, and one that seems most consistent with evidence from the nineteenth-century U.S. railroad industry, is that collusion is more likely to break down in economic downturns. The intuition for this from Green-Porter-type models is that in an economic downturn, even the monopoly or joint-profit-maximizing price will be relatively low, and the payoff to an individual firm from breaking ranks and maximizing own profit will be relatively large.

An alternative view (Rotemberg and Saloner, 1986) is that the temptation to defect from output-restriction will be greatest when demand is high, since that is when the payoff for breaking ranks is the greatest. Haltiwanger and Harrington (1991) extend the Rotemberg and Saloner model and examine the impact of changes in demand (rising or falling) as well as the level of demand (high or low) on firms' incentives to restrict output. Haltiwanger and Harrington's theoretical model "shows that the most difficult point of the cycle for firms to collude is not necessarily when demand is high but rather when demand is falling. Hence ... firms find it toughest to collude during recessions".

Borenstein and Shepard (1996) test the Haltiwanger and Harrington model for the U.S. retail petrol market at the end of the 1980s and start of the 1990s. Their evidence is consistent with breakdowns of tacit collusion during economic downturns (1996, p. 448): they "find lower margins when demand is expected to decline next period than when it is expected to increase", all else equal.

6.3 Collusion

Under certain conditions, a generalized trigger strategy allows firms to restrict output most of the time. It does not, in general, allow firms to restrict output to the joint-profit-maximizing level. The more uncertainty there is about the location of the demand curve, the more the trigger strategy equilibrium output wil exceed the monopoly level.

6.3.1 Collusion Cost

As emphasized above, whether a particular course of conduct constitutes collusion is a judgement to be made by a legal system. Here we suppose that collusion involves the spending of money, a collusion cost K per period per firm, to put a private enforcement mechanism in place. We will discuss examples of enforcement mechanisms that have been employed by real-world cartels.

Suppose for simplicity that collusion allows firms to restrict output to the monopoly level, and that monopoly profit is divided equally among the colluding firms. Then in a world without an antitrust or competition policy prohibition of collusion, a single firm's collusive value is the present value of its per-period share of monopoly profit, minus its contribution toward the cost of running the cartel:

$$V_{\text{col}} = \frac{\pi_m - K}{r},$$
(6.14)

where once again π_m is a single firm's share of monopoly profit.

In an uncertain environment, firms' options are to

(a) tacitly collude and go through occasional episodes of output expansion and low profit, or

(b) explicitly collude and maintain consistent high profit, while helping to pay the cartel's monitoring and enforcement costs.

It is more likely that explicit collusion will be the most profitable strategy if uncertainty about the location of the demand curve is great, which lowers firm value under non-cooperative collusion, and if K is small, so that it does not cost much to collude.

6.3.2 Illegal Collusion

If public policy prohibits collusion, and imposes fines on firms found to have colluded, the value of a colluding firm must allow for the chance that a colluding firm will be caught, and if caught, convicted. Then the expected value of a colluding firm is:

$$V_{\text{col}}^{AT} = \frac{\pi_m - K - \tau_1 \tau_2 \mathcal{F}}{r},$$
(6.15)

where:

$\tau_1 =$ the probability that collusion is detected;

$\tau_2 =$ the probability that colluding firms are convicted, if collusion is detected; and

$\mathcal{F} =$ the fine imposed on a firm convicted of colluding.[5]

---

[5] Not all punishment need be monetary: in the United States, and under some other legal regimes, business executives found to have colluded may be sent to prison.

The expected value of a colluding firm under a legal regime that punishes proven collusion is the present value of the firm's per-period share of monopoly profit, minus its contribution toward the cost of running the cartel, minus the fines it has to pay if convicted of colluding.

The probability that collusion is detected, τ_1, is larger, the greater the resources of enforcement agencies. If a legal system permits private antitrust suits, then τ_1 will be larger, the lower is the cost to private plaintiffs of mounting an antitrust suit, and the greater the reward they receive if they are successful. The probability of conviction if a colluding firm is taken to court, τ_2, depends on the nature of the legal system—not only the economic sophistication of judges (and, in some systems, juries), but also the institutional rules that protect the rights of plaintiffs and seek to guarantee them a fair trial. If public policy punishes collusion, the expected value of a colluding firm is less, all else equal, the more likely it is that collusion is detected, the more likely it is that the legal system will convict a colluding firm, and the greater the fine imposed on a colluding firm.[6]

 BOX **Collusion and Market Performance in the U.S. Indoor Bleacher Industry, 1944–1961**

In the mid-twentieth-century United States, a small number of firms supplied folding seats (bleachers) to institutions, primarily schools, for installation in gymnasiums and other multipurpose rooms. In 1960 the four largest firms supplied 74 per cent of the market; the Herfindahl index was 0.12, roughly the value for a market supplied by eight equally sized firms. The product was differentiated in terms of folding mechanism and number, length, width, depth, and rise of rows, and various extras. Bleachers could be fixed to a wall or mobile. Bleachers typically accounted for a small part of the cost of a school construction project, and demand was insensitive to price.

The four major suppliers colluded, under the auspices of the Gymnasium Seating Council (GSC), from 1944 to 1952. In 1952 Brunswick Corporation purchased one of the leading bleacher suppliers. Initially Brunswick refused to become involved, and the GSC dissolved in 1953. Following personnel changes at Brunswick, it joined other bleacher suppliers to form the Folding Gymnasium Seating Council (FGSC) in 1954. Collusion continued until 1959, when Grand Jury indictments led to guilty pleas and ripple-effect treble-damage suits on behalf of local school districts.

The mechanisms of collusion under the GSC and the FGSC were similar, and similar to other documented cartels. Both had a Chairman and a secretary. The Chairman had access to members' records. "Fair trade practice rules" aimed to standardize price quotations, which were to be "on a delivered and installed basis only" and were not to be made on a combination basis with other products (such sales might have allowed surreptitious price discounts). Field agents—the direct contact with customers—were not to discount prices. The cartels fixed prices and allocated market shares. The Chairmen fine-tuned bids to keep actual shares near the agreed levels. The course of collusion never did run smooth, and both groups were troubled by the pricing of extras, ❯❯

---

[6] It is possible that a firm colludes and the collusion is not detected. It is possible that collusion is detected, but the firm is not convicted. It is also possible that a firm does not collude but is accused of doing so. Then, at least, the firm must cover the cost of defending itself. At worst, a firm that has not colluded may be convicted and fined. See Martin (2006).

>> combination bids, overeager agents willing to cut price to make a sale, cheating, and entry. The FGSC had a kind of internal court to deal with cheating; offending parties would make amends for stealing business by bidding high on and so sacrificing later sales. The FGSC offered targeted price discounts in an unsuccessful attempt to drive one entrant from the market. Sunk cost was apparently a factor: one estimate was that it would have taken a five-year price war to drive an incumbent from the market.

The GSC met three or four times a year through 1949, and monthly thereafter. The direct annual cost of running the conspiracy—the chairman's salary, the cost of providing reports, cost of monthly meetings—was at least $120,000, 1 per cent of industry annual sales. Erickson (1965) estimates that the cartel raised prices 30 per cent, profit 34 per cent, and allowed costs to rise 23 per cent. Technological improvements took place mainly during periods in which collusion had broken down. In one case, a cartel member developed an improved bleacher power operator and at the behest of the FGSC, it was priced so it did not undercut the existing products of other firms.

Source: Based on Erickson (1965, 1969).

6.4 Factors Affecting Cartel Stability

Our simple models suggest that if demand is stable, tacit collusion will be stable, if the interest rate firms use to discount future profit is low enough, and will increase firms' value compared with non-cooperative behaviour. If demand is unstable, firm value under tacit collusion will be reduced by intermittent punishment phases. In that case, firms may increase their value by colluding, even though there are costs associated with implementing and maintaining a collusive scheme. But an efficiently enforced antitrust or competition policy that fines colluding firms enough can reduce the return to collusion enough to make collusion unprofitable.

Other elements of market structure will affect the stability of tacit and overt collusion. Some of these factors relate to the firms that are part of the cartel, others to market conditions external to the cartel.

6.4.1 Internal Factors

Firms are more likely to be able to reach an agreement, all else equal, if they hold similar views about what it is a cartel or non-cooperative group should do. In an account of factors influencing negotiations in Danish cartels, Fog (1956, pp. 19–20) writes:

> What is to be considered the maximum solution depends upon whether you take a short-run or a long-run point of view, whether due regard has to be paid to potential competition, risk of Government interference, etc. When the views as to what is the proper cartel price are extremely divergent, as is often the case, this is more frequently due to divergencies as to what is the best line of policy than to differences in individual optimum prices.

Fog's experience (1956, p. 20) was that larger firms tended to prefer lower prices. One reason was that they took a longer view—maximized value over a longer time horizon—than smaller firms. Another reason was that by holding price below the joint-maximizing level, they reduced the incentive of smaller firms to defect from the cartel.

Cost differences

Cost differences make it more difficult for cartel members to reach an agreement. If firms have constant but different marginal costs, they will have different ideas about the output that makes marginal cost equal to marginal revenue. Firms with high fixed cost will suffer greater losses if the cartel reduces price during economic downturns than will firms with low fixed cost.

If marginal costs are not constant, then in order to maximize joint profit a cartel would have to reallocate output among firms to bring marginal cost at different firms into equality.[7] This would mean reduced output for high-marginal-cost firms and increased output for low-marginal-cost firms. Very high-cost plants might have to be closed down to maximize industry profit.[8] But high-cost firms are unlikely to trust their low-cost colleagues in crime to rely on a non-binding promise of future side-payments to compensate for current output reductions.[9] Collusion is more likely to be successful if cartel members have similar cost functions.

Product differentiation

Extensive product differentiation is likely to lead to different views on what it is the group should do. Producers of high-quality varieties are likely to favour higher prices, all else equal. Producers of low-quality varieties are likely to favour lower prices. With extensive product differentiation, a tacitly or overtly colluding group will need to fix a price schedule, not just a single price. Whatever price schedule is fixed will carry within it its own tensions. Producers of high-quality varieties may go along with lower prices for lower quality varieties. But they will not want the lower prices to be too low; that might tempt customers who would otherwise opt for a higher-quality variety to switch to a lower-quality variety. Producers of lower-quality varieties will be happy to see their own prices go up, but not too high, lest some of their customers switch to higher-quality varieties.

In addition, if products are differentiated, there is an easy way to surreptitiously offer a customer a low price. Ship a high-quality variety, bill at the price of a low-quality variety. If the ruse comes to light, it is easy enough to plead that there has been a clerical error. The upshot of these considerations is that group output restriction is favoured when the product is relatively standardized.

---

[7] Profit maximization requires that marginal revenue equal marginal cost. If the marginal cost of every firm is to be equal to marginal revenue, then each firm must produce an amount that makes its marginal cost equal to the common value of marginal cost of all other firms.

[8] In the pre-Sherman Act golden age of U.S. trust formation, it was far from unheard of for fringe operators to open up new plants for the sole purpose of making a profit by selling out to a trust.

[9] Fog (1956, p. 20) writes that "The cartel negotiations I have been informed about have been characterized by mutual suspicion and distrust ... " Blair (1967) reprints substantial extracts from minutes of quinine cartel meetings (Section 20.2.2); mutual suspicion and distrust is evident.

Rates of time preference

A low discount rate—valuing future income nearly as much as present income—facilitates tacit collusion. If firms have similar rates of time preference, they are more likely to agree on the way to trade off present and future income. It only takes one supplier with a "live for today" attitude to destabilize tacit collusion.[10]

Differences in large country and small country views about what it is oil-producing nations as a group should do have plagued OPEC throughout its existence. Large OPEC members, where size is measured in terms of proven oil reserves, have generally preferred lower prices. This preference is often attributed to the fact that they take a longer view of the world oil market than oil-producing nations with lower reserve levels.

In Section 5.3.4 we encountered the idea that a firm's financial market decisions can impact its product-market decisions. In particular, if a firm faces the possibility of bankruptcy, it will maximize profit only for situations in which bankruptcy does not occur. If the firm is bankrupt, the owners of the firm lose everything in any case. For this reason, a firm facing the possibility of bankruptcy may place greater weight on the short-run income to be gained from output expansion and less weight on tacitly collusive profit to be earned in the distant future. Extra short-run profit might help a firm stave off bankruptcy. If the firm goes bankrupt, high future profits go to some other firm. Thus financially constrained firms are more likely to defect from tacit collusion, all else equal.

Busse (2002) tests this possibility by examining the pricing behaviour of 14 U.S. airlines over the period 1985–1992. She finds that highly leveraged firms—those facing a greater possibility of bankruptcy—were more likely, all else equal, to initiate price wars. This supports the view that financial distress makes it more likely that a firm will defect from non-cooperative collusion.

Multimarket contact

If tacit collusion is stable, the reason is that firms individually find it in their own self-interest to restrain output. If supplying firms are diversified and meet in many product or geographic markets, then tacit collusion in any one of those markets may be reinforced by the calculation that defection and short-run profit in one market would expose the defector to retaliation and loss of future profit in many markets, not just the one in which defection occurs. Multimarket contact can stabilize tacit collusion, all else equal.[11]

Seller concentration

When industry output is produced by a few large firms, it is more likely that they will be able to reach a common view about what it is they should do, all else equal. This makes it easier for them to agree to do it. Further, when there are only a few producers, it is be easier to detect deviations from the agreed or understood line of conduct. We therefore expect that joint exercise of market power is more likely to occur when seller concentration is high. By the same token, if a concentration is low, a trade association may play a vital role in establishing and maintaining a collusive scheme.

---

[10] See Harrington (1989) for a model in which the adhesion of firms with short time horizons to tacit collusion is secured by allocating them larger market shares, all else equal.

[11] Kahn (1950), Edwards (1955), Bernheim and Whinston (1990), Scott (2008a). There is reason to think that multimarket contact affects performance in the crude oil industry, where international majors meet as partners in joint ventures in oilfields around the world, in pharmaceuticals, and in the passenger airline industry. On the latter, see Singal (1991).

Vertical integration

Nocke and White (2007) identify an *outlets effect* and a *punishment effect* of forward vertical integration on the stability of tacit collusion by upstream firms that supply an input to downstream firms in an imperfectly competitive market. The payoff of a defecting upstream firm is the extra profit it makes, until detected, on sales to downstream firms. But a vertically integrated upstream-downstream firm would never buy from a defecting upstream firm—a vertically integrated firm obtains the product at marginal cost; a defecting firm would offer the input for a price above marginal cost, even if below the cartel price. Vertical integration thus reduces the payoff from defection, and so tends to increase cartel stability.

The punishment effect goes in the opposite direction. If tacit collusion is a non-cooperative equilibrium, it is because the difference between collusive and reversion payoffs is large enough to outweigh, in present discounted value, the difference between defection and collusive payoffs. Since the final good market is imperfectly competitive (as most retail markets or markets with a spatial dimension are), a vertically integrated firm will receive some economic profit from its downstream operation even if the upstream market is in a punishment phase. For a defecting upstream firm, vertical integration reduces the difference between collusive and reversion payoffs, so tends to reduce cartel stability.

In the Nocke and White model, the outlets effect dominates the punishment effect, and vertical mergers facilitate tacit upstream collusion, provided the number of upstream and downstream firms is sufficiently large. In particular, a merger between firms in different layers of what had been a bilateral oligopoly of non-integrated firms makes it easier to sustain tacit upstream collusion.

6.4.2 External Factors

Buyer concentration

Demand-side market structure may affect the occurrence or success of output restriction. Large buyers may bargain for lower prices, tempting specific firms to make secret selective price cuts, thus causing rivalry to break out. This is the theory of *countervailing power*.[12] Large buyers may also credibly threaten to vertically integrate backward and produce the cartelized product themselves, effectively entering the supply side of a cartelized market. Similarly, large input suppliers may bargain for higher prices for the inputs they sell, or threaten to integrate forward and begin to compete with their customers. Tacit collusion is more likely to be stable, all else equal, if firms in an industry buy inputs from many small suppliers and sell outputs to many small buyers.

Entry

Entry, by vertical integration or otherwise, may destabilize collusion.[13] Voight (1962, pp. 171–172, p. 184) finds a predominant pattern to the life cycles of legal German cartels in the 1920s and 1930s:[14]

---

[12] See Marshall (1920, Chapter XIV), Galbraith (1952, 1954), and for a critical assessment, Stigler (1954).

[13] There is some indication that this happened with the Joint Executive Committee; see Vasconcelos (2004). See Elzinga and Mills (1999) for a model of price wars triggered by entry, and an application.

[14] Newman (1948, p. 577) writes of the German potash industry, which was cartelized from 1897: "High profits and relatively free entry into the industry tempted new firms; these, after threatening a price war with the cartel, were eventually taken in and given a quota."

1. if cartel members had similar cost curves, they were be able to reach agreement and raise price;

2. entry and expansion of output from firms outside the cartel would lead to cartel collapse;

3. after an interval of "cut-throat competition", the cartel would reform, including entrants from (2);

4. go to (1).

The limited number of exceptions were cartels that could block entry using patent rights, control of essential raw materials, government intervention, or other stratagems.

Collusion is more likely to succeed, and endure, if entry cost is high. If entry cost is low, successful cartelization will either induce destabilizing entry or require the division of cartel economic profit among a larger and larger number of suppliers.

Industry growth rate

Even with a low cost of entry, potential entrants are less likely to expect entry to be profitable if the industry is shrinking. Because of the lower threat of entry, and simply because they have relatively more to gain by restricting output, tacit or overt collusion may be more likely to succeed in industries that are in secular decline.

By contrast, in a growing industry, particularly one where capacity places a limit on the amount of output that can be produced in the short run, overt or tacit collusion may be largely irrelevant until new capacity can be brought on line. If firms are producing at capacity and the quantity demanded at prevailing price levels exceeds the quantity supplied, then in the short run price will rise to ration the available quantity supplied among consumers.

Size and frequency of individual transactions

If the business of an industry involves frequent and relatively small sales, the incremental profit to be gained by short-run defection from output-restricting behaviour will be relatively small. If business comes along infrequently and in large lumps—a contract to supply fighter aircraft to a national air force, for example, or to supply pipes for a metropolitan area sewerage system—the payoff to shading price a little and grabbing a big lump of sales can be great, and retaliation some time in the future. Collusion is less likely to be stable where sales are large and infrequent, all else equal.

Open bidding and other types of public policy

Even so, if the large and infrequent sales are to a unit of government, and the buyer's decisions are made based on sealed bids that are revealed when the contract is awarded, that will tend to chill rivalrous behaviour. If a firm defects from collusion and a government buyer reveals the author of the low bid, it also exposes the low bidder to immediate retaliation. Open bidding facilitates tacit collusion.

Other public policies, adopted in all innocence,[15,16] may facilitate tacit or overt collusion. McMillan (1991, p. 207) suggests that the traditional Japanese government practice of

---

[15] See the discussion in Section 20.3.2 of the effect of a Danish publicity policy on market performance in ready-mixed concrete in the early 1990s.

[16] Some government-facilitated collusion is quite deliberate. Agricultural policy in developed countries provides examples. See Filson *et al.* (2001) for an analysis of U.S. agricultural marketing orders from this perspective.

limiting bids on public-works contracts may be rooted in bureaucratic risk aversion—if an administrator awards a contract to a hitherto unknown bidder, it is the administrator's head that will be on the block if performance is not satisfactory. Since qualified bidders are selected from firms with a history of work in Japan, entry by foreign firms is blocked (McMillan, 1991, p. 207): "Catch-22: you cannot win a contract unless you bid, but you are not allowed to bid unless you have won a contract." Thus public policy with another purpose entirely serves to block entry by firms that might, if allowed on the market, improve market performance.[17]

Knittel and Stango (2003) examine the impact of interest-rate ceilings on interest rates charged in the U.S. credit card market during the years 1979–1989. They investigate the possibility that an interest-rate ceiling can act as a *focal point* that makes clear to an individual firm the price on which other firms are likely to coordinate, thereby facilitating joint exercise of market power as a result of individual decisions. Their results show evidence of a focal-point effect, facilitating tacit collusion, particularly in the early years of their sample.[18] Thus state policies adopted with the goal of improving performance in a particular market actually had the opposite effect.

6.5 Cartels In Practice

6.5.1 15th-century European Alum[19]

In the Middle Ages, alum (a naturally occurring chemical compound) (de Roover, 1963, p. 152) "was extensively used in glassmaking, in tanning, and in the textile industry as a cleanser to remove grease and impurities from the wool and as a mordant to fix the dyes so the fabrics would not discolor". Genovese merchants parlayed their support for the fourth crusade (1202–1204) into control of the richest alum deposits known in the world, on the Turkish coast, and began an almost 200-year near-monopoly of the European alum market.

This near-monopoly came to an end with the Ottoman conquest of Constantinople in 1453. The Turks charged high rents for the right to exploit their alum deposits, and these rents were passed along to the European market in the form of higher prices.

There were minor European sources of alum, the most important located on the island of Ischia, near Naples. But Turkish control of the European alum market was not jeopardized until the discovery, in 1461, of high-quality alum deposits near Civitavecchia, the port city of Rome. The Pope granted the exclusive right to work these deposits to a consortium of merchants, in return for payments that were specified in detail. As part of the contract, the church forbade the sale of Turkish alum in all of Christendom. Ships that were found to have violated this decree were subject to being boarded and to having their cargo confiscated.

But the profitability of the Civitavecchia deposits was reduced by competition from the Ischia mines. In June, 1470, the Medici Bank brokered a 25-year cartel agreement between

---

[17] McMillan (1991, pp. 211–213) also suggests that Japanese public-works cartels are not able to block entry by inefficient Japanese firms, so the fruits of collusion are dissipated by higher than necessary production costs and rent-seeking expenditures as many firms seek the limited number of public contracts available.

[18] Knittel and Stango also find that tacit collusion encouraged entry, causing tacit collusion to weaken by the end of their sample period.

[19] This section is based on Zippel (1907, pp. 35–38), Strieder ([1925] 1971, pp. 168–183), Piotrowski ([1933] 1978, pp. 153–163), de Roover (1963), and Barnikel (1972, pp. 2–3).

the Pope and King Ferdinand I of Naples. Papal participation in the cartel was justified on the ground that the proceeds would finance further crusades. There is evidence (Piotrowski, 1933, p. 163) that Neapolitan businessmen involved in exploitation of the Ischia deposits urged the King of Naples to take part in the cartel agreement. This may be seen as an example of rent seeking on the part of the businessmen.

Under the terms of the agreement, neither party was to make sales without informing the other. Each party was to supply half of any sale. The cartel agreement specified the prices at which sales were to take place. If an agent of either party were to make sales at a lower price, the lost profit of the other party was to be made up. Sales were to be for cash, not barter, with credit to be allowed for not more than one year. The agreement provided for substantial financial penalties for violations of the cartel agreement.

Each party to the agreement had permanent representatives at the mines and warehouses of the other. These representatives had keys to the warehouses, and were entitled to examine accounts recording amounts of alum extracted and shipped.

The agreement appears to have functioned as described for about two years. It was revised on terms more favourable to the Vatican following the election of a new Pope.[20]

Papal decrees against Turkish alum were a barrier to competition. Permitting piracy against ships carrying Turkish alum was an example of raising rivals' costs. The elaborate institutional arrangements specified in the cartel agreement of 1470 had the purpose of making detection of defections from the agreement more rapid, and therefore less profitable. The requirement that sales be for cash, and the strict limitations on credit terms, eliminated methods of giving secret discounts. The penalties that were to be paid if a violation was detected reduced the expected payoff from defection.

6.5.2 18th-century English Copper[21]

Birmingham, England native Matthew Boulton (1728–1809) had diverse manufacturing interests, among which jewellery, silverware, steel sheet, clocks, and coins. He was also an early financial backer of James Watt, inventor of a much improved steam engine. From 1775 their partnership, Boulton & Watt, exploited Watt's patent on his steam engine (a patent first granted for 14 years, from 1768, and later extended until 1800 by special Act of Parliament).

The major early use of the Watt steam engine was to power pumps to extract water from relatively old and deep Cornwall copper mines. The Watt engine was so effective that it made possible an increase in copper output.

The Cornwall mines faced competition from relatively new and easy-to-work mines in Anglesey. Increased supplies from both areas caused the price of copper to collapse, threatening Cornish mines with bankruptcy and jeopardizing the royalty payments due Boulton & Watt under licences for the steam engine. To avoid this, Matthew Boulton became involved in the Cornish copper industry.

Boulton & Watt purchased shares in Cornwall copper mines. Viewed as a stand-alone proposition, these investments lost money. But for a time they enabled the mines to remain

---

[20] de Roover (1963, p. 156) writes that the cartel was probably dissolved "because the Medici discovered that their partner was not as formidable a competitor as they had anticipated and that they had paid too high a price for his cooperation".

[21] This section is based on Allen (1923). See also Roll (1930).

in operation and make royalty payments to Boulton & Watt; overall the firm came out ahead. As the situation of the mines worsened, Boulton was obliged to take a more direct role.

He engineered the formation of a joint sales agency, the Cornish Metal Company, in which he and his friends were major investors. The Company committed itself to buy all Cornish copper ore mined between 1 September 1785 and 1 September 1792, to arrange for the ore to be smelted, and to sell the resulting copper. Ore was to be purchased at prices fixed by the 36 directors of the Company. Two-thirds of the directors were nominated by mineowners.

Having thus unified control of the Cornwall mines, Boulton worked out an agreement with the Anglesey mines (Allen, 1923, p. 78, footnotes omitted):

> [A] minimum price for all the copper produced by the two centres was fixed, and from this price both parties bound themselves not to depart under a penalty of £100,000. Cornwall's share of the total sales was to be three-fifths, while that of [Anglesey] was fixed at two-fifths. ... no attempt was made ... to set any limit to the total amount of production. ... Each party was required to present the other with weekly accounts of its sales ... The operation of the contract was to begin in May 1786, after which date the price of copper was to be £86 a ton. This price ... was about £12 higher than that which had ruled in May 1785 ...

This first version of the scheme floundered, for three reasons. First, the increase in the price of copper metal caused an increase in the price of copper ore, which in turn caused an increase in ore production and the accumulation of copper in cartel warehouses, copper that could not be sold at the high fixed price. Second, copper from sources outside cartel control, some in England and some on the continent, flowed into the English market. Third, the Anglesey interests sold more than their agreed share of total output.

By 1787, the Cornish Metal Company had an estimated two-year supply of copper sitting in its warehouses. Boulton proposed that output from the mines be limited. This led to labour unrest (including threats to destroy the homes of mineowners). Rather than restrict output, mineowners broke their contract with the Company, at which point the Anglesey mines lowered their price.

Open rivalry did not last long: there was a new agreement by the end of the year. A single joint sales agent was set up for Cornwall and Anglesey. Quotas were established for each region, and the price of copper was reduced to £80 a tonne. To bring about the agreed reduction in output, the Company paid an amount per tonne of past output rates to mines that closed.

Labour unrest followed mine closures. The huge accumulation of warehoused copper continued to hang over the market, depressing prices for copper metal and, in consequence, for copper ore. Many of the Cornwall mines were unable to make their agreed royalty payments to Boulton & Watt.

It was only in October 1789 that the copper market recovered to the point that the Company could begin to dispose of its surplus stocks. But Cornish interests were saved, around 1790, when Anglesey copper deposits were exhausted. The price of copper rose, and the situation of the Cornish Metal Company improved—not without further market disorder related to disposing of the accumulated stock of copper metal.

The Cornish Metal Company was closed down, as originally planned, in 1792. The reduction in supply, from Anglese and from closed Cornish mines, meant it was possible to dispose of accumulated stocks at favourable prices. Cornwall copper interests prospered, as the Napoleonic Wars fuelled demand and kept prices high.

What are the lessons of this episode for cartel dynamics? An effective cartel must have ways to monitor members' actions. Further, a cartel can control at most one side of a market—the supply side. It is not enough for a cartel to announce a high price. To make that price effective, the cartel must restrict the total quantity supplied to the quantity demanded at the announced price. If the cartel cannot keep supplies from other sources off the market, it must reduce its own output to neutralize "fringe" output and keep the total quantity supplied down to the quantity demanded at the cartel price.

6.5.3 19th-century British Pin Industry Price Associations

Jones (1973) chronicles the rise and fall of five price associations—two national and three regional—in the relatively concentrated British pin industry in the early century after publication of the *Wealth of Nations*. The first, national, association began at uncertain date around the start of the 19th century. It succumbed in 1820, Jones suggests, as economic downturns in the United States led U.S. firms to default on or defer payment of their debts to British firms, at once making the British firms short of liquid financial assets and obliging them to stock pins that had been intended for the U.S. market. Fixed capital requirements were relatively low, but (Jones, 1973, p. 244) "there was an incentive to retain labour, especially supervisory and skilled workmen, in order that future production might not be jeopardized, and thus the quasi-fixed cost of labour would inevitably increase the pressure on scarce resources". The need to cover short-run costs induced enough firms to maximize short-run profit to lead to the collapse of the association.

The end of 1820 and early 1821 saw a short-lived Birmingham/Warrington price association; it collapsed (not surprisingly, Jones, remarks, given the absence of barriers to entry), in the face of competition from London suppliers.

In 1824, a combination of economic depression and German competition kept British firms out of the U.S. market. Under pressure from Birmingham workers, who took exception to the idea that where prices went, their wages would follow, there was an effort to form a national price association. A major London producer undercut the association's price list, and this association too collapsed by the end of the year. This collapse was followed by tacit collusion in London and another short-lived price association in northern England.

After a year and a half or so of general depression and intense price competition, 1827 saw the formation of a price association by the three firms that supplied the London market. Market structure favoured non-cooperative collusion (Jones, 1973, p. 248):

> This reduction in numbers, the geographical proximity of the participants, and their pre-occupation with a highly concentrated local market fostered a high degree of information flow to and between firms. This militated against deviation and against mistrust, the latter being a real obstacle to earlier associations.

The London firms succeeded in raising prices, and soon faced competition from low-quality pins marketed by Bristol suppliers. The London firms introduced a line of common pins to meet this competition, but maintained prices on their own "best pins". Although unable to drive the country producers from the London market, the London firms were largely successful in maintaining prices in their regional market for several years. Jones attributes this success to entry costs rooted in product differentiation[22] and financial market information advantages of the London incumbents.[23] This price association too fell apart by 1840, its collapse the result of a combination of an economic downtown in the late 1830s, the collapse of export markets, and price-cutting in search of liquid assets as cash reserves were depleted.

6.5.4 Pre-Sherman Act U.S. Railroad Cartels

Before the Sherman Act drove U.S. cartels from the light of day, they operated openly. They had no reason not to: while cartel agreements could not be enforced in court, they were not illegal. Study of the operations of such cartels reveals that they invested costly resources to establish procedures that would reduce the payoff from defecting, and to detect defection if it occurred.

The foundation for a U.S. national railway system had been put in place by 1860, although the national railway system itself lay in the future. Few railroad lines outside New England faced direct competition from another line. Most railroads operated as local monopolists. But by the early 1870s, with the completion of transcontinental lines and the laying down of the first feeder lines, enough regional duopolies or triopolies had been established to make collusion profitable, if it could be made to work.

Entry into regional railway markets was costly. The cost of entry included not only the fixed cost of the railway line itself, but also the cost of assuring connecting outlets at the end of the line (Harley, 1982, p. 804): "Any new entrant had to obtain main line connections either to a port or to the eastern trunk lines—usually at Chicago or St. Louis. ... by the early 1870s there were only two or three railroad companies that could reasonably build in most areas." Colluding firms could not disregard the possibility of entry, but they were able to identify the most likely potential entrants.

The Iowa/Omaha Pool

Railroad cartels were organized on a regional basis. The first, the Iowa or Omaha Pool, was formed in late 1870 by three railroads (Riegel, 1924, p. 570):

> The Omaha Pool was a verbal agreement which sought to remove the tendency toward rate cutting by removing its cause and making the return equal for each line regardless of the amount of traffic carried. All business between Chicago and Council Bluffs was to be pooled. Forty-five per cent of the passenger and fifty per cent of the freight income was to be retained to pay operating expenses, and the remainder was to be divided equally among the three roads. There was no machinery of enforcement except the opportunity given the officials to see each other's books; and the success of the arrangement depended for the most part on the good faith of the parties involved.

---

[22] Jones (1973, p. 251): "[T]he establishment of a permanent sales staff in the city meant that London makers were able to maintain a close and regular contact with wholesale and retail outlets. The continuous service was of especial importance in supplying the retail trade who tended to buy small lots at short intervals ... "

[23] Jones (1973, p. 251): "Monthly settlement of accounts kept small retailers on a fairly tight rein, whilst an intimate knowledge of the mercantile affairs of the City and West End enabled the London houses to assess the credit-worthiness of potential customers very readily."

Yet Harley (1982, p. 812) writes that the "'Iowa Pool' was the most successful American railway cartel and lasted, although not without strains, from 1870 to 1884." Riegel (1931, p. 366) attributes its success to its simplicity. But the early simplicity of the Iowa Pool was disrupted by entry and the need to take shippers' alternative sources of transportation services into account (Riegel, 1924, p. 572): "Omaha, as a Missouri River point, had to have a rate comparable to other Missouri River rates, and this meant that consideration must be given to the rates charged by all roads to the Missouri River and also to the rates of their eastern connections." In 1882 the Omaha Pool put in place a formal cartel structure, with the establishment of the Iowa Trunk Lines Association.[24]

The Southern Railway & Steamship Association

The Southern Railway & Steamship Association (SRSA) began in 1875 (Hudson, 1890a, p. 72): "Any road south of the Ohio and Potomac Rivers and east of the Mississippi could become a member. Any steamship company connecting these roads with Boston, Providence, New York, Philadelphia, or Baltimore was eligible." It sought, apparently with success, to restrain competition. Hudson (1890a, p. 75) reports a single one-month episode (from 14 February 1878 to 15 March 1878) of price competition between 1877 and 1887. Ulen (1978, p. 83) reports that episode and another, in 1884. Thus, in the SRSA's market, competition broke out twice, for short periods, in ten years.

To achieve its purpose, the SRSA established an elaborate, quasi-governmental infrastructure. It had a chief executive officer, the General Commissioner. It had a "legislature", the annual convention, at which each member was represented. It had a judiciary: first, outside referees hired to deal with specific disputes, later a permanent Arbitrator.

Members of the SRSA agreed on the shares of freight traffic that each should carry.[25] The initial arrangement was that any road that carried more than its agreed share would keep one-half cent per tonne-mile to cover its costs and pay anything above that to the General Commissioner. He in turn would distribute these payments to firms that had ended up carrying less than their agreed shares. To permit the Commissioner to perform these transfers, he received daily reports on freight traffic from members. He provided members with monthly summaries of this information.

Goodwill, it turned out, was not enough to ensure compliance with the agreement on traffic shares. Members later agreed that each road would deposit an amount equal to 20 per cent of revenue on pool traffic with the Commissioner, who used these funds to settle accounts arising out of share imbalances. To combat price-cutting by misclassification of goods in a lower rate class, the SRSA authorized the Commissioner to appoint two Inspectors of Weights and Measures, who could ensure that freight was carried at agreed rates.

Placing good-faith deposits in the hands of the Commissioner was a commitment by members that they would not profit from deviations, inadvertent or otherwise. Controlling weight classification served to prevent one kind of under-the-table discount. Reporting rates to the Commissioner, and employing auditors to ensure the accuracy of those reports, meant that deviations from agreed-upon rates would be detected. Rapid detection of deviations was

---

[24] For details, see Riegel (1924).

[25] This description of the Association's operations is based on Hudson (1890a). A copy of the Agreement as of 1886–1887 is printed as an Appendix, Hudson (1890b).

also facilitated by common ownership of the Green Line, the leading fast freight line in the South.

Fast freight companies were independent firms that paid for the use of railway track and then offered shipping services to the public. Common ownership of the highly profitable Green Line facilitated collusion in two ways. First, in the course of managing the Green Line, each firm learned about the operations of the other firms. Second, a railroad considering rate cuts would need to anticipate not only the possibility that a general rate war would follow but also that the operations of the Green Line might be disrupted, meaning that it would lose its share of those profits as well as suffer losses on its railway operations.

To further reduce the possibility of misunderstandings, the SRSA employed a clear focal point for the rates that were to be charged. It based its rates on those of the next best alternative available to its customers, the sum of the rail rate from Chicago to Baltimore, the water rate from Baltimore down the Atlantic coast to the nearest southern port, and the rail rate again for local transport inland. In this way, all firms knew what cartel rates were supposed to be, and the cartel set the highest rates it could without inducing customers to switch to alternative suppliers.

The Joint Executive Committee

The Joint Executive Committee (JEC) was established on 18 April 1879, the successor of previous pools of lines hubbing at Chicago. It operated in a more complex environment than the SRSA or the Iowa Pool. JEC members were more diversified geographically than members of the other cartels, and to the extent that their other operations did not overlap, their overall interests differed. The JEC also faced competition from a combination of Great Lake and eastern rail lines that was more serious, at least when the Great Lakes were not frozen, than the intermodal competition faced by the other two cartels (Lobato and Walsh, 1994; Mariuzzo and Walsh, 2006).

The JEC had a formal structure similar to that of the SRSA.[26] Like the SRSA, the JEC collected detailed information on shipments of individual lines, compiled it, and reported back to members. It had a Board of Arbitrators to settle disputes.[27] If price cuts were detected, its Commissioner could, on his own authority, match the price cuts by reducing rates quoted on the Chicago Board of Trade. JEC members placed good-faith deposits with the Commissioner, to be forfeited in the event of cheating. Members also refused to transfer freight to or from a cheating road. Intermittent price wars resembled the predictions of the trigger strategy model.

Ellison (1994) reports the results of a statistical analysis of the ability of the JEC to approach monopoly profit. He estimates a conjectural variation parameter, during periods when the JEC had not dropped prices to punish a suspected episode of cheating, of 0.85. This approaches the monopoly value (i.e., 1). On this evidence, the JEC succeeded in raising the returns of its members.

---

[26] This description of JEC operations is based on Ulen (1978, p. 92).

[27] One of these was Charles Francis Adams; on Adams' involvement with the JEC, see McCraw (1984, pp. 47–53). Since the amount firms are willing to invest in making collusion work is one indication of its profitability, we note that according to Ulen (1978, p. 102), the Joint Executive Committee paid Adams, David A. Wells, and John Wright each $10,000 a year to serve as arbitrators. This was at a time when the *per capita* annual income in the United States is estimated to have been $204.

Construction

Price and output—in the context of nineteenth-century U.S. railroads, rates, and shipments—are a firm's most important short-run strategic variables. Other strategic variables come into play over the long run. In some markets, firms advertise to cultivate a profitable brand image. In others, firms engage in research and development to develop new products or more efficient production processes. In many markets, investments in capacity must be made before production can be carried out. For nineteenth-century U.S. railroads, capacity decisions concerned the timing and location of railroad track construction.

Railroad construction was a commitment to enter a market, particularly since in the late nineteenth-century, courts refused to let bankrupt railroads go out of business (Ulen,

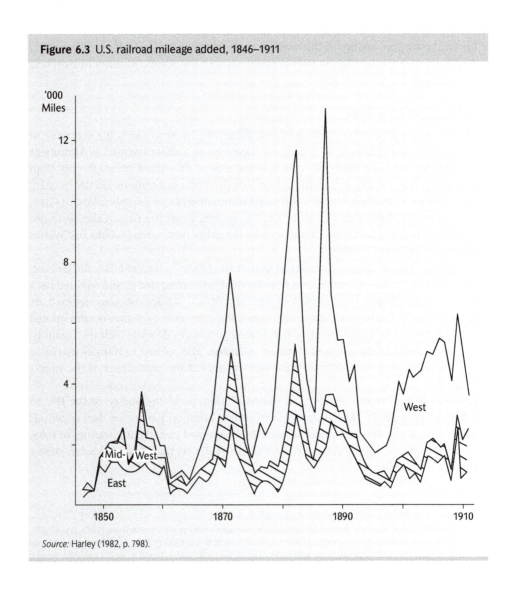

Figure 6.3 U.S. railroad mileage added, 1846–1911

Source: Harley (1982, p. 798).

1978, pp. 70–74). But it could be a short-run equilibrium not to enter a rival's market (Grodinsky, 1962, p. 105):[28]

> Many roads created territorial enclaves: mutually monopolistic areas, where each road agreed not to invade the territory of the other. These agreements were usually verbal understandings and were only infrequently reduced to writing. Sometimes they were examined and approved by the directors of the contracting parties, while other arrangements expressed only understandings reached by executive officers.

A breakdown in price collusion might trigger a breakdown in such a mutual forbearance equilibrium.

Harley (1982) raises the possibility that railroads colluded on the timing of construction. Capacity collusion was a device to facilitate control over rates. It was also profitable to delay construction and allow the settling of frontier areas to go forward, so that a railroad line, once built, would serve a more densely populated area. The profitability of defecting from such an agreement increases as time goes by, settlement proceeds, and the first firm to build gets a strategic advantage in serving a more settled area. Harley attributes the two peaks in railroad construction of the 1880s (Figure 6.3) to breakdowns in oligopolistic agreements to delay construction.

19th-century U.S. railroad cartels:

These relatively high-fixed-cost, low-marginal-cost firms operated in highly concentrated regional markets. Before passage of the Sherman Act made overt collusion illegal, they invested scarce resources to make it easier to detect cheating on collusive agreements and to compel payment of penalties upon detection of cheating. This conduct aimed to reduce the incentive to cheat and sustain the collusive agreements.

6.6 The Effects of Collusion

6.6.1 On Market Performance

Cartel overcharges

How close have cartels come to maximizing joint profit? Connor (2005) examines estimates of cartel overcharges from a variety of sources for 674 national and international private, hard-core cartels that ended between 1780 and 2004. He defines a private, hard-core cartel as (2005, p. 26) "one that by contemporary U.S. standards could be criminally indicted under the Sherman Act". The cartel overcharge is the percentage increase in price over marginal cost, $(p - c)/c$.

The range of estimates assembled by Connor is described in Table 6.1. It shows, for example, that there were 59 observations of national cartels ending in the period 1780 to 1891. The median estimated average overcharge for these cartels during their lifetimes was

---

[28] This is quoted by Harley (1982, p. 810).

Table 6.1 Median average cartel overcharge and number of observations, by time period and type of cartel

End Date	National	International	Overall
		Overcharge/Observations	
1780–1891	22/59	41/5	23.5/64
1891–1919	21/61	48/36	30.4/97
1920–1945	18/9	36–37/147	34.0/156
1946–1973	14/72	26/20	15.0/92
1974–1990	18–20/59	40–43/20	24.0/79
1991–2004	17–18/49	25/137	24.0/186
All Years	17–19/309	30–33/365	25.0/674

Source: Connor (2005, Tables 5, 6).

22 per cent. The overall median average overcharge of national cartels was 17 to 19 per cent, of international cartels 30 to 33 per cent, and of all cartels 25 per cent.

For comparison, Griffin (1989) reports an average Lerner index of 0.31 for a sample of 54 international cartels. This corresponds to an overcharge of 0.45.

Duration

The impact of collusion on market performance depends not only on how high cartels are able to raise price, but also on how long they are able to maintain an increase. The cartels in the Griffin (1989) sample had an average lifespan of 7.3 years. Suslow (2005) studies 71 international cartels that operated between World War I and World War II. For cartels that ended during this period (that is, cartels not in operation at the beginning of World War II), the average lifespan was 3.7 years. The average lifespan for all cartels was 8.3 years. For a sample of 71 international cartels convicted of violating one or both of U.S. antitrust or EU competition policy since 1990, Levenstein and Suslow (2006b) report an average lifespan of 7.5 years, with a range of 1 to 29 years. Cartels may not last forever—very few things do—but they last long enough to cause significant resource misallocation and welfare losses.

6.6.2 On Market Structure

Entry

Additional effects arise if colluding firms succeed in raising price but cannot prevent new firms from coming into the market. Suppose, for example, that in a market with inverse demand curve (6.1) and cost function (6.2), fixed cost F is 550.

Then Cournot duopoly profit per firm per period is positive:

$$\pi_1 = \pi_2 = (40 - 10)(30) - F = 900 - 550 = 350 > 0. \tag{6.16}$$

With three firms in the market, Cournot triopoly profit would be negative:

$$\left(100 - 3\frac{100 - 10}{4} - 10\right)\left(\frac{100 - 10}{4}\right) - 550 = -43.75 < 0. \tag{6.17}$$

With Cournot behaviour, the equilibrium number of firms is two.

If three firms collude on monopoly output, each firm produces 15 units of output. The monopoly price is 55; hence each of the three firms earns positive profit:

$$(55 - 10)(15) - 550 = 675 - 550 = 125 > 0. \tag{6.18}$$

In this particular example, collusion on the monopoly output level makes possible an increase in the number of firms from two to three. More generally, if firms collude and raise price, the higher price may make additional entry profitable, possibly entry by less efficient firms.[29] The result is that output is restricted, so there is a higher price and lost consumer surplus, and at the same time too many resources (from a social point of view) are used to produce the restricted output, dissipating the economic profit that would otherwise have accrued to colluding firms.

In the example, if two incumbent firms collude on the monopoly price and as a result a third firm comes into the market, the first two firms earn less profit than they would as Cournot duopolists: monopoly profit split among three firms is 125 per period, Cournot duopoly profit per firm is 350. It might very well be, however, that firms could find ways to restrict output and raise price without violating anticollusion laws but that actively trying to keep a third firm out of the market would leave evidence of other kinds of anticompetitive behavior (monopolization) against which it would be more difficult to defend. It might simply be, in the oft-quoted words of Hicks (1935, p. 8), that "The best of all monopoly profits is a quiet life".[30]

If a monopoly price would make entry profitable, incumbent firms might non-cooperatively collude to raise price above the Cournot level but below the monopoly level. non-cooperative collusion would still worsen market performance, but not so much as if entry were not possible. Thus we have the possibility that the threat of entry—potential competition, rather than actual competition—might improve market performance. It is also possible that one equilibrium oligopoly price is the highest price that will not induce entry.

A kind of natural experiment generated by United Kingdom competition policy suggests that collusion may in fact result in excess entry (Hannah, 1990, pp. 357–360; Symeonidis, 1998, 2002). Before 1956, the UK rule was that agreements to restrain trade were neither

---

[29] Hudson (1890a, p. 92) writes that without the Southern Railway and Steamship Association "The stronger lines would perhaps have survived . . . , but hardly the weaker." McFadden (1978. p. 470), writing of the late nineteenth-century U.S. barbed wire industry, writes that "The larger and more integrated manufacturing concerns recognized that they actually gained little by adhering to pooling or price agreements, since fixed prices only assured the continued existence of the less efficient processors".

[30] Chandler (1990, Part III) documents the inclination of British industrialists, with whom Hicks would have been most familiar, to avoid tough competition; see in the same vein Howard (1954) and Feldenkirchen (1987, p. 450), who writes about Germany: "During the 1920s, the large German conglomerates . . . assumed functions increasingly recognized as not well suited to cartels and syndicates, since cartels invariably attempted to secure the financial survival of their weakest members."

illegal nor enforceable in courts of law. Trade associations in a number of industries administered elaborate schemes to exchange information about prices and quantities sold. These schemes made it easier for rivals to detect output expansion or price cutting, which in turn increased the stability of tacit collusion.

In 1956 the UK Restrictive Trade Practices Act made restrictive agreements illegal. It required that existing restrictive agreements be registered with public authorities. The Act allowed a Restrictive Practices Court to permit a restrictive agreement, by way of exception to the general prohibition, if it found benefits that outweighed the negative effects.

Immediately after the law went into effect, it was not known what approach the Restrictive Practices Court would take toward permitting agreements, and it appears that most existing restrictive agreements were in fact registered. As it turned out, the Court took a tough approach to applying the law; few agreements were permitted. Information exchange agreements ended, and between 1958 and 1977 the combined market share of the five largest firms in industries affected by the Restrictive Practices Act rose by an average of 15 percentage points. The most likely explanation is that in the United Kingdom, trade association activities supported non-cooperative collusion but did not restrict entry, thus permitting the survival of relatively inefficient firms. When trade association activities were limited by a more vigorous competition policy, rivalry increased and less efficient firms went out of business, freeing resources for use in other markets.[31]

Capacity

Just as firms may be able to collude on price but not restrict entry, so firms may be able to collude on price but find it more difficult to manage investments in capacity. For the nineteenth-century U.S. railroad industry, this is suggested by the pattern of construction shown in Figure 6.3. Individual firms have an incentive to expand capacity, to try to increase bargaining power within the cartel. By creating the possibility of expanding output, excess capacity carried by a leader within the cartel will discourage smaller members from cheating, and provides a way to discipline them if they do cheat.[32] And excess capacity financed while the cartel is working may be good insurance for maintaining market position if the cartel should break down.

The resources devoted to excess capacity are as much a social cost of collusion as is deadweight welfare loss. Loescher, discussing the U.S. cement industry's use of basing-point pricing in the 1920s, writes (1959, pp. 180–181):[33] "Society paid a heavy price for the cement industry's success in stabilizing prices in the face of excess capacity: that success encouraged further excess capacity." Scherer *et al.* (1975, pp. 168–169) similarly report that cartels delayed rationalization of capacity in the U.S. and British cement industries, in the British and Swedish steel industries, and in the British glass bottle, textile, and cotton yarn spinning industries.

---

[31] See Howe (1973) for an account of UK wire rope trade associations. Howe concludes that in this sector, trade association activity did not eliminate pressure for cost minimization, although it may have slowed innovation. Voight (1962, p. 204) suggests that German cartels had the effect of protecting small- and medium-sized firms.

[32] The United States Steel Corporation used its excess capacity in 1909 to expand output and bring home to fringe firms the ill effects of competition. Saudi Arabia similarly used its excess crude oil capacity in 1985 and 1986, bringing other members of the Organization of Petroleum Exporting Countries around to Saudi Arabia's view of sensible policy for the cartel.

[33] See also Waldman (1988), who documents the presence of excess capacity under collusion in three U.S. industries, the cement industry, the cardboard container industry, and the electric turbine industry.

6.6.3 Evidence

From antitrust enforcement

Palmer Palmer (1972) analyses successful U.S. horizontal restraint-of-trade antitrust cases for the period 1966–1970. The distribution of growth ratios of the industries in which the restraint-of-trade cases in his sample occurred are shown in Figure 6.4. For comparison purposes, between 1958 and 1963 the growth ratio of U.S. gross national product was 1.31.[34] Two-thirds of the challenged agreements (49 out of 74) occurred in industries growing less rapidly than the economy as a whole. This is consistent with the view that price fixing is more likely in declining sectors.

Table 6.2 shows the distribution of restraint-of-trade cases by four-firm seller concentration ratio and industry growth rate for the subset of Palmer's sample with concentration ratio observations. For both low-growth and high-growth industries, the number of price-fixing cases rises moving into the middle range of the concentration distribution and falls as concentration reaches very high levels. The peak occurs at a higher concentration level for high-growth industries.

In low concentration industries, there are likely to be too many firms for tacit or overt collusion to work. In intermediate concentration ratios, the payoff to restricting output is great, but there are enough firms that collusion must be overt to succeed. The collusion-prone output range is higher in industries that are growing rapidly, because in growing industries joint output restriction is not privately optimal even if concentration is moderate. At high concentration levels, there are so few suppliers that collusion is unnecessary—above a critical concentration level, leading firms understand where their interests lie without the need to get together and talk about it.

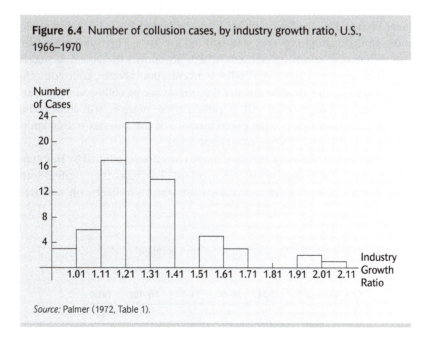

Figure 6.4 Number of collusion cases, by industry growth ratio, U.S., 1966–1970

Source: Palmer (1972, Table 1).

---

[34] That is, 1963 U.S. GNP divided by 1958 U.S. GNP was 1.31, implying a compound annual growth rate of 5.5 per cent. The industry growth ratios also compare industry value of shipments for 1958 and 1963.

Table 6.2 Number of antitrust cases by industry CR4 and industry growth rate

CR4	GR < 1.31	GR ≥ 1.31
0.20–0.29	2	1
0.30–0.39	1	2
0.40–0.49	4	2
0.50–0.59	8	1
0.60–0.69	12	1
0.70–0.79	2	4
0.80–0.89	3	0
0.90–0.99	2	2
Total	34	13

Source: Palmer (1972, Table 2).

Hay and Kelley   Hay and Kelley (1974) study successful U.S. Department of Justice criminal cases under Section 1 of the Sherman Act from the period 1963–1972. Essentially all of the conspiracies in their sample covered standardized products. Their findings on the seller concentration-collusion relationship, some of which are shown in Table 6.3, suggest even more strongly than those of Palmer that seller concentration favours collusion. They also suggest that high seller concentration favours the persistence of collusion (Hay and Kelley, 1974, p. 26): "numbers as large as ten will, in certain circumstances, still allow collusion to continue for long periods of time. ... the preponderance of conspiracies lasting ten or more years were in markets with high degrees of concentration."

Table 6.4 gives the number of firms involved in the conspiracies studied by Hay and Kelley, and indicates whether a trade association was involved. The cases they studied sometimes involved many firms. Trade association involvement was more likely, on balance, if the

Table 6.3 Four-firm seller concentration ratios, 50 U.S. DOJ price-fixing cases, 1963–1972

CR4 (per cent)	0–25	26–50	51–75	76–100	Total
Number of cases	3	9	17	21	50

Source: Hay and Kelley (1974), Table 2.

Table 6.4 Number of conspirators and trade association involvement, 62 U.S. DOJ price-fixing cases, 1963–1972

Number of conspirators	2	3	4	5	6	7	8	9	10	11–15	16–20	21–25	>25	Total
Number of cases		1	7	8	4	10	4	3	5	7	5	2	–	6	62
Trade association involved	–	–	1	–	4	1	–	1	3	1	1	–	6	18

Source: Hay and Kelley (1974, Table 2).

number of firms was large.[35] Seven of the eight cases with 16 or more participants involved a trade association.

Hay and Kelley are also able to shed light on the duration of criminal cartels (1974, p. 26):[36] "[T]here were many situations in which the agreements had been in existence for so long that no one could remember the origins. Several conspiracies had their roots in the [depression-era National Recovery Administration]. Some meetings which began then continued for decades." If market conditions are right, or firms are able to put enforcement mechanisms in place, there is no reason to think that cartels will be ephemeral or ineffective.

Electrical equipment conspiracies   The electrical equipment industry supplies a broad range of products to public and private generators of electricity. Some of these products are standardized. Some are made to order. Some face extensive foreign competition; others do not. For most products, the ratio of fixed to variable cost is high. The industries have high levels of seller concentration. Not surprisingly, since many sales are to governments and therefore affected by government budget constraints, electrical equipment markets are subject to severe cyclical demand fluctuations.

In the United States in the 1950s, the electrical equipment industry was home to an elaborate explicit collusion scheme (Lean *et al.*, 1982, p. 1, footnotes omitted):

> more than 30 electrical-equipment manufacturers engaged in an elaborate conspiracy to fix prices charged utilities. The conspirators' illegal meetings covered 20 product lines (including, for example, steam turbine generators, demand and watt-hour meters, and power circuit breakers) with annual sales approaching $2 billion. After [Tennessee Valley Authority] complaints about identical sealed bids, Justice Department investigations began in 1959, and a grand jury handed down indictments in the next year. As the result of successful prosecution under the Sherman Act's section I, conspiring companies and individual officers received fines exceeding $1 million, and some executives were given jail sentences. Subsequently, State and local governments and privately owned utilities sued the equipment makers for damages imposed by conspiracy-raised prices. The resulting refunds reduced manufacturers' after-tax incomes in the early 1960's by more than $150 million.

---

[35] Fraas and Greer (1977, pp. 42–43) draw a similar conclusion from an analysis of 606 U.S. Department of Justice price-fixing cases from the years 1910–1972.

[36] The National Recovery Administration, which existed over the period 1933–1935, included among other policies a relaxation of antitrust constraints on trade association activities. See Section 20.3.2.

Lean *et al.* (1982) report the results of a statistical analysis of the profitability of eight of the 20 product groups involved in the conspiracies. These eight product groups accounted for some 60 per cent of sales during the conspiracy. One part of their study covers the years 1957–1959, when active conspiracy was underway, and the post-conspiracy years 1960–1970.

During this latter period, there was what appeared to be the use of a facilitating practice in the turbine-generator market. General Electric published a turbine generator price book[37] and adopted a "price-protection" policy: if it granted a discount to any customer, it would grant the same discount to all orders taken in the previous six months. General Electric published details of outstanding orders when it made these policy changes. In short order, Westinghouse imitated General Electric's price policy. The effect of the price guarantee, which was a commitment to its customers, was to raise the cost to General Electric of cutting price, since any price cut would have had to be general rather than selective. The Department of Justice later challenged the price protection policy under the antitrust laws.

Lean *et al.* find that profit rates on sales were about two percentage points higher, on average, during the years of active collusion. Profit rates for turbine generators were between seven and ten percentage points higher during the period of alleged price signalling. Increases in both seller concentration (CR2, the combined market shares of the two largest firms) and own market share both had a positive impact on profitability.[38]

Furthermore, the profit rate was significantly lower for electrical equipment products that were made to order. A good that is made to order is the extreme case of product differentiation, and this finding supports the view that product differentiation makes it more difficult to collude.

Experimental Evidence

Isaac *et al.* Isaac *et al.* (1984) report the results of experiments that explore the results of conspiracy in experimental price-setting oligopoly markets. Their focus is on posted-offer markets, but they report results for double auction markets as well.[39] The experimental markets had four buyers and four sellers, with induced demand and supply curves of the general type shown in Figure 2.12. The competitive equilibrium quantity in the experimental markets was seven units of output, the monopoly or joint-profit-maximizing output was three units of output.

During experiments that allowed for conspiracy, sellers[40] were given four-minute intervals between periods during which (Isaac *et al.*, 1984, p. 196) "they were free to discuss all aspects of the market except that (1) they could not discuss side payments or physical threats, and (2) they could not discuss quantitative information about their payoff tables".

The "side payments" restriction rules out situations in which four sellers agree that three will sell one unit each, one will sell nothing, and that the three who make sales will make a payment to the one who sits on the sidelines of the market. The prohibition on discussion

---

[37] Allen (1976, p. 51) writes that "The vendors have rather openly regarded publication of a price handbook as inter-vendor communication—during the 1950's General Electric's was admittedly copied by its rivals ... "

[38] Profitability was about 1.3 percentage points higher, all else equal, if CR2 was ten percentage points higher. Profitability was about 3 percentage points higher, all else equal, if own market share was 10 percentage points higher.

[39] Isaac and Plott (1981) also report results of double auction conspiracy experiments.

[40] Isaac *et al.* also report the results of experiments in which buyers were allowed to collude.

Figure 6.5 Posted offer No conspiracy-conspiracy experiment

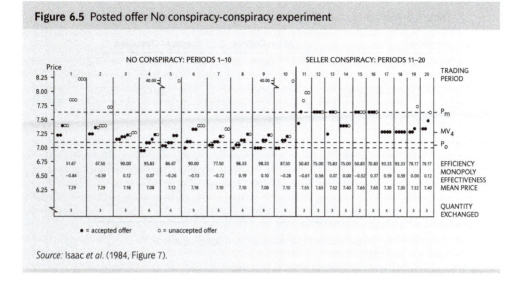

Source: Isaac *et al.* (1984, Figure 7).

of own-payoff tables matches a characteristic of many real-world markets, that firms have a better idea of their own costs than they do of the costs of rivals.

The prohibition of threats is understandable in an experiment involving human subjects. It is worth keeping in mind, however, that violence, threatened or otherwise, is not ruled out as an enforcement mechanism in real-world cartels.[41]

Offered and accepted prices for one of the Isaac *et al.* experiments are shown in Figure 6.5. The first ten columns show results for periods when seller conspiracy was not allowed, the final ten columns show results for periods when seller conspiracy was allowed. On the right side of the figure, P_m is the monopoly price and P_0 marks the range within which the competitive price should fall. $MV4$ is the price (below the monopoly or joint-profit-maximizing price) if each of the four suppliers sells one unit of output.

The first two rows at the bottom of the figure show indices of market performance. The efficiency measure, E, is the sum of actual buyer and seller earnings in the period, as a percentage of same sum at a competitive equilibrium. The monopoly value of E is 85. For colluding sellers to reach this level, they would need to restrict sales to three units and ensure that each of those units is sold by the supplier with the lowest cost.

The measure of market performance, E, takes consumer and supplier welfare—consumer surplus and economic profit—into account. The measure of monopoly effectiveness, M, focuses on performance from the supply-side point of view. M is the excess of actual over competitive profit as a fraction of the corresponding theoretical monopoly value:

$$M = \frac{\pi - \pi_c}{\pi_m - \pi_c}. \tag{6.19}$$

The third and fourth rows at the bottom of the figure show the average price per period and the number of units sold.

---

[41] Violence is, of course, illegal. But so is collusion.

Table 6.5 Average outputs, Binger *et al.* Cournot market experiments

Treatment	Mean Output	Standard Deviation
2-seller without communication	40.61	9.69
2-seller with communication	34.12	8.91
2-seller Cournot equilibrium	40.00	
5-seller without communication	51.53	7.97
5-seller with communication	37.52	11.59
5-seller Cournot equilibrium	50.00	

Note: Competitive equilibrium output is 60, joint-profit maximizing output is 30
Source: Binger *et al.* (1992, Table 1).

In the no-conspiracy periods shown in Figure 6.5, prices start high, although not as high as joint-profit-maximization would require, and drift downward. By period ten, price is within the competitive range, and the quantity sold is the competitive equilibrium quantity. Price begins to drift upward as soon as conspiracy is permitted, with either three or four units sold from period thirteen onward. Price is at the monopoly level in periods 12, 13, 15, and 16, and at or near $MV4$ in periods 17–20. Firms succeed in restricting output, but do not consistently increase profit above the Cournot level (see the figures listed for monopoly effectiveness M). Isaac *et al.* (1984, p. 320) interpret their results as showing that collusion can raise price in experimental markets, but not necessarily to the monopoly level.

Binger *et al.* Binger *et al.* (1992) examine the impact of communication and of differences in the number of sellers in experimental Cournot markets. The markets have linear demand and constant marginal cost.[42] In the sessions without communication, each seller in each period privately decided a quantity to offer for sale, and informed a monitor of the amount. The monitor totalled the quantities supplied by all sellers and determined the market-clearing price from the equation of the inverse demand curve. With price and therefore payoffs determined, the market went on to the next period.

In the sessions with communication, the procedure was similar, except that experimental subjects had the opportunity to discuss the market (Binger *et al.*, 1992, p. 10):

> They could confer for 10 minutes before the experiment began and for 5 minutes at the end of every 10th trading period. All quantity decisions were made in private and no communication of any kind was allowed between conference periods.

---

[42] The equation of the duopoly market inverse demand curve was $P = 26.48 - Q$, with constant marginal cost 2.48 per unit. The equation of the five-seller market inverse demand curve was $P = 62.41 - Q$, with constant marginal cost 2.41 per unit. For comparison purposes, the duopoly results in Table 6.5 are normalized so that competitive and monopoly outputs in both markets are the same.

Since commitments made during the conferences were not binding, the experiment is one of non-cooperative collusion in a quantity-setting market.

There were six duopoly experiments of 40 periods without communication, and six duopoly experiments of 40 periods with communication. There were two five-seller experiments of 47 periods, one with and one without communication. Table 6.5 shows average outputs for the four treatments. The average results for the no-communication treatments are strikingly close to the Cournot equilibrium values. When communication is permitted, output is below the Cournot level, although not, on average, as low as the joint-profit-maximizing level.

SUMMARY

The persistence of collusion—tacit or overt—depends on the relative increase in long-run profit from collective price increase and output restriction and the higher but shorter-run profit from striking out on one's own. Whether output restriction or short-run payoff maximization offers the greater payoff depends on market structure and the ways in which firms trade off economic profits received at different points in time.

Joint price increases and output restriction are easier to maintain where there are few suppliers with similar time horizons, where the product is standardized, and where transaction prices are transparent. Business practices that increase price transparency, and so raise the likelihood of retaliation for a discriminatory price cut, increase the stability of tacit collusion.

The history of legal cartels is that they invested resources to detect and punish defection. Illegal cartels, to the extent that we are aware of the nature of their activities, appear to have done so as well.

Cartels are subject to periodic breakdowns. But they last long enough, and raise price high enough above marginal cost, to impose significant welfare losses on society. Tacit collusion may attract excess entry and so reduce consumer surplus while frittering away economic profits as the restricted amount of output that is produced is divided among a larger number of firms.

STUDY POINTS

- trigger strategy (Section 6.2.1), collusion (Section 6.3)
- cartel stability (Section 6.4)
- cartel practices (Section 6.5)
- cartel effects (Section 6.6)
- collusion or tacit collusion and the survival of inefficient firms (Section 6.6.2)

FURTHER READING

On price wars during booms, in addition to the references in the text, see Kandori (1991). Ivaldi *et al.* (2006) survey the literature on tacit collusion. Connor (2005, pp. 13–23) is a concise and comprehensive guide to the literature on cartels. On cartel stability, see Grossman (2004) and Levenstein and Suslow (2006a). On international cartels, see Barjot (1994), Connor (2006), and on the cement industry, Dumez and Jeunemaître (2000). On interfirm communication and collusion, see Kühn (2001). Engel (2007) surveys experimental tests of collusion.

For single-period models of collusion by some but not all firms, see Selten (1973), d'Aspremont *et al.* (1983), Martin (1990), and Shaffer (1995). For a survey of the literature on multimarket contact, see Scott (2006b), and for a critical view, Thomas and Willig (2006). See Brander and Spencer (1985) for a conjectural-variations model of large-numbers collusion when entry is possible.

For more on the Renaissance-era European alum industry, see Parks (2005, Chapter 6). See Boldrin and Levine (2004, pp. 348–349) for a concise account highlighting the role of intellectual property rights in the commercial fate of Boulton & Watt. For a discussion of cartels in the early 19th-century U.S. Midwest, see Hunter (1970). Belcher (1904) discusses the mechanics of pools in the late 19th- and early 20th-century U.S. Briggs (1989) gives a concise account of the Joint Executive Committee. For accounts of the much-studied electrical equipment conspiracies, see Smith (1961), Walton and Cleveland (1964), or Baker and Faulkner (1993). On trade associations and collusion in the U.S., see Macrosty (1907), and on the UK Restrictive Trade Practices Act, see Stevens and Yamey (1965), Broadberry and Crafts (2001). Brusse and Griffiths (1997b) survey post-World War II European cartels.

PROBLEM

6–1 Suppose that a market has the linear inverse demand curve:

$$p = 100 - Q \qquad (6.20)$$

in every time period and that all firms have constant marginal and average variable cost 10 per unit of output,

$$C(q) = 10q. \qquad (6.21)$$

Find the trigger strategy stability condition if the market is supplied by n firms. How does the stability condition change as n increases?

DOMINANT FIRMS

7

Daniel Striped Tiger: This sandbox doesn't belong to you.

Mr. Allmine: Oh, yes it does. See here in my book. That says sandboxes so that means that sandboxes are all mine. That's my name, ALLMINE.

Mr. Roger's Neighborhood, 6 March 1974

7.1 Introduction

A monopolist is the single supplier of a market into which entry is impossible. Departing from the case of monopoly leads us to consider markets in which a leading firm interacts with actual or potential rivals. The interaction may be one-way, as in a market with a leading supplier that takes the supply decisions of a fringe of price-taking firms into account. The interaction may take place over time, as in a market where one oligopolist makes its decisions before others. The interaction may be between an incumbent and a potential rival, as in a market where a single active supplier faces the threat of entry and takes the anticipated actions of potential entrants into account.

Such markets can be scenes of *strategic behaviour*, business conduct that is profitable because of its effect on rivals, not because of its impact on consumers, and it is strategic behaviour by leading firms that is the topic of this chapter. We first discuss leadership models of oligopoly, in which one firm—by dint of understanding, timing, or commitment ability—is able to alter rivals' behaviour to its own advantage. Leadership models lead naturally to models of entry deterrence, in which the leader alters the behaviour of potential rather than actual rivals, and to models of predatory pricing and broader classes of strategic conduct by which a leader firm may induce an actual rival to leave its market.

7.2 Leadership Models

We begin with four models of markets in which one firm is able to exercise control over output and price, but subject to limitations created by the responses of other firms to its decisions. In a market with a dominant firm and a competitive fringe, one firm knows that it faces a residual demand that depends on how much fringe firms produce, and knows also that fringe firms take price as given and maximize profit. In a durable good monopoly, one firm creates its own future fringe competition: the product it sells today remains usable and can satisfy demand tomorrow, in competition with its own future output. In a quantity-leadership model, all firms are aware of their oligopolistic interdependence, but one firm understands the way other firms adjust their own output to its own, and is able to use this knowledge to its advantage. The standard model of limit pricing is a version of the quantity leadership model, with the difference that the firm with an information advantage is already active, while other firms are potential suppliers that must pay entry costs if they decide to begin production.

7.2.1 A Dominant Firm with a Competitive Fringe

Our first leadership model is of a dominant firm in a market with a fringe of price-taking firms. By adjusting its output, the leader exercises some control over price. Like all firms with market power, the extent to which the dominant firm finds it profitable to raise price is determined by the price elasticity of demand. For a dominant firm with a fringe of price-taking competitors, the price elasticity of its *residual* demand depends on consumer behaviour, as described by the market demand curve, and on fringe behaviour, as described by the fringe supply curve.

Setup

To pursue the implications of fringe behaviour for dominant firm market power, let the demand side of a market be described by the equation:

$$p = 100 - (q_D + q_F). \tag{7.1}$$

Let the market be supplied by one leader and a fringe of small firms. The leader has constant marginal cost 10 per unit of output. It would be able to supply the entire quantity demanded at a price equal to its marginal cost. It knows the market demand equation.

The leader also understands that fringe firms take price as given and maximize their own profits—each fringe firm produces a quantity that makes its marginal cost equal to price. The aggregate supply curve of the fringe is found by adding up the quantities that would be supplied by each fringe firm at different prices. For this example, suppose that this adding-up exercise yields a fringe supply that is positive and increasing in price for prices greater than 10, and zero otherwise:

$$q_F = \begin{cases} 2(p - 10) & p \geq 10 \\ 0 & 0 \leq p \leq 10 \end{cases}. \tag{7.2}$$

The fringe supply curve is drawn as the dotted line in Figure 7.1.

Residual demand

Substituting the fringe supply equation (7.2) into the market inverse demand equation (7.1) and rearranging terms gives the equation of the dominant firm's residual inverse demand curve,

$$p = 40 - \frac{1}{3}q_D. \tag{7.3}$$

If the leader restricts output, price rises and the quantity supplied by the fringe increases. If fringe supply were fixed while the leader produced 1 less unit of output, price would rise

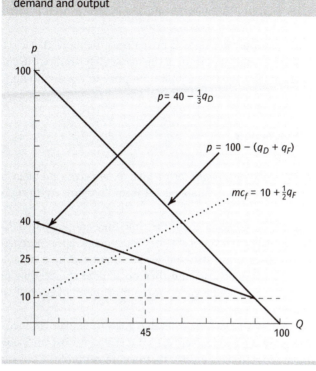

Figure 7.1 Dominant firm with a price-taking fringe: residual demand and output

by 1 (equation (7.1)). But for every unit of output less that the leader produces, fringe supply increases by two-thirds.[1] The net increase in price if the leader reduces output by 1 unit is only one-third (equation (7.3)).

In terms of Figure 7.1, the dominant firm's residual demand curve is drawn by subtracting the quantity supplied by the fringe at any price from the quantity demanded at that price. Residual demand is zero where the fringe supply curve intersects the demand curve (60, 40)—at this price, the fringe supplies the entire quantity demanded. Residual demand equals market demand at the price where fringe supply is zero—for the fringe supply equation (7.2), when $p = 10$. With linear market demand and linear fringe supply, the residual demand curve is also linear, and is the straight line connecting the two points (0, 10) and (60, 40).

Leadership output

The dominant firm maximizes profit by producing the output that makes its marginal revenue,

$$MR = 40 - \frac{2}{3}q_D, \tag{7.4}$$

equal to its marginal cost, 10. The marginal revenue curve is omitted from Figure 7.1 to avoid visual clutter, but setting marginal revenue from (7.4) equal to 10 and solving the resulting equation for q_D gives the dominant firm's profit-maximizing output, 45. The output level

---

[1] Subsitute (7.3) into (7.2) to express fringe supply as a function of dominant firm output, $q_F = 60 - \frac{2}{3}q_D$.

a profit-maximizing monopolist would choose is also 45. But with a competitive fringe the resulting price is 25, not the monopoly price, 55. If price is 25, fringe supply is 30 (equation (7.2)), making the total quantity supplied 75 and keeping price well below the monopoly level.

The more rapidly fringe supply increases as price rises—the more elastic is the fringe supply curve—the smaller is the residual portion of the market left over for the dominant firm at any price and the closer, all else equal, is equilibrium price to the dominant firm's marginal cost.

7.2.2 Durable Goods Monopoly

The commitment problem

Coase (1972a) suggests that the *commitment* or *time inconsistency* problem may prevent a monopolist producer of a consumer durable good from charging anything other than the competitive price.

Buyers consume perishable goods at about the time they are purchased. Consumers of a perishable good return quickly to the market—they must make repeat purchases to continue consuming the product. In contrast, it is the services rendered by a durable good (a car, a software package) that consumers use, and they do so over the lifetime of the product. Consumers of the services of a durable good drop out of the market until what they have purchased must be replaced.

Suppose that a monopolist brings a new durable good to market. To focus on the issues posed by durability, suppose the good never wears out and never becomes obsolete.

To begin with, the monopolist sets a price that maximizes profit. Consumers with sufficiently high reservation values buy the good and leave the market. But if consumers with high reservation prices have dropped out of the market, it is profitable for the monopolist to lower price and sell to a second tranche of consumers, those willing to pay more than the marginal cost of production but less than the first-round monopoly price. In principle, this process might repeat itself, with a sequence of price reductions that allows the durable-good monopolist to squeeze more and more economic profit out of the market.

But if consumers with high reservation prices anticipate that price will decline, and if price changes would be frequent, patient consumers will delay purchasing the durable good early on, even if they have high reservation prices. In effect, if the durable good monopolist cannot commit to holding price up over time, the price it can realize on current sales is reduced because of the competition its early sales face from its own later sales.

The commitment problem cannot be neutralized by simply announcing a policy of no future price reductions. This is the *time inconsistency* aspect of the phenomenon: the interests of the monopolist at any future point in time are inconsistent with the interests of the monopolist over all time. If the durable good monopolist announces today that it will not lower price a year from now, but cannot commit to holding price up, far-sighted current consumers will expect that a year from now, the monopolist will do what is in its best interest *at that time*. The *Coase Conjecture* is that in the absence of commitment mechanisms, a durable-good monopolist will be obliged to set a price equal to marginal cost.[2]

---

[2] At the end of June 2007, Apple, Inc. placed its new iPhone, a durable good, on the market at a price of $599. Ten weeks later it reduced the price to $399, unleashing a wave of outrage from first-round buyers ("Price cut on iPhone angers some users", Associated Press, 6 September 2007) and an eventual Apple decision to offer rebates in

Resolutions

Coase suggests a number of ways to resolve the commitment problem. A durable-good monopolist might agree to buy back any units of output that it sells, at the price at which they were originally sold. Such a buy-back policy would protect early purchasers against suffering capital losses if the monopolist lowers the price of the good after they buy. It would also reduce the incentive of the monopolist to lower prices, since price reductions would oblige it to repurchase previously sold units at the higher price. Alternatively, the monopolist could lease rather than sell the product. Or the monopolist could change the design of its product to make it less durable—the time between successive editions of university textbooks seems to fall over time, and one consequence is to kill the secondhand market.[3]

As suggested by Waldman (2003, pp. 134–135), the *Coase Conjecture* is important for two reasons. It directs attention to "a variety of contractual provisions that allow firms to avoid the time inconsistency problem." It alerts us to time inconsistency in markets that do not involve durable goods.

Secondhand markets

The other side of the durable goods monopoly coin is that early purchasers may resell their units of the durable good, if they find it profitable to do so. What Judge Learned Hand wrote of a firm with a patent-based monopoly applies to producers of durable goods as well (148 F.2d 416 at 425):

> The monopolist cannot prevent those to whom he sells from reselling at whatever prices they please. ... Nor can he prevent their reconditioning articles worn by use ... At any moment his control over the market will therefore be limited by that part of what he has formerly sold, which the price he now charges may bring upon the market, as second hand or reclaimed articles.

The commitment problem arises when a durable good producer's present sales compete with its own future sales. If there is a secondhand market, a durable good producer's present sales compete with its own past sales.

Before World War II, Alcoa (the Aluminum Company of America) was the only U.S. producer of aluminum ingot from ore. Alcoa's dominant market position originated with a patent-based monopoly. After patent protection ended, Alcoa sustained its market position by its control of high-quality bauxite deposits and other conduct to be described presently.[4] Alcoa's primary aluminum production faced marginal competition from imported primary aluminum and from U.S. firms that recycled aluminum scrap into secondary aluminum.

---

the amount of the price reduction to those who had purchased within two weeks of the lower price and credits of \$100 to earlier purchasers (Robertson, 2007). This episode suggests that consumers are often not as prescient or as patient as presumed by Coase's analysis. But it also suggests that consumer reaction to intertemporal price discrimination is something that even a monopoly supplier ignores at its own peril.

[3] These practices may of course serve purposes other than dealing with the commitment problem. A lease-only policy prevents the development of a secondhand market that would compete, to some extent, with new durables (see below). Staggered long-term leases leave only a fraction of the market potentially available for an entrant at any point in time, and may raise the cost of entry. Textbooks must be kept up to date.

[4] Control of bauxite deposits and restrictive contracts with electric power generators may (Krattenmaker and Salop, 1986, pp. 236–238) or may not (Lopatka and Godek, 1992) have been an example of strategically raising rivals' costs (see Section 7.4).

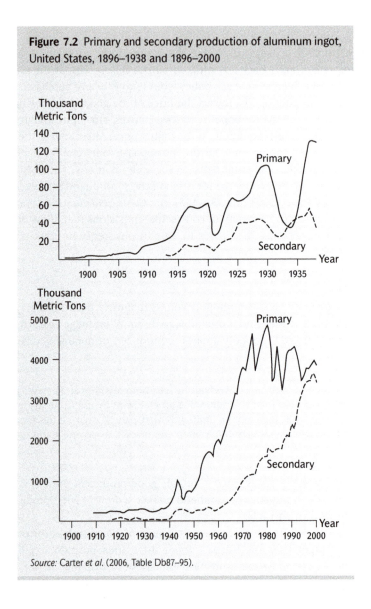

Figure 7.2 Primary and secondary production of aluminum ingot, United States, 1896–1938 and 1896–2000

Source: Carter *et al.* (2006, Table Db87–95).

As shown in Figure 7.2, small amounts of aluminum were sold in the United States at the end of the nineteenth century. When secondary aluminum supplies are first recorded in statistical sources, 1913, they amounted to 5 million metric tonnes per year, compared to 22 million metric tonnes output per year of primary aluminum. Since that time, secondary supply exceeded primary output once, in the depression year 1934, and approached it in 1999.

Static oligopoly models analyse the behaviour of firms that non-cooperatively maximize single-period profit. Static models are ill-suited to analyse behaviour—like that of a durable-good monopolist that by producing today creates its own future competition—with inherently intertemporal consequences. In principle, in setting the level of current output, a far-sighted durable-good producer will anticipate the extent to which future recyclers will recover its current output and return it to the market at a later date. Future lost profit will be discounted and set against current profit. A durable-goods monopolist that seeks to maximize its present-discounted value over all future time will reduce current output, all else equal, relative to the amount that would maximize current profit.

Swan (1980) estimates alternative models of dynamic, value-maximizing behaviour for the U.S. aluminum market for the years 1923–1940. He finds that secondary competition induced Alcoa to reduce its own output, but did not prevent Alcoa from exercising market power and holding price above marginal cost. His findings suggest (1980, p. 94, fn. 20) that Alcoa's markup over cost on primary aluminum, $(p-c)/c$, was 0.83. The corresponding Lerner index, $(p-c)/p$, is 0.45.

 BOX   Ignorance is Bliss (I)

The Aluminum Company of America enjoyed patent protection in its early life, but earned handsome profits even afterward, which raises a puzzle (Wallace, 1937, p. 102):

> During the last few years before expiration of the Bradley patent the Aluminum Company of America apparently received average earnings of somewhere between 30 and 40 per cent upon its total assets. The average annual rate of return seems to have been over 15 per cent in the years 1909–1911 and nearly 20 per cent in the next three years. A tariff of 9 cents per pound until 1909 and 7 cents until 1913 contributed in some measure to this record. It must have been apparent to anyone familiar with the metal industries during the decade 1905–1914 that the increasing use of this new metal was proceeding by great jumps. Here, one would think, was an inviting prospect for new capital and enterprise.

Why, Wallace asks, did entry not occur?

One factor (emphasized in U.S. v. Alcoa (1945)) was Alcoa's expansion of capacity along with, or in anticipation of, growth in demand:

> The answer seems to be found chiefly in the expansion policy, facilitated by tariff protection, upon which the Aluminum Company embarked four years before the patent expired and at the time when the upward swing of demand for the young metal began—an expansion which consisted in the purchase of a large part of the deposits of domestic bauxite economically suitable for aluminum reduction and a tremendous increase in power resources and power plant, reduction cell, and semi-fabricating capacity.

But Wallace points out that Alcoa did not engage in what later would be called limit pricing (1937, p. 113): "Price was still high in the sense that it permitted substantial elements of monopoly profit." Other factors discouraged entry.

One of these factors was ignorance on the part of potential rivals. Alcoa was privately held, and published annual financial reports only from 1926 (1937, p. 113):

> Trade gossip would have indicated that the business was quite profitable, but until some meager data were divulged in the tariff hearings of 1912–1913, the promoter would have been forced to rely upon attempts to reckon the costs of production in order to derive even an approximate guess as ≫

> ⟫ to how profitable. It might have been difficult to discover persons technically competent to perform this task. ... Furthermore, although it must have been clear that the new metal was to enjoy a large and speedy growth, it was doubtless not easy to discern with even approximate sureness how great or how rapid it would turn out to be. And since it requires several years to bring a new power plant and reduction works into operation, any degree of inability to forecast demand is a serious element.

7.2.3 Quantity Leadership

It is plausible to model a fringe of many small firms as being made up of price takers. The price taking assumption is less convincing if there are few firms in the fringe, particularly if, although smaller than the leader, they can no longer be described as small in relation to the size of the market. Once fringe firms are large enough to recognize that changes in their own output levels affect market price, they will interact with the dominant firm as oligopolists, not as price takers.

Setup

Perhaps the first model of dominant firm oligopoly is a model of duopoly in which one firm has an informational advantage over the other. The model is usually attributed to Stackelberg (1934), and it modifies just one of the assumptions of the basic Cournot duopoly model. Instead of supposing that each firm has the same kind of understanding of the conduct of the other firm, the assumptions of the Stackelberg quantity leadership duopoly model are that the follower makes its output decision as in the basic Cournot model, and the leader knows this.

"The follower makes its output decision as in the basic Cournot model" does *not* mean "Firm 2 produces its Cournot equilibrium output". It means that firm 2 produces the output that maximizes its own profit, given the output that firm 1 produces. Firm 1 knows this, and takes firm 2's anticipated output decision into account when it decides how much to produce. This leads firm 1 to produce a different output as a Stackelberg leader than it would produce as a Cournot duopolist. Firm 2's best response to firm 1's Stackelberg leader output is different from firm 2's best response to firm 1's Cournot equilibrium output. But firm 2 produces the output given by its best response function in both cases.

Follower behaviour

If we adapt the previous example to the case of two firms, then the equation of the inverse demand curve is:

$$p = 100 - (q_1 + q_2). \tag{7.5}$$

Let both firms have cost function:

$$c(q) = 10q, \tag{7.6}$$

so there is constant average and marginal cost 10 per unit of output. Then in the usual way firm 2's best response equation is:

$$q_2 = 45 - \frac{1}{2}q_1. \tag{7.7}$$

Residual demand

Stackelberg's second assumption means that the leader, firm 1, is able to work out (7.7) as the relationship between what firm 1 decides to produce and what firm 2 decides to produce.

The equation of firm 1's residual demand curve is:

$$p = (100 - q_2) - q_1. \qquad (7.8)$$

Substituting (7.7) on the right in (7.8) to eliminate q_2 and rearranging terms gives the equation of firm 1's residual demand curve,

$$p = \left[(100 - \left(45 - \frac{1}{2}q_1\right)\right] - q_1 = 55 - \frac{1}{2}q_1. \qquad (7.9)$$

(7.9) shows the market-clearing price for any quantity sold by firm 1, taking into account firm 2's profit-maximizing output choice as described by (7.7).

Leadership output

Firm 1 maximizes profit by setting marginal revenue along the residual demand curve (7.9) equal to its marginal cost, as illustrated in Figure 7.3.

$$MR_1 = 55 - 2\left(\frac{1}{2}q_1\right) = 10. \qquad (7.10)$$

$$q_{SL} = 55 - 10 = 45. \qquad (7.11)$$

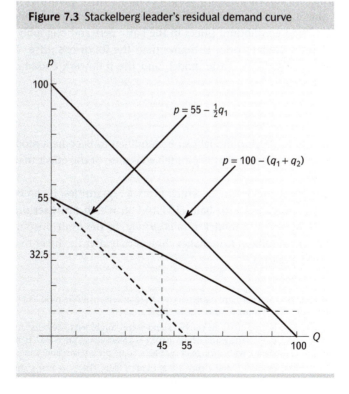

Figure 7.3 Stackelberg leader's residual demand curve

The Stackelberg quantity leader maximizes profit by producing more than its Cournot duopoly equilibrium output level.[5]

Follower output

In the Cournot model, best-response functions slope downward. Since the Stackelberg leader produces more than its Cournot duopoly equilibrium output, the Stackelberg follower produces less than its Cournot duopoly equilibrium output:

$$q_{SF} = 45 - \frac{1}{2}(45) = 22.5. \tag{7.12}$$

Aspects of equilibrium

Total output under Stackelberg leadership exceeds Cournot duopoly output:

$$45 + 22.5 = 67.5 > 60. \tag{7.13}$$

It follows that equilibrium price under Stackelberg leadership is less than Cournot duopoly price:

$$100 - 67.5 = 32.5 < 40. \tag{7.14}$$

The Stackelberg quantity leader earns greater profit than it would in Cournot duopoly equilibrium, and the Stackelberg quantity follower earns less:

$$(32.5 - 10)(45) = 1012.5 > (40 - 10)(30) = 900 \tag{7.15}$$

$$(32.5 - 10)(22.5) = 506.25 < 900. \tag{7.16}$$

These relationships are reversed if firms set prices rather than quantities (Problem 7–3). If firms set prices, the Stackelberg price leader and the Stackelberg price follower both set prices that are higher than equilibrium prices in the basic Bertrand oligopoly with product differentiation model; the leader's price is higher than the follower's price. The payoffs of both firms rise compared with the basic model, and the follower's equilibrium payoff is greater than that of the leader.[6]

7.2.4 Limit Pricing

The Stackelberg quantity leadership model can be modified to become a model of strategic entry deterrence, "business conduct that is profitable because of the effect that it has on the incentives facing rivals".

Although the resulting model is one in which firms set quantities, it can be traced to an earlier informal model, associated with Bain (1949b),[7] in which firms set prices. For that reason it is usually referred to as a model of *limit pricing*. In the limit price model, what is being limited is *entry*: an incumbent firm makes choices that alter the incentives of potential entrants to come into the market.

---

[5] With a linear demand equation and constant marginal cost, the Stackelberg leader produces the same quantity that would be produced by a monopolist in an otherwise identical market.

[6] The leadership and fringe models exposited here can be extended and combined to describe markets of different types. McCalla (1966), for example, models the world wheat market as a Stackelberg price-leadership model (Canada the leader, the United States the follower), with a fringe of suppliers, some price takers and some oligopolistic.

[7] The limit price model is more a child of Modigliani (1958) than of Bain. There are many anticipations of the limit price model, for example Marshall ([1890] 1925, p. 270) or Jones (1921, p. 277).

Setup

To develop the quantity-setting version of the entry-deterrence model, reinterpret the inverse demand equation (7.5) so that firm 1 is an incumbent, already in the market, and firm 2 is a potential entrant, a firm that will come into the market if it expects it to be profitable to do so.

Suppose that entry involves a fixed and sunk entry cost e, an investment that must be made to produce at all and which cannot be recovered by resale of assets if firm should decide to leave the market. Suppose also that if the entrant comes into the market, it operates with constant marginal and average variable cost 10 per unit (as does the incumbent, which is already in the market).

Entrant's value

If the entrant comes into the market, its single-period profit depends on the incumbent's output after entry:

$$\pi_2 = (p - 10)q_2 = (90 - q_1 - q_2)q_2. \tag{7.17}$$

The post-entry market will be a non-cooperative quantity-setting duopoly. If the entrant comes into the market at all, it will maximize profit, and the output that maximizes profit makes its residual marginal revenue equal to its marginal cost. That is, it will produce the output given by its best response equation,

$$q_2 = 45 - \frac{1}{2}q_1. \tag{7.18}$$

From the equation of the market demand curve (equivalently, from the incumbent's residual demand equation, (7.9)), if the entrant is in the market, price minus marginal cost is:

$$p - 10 = 90 - q_1 - \left(45 - \frac{1}{2}q_1\right) = 45 - \frac{1}{2}q_1. \tag{7.19}$$

Then the entrant's present-discounted value if it comes into the market is:

$$V_2 = \frac{1}{r}\left(45 - \frac{1}{2}q_1\right)^2 - e. \tag{7.20}$$

The first term on the right is the value of the entrant's profit over all future time, discounted back to the present at interest rate r. The second term on the right is the sunk entry cost that must be paid to come into the market.

Entry deterrence with output commitment

Suppose now that the incumbent can commit in advance to the output it will produce. Such a commitment would be possible if the incumbent can sign long-term contracts with buyers, contracts that oblige it to deliver specified outputs far into the future.[8] Stepping outside the specific assumptions of the model, effective commitment would be possible if the incumbent can choose a technology that makes most of its cost fixed, and therefore its marginal cost near zero, up to some capacity level. Then if it is profitable for the incumbent to produce at all, it will be profitable for the incumbent to produce at full capacity. In such a case, by picking a capacity level, the incumbent essentially commits to an output level as well.

---

[8] Modigliani's (1958, p. 217) *Sylos' postulate* is that potential entrants believe incumbents will maintain post-entry output at pre-entry levels.

Entry-deterring output   If the incumbent commits to an output level that makes the potential entrant's post-entry profit negative, the incumbent can keep the potential entrant out of the market. The entry-deterring level of output is the one that makes the potential entrant's post-entry value just equal to zero:

$$V_2 = \frac{1}{r}\left(45 - \frac{1}{2}q_1\right)^2 - e = 0 \Longrightarrow q_1 = q_L = 90 - 2\sqrt{re}. \tag{7.21}$$

Whether or not entry deterrence is the most profitable choice for the incumbent depends on the size of entry cost. We can distinguish two extreme cases.

Blocked entry   The first is the case in which entry is *blocked*,[9] so that the market is a *natural monopoly*. If entry cost is so large that the entry-deterring output is less than the monopoly output, then the incumbent can produce the monopoly output and the entrant will not find it profitable to come into the market. This occurs if:

$$q_L = 90 - 2\sqrt{re} \le 45, \text{ which requires } e \ge \frac{1}{r}(22.5)^2 = \frac{506.25}{r}, \tag{7.22}$$

Contestable market   At the other extreme, suppose entry is costless, $e = 0$. This is the *contestable market* of Section 3.3.2. Then to deter entry, the incumbent would need to commit to producing the output that would be produced in the long-run equilibrium of a perfectly competitive market,

$$q_L = 90. \tag{7.23}$$

This follows from (7.21) if $e = 0$. If the incumbent is committed to producing an output level that would make price equal to marginal cost, then if the second firm were to sell anything at all, price would be below marginal cost and both firms would lose money.[10]

In-between   Between these two extreme cases, if the incumbent commits to producing slightly more than the limit output, the entrant will stay out of the market. Price will be slightly less than:

$$p_L = 100 - q_L = 100 - (90 - 2\sqrt{re}) = 10 + 2\sqrt{re}. \tag{7.24}$$

The entry-limiting price p_L is higher, the greater are entry costs.

If entry is neither blocked nor costless, but something in between, the incumbent's limit profit per period if it commits to the entry-deterring output level is:

$$\pi_L = (p_L - 10)q_L = 2\sqrt{re}\,(90 - 2\sqrt{re}). \tag{7.25}$$

The incumbent's present discounted value if it deters entry is:

$$V_L = \frac{2\sqrt{re}\,(90 - 2\sqrt{re})}{r} = 2\sqrt{\frac{e}{r}}\,(90 - 2\sqrt{re}) = 180\sqrt{\frac{e}{r}} - 4e. \tag{7.26}$$

---

[9] Bain refers to this as blockaded entry, and his usage has passed into the literature. It suggests that the incumbent is doing something with the specific purpose of keeping the potential entrant out of the market, just as naval forces blockade a port. But for sufficiently large values of sunk entry cost e, no action by the incumbent is required to render entry unprofitable. It simply *is* unprofitable for one more firm to come into the market, given non-cooperative and non-strategic conduct on the parts of the firms (here, firm) already in the market.

[10] If the potential entrant had a higher unit cost than the incumbent, the incumbent could price just below the entrant's average cost and maintain its single-supplier status indefinitely. See Section 2.3.5.

Incumbent's choice   For the incumbent, the alternative to committing to an entry-deterring output level is to let the entrant into the market and to compete as a (say) Cournot duopolist. The incumbent's Cournot duopoly profit per period would be 900.

If $r = 1/10$, the incumbent's Cournot duopoly value is 9000. If entry cost is 350 and the interest rate used to discount future income is $r = 1/10$, the entry-deterring output level is:

$$q_L = 90 - 2\sqrt{35} = 78.17. \tag{7.27}$$

The incumbent's value if it deters entry is:

$$\frac{2\sqrt{35}\left(90 - 2\sqrt{35}\right)}{1/10} = 9248.9, \tag{7.28}$$

which is greater than the incumbent's Cournot value. For this entry cost and interest rate, the incumbent's value-maximizing option is to expand output and deter entry.

On the other hand, if entry cost is 300, the entry-deterring output level is:

$$q_L = 90 - 2\sqrt{30} = 79.046. \tag{7.29}$$

The incumbent's value as an entry-deterring single supplier,

$$\frac{2\sqrt{30}\left(90 - 2\sqrt{30}\right)}{1/10} = 8659, \tag{7.30}$$

is less than its value as a Cournot duopolist. For this lower value of entry cost, the incumbent's value-maximizing option is to accommodate entry. If entry cost is sufficiently low, it is not in the incumbent's own self-interest to deter entry. Some monopolies are not worth having.

Entry deterrence with imperfect information about the incumbent[11]

If there is complete and perfect information and if the incumbent firm cannot commit in advance to producing a specific output level, then the entry decision ought to depend on the entrant's post-entry equilibrium profit, not on what it sees the incumbent doing before entry. If the entrant knows that firms will compete in quantities in the post-entry market, then it should make its decision based on its anticipated Cournot equilibrium profit.

But this conclusion depends on the entrant being able to work out what its post-entry profit will be. If the entrant is uncertain about the kind of incumbent it will face, or the kind of market it considers entering (about the level of demand or the extent of product differentiation, for example), an incumbent's actions may deter entry.

To illustrate this, suppose that entry cost $e = 8000$, that the interest rate $r = 1/10$, that the entrant's marginal cost is 10 per unit, and that there are two possibilities for the incumbent's unit cost.

High-cost incumbent   The first possibility is that the incumbent's unit cost is also 10 per unit. Then if the entrant comes into the market, the post-entry market is a Cournot duopoly in which the two firms have identical marginal costs. We know from previous discussions of this example that each firm's equilibrium output is 30 units, that equilibrium price is 40, and that the entrant's present discounted value if it comes into the market is:

$$V_2(10, 10) = \frac{1}{r}\pi_2(10, 10) - e = 10(900) - 8000 = 1000 > 0. \tag{7.31}$$

---

[11] This section is based on Milgrom and Roberts (1982).

A profit-maximizing potential entrant that is certain the incumbent's unit cost is 10 will enter.

Low-cost incumbent   The second possibility is that the incumbent's unit cost is 1. The post-entry market is a Cournot duopoly with unequal unit costs. Equilibrium outputs and price are:[12]

$$q_1 = 36 \qquad q_2 = 27 \qquad p = 100 - (36 + 27) = 37. \tag{7.32}$$

Firm 2's value if it enters is negative:

$$V_2(1, 10) = \frac{1}{r}\pi_2(1, 10) - e = 10(37 - 10)(27) - 8000 = -710 < 0. \tag{7.33}$$

A profit-maximizing potential entrant that is certain the incumbent's unit cost is 1 will not enter.

High-cost incumbent's options
Reveal its cost type   Now suppose that the incumbent has marginal cost 10 per unit, but the entrant does not know this. The entrant only knows that the incumbent's marginal cost could be 1 or could be 10.

The incumbent is a monopolist in the pre-entry period. If it produces the monopoly output of a firm with constant marginal cost 10 per unit,

$$q_m(10) = 45, \tag{7.34}$$

price is

$$p_m(10) = 55 \tag{7.35}$$

and its profit is the profit of a monopolist that has a marginal cost 10 per unit and acts as if it has a marginal cost 10 per unit,

$$\pi_m(10, 10) = (55 - 10)(45) = 2025. \tag{7.36}$$

A low-cost incumbent would have no reason to produce output $q_m(10) = 45$: to do so would mean giving up profit in the short run and also misleading the potential entrant into the belief that entry would be profitable. Thus, if the entrant observes a pre-entry output $q_m(10)$, the entrant should realize that the incumbent's marginal cost is 10. The potential entrant would come into the market. After entry, the incumbent would earn Cournot duopoly profit 900 per period.

The incumbent's present discounted value if it reveals its cost and entry occurs in the next period is:[13]

$$\begin{aligned} V_1(10, 10) &= \frac{1}{1+r}(2025) + \frac{1}{(1+r)^2}(900) + \frac{1}{(1+r)^3}(900) + \dots \\ &= \frac{1}{1+r}(2025 - 900) + 900\left[\frac{1}{1+r} + \frac{1}{(1+r)^2} + \frac{1}{(1+r)^3} + \dots\right] \\ &= \frac{1125}{1+r} + \frac{900}{r}. \end{aligned} \tag{7.37}$$

---

[12] The equations of the best response functions are (incumbent) $2q_1 + q_2 = 99$ and (entrant) $q_1 + 2q_2 = 90$. These may be solved to find equilibrium outputs.

[13] For $r = 1/10$, $V_1(10, 10) = 10022\frac{8}{11}$.

Mask its cost type Suppose now that instead of producing 45 units of output in the first period, thus revealing the nature of its marginal cost, the high-cost incumbent mimics a low-cost incumbent and produces the monopoly output of a firm that has marginal cost 1 per unit,

$$q_m(1) = \frac{1}{2}(100 - 1) = 49.5. \tag{7.38}$$

Price is then $100 - 49.5 = 50.5$. The incumbent gives up some profit if it has high cost but produces the profit-maximizing output of a low-cost firm:

$$\pi_m(10, 1) = (50.5 - 10)(49.5) = 2004.75 < 2025 = \pi_m(10, 10). \tag{7.39}$$

But by strategically deviating from the single-period profit-maximizing output, the incumbent keeps the potential entrant in the dark about its cost type. It might have low cost, it might have high cost—the potential entrant gains no information by observing pre-entry output.

Bottom line Whether or not the potential entrant would stay out of the market depends on its beliefs about the incumbent's cost level.[14] If the potential entrant stays out of the market and the incumbent continues to masquerade as a low-cost firm, the incumbent's present discounted value can be greater than its value if it reveals its unit cost, (7.37), depending on the potential entrant's beliefs and on the interest rate used to discount future income.[15] The entrant's uncertainty about the kind of incumbent it faces may make it profitable for the incumbent to expand output and deter entry.

---

[14] Let λ, a number between 0 and 1, be the entrant's prior (before observing the incumbent's output) probability that the incumbent has low unit cost. Then $1 - \lambda$ is the entrant's prior probability that the incumbent has high unit cost. If the entrant learns nothing by observing the incumbent's output, the entrant's expected post-entry value is

$$\lambda(-710) + (1 - \lambda)(1000) = 1000 - 1710\lambda.$$

The entrant's expected profit is positive for $\lambda < 1000/1710 = 0.59$. If the entrant maximizes expected profit, it will come into the market for $\lambda < 0.59$, otherwise not.

[15] Continuing fn. 14, if the incumbent produces 49.5 units of output, one of two things happens. The entrant stays out, with probability λ (the entrant's probability that the incumbent has low cost), and then the incumbent's value is $2004.75/r$. Alternatively with probability $1 - \lambda$ the entrant comes into the market, and then the incumbent's value is:

$$\frac{1}{1+r}(2004.75) + \frac{1}{(1+r)^2}(900) + \frac{1}{(1+r)^3}(900) + \cdots = \frac{1104.75}{1+r} + \frac{900}{r}.$$

For $r = 1/10$, this is $10004\frac{7}{22}$.

The high-cost incumbent's expected value from masquerading as a low-cost incumbent is:

$$\lambda\frac{2004.75}{r} + (1 - \lambda)\left(\frac{1104.75}{1+r} + \frac{900}{r}\right) = \lambda\frac{4419}{4r(1+r)} + \frac{1104.75}{1+r} + \frac{900}{r}.$$

The high-cost incumbent's value if it reveals its costs to be high is given by (7.37). The difference between the incumbent's value if it hides and if it reveals its cost type is:

$$\lambda\frac{4419}{4r(1+r)} + \frac{4419}{4(1+r)} + \frac{900}{r} - \left(\frac{1125}{1+r} + \frac{900}{r}\right) = \frac{4419}{4r(1+r)}\left(\lambda - \frac{81r}{4419}\right).$$

This is positive for $\lambda > \frac{81r}{4419}$, and rises with λ. The more likely the potential entrant thinks it is that the incumbent has low cost, the greater the payoff to a high-cost incumbent from acting as if it has low cost. If $\lambda = 0$, so that the potential entrant is certain the incumbent has high cost, then the entrant will come in to the market, and the incumbent would not gain by pretending that it has high cost.

If the incumbent does expand output and deter entry, market performance is better—greater output, lower price, less deadweight welfare loss—than it would be if entry were blocked. In general, market performance if the incumbent deters entry will be worse than it would be with entry.

7.2.5 Dynamic Limit Pricing

The models of entry-deterring behaviour developed to this point make entry an all-or-nothing phenomenon. Entry either occurs, or it does not. If entry occurs, the entrant maximizes profit (value) according to its information and technology, but is not different from incumbents merely because it is new to the market.

Entry is often merely the first stage in an extended growth process. This process may result in finding and filling a niche in the market, ultimately joining leading firms in the oligopolistic core. It may result in dithering about and ultimately exiting the market. Gaskins (1971) models entry-limiting behaviour in markets where fringe expansion is more rapid, the larger the price-cost margin set by a leading firm. This is plausible if, for example, markets for financial capital are imperfect and fringe firms must finance expansion from retained earnings. Then greater price-cost margins imply that fringe firms have a greater cash flow and are able to expand more rapidly, all else equal.

In such a market, the value-maximizing strategy for the leading firm is to initially set a high price-cost margin, but below the static monopoly level. A high price-cost margin attracts some fringe entry and expansion. As time goes by, the leading firm lowers its price, continuing to give up market share to the fringe, but at a rate that declines over time. Eventually, the leading firm or oligopolistic group loses its commanding position, and oligopolistic interaction takes on a rivalry-among-equals flavour.

The dynamic limit pricing model may well describe the development of the United States' steel and car industries, with in the former industry the United States Steel Corporation the dominant firm that slowly gave up market share (Yamawaki, 1985) and in the latter industry the Big Three U.S. car manufacturers (General Motors, Ford, and Chrysler) giving up market share and collective leadership to foreign suppliers.

 BOX   Dynamic Limit Pricing

The patents for xerographic copying were granted in the 1940s. The firm that is now the Xerox Corporation introduced its 914 office copier in 1959. Xerox copiers competed with electrofax copying at the low-volume end of the market, with thermographic copying for medium-volume copying, and with offset duplicating for high-volume copying.

Xerography had higher fixed cost (a more complex machine) and lower variable cost (ordinary rather than specially treated paper) than electrofax. It also had a quality advantage *vis-à-vis* electrofax.

Xerox Corp. first entered the market for low- and medium-volume copying. It priced relatively high, apparently near the short-run monopoly price. This allowed it to raise funds that it used to finance the expansion of its network of service centres and to enter the high-volume copying market, which it did in 1965. »

>> Taking account of the quality differential, in medium- and high-volume copying Xerox priced above the unit cost of competing processes, making some entry profitable, but below the short-run profit-maximizing price. It gave up market share to other processes, with 25 electrofax firms entering the low-volume copying submarket before 1968, ten entering the medium-volume copying submarket, and three (through 1967) entering the high-volume copying submarket. Thus (Blackstone, 1972, p. 62):

> Xerox, utilizing its market power derived from patents ... has entered each segment, charged a price which attracted entry ... , then lowered its prices after the expected entry had reduced its demand curve. ... In the process, it has allowed itself to be supplanted to a considerable extent in low- and medium-volume copying ... Xerox gradually moved into the high- and very-high-volume segment, where in 1968 it was dominant, obtaining approximately 75 percent of the combined high- and very-high-volume segment's revenue.

Source: Blackstone (1972).

7.2.6 The Persistence of Leadership?

Some of the dominant firms formed during the wave of consolidation that swept U.S. industry at the turn of the nineteenth century endured. Some went into the kind of long decline typified by United States Steel. Some, vastly overcapitalized in markets where size conveyed no advantage and without distinctive assets that might deter entry, simply collapsed of their own weight.[16] The first generation of economists who looked back on the fate of these firms took dominance to be ephemeral (Burns, 1936, p. 142): "It appears to be the common fate of leaders to suffer a decline in their proportion of the total business in the market." Worcester (1957) argued that the dominant firm industry is a transitional form of market structure. In this view, a once-dominant firm may eventually find itself the *barometric price leader* in an oligopolistic group of firms (without or with a fringe of price-taking rivals). In contrast to dominant firm leadership, which is a manifestation of partial monopoly (Nichol, 1930), barometric price leadership is a creature of oligopoly. The barometric price leader—often but by no means always the largest firm—posts prices that serve as an industry focal point and facilitate tacit collusion. An ex-dominant firm may find itself a follower of some other barometric leader. Or the number of roughly equally sized rivals may become so large that the industry becomes one of monopolistic or of effective competition. But, in this view, the dominant firm market structure will evolve into some more rivalrous form.

U.S. firms

Caves *et al.* (1984) find support for dynamic limit pricing model in the profitability and market share loss of 34 once-dominant firms formed during United States First Merger Wave at the turn of the nineteenth century.[17] They find that leading firms enjoyed higher profitability, all else equal, in markets where minimum efficient scale was large relative to market size and the greater the firm's initial market share. Dominant firms gave up market share over time, as predicted by the dynamic limit pricing model, but they gave up market share more

---

[16] See, for example, Navin and Sears' (1954) discussion of the International Mercantile Marine Company.

[17] Edwards (1975) argues that the dominance of firms with leading positions in the early 1920s tended to persist.

slowly, the greater the absolute capital investment required to create an efficient-scale plant. Thus barriers to entry seem to protect profit and slow the rate at which a dominant firm will let its market share decline as it maximizes present-discounted value.

 BOX   Price Leadership

Dominant Firm Price Leadership (Stigler, 1947, p. 444):

> In the one sense [price leadership] refers to a dominant firm that sets the price, allows the minor firms to sell what they wish at this price (subject perhaps to nonprice competition), and supplies the remainder of the quantity demanded.

Barometric Price Leadership (Stigler, 1947, pp. 444–445, pp. 445–446):

> In the other sense, price leadership refers to the existence of a firm that conventionally first announces price changes that are usually followed by the remainder of the industry, even though this firm may not occupy a dominant position. . . .
>   . . . The second type of leader, the barometric firm, commands adherence of rivals to his price only because, and to the extent that, his price reflects market conditions with tolerable promptness.

Price Leadership in Lieu of Overt Agreement (Markham, 1951, p. 901*)

> In industries which possess certain specific features

- supplied by a few large firms, aware of mutual oligopolistic interdependence
- costly entry
- product varieties are close substitutes
- relatively inelastic market demand
- firms have similar cost curves

> price leadership may conceivably be so effective as to serve all the ends of a strong trade association or of a closely knit domestic cartel and, hence, in a political environment where overt collusion is illegal, may be the only feasible means of assuring parallel action among sellers.

* The bullet points are made by Markham in other words on pages 901–903; the words immediately before and after the bullet points are exact quotations, and are parts of a single paragraph.

World firms

Hannah (1999) finds that the 100 largest firms in the world in 1912 held a precarious grip on market leadership (Table 7.1): just more than half survived in any form in 1995; just short of 20 per cent were then among the world's 100 largest firms.[18] Although Hannah's results are consistent with dynamic limit pricing, he is not keen on that interpretation (1999, p. 261):[19]

---

[18] For the firms that disappeared, one might take the view that a lifetime of up to 83 years is a long run. Further, Hannah's topic, although closely related to dominance, is different: a firm may be dominant in its market without being one of the world's 100 largest firms (indeed, a firm may be one of the world's 100 largest firms without being dominant in its market).

[19] Hannah later (1999, p. 269) argues essentially that declining dominant firms may have gone into merger for lack of any better option: "The most promising solution for such firms may have been the absorption into other

Table 7.1 Summary measures of long-run performance of the hundred largest firms of 1912 by 1995

Outcome	Probability of Outcome (%)
Survives in top hundred	19
Survives and larger in 1995 than in 1912	28
Experiences bankruptcy or similar	29
Larger in 1995 or on earlier exit than in 1912	35
Survives in any independent form	52
Disappears	48

Source: Hannah (1999).

Casual inspection of the business histories of the declining firms in this population suggests that planned decline was rarely their explicit objective, though it may have been implicit in their muddled reactions. . . . the general impression in these companies' histories is of depressed profits desperately used by managements to paper over the cracks of declining capabilities, not of generosity to stockholders during a preplanned yielding to competitors of market share they could not have expected to keep.

Decline occurs, he concludes, but is not inevitable (1999, p. 270, emphasis in original): "Dynamic economies—of which the global economy in which most of these firms in varying degrees operated is the largest case—indeed consist of rising and declining industries, but businesses can develop and sustain competitive advantages in *either* kind of industry." Dominant positions persist, he suggests (1999, p. 271) where the dominant firm possesses some intrinsic, inimitable capability. But, he also suggests, it is inherent in the nature of such assets that they can be observed, if at all, only with great difficulty: if it were straightforward to diagnose the firm characteristics that produce dominant positions, rivals would imitate those characteristics, and dominance would decline.

Japanese Firms

Sutton (1999) compares observed changes of market shares of leading firms in 45 Japanese industries over a 23-year period from the mid 1970s with the changes that would be expected if shifts in market share were independently random, with no systematic tendency for dominance to persist and no systematic forces tending to erode leading positions. He classifies the industries in his sample into two groups, one in which the random changes model does a good job matching observed changes, and one in which leading positions seem to persist.

---

firms that many of them suffered, presumably to maximize the value of what few transferable skills they still embodied." It is possible that the decline of many firms, consistent with dynamic limit pricing was not intentional generosity to stockholders, but rather "the most promising", although unpalatable, option to maximize value.

Like Hannah, Sutton is cautious about general explanations that explain which industries fall in which groups. Oligopolistic interactions can be modelled, industry by industry, but the way a general model will play out in any particular industry is likely to depend on industry-specific characteristics that may not be observable at all (firms' beliefs about the way rivals will react). General patterns may be discerned in broad cross-sections of industries; explanations for the observed patterns should be sought in narrow cross-sections of similar industries, or in studies of firms within the same industry.

Resumé

The evidence suggests that dominant firms may, but need not, decline. If dominant positions shrink over time, it may be because that is the dominant firm's value-maximizing position. It may be because rivals imitate (or surpass) the dominant firm. Whether dominance disappears, and if so, at what rate, will depend on oligopolistic interactions that can be modelled. The possibility that dominance will not decline is inherent in oligopolistic interactions. If a dominant firm can commit to a strategy that deters entry, it may retain its dominant position indefinitely. If it can adapt such strategies to expel rivals, it may transform itself into, if not a monopolist in a strict sense, at least a single supplier facing the possibility of entry. In such cases, a dominant firm market structure will evolve into some less competitive form (Geroski and Jacquemin, 1984). It is to the consideration of such strategies that we now turn.

7.3 Predation

7.3.1 Predation in "As If" Perfectly Competitive Markets?

Standard Oil

The classic model of predatory pricing is associated with the rise of the Standard Oil Company in the United States at the end of the 19th century.[20] It considers a leading firm that operates in many geographic or product markets, in some of which it faces rivalry from lesser competitors. Sustained by the economic profit from its overall operations, it is able to sequentially target individual submarkets, cutting price below rivals' average cost and forcing them to exit. It may suffer short-run losses itself, in the target market, but after the predatory campaign succeeds, it is able to raise price to the unconstrained (by fringe competition or the threat of entry) monopoly level, recoup its losses, and (if need be) repeat its predatory tactics elsewhere.

Good approximation

Recall the methodological position of the Second Chicago School that most markets, most often, can be modelled as if they are perfectly competitive. Arguments associated with McGee (1958, 1980) and Telser (1965, 1966) suggest that if the model of perfect competition is applied, predation is not a rational value-maximizing strategy for a leading firm.

---

[20] McGee (1958) argues that there is no convincing evidence of predatory pricing in the records of the 1911 landmark antitrust decision that resulted in the breakup of Standard Oil. This reading of the trial record has been called into question (Dalton and Esposito, 2007). In any case, following Posner (1976b, p. 186), "that a practice is not discovered by the lawyers for a party to a lawsuit is not always compelling evidence that the practice did not occur". It now appears that predation was one factor, but only one, in Standard Oil's rise. See Section 21.2.1.

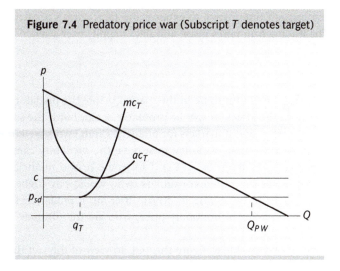

Figure 7.4 Predatory price war (Subscript *T* denotes target)

Predatory campaign

This analysis can be presented using Figure 7.4. It shows cost curves and the demand curve for a market that is supplied by a dominant firm (constant marginal and average cost c per unit of output) and a fringe firm with $\cup$-shaped average and marginal cost curves.[21] To avoid visual clutter, the fringe firm's average variable cost curve is not shown in Figure 7.4, but p_{sd} is the fringe firm's shutdown price, the minimum value of its average variable cost. At price p_{sd}, the fringe firm's losses equal its fixed cost; its (negative) "profit" is the same whether it produces output q_T or shuts down. For lower prices, it minimizes losses by going out of business.

If the leading firm is accommodating, both firms make a profit.[22] Suppose instead the dominant firm cuts price to p_{sd}. Then the small firm loses its fixed cost, every time period, until it exits.

The quantity demanded at price p_{sd} is Q_{PW}. In order to make the predatory price stick, the dominant firm must sell a quantity:

$$Q_{PW} - q_T, \tag{7.40}$$

per time period, q_T being the per-period output of the target firm as long as it continues to operate.

The predatory price p_{sd} is less than the leading firm's unit cost (c), so the leading firm loses money during the price war. In fact, the leading firm's losses are greater than those of the

---

[21] Why, one may ask, do the two firms have different types of cost functions? The dominant firm may be a multiplant firm, able to produce in factories located in other regions and "import" into the target geographic submarket at constant marginal cost. It may be part of a larger industrial group and have access to financial resources that the small firm does not.

[22] "Accommodation" may mean that the rival is a price taker and the leading firm maximizes profit along its residual demand curve; it may mean that the two firms play a Cournot game or a Stackelberg leader-follower game. For purposes of the present discussion, any non-predation scenario that does not involve economic losses for the small firm qualifies as "accommodation".

target firm. But after enough time passes to exhaust the target firm's financial resources, it exits the market. The leading firm raises price, and lives happily ever after.

To the rescue

Or does it?

It was profitable for the small firm to be in the market before the predatory campaign. If the target firm can survive the attack, it will be profitable again. But if the small firm has a profitable future in the market, and if markets for financial capital work well, then the small firm should be able to borrow enough money to survive the predatory campaign (Stigler, 1967, p. 298). Alternatively, (Easterbrook, 1981) if for some reason financial markets will not lend money to the target firm, then consumers (who would pay higher prices in the post-predation period) ought to be willing to do so. After all, if predation is successful, it is consumers, who end up paying a monopoly price, who are the ultimate victims of the predatory campaign.

The dominant firm should be able to figure this out. In view of the fact that a predatory campaign could never succeed, such a campaign would involve avoidable short-run economic losses, with no prospect of eventual economic profits. Thus, it would never be tried.

Re-entry

Further, recall the limit price model. If there are no (or low) entry costs, the incumbent would face the possibility of entry after a successful predatory campaign. It might even face the prospect of re-entry by the target firm. Once again, this would eliminate any prospect of post-predation profits, so a value-maximizing leading firm would not engage in predation in the first place.

Finally, suppose there is imperfect information in capital markets, that customers are short-sighted, and that there are sufficient entry or re-entry costs that a predatory campaign would be profitable. Then there are at least two alternatives that are likely to be more profitable. First, the two firms could collude, sharing monopoly profit. Second, if the return to be had from collusion is not sufficient for the dominant firm, it could simply buy the target firm. That way the incumbent firm could begin earning economic profit right away, rather than waiting until the end of a costly price war.

On these grounds, Chicago-school economists were sceptical about the possibility that predatory behaviour could occur as an equilibrium phenomenon.

7.3.2 Episodes of Predation

Shipping conferences

Mogul Steamship   The landmark British *Mogul Steamship* case,[23] involved a conference of shipping liners that engaged in collusive predation against a firm outside the conference. The members of the shipping conference aimed to control traffic in tea from southeast China ports to the British Empire. Conference members agreed that if non-conference ships appeared in one of the ports the conference wished to reserve for itself, conference members would send as many ships as necessary to the port, and would offer rates as low as necessary,

---

[23] Mogul Steamship Co. *v.* McGregor, Gow & Co. *et al.* 54 L.J.Q.B. 540 (1884/1885); 57 L.J.K.B. 541 (1887/1888); 23 Q.B.D. 598 (C.A.)(1889); [1892] A.C. 25. See Section 19.2.1.

to prevent non-conference ships from taking on cargo. When entry occurred, they did so; conference ships carried freight at rates below cost.[24]

Shipping conferences—of which there were (and are) many, are cartels. The events that led to the *Mogul Steamship* decision were rooted in an episode of failed oligopolistic coordination. Before the conference undertook its predatory campaign, the target shipper sought to be admitted to the conference.[25]

Entry, predation, price wars Attempts to enter shipping conference markets were not uncommon. Some attempted entry evoked a predatory response, some did not. Scott Morton (1997) analyses factors influencing shipping conference responses to entry for episodes of attempted entry into three shipping conferences over the decades covering the end of the nineteenth century and beginning of the twentieth century.

As indicated in the upper rows of Table 7.2, there was no price war for 32 of 47 episodes of entry, yet four of the 32 entrants ultimately left the market. 14 of 47 entry attempts were met with a price war. In eight of these cases, the target firm remained in the market.

Imperfect information Scott Morton's analysis rests on imperfections not only in financial markets but also in the information entrants and incumbents had about each other. During the period covered by her sample, most shippers were privately owned. Some entrants were

Table 7.2 Outcomes of Price Wars, Scott Morton sample

	All Entrants		
	Accept	**Exit**	**Unclear**
War	8	6	0
No War	28	4	1

	New vs. Other Entrants		
	War	**No War**	**Accept**
New	8	5	4 (1 result unclear)
Other	6	27	32

Source: Scott Morton (1997, Table V).

---

[24] The conference also employed a form of loyalty rebate: shippers and agents in the target ports who dealt exclusively with conference ships were entitled to a 5 per cent rebate on annual payments. Use of an independent vessel meant loss of the loyalty rebate for all tea shipped on conference liners that year. The loyalty rebate raised the cost to clients of switching to a conference rival.

[25] Yamey (1972, p. 138). Marriner and Hyde (1967, p. 148) write that Mogul's application was denied because it intended to schedule ships only in periods of peak demand, leaving other conference members to supply transportation services in slack periods, and that after failing to prevail in its court challenge (1967, p. 150) "eventually Mogul ships were readmitted to conference agreements".

part of larger organizations that operated in many ports. A conference might be able to estimate the financial resources of such an entrant fairly accurately, or at least conclude that those resources were not negligible. Other entrants might rely mainly on the financial backing of family and a narrow circle of business connections. Such entrants might appear to be easy targets of a predatory campaign, but conference members could never be entirely certain.

Furthermore, an entrant would itself be to some extent uncertain of its prospects. This would be particularly the case for a *de novo* entrant, without previous experience in the industry. But even a shipper with experience in other ports would have to allow for the possibility that the slings and arrows of outrageous fortune, without any strategic response from the conference, might cause its entry attempt to fail.

Age is one entrant characteristic that might be expected to convey information about expected survivability. In Scott Morton's sample, as indicated in the lower rows of Table 7.2, eight of 13 cases of entry by new firms (less than five years old), were met with a price war. Four or five of these cases resulted in successful entry. By contrast, only six of 33 episodes of entry by older firms were met with price wars, and in only one of these cases did entry fail.

Scott Morton also finds that a predatory response was less likely against a larger firm. She interprets her results as supporting "long purse" theories of predation: imperfect financial markets allow incumbents with substantial resources to resist entry attempts by firms with limited resources.

"Good" entrants Podolny and Scott Morton (1999) extend the analysis by considering the impact of conference anticipation of post-entry behaviour on the conference's reaction to entry. Conference members have an interest in seeing to it that an entrant, if successful, will not disrupt the pre-entry consensus that allowed firms to raise price and collect economic profits. Podolny and Scott Morton find that price wars were less likely against high-social-status entrants, all else equal, and that price wars were less likely against British than against non-British entrants. Conference members tended themselves to be British and of high social status. By using observable characteristics as proxy indicators of post-entry behaviour, conferences sought to promote post-entry consensus.

U.S. sugar refining

Sugar Trust The sugar industry was touched by the wave of consolidation that swept U.S. industry at the end of the nineteenth century. For sugar refining, consolidation first took the form of creating the Sugar Trust, in December 1887. The Sugar Trust unified control of 18 previously independent firms. Seventeen of these were located in the eastern part of the country, and their combined share of that market was about 80 per cent. One firm going into the trust, American Sugar Refining, was located in California and supplied about 20 per cent of the West Coast market. The Sugar Trust also rationalized production, closing ten of its original 20 plants. From 1887 to 1889, the average price of refined sugar rose from $6.013 to $7.640 per hundred pounds (Eichner, 1969, p. 343).

West Coast price war The leading West Coast supplier was the California Sugar Refining Company, owned by Claus Spreckels, Senior. It had an 80 per cent share of the West Coast market, and its position was fortified by Spreckels' control of Hawaiian sugar cane supplies. Spreckels' plantations supplied one-third of the Hawaiian crop, and he had a three-year contract to buy the remainder.

Spreckels was under the impression that he had a mutual forbearance arrangement (each to stay out of the other's area) with the eastern firms. He realized that the entry of American Sugar Refining into the Trust meant that this arrangement had gone by the wayside, and reacted accordingly (Eichner, 1969, p. 154). First, Spreckels cut the price of refined sugar. American was obliged to cut its price as well, to maintain its sales. American quickly received more orders than it could fill with the raw sugar in its warehouses. It turned to the only source of supply for raw sugar convenient to the West Coast at that time of year: Hawaii. But Spreckels controlled the Hawaiian supply of raw sugar. He forced the price of raw sugar up to the price at which American could sell refined sugar.

Spreckels had the Trust's California plant in a price-cost vice. He would lower the price of refined sugar, placing American in the situation of making losses if they took and filled orders for refined sugar. American would stop taking orders. Spreckels would raise the price of refined sugar, and American would begin taking orders again. Spreckels would then lower the price of refined sugar, and the cycle would repeat itself. This continued for several months, until American managed to get supplies of raw sugar from the Dutch East Indies.

East Coast price war   Eichner (1969, pp. 159–160) describes the Sugar Trust's eastern activities as those of a dominant firm with a competitive fringe. In December 1889, Spreckels opened a sugar refinery in Philadelphia, doubling the eastern capacity outside trust control. This entry triggered a two-year price war, during the course of which the Sugar Trust was reorganized as the American Sugar Refining Company (ASRC). The price war ended in the summer of 1891, with the formation of Western Sugar Refining, which was set up to own both Spreckels' and ASRC's West Coast refineries. Spreckels and ASRC each owned 50 per cent of Western Sugar Refining. As part of the same arrangement, Spreckels sold a minority interest, 45 per cent, of his Philadelphia plant to ASRC. The price war ended with the two groups having common interests in California, but Spreckels' controlling interest in the Philadelphia plant gave him a weapon he could use to retaliate against ASRC if need be.[26]

Entry followed by price war   A second price war, triggered by the threat of entry into the sugar industry, broke out in 1896. Arbuckle Brothers was the leading U.S. supplier of roasted coffee, and a sister firm of Arbuckle & Company, a large wholesale grocer and major purchaser of refined sugar from the American Sugar Refining Company. Arbuckle Brothers owed its commercial success to its patent on a process that allowed it to package coffee in one-pound bags. It experimented with buying barrelled ASRC sugar at regular wholesale prices and repackaging it in two-pound bags for further distribution. The package itself was popular with the final consumer, but the resale margin was small. Arbuckle Brothers unsuccessfully sought a discount from ASRC. ASRC first threatened to refuse to sell refined sugar to Arbuckle Brothers for repackaging and resale, then (in September 1896), sought to buy Arbuckle Brothers' patent on the packaging process.

Arbuckle Brothers' reply was to announce that it had decided to enter the sugar refining industry, and it did so in August 1898. ASRC feared that successful entry by one firm would trigger a flood of entry that would erode its dominant position. In December 1896, ASRC bought Arbuckle Brothers' leading competitor and started a price war in the roasted coffee market.

---

[26] Within a few months Spreckels' business activities took his attention elsewhere. In March, 1892, ASRC purchased control not only control of Spreckels' Philadelphia plant, but also of three other Philadelphia-area sugar refineries. It was this acquisition that led to the 1895 *E.C. Knight* decision (Section 18.6.2).

In November 1898, Claus Doscher, former owner of one of the firms that had gone into the Sugar Trust, opened a second independent sugar refiner. Each of the independent plants had a capacity of only 3,000 barrels per day, compared with 49,500 barrels per day of ASRC and its allies. But the entry of a second firm seemed to confirm ASRC's fear of entry by a whole sequence of new rivals, and once again, a period of vicious oligopolistic rivalry began.

The course of the sugar price war is illustrated in Figure 7.5. The horizontal axis in Figure 7.5 shows time. The graph shows the price-average variable cost gap.[27] Their best estimate of average fixed cost is 26 cents per 100 pounds of refined sugar, with a minimum estimate of 16 cents per 100 pounds. If the price-constant average variable cost margin is below average fixed cost, then price is below average cost. It is clear from Figure 7.5 that the price of refined sugar was below average cost in the first part of 1899, and very likely below average cost again at the end of 1899 and through early 1900.

The spike in prices in the summer of 1899 marks a deliberate break in the price war by ASRC. Summer was the period of peak demand and the forgone profits were simply too great for ASRC to maintain the price war. Afterward, ASRC resumed the price war, causing substantial losses to itself, to Arbuckle Brothers, and to the few remaining smaller independents.

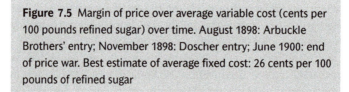

Figure 7.5 Margin of price over average variable cost (cents per 100 pounds refined sugar) over time. August 1898: Arbuckle Brothers' entry; November 1898: Doscher entry; June 1900: end of price war. Best estimate of average fixed cost: 26 cents per 100 pounds of refined sugar

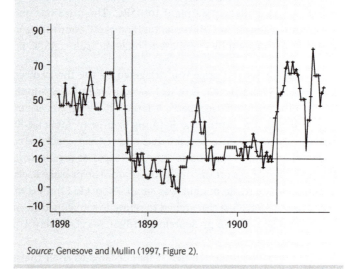

Source: Genesove and Mullin (1997, Figure 2).

---

[27] The technology used to refine sugar was commonly known. The usage of variable inputs, mainly raw sugar produced from sugar cane, was in fixed proportions to output. Genesove and Mullin (1997, 1998) are able to document the constant average variable cost per 100 pounds of refined sugar as 1.075 times the price of raw sugar. Using this relationship, they are able to measure the difference between the price of refined sugar and average variable cost.

Two of the independents contacted ASRC to plead for relief. This contact led to a merger, brokered by ASRC, of the Doscher firm and two small independents, to form the National Sugar Refining Company. Although nominally independent, National was under the effective control of ASRC.

 BOX   Fighting Brands in the Cash Register Industry

John H. Patterson acquired control of a cash register company, which he renamed the National Cash Register Company (NCR), in 1884. By 1911, NCR supplied 95 per cent of the U.S. market for cash registers (Jones, 1922, p. 478). The cash register was a new product, high technology for its day, and NCR's commercial success was due in no small measure to the highly trained sales force that Patterson organized to convince cautious merchants of the merits of its product.

NCR's commercial success was also a result of Patterson's determined efforts to smash competitors. As early as 1888, he wrote (quoted by Friedman, 1988, p. 577):

> We have no serious competitors yet, and we do not propose to have any formidable ones if we can help it. But before any of the weak ones get strong we must crush them out.

Among NCR's tactics to crush competitors, along with running bogus independent companies and teams of "special men" trained to make rivals' machines malfunction, was the use of fighting brands or "knockers" (Friedman, 1998, p. 577):

> [Knockers] were look-alike copies of the [competitor's] machine, built in such a way as to avoid patent violation, and price below the [competitor's] machine. "The intention of introducing this register is not to sell it, but only to prevent the sales of [rival] registers," Patterson explained. "We do not want the 'knocker' sold except where the [customer] won't buy our other registers and insists on buying [a rival] register on account of the price."

Friedman writes (1988, p. 577):

> The use of knockers became a major part of N.C.R.'s marketing strategy and the company even developed knocker catalogs to display their machines side-by-side with the originals. ... The use of "knocker" registers freed Patterson from having to compete on price with his standard line of machines; it was only with these machines that he under-sold his competitors.

Draining entrants' financial resources   ASRC and Arbuckle Brothers broke off the price wars in sugar and coffee in mid 1900. Arbuckle Brothers remained in the sugar refining business.

Genesove and Mullin (1997) point out that sugar refineries are highly specific, sunk investments, and that once the new refineries had come into the market, forcing them to exit was not a realistic possibility. Nor (in contrast to ocean shipping conferences) would predation serve to reveal the entrants' characteristics. The technology involved in sugar refining was a standard one. Spreckels and Claus Doscher were both experienced and well known in the industry. Rather, the price war paid off for ASRC because it tied up financial resources that the entrants might otherwise have used to expand capacity, permanently taking market share away from ASRC. Genesove and Mullin (1997) estimate ASRC's annual rate of return from limiting Arbuckle Brothers' capacity expansion at 5.8 per cent.

There were intangible payoffs to predation as well. By fighting two episodes of entry, ASRC established a reputation as being willing to inflict losses on future entrants. It also ensured its position as the industry price leader (Eichner, 1969, p. 227).

Chewing tobacco: predation to lower purchase price

If firms in an oligopoly do not behave as perfect competitors, the argument that purchase is always a more profitable strategy than predation is not valid (Yamey, 1972, pp. 130–131). In an imperfectly competitive market, the owners of a target firm are likely to ask a higher price for selling out than the dominant firm would wish to pay. A bout of predation may be just the thing to knock down the asking price. Early predation against one firm may bring down the cost of later acquisitions. In contrast, a policy of simply buying rivals out may encourage acquisition targets to ask a high price; it may encourage entry for the specific purpose of selling out to the dominant firm.[28]

Burns (1986) documents the role such considerations played in the rise of the old American Tobacco Company to a dominant position in the U.S. plug (or chewing) tobacco industry at the turn of the nineteenth century.[29] Between 1891 and 1906, American Tobacco acquired 43 rivals and established a near-monopoly position in markets for chewing tobacco and snuff. Many of these acquisitions were preceded by a predatory campaign carried out by means of a "fighting brand", (Burns, 1986, p. 271, fn.12):

> Most allegations of predatory pricing by the American Tobacco Co. describe warfare that was closely tailored to the business of a single rival. Evidently, many of them sold distinctive products in small territories. Hence the trust could attack each one effectively, while substantially limiting its own losses, by selling a close imitation priced below cost only in the competitor's marketing area.

Bogus independent firms—secretly controlled by the trust—were also used to start price wars and drive down acquisition price.

Burns finds that predatory pricing early on created a reputation that reduced the cost of later purchases. He estimates that American Tobacco lost some $200,000 in predatory campaigns from 1899 to 1901, but as a result saved $1.07 million on two later purchases.

***

 BOX   Predatory Conduct in the Market for Chewing Tobacco

From correspondence between Caleb C. Dula, a vice-president of the Tobacco Trust and the heads of two "bogus independents" (located in Louisville, Kentucky and Richmond, Virginia), firms portrayed as independent but actually controlled by the Tobacco Trust. The product in question was plug or chewing tobacco, at the start of the nineteenth century (Burns, 1989, p. 327) "the second-largest branch of the tobacco industry ... ; the trust accounted for 78.6% of total plug output".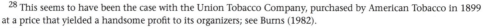

***

[28] This seems to have been the case with the Union Tobacco Company, purchased by American Tobacco in 1899 at a price that yielded a handsome profit to its organizers; see Burns (1982).

[29] The American Tobacco Company was later dissolved in a landmark antitrust decision, U.S. *v.* American Tobacco Co. 221 U.S. 106 (1911).

>> (a) Pricing below unit cost

Louisville to Dula, 27 April 1905: "[I]t was agreed that I should make an active campaign in the State of Ohio, which I am now doing, and losing money in that fight. We have been there about a month, and up to this writing have sold about 19,000 lbs, but we have six men in that field, and of course, this means a loss, but we are making some headway, and I think if the fight is kept up in that field, we will put 'Index' [the plug brand of a genuine competitor] out of business, just as we did in Indiana."

(b) Other regional markets a source of capital:

Dula to Louisville, 27 July 1903: "In view of the fact that we practically control the plug smoking business in Maine on 'Sickle', 'Good Smoke', and 'Peace and Goodwill', ... , it seems to me that it would be well for you now to change your deals some in New England, and try to make some money there to help defray expenses in the fighting territory, such as Michigan, Indiana and the North West."

(c) Raising prices in the post-predation period:

Dula to Richmond, 26 May 1905: "I note what you say in regard to making more money on sun cured [plug], and if there is no competition outside of [the R.J.] Reynolds [Tobacco Company, under secret trust control] and the American Tobacco Co. that makes it necessary to keep prices down, I can see no reason why it should not be immediately adjusted upon a basis that will afford a fair margin."

(d) Predation before acquisition:

Dula to Louisville, 28 July 1903: "In regard to Long Cut Tobacco, I think it is a splendid suggestion you make, that you get out a brand similar to 'Gorman'. If he decides within a few days to trade with you, there can be no harm done in having this brand ready, and in the event that he does not show an inclination to trade, you can probably pound him so hard that he will be willing to trade a little later on."

Source: Burns (1989), based on trial records of U.S. *v.* American Tobacco Co. 221 U.S. 106 (1911).

Bell Telephone

Patent protection   The original Alexander Graham Bell telephone patents expired in 1893 and 1894. While they enjoyed patent protection, American Telephone and Telegraph Corporation (Bell) and its regional operating companies concentrated their efforts on business customers and densely populated metropolitan regions. A 1938 Federal Communications Commission report[30] wrote that "the [Bell] System's attitude toward the public was characterized by arrogance and indifference".

Expiration and entry   At the dawn of the telephone era, business customers were particularly interested in national or trunk-line service, which required relatively costly infrastructure. Residential customers were much more in the market for regional telephone service, which was less expensive to provide. Expiration of the Bell patents made it possible for regional independents to enter the field, and they were quick to do so.

---

[30] Quoted by Gabel (1969, p. 344).

Table 7.3 Bell and independent market shares, 1907

	Bell	Independents Affiliated with Bell	Bell + Affiliated Independents	Non-affiliated Independents
North Atlantic	74.9	3.3	78.2	21.8
South Atlantic	57.2	7.4	64.7	35.3
North Central	33.8	20.5	54.3	45.7
South Central	50.2	18.6	68.9	31.1
Western	71.0	6.7	77.7	22.3
United States	51.2	13.7	64.9	35.1

Source: Gabel (1994, Table 1).

Bell's initial response to entry was (Gabel, 1969, pp. 349–350) a propaganda campaign to portray independents as risky enterprises, to refuse to connect independents with the Bell network, and to refuse to sell equipment to independent telephone companies.[31] Bell also expanded its own network, often reacting when an independent entered a residential area.

Internal expansion proved costly, and Bell was not able to stop the growth of fringe firms. By 1907, Bell's share of the U.S. telephone market had fallen to 51.2 per cent (Table 7.3). Independents were particularly successful in the Midwest and the South.

Strategic responses   Bell changed its management and its policy. The Bell system response to the growth of independent telephone companies in its southern markets was typical of its response nationwide (Weiman and Levin, 1994, p. 105):

- pricing below cost in response to entry, which deprived competitors of the cash flow required for expansion even if it failed to induce exit;
- investing in the toll network ahead of demand, isolating independent companies in smaller towns and rural areas, and forcing them to accept acquisition of sublicensing on terms favorable to [Southern Bell];
- influencing local regulatory policy in large cities to weaken rivals and ultimately to institutionalize the Bell monopoly.

The strategy of cutting price to deny entrants funds that might have been used for expansion was employed outside the South as well (Gabel, 1969, p. 548).

Where it could do so, Bell manipulated the local regulatory process to handicap independents (Gabel, 1994, pp. 561–562):

> When franchises were issued to the Independents ... they typically included stipulations that set maximum rates, required free telephone service to the city government, free use of the telephone poles and underground conduits for fire and police lines, and royalty fees.

---

[31] This last strategy encouraged the development of independent equipment manufacturers, as Bell equipment patents expired.

No such requirements were imposed on Bell, which operated under previously established franchise agreements.

Bell also undertook an aggressive campaign to portray the telephone industry as a natural monopoly. This was not the case,[32] but Bell turned to regulation as a way of getting government to block competition. In 1910, the U.S. government gave the Interstate Commerce Commission authority to regulate interstate telephone companies. Many states undertook regulation of intrastate telephone service, and local Bell franchises were often exclusive. The result was an artificial monopoly that lasted until technological change prompted the breakup of the Bell System in 1984 (Gabel, 1969, pp. 358–359).

 BOX **Predatory Pricing in the Refined Oil Market**

Bringhurst (1979, pp. 72–73):

In October 1903 a salesman for the Evansville Oil Company visited Gallatin. Evansville Oil was an independent firm with headquarters in Indiana and a refinery at Oil City, Pennsylvania. The salesman offered Gallatin consumers high-quality Pennsylvania coal oil for $.145 per gallon, only a cent per gallon more than the inferior Standard product. Since many Tennesseans were dissatisfied with the quality of Standard coal oil, the Evansville representative had little difficulty securing orders for a railroad tankcar of his product.

Standard agents quickly learned of the Evansville Oil contracts through their informants, who worked for the railroads. The agents promptly relayed this information to Comer [Kentucky Standard's superintendent for north central Tennessee], and he promptly ordered Holt [Standard's regional sales representative for Gallatin] "to go to Gallatin and hold his trade, and procure the orders that had been given to the Evansville Oil Company countermanded. Holt visited the Evansville customers and offered free oil to those who would cancel their orders. Several merchants agreed, and they received a total of three hundred gallons of free oil for their cooperation. One of the merchants . . . sent a telegram to Evansville Oil, at Holt's expense, cancelling the orders. But the cancellation came too late. The oil was already in transit.

Comer then informed the comptroller of Tennessee that Evansville Oil was shipping petroleum into the state. . . . As originally contracted, the Evansville Oil shipment was not taxable because it was a direct interstate transaction. But since a substantial part of the order had been cancelled, much of the oil would have to be stored at Gallatin and subsequently resold, thus becoming liable to state taxation. . . .

When Evansville Oil's cargo arrived at Gallatin, [the merchants who had ordered it] refused delivery. The company therefore had to store the oil and find new buyers, which meant storage expenses and state taxes. Evansville Oil consequently lost a substantial sum on the transaction and decided to abandon further attempts to market oil in the area. After the independent oil company had withdrawn, Kentucky Standard increased the price of its low-quality coal oil to $.145 per gallon.

Recapitulation

A market system presumes that firms compete for the favour of customers. In oligopoly, firms compete as well with strategies that aim to block rivals from competing for the favour of

---

[32] The evidence is that unit cost went up, not down, as a regional network expanded, and that rates for a single phone line increased when Bell took over providing service in an area.

customers. Such strategies include loyalty rebates, price-cutting to deny rivals cash flow that might otherwise be used for expansion, and rent-seeking solicitation of regulation to shackle competitors.

A single episode of predatory conduct may be a money-losing proposition, if considered in isolation. But predation in one market may create a reputation that discourages entry in other markets, starves entrants of financial capital, or drives down the cost of buying rivals in other markets. It may encourage rivals in other markets to tacitly collude with the predator. For a dominant firm that operates in many regional or product markets, predation can be a value-maximizing strategy.

7.3.3 Models of Predation in Imperfectly Competitive Markets

Chain store paradox

Selten's (1978) *chain-store paradox* model hammers home the point that predation (like limit pricing) does not work if there is complete information, if entrants have unlimited reasoning ability, and if the dominant firm cannot commit to an aggressive strategy. In the chain store model, a dominant firm—the incumbent—operates a chain of stores in 20 separate local markets. In each market, one after another, it faces the prospect of entry by a single rival. A game tree and payoff matrix for one such stage game are shown in Figure 7.6. Each entrant earns a payoff that is determined in the single market in which it operates. The incumbent's payoff is the sum of its earnings in each of the 20 markets.

In each market, the entrant's choices are to enter or to stay out. If the entrant stays out, it earns $1 (the return from the best alternative investment); the incumbent earns $5. If the entrant comes in, then the incumbent must decide whether to cooperate with the entrant (both earn a return of $2) or to fight entry (both earn a zero return). A cooperative incumbent restricts output and shares the market; an aggressive incumbent expands output, even at the cost of lost profit.

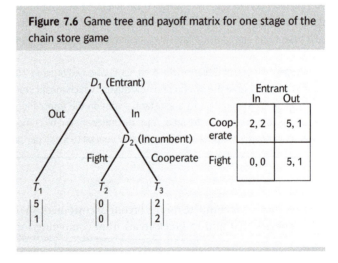

Figure 7.6 Game tree and payoff matrix for one stage of the chain store game

Deterrence If the dominant firm follows a deterrence strategy, it announces its intention to react aggressively to entry. If an entrant believes the announcement, then the entrant is better off staying out of the market. If entry occurs, it is likely to occur early on, and the incumbent will have to give up some short-run profit by carrying out the threat to deter entry. But later potential entrants will learn of the incumbent's aggressive behaviour and become convinced that the incumbent will react aggressively to entry. The incumbent will earn more than enough profit in later markets to make up for losses in early markets.

The final period However, deterrence will not work in the final market. If predation is attractive at all for the incumbent, it is because predation generates future benefits. What the incumbent does in the final period cannot generate future benefits. An aggressive reaction in the final period would mean a loss for the incumbent without the prospect of any later gain; thus the threat of an aggressive reaction in the final market would be an empty one. If the potential entrant to the final market believes the incumbent acts to maximize its own payoff, then the potential entrant to the final market would not believe a threat by the incumbent to react aggressively to entry.

Backward induction But if a threat to react aggressively to entry in the final period would not be credible, then neither would a threat to react aggressively to entry in the next-to-last period. Aggressive behaviour in the next-to-last period would be attractive to the incumbent only because of the benefits it would yield in the final period. Since the potential entrant in the final period would not believe a threat to react aggressively to entry, there is no last-period payoff to acting aggressively in the next-to-last period.

The *backward induction argument* pushes the reasoning that the incumbent could not credibly threaten to react aggressively to entry in the final period to its logical conclusion. If the incumbent could not credibly threaten to deter entry in the final period, then it would have nothing to gain from reacting aggressively to entry in the next-to-last period. But in this case, it would have nothing to gain from reacting aggressively to entry in period 18, and so on back to period 1. No fully informed entrant with unlimited reasoning would ever believe a threat to react aggressively. The only logically consistent equilibrium under conditions of complete and perfect information and unlimited computing ability has each entrant enter and the incumbent accommodate all entry: the incumbent's payoff is $40.[33]

Paradox Why does Selten call this result a *paradox*? Because the logical result is not believable (Selten, 1978, pp. 132–133):

> If I had to play the game in the role of [the incumbent], I would follow the deterrence theory. I would be very surprised if it failed to work. From my discussions with friends and colleagues, I get the impression that most people share this inclination. ... mathematically trained persons recognize the logical validity of the induction argument, but they refuse to accept it as a guide to practical behaviour. ...
>
> The fact that the logical inescapability of the induction theory fails to destroy the plausibility of the deterrence theory is a serious phenomenon which merits the name of a paradox.

---

[33] The outcome in which each entrant comes in and the incumbent accommodates entry is a *subgame perfect equilibrium*, which in the context of this model means that it is an equilibrium if the game starts in period 1, or in period 2, ... , or in period 20.

The conclusion that predation would not be a credible strategy in the chain store model depends on the assumptions that there is complete information and that all the entrants have sufficient calculating ability to work out the subgame perfect equilibrium of the game. Abandoning these assumptions makes it possible to resolve the chain store paradox.

Bounded rationality   Selten's (1978, Section 5) resolution of the chain store paradox relies on a model of boundedly rational human decision making. Rather than conceiving of individuals as acting with complete information and unlimited analytical ability, he suggests thinking of decisions as being taken at one of three levels:

1. The level of routine: "decisions are made without any conscious effort" based on "experience with similar decision problems in the past".

2. The level of imagination: "the decision maker tries to visualize how the selection of different alternatives may influence the probable course of future events. ... The decision maker does not know why he imagines one scenario rather than another. The imagination process is governed by a multitude of procedural decisions which are made on the routine level. ... The imagination process is similar to a computer simulation. The program of this simulation is determined on the routine level."

3. The level of reasoning: "a conscious effort to analyse the situation in a rational way on the basis of explicit assumptions whose validity is examined in the light of past experience and logical thinking. ... The level of reasoning needs the help of the lower levels of imagination and routine. Ordinarily logical analysis is based on some kind of simplified model whose assumptions are the products of imagination. Moreover, the results of the imagination process are used as heuristic hints which guide the process of reasoning."

For Selten, the backward induction argument is made at the level of reasoning, while the deterrence theory is plausible at the level of imagination (1978, p. 153):

> On the level of imagination a clear and detailed visualization of a sequence of two, three, or four periods is possible—the exact number is not important. ... For a large number of periods the scenarios will either be restricted to several periods, e.g. at the end of the game or the visualization will be vague in the sense that the individual periods are not seen in detail. ...
>   On the level of imagination, one cannot find anything wrong with the deterrence theory ...

Imperfect information about the incumbent's payoffs   Kreps and Wilson (1982) show that if there is imperfect information, deterrence may be an equilibrium strategy, even if firms have unlimited computing ability.

Game trees for a single stage of the Kreps and Wilson extension of the chain store game are shown in Figure 7.7. The entrant earns nothing if it stays out, loses money if it comes in and the incumbent fights ($b - 1 < 0$), makes a profit ($b > 0$) if it comes in and the incumbent cooperates. If the potential entrant stays out, the incumbent's payoff is $a > 1$.

But the entrant is uncertain about the incumbent's payoffs in the event of entry. There are two possibilities. If the incumbent is weak, it earns more by cooperating than by fighting entry (Figure 7.7(a)). If this game tree holds for every stage of the game, and entrants know it holds for every stage of the game, the backward induction argument applies. In equilibrium entry occurs and the incumbent cooperates in every period. If the incumbent is strong, it earns more by fighting than by cooperating (Figure 7.7(b)).

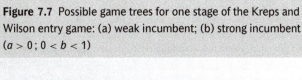

Figure 7.7 Possible game trees for one stage of the Kreps and Wilson entry game: (a) weak incumbent; (b) strong incumbent $(a > 0 ; 0 < b < 1)$

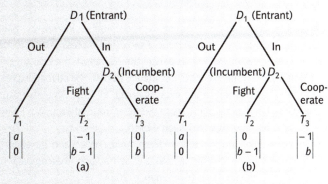

A weak incumbent will always cooperate in the last period. Depending on beliefs, it may be a value-maximizing strategy for a weak incumbent to pretend to be strong in early periods, creating a reputation for being strong that will keep entrants out of the market in the middle and toward the end of the game. If information is imperfect, predation may be an equilibrium strategy.

Signal-jamming In the Kreps and Wilson model, predation may pay because predation prevents the entrant from learning something about the incumbent—whether it is likely to fight or not. Similarly, in the entry-limitation model of Section 7.2.4, the incumbent alters its output to prevent the entrant from learning whether the incumbent's costs are high or low. In the signal-jamming model of Fudenberg and Tirole (1986), predation can pay because it prevents an entrant from learning something about the market. Secret price cuts, particularly price cuts targeted at an entrant's most likely customers, may lead the entrant to conclude that the market is too small for it to profitably continue. If a predatory campaign induces one entrant to leave the market, later potential entrants may be discouraged and stay out of the market.

 BOX **Ignorance is Bliss (II)**

American Express money orders (MO), introduced in 1882, and Travellers Cheques (TC), introduced in 1890, began as small but lucrative sidelines to the company's primary activity as the leading member of a reclusive five-member cartel that controlled express shipping in the United States (Grossman, 1987, pp. 136–137):

> ❯❯ ... the express companies succeeded in maintaining a policy of almost total secrecy into the twentieth century. ... no other industry imposed the kind of blackout on information managed by the express companies. As unincorporated associations, they could legally deny shareholders and anyone else information about the size and profitability of their business. In 1880, the companies even refused (and were not challenged) to give information to the U.S. Census Bureau.
>
> The collusive monopoly over express shipping was eventually undone by publicity from Progressive-era muckrakers. In 1906 the U.S. government subjected express carriers to regulation by the Interstate Commerce Commission. In 1917, as part of the war effort, the U.S. government took control of American railroads, and while in control declined to honour the railroad-express company contracts that had been the exoskeleton of the express cartel. In 1918, American Express (along with its erstwhile rivals) ceded its express activities to the newly formed American Railway Express Company, and was out of the business that had given it birth.
>
> But the float—interest earned on funds held to redeem money orders and Travellers Cheques—sustained the company while it found its way. True to it early tradition, the company made every effort to hide just how profitable the float was (Grossman, p. 206):
>
>> ... the company made money each year. The profits came exclusively from the TC and the money order, particularly the former; TC volume hit $200 million in 1926. Of course, the company made its money, not on the sales of TCs, but on the float .... The short- and long-term TC floats reached a total of more than $50 million and produced regular profits, not huge amounts, but enough to pay through 1928 about $1 million a year in dividends and add another million to surplus.
>>
>> The strangest aspect of the float was that few outside the company knew about it and fewer still appreciated its importance. Nearly every Amexco employee worked in travel, which made no money, while a handful of staffers ... made all the money and labored in total obscurity as far as stockholders and the general public were concerned ... For the next thirty-five years, no one in the company talked about the float publicly for fear that banks and other travel companies, realizing how lucrative it was, would get into the business and take Amexco's market share. That share was substantial: in the 1920s, around 50 percent.
>
> *Source:* Grossman (1987).

The prevalence of "bogus independents" and "fighting brands" in known episodes of predation is consistent with the signal-jamming model. So are instances in which profitable firms went to great lengths to disguise just how profitable they were; see the discussion of American Express in the accompanying box, and the discussion of Alcoa in Section 7.2.2.

The long purse A mainstay of early arguments that predation against entrants and small incumbents could be a successful and profitable strategy for an incumbent was that the predating firm would have the financial resources to survive a period of predatory losses, and the target firm would not. A mainstay of the hard-core Chicago argument that predation could never be profitable and therefore would never be tried was that consumers or financial markets would willingly provide funds to a target of predation. In practice, however, there is imperfect information in financial markets, as there is in product markets. Small firms may need funds because they are targets of predation; they may need funds because they are inefficient. If a firm portrays itself to either financial markets or final consumers as a target of predation, the potential source of funds cannot be certain the portrayal is accurate (even if it is). Because information about the target firm's viability is not only imperfect but impacted on the borrowing side of the market, targets of predation will be less able to raise funds from outsiders. If they are able to do so at all, they will face a higher cost of capital because of the risk of default perceived by lenders.

Free riding A target of predation would also confront a free rider problem in attempting to raise funds from consumers. All consumers benefit if the target firm lives to compete another day. But if the number of final consumers is at all large, the benefit to any one consumer will be small, absolutely and relative to the amount sought by the target firm. Even if repayment would be reasonably secure, provided enough funds are raised, risk-averse final consumers will have every incentive to stand back and let others shoulder the burden—and the risk—of lending to the target of predation.

Entry deterrence:

If potential entrants are uncertain about an incumbent firm's costs, or its payoffs, or the size of the market, an incumbent firm may be able to discourage entry by acting as if it has low unit costs or in ways that make the market appear to be less profitable than it really is. If potential entrants make decisions in a boundedly rational way, an incumbent may maximize its value by engaging in periodic episodes of predation, unprofitable in isolation, that establish a reputation that discourages entry in other times and places. Imperfect and impacted information in financial markets makes it doubtful that lenders will provide targets of predation with the wherewithal to withstand a sustained campaign.

7.3.4 Experimental Tests

Isaac and Smith (1985) examine whether or not predation occurs in the experimental posted-offer market shown in Figure 7.8. The market has one large supplier, with marginal and average cost decreasing up to 7 units of output, then sharply increasing to maximum output of 10. There is also one small supplier, with marginal and average cost decreasing up to 3 units of output, then sharply increasing to maximum output of 4.[34]

The demand and supply curves overlap for prices between $2.66 and $2.76. Outcomes in this range are competitive equilibria, in that each firm produces an output on the vertical segment of its marginal cost curve, the output it would produce if acting as a price taker, and the quantity supplied equals the quantity demanded.

The most obvious form of predatory pricing has the large firm selling 10 units at a price between $2.60 and $2.65.[35] To impose a lower price, the large seller would need to supply 11 units of output, but this exceeds its capacity of 10 units. $2.65 is the highest price that is

---

[34] From Harrison (1988, p. 406, fn.3): "The marginal costs for seller A are $2.58, 2.54, 2.52, 2.50, 2.48, 2.46, 2.44, 2.80, 2.80, and 2.80 for units 1–10 respectively, and for seller B they are $2.76, 2.66, 2.56 and 3.32 for units 1–4. The demand schedule is $3.92, 3.72, 3.52, 3.35, 3.21, 3.07, 2.97, 2.90, 2.84, 2.76, 2.59, 2.50, 2.32, 2.10, 1.88, 1.66, 1.44, 1.22, 1.11, and 1.00 for units 1–20 respectively." The fourth unit of the small firm's marginal cost curve and the upper and lower segments of the demand curve are not shown in Figure 7.8.

[35] Harrison (1988, pp. 406–409) discusses other price-output combinations for this experimental design that have predatory aspects.

Figure 7.8 Cost, demand, and supply curves, Isaac and Smith (1985) predatory pricing experiment (Subscript L denotes large firm, subscript S denotes small firm)

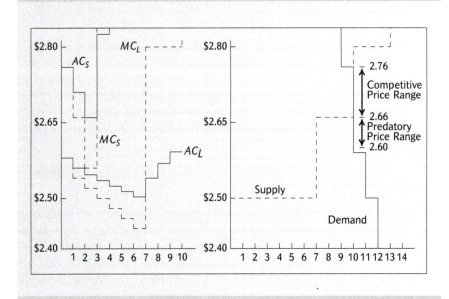

below the small seller's average cost if it produces 3 units. As the marginal cost of the large seller's eighth through tenth units of output is $2.80, an offer to sell 10 units at price (say) $2.65 means the large firm sets a price below its marginal cost.

Within the basic demand-and-supply structure of Figure 7.8, Isaac and Smith (1985) consider variations in which the large firm has a "deep pocket" (an initial endowment twice that of the small firm), in which there is a sunk entry cost,[36] and alternative information conditions. They find no evidence of predation, and write (1985, p. 321, fn.1):

> While the negative results of the 11 experiments we report cannot prove that predatory pricing does not exist, we feel that they alter the burden of proof for those who would design public policy as though predation were a robust phenomenon. We invite antitrust scholars to scrutinize our experimental design, to suggest specific ways in which they would alter it, and to state the corresponding outcomes they are prepared to predict.

Harrison (1988) accepted this invitation. His experimental design involved the simultaneous operation of five markets, each with a demand side like that of the Isaac and Smith (1985) experimental market. Experimental subjects were able to choose the market in which they would operate. Four experimental subjects were given the Isaac and Smith (1985) large-firm cost function, for one of the markets, and the small-firm cost function for any other market. The seven other subjects were given the Isaac and Smith (1985) small-firm cost function, no matter which market they chose to enter.

---

[36] As in Coursey *et al.* (1984b), entry required purchase of a permit that was valid for 5 periods; see Section 5.2.3.

With this experimental structure, the efficient pattern of market structures has four markets supplied by two firms, one large and one small, while three small firms enter the remaining market.[37]

Harrison observed several episodes of predatory behaviour. For example, in one case, a large firm offered to sell 10 units at prices 2.64 and 2.60 in two successive periods. The small firm that had been in the market exited. The large firm then sold 7 units at prices 2.65, 2.85, and 3.15 in the three following periods. Harrison concludes (1988, p. 416) that extending the Isaac and Smith framework to a multiple-market environment is sufficient to "bring alive" the reputation effects that theory underlie equilibrium predation in markets with incomplete information.[38]

7.4 Raising Rivals' Costs

The gist of the McGee–Telser argument that one should not expect to observe predation as an equilibrium phenomenon is that there is always some more profitable alternative, either collusion with or purchase of an inconvenient rival. Salop and Scheffman (1987, 1993) point out a third alternative: imposing higher costs on a rival can tame or kill it as effectively as lowering price, and at lower cost to the dominant firm. This is the theory of *raising rivals' costs (RRC)*.

A rival that has higher cost will typically reduce output (in a quantity-setting market) or raise price (in a price-setting market with product differentiation). This will permit a dominant firm to expand its own output or raise its own price. If a rival's costs are made high enough, it may shut down entirely. A firm that suffers the cost increase will react quickly, since it is in its own interest to do so. Hence a dominant firm that strategically engineers a cost increase for its competitors will benefit quickly, rather than having to go through an initial period of losses.

7.4.1 A Stackelberg Leader RRC Model

It may even be profitable for a dominant firm to accept some increase in its own cost, if by so doing it can inflict an even larger cost increase on smaller rivals. To see this, return to the Stackelberg quantity-leadership model of Section 7.2.3, where the equation of the inverse demand curve is:

$$p = 100 - (q_1 + q_2)$$

and both firms have constant marginal cost 10 per unit of output.

Assume now that both firms have a fixed cost of 300 per period. Then from expressions (7.15) and (7.16), the per-period profits of the Stackelberg leader and of the Stackelberg follower are $1012.5 - 300 = 712.5$ and $506.25 - 300 = 206.25$, respectively.

---

[37] The supply curve in the fifth market is then different from that shown in Figure 7.8. Three small price-taking firms will each supply 3 units, total supply 9 units, for prices greater than or equal to $2.56 and less than $3.32. Nine units of output will be demanded for prices less than or equal to $2.84 and greater than $2.76. The supply curve coincides with the demand curve for $2.76 < p \leq 2.84$, which is the range of competitive prices.

[38] Gomez *et al.* (undated) report results of three replications of Harrison's experiment that show little evidence of predatory pricing, and variations (making entry and price decisions sequential rather than simultaneous) that "resulted in a consistent pattern of predatory pricing in most markets …"

How does the Stackelberg leadership outcome change if firm 1 can arrange an increase in firm 2's marginal cost to $c_2 = 25$, although to do so its own marginal cost must rise to $c_1 = 20$?

In this case, the equation of firm 2's best response function is:

$$q_2 = \frac{1}{2}(100 - 25 - q_1) = \frac{1}{2}(75 - q_1). \tag{7.41}$$

The equation of firm 1's residual demand function is then:

$$p = 100 - q_1 - \frac{1}{2}(75 - q_1) = 62.5 - \frac{1}{2}q_1. \tag{7.42}$$

Firm 1 maximizes its profit if it produces the output that makes marginal revenue for this residual demand equation equal to its marginal cost,

$$62.5 - 2\left(\frac{1}{2}\right)q_1 = 20. \tag{7.43}$$

The Stackelberg leadership output is therefore:

$$q_{SL} = 42.5. \tag{7.44}$$

From (7.41), firm 2's Stackelberg follower output is:

$$q_{SF} = \frac{1}{2}(75 - 42.5) = 16.25. \tag{7.45}$$

The Stackelberg follower's equilibrium profit, if it stays in the market, is:[39]

$$\pi_2 = q_{SF}^2 - 300 = (16.25)^2 - 300 = -35.9375. \tag{7.46}$$

Firm 2 will lose money if it stays in the market. To maximize its own payoff, it will exit, leaving firm 1 as a monopoly supplier with higher unit cost. Firm 1's profit-maximizing monopoly output satisfies the equation:

$$100 - 2q_1 = 20, \tag{7.47}$$

so its monopoly output is:

$$q_m = 40. \tag{7.48}$$

Firm 1's monopoly profit per period with higher marginal cost 20 per unit is:

$$(40)^2 - 300 = 1600 - 300 = 1300, \tag{7.49}$$

nearly twice the Stackelberg leader profit per period of 712.5 at the lower marginal cost 10 per unit.[40]

---

[39] There are different ways to work out the follower's profit. One is to note that from the equation of the follower's best response function, (7.41), $100 - q_1 - q_2 - 25 = q_2$. But from the equation of the inverse demand curve, $100 - q_1 - q_2 = p$, so $p - 25 = q_2$. The follower's per-period profit is $(p - 25)q_2 - 300$, and $p - 25 = q_2$ leads to (7.46).

[40] Strictly speaking, to compare payoffs under the two strategies (Stackelberg leadership and raising the rival's cost) one should take the present discounted value of the two income streams, 712.5 and 1300 respectively, and subtract the cost to the leader of engineering higher unit costs for both firms from the value of the second income stream. But unless a raising rivals' cost strategy is very costly, it is likely to maximize the dominant firm's value. At an interest rate of 10 per cent, firm 1's value under a raising rivals' cost strategy would be 13000, while its value as a Stackelberg leader would be 7125. As long as the cost of implementing a raising rivals' cost strategy is less than $13000 - 7125 = 5875$, more than eight times the per-period profit of a Stackelberg leader, raising rivals' cost will be the value-maximizing choice.

7.4.2 Examples

Cost-raising strategies may involve the strategic manipulation of input requirements or of input prices. The cost of pollution control equipment for a factory, for example, will be largely a fixed cost. If public policy mandates the use of such equipment, larger firms will be able to spread this fixed cost over a greater number of units of output than will smaller firms. Such an increase in fixed cost may be sufficient to cause some small firms to shut down. The cost of implementing this kind of cost-raising strategy would be the expense of lobbying the government to obtain the indicated type of regulation.

Williamson (1968a) discusses the facts underlying the U.S. Supreme Court decision in the *Pennington*[41] case. The issue there was an industry-wide labour contract and an alleged conspiracy between a union and a group of owners of larger mines to strategically disadvantage smaller mines. High wages raised the costs of both large and small mines. But the impact was greater on small mines, which tended to use more labour-intensive production techniques, than on larger mines, which tended to use more capital-intensive production techniques. Industry-wide higher wages raised the costs of small mines relatively more than the costs of large mines.

Similarly, U.S. airline pilot unions negotiated contracts in the 1990s that restricted the use of regional jets. Such restrictions protected the pilots' wage structure. They also raised the costs of regional airlines more than the cost of national carriers, which relied more on larger planes (Swoboda, 1999). An industry-wide cost increase differentially disadvantaged small firms because large and small firms employed different technologies.[42]

 BOX **Rackets, Raising Rivals' Costs, and Collusion**

The U.S. pasta noodle industry of the 1930s included firms with up to 25 presses and capacity of 500 pounds an hour, along with screw-type presses with a capacity of 40 pounds per hour. The Chicago-area pasta market included 14 to 17 large firms and many fringe producers. Some of the latter appear to have been enterprises of last resort, as workers thrown into the ranks of the unemployed by the Great Depression pulled small presses out of storage and put them to use, for lack of any better opportunity.

In 1931, a certain Gennaro Calabrese organized the Chicago Macaroni and Noodle Manufacturers Club. Membership in the Club entailed a *two-part tariff*: monthly dues of $25, plus charges of one-quarter cent per pound of pasta sold (Alexander, 1997, p. 180):

> Calabrese collected the "sales tax" part of his extortion receipts by selling package "labels" at a fee of 0.25¢ per pound of pasta products. The labels were not decorative product labels but were more akin to tax stamps. Manufacturers were required to put the labels on each package of pasta sold within a 50-mile radius of Chicago.

Physical violence (bombings and beatings) were used to encourage compliance with Club policy. ❯❯

---

[41] United Mine Workers of America *v.* Pennington *et al*. 381 U.S. 657 (1965).

[42] Strategic raising of rivals' costs played a role in the Standard Oil's acquisition of a dominant position in the U.S. oil industry at the end of the nineteenth century. We discuss this in Section 21.2.1.

>> The Club "dues" were, of course, a racket. But the Noodle Manufacturers Club seems to have been something other than a run-of-the-mill episode of organized crime. Club dues raised the unit costs of small firms much more than of large firms (Alexander, 1997, p. 181):

> Calabrese's monthly press tax of $25 would impose a negligible burden on 500-pound-per hour presses (around 0.02¢ per pound), as long as they were producing near capacity. Meanwhile, the press tax would roughly double the 0.25¢ per-pound sales-tax burden for a 40-pound per hour press.

There is evidence that two leading Chicago pasta-producing firms cooperated with Calabrese, and that his activities were part of a wider scheme to enforce collusion during an economic downturn. Calabrese very likely was hired by the collusive core of the industry to keep down fringe competition and to guard against defections from the cartel (Alexander, 1997, p. 198):

> Most incumbents used large presses while targeted entrants were trying to produce with low-output equipment. Loading a portion of the racketeer's fee onto a lump-sum press tax created what appeared to be nondiscriminatory "club dues" but could block entry while imposing a relatively small burden on most incumbents. Calabrese's fee was too low to eliminate incentives for large-press firms to overproduce . . . Hence he relied on labels to aid in monitoring output. Individual producers were probably restricted in the number of labels they could buy and constrained to the "after-tax" profits they could generate from filling their own production quotas.

Source: Alexander (1997a); see also Alexander (1997b).

7.5 Strategic Bundling

7.5.1 Bundling to Induce Exit

Bundling is the practice of selling two or more products for one price. One example is block-booking of movie films, the distribution of packages of films of varying quality to movie theatres (Stigler, 1963). The telecommunications sector is rife with bundling, including cable-TV suppliers that offer packages of channels for a single monthly rate, and companies that offer cable TV, internet access, and cell-phone service at one price. Other examples of bundling include round-trip airline tickets and software packages that combine a personal computer operating system with applications (word processor, spreadsheet, and the like).[43]

Bundling and related marketing practices have sometimes been viewed as constraining customer choice, requiring customers to "buy things they don't want to get what they do want". We will see in Section 8.3 that this aspect of bundling is best understood as a means for a firm to engage in price discrimination. Bundling has also been viewed as a foreclosure device, one that permits a firm with control over price and output in the market for one good, by bundling, to establish or re-enforce control over price and output in the market for some other good, at the expense of rivals whose operations would be rendered unprofitable in ways that were not "competition on the merits".

---

[43] Bundling is relating to tying, the practice of agreeing to sell one good ("the tying good") only on the condition that the purchaser takes such supplies as it needs of some other good ("the tied good") from the same seller. Tying contracts, in contrast to bundles, do not require that tying and tied good be taken in fixed proportions. We discuss tying contracts in Chapter 12.

Demand

Bundling may create substitutability relationships, even if the components of the bundle products are unrelated in demand. By so doing, bundling may render some equally efficient firms unprofitable. Strategic bundling can be profitable because it drives rivals from the market, not (directly) because of its demand-side effects.

No bundling   Recall from Section 3.3.3 the linear demand for differentiated products specification. Let there be two firms, A and B, and two goods, 1 and 2, that are independent in demand, with inverse demand equations:

$$p_1 = 100 - Q_1 = 100 - q_{1A}. \tag{7.50}$$

$$p_2 = 100 - Q_2 = 100 - (q_{2A} + q_{2B}). \tag{7.51}$$

Firm A sells product 1 and product 2. Firm B sells only product 2. For concreteness, let all marginal and average variable costs be 10.

Without bundling, market 1 is a monopoly and market 2 is a Cournot duopoly. The monopoly output and price for good 1 are:

$$q_{1m} = 45 \text{ and } p_{1m} = 55. \tag{7.52}$$

Profit, before taking any fixed cost into account, is $(45)^2 = 2025$.

In the good 2 Cournot duopoly equilibrium, each firm produces 30 units. Duopoly equilibrium price is 40, and each firm earns profit $(30)^2 = 900$, before taking fixed costs into account. As long as firm 2's fixed costs are less than 900, it will be profitable for firm 2 to remain in the market.

Bundling   Suppose now that firm A sells its products only in bundles that contain one unit of good 1 and one unit of good 2. That is, firm A offers b_A bundles:

$$(1,1). \tag{7.53}$$

Firm B, which does not produce product 1, sells a "bundle" that consists only of one unit of good 2,

$$(0,1). \tag{7.54}$$

The relationships between the bundles and the underlying variables are:

$$Q_1 = b_A \tag{7.55}$$

and

$$Q_2 = b_A + b_B, \tag{7.56}$$

respectively, where b_A is the number of bundles sold by firm 1 and b_B is the number of bundles sold by firm 2.

From Problem 7–5, the equations of inverse demand curves for bundles are:

$$p_A = 200 - 2\left(b_A + \frac{1}{2}b_B\right) \tag{7.57}$$

and

$$p_B = 100 - (b_A + b_B). \tag{7.58}$$

Bundles are substitute goods even though the underlying products are completely independent in demand. Bundle A is a perfect substitute for bundle B: both contain one unit of good 2. Bundle B is an imperfect substitute for bundle A, since one element of Bundle A is absent from bundle B. The strategic implication is that any customer who buys the A bundle at price p_A picks up one unit of good 2 as part of the bundle, so is out of the market for bundle B.

Payoffs   If firm 1 attracts enough customers for the A bundle, the number of potential customers left for firm 2 can be so small that it is unable to cover its fixed costs. For this example (see Problem 7–6), non-cooperative equilibrium payoffs, before allowing for fixed costs, if firm A follows a bundling strategy, are:

$$\pi_A = 2\left(\frac{3}{7}\right)^2 (90)^2 = 2975.6 \qquad \pi_B = \left(\frac{2}{7}\right)^2 (90)^2 = 661.2. \qquad (7.59)$$

If firm B stays in business, firm A's profit rises from $2025 + 900 = 2925$ to 2975.6 (before allowing for fixed cost). But firm B's profit, before allowing for fixed cost, falls from 900 to 661.2. If firm B's fixed cost is between 661.2 and 900, say 700, then it will lose money because firm A opts for a bundling strategy. For such values of fixed cost, firm B will exit the market. Firm A's profit, selling the number of bundles that makes B lose money, is 1738.8, more than the 2925 firm A would make (before allowing for fixed cost) without bundling.

Bakos and Brynjolfsson (1999, 2000) emphasize the strategic impact of bundling in markets for high-technology information goods, in particular those sold over the internet, that are characterized by costs that are predominantly fixed, so that marginal cost for such goods is near zero. In their model, (Bakos and Brynjolfsson, 2000, p. 78) "even when [a firm that does not bundle] has lower fixed costs, lower marginal costs, or higher quality than the entrant, it may be forced to exit when the entrant uses the bundling strategy" if bundling changes substitutability relationships in such a way that the non-bundling firm cannot cover its fixed costs.

Academic journals   A distinctive aspect of the market for academic journals is that for most consumers, access to academic journals is mediated by a research, and usually university, library. University libraries operate under budget constraints that all too often tightly constrain subscription/purchasing decisions.

The supply side of the academic journal market is highly concentrated. By offering subscriptions to bundles of large numbers of journals—the "Big Deal"—leading publishers are able to raise the cost of entry (Edlin and Rubinfeld, 2005, p. 443):

> The immediate effect of the introduction of Big Deal arrangements has been to move competition from individual journals to large bundles of journals. This move has created a very substantial strategic barrier to entry into markets for journals. Apart from the necessity of achieving viable scale in an industry where founding even a single journal requires the daunting task of creating a new coordination equilibrium, a new entrant needs to compete for library subscriptions in an industry where a substantial share of library budgets is committed in long-term contracts with existing publishers.

BOX   Exclusionary Bundling by a Frm with Market Power

Ortho Diagnostic Systems, Inc. *v.* Abbott Laboratories, Inc. 920 F. Supp. 455 (1996), at 467:

> Assume for the sake of simplicity that the case involved the sale of two hair products, shampoo and conditioner, the latter made only by A and the former by both A and B. Assume as well that both must be used to wash one's hair. Assume further that A's average variable cost for conditioner is $2.50, that its average variable cost for shampoo is $1.50, and that B's average variable cost for shampoo is $1.25. B therefore is the more efficient producer of shampoo. Finally, assume that A prices conditioner and shampoo at $5 and $3, respectively, if bought separately but at $3 and $2.25 if bought as part of a package. Absent the package pricing, A's price for both products is $8. B therefore must price its shampoo at or below $3 in order to compete effectively with A, given that the customer will be paying A $5 for conditioner irrespective of which shampoo supplier it chooses. With the package pricing, the customer can purchase both products from A for $5.25, a price above the sum of A's average variable cost for both products. In order for B to compete, however, it must persuade the customer to buy B's shampoo while purchasing its conditioner from A for $5. In order to do that, B cannot charge more than $0.25 for shampoo, as the customer otherwise will find A's package cheaper than buying conditioner from A and shampoo from B. On these assumptions, A would force B out of the shampoo market, notwithstanding that B is the more efficient producer of shampoo, without pricing either of A's products below average variable cost.

There is an additional strategic effect of bundling that operates through the purchasing library's budget constraint (Jeon and Menicucci, 2006, p. 1041):

> Second, a publisher's bundling has an indirect effect of inflicting negative pecuniary externalities on all other publishers. The very fact that bundling allows a publisher to increase its own profit implies that, after a publisher's bundling, there is less budget left for books and for all the other publishers' journals.

7.5.2 Bundling to Alter Rivals' Conduct

Price-setting oligopoly

Bundling alters demand-side substitution relationships. If in the model outlined above, the two firms supplying market 2 (without bundling) compete in prices rather than quantities, then in equilibrium, price equals marginal cost. By bundling, the first firm makes its product an imperfect substitute for the product of the second firm. When firms sell differentiated products in price-setting markets, equilibrium prices are above marginal cost. Thus bundling can be profitable for both firms in price-setting duopoly (Carbajo *et al.*, 1990, p. 285).

To facilitate tacit collusion

Since bundling affects demand-side substitutability relationships, it is not surprising that bundling has an impact on the conditions that must be satisfied for non-cooperative collusion to be an equilibrium in a repeated game. An individual firm's incentive to adhere to tacit-collusion pricing and output, period after period, depends on the relative size of the increased profit that comes from short-run best-response behaviour and the present-discounted value of longer-run lost profit once other firms respond in kind. Spector (2007) points out that by engaging in mixed bundling, so that both components can be purchased at the bundle price or either component can be purchased separately at a component price, a firm with unilateral market power in one market (call it "the leveraging firm") places some customers—those who prefer the bundle to the second component alone—out of reach of a rival in the second market that contemplates defecting from tacit collusion. By cutting price, a competitor in the second market can attract customers who would otherwise purchase only the second good from the leveraging firm, but since it does not produce the first good, it cannot get the business of customers who buy the bundle. By reducing the short-run gain from defection, bundling increases the range of discount rates for which tacit collusion will be a non-cooperative equilibrium. Both firms earn more profit than they would in one-period non-cooperative equilibrium.

SUMMARY

A monopolist has a 100 per cent share of its market and does not face the possibility of entry. A dominant firm may have a near-100 per cent share of its market, but actual or potential competition means that equilibrium performance in dominant-firm markets can be quite different from economic performance under monopoly. Such competition may be by potential entrants, by a price-taking fringe, by recyclers of a durable good, or by oligopolist followers of the dominant firm's lead.

A Stackelberg quantity leader increases its own profit, industry output, and consumers' surplus, compared with non-cooperative oligopoly. Depending on entry costs and rivals' reasoning ability, a quantity leader may find it profitable to expand output, lower price, and preserve a dominant market position. The result is improved market performance, although an incumbent's reaction to potential competition does not generally bring as much of an improvement in market performance as would entry and an increase in the number of independent rivals.

Strategic behaviour may allow a firm to obtain or maintain a dominant position. Predation in selected product or geographic markets may allow a firm to establish a reputation that will cause potential rivals to back off in other markets, or starve rivals of capital they need to expand and cannot obtain on imperfect real-world financial markets. Less extreme forms of strategic behaviour include contracts and marketing arrangements that raise the cost to rivals of getting their products in front of consumers.

STUDY POINTS

- dominant firm with a price-taking fringe (Section 7.2.1)
- durable good monopoly (Section 7.2.2)
- Stackelberg leadership model (Section 7.2.3)
- strategic behaviour, limit pricing (Section 7.2.4)
- entry deterrence (Section 7.2.4)
- predation by dominant firms (Section 7.3.2)
- the chain store paradox (Section 7.3.3)
- predation in experimental markets (Section 7.3.4)
- raising rivals' costs (Section 7.4)
- strategic bundling (Section 7.5.1)

FURTHER READING

The model of a dominant firm with price-taking fringe is usually attributed to Forchheimer (1908). It was earlier exposited by Auspitz and Lieben (1889). On its properties, see Reid (1977). The Stackelberg leadership model is due to Sting (1931). On these points, see Schmidt (undated). Rosenbaum (1998) is a useful collection of case studies of dominant firms.

See Ausubel and Deneckere (1987) and Reynolds (2000) for concise reviews of the literature on durable good monopoly, and Waldman (2003) for a comprehensive discussion. For models that endogenize the choice of leader–follower roles, see Dowrick (1986), Hamilton and Slutsky (1990), Van Cayseele and Furth (2001), and van Damme and Hurkens (2004). On strategic entry deterrence generally, see Geroski (1991, pp. 111–121). On limit pricing, see Kamien and Schwartz (1971), for a qualification to Gaskins (1971), see Ireland (1972). Rassenti and Wilson (2004) report the results of experimental tests of the static quantity leadership model, Geroski and Toker (1996) give some evidence of persistence of leadership positions among UK firms. Lieberman and Montgomery (1988, 1998) give a management-literature perspective on factors that may or may not contribute to the persistence of dominance.

On the "long purse" model of predation, see Telser (1966). Lerner (1995) tests the "long purse" theory of predation for the disk drive industry.

Schmalensee (1984) reports suggestive profitability and welfare results based on numerical analysis for monopoly bundling when reservation prices are normally distributed. For a survey of the bundling literature, see Nalebuff (2003), and for a compact presentation, Crawford and Cullen (2007, Section 2).

The facts of *Mogul Steamship* are discussed by Taft (1914, p. 19), Letwin (1965, pp. 49–51), and Yamey (1972). Robinson (1941, pp. 69–72) and Sjostrom (1988) discuss loyalty rebates. Marshall (1919, Book III, Chapter III), McGee (1960), Scott Morton (1997), and Sicotte (1997) discuss shipping conferences in general. Shipping conferences have also been used as an example in the "empty core" literature, on which see Telser (1988), Sjostrom (1989), Pirrong (1992), and McWilliams and Keith (1994).

On the Sugar Trust, see Eichner (1969), on which the narrative discussion of Section 7.3.2 is largely based, as well as Zerbe (1969, 1970) and Eichner (1971). Porter (1969) discusses the early years of American Tobacco. On the early history of the telephone industry, in addition to the references cited in the text, see Bornholz and Evans (1983). Predation, or the lack of it, by the Gunpowder Trust, is discussed by Stevens (1912) and Elzinga (1970). Brevoort and Marvel (2004) discuss predation by the National Cash Register Company.

Kaldor (1950–51, p. 24, fn. 3), Director and Levi (1956, p. 290) and Nelson (1957) anticipate the theory of raising rivals' costs.

PROBLEMS

Asterisks indicate advanced problems.

7-1[44] (Dominant firm with price-taking fringe, raising rivals' costs)

Suppose the demand side of the market for pasta is described by equation

$$P = 11 - \frac{1}{5}Q.$$

(a) Find the profit-maximizing output, price, and profit if the market is supplied by a single firm with constant marginal cost 6.5 per unit of output.

---

[44] Based on Alexander (1997a, Table 4).

(b) Suppose now that the market is supplied by one firm with constant marginal cost 6.5 per unit of output, and by two types of fringe firms, efficient and high-cost. The marginal cost equations of the two types of fringe firms are:

$$c_e = \frac{11}{2} + q_e$$

and

$$c_h = 6 + q_h,$$

respectively, and there are seven fringe firms of each type.

Find equilibrium price, outputs, and the profit of the dominant firm if the fringe firms act as price takers and the dominant firm maximizes profit as a quantity leader, taking fringe firm behaviour into account.

(c) Find equilibrium outputs and the profit of the dominant firm if the fringe firms act as price takers and the dominant firm sets a price $P = 8.75$ while imposing a "tax" of 2.75 per unit of output on efficient fringe firms and a "tax" 2.5 per unit of output on high-cost fringe firms.

7–2[45] (Dominant firm with price-taking fringe, raising rivals' costs) Suppose there is a monopoly supplier of a market with inverse demand equation:

$$p = 31 - \frac{1}{100}q$$

and constant marginal and average cost 1 per unit.

(a) Find the firm's profit-maximizing monopoly output and the resulting price. Illustrate graphically.

(b) Suppose there is a fringe of firms that produce a combined output of 750 (no matter what the market price).

Find the (now) dominant firm's profit-maximizing output and the equilibrium price. Illustrate graphically.

(c) Suppose that instead of producing a constant output 750, the fringe firms are price takers with combined supply curve:

$$mc_f = 1 + \frac{1}{100}q_f.$$

Find the dominant firm's profit-maximizing output and the equilibrium price. Illustrate graphically.

7–3 (Price leadership with product differentiation) For a price-setting duopoly with product differentiation, let the equations of the inverse demand curves be:

$$p_1 = 100 - \left(q_1 + \frac{1}{2}q_2\right) \qquad p_2 = 100 - \left(\frac{1}{2}q_1 + q_1\right), \qquad (7.60)$$

with corresponding demand equations

$$q_1 = \frac{2}{3}(100 - 2p_1 + p_2) \qquad q_2 = \frac{2}{3}(100 + p_1 - 2p_2). \qquad (7.61)$$

Let marginal cost be constant at 10 per unit.

Find equilibrium prices and profits if firm 2 sets its price p_2 non-cooperatively to maximize its own profit, if firm 1 knows this, and if firm 1 maximizes its own profit, taking firm 2's behaviour into account.

---

[45] Based on numerical examples of Forchheimer (1908).

7–4 (Limit pricing) For the price-setting market of Problem 7–3, let firm 1 be an incumbent and firm 2 a potential entrant that must pay a fixed and sunk entry cost e if it comes into the market. If firm 1 can commit to a post-entry price, what price must it set to make entry unprofitable? Under what circumstances (for what values of re, where r is the interest rate used to discount income) would firm 1 prefer to deter entry (a) if the post-entry market would be a Bertrand (non-cooperative) duopoly and (b) if firm 1 would be a Stackelberg price leader in the post-entry market?

7–5* (Bundling and inverse demand) Suppose that (7.50) and (7.51) are derived by maximizing the representative consumer utility function:

$$U = m + 100Q_1 - \frac{1}{2}Q_1^2 + 100Q_2 - \frac{1}{2}Q_2^2 \qquad (7.62)$$

subject to the budget constraint:

$$Y = p_1Q_1 + p_2Q_2 + m \qquad (7.63)$$

(see Problem 3–11). Show that the equations of the aggregate demand curves for bundles are (7.57) and (7.58).

7–6* (Strategic bundling) For the example of Section 7.5.1, let F_2 denote the fixed cost of producing good 2. If product market competition takes the form of Cournot duopoly, show that there are values of F_2 for which firm B makes a profit if goods are not bundled and loses money if they are bundled. Show that if bundling causes firm B to lose money and exit, it is privately profitable for firm A to bundle.

PRICE DISCRIMINATION (8)

This is the worst kind of discrimination. The kind against me.

Bender (*Futurama*)

8.1 Introduction

Businesses routinely charge different consumers different prices for identical units of a good or service. Imperfect information sustains persistent price discrimination in fish markets around the world. In the United States, in-state residents and out-of-state residents pay different tuition to attend the same public university. Airline passengers sitting next to each other on the same flight pay vastly different prices for their tickets. Senior citizens and students obtain discounts that are not available to those in the so-called prime of life.

From the work of Pigou ([1920] 1950) onward, it has been customary to distinguish three types of price discrimination:

(1) *First-degree* price discrimination: each consumer pays his or her *reservation price*—the maximum price the consumer is willing to pay—for each unit of the good consumed.

(2) *Second-degree* price discrimination: output is divided into lots, each lot being sold for the highest price at which the whole lot will be purchased.

(3) *Third-degree* price discrimination: consumers are be partitioned into groups, each of which is supplied at a different profit-maximizing price.

There is no first-degree price discrimination in the modern mall, but it is the rule rather than the exception in the open-air market (see the accompanying box). A practical impediment to first- and second-degree price discrimination is that customers do not wear their reservation prices on their sleeves. Much real-world second-degree price discrimination depends on the seller being able to devise price- and product-structures that induce customers to sort themselves into groups with different reservation prices. Our topics in this chapter are the economics of first-, second-, and third-degree price discrimination and their impact on market performance.

8.2 Price Discrimination Toward Final Consumers

8.2.1 First-Degree Price Discrimination

If first-degree price-discrimination is impossible or prohibited, a monopoly supplier of the market shown in Figure 8.1 maximizes profit by producing 45 units of output and selling them at a price 55 per unit. The resulting profit is 2,025. With first-degree price-discrimination, the monopoly supplier sells 90 units of output, each to the consumer willing to pay the highest price for that particular unit. The discriminating monopolist captures all consumer surplus on the first 45 units of output. It also produces an additional 45 units of output, bringing output to the long-run perfectly competitive equilibrium level, and eliminating deadweight welfare loss from output restriction.

First-degree price discrimination permits the monopolist to wring the maximum possible profit out of the market. Consumers enjoy no surplus—each consumer pays his or her reservation price for every unit purchased. Nor do consumers suffer deadweight welfare loss. There is no monopolistic output restriction, and output is the same as it would be in long-run perfectly competitive equilibrium.

The extra profit collected by the monopolist does not come out of thin air. It is consumer income that would, without price discrimination, be spent in other industries. Thus along with the output increase from first-degree price discrimination shown in Figure 8.1 come output reductions in other markets.

  BOX   First-degree Price Discrimination in Practice

It was in [the] context of providing vocational training and supplying the orphanages that [Gardiner C.] Means applied his energy while in Turkey [in 1919]. He developed a putting-out system of children knitting wool stockings, sweaters, and caps on machines sent from the States; he also supervised shoe shops, hand-weaving and hand-spinning shops, a dye shop, a tailor shop, a blacksmith shop, a tin shop, and a carpentry shop; and finally he developed a putting-out system for cotton and wool spinning. . . . Besides developing and supervising these activities, Means had to work with the local merchants who imported the raw materials for the shops, and with the merchants in Halab and Damascus. . . . The Near East merchants with whom Means dealt operated within the context of an "oriental" bazaar . . . in which . . . there were no established prices prior to the actual transaction. Consequently, Means had to bargain with the individual merchants as to both price and quantity, and the particular figures arrived at were specific only to that transaction. Thus, a buyer following on the heels of Means (or if Means returned the following day to the same seller) would have to engage in the bargaining process anew and arrive at his own price and quantity relationship. For the tourist who bargains only over a few goods, this process of establishing a selling price can be enjoyable; but for Means who had to purchase a vast array of raw materials, the process was long and exhausting, particularly when he had to bargain with more than one seller of a particular item in order to get it at a reasonable price . . . .

Source: Lee and Samuels (1992, p. xvii).

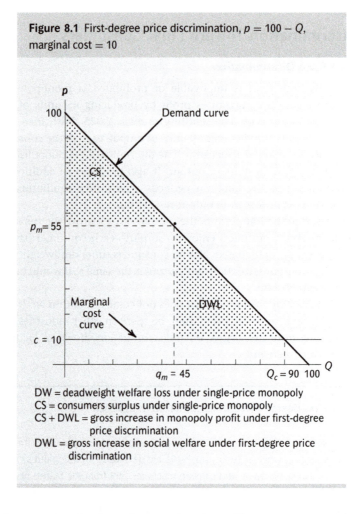

Figure 8.1 First-degree price discrimination, $p = 100 - Q$, marginal cost $= 10$

DW = deadweight welfare loss under single-price monopoly
CS = consumers surplus under single-price monopoly
CS + DWL = gross increase in monopoly profit under first-degree
price discrimination
DWL = gross increase in social welfare under first-degree price
discrimination

The usual assumption that is made to analyse the welfare consequences of price discrimination is that all these other markets are in long-run perfectly competitive equilibrium. In that case, the prices in those markets equal the marginal costs of supplying those markets. Then the output reductions in other markets are valued at their marginal costs of production, while the output increases in the market where price discrimination takes place are valued at more than the marginal cost of production. Under these conditions, the increase in output due to first-degree price discrimination represents an overall increase in welfare, even taking reduced output in other markets into account. If the other markets from which spending is transferred are *not* perfectly competitive, then there is a net welfare gain in the market where discrimination occurs, a net welfare loss in the other markets, and the overall welfare effect of first-degree price discrimination is ambiguous.[1]

---

[1] This is the slippery world of *second-best* welfare economics (Lipsey and Lancaster, 1956–1957). To deal formally with these issues requires making the jump from the partial-equilibrium models most common in industrial economics to a general equilibrium framework.

8.2.2 Second-Degree Price Discrimination

Shakespeare makes Duncan say[2] "There's no art to find the mind's construction in the face." But where customers differ in the value they attach to various product characteristics, profit-maximizing businesses have learned to fix structures of prices and product characteristics in ways that lead utility-maximizing consumers to reveal something about one aspect of their minds' construction—the upper limit of the amount they will pay for a particular type of product.

Intertemporal price discrimination

Although the idea of a bicycle as a luxury consumer durable good may today strike one as a little odd, the phenomenon shown in Table 8.1 is a familiar one. The latest, trendiest gizmo—high-definition TV, pocket calculator, mobile phone—is introduced at a relatively high price. Over time, the price falls and eventually stabilizes at a level much below the initial price.

There are many reasons one might expect to see such a price pattern. If production expands and there are economies of scale, marginal cost will fall. The same may happen if learning-by-doing is a factor, so that unit cost falls as cumulative production increases. In either case, a profit-maximizing firm with lower marginal cost would charge a lower price. Alternatively, second-movers may enter what began as a monopoly market. With or without entry, used versions of consumer durables may find their way into a secondhand market that offers imperfect substitutes for the most up-to-date new model. The oligopoly price will be less than the monopoly price.

Setup   But one reason behind new-product prices that fall from an initial high level might be intertemporal price discrimination. Suppose, for example, that there are two groups of consumers, N_t techies and N_e others, and two time periods. Techies get utility α_t per time period from using the latest model cell phone, while everyone else gets a lower utility $\alpha_e < \alpha_t$. A cell phone is a durable good, so each consumer buys at most one.

Reservation prices   If a techie buys a cell phone in the first period at price p_1, net discounted utility is:

$$\alpha_t + \frac{\alpha_t}{1+r} - p_1 = \frac{2+r}{1+r}\alpha_t - p_1. \tag{8.1}$$

Thus,

$$R_{t1} = \frac{2+r}{1+r}\alpha_t \tag{8.2}$$

is the first-period techie reservation price, the price at which the seller leaves no surplus value for the techie buyer. Similarly, the first-period reservation price for non-techies is:

$$R_{e1} = \frac{2+r}{1+r}\alpha_e < R_{t1}. \tag{8.3}$$

The highest price that will sell to everyone in the first period is R_{e1}. This price is less than the techie reservation price, so at this price techies will certainly buy in the first period. Everyone else will be indifferent between buying and not buying. For concreteness, we assume consumers buy if the price leaves them no surplus value.

---

[2] *Macbeth*, Act I, Scene 4.

Table 8.1 Catalogue price (in francs) of Hirondelle bicycle, France, 1892–1908

	Most expensive model	Least expensive model
1892	500	360
1893	420	275
1894	380	250
1895	365	209
1896	318	180
1897	256	214
1898	275	214
1899	300	237
1902	300	190
1903	300	190
1904	300	190
1905	300	190
1907	350	130
1908	350	130

Source: Phlips (1983, Table 5.3), based on Fourastié (1959).

No intertemporal price discrimination   Assume that marginal and average cost is constant, and normalize them to be zero. Then the firm's value if it sets a price to maximize value selling to all consumers in the first period is:

$$V_1 = \frac{2+r}{1+r} \alpha_e \left(N_t + N_e\right). \tag{8.4}$$

Techies enjoy some consumer surplus, in the amount:

$$S_{t1} = \frac{2+r}{1+r} \left(\alpha_t - \alpha_e\right) N_t. \tag{8.5}$$

Net social welfare if the firm sells to all consumers in the first period is the sum of the firm's value and techies' consumer surplus,

$$NSW_1 = \frac{2+r}{1+r} \left(\alpha_t N_t + \alpha_e N_e\right). \tag{8.6}$$

Intertemporal price discrimination An alternative strategy for the firm is to set a high price in the first period, selling only to techies, and a lower price in the second period, selling to everyone else. If it does this, it will set a second-period price that captures all second-period surplus,

$$p_2 = \alpha_e. \tag{8.7}$$

It will set the highest price it can in the first period, to capture as much techie surplus as possible, without inducing techies to wait one period and take advantage of a lower price. Techies will buy in the first period if the net surplus they get by so doing is at least as great as the discounted surplus from waiting one period. This price must satisfy the inequality:

$$\frac{2+r}{1+r}\alpha_t - p_1 \geq \frac{1}{1+r}(\alpha_t - p_2) = \frac{1}{1+r}(\alpha_t - \alpha_e). \tag{8.8}$$

The highest price that satisfies this no-delay constraint is:

$$p_1 = \frac{2+r}{1+r}\alpha_t - \frac{1}{1+r}(\alpha_t - \alpha_e) = \alpha_t + \frac{1}{1+r}\alpha_e. \tag{8.9}$$

This price is greater than the reservation price of non-techies, so they would not buy in the first period.

The resulting techie surplus is:

$$\left[\alpha_t + \frac{\alpha_t}{1+r} - \left(\alpha_t + \frac{\alpha_e}{1+r}\right)\right]N_t = \frac{\alpha_t - \alpha_e}{1+r}N_t \tag{8.10}$$

The firm's value with two-period pricing is:

$$V_{12} = \left(\alpha_t + \frac{1}{1+r}\alpha_e\right)N_t + \frac{1}{1+r}\alpha_e N_e. \tag{8.11}$$

Value maximization Comparing V_{12} and V_1, the firm has a greater value spreading sales over time if the proportion of techies in the population is sufficiently great, given the relative utility of the two groups, or equivalently if the relative utility of techies is sufficiently great, given the proportion of techies in the population:

$$\frac{N_t}{N_t + N_e} > \frac{\alpha_e}{\alpha_t}. \tag{8.12}$$

At the same time, consumer surplus (which goes to techies under either price policy) and net social welfare are both greater without intertemporal price discrimination. If condition (8.12) is satisfied, intertemporal price discrimination is privately profitable but socially harmful.

Quality price discrimination

Customers may be induced to sort themselves according to their preferences for quality. The classic example is the pricing—and product design—of seats in first- and second-class train cabins of a train going between two cities. A contemporary equivalent would be first-class, business-class, and economy airline seating.

Setup Suppose there are three types of cabins—high, medium, and low quality—on a passenger flight. Assume that marginal and average variable costs are constant and rise with quality:[3]

$$c_H > c_M > c_L. \tag{8.13}$$

---

[3] In the rest of this section, expressions for profit are before allowing for fixed cost.

There are N_H quality-conscious customers with reservation prices r_H, r'_M, and r_L, respectively, for the three different types of seats. There are N_M customers with reservation prices r_M, r_M, and r_L respectively, for the three different types. These customers are indifferent to, or at least, unwilling to pay for, the difference between high and medium quality. The quality-conscious group will pay more for a medium-quality variety than will the other group:

$$r'_M > r_M. \tag{8.14}$$

But we assume, as seems reasonable, that if a customer gets the same net utility from seats in two different cabins, the customer travels in the highest-quality cabin.

Finally, assume that the airline makes a greater profit on seats in higher-quality cabins:

$$r_H - c_H > r'_M - c_M > r_M - c_M > r_L - c_L. \tag{8.15}$$

One cabin

High quality   One strategy for the airline would be to offer only one quality service on a flight. If it is high-quality seating that is offered, only quality-conscious passengers would travel. The airline would set price r_H, leaving no surplus for passengers. The profit from this high-price, high-quality strategy is:

$$(r_H - c_H)\,N_H. \tag{8.16}$$

Medium quality   If only medium-quality seating is offered, the firm would set price set either price r_M or price r'_M. If the airline were to set price r'_M, only quality-conscious passengers would travel, and profit would be:

$$(r'_m - c_M)\,N_H. \tag{8.17}$$

We have assumed that the profit margin is greater on high- than on medium-quality goods, $r_H - c_H > r'_M - c_M$. Hence if the airline is going to sell only to quality-conscious passengers, it will do so by offering first-class service. If the airline sells only the medium quality variety, it will set price r_M and sell to all customers. Profit following this pricing strategy is:

$$(r_M - c_M)\,(N_H + N_M). \tag{8.18}$$

 BOX   Dupuit on Second-Degree Railroad Rate Discrimination

Only too often does the sight of third-class passengers traveling in open or poorly sprung carriages, and always badly seated, raise an outcry against the barbarity of the railway companies. It wouldn't cost much, people say, to put down a few yards of leather and a few pounds of horsehair, and it is worse than avarice not to do so. . . . It is not because of the few thousand francs which would have to be spent to put a roof over the third-class carriages or to upholster the third-class seats that some company or other has open carriages with wooden benches. . . . What the company must try to do is to prevent the passengers who can pay the second-class fare from traveling third class; it hits the poor, not because it wants to hurt them, but to frighten the rich. . . . For the same reason leather and horsehair are meted out so sparingly in the second-class carriages; it is to keep in the first class all passengers who would be willing to pay the price in the absence of a second class. And it is again ⓥ

> ⟫ for the same reason that the companies, having proved almost cruel to third-class passengers and mean to second-class ones, become lavish in dealing with first-class passengers. Having refused the poor what is necessary, they give the rich what is superfluous.
>
> *Source:* Dupuit [1849] 1962, quoted by Ekelund and Hébert (1999, p. 223).

Low quality (not) If the airline offers only low-quality service, the profit-maximizing price is r_L and profit is:

$$(r_L - c_L)(N_H + N_M). \tag{8.19}$$

But we have assumed $r_M - c_M > r_L - c_L$, so this would never be the most profitable option.

One-cabin choice If the airline offers only a single quality service, it will find it most profitable to offer the medium quality if the marginal profit on the medium-quality variety is sufficiently great, given the share of H-customers in the population, or equivalently if the share of H-customers in the population is sufficiently small, given the relative marginal profitability of medium and high-quality varieties:

$$(r_M - c_M)(N_H + N_M) > (r_H - c_H)N_H \Leftrightarrow \frac{r_M - c_M}{r_H - c_H} > \frac{N_H}{N_H + N_M}. \tag{8.20}$$

We go forward supposing that this condition is met, which is reasonable if those willing to pay for high quality are a relatively small fraction of the population. Then if the airline offers only one quality, it offers the medium quality to everyone at price r_M.

Two cabins

High and medium But the airline need not confine itself to offering a single quality service. It might offer high and medium quality varieties, at prices p_H and p_M, respectively. If it does this, it will set $p_M = r_M$ and capture all surplus from M-customers. The price offered H-customers if they buy the H variety must leave them at least as much surplus as they would get buying the medium quality at price r_M,

$$r_H - p_H \geq r'_M - r_M. \tag{8.21}$$

The highest price that will satisfy this inequality is:

$$p_H = r_H - (r'_M - r_M). \tag{8.22}$$

Some surplus remains with quality-conscious consumers, so they won't switch to a lower-quality cabin. The amount of this surplus is:

$$(r_H - p_H)N_H = (r'_M - r_M)N_H. \tag{8.23}$$

If the airline offers high and medium qualities at these prices, its profit is:

$$[r_H - (r'_M - r_M) - c_H]N_H + (r_M - c_M)N_M. \tag{8.24}$$

Net social welfare is surplus plus profit, and this works out to be:

$$(r_H - c_H)N_H + (r_M - c_M)N_M. \tag{8.25}$$

High and low   But there is another option open to the firm: if can offer the high and the low quality varieties. If it does that, the price for the low-quality variety will be r_L. This leaves any passengers, including quality-conscious passengers, with no surplus if they fly economy class. Quality-conscious passengers also have no surplus if they fly first-class at price r_H. We have assumed that if consumers would get the same net surplus flying in two different cabins, they opt for the higher-quality cabin.[4] This means the airline can set a price $p_H = r_H$ for a first-class ticket, sell to quality-conscious travellers at this high price, and earn overall profit:

$$(r_H - c_H) N_H + (r_L - c_L) N_M. \tag{8.26}$$

Quality degradation condition   Comparing payoffs in the two cases (H and M versus H and L), the quality-degradation strategy is the most profitable if:

$$(r'_M - r_M) N_H > [r_M - c_M - (r_L - c_L)] N_M. \tag{8.27}$$

The expression on the left is the profit that has to be given up to keep quality-conscious passengers from switching if medium- and high-quality varieties are offered. The expression on the right is the profit lost selling low rather than medium quality to M-passengers. If less profit is lost selling low- rather than medium-quality rides to M-passengers than has to be left as surplus value to H-passengers to induce them not to switch if medium-quality rides are offered, then the airline will opt for the maximum quality difference between cabins.

If this second strategy is followed, there is no surplus left to consumers— profit and net social welfare are the same amount. Net social welfare without and with quality degradation, respectively, are:

$$(r_H - c_H) N_H + (r_M - c_M) N_M \tag{8.28}$$

and

$$(r_H - c_H) N_H + (r_L - c_L) N_M, \tag{8.29}$$

respectively. By the assumptions we have made, net social welfare is greater without quality degradation, even if the airline finds quality degradation profitable.

8.2.3 Third-Degree Price Discrimination

The prerequisites for third-degree price discrimination to be *possible* are that consumers can be segmented into groups, and that consumer arbitrage—resale from one group to another— is not possible. Consumer arbitrage will generally not be possible for services. Transportation cost will often make consumer arbitrage effectively impossible for consumer goods that are sold in different regional markets. Impediments to consumer arbitrage may be a consequence of product design, as for example the denaturing of alcohol that blocks arbitrage between the market for industrial use of alcohol and the alcoholic beverage market.

If the two conditions for third-degree price discrimination to be possible are met, the prerequisite for third-degree price discrimination to be *profitable* is that different groups of consumers have different price elasticities of demand. We know from our review of the basic monopoly model that a monopolist's profit-maximizing price for a market makes its Lerner index equal to the inverse of the price-elasticity of demand. If different groups of consumers

---

[4] If the airline offered a price slightly below r_H, quality-conscious passengers would get greater surplus by flying first class.

Figure 8.2 Group demand curves

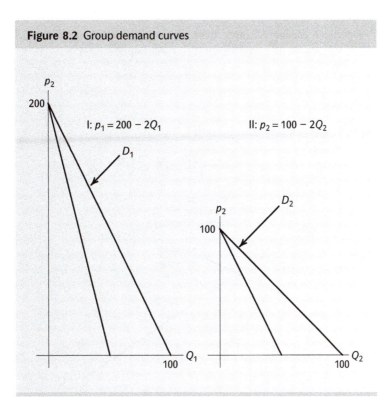

have different price elasticities of demand, a monopoly supplier will find it profitable to charge them different prices.

Setup Figure 8.2 shows a pair of demand curves for two markets. If the markets cannot be segmented, the two group demand curves:

$$p_1 = 200 - 2Q_1 \tag{8.30}$$

and

$$p_2 = 100 - Q_2 \tag{8.31}$$

add up to the combined inverse demand curve with equation[5]

$$p = \begin{cases} 200 - 2Q & 0 \le Q \le 50 \\ \frac{400}{3} - \frac{2}{3}Q & 50 \le Q \le 200 \end{cases}. \tag{8.33}$$

---

[5] For prices higher than 100 (that is, for quantities less than 50), only group 1 makes purchases, and the "combined" demand curve is just the demand curve of consumers in group 1. For prices lower than 100, some members of both consumer groups make purchases, and the quantity demanded at any price is the sum of the quantities demanded by each group,

$$Q = \frac{200 - p}{2} + 100 - p. \tag{8.32}$$

Solving (8.32) for price p as a function of Q gives the expression in the lower row of (8.33).

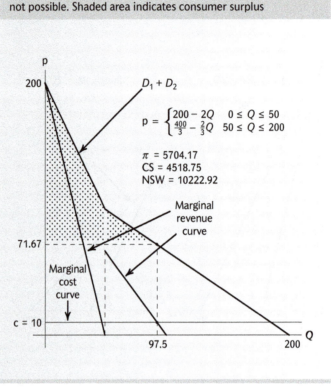

Figure 8.3 Monopoly output, third-degree price discrimination not possible. Shaded area indicates consumer surplus

$D_1 + D_2$

$$p = \begin{cases} 200 - 2Q & 0 \le Q \le 50 \\ \frac{400}{3} - \frac{2}{3}Q & 50 \le Q \le 200 \end{cases}$$

$\pi = 5704.17$
$CS = 4518.75$
$NSW = 10222.92$

Marginal revenue curve

Marginal cost curve

The no-discrimination aggregate demand curve is shown in Figure 8.3. The equations of the two segments of the marginal revenue curve can be derived from the equations of the two segments of the inverse demand curve in the usual way.

No discrimination: profit maximization and market sizes The marginal cost curve in Figure 8.3 cuts both segments of the marginal revenue curve. The first intersection has the non-discriminating monopolist set a high price and sell only to group 1, the second calls for a sufficiently lower price that the monopolist makes some sales to both groups. In general, one must compare profits at the two output levels to determine which is the most profitable.

For this example, the profit equation is

$$\pi = \begin{cases} (200 - 10 - 2Q)\,Q & 0 \le Q \le 50 \\ \left(\frac{400}{3} - 10 - \frac{2}{3}Q\right) Q & 50 \le Q \le 200 \end{cases} \tag{8.34}$$

As shown in Figure 8.4, group 2 is large enough, relative to group 1, to make selling to both groups at a relatively low price the most profitable option for the nondiscriminating monopolist.

If group 2 is much smaller than group 1, a profit-maximizing firm that is not allowed to price discriminate might make a greater profit by setting a high price and making no sales to group 2. Such a case is shown in Figure 8.5 (drawn for a second group that is half the size implied by equation (8.31), with inverse demand equation $p_2 = 50 - Q_2$).

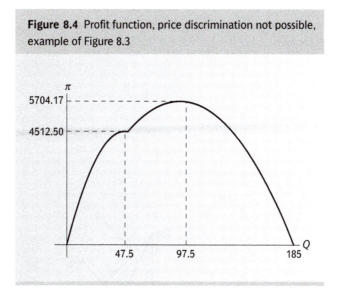

Figure 8.4 Profit function, price discrimination not possible, example of Figure 8.3

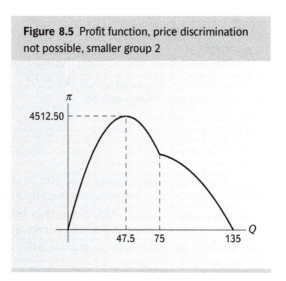

Figure 8.5 Profit function, price discrimination not possible, smaller group 2

Discrimination   If it is possible to segment the two groups of consumers, the monopolist will find it profitable to do so. This is shown in Figure 8.6, which is drawn for the example of Figure 8.2. The profit-maximizing monopolist will charge a higher price to group 1, and a lower price to group 2, compared with the no-price-discrimination value.

Price discrimination is profitable: with price discrimination the monopolist earns profit 6,537.5, without price discrimination only 5,704.17. Price discrimination also leaves consumers worse off (consumer surplus 3,268.75 with price discrimination, compared with

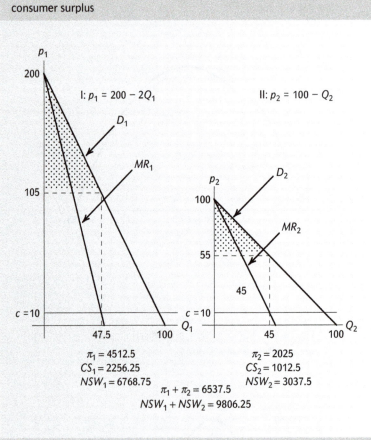

Figure 8.6 Third-degree price discrimination. Shaded areas indicate consumer surplus

I: $p_1 = 200 - 2Q_1$

II: $p_2 = 100 - Q_2$

$\pi_1 = 4512.5$
$CS_1 = 2256.25$
$NSW_1 = 6768.75$

$\pi_2 = 2025$
$CS_2 = 1012.5$
$NSW_2 = 3037.5$

$\pi_1 + \pi_2 = 6537.5$
$NSW_1 + NSW_2 = 9806.25$

4,518.75 without). The loss of consumer surplus exceeds the gain in economic profit: net social welfare falls if there is price discrimination (9,806.25 versus 10,222.92).

The result of this example—that price discrimination is privately profitable but reduces social welfare—holds if demand curves are linear. If demand curves truly curve, then the welfare effects of price discrimination are ambiguous. In general, price discrimination may increase or decrease social welfare.

Supply to small markets Price discrimination may make it profitable to sell in some markets that would not otherwise be supplied. The example of Figure 8.5 shows such a case. All consumer surplus and profit from markets that are profitably served only with third-degree price discrimination is an increase in social welfare.

Misallocation between consumers Price discrimination brings with it a source of welfare distortion that is distinct from the familiar deadweight welfare loss due to output restriction. Figure 8.7 compares prices and outputs for the two groups if price discrimination is and is not possible. With price discrimination, group I consumers are faced with a higher price, and

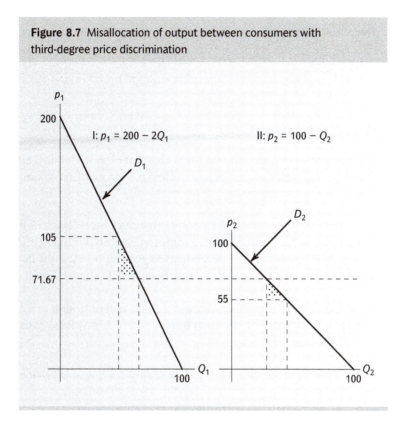

Figure 8.7 Misallocation of output between consumers with third-degree price discrimination

some of them drop out of the market. The lost consumer surplus on purchases that would have been make by group I consumer at a non-discriminatory price is the area of the shaded region on the left in Figure 8.7. At the same time, with price discrimination, group II consumers are faced with a lower price, and some of them make purchases that would not have been made at a non-discriminatory price. The incremental consumer surplus on these sales is the area of the shaded region on the right in Figure 8.7. The group I consumers who drop out of the market have higher reservation prices than the group II consumers who come into the market. If (contrary to the assumption that consumer arbitrage is not possible), group 2 consumers who buy at the low price of 55 could resell to group 1 consumers whose reservation prices are more than 55 but less than 105, both groups would be better off. That consumers with lower reservation prices are able to obtain the product, while other consumers with higher reservation prices are not, is a welfare distortion due to price discrimination.

Long-haul/short-haul rate discrimination

It seems only commonsense that it should cost more to ship cargo or a passenger a longer distance than a shorter distance. That railroad rates were often higher for short hauls than for long hauls was a frequent complaint in the glory days of railroads. Yet commonsense, as Hotelling (1932, p. 578) reminds us, is often singularly unreliable in such matters. Cost may well rise with distance, and if price tracks cost, as it will in the long-run equilibrium of

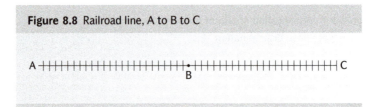

Figure 8.8 Railroad line, A to B to C

a perfectly competitive market, so price should rise with distance as well. But if a market is imperfectly competitive, this logic fails, and a lower price for a longer distance can be a sign of better market performance, not worse.

Setup To show this by example, consider the case of three cities—A (Lafayette), B (Bloomington), and C (Terre Haute)—on a railroad line, as shown in Figure 8.8. Suppose the railroad can prevent consumer arbitrage: a traveller who wishes to go from A to C must buy a ticket for that route, not two tickets, one for travel from A to B and one for travel from B to C, and so on.[6]

Let the average variable cost of providing transport from A to B or from B to C be 1, and let the average variable cost of providing transport from A to C be 2. Any fixed costs are sunk costs that were paid in the past.

Third-degree price discrimination possible (I) As a first example, suppose the demand equations for the three routes are:

$$p_{AB} = 19 - 9q_{AB} \qquad p_{BC} = 19 - 9q_{BC} \qquad p_{AC} = 8 - \frac{1}{4}q_{AC}, \qquad (8.35)$$

where footnotes denote the endpoints of a voyage and the demand equations show price-quantity relations for travel in both directions.

If the railroad is the only supplier of transportation services along these routes, the monopoly prices and outputs are:

$$p_{AB}^* = p_{BC}^* = 10, q_{AB}^* = q_{BC}^* = 1 \qquad p_{AC}^* = 5, q_{AC}^* = 12. \qquad (8.36)$$

So far, this is simply an example of third-degree price discrimination. There will be deadweight welfare loss in each market. But price discrimination is only a symptom of the fundamental cause of welfare loss, which is imperfect competition.

Third-degree price discrimination prohibited If price discrimination is forbidden, the firm must charge a through fare that is the sum of the two segment fares:

$$p_{AC} = p_{AB} + p_{BC}. \qquad (8.37)$$

The firm's profit if it is not allowed to discriminate is:

$$\pi = (p_{AB} - 1)\,q_{AB} + (p_{BC} - 1)\,q_{BC} + (p_{AB} + p_{BC} - 2)\,q_{AC}, \qquad (8.38)$$

---

[6] If the price of a ticket from A to C were sufficiently low, a passenger who wished to travel from A to B might purchase a ticket to travel from A to C and simply get off the train at B. Passenger airlines have rules intended to prevent this, although their ability to enforce the rules is limited. If instead of passenger travel we discuss the shipment of cargo, then this sort of arbitrage is ruled out—the railroad can simply refuse to unload the cargo until arrival at the destination for which a ticket has been purchased.

Figure 8.9 On the banks of the Wabash

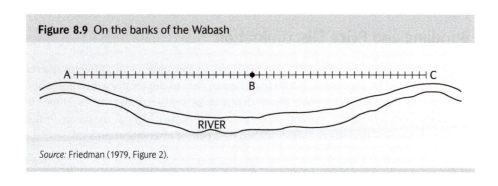

Source: Friedman (1979, Figure 2).

where expressions for the quantities demanded in terms of prices are found from the inverse demand equations in (8.35). The first-order conditions to maximize (8.38) with respect to p_{AB} and p_{BC} give two linear equations in the two prices, and these equations can be solved for the profit-maximizing no-discrimination prices,

$$p_{AB} = p_{BC} = \frac{190}{73} = 2.60. \tag{8.39}$$

The fare for travel from A to C is twice this, $p_{AB} + p_{BC} = \frac{380}{73} = 5.20$. Rates rise for long-haul customers, fall for short-haul customers, but remain above marginal cost in all three markets.

Third-degree discrimination possible (II) As a second example, change the inverse demand equation for the AC market to:

$$p_{AC} = 38 - \frac{1}{4} q_{AC}. \tag{8.40}$$

With this inverse demand equation, if rate discrimination is possible, the profit-maximizing price and quantity sold in the AC market are:

$$p^*_{AC} = 20 \qquad q^*_{AC} = \frac{1}{2} \frac{38 - 2}{1/4} = 72. \tag{8.41}$$

Even if rate discrimination is possible, the profit-maximizing firm does not discriminate: the price in the long-haul market is the sum of the prices in the short-haul markets. But price is above market cost in all three markets. Once again, the fundamental problem is imperfect competition, not price discrimination (or its absence).

Rival means of transportation Second, (following Friedman, 1979) suppose (a) there are competing transportation companies that operate along the Wabash (Figure 8.9), (b) that river transportation is a perfectly competitive market, (c) that the constant average and marginal cost of river transport from A to C is 5, and (d) that as far as travellers between A and C are concerned, river transport and rail transport are perfect substitutes.

The railroad then finds itself in the situation of the single supplier facing competition if it raises price above a certain level. To maximize profit in the AC market, it should set a price just below 5 (the resulting quantity sold will be slightly more than 132). Once again, there is price discrimination. But compared with the previous example, the price discrimination is an indication of greater rivalry, not less. Price discrimination improves market performance in the AC market without worsening performance in either the AB or the BC markets.

8.3 Bundling and Price Discrimination

Bundling may allow a firm to charge different net prices to consumers with different reservation values, and so can be a means for a firm to engage in second-degree price discrimination.
To see this, consider a producer of two goods that may be sold separately or together.[7] To
describe the demand side of the market, suppose each consumer buys at most one unit of
each good. A consumer's preferences are described by a pair of reservation prices:

$$(r_1, r_2) \tag{8.42}$$

that are the maximum amount the consumer will pay for each good. The reservation price
for each good is less than some upper limit, α, which for simplicity we take to be the same
for both goods.

Assume also that an individual's demand for the two goods is independent and that the
maximum amount a consumer will pay for a bundle consisting of both goods is the sum of
the reservation prices for the two goods if purchased separately,

$$r_1 + r_2. \tag{8.43}$$

8.3.1 Pure Components

Figure 8.10 shows a plane with reservation prices for good 1 on the horizontal axis and
reservation prices for good 2 on the vertical axis. One can think of consumers being distributed along the horizontal axis according to their reservation prices for good 1 and along
the vertical axis according to their reservation prices for good 2. This implies a distribution
of consumers' reservation-price pairs throughout the plane.

If the firm sets a price p_1^* for good 1 and a price p_2^* for good 2, consumers are divided into
four groups. Those in region A have high reservation prices for both goods and buy both
components. Those in region B have a high reservation price for good 2, not for good 1; they
buy only good 2. Consumers with reservation price pairs in region C have a high reservation
price for good 1, not for good 2, and buy only good 1. Consumers in region D have low
reservation prices for both goods and don't buy either good.

Under a pure components marketing strategy, the demand for each good depends only on
the distribution of reservation prices for that good. If n consumers have reservation prices for
each good that are uniformly distributed between 0 and α, the resulting aggregate demand
equation, of a linear demand curve, is:

$$p_i = \alpha - \frac{\alpha}{n} q_i, \tag{8.44}$$

for $i = 1,2.$[8] If each good is produced with constant marginal and average cost c per unit,
monopoly profit for each good is:

$$\pi_i = \frac{n^2}{4} \left(\frac{\alpha - c}{\alpha} \right)^2. \tag{8.45}$$

---

[7] An example would be a restaurant that offers items *à la carte* and also complete meals with predetermined
courses at a *prix fixe*.

[8] See Problem 7–7. Schmalensee (1984) examines the case in which reservation prices are normally distributed.

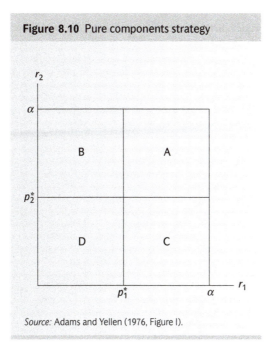

Figure 8.10 Pure components strategy

Source: Adams and Yellen (1976, Figure I).

8.3.2 Pure Bundling

The demand situation if the firm sets a pure bundling strategy is shown in Figure 8.11. Consumers are now divided into two groups—those whose combined reservation price $r_1 + r_2$ is at least as great as the bundle price p_B^*, who purchase the bundle, and all others, who do not.

Aggregate demand for the bundle depends on the distribution of the sum of reservation prices. For the case previously considered, n consumers with reservation prices for each good that are uniformly distributed between 0 and α, the aggregate demand equation for bundles is:[9]

$$q_B = \begin{cases} \frac{n}{\alpha^2}\left(\alpha^2 - \frac{1}{2}p_B^2\right) & 0 \le p_B \le \alpha \\ \frac{n}{2\alpha^2}\left(2\alpha - p_B\right)^2 & \alpha \le p_B \le 2\alpha \end{cases} \tag{8.46}$$

(Figure 8.12). The effect of bundling on demand is to collect consumers with diverse types of reservation prices in the middle of the bundle demand curve. Consumers with high reservation prices for good 1 and low reservation prices for good 2, with intermediate reservation prices for both goods, and consumers with low reservation prices for good 1 and high reservation prices for good 2 all have intermediate reservation prices for the bundle, and their quantities demanded are all in the central portion of bundle aggregate demand.

Depending on the relation between the maximum reservation price α and marginal cost (c), the profit-maximizing bundle price can occur on either the upper or the lower portion of

---

[9] One way to work out the aggregate demand equation is to measure the area A' within the $(0,\alpha) \times (0,\alpha)$ rectangle in Figure 8.11; see Problem 7–7. Alternatively, note that the sum of the reservation prices has a distribution that is the convolution of two uniform distributions, hence a symmetric triangle density function over $(0,2\alpha)$. Salinger (1995) derives a number of properties of the bundle demand curve.

Figure 8.11 Pure bundling strategy

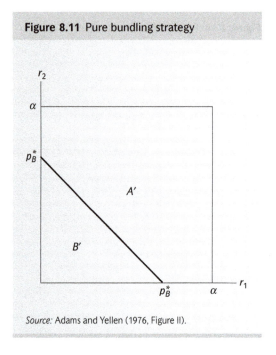

Source: Adams and Yellen (1976, Figure II).

the demand curve. Pure bundling can be either more or less profitable than selling pure components. Pure bundling is more profitable than marketing pure components when marginal cost is low. If marginal cost is low, the profit-maximizing bundling price is low enough so that the firm makes sales to, and captures consumer surplus from, the mass of consumers located in the central part of the aggregate demand curve. Some of those sales (low reservation prices for one or the other of the two goods) are not made under a pure components sales strategy.[10]

8.3.3 Mixed Bundling

Figure 8.13 illustrates the way consumers split themselves up if faced with a mixed bundling strategy—the bundle can be purchased at price p_B^*, or either component can be purchased separately at a stand-alone price. Figure 8.13 is drawn for the interesting case,[11]

$$p_B^* < p_1^* + p_2^*, \tag{8.47}$$

when the structure of prices makes it cheaper for a consumer who wants both goods to purchase the bundle rather than the components. Once again, there are four groups of consumers.

---

[10] See Problem 7–7 and Bakos and Brynjolfsson (1999). Pure bundling may increase or decrease consumer surplus, compared with pure components marketing. The result is sensitive to the distribution of reservation values (Salinger, 1995, p. 94).

[11] In the contrary case, $p_B^* \geq p_1^* + p_2^*$, sometimes called "constructive refusal", there is at best no advantage to buying the bundle over purchasing the components separately (if $p_B^* = p_1^* + p_2^*$), and if the bundle costs strictly more than the sum of the prices of the components ($p_B^* > p_1^* + p_2^*$), a buyer would incur needless expense by purchasing the bundle rather than the components.

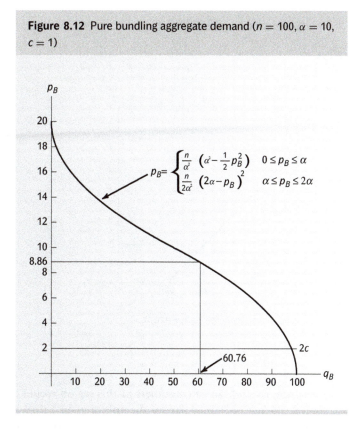

Figure 8.12 Pure bundling aggregate demand ($n = 100$, $\alpha = 10$, $c = 1$)

$$p_B = \begin{cases} \frac{n}{\alpha}\left(\alpha - \frac{1}{2}p_B^2\right) & 0 \le p_B \le \alpha \\ \frac{n}{2\alpha}\left(2\alpha - p_B\right)^2 & \alpha \le p_B \le 2\alpha \end{cases}$$

Consumers with reservation price pairs in region $Op_2^*XYp_1^*$ have $r_1 + r_2 < p_B^*$, $r_1 < p_1^*$, and $r_2 < p_2^*$. They don't buy the bundle and they don't buy either component.

There are two parts of the region $p_2^*\alpha WX$. Consumers with reservation price pairs in the triangle $p_2^*p_B^*X$ have $r_1 + r_2 < p_B^*$ and $r_2 \ge p_2^*$: they buy component 2, not the bundle. Consumers in the region $p_B^*\alpha WX$ have $r_1 + r_2 \ge p_B^*$, $r_2 \ge p_2^*$ and:

$$r_2 - p_2^* > r_1 + r_2 - p_B^*. \tag{8.48}$$

These consumers would buy the bundle under a pure bundling strategy (if only the bundle were offered at price p_B^*), but they get greater surplus by buying only component 2. Hence all consumers in region $p_B^*\alpha WX$ buy component 2. By similar arguments, all consumers with reservation price pairs in $p_1^*YZ\alpha$ buy component 1.

Consumers with reservation price pairs in $XWLZY$ buy the bundle.

Price discrimination Consumers in regions $XWIJ$ have $r_2 \ge p_2^*$, so would be willing to pay p_2^* for one unit of good 2. But for consumers with reservation price pairs in this region:

$$r_1 + r_2 - p_B^* > r_2 - p_2^*, \tag{8.49}$$

so they get an even greater surplus by buying the bundle than by buying only component 2. By buying the bundle, they acquire a unit of good 1, even though their reservation prices

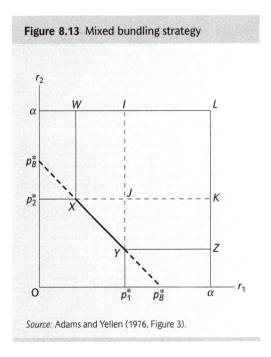

Figure 8.13 Mixed bundling strategy

Source: Adams and Yellen (1976, Figure 3).

for good 1 are below its price, $r_1 \leq p_1^*$. Since consumers in this region would be willing to pay p_2^* for a unit of good 2, the net price they pay for the unit of good 1 they get as part of the bundle is $p_B^* - p_2^*$, and from (8.49), $p_B^* - p_2^*$ is less than good 1 reservation prices in this region.

$$r_1 > p_B^* - p_2^*. \tag{8.50}$$

It is in this sense that mixed bundling involves an element of price discrimination: some consumers with relatively low reservation prices for one of the goods have the chance to pick up the good, as part of a bundle, at a lower effective price than they would have to pay to buy the low-value good as a component. A similar argument applies to region *YJKZ*.

Consumers with very low reservation prices for good 1 will not buy a bundle even though it offers them a chance to get a unit of good 1 at a low price. These are consumers with reservation-price pairs in region $p_B^*\alpha WX$.

Resumé

Venkatesh and Kamakura explain the demand-side benefits of mixed bundling—for the bundler—when reservation prices for the goods that are the components of the bundle are independent (2003, p. 217): [12]

> Conventional wisdom ... suggests that pure bundling works by reducing buyer heterogeneity and focusing on consumers who value both products; pure components is attractive in tapping

---

[12] "Optimal" here should be understood as "privately profit maximizing", not as "optimal from a social welfare point of view".

consumers who are willing to pay a high price for one product but not for the other; and mixed bundling typically emerges as the optimal strategy, as it blends the advantages of pure components and pure bundling.

There can be cost-side consequences of bundling for profitability as well. Pure bundling raises the possibility that one good or the other will be sold to a consumer at an effective price below its marginal cost (Crawford and Cullen, 2007, p. 381). In Figure 8.11, for example, consumers with reservation price pairs in the upper-left region of the reservation price square—near $(0, \alpha)$—have a low reservation price for good 1, a high reservation price for good 2, and a high-enough reservation price for the bundle, $r_1 + r_2$, so that they buy the bundle. But since the effective price for good 1, $p_B^* - p_2^*$, is less than the reservation price for good 1 (see (8.50)), all consumers in this region with r_1 less than good 1's marginal cost pay an effective price for good 1 that is below marginal cost. The firm can increase profit if it can sell only good 2 to consumers with this kind of reservation-price pair, and mixed bundling makes this possible. By appropriate choice of component prices, a monopoly mixed bundler can place some such consumers in $p_B^* \alpha WX$ of Figure 8.13: they are offered the chance to buy the bundle, but get greater surplus buying good 2 alone. Mixed bundling allows the firm to eliminate some[13] below-marginal-cost sales, and is never less profitable than pure bundling.

General results for the impact of monopoly bundling on consumer welfare and on net social welfare are also few and far between. Bakos and Brynjolfsson (1999, Proposition 1) show that with independent reservation prices and zero marginal cost, deadweight welfare loss and consumer surplus both go to zero as the number of components in the bundle increases. But if marginal cost is sufficiently high, all else equal, pure bundling is less profitable, and leads to greater deadweight welfare loss than pure components marketing.

8.3.4 Bundling by Cable-TV Systems

As we have seen, the consequences of bundling for market performance are, in general, ambiguous. Mixed bundling—one package of networks offered as basic service, additional bundles offered for an additional monthly fee, and specialty channels offered on a stand-alone basis—has been a controversial feature of the U.S. cable television market.[14]

Crawford (2005) examines the welfare impact of bundling for a sample of 1159 U.S. cable TV systems in the late 1990s. His results support the idea that cable-TV systems bundle as a way to engage in profitable price discrimination. Bundling of the top-15 networks (such as CNN or ESPN, ranked by number of subscribers) is estimated to increase the cable provider's profit by 6 per cent. It is also estimated to reduce consumer surplus 5.5 per cent, and to increase net surplus 2.5 per cent. In the same vein, Crawford and Cullen (2007, p. 402) find that if cable systems were obliged to unbundle their offerings and charge for each network separately ("à la carte" pricing), consumer surplus in a typical market would increase 65.6 per cent, profit would fall 44.2 per cent, and net social welfare would fall 7.4 per cent. On these

---

[13] But not all; see Adams and Yellen (1976, pp. 481–484).

[14] Cable-TV systems face competition from satellite providers. The degree of substitutability between the two types of providers is a matter of lively dispute.

estimates, mixed bundling improves net social welfare, but is less likely to be found to have a positive impact on market performance, the more weight is given to consumer welfare.

In late 2007, the U.S. Federal Communications Commission concluded that cable TV systems were available to at least 70 per cent of U.S. households, and that at least 70 per cent of those households subscribed to cable service (Labaton, 2007). The FCC therefore prepared to issue rules regulating cable TV rates and mandating à la carte pricing. The FCC's proposals were justified not only (it might be more accurate to write, not primarily) by a concern for static market performance in the usual sense of consumer surplus and producer surplus, but by a concern to maintain a diversity of viewpoints in the arena of public discourse.[15]

8.4 Price Discrimination and Market Performance

Antitrust and competition authorities have been concerned with *primary line* injury to competition—injury to competition in the market supplied by the discriminating firm and with *secondary line* injury to competition—injury to competition in the market supplied by the customer-firms of the discriminating producer of an intermediate good. In this section we consider two examples of price discrimination in the sale of intermediate goods. The first example is of price discrimination by a monopolist producer of an input that is purchased by downstream firms and used to manufacture a finished product that is sold to final consumer demand. The second example is of price discrimination by duopolist producers of such an input. The two examples together suggest that there is no unique relationship between the impact of price discrimination on competition and the impact of price discrimination on market performance.

8.4.1 Price Discrimination by a Monopolist Input Supplier

Setup

Suppose that an upstream monopolist produces an input that is purchased by two downstream firms. The constant marginal and average cost of the input is 10. The downstream firms compete as Cournot duopolists. They process the input, in combination with some other inputs, to make a product that is sold to final consumers. One unit of the input is required to produce one unit of final good output. The equation of the inverse demand curve for the final good is:

$$p = 100 - (q_1 + q_2). \tag{8.51}$$

Leaving aside the cost of the input produced by the upstream monopolist, the downstream firms, which differ in efficiency, have marginal costs 10 and 20 per unit of final good output, respectively.

No price discrimination

To provide a basis for comparison, we first examine the profit-maximizing strategy for the upstream firm if it charges the same price, ω, to both downstream firms. The downstream

---

[15] The U.S. Cable Communications Act of 1984 gives the FCC the authority to adopt rules to promote "diversity of information sources" if the market for television services passes the seller concentration level indicated by the "70/70 rule". The same concern for media diversity has been an issue in other countries besides the United States (Italy, for example).

market is then a Cournot duopoly with cost differences. The cost functions of the two down-stream firms are:

$$c_1(q_1) = (10 + \omega) q_1 \text{ and } c_2(q_2) = (20 + \omega) q_2, \tag{8.52}$$

respectively.

Downstream outputs (I) For $\omega \leq 70$, equilibrium downstream outputs are

$$q_1^d = \frac{1}{3}(100 - \omega) \qquad q_2^d = \frac{1}{3}(70 - \omega). \tag{8.53}$$

For $\omega > 70$, firm 2's equilibrium output is zero, and firm 1 supplies the downstream market as a monopolist with marginal cost $10 + \omega$. Firm 1's profit-maximizing output is:

$$q_1^m = \frac{1}{2}(90 - \omega). \tag{8.54}$$

For $\omega \geq 90$, firm 1's equilibrium output is zero.

Upstream Since one unit of the input is required for every unit of output, the upstream firm's derived demand and profit functions are:

$$U = \begin{cases} \frac{1}{3}(100 - \omega) + \frac{1}{3}(70 - \omega) & \omega \leq 70 \\ \frac{1}{2}(90 - \omega) & 70 < \omega \leq 90 \end{cases} \tag{8.55}$$

and

$$\pi = \begin{cases} \frac{1}{3}(\omega - 10)(170 - 2\omega) & \omega \leq 70 \\ \frac{1}{2}(\omega - 10)(90 - \omega) & 70 < \omega \leq 90, \end{cases} \tag{8.56}$$

respectively.

The upstream firm's profit function is shown in Figure 8.14. The upstream firm maximizes profit by setting $\omega = 47.5$,[16] and this payoff is:

$$\pi^u = \frac{1}{3}\left(\frac{95}{2} - 10\right)(170 - 95) = 937.5. \tag{8.57}$$

Downstream outputs (II) Substituting $\omega = 47.5$ into (8.53) gives the equilibrium outputs of the downstream firms,

$$q_1^d = 17.5 \qquad q_2^d = 7.5. \tag{8.58}$$

For this linear inverse demand, constant marginal cost example, each firm's downstream payoff is the square of its output.

Price discrimination

If the upstream firm price discriminates, it charges a price ω_1 per unit to downstream firm 1 and a price ω_2 per unit to downstream firm 2. The cost functions of the downstream firms are therefore:

$$c_1(q_1) = (10 + \omega_1) q_1 \qquad c_2(q_2) = (20 + \omega_2) q_2. \tag{8.59}$$

---

[16] The derived demand equation is $U = \frac{1}{3}(170 - 2\omega)$, in inverse form $\omega = 85 - \frac{3}{2}U$. Set derived marginal revenue equal to marginal cost, 10, to find the upstream firm's profit-maximizing output, $U = 25$. The corresponding input price is found from the inverse input demand equation. Alternatively, and directly, solve the first-order condition to maximize the lower segment of the upstream firm's profit function with respect to ω.

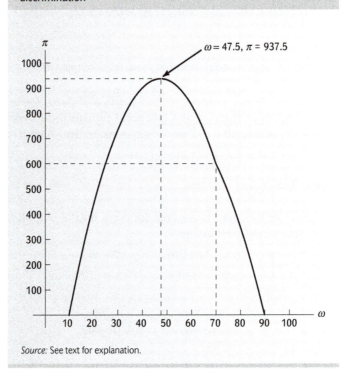

Figure 8.14 Monopoly input supplier's profit function, no price discrimination

Source: See text for explanation.

Downstream outputs (I)   The downstream firms compete as Cournot oligopolists. The downstream market is once again a Cournot duopoly with cost differences, and the equilibrium outputs of the two downstream firms are:

$$q_1(\omega_1,\omega_2) = \frac{1}{3}(100 - 2\omega_1 + \omega_2) \text{ and } q_2(\omega_1,\omega_2) = \frac{1}{3}(70 - 2\omega_2 + \omega_1), \qquad (8.60)$$

respectively.[17]

Upstream   These are also the derived demand equations facing the monopoly input supplier. It thus sells $q_1(\omega_1,\omega_2)$ units of the input to firm 1 at price ω_1, and $q_2(\omega_1,\omega_2)$ units of the input to firm 2 at price ω_2. The upstream firm's payoff is:

$$\pi^u(\omega_1,\omega_2) = (\omega_1 - 10)q_1(\omega_1,\omega_2) + (\omega_2 - 10)q_2(\omega_1,\omega_2). \qquad (8.61)$$

Substituting from (8.60) into (8.61), the upstream firm picks ω_1 and ω_2 to maximize:

$$\pi^u = \frac{1}{3}[(\omega_1 - 10)(100 - 2\omega_1 + \omega_2) + (\omega_2 - 10)(70 - 2\omega_2 + \omega_1)]. \qquad (8.62)$$

---

[17] The output levels indicated in (8.60) are valid provided both quantities are non-negative. This requirement corresponds to the restriction that $\omega \leq 70$ for (8.53) to be valid in the no-price-discrimination case. There are then some restrictions on the values of ω_1 and ω_2 that can be used for the example to make sense. We do not work out the details of these restrictions, but they are satisfied for the cases of interest here.

The profit-maximizing input prices are:[18]

$$\omega_1 = 50 \qquad \omega_2 = 45. \tag{8.63}$$

When price discrimination is possible, the upstream firm sets a higher price for the low-cost downstream firm, and a lower price for the high-cost downstream firm, compared with the no-price-discrimination case. In this sense, one can say that price discrimination distorts competition in the downstream market, to the advantage of the high-cost downstream firm and to the disadvantage of the low-cost downstream firm.

Downstream outputs (II) With price discrimination, the outputs of the downstream firms are:

$$q_1 (\omega_1, \omega_2) = 15. \qquad q_2 (\omega_1, \omega_2) = 10. \tag{8.64}$$

From this perspective as well, price discrimination disadvantages the low-cost downstream firm, which ends up producing less than it would if price discrimination were forbidden.

Equilibrium With price discrimination, the upstream firm's payoff is:

$$\pi^u = (50 - 10)(15) + (45 - 10)(10) = 950, \tag{8.65}$$

and this is greater than its payoff if it cannot price discriminate, 937.5.

Thus price discrimination leaves the upstream firm better off, the low-cost downstream firm worse off, and the high-cost downstream firm better off. But total output is the same with or without price discrimination:

$$15 + 10 = 17.5 + 7.5 = 25. \tag{8.66}$$

Since price discrimination does not change total output, it does not change the price consumers pay for the final good and it does not change consumer surplus. In this example, price discrimination distorts competition but has no effect on consumer welfare.

Two-part tariffs

A non-discriminatory *two-part tariff*—a fixed fee no matter how much a downstream firm buys and a price per unit—can yield the upstream firm an even greater payoff and result in increased output. Continuing the previous example, suppose the upstream monopolist charges a franchise fee of 1600 (per time period) and a per-unit price $\omega = 10$.[19] The less efficient, high-cost downstream firm will not purchase the input. As either a duopolist or a higher-cost single supplier in the downstream market, it would not earn enough to pay the franchise fee.

---

[18] The equations of the first-order conditions to maximize (8.62) are:

$$3\frac{\partial \pi^u}{\partial \omega_1} = 110 - 4\omega_1 + 2\omega_2 \equiv 0 \qquad 3\frac{\partial \pi^u}{\partial \omega_2} = 80 - 4\omega_2 + 2\omega_1 \equiv 0.$$

Solving these two linear equations gives (8.63).

[19] Here we assume that contract offers are public or that the upstream firm can commit to supply only the low-cost upstream firm. If not, once the low-cost firm had agreed to the two-part tariff, it would be profitable for the upstream firm to supply the high-cost downstream firm on better terms. But this would make the final-good price less than the monopoly price and the franchise agreement unprofitable for the low-cost downstream firm. Anticipating this, the low-cost downstream firm would not accept the (1600,10) two-part tariff. Such a holdup problem creates an incentive for the upstream monopolist to integrate forward; see Section 10.4.3

If the low-cost downstream firm accepts the franchise contract, it will maximize profit with marginal cost 20, and produce the monopoly output, 40, which final consumers will demand at price 60:

$$MR_{dL} = 100 - 2Q = 20 \qquad Q = 40 \qquad p = 60. \qquad (8.67)$$

Gross economic profit in the final good market is:

$$(p - 20)(40) = (40)^2 = 1600. \qquad (8.68)$$

This is just enough to pay the franchise fee.

The low-cost downstream firm breaks even, meaning it earns a normal rate of return on investment. The upstream firm earns 1600 per time period, rather than 950. Consumers are not as well off as they would be in long-run perfectly competitive equilibrium (price would be 20, output 80). But output with the two-part tariff is 40, rather than the 25 units sold with per-unit pricing. The reason is that with a two-part tariff, the upstream firm sets a low per-unit price. This reduces the marginal cost of the downstream firm that actually purchases the input, making its profit-maximizing output larger, all else equal.

8.4.2 Price Discrimination to Support Collusion

Setup

Suppose now that there are two producers of the upstream good and that they produce identical versions of the input. The average and marginal cost of producing the input is constant, and for simplicity we normalize this cost to be zero. The two upstream firms compete as Bertrand duopolists.

There are n firms in the downstream market. One unit of the input is needed to produce one unit of the final good. For all inputs except the one produced by the upstream firms, the constant marginal and average cost of the downstream firms is c per unit. The downstream firms also compete as Bertrand oligopolists.

Derived demand

We begin by working out the equation of the derived inverse demand curve facing the upstream firms. The equation of the demand curve for the final good, written in inverse form, is:

$$p = 100 - Q. \qquad (8.69)$$

Suppose for the moment that price discrimination does not take place. Let ω denote the input price. Then marginal cost of the downstream firms, taking all inputs into account, is

$$c + \omega \qquad (8.70)$$

per unit. Since the downstream firms compete as Bertrand oligopolists and the final good is a homogeneous product, the equilibrium price is marginal cost. In equilibrium, the quantity demanded in the final good market satisfies:

$$c + \omega = 100 - Q. \qquad (8.71)$$

With modest rearrangement of terms, the equation of the derived inverse demand curve for the upstream good is seen to be:

$$\omega = 100 - c - U, \qquad (8.72)$$

where $U = Q$ is the quantity demanded of the upstream good.

No upstream collusion

Since the upstream firms also compete à la Bertrand, the equilibrium input price equals the marginal cost of producing the upstream good, $\omega_B = 0$. The equilibrium price in the final good market is $p_B = c$. Upstream and downstream firms earn zero economic profits.

Upstream collusion

How would the outcome change if the upstream firms were able to collude and obtain the monopoly profit? Monopoly output for the inverse demand curve (8.72) is:

$$U_m = \frac{1}{2}(100 - c).$$ (8.73)

This makes the monopoly input price:

$$\omega_m = 100 - c - \frac{1}{2}(100 - c) = \frac{1}{2}(100 - c).$$ (8.74)

Monopoly profit would be:

$$\pi_m = \frac{1}{4}(100 - c)^2,$$ (8.75)

and this is the prize (per period) for successful collusion.

Downstream enforcement[20]   The upstream firms (call them U_1 and U_2) set the monopoly input price (8.74) for all downstream firms except the first, D_1. D_1, publicly or privately, is quoted the discriminatorily low price:

$$\omega_1 = \frac{1}{3}(100 - c) < \omega_m.$$ (8.76)

The downstream market is a Bertrand oligopoly. D_1 can undersell its rivals slightly and drive them out of business. D_1 may buy out its rivals; they may simply pack their tents and disappear into the night (to invest their assets in some other industry). Whatever the means of their exit, the outcome is not in doubt. Leaving the details of the transition period aside, D_1 will set a price slightly less than ω_m and sell a quantity of the final good slightly greater than $Q_m = U_m$.

As its contribution to the collusive scheme, D_1 buys half its inputs from U_1 and half its inputs from U_2. Leaving aside the small discrepancy due to the fact that D_1 sets a price just below $c + \omega_m$, each of the three firms (U_1, U_2, and D_1), collects profit per period:

$$\frac{1}{12}(100 - c)^2.$$ (8.77)

That is, the three firms evenly divide the monopoly profit.

The price ω_1 has been chosen in this example to result in equal division of the monopoly profit. While equal division has a certain innate charm, in practice one would expect the division of collusive profit to depend on a bargaining process, from which an unequal division of profit might result.[21]

---

[20] See the discussion in Section 21.1.1of the South Improvement Company/Standard Oil episode.

[21] In theory, the upstream firms could obtain virtually all the monopoly profit for themselves, by playing off the downstream firms one against the other. If D_1 will police the cartel for one-third of the monopoly profit, leaving D_2 and all the other downstream firms with nothing, then D_2 ought to be willing to police the cartel for (say) one-quarter of the monopoly profit. And so on. This did not happen in the South Improvement Company/Standard Oil episode, and Standard Oil's speedy acquisition of its competitors may well be explained by a desire to secure its negotiating position vis-à-vis its railroad "partners".

Here, as in Section 8.4.1, price discrimination distorts competition in the downstream market, which is transformed into a monopoly. Here, and in contrast to the situation considered in Section 8.4.1, price discrimination worsens market performance and reduces consumer welfare.[22]

8.4.3 Postscript

In the first example, price discrimination by a monopolist distorted downstream competition and increased the monopolist's profit, but left consumer welfare unchanged. In the second example, collusive price discrimination distorted downstream competition and served as a method to restrict output and extract monopoly profit, leaving consumers worse off. The two examples together suggest that the answer to the question "Does price discrimination distort competition in market X?" is a poor guide to the answer of the question "Does price discrimination worsen market performance in market X?"

SUMMARY

Price discrimination is a symptom of imperfect competition. Price discrimination toward final consumers can allow a firm with market power to increase its economic profits. Firms may establish price structures and choose product characteristics to effect second-degree price discrimination; they may block consumer arbitrage to make third-degree price discrimination possible. If price discrimination is not too costly to put in place and it results in increased output of a standardized product, it increases net social welfare (although it may leave consumers worse off). Price discrimination may also make it profitable for a firm to serve markets that it would not otherwise be profitable to serve. The welfare consequences of price discrimination toward final consumers are, in general, ambiguous.

Price discrimination by an upstream firm with market power over an essential input can distort competition among downstream firms. In a dynamic perspective, price discrimination may support collusion, which would worsen market performance.

STUDY POINTS

- price discrimination: first degree (Section 8.2.1), second degree (Section 8.1), third degree (Section 8.2.3)
- commodity bundling (Section 8.3)
- price discrimination and market performance (Section 8.4)

FURTHER READING

On second-degree price discrimination by marketing packages of differing sizes at differing prices per unit, see Pigou (1904). On price discrimination, see Robinson (1933), Schmalensee (1981), Phlips (1983), Borenstein (1985), Katz (1987), Holmes (1989) and Varian (1989).

---

[22] This example is not meant to suggest that price discrimination by oligopoly suppliers everywhere and always supports collusion. It may do so; Standard Oil and the Sugar Trust are cases in point. But surreptitious price cuts may destabilize tacit or overt collusion.

PROBLEMS

An asterisk indicates an advanced problem.

8–1. (Third degree price discrimination) Let there be two groups of consumers. Both are supplied by the same firm, which produces with average and marginal cost 1 per unit of output.

The inverse demand equation for the first group is:

$$p_1 = 25 - q_1.$$

(a) If the inverse demand equation for the second group is:

$$p_2 = 17 - 2q_2,$$

find the profit-maximizing output levels and prices if the firm is able to charge different prices to the two groups.

Find the profit-maximizing output level, price, and quantity sold to each group if the firm is not able to charge different prices to the two groups.

What are the implications of price discrimination for consumer welfare and market performance for this example?

(b) Answer the same questions if the inverse demand equation for the second group is:

$$p_2 = 11 - 2q_2.$$

8–2. (Monopoly input supply) An upstream firm is the monopoly supplier of an input which it produces at constant marginal and average cost 50 per unit and sells to two downstream firms.

The downstream firms use one unit of the input, in combination with other inputs, to produce a final good that they supply to a market with inverse demand equation:

$$p = 1100 - \frac{1}{2}(q_1 + q_2).$$

The two downstream firms compete as Cournot duopolists.

Downstream firm 1 has constant marginal and average cost 100 per unit of output for all inputs except the input produced by the upstream monopolist.

Downstream firm 2 has constant marginal and average cost 200 per unit of output for all inputs except the input produced by the upstream monopolist.

(a) Find the profit-maximizing input price ω if the upstream firm must charge an identical price to both downstream firms.
Find the equilibrium outputs of the downstream firms, the final good price, and the profits of all three firms.

(b) The profit-maximizing input prices if the upstream firm is allowed to price discriminate are $\omega_1 = 525$ to the first downstream firm and $\omega_2 = 475$ to the second downstream firm.
Find the equilibrium outputs of the downstream firms, the final good price, and the profits of all three firms.

8–3* (Commodity bundling) Suppose n consumers purchase either 0 or 1 units of two homogeneous products. Let r_i denote a consumer's (gross) utility from consuming 1 unit of good i, for $i = 1, 2$. Different consumers have different r_is. Assume that the distribution of r_i is uniform on the interval $0 \le r_i \le \alpha$, for $i = 1, 2$. For simplicity, refer to a consumer with reservation prices (r_1, r_2) as "a consumer at (r_1, r_2)".

If a consumer at r_i purchases one unit of product i at price p_i, that consumer obtains net utility:

$$r_i - p_i. \tag{8.78}$$

If the marginal and average cost of producing a unit of either good is c, find the profit-maximizing prices of a monopoly supplier under a pure component pricing strategy and under a pure bundling strategy. Compare the resulting payoffs for $n = 100$, $\alpha = 10$, $c = 1$.

MARKET STRUCTURE

[W]hether the law [of competition] be benign or not, we must say of it ... : It is here; we cannot evade it; no substitutes for it have been found; and while the law may be sometimes hard for the individual, it is best for the race, because it insures the survival of the fittest in every department. We accept and welcome, therefore, as conditions to which we must accommodate ourselves, great inequality of environment, the concentration of business, industrial and commercial, in the hands of a few, and the law of competition between these, as being not only beneficial, but essential for the future progress of the race.

Carnegie (1889, p. 655)

9.1 Introduction

The topic of this chapter is whether or not Andrew Carnegie's views on equilibrium market structure, quoted above, are correct. Does modern technology imply that the control of production will inevitably be concentrated in the hands of a few producers? Many have thought so, including Karl Marx, but today economists' judgement is more nuanced, expecting high seller concentration in industries with some technological and demand characteristics, not others, and leaving room for a certain element of chance as well.

We begin this chapter with a brief treatment of the evolution of the structure of overall economic activity in developed economies, then turn our attention to the analysis of the determinants of market structure, which the structure-conduct-performance school explained in terms of entry conditions. Entry conditions in turn were seen as depending on the nature of economies of scale, on product differentiation, and on the absolute capital investment required for efficient operation (see Section 5.3.2). Later scholars have drawn attention to the impact of the internal organization of firms on productive efficiency and to the quality-enhancing effects of sales efforts and research and development on entry costs.

We then examine dynamic models of market structure. Unlike static models, which picture entry and exit as more or less automatic flows of firms drawn to economic profits and repelled by economic losses, dynamic models picture entry and exit as parts of a triage that selects more efficient and/or more profitable firms into the set of surviving firms and selects most entrants into the set of short-lived also-rans.

9.2 The Structure of Industries Within the Economy

The structure of economic activity in developed countries has changed sharply over time. The manufacturing sector generates much less of U.S. gross domestic product than was once the case. Between 1947 and 2007, the combined share of manufacturing, wholesale and retail distribution, and transportation and warehousing—roughly, the sectors involved in producing and delivering manufactured goods to final consumers—fell from 47.31 per cent to 26.77 per cent of U.S. gross domestic product (Table 9.1). Over the same period, the

Table 9.1 U.S. industry value added as per cent of gross domestic product, 1947 and 2007

Sector	1947	2007
Agriculture	8.17	1.17
Mining	2.34	1.99
Utilities	1.36	2.14
Construction	3.67	4.07
Manufacturing	25.60	11.67
Wholesale	6.34	5.77
Retail	9.39	6.41
Transportation & warehousing	5.98	2.92
Information	2.53	4.66
Finance, insurance, real estate, rental, and leasing	10.41	20.67
Professional and business services	3.71	12.17
Educational services, health care, and social assistance	1.88	7.88
Arts, entertainment, recreation, accommodation, food services	3.21	3.65
Other services, except government	2.95	2.29
Government	12.47	12.58

Source: U.S. Bureau of Economic Analysis.

Table 9.2 Sectoral share of gross value added, EU-27, 2006

Sector	%
Business activities and financial services	27.9
Other services	22.6
Trade, transport, and communications	21.6
Industry	20.2
Construction	6.2
Agriculture, hunting, and fishing	1.8

Source: Eurostat Statistical Yearbook 2008, Table 1.4.

combined shares of service sectors[1] in gross domestic product rose from 22.16 per cent to 46.66. In real terms, manufacturing-sector GDP per capita nearly doubled between 1947 and 2007. But real GDP per capita in the service sectors grew more than seven-fold over the same period, so that manufacturing declined in importance relative to services.

There is a similar pattern of overall economic activity in the European Union (Table 9.2). In 2007, value added in service sectors for the EU-27 was 50.5 per cent, value added in industry 20.2 per cent. In developed economies, productivity increases in capital-intensive manufacturing sectors have permitted the shift of resources to high-value-added, labour-intensive service industries.

9.3 Supply-Side Market Structure

Among the many market characteristics thought to influence market performance, industrial economists have given pride of place to the number and size distribution of firms on the supply side of the market. A single measure of seller concentration (early on, an n-firm concentration ratio, later the Herfindahl index) was treated as a summary statistic of the distribution of relative firm sizes, a measure of "fewness" on the supply side of a market. A concentration ratio closer to 100 per cent or a Herfindahl index closer to 1 meant an industry structure closer to monopoly, a concentration ratio or a Herfindahl index closer to zero meant an industry structure closer to the "many small firms" of perfect competition.

Most often, it was supply-side market structure in manufacturing industries that was analysed, and this for two reasons. The formation of trusts in the United States at the turn of the nineteenth century drew attention to the manufacturing sector. This emphasis on

---

[1] The rows of Table 9.1 from finance, insurance, real estate, rental, and leasing to other services, except government, inclusive.

manufacturing was re-enforced by the worldwide collapse of manufacturing activity during the Great Depression of the 1930s. Manufacturing was the most important sector of the economy, and the first studies of supply-side market structure were of manufacturing. On a more pragmatic level, although this is hardly a justification, government agencies tended (as they still do) to collect and report more detailed information about manufacturing than about other sectors of the economy. Industrial economists pushed the analysis of the manufacturing sector farther than they did that of other sectors because it was easier to obtain data about the manufacturing sector.

9.3.1 Manufacturing: Description

United States

The relative decline of manufacturing in overall economic activity for developed economies suggests that the emphasis on the structure of manufacturing industries is no longer appropriate (if ever it was). But that is where we begin. Table 9.3 gives an indication of the distribution of four-firm seller concentration ratios, the combined U.S. market shares of the four largest U.S. suppliers, as reported in the 2002 U.S. Economic Census, for 413 six-digit NAICS manufacturing industries.

Table 9.3 Six-digit NAICS manufacturing industry share of value of shipments, by four-firm seller concentration ratio decile, 2002

Concentration Range	Number of Industries	Per Cent of Total Value of Shipments
$90 \leq CR4 \leq 100$	11	6.30
$80 \leq CR4 < 90$	15	3.89
$70 \leq CR4 < 80$	31	8.48
$60 \leq CR4 < 70$	44	6.53
$50 \leq CR4 < 60$	60	15.97
$40 \leq CR4 < 50$	77	20.83
$30 \leq CR4 < 40$	61	15.37
$20 \leq CR4 < 30$	73	12.97
$10 \leq CR4 < 20$	28	6.02
$0 \leq CR4 < 10$	13	3.66
Total	413	100.00

Manufacturing industries are made up of (U.S. Department of Commerce, 2006, p. ix) "establishments engaged in the mechanical, physical, or chemical transportation of materials, substances, or components into new products". An "establishment" is a plant or location at which productive activity takes place. For each industry, the Economic Census reports the share of value of shipments supplied by the largest 4, 8, 20, and 50 firms, as well as a Herfindahl index computed using the market shares of the largest 50 companies.[2] The n-firm seller concentration ratio is the combined share of the shipments of the largest n U.S. firms in the shipments of all such firms. The concentration ratio understates the place of the largest firms in economic markets if an industry's geographic markets are smaller than the whole United States. The concentration ratio misstates the place of the largest suppliers in economic markets in that it does not include imported sales.

The simple average four-firm seller concentration ratio for the industries described in Table 9.3 is 45.1 per cent; the value-of-shipments weighted average is 47.6 per cent. 161 of the 413 industries described in Table 9.3 have four-firm seller concentration ratios 50 per cent or more; these industries account for 41.17 per cent of the value of shipments of industries in the sample.[3] 175 industries have four-firm seller concentration ratios less than 40 per cent; these industries account for 38.02 per cent of the value of shipments of industries in the sample. In 2002, the typical six-digit NAICS U.S. manufacturing industry had the supply-side structure of a moderately concentrated oligopoly, with a dispersion of less and more concentrated industries and an upper tail of highly concentrated industries.[4]

European Union

Table 9.4 reports approximate concentration measures for several EC two-digit NACE industries. The concentration measures are constructed using data for a sample of 309 large EC firms. Despite that fact that few industrial economists would consider two-digit classifications to represent industries in an economic sense, concentration measures were calculated at the two-digit industry level to allow for the fact that most of the firms are diversified into several less aggregated (three- or four-digit) industries. The concentration measures given in Table 9.4 suggest that even for highly aggregated industry categories, there is a substantial variation in concentration across industries. They also suggest that there is typically substantial inequality in firm size among firms in the same industry. In NACE industry 22, for example, the largest of the 28 large firms in the sample has a market share of slightly more than 17 per cent. The ten largest firms have a combined market share of nearly 70 per cent, indicating that the smallest 18 firms divide the remaining 30 per cent of sales. The numbers-equivalent measure for industry 22 is 14.4, roughly half the number of firms in the sample. The numbers-equivalent measures reported in Table 9.4 are all substantially less than the actual number of firms. Industries 25 and 47 are the least concentrated, and industries 24 and 34 the most concentrated.

---

[2] The Economic Census does not report aggregate figures if doing so would make it possible to infer information about individual firms. The 413 industries described in Table 9.3 are all those for which data were reported, excluding industries that are residual categories (to which were assigned establishments producing "miscellaneous" or "not elsewhere classified" products).

[3] The Table 9.3 industry with the largest four-firm seller concentration ratio is industry 331411, primary smelting and refining of copper, with CR4 = 99.2 per cent.

[4] A very similar picture emerges if one looks at the inverse of the Herfindahl index, the number of equally sized firms that would result in the reported value of the Herfindahl index.

Table 9.4 Concentration statistics for selected NACE industries, EC, 1994

NACE code	Title	C1	C4	C10	H	1/H	n
34	Electrical engineering	24.9	62.1	87.4	0.127	7.9	22
24	Manufacture of non-metallic mineral products	25.2	59.3	86.7	0.119	8.4	16
35	Manufacture of motor vehicles and of motor vehicle parts and accessories	19.5	56.7	89.5	0.108	9.2	22
31	Manufacture of metal articles	20.3	54.5	82.0	0.105	9.5	18
32	Mechanical engineering	21.0	47.1	69.9	0.089	11.3	27
41/42	Food, drink, and tobacco industry	16.1	43.2	62.2	0.067	15.0	51
22	Production and preliminary processing of metals	17.2	41.6	69.4	0.069	14.4	28
50	Building and civil engineering	17.0	41.5	62.6	0.063	15.8	40
25	Chemical industry	9.0	29.9	53.5	0.040	24.7	50
47	Manufacture of paper and paper products, printing and publishing	7.9	28.2	55.5	0.043	23.3	32

Note: n is the number of firms assigned to the industry
Source: EC Commission (1997).

Using 1987 data, Davies and Lyons (1996) compare four-firm seller concentration ratios at the three-digit manufacturing industry level for Japan, the European Union, and the United States. They find that Japanese manufacturing industries are most concentrated, on average and EU manufacturing industries least concentrated (Davies and Lyons, 1996, p. 58, fn. omitted): "Using the midpoint US and Japan estimates, EU market concentration is 14 points lower than the USA and 34 points lower than Japan." This is the result one would expect if the process of European market integration is not yet complete, so that the number and size-distribution of firms in the typical EU manufacturing industry have not yet adjusted to long-run levels.

There are wide variations in the supply-side market structure of manufacturing and other industries, and such variations persist for less broadly-defined groups of industries. Table 9.5 describes concentration levels for six-digit NAICS industries, grouped by three-digit subsectors. Within most subsectors, some six-digit industries are relatively unconcentrated, some highly concentrated. But there are also general patterns: the minimum four-firm concentration ratio in what is on average the most highly concentrated subsector, beverage and

Table 9.5 Average six-digit NAICS industry CR4, by three-digit NAICS industry, 2002

NAICS Code	Title	Number of Six-digit Industries	Per Cent of Total Value of Shipments	CR4		
				min	mean	max
312	Beverage & tobacco products	8	3.00	42.9	74.3	95.3
336	Transportation equipment	25	16.20	26.3	73.1	96.0
314	Textile product mills	6	0.58	12.4	55.2	79.7
334	Computer & electronic products	26	9.44	20.1	52.5	76.8
335	Electrical equipment, appliances, & components	18	2.34	24.1	50.7	93.4
316	Leather & allied products	8	0.15	35.0	50.4	96.8
311	Food	41	12.01	3.7	47.6	91.4
322	Paper	19	4.40	21.7	47.4	71.2
325	Chemicals	31	11.32	23.5	47.3	92.9
331	Primary metals	21	3.78	13.2	45.8	99.2
333	Machinery	44	6.06	7.0	42.4	88.0
315	Apparel	19	0.90	5.9	41.8	83.5
324	Petroleum & coal products	4	6.30	24.9	41.1	60.0
326	Plastics & rubber products	15	2.76	20.6	40.2	84.6
327	Nonmetallic mineral products	20	2.34	10.3	36.5	88.3
313	Textile mills	11	1.29	19.5	34.0	64.4
337	Furniture & related product	13	2.24	10.1	31.5	64.4
321	Wood products	12	2.31	6.9	27.3	66.6
332	Fabricated metal products	38	6.54	2.2	22.3	83.0
323	Printing & related support activities	11	2.74	7.5	18.2	63.9
		390	96.7	2	47.7	99.2

Source: 2002 Economic Census.

tobacco products, 42.9 per cent, is larger than the weighted[5] average four-firm concentration ratio of the ten least-concentrated subsectors. Concentration varies within subsectors, but tends to vary in a systematic way from subsector to subsector.

9.3.2 Explanation

Supply-side market structure is a product of economic forces—firms decide to enter or leave a market, to expand or contract the scale of their operations. By analysing these economic forces, one can hope to explain the differences in the size distributions of firms in different industries. Such explanations fall in three generally complementary categories.

Entry conditions

Industrial economists first explained differences in market structure in terms of differences in entry conditions. Entry conditions were seen as depending directly on basic demand and supply conditions, and indirectly on firm conduct, some of which could influence basic demand and supply conditions (Figure 1.1). Markets into which entry was difficult would be concentrated, and markets into which entry was easy would be unconcentrated.

Organizational capabilities

The contribution of the business historian Alfred D. Chandler, Jr. was to highlight the impact of firm structure on entry conditions, market structure, and market performance. In industries with some types of technology and demand characteristics, there are potential efficiency advantages to large-scale operation. In industries with other types of technology and demand characteristics, there are few or no advantages to large-scale operation. The former type of industry had become concentrated—Chandler looked at the past to try to understand the present—if and when firms developed organizational techniques that made it possible to realize potential efficiencies. The latter type of industry had not become concentrated.

Endogenous sunk costs

John Sutton has emphasized that in some industries, technology and demand characteristics depend in an intrinsic way on firms' decisions—in R&D, in product design, in marketing. In this perspective, there are some kinds of markets in which firms can create and sustain efficiency and strategic advantages of large-scale operation. Such markets can be characterized by the extent to which consumers regard the products of different suppliers as homogeneous or differentiated, and, if differentiated, on the balance between horizontal and vertical product differentiation. Markets in which vertical product differentiation can be enhanced by marketing and product development efforts tend to be supplied by a few larger firms; other markets do not.

9.3.3 Models of Cournot Market Structure

Static models of market structure explain equilibrium market structure in terms of market size and entry cost by making the assumption that the number of firms adjusts so that firms earn only a normal rate of return on investment.

---

[5] The mean concentration ratio reported in Table 9.5 is the average of four-firm concentration ratios of six-digit industries within the subsector, weighted by industry value of shipments.

Cournot oligopoly, single-plant firms

Setup

We consider a market with linear inverse demand,

$$p = a - Q. \tag{9.1}$$

The cost function is:

$$c(q) = F + cq + dq^2, \tag{9.2}$$

for $q > 0$ (and $c(0) = 0$), with F, c, and d all positive, For the moment interpret (9.2) as the cost function of a single firm.

Fixed cost F must be paid if the firm operates at all; it can be avoided by shutting down. The average variable and marginal cost functions for the cost function (9.2) are linear, with equations:

$$AVC(q) = c + dq \tag{9.3}$$

and

$$MC(q) = c + 2dq \tag{9.4}$$

respectively. c is the minimum value of marginal cost. d determines the extent of diseconomies of scale: for every unit increase in output, average cost rises by d, marginal cost by $2d$.

In the short run, diseconomies of scale are a consequence of larger and larger amounts of variable factors of production (labour, materials) "crowding" a fixed capital stock. Over the long run, when the stock of physical capital is variable, one might still regard "management" as a fixed factor of production and expect to observe diseconomies of large firm scale.

Cost curves

(9.2) implies an average cost equation:

$$AC(q) = \frac{F}{q} + c + dq. \tag{9.5}$$

A few average cost curves, for $c = 10$, $d = 1$ and different values of F, are shown in Figure 9.1.[6] Considering the first term on the right in (9.5), F/q, when output is small, fixed cost per unit of output is large. As output increases, fixed cost is spread over more units of output and fixed cost per unit of output falls. Considering the third term on the right in (9.5), as output increases, variable cost per unit of output rises. For low output levels, the spreading-of-fixed-cost effect predominates, average cost falls as output rises, and the average cost curve exhibits economies of scale. For large output levels, diseconomies of scale predominate, average cost rises as output rises, and the average cost curve exhibits diseconomies of scale. Over the whole range of output, the result is a roughly ∪-shaped average cost curve.

Minimum efficient scale

The minimum point on the average cost curve occurs where the marginal cost curve and the average cost curve intersect. Solving equations (9.4) and (9.5), we find the output level at which the average cost and marginal cost curves intersect, the *minimum efficient scale* output level, so called because it yields the lowest value of average cost:

$$q_{mes} = \sqrt{\frac{F}{d}}. \tag{9.6}$$

---

[6] For an explanation of the particular values of F that are used in Figure 9.1, see Figure 9.2 and the associated text.

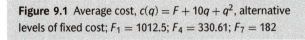

Figure 9.1 Average cost, $c(q) = F + 10q + q^2$, alternative levels of fixed cost; $F_1 = 1012.5$; $F_4 = 330.61$; $F_7 = 182$

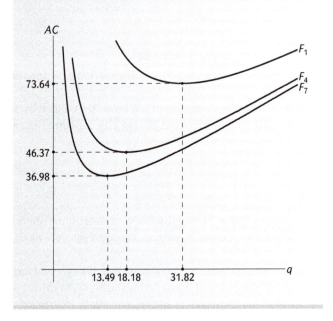

The minimum efficient scale output is determined by the technology, as described by the cost function. It rises as fixed cost F rises and as the diseconomies of scale parameter d falls.

Substituting (9.6) in either (9.4) or (9.5), the minimum value of average cost is:

$$AC_{min} = c + 2\sqrt{dF}. \tag{9.7}$$

The minimum value of average cost rises as F or d rises.

Equilibrium number of firms

From this model of the costs of a single firm, we can obtain a basic model of market structure. Suppose that there are n firms, each with cost function of form (9.2), and that they behave as Cournot oligopolists. Then firm 1 (for example) maximizes profit along its residual demand curve by picking an output level that makes marginal revenue equal to marginal cost,

$$a - (q_2 + q_3 + \ldots + q_n) - 2q_1 = c + 2dq_1, \tag{9.8}$$

leading to the expression:

$$q_1 = \frac{1}{2(1 + d)} [a - c - (q_2 + q_3 + \ldots + q_n)] \tag{9.9}$$

for firm 1's best-response output when the cost function implies that there are diseconomies of large scale.[7]

---

[7] Strictly speaking, (9.9) is the equation of firm 1's best response function only if the resulting output means that firm 1 does not make losses that exceed its fixed cost. If firm 1 were to make losses that exceed its fixed cost, its profit-maximizing output would be zero (that is, its profit-maximizing choice would be to shut down).

Because we have assumed that firms are identical, in equilibrium all firms produce the same output.[8] Setting $q_1 = q_2 = \cdots = q_n = q_{Cour}$ in (9.8) and rearranging terms gives an expression for equilibrium output per firm,

$$q_{Cour} = \frac{a-c}{n+1+2d}. \tag{9.10}$$

If $d = 0$ this reduces to (3.42), the result when returns to scale are constant.

Equilibrium profit per firm when there are n firms supplying the market is:

$$\pi_{Cour} = (1+2d)q_{Cour}^2 - F = (1+2d)\left(\frac{a-c}{n+1+2d}\right)^2 - F. \tag{9.11}$$

From a theoretical point of view, we can close the model by assuming that in the long run, new firms enter the market if short-run equilibrium profit is positive, incumbent firms exit the market if short-run equilibrium profit is negative. The long-run equilibrium number of firms n_{Cour} is then the number that makes $\pi_{Cour} = 0$; from (9.11),

$$n_{Cour} = (a-c)\sqrt{\frac{1+d}{F}} - (1+2d) = \frac{a-c}{q_{mes}}\sqrt{1+\frac{1}{d}} - (1+2d). \tag{9.12}$$

$a - c$ is the quantity that would be demanded in this market if price were equal to the smallest value of marginal cost (c). In this sense, $a - c$ is a measure of market size; the market is larger, the larger is a, the maximum about any consumer would pay for the product, is larger, and the smaller is c, the lowest value of marginal cost.[9] What (9.12) says is that the long-run Cournot equilibrium number of firms n_{Cour} is larger, the larger is the market and the smaller is minimum efficient scale output.[10]

For concreteness, let $a = 100$, $c = 10$, and $d = 1$. Then from the expression after the first equals sign in (9.12), the relation between fixed cost and the long-run equilibrium number of firms is:

$$n_{Cour} = 90\sqrt{\frac{2}{F}} - 3, \tag{9.13}$$

which is shown in Figure 9.2.

If $F > 1{,}012.5$, the equilibrium number of firms is zero. If fixed cost is very high, relative to market size, it is not profitable even for a monopolist to supply the market. For lower values of fixed cost, $648 < F \le 1{,}012.5$, it is profitable for one firm to supply the market, but not two (the market is a natural monopoly). If $450 < F \le 648$, the Cournot equilibrium market structure is duopoly, and so on. The lower the value of fixed cost, the larger the equilibrium number of firms.[11]

---

[8] We make the assumption that firms are identical for expositional simplicity. Examining the case of different firms makes the algebra more complicated but does not change the qualitative nature of the results; see Section 3.2.4.

[9] For simplicity, we have written the market demand equation (9.1) with slope -1. If a generalized linear demand equation is $p = a - bQ$ is used, the natural measure of market size is $(a-c)/b$, the quantity that would be purchased if price were equal to c.

[10] For simplicity, we have ignored the fact that the number of firms must be an integer. To be precise, the equilibrium number of firms is the greatest integer less than the value of n_{Cour} given by (9.12). In the long run, entry and exit will reduce profit to a level so low that if one additional firm were to come into the market, all firms would lose money.

[11] These figures are derived in the following way. Solve (9.13) for F to obtain $F = 16200/(n+3)^2$. The value of F that makes $n = 1$ is $16200/16 = 1012.5$, the value of F that makes $n = 2$ is $16200/25 = 648$, and so on.

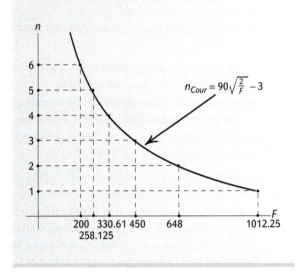

Figure 9.2 Equilibrium number of firms and fixed cost relationship, Cournot oligopoly, $p = 100 - Q$, $c(q) = F + 10q + q^2$

$$n_{Cour} = 90\sqrt{\frac{2}{F}} - 3$$

Cournot oligopoly, multiplant firms

To this point, we have interpreted (9.2) as the equation of a cost function for a firm. If, instead, we take it to be the cost function of a single plant, then a firm with a high profit-maximizing output can avoid the effect of plant-level diseconomies of scale by operating more than one plant (Joseph, 1933; Dewey, 1969, Chapter 3).

If a firm decides to produce all its output in a single plant, its cost function is (9.2). If all plants have the same cost function, and a firm opens a second plant, the efficient (cost-minimizing) allocation of output is to produce the same amount in each plant.[12] Thus, if a firm operates two identical plants, the firm-level cost function is:

$$c_2(q) = 2\left[F + 10\left(\frac{1}{2}q\right) + d\left(\frac{1}{2}q\right)^2\right]. \tag{9.14}$$

The firm must pay a second set of fixed costs for the second plant, but as a result it is able to produce half its output in each plant, reducing the impact of diseconomies of scale. If output rises above the level at which the cost of producing all output in one plant is the same as the cost of producing half of firm output in each of two plants, an output level defined by the condition:

---

[12] If plants are identical, and output is not the same in both plants, then since the firm will be operating plants on the upward-sloping segments of the average cost curves, marginal cost must be higher in the plant producing more output, and lower in the plant producing less output. But then the firm can reduce cost, keeping total output unchanged, by shifting some production from the high-marginal cost plant to the low-marginal cost plant. With identical plants, cost-minimization requires the same output level in all plants.

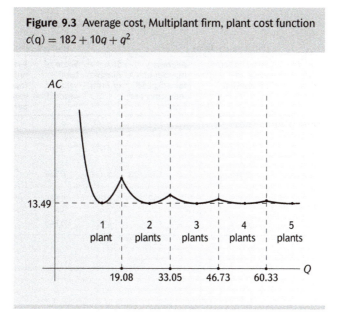

Figure 9.3 Average cost, Multiplant firm, plant cost function
$c(q) = 182 + 10q + q^2$

$$c(q) = F + 10q + dq^2 = 2\left[F + 10\left(\frac{1}{2}q\right) + d\left(\frac{1}{2}q\right)^2\right] = c_2(q),\qquad(9.15)$$

then the firm will minimize its cost by opening a second plant. If output rises further still, the firm will minimize its cost by opening a third plant, producing one-third of its output in each plant, and so on. In this way, as shown in Figure 9.3, the firm-level average cost curve exhibits approximate constant returns to scale for output above q_{mes}. The firm's average cost never rises too much above the minimum value of average cost given by (9.7), because if firm output reaches a level that drives up average cost in existing plants, in the long run the firm can open an additional plant, redistribute output among plants, and bring average cost down toward the minimum level.

Multiplant firms in practice

This theoretical story pictures multiplant operation as a way of organizing production that avoids diseconomies of scale at the plant level. Each plant produces an output that is not too different from the cost-minimizing level, and over the long run a firm expands output by opening up additional plants.

In the U.S. manufacturing sector, multiplant firms tend to be larger and more diversified than single-plant firms (Table 9.6). Although they are a small fraction of the total number of firms, they account for the bulk of manufacturing output. Evidence suggests (Scherer *et al.*, 1975) that multiplant firms frequently operate plants that appear to produce less than minimum efficient scale outputs. In some cases, this may reflect the fact that markets have a spatial aspect. A firm may operate a plant that is of suboptimal size from the point of view

Table 9.6 Descriptive statistics, single-plant and multiplant manufacturing firms

Year	Single-plant firms				Multiple-plant firms			
	Number of firms	Share of number of firms	Share of total value of production	Average number of four-digit SIC industries per firm	Share of number of firms	Share of total value of production	Average number of four-digit industries per firm	Average number of plants per firm
1963	265,779	0.945	0.215	1.23	0.055	0.785	2.75	3.72
1967	265,599	0.942	0.194	1.15	0.058	0.806	2.69	3.59
1972	263,169	0.926	0.146	1.13	0.074	0.854	2.70	3.54
1977	295,687	0.928	0.150	1.12	0.072	0.850	2.55	3.59
1982	294,394	0.927	0.152	1.52	0.073	0.848	2.52	3.50

Source: Dunne *et al.* (1988, Table 1).

of production cost alone, but at a location that allows the firm to save transportation costs to a particular group of consumers.

9.3.4 Production Scale Economies and Seller Concentration

Seller concentration is likely to be larger, the larger are plant- or firm-level economies of scale, relative to market size. But unless a market is very small, observed levels of supply-side concentration are typically much larger than required to fully realize economies of scale.

The second, third, and fourth columns of Table 9.7 show, for 12 U.S. industries, estimates of minimum efficient plant scale, the maximum number of plants per firm required for efficient operation, and the observed 1967 four-firm seller concentration ratio, respectively. Four-firm seller concentration ratios substantially exceed the level required for single-plant efficiency for all 12 industries. If one makes the maximum possible allowance for economies of multiplant operation (the final column of the table), seller concentration exceeds the efficiency-dictated level for all industries except beer brewing and household refrigerators. Scale economies alone do not explain observed concentration levels.

9.3.5 Network Externalities

Models of markets without network externalities explain the long-run number of firms that will supply a market in terms of fixed cost, market size, and the degree of product differentiation. Differences in firm size are explained in terms of differences in firms' costs.

Equilibrium market structure and market structure-performance relations are quite different in the presence of network externalities (Economides and Flyer, 1997). If there are direct network externalities, consumers value a product more, the greater the number of consumers that use the product. If there are indirect network externalities, consumers value a product that serves as a platform more, the greater the availability of complementary products

Table 9.7 MES plant size and four-firm seller concentration industry, 12 U.S. industries, 1967

Industry	MES plant size as percentage of 1967 U.S. consumption	Plants	1967 four-firm seller concentration ratio	$\dfrac{CR4}{4\,(Plants * MES)}$
Beer brewing	3.4	4	40	0.74
Cigarettes	6.6	2	81	1.5
Broad-woven cotton and synthetic fabrics	0.2	6	36	7.5
Paints, varnishes, and lacquers	1.4	1	22	3.9
Petroleum refining	1.9	3	33	1.4
Shoes (other than rubber)	0.2	6	26	5.4
Glass containers	1.5	4	60	2.5
Cement	1.7	1	29	4.3
Integrated wide strip steel works	2.6	1	48	4.6
Ball and roller bearings	1.4	5	54	1.9
Household refrigerators and freezers	14.1	8	73	0.16
Storage batteries	1.9	1	61	8.0

Note: "Plants" is the maximum number of MES-scale plants required to have no more than a slight cost or price handicap
Source: Scherer (1974, Table 3, Table 6).

designed for compatibility with the platform standard. Equilibrium market structure will often involve a single firm, dominant in the sense that it supplies most consumers, but also (and for the same reason) delivering the product that consumers value most. A fringe of smaller firms may operate in the market as well, but they will not be able to compete away the economic profits of the leading firm: since their products have smaller networks, their products deliver less value to the bulk of consumers. If network economies are important, market performance is best when a single leading firm supplies most of the market.

BOX   Format Wars

Sony Corporation introduced a Betamax-format video cassette recorder in Japan in April 1975, and in the United States in February 1976. JVC entered the U.S. market with a VHS (Video Home System)-format VCR 19 months later, in September 1977. Although the matter is unavoidably subjective, it is widely believed that Betamax was technically superior to VHS. Yet by 1984, VHS-format VCRs accounted for 80 per cent of the market, Betamax only 20 per cent (Figure 9.4). In 1988, Sony conceded defeat and began producing VHS-format VCRs.

The decline and fall of Betamax was the result of decisions by Sony and JVC that enabled JVC to leverage network externalities and overcome Sony's first-mover advantage.

Neither Sony nor JVC had the capacity to supply anticipated demand for video cassette recorders; each sought to enlist other firms to produce VCRs compatible with its format. Sony did so in a way that limited its maneuverability (Cusumano *et al.*, 1992, p. 70):

> When it approached the other firms, Sony had already begun tooling up for the Betamax, signaling to prospective partners a commitment to proceed with mass production irrespective of their support. Sony thus acted as a true first mover, perhaps believing that its lead in the market would convince other firms to follow. At the same time, having begun manufacturing preparations also made Sony less flexible, because altering the design of its machine would require expensive changes in manufacturing equipment.

JVC, perhaps of necessity, took a less rigid approach (Cusumano *et al.*, 1992, p. 72, p. 74; fns. omitted):

> [T]o entice other firms to support VHS, JVC was willing to let other companies participate in refining the standard, such as moving from two hours to longer recording times or adding new features. ... One outcome of JVC's approach was that prospective manufacturing partners truly believed they would have some stake in the future evolution of VHS features. Allowing partners to share in development also improved the VHS in ways that JVC might not have pursued itself.

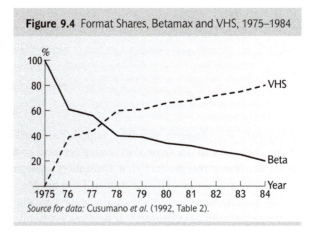

Figure 9.4 Format Shares, Betamax and VHS, 1975–1984

Source for data: Cusumano *et al.* (1992, Table 2).

>> Betamax's technical superiority not to the contrary, consumers appreciated the longer playing time and more elaborate programming features of early VHS-format VCRs. Sony might have confronted the judgement of the marketplace by lowering price and holding on to its market share while it adapted the features of Betamax VCRs (which it eventually did). If it had done so, the outcome of the format wars might have been different; one set of estimates suggests that (Ohashi, 2003, p. 480) "[I]f Beta had cut its price in the first three years of the VHS introduction, the format could have achieved more than 98% of the market by 1985." The inability or unwillingness to recognize the importance of network externalities was the death-knell for Betamax (Ohashi, 2003, p. 449): "[T]he format war between VHS and Beta was already over in 1981–1982; by the time Sony realized they were falling behind, it was too late to overcome their disadvantage."

Sources: Cusumano *et al.* (1992), Ohashi (2003).

9.3.6 Path Dependence (I)

There remains the question how, if network externalities are present, the market will select the firm that ends up with the largest network. Whether we should expect markets to select a leading variety that is in any sense optimal is the subject of vigorous debate. The *path dependence* literature argues that when network externalities are present, chance historical events can have a critical impact on which among early products reaches a leading position.

David (1985) points to the example of the basic QWERTY keyboard layout, developed by engineers for one of the early typewriter manufacturers (Remington) to slow touch typists down and reduce the frequency of jamming in the physical mechanism of the typewriter keys. Once it became standard to teach touch typing according to the QWERTY layout, the dominant position of the QWERTY keyboard was secure. In this instance, the compatible good that creates network externalities in the keyboard market is the training—the human capital—of those who use the keyboards.

In David's view, the QWERTY keyboard became standard largely because it happened to accumulate a large pool of trained users before other keyboard layouts. Thus, the QWERTY layout continues to be used, long after the problem of jamming typewriter keys (indeed, the keys themselves) has vanished. Other keyboard layouts—David mentions the so-called Dvorak keyboard—might be more efficient in a time-and-motion study sense, but they are out of luck.

Liebowitz and Margolis (1990) question the claim that the Dvorak keyboard allows more efficient typing. They also make the more general point (1990, p. 4, fn. 4) that once a particular standard is in place as the largest network, the interesting question from an efficiency point of view is not "Would society have been better off if a different standard had been chosen from the beginning?", but rather "Given that the existing standard is now in place, will society be better off with a different standard, taking switching costs into account?" In the context of the keyboard example, switching costs would include retraining all the touch typists previously trained on the QWERTY layout.

9.3.7 Horizontal Production Differentiation: The Circle Model

Mobile firms, no price discrimination

Setup Product differentiation is another factor that determines the extent of supply-side concentration. We examine the horizontal product differentiation-concentration link using the circle spatial oligopoly model introduced in Section 4.2.3. We retain from that model the assumptions that l consumers are evenly distributed around a circle of circumference l, that firms are able to relocate at will along the circumference, and that there is a transportation cost t to move one unit of output one unit of distance along the circumference. We make two changes in the model of Section 4.2.3, one regarding the demand side of the market and one regarding the supply side of the market. For simplicity, we consider the case of consumers without a reservation price: each consumer buys one unit of the good from the firm that offers the lowest delivered price. As for the supply side, we suppose that in addition to constant marginal cost c per unit of output, each firm has a fixed cost F.

As in the previous discussion (although it was not emphasized there), firms cannot price discriminate: firm 1 sets a price at its location, p_1, and the delivered price quoted by firm 1 to a consumer a distance x from firm 1's location is:

$$p_1 + tx. \tag{9.16}$$

Prices   The analysis of equilibrium prices is a simplified version of that given in Section 4.2.3. Since firms can shift locations, in equilibrium firms will be spaced evenly around the circle—if there are n firms, with each firm an arc-distance l/n from its neighbor on either side.

Suppose firm 1's neighbours both charge the same price (which they will do in equilibrium), and call that price p_{circ}. The right-hand-side boundary of firm 1's market is the location of consumers, at distance x, who are quoted the same price by firm 1 or firm 2:

$$p_1 + tx = p_{circ} + t\left(\frac{l}{n} - x\right). \tag{9.17}$$

Solving (9.17) for x, the quantity demanded of firm 1 on its right is:

$$x = \frac{l}{2n} + \frac{p_{circ} - p_1}{2t}. \tag{9.18}$$

By symmetry, the total quantity demanded of firm 1 is $2x$. Firm 1's payoff is:

$$\pi_1 = (p_1 - c)\left(\frac{p_{circ} - p_1}{t} + \frac{l}{n}\right) - F. \tag{9.19}$$

The first-order condition to maximize (9.19) is:

$$-\frac{1}{t}(p_1 - c) + \left(\frac{p_{circ} - p_1}{t} + \frac{l}{n}\right) = 0. \tag{9.20}$$

Hence if the firm is maximizing profit (if (9.20) holds),

$$\frac{p_{circ} - p_1}{t} + \frac{l}{n} = \frac{1}{t}(p_1 - c) \tag{9.21}$$

and firm 1's payoff is:

$$\pi_1 = \frac{1}{t}(p_1 - c)^2 - F. \tag{9.22}$$

Because the firms are identical, in equilibrium all firms will charge the same price. Set $p_1 = p_{circ}$ in the first-order condition (9.20) and solve for the equilibrium price,

$$p_{circ}^* = c + \frac{tl}{n}. \tag{9.23}$$

Payoffs and number of firms   Substituting (9.23) into (9.22), equilibrium profit per firm is:

$$\pi^*_{circ} = \frac{1}{t}\left(p_{circ} - c\right)^2 - F = t\left(\frac{l}{n}\right)^2 - F. \tag{9.24}$$

If there is free and easy entry and exit, the number of firms n adjusts until equilibrium profit is zero. Setting $\pi^*_{circ} = 0$ and solving for n, the equilibrium number of firms (ignoring the fact that the number of firms must be an integer) is:

$$n^*_{circ,1} = \frac{l}{\sqrt{F/t}}. \tag{9.25}$$

There are more firms, in equilibrium, the larger the market (l), the lower are fixed costs, and the higher is transportation cost. In the figurative interpretation of this model, larger transportation cost corresponds to greater product differentiation, suggesting that the number of single-brand firms should be larger in markets where horizontal product differentiation is greater, all else equal.

Mobile firms, price discrimination

A modification of the model shows that the equilibrium number of firms depends not only on technology (the cost function) and demand (the extent of product differentiation), but also on firm conduct. Consider the same circle model, but change firm price-setting behaviour. Suppose that instead of setting a non-discriminatory price to maximize profit, taking the prices of its neighbours as given, firms are able to price discriminate—to charge a different price, net of actual transportation cost, to consumers at different locations.

If there are n firms that can costlessly relocate on the circumference of the circle, there is an arc-length l/n between firms. Because firms compete in price, firm 1's price for a consumer located a distance $l/2n$ to (say) its left must equal the marginal cost of its left-hand neighbour, firm n, of delivering to that point,

$$p_1\left(\frac{l}{2n}\right) = c + \frac{1}{2}t\frac{l}{n}. \tag{9.26}$$

This is the usual result of price-setting (Bertrand) competition, applied in a circular spatial market: if two price-setting firms supply products that are perfect substitutes to the same market, the equilibrium price is marginal cost. If firm 1 charged a price greater than $p_1\left(\frac{l}{2n}\right)$ to consumers at distance $\frac{l}{2n}$ from its location, firm n could profitably undercut firm 1's price and get the business at that location. If firm 1 were to charge a price lower than $p_1\left(\frac{l}{2n}\right)$ to consumers at distance $\frac{l}{2n}$ from its location, it would be needlessly giving up profit—it could raise price without losing the sale.

Closer to its location, firm 1's profit-maximizing strategy is to charge the highest price it can without losing sales to the neighbour on the left. At distance x from firm 1's price is the delivered price from firm n,

$$p_1(x) = c + t\left(\frac{l}{n} - x\right).$$

Firm 1 sets prices in the same way in its right-hand market. Equilibrium prices are shown by the solid line in Figure 9.5. Firm 1's profit is the shaded area in Figure 9.5, minus fixed cost:

$$\pi_1 = 2\left(\frac{1}{2}\right)\left(\frac{l}{n}\right)\left(\frac{tl}{2n}\right) - F = \left(\frac{1}{2}\right)t\left(\frac{l}{n}\right)^2 - F. \tag{9.27}$$

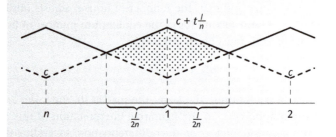

Figure 9.5 Extent of the market, circle model with price discrimination

Notes: Horizontal axis, arc distance along circumference; vertical axis, cost and delivered price. n = number of firms, c = marginal production cost, t = transportation cost per unit distance, l = circumference. Shaded area indicates firm 1's profit (before allowing for fixed cost).

If firms are mobile and there is free entry and exit, the number of firms will adjust until profit is zero:

$$n^*_{circ,2} = \frac{1}{\sqrt{2}} \frac{l}{\sqrt{F/t}} = \frac{1}{\sqrt{2}} n^*_{circ,1} < n^*_{circ,1}. \tag{9.28}$$

The equilibrium number of firms depends not only on the size of the market and technology (the parameters of the cost function), but also on conduct. When firms price discriminate, competition is tougher at boundary locations, profit per firm is less for any given number of firms than if firms do not price discriminate, and there is room for fewer firms in the market.

Immobile firms

Return now to a market in which each firm sets a price at its plant and the delivered price to a customer is the price at the plant plus transportation cost. Firms can set a different price for their left- and right-side markets.

There are n firms evenly spaced around the circle. What is the profit of a firm that locates midway between firms 1 and 2 *if they do not relocate*?

The entrant will play a pricing game with firms 1 and 2. In equilibrium, it will supply customers out to an arc-distance $l/4n$ on its left from its location, leaving and arc-distance $l/4n$ for firm 1, and similarly on its right. It supplies a segment of arc-length $l/2n$, half the arc-distance supplied by each of the n incumbents before the entrant arrived on the scene. Because its neighbours do not move, the entrant's share of the arc is $l/2n$.

The entrant's profit in this pricing game is:

$$\pi_E = \frac{t}{2}\left(\frac{l}{2n}\right)^2 - F, \tag{9.29}$$

and the equilibrium number of firms (once again, ignoring the fact that the number of firms must be an integer) is the value that makes $\pi_E = 0$:

$$n^*_{circ,3} = \frac{1}{2\sqrt{2}} \frac{l}{\sqrt{F/t}} = \frac{1}{2} n^*_{circ,2}. \tag{9.30}$$

If firms are immobile, the equilibrium condition for market structure is not that incumbents earn zero profit, but that a potential entrant would earn zero profit if it should come into the market. By confining an entrant to a smaller segment of the market than they themselves enjoy, incumbents can earn economic profits without attracting entry.

If location on the circular market is taken to represent a particular product characteristic, or a brand image established by advertising and/or previous consumer experience, then it may well be that location cannot be easily changed. In such markets, firms clever enough or lucky enough to produce varieties with favorable brand images may be able to earn economic profits even though an entrant would not make enough profit to cover fixed costs. Such firms would enjoy larger market shares, all else equal, than producers of less-favoured varieties. Markets supplied by such firms would be more concentrated, all else equal, than suggested by models in which entrants can approach the "locations" of established brands.[13]

9.3.8 Empirical Studies of Concentration I: Cross-Section and Industry Studies

Industry Cross-Section Studies

Table 9.8 describes changes in seller concentration for a sample of 167 U.S. manufacturing industries over the quarter-century from 1947 to 1972. There is a modest increase (1.5 percentage points) in overall average concentration. This stable overall average masks disparate trends in concentration in different types of industries. Over the time period covered by the study, producer good industries became modestly less concentrated, and consumer good industries with a low degree of product differentiation became modestly more concentrated (as did consumer good industries overall). Concentration in moderately differentiated

Table 9.8 Levels and changes in four-firm seller concentration ratio (per cent), 167 U.S. manufacturing industries, 1947–1972

	Producer Good Industries	Consumer Good Industries				All (167)
	(97)	Low (21)	Moderate (33)	High (16)	All (70)	
1947	44.7	25.9	36.2	47.7	35.7	40.9
1972	42.8	28.3	41.4	60.6	41.8	42.4
Change	−1.9	2.4	5.2	12.9	6.1	1.5

Source: Mueller and Rogers (1980).

[13] Along these lines, Schmalensee (1978), Scherer (1979), and Wildman (1984) discuss strategic brand proliferation to discourage entry in the U.S. breakfast cereal market.

consumer good industries increased 5.2 percentage points (a 14 per cent increase over the 1947 level). Concentration in highly differentiated consumer good industries increased 12.9 percentage points (a 27 per cent increase over the 1947 level).

For the same sample of industries, Mueller and Rogers (1980) estimate an equation showing the average relation between industry concentration in 1972 ($CR4_{1972}$) and industry concentration in 1947 ($CR4_{1947}$), the industry growth rate (GR), industry size, and the industry-average advertising sales ratio (ASR):[14]

$$CR4_{1972} = 23.48 - 0.003GR - 0.155Size + 1.06ASR + 0.77CR4_{1947}. \tag{9.31}$$

Their results suggest that the 1972 four-firm concentration ratio is significantly smaller in larger industries and significantly larger in industries with larger advertising-sales ratios. They estimate an alternative specification, breaking advertising spending into two types, spending on television and radio advertising and spending on other media, and examine the distinct impact of advertising on these alternative types of outlets on seller concentration. In this alternative equation, it is television and ratio advertising that has a significant positive impact on concentration; the estimated coefficient of spending on other types of advertising is negative and statistically insignificant.[15]

Equation (9.31) estimates the impact of the growth rate of industry sales, industry size, and industry advertising intensity on changes in concentration over time. In the long run, and in the absence of disturbances or structural changes, equation (9.31) implies that industry concentration will be a function of GR, $Size$, and ASR, a function that can be found by setting $CR4_{1972} = CR4_{1947} = CR_{LR}$ in (9.31) and solving for the long-run seller concentration ratio CR_{LR}. Equation (9.31) also implies that the expected time for industries in this sample to reach the long-run concentration level is $(1972 - 1947) \times \frac{0.77}{1-0.77} \approx 84$ years.

Industry studies: brewing

Small firms once prospered in the U.S. brewing industry, in part due to vertical integration into distribution and in part because of an ability to underprice national breweries (Stack, 2000, p. 435): "From the mid-1890s until Prohibition, hundreds of regional and local breweries reasserted themselves in the market for beer. These firms often were able to provide less expensive beer and to sell it in saloons that they owned or controlled. Together, these two factors enabled regional and local breweries to present a competitive challenge to national firms in the years leading up to Prohibition."

---

[14] GR is the percentage change in industry value added between 1947 and 1972. $Size$ is the natural logarithm of 1972 industry value added. Advertising spending used to construct ASR covers expenditures in six different types of advertising media.

[15] In yet another specification, they omit the advertising-sales ratio as an explanatory variable and employ in its stead dummy variables for low, moderate, and high product differentiation in consumer good industries, defined as for Table 9.8. As one would expect from Table 9.8, there is no significant difference in concentration between producer good industries and low-differentiation consumer good industries; concentration is higher in moderate-differentiation consumer good industries, and higher still in high-differentiation consumer good industries. Confirmation of the importance of television advertising is provided by Jenny and Weber (1978), who analyse the determinants of concentration in French manufacturing industry for a period, the 1960s, when there was no television advertising in France; they find no significant impact of product differentiation on changes in concentration.

Table 9.9 Seller concentration measures, U.S. domestic beer producers, 1950–2000, by decade

Year	CR4 (%)	H	1/H
1950	22.03	0.0203671	49.10
1960	26.97	0.0343296	29.13
1970	72.46	0.0709531	14.09
1980	90.36	0.155566	6.43
1990	98.30	0.285261	3.51
2000	95.50	0.36179	2.76

Source: Tremblay and Tremblay (2005, Chapter 4).

But the supply side of the post-World War II U.S. beer industry became increasingly concentrated (Table 9.9).[16] Table 9.10 shows that in 1950 there were only 350 firms supplying an industry that could have supported 829 efficiently sized breweries. But by 2000, 24 brewers operated in an industry large enough for 11 minimum efficient scale brewers. Along with the increase in supply-side concentration had come a proliferation of small-scale brewers supplying niche markets.[17]

Table 9.10 suggests that changes in minimum efficient plant scale—which rose from 0.1 per cent of industry production in 1950 to 9.9 per cent in 2000—drove part of the increase in seller concentration. Between 1950 and 2000, the combined market shares of the largest four breweries rose by more than a factor of four; over the same period, the minimum efficient plant percentage of industry output rose by a factor of almost 100. But advertising was a factor as well. Tremblay and Tremblay (2005, Table 3.4) estimate the following equation for the U.S. brewing industry over the years 1950 to 2000:[18]

$$CR4_t = -2.1652 + 0.0070ADV_t + 0.6388\frac{MES_t}{S_t} + 0.9035CR4_{t-1}, \tag{9.32}$$

---

[16] In 2002, the U.S. Economic Census reported a four-firm seller concentration ratio for breweries of 90.8 per cent. The 1997 and 2002 Herfindahl indices for the industry, NAICS code 312120, were suppressed to preserve individual-firm confidentiality.

[17] Without product differentiation, one expects excess entry, from a social point of view, in imperfectly competitive markets (Mankiw and Whinston, 1986). In making the entry decision, a firm considers only whether or not it can (expects to) earn a profit in the post-entry market. It does not take into account the lost profit entry will impose on incumbents. The post-entry change in social welfare is then less than the entrant's profit (and increased surplus). Product differentiation will mitigate and may reverse the excess entry effect, as new varieties may better match preferences of some consumers than do existing varieties.

[18] The estimated coefficient of advertising is statistically significant at the 1 per cent level. In an otherwise identically specified equation using the Herfindahl index as a dependent variable, the coefficients of advertising and minimum-efficient-pant share of industry output are both statistically significant at the 1 per cent level.

Table 9.10 *MES* = minimum efficient plant scale as a percentage of total beer production; n^* = number of MES-scale plants required to supply total beer production; n = number of independent mass-producing beer companies

Year	MES (%)	n^*	n	n/n^*
1950	0.1	829	350	0.42
1960	1.1	88	175	1.99
1970	6.4	15	82	5.47
1980	9.1	11	42	3.82
1990	8.5	12	29	2.41
2000	9.9	11	24	2.18

Source: Tremblay and Tremblay (2005, Table 3.1).

where ADV_t is industry spending on advertising in year t. During this half-century, greater industry advertising significantly increased industry concentration, all else equal. Like equation (9.31), equation (9.32) implies a long-run relationship between $CR4$, ADV, and MES/S that can be found by setting $CR4_t = CR4_{t-1} = CR_{LR}$ in (9.32) and rearranging terms. The estimated mean time for adjustment to the long-run equilibrium concentration level is 9.36 years.[19]

9.3.9 Chandler[20]

The creation of a continent-wide single market in the United States in the aftermath of the U.S. Civil War set the stage for a massive transformation of U.S. industrial structure. An orgy of horizontal mergers at the turn of the nineteenth century consolidated control of supply in many industries in the hands of a few large firms. In some industries, this control was ephemeral. In others, it endured. Chandler identified three factors that, in tandem, produced enduring dominance.

Economies of scale

The first factor was production economies of scale. Large size implied cost advantages particularly in industries that involved processing—steel, whiskey, flour, sugar, cigarettes. With capital-intensive production techniques, continuous operation at maximum capacity meant economies of throughput that spread high fixed costs over the maximum possible output,

---

[19] Tremblay and Tremblay obtain similar qualitative results using the Herfindahl index rather than CR4 as a concentration measure. The estimated mean time for adjustment to the long-run equilibrium concentration level is 3.04 years for the Herfindahl index equation.

[20] We defer consideration of Alfred D. Chandler's work on firm structure to Section 10.3.1, but here consider the implications of his analysis of firm structure for market structure.

reduced average cost to a minimum, and made it possible for the large firm to undersell any and all competitors.

Vertical integration

The second factor was vertical integration, backward to ensure access to essential inputs or forward into distribution, to ensure access to the final consumer. Where products were perishable (dressed meat), or high-technology consumer durables that required point-of-sale demonstration (the sewing machine), or differentiated by design (industrial sandpaper) or advertising (breakfast cereal), producers moved into wholesale distribution and sometimes retail distribution as well. Arms-length transactions could not be relied upon to deliver a steady stream of supplies or to secure outlets for the finished product, and disruption of either input or output streams would mean that production would slow or stop, driving up average cost. Backward and forward integration was essential if economies of throughput were to be realized. But integration also meant an increase in the cost of successful entry, which would have to be made on an integrated basis, and so reduced the threat of potential entry.[21]

Organizational capabilities

Third, Chandler emphasized, low unit cost and enduring market leadership did not follow automatically from the first two conditions. Coordination of input flows, production, and output flows required the development of managerial techniques uncalled for and unheard of in an earlier age. The industries that became concentrated were those where vertical integration sustained economies of scale. The firms that endured on the supply sides of those concentrated markets were the ones that were first able to coordinate vertical and horizontal operations.

9.3.10 Sutton

In analysing the determinants of market structure, Sutton distinguishes between type I industries, in which the nature of demand is given, and type II industries, in which a firm can shift the demand for its variety by investing by making fixed and sunk investments in advertising or product design in a preliminary stage that comes before competition in the marketplace.[22] Type I industries deal in products with no or slight horizontal product differentiation. The products of type II industries may be horizontally differentiated, but they are vertically differentiated as well. In contrast to type I industries, in type II industries the degree of vertical differentiation is influenced by firms' investments in sales efforts and product design that aim to increase consumers' reservation prices for their varieties.

Type I industries

In type I industries, the fixed investment required to establish a minimum efficient scale plant is determined by technology. If market size increases, the equilibrium number of firms increases as well. In this class of model, firms have identical output levels in equilibrium;

---

[21] In terms of the Cournot-model long-run equilibrium number of plants and equation (9.12), vertical integration increased fixed cost F, increased minimum efficient scale q_{mes}, and reduced the equilibrium number of plants.

[22] The "type I, type II" terminology is due to Schmalensee (1992).

one can then think of the inverse of the equilibrium number of firms as a measure of seller concentration. In the limit, if market size goes to infinity, equilibrium seller concentration approaches zero.

Type II industries

In type II industries, the fixed investment required to establish a minimum efficient scale operation must cover not only the cost of an efficient-scale plant but must also match incumbents' spending on quality-enhancing marketing and product development. In Sutton's framework, what determines incumbents' incentives to invest in consumers' appreciation of quality is an *escalation parameter*, α, the ratio between the incremental profit a firm can get by investing in sunk demand-shifting strategies and the size of the quality increase needed to get that incremental profit. If α is large, a firm can profit by increasing the quality of its variety.

The escalation parameter describes the relative profitability of a quality increment. The quality cost elasticity parameter[23] β indicates how quickly cost rises with quality. In high-α, low-β industries, it is profitable to have a variety for which consumers have high reservation prices, and the fixed cost of enhancing quality is modest. In high-α, low-β industries, increases in market size lead incumbents to invest in endogenous fixed and sunk costs, shifting their demand curves up. The endogenous increase in fixed cost neutralizes the tendency of market expansion to induce entry that is present in type I industries. In type II industries, seller concentration is bounded away from zero even as market size increases.

Empirical Studies of Concentration II: The Bounds Approach

Comparative[24]   A central prediction of Sutton's analysis is that seller concentration will approach zero as market size increases in industries where the level of fixed cost is technologically given, but be bounded away from zero in industries where incumbent firms can make fixed and sunk investments to enhance consumers' willingness to pay for their varieties.

Sutton estimates the lower bound of the concentration-market size relationship for six low-advertising food-and-drink industries in six countries, for 1986.[25] The result is shown in Figure 9.6. What is measured on the vertical axis is a logarithmic transformation of the four-firm seller concentration ratio.[26] The horizontal axis measures the natural logarithm of the ratio of market size (S) to the amount of investment required to set up a plant of minimum efficient scale (σ); this amounts to measuring market size in terms of the number of minimum-efficient-scale plants for which there is room in the market. Each dot in Figure 9.6 represents a market size-concentration observation for one of the six industries in one of the six countries. As Sutton's analysis predicts for industries dealing in what he describes as "commodity products", where neither vertical product differentiation nor endogenous

---

[23] In some models, Sutton writes ρ^β as the fixed cost of a quality level ρ. See Section 17.2.3.

[24] See also the discussion of market integration and seller concentration in the European Union in Section 17.3.2.

[25] "Low-advertising" is defined as a median industry advertising-sales ratio less than 1 per cent. The low-advertising industries are salt, sugar, bread, flour, canned vegetables, and processed meat. The six countries are France, Germany, Italy, Japan, the United Kingdom, and the United States. Some industries were omitted for some countries; some data was for a time near 1986. For details of measurement issues, see Sutton (1991, Chapter 4).

[26] Measuring the concentration ratio C_4 from zero to one, the transformed seller concentration ratio $\tilde{C}_4$ is the natural logarithm of the ratio $C_4/(1 - C_4)$. The transformed variable takes negative values for $C_4 < 1/2$, positive values for $C_4 > 1/2$.

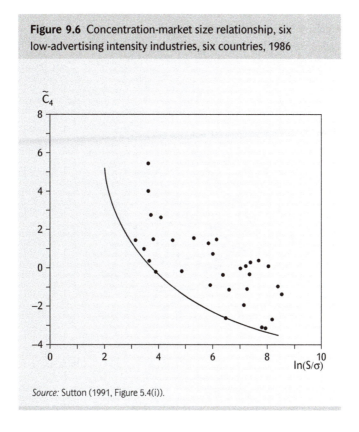

Figure 9.6 Concentration-market size relationship, six low-advertising intensity industries, six countries, 1986

Source: Sutton (1991, Figure 5.4(i)).

investment in vertical product differentiation come into play, the lower bound of concentration declines as market size increases.

Sutton estimates the same type of concentration-market size relationship for 14 high-advertising food-and-drink industries, for the same six countries. In this type of market, advertising is a fixed (with respect to output) and largely sunk investment in an intangible asset, the brand image of a high-quality product. For this type of market, Sutton's analysis predicts that concentration will be bounded from below as market size increases, and this is the kind of relationship shown in Figure 9.7.[27] The lower bound for high-advertising industries flattens out more or less at $\ln \frac{C_4}{1-C_4} = -1$, corresponding a value of C_4 around 27 per cent.

EU Car Industry The size distribution of firms supplying the EU new car and light truck market in 2007 is shown in the *Lorenz curve* of Figure 9.8.[28] The Lorenz curve shows the combined market shares of the largest 20 per cent of firms, the largest 40 per cent of firms, and so on. If all firms were of equal size, the largest 10 per cent of firms would have a combined market share of 10 per cent, the largest 20 per cent of firms would have a combined market share of 20 per cent, and so on: the Lorenz curve would coincide with the diagonal.

---

[27] For comparison purposes, the lower bound from Figure 9.6 is reproduced in Figure 9.7.

[28] The market shares are given in Table 9.15, and shown individually in Figure 9.10.

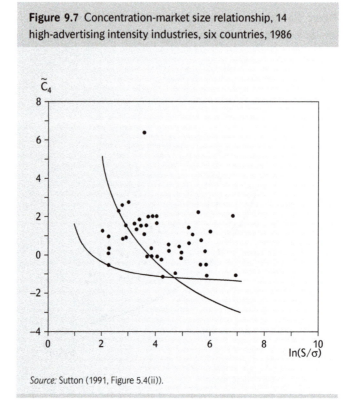

Figure 9.7 Concentration-market size relationship, 14 high-advertising intensity industries, six countries, 1986

Source: Sutton (1991, Figure 5.4(ii)).

In the EC market for cars and light trucks, the largest 20 per cent of firms in 1997 had a combined market share of nearly 60 per cent, the largest 40 per cent of firms had a combined market share of nearly 90 per cent, while the smallest 60 per cent of firms divided up little more than 10 per cent of the market. The bulge of the cumulative market share curve away from the diagonal is an indication of the unequal distribution of firm sizes in the EC market for new cars and light trucks.[29]

Sutton (1998, Chapter 10) shows that under mild conditions, the m-firm seller concentration ratio CRm, the sum of the market shares of the largest m firms, in endogenous sunk cost industries should not be less than a lower bound:

$$CRm \geq \frac{m}{N}\left(1 - \ln\frac{m}{N}\right), \tag{9.33}$$

(where ln denotes the natural logarithm and the concentration ratio is measured for the largest m of a total of N firms), independent of industry size. The argument is that where firms can influence demand by endogenous sunk expenditures, firms in larger markets will spend more on advertising and/or research and development, increasing F endogenously so that the equilibrium concentration ratio remains above a minimum level. In terms of the kind of Lorenz curve shown in Figure 9.8, the prediction is that in industries where endogenous

---

[29] The ratio of the area between the diagonal and the Lorenz curve to the area of the triangle below the diagonal is the *Gini coefficient*, an alternative measure of seller concentration.

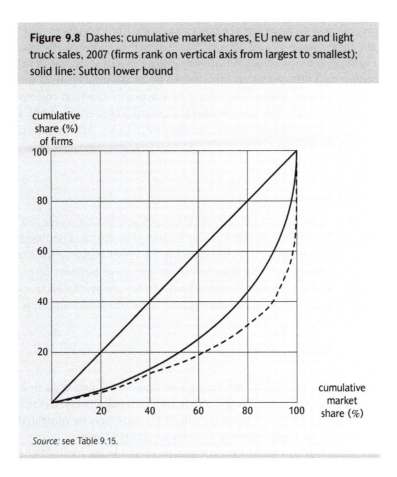

Figure 9.8 Dashes: cumulative market shares, EU new car and light truck sales, 2007 (firms rank on vertical axis from largest to smallest); solid line: Sutton lower bound

Source: see Table 9.15.

spending can promote product differentiation, the Lorenz curve will lie farther from the diagonal than the limit given by the right-hand side of inequality (9.33). The Sutton lower bound is shown as a solid line in Figure 9.8. The inequality is satisfied for all m/N.

9.3.11 Overall

The classical, business history, and bounds approaches to the analysis of market structure have much in common. All emphasize efficiency as one factor that explains supply-side market structure; the classical and bounds approaches highlight productive efficiency—efficient plant size relative to market size. Chandler adds as well consideration of efficient operation within the firm. All three highlight product differentiation as a factor that explains market structure.

Empirical studies carried out in the structure-conduct-performance tradition or motivated by explicit oligopoly models aimed to estimate equations that would explain differences in the levels of concentration in different industries. Sutton deliberately eschews this approach. He accepts as an implication of the game-theoretic approach that equilibrium market structure in any industry will depend on subtle factors—Do firms set prices or quantities? What is the timing of moves? How do firms form beliefs about rivals' likely conduct?—that are often unobservable and incapable of being compared from industry to industry. His less ambitious approach is to estimate a lower bound on the way seller concentration varies with market size. Endogenous product differentiation turns out to be an essential element in determining the location of this lower bound. Understanding the extent to which concentration in any particular industry exceeds the lower bound is a question best examined by looking at changes in concentration, and market shares, industry-by-industry, so that industry-specific factors can be taken into account.

9.3.12 Retail Distribution

For the purposes of its Economic Census, the U.S. Department of Commerce (2005a, p. ix) defines retail establishments as "fixed point-of-sale locations, located and designed to attract a high volume of walk-in customers.... They typically sell merchandise to the general public for personal or household consumption, but some also serve business or institutional clients." Retailers are suppliers to final consumer demand; they are purchasers from the manufacturers that produce or from wholesale distributors[30] who warehouse and ship the goods in which retailers deal.[31]

The grocery trade

National concentration ratios for U.S. retailing for several NAICS four-digit industries are given in Table 9.11. Five-firm concentration ratios for the retail grocery sector for six EU member states from 1988 to 1996 are given in Table 9.12; these may be compared with the 31 per cent national four-firm concentration ratio for the United States.

The markets in which final consumers purchase retail goods are local. The markets in which retailers compete are regional, with configuration that depends on what by way of shorthand it is tempting to call transportation cost (and we succumb to that temptation here), but which includes as well the cost of the entire distribution operation.[32] The markets in which retailers acquire the goods they sell to final consumers will most often be national.

For local or regional markets, the concentration figures of Tables 9.11 and 9.12 are misleadingly small. Keeping this in mind, there are surprisingly large four-firm seller concentration levels in some U.S. retail industries, suggesting the presence of chain stores that operate

---

[30] For statistics on supply-side concentration in U.S. wholesale industries, see U.S. Department of Commerce (2005b).

[31] We gloss over two points here. First, manufacturers may integrate forward into wholesale or retail distribution. We have alluded to such integration, which plays a central role in Alfred Chandler's analysis of the rise of large firms, in Section 9.3.9, and return to the topic in Chapter 10. Second, instead of purchasing the goods they wholesale or retail, distributors may hold goods on consignment from manufacturers. The policy implications of this distinction for contracts between manufacturers and distributors, which we discuss in Chapter 24, have been controversial.

[32] In his study of U.S. supermarkets, Ellickson (2007) takes geographic markets to be distribution areas, of which he delineates 51, noting that (2007, p. 49) "Although quite large in population, even the largest [Metropolitan Statistical Areas] are not independent on the cost side: supermarket firms routinely serve stores in several [Metropolitan Statistical Areas] from the same distribution center. For example, the top four firms in Southern California serve stores in the San Diego, Riverside, Ventura, and Orange Country [Metropolitan Statistical Areas] from distribution centers in east Los Angeles." See also Raff and Temin's (1999) description of the Chicago distribution facility from which, from 1906, Sears, Roebuck & Co. filled mail orders from the entire United States.

Table 9.11 Four-firm seller concentration ratio, U.S. retailing, by four-digit NAICS industry, 2002

NAICS Code	Title	%
4411	Automobile dealers	5.3
4413	Automotive parts, accessories, & tire stores	21.2
4421	Furniture stores	8.1
4422	Home furnishings stores	20.9
4431	Grocery stores	31.0
4441	Specialty food stores	6.8
4442	Beer, wine, & liquor stores	8.3
4451	Grocery stores	31
4452	Specialty food stores	6.8
4453	Beer, wine, & liquor stores	8.3
4461	Health & personal care stores	45.7
4471	Gasoline stations	8.2
4481	Clothing stores	28
4482	Shoe store	39.9
4483	Jewelry, luggage, & leather goods stores	22.3
4511	Sporting goods, hobby, & musical instrument stores	24.2
4512	Book, periodical, & music stores	48.3
4521	Department stores	66.4
4531	Florists	1.7
4532	Office supplies, stationery, & gift stores	45.9
4533	Used merchandise stores	9.9
4541	Electronic shopping & mail-order houses	18.7
4542	Vending machine operators	20.7
4543	Direct selling establishments	11.0

Source: 2002 Economic Census.

Table 9.12 National retail grocery five-firm concentration ratios, 1988–1996

	1988	1992	1996
Belgium	52	53	56
France	42	49	52
Germany	27	37	41
Netherlands	59	59	61
Spain	19	23	25
United Kingdom	53	60	64

Source: Dobson and Waterson (1999, Table 1).

in many local markets. Grocery concentration seems higher on average in the EU member states than in the U.S. (Dobson and Waterson, 1999, p. 137). As a structural indication of oligopsony power, influence over price in the markets in which retailers purchase, the concentration ratios of Tables 9.11 and 9.12 are probably what one wishes to look at.

Structural changes in distribution industries are a perennial policy concern.[33] Some of this concern arises from the desire of some classes of retailers to be protected from the competition of other classes of retailers.[34] Another question involves the consequences of increasing concentration in distribution for the bargaining (countervailing) power of distributors *vis-à-vis* manufacturers, and the implications for final market performance. All else equal, greater concentration in distribution should allow distributors to bargain for lower prices in the imperfectly competitive markets in which they acquire supplies. Taking it for granted that competition in retail markets is also imperfectly competitive, one question is whether there is enough rivalry in final good markets so that lower prices are passed on to final consumers. An alternative scenario is that if a few distributors traffic in the products of a few large manufacturers, in regional market after regional market, they will be able to work out symbiotic relationships that raise the cost of entry and worsen market performance.

Chain stores Ellickson (2007, pp. 45–46; see also Brown *et al.*, 2005) distinguishes three regime shifts in the U.S. grocery trade. From the 1920s, chain stores (exemplified by A&P) cut their own costs where they integrated backward into manufacturing (of store brands)

---

[33] Clarke points out that in his 1890 *Principles of Economics*, Alfred Marshall wrote of small retailers being displaced by large because of (2000, p. 975) "the better terms negotiated by larger retailers; the ability of larger organizations to arrange for goods to be transported more cheaply than smaller firms; and the added attraction of large stores to customers because of the variety of products they offer".

[34] As noted by Lewis (1945, p. 202), Adam Smith remarks on grocers' quest for protection in *The Wealth of Nations* ([1776] 1937, p. 341). In the U.S., protection of small retailers from chain store competition was the purpose of the Robinson-Patman Act of 1936 (Section 23.2.2).

and wholesale distribution. They passed the lower costs on to consumers in the form of lower prices, saw their market shares grow, and were able to bargain for lower prices from manufacturers of products they purchased rather than produced. The market shares of chain stores increased at the expense of small grocers.

Supermarkets   The 1950s saw the rise of suburban supermarkets, which (Ellickson, 2007, p. 45) "competed on the basis of both price and variety, linking stores to firms through both advertising and distribution. ... it was the new focus on product variety that distinguished the dominant supermarket firms from the competitive fringe of independent grocers. Supermarkets were now vertically differentiated". As population moved out of city centres, small grocers once again lost ground.

Supermarket chains   At the end of the twentieth century, supermarkets invested in (Ellickson, 2007, p. 46) "proprietary information technology and logistical systems aimed at increasing variety while minimizing storage and transportation costs" that permit a substantial increase in the variety of products available for consumers. These investments in endogenous sunk quality-enhancing investments, Ellickson argues, made the U.S. retail grocery market the kind of market shown in Figure 9.7, where seller concentration remains at oligopoly levels even if market size increases. His empirical results show the presence of a fringe of small firms, but confirm the "endogenous sunk cost" nature of the oligopoly core of large supermarkets chains.

 BOX   **Static models of market structure**

Begin with the premise that entry and exit will adjust the number of firms in a market until incumbents earn zero economic profit, or at most so little profit that further entry would be unprofitable. Such models highlight large economies of scale, small markets, and low transportation cost (little horizontal product differentiation) as factors associated with fewness and concentration on the supply side of a market. Chandler's work emphasizes the importance of efficient firm organization as a prerequisite for taking operating efficiencies to the market. Sutton's bounds approach emphasizes that in markets susceptible to endogenous vertical product differentiation, firms can raise entry cost by investing in quality improvements.

9.4 The Dynamics of Market Structure

The most elementary theoretical story about entry and exit is that in the long run, the number of firms adjusts until equilibrium profit per firm is zero. Potential entrants have a more or less virtual existence, until they manifest themselves via the act of entry. Once a firm comes into the market, it is an incumbent and indistinguishable from other incumbents. If the rate of return on investment in the industry is below normal, some firms leave the market, but the model is agnostic as to which firms leave first.

Real-world entry and exit is rather more complex than its elementary theoretical counterpart. Table 9.13 gives some descriptive statistics about entry and exit rates for (primarily) manufacturing industries in eight countries. The number of firms entering and the number

Table 9.13 Average rates gross entry and exit, by industry, eight countries (per cent)

Country	Time period	Entry rate		Exit rate		Sample, Industry Level
		Number of firms	Market share	Number of firms	Market share	
Belgium (manufacturing)	1980–84	5.8	1.6	6.3	1.9	130, 3-digit
Belgium (services)	1980–84	13.0	4.4	12.2	4.1	79, 3-digit
Canada	1971–79	4.0	3.0	4.8	3.4	167, 4-digit
Germay	1983–85	3.8	2.8	4.6	2.8	183, 4-digit
Korea	1976–81	3.3	2.2	5.7	n.a.	48, 4-digit; 14, 5-digit
Norway	1980–85	8.2	1.1	8.7	1.0	80, 4-digit
Portugal	1983–86	12.3	5.8	9.5	5.5	234, 5-digit
UK	1974–79	6.5	2.9	5.1	3.3	114, 3-digit
US	1963–82	7.7	3.2	7.0	3.3	387, 4-digit

Note: n.a. indicates data not available. Statistics refer to manufacturing industries unless otherwise noted
Source: Caves (1998, Table 2), Cable and Schwalbach (1991, Table 14.1).

of firms exiting is typically about the same fraction of the number of incumbent firms. The combined market shares of both groups is typically small. For the eight countries, the number of entrants per year is about 6.5 per cent of all firms, and for manufacturing industries their combined market share is about 2.8 per cent. Entrants average about one-fifth the size of incumbents (Cable and Schwalbach, 1991, p. 258).

There are substantial simultaneous entry and exit flows. Studies often show that entry and exit rates are positively correlated, meaning that entry and exit rates into any specific industry tend to be either both high or both low (Dunne *et al.*, 1988, Table 6). This is not what neoclassical models predict. If entry occurs when profits are above normal, and exit occurs when profits are below normal, then one would expect to see either entry or exit at any point in time for a single industry, but not simultaneous entry and exit.

9.4.1 Entry and Exit as a Selection Mechanism

Dynamic models of entry and exit flows picture them as parts of a selection mechanism, involving firms that explore (Jovanovic, 1982) and develop (Ericson and Pakes, 1995) their own abilities and test their ideas about segments of a market that might be up for grabs. Evidence suggests that the way this selection mechanism plays itself out is related to industry and entrant characteristics.

Industry life cycle

At the beginning of an industry's existence, all segments of the market are up for grabs. Figure 9.9[35] shows the pattern of entry, exit, and number of incumbents that is observed, with many variations, over the life of a typical industry (Agarwal and Gort, 1996, pp. 489):[36]

- Stage 1 corresponds to the initial period when there are at most only several sellers.

- Stage 2 is the immediately following period of high net entry. . . .

- Stage 3 is a transitional plateau in the number of sellers. This stage, unlike stage 2, does not occur for many new product markets.

- Stage 4 . . . is the period of negative net entry and may also be subdivided into phases of acceleration and deceleration in negative net entry.

- Stage 5 corresponds to maturity in the market and no strong consistent trends in net entry . . .

Initial entrants may come from related industries;[37] they may be users that integrate backward, or input suppliers that integrate forward. Stage 2 involves substantial experimentation with alternative designs, as firms that are not quite sure what they are capable of doing try to meet the needs of consumers who are not quite sure what it is they want at a price they are willing to pay. In stage 4, the industry standardizes on a dominant design. The transition from experimentation to standardization will occur more rapidly, the freer the flow of information in the industry and the easier it is for later entrants to imitate earlier entrants (Clark, 1983, p. 109). Such imitation is likely to be easier, all else equal, in rapidly growing markets (Agarwal and Gort, 2001).

In stage 4, innovative activity shifts to improving productive efficiency within the "natural trajectory" (Nelson and Winter, 1977) defined by the dominant design. Production is mechanized, with the development of capital assets, specific to the natural trajectory, that combine previously distinct steps in the production process. Firms with a lead in the efficiency race gain market share. There is a "shakeout" of minor producers and the bulk of industry supply is concentrated in an oligopolistic core. In stage 5, firms in the core compete oligopolistically among themselves, while an ever-changing group of small firms circle precariously on the edge of the market. The identities of the small firms change over time, but the nature of the fringe group as a whole does not change very often. It is the rare fringe firm that has a cost or quality advantage sufficient to permit it to make the leap from the fringe to the inner circle. And fringe firms that seem on the verge of making the leap may find themselves the target of strategic entry-deterring behaviour.

Stage 5 continues until there is (Clark, 1983, pp. 112–113) "epochal innovation", a technological end run around the trajectory-specific assets and abilities of industry leaders that defines a new dominant design and a new natural trajectory. Epochal innovation may arise out of a change in the way production is organized (Toyota's use of "just-in-time" coordination with input suppliers to reduce inventory carrying costs). It may involve a completely

---

[35] See similarly Klepper (1996, Figure 1).

[36] What are made bullet points here are not set off as a list in the original.

[37] Klepper and Simons (2000) document the role of producers of radio receivers in the U.S. television receiver industry.

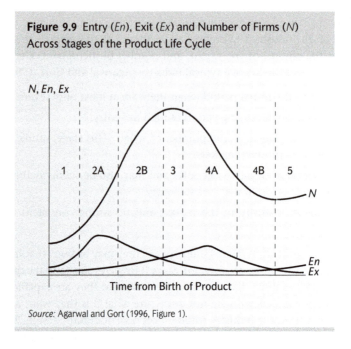

Figure 9.9 Entry (*En*), Exit (*Ex*) and Number of Firms (*N*) Across Stages of the Product Life Cycle

Source: Agarwal and Gort (1996, Figure 1).

new way to meet an existing set of consumer needs (the pocket calculator compared with the slide rule). It may happen because of changes in the prices of substitute or complementary goods (the sharp increase in energy prices in the first decade of the twenty-first century promises to disrupt the market structures of many industries in which established technological trajectories are premised on the availability of inexpensive energy).

 BOX   Shakeout in the U.S. Car Industry

Clark (1983, p. 103):

> Anyone trying to buy a car in 1900 was confronted with a bewildering array of products and technologies. There were cars powered by steam, electricity, or gasoline; cars with three wheels or four; cars with open air cabs or closed carriages. Nor were these differences merely cosmetic. Structural features, mechanical principles, and performance characteristics varied widely from car to car.
>
> Seventy-three years later, before the oil crisis of 1973, that technological diversity had all but disappeared.

Klepper and Simons (1996, p. 82):

> The first commercial sale of a U.S.-made automobile occurred in 1896. Subsequently the output of the industry grew exponentially, with production of automobiles reaching 23,000 by 1904 and climbing to 5.3 million by 1929. ... four producers enter[ed] production in 1895, with the number of firms climbing sharply to a peak of 274 in 1909, then falling to 121 by 1918 and continuing to fall to an eventual low of seven firms in 1955. We date the shakeout of producers as starting in 1909 when the number of firms peaked. ≫

>> Entry was concentrated in the years preceding the peak number of firms. Entry averaged 48 firms per year from 1902 to 1910 and then dropped at the start of the shakeout by two-thirds, averaging 16 firms per year from 1911 to 1921. Thereafter entry became negligible, with only 22 entrants in the entire period from 1922 to 1966. In contrast to these fluctuations in entry, exit rates remained remarkably stable over time. From 1900 to 1918, the percentage of firms exiting averaged about 16% per year. It decreased to 9% per year in 1919 to 1922 and then rose to 28% per year in 1923 to 1925, after which it fell back to an average of 12% per year from 1926 to 1939.

Industry characteristics matter

Simultaneous entry and exit takes place throughout the industry life cycle, with entry peaking early in stage 2, exit early in stage 4. The nature of entry and exit flows varies with industry characteristics.

For a cross-section of four-digit U.S. manufacturing industries in the late 1970s and early 1980s, Kessides (1991) finds that entry is greater, the greater is incumbent profitability and lower, the greater the sunk investment required of an entrant. For a sample of industries from 36 countries during the 1980s, Gschwandtner and Lambson (2002) similarly find that variation in the number of firms in an industry is less, the larger are sunk costs. This result suggests that the need to cover sunk entry cost discourages entry, all else equal, but that once such costs have been paid, the size of losses needed to induce exit is greater.[38]

Market size is a critical factor. Asplund and Nocke (2006) report that the entry rate rises with market size in Swedish regional hair salon markets. Audretsch (1995) tests Winter's (1984) distinction between industries with an entrepreneurial technological regime (small firms have a comparative advantage in innovation) and industries with a routinized technological regime, in which they do not. The need to invest in innovation would be a barrier to mobility in industries with a routinized technological regime. Audretsch's results suggest that (1995, pp. 446–447) new firms are significantly more likely to survive in industries with an entrepreneurial technological regime, all else equal. Troske (1996), in a study analysing entry, growth, and exit for firms in the Wisconsin manufacturing and finance, insurance, and real estate (FIRE) sectors from 1978 to 1987, finds that FIRE entrants come in at larger scale and suffer smaller reductions in relative size than do manufacturing entrants.[39]

Entrant characteristics matter

In their study of entry to and exit from U.S. manufacturing industries in Census years between 1963 and 1982, Dunne et al. (1988) categorize entrants into three groups: new firms, firms that entered by diversifying from another industry and built a new plant to carry out entry, and firms that entered by diversifying from another industry and did so by altering the mix of products from an existing plant. Firms that entered by diversifying and building a

---

[38] Cabral and Ross (2008) make the argument that large-scale sunk investment may facilitate entry by making clear to incumbents that the entrant is committed to remain in the industry. One of their motivating examples is Archer Daniels Midland's 1991 entry into the lysine industry, on a scale that doubled industry capacity (Section 20.2.3). The need to make sunk investments may well have a negative effect on small-scale exploratory entry and yet be capable of having a positive effect on large-scale entry by a firm that is thoroughly acquainted with technology and demand in the target market.

[39] Ericson and Pakes (1998) report comparable results for manufacturing and retailing.

new plant (very likely a sunk investment) came in at larger scale than other types of entrants, in fact beginning production (1988, p. 512) "at an output level larger than the average size firm in the industry". Ten years after entry, surviving diversifying new-plant entrants were of average industry size; other types of entrants were below average size.

These findings are reminiscent of those of Beesley and Hamilton (1984), who analyse births and deaths of establishments in Scotland in the late 1970s. They find that it is diversifying entry that resembles the profit-erosion driven entry of static models (1984, p. 228: "[W]e would argue that the more serious competitive threat to dominant suppliers is from the strategic entry moves of other large companies rather than the activities of the archetypal small entrepreneur"). Independent (that is, non-diversifying) entry is much more a proving ground (a seedbed, as Beesley and Hamilton describe it) for new products or processes, and more often followed by exit than enduring market success (1984, p. 229: "Our data reveal many independent entrepreneurs prepared to try something out of the ordinary—and that many fail in the attempt").

Dunne *et al.* (1989) find that growth rates fall, and survival rates rise, as plant age and size go up. For single-plant firms, the increase in survival rates is insufficient to counterbalance the decline in growth rates; the net growth rate of single-plant firms falls as plant age and size go up. For plants owned by multiplant firms, the increase in survival rates more than outweighs the decline in growth rates; the net growth rate of plants owned by multiplant firms rises as plant age and size go up. Dunne *et al.* (2005) examine entrant survival for 181 regional U.S. markets and seven products between 1963 and 1967. They report that entrants with experience in other regional markets, and who built a new plant, were least likely to exit for six of the seven product markets.

Eriksson and Kuhn (2006) similarly report results suggesting the importance of industry-specific experience for entrant survival. They examine the fate of entrants that were spun off from existing Danish firms between 1981 and 2000, and find that spin-offs from continuing parent firms were less likely to exit. The survival rate of spin-offs from parent firms that had themselves gone out of business was indistinguishable from that of run-of-the-mill entrants.

9.4.2 Turbulence, Turnover, and Mobility

Static oligopoly models point to static measures of market structure—market share, concentration, the Herfindahl index—as factors that determine market performance. Dynamic models offer a rationale for considering changes as well as levels in such variables in trying to understand what drives market performance (Hart and Prais, 1956, p. 161):

> If the firms in two industries ... have the same size distribution—and hence the same measure of concentration—it is still possible that their condition is very different from the economic point of view. For in one industry it may be that the largest firm at present was also the largest firm a century ago, and so on all along the size range; but in the other industry ... the state of competition and rate of innovation may be such that no firm holds its rank in the size distribution for very long. One may thus speak of industries that have a *rigid* structure and others that have a *mobile* structure; industries that have both a high degree of concentration and a rigid structure are those in which one may suspect the existence of monopoly elements.

Davies and Geroski (1997) examine changes between 1979 and 1986 in the market shares of the leading five firms in each industry for a sample of 54 three-digit UK industries. Industry concentration was stable (falling 3 per cent, on average, between 1979 and 1986), and membership in the club of leading firms was relatively secure (1997, p. 384): "the typical industry had just one entrant or exitor" [into or out of the top five]; "entry and exit usually occurred at the fourth or fifth place in the top five ranking." Beneath this surface stability, however, there were substantial shifts in leading firms' market shares. Advertising clearly and spending on research and development "to a lesser extent" increased leading-firm market share turbulence.[40] Matraves and Rondi (2005) show that market shares of leading firms in EU manufacturing industries fluctuate more rapidly, all else equal, in larger markets.

9.4.3 Path Dependence (II)

Static models paint a deterministic picture of equilibrium market structure. For a given relation between minimum efficient firm scale and market size, and given degrees of horizontal and vertical product differentiation, the number and size distribution of firms is in equilibrium when further entry would be unprofitable. Dynamic models, which depict entry as a learning and selection process, emphasize that chance events early in an industry's history can have long-run consequences for its eventual market structure. If stage 2 entrants are unlucky or inept, incumbents will have leeway to reduce their own costs (improving efficiency along the natural trajectory) and consolidate their market position. In stage 5, such markets will be small-numbers oligopolies. Stage 2 entrants that are lucky or skillful will be able to improve their own efficiency along the natural technological trajectory and make a home for themselves in the oligopoly core. In stage 5, such markets will be large-numbers oligopolies. In the same way, there may be elements of path-dependence in early idiosyncratic choices of dominant design that set a market on one technological trajectory rather than another. Light-water nuclear reactors and petrol- rather than steam-engine cars may be examples (Arthur, 1989). All of this lends credence to the analytical approach of the structure-conduct-performance approach: if the link from underlying demand and technology conditions to market structure is mediated by chance effects, it makes a certain amount of sense to look at the impact of market structure on firm conduct and market performance.

Dynamic models of market structure

These picture entry and exit flows as a triage mechanism, a proving-ground for new products and processes. Once an industry settles on a dominant technological trajectory, exit is the most common result of independent entry. To the extent that entry has any impact on the conduct of leading incumbents, it is entry by firms that diversify from other industries, not *de novo* entry. But the relative invulnerability of leading firms to fringe competition, and consequent stability of concentration, masks changes in market share rankings within the oligopolistic core.

9.4.4 Firm Size Distributions

In elementary models of oligopoly, it is common (largely for expositional reasons), to make assumptions that imply that all firms are the same size (produce the same amount of output)

---

[40] These results are consistent with earlier evidence that the costs of moving from the fringe to the inner circle of established oligopolistic firms depends on *barriers to mobility* (Caves and Porter, 1977) that are higher the larger is minimum efficient scale output in relation to market size, the greater the fraction of operating investments that are sunk costs, and the more important is spending on advertising and on innovation. In the same vein, see Oster (1982) and Thomas (1995).

Table 9.14 Selected U.S. Manufacturing Concentration Statistics, 2002

2002 NAICS code	Largest firms →	4	8	20	50	H index	$\hat{n}$	n
311	Food	16.8	25.4	39.8	53.1	118.7	84.2	23,334
3111	Animal food	29.8	40.9	59.0	73.0	364.9	27.4	1,211
311111	Dog and cat food	64.2	81.3	93.2	98.0	1,845.4	5.4	176
31123	Breakfast cereal	78.4	91.1	98.8	100.0	2,521.3	4.0	45
32411	Petroleum refineries	41.2	63.5	89.3	99.3	639.7	15.6	88
331111	Iron and steel mills	44.4	58.5	77.7	93.0	656.7	15.2	285
331312	Primary aluminum production	85.3	97.9	99.9	100.0	D	—	26
333111	Farm machinery and equipment	57.6	64.7	73.2	81.5	1,656.8	6.0	1138
336111	Automobiles	75.5	94.2	99.3	99.8	1,910.9	5.2	164

Notes: "H index"is 10,000 times the Herfindahl index; $\hat{n}$ is the inverse of the H index; n is the actual number of companies. "D" indicates information suppressed to maintain confidentiality of individual company data
Source: U.S. Census Bureau, 2002 Economic Census.

in equilibrium. But in most industries, there are substantial and persistent inequalities in firm size. The statistics in Table 9.14 are for a few U.S. manufacturing industries, but the nature of the results is typical. Comparing the actual number of firms with the inverse of the Herfindahl index, a numbers-equivalent measure of seller concentration, suggests that in most industries, even highly concentrated industries, there are a large number of firms with small market shares. Such differences also appear in Table 9.15, which lists 2007 sales revenue and market shares of cars and light trucks by supplier in three regional markets—Western Europe, Japan, and North America.

Figure 9.10 shows the individual market shares of the 22 largest European firms identified by name in Table 9.15.[41] Five firms have market shares of more than 11 per cent each, after which market shares fall off sharply.

Gibrat's Law

Gibrat (1931) put forward the descriptive hypothesis, which he called the *law of proportionate growth* (and which has come to be known as *Gibrat's Law*) that the probability of a given

---

[41] Market shares for the three smallest EU suppliers are omitted from the figure because their market shares are so small as to be visually indistinguishable from the horizontal axis.

Table 9.15 2007 new car and light truck sales (1000s) and regional shares, Herfindahl indices, and numbers equivalents

Europe	Sales	%	Japan	Sales	%	North America	Sales	%
Volkswagen	3,214	19.67	Toyota	2,224	42.39	General Motors	4,451	23.54
PSA/Peugeot	2,068	12.66	Nissan	718	13.69	Ford	2,952	15.62
Ford	1,748	10.70	Suzuki	670	12.76	Toyota	2,888	15.28
General Motors	1,681	10.29	Honda	622	11.85	Chrysler	2,438	12.90
Renault	1,444	8.84	Mazda	254	4.84	Honda	1,777	9.40
Fiat	1,286	7.87	Mitsubishi	227	4.32	Nissan	1,359	7.19
Toyota	1,034	6.33	Subaru	226	4.30	Hyundai-Kia	882	4.67
BMW	861	5.27	Daimler	76	1.44	Volkswagen	527	2.79
Daimler	830	5.08	Volkswagen	68	1.29	Mazda	399	2.11
Hyundai-Kia	597	3.65	BMW	61	1.17	BMW	374	1.98
Honda	336	2.05	Isuzu	41	0.79	Daimler	280	1.48
Nissan	320	1.96	Ford	19	0.37	Subaru	204	1.08
Suzuki	290	1.77	PSA/Peugeot	11	0.20	Mitsubishi	163	0.86
Mazda	242	1.48	General Motors	9	0.18	Suzuki	120	0.63
Mitsubishi	144	0.88	Fiat	7	0.13	Porsche	37	0.20
Chrysler	120	0.73	Chrysler	6	0.12	Renault	19	0.10
Subaru	49	0.30	Porsche	4	0.08	PSA/Peugeot	14	0.07
Porsche	46	0.28	Renault	2	0.05	Fiat	8	0.04
Ssangyong	24	0.15	Hyundai-Kia	1	0.02	Isuzu	7	0.04
Aston Martin	2	0.01	Lotus	0.4	0.01	Lotus	3	0.01

(Continued)

Table 9.15 (Continued)

Europe	Sales	%	Japan	Sales	%	North America	Sales	%
Proton	2	0.01	Aston Martin	0.3	0.01	Aston Martin	1	0.006
Isuzu	1	0.009	Lamborghini	0.2	0.003	Lamborghini	1	0.005
Lotus	1	0.008	MG Rover	0.1	0.002			
Lamborghini	0.8	0.005	Proton					
MG Rover	0.3	0.002	Ssangyong					
Other	21		Other	2,447				
H		0.1029			0.2354			0.1380
1/H		9.72			4.25			7.24

Notes: Herfindahl indices exclude "Other" sales
Source: *Automotive News 2008 Global Market Data Book*.

percentage change in the size of a firm over a given time period for firms in an industry is independent of the firm's initial size.[42] In other words (Ijiri and Simon, 1977, p. 141): "a firm randomly selected from those with a billion dollars in assets has the same probability of growing, say, 20 percent, as a firm randomly selected from those with a million dollars in assets".

Gibrat's Law, implausible though it may be in its strict form,[43] implies that firm size distributions will be lognormal,[44] exhibiting the kind of inequality shown in Figure 9.11, which is commonly observed in a wide variety of industries.

---

[42] The apparently stochastic emergence of unequal size distributions has been discussed in many contexts; Simon (1955) considers distributions of words in prose samples by their frequency of occurrence; distributions of scientists by numbers of papers published; distributions of cities by population; distributions of incomes by size; and distributions of biological genera by number of species (although he does so in connection with the Yule distribution, not the lognormal).

[43] *Gibrat's Law* in its strict form has the counterfactual implications that the mean and variance of firm size increase without limit over time. Many modifications of *Gibrat's Law* have been explored with the purpose of circumventing these implications, among which making firm growth rates negatively related to firm size, allowing for entry and exit, and introducing a minimum efficient scale, above which a firm must operate if it is to operate at all. For a survey, see de Wit (2005). One of Herbert Simon's variations on the *law of proportionate growth* is an intellectual antecedent of John Sutton's submarkets approach; see Sutton (1997b, Section II).

[44] This derivation appears in Kalecki (1945), Aitchison and Brown (1957, Ch. 3), Scherer (1970, p. 127), and Sutton (1997): let x_t be the size of a firm at time t (size may be measured by assets, sales, employees). Let the proportionate rate of growth be random

$$\frac{x_t - x_{t-1}}{x_{t-1}} = \varepsilon_t;$$

then $x_t = (1 + \varepsilon_t) x_{t-1}$ and

$$\ln x_t = \ln (1 + \varepsilon_t) + \ln x_{t-1} \approx \varepsilon_t + \ln x_{t-1}$$

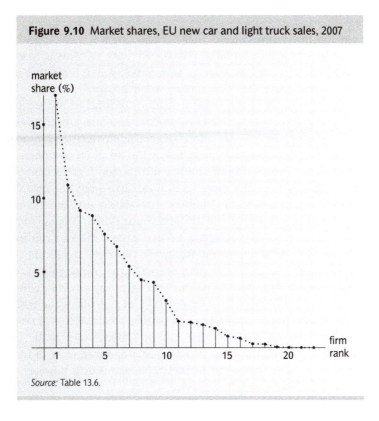

Figure 9.10 Market shares, EU new car and light truck sales, 2007

Source: Table 13.6.

Figure 9.11 Frequency distribution of quoted UK companies, 1950, with fitted two-parameter lognormal distribution

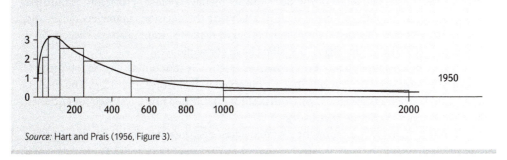

1950

Source: Hart and Prais (1956, Figure 3).

(if the length of a time period is sufficiently short that ε_t can be taken to be small). Solving recursively backward,

$$\ln x_t = \ln x_0 + \sum_{\tau=1}^{t} \varepsilon_\tau.$$

Assume the random terms ε are independently distributed with mean m and variance σ^2. Then the central limit theorem implies that for large enough t, $\ln x_t$ is distributed as a normal random variable with mean mt and variance $mt, \sigma^2 t$, $\ln x_t \sim N\left(mt, \sigma^2 t\right)$. That is, the limiting firm size distribution is lognormal.

On balance, empirical evidence suggests that Gibrat's Law is a good approximation to the way firm sizes change over time for large, established firms. Entrants tend to exit more frequently than would be predicted by Gibrat's Law. Small, young firms that do not exit quickly tend to grow more rapidly than Gibrat's Law would predict.

Cabral and Mata (2003) examine the size distributions of firms in two samples of Portuguese data, one covering 587 large, publicly listed firms and one covering nearly 34,000 manufacturing firms. The lognormal distribution is a good approximation for the size distribution of firms in the large-firm sample, as predicted by the law of proportionate effect. The other sample includes small firms, and the firm size distribution for this sample is skewed to the right, containing proportionally more small firms than would be predicted by the lognormal distribution. Cabral and Mata (2003, pp. 1079–1080) attribute this observation to financial market constraints that differentially bind young firms: "Suppose that financing constraints are especially relevant for young firms. Then, even if the long-run size distribution for a given cohort is close to symmetric, we should observe a significant skew to the right during the first periods, that is, a large mass of small firms. Among this mass of small firms, some are small because they want to be small on efficiency grounds, whereas others are small because they are financially constrained." This result explains the observed deviation of small-firm growth rates from the random pattern predicted by Gibrat's Law. It is also consistent with the idea, noted above, that entrant characteristics matter for whether an entrant dithers around a bit on the fringe of an industry and then exits, or transitions to a long-term presence in its industry. Binding financial constraints may, however, induce the exit of firms that would otherwise be able to survive.

9.5 Reconciliation[45]

Static models of market structure are deterministic—how a firm fares in the marketplace, for better or worse, is a consequence of the decisions its managers make. Professors at business schools spend a fair amount of time and effort analysing the decisions managers make, and teaching courses about what decisions managers ought make to attain business success. So it is comforting to think that managers' decisions have consequences.

Yet dynamic models that picture firm growth as essentially random do a good job predicting the kinds of firm size distributions that are observed in real-world industries. The models are a little rough around the edges; they work best for established firms, less well for entrants. But on balance, they do not do that badly.

What is one to make of the argument that managers' decisions determine firms' outcomes if models that predict outcomes as largely random fit the data pretty well? There is less of a contradiction between the two world views than meets the eye. Of course managers' decisions have an impact on firms' performance. Of course there is a chance element to the outcomes that result form managers' decisions. No manager approves an advertising campaign expecting that it will repel consumers. No manager approves a change in product design expecting that buyers will think that the "new, improved" version is of lower quality than the "old, unimproved" version. No pharmaceutical company pursues years of investment in

---

[45] See Geroski (2005).

a new drug, anticipating that it will be no more effective than a placebo. Managers make decisions under conditions of uncertainty; there is a chance element in how those decisions turn out. Static models neglect such considerations. One may rationalize this neglect on expositional grounds, or on the argument that the results of static models suggest what ought to happen in a run that is sufficiently long for all uncertainty to resolve itself. One may also take the view that static models are only a foundation, upon which dynamic models are to be built. But there is no fundamental contradiction between the two sets of results.

SUMMARY

In a time period so long that entry and exit have driven economic profit to zero, supply-side concentration should be greater, the greater is minimum efficient scale and the more effectively firms are organized to realize maximum potential efficiency. If incumbent firms can enhance vertical product differentiation by investing in sales efforts and product design, seller concentration can be bounded away from low levels even if the market becomes large.

Markets without network externalities work well if equilibrium firm size is small, relative to the market, if barriers to entry and mobility are small, if such sunk costs as are present tend to be exogenous rather than endogenous, and if the carrying out of transactions across markets does not involve too much investment in specific assets. Markets with network externalities work well when most consumers are connected to the network of a single firm, which then supplies them with the highest-value product.

Real-world entry is a hazardous process. Although entry does seem to respond to profit opportunities, this response is much less automatic than it is often taken to be in theoretical discussions. Entry and exit are as much elements of a screening mechanism that selects firms that are able to meet a market test as they are an equilibrating mechanism that drives economic profit to zero. There are chance elements to the outcomes of business decisions, and these chance elements contribute to persistent inequalities in firms size distributions.

STUDY POINTS

- Structure of economic activity in developed economies (Section 9.2)
- Market structure, descriptive (manufacturing, Section 9.3.1; retail, Section 9.3.12)
- Static models of market structure (Section 9.3.3)
  - Long-run equilibrium number of plants in a Cournot market (Section 9.3.3)
  - Multiplant firms (Section 9.3.3)
  - Circle model (Section 9.3.7)
- Network externalities (Section 9.3.5)
- Firm organization and market structure (Section 9.3.9)
- Exogenous sunk cost industries v. endogenous sunk cost industries (Section 9.3.10)
- Empirical studies of market structure (Section 9.3.8, Section 9.3.10)
- Dynamic models of market structure (Section 9.4)
- Gibrat's Law (Section 9.4.4)
- Path dependence (Section 9.3.6, Section 9.4.3)

FURTHER READING

For a discussion of changes in the structure of economic activity in the U.S. economy, see Carter (1967). On price discrimination in spatial models, see Hoover (1937), MacLeod *et al.* (1988), and Anderson and Engers (2001). For spatial models with fixed locations, see Eaton and Lipsey (1978) and Eaton and Wooders (1985); for such models where firms enter in sequence, see Hay (1976) and Prescott and Visscher (1977).

See Matutes and Regibeau (1996) on network externalities, and Gandal (2002) for a discussion that draws policy implications. For an entree to Alfred Chandler's vast work, see McCraw (1988) and Chandler (1992).

For introductions to Sutton's work, see Sutton (1990, 1996, 2007) and the reviews by Bresnahan (1992), Schmalensee (1992), and Scherer (2000). For empirical tests of the bounds approach, see among others Robinson and Chiang (1996), Matraves (1999), Rogers (2001), Bakker (2005), and Marin and Siotis (2007). On market structure in the U.S. beer industry, in addition to Tremblay and Tremblay (2005), see Sutton (1991, Chapter 13) and McGahan (1991).

For more on the U.S. supermarket sector, see Cotterill (1986) and Betancourt and Malanoski (1999). On the impact of high-technology distribution systems on the structure of retail trade generally, see Holmes (2000).

On entry and exit, see Geroski (1991), Geroski and Schwalbach (1991), Audretsch (1995); Troske (1996, Section II) is a concise survey, and for comprehensive reviews, Geroski (1995), Caves (1998). The discussion in the FTC's 1999 *Study of the Commission's Divestiture Process* of factors affecting the success or failure of entrants is instructive. On entry and exit over the product life cycle, see Gort and Klepper (1982), Klepper and Graddy (1990), Agarwal and Gort (1996), and Klepper (1997). On shakeouts, see Klepper and Simons (1996, 2005). The seminal model of entry as a selection mechanism is Jovanovic (1982); more recently, see Asplund and Nocke (2006). On exit from declining industries, see Ghemawat and Nalebuff (1985, 1990), Whinston (1988), and Lieberman (1990). On changes in market share rankings as an index of competition, see Baldwin and Gorecki (1994), Geroski and Toker (1996), and Sutton (2007). For references to and a critique of an older literature, see Hymer and Pashigian (1962). For good brief discussions of the literature on Gibrat's Law, see Boeri (1989), McCloughan (1995), and for a survey, Sutton (1997b).

PROBLEMS

9–1 (Fixed cost, sunk cost, market structure I) Let firms operate with production function

$$q = \min\left[\frac{K - 160}{1}, \frac{L - 20}{1}\right]$$

for $K \geq 160$, $L \geq 20$, and $q = 0$ otherwise, so that to produce at all requires hiring at least one hundred and eighty units of capital and twenty units of labor, and that each unit of output requires one additional unit of capital and one additional unit of labour over these minimum amounts.

Firms hire labour at wage rate $w = 5$ per period and purchase physical capital at price $p^k = 50$; for simplicity, assume both input prices are constant over time, and assume also that physical capital does not depreciate.

The rental rate of the services of one unit of physical capital is rp^k, where $r = 1/10$ is the rate of return on a safe asset (the opportunity cost of investing financial capital in the firm).

If the firm wishes to resell a unit of physical capital, it can do so at price αp^k, where the cost-sunkenness parameter α is a number that lies between 0 and 1. If $\alpha = 0$, investments in the industry are completely sunk, in the sense that if the firm should wish to exit the industry, it would not be able to recover any of its investment in physical capital. If $\alpha = 1$, investments in the industry are not sunk at all.

(a) Assume that production is efficient, in the sense that firms minimize cost. Find the equation of the cost function of a firm. Identify fixed cost, variable cost, marginal cost, and sunk cost.

(b) In a market with inverse demand curve:

$$p = 100 - Q,$$

what is the long-run equilibrium number of firms in Cournot oligopoly if firms produce efficiently? How does the level of fixed cost affect the long-run equilibrium number of firms?

(c) Now suppose that the rental cost of capital services rises, the more are investments in the industry sunk, that is, that the rental cost of capital services is:

$$\rho = \rho(\alpha), \text{ with } \rho(1) = r, \rho' < 0.$$

The opportunity cost to a firm of investing in an industry is the amount it must pay to borrow financial capital. The resale value of physical capital is collateral that secures the value of loans (or that reverts to bondholders, if a firm should go bankrupt). The more are costs sunk (the lower is α), the lower the value of this collateral, all else equal, and the greater the interest rate that financial markets will require to finance investments in the industry.

How do changes in the extent to which an industry's costs are sunk affect the equilibrium long-run number of firms?

9–2 (Sunk cost and market structure II) Continuing Problem 9–1, let $\alpha = 1/2$, so that half of a firm's investment in physical assets is sunk. Suppose the firm is supplied by one firm that produces the monopoly output.

(a) What is the firm's monopoly profit?

(b) If a second firm comes into the market, what is the first firm's marginal cost? (Hint: calculate the present-discounted value of the first firm's cost if it sells its excess capital at the start of the period in which entry occurs.)

(c) If the post-entry market is a Cournot duopoly, what is the second firm's equilibrium profit? How do changes in the extent to which costs are sunk affect the second firm's post-entry profit?

9–3 Consider a market with linear inverse demand function:

$$p(Q) = a - bQ,$$

where Q is total output. Let the firm-level cost function be cubic,

$$C(q) = F + cq - dq^2 + eq^3.$$

Here $F, a, b, c, d \geq 0, e > 0$. Assume also that $a - c > 0$ and $d > b$.

Find the long-run equilibrium number of firms if the market is a Cournot oligopoly and entry occurs until profit per firm is zero.

9–4 (Equilibrium number of firms, Cournot oligopoly, differentiated products) For a price-setting oligopoly with product differentiation, let the equations of the inverse demand curves be:

$$p_i = 100 - (q_i + \theta Q_{-i}),$$

for $i = 1,2,...,n$ and $Q_{-i} = \sum_{j\neq i}^{n} q_j$, with the equation of the firm-level cost function:

$$c(q) = F + 10q.$$

Find the equilibrium number of firms if the long-run equilibrium number of firms adjusts until Cournot equilibrium profit per firm is zero. How does the equilibrium number of firms change as θ changes?

9–5 (Measuring market share with differentiated products) Show that if (for example, for duopoly) inverse demand curves have equations (3.45) and (3.46),

$$p_1 = 100 - (q_1 + \theta q_2),\tag{9.34}$$

$$p_2 = 100 - (\theta q_2 + q_1),\tag{9.35}$$

the expression for the Lerner index of market power that corresponds to (3.22) is:

$$\frac{p_1 - c'(q_1)}{p_1} = \frac{s_1}{\varepsilon_{Q_1 p_1}},\tag{9.36}$$

where:

$$s_1 = \frac{q_1}{q_1 + \theta q_2} \equiv \frac{q_1}{Q_1}\tag{9.37}$$

(so that $Q_1 = q_1 + \theta q_2$) is firm 1's market share, taking account of the imperfect substitutability of variety 2 for variety 1, and:

$$\varepsilon_{Q_1 p_1} \equiv -\frac{Q_1}{p_1}\frac{dp_1}{dQ_1}.\tag{9.38}$$

9–6 (Cournot duopoly, horizontal and vertical product differentiation, generalizing Problem 3–11)

Let there be two varieties of a good, variety 1 and variety 2, of which quantities q_1 and q_2 are sold at prices p_1 and p_2, respectively, and a homogeneous good m sold at price 1. Preferences are described by the representative consumer welfare function:

$$U(q_1,q_2,m) = \alpha_1 q_1 + \alpha_2 q_2 - \frac{1}{2}\beta(q_1^2 + 2\theta q_1 q_2 + q_2^2) + m,\tag{9.39}$$

which is valid for $q_1 \geq 0$, $q_2 \geq 0$, $m \geq 0$. The aggregate budget constraint is:

$$Y = p_1 q_1 + p_2 q_2 + m.\tag{9.40a}$$

α_1, α_2, and β are positive parameters. Without loss of generality, let $\alpha_1 > \alpha_2$. θ is a parameter with $0 \leq \theta \leq 1$, and Y is aggregate income. Aggregate demand for q_1 and q_2 and m is found by maximizing the representative consumer welfare function (3.84) subject to the budget constraint (3.85a).

(a) Find the equations of the inverse demand functions for q_1 and q_2.

(b) Suppose each variety is produced by a Cournot duopolist at constant marginal cost c per unit. Find equilibrium outputs, prices, and payoffs. Discuss restrictions on parameter values that must be satisfied for equilibrium outputs to be non-negative.

FIRMS AND FIRM STRUCTURE

10

> Long before a factory has reached this extent, it will have been found necessary to establish an accountant's department, with clerks to pay the workmen, and to see that they arrive at their stated times; and this department must be in communication with the agents who purchase the raw produce, and with those who sell the manufactured article.
>
> Babbage ([1835] 1963, p. 216)

10.1 Introduction

In *The Wealth of Nations*, Adam Smith ([1776] 1937, p. 700) took a critical view of the impact of corporations on market performance:

> The directors of [joint-stock] companies, ... being the managers rather of other people's money than of their own, it cannot well be expected that they should watch over it with the same anxious vigilance with which the partners in a private copartnery frequently watch over their own. Negligence and profusion, therefore, must always prevail, more or less, in the management of the affairs of such a company.

Despite this early attention, economists came slowly to the idea that it was necessary to look at the organization of economic activity within firms to fully understand the organization of economic activity within markets.[1] There are abstract versions of firms in the neoclassical theory of perfectly competitive markets. But those "firms" operate under conditions of complete and perfect information, purchase inputs in markets that are themselves perfectly competitive, and independently maximize their own profit, taking price as given:

---

[1] Some simply rejected the firm as a central concern of economics (Demsetz, 1983, p. 377, footnote omitted; p. 378) "The chief mission of neoclassical economics is to understand how the price system coordinates the use of resources, not to understand the inner workings of real firms", and "[T]he firm is defined, not to approximate the activities of a real firm, pre- or postcorporate organization, but as the theoretical institution in which production (for others) takes place."

there is no scope for inefficiency, no discretion as to goals pursued or methods chosen to reach those goals. In the perfectly competitive market, there is no firm behaviour to explain, no place for entrepreneurship, nothing for a manager to do.[2]

As early as 1890, Alfred Marshall recognized that there were markets that did not fit the assumptions of the perfectly competitive model.[3] There was an initial round of analyses of such markets in the 1920s,[4] but this literature focused on the consequences of fewness of firms and product differentiation for market performance. As far as internal organization was concerned, the "firms" of these models of imperfect or monopolistic competition remained black boxes.

Early in the economic train wreck that was the Great Depression, Berle and Means' *The Modern Corporation and Private Property* (1932) picked up where Adam Smith had left off and highlighted the separation of ownership and control in large corporations with widely dispersed ownership as a phenomenon worthy of economists' attention. It was not merely the existence of large firms in important sectors of the economy that drove economists of this period to look within the firm. There had been large firms before—the Standard Oil Company, for example, or the Ford Motor Company—but with a little effort one could persuade oneself that these were simply the owner-operated, profit-maximizing firm of neoclassical economic theory, writ large. What drove economists to look inside the firm was the presence of large firms for which internal organization seemed to matter, in ways there were not understood, for market performance.

Some economists sought to understand firm organization-market performance relationships by asking businessmen what it was they did, and how they did it (Hall and Hitch, 1939). Some economists developed models of firms that maximized sales, or growth, or managerial perquisites (Baumol, 1958; 1959/1967; Williamson, 1964; Marris, 1968). Some scholars abandoned the maximization assumption entirely (Simon, 1959; Cyert and March, 1963), visualizing firms as organizations that (Simon, 1987, p. 223) "ordinarily settle for 'satisfactory' profits, and . . . only when they fail to achieve these . . . search for improved products or methods of operation".

---

[2] One should not be too hard on the neoclassical microeconomic theories of perfectly or imperfectly competitive markets. They are, after all, theories of *equilibrium* market performance, and in equilibrium, the tasks reserved for management are routine. It is in disequilibrium that the efforts of the entrepreneur (in the sense of Joseph A. Schumpeter; see Chapter 14), come to the fore.

[3] See Marshall (*Principles*, [1890] 1920, p. 501; this is mentioned by Robinson, 1934, p. 246) "in many industries each producer has a special market in which he is well known, and which he cannot extend quickly . . . [;] though it might be physically possible for him to increase his output rapidly, he would run the risk of forcing down very much the demand price in his special market . . . " See also Marshall's ([1890] 1925) remarks on trusts.

[4] See Hicks (1935) for a contemporary survey. One may date this literature from Sraffa, whose (1926, p. 543) "The chief obstacle against which [firms] have to contend when they want gradually to increase their production does not lie in the cost of production—which, indeed, generally favours them in that direction—but in the difficulty of selling the larger quantity of goods without reducing the price, or without having to face increased marketing expenses" sounds the same theme as Marshall.

The prevailing assessment of these works is that (Hart, 1989, p. 1757) "theories that attempt[ed] to incorporate real world features of corporations, partnerships and the like often lack precision and rigor, and ... therefore failed, by and large, to be accepted by the theoretical mainstream". But the issues they raised remain.

A later round of efforts to analyse the internal organization of firms and draw implications for market performance promises to have an enduring impact. It can be traced to two sources. The first is the demands of policymakers with responsibility for antitrust and competition policy toward mergers (a topic we take up in Chapter 22). Businesses are wont to defend proposed mergers with the prospect of the efficiency gains they will bring. Williamson (1968b, 1977a) put forward a general framework, which we discuss in Section 11.3.2, within which the net welfare impact of a merger is the difference between welfare losses from increases in market power (if any) and welfare benefits from increases in efficiency (if any). It is difficult to satisfactorily analyse the kinds of efficiency gains that might flow from a merger using as a model of the firm a black box that always operates at maximum efficiency. Policy needs for a framework within which differential firm efficiency can be analysed is one source of the demand for economic models of the internal organization of firms. On the supply side, economic historians, building on Alfred D. Chandler, Jr.'s studies of large firms in American and world business history, provided much descriptive material, and not a little analysis, documenting the development of prevailing forms of firm structure and making it undeniably clear that firm structure does matter for market performance.

Prompted by the policy-driven demand for a framework that would permit the analysis of the impact of changes in firm structure on market performance and by the supply from business historians of the raw material against which such analysis might be tested, economists delved within the firm. Along the way, they rediscovered Coase (1937), a neglected work that contained the seeds of much later work.

We begin this chapter by describing the presence of large firms in modern economies. We discuss their rise and the link between internal organization and the kinds of markets in which large firms not only rose but also endured. We examine Berle and Means' topic, the separation of ownership and control. We examine the Coase question ("Why are there firms?"), review some of the answers economists have given to that question, and examine evidence on factors influencing the kinds of activities that take place within firms.

10.2 Large Firms

10.2.1 Their Presence

U.S.

Seller concentration is typically measured by a concentration ratio, the combined share of some specified number of the largest firms in industry sales, or by a Herfindahl index that summaries the entire size distribution of firms. *Aggregate concentration*, in contrast, is typically measured by the combined share of the largest 50, or 100, or 200 firms in some variable, such as assets, employment, value of shipments, or value added, for an economy as a whole.

Berle and Means (1932) founded a literature with their estimates of the share of U.S. national wealth controlled by corporations early in the Great Depression.[5] By their calculations, this share ranged from 22 per cent to nearly 50 per cent, depending on what category of wealth was being considered (Table 10.1). They suggested (1932, pp. 41–42) that large corporations had been growing "two and three times as fast as all other non-financial corporations" and would "absorb a larger and larger share of overall economic activity".

The increase in US aggregate concentration feared by Berle and Means has not materialized (Table 10.2). Table 10.1 measures aggregate concentration in three different samples, Table 10.2 in manufacturing, but the consensus interpretation of these and other estimates is clear: aggregate concentration in the United States rose from the late 1940s to the 1970s, fell through the late 1990s, and may have increased since then (White, 2002, p. 156).

As a kind of half-way house between aggregate concentration and market concentration, one might look at the combined share of large firms in broad sectors of the economy, narrower than the economy as a whole but including many distinct markets. Table 10.1

Table 10.1 Relative importance of large corporations in the U.S. economy on or about January 1, 1930

	%	Probable Range (%)
Proportion of corporate wealth (other than banking) controlled by the 200 largest corporations	49.2	45–53
Proportion of business wealth (other than banking) controlled by the 200 largest corporations	38.0	35–45
Proportion of national wealth controlled by the 200 largest corporations	22.0	15–25

Source: Berle and Means ([1932] 1991, p. 33).

Table 10.2 Share of largest 200 companies in U.S. manufacturing sector value added, 1947–2002

Year	1947	1954	1958	1963	1967	1972	1977	1982	1987	1992	1997	2002
Per Cent	30	37	38	41	42	43	44	43	43	42	41	42

Source: Atack and Bateman (2006); U.S. Census Bureau (2001, 2006).

---

[5] Guinnnane *et al.* (2007) argue that Berle and Means' focus on the corporation is misplaced. They point to the private limited liability company (PLLC) as an important form of business organization that combines aspects of the partnership and the corporation and has distinctive advantages, particularly for small- and medium-sized enterprises.

Table 10.3 Share of largest 50 firms in sector revenue/receipts/sales, U.S., 2002

Sector	%
Utilities	69.0
Information	62.0
Finance, insurance	44.9
Transportation & warehousing	33.0
Retail	31.7
Wholesale	27.2
Manufacturing	24.5
Real estate, rental, and leasing	24.4
Accommodation and food services	23.1
Administrative, support, waste management, and remediation services	21.9
Educational services	21.4
Arts, entertainment, and recreation	19.6
Professional, scientific, and technical services	16.2
Health care, and social assistance	14.7

Source: 2002 Economic Census.

shows that in 2002 the 200 largest U.S. manufacturing firms accounted for 42 per cent of value added in manufacturing. Table 10.3 shows that in 2002 the largest 50 manufacturing firms accounted for 24.5 per cent of manufacturing sales. Aggregate concentration in U.S. manufacturing is, if anything, low relative to aggregate concentration in most other sectors of the U.S. economy.

EU

The successive expansions of the European Union, and the ongoing process of economic integration that accompanies them, make the EU a moving target for many purposes, not least of which the measurement of aggregate concentration. Whatever one might mean by "an equilibrium level of aggregate concentration", one might suppose that the U.S. figure approximates it. There can be no such presumption for the EU.

Davies and Lyons (1996) construct estimates of aggregate EU manufacturing concentration for 1987, and compare it with aggregate concentration in Japan and the U.S.

Table 10.4 Shares of largest 50 (C50) and 100 (C100) firms in aggregate manufacturing

	C50	C100
EU	22	28
Japan	19	n.a.
U.S.	24	34

Source: Davies and Lyons (1996, Table 9.1, based in part on White, 1981, Doi , 1991.

(Table 10.4).[6] As they observe, aggregate 50-firm concentration is similar for the EU and the U.S. Since the 1987 EU was a union of partially integrated regional markets, one would expect aggregate concentration to be lower in the EU than in the U.S. This may explain why the aggregate share of the 51st through 100th firms in the U.S. is twice the corresponding figure for the EU If second-tier large EU firms increase their scale as market integration proceeds, 100-firm aggregate EU concentration will approach the U.S. level.

10.2.2 What to Make of It

Economic power

Berle and Means were concerned with the discretionary power that large size might bring (1932, p. 34):

> Smaller companies which sell to or buy from the larger companies are likely to be influenced by them to a vastly greater extent than by other smaller companies with which they might deal. In many cases the continued prosperity of the smaller companies depends on the favor of the larger and almost inevitably the interests of the latter become the interests of the former. The influence of the larger company on prices is often greatly increased by its mere size, even though it does not begin to approach a monopoly. Its political influence may be tremendous.

In the same vein, Chandler (1967, p. 101) writes of "[t]he extreme concentration of power" in large corporations as an issue "in a society committed to democratic values" that is "still totally unresolved".

Livermore (1940) argued that national corporations had opened local and regional markets to competition and very likely improved market performance, not worsened it. But Livermore's critique of Berle and Means was merely an early entry in a continuing dialogue at cross-purposes. Berle and Means argued that size alone would bring large firms discretionary power; Livermore argued that entry by large firms had reduced the ability of firms with large shares of small markets to exercise market power. Both claims may be correct, because they address different issues.

---

[6] The U.S. data in Table 10.4 refer to 1976, the Japanese data to 1988.

Despite the increased attention economists give to the firm as a framework for organizing transactions, they tend still to assess a firm's impact on economic performance in the context of the markets within which it operates. If more efficient internal organization allows a firm to reduce its marginal cost, that makes it profitable for the firm to lower price *in the markets within which it operates*. If vertical integration, while permitting reduced marginal cost, raises the fixed and sunk cost of entry *into the markets within which a firm operates*, that permits it to profitably raise prices *in those markets*.

In analysing the consequences of firm structure for performance, therefore, many economists tend also to measure firm size relative to market size, to hold that (Adelman, 1964, p. 228) "absolute size is absolutely irrelevant". In this view—consistent with most models of and much evidence about imperfectly competitive markets—market share and market concentration matter for market performance, aggregate concentration does not. A firm that is large in an absolute sense will have no differential ability to hold price above marginal cost merely because it is large.

An alternative view is that absolute size has implications for market performance even if a firm that is large in an absolute sense is small in its markets (Edwards, 1964, p. 42):

> A big firm has advantages over a smaller rival just because it is big. Money is power. A big firm can outbid, outspend, and outlose a small firm. It can advertise more intensively, do more intensive or extensive research, buy up the inventions of others, defend its legal rights or alleged rights more thoroughly, bid higher for scarce resources, acquire the best locations and the best technicians and executives. If it overdoes the expenditures it can absorb losses that would bankrupt a small rival.

Another reaction to the "absolute size is absolutely irrelevant" position is that although *in principle* a firm might be large in an absolute sense but small in relation to the markets in which it operates, *in practice* firms that are large in an absolute sense tend to have large shares of their markets. If this is so, then where high aggregate concentration leads, high market concentration will follow.

There is some indication that high aggregate concentration and high market concentration go together. Utton identifies the leading firms in a 1963 sample of 30 broadly-defined UK product groups, and reports that leading firms in many product groups were also among the top 100 firms in UK manufacturing as a whole (1974, pp. 152–153):

> [I]n half of the sample product groups at least one of the three largest firms was among the largest 100 firms in the whole manufacturing sector and in about 23% of all product groups the leading 2 or 3 suppliers were also among the largest firms overall.

Blair (1972, pp. 53–55) finds that for U.S. manufacturing industries in 1958 "In more than half of the 1,014 product classes in manufacturing as a whole, at least one of the 100 largest [firms] was among the 4 largest producers, and in 31 percent at least 2 came from the 100 largest." Clarke and Davies (1983) find that 10 per cent of the increase in UK manufacturing aggregate concentration between 1963 and 1968 was due to increases in diversification of firms across industries.

Political power

If one wishes to explain market performance, and if the reason to be concerned about high aggregate concentration is because it is associated with high market concentration, then this leads back to market concentration as an immediate factor affecting market performance. But there may be other reasons to be concerned about aggregate concentration than its impact, direct or indirect, on market performance. Aggregate concentration may be a concern because large firms, by means of lobbying and financial contributions, are able to influence the democratic political process to promote economic policies that favour their own interests.

Edwards (1955, pp. 346–347, emphasis added) argues forcefully that "the campaign contributions of large companies and the occasional case of direct and indirect bribery are probably the *least* significant sources of the large company's political power". Rather, the cost of maintaining an office in Washington or Brussels is for the most part a fixed cost. There is nothing illegal or immoral about maintaining staff to keep track of legislative and administrative activity, to prepare studies that put a company's position in the best possible light, or to employ consultants and lobbyists to present those studies to the right government department at the right time. But such activities can determine the outcome of political processes, and large firms are better able to cover their costs than are small firms.

Here anecdotes abound but systematic evidence is scarce. Using data for U.S. industries in 1963, Salamon and Siegfried (1977) find that the federal corporate income tax rate, adjusted for targeted deductions and exemptions, was lower the larger the asset size of the median firm in an industry. In another test, they find that U.S. state taxes on motor vehicle fuel are lower in states with a large petroleum refining industry that is dominated by large firms. These results suggest that large firms are able to influence the design of public policy to reduce their own tax burden or promote their industry's economic interest.

Kim (2008) finds that firm size as measured by sales has a positive impact on both lobbying expenditures and political contributions.[7] Firm size as measured by number of employees has a negative impact on corporate lobbying expenditures, but no significant effect on political contributions. He also reports some findings showing a positive impact of lobbying on stock-market returns. On balance, Kim's results support the existence of a firm size-political influence link.

10.3 Their Rise

Chandler (1984) documents the rise of large firms in the United States and developed economies generally. Large firms did not spring up chance here in one industry, there in another. Large firms clustered in a few specific sectors (Table 10.5). These were the sectors where changes in technology made economies of speed possible, and where realization of those economies required vertical integration and effective management of input-output flows.

10.3.1 U.S.

We have seen that the analysis of market structure divides industries into two broad categories. In type I industries, production requires firms to make fixed and sunk investments that are exogenously determined by the technology. In such industries, market expansion makes entry by additional firms profitable, and concentration falls as the size of the market increases. In type II industries, those with endogenous sunk costs, market expansion

---

[7] Kim's analysis is for firms in the S&P 500 stock market index for the years 1998–2004.

Table 10.5 Number of 200 largest national manufacturing firms, four industrialized countries

	19–	1930	1948	1973
Germany	138 (1913)	130 (1928)	126 (1953)	121
Japan	70 (1918)	76	120 (1954)	128
United Kingdom	88 (1919)	69	88	99
United States	117 (1917)	112	122	117

Note: SIC industries 28 (chemical), 29 (petroleum), 33 (primary metal), 35 (machinery), 36 (electrical machinery), 37 (transportation equipment).
Source: Chandler (1984, Tables 2–5).

makes it profitable for incumbent firms to sink investments in cost-reducing or product-differentiating technology, raising entry cost and sustaining high levels of concentration.

Market integration

The decades immediately following the U.S. Civil War saw a general expansion of U.S. market sizes, as railroads reduced transportation costs and forged what had been independent regional markets into unified continent-wide markets, while at the same time the first waves of immigration created mass markets in the great eastern cities. As markets expanded, first-mover firms in type II industries took advantage of economies of continuous operation to sharply reduce average cost and increase market share. But maintaining continuous operations required both secure input supplies and secure access to distribution channels. Firms in type II industries integrated backward, or forward, or both, depending on specific market characteristics, raising the cost of entry.

Great Merger Wave

A recession in the mid 1890s was one trigger for the Great Merger Wave of 1893–1903, the first of a series of merger waves that periodically transformed the structure of the U.S. and other developed economies (Section 11.2). Beyond the creation of dominant firms in many industries, this first merger wave had two significant consequences for the evolution of firm structure. First, the acquisitions behind these mergers were financed largely by shares of stock in the acquiring firm. This method of paying for acquisitions was a prerequisite for the dispersed ownership decried by Berle and Means thirty years later. Second, as vertically integrated firms moved (by merger or internal growth) into new regions or product markets, they incorporated new activities in their existing administrative structures, originally developed for a single product and area.

The U-form firm

This type of *functional* (or *unitary*) administrative structure is illustrated in Figure 10.1.[8] It is natural that in a small firm that deals primarily in one product or one region, there is one

---

[8] Figures 10.1 and 10.2 are simplified versions of Figures 1 and 2, respectively, of Chandler (1990).

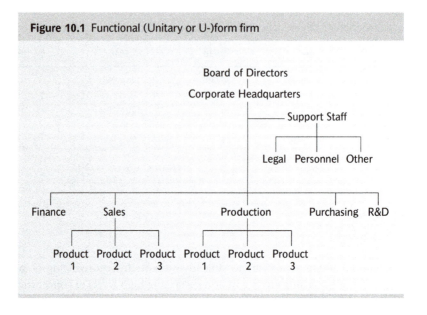

Figure 10.1 Functional (Unitary or U-)form firm

purchasing department, one production department, one sales department, and so on. In very small firms, these "departments" may well all be the responsibility of a single owner-manager. As the size of the firm increases, by adding new products or extending operations to other regions, it is equally natural to simply scale up the functional operating divisions, at a certain point adding support staff and (in some industries) a formal R&D operation.

Bounded rationality, however, places limits on the size of firm that can be effectively managed with a functional administrative structure. Department managers naturally tend to pursue the interests of their functional divisions, rather than those of the firm as a whole, while corporate executives must deal with day-to-day operating decisions as well as with long-term, strategic planning, even as the quantity of information reaching them from the operating level increases and the quality of information reaching them from the operating level decreases.

The M-form firm

The DuPont company's involvement in the United States' World War I war effort set it on a path that led to organizational innovation (Chandler 1960; Chandler and Salsbury, 1971). Even before the end of World War I, DuPont anticipated that without a deliberate strategy of diversification, substantial parts of the physical and human capital in which it had invested to meet wartime demand for explosives would become excess capacity, entailing considerable loss of sunk investment.[9] In a simpler age, such losses might have been avoided by setting up cartels. But from 1890 onward, U.S. antitrust law exposed firms that divided markets or colluded on price to harsh sanctions, and contributed to a climate of vigorous competition that

---

[9] Such losses occurred in the U.S. Appalachian coal industry after World War I (Section 20.2.1) and in the European coal industry after World War II (the rise of oil as a substitute for coal was a factor in the second case).

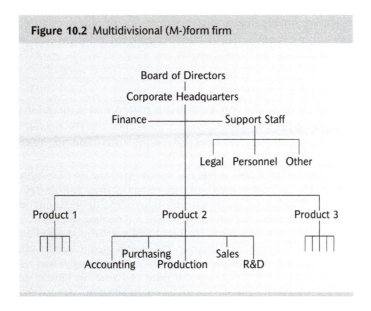

Figure 10.2 Multidivisional (M-)form firm

encouraged firms to seek efficiency within their own operations, not through cooperation with rivals.

The policy of deliberate diversification pushed the U-form administrative structure to its limits, and beyond. Necessity is the mother of invention, and necessity led DuPont to develop the multidivisional or M-form firm illustrated in Figure 10.2 (Chandler, 1960, pp. 272–273, footnote omitted):

> Du Pont's first step in this pioneering change was, in the words of its annual report, "to segregate its five principal industries ... , placing each in charge of a general manager" ... Each departmental manager had his own staff and full responsibility and authority for the development, manufacturing, and sale of his products and for the financial performance of his unit. Next, the functional departments—research, engineering, purchasing and accounting—became advisory or service departments whose staff officers audited, advised, and helped to coordinate the work of the operating departments; and they also assisted the new general office. The creation of this office, the final step in the reorganization, was brought about by relieving the president and the Executive Committee of all day-to-day operating duties and so permitting them to concentrate on making over-all company policy.

The principle of the M-form organizational structure is to delegate day-to-day operating decisions to divisions, each responsible for a specific region or product, with senior management responsible for monitoring[10] division performance and for strategic decisions that determine plans for the long run. The M-form recognizes limits imposed by bounded rationality—division managers have neither the information nor the perspective to effectively contribute to strategic decisions; senior management who end up bogged down

---

[10] Following Jensen and Meckling (1976, p. 308, fn. 9), "the term monitoring includes more than just measuring or observing the behavior of the agent. It includes efforts on the part of the principal to 'control' the behavior of the agent through budget restrictions, compensation policies, operating rules etc."

in operating decisions are unable to attend to the firm's long-run concerns. Monitoring by senior management limits *subgoal pursuit* by middle managers, inducing them to pursue the company's rather than their own private goals.[11]

Three-pronged investment

In Chandler's view, large-scale production, vertical integration, and the multidivisional management structure make up the *three-pronged investment* that creates the organizational capabilities[12] that are the essential characteristic of the leading firm (Chandler, 1992, p. 84):

> These learned capabilities resulted from solving problems of scaling up the processes of production, from acquiring knowledge of customers' needs and altering product and process to services needs, coming to know the availabilities of supplies and the reliability of suppliers, and in becoming knowledgeable in the ways of recruiting and training workers and managers. Such learned knowledge manifested itself in the firms' facilities for production and distribution. It was even more evident in the firms' product- and process-specific human skills. Of these skills the most critical were those of the senior executives—the top managers who recruited and motivated the middle and lower level managers, defined and allocated their responsibilities, monitored and coordinated their performance, and who, in addition, planned and allocated resources for these enterprises as a whole.

10.3.2 EU

Chandler's extension of this analytical framework from the U.S. to other industrialized countries has proven controversial. Although, Chandler wrote that (1980b, p. 35)[13] "The modern multiunit industrial enterprise first appeared in Europe at about the same time—the late nineteenth century—as it did in the United States", the interactions of economies of scale and scope, multiunit management, and organizational capabilities were different in Europe than in the United States (1985b, p. 35):

> The manufacturers in these industries ... made less extensive use of mass-production techniques, particularly the manufacture of machinery through assembling interchangeable parts, than those in the United States. Because coordination of the flow of goods was less complex, middle management was leaner than in United States firms. Even more important, owners continued to manage enterprises at the highest level. In Europe, entrepreneurs, their families, and representatives of banks and other large investors continued to make critical policy decisions about coordination of production and allocation of resources. As a result, the managerial class remained much smaller than in the United States and fewer signs of professionalism, such as schools, associations, and journals, appeared.

---

[11] In the 1920s DuPont acquired an interest in General Motors, and was instrumental in GM's adoption and perfection of the M-form (Chandler, 1977). Freeland (2005) argues that GM implemented a compromise version of the M-form, permitting some involvement of division managers in strategic decisions. The compromise was the work of GM President Alfred P. Sloan, Jr., who held that such participation was a price that had to be paid to elicit adherence to upper-level decisions.

[12] Langlois (2003) attributes the term "organizational capabilities" to Richardson (1972).

[13] In Germany, Siemans (Kocka, 1971, p. 154; see also Kocka, 1990, p. 713) "developed the specific decentralization pattern of the highly diversified, multi-divisional enterprise ten to twenty years before du Pont and General Motors first adopted it ... during the early 1920's". The French glass and chemical firm Saint-Gobain had a multi-divisional structure in 1905 (Lévy-Leboyer, 1980, p. 199).

Absolute advantage?

It is not these facts that are controversial, but their interpretation. Chandler sometimes seems to suggest that the multidivisional corporation is the be-all and the end-all framework for resource allocation within the firm (1980b, p. 35):

> Because the managerial enterprise and the class that managed it first flourished there, the United States experience often provided models and precedents for their evolution in other parts of the world.

Comparative advantage depends environment

UK: the family firm   Or is it possible that the multidivisional firm might have had fewer profitability advantages outside the U.S. than within it? Hannah argues that UK firms had less reason to vertically integrate than U.S. firms supplying the same kinds of goods, because UK markets were more efficient than U.S. markets (1980, pp. 63–64):[14]

> Chandler has argued that energy- and capital-intensive industries require hierarchical structures for scheduling in order to ensure a steady flow of work, but similar changes in nineteenth-century Britain ... did not lead to an equally noticeable growth of large corporations. This difference resulted at least in part from the highly developed and efficient British system of markets for commodities, skills, and distributive and financial services, as well as for final products; thus efficient scheduling by market mechanisms was often possible.

It is also possible that different management structures most efficiently serve different types of final consumer demand. Not only was the American market large, but the tastes of the American consumer made run-length economies possible (Payne, 1967, p. 524): "Perhaps the most significant feature of the American national market was its willingness to accept a mass-produced standardized product." British firms, in contrast, cultivated product differentiation as a way of insulating themselves from competition.[15]

Another factor in Britain was the role of the family firm (Chandler, 1980a, p. 410). Urbanization took place a generation or more earlier in the UK than in the U.S., and before the industrial revolution; (Payne, 1967, p. 524; emphasis in original) "By the time that all the essential prerequisites for the massive growth of the firm *were* present, the industrial structure of the United Kingdom had become so well established that further change was rendered extremely difficult. Industrial organization—characterized by the family firm—had partially ossified at a relatively low level of development, and this structure remained largely undisturbed even when the legal obstacles to firm growth were finally removed in the mid-[1850s]." Family-run firms, in this analysis, were not strong on entrepreneurship. If forced to choose between independence and value-maximization, they would choose independence.

---

[14] See similarly Chandler (1980a, p. 402, emphasis added): "Thus, the continuance of the family firm in Britain was encouraged by the existence of a well-established distribution network both at home and in the long-distance trades serving small but fast-growing overseas markets and sources of supply. *The invisible hand of the market worked more effectively in the United Kingdom than in the United States.* Nevertheless, these factors cannot alone account for its longevity."

[15] But see Hannah (1980, p. 61) "Regional and class tastes generally varied more widely in Great Britain than in the United States, although radio, national advertising, and national brands were already reducing these differences by the 1920s. ... in business sectors in which tastes were probably more standardized ... in Britain than in the United States ... —in the food industry, for example—mass production and mass retailing grew rapidly and probably faster than in the United States."

If an economic downturn made independence fatal, the preference was for (Payne, 1967, p. 526) "temporary co-operation with rivals through a trade association until better times came round". The UK's relaxed common law treatment of agreements in restraint of restraint of trade did nothing to discourage this tendency. When British firms did merge, it was frequent for the post-merger firm to be run as a collection of largely autonomous fiefdoms, without the reorganization and rationalization required to realize potential efficiency gains.[16]

Germany: cooperative managerial capitalism   In Germany, cartels and tariffs made it profitable for firms to integrate vertically. A vertically integrated steel firm could extract its own iron ore at a cost below the cartel price; a vertically integrated firm could produce its own supplies at a cost below the price of tariff-burdened imports (Stigler, 1951, p. 191; Kocka, 1980, p. 87, p. 107; Feldenkirchen, 1987, p. 419).

Chandler emphasizes other factors that encouraged the emergence in Germany of what he calls "cooperative managerial capitalism". One was the German legal system's cordial approach to cartels. Another was the role of banks in German industry (Chandler, 1990, p. 395):

> [I]n Germany, . . . unlike Britain and the United States, large multipurpose banks played a major role in providing funds for the initial investment in the new, capital-intensive industries—investment that was essential to achieve the economies of scale and scope. Such a role meant that the representatives of banks sat on the boards of many enterprises and so participated in top-level decisions more than was the case in either Britain or the United States.

Bank representatives, Chandler notes (1990, p. 427) "normally preferred cooperation to competition, particularly when competition threatened profits".

U.S. firms were able to achieve economies of scale by serving a large domestic market, British firms by supplying the Empire and their long-standing overseas markets. German firms depended on sales in European markets outside Germany to reach output levels that permitted the realization of economies of scale. They faced competition from local producers (not to mention U.S. and British firms) in these markets, and they cooperated on export markets. Cooperation on export markets facilitated cooperation within Germany.

In Chandler's view, cooperative managerial capitalism permitted German firms to develop organizational capabilities that permitted industrial rationalization and recovery in the aftermaths of World Wars I and II, in a way that British family capitalism did not. This assessment too is controversial, with some arguing that there was less to cooperative managerial capitalism than meets the eye. Some hold that such consolidation as took place in Germany in the 1920s was more an attempt to deal with systemic development of excess capacity than the outcome of a process of cooperative competition, and was singularly unsuccessful in rationalizing the organization of industry (Kleinschmidt and Welskopp, 1993, p. 274, pp. 282–283).

---

[16] Thus, the firm that became Metal Box, formed by merger in 1922, was (Reader, 1976, p. 39, p. 40) "a very cosy affair". For the Board of Directors, "It was no part of their purpose to interfere in the management of each others' enterprises: far less to extinguish their independence in the manner of the 'rationalizers' of the day . . . " Rationalization did not occur until the 1930s, in face of the dual threats of depression and American competition.

10.3.3 Backlash

One reaction to Chandler's analytical framework has been to accept the suitability of the multidivisional firm for the United States, without accepting that this implies unsuitability of the alternative forms that arose in other countries, industries and at other times (Fligstein, 1990, p. 733):[17]

> The decisive difference between the strategies and structures of British, American, and German firms ... hinged on their local political and legal systems and on their moment of entry into the modern capitalist world. The types of routines that they created were quite different precisely because of the different conditions faced by their respective managers and entrepreneurs. But, once each chose to produce a given set of organizational routines, those organizations persisted for long periods.

Another reaction is more fundamental. Chandler sometimes seems to assume away the possibility of strategic behaviour by large firms. Thus he defines capitalism as (Chandler, 1980b, p. 12) "an economic system in which the means of production and distribution are operated by privately rather than publicly owned enterprise and in which decisions within individual enterprises are motivated by consumer demand". But in a capitalist system, the motivation of the firm is to maximize its own value. Value maximization includes satisfying consumer demand; it may also include actions intended to raise the cost to rivals of satisfying consumer demand. That large firms endure does not imply that they allocate resources efficiently from a social point of view. In this harsher view, Chandler's analysis is only the first stage in the analysis of the resource allocation implications of the multidivisional business form (Alford, 1990, p. 642).

10.4 The Separation of Ownership and Control

10.4.1 The Berle-Means Analysis

Management control

In *The Modern Corporation and Private Property* (1932), Berle and Means analysed the control (which they defined as the ability to select the majority of the board of directors) of the 200 largest U.S. non-financial institutions. They placed firms in five control categories—(a) control through almost complete ownership, (b) majority control, (c) control through such legal devices as stock pyramids, non-voting stock, and voting trusts, (d), minority control, and (e) management control—and concluded that 44 per cent of the firms in their sample were under management control.[18] For Berle and Means, this raised the prospect of an economy in which (Berle, 1954, p. 180)[19]

> corporations are guided by tiny, self-perpetuating oligarchies. These in turn are drawn from and judged by the group opinion of a small fragment of America—its business and financial

---

[17] Chandler himself writes similarly (1992, p. 89) "The point is that an understanding of the changing boundaries of the firm required an awareness of the specific capabilities of the firm and the characteristics of the industry and market in which it operates at the time the changes were made."

[18] See Leech (1987b, Section I) for a careful discussion of Berle and Means' methodology.

[19] This is quoted by Mason (1958).

community. Change of management by contesting for stockholders' votes is extremely rare, and increasingly difficult and expensive to the point of impossibility. The legal presumption in favor of management, and the natural unwillingness of courts to control or reverse management action save in cases of the more elementary types of dishonesty and fraud, leaves management with substantially absolute power.

Principal-agent problem

Nearly a century later, there are two contrasting views about the separation of ownership and control in corporate enterprise. One is that Berle and Means identified a genuine negative feature of the broadly held, publicly quoted corporation, what economists now call a *principal-agent problem*. Collectively, the owners of the firm hire managers to maximize the firm's value. The owners are the principals, the manager is their agent. But it requires time and effort for any one shareholder to monitor management, while any increase in firm value that results from careful, costly monitoring must be shared with all stockholders. It is rational for the individual stockholder to free-ride on the monitoring efforts of others, with the result that monitoring does not occur. Management is left to its own devices, and its own devices lead it down paths that maximize management utility, not shareholder value.[20] Those paths need not involve anything so crass as conspicuous consumption (a fleet of private jets at management disposal, for example). Management may engage in empire-building, diversifying the firm into sectors for which its organizational capabilities are ill-suited. Management may pursue the quiet life—paying workers a little more than the market rate, to maintain labour peace, keeping outmoded plants in operation after their time, to promote community relations (Bertrand and Mullainathan, 2003). Senior management may involve simply hanging on too long, keeping themselves in place when maximization of shareholder value would require passing the baton to their successors.[21]

Corporate governance

Large corporations do not exist in a vacuum. If it is profitable to monitor management, one might anticipate the development of *corporate governance* mechanisms that reduce the incentives or ability of managers to pursue their own interests. There is a market for the services of managers; competition from potential replacements may induce managers to maximize shareholder value (Fama, 1980). Product-market competition may lead to a Prisoners' Dilemma outcome, in which the managers of each firm fully exert themselves to match the efforts of managers of other firms, even though managers as a group would be better off if they could coordinate on (lack of) effort (Hart, 1980). Debt may encourage value-maximization, not only because a failure to repay debt would threaten managers' employment, but also because lenders have an incentive to monitor managers (Jensen, 1986). Managers who deviate too much from value-maximization open their firm up to

---

[20] This is the central theme of the managerial theories of the firm cited in Section 10.1.

[21] The example of the first Henry Ford comes to mind. See also Demsetz and Lehn (1985, p. 1162, fn. 4): "The share prices of Disney, Gulf and Western, and Chock Full O'Nuts all rose dramatically on the deaths of their dominant owners. Allegedly the prices of these stocks had been depressed by the policies of Walt Disney to keep a considerable library of Disney films from television, of Charles Bluhdorn to use Gulf and Western to hold a large portfolio of stocks in other companies, and of Charles Black to use Chock Full O'Nuts to maintain large real estate investments. All three policies are associated by the financial community with the personal preferences of the then dominant owner-managers of these companies. Shortly after the deaths of Disney, Bluhdorn, and Black, share prices rose, respectively, 23 percent, 42 percent, and 22 percent."

the possibility of takeover by an insurgent management team that promises owners better performance.[22] Owners might tie what managers are paid to the value of the firm, so that managers maximize firm value because by so doing they maximize their own payoffs. One way to do this is to make part of the manager's compensation in the form of shares of stock in the firm, so that the manager becomes an owner. Another way is to make part of the manager's compensation in the form of bonuses that are contingent on the firm's performance.

That such corporate governance mechanisms *might* lead managers to maximize shareholder value does not mean that they *will* do so. It is the essence of the principal-agent problem that although the firm's performance can be observed, the agent's (manager's) effort cannot. Managers are in a position to control the flow of information about their own performance, not only to principals (owners), but also to potential rival managers. One expects product-market competition to encourage value maximization if product markets are effectively competitive (Mason, 1958, pp. 10–11)—but if the separation of ownership and control is an issue, it will often be for firms that supply markets that are not effectively competitive. There is a free riding problem in the market for corporate control (Grossman and Hart, 1980): not only will a team of outside managers have to bear the administrative costs of mounting a takeover attempt, but it will have to share any increase in firm value with the owners of the firm, reducing their own payoff from a successful takeover. Further, in the United States, antitakeover provisions of state laws come close to effectively blocking takeovers (Grundfest, 1990, p. 92).

Morck *et al.* (1988) find[23] that firm performance improves as management ownership rises from zero to 5 per cent. But firm performance worsens as management ownership rises from 5 per cent to 25 per cent, above which level there is again some improvement with increases in management ownership. The fundamental weakness with the managerial incentive argument is that although it is easy to write "owners structure management compensation to induce managers to maximize the firm's value", in large measure it is managers who propose their own compensation to boards of directors. Owners have no direct role (Shleifer and Vishny, 1997, p. 745):

> The more serious problem with high powered incentive contracts is that they create enormous opportunities for self-dealing for the managers, especially if these contracts are negotiated with poorly motivated boards of directors rather than with large investors. Managers may negotiate for themselves such contracts when they know that earnings or stock price are likely to rise, or even manipulate accounting numbers and investment policy to increase their pay.

Becht *et al.* (2005, p. 63) conclude that "[I]t has become difficult to maintain the view, based on data from the bull market of the early 1990s, that U.S. pay practices provide explicit and implicit incentives for aligning the interests of managers with those of shareholders. Instead, the rival view that U.S. managers have the ability, the opportunity and the power to set their own pay at the expense of shareholders ... increasingly prevails."

Large industrial corporations are not the only form of large private enterprise; corporate management might be monitored by the management of specialized financial institutions.[24]

---

[22] This is the *market for corporate control*, which we consider in Chapter 22.

[23] For a sample of 371 *Fortune 500* firms for 1980.

[24] "Quis custodiet ipsos custodes?"—large financial institutions may themselves be afflicted by a separation of ownership and control; it might be privately profitable for the management of the monitoring firm and the man-

But in the United States, at least, there are legal impediments to institutional monitoring (Roe, 1990, p. 20):[25]

> [L]aw constrains financial institutions' role in the corporate structure. ... law prohibits banks and bank holding companies—the institutional players with half of the money—from owning and controlling corporations; law prohibited insurance companies from owning stock for a half-century (and now limits their ownership); and law exacts tax penalties from mutual funds owning control blocks.

Thus, one view of the separation of ownership and control is that it is a characteristic of corporate enterprise, certainly for the United States and perhaps, or perhaps in due time, for other developed economies as well.

10.4.2 The Dominant-Shareholder Revision

A contrasting view is that Berle and Means got it wrong, certainly for corporations outside the United States, and perhaps for the United States as well. This assessment is that there *is* a principal-agent problem associated with corporate enterprise, but it is not the principal-agent problem pointed to by Berle and Means. Rather, most corporations have a controlling shareholder or group of shareholders, and the challenge for corporate governance is to design a framework that protects shareholders outside the controlling group (La Porta *et al.*, 1999, p. 474, emphasis added):[26]

> [T]he Berle and Means corporation is far from universal, and is quite rare for some definitions of control. Similarly, the so-called German model of bank control through equity is uncommon. Instead, controlling shareholders—usually the State or families—are present in most large companies. These shareholders have control rights in firms in excess of their cash flow rights, largely through the use of pyramids, but they also participate in management. The power of these controlling shareholders is evidently not checked by other large shareholders. *The results suggest that the theory of corporate finance relevant for most countries should focus on the incentives and opportunities of controlling shareholders to both benefit and expropriate the minority shareholders.*

Table 10.6 reports a comparison by countries, due to Becht and Mayer (2001), of the median size of the largest and second-largest voting blocs in publicly listed firms in 10 countries.[27] The United Kingdom and the United States are atypical, with median largest voting blocs noticeably smaller than those of other countries. It is also striking that for most countries, the median size of the second-largest voting bloc is substantially less than the median size of the largest voting bloc.

---

agement of the monitored firm to collude at the expense of the owners of both firms; Gadhoum *et al.* (2005, p. 351) refer to this as a "second-order agency problem". The (alleged) relationship of Arthur Andersen LLP and Enron Corporation comes to mind.

[25] The U.S. Glass-Steagall Act, passed in 1933 in the wake of the Great Depression, mandated a separation of commercial and investment banking. It was repealed in 1999. Commercial banks subsequently invested heavily in derivatives and other assets key to the financial side of the Great Recession of 2009.

[26] Hilt (2008) documents the use of limitations on the voting rights of large shareholders in 1820s New York as a corporate governance device to mitigate exploitation of small shareholders.

[27] Data are for 1992 (UK), 1995 (Belgium), 1998 (Sweden), otherwise for 1996.

Table 10.6 Median size (per cent) of largest and second-largest voting bloc, by country, mid 1990s

	Number of Companies	Largest	Second-largest
Austria	50	52.0	2.5
Belgium	140	56.0	6.3
Germany	372	57.0	< 5
Spain	193	34.5	8.9
France	CAC 40	20.0	5.9
Italy	214	54.5	5.0
Netherlands	137	43.5	7.7
Sweden	304	34.9	8.7
UK	207	9.9	6.6
U.S.: NYSE	1309	5.4	< 5
U.S.: NASDAQ	2831	8.6	< 5

Source: Becht and Mayer (2001, Table 2.2).

Gadhoum *et al.* (2005) examine control of 3607 publicly listed U.S. firms for 1996. They trace ownership amounts through the veil of chains of ownership,[28] and alternatively define a controlling shareholder as having 10 per cent or, more restrictively, 20 per cent of outstanding shares.[29] A portion of their results is reproduced in Table 10.7, along with comparable

---

[28] So that if family A owns 5 per cent of the shares of company B and 10 per cent of the shares in company C, while company C owns 50 per cent of the shares in company B, family A directly and indirectly holds 10 per cent of the shares in company B.

[29] To place this in perspective, Berle and Means used a 20 per cent threshold for minority control; they discuss in some detail a proxy fight in which a 14.9 per cent ownership share enabled John D. Rockefeller (apparently at some expense) to exert control of the Standard Oil Company of Indiana. *Fortune Magazine* (1940; see the accompanying box) refers to a "Wall Street rule of thumb" "that 15 to 20 per cent is working control if you are already in the saddle". Larner (1966, p. 780) cites a Wall Street Journal report that the management of Trans World Airlines considered 10 per cent ownership the threshold for effective control. Shleifer and Vishny (1986, p. 462, footnote omitted) write that "Empirically, large shareholdings are extremely widespread and very substantial where present. In a sample of 456 of the Fortune 500 firms, 354 have at least one shareholder owning at least 5 percent of the firm. In only 15 cases does the largest shareholder own less than 3 percent of the firm. The average holding of the largest shareholder among the 456 firms is 15.4 percent." La Porta *et al.* (1999, pp. 475–476) write that "To describe control of companies, we generally look for all shareholders who control more than 10 percent of the votes. The cutoff of 10 percent is used because (1) it provides a significant threshold of votes; and (2) most countries mandate disclosure of 10 percent, and usually even lower, ownership stakes."

Table 10.7 Ownership and control of corporations in the USA, Western Europe, and East Asia, 10 per cent control threshold

	10 per cent threshold			20 per cent threshold		
	U.S.	East Asia	Western Europe	U.S.	East Asia	Western Europe
Corporations with controlling shareholder	59.74	79.72	86.28	28.11	56.40	63.07
Family controlled	36.60	45.05	55.87	19.82	37.86	44.29
Family controlled and managed	24.57	24.57	37.32	76.22	57.10	68.45
Controlled by widely-held financial institution	16.33	17.80	18.34	4.66	4.94	8.73
Controlled by widely-held corporation	3.91	10.61	1.32	2.41	9.02	1.97
State controlled	0.17	6.26	4.12	0.00	4.58	4.14
Widely-held	40.26	20.28	13.72	71.89	43.60	36.93

Source: Gadhoum, Laing, and Young (2005, Table 1).

figures for East Asia and Western Europe.[30] Even on the conservative 20-per cent control definition, they find that 28.11 per cent of U.S. corporations have a controlling shareholder; with the 10-per cent control definition, the figure is nearly 60 per cent. Family control is noteworthy in Western Europe. In the United States, family control exceeds control by financial institutions.

 BOX   **"The Greatest Problem Before Executives"**

We return now to the greatest problem before executives—the fact that they are not masters in their own houses—a problem not concerned with Washington, with labor, with markets, but with that other half of management: the directors—and, through the directors, with the stockholders they represent. The number of stockholders is about 4,000,000 according to the most cautious estimates: about 20,000,000 according to the most glowing guesses. A figure of about 6,000,000 stockholders has been derived from a special unpublished FORTUNE Survey, and this is probably the closest to a reliable estimate that has yet been made. With stockholders in any such numbers scattered all over the country, with their notorious disregard for annual meetings and proxies, it is easy to conclude that the stockholder has become a negligible factor in our "publicly owned" companies. But . . . »

---

[30] The latter are due to Claessens *et al.* (2000) and Faccio and Lang (2002), respectively.

> ❯❯ it makes very little difference how many stockholders there are for the simple reason that relatively few of them own a large portion of all stock outstanding. Only 55,794 people had dividend income of $10,000 or more in 1936, and this group may properly be called the core of capitalism. These people are not even 1 per cent of the estimated number of stockholders, but they share among them the ultimate control over the leading companies.
>
> Within this group holdings are so concentrated that control is usually in a few hands. The SEC found that the 1,736 corporations with equity securities listed on national exchanges had 2,054,000,000 shares of stock outstanding. Five and a half per cent of these shares were directly owned by officers and directors. Directly and indirectly, these men, together with the so-called "principal stockholders" (those holding 10 per cent or more), owned 22.3 per cent of all the stocks listed. Since Wall Street rule of thumb has it that 15 to 20 per cent is working control if you are already in the saddle, it is clear that the idea of absentee ownership as usually interpreted is largely a fiction. What happens is that the small stockholder gets a free ride because of the vigilance of a small group of those more heavily interested …
>
> All of this adds up to an extremely powerful force constantly exerted on corporation officers. They must constantly struggle to square their conception of proper modern operating policies with the stubbornly held views of the highly articulate owners.
>
> Source: Fortune Magazine February 1940, p. 108.

In short, the managers of large, publicly quoted corporations may not lead quite the independent lives visualized by Berle and Means. That does not imply that the issues raised by the separation of ownership and control can be dismissed out of hand. Becht and Mayer (2001, p. 38) write that "Even in countries with dominant shareholders, we have observed a variety of mechanisms that management can employ to protect itself from external investor interference", and suggest at least the possibility that:

> If, as a consequence, corporations are run by managers who are able to shield themselves from external influence by investors then control by owners will be largely irrelevant. The Berle and Means view of strong managers/weak owners may therefore be applicable even in the presence of dominant blockholders and the formal distinction between patterns of corporate control may be of little relevance in the face of a class of largely unaccountable management.

10.5 Why Are There Firms?—and Why Is There More Than One?

10.5.1 Transaction Costs

Coase (1937) is the progenitor of the modern theory of the firm. He contrasted the neoclassical vision of resource allocation in markets by the invisible hand of the price mechanism with the directed allocation of resources within firms.[31] Coase traced the organization of productive activity within firms to the costs of using markets, particularly the costs of learning

---

[31] Simon (1991, pp. 40–41) makes the point that real-world markets rely as much on quantity adjustment as on price adjustment as an equilibrating mechanism. Inventory changes are one example; delivery delays are another. It is also true that large modern corporations may use transfer prices to allocate resources within the firm. Thus the distinction between resource allocation by price within markets and by quantity within firms is not as clear-cut as might at first appear.

relevant prices (1937, p. 390) and the costs of negotiating contracts (1937, pp. 390–391). When such *transaction costs* are sufficiently high, it becomes efficient to bring the transactions within a firm and carry them out under the authority of a manager rather than on a market by means of the price mechanism.

Limits to firm size, among which *managerial loss of control*, make it uneconomic to bring all transactions within the firm. By "managerial loss of control" Coase (1937, pp. 394–395) designates what are now regarded as two distinct phenomena, an increasing minimum marginal cost of organizing transactions within the firm and X-inefficiency, the failure to minimize the cost of organizing transactions within the firm.[32] In the Coasian story, the distinguishing characteristic of the firm is the suppression of the price mechanism,[33] and firm size is determined by a balance between the marginal cost of using the market and the marginal cost of production within a firm.[34].

For Coase, the central point of *The Nature of the Firm* was straightforward (Coase, 1988b, p. 19):[35]

> All that was needed was to recognize that there were costs of carrying out market transactions and to incorporate them into the analysis, something which economists had failed to do. A firm had therefore a role to play in the economic system if it were possible for transactions to be organized within the firm at less cost than would be incurred if the same transactions were carried out through the market. The limit to the size of the firm would be set when the scope of its operations had expanded to the point at which the costs of organizing additional transactions within the firm exceeded the costs of carrying out the same transactions through the market or in another firm.

Once this point has been made (Coase, 1988c, p. 47):

> Like galaxies forming out of primordial matter, we can imagine the institutional structure of production coming into being under the influence of the forces determining the interrelationships between the costs of transacting and the costs of organizing. These interrelationships are extremely complex, involving ... pricing practices, contractual arrangements, and organizational forms.

10.5.2 Information

If Coase made the point that the choice between firm and market depends on the cost of carrying out a transaction within a firm or across a market, it is to Arrow that we owe the observation that transaction costs depend in an essential way on how firms and markets deal with the failure of the "complete and perfect information" assumption of the neoclassical

---

[32] Coase (1937, pp. 394): "It may be that as the transactions which are organised increase, the entrepreneur fails to place the factors of production in the uses where their value is greatest".

[33] Coase (1937, pp. 393): "A firm ... consists of the system of relationships which comes into existence when the direction of resources is dependent on an entrepreneur."

[34] Coase (1937, p. 395): "A firm will tend to expand until the costs of organising an extra transaction within the firm become equal to the costs of carrying out the same transaction by means of an exchange on the open market or the costs of organising in another firm".

[35] Coase (1988b, p. 23): "What strikes me in rereading this article is its extreme simplicity. There is no subtle or complicated argument to tax the brain and no concepts difficult to understand." It may nonetheless be that the full implications of the concepts have been difficult to understand.

model of perfect competition.[36] Later "new theories of the firm" can be seen as elaborations of this point.

Arrow (1969, p. 48) characterizes transaction costs as the "costs of running the economic system". He has been clear (as was Coase) that there are costs of organizing transactions within firms as well as across markets. "Moral hazard", which Arrow (1969, p. 55) suggests might better be termed "the confounding of risks and decisions", owes its name to a characteristic of insurance markets: that the care an individual takes to guard against injury or damage depends on the kind of insurance against injury or damage that is available, while the cost of offering insurance against injury or damage depends on individuals' efforts to reduce the risk of injury or damage. But moral hazard also manifests itself within firms, and is the basis for the principal-agent problem that is central to the design of institutions of corporate governance: the owners of the firm hire managers to maximize firm value, cannot observe managers' efforts, and cannot distinguish the impact of managers' efforts and the slings and arrows of outrageous fortune on firm value.

Arrow (1975) observes that manufacturers may have an incentive to integrate forward into distribution as a means of acquiring information about final goods markets. More generally, (1981, p. 37) "the scarcity of information-handling ability is an essential feature for the understanding of both individual and organizational behavior". Because it is costly to transmit information, firms create internal communication channels.[37] The kind of communication channels that arise in a firm will be path-dependent, sensitive to chance historical events during the firm's development. Firms will develop codes, efficient short-hands, for information transmission. Because the development of communication channels is path dependent, the codes that develop in different firms may be quite different, and incompatible, yet equally efficient.[38]

10.5.3 Vertical Integration

Asset specificity and the fundamental transformation

In a series of publications,[39] Oliver Williamson lays out a transaction-cost framework to analyse the division of activity between firms and markets. He assumes (in contrast to neoclassical economic theory) that the parties to transactions have only imperfect information and limited reasoning power: that, in the words of Simon (1947), economic agents are *boundedly rational*. Williamson also assumes that the parties to transactions behave *opportunistically*: that they pursue their own self-interest, and that in so doing they behave in a way that is

---

[36] Spence (1975, p. 164) concurs: "There is an impressive and growing body of literature that suggests the firm, in large part, consists of nonmarket institutions whose function is to deal with resource allocation in the presence of informational constraints that markets handle poorly or do not handle at all".

[37] The unitary-form and multidivisional-form administrative structures are alternative kinds of communication channels.

[38] The vision of the firm as embodying a unique network of information-processing channels, a network that results from path-dependent sunk investments, anticipates later resource-based views of the firm, on which see Penrose (1959), Wernerfelt (1984, 1995). It also brings to mind Chandler's (1992) emphasis on organizational capabilities as a determinant of corporate performance. The observation that different firms have different communication codes leads into the idea of corporate cultures (Kreps, 1990; Crémer, 1993), and has implications for the extent to which a merger can be expected to yield efficiency gains if it involves firms with vastly different corporate cultures.

[39] Williamson (1970, 1975, 1981, 1985, 1993), among others.

devious if devious behaviour is privately optimal. In this analysis, it is the combination of bounded rationality, opportunism, *and the need to invest in highly specific assets* that make it relatively inefficient to use markets for transactions that occur frequently and under conditions of uncertainty.

If an asset is highly specific to a particular transaction, it may be quite valuable (the present discounted value of the income stream it generates will be large) if used in that transaction, but impossible to transfer to other uses, so that investment in the asset is sunk.[40] In a world of uncertainty and bounded rationality, investment in specific assets can lead to a *fundamental transformation* in the relative bargaining positions of the parties to a transaction. If a buyer[41] awards a contract to one of a large number of potential suppliers, it will be able to play one potential supplier off against another and extract the best possible terms for itself. If, after the contract is awarded, it makes sunk investments to support the contract,[42] the *ex ante* large-numbers bargaining situation is transformed into an *ex post* small-numbers bargaining situation in which the buyer is *held up* as the supplier opportunistically tries to revise the terms of an agreement in its own favour.[43] Legal protection against such behaviour may not be available, or costly to obtain: bounded rationality will make it difficult for a court to determine if devious behaviour has taken place, or to devise appropriate remedies if it has taken place. In circumstances of this kind, a firm may well conclude that the best way to avoid holdup is to integrate vertically, bringing the transaction within the firm, so that the potentially opportunistic independent trading partner becomes an employee. By internal monitoring and an appropriate compensation system, the interests of an employee can be made more allied with those of the firm than can the interests of an outsider.

But merely because sunk investments make opportunistic behaviour possible does not mean that opportunistic behaviour will, on balance, be profitable. Against the short-term gain from revised bargaining terms must be set longer-run losses (Coase, 1988c, p. 44):

> Opportunistic behavior is not necessarily fraud, although it may be, but in estimating the likelihood of opportunistic behavior the same approach can be used. A defrauding firm may make immediate gains but if it can be identified, future business is lost and this ... would normally make fraud unprofitable. A similar argument suggests that opportunistic behavior of the type we are discussing would also normally be unprofitable and this argument has added force since a firm acting in this way will certainly be identified. That the implementation of long-term

---

[40] Williamson (1983, p. 526) distinguishes four categories of asset specificity: site specificity ("where successive stations are located in a cheek-by-jowl relation to each other so as to economize on inventory and transportation expenses"); physical asset specificity ("such as specialized dies that are required to produce a component"); human asset specificity ("arises [from] learning-by-doing"); and dedicated assets ("put in place contingent upon particular supply agreements and, should such contracts be prematurely terminated, would result in significant excess capacity"). The common element, and defining characteristic of transaction-specific assets is that they "lose value if employed in alternative uses".

[41] For example, a chain of hospitals that invites bids on a long-term contract covering its needs for medical-surgical supplies.

[42] Some such investments might be in physical assets, as, computer hardware and software to permit direct orders from hospital purchasing departments to the favoured supplier. Other sunk investments might be in human capital, such as the training of hospital employees to use the computer order-entry systems.

[43] Marshall (1920/1890, Book V, Chapter XI, § 33) writes "For instance, at Pittsburgh when manufacturers had just put up furnaces to be worked by natural gas instead of coal, the price of the gas was suddenly doubled. And the history of mines affords many instances of difficulties of this kind with neighbouring landowners as to rights of way, etc., and with the owners of neighbouring cottages, railways and docks".

contracts is commonly accompanied by informal arrangements not governed by contract ... and that this approach seems to work suggests to me that the propensity for opportunistic behavior is usually effectively checked by the need to take account of the effect of the firm's actions on future business.

Transaction costs arising from the fundamental transformation that accompanies the investment of specific assets are part of the explanation for the inclusion of particular transactions within the firm, but they are not the whole story.[44]

Property rights

The property rights approach[45] emphasizes the relationship of inputs in production as a factor determining which assets it is efficient for a single firm to own, and the incentives that combining assets under the ownership of a single firm creates for employee decisions. It is more likely that common ownership will be most efficient if inputs are highly complementary, so that they are more productive in combination than if used separately. If the investment decisions of one party to a transaction are more important for efficient operation, then it is more likely to be efficient to make that party the owner of the firm: when unforeseen events occur, the owner's (more important) investment decisions will be taken in a way that is value maximizing, since the owner's interests and those of the firm largely overlap.[46,47]

Price discrimination

Vertical integration may be profitable because it permits a firm to price discriminate, so exercising market power (Stigler, 1951, p. 191; Perry, 1978, 1980). If a firm has market power, it is profitable to discriminate in price between classes of customers with different price elasticities of demand. A necessary condition for such third-degree price discrimination to be possible is that higher-elasticity consumers, who are offered a lower price, be unable to engage in arbitrage—unable to purchase for resale to lower-elasticity consumers. If an input-producing firm supplies market segments with different elasticities, it can effectively price discriminate by selling to low-elasticity market segments through independent distributors, to which it charges a high wholesale price, while integrating forward and supplying high-elasticity market segments itself at a lower price.

Avoid countervailing power

Vertical integration may also be profitable because it permits a firm to avoid the exercise of market power by its trading partners. A firm that is offered inputs at a price above marginal

---

[44] Coase (July 1988, quoted by Helper *et al.*, 2000, p. 474, fn. 43): "Some people acquire resources by theft, but mainly they buy them. People do take precautions against being robbed, but it would be a mistake to analyze the system by focusing exclusively on the precautions."

[45] See Grossman and Hart (1986), Hart and Moore (1990), and Hart (1995).

[46] As noted by Hart (1989, p. 1767; see also p. 1773), the property rights approach assumes that ownership and control go together. To the extent that corporate management is monitored by a dominant shareholder or shareholder group, this might not be as unrealistic an assumption as the separation of ownership and control literature suggests.

[47] The property-rights approach is akin to the Alchian and Demsetz (1972) view of team production as the essential characteristic of the firm, with the owner of the firm monitoring the efforts of team members and in return receiving the residual (not paid to other team members) income of the firm.

cost can profit by integrating backward, producing the good itself and so obtaining it for internal use at the cost of production. Thus, as noted in discussion of German cooperative managerial capitalism, the avoidance of cartel prices was one factor in the early backward integration of German steel firms into the production of coal and iron.

 BOX   Trade Secrets, Monopoly, and Vertical Integration

There were about 600 tapestry weavers in Brussels at the start of the seventeenth century, and 160 around 1705. Tapestry production declined, as trade barriers blocked export markets and subsidies created competitors in markets where there had once been only customers.

In 1672, Gaspar Leyniers paid 200 guilders to an outside dyer for training in use of a red dyestuff hitherto little used in Brussels. There were three other workshops in Brussels that supplied red dyes to tapestry studios. By 1699 only the Leyniers workshop remained active, the high-technology survivor and monopoly supplier of dyes to a declining industry.

In 1690, a certain Jan Brinck moved from Utrecht to Brussels. In 1702, having worked for the Leyniers workshop for some time, he signed a contract committing to work there as manager. After 20 years, he could leave the workshop, provided he did not establish his own shop in Brussels or nearby towns, and would be entitled to a pension of 200 guilders a year. This contract, writes Brosens (2004, p. 37) "clearly aimed at ensuring strict secrecy about the Leyniers dyeing processes".

In 1710, Brinck sought to join the dyers' guild, with a view to establishing his own workshop. Legal wrangling ensued, but in 1711, and after a settlement between Leyniers and Brinck, Brinck opened a dye shop.

Brosens suggests the following chain of causality. In 1709, Leyniers planned to integrate forward and open a tapestry workshop. In view of Leyniers' position as the single supplier of dyestuffs, this would leave Brussels tapestry weavers in the uncomfortable position of competing with a supplier of an essential input. Several tapestry producers (Brosens, 2004, p. 38) "lured [Brinck] away from the Leyniers dye works … in their attempts to counter a total Leyniers monopoly on tapestry production …"

This is not, however, the end of the story. Brinck, who had been backed by the lion's share of the tapestry weavers, appears to have attracted most of Leyniers' customers. In consequence, and despite the long-run decline in the Brussels tapestry industry, in 1712 the Leyniers enterprise entered into a joint venture to produce tapestries. The Leyniers' catalogue (Brosens, 2004, p. 130) "stylistically outclassed the catalogues of … competitors", and the firm prospered at least until 1747.

Source: Brosens (2004).

Double marginalization

A firm with market power that sells to final consumer demand maximizes profit by picking an output or setting a price that makes its marginal cost equal to marginal revenue from the market demand curve. The result is a price above marginal cost. If a monopolist manufacturer sells to oligopolist distributors, it will maximize profit by picking an output or setting a price that makes its marginal cost equal to the derived marginal revenue that results from oligopolistic interactions. Left to their own devices, oligopolist distributors will pick an outputs or set prices that make their marginal cost, the wholesale price set by the manufacturer, equal to residual marginal revenue. The result is double marginalization, a further increase in price above the combined marginal cost of getting the product to the final consumer. Vertical integration avoids double marginalization, making the distributor an employee and endowing the manufacturer with the authority to pick an output that makes the marginal cost of production and distribution equal to marginal revenue from final demand.[48]

Barron and Umbeck (1984) analyse the impact on retail petrol prices of legislation adopted by the state of Maryland that obliged vertically integrated oil companies to divest themselves of their retail outlets, making double marginalization possible where single marginalization had been the rule. They find an increase in retail petrol prices and a reduction in operating hours at stations affected by the divestiture legislation.

Commitment

Hart and Tirole (1990) outline a model in which a commitment problem makes vertical integration a prerequisite for an upstream monopolist producer of an essential input to extract full monopolist profit.[49] To illustrate, suppose a single upstream firm (U_1) supplies a downstream market that is served by two distributors (D_1 and D_2). Let the equation of the inverse demand curve be:

$$p = 150 - q_1 - q_2. \tag{10.1}$$

Suppose the upstream firm produces at constant marginal and average cost 20 per unit, while the dealers have a constant marginal and average cost 10 for every unit they sell.

The upstream firm could obtain monopoly profit by offering (say) D_1 a contract to buy (for resale) 60 units of output at a wholesale price of 80 per unit. 60 units of output would command a price 90 from final consumers. This would allow D_1 to earn zero economic profit ($90 - 80 = 10$), which includes a normal return on investment. U_1 would be paid 4800 by D_1 and earn the monopoly profit, 3600.

If D_1 is offered such a contact, should it accept? If it does, then D_2 faces a residual demand curve:

$$p = 150 - 60 - q_2 = 90 - q_2. \tag{10.2}$$

Having signed a contract with D_1, U could turn around and offer D_2 a contract for 30 units of output at a wholesale price 50 per unit. The total quantity supplied would be 90, price would be 60, and D_2 would earn a normal rate of return on its investment. U would earn $3600 + 900 = 4500$.

D_1, of course, would be out of luck. If it signs a contract that just allows it a normal rate of return without a commitment from U_1 not to later flood the market, D_1 exposes itself to the risk that it would lose $90 - 60 = 30$ on every unit it sells, leaving it a loss of 1800. Because of the risk of being *held up* in this way, D_1 would not accept an offer to buy 60 units from U at a price of 80. *In order to fully exploit its monopoly position, U needs some way to make a commitment to D_1 that it will not hold D_1 up.*[50]

---

[48] Other considerations arise if (as is commonly the case) manufacturing and distribution are both imperfectly competitive. See Section 12.2.2.

[49] The argument has much in common with that made by Coase (1972a) for durable good monopoly; see Section 7.2.2. See also the discussion of two-part tariffs in Section 8.4.1.

[50] The Chicago School "no leverage of market power" argument (Director and Levi, 1956) is that a firm with monopoly power cannot profitably leverage that power to another market. The analysis of the holdup problem in manufacturer-distributor relations shows that vertical restraints can be a *precondition* for the full exercise of market power by the manufacturer.

U could extract the full monopoly profit by integrating vertically. It could take over one of the two downstream firms, or it could set up a new distribution operation. It would then carry out its own distribution services. If it were as efficient as D_1, vertical integration would be as profitable as distributing through D_1 if commitment were not an issue.

Foreclosure

Now extend this example from upstream monopoly to upstream duopoly. Suppose there is a second upstream firm, U_2, able to produce a perfect substitute for U_1's product, but at a higher cost, 32 per unit.[51] Suppose also that if U_1 and U_2 both supply the downstream market, they compete as price-setting firms.

If upstream and downstream firms are independent, the profit-maximizing strategy for U_1 is to sell each downstream firm 40 units of the input for a lump-sum payment 1244.[52] 40 is the Cournot equilibrium output if downstream firms have marginal cost 30, the sum of their own marginal cost and U_1's marginal cost. If downstream firms accept this offer, price is 70, each downstream firm earns gross profit $(70 - 10)(40) = 2400$, pays 1244 to U_1, and is left with 1156 economic profit. U_1 earns economic profit $2(1244 - 800) = 888$.

What makes it an equilibrium for U_1 to offer the downstream firms contracts that leave them with some economic profit? The downstream firms have U_2 as an alternative supplier. If D_1 accepts U_1's offer, D_2 could turn to U_2 and obtain a perfect substitute for U_1's product at U_2's marginal cost, 32 per unit. Under this scenario, D_2's marginal cost would be 42 per unit, its best response output D_1's output (40) would be 34, price would be 76, and D_2's profit $(76 - 42)(34) = 1156$. To make the downstream firms indifferent between accepting D_1's offer and buying inputs from the higher-cost firm, D_1's offer must leave the downstream firms as much profit as they could get by defecting to U_2.

How would market performance change if U_1 merged with D_1 and the postmerger firm could produce the input at constant marginal and average cost 20 per unit, the final product at constant marginal and average cost 30 per unit? If U_1-D_1 were to refuse to supply D_2, D_2 could buy the input from U_2 at U_2's marginal cost, 32. By supplying D_2 with the input at a price a negligible amount below 32, U_1-D_1 can at least keep D_2's business for itself. Further, from a social point of view, if D_2 is to be supplied at a price of 32, it is more efficient that D_2 by supplied by U_1 than by U_2, since U_1 has lower marginal cost than U_2.

Effectively, then, the downstream market is a Cournot duopoly supplied by firms with marginal cost 30 (U_1-D_1) and 42 (D_2) respectively. Equilibrium outputs are 44 and 32 for the integrated and nonintegrated downstream firms, respectively. Total output is lower $(76 < 80)$ and price higher $(74 > 70)$ compared with the no-integration case. U_1-D_1's profit (1936 on its own sales of the final good, 1024 on input sales to D_2, 2960 in all) is greater than the sum of U_1 and D_1's profits without integration $(888 + 1156 = 2044)$. Vertical integration is privately profitable but leaves consumers worse off. Net social welfare also falls.

D_2 (competing as a quantity-setting duopolist) earns some economic profit whether or not U_1 and D_1 are vertically integrated. For D_2, however, integration of U_1 and D_1 means that it

---

[51] U_2 might produce elsewhere and incur a transportation cost 12 per unit to deliver the product to D_1 or D_2. This discussion is thus related to that of Section 2.3.5.

[52] For a complete statement of assumptions and proofs that the outcomes described are equilibrium outcomes, see Hart and Tirole (1990).

pays more per unit for an essential input ($1244/40 = 31.1$ per unit before integration, slightly less than 32 per unit afterward), while its competitor, now integrated, in effect obtains the input at the marginal cost of production ($20 < 31.1$). These price differences in the model correspond to what in real-world markets is sometimes called a *price squeeze* by a vertically integrated firm that competes with non integrated rivals.[53]

Evidence

Fisher Body[54]   As indicated in the accompanying box, in September 1919 the General Motors Corporation purchased a 60 per cent interest in the Fisher Body Corporation. Some five years later, General Motors purchased the remaining 40 per cent of Fisher Body, which became a division of General Motors. Efforts to understand the initial investment and the eventual acquisition have made this the most thoroughly examined testing ground for transaction cost theories of the boundaries of the firm.

Holdup   Klein *et al.* (1978, pp. 308–310) devote not quite two full pages to discussion of this episode, which in their view is consistent with the asset-specificity/holdup problem motive for vertical integration. Under the 1919 contract, General Motors could not hold up Fisher Body by threatening to take its business elsewhere; General Motors had agreed (Coase, 2000, p. 23) "to give to Fisher Body such of its closed body business as Fisher Body was able to handle". Nor could Fisher Body hold up General Motors by raising its price, which was specified (relative to cost) in the contract. Costs might change, of course,[55] but the contract also provided that General Motors could not be charged more than the price of similar car bodies to other customers.

But Klein *et al.* draw attention to the fact that the early years of the contract saw a substantial increase in demand for cars with closed bodies. Despite requests from General Motors (in search of efficiency gains), Fisher Body refused to open up body plants near General Motors' assembly plants.[56] To resolve the impasse, General Motors purchased that part of Fisher Body that it did not already own.

Reconsideration   Subsequent research suggests that the evidence upon which Klein *et al.* base these conclusions was incomplete. The case that Fisher Body held back from locating plants near General Motor's assembly plants is not compelling. In at least one case, General Motors financed construction of a car body plant (Coase, 2000, p. 28). Further, the string of appointments of Fisher brothers to key positions at General Motors during the early 1920s is difficult to reconcile with the idea that Fisher Body was actively engaged in holding up General Motors.

---

[53] A price squeeze is often thought to involve a reduction in the final good price as well as an increase in input price. In the example presented here, the final good price rises rather than falls with vertical integration.

[54] This section is based on Klein *et al.* (1978) and the sources listed in the accompanying box.

[55] Klein (1998) suggests that Fisher Body adopted high cost, inefficiently labour intensive production techniques. There is, however, reason to think that the cost-plus aspects of the GM-Fisher Body contract ended in 1924 (Freeland, 2000, p. 47). This would have eliminated any profit to Fisher Body from high-cost operations.

[56] As Klein *et al.* note, such transaction-specific sunk investments might heave exposed Fisher Body to holdup by General Motors.

BOX   Body By Fisher

- 1916: Fisher Body Corporation formed by combination of three companies of the six Fisher brothers.

- November 1917, General Motors agrees to purchase car bodies from Fisher Body under a "cost plus 17.6 per cent" contract.

- Fisher negotiations with car makers in Cleveland about possible formation of a Fisher-controlled partnership.

- 25 September 1919

  - GM buys 60 per cent of Fisher; GM to name half of the Board of Directors; until 1 October 1924, shares voted by a trust with two GM and two Fisher trustees, unanimity required to act;

  - ten-year contract, Fisher Body to supply GM with closed car bodies, at cost plus 17.6 per cent;

  - Fisher brothers given five-year employment contracts, to end 1 October 1924.

- 1921: Fred Fisher becomes a director of GM.

- 1922: Fred Fisher becomes a member of GM executive committee.

- 1924: Charles and Lawrence Fisher join Fred Fisher on the GM board of directors and executive committee; Fred Fisher appointed to GM finance committee.

- 1925: Lawrence Fisher becomes head of GM's Cadillac division.

- 1 February 1922: former Ford executive William Knudsen hired by GM; becomes vice-president of Chevrolet operations; January 1924, president and general manager of Chevrolet; reorganizes production of Chevrolet K Model to make it quality and cost competitive with Ford Model T.

- May 1926: GM purchases remaining 40 per cent of Fisher Body; William Fisher becomes head of the Fisher Body division, joins the GM board of directors.

Sources: Hounshell (1984), Coase (2000), Freeland (2000), Casadesus-Masanell and Spulber (2000), Helper *et al.* (2000), Baird (2003).

Human capital   If the avoidance of hold up was not the motive for the merger, what was? Valuable human capital, as embodied in the Fisher brothers, was one factor. Freeland (2000, p. 44) emphasizes that although General Motors had a ten-year contract with Fisher Body, the Fisher brothers' employment agreements and the voting trust that gave them effective control of Fisher Body, despite a minority ownership position, ended after five years. Chandler and Salsbury describe the Fisher Brothers as (1971, pp. 575–576) "independent-minded", "they hated to see the family business disappear" and "[i]n this they were emphatically supported by their strong-willed mother". By completing the takeover of Fisher Body, General Motors ensured that it would benefit from the Fishers' services, and that its rivals would not.

Organizational capabilities   Cost minimization was another factor. General Motors' Chevrolet Division developed its K Model to target the Ford Model T's lead in the low-price car market segment. The K Model was a high-quality vehicle, but the Model T held a 70 per cent market share. General Motors had to cut the K Model's cost, so it could profitably lower price and take market share away from the Model T (Chandler and Salsbury, 1971, Chapter 20;

Table 10.8 Value of purchased components as a percentage of value of finished vehicles, U.S. auto industry, early 1920s

Year	Value Finished Vehicles ($)	Value Purchased Components ($)	Per Cent
1922	1,787,122,708	982,952,384	55
1923	2,582,398,876	1,270,000,000	49
1924	2,328,249,632	900,321,000	39
1925	2,957,368,637	1,128,648,000	38
1926	3,163,756,676	823,394,000	26

Source: Casadesus-Masanell and Spulber (2000, Table 4 (based on Seltzer, 1928)).

Baird, 2003, pp. 26–27). Assuring supplies of an essential input, car bodies, and coordinating input flows with the rest of the assembly process, were essential for cost minimization.

This aspect of the GM-Fisher Body merger is consistent with Chandler's "three-pronged investment" analysis of the basis for enduring market leadership. In the same vein, there was at this time a trend toward vertical integration in the U.S. car industry (Casadesus-Masanell and Spulber, 2000; Helper *et al.*, 2000; Table 10.8). A general trend to vertical integration, viewed through the lens of transaction cost analysis, suggests that during this period U.S. car manufacturers found internal organization of inputs more profitable than input acquisition from independent suppliers. That the Fisher Body acquisition was part of a general trend to vertical integration does not lend plausibility to the idea that it was carried out to avoid holdup.

Assessment   One lesson that can be drawn from the Fisher Body episode is that "firm" and "market" are not a mutually exclusive and exhaustive list of ways to organize transactions (Coase, 1988b, p. 27; Helper *et al.*, 2000). In 1919, a ten-year contract was the most profitable feasible option for General Motors to assure its supply of car bodies. Market conditions changed (among such changes, an increase in demand for closed-body cars and the introduction of annual model changes). Five years into the contract, it had become more important for General Motors to coordinate the supply of Fisher car bodies with its assembly operations, and the Fisher brothers' experience with a successful five-year "trial marriage" (Coase, 2000, p. 23) made them more amenable to a full merger. No doubt the 1919 contract had formal provisions that might have allowed either party, under some circumstances, to hold up the other. Hold up does not seem to have occurred, and the 1926 merger is best interpreted as a profit-maximizing response to changed market conditions, not as a way to avoid the loss of sunk investment in highly specific assets.

Great Northern[57]

In October, 1906, the United States Steel Corporation and the Great Northern Railway signed a contract for an indefinite lease governing U.S. Steel's exploitation of Great Northern iron

---

[57] This section is based on Mullin and Mullin (1997).

ore deposits in the Minnesota Western Mesabi range. Mullin and Mullin (1997) make a compelling case that the terms of the contract aimed to protect the interests of both parties as they made sunk investments to carry it out.

The Mesabi deposits were of high quality and capable of being worked at relatively low cost, and they were the last major iron ore deposits outside mining company control. After concluding the contract, U.S. Steel made substantial investments in mine development and in the construction of steel plants that would be most efficiently supplied from the Great Northern deposits. Great Northern constructed dedicated railroad lines to connect mines to Lake Superior docks, and invested in special-purpose freight cars to ship ore.

One provision of the lease was a "take-or-pay" clause: U.S. Steel was to pay for a minimum amount of ore per year, an amount that increased over time, whether it was mined or not. The effect of this clause was to guarantee that Great Northern would not be held up after making sunk investments.[58]

U.S. Steel agreed to ship iron ore taken under the lease exclusively with Great Northern. Great Northern was entitled to advance notice if more than the minimum amount of ore was to be shipped, suggesting that a capacity constraint limited the amount of ore it could ship (without additional investment). U.S. Steel agreed to pay what appears to have been an above-market (although still profitable) royalty rate per tonne of ore extracted over the minimum amount. U.S. Steel's excess royalty payments, in such circumstances, would compensate Great Northern for the need to expand capacity. The freight rate to ship ore was not covered by the "take-or-pay" clause, and the rate U.S. Steel agreed to pay for shipping its ore promised to be very profitable for Great Northern, giving Great Northern an incentive to efficiently manage its part of the operations needed to work the iron ore deposits.

The U.S. Steel-Great Northern arrangement was (Mullin and Mullin, 1997, p. 75) the "effective equivalent" of full vertical integration, "since the lease was of indefinite duration, and the parties expected the iron ore to be substantially exhausted upon reversion". The lease was different from a purchase to the extent that U.S. Steel retained the right to cancel to lease with two years' notice.[59] Like the General Motors-Fisher Body episode, therefore, the U.S. Steel-Great Northern suggests that firms can reach agreements that control transaction costs while falling short of full integration.

Foreclosure

Cable television   Chipty examines the impact of vertical integration on market performance in the U.S. cable television industry, where (2001, p. 431, footnote omitted) "In 1991, there were approximately 11,000 cable systems, 1,600 cable system operators, and 140 national and regional program services ... About 50 of these 140 program services were vertically integrated with cable operators. About 2,300 cable systems, or about 60 percent of all homes with cable access, were controlled by vertically integrated operators."

---

[58] The "take-or-pay" clause transformed what U.S. Steel paid for iron ore, up to the minimum level, from a variable to a fixed cost. The effect of this clause on market performance, as Mullin and Mullin point out, was to give U.S. Steel an incentive to take at least the agreed minimum amount of iron ore every year, placing a floor under subsequent steel output.

[59] U.S. Steel did cancel the lease, in October 1911, apparently in an unsuccessful attempt to avoid antitrust prosecution. See Mullin and Mullin (1997) for details.

Farthest upstream in this vertical chain are the programme producers—movie and television studios. Programme services (like HBO and American Movie Classics) deliver their product to the final consumer through cable systems. Cable systems may or may not be vertically integrated with programme services.

In this market (as indeed in others), vertical integration may bring foreclosure, reduced costs, or higher quality, and the possibilities are not mutually exclusive (Chipty, 2001, p. 433):

> If vertical integration results in market foreclosure, then integrated operators will tend to exclude program services, particularly those that directly rival their upstream affiliates. If vertical integration results in efficiency gains, then integrated operators will prefer to carry their own programming and will tend to offer more program services.

Chipty studies a sample of 1,919 cable television systems managed by 340 operators in 1991. She finds evidence of foreclosure (2001, p. 429, footnote omitted): "Operators who own premium services offer, on average, one fewer premium service and one to two fewer basic services than do other operators. In particular, operators who own premium movie services are less likely to carry the rival basic movie service, American Movie Classics (AMC). In addition, [Tele-Communications Inc.] and Comcast, two operators who own the basic shopping service QVC, are less likely to carry rival shopping service Home Shopping Network (HSN), and they are less likely to carry both QVC and HSN."

At the same time, vertical integration promotes sales, an indication of greater perceived quality, all else equal Chipty (2001, p. 450):[60] "Integrated operators are better at promoting their products than are unintegrated operators. Basic operators offer more basic services and achieve higher basic penetration rates, while premium operators offer fewer basic services and achieve higher premium penetration rates." To this point, Chipty's findings are ambiguous as far as the net impact of vertical integration on market performance is concerned. Foreclosure, which is present, reduces the choices available to final consumers. But there is also evidence that vertical integration increases the quality of the reduced range of choices that is available. Chipty estimates the relation between consumer surplus and vertical integration and concludes that the net impact is neutral or positive (Chipty, 2001, pp. 448–449).

Cement/concrete Cement is an input to the production of concrete (Hortaçsu and Syverson, 2007, p. 251):

> Cement—made by baking limestone and clay or shale together in a kiln and grinding the result into a powder—is a single but important ingredient in the production of concrete. Ready-mixed concrete is produced by mixing cement with sand, gravel, water, and chemical admixtures and is what is contained in the familiar trucks with the spinning barrels on their backs. Thus cement is the upstream industry and ready-mixed the downstream industry.

Hortaçsu and Syverson study the impact of vertical integration on plant-level performance for the eight U.S. Census of Manufactures years between 1963 and 1997, inclusive. They find no evidence of foreclosure: "Instead, vertical integration is associated with lower prices at both the plant and market levels. We do find evidence that this negative relationship is not driven by vertical integration per se, but rather because vertical integration is tied to larger,

---

[60] "Penetration rates", loosely, are measures of market share. See Chipty (2001, pp. 440–441) for definitions.

more productive firms (2007, p. 273)." Vertical integration may cause less-efficient firms to exit (Hortaçsu and Syverson, 2007, p. 287).

Exit of less efficient firms due to a lower price level is a sign of improved market performance. Hortaçsu and Syverson point to coordination economies as the underlying source of vertical integration efficiencies (2007, p. 291, footnote omitted):

> Operating in the ready-mixed industry requires delivering a perishable product to time-sensitive buyers in multiple locations. Having several plants in a local area and coordinating deliveries through a central office could benefit a firm by consolidating overhead (one dispatcher might handle deliveries from several plants that would each have separate dispatchers in single-unit firms) and allowing more efficient use of available resources through cross-plant substitution.

This conclusion has Coasian, Chandlerian, and old-style industrial economics aspects. It is less costly to coordinate regional deliveries within a firm (transaction costs), firms that integrate vertically and are able to realize coordination economies (organizational capabilities), and there is sufficient market rivalry (competition) that savings are passed on to final consumers. The result is improved market performance.

Vertical competition and market performance

Leverage   A tenet of the Second Chicago School was the "no leverage of market power" argument, that a firm with a monopoly position in one market could realize maximum economic profit in that market. It follows that horizontal intermarket links like tying or bundling or vertical integration (by merger or contract) of a firm with market power should not be a policy concern: since a firm with monopoly power can fully exploit that power in one market, horizontal or vertical links must have efficiency motivation and effects, or at worst be neutral for market performance.

To test the hypothesis that competition between vertically integrated and non-integrated firms has no impact on market performance, Grimm *et al.* turn to the U.S. railroad industry, about which they write (1992, p. 298, footnote omitted):

> The meaning of vertical foreclosure in the railroad industry can be represented graphically, as in Figure [10.3], where carriers A and B have a dual cooperative/competitive relationship. Carrier A's TD line is essential for B to serve the OD market. Because A is vertically integrated from O to D while B is not, A's single-line service competes with the A/B joint-line service. Under these circumstances, B is potentially subject to vertical foreclosure. Railroad A may effectively refuse to deal with B on the interline route, thereby tying its monopoly TD service to its OT service.

They analyse shipments of manufactured goods for intercity routes that were served by one single-line railroad and differing numbers of interline railroads. For a sample of intercity shipments of manufactured goods, they estimate the difference between actual and optimal shipper welfare of intercity shippers, allowing for the fact that railroads compete with trucking companies and private trucks in the provision of shipping services. Their results are that if a single-line railroad faces competition from one or more interline railroads, shipper welfare is significantly closer to the optimum.[61] This effect appears whether the interline carriers are at the origin or the destination of the single line.

---

[61] Intuitively, that price is closer to marginal cost: they estimate welfare is about 3 cents per tonne-mile closer to the optimum if there is one additional interline shipper.

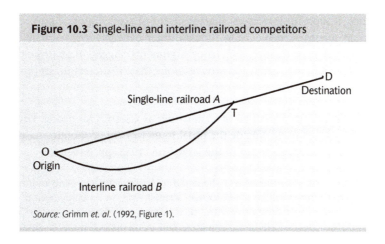

Figure 10.3 Single-line and interline railroad competitors

Single-line railroad A

D
Destination

T

O
Origin

Interline railroad B

Source: Grimm *et. al.* (1992, Figure 1).

If the "no leverage of market power" doctrine were valid for U.S. railroad markets, the number of interline rivals would have no impact on market performance: the single-line railroad would extract full monopoly profit for the intercity route on the segments where it had a monopoly; the extent of rivalry on other segments would be irrelevant. The finding that rivalry between integrated and nonintegrated firms improves market performance is evidence against the "no leverage of market power" doctrine.

Raising rivals' costs   Hastings and Gilbert (2005) use a 1996 merger in the U.S. West Coast oil refining and distribution industries to test the hypothesis that a vertically integrated upstream firm that supplies independent downstream firms in a price-setting market has a strategic incentive to raise its wholesale price. The incentive to raise downstream rivals' input prices arises in price-setting markets because prices in differentiated-good markets are strategic complements. If rivals' costs increase, their profit-maximizing response is to increase their prices. When rivals' prices increase, it becomes profitable for the retail outlets of the vertically integrated firm to increase their retail prices.

Post-merger changes in the vertically integrated acquiring firm's retail market share in different metropolitan areas ranged from near zero to 16 per cent. Hastings and Gilbert report larger wholesale price increases in areas where the acquiring firm faced greater competition from non-integrated petrol stations, particularly if the non-integrated firms were located near the integrated firm's retail outlets. They conclude that (2005, p. 489) "in the presence of upstream market power, changes in vertical market structure can have significant impacts on upstream firm conduct and equilibrium prices".

10.5.4 Diversification

Motives

Large firms typically operate in many markets—they are diversified geographically or across product lines, or both.[62] Market power arguments suggest that firms diversify in a search for

---

[62] Diversification is measured in various ways for various purposes. Focusing for specificity on product diversification, if a firm produces n different products, we write s_i for the sales or employment share of product i in the firm's sales, and order shares so that $s_1 \geq s_2 \geq ... \geq s_n$. One measure of product diversification is simply n, which

private profit that, if successful, worsens market performance. Corporate governance arguments suggest that managers diversify to increase their own payoffs, reducing firm value and worsening market performance. Efficiency arguments suggest that firms diversify to fully exploit fixed assets, in a search for private profit that, if successful, improves market performance.

Power   Two arguments have explained diversification as a search for power. Edwards, who was explicit that he was stepping outside the usual framework of economic analysis,[63] identified the diversified firm as one species of the large firm (1955, pp. 344–345):

> [T]he large enterprise has advantages over the small in its capacity to spend money or take losses at any selected point at which it encounters a small rival, in its enjoyment of discriminations and preferences, in its ability to control distributors, customers, and sources of supply by tie-in sales and exclusive dealing arrangements, and in its opportunities to strengthen its position through exchange of favors with other large enterprises. These various advantages may be important enough to assure the survival and growth of big concerns, relative to small ones, whether or not the big are functionally as efficient as the small.

The issues raised by Edwards' argument substantially overlap with the debate about aggregate concentration (Section 10.2.2), and that discussion need not be repeated here.

Scott (1989b, 1991) has elaborated another of Edwards' arguments, one that does fit it the market-oriented framework: that multimarket contact among diversified firms will support tacit collusion in each of the markets in which the firms meet.

Efficiency   Chandler documents the deliberate diversification of DuPont in the immediate aftermath of World War I, to ensure continued employment of fixed and sunk assets it had accumulated as part of the war effort (Section 10.3.1). Along these lines, the resource view of diversification (Montgomery, 1994, p. 167, footnote omitted) "argues that rent-seeking firms diversify in response to excess capacity in productive factors ... "

Finally, as suggested by our discussion of the separation of ownership and control (Section 10.4), diversification may be a form of empire building for which managers opt if corporate governance fails and they have discretion to pursue their own interests rather than those of the firm's owners.

Nature

Sunk assets   Lemelin (1982) examines patterns of vertical and conglomerate diversification among more than 2,000 Canadian firms in the early 1970s. For firms in producer good

---

(Gort, 1962, p. 9) "might ... throw light on the extent to which an enterprise is likely to enter activities unrelated to its primary operations". Another is to measure diversification as the inverse of specialization, $1 - s_1$. The first measure takes no account of the distribution of the firm's activities across markets, the second takes no account of the distribution of the firm's activities in its second through nth markets. Perhaps the most common measure (Montgomery, 1994, p. 169) is some variation of the Herfindahl index $\sum_{i=1}^{n} s_i^2$. 1 minus the Herfindahl index, $1 - \sum_{i=1}^{n} s_i^2$, takes the value 0 for a firm that operates in one product market, $1 - \frac{1}{n}$ for a firm that has operations evenly distributed across n markets. See Gollop and Monahan (1991), Montgomery (1994) for discussions of the measurement of diversification.

[63] Edwards (1955, p. 332): "Thus the term conglomerate becomes a device for examining problems of size and power apart from the traditional focus upon monopoly and efficiency."

industries, he finds a tendency to diversify laterally into sectors where they can use fixed and sunk assets, and forward into distribution, to ensure outlets for their products. Firms in industries that manufacture consumer convenience goods, with fixed assets that are less sunk than those of producer good industries, tend to diversify into other consumer convenience good industries. In Lemelin's apt phrase, manufacturers of producer goods must sell what they make, while manufacturers of consumer convenience goods are able to make what sells.

R&D capabilities   Assets may be tangible or intangible. Scott and Pascoe (1987) study the diversification of 352 large U.S. manufacturing firms across four-digit industries in the early 1970s. They identify groups of firms that are diversified into the same industries, in which they engage in research and development, significantly more often than would be the case if diversification were random. Then examining the level of R&D spending by firms in such purposively diversified groups, industry by industry, Scott and Pascoe find that they spend more on R&D than firms in the same industries that are not part of diversified groups. They conclude that firms that tend to diversify into the same industries to exploit R&D capabilities make a greater R&D effort in industries where imitation is less rapid, all else equal.[64] These results, like those of Lemelin, are consistent with the efficiency view of diversification.

Rondi *et al.* (1996) examine patterns of diversification of 313 leading EU manufacturing firms across three-digit and alternatively two-digit NACE industries (Table 10.9). The average firm in the sample operates in 2.9 two-digit industries, with 17.1 per cent of sales outside its primary two-digit industry, and in 4.9 three-digit industries, with 28.3 per cent of sales outside its primary industry. About 30 per cent of the firms in their sample are not diversified outside their primary three-digit industry. Among firms in their sample from large EU member states, UK firms appear to be the most diversified, and Italian firms the least diversified. A statistical analysis shows that large firms tend to be more diversified, all else equal, as do firms from member states with highly developed financial markets. The latter results, they

Table 10.9 Two diversification measures, 313 leading EU manufacturing firms, 1987

	N		$1-s_1$ (%)	
	3-digit	2-digit	3-digit	2-digit
Minimum	1	1	0	0
Mean	4.9	2.9	28.3	17.1
Maximum	33	13	84.8	75.0
Standard Deviation	4.8	2.3	26.0	20.4

Note: N = number of NACE industries in which a firm operates; $1 - s_1$ = share of firm's production outside its primary industry.
Source: Rondi et al. (1996, Table 10.1).

---

[64] On the impact of firm's ability to appropriate the fruits of R&D effort on innovative performance, see Section 14.3.1.

suggest, may indicate that the separation of ownership and control favours diversification. They also find that firms from high-R&D or high-advertising primary industries tend to diversify into industries with similar R&D- or advertising-sales ratios. This may result from firms diversifying to exploit intangible assets (know-how, brand name) that are not industry-specific.

New products in new plants   Gollop and Monahan (1991) study the diversification of U.S. manufacturing between 1963 and 1982. They observe an increase in the diversification of firms and a decrease in diversification of production at the plant level. This implies, they suggest, that firms diversify by adding plants that produce products that are new for the firm, not by producing new products in existing plants.[65]

The Gollop and Monahan sample period includes all of the Third Merger Wave, a period of extensive conglomerate diversification, and about half of the Fourth Merger Wave, which largely undid the conglomerate unions of the Third (Section 11.2.3). The increase in firm diversification documented by Gollop and Monahan was reversed by the end of the 1980s (Lichtenberg, 1992).

Impact

Multimarket contact   There is some evidence that diversification supports economic profit, by creating multimarket contact. Thus Scott (1991) reconstructs and extends a firm-level version of the sample used by Bain in his 1956 study of seller concentration, entry conditions, and profitability.[66] Scott's results are that (1991, p. 236) "when multimarket contact of diversified oligopolists was low, profits averaged roughly what they were for the essentially competitive industries. ... But given significant multimarket contact, the diversified oligopolists' profits were much higher on average—significantly higher statistically and in actual magnitude."[67]

Diversification discount   But on balance, the evidence is that diversification reduces firm value, all else equal. This is the so-called diversification discount: financial markets value more diversified firms less, all else equal, than less diversified firms.

Lang and Stulz (1994) examine the impact of diversification on a measure of firm value, Tobin's q, the ratio of a firm's stock market value to the replacement cost of its assets. In principle, a firm in a perfectly competitive market would have a q-ratio equal to 1: if ever the market valued a firm more than the cost of its assets, new firms enter; if ever the market valued a firm less than the cost of its assets, the firm would takes its assets to some other market where they would be valued at a normal rate of return. Values of the q-ratio greater than 1 suggest the firm earns economic profit or possesses intangible assets (perhaps,

---

[65] An implication, they note, is that (1991, p. 329) "technical economies of scope appear to play little role in explaining the measured increase in enterprise diversification. If such technical economies exist and are actively pursued by firms, the economies most likely would be realized at the establishment level, but it is precisely here that diversification has decreased."

[66] See Figure 1.2 and the associated text.

[67] Caves (1981) finds little evidence of an impact of diversification on seller concentration, results that weigh against an indirect effect of diversification on economic profits through its effects on concentration.

organizational capabilities). Values of the q-ratio less than 1 suggest the firm's assets are not being employed to maximum advantage or are to some extent sunk and cannot costlessly be shifted to other markets.[68] For a sample of U.S. firms, Lang and Stulz find that (1994, p. 1278) "highly diversified firms have mean and median q ratios below one and below the sample mean and median every year in our sample period. This is strong evidence that highly diversified firms are consistently valued less than specialized firms." Their analysis also suggests that (1994, p. 1251) "firms that diversify are poor performers relative to firms that do not, lending support to the view that poor performers diversify in search of growth opportunities".[69] Rajan *et al.* (2000), on the other hand, find some indication that diversified firms allocate resources internally toward less efficient divisions.

Productivity   Lichtenberg (1992) examines the impact of parent firm diversification on plant-level productivity for some 17,000 U.S. manufacturing plants in 1980. His findings are that (1992, p. 436) "holding constant the number of the parent firm's plants (and other variables), the greater the number of industries in which the parent firm operates, the lower the productivity of its plants". Schoar (2002) similarly finds that when a firm diversifies, the plants it acquires increase in productivity, its existing plants go down in productivity, with a net reduction in overall productivity. Lower productivity may be one factor behind the diversification discount.

SUMMARY

Coase (1972b, 1988c) has insisted that the proper subject of industrial organization, as a field, is the organization of industry. "The organization of industry" includes not only "the organization of industries" (which we have considered in the previous chapter), but also the organization of economic activity within firms, and that has been our topic here.

In market economies, it is relative profitability that guides private-sector resource allocation, and so it is with the division of activities between firms and markets. Chandler emphasized market size and technology as a determinant of firm size — where the market is sufficiently large and the technology implies that there are potential economies of scale or scope, efficiently organized firms can deliver lower unit costs; it will then be profitable to integrate vertical chains of economic activity within firms.

Chandler's three-pronged investment is part of the explanation for division of activity between firms and markets, but only part. There are costs of organizing transactions across markets. There are costs of organizing transactions within firms, almost all tied in some way to the facts that information is limited and costly to process.

Internal corporate governance mechanisms seem poorly to protect the interests of shareholders as a whole. Large blocks of shareholders may bring management to account. There remains the question precisely to whose account management is brought: firms that expand by diversification seem not to maximize shareholder value. This leads to one topic, the market for corporate control, that we take up in the following chapter,

---

[68] See Smirlock *et al.* (1984) for further discussion.

[69] Lins and Servaes (1999) find evidence of a diversification discount for UK firms, but not for German firms.

STUDY POINTS

- Aggregate concentration
  - Extent (Section 10.2.1)
  - Impact (Section 10.2.2)
- Three-pronged investment
  - U.S. (Section 10.3.1)
  - Elsewhere? (Section 10.3.2)
- Separation of ownership and control
  - Berle & Means (Section 10.4.1)
  - Or not? (Section 10.4.2)
- Theory of the Firm (Section 10.5)
  - Transaction costs (Section 10.5.1)
  - Information (Section 10.5.2)
- Vertical integration (Section 10.5.3)
  - Fundamental Transformation
  - Fisher Body, Great Northern
  - Property rights
  - Market power
- Diversification (Section 10.5.4)

FURTHER READING

For references to and discussion of the early literature on non-neoclassical approaches to the theory of the firm, see Cyert and March (1963, Chapter 2), Cyert and Hedrick (1972), and on the later literature, Milgrom and Roberts (1988), Hart (1989), Holmström and Tirole (1989), and Gibbons (2005). For an introduction to formal principal-agent models, see Sappington (1991).

The literature on aggregate concentration is contentious. In addition to the works discussed in the text, see for the U.S. Means (1939), Gordon (1945/1961), Collins and Preston (1961), Preston (1971), Blair (1972, Chapter 4), Weiss (1983), Caswell (1987), O'Neill (1996), and White (1981, 2002), and for the EU, Jacquemin and Cardon de Lichtbuer (1973), Jacquemin (1974). White (2002) gives a careful discussion of issues arising in the measurement of aggregate concentration.

For an introduction and references to Chandler's work, see McCraw (1988), the review colloquium in the Winter 1990 issue of *Business History Review*, Hannah (1991), Supple (1991), and Chandler (1992). On the spread of the M-form firm, see Kogut and Parkinson (1998). On the family firm in Britain, see Payne (1967, 1984), Church (1993). Another contribution to the literature on the separation of ownership and control is Hannah (2007), who suggests it was visible earlier Britain and France than in the United States.

On vertical integration and price discrimination, Gould (1977), Perry (1978), and Romano (1988). Lafontaine and Slade (2007) survey empirical studies of vertical integration.

PROBLEM

10–1 At most two upstream firms, U_1 and U_2 supply an input to a downstream market supplied by two firms, D_1 and D_2. One unit of the input is required to produce one unit of the output. U_1 and U_2 have constant marginal and average cost c_1 and $c_2 > c_1$ per unit of output, respectively. If U_1 and U_2 are both active, they compete as price-setting firms. D_1 and D_2 have identical constant marginal and average cost x per unit (plus whatever they pay to acquire the input). D_1 and D_2 compete as Cournot oligopolists.

The inverse demand equal for the final good market is

$$p = a - q_1 - q_2,$$

where q_1 and q_2 are the quantities supplied by D_1 and D_2, respectively.

Verify the results stated in Section 10.5.3.

MERGERS

Many small make a great.

Chaucer, *The Manciple's Tale*

11.1 Introduction

Mergers impact market structure and firm structure. A horizontal merger may create a market leader; a series of horizontal mergers in the same market may concentrate supply in the hands of a few firms. Vertical mergers have the potential for cost-saving efficiencies and for strategic foreclosure that raises rivals' costs. Conglomerate mergers may allow a firm to diversify risk by evening out fluctuations in income, may permit privately profitable tying and bundling, or may be simple empire-building. Horizontal, vertical, and conglomerate mergers might all, in principle, be manifestations of the market for corporate control, as a better management expels a worse management to the benefit of the owners of the firm.

We begin with a consideration of the five merger waves have rippled through the supply-side structure of the U.S. economy since passage of the Sherman Act (Figure 11.1). Like waves in an ocean, each is different, yet they have common elements, and it is upon these that we focus. The review of merger waves leads to a discussions of theory and evidence about the implications of mergers for market performance.

11.2 Merger Waves

11.2.1 First: Turn of the 19th Century

The First Merger Wave began with one depression, in 1893, peaked in 1901 with the formation of United States Steel, and ended in 1903 with another depression. There were merger waves at about the same time in Britain[1] and Germany.[2] The mergers that were part of the

---

[1] Utton (1972, p. 52) has the British merger wave peaking between 1895 and 1902. Hannah (1974, Figure 1, Table IV) identifies a trough in British merger activity in 1892 or 1893, a peak in 1898 or 1899, and another trough in 1901.

[2] Kling (2006) dates a German merger wave beginning in 1898 and (2006, p. 675) "centered on a peak in 1906".

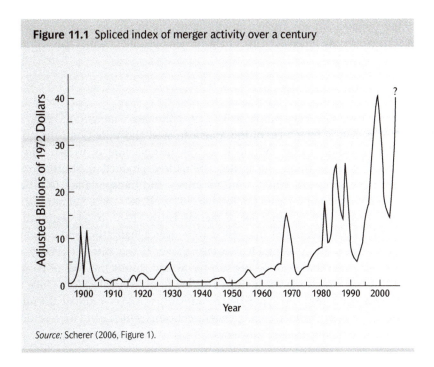

Figure 11.1 Spliced index of merger activity over a century

Source: Scherer (2006, Figure 1).

First Merger Wave were mainly horizontal, typically combined many firms, and created firms that were dominant in their industries (Butters *et al.*, 1951, p. 288, footnote omitted):

> By [early 1904] over 300 industrial combinations, representing consolidations of about 5,000 distinct plants and covering most major lines of productive industry, had been formed. ... with 78 of these consolidated corporations controlling one-half or more of the country's total production in their respective fields, and with 26 controlling 80% or more.

Market integration

Market integration was one force behind the First Merger Wave. But the timing of the First Merger Wave cannot be explained by market integration alone; U.S. market integration was substantially complete a decade or more before the First Merger Wave began. The integration of regional markets naturally suggests the possibility that firms operating in industries with technologies that permitted economies of large scale production would expand output, lower operating cost, and supply a larger geographic market. But evidence is that economies of scale had been largely realized before the merger wave began; O'Brien (1988, p. 645) writes that "average factory size doubled between 1869 and 1899 and increased by about 25 percent between 1899 and 1919 ..."

Competition and competition policy

The intense price competition that accompanied the 1893 depression played a role in the First Merger Wave,[3] as did early U.S. antitrust policy. In an infancy of listless enforcement,

---

[3] Lamoreaux (1985, p. 87). Cook and Cohen (1958) cite intense short-period competition as a cause of mergers in three of their case studies of mergers in six UK industries. Their time periods include that of the first U.S. merger

Section 1 of the Sherman Act was applied strictly against collusion, Section 2 was rendered impotent against large-scale mergers.[4] Firms took the avenue, merger, that was left open to them.

Efficiency (or not)

A merger might pursue efficiency while seeking to eliminate competition. One motive behind the 1899 formation by merger of the American Steel and Wire Company, to create (McFadden, 1978, p. 483) "a near monopoly in the manufacture of barbed wire", was to escape the press of competition. But it also rationalized production, shutting obsolete plants, vertically integrating coal mines, iron ore mines, and transportation facilities, and expanding wire rod production capacity (McFadden, 1978, pp. 486–487). But rationalization was by no means a necessary consequence of merger. Utton (1972, p. 54) writes that two persistent problems of UK mergers of the period were overcapitalization and coordination of post-merger activities. The two problems were related. It was often necessary to pay generously to attract firms that were poorly run but would thwart the goal of containing competition if they stayed outside the merger. This led to overcapitalization. Once the bit players were in, however (Utton, 1972, p. 54) "The difficulty was to co-ordinate the price and production policies of many formerly independent concerns which were used to different methods and were of differing levels of efficiency."

Financial markets

By the late 1890s, New York City had become a financial center that facilitated mergers (Navin and Sears, 1955; Nelson, 1959, pp. 89–100). With the First Merger Wave, industrial securities became an effective device to raise large amounts of financial capital from the private sector. In addition, the existence of a market for securities made it possible to carry out mergers while using a minimum amount of cash, as the owners of firms being purchased accepted payment mainly in shares of stock in the post-merger firm.[5]

Financial promoters played a key role in whipping merger waves along. Markham (1955, p. 162) writes that "the abnormally large volume of mergers formed in 1897–1900 stemmed largely from a wave of frenzied speculation in asset values". Hannah (1974a, p. 8) argues similarly, as regards the parallel U.K. merger movement, that a promoter on the London financial market could "boost expectations from merger issues artificially and ... increase his own profits accordingly", and "There is ample evidence of the major role of the promoting houses in creating excessively optimistic expectations among the investing public, most notably in the case of merger issues ..."

---

wave, but are generally much longer, with exact periods varying from case study to case study. Utton (1972, p. 2) refers to "severe short term price competition" and the presence of excess capacity as "an argument which recurs again and again" in the run-ups to mergers during the first British merger wave.

[4] Until the 14 March 1904 *Northern Securities* decision, a factor halting the First Merger Wave (Stigler, 1950, p. 27; Butters *et al.*, 1951, p. 288).

[5] Stigler (1950) cites the development of a modern market for financial capital, which made it possible to raise funds needed to effect mass mergers, as one of two institutional innovations that explain the timing of the First Merger Wave. The other is the limited-liability corporation, which overcame the "unlimited liability [that] was a major obstacle to the formation of partnerships" (Stigler, 1950, p. 28). Hannah (1974, p. 2) names the same two factors as preconditions for the turn-of-the-nineteenth century UK merger wave.

Summing up

Nelson (1966, pp. 65–66) describes the First Merger Wave as "a record of overcapitalization and the wholesale issuance of stock" and endorses the contemporary conclusion of Arthur Stone Dewing that "the trusts turned out ill".

11.2.2 Second: The Roaring 20s

The Second Merger Wave may have started as early as 1919, the first full year after World War I, or after the economy recovered from a brief 1921 depression. It ended with the October 1929 stock market crash. Most merger activity in the Second Merger Wave took place in food industries, primary metals, petroleum refining, chemicals, and transportation equipment (Eis, 1969, p. 273, p. 275). Where the First Merger Wave transformed industries that had been structurally competitive into dominant firm industries, the Second transformed declining-dominant-firm industries into oligopolies (Stigler, 1950).

Market expansion

Like the First Merger Wave, the Second was preceded by technological change—the arrival of the automobile and commercial radio—that permitted competition on a larger stage, and, for consumer goods, the cultivation of product differentiation (Markham, 1955, p. 172):

> This new transportation system tended to break down small local markets in two ways: it provided sellers with a new means for extending their sales area, and it made consumers considerably more mobile. The 1920's also marked the rise of the home radio, a medium particularly amenable to advertising national brands.

Financial markets

Financial markets contributed to the 1920s merger movement (Thorp, 1931, p. 85): "In periods like 1928 and early 1929, when there is almost an insatiable demand for securities, the merger movement will be certain to flourish. Its most active sponsor is the investment banker." The relaxed attitude of antitrust enforcement agencies during this period was also a factor (Watkins, 1935; Eis, 1969, p. 290; Martin, 2008a, Section 2.3).

11.2.3 Third and Fourth: The Conglomerate 60s and the UnConglomerate 80s

Third Merger Wave

The Third Merger Wave took off in 1965, peaked in 1968, and fell back to the 1965 level by 1972 (Steiner, 1975, p. 5). Not only was it compressed in time, but its composition—pure conglomerate mergers, combining firms with neither horizontal nor vertical relationships—differed from that of other merger waves (Table 11.1).

Antitrust policy   U.S. antitrust policy was a partial explanation for the rise of conglomerate mergers. Early applications of Section 7 of the Clayton Act, as amended in 1950 by the Celler-Kefauver Act, substantially restricted horizontal and vertical mergers, leaving conglomerate mergers and internal growth as avenues for corporate expansion (Mueller, 1969, p. 657; Shleifer and Vishny, 1991). Many corporate managers opted for conglomerate mergers.

Table 11.1 Assets acquired in pure conglomerate mergers as percentage of large U.S. mergers, 1960–1972

1960–63	17.1
1964–67	21.2
1968	43.6
1969	38.1
1970	32.5
1971	43.4
1972	17.9

Source: Steiner (1975, Table 1-4).

Market power Conglomerate mergers, like all others, might be pursued in the search of market power or efficiency or both. To the extent that conglomerate mergers bring the same firms together in many markets, multimarket contact can stabilize tacit collusion (Edwards, 1955, p. 335):

> The interests of great enterprises are likely to touch at many points, and it would be possible for each to mobilize at any one of these points a considerable aggregate of resources. The anticipated gain to such a concern from unmitigated competitive attack upon another large enterprise at one point of contact is likely to be slight as compared with the possible loss from retaliatory action by that enterprise at many other points of contact.

Reciprocity—making purchases by one division of a conglomerate conditional on the seller buying from some other division of the conglomerate—may also be an issue in the effects of conglomerate mergers. With reciprocal buying, purchasing and selling decisions are based on factors not directly related to competition on the merits.[6]

Efficiency The perceived efficiency advantages of the conglomerate firm were largely related to external and internal capital markets. Conglomerate diversification, it was said, would allow a firm to even out fluctuations in its income stream. This would make the conglomerate firm less risky, and it would enjoy a lower cost of capital. Further, conglomerate diversification, particularly if conglomerate firms were organized as multidivisional-form firms, favoured the operation of the market for corporate control (Williamson, 1975, pp. 159–160). If an M-form conglomerate firm takes over a poorly run firm or poorly run division of some other conglomerate, the new owner can just add the acquisition as a new division in its

---

[6] Reciprocal buying was involved in FTC *v.* Consolidated Foods Corporation 380 U.S. 592.

existing multidivisional structure. Finally, the corporate management of an M-form conglomerate firm could operate an internal capital market, harvesting cash flows generated by high-profit, slow-growth divisions and investing them in cash-starved divisions with bright prospects for the future (Williamson, 1975, pp. 158–159; 1981, p. 1556).

We consider the market for corporate control in Section 11.4. Internal capital markets, in operation, seemed to suffer from handicaps. Stewart and Glassman (1988a, p. 86) include among these "unproductive reinvestment of cash flow" and "subsidies for underperforming businesses", which would seem to cut out the heart of the original argument for an internal capital market as a resource allocation mechanism. Rajan *et al.* (2000) find for a sample of U.S. firms in the 1980s and early 1990s that as diversification increases, firms may channel resources toward less efficient divisions.

In order for conglomerate diversification to reduce risk and so lower a firm's cost of capital, financial markets must be able evaluate conglomerate performance. There is some doubt about this (Stewart and Glassman, 1988b, p. 81):

> Several years ago, at a roundtable discussion our firm sponsored covering effective financial communication with investors, an investment banker suggested that conglomerates sold at a discount because securities analysts found them difficult to follow. Michael Sherman, head of investment strategy for Shearson Lehman Brothers, bristled. "It's not that conglomerates are difficult for analysts to understand. We worry that conglomerates are difficult for management to understand," he countered.

This would seem to leave two possibilities, which are not mutually exclusive. The first is that financial analysts had difficulty understanding conglomerate operations, the second that business executives had difficulty managing them. Neither possibility speaks well for the conglomerate firm as a way of organizing economic activity.

Management by the numbers   For Alfred D. Chandler, the Third Merger Wave was a time during which managers lost touch with the importance of organizational capabilities, relying instead on a flawed (1994, p. 18) "view of management as a set of skills unrelated to specific products or industries". As conglomerate managements added divisions, they lost touch with middle management and suffered from information overload. The effect was to neutralize the efficiency advantages of the M-form firm (Chandler, 1994, p. 20):[7] "Top management was basing decisions on numbers, not on knowledge, a practice that made it all the more difficult for the corporate office to carry out the basic functions of monitoring current operations and allocating resources for future activities . . . ."

Fourth Merger Wave

The Fourth Merger Wave, which (Hogan and Huie, 1992, Section II.D) "developed slowly in the late 1970's and reached full flower a decade later", undid the conglomerate mergers of the Third (Hubbard and Palia, 1999, p. 1131, footnote and references omitted):[8]

---

[7] See also Malkiel (2007, p. 57): "[T]he managers of conglomerates tended to possess financial expertise rather than the operating skills required to improve the profitability of the acquired companies."

[8] Hall (1994, pp. 127–130) discusses specific mergers and takeovers of the Fourth Merger Wave.

In the post-1980 period, diversified firms had ... a lower imputed stand-alone value of assets, sales, and earnings than a portfolio of stand-alone firms ... and a lower level of total factor productivity. ... [There was] a return to firm focus and specialization in the 1980s, ... diversifying bidders earned lower abnormal returns on announcement of an acquisition than bidders making related acquisitions. Further, divesting firms in the 1980s earn positive abnormal returns on announcement of the divestiture ..., and are more likely to divest unrelated businesses ...

Reverse course   There remains the question why firms and financial markets participated in a conglomerate merger wave in the 1960s and a deconglomerate merger wave in the 1980s. Matsusaka (1993, pp. 376–377) suggests three possibilities. The first is that conglomerate mergers were value-maximizing in the 1960s and that something changed between the 1960s and the 1980s, so that bust-up mergers were value-maximizing in the 1980s. One such change may have been "lax [antitrust] enforcement in the 1980s under the Reagan administration". Another is that financial markets became more efficient between the 1960s and the 1980s. Or the conglomerate industry may have been like any other profitable new industry that is not protected by barriers to entry. Early conglomerates had latched on to a good thing, and for a while it was very profitable to be a conglomerate. Imitators followed, and the rate of return to being a conglomerate went down.

The third possibility is that (Matsusaka, 1993, p. 377) "the market simply made a mistake about diversification". The typical conglomerate firm may have been just as inefficient, relative to more focused enterprises, in the 1960s, as it came to be perceived as being in the 1980s. On this view the conglomerates, as Arthur Stone Dewing said of the trusts, "turned out ill".

 BOX   Diversification and Divestiture

General Mills emerged from a 1928 merger that combined the operations of 27 companies to form the largest flour company in the world, a vertically integrated company that combining milling, marketing, and distribution. During World War II, it became involved in the production of high-precision ordnance equipment. In the 1950s, it added small household appliances, military electronics, chemicals (along with two-man midget submarines and high-altitude balloons) to its corporate umbrella. By the 1960s, flour had become a very low-profit business. General Mills closed nine of seventeen of its flour mills, reorganized its activities around brand-name consumer food and other consumer products, and divested several other lines of business entirely. In the 1970s, under James McFarland, diversification resumed as the firm acquired interests in toys and games, apparel, restaurants, travel services, and rare coins and stamps. The firm grew, but the rate of return on investment in the new lines of business was low. When E. Robert Kinney became president in 1976, General Mills operated in 13 industries.

By the time Bruce Atwater became president in 1981, it had become (Donaldson, 1990, p. 129) "difficult to manage and monitor performance across industries with large cultural differences: mass distribution foods versus fashion clothing versus the toy and game fads". Atwater had a study carried out comparing General Mills with a "peer group" of 88 similar companies, and the study showed (Donaldson, 1990, p. 131) ≫

>> that the more diversified the company, the more 'average' the performance. Most leading performers, in contrast, were concentrated in one or two industries. ... Only five companies were in five or more industries, as was General Mills at the time.

General Mills revised its business strategy accordingly. By 1988, it had divested extraneous lines of business and reorganized its activities into consumer goods lines and restaurants.

General Mills' management recognized the weaknesses of extreme diversification, and Donaldson (1990) gives them credit for having the foresight to adapt before crisis forced change. Other conglomerates were not so prudent.

Source: Donaldson (1990).

Figure 11.2 General Mills, Inc.: time line of diversification, by term of Chief Executive, 1968–1989

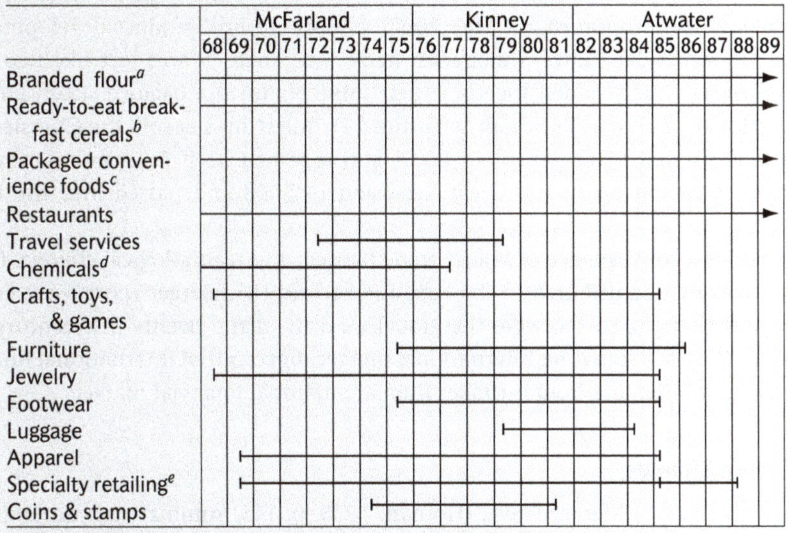

	McFarland	Kinney	Atwater
	68 69 70 71 72 73 74 75	76 77 78 79 80 81	82 83 84 85 86 87 88 89

Branded flour[a]
Ready-to-eat breakfast cereals[b]
Packaged convenience foods[c]
Restaurants
Travel services
Chemicals[d]
Crafts, toys, & games
Furniture
Jewelry
Footwear
Luggage
Apparel
Specialty retailing[e]
Coins & stamps

[a] Gold Medal since 1896.   [b] Wheaties first sold in 1924.
[c] Betty Crocker since 1921; Bisquick first sold in 1930.
[d] Begun in 1924.   [e] Three significant divestitures in 1985.

Source: Donaldson (1990, Table 2).

11.2.4 Fifth: Turn of the 20th Century

The early 1990s were a low point in U.S. merger activity, from which it rose continuously through 11 September 2001, dropped sharply, and rose just as abruptly to its previous level. The Fifth Merger Wave, like the First, will be regarded as one merger movement with two peaks. The worldwide collapse of financial markets at the end of 2008 will end the Fifth Merger Wave, although it will result in mergers in the financial sector and elsewhere.

Great expectations

Yellen (1998) highlights falling regulatory barriers, technological change, a high stock market, and globalization as factors behind the Fifth Merger Wave. Black emphasizes its the worldwide scope (2000, p. 800):

> [T]he current wave has a distinctly international flavor. Many of the signature transactions—including Daimler's acquisition of Chrysler to form DaimlerChrysler and Vodafone's acquisition of Mannesmann—were either entirely outside the United States or involved a non-U.S. party. The $ 180 billion Vodafone-Mannesmann transaction, between two non-U.S. firms, is the largest in history.

DaimlerChrysler was formed by the 1998 takeover of Chrysler by Daimler-Benz AG, a merger billed at the time as "a marriage made in heaven". The combination never lived up to the promise of savings that would justify its $36 billion price tag. The product lines of the two companies overlapped very little, meaning that there were few savings to be had by eliminating duplication. Cultural differences at the two firms scuttled plans for joint product development (The Economist, 17 May 2007): "Efforts to link product development at Chrysler and Mercedes-Benz always met with fierce resistance. 'It was just like two independent companies simply added together their numbers on the balance sheet, and not much else,' [said] an analyst at Burnham Securities." DaimlerChrysler sold the Chrysler division to Cerberus Capital Management in 2007, and renamed itself Daimler AG. Chrysler subsequently was caught up in the Great Recession of 2008 and passed into the hands of Fiat.

Globalization is a consequence of falling trade barriers and technological change. Just as the wider markets that contributed to the First and Second U.S. merger waves were created by technological changes, so too were the global markets of the twenty-first century. The dramatic unravelling of a signature international merger suggests that international financial markets are no more immune from mistakes than are national financial markets.

11.2.5 Common Themes

Looking back on the First Merger Wave, (Homan, 1935, p. 115) summarized contemporary explanations:

- antitrust law was cordial to merger, hostile to collusion;
- business experience with harsh competition during the recent depression;
- development of a financial market that "could absorb securities upon an unprecedented scale";
- imitation of the success of a few early mergers;[9] and
- the role of "promoters and financiers who stood to gain from promoters' fees and underwriting operations".

These themes have been repeated, with variations in emphasis, for later merger waves.

---

[9] Hannah (1974, p. 2) suggests that UK demand for stock was promoted by prominant early combinations and that "the spectacular success of promotions such as the Guinness and Coats flotations, of 1886 and 1890 respectively, further boosted public demand for manufacturing issues".

Antitrust (or the lack of it)

It is easy to point to a cordial antitrust regime as a factor in merger waves. U.S. experience in the First, Second, and Fourth Merger Waves suggests there is an element of truth in this, and the tough U.S. antitrust stand of the 1960s toward horizontal and vertical mergers no doubt contributed to the conglomerate nature of the Third Merger Wave. But other countries have had merger waves without a U.S.-style antitrust policy; waves in antitrust philosophy cannot be more than a partial explanation for merger waves.

Excess capacity

If markets become larger, through expansion, integration, or technological progress, the equilibrium number of firms rises, but less than proportionately to the increase in market size. As markets expand, some firms expand with them, realizing economies of scale, lowering cost—and rendering the productive capacity of some other firms excess. Mergers are a way to rationalize excess capacity. It is not so much harsh, depression-induced competition that induces mergers, but excess capacity that leads to harsh competition in high-sunk-cost industries and then to mergers. Dealing with excess capacity was a factor in the First and Second Merger Waves, and in the restructuring aspects of the Fourth Merger Wave.

Financial markets

Financial markets have their share of responsibility as well. Their performance has been a mix of efficient resource reallocation—making it possible to amass large amounts of financial capital and shift it from one investment to another—and "I'm forever blowing bubbles." When a bubble bursts, a merger wave ends.

11.3 Horizontal Mergers

Mergers may increase market power and/or permit cost savings and quality improvements. As we will see, the crux of merger policy is to maximize the efficiency gains that flow from mergers while minimizing increases in market power. Reaching this goal may require blocking some mergers entirely, and modifying others before they are allowed to go forward. Here we examine basic models of and evidence about horizontal mergers (and in so doing, lay the foundation for the discussion of merger policy in Chapter 22).

11.3.1 A Cournot Model

A first and natural approach to modelling horizontal mergers turns out to miss essential aspects of the phenomenon. It is instructive to understand why. Following Salant *et al.* (1983), consider an n-firm Cournot oligopoly with a homogeneous product, market inverse demand curve:

$$p = a - b(q_1 + q_2 + \ldots q_m + q_{m+1} + \ldots + q_n), \tag{11.1}$$

and constant marginal and average cost c per unit. In the usual way for the Cournot model, the equation of the best-response function for (say) firm 1 is:

$$2q_1 + q_2 + \ldots q_m + q_{m+1} + \ldots + q_n = \frac{a-c}{b}. \tag{11.2}$$

Equilibrium price, output per firm, and profit per firm are:

$$p = c + \frac{1}{n+1} \frac{a-c}{b} \qquad q = \frac{1}{n+1} \frac{a-c}{b} \quad \text{and} \quad \pi = b\left(\frac{1}{n+1}\frac{a-c}{b}\right)^2, \tag{11.3}$$

respectively.

Suppose firms 1 through m, for $m < n$, merge. The new firm picks outputs $q_1, q_2, \ldots,$ and q_m to maximize profit:

$$\pi(m) = \sum_{i=1}^{m} (p-c)q_i = (p-c) \sum_{i=1}^{m} q_i = (p-c)Q_m, \tag{11.4}$$

where $Q_m = q_1 + q_2 + \ldots + q_m$ is total output of the post-merger firm. The equation of the post-merger inverse demand curve can be written:

$$p = a - b(Q_m + q_{m+1} + \ldots + q_n). \tag{11.5}$$

It follows that the best-response function of the post-merger firm is:

$$2Q_m + q_{m+1} + \ldots + q_n = \frac{a-c}{b}. \tag{11.6}$$

But this is just the best-response function of a single firm in an $(n - m + 1)$-firm Cournot oligopoly. The best-response functions of the independent firms are unchanged by the merger, and the post-merger equilibrium is that of Cournot oligopoly with $n - m + 1$ equally-sized firms. Selected equilibrium characteristics of the post-merger market are shown in Table 11.2.

Firms that are outside the merger are better off because of the merger—they produce more, and (price being higher) they earn a greater profit on every unit they sell. But the firms that merge are better off only if:

$$\frac{b}{m}\left(\frac{1}{n-m+2}\frac{a-c}{b}\right)^2 > b\left(\frac{1}{n+1}\frac{a-c}{b}\right)^2 \tag{11.7}$$

or if

$$(n+1)^2 > m(n-m+2)^2. \tag{11.8}$$

This condition is quite restrictive. As shown in Table 11.3, if there are six or fewer firms, a merger must include all firms to be profitable for participating firms. If there are seven through 11 firms, at most one firm can be excluded from a merger if it is to be profitable for participating firms.

Salant *et al.* characterize their result as "puzzling" and "paradoxical". On one level, it reflects the fact that in quantity-setting oligopoly, firms' decision variables are strategic

Table 11.2 Post-merger equilibrium, Salant-Switzer-Reynolds model

Price	$c + \frac{a-c}{n-m+2}$	
	"Firms" $1, \ldots, m$	Firms $m+1, \ldots, n$
Output	$\frac{1}{m}\frac{1}{n-m+2}\frac{a-c}{b}$	$\frac{1}{n-m+2}\frac{a-c}{b}$
Profit	$\frac{b}{m}\left(\frac{1}{n-m+2}\frac{a-c}{b}\right)^2$	$b\left(\frac{1}{n-m+2}\frac{a-c}{b}\right)^2$

Table 11.3 Smallest profitable merger size, Cournot oligopoly

n	3	4	5	6	7	8	9	10	11	12
m	3	4	5	6	6	7	8	9	10	10

Note: n = number of firms in industry; m = smallest number of firms for which a merger would be privately profitable

substitutes—when a post-merger firm reduces output, it is profitable for firms outside the merger to expand outputs. In price-setting oligopoly with linear demand and product differentiation, firms' decision variables are strategic complements—when a post-merger firm raises prices, it is profitable for other firms to raise prices. In such markets, mergers are always profitable (Deneckere and Davidson, 1985).

But "merger" as it appears in the linear inverse demand, constant marginal cost Cournot model is decidedly unlike real-world merger. m firms combine and in the post-merger market produce together as much as a firm that does not participate in the merger. It is more realistic to expect that merging firms will produce more, after the merger, than firms that do not combine.

Perry and Porter (1985) model this type of merger. In their model, a firm's cost function depends on the amount of capital it owns, and capital is in fixed supply to the industry. A merger combines the capital of the constituent firms in the survivor firm. In equilibrium, the survivor firm is larger than firms not involved in the merger.

11.3.2 Empirical Evidence

Market power/efficiency tradeoff

A merger might be profitable because the survivor firm, without being more efficient than parent firms, has greater market power. Such a merger is likely to reduce consumer welfare and social welfare. Or a merger might be profitable because the survivor firm is more efficient than parent firms. Even if such a merger increases market power, cost savings create the possibility that the overall effect of the merger on market performance will be positive.

The issues raised by horizontal mergers that have market power and efficiency effects are illustrated in Figure 11.3, which follows Williamson (1968b).[10] The figure illustrates a single market for a homogeneous good. For simplicity, the initial situation is taken to be one in which price p_1 equals constant average and marginal cost AC_1. A merger takes place and results in two changes: price and output change from (p_1,Q_1) to (p_2,Q_2), and constant average cost falls from AC_1 to AC_2.

Because of the price increase, consumers suffer a deadweight welfare loss, in amount given by the area A_1. Economic profit goes from zero (i.e., a normal rate of return on investment but no more than that) to $(p_2 - AC_2)Q_2$. All of this is economic profit, and a transfer from consumers to producers. Of this transfer, the amount $(AC_1 - AC_2)Q_2$, the area A_2, is a real

---

[10] There are comments and replies in the 1968 and 1969 *American Economic Review*, and further discussion in Williamson (1977a).

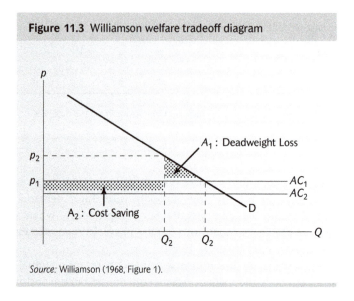

Figure 11.3 Williamson welfare tradeoff diagram

Source: Williamson (1968, Figure 1).

economy, the value of resources that are freed for use elsewhere in the economy. Less is produced after the merger, but fewer social resources are required to produce remaining output than would have been required before the merger. If the income transfer from consumers to the owners of the firm, $(p_2 - AC_1) Q_2$, is considered a wash, the net welfare impact of the merger is $A_2 - A_1$.

Deadweight welfare loss is exactly proportional to the square of the reduction in output if the demand curve is linear, approximately so if the demand curve is non-linear. The cost saving is proportional to post-innovation output. The reduction in output and the level of post-merger output both depend on the price elasticity of demand, but for a wide range of configurations, even modest cost reductions will translate into real economies that exceed deadweight welfare loss.

There are a number of qualifications that might reasonably be made to this basic model (and Williamson makes them). For one, as drawn in Figure 11.3 the post-merger firm is not maximizing profit.[11] This keeps the deadweight welfare loss down and boosts that amount of post-merger output, to which the cost reduction is applied. Here one might suppose that a post-merger monopolist would face the possibility of entry if it raised price above some threshold level.

A related point is that, in application, merger would not be to monopoly. The post-merger market would be an oligopoly, and competition from firms outside the merger would limit the profitable post-merger price increase. Further, if products are differentiated, price changes are no longer a complete guide to changes in consumer welfare, which depends on the levels of consumption of imperfectly substitutable varieties.

---

[11] That is, marginal revenue along the demand curve drawn in Figure 11.3 for output Q_2 is less than marginal cost AC_2.

Let us take it that $AC_1 - AC_2$ is the reduction in unit cost if production is efficient. If market power permits X-inefficiency, not all possible cost savings may be realized. In addition, Figure 11.3 shows static cost savings. It may be that market power slows innovation. The contrary argument has been made, and we return to the question in Chapter 14.[12] But if merger delays innovation, that translates into long-term losses that must be set against the gains shown in Figure 11.3.

Williamson's welfare tradeoff analysis, then, highlights the following questions. To what extent do mergers create or re-enforce market power? To what extent do they permit cost savings? How, if at all, do mergers impact the rate of technical progress? It is to evidence on these points that we now turn.

Market power

A merger that creates a firm with a large market share can make it possible for the firm to profitably raise price, so exercising market power, within the limit implied by the inverse of the price elasticity of demand. If the price elasticity of demand is low, price increases can be substantial.

Microfilm Barton and Sherman (1984) examine the effects of two successive mergers on the relative price of differentiated brands of microfilm. A 1976 merger increased the market share of the industry's dominant firm in the diazo microfilm market from 40 to 55 per cent, and the price of diazo microfilm products rose nearly 10 per cent, relative to the price of vesicular microfilm products. In 1979, a second merger increased the dominant firm's share of the vesicular microfilm market from 67 to 93 per cent, and the price of vesicular microfilm products rose more than a third relative to the price of diazo microfilm products.

The microfilm merger and the pharmaceutical merger described in the accompanying box are mergers of close substitutes that created near-monopolies in markets where the price elasticity of demand was low. In markets for differentiated products, the market-power consequences of a merger depend on the substitutability between brands that are merged under the control of a single firm and on the substitutability between those brands and brands outside a merger. Evidence is that even if there are a number of substitutes, product differentiation makes it possible for firms to hold price above marginal cost, and mergers increase the extent to which they can do so.

US beer Baker and Bresnahan (1988) estimate residual demand curves for Anheuser-Busch, at the time the leading US beer brewer, and two smaller firms in the same industry, Pabst and Coors. These estimated demand curves summarize substitutability relationships. Combined with data on the costs of major inputs, their estimates imply that a merger between either of the smaller firms and Anheuser-Busch would increase market power for Anheuser-Busch, without increasing market power for the other party to the merger. Similarly, a merger between the two smaller firms is not predicted to yield an increase in market power. These

---

[12] But as Williamson (1968b, footnote 10) quotes Hadley (1897, p. 383), we take the liberty of doing so here: "The tendency of monopoly to retard the introduction of industrial improvement is...a more serious thing than its tendency to allow unfair rates. This aspect of the matter has hardly received proper attention. We have been so accustomed to think of competition as a regulator of prices that we have lost sight of its equally important function as a stimulus to efficiency. Wherever competition is absent, there is a disposition to rest content with old methods, not to say slack ones. In spite of notable exceptions this is clearly the rule."

results suggest that competition from these smaller firms limits the ability of Anheuser-Busch to exercise market power.

 BOX   **Merger for Market Power**

- In 1985, the U.S. Food and Drug Administration (FDA) approved the pharmaceutical Indocin for treatment of a congenital heart defect (PDA) that affects about 30,000 premature infants per year in the U.S.

- In August 2005, Ovation Pharmaceuticals, Inc. purchased the rights to Indocin, and raised the price per vial from about $26 to about $36.

- In January 2006, Ovation purchased the rights to NeoProfen, the only pharmaceutical substitute for Indocin.

- The only alternative to pharmaceutical treatment of PDA is risky and expensive surgery.

- Entry of a pharmaceutical substitute requires FDA approval, which for a generic substitute takes on average 18 months and can take more than two years. A generic substitute for Indocin was approved in July 2008; it had not entered the market as of December 2008. The Orphan Drug Act protects NeoProfen against generic entry until 2013; it also has patent protection until 2021.

- After Ovation acquired NeoProfen, it raised the price per vial of Indocin from about $36 to about $500.

- When Ovation began marketing NeoProfen in July 2006, the price per vial was about $483.

- On 16 December 2008, the U.S. Federal Trade Commission filed a complaint in the U.S. District Court for the District of Minnesota, alleging that Ovation's acquisition of NeoProfen was a violation of the Clayton Act Section 7 prohibition of acquisitions that may substantially lessen competition or tend to create a monopoly and an unfair method of competition in violation of Section 5 of the FTC Act.

Breakfast cereal   Nevo (2000) estimates demand equations and marginal costs for 24 brands of ready-to-eat breakfast cereal, using data for 45 cities covering 1988–1992. He uses the estimates to analyse the impact of three proposed mergers, two of which took place.[13]

In 1992, General Mills proposed to acquire ready-to-eat cereals produced by Nabisco. The merger was dropped when antitrust objections were raised. Nevo estimates that if the merger had gone forward, the equilibrium price increase for Nabisco Shredded Wheat cereal would have been 7.5 per cent. A marginal cost reduction of 10.4 per cent would have been needed to keep the price of Shredded Wheat at pre-merger levels.

Nabisco's cereal line was subsequently acquired by Post Cereals.[14] Nevo's estimates imply post-merger price increases of 3.1 per cent (Shredded Wheat) and 1.5 per cent (Post Grape-Nuts) for close-substitute brands of the two lines, and that cost savings of 5 per cent would be sufficient to keep post-merger prices at the pre-merger level.

---

[13] He also analyses two entirely hypothetical mergers.

[14] At the time, part of the Kraft General Foods division of Philip Morris, Inc.

In 1997, General Mills purchased Chex cereals from Ralcorp Holdings. Nevo estimates a 12.2 per cent post-merger price increase for Chex, with a 22.1 per cent cost saving required to keep price at the pre-merger level.

Retail petrol In 1997, the Atlantic Richfield Company (ARCO) acquired control of a large chain of independent California petrol stations and switched them to carrying ARCO-brand petrol. Hastings (2004) finds that prices at competing stations rose 5 cents per gallon, on average, when an independent converted to a branded station, controlling for other factors. Mergers that reduce the number of independent competitors increase equilibrium prices (Hastings, 2004, p. 328):

> [I]ndependent competitors decrease prices through increased price competition. When they are replaced with branded competitors, in a market with consumer brand loyalty, prices competition will be softened, and equilibrium prices will increase. Prices increase more at stations whose brand is less differentiated from other types of gasoline, and prices increase less at stations whose brand is more differentiated from other types of gasoline. Therefore, the identity of the competitors, and not just the number of competitors, is an important determinant of market concentration and firm conduct in retail gasoline.

Retail fast food Thomadsen (2005) estimates equilibrium demand-cost relationships for the retail fast food market (Burger King and McDonald's franchisees), in Santa Clara County, California in July, 1999. His results imply substantial market power (Lerner index 0.3773 for the 39 Burger King outlets in his sample, 0.5779 for the 64 McDonald's outlets). He finds that common ownership of outlets raises prices,[15] that the effect is significant, and larger for outlets that are near rather than far apart. He also finds that hypothetical mergers of outlets of the leading franchise (McDonald's) raise prices more than mergers of Burger King outlets.

Soft drinks Dubé (2005) examines the Denver retail market for carbonated soft drinks using data on the purchases of 2,108 households at 58 supermarkets. He finds Lerner indices ranging from 30 per cent (Dr. Pepper) to 50 per cent or more (Pepsi, the market leader), with Coke and 7 Up around 40 per cent each. He uses the results to simulate the effects of three mergers, two of which were proposed but withdrawn (Coke and Dr. Pepper, Pepsi and 7 UP) and one hypothetical (Coke and Pepsi). The results for the Pepsi-7 Up merger (which are typical), illustrate channels through which mergers in price-setting markets with differentiated products affect market performance and consumer welfare (Dubé, 2005, p. 901):

> For the merger between Pepsi and 7 UP, cola prices did not rise by much more than 2%. However, the price of 7 UP rises between 14% and 16%. The joint profits of 7 UP and Pepsi rose by about 1.5%, mainly because increasing 7 UP product prices improved the profitability of Pepsi products. Profits also rise at both Coke and Dr. Pepper by 6% and 9%, respectively. At the same time, consumer surplus fell by almost $2 million. Overall, the merger led to roughly $1.5 million in lost surplus for the Denver market in each quarter.

---

[15] What is meant is ownership of more than one McDonald's franchise by the same firm or more than one Burger King franchise by the same firm, not the ownership of a McDonald's franchise and a Burger King franchise by the same firm.

Efficiencies

Union Pacific/Southern Pacific   The 1996 merger of the Union Pacific Railroad Company and the Southern Pacific Transportation Company illustrates the difficulty of making the kind of comparison suggested by Figure 11.3. The merger of two competing railroads required the approval of a regulatory agency,[16] and this procedure generated about as much documentary material about projected cost savings as could be hoped for. An impartial analyst took the trouble to go back, after the merger was consummated, and compare realized cost savings with those that had been predicted.[17] Yet the case that the merger generated net benefits is ambiguous at best.

The operating areas of the two companies overlapped substantially. This created the opportunity to integrate the two route systems to make a more complete network, while at the same time eliminating parallel lines, reducing workforce and scrapping duplicate administrative facilities. The sources of some of these potential savings carried with them problems for market performance: the merger reduced the number of lines connecting some cities from three to two, others from two to one.

Union Pacific projected a five-year transition period to implement the merger. During this period operating cost savings—about half savings on labour—of $2,125.6 million were expected.[18] Part of this saving ($628.1 million) is described as "general/administrative" savings. This category includes, in unknown amount, "discounts on fuel and materials, and similar savings on supply/service contracts". As Breen points out (2004, p. 307), to the extent that the railroad's suppliers enjoy cost savings because of the merger and pass those savings on to the railroad in the form of lower prices, that is a real saving of resources and properly counted as a benefit of the merger. It is equally the case that to the extent that the merger gives the railroad greater bargaining power and it is able to negotiate lower prices from its suppliers, there is no real saving of resources, but an income transfer from the suppliers to the railroad. Such an income transfer is a benefit to the railroad but not a social benefit, and should not be counted as a benefit of the merger. It seems likely that treatment of reduced input cost results in an overstatement of cost savings to be realized in the first five years after the merger, but more than that we cannot say.

Against the $2,125.6 million savings must be set transition expenses of various kinds—labour separation expenses, for example—in the amount of $1,456.9 million, yielding a net cost saving for the first five years of $668.7 million. To this amount the companies added two categories of projected benefits.

The first was revenue gains "from merger-induced increases in rail traffic", minus revenue lost to other railroads under policies designed to address competition concerns, a net revenue gain of $281.2 million.[19] This revenue is a benefit to the railroad; it is not a cost

---

[16] The Surface Transportation Board, successor of the Interstate Commerce Commission.

[17] Breen (2004), upon which this discussion is based.

[18] For annual breakdowns, see Breen (2004, Table 1). The totals presented here are not discounted. Union Pacific's benefit estimates were reduced somewhat by the Surface Transportation Board; see Breen (2004, Table 3 and the associated text).

[19] Union Pacific granted a competing line the right to use (for a fee) Union Pacific track where the merger would reduce the number of railroad lines from 2 to 1. See Breen (2004, fn. 6).

reduction.[20] The other projected benefit was cost savings to shippers using the improved facilities of the post-merger railroad, in the amount of $336.2 million. Such savings would be a benefit to shippers, if realized; the amount of this estimate was subject to criticism during regulatory proceedings. One argument was that such saving would occur in any case with general industry productivity increases.[21]

The projected benefits from the merger were, then, a mix of cost savings and revenue gains, including elements that might be transfers from suppliers to the railroad and cost savings to shippers.

After the transition period, Union Pacific projected operating cost savings of $507.8 million per year, of which $261.2 million in reduced labour cost and $138 million in reduced general/administrative expense. Union Pacific anticipated $76 million per year in net revenue gain and $90.8 million per year in cost savings to shippers. Based on these projections, it was expected that the post-merger railroad's ratio of operating expenses to operating revenue would fall from 82.9 per cent to 78.9 per cent during the transition period.[22]

The merger took place in September 1996. Serious service disruptions occurred from July 1997, related to Southern Pacific's aging infrastructure, delays in workforce integration and in installation of a computer system to manage the post-merger system. The disturbances apparently lasted at least two years.[23] The value of losses due to these service disruptions has not been quantified,[24] but should be subtracted from any gains from the merger.

Evidence on actual, as opposed to projected, savings is contradictory. Internal Union Pacific documents suggested greater realized cost savings than had been expected. Union Pacific railroad rates fell after the merger. Railroad rates had been falling generally, so Union Pacific's rate reductions might not have been tied to the merger. But that rates fell is consistent with the idea that the merger generated net savings. On the other hand, Union Pacific's operating ratio, expected to fall four percentage points, (Breen, 2004, p. 308) "rose from 79.1% in 1996 to 87.4% in 1997, and to 95.4% in 1998 before falling to 82.0% in 1999, 82.3% in 2000, and 80.7% in 2001", and this suggests rising rather than falling costs.

To be sure, the regulatory balancing of anticipated costs and anticipated benefits does not map one-to-one into the market power vs. efficiency tradeoff depicted in Figure 11.3. But the best that can be said is that it is impossible to know if the net benefits from the Union Pacific/Southern Pacific merger should have been expected to be positive before the fact, or were positive after the fact. The estimates of costs and benefits that were made going into

---

[20] The revenue increase might be fitted into the Figure 11.3 framework as a post-merger shift in the demand curve, against which would need to be set losses of the firms that would have supplied transportation services in the absence of the merger. It might be analysed in a model of merger in an oligopoly supplying a market with demand for differentiated products.

[21] See Breen (2004, fn. 14 and the associated text).

[22] In 1995, Union Pacific's operating ratio was 79.2 per cent and Southern Pacific's was 96.7 per cent (Breen, 2000, fn. 15).

[23] According to Breen (2004, p. 303, emphasis added), in a December 1998 assessment, the Surface Transportation Board "concluded that the UP/SP service situation had improved considerably *and was expected to continue to improve*" and (2004, fn. 29) in August 1999 the U.S. Department of Transportation stated "that UP rail service had returned to normal levels".

[24] White (2002b, p. 170) writes of "an extraordinary number of train crashes and crew deaths" and notes that "Cutbacks in management, crews, and equipment—which had been part of the projected cost savings from the merger—worsened the problems."

the merger were fragile at best.[25] One can make a case that the integration difficulties that led to the post-merger deterioration in service ought to have been anticipated, and the cost to consumers of the deterioration in service factored into the regulatory calculus. This did not happen, but the deterioration in service did, and makes it difficult to conclude that the realized benefits of the merger were, on balance, positive.

USAir/Piedmont   One point to be taken from the discussion of the Union Pacific/Southern Pacific merger is that in application the outcome of the market power/efficiency assessment depicted in Figure 11.3 can be genuinely ambiguous. A second is that the integration of once-independent companies can be a disruptive and costly process. Sometimes these integration costs can wreck a merger. One example, due to Kole and Lehn (2000), is from the U.S. passenger airline industry. USAir Group acquired Piedmont Aviation in November 1987, paying $1.6 billion. The two were highly profitable regional airlines, but after the airlines were integrated in August 1989 (Kole and Lehn, 2000, p. 240) "USAir's costs rose, productivity and customer service deteriorated, and in the year following August 1989, USAir's stock price fell from $54 to $21.375. Within five years of the completion of the Piedmont merger, USAir had destroyed more than $2.5 billion of shareholder value." The post-merger airline's costs were out of control, because it upgraded Piedmont employees, and the employees of a smaller California airline it acquired around the same time, to the higher pay levels of the acquiring firm. The result was a substantial increase in cost (Table 11.4) that proved disastrous for the merger.[26]

Restructuring, productivity, and innovation   Mergers may facilitate industrial restructuring that increases productivity.[27] In general, such restructuring may occur as firms match themselves with assets that are best suited for their organizational capabilities (Lichtenberg and Siegel, 1987). In declining industries, merger is a way to combine the most-efficient assets of several firms to form the least-cost-possible survivor in a situation where capacity must be reduced to match shrinking demand.[28]

Mergers and R&D output   Dutz (1989) gives examples of mergers in the U.S. steel and railroad industries, among others, that seem to involve the matching of complementary assets.[29] McGuckin and Nguyen (1995) analyse productivity changes for U.S. food manu-

---

[25] See Breen (2004) for a discussion of merger-related benefits that were not (and perhaps could not be) quantified.

[26] Kole and Lehn offer suggestive evidence that the standardization of work rules on the USAir model led to dissatisfaction and lowered productivity of the employees of the acquired airlines.

[27] Weiss (1965) examines the impact of mergers on changes in concentration of six U.S. industries from the 1930s to the 1950s. He finds that all capacity acquisitions in cars and steel, and more than half the capacity acquisitions in the other industries, were below minimum efficient scale. This is consistent with the "merger as a means of rationalization" hypothesis.

[28] We have seen that real-world mergers often fail to rationalize production. The difference, if there be one, between mergers in general circumstances and mergers in declining industries is that inefficient production techniques can survive for a long time in imperfectly competitive industries for which demand is stable or growing. If demand is declining, a firm that is the product of a merger will be obliged to retire some capacity; the question is what capacity it will be most profitable to retire. See Ghemawat and Nalebuff (1990), Dierickx *et al.* (1991) for models of changes industries in the structure of declining industries.

[29] He also emphasizes that simply because a merger occurs in a declining industry does not mean the motive for or effect of the merger is to obtain matching efficiencies. Firms may merge to support the exercise of market power on the way down (Dutz, 1989, p. 30, citation omitted) "In the decline of the U.K. jute industry, especially rapid

Table 11.4 Pre- and post-merger cost indicators, USAir

Year	Cost per Air Seat Mile (cents)	Personnel Cost (per cent of operating revenue)
1984	9.1	33
1985	9.0	32
1986	8.8	33
1989	10.5	36
1990	10.8	40
1991	10.8	39
1992	10.8	39
1993	11.0	40
1994	11.0	41
1995	11.4	30

Source: Kole and Lehn (2000, Table 5.6).

facturing plants that changed ownership during the years 1977–1982 (the first half of the Fourth Merger Wave). Their results are that high-productivity plants were most likely to change hands, and that meant increased productivity five to nine years later. They conclude (1995, p. 274) that "ownership transfers are associated with the purchase and integration of good properties into new firms", with high-productivity plants that are sold being either kept or resold and low-productivity plants being shut down.

Mergers and R&D input   Productivity change is a measure of the output of the R&D process. Hall (1990) examines the impact of the corporate restructuring of the Fourth Merger Wave on U.S. manufacturing firms' spending on research and development. She finds a reduction in R&D by firms involved in acquisitions, but qualifies this with two other findings. First, the decline in R&D spending is related more to the taking on of debt than to being involved in a merger as such. Second, and especially toward the end of the period, mergers and takeovers were more common in low-tech than in high-tech industries; the decline in R&D was less important in the most R&D intensive manufacturing sectors.

As Hall notes (1990, p. 87), there are two possible explanations for a negative debt R&D relationship. The first is a corporate governance story—the duty to meet the fixed interest

during the period 1967–77, mergers were a characteristic of the industry. However, the process of takeover of small firms and their subsequent closure is felt to have been motivated exclusively by a desire to keep prices from falling faster than they otherwise would have."

payments that come with debt disciplines managers and keeps them from making R&D investments with stockholders' money that would be better spent in other ways. In this view, a negative debt-R&D relationship is an indication of good performance. The second explanation is that financial capital markets are imperfect, so not all objectively desirable R&D projects are funded. Then when debt obliges managers to shift funds from R&D projects to interest payments, some privately profitable R&D projects are choked off. Hall (1999, p. 5) writes that "one can interpret the evidence from this period as saying that leveraging occurred where R&D was unprofitable, rather than leveraging taking place and 'causing' R&D cuts".

R&D rationalization   Cassiman *et al.* (2005) suggest that the way mergers affect R&D depends on the nature of the R&D and on the product-market activities of the merging firms. They study 31 mergers that took place after 1990 involving mostly EU firms. They expect that if a merger combines firms doing research in similar technological areas, the post-merger firm will be able to eliminate duplicate inputs and realize economies of scale in R&D. Since firms supplying related product markets are likely to have similar innovation goals, the economies of scale effect should be stronger for merging firms that were product-market competitors. If a merger combines firms doing research in different technological areas, economies of scope from the combination of complementary R&D assets might be possible.

   BOX   **Mergers and Innovation**

IBM is the leading supplier of mainframe computers and the only supplier of new mainframes, which are widely used in business, government, and industry. Users are effectively locked in to IBM-compatible operating systems by existing software written to use IBM mainframe application programming interfaces.

In 2005, the small California firm Platform Solutions, Inc. (PSI) developed software that promised to emulate IBM mainframes on standard servers with an eight-fold increase in speed over existing emulation software.

In 2006, IBM sued Platform Solutions for patent infringement and violation of intellectual property licence agreements. Platform Solutions countersued, denying the violations and alleging unfair competition by IBM. Platform Solutions also complained to the European Commission that IBM had abused its dominant position in violation of the EC Treaty.

On 2 July 2008, IBM announced that it had purchased Platform Solutions, ending private litigation. An IBM press release included the statement that:

> PSI's technologies and skills, along with its intellectual capital, will become part of IBM's long-term mainframe product engineering cycles and part of IBM's future product plans.

IBM "promptly terminated" Platform Solutions' emulation software (Vance, 2009).

In their sample, merging firms that had carried out R&D in similar technological areas reduced R&D after the merger (2005, p. 197): "when merged firms are technologically substitutive, key employees tend to leave more often, the R&D portfolio becomes more focused, the R&D horizon becomes shorter and internal funds available to R&D decrease." As expected, these effects are stronger if the firms were product-market competitors before the merger. In contrast, if a merger combined firms that had done complementary research, R&D spending increased and became more efficient.

In principle, it might be privately and socially optimal for merging firms to shut down largely duplicative R&D operations, although there is less to this argument than might first appear.[30] But for the Cassiman *et al.* sample, merger did not, in practice, allow firms doing substitute R&D to realize scale economies. Rival firms, they conclude (2005, p. 197) "reap little technology gains from [mergers and acquisitions]".

11.4 The Market for Corporate Control

Behind the idea of a "market for corporate control" is the belief that financial markets efficiently distill all available information about firm's investments, so that a firm's stock market value is the best possible estimate of the present discounted value of a firm's income stream. Then if the management of one firm believes it can run a second firm (the target) more effectively than the incumbent management, it can launch a takeover bid. There are some transaction costs to mounting a takeover bid, and within the limits of such costs, incumbent managements will have leeway to pursue their own objectives rather than maximize firm value.[31] But if an incumbent management is "too managerial", pursuing growth for its own sake, empire building, or the quiet life, it will expose itself to takeover attempts, the merits of which will be recognized by efficient financial markets. The value of the target firm will rise, to the benefit of the firm's owners.[32]

The phrase "financial market efficiency" gives a disarmingly precise impression of the accuracy with which financial markets assess firm value. Scherer (2002) quotes Fischer Black's (1986, p. 533, footnote omitted) characterization:

> [W]e might define an efficient market as one in which price is within a factor of 2 of value, i.e. the price is more than half of value or less than twice value. The factor of 2 is arbitrary, of course. Intuitively, though, it seems reasonable to me, in the light of sources of uncertainty about value and the strength of the forces tending to cause price to return to value. By this definition, I think almost all markets are efficient almost all of the time. 'Almost all' means at least 90%.

If the value efficient financial markets place on a firm ranges from one-half to twice its expected value, that opens up the possibility that takeovers might be based on information differences that have nothing to do with efficiency. The managers of a firm mounting a takeover attempt might understand that shares of the firm they manage are momentarily overvalued, allowing them to pay for control of another firm with assets that will go down in value. The managers of a firm mounting a takeover attempt might understand that shares

---

[30] In practice, R&D activities that seek the same goal will try different paths, and in a world of uncertainty, it cannot be known which of several approaches is mostly likely to succeed. See Section 15.5.3.

[31] Smiley (1976) estimates that a firm's market value can fall 13 per cent below the maximum value, on average, without provoking takeover attempts.

[32] If the market for corporate control explanation is to apply, the less efficient management of the acquired firm must be replaced by a more efficient management team. During the Third Merger Wave, this seemed often not to happen (Mueller, 1969, p. 659).

of the target firm are momentarily undervalued, allowing them to buy control of assets that will go up in value.[33]

Financial economists have analysed the effects of mergers on performance by examining the impact of a merger on the stock market value of the merging firms during a narrowly defined "event window" around the time the merger becomes public knowledge.[34] Such studies show that (Caves, 1989, p. 153):

> Acquisitions always entail a large gain for the target firm's shareholders ... The proportional gain if anything has been rising over time and amounts to a premium of 30 percent for the change in corporate control via tender offer or takeover, 20 percent via merger. ... The average return to the bidding firm's shareholders is less clear. Some studies have found small but statistically significant gains, others small losses. It seems safe to conclude that the bidder's shareholders approximately break even. Indeed, they have been doing worse and worse over time.

The finance literature conclusion has been that if the acquired firm's shareholders gain substantially from a merger while the acquiring firm's shareholders more or less break even, the net effect of the merger on a shareholders' wealth is positive (Caves, 1989, p. 153; Scherer, 2006, p. 331).[35]

Two types of evidence raise doubts about this conclusion. The first comes from studies that examine stock-market returns over a longer post-merger period. These find overwhelmingly (Scherer, 2002, p. 9) "that, although the acquiring company's common stock prices experience on average zero cumulative abnormal change in short time 'windows' around merger announcements, they tend, relative to market movements generally, to decline by impressive and statistically significant magnitudes in the one to three years that follow substantial merger activity."[36]

The results of direct studies of the effects of mergers on sales, on profit, and on efficiency also make it difficult to conclude that mergers improve market performance. Gugler *et al.* (2003) examine the impact of mergers around the world between 1981 and 1998 on profit and sales. Their premise is straightforward (2003, p. 643) "Mergers that increase the efficiency of the merging firms should increase both their profits and their sales. Mergers that increase market power should increase profits and reduce sales. A merger which reduces efficiency should reduce both profitability and sales." By these standards, they find that the average profitable merger increased market power and the average unprofitable merger reduced efficiency (roughly 57 per cent of the mergers in their sample were profitable; see their Table 3A). The average profitable merger by small firms, however, increased efficiency. Vertical mergers did not decrease efficiency, and mergers in the chemical and insurance sectors increased market power. The results are broadly similar for the United States, the United Kingdom, and continental Europe.

---

[33] Malkiel (2007, Chapter 3) gives many case studies that seem best explained by differential awareness of market misvaluations.

[34] For discussion of the event study methodology, see Magenheim and Mueller (1988).

[35] One might then question whether acquiring firms are, on average, being managed in *their* shareholders' interest.

[36] Among the conclusions that Rau and Vermaelen (1998) draw from their study of shareholder returns in 3169 mergers and 348 tender offers that took place between January 1980 and December 1991 is that it (p. 252) "adds to a growing body of evidence that short-term measurements of abnormal performance do not capture the full effects of the market reaction to an event, a common assumption in many event studies".

As Mueller (2003, p. 195) observes, in the broad category of changes of corporate owner-ship, it is hostile takeovers that most resemble the theoretical efficiency-enhancing market for corporate control. But hostile takeovers are a small portion of total mergers.[37] As Mueller concludes, "Even if one feels confident that tender offers generate wealth by replacing bad managers, one is left with a lot of other mergers to account for both with respect to their effects on wealth and their underlying motivation."

SUMMARY

Mergers as a class seem often motivated by pursuit of managerial goals that take advantage of special knowledge, do not maximize shareholder wealth, and are susceptible to waves of financial euphoria. Evidence that the market for corporate control works to ensure that management acts in shareholders' interests is not robust. On balance, evidence about the causes and effects of mergers justifies scepticism about their general effectiveness as a resource allocation mechanism.

STUDY POINTS

- Merger waves (Section 11.2)
  - Conglomerate mergers (Section 11.2.3)
  - Generalizations (Section 11.2.5)
- Horizontal mergers (Section 11.3)
  - Cournot model (Section 11.3.1)
  - Market power, efficiency (Section 11.3.2)
  - Innovation (Section 11.3.2)
- Market for corporate control (Section 11.4)

FURTHER READING

I have drawn on Martin (2008) for some of the discussion in Section 11.2. For models of merger in markets where the assets a firm owns determine its costs, and a post-merger firm inherits the assets of its prede-cessors, see Farrell and Shapiro (1990), McAfee and Williams (1992). Hermalin and Katz (2004) model the impact of diversification on the ability to evaluate managerial performance.

---

[37] On the order of 10 per cent for the sample of Rau and Vermaelen (1998).

INTERFIRM CONTRACTS (12)

I have a contract but it's not a commitment in the ordinary sense. It's our ongoing conversation.

Diane Sawyer

12.1 Introduction

Outside the retail sector, most transactions of most firms are with other firms, not with final consumers. Most firms in most markets are involved in (Sraffa, 1960) "the production of commodities by means of commodities"—they buy raw materials, refined and processed goods, and components from other firms, further refine and process them, and sell them to other firms; they outsource or collaborate in the "development" part of "research and development". Firms are embedded in (Richardson, 1972, p. 883) a "dense network of co-operation and affiliation", and transactions in this network of interfirm organization are governed by a wide range of contractual arrangements, from the anonymous, spot-market, arm's-length transaction of the organized currency or commodity market to the 20-year contract for supply of coal to an electric power plant to full vertical integration. Rather than "either market or firm", we confront varying degrees of contractual integration.

The term "contract" conjures up a vision of legal documents that specify all aspects of an arrangement in excruciating detail. This is too narrow a concept for our purpose, which is to understand the kinds of institutional frameworks that organize economic activity. "Contracts" in this sense may be unwritten. They may be extralegal, unenforceable in a court of law, and understood to be extralegal by all involved, yet useful as a record of a common understanding. "Governance", (Palay, 1984, p. 265) "a shorthand expression for the institutional framework in which contracts are initiated, negotiated, monitored, adapted, enforced, and terminated" better describes our topic.

12.2 Contracts: Determinants and Effects

Economic explanations of the determinants of contractual arrangements fall into two broad groups. The first views contracts as a way of accommodating transaction costs through what amounts to partial integration. Very much in the spirit of the transaction cost theory of the firm, this approach emphasizes efficiency aspects of contractual arrangements. The second approach builds on principal-agent analysis, and emphasizes contracts as governance structures that establish necessarily imperfect incentives for those involved to pursue contractual objectives.

12.2.1 Transaction Costs

Williamson (1985) classifies transactions according to the frequency (occasional or recurrent) with which the buyer comes to market and the specificity of investments (nonspecific, intermediate, and highly specific) required of the supplier from which the purchase is made. Following Macneil (1978), he distinguishes between classical, neoclassical, and relational contracts.

Classical contracts

Classical contracts fully specify the details of a stand-alone exchange, with (Williamson, 1985, p. 69) "emphasis ... on legal rules, formal documents, and self-liquidating transactions". This is "contract" in the traditional sense, and is the legal equivalent of the economic model of exchange in a market with complete and perfect information by rational buyers and sellers with unlimited calculating ability. Classical contracting is the efficient governance mechanism, and the market the efficient institutional framework, for occasional transactions and for recurrent transactions that do not require transaction-specific investments.

Neoclassical contracts

For transactions that are not stand-alone events, the reality of imperfect information and limited calculating ability intrudes. This is the neoclassical contract, in which (Macneil, 1978, p. 873, footnote omitted) "specific planning in contractual relations governs in spite of changes in circumstances making such planning undesirable to one of the parties". If transactions are occasional and involve moderate or large investment in transaction-specific assets, buyer and seller may agree to involve a third party who resolves disputes and deals with uncertainty as it arises. Macneil's examples (1978, pp. 866–867) of what Williamson calls trilateral (three-party) governance are of an architect to whom client and construction company delegate the right to decide issues that arise in the course of erecting a building, and contracts that provide for compulsory arbitration if unforeseen contingencies are not resolved by mutual agreement.

Relational contracts

For recurrent transactions that require the supplier to make moderate or large transaction-specific investments, the fundamental transformation and possibility of contractual failure due to potential holdup enter the scene (Goldberg, 1980, p. 339):

> First, people are not omniscient; their information is imperfect and improvable only at a cost.
> Second, not all people are saints all of the time; as the relationship unfolds there will be

opportunities for one party to take advantage of the other's vulnerability, to engage in strategic behavior, or to follow his own interests at the expense of the other party. The actors will, on occasion, behave opportunistically. Third, the parties cannot necessarily rely on outsiders to enforce the agreement cheaply and accurately.

This is the world of relational contracting, which Baker *et al.* (2002, p. 40) characterize in terms of flexibility in dealing with unforeseen circumstances:

> Relational contracts within and between firms help circumvent difficulties in formal contracting (i.e., contracting enforced by a third party, such as a court). . . . A relational contract . . . allows the parties to utilize their detailed knowledge of their specific situation and to adapt to new information as it becomes available. For the same reasons, however, relational contracts cannot be enforced by a third party and so must be self-enforcing: the value of the future relationship must be sufficiently large that neither party wishes to renege.

A relational contract is self-enforcing, but involves a deeper commitment (Macneil (1978, p. 901): "Somewhere along the line of increasing duration and complexity . . . the contractual relation escapes the bounds of the neoclassical system. . . . the substantive relation of change to the status quo has now altered from what happens in some kind of a market external to the contract to what can be achieved through the political and social processes of the relation, internal and external. This includes internal and external dispute-resolution structures." Nineteenth-century cartels seem clearly to have been relationship contracts in this sense.

Integration

Relational traders may maintain independence (bilateral governance) and make investments to support ongoing exchange. If the need to sink transaction-specific investments exposes the supplier to holdup, contractual failure may be avoided if the buyer makes transaction-specific sunk investments as well. If both parties understand that each would lose sunk investments should the exchange relationship go up in smoke, each has effectively committed not to hold up the other and exchange will work. In the extreme, if two-sided sunk investments are infeasible or insufficient, then for transactions that require large transaction-specific sunk investments, the efficient (unified) governance mechanism will be integration, bringing the transaction inside the firm (Section 10.5.3).

Quasi-vertical integration

The world car industry, with a rich and varying web of interfirm contracts linking component suppliers and vehicle assemblers, has been a proving ground for transaction-cost theories of interfirm contract. Monteverde and Teece (1983) focus on a particular institutional feature of the U.S. car industry, the common practice that a car assembler own specialized tools and fabricating equipment that are located and utilized in a supplier's premises. This kind of equipment is highly transaction-specific, designed to produce components suited for models of one car company. Absent some institutional arrangement, a component producer that made a sunk investment in such specialized equipment would expose itself to the possibility of holdup. "Quasi-vertical integration" (assembler ownership of dedicated tools used in the supplier's shop), hypothesize Monteverde and Teece, relieves the supplier of the threat of holdup and so facilitates ongoing exchange. For a sample of car components, they find that quasi-vertical integration is more likely, the greater the investment in transaction-specific equipment required to produce a component.

It should be understood that for exchange relations of this kind, quasi-vertical integration does not eliminate the possibility of holdup. Rather, quasi-vertical integration shifts the possibility of holdup from the component supplier to the car assembler (Monteverde and Teece, 1983, footnote 13, emphasis added):

> [W]e discovered through interviews that there exists some ambiguity and dispute between suppliers and assemblers concerning the extent of ownership rights conveyed by assembler outlay to cover tooling costs. Suppliers insist that tooling is technically owned by them even when paid for by assemblers. On the other hand, assemblers insist that tooling payment conveys to them the right, at minimum, to transfer tooling when the original production agreement cannot be met (the prominent example being when the supplier is struck by its union). Nevertheless, it should be noted that, as far as the supplier is concerned, up-front payment for tooling is all that is required to alleviate the threat of quasi-rent appropriation by the assembler. *However, it is doubtful that an assembler—in order to allay supplier fears of appropriation—would make such an up-front payment if it conveyed no ownership rights, for, in so doing, he would put himself in a position of being subject to supplier opportunism.*

Reputational factors are one reason why such "reverse holdup" seems not to occur (Helper, 1991, fn. 77):

> ... I interviewed in October 1984 a supplier who had GM-owned tooling at his plant that would take nine months and cost $4-5 million to move to another supplier. When asked why he did not try to raise his price at contract renegotiation time, he said, "Because our reputation would be shot to hell. We might get away with it once, but nobody in the business would ever deal with us again; they'd say, 'You're nothing but a bunch of dishonest crooks'."

Relational cycles

Symbiosis   Helper (1991) documents extended cycles in the nature of U.S. car industry supplier-assembler relationships. In the early years of the U.S. car industry, the years of turbulent market structure (Section 9.4.1), suppliers were often better-established firms than assemblers. Suppliers provided car assemblers with financial support and made important contributions to technological progress. Supplier-assembler "contracts" were relational.

Separation   With the consolidation of car assembly in a small-numbers oligopoly, however, came the deliberate reengineering of the structure of supplying industries (Helper, 1991, pp. 806–807, footnote omitted):

> The automakers made huge investments in engineering and management staffs whose work simplified the task of being an auto supplier, thereby reducing the barriers to entry into supplier industries. This task simplification took two main forms: 1) automaker-provided blueprints, obviating the need for design capability for firms in the simple exit mode; and 2) automaker coordination of subassembly, in which each supplier provided only a very small piece of the automobile, so that each firm had to procure, manage inventory for, and assemble only a few parts.

Supplier-assembler contracts were transformed from a long-term, symbiotic relationship to (Helper, 1991, p. 781) "short-term contracts (usually one-year), arms'-length relationships, and many (usually six to eight) suppliers per part". By making supplying industries more competitive, assemblers obtained inputs at close to the lowest feasible prices, keeping as much as possible of the economic profit earned in the final goods market for themselves.

The shift from relational to classical contracting also ended suppliers' contributions to technological progress and contributed to the gradual deterioration in the perceived quality of U.S. car (Mannering and Winston, 1991).

Back again   In the last quarter of the twentieth century, U.S. car manufacturers came under increasing challenge from imports and transplants—foreign-owned car factories located within the United States. Supplier-assembler contracts moved from the classical toward the relational mode; from the 1980s (Helper, 1991, p. 782):

> Only a few suppliers provide each type of part, and information is interchanged extensively between buyer and supplier. Contracts with outside suppliers are increasing in length (three- to five-year contracts are now common), and the automakers are reducing their commitment to their own components divisions, ending such practices as guaranteeing them business and in some cases divesting them completely.

One conclusion that Helper draws from this analysis is that history matters. The choices made by leading U.S. car firms in the 1920s and 1930s constrained the choices open to them in the 1980s (and, as the fate of indigenous U.S. car manufacturers in the Great Recession of 2009 suggests, after that).

Presumptive efficiency   This aspect of the history of the U.S. car industry may suggest another lesson. It has been a rebuttable presumption of the transaction cost approach to the organization of economic activity that institutional arrangements should be taken to be efficiency-enhancing, unless the contrary can be shown.[1] It may often be the case that privately designed institutional arrangements are, on balance, efficiency-enhancing. But the *presumption* that firm and market structures are efficiency-enhancing sits oddly with the usual economic assumption, which is that economic agents seek to maximize their own pay-offs, and that if the choices they make turn out to be efficient from a social point of view, it is because of constraints imposed by the marketplace.[2] The course of twentieth century U.S. car manufacturer-supplier relations suggests that privately profitable institutional arrangements need not be devoid of strategic purpose and need not be efficient from a social point of view.

Japan's car industry

Miwa and Ramseyer (2000) find little evidence that relationship-specific investments explain subcontracting contracts in the Japanese car industry. Small suppliers (2000, p. 2652) "invest little in human capital at all", much less in relationship-specific human capital. Similarly, they have low levels of investment in physical assets, relationship-specific or otherwise. They sell to firms in different industries.

If a car assembler were to invest in its suppliers, that might provide a way to support exchange outside the context of a classic contract. But Miwa and Ramseyer report low levels such ownership shares (2000, p. 2662): "We have equity ownership data on 462 suppliers (162 listed firms and 300 unlisted). In 57% of the suppliers (262 firms) the lead car assembler

---

[1] Williamson (1979a, p. 956 and Section I. C.; 1981, p. 1540; 1985, p. 28; 1983b, p. 127). But see Williamson, (1979a, fn. 5, emphasis added) "*Strategic purposes aside*, the more general purpose of economic organization is to devise arrangements that economize on the sum of production and transaction costs." Williamson (1979, p. 960) is sceptical that organizational arrangements might have strategic purpose or effect ("anticompetitive effects can appear only if rather special structural conditions exist") but it may also be that his assertion of an efficiency presumption was itself strategic ("An efficiency presumption is needed to remedy the distortions that earlier traditions have introduced into the [antitrust] enforcement process").

[2] This is no more than Adam Smith's invisible hand. See also Boyer and Jacquemin (1985).

buyer owns no equity. In an additional 15% (sixty-eight firms), it owns under 10%. In only a quarter of the suppliers does it have at least a 10% interest, and in only 5% does it own a majority interest." They similarly find that suppliers diversify their sales (2000, p. 2662): "We have sales data on 249 suppliers (firms with 67 to 11,574 employees; mean employees of 1,260). In only 127 of these firms (51%) did the lead assembler buyer buy 50% or more of the supplier's output. In only seventy-four (30%) did it buy 70% or more."

Miwa and Ramseyer caution against relying too much on the need to avoid holdup as an explanation for interfirm relationships (2000, p. 2667):

> Through this, we do not purport to disprove [relationship-specific investment] theory as theory. After all, the theory predicts that firms will create distinctive governance mechanisms when [relationship-specific investments] are large and contractual solutions infeasible. If production technology is standard and contracting straightforward, they will solve any problems by contract. And in the end, that is pretty much what we show in Japan. Our claim is instead more modest: that perhaps [relationship-specific investment] theory explains a narrower band of phenomena than we have thought.

12.2.2 Monitoring and Incentives

The principal-agent approach to vertical contracting emphasizes the tradeoff between agent risk-bearing and the provision of incentives when performance depends on both the agent's effort, which is imperfectly observable, and on random fluctuations in market conditions. It has been the analytical framework for empirical studies of contract types, in particular in retail petrol distribution.

In that context, full integration of refining, wholesale and retail distribution (a company-owned outlet) makes the station operator an employee. Vertical integration has the advantage for the company of eliminating double marginalization and the advantage for the station operator of eliminating risk due to business fluctuations—as an employee, the station operator receives a salary. Vertical integration has the disadvantage, for the company, of providing weak incentives for the station operator to maximize effort. Not all operator effort can be monitored; making some or all of the station operator's income dependent on station performance creates an incentive for the station operator, the agent, to act in the interests of the oil refiner, the principal. At the opposite extreme from full integration, complete vertical separation—a dealer-operated station—provides the maximum incentive for dealer effort, obliges the dealer to bear all risk of income fluctuations, and limits refiner income to profit on wholesale sales of refined petrol.

Between full integration and complete separation lie intermediate degrees of vertical connectedness. An oil refinery may retain ownership of a retail station and its petrol (and so the right to set the retail price), but delegate operation of the station to a commissioned agent. The commissioned agent receives a small fixed payment and a payment per unit of petrol sold, and owns and manages non-petrol operations, such as a car wash, a repair service, or a convenience store. In contrast to commissioned agents, lessee-dealers buy petrol at wholesale, set the retail price, and rent the station from the refiner. Like commissioned agents, lessee-dealers operate associated services and bear the risk of income fluctuations from those operations.[3]

---

[3] Slade (1996, 1998) gives clear accounts of types of retail petrol contracts. The commissioned agent form was found to constitute resale price maintenance, until 2007 a *per se* violation of U.S. antitrust law, and does not appear in the United States (Slade, 1996, p. 476).

Slade (1996) uses data from the Fall of 1991 to examine factors affecting distribution contract type for petrol stations in Vancouver, British Columbia. Her particular interest is the impact of ancillary station activities on the risk-incentive tradeoff highlighted by the principal-agent model. Her expectation is that petrol sales and revenue from a convenience store will be complementary, since high petrol sales are likely to go with high convenience store sales. This is less likely to be the case with repair services. If a petrol station is combined with a convenience store, the income a commissioned agent or lessee-dealer receives from the convenience store should motivate effort on the petrol side of the operation. Hence (Slade, 1996, p. 483) "For stations that are operated under contract, gasoline-sales incentives should be higher powered if the second activity is a repair shop and not a convenience store. This is true because gasoline and convenience-store sales are more complementary. Moreover, when one contrasts single and multiple-task stations, it is likely that incentives for selling gasoline will be higher if the second activity is a service bay but not if it is a convenience store. All of these predictions are confirmed by the data."

12.2.3 Vertical Separation

Slade (1998) tests the theory that despite the double marginalization issue, upstream suppliers (in this context, oil refiners) may find it profitable to delegate price-setting authority to the retail level in price-setting markets, given that in such markets, prices are strategic complements. If an independent retail outlet raises its price, the profit-maximizing reaction of nearby outlets is to raise their own price. If the price elasticity of demand at a station is low, and rivals' best response is a large increase in their price, profit at the retail level may increase. By appropriately adjusting the fixed component (rent) of a two-part tariff, the refiner can capture the lion's share of such a profit increase. Slade finds that stations with demand characteristics that make delegation of the price-setting decision profitable are more likely to be run by lessee-dealers or independent owners, less likely to be vertically integrated or run by commissioned agents.[4]

12.3 Vertical Contracts

A central tenet of the Second Chicago School was that horizontal and vertical contracts could not exclude efficient competitors, that applications of antitrust provisions to interfirm contracts on the ground that they were exclusionary were mistaken, of necessity worsened market performance. That horizontal contracts (such as tying or bundling) could not be exclusionary followed from the "no leverage of market power" doctrine. Leaving aside the possibility of raising rivals' costs (Director and Levi, 1956, p. 289, p. 293), a firm with the ability to control price in one market could profit fully from that ability in the market where the power originated. Such a firm could "buy" exclusionary restrictions in other markets, but only at the cost of giving up some of the economic profit it would otherwise enjoy in its home market, in the end reducing its overall profit.

---

[4] See also Slade (1988b, p. 584), who reports that retail beer prices were higher in UK public houses that were owned by a brewer rather than by a publican.

That vertical contracts and vertical integration could not be exclusionary followed from the "one monopoly profit" doctrine. Starting from good approximation assumption (most industries, most of the time, can be treated as if they are perfectly competitive), the Chicago School conclusion was that a firm with market power at some stage in the production process between raw materials and sale of final goods could fully profit from that power by setting a profit-maximizing price in its vertical market segment. Vertical contracts involving exclusive dealing, exclusive territories, resale price maintenance, and the like *could not* be exclusionary. Antitrust prohibitions of such practices were, to paraphrase Bork (1954) "the legal application of an economic misconception".

We have seen (Section 10.5.3) that for an upstream monopolist distributing its product through an imperfectly competitive downstream industry, vertical integration is one way to *make it possible* to fully exploit market power. Much recent economic analysis of vertical contracts suggests that vertical contracts, which may serve efficiency purposes, may also exclude equally or more efficient potential entrants. This does not mean that such practices are everywhere and always exclusionary. It does mean that the Second Chicago School position that they are nowhere and never exclusionary is wrong.

 BOX   Vertical Exclusion in Related Horizontal Markets

In the 1930s United States, carburetors were sold in two markets: as original equipment to car manufacturers and in the aftermarket as replacement equipment for privately owned vehicles. Manufacturers supplied the aftermarket mainly though some 7000 service stations that specialized in the distribution of carburetors. Such a service station would typically stock and service all types of carburetors installed as original equipment. The original equipment market and the aftermarket were linked in that car manufacturers expected full aftermarket service to be available for carburetors used as standard equipment on new vehicles.

Thus to supply the original equipment market, an entrant would need to arrange distribution of its carburetors in the aftermarket. Since original equipment carburetors on new vehicles required little service or replacement, there would be little aftermarket business for two or three years after entry into the original equipment market.

Carter Carburetor Corporation's carburetors were standard equipment on more than half the new cars and trucks sold in the United States in 1934–1936, and more than 60 per cent of those sold in 1937. It supplied most service stations specialized in carburetors, in particular some 1,000 "official contract" stations to which it offered advantageous discounts from list price and from which it expected adherence to a resale price maintenance program.

The Chandler-Groves Company entered the original equipment market in 1935. In 1937, Carter adopted the policy that a distributor who handled any line of carburetors that entered the market after June, 1934 would no longer receive a preferential discount and would lose official contract status, if it had had it in the past. Service stations were thus faced with the choice of continuing to service Carter carburetors, more than half of the aftermarket, or to drop Carter carburetors and carry Chandler-Groves carburetors, which would not generate a significant amount of business for two to three years. Carter vigorously enforced its policy, and many service stations dropped Chandler-Groves carburetors. »

>> The Federal Trade Commission condemned Carter's policy as a violation of Section 3 of the Clayton Act, which prohibits contracts that preclude a distributor from carrying competing products "where the effect …may be to substantially lessen competition or tend to create a monopoly in any line of commerce". The FTC decision was confirmed as follows by the Eighth Circuit Court of Appeals (112 F. 2d 722 at 733):

> [P]ractices of a dominant carburetor manufacturer which are designed to and do prevent a new manufacturer from obtaining a foothold in the service field will handicap the new manufacturer in selling his carburetors for original equipment and may prevent him from marketing a superior product at an equal or lower price. [Carter's] restraint upon competition works in a vicious circle, since service sales on any carburetor normally depend upon the number of automobiles equipped with that carburetor, and loss of service sales and distribution by the carburetor manufacturer in turn affects his ability to meet price competition and service requirements in offering his product for original equipment.

Source: Carter Carburetor Corp. *v.* FTC 112 F. 2d 722 (1940).

12.3.1 Exclusive Territories

Exclusive territories, like vertical integration, are a strategy an upstream firm can use to deal with the commitment problem that would otherwise prevent it from extracting full monopoly profit while selling through downstream distributors. By legally binding itself that it will not supply a downstream firm's rivals, an upstream supplier assures the downstream firm that the market price will allow it to earn a normal rate of return on investment. Given this assurance, the downstream firm will be willing to pay a wholesale price that allows the upstream firm to take the full monopoly profit out of the market.

Alternatively, the upstream firm could supply several downstream firms, but use a retail price maintenance scheme, specifying the retail price to be paid by the final consumer. For such a scheme to be effective, it would have to be possible for the downstream dealers to return unsold units to the upstream firm. The upstream firm could also retain ownership of the product itself, so that downstream firms would act as its agents. In this case, principal-agent considerations come into play.

12.3.2 Exclusive Dealing

Rasmussen *et al.* (1991) and Segal and Whinston (2000) model exclusionary exclusive dealing contracts in a market where an entrant must reach a certain minimum efficient scale to be profitable. If an incumbent firm can sign exclusive dealing contracts that cover a large enough portion of demand, it can make it impossible for entrants to attain minimum efficient scale and exclude potential entrants with a command of the technology equal to its own. Such behaviour need not occur in equilibrium. It may, if buyers cannot coordinate their actions and if individual buyers believe others will sign. Alternatively, if the incumbent can price discriminate, it can sign exclusive dealing contracts with a fraction of buyers, rendering entry unprofitable, and charge a higher price to customers who are not offered exclusive dealing contracts.

Sleeping cars

Frasco (1992) points out elements of a 1943 U.S. antitrust decision[5] that found the Pullman Sleeping Car Corporation in violation of Section 2 of the Sherman Act that seem consistent with the model of exclusion by denial of efficient scale. Pullman was the monopoly supplier of sleeping cars to U.S. railroads. Its contracts specified that it would be the exclusive supplier of sleeping cars and of sleeping car service. At the time of the antitrust case, contracts typically lasted five years; earlier, contract periods had been much longer. Contract expiration dates were staggered, so a potential entrant could compete for the business of only a fraction of the total market at any one time. Entry costs were sufficiently great (Frasco, 1992, p. 234) for the sequential expiration of contracts to deter entry.

Frasco also notes that Pullman made a substantial and transaction-specific investment in assets that had little use outside its dealing with railroads. Along with their impact on the profitability of entry, exclusive-dealing contracts may have served to protect Pullman from the possibility of holdup.

12.3.3 Tying

To enable price discrimination

If downstream firms use a product with different degrees of intensity and there is some essential input that must be used with the product, tying can allow an upstream firm to discriminate among consumers in the price it charges for the product/input package.

Punch cards   Before the dawn of time,[6] IBM required users of its tabulating machines (which it leased but did not sell) to use only IBM punch cards. IBM's rationale was that cards which did not meet the required technical specifications (thickness, cleanliness) would cause the tabulating machines to jam, damaging IBM's reputation. The tying requirement thereby aimed to protect a valuable, if intangible, corporate asset—reputation.

But there was another consequence. By setting a low rental rate for its tabulating machines, IBM encouraged their use. Businesses that used the tabulating machines more intensely used more punch cards. By setting a price above marginal cost for punch cards, IBM collected more for use of the tabulating machine-punch card package from customers who used tabulating machines more intensely, effectively discriminating in price.[7]

To further tacit collusion

The 1956 *Northern Pacific* U.S. antitrust case[8] involved tying the sale of a product (land) and a service (transportation) in a way that had the effect of facilitating tacit collusion. Like many U.S. railroads, the Northern Pacific Railway Company received by way of encouragement at the time of its construction a government grant of alternating tracts of land along its right-of-way. Much of this land it later sold or leased to timber, cattle, mining, and industrial

---

[5] U.S. *v.* Pullman Co. 50 F. Supp. 123 (1943). See also the discussion of Bork (1954).

[6] See IBM Corp. *v.* U.S. 298 U.S. 131 (1936).

[7] To the extent that this marketing strategy increases output, it (like costless first-degree price discrimination) increases net social welfare.

[8] U.S. *v.* Northern Pacific Railway Co. 142 F. Supp. 679 (1956).

companies. As a condition of sale, the buyer agreed to ship its product with Northern Pacific, all else equal. A typical timber contract provision was:[9]

> The purchaser agrees as one of the material considerations of this contract that *rates being equal* it will ship via the Northern Pacific Railway Company all logs, poles, timber and other products manufactured by it from the timber cut under this contract. ... Where the destination of the manufactured product is not on the line of the Northern Pacific Railway Company, such shipments shall be routed to favor said Railway Company with the longest haul, *if the expense to the purchaser is not increased* over the cost of shipment over another rail line. The purchaser shall make monthly reports to the vendor of shipments under this provision, and shall permit the vendor to examine the purchaser's records at any convenient time or place for the purpose of verifying such reports.

Similar clauses were part of other Northern Pacific land contracts. Since the contracts required the buyer or lessee to ship on Northern Pacific only "all else equal"—if no cheaper transportation rates were available elsewhere—it seems unlikely that the contract was a way for Northern Pacific to price discriminate or to make some competitors unprofitable and cause them to leave the market.

One of the problems of tacit collusion is to detect price-cutting or output expansion promptly, thus reducing its profitability. Cummings and Ruhter (1979, p. 342) point out that the tying clauses at issue in *Northern Pacific* effectively obligated land users to provide Northern Pacific with up-to-date information about the rates charged by competing carriers:

> The traffic clauses referred to in the case permitted buyers and lessees to ship on other carriers, and the use of the escape provisions gave Northern Pacific an opportunity to obtain information on other carriers' rates and services. ... Northern Pacific officials regularly visited land users to discuss shipments. When a buyer or lessee did not use Northern Pacific, the contract compelled him to disclose the lower rates or better service available elsewhere.

By increasing the transparency of transaction prices, Northern Pacific reduced the time period over which a more-competitive rival could hope to profit by cutting rates and attracting business—the very customers the rival might hope to attract would have to go to Northern Pacific and inform Northern Pacific of the pricing change. By making more-competitive pricing less profitable, the tying clauses made it less likely that more-competitive pricing would occur.

To leverage market power

Whinston (1990, p. 838, footnote omitted) makes the point that the "no leverage of market power" doctrine depends fatally on the good approximation assumption:

> In an important sense, however, the existing literature does not really address the central concern inherent in the leverage theory, namely, that tying may be an effective (and profitable) means for a monopolist to affect the market structure of the tied good market (i.e., "monopolize" it) by making continued operation unprofitable for tied good rivals. The reason lies in the literature's pervasive (and sometimes implicit) assumption that the tied good market has a competitive, constant returns-to-scale structure.

---

[9] This is quoted by Cummings and Ruhter (1979, p. 330). Emphasis added, footnote omitted.

Whinston develops models in which it can be profitable for a monopolist supplier of one good to commit to tying its monopolized product to another good where it faces actual or potential competition because of a strategic foreclosure effect (1990, p. 840): "once the monopolist has committed to offering only tied sales, it can only reap its profit from its monopolized product by making a significant number of sales of the tied good." This in turn reduces the equilibrium price and profit a competing supplier of the tied good can earn. If a rival's fixed cost is sufficiently large, tying can force it to make losses, inducing exit (or, for a potential entrant, precluding entry).

Whinston emphasizes that the net impact of exclusionary tying is uncertain. If strategic tying occurs, it is because it is profitable; the tying firm is better off. But (Whinston, 1990, p. 839):

> When tied market rivals exit, prices may rise and the level of variety available in the market necessarily falls. Indeed, in the models studied here, tying that leads to the exit of the monopolist's tied market rival frequently leads to increases in all prices, making consumers uniformly worse off. More generally, though, as is common in models of price discrimination, some consumers may be made better off by the introduction of tying.

 BOX **Tying to Transfer Market Power from One Market to Another**

In 1924, the Waugh Equipment Company was a fringe supplier of railroad draft gears, with less than one per cent of the U.S. market.

Waugh was controlled by leading executives of Armour and Company, which shipped around 275,000 railroad carloads of packed meat per year. According to the U.S. Federal Trade Commission, the Armour executives

> ...by promises of freight traffic to be shipped by Armour and Company, and by threats of withdrawal of traffic, ...used the large volume of the Armour traffic to secure the sale of [Waugh's] draft gears to the various railroads in preference to draft gears sold by companies who did not have any appreciable traffic to offer as an inducement.

Waugh's share of the U.S. draft gear market was 25 per cent in 1929 and 35 per cent in 1930. The FTC condemned the tying of traffic and draft gears as an unfair method of competition "which would more than offset the higher efficiency in production and sales methods of competing concerns controlling no such traffic" and ordered that the tying end.

Source: Stigler (1942), TNEC Hearings 5-A (1939, p. 2307).

Evidence suggests that if tying (and vertical restraints in general) does not result in exclusion, the net impact on market performance is positive (Lafontaine and Slade, 2005, p. 21):

> While different theoretical models often yield diametrically opposed predictions as to the welfare effects of vertical restraints, we find that in the setting that we focus on, namely manufacturer/retailer or franchisor/franchisee relationships, the empirical evidence concerning the effects of vertical restraints on consumer well-being is surprisingly consistent. Specifically, it appears that when manufacturers choose to impose such restraints, not only do they make themselves better off, but they also typically allow consumers to benefit from higher quality products and better service provision.

In contrast, when restraints and contract limitations are imposed on manufacturers via government intervention, often in response to dealer pressure due to perceptions of uneven bargaining power between manufacturers and dealers, the effect is typically to reduce consumer well being as prices increase and service levels fall.

Where tying affects market structure, however, the results may be different. Thus, Slade (1998c, p. 205) finds an association between tying and monopoly in Canadian newspaper advertising markets: "whereas over 85% of the newspapers that are published in cities where there is no direct competitor tie the provision of advertising services to the purchase of advertising space, only half of the newspapers that are published in multi-newspaper cities impose a similar restriction."

12.3.4 Resale Price Maintenance

Maximum resale prices to prevent double marginalization

Consider the situation of a monopolist supplying a market with final demand equation:

$$p = 100 - (q_1 + q_2) \tag{12.1}$$

through two downstream firms that compete as Cournot oligopolists.

The monopolist's constant marginal cost is 10 per unit. Firms 1 and 2 have constant marginal cost (for all inputs except that produced by the monopolist) 10 and 20, respectively. Without price discrimination, we have seen (Section 8.4.1) that the monopoly supplier will set a wholesale price:

$$\omega = 47.5. \tag{12.2}$$

This wholesale price becomes part of the marginal cost of the downstream firms. The Cournot equilibrium price is 75, above the monopolist's most profitable price (60) if the lowest marginal cost of serving final consumers is 20 (10 for the manufacturer, 10 for the low-cost distributor).

If the monopolist specifies a maximum resale price $p = 60$ as well as a wholesale price $\omega = 40$, the most efficient distributor would earn an economic profit of 10 on each unit it sells, and the less efficient distributor would just break even (earn a normal rate of return on investment).

Firm 2, earning only a normal economic rate of return, might exit the market. The manufacturer might get rid of it by awarding an exclusive territory to firm 1. In any case, if 40 units of output are sold, the manufacturer earns $40 \times (40 - 10) = 1200$, which is less than the maximum profit of 1600 but more than the 950 that the monopoly supplier collects if it price discriminates and sells to both suppliers. Of course, if the monopolist awards an exclusive territory to the more efficient downstream firm, then the monopolist could fix the wholesale price at $\omega = 50$ and get the maximum possible profit for itself.

Minimum resale prices to combat market failure due to free riding

Consider a consumer good that a manufacturer wishes to put on the market with a high level of pre-sales service. Suppose also that it is not possible to charge for the product and the service separately.[10]

---

[10] At one time, personal computers might have fit this scenario for most consumers. Another example might be a complex home-entertainment system.

It is costly to provide a high-level of pre-sales service. Thus, dealers who agree to provide the level of service that the manufacturer wants will for that reason need to charge higher prices, all else equal, to earn a normal rate of return on their investment.

A dealer who (regardless of contractual obligations) provides a lower level of pre-sales service will have lower costs. Such a dealer might set lower prices and attract the patronage of customers who have "consumed" pre-sales service at another outlet: the cut-rate dealer will *free ride* on the services provided elsewhere. But then the dealers who provide high levels of pre-sale service will lose money. In equilibrium, a high level of pre-sales service will not be provided. Free riding means that the market for distribution services will fail to exist.

A manufacturer can avoid this outcome by specifying a minimum resale price that is high enough to cover the cost of providing the level of pre-sale service that the manufacturer wants. No dealer would then be able to obtain an advantage over its fellows by cutting price; dealers would compete to attract final consumers by offering pre-sales service, which is what the manufacturer wants.

 BOX   Are Books Different?

Curiously, the first important book marketed under the UK *net book agreement*, a retail price maintenance scheme for books, was Alfred Marshall's 1890 *Principles of Economics*. Guillebaud (1965) publishes correspondence between Alfred Marshall and his publisher, Sir Frederick Macmillan, regarding the net book agreement.

Macmillan to Marshall, 15 April 1890:

> At present, as you are aware, it is usual for booksellers to allow their customers a discount ... from advertised prices. This system is the cause of two evils: in the first place books have to be made (nominally) ridiculously expensive in order that there may be plenty of margin for taking off discounts, and in the second place the system of allowing discounts to retail purchasers has fostered a spirit of competition among booksellers so keen that there is not enough profit in the business to enable booksellers to carry good stocks or to give their attention to bookselling proper. ...
>
> Our theory is that the proper thing to do is only to allow the retail bookseller such a discount from the published price as will give him a fair profit if he gets full price for a book. This, of course, would enable publishers to make books, nominally, cheaper. We have adopted the plan in isolated cases ... We should like to try the same plan with a book of general interest intended for wide sale, and it has occurred to us that your *Principles of Economics* is well suited for the purpose. ... It would, however, be an experiment, and we should not like to make it without your full approval. ...

One of Marshall's objections to fixing retail prices was that doing so obliged the bookseller to take the same margin whether sales were for cash or for credit (Marshall to Macmillan, 9 September 1898):

> I feel rather more strongly on the question of coercing the bookseller into charging equal prices for unequal services, those which he renders to the customer who pays cash & involves him in no risk; and those which he renders to the customers who pays once a quarter.   »

> ❯❯ Macmillan's reply highlighted the possibility that reintroducing discounts, on any basis, would cause the whole scheme to unravel (Macmillan to Marshall, 15 September 1898):

> As to the second point about a discount for cash, you will see that as the competition which has brought retail bookselling to the verge of ruin came about through the pretence of giving discounts for ready money, it would be very dangerous to begin the same system with *net* books, as it would doubtless lead to the same result in a short time. The only safe plan is to treat all bookselling as if it was a cash business (which for the most part it is) & to make no provision for long credit.

> One of the standard defences of retail price maintenance in books is that by guaranteeing the retailer an ample profit margin on more popular books, the retailer is enabled to carry in stock books of a higher literary quality that turn over less rapidly. One of Marshall's remarks touched, indirectly, on this subject (Marshall to Macmillan, 17 September 1898):

> [T]he percentage allowed to the bookseller on expensive scientific books should, in the interest of the advance of knowledge be kept lower than on most other kinds of books. They give the bookseller no trouble because he never knows anything about them, and he never stocks them: his services are to be compared in this matter to those of a news agent rather than to those of a skilled tradesman. In books on light literature & art, and especially such as are suitable for presents, it is different. There he can be of use as a counsellor, and his stock is almost an essential.

> Marshall did not convince Macmillan. Retail price maintenance was formalized in the Net Book Agreement of 1899, an agreement between publishers and booksellers that was in force for almost a century. The Net Book Agreement had largely collapsed by 1995, and was found to be a violation of UK competition law in 1997.
> In addition to Guillebaud (1965), see Tosdal (1915), Grether (1934), Barker and Davies (1966), and Utton (2000), and for the treatment of the Net Book Agreement under E.C. competition policy, Section 16.5.4.

Caveats are in order. First, a profit-maximizing manufacturer who imposes minimum resale price maintenance does so expecting greater profit, all else equal. But increased profit and improved market performance are not the same thing. The net welfare effects of minimum resale price maintenance are ambiguous. Some consumers may be quite happy to consume, and to pay for, a high level of pre-sales service. Others may not. The latter either stay in the market and pay for a level of pre-sales service that they do not want, or they drop out of the market. The net welfare effect of vertical restraints that eliminate low-service, low-price outlets depends on the relative number of consumers who want and do not want a high level of sales efforts (Scherer, 1983; Comanor and Kirkwood, 1985).

Second, it is not clear how applicable the free-riding story is. It does not apply, for example, to post-sales service at a car dealership, since post-sales service can be charged for separately.

Third, it is not clear that the presence of low-price, low-service suppliers necessarily drives higher price, high services outlets from the market. Lower-price internet bookstores and higher-price brick-and-mortar bookstores coexist, offering varieties that are differentiated by ambiance and speed of delivery. But if publishers can buy distribution services from high-sales-effort bookstores even in the presence of internet competition, then market failure justification for resale price maintenance in the book trade is invalid.

Minimum resale prices to enforce dealer collusion

Vertical restraints may stabilize tacit or overt collusion among wholesale or retail distributors. For example, Eichner (1969, p. 191) writes of the late nineteenth century U.S. sugar refining industry:

> The sale of refined sugar constituted approximately 40 per cent of the wholesale grocers' business, but since sugar was an item of uniform quality, the wholesale grocers generally found themselves forced to handle it "without getting back the actual cost of distribut[ion]." It seemed that some jobber was always willing to cut his price in order to make a sale to a new customer, and since the wholesale grocers' costs were almost entirely overhead in nature, the price at which they found themselves forced to sell often was no higher than the price at which they had bought the sugar from the refiner.

In June, 1891, New York and New England wholesale grocers went to the industry's dominant firm, the American Sugar Refining Company, and asked it to police a wholesale cartel:

> [W]hat the ... wholesale grocers wanted was for the American Sugar Refining Company to force all jobbers to adhere to a single price for sugar, a price that would enable the wholesale grocers to handle sugar at a profit. This was to be accomplished through a system of rebates paid only to those wholesaler grocers who honored a pledge not to sell refined sugar for less than the prices posted by American.

Exclusive dealing contracts to raise the cost of entry Vertical restraints may have the effect of raising entry cost. In the episode considered just above, the American Sugar Refining Company adopted a rebate system at the request of its wholesale distributors in New York and New England. It quickly realized, however, that in return for its services as cartel policeman, it could require that the wholesale grocers deal only in ASRC refined sugar. The result would be to raise the cost of entry for prospective rivals in sugar refining, who would be foreclosed from existing distribution channels.

By September 1894, most wholesale grocers east of the Missouri River had signed on to the rebate scheme, which for propaganda purposes was rebaptized "the equality plan". In its late 1890s entry into the U.S. sugar refining market, Arbuckle Brothers (an established coffee roasting firm) had to go over the heads of New England wholesale grocers, and distribute direct to retailers.

Minimum resale prices to facilitate manufacturer collusion

Vertical restraints may stabilize tacit or overt collusion by producers. It is the prospect of additional profit that tempts a (tacitly or overtly) colluding firm to shade price and steal sales from its fellows. If industry-wide resale price maintenance is effective, then a wholesale price-cutting manufacturer would simply be making a gift to its distributors. Given minimum resale price maintenance, retailers would not cut price, and industry sales would not increase.

A price-cutting manufacturer might nonetheless benefit, to the extent that dealers shifted orders from other cartel members to the manufacturer who offered them a larger distributing margin. But this loss of sales would be a signal to other manufacturers that prices were being cut, and the involvement of dealers would make it relatively easy to identify the offending manufacturer.

If industry-wide resale price maintenance is ineffective, then a wholesale price cut might be passed on to the final consumer. But a retail price cut, when none ought to take place, would be a signal of either dealer or manufacturer misbehaviour, and would invite retaliation by other manufacturers. Thus industry-wide resale price maintenance can facilitate manufacturer collusion.

SUMMARY

The organization of industry encompasses market structure, firm structure, and a dense network of interfirm contracts. A "contract", in this context, sets out an institutional framework within which one or more transactions take place. For all except the most straightforward transactions, contracts will by incomplete, and include formal or informal mechanisms for determining actions as uncertainty resolves itself.

Contracts create incentives for those who are parties to them. Some features of some contracts respond to transaction costs. Some features of some contracts have strategic effects, raising entry costs. Under the influence of transaction cost analysis, the economics literature concludes that interfirm contracts in general and contracts between vertically related firms in particular may promote efficiency and improve market performance and may also have strategic effects that are privately profitable because they make entry unprofitable or soften competition among incumbents, worsening market performance.

STUDY POINTS

- Contracts
  - transaction cost influences (Section 12.2)
  - principal-agent issues (Section 12.2.2)
- Vertical contracts
  - exclusive territories (Section 12.3.1)
  - exclusive dealing (Section 12.3.2)
  - tying (Section 12.3.3)
  - resale price maintenance (Section 12.3.4)

FURTHER READING

On vertical contracts generally, see Katz (1989). On the holdup problem, see Hart and Tirole (1990), Rey and Tirole (2005). For a review of the early literature on vertical integration to avoid double marginalization, see Machlup and Taber (1960). For empirical studies of transaction cost influences on contracting, see Masten (1984) (aerospace procurement), Anderson and Schmittlein (1984) (human asset specificity in sales), Joskow (1985, 1987, 1990) and Kerkvliet (1991) (coal). Shepard (1993) and Blass and Carlton (2001) study contract choice in retail petrol distribution. On block booking of movie films, see Hanssen (2000) and Kennery and Klein (2000); on motion picture distribution, see DeVany and Walls (1996) and Corts (2001). On franchising, see Lafontaine (2005); on business groups, see Chandler (1982), Encaoua and Jacquemin (1982), and Goto (1982).

PROBLEM

Asterisk indicates an advanced problem.

12–1* There are two varieties of a differentiated product. Linear inverse demand equations are:

$$p_1 = a - b(q_1 + \theta q_2) \tag{12.3}$$

$$p_2 = a - b(\theta q_1 + q_2), \tag{12.4}$$

where $0 \le \theta \le 1$ and larger values of θ mean that the varieties are closer substitutes.

Show that the demand equations are:

$$q_1 = \frac{(1-\theta)a - p_1 + \theta p_2}{b(1-\theta^2)} \tag{12.5}$$

$$q_2 = \frac{(1-\theta)a - p_2 + \theta p_1}{b(1-\theta^2)}. \tag{12.6}$$

Variety i is produced by manufacturer i at constant marginal and average cost c per unit.

(a) Case 1 (Vertical integration): Manufacturers compete as non-cooperative price-setters, selling direct to final consumer demand.

Find equilibrium prices and payoffs.

Remark: there are computational advantages to writing the demand equations in terms of deviations of the intercept and prices from marginal cost, i.e., $b(1-\theta^2)q_1 = (1-\theta)(a-c) - (p_1-c) + \theta(p_2-c)$.

(b) Case 2 (Two-stage game; vertical separation; linear pricing): Manager i sells to retailer i at wholesale price ω_i per unit. Retailers have no variable costs other than the wholesale price, and no fixed costs. Retailers compete as non-cooperative price-setters. Manufacturers non-cooperatively set wholesale prices to maximize their own payoff, taking into account equilibrium retailer behaviour.

Find equilibrium prices and payoffs. Show that manufacturers make a greater profit in case 2 than in case 1 for $\theta > 0.62$.

(c) Case 3 (Two-stage game; vertical separation; two-part tariff): Manager i sells to retailer i at wholesale price ω_i per unit and a lump-sum payment F_i that equal's retailer i's . Retailers have no variable costs other than the wholesale price, and no fixed costs other than the lump-sum payment. Retailers compete as non-cooperative price-setters. Manufacturers non-cooperatively set wholesale prices, taking into account equilibrium retailer behaviour.

Find equilibrium prices and payoffs. Show that manufacturers make a greater profit in case 3 than in case 1 for $\theta > 0.77$.

ADVERTISING, INFORMATION, AND SALES

When action grows unprofitable, gather information; when information grows unprofitable, sleep.

Ursula K. Le Guin, *The Left Hand of Darkness*

13.1 Introduction

In real-world markets, information is imperfect. The extent of the imperfection varies—from the nearly complete and perfect current information of highly organized currency and commodity markets to the veils of obscurity that seem to characterize wholesale fish markets—but that information is sufficiently imperfect in most markets to matter for market performance is not in doubt.

If information is imperfect, it may be profitable for firms to provide consumers with information, and advertising is one way to do so. But advertising can affect market performance in different ways in different markets. To the extent that advertising informs, it lowers entry costs, increases price elasticities of demand, and improves market performance. To the extent that advertising persuades, it raises entry costs, lowers price elasticities of demand, and worsens market performance.

We begin this chapter by considering basic models of monopoly and oligopoly advertising. We then turn to empirical evidence about the impact of advertising on market performance.

One of the things that firms advertise is sales—periods of low prices that are followed by a return to "normal" prices. A firm that holds occasional sales varies the prices it charges, for the same goods, over time. If different firms in a market hold sales at different times, then there will be times when different firms charge different prices for the same good in the same market. Economists are wont to work with models that predict a single equilibrium market price. Such models imply that if two firms charge different prices for the same good in the same market, all consumers purchase from the firm that sets the lower price. Yet it is clear that there are markets in which prices for identical units of one and the same good differ over time, over space, and over the internet, with simultaneous sales by high-price and low-price firms.[1] The role of sales—intermittent episodes of low prices—in clearing markets where information is imperfect and consumer search costly, is also a topic for this chapter.

13.2 Models of Advertising

13.2.1 Monopoly Advertising: The Dorfman-Steiner Condition

Beginning with the case of monopoly, suppose the quantity demanded from a firm depends not only on its price (p), but also on the amount (A) of its advertising:

$$\pi\,(p, A) = (p - c)\,Q\,(p, A) - F - p_A A. \tag{13.1}$$

Here c is the constant marginal and average variable cost of production, and F is fixed cost. To focus on the impact of advertising on product market performance, not the market for advertising itself, we suppose that the firm can buy advertising messages in a perfectly competitive market for advertising services. p_A is the price of a unit of advertising in that market. $p_A A$ is therefore the firm's cost of advertising.

Profit-maximizing price and advertising levels satisfy two relationships. One is the familiar Lerner index, that the profit-maximizing price-cost margin equal the inverse of the price elasticity of demand:

$$\frac{p - c}{p} = \frac{1}{\varepsilon_{Qp}}. \tag{13.2}$$

The other relationship is the *Dorfman-Steiner* condition:[2]

$$\frac{p_A A}{pQ} = \frac{p - c}{p}\varepsilon_{QA}, \tag{13.3}$$

A monopolist's advertising level maximizes its profit if the advertising-sales ratio equals the product of the price-cost margin and the elasticity of demand with respect to advertising.[3]

The Dorfman-Steiner condition implies that if demand for a firm's product is completely insensitive to advertising ($\varepsilon_{QA} = 0$), it will not advertise, and this is what we should expect. It also implies the advertising is a creature of imperfectly competitive markets. In the long-run

---

[1] One might, of course, take the view that there is never *really* price dispersion because products are never *really* homogeneous. Stigler's (1961, p. 214) response to this argument is "there is never absolute homogeneity in the commodity if we include the terms of sale within the concept of the commodity. Thus, some car dealers might perform more service, or carry a larger range of varieties in stock, and a portion of the observed dispersion is presumably attributable to such differences. But it would be metaphysical, and fruitless, to assert that all dispersion is due to heterogeneity."

[2] (13.3) is implied by the work of Dorfman and Steiner (1954), and made explicit by Cable (1972) and Schmalensee (1972).

[3] Formally, set the derivatives of (13.1) with respect to price and advertising equal to zero, to obtain:

$$\frac{\partial \pi\,(p, A)}{\partial p} = (p - c)\frac{\partial Q\,(p, A)}{\partial p} + Q\,(p, A) \equiv 0 \tag{13.4}$$

and

$$\frac{\partial \pi\,(p, A)}{\partial A} = (p - c)\frac{\partial Q\,(p, A)}{\partial A} - p_A \equiv 0. \tag{13.5}$$

The former leads to the Lerner index by the usual manipulations. From the latter, multiply both sides of $p_A = (p - c)\frac{\partial Q(p, A)}{\partial A}$ by $\frac{A}{pQ}$ to obtain (13.3).

equilibrium of a perfectly competitive market, price equals marginal cost, $p = c$, so that the profit-maximizing advertising-sales ratio is zero. This result should also be expected: if a firm can sell as much or as little as it wants at a price that includes a normal rate of return on investment, and no customer would buy from the firm at any higher price, then the firm cannot profit by advertising.[4]

13.2.2 Goodwill

We derived the Dorfman-Steiner condition in a static model: the monopolist sets price, decides how much it will advertise, makes sales, and the market is over. We might use such a model because we want to study a market that is going to take place just once (an estate sale, for example), or to develop intuition. Alternatively (and following Nerlove and Arrow, 1962), we might wish to consider the advertising decision of a firm that operates over many time periods, and by advertising builds up goodwill that benefits it not only in the present but also in the future.

Suppose goodwill is built up by advertising, but depreciates at rate δ per time period. Goodwill may depreciate because consumers forget the content of past advertising messages or because model changes or technological progress make part of the content of past advertising messages obsolete.

Then if G_0 is the stock of goodwill inherited from the past, and the firm advertises A_1 at the start of the first period, the stock of goodwill at the start of the first period is $G_1 = (1 - \delta) G_0 + A_1$. If the firm advertises A_2 at the start of period 2, the stock of goodwill at the start of period 2 is $G_2 = (1 - \delta) G_1 + A_2 = (1 - \delta)^2 G_0 + (1 - \delta) A_1 + A_2$, and so on. The stock of goodwill at the start of period t is then the undepreciated part of goodwill inherited from the past, the undepreciated part of goodwill greater by advertising in periods 1 through $n-1$, and goodwill created by advertising in period t:

$$G_t = (1 - \delta)^t G_0 + \sum_{\tau=1}^{t} (1 - \delta)^{t-\tau} A_\tau. \tag{13.6}$$

If the quantity demanded in period t depends on price and the stock of goodwill,

$$Q(p_t, G_t), \tag{13.7}$$

the firm's profit in period t is:

$$\pi(p_t, G_t) = (p_t - c) Q(p_t, G_t) - F - p_A A_t,$$

where c is constant marginal and average variable cost, F is the fixed cost that must be paid if the firm operates at all, A_t is the amount of advertising in period t, and p_A is the cost of a unit of advertising. Although goodwill depreciates over time, the advertising that the firm purchases in period t adds something to the stock of goodwill that the firm enjoys in every subsequent period.

The value of the firm is the present-discounted sum of its profit in each future period,

$$V = \sum_{t=0}^{\infty} (1 + r)^{-t} \left[(p_t - c) Q(p_t, G_t) - F - p_A A_t \right]. \tag{13.8}$$

---

[4] One sometimes encounters what are described as models of advertising in competitive markets, but in such cases "competitive" is used in the sense of "rivalry", not to designate the model of perfect competition. Thus, in Stegeman (1991), consumers are able to buy from a firm only if they have received an advertising message from the firm; the "complete and perfect information" assumption of the model of perfect competition fails.

In the static model that yields the Dorfman-Steiner condition, the payoff from advertising is the profit on incremental sales due to advertising in the one-period market. In the extended model, advertising today increases goodwill over all future time—although the goodwill created in the current period depreciates, it never disappears entirely. In this dynamic model, the optimality condition for advertising is that advertising in the current period be purchased until the price of a unit of advertising purchased today equals the discounted and depreciated profit over all future time from having an extra unit of goodwill in the current period,

$$p_A = \sum_{\tau=0}^{\infty} \left(\frac{1-\delta}{1+r} \right)^{\tau} (p_{t+\tau} - c) \frac{\partial Q_{t+\tau}}{\partial G_{t+\tau}}, \tag{13.9}$$

where $\frac{\partial Q_{t+\tau}}{\partial G_{t+\tau}}$ is the change in quantity sold in period $t + \tau$ due to a small change in the amount of goodwill in period $t + \tau$. (13.9) is the dynamic-model equivalent of the Dorfman-Steiner condition.

13.2.3 Advertising and Entry (I)

Now suppose there is a potential entrant. As long as the entrant stays out of the market, the quantity demanded of the incumbent depends on its own price and its own goodwill, as indicated by (13.7). If the entrant comes into the market in period t, then as usual in price-setting oligopoly, the quantity demanded of each firm depends on the prices set by both firms. In a market where goodwill affects demand, the quantity demanded of each firm also depends on the accumulated goodwill of the incumbent (superscript I), and the current advertising of the entrant (superscript E). General expressions for the quantities demanded are:

$$Q^I \left(p_t^I, p_t^E, G_t^I, A_t^E \right) \text{ and } Q^E \left(p_t^I, p_t^E, G_t^I, A_t^E \right). \tag{13.10}$$

The incumbent's stock of goodwill is built up from past advertising expenditures, while the entrant's stock of goodwill in the first period after entry is the goodwill that its advertising creates in that first period. The entrant will build up goodwill with time. But while that process is going on, it will benefit less from accumulated goodwill than the incumbent.

Advertising-demand relationships are different in different types of markets. One possibility is that the incumbent's accumulated goodwill increases its quantity demanded and reduces the quantity demanded of the entrant, all else equal, while the entrant's advertising increases its quantity demanded and reduces the quantity demanded of the incumbent, all else equal. Advertising then has a *business-stealing effect*, with sales efforts by one firm attracting customers from the other. Alternatively, advertising by one firm may have a *market-expansion effect*, increasing the general level of sales without higher sales by one firm coming at the expense of lower sales by other firms. In markets where the business-stealing effect dominates, incumbents' accumulated stocks of goodwill reduce entrants' expected profitability, and may make entry unprofitable.

13.2.4 Advertising and Welfare

The welfare impact of advertising by a monopolist can be discussed in terms of Figure 13.1. Following Dixit and Norman (1978), suppose a small change in the level of advertising, ΔA, shifts the demand curve from D to D'. On demand curve D, the monopolist maximizes profit selling quantity q_m at price p_m. In Figure 13.1(a), on demand curve D', the monopolist maximizes profit selling the larger quantity q'_m at the higher price p'_m.

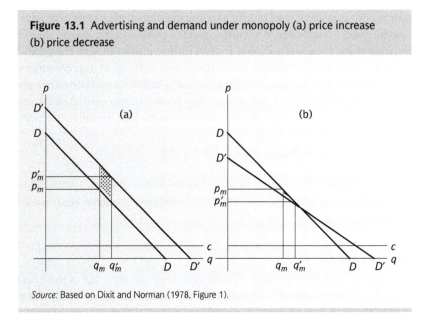

Figure 13.1 Advertising and demand under monopoly (a) price increase (b) price decrease

Source: Based on Dixit and Norman (1978, Figure 1).

The monopolist must earn a greater profit by advertising: otherwise, it would not advertise. Consumers, however, pay a higher price. These parts of the net change in welfare due to advertising add up to:

$$\Delta W = \Delta \pi - Q \Delta P. \qquad (13.11)$$

There is also some consumer surplus on the additional output that is sold because of advertising. For small changes in advertising, this change in consumer surplus is small enough relative to the other parts of the change in welfare that it can be neglected without affecting the results.

Divide both sides of (13.11) by ΔA, to obtain the change in welfare per unit change in advertising:

$$\frac{\Delta W}{\Delta A} = \frac{\Delta \pi}{\Delta A} - Q \frac{\Delta P}{\Delta A}. \qquad (13.12)$$

But if the monopolist maximizes profit, the first term on the right is zero: a profit-maximizing firm will advertise until the marginal revenue from advertising equals the marginal cost of advertising, so that the change in profit from a small change in advertising is zero. Then (13.12) implies that advertising affects welfare and price in opposite ways:

$$\frac{\Delta W}{\Delta A} = -Q \frac{\Delta P}{\Delta A}. \qquad (13.13)$$

In the Dixit-Norman model, if advertising leads to a higher price, as drawn in Figure 13.1(a), it is excessive from a social point of view: welfare would increase if firms advertised less, which would mean a smaller price increase. If advertising leads to a lower price, as drawn in Figure 13.1(b), it is insufficient from a social point of view: welfare would rise if firms advertised more, which would mean a greater price decrease.

13.3 Empirical Evidence

13.3.1 Advertising Impact

Our discussion of the welfare impact of advertising directs attention to two features of advertising's impact on consumer behaviour and market performance: the extent to which advertising shifts demand, and whether more advertising goes with higher or lower prices.

On the quantity sold

Mela *et al.* (1997) study the impact of advertising and sales promotions (temporary price reductions, coupons, displays) on the quantity sold using more than eight years of scanner data for brands sold by a major U.S. consumer packaged good company through 11 stores in one U.S. market. They categorized the 1,590 households whose purchasing patterns were tracked as either brand-loyal or non-loyal, based on a household's purchasing history. They find two effects of advertising:

- more advertising decreases consumers' price sensitivity, particularly for consumers who are not brand loyal;

- the size of the non-loyal segment of the market falls if there is more advertising.

The two effects together, they conclude, show (1997, p. 257) "a powerful role of advertising in reinforcing consumer preferences of brands".[5] They also find that price promotions make consumers more price sensitive. Non-price promotions make brand-loyal consumers less price sensitive, but have the opposite effect on consumers who are not brand loyal.

Duration of effect

The unique product of the Lydia E. Pinkham Medicine Company was its Vegetable Compound, a home remedy first concocted by the firm's homonymous founder, Lydia E. Pinkham.[6] The Vegetable Compound was first sold in 1873. It was promoted exclusively by advertising, primarily newspaper advertising. Advertising was extensive, generally between 40 and 60 per cent of sales, peaking at nearly 85 per cent of sales in the 1934 (Figure 13.2). If that advertising was to be believed, the Vegetable Compound was proof against essentially all the ills that flesh is heir to, particularly those ills which afflict the distaff side of humanity.

The Medicine Company had no direct competitors,[7] so its advertising was directed toward the final consumer, not at oligopolistic rivals. There were occasional run-ins with the U.S. Food and Drug Administration, which regarded some advertising claims as false or misleading. In 1914 the U.S. Internal Revenue Service threatened to tax the Vegetable Compound as an alcoholic beverage, and the Vegetable Compound's alcohol content was reduced to about 15 per cent. But by and large, the Medicine Company could advertise its product as it wished.

---

[5] This effect of advertising was identified by Kaldor (1950–1951); see Section 5.3.2.

[6] The company maintained its independence until 1968, when it was sold to Cooper Laboratories, Inc., which moved production to Puerto Rico. As recently as 2003, an herbal medicine was marketed under the Lydia Pinkham name by a successor of Cooper Laboratories.

[7] See, however, Pollay's (1984, fn. 2) discussion of a patent medicine, Wine of Cardui, that enjoyed a certain success in the southern United States.

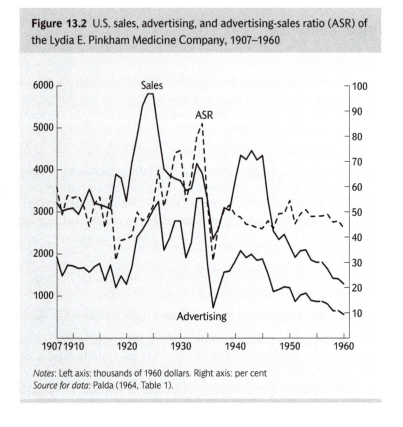

Figure 13.2 U.S. sales, advertising, and advertising-sales ratio (ASR) of the Lydia E. Pinkham Medicine Company, 1907–1960

Notes: Left axis: thousands of 1960 dollars. Right axis: per cent
Source for data: Palda (1964, Table 1).

It wished to advertise a lot,[8] and the records of its advertising have been a proving ground for the estimation of the duration of advertising's effect on sales.

This estimation turned out to be a minefield of statistical difficulties. First estimates, based on yearly data, suggested that it took nearly five years for current advertising to have 90 per cent of its eventual total effect on sales, the "90 per cent duration interval". Subsequent estimates, using monthly data, reduced the estimate of the 90 per cent duration interval to three or four months.

Later estimates tend find shorter duration intervals. Clarke (1976) surveys studies of the duration on advertising impact on a wide variety of products (food products like catsup, patent medicines, cleaning products, petrol, alcohol, cigarettes). His main finding is (1976, p. 355):

> [T]he published econometric literature indicates that 90% of the cumulative effect of advertising on sales of mature, frequently purchased, low-priced products occurs within 3 to 9 months of

---

[8] Here the story complicates itself. From 1927 through 1934, company advertising policy was set by a grand-daughter of Lydia E. Pinkham. At this point another branch of the family asserted control, with two results. One result was a sharp decline in advertising in 1935 (Figure 13.2). A second result was an inter-family lawsuit that resulted in much of the information about the company's advertising policy being made public.

the advertisement. The conclusion that advertising's effect on sales lasts for months rather than years is strongly supported.

This suggests that the entry-deterrence effect of accumulated goodwill is likely to be small for frequently purchased consumer goods.

On price

The welfare analysis given above suggests that there will be too much advertising, from a welfare point of view, if advertising raises prices, and too little advertising, from a welfare point of view, if advertising lowers prices. Here we review studies that have examined the impact of advertising on prices in specific markets.

Here's looking at you, kid.

Eyeglasses Benham (1972) compares the price of eyeglasses and eye examination/ eyeglass bundles for states that (in 1963) restricted and did not restrict advertising by opticians and optometrists. Rows (1) and (3) of Table 13.1 show average prices for his whole sample. Rows (2) and (4) compare average prices in jurisdictions with extreme opposite approaches to advertising these products: Texas and the District of Columbia (with no restrictions on advertising) with North Carolina (long-standing severe restrictions). Both

Table 13.1 Average cost of eyeglasses and average combined cost of eye examination plus eyeglasses (in dollars) as a function of state restrictions on advertising, 1963

Population Group	States with Complete Advertising Restrictions		States with No Advertising Restrictions		
	$\overline{X}_1$	N	$\overline{X}_2$	N	$\overline{X}_1 - \overline{X}_2$
			Eyeglasses		
1) All individuals	33.04	50	26.34	127	6.70
2) All individuals in Texas, North Carolina, and the District of Columbia	37.48	21	17.98	27	19.50
			Eyeglasses and Eye Examinations		
3) All individuals	40.96	121	37.10	261	3.86
4) All individuals in Texas, North Carolina, and the District of Columbia	50.73	37	29.97	72	20.76

Source: Benham (1972).

comparisons show lower prices where advertising was permitted than where it was not.[9] Benham concludes that his results (1972, p. 349, footnote omitted) "are consistent with the hypothesis that, in the market examined, advertising improves consumers' knowledge and that the benefits derived from this knowledge outweigh the price-increasing effects of advertising".

Optometrics Historically, professional associations (of lawyers, physicians, dentists, and so on) prohibited advertising, particularly of prices, as unprofessional. The two-part argument behind banning price advertising was that (Kwoka, 1984, p. 211):

(a) consumers recognize lower prices and shift their business accordingly, but cannot judge the quality of professional services that they receive; professionals who advertise will accommodate the increase in business by reducing the quality of the product they provide, namely, their own service;

(b) competition from low-price, advertising practitioners will confront non-advertisers with the choice of lowering price and quality themselves or else seeing the size of their practices decline.

The second point is a version of the *free-riding argument*, in this context that rivalry of low-price, low-quality professionals will make it impossible for high-price, high-quality professionals to maintain their place in the market.

Kwoka analyses price and examination time in three cities that prohibited the advertising of optometric services and four cities that permitted the advertising of optometric services. Within cities that permitted optometrists to advertise, he classified optometrists into four groups:

- non-advertisers, who listed their business in the Yellow Pages but did not otherwise announce their presence to the world,

- optometrists who advertised to the extent of storefront publicity at their place of business,

- optometrists affiliated with local firms who engaged in local media advertising, and

- heavy advertisers, affiliated with regional or national chain stores.

In markets that permitted advertising, small-firm affiliated and chain-store affiliated opticians charged $11–$12 less than similar firms in non-advertising markets. Non-advertisers in markets that permitted advertising also set lower prices, presumably to meet competition from advertising suppliers in the same market. Thus the argument that competition from low-price, advertising professionals would induce non-advertisers to reduce price finds support.

Kwoka also finds that chain-store-affiliated opticians in advertising markets spent about five minutes less, per exam, than chain-store affiliates in non-advertising markets. But he found that non-advertising opticians in advertising markets spent about 11 minutes *more* per exam than non-advertising opticians in non-advertising markets. In a market in which consumers differ in the value they place on quality of service, non-advertising opticians were

---

[9] Price differences might also reflect differences in market structure, or differences in quality of service and product. Benham makes some attempts to control for these factors, without overturning the basic picture of Table 13.1.

able to compete with low-price, low-quality rivals by offering a higher-quality product. In this case, it is the free-riding argument that fails, not the market.

Read all about it! (Not)   On 10 August 1979, a strike reduced New York City newspaper circulation, and along with it the major source of food advertisements, by 95 per cent. In neighboring Nassau County, east of New York City, newspaper circulation fell only 45 per cent. On 20 August 1979, interim newspapers appeared in the New York City borough of Queens, restoring about half the pre-strike circulation. There were fewer food advertisements in the interim newspapers than normally appeared in regular newspapers. The newspaper strike ended on 5 October 1979.

Glazer (1981) compares changes in food prices (grapes, lettuce, watermelon, chicken, beef) in Queens and Nassau County over the course of the strike. He finds that during the first week of the strike prices in Queens supermarkets, where there was less advertising, rose relative to prices in Nassau County, where there was more advertising. This are some signs of a relative price decline in Queens when interim newspapers appeared. With the end of the strike and the resumption of conventional advertising levels, food prices in Queens fell relative to those in Nassau county. Throughout, there was little impact of the strike on prices at Queens food outlets that did not normally advertise, such as fruit and vegetable stands. In this market, therefore, advertising appears to lower prices.

I'll drink to that   At one time, the state of Rhode Island prohibited the advertising of alcoholic beverages. An alcoholic drinks outlet could not place a sign in its window listing prices, it could not advertise prices in newspapers. On 13 May 1996, with its decision in the *44 Liquormart* case,[10] the U.S. Supreme Court found that this prohibition violated the right to free speech guaranteed in the U.S. constitution.

Milyo and Waldfogel (1999) collected a sample of 6,480 observations of the retail prices of 33 alcoholic beverage products at 115 stores in Rhode Island and Massachusetts over a time period from roughly a year before to a year after the *44 Liquormart* decision. Advertising of alcoholic beverages was legal in Massachusetts throughout the sample period, and, given the geographic proximity of the two states, inclusion of Massachusetts data in the study made it possible to control for factors unrelated to advertising that affected the market for alcoholic beverages.

They show that Rhode Island stores that choose to advertise, when it became legal to do so, had lower prices before advertising became legal than Rhode Island stores that did not choose to advertise, when it became legal to do so (Milyo and Waldfogel, 1999, p. 1087): "Stores that eventually advertise in the newspaper had prices which were 7.71 percent lower than prices at non-advertising stores prior to June 1996 . . . " This result is consistent with the view that one role of advertising is to provide information: retail outlets that had low prices advertised to let consumers know they had low prices.

Milyo and Waldfogel find no significant impact of advertising on the overall level of prices for alcoholic beverages. It does not appear that advertising increased the price elasticity of demand for alcoholic beverages in general. But they do find specific effects of advertising on prices. Stores that advertised individual products reduced the prices *of those products* by about

---

[10] 44 Liquormart *v.* Rhode Island 517 U.S. 484 (1996).

20 per cent. If a product was advertised by a store and by other outlets within a two-mile distance, prices were 23 per cent lower than in the absence of rival advertising. There is thus evidence of a targeted price-lowering effect of advertising, and also evidence that advertising is an element of oligopolistic rivalry.

13.3.2 Informative Advertising

Advertising that directly conveys information about available products and services may lower consumer search costs and increase consumers' price elasticity of demand. This in turn may induce profit-maximizing firms to reduce price and so improve market performance.

Classified newspaper advertisements, which typically describe an item that is for sale and often indicate the price at which it is for sale, are an example of directly informative advertising. Advertising may convey other information in addition to price. Table 13.3.1 indicates some of the information content categories used by marketing professionals to evaluate the information content of advertisements.

Table 13.2 Types of information that might be communicated by advertising.

Price-value. What does the product cost? What is it worth to potential buyers?	*Nutrition.* Are specific data given concerning nutritional content? Are specific comparisons made with other products?
Quality. What characteristics distinguish the product from competing products in terms of workmanship, engineering, durability, excellence of materials, structural superiority, superiority of personnel, attention to detail, or special services?	*Packaging or shape.* In what packages is the product available? In what special shapes is the product available?
Performance. What does the product do and how well does it do it, compared with competing products?	*Guarantees or warranties.* What post-purchase assurances accompany the product?
Components or contents. What is the product made of? What are its ingredients? What ancillary items come with it?	*Safety.* What safety features are available? How do they compare with those of competing products?
Availability. Where when can it be purchased?	*Independent research.* Are there results of research by an "independent" research firm?
Special offers. Are there any limited-time non-price deals?	*Company research.* Are there data gathered by a company to compare its product with those of competitors?
Taste. Is there evidence potential customers perceive the taste of a particular product to be superior?	*New ideas.* Is a totally new concept introduced in the advertisement?

Notes: Based on Abernethy and Butler (1992, Figure 1), which is in turn based on Resnik and Stern (1977) and Stern *et al.* (1981)

Yet analysis of the information content of media advertising will surprise no one who has been exposed to it: the information content is often vanishingly small.[11] In a survey of studies using the fourteen information categories outlined in Table 13.3.1, Abernethy and Butler write (1992, p. 400; citations omitted):

> Four studies have examined U.S. television ads for information strategy . . . . . . these four studies found an average of only 1.06 information cues per ad with 37.5 percent of the ads having no information (total of 1,655 ads . . .). Seven studies of U.S. magazine advertising . . . coded a total of 14,554 ads and found an average of 1.59 cues per ad with 15.6 percent of the ads having no information cues . . .

Their own study of newspaper advertising finds that (1992, p. 415) "service advertising has less information overall than advertising for products and product/service combinations". Suppliers of services often failed to advertise price, availability, and means of payment.

The best to you each morning (I)

In the early 1980s, the U.S. Food and Drug Administration (FDA) prohibited cereal manufacturers from advertising health claims for their products. In the 1970s and the early 1980s, scientific research produced substantial evidence that a high level of fiber in the diet significantly reduces the incidence of colon cancer. The U.S. Surgeon General recommended an increase in fiber consumption.

Beginning in October 1984, Kellogg Company, with the support of the National Cancer Institute, began an advertising campaign, publicizing the link between fibre and colon cancer, and emphasizing the high fibre content of its All-Bran cereal. One result was a reconsideration and eventual reversal of FDA policy. A second was that other cereal producers began their own advertising campaigns, also promoting the consumption of high-fibre cereal.

Figure 13.3 shows the weighted (by market share) average fibre content of cereals on the U.S. market during this time period. Average fibre content rises after the health benefits of a high-fibre diet began to be advertised. Some of this increase is due to increased consumption of existing high-fibre cereal brands, some to the introduction of new high-fibre cereal brands after the change in policy about advertising health claims. The change in consumption patterns is consistent with the idea that one role of advertising is to convey information.

13.3.3 Advertising as a Signal

Nelson (1974) makes an argument to explain some advertising that does not directly convey information. Some goods are *experience goods*: their quality cannot really be appreciated before purchase and consumption. One cannot gauge the likely quality of a meal at a restaurant without having sampled the cuisine (and likely more than one time). The chatter of

---

[11] Information content seems also to vary systematically with the type of advertising media that delivers the message. Abernethy and Franke (1996) analyse 118 studies of the information content of advertising messages and report that newspaper, magazine, and radio advertisements had the greatest information content, in that order. Outdoor and television advertising had essentially the same information content, much less than the other three. They comment that (Abernethy and Franke 1996, p. 10) "Magazines [provided the most information about] quality, performance, nutrition, packaging, and research information. Radio led in providing information on components and special offers. Outdoor gave the most information on availability and taste. Television did not lead in any category".

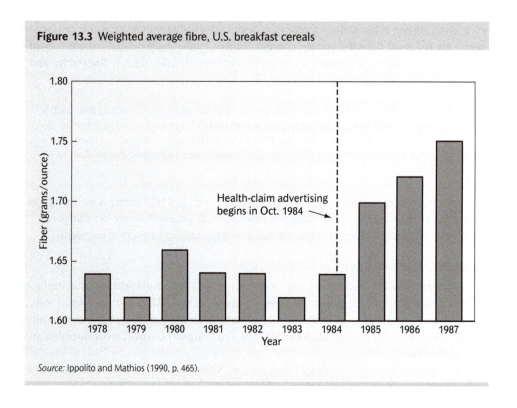

Figure 13.3 Weighted average fibre, U.S. breakfast cereals

Source: Ippolito and Mathios (1990, p. 465).

friends in the hallway may provide some indication, but tastes differ enough so that this sort of information is an imperfect guide.[12] Nelson suggests that for experience goods, the mere fact that a product is advertised conveys the information that it will be satisfactory—that advertising is a signal of product quality.

The argument can be made starting with the Dorfman-Steiner condition, that spending on advertising, relative to sales revenue, will be more for more profitable varieties. High-quality varieties will be more profitable, all else equal: in an imperfectly competitive market, the higher is quality, the higher the price that will maximize the producer's profit. If advertising is viewed as a signal, then without conveying any information about the details of product characteristics, the mere fact that much is spent on advertising an experience good delivers the message that it is of high quality.

This signalling hypothesis is most plausible, however, for new goods. Once a product is established, it will enjoy the level of brand loyalty, high or low, that experience generates. Hence advertising as a signal of quality should fall over time. Correspondingly, price should rise over time, as producers increase the price of varieties that have demonstrated their high quality in the marketplace.

---

[12] See, however, Bikhchandani *et al.* (1998), who discuss the impact of information transmission among consumers on demand.

Yogurt Ackerberg (2001) finds that television advertising has a significant impact on purchases of a new brand of yogurt by inexperienced consumers, but little effect on purchases by experienced consumers. In this case—a consumer non-durable good—the role of advertising seems to be to inform rather than to persuade. Television advertising informs the consumer that the good exists. Once the good has been sampled, it is the consumer's experience that determines whether or not there are repeat purchases.

Quality rankings Caves and Greene (1996) analyse the determinants of *Consumer Reports* quality rankings published from August 1988 through September 1990, for brands in 196 product groups. They relate rankings to the importance of alternative sources of information for different product groups. Possible sources of information include advertising, friends and other advisers (but not sales personnel), own past experience, evaluations by independent parties (such as *Consumer Reports*), and own search. They also take product group characteristics, such as time between purchases, into account. Among other results, they find that advertising rises with quality for brands in product groups that are subject to frequent design changes and where past experience and search influence choice among available brands. The importance of past experience and search is inconsistent with consumer reliance on advertising as a signal of quality. Rather (Caves and Greene, 1996, p. 50) "advertising tends directly to provide verifiable information on goods that are innovative or otherwise strongly differentiated vertically".

Compact disc players Horstmann and MacDonald (2003) test the signaling model for the first decade of the compact disc player market, 1983–1992. As a new type of product, consumers could not have experience with the way different varieties would perform, or indeed how CD players would interface with existing sound systems. For a sample of 1,667 CD players produced by 115 firms, Horstmann and MacDonald's findings are inconsistent with the signalling model. In their sample, price declines and advertising rises with experience. This result, they suggest, implies that consumers remain uncertain about the quality of experience goods even after consuming them. Advertising, to inform or persuade, continues to be profitable because consumers, after consumption, have imperfect impressions of the nature of the products they have consumed.

13.3.4 Persuasive Advertising

The best to you each morning (II)

Some advertising may inform. But it is difficult to accept that the producers of Wheaties or Cheerios pay for large amounts of advertising with the intent to inform potential consumers about their products' characteristics. Most consumers have personal experience with long-established brands.

Advertising may also have an impact on brand loyalty, but the nature of the effect is ambiguous. Accumulated goodwill, of the kind pictured in Section 13.2.2, may build brand loyalty and raise the cost of entry. But if the brand loyalty of established varieties is based on the experience of actual consumers, then advertising may be much more a tool to entice consumers to try a variety for the first time. In this case, advertising serves more to break down consumers' loyalty to other varieties than to build up loyalty to the advertised variety.

Shum (2004) studies a sample of scanner data on cereal purchases of 1,010 Chicago-area households at six supermarkets between June 1991 and December 1992. One of his findings is that brand loyalty, which he measures by recent consumption experience, is a significant factor in the breakfast cereal market (Shum, 2004, p. 258):

> [H]ouseholds are much more likely to repurchase brands they have purchased recently: ... recent purchase of a brand raises the median household's purchase probability from 0.26% to 5.66%, which is about a 20-fold increase.

Here "recent purchase" means having purchased the brand in the previous 12 weeks.

Shum's analysis permits him to estimate how much a household would have to be paid to make it as likely that it would purchase a brand to which it is *not* loyal as would a household loyal to the brand. This is also a measure of brand loyalty: the larger the payment required, the greater the household's preference for a variety with which it is familiar. The estimates are large: a household loyal to Cheerios, for example, would require an average subsidy of $3.66 to neutralize the loyalty disadvantage of other brands. For ten leading brands, the average figure is $4.33.

Shum also finds that advertising and the estimated switching subsidies are negatively related: a 25 per cent change in advertising in one direction causes the switching subsidy to change by almost 16 per cent in the other direction. This suggests that advertising can be a device for a firm to attract consumers who are loyal to other brands. Advertisements for Cheerios, in this view, aim to lure consumers who are loyal to other breakfast cereals.

It also appears that higher advertising is a profitable substitute for lower prices. Shum finds that if advertising expenditures were reduced 25 per cent, and prices lowered enough to keep firms' market shares unchanged (2004, p. 262), "the price discount would 'cost' about $3.77 ... million ... more than the reduction in advertising expenditures".

 BOX   Sapolio: the Advertising of Experience Goods

In 1869 New York City firm Enoch Morgan's Sons began to promote one of its line of soap products, Sapolio, with an extensive advertising campaign. Commercial success followed. By 1900, the time of the "Spotless Town" campaign, Sapolio was (Tull, 1955, p. 128) "as well known as any product then on the market".

Sapolio was a scouring cleanser in cake form. Early on it faced competition from heavily advertised rival cake cleansers, and later from powdered cleansers, important among these being the brands of industrial meat-packers that entered the cleanser market with by-products of their primary activity. Sapolio's advertising budget fell from 1905, and with it Sapolio sales.

But other forces were at work. In the face of increasing sales of powdered cleansers, Enoch Morgan's Sons banked on the fact that (Tull, 1955, p. 136) "a cake cleanser was more economical than a powdered cleanser. As soon as housewives recognized this, powder sales would begin to fall". While other cake producers introduced powdered cleansers, Sapolio advertising emphasized its "economy" aspects.

Since Sapolio's rise was based on advertising, it is tempting to attribute its fall to its reduction in advertising after 1905. But cleanser is an experience good; once induced by advertising to try the product, consumers will continue only as long as experience is satisfactory. Sapolio's fall is »

>> more the failure of a dominant firm to innovate than a failure of marketing (Pollay, 1984, p. 18): "the decline of Sapolio not to a reduction in advertising expenditures, but to a failure on the part of management to recognize the shift in consumer preference from caked soaps to powders".

Source: Tull (1955).

Figure 13.4 The butcher of Spotles Town

13.3.5 Advertising and Entry (II)

Strategic advertising to deter entry

Bagwell and Ramey (1988) develop a model of strategic entry-deterring advertising that is similar to the Kreps and Wilson (1982) generalization of the chain store game (Section 7.3.3). For simplicity, consider the case of a potential entrant into a market supplied by one incumbent, and suppose there is no goodwill: advertising in the current period affects demand only in the current period.

In most kinds of oligopoly, an entrant will earn less profit, the lower an incumbent's (or incumbents') marginal cost. From (13.2) and (13.3), we know that the profit-maximizing pre-entry prices depend on the incumbent's marginal cost. If the entrant is uncertain about the incumbent's cost, a high-cost incumbent may find it profitable to set a price and advertise at a level that would maximize the profit of a lower-cost firm, keeping alive for the entrant the possibility that the incumbent has lower marginal cost than is actually the case. This will generally lead a higher-cost incumbent to set a lower price and a higher advertising level than it would if it were not mimicking a lower-cost firm. As with the basic limit-pricing model, the price reduction leaves consumers better off, all else equal. The welfare impact of additional advertising is ambiguous.

The best to you each morning (III)

Thomas (1999) studies rivals' price and advertising response to the introduction of new brands of breakfast cereal. His sample covers 129 cereals for the years 1971–1989. 112 of the 129 cereals appeared on the market for the first time during his sample period. He divides the cereals into 13 market segments (bran/high fibre, shredded wheat, etc.) and studies the price and advertising response to the introduction of new brands.

The price response to the arrival of a new cereal brand depends on whether the firm producing the brand is already active in the market segment. If an incumbent introduces a new brand, the response of other incumbents is to raise price. If the new brand is produced by an entrant, incumbents react by lowering price. But the advertising response to entry is to increase advertising, whether the new brand is produced by an incumbent or an entrant. In the breakfast cereal industry, advertising is a device to strategically react to entry.

Generic pharmaceuticals

The market for prescription medicines is distinctive in a number of ways. On the demand side, the consumption decision is made by a physician, not by the consumer. Thus one would expect advertising to be directed toward the physician as much or more than to the final consumer, and this has historically been the case. Prescription medicines have been intensely advertised in medical journals, and pharmaceutical company "detail men" engage in individual sales efforts to physicians.

Further, payment for the product is often made by an insurance company rather than the consumer. This suggests that a policy of setting a low price with the goal of building a loyal customer base is unlikely to be an attractive one in the pharmaceutical market.

On the supply side, prescription medicines marketed in the United States must undergo a lengthy and expensive process to obtain approval by the Food and Drug Administration (FDA) before they can be put on the market. They also enjoy patent protection (and for a period that is extended to allow for the time needed to obtain FDA certification). Once a patent expires, entrants may offer a generic substitute.

A generic substitute must also obtain FDA approval, but it may do this by showing that the generic product is equivalent to the patented drug. Obtaining FDA approval for a general drug is typically quicker (18 months) and less expensive ($250,000 to $20 million in the early 1990s) than for a patented product (Scott Morton, 2000, p. 1090).

Scott Morton (2000) studies the impact of advertising and sales efforts on the generic entry decision for a sample of 98 drugs that lost patent protection between 1986 and 1991. In half of these cases, a generic entrant was approved to enter the market at the moment of patent expiration. The average number of generic entrants within the first year was 1.27, and within two years, 2.09.

Scott Morton finds that the most important inducement to entry is market size, measured by sales revenue in the year before the patent expires: entry is more likely into larger markets. But sales revenue loses its entry-attracting effect if there is a duopoly producing the patented product (which may happen if two firms share a patent). These results suggest that it is the lure of economic profit that attracts entry. Advertising, however, whether in medical journals or by detailing to physicians and hospital purchasing agents, has no significant impact on the entry decision. Sales efforts by patented drugs may increase revenue before the patent expires, but do not appear to raise the cost of entry after the patent expires.

13.4 Advertising Competition in Oligopoly

Section 13.2.3 contains expressions for the quantities demanded from two firms as functions of their prices and accumulated stocks of goodwill. There we thought of one firm as an incumbent, one as an entrant. In general, however, we might think of the demand expressions in (13.10) as typical of oligopoly markets in which the quantity demanded of each firm depends on the prices charged and the goodwill accumulated by all firms. Again in the most general case, a firm's goodwill might depend not only on its own current and past advertising, but also on its own current and past prices—lower values building goodwill—and on rivals' current and past prices and advertising. The result is a vision of imperfectly competitive markets where rivalry involves a complex interaction of price and advertising, and may have the market-expansion and business-stealing effects introduced in Section 13.2.3.

13.4.1 Crackers!

Slade (1995) studied price and advertising competition in the market for saltine crackers in Williamsport, Pennsylvania. Her weekly data was for 1984–1985 and allowed her to trace the impact of changes in prices, advertising in local newspapers, coupons, and in-store displays on sales of three national brands and of private label brands.

She reports from interviews with grocery marketing managers that customers were divided into searchers and loyalists, much like the Marseille wholesale fish market of Section 3.5.4 (Slade, 1995, p. 457): "less than ten percent of households contain comparison shoppers who visit several stores in a week to search for the lowest-priced items. The remaining 90 percent frequent the same store each week. Their choice of store is determined by location (often proximally to work or home) and by the quality of the store (freshness of produce and meat, product offerings, overall pricing policies, etc.)". Prices are changed slightly less than once every five weeks, and a grocery chain advertises a specific brand "five or six percent of the time". Lower prices and greater sales efforts—advertising and displays—go together in her sample; the role of advertising "is to provide information about grocery-store specials".

Her statistical analysis suggests that lower prices and greater advertising increase a brand's sales, and reduce rivals' sales. The results for price thus show that different brands of saltine crackers are substitutes. The results for advertising suggest the presence of business-stealing effects. There is some market-expansion effect as well: if all firms advertise, combined sales go up. Advertising appears to create a stock of goodwill, but a short-lived one: advertising affects demand in the week it occurs and two weeks thereafter, suggesting that (Slade, 1995, p. 463) "consumers must be constantly reminded of products".

As for the nature of oligopolistic competition, she finds that stores (Slade, 1995, p. 448) "compete vigorously on the advertising front and accommodate one another on the price front. The net result is more advertising and higher prices than what would be observed if they were engaged in a static game". Market equilibrium resembles a collusive outcome, but results from independent behaviour (Slade, 1995, p. 474): "The end result, higher prices, while giving the appearance of overt collusion in a static framework, is a natural outcome of noncooperative behavior in a more comprehensive game".

13.5 Sales

Standard economic models predict that there will be a single equilibrium price for a good, and that this price will persist until there is some change in underlying conditions on either the demand side or the supply side of the market. Casual observation suggests that this prediction must be qualified for many markets, markets in which periods of "normal" prices are regularly or irregularly interrupted by intervals of low prices.

Some explanations for low-price promotions flatly contradict the "law of one price". These explanations describe models in which there are persistent differences between consumers, and sales are a device to engage in second-degree price discrimination. Other explanations for sales are consistent with the "law of one price", and rely on periodic changes in consumer behaviour or cost conditions that make a brief, temporary reduction in price optimal. Periodic low prices may also have a strategic element, as a response to entry.

13.5.1 Second-Degree Price Discrimination

Varian (1980) models sales in a market for a product about which individual consumers are either informed (perhaps having been exposed to an advertisement) or uninformed about the prices offered at different stores. The sequence of events envisaged is that firms first set and advertise prices. Informed consumers then go to the lowest-price store. Uninformed consumers go to some store at random. Each consumer buys one unit of the good, provided the price at the store visited is below the consumer's reservation price. The reservation price is the same for all consumers.

If any firm were to set a predictable price, other firms could undercut it slightly and it would sell only to uninformed consumers. In equilibrium, firms set prices randomly, so that every firm has some chance of charging the lowest price and making sales to informed consumers. Firms with low prices appear to be holding a sale, compared with their own past prices and with prices at other stores. The identity of the low-price seller changes over time, but it is the low-price seller that supplies the informed segment of the market.

13.5.2 Durable Goods

Conlisk *et al.* (1984; see also Sobel, 1984) describe a market in which the nature of the pool of potential customers changes over time, making occasional periods of low prices a value-maximizing policy. The market is supplied by the producer of a durable good for which consumers have different reservation prices, some high and some low. New consumers enter the market over time; consumers who purchase the product leave the market. If the durable good producer sets a high price most of the time, it takes the maximum profit from consumers with high reservation prices. Consumers with low reservation prices are not willing to pay the high price, and remain in the market. Eventually, the stock of low-reservation-price consumers has built up so much that it becomes profitable for the producer to lower price, supply the relatively large low-valuation segment of the market, then raise price again.

The equilibrium of their model matches common features of sales in retail markets (Conlisk *et al.*, 1984, p. 489): "For many products, low price sales seem to display three properties. The sales come as no surprise to consumers; they are followed quickly by substantial price rises; and they induce increased purchases".[13]

13.5.3 Retailer Inventories

Aguirregabiria (1999) studies the interaction of retailer inventory holding patterns and retail pricing. If there are fixed costs to placing orders, retailers will replenish inventory only

---

[13] Similar effects appear in Gallini and Karp (1989).

intermittently. If there are fixed costs to changing posted prices—*menu costs*—retailers will change prices only intermittently.

Between orders, supplies on hand in inventory decline. An unexpected surge in demand can cause a retailer to stockout, requiring an immediate order for new supplies and leaving the retailer unable to satisfy demand until new supplies arrive. Immediately after inventories have been replenished, demand is most elastic: with full inventories, there is little risk of stockout, the retailer is almost certain to be able to supply any quantity demanded. When demand is most elastic, profit-maximizing prices are relatively close to marginal cost. As the amount in inventory falls, the expected price elasticity of demand falls—there is a higher probability that a low price will lead to a stockout rather than increased sales. As the expected price elasticity of demand falls, the profit-maximizing price rises. The resulting price pattern involves low prices just after inventories have been resupplied, with occasional price increases thereafter as the difference between posted prices and profit-maximizing prices becomes large enough to cover the menu costs of implementing a price change.

Aguirregabiria tests his model using data on sales of 534 brands sold by a supermarket chain in the Basque region of Spain between January 1990 and May 1992. There is evidence of the cyclical ordering pattern predicted by the model, that prices are lowest after orders, and rise between orders.

13.5.4 Fashion

The possibility of retailer stockouts provides one explanation for end-of-season clearance sales, a common phenomenon for seasonal goods such as "fall fashions" or skiing equipment (Nocke and Peitz, 2007). The explanation also has aspects of intertemporal price discrimination. At the start of a season, a retailer is uncertain precisely what quantity will be demanded, and will arrange to have on hand a supply that balances expected profit from realized sales, expected lost profit if supplies should run out before the season ends, and the expected loss if goods remain unsold at the end of the season and must be discarded or remaindered.

In this kind of market, by setting a high price at the start of the season, the seller can make high-profit sales to customers least willing to run the risk of being unable to buy at all toward the end of the season. Low prices at the end of the season—a clearance sale—allow the seller to dispose of stocks before they cannot be sold at all. Customers who wait until the end of the season run the risk of not being able to buy the product at any price.

An alternative explanation for sales of high-fashion items rests on the argument that the seller of a unique good (a designer dress) or a kind of good that goes on the market only infrequently (the biggest house in town) will be uncertain precisely what the market will bear (Lazear, 1986). The initial profit-maximizing price for such a good is relatively high: it balances out the expected chance of making an extremely profitable sale right away against the chance that the good will remain unsold for some time. If the good does not sell, the seller learns something: that the initial price was too high. This information is used to adjust the price, downward, until a buyer appears.

13.5.5 Consumer Shopping Behaviour

Brand loyalty

Sales may be a response to product characteristics or to consumer characteristics. They may also be a response to consumer behaviour (Raju *et al.*, 1990). Compare the relative costs

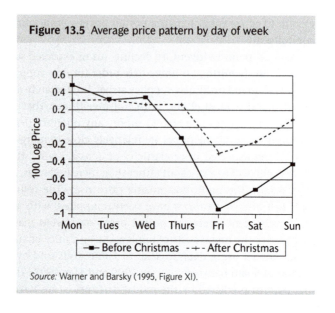

Figure 13.5 Average price pattern by day of week

Source: Warner and Barsky (1995, Figure XI).

and benefits of low sales prices for a national brand that has a large following of loyal consumers and for a store brand. If a brand with a pool of loyal (low price elasticity of demand) customers lowers price, it may attract some buyers who would otherwise purchase a store brand, but in doing so, it gives up a relatively large amount of revenue from sales to its loyal customers that it could have made at its regular price. Store brands compete on a price basis in any case; by holding prices down, they keep the patronage of customers who might otherwise be tempted by sale prices or the national brand.

Raju *et al.* (1990) develop a model in which products with less brand loyalty have more to gain from low prices. They examine the frequency of low prices for 59 national brand-store brand pairs of retail items sold by a major grocery chain over a period of 24 weeks, and report that for 31 pairs, the store brand offered discount prices more often than the national brand. In 11 cases, low prices occurred about as often for both brands, and for 17 pairs, the national brand offered low prices more often than the store brand. This evidence suggests that brand loyalty does discourage promotional pricing.[14]

Shopping times

The "fashion" explanation of sales points to the fact that markets for some goods are thin, with few potential customers (and the valuations of those customers highly uncertain. Warner and Barsky (1995) point to markets that are intermittently thick, with many potential customers, to explain a commonly observed pattern of retail prices for a different type of product.

The pricing pattern they observe—for sales of eight goods at 17 retail stores in Ann Arbor, Michigan from November 1 to February 28, 1988—is shown in Figure 13.5. On average, prices are highest on Mondays, fall steadily and bottom out on Friday, then recover somewhat

---

[14] But see Berck *et al.* (2008), who find no evidence of a brand loyalty effect in an analysis of scanner data on retail orange juice sales.

on Saturday and Sunday. The decline in prices is greater in the period immediately before Christmas, all else equal.

The kinds of goods Warner and Barsky study—among which, action figures, bath towels, bicycles—are not products for which the demand side of the market is thin; retailers should have a good idea of the nature of demand. Nor, with one possible exception (a man's crewneck sweater), are they fashion goods. The fashion and clearance sale explanations for low prices do not apply to this kinds of products. Nor would those models explain a price increase after low Friday prices.

Warner and Barsky instead rely on regular shopping patterns to explain the pattern of prices they observe. For some goods, consumers systematically defer "trips to the mall" until the weekend, when the opportunity cost of time spent shopping is less. End-of-week buyers consolidate purchases. The marginal benefit of searching for lower prices is greater, because they plan on spending more. If consumers search more intensely for low prices—if their price elasticity of demand is higher—the profit-maximizing response of retailers is to lower price.

A Hotelling model   To make this point in a simple model, we adapt the Hotelling linear market model of Section 4.2.2,[15] which we take to describe a retail market. In the standard exposition of the Hotelling linear model, firm's locations are fixed (firm A is a distance a from the left end of the market, firm B is a distance b from the right end of the market). The line is l units long, and there is one consumer per unit distance. There is a transportation cost t per unit distance. "Transportation cost" may be interpreted literally, or it may represent lost utility because a consumer cannot purchase a version of the good with his or her most-preferred combination of product characteristics. Each consumer buys one unit of the good from the store that offers the lowest full price, purchase price plus transportation cost.

To investigate the impact of market thickness on equilibrium prices, suppose each consumer buys q units of the good, rather than 1 unit, from the store that offers the lowest full price. Proceeding as in Section 4.2.2, there is a boundary location at distance x from firm A and distance y from firm B. Consumers whose preferences place them at the boundary location have the same delivered price from either firm. x and y satisfy the equal-full-price condition,

$$p_A q + tx = p_B q + ty. \tag{13.14}$$

Equation (13.14) and the length-of-line condition $(a+x+y+b = l)$ determine the quantities demanded of each firm at prices p_A and p_B. Equilibrium prices, if each firm pays a wholesale price c per unit for goods it resells to final consumers, are:[16]

$$p_A^* - c = \frac{t}{q}\left[l + \frac{1}{3}(a - b)\right] \text{ and } p_B^* - c = \frac{t}{q}\left[l + \frac{1}{3}(b - a)\right]. \tag{13.15}$$

That is, the profit-maximizing markup of price over marginal cost is less, the greater the quantity sold to each consumer. The greater the quantity sold at a given price, the greater the price elasticity of demand, all else equal, and the closer is the profit-maximizing price to marginal cost.

---

[15] Warner and Barsky (1995) make the same point starting from the Salop (1979) circle model.

[16] Assume also that a and b are sufficiently small (each firm is sufficiently close to its end of the line) that in equilibrium firms share the centre of the market.

Consumer inventories

Some goods are stored in consumer inventories for consumption between shopping trips. Hendel and Nevo (2006a, b) examine the implications of consumer inventories for price promotions and consumer response to low prices. For the goods they study—laundry detergent, soft drinks, and yogurt—they find that households purchase more when goods are on sale, and delay later purchases. When the goods are not on sale, the quantity purchased increases, all else equal, with time from the most recent sale. Stores tend to offer low prices more often, and on smaller sizes, for a storable but perishable good like yogurt and less often and on larger sizes for a storable, non-perishable good like detergent.

13.5.6 Strategic

Lal (1990) describes a market supplied by three firms, two of which have a national following (brand preference). Some consumers are loyal, and some are potential switchers. Loyal consumers always buy from the same national firm, if they buy at all. Switchers will buy from the third firm if its price is sufficiently below the prices of the national firms. Lal works out conditions under which the two national brands alternate holding sales, in a strategy that has the effect of keeping the third firm from attracting a large number of switching consumers.[17] He suggests that this kind of outcome occurs in the U.S. soft drink market, with Coke and Pepsi playing the roles of the national brands.

13.5.7 Recapitulation

Price promotions—sales—are common in many markets, but the explanations for sales differ from market to market. Sales in some markets are a response to unobservable differences in consumer characteristics, and a marketing device to permit second-degree price discrimination. The pricing of durable goods (sorting out high-reservation and low-reservation price buyers) and the time-pattern of pricing of seasonal goods (sorting out consumers who will pay to avoid being unable to buy the product at all) are examples. A declining price for high-fashion goods and goods sold in thin markets is a device for a seller to learn about the nature of demand. Weekend sales, on the other hand, are a profit-maximizing response to consumer shopping patterns that make markets cyclically thick, increasing the price elasticity of demand in a regular pattern.

Some sales are a result of profit-maximizing retail inventory management when there is a fixed cost to replenishing supplies, combined with a fixed cost of changing posted prices. The timing of sales will differ if consumers can store the product in their own inventories.

The nature of sales in some markets is determined by oligopolistic interactions. If a product enjoys substantial brand loyalty, the cost in terms of lost profit on sales to loyal customers makes it less profitable to put the product on sale, all else equal. But periodic sales by an established firm reduce expected post-entry profit, allowing incumbents to exercise greater average market power.

---

[17] Formally, the model has much in common with the non-cooperative collusion models of Chapter 6.

13.6 Price Dispersion

13.6.1 Online Book Market

Internet search costs are extremely low—with a click or two of the mouse, one can compare the price of an item at different web sites; a shopbot can make the comparison for you. The model of perfect competition (or the model of Bertrand competition with homogeneous products) would lead one to expect a single equilibrium price, equal to marginal cost. Common experience, however, suggests that this expectation is not fulfilled. Not only do identical products sell for different prices at different web sites, it is not all uncommon for different prices to be charged for identical products on the same web site. It is not uncommon to find a used book listed at a higher price than a new copy of the same book, either at the same web site or different web sites.

Consumer search behaviour

Clay *et al.* (2001) study the pricing of 399 books at 32 online bookstores over a 25-week period from late 1999 to early 2000. They observe that despite low internet search cost, (2001, p. 526) "Many consumers routinely go to Amazon without checking prices at other stores". They estimate maximum savings missed by buying from Amazon without search at between 10 and 25 per cent of the Amazon price, depending on the type of book.

They analyse prices at the "big three" bookstores (Amazon, Barnes & Noble, and Borders) and at smaller fringe stores. For both groups, price dispersion at the title- and store-level was lower if a sufficiently large number of rivals sold the same title in the same week. This narrowing of price dispersion did not always show up for small increases in the number of rivals offering the same title. The prices of more heavily advertised books were lower, all else equal. They also note that some fringe firms appear to do little to establish a brand name, while setting prices just below Amazon's prices. At the time of the Clay *et al.* (2001) study, two out of eight such stores had gone out of business. A slightly lower price captures the entire market in the Bertrand model with homogeneous product, but not, it would appear, on the internet.

Endogenous sunk cost

Latcovich and Smith (2001) find that the structure of the internet book market is consistent with the hypothesis that it is a Sutton "type II", endogenous sunk cost industry, with the leading firms investing in advertising and web site quality to maintain market share even as market size expands. In this market, although a book is a standardized product, there are quality differences based on (2001, p. 232) "reliability, security, and ease of use". Sunk investment can improve performance in these dimensions, and advertising can inform buyers about the improvements.

They examine prices for a time period similar to that of Clay *et al.* Among other results, they find that prices do not appear to fluctuate randomly at a particular internet seller, ruling out random pricing as a means of second-degree price discrimination as an explanation of price dispersion. They note that the big three internet sellers set similar prices and change prices for specific titles at about the same time. They suggest tacit collusion or "loss leader" pricing of best sellers as possible explanations. Since each firm can use the internet to monitor rivals' prices, the similarity of book prices set by leading internet sellers may simply be price-matching behaviour in a market with highly transparent prices.

13.6.2 Experimental Evidence

The model

Morgan *et al.* (2005) report the results of experimental tests of a consumer search model with advertising. The model is designed to explain the robust observation of persistent price differences in internet markets. In contrast to the basic search model, the Morgan *et al.* model allows a firm to advertise, to inform consumers of its price. Firms that advertise set a price below the reservation price. Different firms that advertise set different prices. Firms that do not advertise set the reservation price; there would be no reason for such a store to set a lower price, since any consumer it sells to is not going to search elsewhere.[18] Although some firms advertise and some firms do not, and firms that advertise set different prices, in equilibrium all firms maximize their expected values. In equilibrium, all firms have the same expected value (otherwise, some firms would change their decisions).

Advertising leaves consumers better off: when firms advertise, they set a lower price, hoping to attract searching consumers. But in the Morgan *et al.* model, advertising is costly. The more expensive is advertising, the smaller is the number of firms that advertise and the lower is the level of advertising by such firms. More expensive advertising, therefore, leaves consumers worse off (paying higher prices) and firms better off (greater expected profit).

The experiment

Morgan *et al.* (2005) report the results of experiments with two and with four experimental subjects acting as sellers. Twenty-four computer-programmed buyers make up the demand side of each experimental market. Twelve buyers were programmed to buy one unit from the store with the lowest advertised price, 12 buyers were programmed to buy from the first store they contacted.[19] In half of the experimental sessions, the cost of advertising was 200, in the other half 400.

Table 13.3 describes the results of the four-seller experiments. Theoretical predictions are that the level of advertising will fall, and price will rise, as the cost of advertising goes up. This is the result that was observed in the experiments. But the experimental subjects advertised more than predicted, whether the cost of advertising was low or high. Thus the other prediction of the model, that firms' expected profits rise with the cost of advertising, is not confirmed experimentally. In Table 13.3, predicted profits are 367 and 433 with advertising cost 200 and 400, respectively, while the corresponding observed profits are 290 and 302.[20]

The model predicts what is observed in real-world (for example) internet markets: price dispersion, the failure of the law of one price. Advertised prices in the Morgan *et al.* experiments differ. Especially for the high-advertising-fee sessions, the experimental price distribution shows more low prices than predicted by theory.

In these experimental markets, advertising lowers price, thus leaving consumers better off. But since sellers advertise more than the predicted profit-maximizing levels, higher advertising fees do not lead to the higher profits predicted by the model.

---

[18] This is the kind of argument that underlies the Diamond Paradox; see Section 3.5.

[19] Consumers would only buy if a price were below the reservation price; sales would be equally divided among low-price advertisers if two or more firms posted identical low prices, and sales would be equally divided among all sellers if no sellers advertised. See Morgan *et al.* (2005) for other details of the experimental design.

[20] The model also predicts that equilibrium advertising levels and advertised prices will both be less with four sellers than with two sellers, and experimental results match this prediction.

Table 13.3 Results, Morgan *et al.* four-seller advertising experiments

Advertising fee	200		400	
	Predicted	Observed	Predicted	Observed
Advertising propensity (%)	39	53	24	39
Expected advertised price	64	63	75	69
Expected unadvertised price	100	98	100	97
Expected profits	367	290	433	302
Expected price to loyal buyers	86	80	94	86
Expected price to bargain-hunters	63	52	82	66

Source: Morgan *et al.* (2005, Table 2, Table 3).

SUMMARY

Advertising and other kinds of sales efforts may inform, so that consumers consider a wider range of possibilities when they make purchasing decisions. Sales efforts may persuade, tilting a purchasing decision toward one brand and away from others. Or sales efforts may simply reenforce established consumption patterns.

Advertising may have the purpose or effect (or both) of altering the cost of entry. Incumbents may advertise in part because their own accumulated goodwill requires entrants to advertise more to carve out a niche in the market. Incumbents may advertise to signal (accurately or otherwise) that they have low costs, or produce a high-quality variety.

Sales efforts increase social welfare if prices are lower when products are advertised, and reduce social welfare if prices are higher when products are advertised. Case studies suggest that the welfare effect of advertising may be positive in some markets, negative for others. There is evidence that consumption patterns change if advertising informs consumers that a product has characteristics consumers find beneficial (high fibre cereal). For some products, advertising weakens loyalties to other brands. And the signalling role of advertising, for products with which most potential buyers have previous consumption experience, presupposes a kind of depreciation of experience over time. In this case, the advertising signal reminds consumers of (or reinterprets for them) the nature of their consumption experience.

STUDY POINTS

- Dorfman-Steiner condition (Section 13.2.1)
- Advertising and goodwill (Section 13.2.2)
- Advertising and welfare, advertising and price (Section 13.2.4, Section 13.3.1, Section 13.6.2)
- Advertising as information source (Section 13.3.2, Section 13.3.4)

- Advertising as a signal (Section 13.3.3)
- Strategic advertising (Section 13.3.5, Section 13.4)
- Advertising and entry (Section 13.3.5)
- Price promotions (sales) (Section 13.5), price dispersion (Section 13.6)

FURTHER READING

Farris and Albion (1980) give a concise review of Chicago School—structure-conduct-performance school controversies over the impact of advertising on market performance. Cady (1976), Feldman and Begun (1980), and Kwoka (1984) employ the cross-jurisdiction comparison approach of Benham (1963) and obtain qualitatively similar results. For breakfast cereal industry studies, see Schmalensee (1978), Scherer (1979) and Wildman (1984), and Hausman (1997). On the Lydia E. Pinkham Medicine Company and the analysis of its sales and advertising data, see Palda (1964), Clarke (1976), Pollay (1979, 1984), Berndt (1991, pp. 400–404), and Munsey (2003). For discussion of pricing patterns for fashion goods, see Pashigian (1988), Pashigian and Bowen (1991).

INNOVATION

14

If we knew what it was we were doing, it would not be called research, would it?

Albert Einstein (attributed)

14.1 Introduction

The term "Schumpeterian competition" is used to denote rivalry in the development and commercialization of new products or production processes, in contrast with product market rivalry. It is often associated with the view that static market power can lead to improved market performance if (in some versions, since) it leads to more rapid technological progress. That is one of the possible relationships between static market power and technological performance conceived of by Joseph Schumpeter (1883–1950), one of the great economists of the first half of the twentieth century.

The questions Schumpeter asked are still with us, and are the subject of this chapter. Are large firms better innovators than small firms? What kind of market structure is most conducive to rapid technological progress? Is there is a tradeoff between static and dynamic market performance? Is there a feedback effect from technological rivalry to market structure?

In this chapter, after a review of what Schumpeter actually said about the topics that are debated in his name, we consider first theory and evidence on the firm size/market structure-innovation relationship, and second the impact of other market characteristics on innovative performance.

14.2 Schumpeterian Competition

Schumpeter conceived of innovation in a broad sense, as (1939, p. 84) "doing things differently". As examples of innovation, he gave (Schumpeter, 1947, p. 153) the introduction of new commodities, the introduction of new ways of producing old commodities, "the opening up of new markets for products or new sources of supply of materials", and "reorganizing an industry, for instance, by making a monopoly out of it". He made a distinction between invention, which involved (1939, p. 84) "scientific novelty" and innovation, which might or might not be directly related to invention. Similarly, he made a distinction between the inventor and the entrepreneur (Schumpeter, 1947, p. 152): "The inventor produces ideas, the entrepreneur 'gets things done,' which may but need not embody anything that is scientifically new."

14.2.1 Schumpeter Mark I

Schumpeter's views about market structure-innovation relationships changed over time. His early approach, modelled after the rough-and-tumble large-numbers oligopolies of early industrialization, was that the entrepreneur was central to innovation (1947, p. 154):

> The typical industrial entrepreneur of the nineteenth century was perhaps the man who put into practice a novel method of production by embodying it in a new firm and who then settled down into a position of owner-manager of a company, if he was successful, or of stockholding president of a company, getting old and conservative in the process.

In this vision, which Schumpeter called Competitive Capitalism and which we now call *Schumpeter Mark I*, it was the new firm that carried out innovation (1934b, p. 66):[1]

> it is not essential to the matter—though it may happen—that the new combinations should be carried out by the same people who control the productive or commercial process which is to be displaced by the new. On the contrary, new combinations are, as a rule, embodied, as it were, in new firms which generally do not arise out of the old ones but start producing beside them; ... in general it is not the owner of stage-coaches who builds railways.

14.2.2 Schumpeter Mark II

Schumpeter's later analysis was suggested by the concentrated market structures of the early twentieth century, which he called Trustified Capitalism. In this *Schumpeter Mark II* vision of innovation, it is the established firm that drives technological progress (1943, p. 82):

> As soon as we go into details and inquire into the individual items in which progress was most conspicuous, the trail leads not to the doors of those firms that work under conditions of comparatively free competition but precisely to the doors of the large concerns ... and a shocking suspicion dawns upon us that big business may have had more to do with creating that standard of life than with keeping it down.

In this possibly less romantic and probably more orderly world, innovation would be almost a matter of routine; in the words of John Kenneth Galbraith (1952, p. 86; see also Schumpeter, 1947, p. 157):

> Technical development has long since become the preserve of the scientist and the engineer. Most of the cheap and simple inventions have, to put it bluntly, been made. Not only is development now sophisticated and costly but it must be on a sufficient scale so that successes and failures will in some measure average out. Few can afford it if they must expect all projects to pay off.

---

[1] Schumpeter (1939, p. 96) regarded an old firm that underwent a complete change of management as a new firm.

14.3 Market Structure, Firm Size, and Innovation

14.3.1 Theory

Market Structure

Monopoly vs. Competition   Arrow's (1962) seminal contribution compares the profitability to be gained by cost-reducing or *process innovation* under monopoly, all else equal, with the profit to be gained by making the same innovation in an otherwise identical perfectly competitive industry. To illustrate Arrow's approach, consider a monopoly market with inverse demand equation:

$$p = 100 - Q, \tag{14.1}$$

as shown in Figure 14.1.

If marginal and average cost are $c_1 = 50$ per unit of output, the monopolist maximizes profit by producing 25 units of output, and the resulting monopoly profit is 625. If, on the other hand, marginal and average cost are $c_2 = 25$ per unit of output, the monopolist maximizes profit by producing 37.5 units of output, and monopoly profit is 1406.25. The profit a monopolist can gain by developing a new production process that reduces marginal and average cost from 50 to 25 is:

$$\pi_2 - \pi_1 = 1406.25 - 625 = 781.25. \tag{14.2}$$

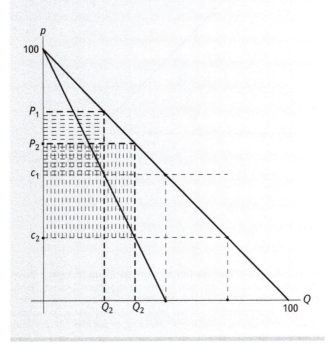

Figure 14.1 Profit to be gained by innovation under monopoly; $p = 100 - Q$; $c_1 = 50$; $c_2 = 25$; $Q_1 = 25$, $P_1 = 100 - 25 = 75$, $Q_2 = 37.5$, $P_2 = 62.5$

This is shown in Figure 14.1 as the difference between the area $(P_2 - c_2)Q_2$, profit after the innovation, and the area $(P_1 - c_1)Q_1$, profit before the innovation. A fully informed, profit-maximizing monopolist would be willing to spend up to 781.25 on a project to reduce unit cost from 50 to 25.

Now suppose that an otherwise identical industry is perfectly competitive.[2] If marginal and average cost are 50 per unit, then in long-run equilibrium price is also 50 per unit, the quantity supplied is 50 units, and firms earn zero economic profit, $\pi_1 = 0$. If a single firm develops a cost-reducing innovation for which it receives a completely effective patent (excluding all other firms from use of the new technology) and is able to produce at constant marginal and average cost 25 per unit, it can supply the entire market—sell slightly more than 50 units of output at a price slightly less than 50—and earn an economic profit/efficiency rent $\pi_2 = (50 - 25)(50) = 1250$. This is shown in Figure 14.2 as the area

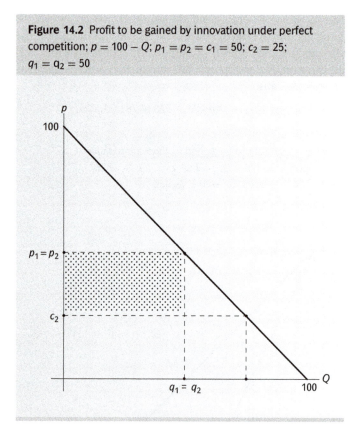

Figure 14.2 Profit to be gained by innovation under perfect competition; $p = 100 - Q$; $p_1 = p_2 = c_1 = 50$; $c_2 = 25$; $q_1 = q_2 = 50$

---

[2] Arrow's comparison is of the profit to be gained by an innovating firm in a given industry depending on whether the pre-innovation market structure is monopoly or perfect competition. Demsetz (1969, pp. 14–19) shows that a monopolist innovator will gain more than an innovator in a perfectly competitive market if the monopolist supplies a market in which the quantity demanded, at any price, is twice that demanded in the perfectly competitive market. It is not obvious why Demsetz' comparison is interesting; in any event, it says nothing about Arrow's analysis.

$(p_1 - c_2)q_1$. The profit a firm in a competitive industry can gain by first developing a new production process that reduces marginal and average cost from 50 to 25 is more than the payoff to a monopolist that develops the same innovation:

$$\pi_2 - \pi_1 = 1250 - 0 = 1250 > 781.25. \tag{14.3}$$

The result that cost-reducing innovation yields greater profit in a perfectly competitive industry than in an otherwise identical monopoly is a general one, and does not depend on the particular example that we have used here. For the innovating firm in a competitive industry—a firm that innovates to escape the constraints of static product market competition—all of the profit that flows from successful innovation is a net gain. For an identically situated a monopolist, part of the payoff from new process innovation replaces profit that would have been earned in any case with the existing technology. This *replacement effect* (Tirole, 1988, Chapter 10) means that the profit from cost-reducing innovation in a competitive industry is greater than it would be if the industry were monopolized.

By developing a lower-cost way of producing a homogeneous product, an innovating competitive firm can capture the entire market, and collect an efficiency rent equal to the cost-saving per unit output times the quantity demanded at the pre-innovation unit cost. But most manufacturing R&D aims to commercialize new (that is, differentiated) products, not new processes.[3] If a firm develops a new product and some consumers opt for old varieties in the post-innovation market, the profit earned by producers of the old varieties, like the replacement effect, reduces the profit of the successful innovator. A monopolist producer of all varieties, taking demand interactions into account, may earn a greater incremental profit from *product innovation* than would an otherwise identically situated producer of a single variety.[4]

 BOX **The Art Biz in 17th-century Netherlands: Process Innovation, Product Innovation, and Diffusion**

There are general economic laws, of innovation as with other aspects of economic activity. The details of the application of those laws differ from market to market (Montias, 1990, pp. 51–52):

> A product innovation introduces a totally new commodity (e.g. a horseless carriage) or changes the outward characteristics of an old one (color TV replacing the old black-and-white one). A process innovation reduces the cost of turning out an existing product (e.g. as where an automatic machine replaces a hand-powered weaving loom). In industry the two types of innovation can often be kept distinct, if only because many process innovations increase the productivity and lower the costs of the machines that make the products, rather than the products themselves ... Not so in art, where almost any cost-cutting process innovation will change the appearance of the product. Here the two types of innovation may be thought of as proceeding simultaneously.

Even in art, production is a process (Vermeylen, 2001, p. 52):*

> [W]orkshops produced art in a semi-industrial fashion, applying process-innovation strategies to cut costs. ... In painting, this resulted in the serial production of a few well-chosen compositions. ... The

---

[3] For the Scherer (1982b, p. 229; 1984, pp. 419–420) sample of large U.S. manufacturing firms for the early 1970s, about one-quarter of R&D aimed to develop new processes, three-quarters to develop new products.

[4] See Greenstein and Ramey (1998) for an analysis in the context of vertical product differentiation.

use of patterns and models was widespread in the southern Netherlands from the fifteenth century onward, and a rich collection of prints and drawings was essential to the success of any workshop. . . . techniques such as pouncing and tracing enabled artists and their assistants to duplicate existing compositions countless times.

Techniques that permitted the realization of economies of scale were combined with product differentiation in the pursuit of profit (Montias, 1990, p. 52):

[P]roductivity-increasing, cost-cutting process innovations that artists introduced in the 16th century . . . , which included ready-made patterns and pumices in painting and interchangeable, mechanically made figures and decorative trimmings in carved altarpieces, at least attempted to maintain the overall appearance of the products . . .

In the first half of the 17th century . . . an unprecedented phenomenon occurred: a popular new style developed in painting that also happened to reduce the time and effort to execute a work. The innovation was both 'process' and 'product'. . . . the gradual abandonment of the linear, minutely descriptive approach, characteristic of late 16th century 'manneristic' painters, and its replacement by a painterly, broadly evocative style, which reached its culmination in the tonal or 'monochromatic' paintings of the late 1640s. This evolution was perhaps most evident in landscape painting, but it also played a distinct role in still-life . . . and in history painting[.]

*Vermeylen (2001, p. 52): "Pouncing most often involved tracing the original composition on paper, and subsequently transferring the sketch—and, hence, the composition—through pricking, onto another canvas or panel."

The diffusion of product and process innovation (that is, spillovers) improved market performance (Montias, 1990, pp. 54–55):

Was it economic or artistic factors that had motivated artists to adopt these productivity-enhancing innovations in the first place? I don't think we shall find the answer to this question in the case of the first innovators . . . But I am fairly sure that the imitators of the products of these innovators had no choice: if they wanted to match the relatively low prices that this kind of modern painting brought, they had to paint more quickly and turn out more paintings every week or month to make a tolerable living. What happened, in other words, is that as a result of competition, the beneficial effects of the cost-cutting innovation accrued, neither to the innovators nor to their imitators, but to the consumers of the new products who could now more easily afford them.

Oligopoly   The Arrow analysis is that the replacement effect means that firms earning economic profit will have less to gain from innovation than firms that do not earn economic profit, all else equal. On the other side of the question, four main reasons for expecting large firms to have advantages in carrying out R&D appear in the literature:[5]

- large firms are able to spread fixed cost of research over a larger sales base;

- large firms have advantages in financial markets;

- large firms are better able to exploit economies of scale and scope in research, if such economies exist;

---

[5] Galbraith (1952, p. 86, quoted in Section 14.2.2); Nelson (1959); Mansfield (1963, p. 557); Henderson and Cockburn (1996, p. 33).

- (the serendipity effect) a large, diversified firm is more likely to be able to exploit an unexpected discovery.

The Schumpeter Mark II view of innovation has been taken to imply that concentrated supply-side market structure favours innovation, and this for at least two reasons. First, leading firms in concentrated industries will earn economic profits, and so be able to finance costly R&D efforts.

Appropriability Second, with few significant rivals, a large firm deciding whether or not to invest in innovation can be reasonably confident that it would be able to *appropriate* the profits flowing from success—that the innovation would not be imitated by numerous small rivals and the profits competed away.[6] Arrow's competition vs. monopoly comparison makes the assumption that the successful innovator in a perfectly competitive market receives a completely effective patent. As we will see, this assumption is often at odds with reality. In many technology areas, patents are not particularly effective at excluding rivals.

 BOX The Cotton Gin

A classic example of inability to appropriate the profit from successful innovation is Eli Whitney and the cotton gin. The cotton gin made the cultivation of cotton profitable and revolutionized the economy of the early nineteenth-century southern United States. But once its basic idea was understood, it could be copied by any reasonably competent craftsman. At considerable expense, Whitney succeeded in some legal efforts to enforce his patent rights. But imitation made his initial business plan of producing and selling cotton gins unprofitable. He fell back on the plan B of licensing the use of his technology to others rather than exploiting it himself.

See Mirsky and Nevins (1952), Hirshleifer (1971, pp. 570–571).

Market structure It is an old idea in industrial economics that innovation will rise with concentration from low to intermediate concentration levels, then fall as concentration rises from intermediate to high levels, so that a graph of R&D effort or results against concentration would have an inverted-∪ shape.[7]

 BOX Stick-to-it Serendipity

3M Company began life as the Minnesota Mining and Manufacturing Co. It was long best known to the general public as the manufacturer of Scotch® Tape. But business clients knew it as the source of a wide variety of abrasive products, and in this regard 3M invested heavily in the development of

---

[6] For a formal treatment of the impact of easy imitation on innovation in oligopoly, see Baldwin and Childs (1969), and from a somewhat different perspective, Teece (1986).

To fully appropriate the social benefit of a new product innovation, an innovating firm would have to be able to first-degree price discriminate, and this will not normally be feasible. Imitation—what we will call R&D output spillovers—further reduces the payoff of an innovator that cannot price discriminate.

[7] An inverted-∪ relation between market structure and other types of non-price competition, such as advertising, was also expected (and often found).

adhesives that might be used in the production of industrial sandpaper and other products. In 1968 a 3M researcher developed an adhesive that was not very sticky:

> It was an adhesive that formed itself into tiny spheres with the diameter of a paper fiber. The spheres would not dissolve, could not be melted, and were very sticky individually. But because they made only intermittent contract, they did not stick very strongly when coated onto tape backings.

3M researchers worked for years to find commercial applications for the moderately sticky adhesive. The break came when 3M researcher Art Fry, frustrated "at how his scrap paper bookmarks kept falling out of his church choir hymnal . . . realized that [the] adhesive could make . . . a wonderfully reliable bookmark". Considerable work remained to build on this insight, but the end result, brought to market in 1980, was the now-ubiquitous Post-it® sticker, the product of a research programme that paid off in an unexpected way.

Source: "Art Fry and the invention of Post-it® Notes", <http://www.3m.com/about3m/pioneers/fry.jhtml>, downloaded 26 November 2006. On 3M generally, see Huck (1955).

Expecting that appropriability would be weak, that public policy would compel the licensing of really fundamental innovations to competitors, and that financing would[8] be scarce in low-concentration industries, while firms in high-concentration industries might opt for the quiet life, Villard (1958, p. 491) suggested that:

> [I]ndustries where "competitive oligopoly" prevails are likely to progress most rapidly and that therefore "competitive oligopoly" may well be the best way of organizing industry. The basic point is that progress is likely to be rapid (1) when firms are large enough or few enough to afford and benefit from research and (2) when they are under competitive pressure to innovate—utilize the results of research.

Another reason to expect reduced investment in innovation in high-concentration industries is the *replacement effect*: the incremental profit from innovation is less, all else equal, to the extent that potential innovators earn oligopoly profits in the pre-innovation market.

Arrow: large firms vs. small

Arrow (1983) draws on the theory of information flows to conclude that large firms and small firms will have comparative advantages in different types of innovation.

Transaction costs in the transmission of information will affect R&D funding decisions for large and small firms alike, but the nature of the effects differs. Small firms, with little if any financial reserves, will be obliged to seek external funding for large-scale innovation projects. Financial markets, with limited ability to distinguish more promising from less promising projects, will raise the cost of financial capital for all small borrowers, to compensate for the perceived risk of default. Small firms will pay a higher interest rate for what they are able to borrow, and it will often be impossible for small firms to obtain substantial amounts of external funding at *any* interest rate.

Large, established firms will be able to raise funds externally at lower interest rates than small, new firms. Large firms will generate more internal funds than small firms. Indeed,

---

[8] For a more formal argument to the same effect, see Scherer (1967b, p. 391).

one of the advantages of diversification was thought to be that corporate management could harvest cash from profitable divisions with low growth prospects and invest it sectors that promised greater long-run returns. But to obtain funding for an investment project, an operating division will have to defend the project to a corporate management that is less informed and less expert than it is. There will also be competing demands for corporate management attention; corporate management will see the merits of a proposed innovation, whatever those merits are, less clearly than those at the operating level. Such managerial diseconomies of scale imply that large-firm investment in innovation, like small-firm investment in innovation, will be handicapped by information-transmission transaction costs. But large firms will have a comparative advantage, relative to small firms, in funding large-budget R&D.

If corporate management's world view is conditioned by established technologies, (Arrow, 1983, p. 24) "there may be a bias against greater originality in large firms". This is the Schumpeter Mark I analysis. But large firms, with funds to invest, will be well-positioned to purchase the R&D results of small firms, or the small firms themselves, once a project has been carried as far as a small firm's resources permit (Arrow, 1983, p. 27):[9]

> Smaller firms will tend to specialize more in the research phase and in smaller development processes; larger firms will devote a much smaller proportion of their research and development budget to the research phase. They will specialize in the larger developments and will buy a considerable fraction of the research basis for their subsequent development of innovations.

14.3.2 Evidence[10]

Firm Size and innovation

The Schumpeter Mark II approach makes two distinct but related claims. The first is that large firms have a comparative advantage in innovation, compared with small firms. The second is

---

[9] See Mowery and Rosenberg (1993, p. 32, internal citations and footnote omitted): "[E]arly [19-century] research laboratories focused in part on developing inventions created by in-house research, but also monitored the environment for technological threats and opportunities for the acquisition of new technologies, in many cases through the purchase of patents or firms. Many of Du Pont's major product and process innovations, for example, were obtained by the firm at an early point in their development, often on the advice of the central research laboratory. For much of the pre-1940 period, Du Pont research focused on developing inventions acquired from external sources; nylon and neoprene were exceptions to this rule. The research facilities of AT&T, General Electric, and, to a lesser extent, Eastman Kodak, performed similar monitoring roles during this period."

[10] The empirical literature on innovation brings to mind Frank H. Knight's (1940, fn. 10) admonition that "Insistence on a concretely quantitative economics means the use of statistics of physical magnitudes, whose economic meaning and significance is uncertain and dubious. ... In this field, ['where you cannot measure your knowledge is meagre and unsatisfactory'] very largely means in practice, 'if you cannot measure, measure anyhow!'" Thus, some empirical tests of the extent to which innovation is related to firm size and seller concentration examine the way firms' use of R&D inputs, such as spending on R&D or employment of scientists and engineers, varies with firm size and seller concentration (and other factors). Other studies examine the way some measure of R&D output (most often patents) varies with firm size and seller concentration (and other factors). But not all innovations are the fruit of budgeted R&D programs; not all corporate patents are due to technical personnel. A firm's R&D output depends not only on its own R&D inputs but on the accumulated intellectual soup of its technology area; R&D inputs generate innovation, if at all, with a lag that will vary from firm and sector to sector. Not all innovations are patented. If one presumes that the patent office does its job, all patents represent innovations, but some innovations are more innovative than others. Nowhere more than here is attention to the details and limitations of measurement called for; see Scherer (1965a), Cohen *et al.* (1987), Acs and Audretsch (1987), and Griliches (1979, 1989, 1990).

that supply-side market concentration favours innovation, all else equal. On balance, neither claim has fared well in empirical tests.

Patenting Nicholas (2003) examines the relationship between firm size and patenting for publicly listed U.S. firms for 1908–1918 and 1919–1928.[11] Particularly for the second time period, he finds that large firms and firms with intermediate or high market shares (more than 40 per cent) have significantly more patents, all else equal. Firms with higher patent counts also had higher stock-market values than would otherwise have been the case. This supports the Schumpeter Mark II version of the firm size, market structure relationship (Nicholas, 2003, pp. 1054–1055): "firms with high levels of market power tended to innovate more because they had strong incentives to do so pre-emptively: the threat of creative destruction loomed in the product market, and financial markets rewarded innovators with large payoffs".

Employment Mowery (1983b) examines the U.S. firm size-R&D employment relationship for 1921–1946, for samples that include firms among the 200 largest U.S. manufacturing firms and for some smaller firms. In this later period, larger firms outside the chemical industries did *not* employ disproportionately more scientific personnel than smaller firms, all else equal, a finding that supports the Schumpeter Mark I hypothesis. After 1933, R&D employment is associated with more rapid firm growth, for firms of all sizes. Mansfield (1963), who studies the periods 1919–1938 and 1939–1958, gives some comfort to Schumpeter Mark I, finding that the largest U.S. steel producers had a smaller share of steel industry innovations than of steel industry capacity, and some comfort to Schumpeter Mark II, finding that the largest U.S. coal and petroleum producers had a larger share of their industry's innovations than of its output (coal) or capacity (petroleum).

Fortune 500 Scherer (1965b) looks at the relation between firm and market characteristics in 1955 and the number of patents per firm in 1959, for 448 firms from the 1955 *Fortune* list of the largest U.S. corporations. The four-year lag is because (Scherer, 1965b, p. 1097, reference omitted) "on the average nine months pass between the conception of an industrial invention and the filing of a patent application and because during the 1950's three and one-half years were required for the Patent Office to process an average application to the point of issue". For these firms (1965b, p. 1103) "sales volume is persistently more concentrated among the largest firms than R&D employment, which in turn tends to be slightly more concentrated than patenting". That is, among firms large enough to be listed among the Fortune 500, smaller firms have a greater share of patents than they do of R&D employment, and a greater share of R&D employment than they do of sales. Firms in high-technology sectors (of the day: mostly chemical and electrical industries) patented more, all else equal, than firms in other sectors. Market concentration had little impact on patenting.

U.S. manufacturing Beginning with firms listed in Standard and Poor's Compustat financial reporting services for publicly listed firms, Bound *et al.* (1984) construct a comprehensive database describing about 2600 U.S. manufacturing firms for 1976. For this later and much

---

[11] Both samples of firms, he notes (2003, p. 1028) "are dominated by firms incorporated during the great merger wave ... "

larger sample, the results for technological opportunity are qualitatively similar to those of Scherer (Bound *et al.*, 1984, p. 48): "research and development is done across all manufacturing industries with much higher intensities in such technologically progressive industries as chemicals, drugs, computing equipment, communication equipment, and professional and scientific instruments". Over the whole range of firm sizes, R&D spending is more-or-less proportional to firm size, but there is evidence that small firms and large firms both invest more in R&D than intermediate-size firms.[12] As Bound *et al.* note (1984, pp. 51–52), the small firms in their sample are distinctive, in the universe of all small firms, in the sense that they are successful enough to be listed on organized financial markets.

Innovative output   Acs and Audretsch (1988) analyse the impact of firm size on innovation for U.S. manufacturing industries using a U.S. government census of manufacturing industry innovations, classified by originating firm and industry, for 1982. Descriptively (Table 14.1), their results confirm those of Mansfield (1963): small firms have a greater share of innovations than of employment in some sectors, a smaller share of innovations than of employment in other sectors. Analytically, they find that (1988, pp. 687–688) "the number of small-firm innovations tends to be small relative to that in the entire industry in industries which are high in R&D, capital-intensive, and which are concentrated. ... the innovation activity of small firms is high relative to the industry level in industries in which there is only a small share of small firms, and in which skilled labor plays an important role".

Summary   Cohen and Klepper (1996b) summarize empirical studies of the firm size-R&D relationship as showing:

(a) the probability that a firm does R&D at all rises with firm size;

(b) for most industries, among firms that do R&D, R&D is roughly proportional to firm size;

(c) among firms that do R&D, R&D productivity—the number of innovations per unit of spending on R&D—falls as firm size rises.

They explain these results in terms of large firms' ability to spread the cost of R&D over greater output (Cohen and Klepper, 1996, p. 933):

> Intuitively, larger firms pursue more marginal R & D projects than smaller firms because they have a bigger output over which they can apply the results of the projects ... Consequently, the average project they pursue has a lower return, measured in terms of the number of patents or innovations, than smaller firms. ... The greater output over which larger firms can apply their R & D enables them to profit more from R & D than smaller firms, which leads them to undertake more R & D projects at the margin than smaller firms. By undertaking more R & D, larger firms achieve a lower average cost of production and/or higher product quality and hence greater profits than smaller firms. This explains why larger firms can prosper despite the lower average productivity of their R & D.

Cohen and Klepper expect—and their own empirical results show—that the size-R&D relationship should be weaker for high-growth industries and for industries where much of the profit from innovation can be realized by licensing use of the innovation to others,

---

[12] Scott (2009) outlines conditions under which one might observe such a ∪-shaped competition/R&D relationship at the firm level.

Table 14.1 Number of innovations and the relative innovative activity of large and small firms in the most innovative U.S. industries, 1982

	Small-firm innovation share	Small-firm employment share	Innovation share / Employment share
Petroleum	0.400	0.113	3.540
Electrical Equipment	0.411	0.164	2.506
Instruments	0.506	0.221	2.290
Transportation Equipment	0.149	0.075	1.987
Machinery (non-electrical)	0.485	0.289	1.678
Primary Metals	0.276	0.227	1.216
Food	0.228	0.220	1.036
Fabricated Metal Products	0.388	0.524	0.740
Paper	0.161	0.234	0.688
Leather	0.273	0.422	0.647
Stone, Clay, and Glass	0.219	0.347	0.631
Furniture	0.365	0.596	0.612
Textiles	0.133	0.325	0.409
Printing	0.191	0.524	0.365
Chemicals	0.313	0.135	0.319
Apparel	0.099	0.565	0.175
Lumber	0.088	0.564	0.156

Source: Acs and Audretsch (1988).

as opposed to direct exploitation.[13] In companion work (Cohen and Klepper, 1996a), they point to the relative advantage of large firms for innovations where profitability is tied to output levels to explain the predilection of large firms for process innovation, while smaller firms are more inclined to product innovations.

---

[13] Cohen and Klepper identify four high-growth industries (industrial controls and motors and generators, cleaning agents, industrial organic chemicals, and miscellaneous plastic products), and, one, drugs, as an industry where licensing is an effective way to profit from innovation.

Market structure and innovation

Scherer (1967) found an inverted-∪ relationship between concentration ratios and employment of technical personnel in 56 U.S. manufacturing industries in 1960: employment of technical personnel rose with the four-firm seller concentration through values between 50 and 55 per cent, and fell thereafter. When Scott (1984) examines the relation between R&D spending per dollar of sales and seller concentration for 3,388 lines of business[14] of 437 U.S. manufacturing firms, he finds an inverted-∪ with a peak at a four-firm seller concentration ratio of 64 per cent. When he controls for unobserved firm and industry effects, however, the inverted-∪ relationship disappears.

Seller concentration is a central aspect of market structure, and it is the seller concentration-innovation link that has been most subject to empirical testing. Market share is another aspect of market structure. One might think that a firm with a larger market share would be better able to finance innovation and better able to appropriate profit from successful innovation, holding the effect of seller concentration constant. Blundell *et al.* (1999) examine the impact of market share, market concentration, and other industry characteristics on innovation for 340 UK manufacturing firms for the years 1972–1982. In their sample, more concentrated industries had fewer innovations, as did industries facing less import competition. But within an industry (1999, p. 550), "it was the high market share firms who tended to commercialize more innovations ... " Further, innovating firms with high market shares had greater stock-market values than high-market-share firms that did not innovate.

Rivalry and innovation[15]

Schumpeter Mark II holds that there will be a positive impact of market concentration on innovation *because* the leading firms in concentrated markets will be shielded from rivalry—thus, they will earn economic profits that will allow them to finance innovation, and (having few rivals), they will be able to act in confidence that they will be able to collect whatever profit flows from successful innovation. Some studies look directly at the impact of rivalry on innovative performance.

Productivity   Baily and Gersbach (1995) examine the impact of rivalry on productivity for nine industries in Germany, Japan, and the United States. They emphasize the importance of international rivalry as a promoter of competitivity (1995, p. 308):

> [I]t is the nature of competition facing companies that strongly influences the productivity of the production processes used in a given industry in a given country and hence whether that industry is a leader or a follower or is becoming a leader. In particular, it is vital that industries in a given country compete against companies with the best manufacturing processes, wherever these leaders are located, so that they themselves become best-practice producers. Vigorous global competition against the best-practice companies not only spurs allocative efficiency, it can also force structural change in industries and encourage the adoption of more efficient product and process designs.

---

[14] A "line of business" was an operation of a diversified firm in a particular industry; the data was collected by the now-defunct Line of Business Program of the U.S. Federal Trade Commission.

[15] There is a direct analogy between the decision to invest in process innovation and efforts to increase operating efficiency: both involve current spending in hopes of lower future cost (Vives, 2008, p. 421). The literature on the impact of rivalry on X-inefficiency (Section 2.5.3) therefore provides indirect evidence about the impact of rivalry on firms' incentives to invest in process innovation.

They also find (1995, p. 345) that competition by foreign firms, not bound or blinded by traditional ways of doing things, has a much greater impact on performance than competition by domestic firms.

Concentration   Broadberry and Crafts (2001) look at the impact of market structure and trade association activity on innovation in the UK in the 1950s. They find little evidence that trade association activity affected innovation,[16] but there is a negative impact of seller concentration on innovation. They conclude that (2001, p. 112) "On balance, the evidence . . . goes against the claim that market power promotes innovation."

Lerner index   Aghion *et al.* (2005) find an inverted-$\cup$ relation between patents, a measure of R&D output, and the Lerner index, a measure of market performance that they interpret as an index of competition, for a sample of UK firms between 1973 and 1994. They model the incentive to innovate as depending on the difference between pre-innovation and post-innovation profits.[17] At intermediate levels of rivalry, they argue, the successful innovator will have the most to gain, so the incentive to escape competition will induce greater investment in innovation, all else equal.

Summary   Gilbert (2006, pp. 205–206) concludes his survey with the observation:

> The empirical literature does not support a conclusion that large firms promote innovation because they provide large and stable cash flows, economies of scale (above some threshold), or risk diversification. This is contrary to Schumpeter's argument that monopoly can promote innovation by providing a "more stable platform" for R&D. At the same time, neither theory nor empirical evidence supports a strong conclusion that competition is uniformly a stimulus to innovation.

It remains possible to argue that Villard's (1958) "competitive oligopoly" is the most hospitable environment for technological advance.[18]

   BOX   **The Sailing Ship Effect**

The greatest technological refinements of sailing technology were achieved after the introduction of steamships, when it was clear that sail power, for commercial use at least, was a dying technology (Gilfillan, 1935, p. 157):   »

---

[16] In other work (Broadberry and Crafts, 1996) they identify a negative impact of trade association activity on productivity growth.

[17] That innovation depends on this difference in profit is part of Arrow (1962), and is a standard result of innovation-race models (Section 15.11; for a review, see Martin (2002a, Section 14.4)). It explains the sailing ship effect, that the fear of profit to be lost if a firm does not innovate can be as great an incentive as the prospect of profit to be gained if a firm does innovate. See the accompanying box.

[18] Saul (1960) is an interesting study of the impact of American competition on British industrial performance at the end of the nineteenth and start of the twentieth centuries. After reviewing difficulties of British industry, he concludes (p. 36, footnote omitted) "Yet it would have been a serious mistake to have attempted to cure all this by restricting foreign competition. In all the industries we have discussed imports from overseas helped to create new demands and to stimulate British industry to action."

> ➤ Large size was 5- to 800 tons in 1800, and for three centuries previously; by mid-century it was 2,000, carrying hundreds, even 1,000 emigrants; and today 3- to 5,000 tons register. Iron was used first for bolts, then in diagonal strips for strengthening the hull, then in knees (1810), breast-hooks and pillars, then for frames (composite build, 1850), and for the whole hull, 1838, followed much later by steel, and in time by iron (1840) and steel ('63) in masts, spars and standing and even running rigging.

In part, sail technology benefited from the same rise of new materials that permitted the development of steamships. In part, refinements in sail technology became possible *because of* the development of steam technology (Gilfillan, 1935, p. 157):

> For the steam tug, taking them in and out of harbor, relieved the windjammers of need for handiness, enabling greater length and fine lines, and enabling guaranteed sailings out of a harbor.

Taking advantage of these opportunities, firms invested substantial resources to improve a technology that was doomed to obsolescence.

See also Cooper and Schendel (1976) and De Liso and Filatrella (2004).

14.3.3 Beyond Schumpeter

Schumpeter painted with a broad brush, and for non-economists, what he wrote is often seen as the beginning and end of the economics of innovation. The economics literature has long since moved beyond the big firm versus small firm, monopoly versus competition terms of the Schumpeter Mark I/Schumpeter Mark II debate to the analysis of firm, industry, and technology characteristics that facilitate or impede innovation.

Demand-pull/technology-push

Much of this analysis builds on an early post-Schumpeter literature disputing the relative importance of demand and technology—supply—in commercializing technical advance.[19] Jacob Schmookler (1962, 1966) put forward the idea that in a market system, more resources would be invested in innovations that were expected to be more profitable, all else equal, and that expected profit would be positively related to output. Thus private investment in innovation would be pulled toward sectors with high or growing demand. Schmookler found

---

[19] A simple model of process innovation, based on Nordhaus (1989, pp. 321–322), illustrates the interaction of demand and technology (supply) to jointly determine profit-maximizing innovation levels. Let pre-innovation unit cost be c and post-innovation unit cost $(1 - \rho)c$, where the proportional cost reduction ρ lies between zero and one. Let annual market sales be S. Abstract from the fact that in general one would expect lower cost to result in a lower price, and a lower price to result in greater sales, and assume that S is unchanged by innovation. Assume also that sales are to final consumer demand. (If the product is an intermediate good, welfare changes in using industries due to cost reduction in the supplying industry would need to be taken into account.) Then the annual social benefit of cost-reducing innovation is ρcS. Using an interest rate r to discount annual values, the present value of the social benefit from innovation is $\rho cS/r$. Let α be the degree of appropriability, with $0 \leq \alpha \leq 1$. If first-degree price discrimination is not possible, $\alpha < 1$. The present value of the private benefit from innovation is then $\alpha\rho cS/r$. Suppose there is a Cobb-Douglas cost-reduction production function, $\rho = AR^x$, $0 < x < 1$, where R is input of R&D resources and A an R&D productivity shift parameter. If R&D inputs are hired at unit cost w_R, an innovating firm selects R to maximize $V = \frac{\alpha cS}{r}AR^x - w_R R$. From the first-order condition to maximize V, the value-maximizing level of R&D inputs is $R^* = \left(A\frac{\alpha cS}{r}\frac{x}{w_R}\right)^{\frac{1}{1-x}}$. R^* rises with demand (S), with technological productivity (A), and with appropriability α. R^* is also larger as R&D inputs are less expensive (w_R smaller).

that the number of patents taken out in an industry tracked demand measures like output or capital good investment, usually with a lag. He concluded that (1962, p. 18, footnote omitted) "expected profits from invention, the ability to finance it, the number of potential inventors, and the dissatisfaction which invariably motivates it—are all likely to be positively associated with sales". In other words, Schmookler argued, in a market system it is the lure of profit that directs the allocation of resources to innovation (as it directs the allocation of resources to other activities).

Others argued that largely exogenous technological advance is a prerequisite to profitable innovation (Rosenberg, 1974, p. 97):

> It is certainly true that the progress made in techniques of navigation in the sixteenth and seventeenth centuries owed much to the great demand for such techniques in those centuries. ... But it is also true that a great potential demand existed in the same period for improvements in the healing arts generally, but that no such improvements were forthcoming. The essential explanation is that the state of mathematics and astronomy afforded a useful and reliable knowledge base for navigational improvements, whereas medicine at that time had no such base. Progress in medicine had to await the development of the science of bacteriology in the second half of the nineteenth century.

In this view, the quest for profit can play its role only after technical progress has laid the necessary foundation.

It is useful here to distinguish between fundamental and incremental innovation.[20] Fundamental innovations, like the steam engine or the semiconductor, make innovative applications possible in many sectors of the economy.[21] Fundamental innovations are fundamentally unpredictable, but when a fundamental innovation occurs, it triggers the cornucopia of progress that characterizes high-technology sectors of the economy (Klevorick *et al.*, p. 188):

> A striking characteristic of industries that are commonly thought to be rich in technological opportunities is that high R&D intensities and high rates of technical advance tend to be sustained over time. They do not fall off as one would expect if the most productive opportunities were being exhausted and no new ones were being added.

Once a fundamental innovation sets the stage for further progress, private investment follows expected profit to commercialize incremental innovations (Schmookler, 1962, p. 16): "Even if the germinal ideas for inventions occur costlessly and at random ..., it often takes talent, hard work and money to carry them out. These are not likely to be forthcoming in volume without commensurate prospective rewards in income or prestige. Clearly, prospective rewards will be favorably affected by high volume of sales of the commodity to be improved."

Incremental innovation occur in small steps, but those steps combine to generate substantial progress (Baily and Chakrabarti, 1985, p. 612):

> [S]mall, incremental innovations can be ... important. A breakthrough innovation—the shuttleless weaving machine—was available by the 1970s, but could not be used throughout the textile industry until successive generations of new machinery had been developed that both perfected

---

[20] Wilson (1974) adds a third category, "imitative innovation", of which he mentions reverse engineering and inventing around a patent as examples. See our discussions of appropriability and spillovers.

[21] See Bresnahan and Trajtenberg (1995), Jovanovic and Rousseau (2005).

the technology and adapted it to produce the great variety of fabrics that the industry makes. The new machinery developed over fifteen years or more made up a near-constant flow of equipment innovations that contributed to productivity growth.

A substantial literature tests the demand-pull and technology-push theories of innovation. Most often, these studies measure innovative activity by some index of patents taken out,[22] and control for differences in technological opportunity by subjectively identifying some sectors as "high-technology". [23] This work finds that demand and technology interact to determine interfirm and interindustry differences in innovation. Thus Scherer (1982a)[24] relates patenting activity by 443 large U.S. firms to variables describing demand in industries where the patents would be used and to industry groupings that differed in technological opportunity. Patenting activity responded immediately to demand fluctuations, giving some comfort to Schmookler, but technology regime also played a role. In comparison to industries using mechanical technologies, patenting responded more to differences in sales in areas like chemicals and electronics, less in sectors using traditional technologies.

Uncertainty

Uncertainty impinges on innovation in two fundamental ways. First, the creative process is inherently uncertain. Even in sectors where there is a strong link between scientific analysis and commercial applications, as in pharmaceuticals, exactly how a particular approach will turn out cannot be foreseen with certainty. In the words of one drug-industry researcher (quoted in Tapon and Cadsby, 1996, pp. 389–390):[25]

> I think that rational drug design is obviously very admirable. It's more than a great idea, it's a move in the right direction. It applies as much rationality to your programs as possible. But, you're not going to be able to predict 100% … of the outcome. You're always going to have things that happen that nobody really foresaw and you look back in hindsight and say that there is no way that we could have predicted that outcome … There is a certain amount of good luck involved … you have to have the breaks; if you don't have the breaks in drug development you may have great difficulty in getting any compound.

---

[22] Patents are an imperfect measure of innovation; on this point, see fn. 10 as well as the discussion of patent effectiveness in Section 15.6.2.

[23] Scherer classifies industries (1982, p. 235) "into seven groups according to the perceived richness of their knowledge bases: organic chemicals, other chemicals, electronic systems and devices, other electrical equipment, the metallurgical trades, industries with 'traditional' technologies (such as sugar refining, textile weaving, and cement making), and a base case consisting mostly of industries with mechanical technologies". Wilson classifies industries into three groups (1988, p. 176): "There are eight industries classified as high opportunity—basic chemicals, plastics, synthetics; pharmaceuticals; computers; electronic equipment and components; aircraft and missiles; scientific instruments; optical and photographic equipment; and medical instruments and supplies. Low opportunity industries are primarily food, textile, wood, paper, stone, clay, glass, and metals industries. All others are classified as medium opportunity." The subjective classification of industries by technological opportunity can be justified by the fact that (Klevorick *et al.* 1995, p. 189, fn. 2; see similarly Mowery, 1995b, p. 155) "The ranking of industries by R&D intensity is remarkably stable over relatively short historical periods, such as a decade. In the United States the rank correlation between 1978 and 1988 industry R&D intensities (measured at the 2-1/2 digit level by the National Science Foundation) is 0.956."

[24] See also Stoneman (1979), Jaffe (1988), Kleinknecht and Verspagen (1990).

[25] In this regard, not much has changed since Nelson (1959a, p. 112, p. 113) observed that "There is considerable uncertainty as to the outcome of a research and development program, the uncertainty being, of course, closely related to the degree of knowledge in the relevant fields and to the advance sought in the program" and "What looks good on paper may not look so good in practice."

Second, market uncertainty must be added to technical uncertainty. What is the target market? How will it respond to a new product or design? While market uncertainty is present even for new varieties of an existing product,[26] trying to predict the nature of demand for a genuinely new product is a major hurdle for the aspiring entrepreneur.[27]

Technical and market uncertainty reduce firms' incentives to invest in R&D, all else equal.

Spillovers, absorptive capacity, appropriability

We return to the topics of spillovers and appropriability, and introduce the concept of absorptive capacity. R&D input spillovers mean a firm's R&D efforts reduce the cost of rivals' R&D. R&D output spillovers mean that imitation prevents a successful innovator from appropriating the full social benefit, or even the potential monopoly profit, that flows from its discovery. "Absorptive capacity", a minimum level of pertinent expertise, may be necessary for a firm to take advantage of information flows that come its way. The more rivals must invest in absorptive capacity to profit from spillovers, the less input or output spillovers take place, and the greater is appropriability. There is reason to think that the nature of spillovers, and firms' incentives to invest in absorptive capacity, vary in a systematic way depending on the type of R&D that is in play.

Spillovers Investment in innovation is characterized by input spillovers and output spillovers, both of which make the private return to R&D less than the social return (Arrow, 1962, p. 615):

> [N]o amount of legal protection can make a thoroughly appropriable commodity of something so intangible as information. The very use of the information in any productive way is bound to reveal it, at least in part. Mobility of personnel among firms provides a way of spreading information. Legally imposed property rights can provide only a partial barrier, since there are obviously enormous difficulties in defining in any sharp way an item of information and differentiating it from similar sounding items.

Schumpeter recognized that a fundamental innovation would trigger a follow-on cycle of incremental innovation (1935, p. 6):

> [A]s soon as the various kinds of social resistance to something that is fundamentally new and untried have been overcome, it is much easier not only to do the same thing again but also to do similar things in different directions, so that a first success will always produce a cluster. (See, e.g., the emergence of the motor-car industry.)

There are references here to two distinct phenomena. The first is innovation spillovers, "doing the same thing again". An entrepreneur commercializes knowledge in search of economic profit. Followers imitate the innovation and erode that economic profit. The innovator is worse off. Looking at one round of innovation in isolation, spillovers improve static market performance, because the innovative product is supplied (the innovative process is

---

[26] The Ford Motor Company's 1957 introduction of the Edsel is a prominent but by no means unique example of firms' inability to predict how the market will react to a new variety.

[27] IBM president Thomas J. Watson is supposed to have said in 1945 that "I think there is a world market for about five computers" (Salus, 1994, p. 16). Very likely he was describing the market for large mainframe computers. Even with that qualification, the market turned out to be substantially larger than seems to have been anticipated.

applied) in a more competitive market. But if potential entrepreneurs who follow anticipate that their profits too would be reduced by imitators, they will be less willing to make the investments that would trigger later waves of innovation.

The second is that an innovation may extend beyond the original field of application. Doing "similar things in different directions", Toyota developed "just-in-time" production in the car industry. This was certainly an innovation[28] in Schumpeter's sense—a new way of producing old commodities.[29] As a way of organizing production, it could be applied to many different products, not just automobiles. More generally, as suggested by Schumpeter's reference to the motor car industry, innovation is cumulative. Henry Ford's fundamental innovation, the commercial application of mass production techniques, made possible an uncountable number of product and process innovations. To the extent that the anticipation of R&D output spillovers reduces the expected profitability of investing in innovation, such spillovers reduce the rate of technological advance. To the extent that R&D output spillovers are the basis for future innovation, they speed the rate of technological advance. Moderate levels of R&D output spillovers will leave firms some reason to invest in innovation and support later innovation.

R&D input spillovers occur when the R&D efforts of one firm help rivals reach their own research goals. For example, Henderson and Cockburn (1996, pp. 35–36) write of the pharmaceutical industry that it:

> is characterized by high rates of publication in the open scientific literature, and many of the scientists ... stressed the importance of keeping in touch with the science conducted both within the public sector and by their competitors. Nearly all of them had a quite accurate idea of the nature of the research being conducted by their competitors, and they often described the ways in which their rivals' discoveries had been instrumental in shaping their own research.

Effective R&D effort in high science-content sectors like pharmaceuticals requires that researchers keep abreast of the knowledge frontier in their field. The interactions this requires reveal what they are doing to researchers working in other places, just as they learn what other researchers are doing.

R&D output spillovers occur when first-discoverers are not able to collect all of the economic profit generated by their innovation. In a study of 48 US new product innovations, Mansfield et al. (1981) report that 60 per cent of successful patented innovations were imitated within four years of introduction. For a sample of 100 U.S. manufacturing firms, Mansfield (1985) reports survey evidence indicating that rivals have information about R&D decisions in 12–18 months, and information about new products or processes in 12 months or less.[30] Such leakages occur (Mansfield, 1985, p. 221) because:

---

[28] But see Schwartz and Fish (1998), who document use of a "hand-to-mouth" industrial organization in 1920s and 1930s Detroit that had the essential characteristics of just-in-time production.

[29] The importance of "ways of doing things" is emphasized by Baily and Gersbach, who conclude from an international comparison of productivity differences in nine industries (1995, p. 308) that "The major part of the productivity differences ... can be attributed to the way functions and tasks are organized and to the fact that some companies have designed the products they make so that they require less labor and material to manufacture."

[30] Cabellero and Jaffe analyse patent citation patterns, conclude that the diffusion of information about innovations is essentially instantaneous, and note (1993, pp. 68–69) that this finding is consistent with the results of Mansfield (1985).

input suppliers and customers are important channels (since they pass on a great deal of relevant information), patent applications are scrutinized very carefully, and reverse engineering is carried out. In still other industries, the diffusion process is accelerated by the fact that firms do not go to great lengths to keep such information secret, partly because they believe it would be futile in any event.

"Copycat" innovation may involve simply replicating another firm's invention, but need not be so crude. Simply knowing that some lines of research work, while others do not, will allow follow-after firms to carry their own independent work forward more rapidly and at a lower cost than first innovators.

 BOX   Innovation Spillovers

There was a web of connections between the pioneers of the steamboat: Rumsey, Fitch, Miller, Fulton, Stevens, Symington, Bell and Livingston. James Rumsey had demonstrated a steamboat, driven by a jet, on the Potomac in 1785 and John Fitch ran a paddle-boat on the Delaware in 1787. Fulton and Stevens knew of these experiments. Patrick Miller built the first steamboat in Britain in 1788 using engines designed by Symington. This proved impractical, but Symington built Britain's first successful steamboat in 1801. Stevens experimented with steamboats at Hoboken from 1802 onwards. Fulton was also experimenting with steamboats in France in 1802, where he met Livingston, Steven's brother-in-law. In 1804 Fulton visited Scotland and met Symington and Bell, who later built the *Comet*. When Fulton returned to America he was in correspondence with Bell about the details of Miller's boat.

The development of practical steamboats was thus the work of men who profited from the ideas and mistakes of others.

Source: Jewkes *et al.*, 1969, p. 45.

R&D spillovers have positive (input spillovers reduce the cost of R&D) and negative (output spillovers reduce the expected payoff from R&D) effects on firm investment in R&D. Whether the net impact is positive or negative is an empirical question. Jaffe (1988) analyses the R&D activity in 1976 of 573 publicly listed U.S. firms in 49 technology areas. He finds that the R&D activity of an individual firm is positively affected by spillovers from firms with similar patterns of R&D activity (1988, pp. 436–437): "[T]he positive externalities apparently [outweigh] any negative competitive effects on average. When R&D in a firm's vicinity increases, the firm does more R&D itself and its productivity grows faster, even controlling for the increased R&D."

Absorptive capacity Notwithstanding Arrow's (1962) emphasis on the intangible nature of information, the view the information flows costlessly has been challenged on both theoretical and empirical grounds. Cohen and Levinthal (1989, pp. 569–570) emphasize that information often does *not* flow freely from an innovator to other users:

[W]e argue that while R&D obviously generates innovations, it also develops the firm's ability to identify, assimilate, and exploit knowledge from the environment—what we call a firm's 'learning' or 'absorptive' capacity. While encompassing a firm's ability to imitate new process or product innovations, absorptive capacity also includes the firm's ability to exploit outside knowledge of a more intermediate sort, such as basic research findings that provide the basis for subsequent applied research and development.

Vonortas emphasizes the tacit nature of some kinds of knowledge (1994, p. 415):[31]

technological knowledge involves a combination of poorly-defined, and often incomplete, know-how and a set of highly codified information which is hard to acquire and utilize effectively.

In sectors of the economy where knowledge has a tacit component, appropriability of the economic profit that flows from successful innovation will typically not be limited by the free flow of knowledge. Where knowledge is tacit, firms need to maintain their own stock of knowledge and technical ability to absorb knowledge generated elsewhere in the economy. This is a major incentive for firms to engage in basic research (Rosenberg, 1990, p. 171):

[S]cientific knowledge and research in general ... is regarded by economists as being "on the shelf" and costlessly available to all comers once it has been produced. But ... it frequently requires a substantial research capability to understand, interpret and to appraise knowledge that has been placed upon the shelf—whether basic or applied. The cost of maintaining this capability is high, because it is likely to require a cadre of in-house scientists who can do these things. And, in order to maintain such a cadre, the firm must be willing to let them perform basic research. The most effective way to remain effectively plugged in to the scientific network is to be a participant in the research process.

Appropriability   Levin *et al.* (1985) augment an industry-level version of the kind of sample used by Scott (1984) with survey-based measures of technological opportunity, appropriability, and innovative output.[32] They find higher R&D spending per dollar of sales in industries with a larger share of investment and equipment in the previous five years,[33] with a stronger science base, and with more related research by government agencies and laboratories. Neither seller concentration nor appropriability conditions have a significant effect on R&D spending per dollar of sales once technological opportunity and industry effects are taken into account.

Seller concentration again has an insignificant impact on industry innovation. But innovation is significantly greater, the more effective are appropriability mechanisms and the longer the time it takes a rival to duplicate an innovation. Levin *et al.* conclude that (1985, p. 24) "To explain interindustry variation in R&D incentives and the productivity of innovative effort, we must look to underlying differences in technological opportunities and appropriability conditions."

Like Levin *et al.* (1985), Angelmar (1987, pp. 73–74) uses business responses to a question "whether it benefits to a significant degree from patents, trade secrets, or other proprietary methods of production or operation" to measure industry appropriability conditions. For his

---

[31] See also Teece (1996).

[32] See the discussion of Scott (1984) in Section 14.3.2. The survey data is discussed in Section 15.6.2.

[33] They interpret more investment in the most recent five years as indicating an immature technology, hence greater technological opportunity. This may be so. Greater recent investment might also indicate growing demand, and the kind of demand-push effect studied by Jacob Schmookler.

sample of 160 business units (parts of large firms) in 1978, R&D spending per dollar of sales was consistently higher, the greater appropriability. He also finds a positive impact of seller concentration on R&D spending in industries with low appropriability and low customer switching costs, but a negative impact of seller concentration on R&D spending in industries with high appropriability and high customer switching costs. That is, where other market conditions do not favour private investment in innovation, high seller concentration has the effects envisaged by Schumpeter Mark II. Where market conditions favour private investment in innovation even by small firms, the inclination of large firms to pursue the quiet life makes Schumpeter Mark I a better explanation for market structure-dynamic market performance relationships.

Division of Labour (?)   At first glance, the distinction between basic research and applied research is clear enough (David *et al.*, 1992, p. 74, footnote omitted):

> The goal of basic research is increased understanding of a subject or natural phenomenon, rather than the creation of specific applications with economic value; such application-oriented research activities are categorized here as applied research. Basic research generally has been conducted in conformity with the traditions of "open science," with complete disclosure of results and methods through rapid publication. Applied research activities are more often organized to create information whose benefits are privately appropriable, through patents or other institutional devices such as trade secrets.

As shown in Table 14.2, spending on basic research in the United States accounts for just under 18 per cent of total R&D spending. More than half of U.S. basic research takes place in universities, and basic research accounts for the overwhelming share of research carried out at universities (75.4 per cent in 2006). Applied research has historically taken place mostly within the Federal government and within industry, and spending on development is overwhelmingly in industry.

The appearance of a neat division of labour masks fuzzy boundaries.[34] Universities emphasize basic research, but much of that basic research is directed toward informing

Table 14.2 Spending on R&D type by sector, 2006 (millions of 2006 dollars)

	Federal Government	Industry	Universities & Colleges	FFRDCs	Other Nonprofit	Total
Basic R	4,952	8,384	35,413	5,292	7,680	61,721
Applied R	7,692	51,173	9,623	3,666	4,635	76,789
D	12,682	188,112	1,951	4,424	2,192	209,361
Total R&D	25,326	247,669	46,987	13,382	14,507	347,871

Source: NSF (2008). FFRDC indicates Federally Funded Research and Development Center.

---

[34] See Nelson (1956b, 2006), Rosenberg (1990), Pavitt (1991), Brooks (1993), Rosenberg and Nelson (1994), and Dasgupta and David (1994).

applied research.[35] It is with basic research that Arrow's views on the public good nature of information have the greatest force. It is spillovers of basic research that yield the greatest social benefit, increasing the pool of public knowledge available to be applied to specific problems. Correspondingly, increases in the appropriability of the output of basic research have little potential social benefit (basic research is without commercial objectives) and great potential for social harm (by restricting cumulative innovation). Applied research, and even more development, take place mainly in the private sector because it is the private sector that has the complementary assets needed to massage the fruits of basic research into something that will stand the test of the marketplace—in particular, knowledge of the commercial environment in which the knowledge will be applied (Nelson and Rosenberg, 1993, p. 10). It is with applied research and development that Cohen and Levinthal's emphasis on absorptive capacity gains relevance.

 BOX   **A Taxonomy of Research and Development**

- *Research and development* (R&D): "Creative work undertaken on a systematic basis in order to increase the stock of knowledge, including knowledge of man, culture, and society, and the use of this stock of knowledge to devise new applications."

- *Basic Research*

  – Federal, university, and nonprofit Sectors: "research directed toward increases in knowledge or understanding of the fundamental aspects of phenomena and of observable facts without specific application toward proccesses of products in mind."

  – Industry: "original investigations for the advancement of scientific knowledge . . . which do not have specific commercial objectives, although they may be in fields of present or potential interest to the reporting company."

- *Applied Research*

  – Federal, university, and nonprofit sectors: "research directed toward gaining knowledge or understanding necessary for determining the means by which a recognized and specific need may be met."

  – Industry: "research projects which represent investigations directed to discovery of new scientific knowledge and which have specific commercial objectives with respect to either products or processes."

- *Development*: "the systematic use of the knowledge or understanding gained from research directed toward the production of useful materials, devices, systems or methods, including design and development of prototypes and processes . . ."

Source: National Science Foundation (2001, p. 2).

---

[35] In the United States, there is a long-standing tradition of university-private sector cooperation to promote innovation and apply it in a productive way. This is the philosophy behind the Morrill Act of 1862, which established the land-grant college system. Much useful innovation comes out of the Agricultural Extension Service, which was tied to land-grant colleges in 1914. In Germany, the Fraunhofer Laboratories serve a similar role as regards applied industrial research.

Feedback: innovation and market structure

The Schumpeter Mark I/Schumpeter Mark II literature is usually cast as a debate about the determinants of dynamic market performance, and properly so. But it is as much a debate about market structure as about market performance. In a Schumpeter Mark I industry, there is sequential turnover of leading firms—today's dominant firm is displaced by an innovative entrant, which reigns until it in its turn is displaced in a subsequent wave of creative destruction. In a Schumpeter Mark II world, a dominant firm has a comparative advantage in innovation that allows it to maintain its dominant position—and in a Schumpeter Mark II industry, persistent dominance goes hand in hand with good dynamic market performance.

Stepping back from the Schumpeter/Schumpeter debate, there are other avenues by which one might expect firms' R&D activities to affect equilibrium market structure. The cost of R&D is fixed with respect to output fluctuations. Where fixed cost is greater, the equilibrium number of firms is typically smaller, all else equal. In R&D-intensive endogenous sunk cost industries, it is quality-enhancing R&D that maintains a lower bound on concentration.

R&D may also lend itself to strategic entry-deterring behaviour. A dominant firm may invest in new technologies less with the intention of using them itself and more with the intention of preventing rivals from using them—or, in a world of imperfect appropriability, with the intention of making it more costly for rivals to develop competing technologies.

Arrow (1962) compares the profit to be gained from innovation by the monopolist of a market into which entry is blocked and an innovating firm in an otherwise identical perfectly competitive market. Because of the replacement effect, the monopolist has less to gain from innovation than the competitive firm. Gilbert and Newbery (1982) ask how this result is affected if an innovating entrant could make the monopolist's market a duopoly, while the monopolist could block entry by preemptively developing and patenting the technology.[36] In this case, the payoff to the entrant from developing the new technology is the discounted present value of post-entry duopoly profit. The net payoff to the incumbent from pre-emptively developing the new technology is the present discounted value of the difference between post-innovation monopoly profit and post-entry duopoly profit, if the entrant develops the new technology. The precise amounts of the respective duopoly profits will depend on the nature of competition in the post-innovation market. But for most duopoly models, the value the entrant would gain by successful innovation would be less than the value the monopolist would lose by permitting entry. It follows that if the incumbent can be sure of innovating first by spending more than the entrant to develop the new technology, it will be profitable for the incumbent to do so, thus blocking entry.[37]

---

[36] As Gilbert and Newbery (1982, p. 515) note "The existence of patent rights is neither necessary nor sufficient for preemptive activity", what is required for preemption to be feasible is that the incumbent has a way of appropriating the economic profit that flows from innovation. We will see (Section 15.6.2) that patents are but one of several appropriability mechanisms, and by no means the most effective.

[37] In October, 2008, the U.S. Court of Appeals for the Federal Circuit ruled that payments by the holder of a pharmaceutical patent to a firm that had developed a generic substitute that agreed to drop a patent challenge and hold its generic substitute off the market until the patent expired do not violate U.S. antitrust law (*In Re Ciprofloxacin Hydrochloride Antitrust Litigation S44 F.3d 1323 (Fed. Cir. 2008)*). With such a *reverse payment patent settlement agreement*, the incumbent can be certain of blocking entry until the expiration of its patent. The Federal Trade Commission has a track record of challenging such agreements, and in the early days of the Obama administration,

Reinganum (1983) shows that the replacement effect can come back into play if there is uncertainty in the R&D-input/R&D output relationship. This is easiest to see if the innovation is *drastic*, so that if the entrant patents the new technology, the incumbent, using the old technology, would lose money at the monopoly price for the new technology. This is the Schumpeter Mark I cycle—challenger displaces incumbent. Then the post-innovation payoff is the same for both firms—monopoly profit using the new technology. But the incumbent has less to gain—before innovation, it collects monopoly profit using the old technology, the challenger earns nothing. This is the replacement effect, and as before, it means that the incumbent spends less than the challenger in pursuit of the uncertain innovation. By extension, the same result will hold for innovations that are nearly drastic.

SUMMARY

The views that have been attributed to Schumpeter Mark II are a study in black-and-white—innovation is favoured in concentrated markets that are supplied by large firms, disfavoured in unconcentrated markets that are supplied by small firms. The post-Schumperian literature is shades of grey. Adequate pure and applied scientific knowledge is a prerequisite for technological advance. Given an adequate knowledge base, innovating individual and firms will direct their efforts in directions expected to be most profitable. Expected profitability depends not only on the size of the market to be served by the innovation, but also by R&D input and output spillovers. Where appropriability conditions are otherwise weak, market concentration may favour innovation as envisaged by Schumpeter Mark II. These considerations give some explanation for variations in R&D efforts from market to market. As for R&D output, "the race is not [always] to the swift, ..., nor yet favour to men of skill; but time and chance happeneth to them all".

STUDY POINTS

- Schumpeter Mark I, Schumpeter Mark II (Section 14.2)
- Incremental profitability and the incentive to invest in innovation (Section 14.3.1)
- Demand-pull, technology-push (Section 14.3.3)
- Uncertainty (Section 14.3.3)
- R&D spillovers (Section 14.3.3)
- Absorptive capacity (Section 14.3.3)
- Appropriability (Section 14.3.3)
- Innovation and market structure (Section 14.3.3)

---

the U.S. Department of Justice has indicated a willingness to do so as well. Legislation has been proposed in the U.S. Senate to make them illegal; see 3 February 2009 press release "Kohl, Grassley introduce bill to stop industry 'payoffs' that delay generic drugs", downloaded 20 February 2009 from URL <http://kohl.senate.gov/newsroom/pressrelease.cfm?customel_dataPageID_1464=2126>.

FURTHER READING

On the distinction between Schumpeter Mark I and Schumpeter Mark II, see Kamien and Schwartz (1982), Winter (1984). For a useful contemporary discussion, see Mason (1951), and more recently McCraw (2008). For contributions to the large theoretical literature on market structure-innovation relationships in oligopoly, see among others Scherer (1967b), Barzel (1968), Loury (1979), Lee and Wilde (1980), Reinganum (1982), Spence (1984), Beath *et al.* (1988), d'Aspremont and Jacquemin (1988), Kamien *et al.* (1992), Katsoulacos and Ulph (1998), and Amir (2000). For surveys, see Van Cayseele (1998), Gilbert (2006) and Vives (2008, pp. 419–425). For surveys of empirical studies, see Kamien and Schwartz (1982), Baldwin and Scott (1987), Cohen and Levin (1989), Cohen (1995), and Symeonidis (1996). On R&D spillovers, see Kamien and Zang (2000), Martin (2002a), Hinloopen (2000, 2003), and for surveys, Griliches (1992), De Bondt (1997). Dasgupta and Stiglitz (1980) emphasize the reverse impact of R&D on equilibrium market structure.

PROBLEMS

Asterisks indicate advanced problems.

14–1* (KMZ-equivalent model) A Cournot duopoly product market has inverse demand equation:

$$p = 100 - (q_1 + q_2). \tag{14.4}$$

Constant marginal and average cost with an initial technology is the same for both firms, 10 per unit of output.

In a first stage, firms 1 and 2 select own-financed cost reductions x_1 and x_2. Constant marginal and average costs in the second stage are:

$$c_1 = 10 - (x_1 + \sigma x_2) \tag{14.5}$$
$$c_2 = 10 - (\sigma x_1 + x_2), \tag{14.6}$$

where the spillover parameter σ lies between 0 and 1.

The cost of an own-financed cost reduction x_i is:

$$\frac{1}{2}\gamma(1+\sigma)x_i^2, \tag{14.7}$$

for $\gamma > 0$ and $i = 1,2$.

In the first stage, firm i non-cooperatively selects x_i to maximize its payoff:

$$\Pi_i = \pi_i - \frac{1}{2}\gamma(1+\sigma)x_i^2,$$

where π_i is the second-stage Cournot equilibrium profit.

Find the best-response equations for x_1 and x_2 and the equilibrium cost reductions. How do equilibrium cost reductions change as σ changes?

14–2* (KMZ model, no spillovers) For a two-stage game with inverse demand equations:

$$p_1 = a - b\left(q_1 + \theta q_2\right) \tag{14.8}$$

$$p_2 = a - b\left(\theta q_1 + q_2\right), \tag{14.9}$$

suppose that a firm spending y_i in a first-stage obtains a cost reduction $\sqrt{\frac{2}{\gamma} y_i}$. Show that equilibrium cost reductions are the same as those obtained for Problem 14–1 when $\sigma = 1$.

PROMOTING INNOVATION ⬤15

Its getting better all the time.

The Beatles

15.1 Introduction

From a social point of view, resource allocation is efficient when the expected rate of return on investment is the same in all activities. Since research and development produces knowledge, which often requires some investment in absorptive capacity to be accessed but nonetheless has many of the aspects of a public good, it is to be expected that the social rate of return to investment in R&D will exceed the private rate of return to investment in R&D.[1] A large literature suggests that this is the case. Further, information imperfections in financial markets mean it is to be expected that private returns to research and development will be greater than private returns to investment in other activities. That the social and private returns to investment in innovation exceed the private return to investment in innovation means that private investment in innovation is insufficient, from a social point of view, and makes a case that public policy should promote private investment in innovation.

In this chapter, we first review evidence on the rate of return to investment in research and development, then consider policies put forward to increase private sector R&D. These include using public procurement to increase the demand for innovative goods, tax breaks and subsidies to lower the cost of R&D, encouraging R&D cooperation (so making

---

[1] Hirshleifer (1971) notes that an innovator with foreknowledge of the consequences of a major technological change could in principle invest in assets the value of which would increase after diffusion of the innovation. Hirshleifer's example is Eli Whitney and the cotton gin: Whitney, knowing that land suited to the growing of cotton would increase sharply in value, might have invested in such land and made tremendous capital gains on his investment. Hirshleifer himself acknowledges that real-world difficulties (1971, p. 573) may block this path to riches. Either an innovator's investments in capital gains will be limited by his personal wealth, or an innovator with foreknowledge will have to turn to financial markets for investment funds. Here the lemons problem rears its ugly head. Supposing that the lemons problem is neutralized in some way, in the process of arranging financing, an innovator with foreknowledge must share the knowledge with a lender who has greater financial assets than he does. Rather than lending to the innovator, the lender could simply thank the innovator for bringing an investment opportunity to his attention and make the investments for his own sake. It seems unlikely that foreknowledge will, in practice, offer an avenue for excess returns to the successful innovator.

it possible for firms to share the cost of R&D), and establishing intellectual property rights that support temporary market power over innovative products and processes. As will be seen, the case is far from clear that the general effect of any of these policies is to promote innovation.

15.2 The Rate of Return to R&D

Mansfield *et al.* (1977) report the results of case studies of 17 innovations—13 new product innovations, 4 new process innovations. For each innovation, they estimate the present-discounted value of consumers' surplus, incremental firm profit, and the social return (from the time of discovery through 1973). The median private and social rates of return were 25 and 56 per cent, respectively.[2] In about 30 per cent of the cases, they estimate a private rate of return so low that no profit-maximizing firm, with perfect foresight, would have invested in the innovation, although the social rate of return was so high that the investment was socially beneficial.

Griliches (1992) reports estimates of the rate of return to public R&D in agriculture that range from 28 to 67 per cent. Jones and Williams (1997) survey the literature that examines the impact of R&D on productivity growth, and indicate that typical results are a rate of return of about 30 per cent if attention is limited to the returns to R&D within the industry carrying out the R&D, with the rate of return rising as high as 100 per cent if returns in other industries that use R&D are taken into account. Hall (1993b, pp. 316–318; see also Hall, 1996) finds that increased competition in some sectors of U.S. manufacturing (electrical, instruments, computing, and electronics) in the 1970s and early 1980s triggered restructuring and more rapid reductions in the returns to past R&D investments than might have been expected. But the rate of return on R&D continued to be high in the pharmaceutical and chemical sectors over the same period, and the social rate of return to investment in innovation exceeded the private rate of return.

***

 BOX   **Innovation in a market system**

The incentives for profit-maximizing firms to invest in new products and processes are reduced by R&D input and output spillovers and by the inherent uncertainty of the innovative process. The social rate of return to investment in R&D is greater than the private rate of return to investment in R&D, and in some sectors, the private rate of return to investment in R&D is greater than the private rate of return to investment in other types of business assets.

***

[2] In some cases, the main effect of innovations they studied was to increase profit (Mansfield *et al.*, 1977, p. 231): "In the case of three of the four process innovations included in our sample, there was no apparent effect on product prices. By lowering the costs of the innovators, these process innovations increased the innovator's profits. Also, since they were imitated (or used at nominal cost) by other firms, they soon increased the profits of other firms as well." The fourth process innovation in their sample led to a reduced price to consumers, which would mean an increase in consumers' surplus.

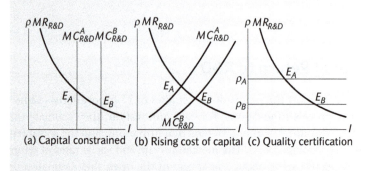

Figure 15.1 Marginal revenue, marginal cost of investment in R&D. ρ = rental cost of R&D capital services, I = investment in R&D capital

(a) Capital constrained (b) Rising cost of capital (c) Quality certification

15.3 Financial Incentives

15.3.1 The Firm's R&D Investment Decision

If the private sector underinvests in innovation from a social point of view, then government might employ other policy approaches to promote R&D. What can be said about such policies? As is often the case in economics, one can go a long way with demand and supply. In the context of the R&D investment decision of an individual firm, "demand" is the marginal revenue from purchase of an additional bit of R&D capital, and "supply" is the marginal cost of funds invested in R&D capital.[3] Figure 15.1(b) shows a downward-sloping marginal revenue from R&D investment curve and an upward-sloping marginal cost of investment funds curve. Investing more in R&D capital—hiring more scientific personnel, investing in equipment to support their work—increases the firm's absorptive capacity and shortens the time needed to bring more efficient production processes on line or higher-quality products to market. The present value of the resulting changes in future profit is the marginal revenue from current investment in R&D assets. If the firm invests in its most profitable R&D opportunities first, then the greater its level of R&D investment, the lower the marginal rate of return on the last bit of R&D investment.

Demand-side effects

Government may promote private investment in R&D by increasing public demand for the products of R&D-intensive sectors. Government may contract with commercial or university laboratories directly to have specific R&D projects carried out.[4] In terms of Figure 15.1(b), this would shift the R&D marginal revenue curve to the right, increasing the equilibrium amount of R&D and raising the equilibrium marginal rate of return to investment in R&D.

---

[3] Here I follow David *et al.*'s (2000) discussion of their Figure 1, upon which Figure 15.1 is based. They give credit to Howe and McFetridge (1976) for elaborating the marginal revenue, marginal cost approach to analysis of the R&D investment decision. See Howe and McFetridge (1976, fn. 1) for references to antecedents.

[4] On distinctions between the impacts of public procurement and public R&D contracts on private R&D investment, see Mowery and Rosenberg (1993, pp. 43–47), David *et al.* (Section 2.4). On contract R&D, see Mowery (1983a), Mirowski and Van Horn (2005).

The upward slope of the marginal cost of R&D investment means that the increase in R&D investment is less than the rightward shift in the marginal revenue of R&D curve.

Limitations of the model need to be kept in mind. A presumption of the model is that the current purchase price of R&D assets does not change with the firm's purchases of R&D assets. In practice, such changes might occur. Suppose, for example, that the marginal revenue from investing in R&D assets specific to nuclear power generation increases because governments expand programmes that rely on nuclear power as a source of electricity. In the short and medium run, the equilibrium wage rate of nuclear engineers would go up, and an increase in R&D demand will induce an increase in the marginal cost of R&D. This would tend to make the increase in R&D smaller, all else equal.

Working in the other direction, public procurement might subsidize R&D performed by a supplying firm. This would tend to lower the cost of R&D, all else equal. If learning-by-doing is a factor, the experience the firm's employees gain satisfying government demand will increase their productivity in other work. That is, there might be spillovers from such publicly funded R&D to a supplying firm's other products.[5] The net effect on the rate of return to R&D of these cost-side ramifications of an expansion in demand is ambiguous; the equilibrium amount of R&D investment should in any case increase.

Cost-side effects

By its policy choices, government can influence shift the marginal cost of capital curves shown in Figure 15.1. In Appendix I we derive an expression for the rental cost of R&D capital services, ρ_1^C:

$$\rho_1^C = r + \delta_C - (f_C + td_C) - (1 - \delta_C)\frac{p_2^c - p_1^c}{p_1^c}. \tag{15.1}$$

Equation (15.1) is analogous to the standard expression for the rental cost of the services of physical capital, a difference being that here the asset is intangible, the technical competence of the firm. The conceptual framework models the firm as inheriting a stock of R&D capital from the past. R&D capacity depreciates at rate δ_C—knowledge becomes out of date (the ability to use a slide rule does not contribute to technological performance in the way that once it did) and this depreciation is part of the cost of using the services of the stock of R&D capital.

At the start of the period, the firm purchases R&D assets at price p_1^c. The opportunity cost of purchasing a unit of R&D assets at price p_1^c is rp_1^c, where r is the firm's marginal cost of investment funds. In general, one expects the marginal cost of funds to rise with the firm's investment in R&D (and other) assets.[6] As investment rises, the firm will pursue riskier projects, and lenders will require a greater risk premium before agreeing to provide funds.

At the end of the period, $1 - \delta_C$ of a unit of R&D assets purchased (or on hand) at the start of the period remains. Its replacement cost, per unit, is the cost of a unit of R&D capital at the start of the following period, p_2^c. If the price of R&D capital has risen, $(p_2^c - p_1^c)/p_1^c > 0$ is the rate of appreciation in unit value of the firm's stock of R&D capital, and the increase in value of the stock while the firm was using it reduces the rental cost. If the price of R&D capital has fallen, $(p_2^c - p_1^c)/p_1^c < 0$ is the rate of depreciation in unit value of the firm's stock

---

[5] There might be spillovers from publicly funded R&D to the R&D efforts of other firms in the industry. Such firms (thinking that their own marginal revenue of R&D investment curves have shifted to the left) might also redirect their R&D efforts away from sectors where public-sector support has gone to a competitor.

[6] See Martin (1989) for a model of a firm that raises funds by the sale of stocks and bonds on financial markets that have a rising marginal cost of capital.

of R&D capital, and the decrease in value of the stock while the firm was using it increases the rental cost.

t, f_C, and d_C are policy variables. t is the tax rate, which for simplicity we take to be constant. d_C is the rate of depreciation allowed on R&D capital for tax purposes. d_C need have no particular relationship with the actual rate at which R&D capital depreciates. If R&D capital does not depreciate at all ($\delta_C = 0$), a government might nonetheless allow a firm to treat all of its R&D investment as a current expense ($d_C = 1$), reducing tax payments owed by the full amount of R&D investment and correspondingly reducing the rental cost of a unit of services of R&D assets. If the tax code provides for an R&D investment tax credit, f_C per unit of R&D capital, this too reduces the rental cost of a unit of R&D services.

Of course, an R&D tax credit can benefit a firm only to the extent that it would otherwise have a tax bill. High-tech start-ups often have no sales, no profit, no tax bill, and nothing to gain from R&D tax credits.[7] Another problem is that tax-based support for private R&D gives firms an incentive to reclassify activities to reduce tax payments, without in fact changing the amount of R&D investment (Mansfield, 1993, p. 333).[8]

Public support for private R&D may have a certification effect, convincing financial markets that it is less risky to fund private R&D projects.[9] Such a certification effect will reduce the risk premia required by lenders and lower the firm's cost of financial capital (r). In terms of Figure 15.1(c), some kind of public support (subsidies; procurement contracts) reassures financial markets and reduces the firm's rental cost of R&D capital services from ρ_A to ρ_B. Even in the extreme case shown in Figure 15.1(c), where the firm is able to fund as much investment as it wishes at a given rate, certification increases private investment as the firm moves down its marginal revenue of R&D investment curve. This increase is over and above any increase due to a shift in the R&D marginal revenue curve (not shown in the figure).

15.3.2 Subsidies[10]

Government may promote private R&D by granting R&D subsidies. If a firm is unable to borrow funds for R&D at any interest rate, as illustrated in Figure 15.1(a),[11] a government grant permits the firm to undertake R&D that would not otherwise be possible. The increase in R&D performed should equal the amount of the grant.

In practice, whether public subsidies increase private R&D investment in this one-for-one way is an empirical question. It will be profitable for a firm that receives a grant to take the grant and use it to fund R&D that the firm would have done anyway. Given the gap between the private and the public rate of return to R&D investment, it would be optimal for public money to support R&D projects that have low private and high public rates of return. One may question the ability of public agencies to identify such projects.[12] As important, one

---

[7] Even for an established firm, the immediate benefit of an R&D tax credit will be reduced during recession. It will often be possible to carry an unused tax credit forward to a more prosperous tax year.

[8] But see Hall (1993a, p. 29) for a more sanguine view of the relabelling issue.

[9] Lerner (1999) finds evidence of a certification effect for grants by the U.S. Small Business Innovation Research Programme.

[10] We do not address the possibility that if a government subsidizes R&D by its firms, and those firms operate in international markets, it may find itself playing an R&D subsidy game with the governments of other countries. See Spencer and Brander (1983).

[11] Small start-up firms in high-technology sectors in particular may find themselves cash-constrained in this way.

[12] But see Trajtenberg's (2002, pp. 85–86) discussion of an Israeli venture capital programme. An approach that would reduce the need to rely on government perspicacity would be to have government subsidize venture capital

may question their incentives to do so. A government agency has its own life to lead; it must periodically justify its budget at least, and its existence perhaps, before the elected masters of the public purse. "The projects we funded had high expected rates of return, unfortunately none of them panned out" is not the most powerful argument for continued funding.[13] Given these public and private incentives, direct government grants for R&D may increase private-sector profitability but not private-sector investment in R&D.

15.3.3 Evidence

R&D spending elasticity

A number of studies suggest that tax credits for private R&D have a modest net positive effect on the amount of R&D done in the private sector. Hall (1993a, p. 29) estimates that in the 1980s, U.S. tax incentives increased private R&D spending about $2 billion dollars per year, at a cost of $1 billion (in 1982 dollars).[14] Hall and Van Reenen (2000) find ambiguous results in empirical studies of the impact of tax credits on private R&D, and suggest the conclusion that a one-for-one effect—a one dollar tax credit translates into one more dollar private R&D as "a good ballpark figure". Bloom *et al.* (2002) estimate that a 10 per cent reduction in the cost of R&D leads to a 1 per cent short-run, and 10 per cent long run, increase in private R&D.

There has been a proliferation of empirical studies of the impact of R&D subsidies on private R&D in the early 2000s. Like empirical studies of the impact of tax credits, the most positive interpretation that comes out of this literature is that subsidies have their greatest impact on R&D by small firms, and at most increase R&D investment by the amount of the subsidy.

Displacement

Evidence on the displacement effect of R&D subsidies is similarly mixed.[15] Wallsten (2000) finds that grants made under the U.S. Small Business Innovation Research Programme replace

---

firms, lowering their cost of capital and allowing them to fund more private R&D. The argument in favour of this approach is that it is the business of venture capitalists to identify promising investment opportunities in the early stages (see Martin and Scott, 2000). One would expect venture capitalists to pursue R&D projects with high expected private rates of return. Thus subsidizing venture capitalists would increase the amount of private R&D but not direct funds to the projects with the largest public-private rate of return gap.

[13] Yet, if the public agency is doing its job properly it might be that this would be the result. Scherer and Harhoff (2000) argue that the distribution of R&D outcomes implies that many projects fail, and many others have low returns, with a small fraction of R&D projects that are extremely successful. Public support for private R&D should aim to fund the needle in the haystack; if hay comes up most of the time, that is not an indication that public support is being mismanaged.

[14] She also cautions that (1993a, p. 30) "it may not be possible to achieve a long-term investment strategy with a short-term tax policy".

[15] Buson (2000, p. 131) finds that "public funding induced an additional 20 % of private expenditure" in her sample of Spanish firms, but cannot rule out complete crowding out of private by public funding for 30 per cent of the firms she studies. Lach (2002) finds a strong effect of public support on R&D spending of small Israeli firms, but as most aid went to large firms, the overall impact of subsidies on private R&D spending was not statistically significant. González *et al.* (2005, p. 946) report that for their sample of Spanish firms "Subsidies during the period are thus estimated to increase total R&D expenditure by more than their amount, with almost half of the effect coming from the firms stimulated to perform R&D, which are mainly small firms." Almus and Czarnitzki (2003) find that Eastern Germany firms receiving R&D subsidies spend more on R&D in proportion to sales than firms that do not receive subsidies; Czarnitzki and Licht (2006) report that subsidies stimulate additional private R&D spending in both Eastern and Western Germany, with a larger effect in Eastern Germany.

private R&D spending one-for-one, without increasing total R&D spending. González and Pazó (2008) study the impact of R&D subsidies to 2,214 Spanish firms in the 1990s. For firms that already do R&D, their results are similar to those of Wallsten (González and Pazó, 2008, p. 384): "firms do not substitute public funds with private R&D investment, but public funds do not significantly stimulate private expenditures of firms that would carry out R&D activities in the absence of subsidies". They do find evidence that R&D subsidies may encourage R&D by small firms and by firms in low-technology sectors that would not otherwise undertake R&D.[16] This would be expected, for example, if small firms are cash-constrained (Figure 15.1(a)) and R&D subsidies cover the fixed cost of starting up an R&D operation.

15.4 Indirect Support

In the period before World War II, the U.S. federal government participated in the national research effort, but in a circumspect way (Mowery and Rosenberg, 1993, pp. 38–39): "Closely linked with the rise of the giant multiproduct corporation that began at the turn of the century, industrial research contributed to the stability and survival of these firms. Before 1940 federal support for research that was not agricultural was very limited and may well have been exceeded by state government support. . . . As research within industrial establishments grew in importance, university research during this period often involved various forms of collaboration with private industry."

This limited involvement changed entirely moving into the Cold War, as (Mowery, 1998, p. 640): "The federal government assumed a role as a financial supporter that dwarfed its pre-1940 presence, as the federal share of national R&D spending rose from roughly 20% in 1939 to more than 50% by 1962. Federal spending supported R&D activity in industry and universities, rather than being concentrated in federal government laboratories . . . "

The bulk of this national-government spending on R&D was defence-related.[17] It is sometimes said that this defence-related support for business research, along with defence-sector purchases of the military hardware that was the fruit of that research, had spillovers to the development of civilian products that amounted to an indirect subsidy of private R&D carried out for private profit.[18] There may have been such an effect early on; Nelson (1993, p. 513) argues that U.S. military spending helped U.S. electronics and aircraft firms in the 1960s, but not since then.[19] These spillovers had an opportunity cost: the resources bid away for defence-related work drove up the cost of civilian research. For Nelson (1993, p. 514),

---

[16] Mohnen and Röller (2005) similarly suggest that the appropriate policy mixes to induce firms to start R&D and to induce firms that already do R&D to increase their R&D investment differ.

[17] Between 1960 and 1988, the share of defence spending in U.S. federal government R&D spending rarely fell below 50 per cent (Mowery and Rosenberg, 1993, Table 2.4).

[18] Another matter is the performance of defence-related R&D in terms of its stated purposes (Nelson, 1993, p. 323): "There are various issues about the efficacy of the post-Second World War military R & D programs that can be raised. . . . a strong case can be, and has been, made that many of these programs have been frighteningly misguided and disgracefully mismanaged. One major alleged problem is lack of a sophisticated mechanism for appraisal of objectives, of the sort provided by customer markets. Another is lack of serious competition among producers, once an R & D contract has been let."

[19] But see Rosenberg (1990, Section 7), who emphasizes that small firms have an incentive to engage in basic research as a way of demonstrating their capacity to fulfil government contracts.

"since 1972 it is arguably the case that military R & D has cost the US considerably in terms of foregone civilian alternatives".

15.5 R&D Cooperation

Diverse forces converged to bring the subject of R&D cooperation to the centre of the academic and policy stage in the 1980s. On the academic side, one can point to those characteristics of innovation (R&D input and output spillovers) that raise the spectre of market failure in the allocation of resources to innovation. To these sources of possible market failure one may add the more conventional industrial economics concern with the nature of market structure in high-fixed cost industries, and the implications for static market performance. Where fixed cost per firm is high, relative to market size, the equilibrium number of firms is small. Much of the cost of research and development is fixed, leading one to suspect that high-technology industries will be supplied by a few large firms. Small numbers-oligopoly does not hold out the prospect of good static market performance. The Schumpeter Mark II argument is that one should not dwell on static welfare losses because they will be trumped, in the long run, by welfare gains from technological progress. But in the words of Koopmans in another context (1957, p. 139) "One cannot help but feel uneasy in the face of so much ingenuity." It would be nice, if it were possible, to combine good static market performance *and* rapid technological progress.

Interfirm R&D cooperation may address both sets of concerns. (It may raise other concerns. But let us take things in order.) A problem with R&D input spillovers is that a firm pays for something and its competitors get part of the benefit. Cooperative R&D, appropriately structured, can allow firms to share costs *and* results. In the best of all possible worlds, rivals who benefit from a firm's R&D efforts will contribute to the cost of those efforts, and every firm will be sure of having access to all firms' research results. These aspects of R&D cooperation address innovation market failure issues. Cost sharing means fixed cost per firm will be lower than would be the case without R&D cooperation; the equilibrium number of firms should be larger, all else equal. And since innovative results are shared by cooperating firms, conventional product-market rivalry will be facilitated in the post-innovation market.

If it had been only the possibility of innovation market failure on the table in the last part of the twentieth century, very likely the consequences of R&D cooperation would have remained strictly an academic matter. But that was decidedly not the case. Policy-makers around the world looked askance at the economic performance of their respective economies.[20]

In the United States, annual productivity growth, which had averaged 1.91 per cent between 1959 and 1973, fell to an average annual rate of 0.4 per cent for 1973–1995.[21] An era ended (Nelson, 1990, p. 117, footnotes omitted):

---

[20] In Japan, with the lost decade of 1990s still in its future, anxiety was rather about formal or informal trade barriers raised against its exports. See Chapter 16.

[21] Steindel and Stiroh (2001, Table 1). The figures are the average non-farm business total factor productivity growth rate over the indicated periods. Total factor productivity growth (Steindel and Stiroh, 2001, p. 4) "reflects phenomena such as general knowledge, the advantages of particular organizational structures or management techniques, reductions in inefficiency, and reallocations of resources to more productive uses". (In a cautionary remark, however, O'Sullivan (1995, p. 235) describes total factor productivity as "the concept that is to the macroeconomist what the firm is to the microeconomist".) Annual TFP growth recovered to 1.26 per for 1995–1999; that recovery lay in the future in the 1980s, as policymakers considered policies to promote R&D.

During the quarter century following the Second World War, the United States was the world's most productive economy, by virtually all measures. U.S. output per worker was higher than anyone else's by a considerable amount; so too total factor productivity. These differences held not just in the aggregate but in almost all industries.

Many factors lay behind the U.S. edge in total factor productivity, but it seems clear that more advanced technology was prominent among these. U.S. firms were in the forefront of developing the leading-edge technologies, their exports in these accounted for the lion's share of world markets, and their overseas branches often were dominant firms in their host countries. The U.S. R&D and educational systems were the object of envy and emulation by other nations.

No longer. The U.S. technological lead has badly eroded in many industries and in some the U.S. now is a lagger.

Similar concerns were present on the other side of the Atlantic (Sharp, 1991, p. 63):[22]

[I]n the late 1970s ..., emerging from the traumas of oil crisis and recession and beset by problems of adjustment in older industries such as steel, shipbuilding, even chemicals, Europe suddenly became aware of the very fast advances being made by American and Japanese firms in micro-electronics and associated technologies. European firms seemingly blind to many of these developments were now suddenly faced by the prospect of American and Japanese competitors picking off markets which they had long regarded as theirs. Many businessmen despaired of their ability to regain lost ground—hence the term 'Europessimism' which came to describe the era.

The reaction of U.S. policymakers was to fall back on what Nelson and Rosenberg (1993, p. 3) call "technonationalism", combining support for high-technology industries (without thinking very deeply about how to make such support effective) with elements of imitation, protectionism, and mercantilism. Observing a substantial number of R&D joint ventures in (particularly) the Japanese semiconductor industry, and the increasing importance of Japanese firms in the world semiconductor market, U.S. policymakers relaxed antitrust coverage of R&D joint ventures; this approach was later extended to R&D joint ventures that included production. The cordial approach to R&D cooperation was combined with a general strengthening of intellectual property rights (Katz and Ordover, 1990, p. 141; Mowery and Rosenberg, 1993, p. 60). Both initiatives—promoting R&D cooperation and strengthening intellectual property rights—might also be ways to narrow the gap between the private and social return to investment in innovation. We defer consideration of the relationship between intellectual property rights and technological performance to Section 15.6 and here consider the implications of R&D cooperation for market performance.

15.5.1 Types of R&D Cooperation

There are definitions of R&D cooperation to suit every taste and purpose. The alternative definitions of Kamien *et al.* (1992) (see the accompanying box) characterize R&D cooperation in terms of what a firm maximizes when it sets its R&D effort and in the treatment of R&D input spillovers. The reference case is non-cooperative R&D and input spillovers as determined by the technological ambiance—this is the absence rather than the presence of R&D cooperation. In the Kamien *et al.* taxonomy, the distinguishing characteristic of

---

[22] Sharp continues "In fact things were by no means as bad as the pessimists made out."

research and development *cartelization* is that each firm sets its R&D effort to maximize joint profit.[23] The distinguishing characteristic of a research joint venture (RJV) is that firms maximize spillovers. Thus R&D cartelization implies firms set R&D efforts to maximize joint profit, RJV cartelization implies firms set R&D efforts to maximize joint profit and also maximize R&D input spillovers. With RJV competition, each firm sets its own R&D effort to non-cooperatively maximize its own profit, and firms maximize R&D input spillovers.[24] The Kamien *et al.* classification abstracts from tacit or overt product-market collusion.

Ouchi (1989) and Vonortas (1994) make a distinction between *operating entity* R&D joint ventures and *secretariat* joint ventures. With an operating entity R&D joint venture, parent firms set up a stand-alone laboratory and share full and complete access to its results.[25] The secretariat R&D joint venture is a subcontractor or coordinator Ouchi (1989, p. 1321):

> The secretariat is a small administrative body that coordinates research tasks among a set of entities, which may include companies, universities, and government laboratories. The secretariat may collect funds and then allocate these to chosen projects, or it may serve as the coordinative body through which member institutions jointly apply for external funds or agree to commit their own resources to work in their own laboratories in a manner that fits a joint plan. The distinguishing feature of the secretariat is what it does not have: ... its own facilities and laboratories in which R&D tasks are performed. Instead, all such tasks are undertaken either in member-owned facilities or in other external facilities that perform as contractors to the secretariat.

This is akin to Kamien *et al.*'s R&D cartelization (see also Vonortas, 1994, p. 416).

 BOX Types of R&D Cooperation

Kamien *et al.* (1992)

- R&D competition: non-cooperative R&D and product-market behaviour, spillovers as determined by technological environment;

- R&D cartelization: joint-profit-maximizing R&D decisions, non-cooperative product-market behaviour, spillovers as determined by technological environment; »

---

[23] "Cartelization" is perhaps an unfortunate usage, since it does not, in this context, indicate product-market collusion.

[24] There is evidence that firms sometimes set spillovers strategically; see the discussion, below, of the VLSI Project. At the level of theory, one might wish to model the choice of spillovers, to the extent that spillovers are a choice variable, rather than compare the case in which the spillover rate is exogenous with the case in which it is maximal. Kamien and Zang (2000) take a step in this direction by making spillover rates depend on absorptive capacity, which is endogenous. Adams (2000) similarly has a learning model of spillovers. Piga and Poyago-Theotoky (2005) make spillovers depend on location, the choice of which is endogenous. Grünfeld (2006) allows a firm's decision to become a multinational affect the degree of spillovers.

[25] Reality can be more complex than theory (and usually is). Katz and Ordover (1990, pp. 186–189) discuss an operating-entity joint venture, the Microelectronics and Computer Corporation (MCC), that charted its own research path, leading parent firms to exercise their rights of legal control to force MCC research into the lines desired by the parents.

> - RJV competition: non-cooperative R&D and product-market behaviour, spillovers made as large as possible;
>
> - RJV cartelization: joint-profit-maximizing R&D decisions, non-cooperative product-market behaviour, spillovers made as large as possible.

Katz and Ordover (1990, p. 143):

- "[A] traditional joint venture, in which two or more parties create a separate entity in which they all have equity interests to conduct well-defined R&D projects for their benefit."

- "[T]he research consortium, which may pursue broad programs in basic R&D in those areas where appropriability and spillovers are especially pervasive ... "

- "[V]enture capital investment by market leaders in a stand-alone startup company."

- "A royalty-free cross-licensing agreement, under which firms agree in advance to share R&D results but not R&D costs ... "

- "Agreements among firms to let their research personnel share ideas or to let the employees of one firm tour the plant of another ... "

Ouchi (1989)/Vonortas (1994, p. 416):

- "Secretariat RJVs enable member firms to set the levels of generic research expenditures collectively ex ante. The research is conducted independently, however, and the degree of knowledge externalities inherited from the non-cooperative setup remains unaffected."

- "Operating entity RJVs ... generic research is ... jointly performed and the resulting information is fully and instantaneously disseminated to member firms."

Nelson (1988, p. 318):

the practice of implicit patent pooling, which exists in a number of industries, under which rivalrous firms apparently have an agreement not to sue each other for infringements. Such arrangements reflect an apparent agreement among a group of firms that they are all better off if they make a common, big pool of at least some of their technological knowledge, than if they all try to keep their individual pools strictly private.

Hagedoorn (2002, pp. 478–479):

[N]on-equity, contractual forms of R&D partnerships, such as joint R&D pacts and joint development agreements ... cover technology and R&D sharing between two or more companies in combination with joint research or joint development projects. Such undertakings imply the sharing of resources, usually through project-based groups of engineers and scientists from each parent-company. The costs for capital investment, such as laboratories, office space, equipment, etc. are shared between the partners. ... these contractual R&D partnerships have a limited time-horizon, due to their project-based organization ...

Katz and Ordover (1990) consider a range of formal and informal cooperative R&D arrangements. Their "traditional joint venture" is the Ouchi/Vonortas operating entity R&D joint venture, and what they call a research consortium corresponds to a secretariat joint venture. A venture capital arrangement is akin to an operating entity joint venture, with ultimate authority resting on financial leverage rather than ownership. They also describe formal arrangements to cross-license patents, so that each firm party to the agreement will have access to the technology of other firms. Nelson's (1988) "implicit patent pool" goes in the same direction. Formal and informal cross-licensing agreements correspond in a practical sense to "maximizing R&D output spillovers" among the firms that are parties to the agreement. Arranging for interaction among research employees of different firms corresponds to "maximizing R&D input spillovers". The contractual R&D joint ventures highlighted by Hagedoorn (2002) are transient cooperative arrangements in pursuit of a specific goal.

15.5.2 Cooperation Between?

R&D cooperation may involve firms that are competitors in the same product market, as when General Motors and Toyota established a jointly owned venture (NUMMI, New United Motor Manufacturing, Inc.) to produce small cars to be marketed separately by the parent firms.[26] R&D cooperation may involve firms that are vertically related, as when a manufacturer and its suppliers collaborate on input design and development (Bidault *et al.*, 1998) or a new-product innovator collaborates with prospective lead users during the development process (Von Hippel, 1986). Firms may collaborate with university laboratories.

Cooperative research may be contractual, as when a pharmaceutical company subcontracts a step in the drug development process to a specialized contract research organization (CRO), or a car company subcontracts research on some aspect of emission control systems to an independent laboratory.[27] Arrow's paradox of knowledge (Dosi *et al.*, 2006, p. 892), "if the potential buyer does not know the content of the information, he cannot appreciate its value, but if he knows it, he does not need to buy it any longer", is a reason to expect the market for innovation to fail. But the existence of independent research laboratories suggests that independent researchers and their clients are able to fashion contracts that allow CROs to collect income from clients while assuring clients they will receive the knowledge for which they have contracted.[28]

15.5.3 The NCRA and Extensions

In 1984, the U.S. Congress adopted the National Cooperative Research Act (NCRA), which altered the treatment of R&D joint ventures under U.S. antitrust law.[29] The principal changes were (Scott, 2008b) to prescribe application of the rule of reason rather than the *per se* rule in hearing antitrust challenges to R&D joint ventures, reducing the maximum penalty in private antitrust suits involving R&D joint ventures from treble to single damages, provided

---

[26] This production joint venture, started in 1984, involved innovation in the broad Schumpeterian sense. It gave General Motors the opportunity to master "just-in-time" production techniques, and it gave Toyota the opportunity to familiarize itself with the U.S. car market (including U.S. workers).

[27] It may happen that a research project is contracted out to a university laboratory, so contract research can also be university-industry collaboration.

[28] On contact research, see Mowery (1983a).

[29] In 1993, the provisions of the NCRA, renamed the National Cooperative Research and Production Act, were extended to joint production. In 2004, the Standards Development Organization Advancement Act extended NCRPA coverage to standards development organizations.

a joint venture was registered with U.S. antitrust authorities, and (contrary to typical U.S. practice), obliging losing plaintiffs to pay all litigation costs.

Alleged benefits of R&D cooperation

Passage of the NCRA was a response to the perceived deterioration of U.S. performance on world markets, with rising trade deficits and declining world shares of high-technology markets (Wright, 1986, p. 138; Brod and Link, 2001, pp. 105–106). The kinds of economic arguments that were put forward in favour of encouraging R&D cooperation are summarized by Katz and Ordover (1990, pp. 144–145; bullet points not set off as a list in the original):

> A simplistic view of the R&D process identifies two primary benefits of ex ante cooperation:
>
> (1) Greater amount of R&D investment. An ex ante cooperative R&D agreement can serve as a mechanism that internalizes the externalities created by technological spillovers while continuing the efficient sharing of information. ... By internalizing positive R&D spillovers across firms, R&D cooperation may raise the incentive to conduct R&D and hence the total amount of R&D investment.
>
> (2) Greater efficiency of R&D investment. To the extent that cooperative R&D is more widely disseminated than individually conducted R&D, ex ante cooperation increases the efficiency of R&D efforts because a single investment benefits a greater number of firms. This efficiency gain has three types of positive effects.
>
> • First, sharing lowers the cost of investment for each firm, which may induce them to conduct more R&D.
>
> • Second, even if ex ante cooperation leaves the total amount of R&D investment unaffected or slightly reduced, it might increase the effective amount of R&D.
>
> • Third, cooperative R&D eliminates the wasteful duplication that would occur if several firms separately undertook the same projects.

They continue "The problem with this view is that it is simple-minded".

Joint R&D and product-market performance Regarding the first point, there is good reason to think that R&D cooperation will improve market performance, but it may or may not increase the level of R&D investment. A firm's incentive to invest in R&D is not only the lure of profit to be gained from early innovation, but the fear of profit to be lost from later innovation. In oligopoly, R&D by one firm is widely thought to stimulate R&D by other firms.[30] When firms carry out joint R&D, this stimulus is removed, and equilibrium R&D levels fall.[31]

But R&D cooperation will likely improve market performance, provided it does not facilitate tacit collusion, because of its impact on static market performance in the post-innovation market. With R&D cooperation, it is typically the case that all cooperating firms have access to discoveries on identical terms, meaning that they compete on equal terms

---

[30] This is the heart of Villard's (1958) argument that it is intermediate levels of concentration that are most conducive to technological progress, all else equal.

[31] For formal models with this effect, see d'Aspremont and Jacquemin (1988), Martin (2002b).

after discovery. R&D cooperation means greater rivalry, and therefore improved market performance, after discovery.[32]

The qualification "provided it does not facilitate tacit collusion" is important (Fisher, 1990, p. 194):[33]

> I take a very skeptical view of a policy of allowing cooperation where one is unsure that it is a good idea. Firms cooperating in R&D will tend to talk about other forms of cooperation. Further, in learning how other firms react and just in living with each other, each cooperating firm will get better at coordination. Hence competition on the product market is likely to be harmed.

R&D cooperation and investment in R&D   As for the increased efficiency of R&D, the first point fails for reasons suggested by Figure 15.1(b). It is correct that R&D cooperation will reduce the cost of doing R&D, and that, all else equal, this will induce firms to invest more in R&D. But all else is not equal: R&D cooperation means more intense rivalry in the post-innovation market. R&D cooperation shifts the marginal revenue curve as well as the marginal cost curve down. As far as theory is concerned, the net effect of R&D cooperation on R&D investment per firm is ambiguous.

Wasteful duplication   The argument that R&D cooperation is beneficial because it eliminates "wasteful duplication" is particularly egregious, having been discredited both theoretically (Dasgupta and Maskin, 1987) and empirically (Nelson, 1982, pp. 455, reviewing case studies):

> From a social point of view, effective pursuit of technological advance seems to call for the exploration of a wide variety of alternatives and the selective screening of these after their characteristics have been better revealed—a process that seems wasteful with the wonderful vision of hindsight.

When the outcome of R&D projects is uncertain, it is socially beneficial, and frequently privately beneficial as well, to pursue multiple research paths toward a common target.

Antitrust and R&D cooperation

If one wishes to encourage R&D cooperation, there are many ways to do it—one could subsidize joint R&D, or give favourable tax treatment to spending on joint R&D. If one wishes to encourage R&D cooperation by relaxing the application of antitrust law to R&D cooperation, then one ought to be able to make the case that concerns about antitrust liability led firms to refrain from setting up R&D joint ventures. No such case was convincingly made (Katz and Ordover, 1990, p. 169, footnote omitted):

> The National Cooperative Research Act of 1984 was enacted as a partial response to antitrust constraints on cooperative R&D agreements among firms. While the adverse effects of the constraints have never been rigorously demonstrated, either theoretically or empirically, the notion

---

[32] But one should also keep in mind, with Baumol (1992, p. 135), that "The members of a technology cartel acquire an enormous competitive advantage over nonmembers." The overall effect of R&D cooperation on post-innovation product-market performance will combine competition on more equal terms among parties to the cooperation and competition on unequal terms with firms outside the cooperation.

[33] For a formal treatment, see Martin (1996).

that the threat of antitrust litigation might reduce the extent of cooperation seemed quite plausible to many observers despite the fact that such agreements have been treated more and more leniently by the courts and by the antitrust enforcement authorities.

At least in its first 80 years, the annals of U.S. record one antitrust result—not a judgment, but a consent decree—involving an R&D joint venture (see the accompanying box). This consent decree following a U.S. government antitrust suit alleging that major U.S. car manufacturers had used an R&D joint venture to collectively delay the development and commercialization of emission control devices. Firms considering formation of an R&D joint venture to promote innovation would have no reason to be concerned about antitrust penalties against an R&D joint venture formed to delay innovation.

In short, (Scott, 2008b, p. 1300, footnotes omitted): "[A]lthough some joint ventures had been found to be *per se* unlawful prior to 1984, none of them were research joint ventures. The fear of *per se* illegality may have stopped some firms from forming procompetitive research joint ventures, but the fear could not have been based on actual antitrust attacks on such ventures."

 BOX   **R&D Cooperation**

Scientific evidence existed from 1950 that petrochemical smog was the result of a sunlight-induced chemical reaction between car exhaust fumes and nitrous oxide. The attitude of the U.S. car industry was that this was not a problem, or at least, not its problem:* "The Ford engineering staff, although mindful that automobile engines produce exhaust gases, feels these waste vapors are dissipated in the atmosphere quickly and do not present an air pollution problem. Therefore, our research department has not conducted any experimental work aimed at totally eliminating these gases."

In 1953, after Los Angeles-funded research documented car exhaust as the major source of smog, car manufacturers established an R&D joint venture, the Vehicle Combustion Products Committee, to develop emission-control devices. In 1954, car industry representatives assured Los Angeles officials that emission control devices would be ready for the 1958 model year. 1958 came and went without emission control devices. While car companies dragged their feet, firms outside the industry responded to a California law that would make exhaust controls mandatory once the state had certified two or more emission control devices. Confronted with the prospect that they might be required to install other firms' products on their vehicles, the car industry announced that it would have emission control devices available by 1967. Four independent emission control devices were approved in 1964, meaning their use would have been mandatory in 1966. As luck would have it, the car industry had its own emission control devices ready for the 1966 model year.

In 1965, in response to a request by the Los Angeles Country Board of Supervisors, the Antitrust Division of the U.S. Department of Justice began an investigation of the U.S. car industry's R&D cooperation. In January 1969, the Department of Justice filed an antitrust suit against the firms involved and their trade group, the Automobile Manufacturers' Association.

According to a Department of Justice press release,

> The suit alleged that the defendants and others have agreed since as early as 1953 to eliminate all competition among themselves in the research, development, manufacture, installation and »

>> publicity of air pollution devices and in the purchase of patents and patent rights covering such equipment. The complaint also alleged that the defendants agreed to install anti-pollution devices only upon a uniform date. Three agreements involving attempts to delay installation were also cited . . .

and,

The suit asserted that the defendants also agreed to restrict publicity on advances in air pollution technology. In addition, the defendants agreed among themselves, through a patent cross-licensing agreement, to restrict the price they would pay for patents developed by outsiders.

In September, 1969 the Department of Justice and the firms involved entered into a consent decree (again from a Department of Justice press release):

. . . prohibiting the four major auto manufacturers and the Automobile Manufacturers Association from conspiring to delay and obstruct the development and installation of pollution control devices for motor vehicles.
The decree also requires them to make available to any and all applicants royalty-free patent licenses on air pollution devices and to make available technological information about these devices.

*From the reply of a Ford engineer to a Los Angeles County Supervisor, March 1953, quoted by Nader (1965) and reproduced in Jaffe and Tribe (1971, p. 144).

Source: Jaffe and Tribe *Environmental Protection*. Chicago: Bracton Press, 1971, Part 2, Chapter 1: "U.S. v. Automotive Manufacturers' Association"; United States v. Automobile Manufacturers' Association, 1969 Trade Cas. (CCH) Para. 72,907 (C.D. Cal. 1969), modified, 1982 Trade Cas. (CCH) Para. 65,088 (C.D. Cal.).

NCRA in practice

The response of American enterprise to the NCRA and successor legislation has been underwhelming, with annual registrations rising from 17 in 1986 to 115 in 1995, falling to 22 in 2003, spiking to 226 in 2004 but falling again to 17 in 2006 (Figure 15.2), an average of just under 65 registrations per year between 1985 and 2006.[34] Circumstantial evidence suggests that only a minority of R&D joint ventures opt for NCRA registration.[35]

Röller *et al.* (2007) analyse the characteristics of firms that formed and registered R&D joint ventures under the NCRA during the years 1990–1994. Their findings suggest that

---

[34] The CORE (COoperative REsearch) database, upon which Figure 15.2 is based, is described by Brod and Link (2001).

[35] Hagedoorn (2002, pp. 479–480), commenting on the MERIT-CATI database of all R&D joint ventures that can be traced from public records, writes that "[The 1980s] mark a steep increase from about 200 annually made partnerships to over 500 new R&D partnerships made each year at the end of the 1980s and the turn of the decade. The first couple of years of the 1990s show a drop in the newly made partnerships to about 350 and 400, but in 1995 there is another peak with a record of nearly 700 new R&D partnerships. At the end of the nearly 40 years on which I have been able to find data, the number of new R&D partnerships is decreasing again, to about 500 new partnerships." Table 1 of Duysters and Hagedoorn (1996) covers 4192 strategic technology alliances over the years 1980–1989. Of these, about 60 per cent involved U.S. firms (62.6 per cent for 180–184, 59.5 per cent for 1985–1989). Making a bold back-of-the envelope calculation, if 60 per cent of the 700 research partnerships recorded in the MERIT-CATI database for 1995 involved U.S. firms, that is 420 research partnerships formed involving U.S. firms. In 1995 115 firms, 27 per cent of 420, registered with U.S. antitrust authorities under the provisions of the NCRA.

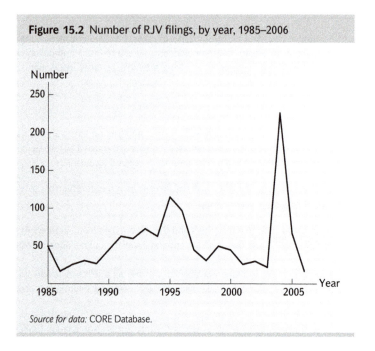

Figure 15.2 Number of RJV filings, by year, 1985–2006

Source for data: CORE Database.

R&D joint ventures are more likely to be formed by firms of the same size, and that the more R&D joint ventures a firm participates in, the more likely it is to participate in additional R&D joint ventures. There is also evidence that firms in the transportation equipment industry are differentially likely to form R&D joint ventures with firms in vertically related industries (primary metals and instruments and related products).

But the kinds of industries in which R&D joint ventures were registered do not seem to be those for which one would expect innovation market failure. Scott (2008b, pp. 1312–1313) reports that early R&D joint ventures were more common in concentrated industries, not the unconcentrated industries where spillovers and low appropriability would be anticipated. R&D joint ventures were formed more in high-productivity-growth industries than in low-productivity-growth industries. Industries with more NCRA R&D joint ventures had higher company spending on R&D than those that did not. There were no obvious appropriability differences between industries with more joint ventures and industries with fewer joint ventures.[36]

R&D cooperation in the semiconductor industry[37]

VLSI   In the late 1970s a cooperative R&D effort in the Japanese semiconductor industry generated much attention for the idea that R&D cooperation might promote innovation. The VLSI (Very Large Scale Integrated Circuits) Project was an Engineering Research Association organized by the Japanese Ministry of International Trade and Industry (MITI). The VLSI

---

[36] There was some indication that registered R&D joint ventures were more common in specific sectors where appropriabililty might be limited, such as environmental research and safety-related research.

[37] For a formal model of R&D cooperation, see Problem 15–1. But there are fundamental limitations to the theoretical treatments of R&D and R&D cooperation in the literature. In part this reflects the multifaceted nature of R&D in a market economy; there is no unified field theory of R&D, and none is on the horizon. In the library of

project included five companies (Fujitsu, NEC, Hitachi, Mitsubishi, Toshiba) and over the four years of its existence (1976–1979), it generated more than a thousand patents.

Limited joint R&D The VLSI project is rich in lessons for the public support of cooperative research, although those lessons are not necessarily those that are usually drawn. The VLSI project involved six joint laboratories. One of the 6 was a genuine joint laboratory, in the sense that it involved balanced participation of representatives from all the partner companies.[38] Each of the other laboratories was dominated by one or another of the specific companies. Of the patents generated by the project, 59 per cent were taken out by a single applicant; only 16 per cent were taken out by applicants from more than one of the VLSI partner firms (Sigurdson, 1986, p. 50).

Subsidies The VLSI project, like most Japanese R&D joint ventures, seems mainly to have been a mechanism for administering government subsidies (Odagiri and Goto, 1993, p. 88; Sigurdson, 1986, p. 110). The VLSI budget was 60 million yen, half provided by the companies and half by MITI.

Commodity chips The VLSI project is often said to have established a leading Japanese presence in the world semiconductor market, but it is important to understand the nature of that presence. Duysters and Hagedoorn compare the performances of EU, Japanese, and U.S. microelectronics firms in the 1980s and conclude that EU and U.S. firms outperform the Japanese from a technological point of view (1995, p. 219):

> Aggressive price competition and low cost production enabled Japanese firms to drive US competitors out of 'commodity' markets such as DRAMs [Dynamic Random Access Memory chips]. The inability to compete with Japanese companies in price-sensitive mature markets induced European and US firms to upgrade their product line and move into high-end growth markets such as microprocessors and custom chips.

Sematech In the United States, Sematech (Semiconductor Manufacturing Technology) was formed in 1987 as a joint industry-government sponsored research consortium intended to revitalize the US semiconductor industry, in no small measure as a strategic response to the rise of Japanese semiconductor manufacturers. Sematech was founded with 13 corporate members. A 14th joined in short order; 3 of the 14 later withdrew.

---

specific models of R&D, many, in search of tractability, abstract entirely from uncertainty. Those that incorporate uncertainty do so by assuming outcomes can be described in terms of a probability distribution over known possible outcomes: if I spend so much on my R&D project, I don't know when it will be complete, but I know the expected time at which it will be complete, and I know the way changes in the amount I spend affect the expected time of completion (see Appendix II for an example). One may argue that not only is uncertainty an essential aspect of innovation, but that the kind of uncertainty in play cannot be analysed in terms of known possible outcomes. This is the Knightian uncertainty of Frank H. Knight's *Risk, Uncertainty and Profit* (1921), and implies that (Nelson, 2006, p. 2) "neoclassical modeling ... which did take aboard risk, in the sense of the agents knowing only a probability distribution of outcomes given any action they would take, missed the point that in many empirical cases the agents did not even imagine the path that actually unfolded, much less being able to assign *ex ante* a probability to it."

[38] Mowery (1995, p. 527) argues that the role of most cooperative Japanese joint ventures was not so much to generate new knowledge as to circulate and diffuse existing knowledge. The VLSI project was exceptional in having one genuinely joint research laboratory; for the most part, it followed the general pattern.

Joint R&D   Sematech maintains its own research facility, in which it seeks to simulate manufacturing conditions. It signs contracts with outside laboratories to carry out research in specified areas. That Sematech has its own research facility makes it exceptional among U.S. joint R&D projects (Peck, 1986, p. 219):

> the most common pattern in . . . U.S. R&D joint ventures has been for the research to be carried out by participants in their own facilities or by contract with universities and independent organizations . . .

Sematech is widely credited with enabling the US industry to regain world market share, reversing losses to Japanese suppliers. In 1994, it announced its intention to give up US government support at the end of the 1996 fiscal year, and weaned itself from direct subsidies.

Reduced R&D spending   From a policy point of view, it is important not only to ask if Sematech was successful but also what results might have been obtained without cooperative R&D. Irwin and Klenow (1996) estimate that Sematech member firms reduced their overall R&D spending, inclusive of their contributions to the consortium, by $300 million per year. Sematech's research budget during this period was $200 million per year, of which the member firms contributed about half of the funds. If this result is accepted, the net effect of Sematech was to reduce industry spending on R&D. The member firms put about $100 million a year into the consortium and reduced their own R&D spending apart from their contributions to the consortium by four times that amount, yielding a net reduction in their overall R&D spending of $300 million.

Postmortem

In retrospect, it is not surprising that the NCRA and its successor legislation did not obviously stimulate the formation of R&D joint ventures by U.S. firms. U.S. firms were not discouraged from forming R&D joint ventures by the prospect of public or private antitrust challenges, so making that prospect more remote had little effect. The stated premise of the NCRA, that the U.S. had fallen behind other industrial countries because of differentially poor technological performance, and that this poor performance was somehow due to misguided antitrust policy, was wrong on both counts. The U.S. did not fall behind other industrialized countries; other industrialized countries caught up with the U.S.[39]

The effect of the NCRA and its progeny has been to weaken competitive pressure on U.S. firms. The ultimate impact on technological performance may be opposite that hoped for (Mowery and Rosenberg, 1993, p. 60, reference omitted):[40]

---

[39] Nelson (1990) makes this case in a compelling way.

[40] Mowery (1995b, p. 148) writes "A 'national innovation system' is the network of private- and public sector institutions that exert the primary influence on the creation and adoption of new technologies." See Nelson (1993b) for a comparative study of national innovation systems. It is a lesson of modern industrial economics that institutions matter, and that is surely the case for innovation. It is not so clear that the boundaries of innovation-related institutions are national. As Nelson and Rosenberg (1993, p. 5) remark, "National governments act as if [the concept of a 'national' system makes sense today]. However, that presumption, and the reality, may not be aligned." Mowery (1995, p. 148) raises the possibility that national innovation systems, like the Holy Roman Empire, may be neither national, nor innovation, nor system.

In both antitrust and intellectual property policy, the Reagan and [George H. W.] Bush Administrations are strengthening the returns to innovators. The policy initiatives in antitrust have also been influenced by the example of Japanese success in cooperative research and technology development, although the recent antitrust legislative proposals extend the scope of cooperation well beyond the precompetitive research stage in which Japanese firms most often collaborate. This policy focus, however, fails to address one of the most serious weaknesses of the U.S. national innovation system, the slow pace of domestic adoption of new technologies in manufacturing. Policies designed to increase the rewards to innovators in some instances will increase the costs associated with the adoption of the technologies produced by the innovators, and thereby may hamper diffusion . . . Moreover, the "lessons" drawn from the Japanese experience by US policymakers appear to overlook the emphasis within Japanese industry and technology policies on support for domestic technology adoption and on strong domestic competition in technology commercialization.

15.5.4 EU

We will see (Section 20.5.2) that although Article 101(1) of the EC Treaty prohibits agreements that distort competition and affect trade between the Member States, Article 101(3) provides an exception to this prohibition, subject to some conditions, for agreements that promote technical or economic progress. On one level, therefore, EU competition policy has always accepted the idea the R&D cooperation can improve market performance. In contrast to the panglossian world view behind the NCRA, EU competition policy has also always recognized that R&D cooperation has the potential to adversely affect static market performance (Jacquemin and Spinott, 1986, pp. 498–499, footnote omitted):

> [Economic] analyses imply that the full exploitation of the results of cooperative research very often require concerted manufacturing, development, and marketing to sell products which embody these results. If this is true, a regulation of R&D cooperation excluding any cooperation at the level of the products could discourage or destabilize many valuable agreements. However, allowing an extension of cooperation from R&D to manufacturing and distribution encourages collusive behavior which could impede competition. This is precisely the dilemma faced by the European antitrust authorities.

EU policy on R&D (and other) cooperation, while marked by what Sharp (1991, pp. 60–61) describes as schizophrenic tension between free marketeers and mercantilists, has kept in mind the idea that product-market competition promotes good technological performance (Sharp, 1991, p. 63):

> [In the late 1970s], observers began to question whether . . . promoting 'national champions' in each individual member state was not diverting European companies from taking advantage of the Community's major asset, its common market of 320 million and instead fragmenting effort between the various national markets. Increasingly, too, the lack of competition was questioned. Large companies might be necessary to achieve the relevant economies of scale and scope, but such benefits were rapidly negated if the companies concerned made insufficient effort to keep up with new technologies, complacent in their protected position in home markets.

Thus, the European Commission's 2000 Block Exemption Regulation for R&D agreements includes as conditions for the block exemption to apply that all cooperating parties be able to exploit joint research results, that they be able to engage in unrelated R&D, alone or jointly with third parties, and that they be able to engage in related R&D after the agreement has run its course. Consistent with the EU's general structural approach to maintaining product-market rivalry, if cooperating firms are competitors, the block exemption applies if their combined market shares is not greater than 25 per cent. Joint R&D by firms that are not competitors is not subject to market share limitations.

15.6 Intellectual Property Rights

Intellectual property laws attempt to make it possible to own the right to use ideas, to make appropriable that which Arrow (1962, p. 615, quoted above) asserts cannot be made thoroughly appropriable, information. The main categories of intellectual property rights are patents, trademarks, and copyright.[41] It is the line of least resistance to describe patents as seeking to confer monopoly in a new product or process. This is imprecise. A patent grants the right to exclude others (in the United States, generally for a period of 20 years from the date a patent application was filed) from using an innovation. The holder of a patent on an improvement of a previously patented innovation may exclude others from using the improvement, while being him- or herself excluded from using the base innovation.

A trademark protects a business' investment in building a publicly familiar commercial identity.[42] A copyright protects the words in which an idea (song, music, image) is expressed, not the underlying concept. Others may express a concept in their own way without violating copyright.

A trade secret is not, strictly speaking a form of intellectual property. It is a way for a firm to safeguard the income that flows from a piece of knowledge. Potentially, this protection can last forever. But the protection is fragile. If the basis of a firm's business is a secret egg salad recipe, and through neglect or chance the recipe becomes public, the firm has no recourse. If, on the other hand, an employee who in the course of his or her duties acquires knowledge of the recipe reveals the information, in violation of a previous agreement not to do so, the firm can sue the employee for breach of contract.[43] But the right of the firm to recover damages is rooted in contract law, not a property right in the secret.

15.6.1 Background[44]

Mercantilism

Although the currently most fashionable rationale for the institution of intellectual property is that the public good aspects of information mean some legal support for appropriability is necessary to (Lincoln, 1858, 1859) "[add] the fuel of interest to the fire of genius" and encourage private investment in innovation in a market system, the origin of intellectual property laws was fundamentally mercantilist. The earliest patents, which developed first

---

[41] See the United States Patent and Trademark Office web site, URL <http://www.uspto.gov/web/offices/pac/doc/general/whatis.htm>. Specialized types of intellectual property rights include plant breeder rights, geographic indications ("champagne"), industrial design protection, and protection for integrated circuit layout designs.

[42] Subtle problems arise if markets converge and make competitors of firms that have cultivated overlapping trademarks in what had been distinct markets. See Flynn (2007), discussing the resolution of a legal dispute between the computer company Apple Inc. and the Beatles-founded music company Apple Corps Ltd.

[43] See, for example, Associated Press "Ex-secretary found guilty of stealing Coke secrets", 2 February 2007.

[44] See Machlup and Penrose (1950), Machlup (1958), and David (1993).

in late 15th-century Venice, later in Elizabethan England and then elsewhere in Europe—were granted to skilled craftsmen from foreign parts who would agree to train residents in a hitherto locally unknown art (as, the production of specialized textiles). The patent was a protection of the skilled craftsman against too-prompt competition from those he trained. Thus the first English patents were for a period of 14 years, twice the standard seven-year apprenticeship. Similarly, the earliest copyrights were not granted to establish an author's right to control his own work. They were sought by publishers in early sixteenth-century England and the Netherlands to control (that is, prevent) ruinous competition.

"Inventor" ≈ "importer"

It was the English Statute of Monopolies of 1623 that established the principle that it should be the "true and first inventor" that received a monopoly patent (Machlup and Penrose, 1950, p. 2). The word "inventor" continued to be read to include importers of machines used and introducers of processes known elsewhere (MacLeod, 1996, p. 18).[45] The revolutionary French Constitutional Assembly adopted a patent law in 1791. The right of the U.S. Congress to pass laws regulating intellectual property is established in the Constitution,[46] and the first such law was passed in 1793.[47]

The desirability of a patent system was vigorously debated throughout the nineteenth century. In the 1860s, it seemed reasonable to expect that patent protection, where it had been established, would be abolished.[48] Opposition to patents, which was shared by most economists, was tied to opposition to monopoly and support for free trade.

 BOX   A Tale of Two Patents

(1) The Selden Patent

In 1879, when it was a good bet that there would some day be an important horseless carriage industry but unclear whether such vehicles would be powered by steam, electricity, or petrol, patent attorney George B. Selden filed an application for a patent on a hydrocarbon-powered motor vehicle. U.S. Patent Office regulations required an applicant to reply to communications within two years. By taking the maximum amount of time to respond to official communications, Selden delayed the granting of his patent until 5 November 1895. Selden, who never built a machine based on the patent, found himself in a position to demand royalties from—as he asserted—any type of car, provided he could cover the cost of enforcing the rights he claimed under the patent.   »

---

[45] This interpretation persisted in France through the mid-nineteenth century (Moser, 2005, p. 1217).

[46] Article I, Section 8, Clause 8 of the U.S. Constitution (emphasis added): "Congress shall have power ... *to promote the progress of science and useful arts*, by securing for limited times to authors and inventors the exclusive right to their respective writings and discoveries."

[47] To be patented, an invention must be novel, useful, and not obvious. At this writing, a patent is granted to the first to invent, not (in contrast to much of the rest of the world) to the first to file for a patent.

[48] The Netherlands abolished its patent system in 1869 (Moser, 2005, p. 1229). Moser (2005, p. 1218) notes that Switzerland and Denmark did not have patent systems in 1851, Switzerland and the Netherlands did not have patent systems in 1876.

>> Meanwhile, the Electric Vehicle Company, which had its origin in a failed scheme to monopolize the taxicab market in major U.S. cities, took note of the progress made by petrol-powered cars. As an insurance policy of sorts, it purchased the Selden patent and proceeded to organize the Association of Licensed Automobile Manufacturers (ALAM), from the members of which it asked a royalty of 1.25 per cent on the list price of each car produced.

The strength of the Selden patent was open to question, but most car manufacturers went along with it, perhaps because it appeared to be a tool they might be able to use to control competition from fringe producers. Unfortunately for ALAM and the Electric Vehicle Company, one of the few car manufacturers who declined to pay royalties was Henry Ford, who (after an initial loss in District Court), obtained a ruling from the Second Circuit Court of Appeals* to the effect that the Selden patent, although valid, applied only to cars powered by two-cycle engines, and so was not infringed by Ford's vehicle, powered by a four-cycle engine. Thus (Rae, 1955, p. 308):

> Ford ... was cast by public opinion in the role of David battling the monopolistic Goliath—a role, needless to say, worth millions of dollars in advertising value to the Ford Motor Company.

Note: *Columbia Motor Car Co. *et al.* v. C. A. Duerr & Co. *et al.* 184 F. 893 (1911).
Sources: Welsh (1948), Greenleaf (1961), Rae (1955).

(2) The Kearns Patent

In 1962, Wayne State University engineer Robert Kearns, while driving through a light rain, had the idea of controlling windshield wipers so they would move intermittently rather than at a constant rate. He developed a prototype by mid 1963, demonstrated it to Ford Motor Company engineers, who expressed some interest in the idea, and obtained the first of many patents in 1967. Ford began commercializing intermittent windshield wipers in 1969, using (Seabrook, 1993, p. 47) "a transistor, a resistor, and a capacitor in the same configuration that Kearns had designed". Ford took the view that it was not infringing Kearns' patents, which in any case, it asserted, were invalid. Kearns filed a patent-infringement suit against Ford in 1978, and in 1989 declined an offer from Ford to settle for a reported $30 million. After a jury verdict awarding Kearns $5.2 million, Ford settled for $10.2 million. A later suit against produced a finding that Chrysler Corporation had unintentionally infringed Kearns' patents, and awarded Kearns more than $20 million.

Kearns' marriage broke up during his protracted patent litigation. Despite his eventual monetary recovery, he never succeeded in what he always asserted was his fundamental ambition, to produce and supply windshield wipers to car manufacturers. He died in 2005 and according to one obituary (Schudel, 2005) "In his final years, he drove around in two aging vehicles: a 1978 Ford pickup and a 1965 Chrysler. Neither had intermittent wipers."

Source: Seabrook (1993).

Pros and cons

Four main arguments were put forward to support the idea of intellectual property rights (Machlup and Penrose, 1950, p. 10; Machlup, 1958, p. 21):

- "A person has a natural property right in his or her own ideas."
- "Justice requires that a person receive, and therefore that society secure to him, reward for his services in proportion as these services are useful to society. ... The most appropri-

ate way to secure to inventors rewards commensurate with their services is by means of exclusive patent rights in their inventions."

- Monopoly profit is an incentive to induce private investment in innovation (that would otherwise be insufficient from a social point of view).
- Patent rights are a *quid pro quo* for disclosure of inventions.

Natural property right If the first argument is accepted, one is bound to ask why patent rights are granted for only a limited period of time. Another way to state this point is to observe that the first and fourth arguments are inconsistent, since the fourth implies that whatever right the inventor has in the protected ideas is given up upon expiration of the patent.

Justice There are really two separable propositions in the second argument. The first is justice requires a person to receive reward for his services in proportion as these services are useful to society. While this may be so, the economist must note that the rewards to other types of labour—butcher, baker, candlestick maker, as well as nurse, librarian, and college professor—are not determined by an evaluation of the social usefulness of the services rendered but by the relationship between the supply of and the demand for each particular type of labour. The second is that if for whatever reason society wishes to increase the income that flows from invention, patents are the best way to accomplish that goal. As we shall see, the evidence is against this proposition.

Inducement The third point is closest to the modern rationale for a system of intellectual property rights. Against the argument that the lure of economic profit is needed to induce firms to invest in commercialization is the counterargument that the threat of the economic losses that will be suffered if a rival firm commercializes first is also a powerful an incentive for business innovation—that (Villard, 1958, p. 493) "what is needed for innovation is a situation in which firms that fail to innovate get hurt and get hurt severely". [49]

Disclosure As for the fourth point, keeping an innovative product or process secret is always an alternative to applying for a patent. One might suspect, therefore, that innovators who believe they will be able to maintain the secrecy of their discovery will do so. Inventors who think their discovery is likely to leak out, or be independently rediscovered in short order by a rival, will have the strongest incentive to take out a patent. But then society grants the right to exclude rivals, for the length of the patent, precisely for those innovations that are most likely to be disclosed in any event. In such cases, the effect of patent protection is to slow diffusion of the innovation.[50]

---

[49] This might be termed the *Red Queen principle* (it takes all the running you can do to keep in the same place). It is at least in part an explanation of the sailing ship effect: doomed technology or not, firms will invest in improvements if the losses to be avoided before extinction exceed the cost.

[50] Some confirmation appears in the work of Moser (2005). She analyses the relation between patent laws and innovations for Northern European countries using innovations exhibited at the 1851 Crystal Palace World's Fair or the 1876 Centennial Exhibition, and concludes (2005, p. 1231) that "Innovators in countries without patent laws concentrated in industries where secrecy was an effective alternative to patent grants . . . ." This is evidence that patent laws encourage private investment in innovation in sectors where appropriabililty would otherwise be weak. It is also evidence that for such innovation as occurs in those sectors, patent laws delay diffusion.

That dynamic market performance be improved by the disclosure component of the patent package is conditional on patents, which are publicly available, serving as a source of information. Cowan and van de Paal (2000, p. 66) report that European innovating firms with between 10 and 499 employees ranked patent disclosures 10th out of 11 external sources of innovation information; only consultants were less important. About one-third of large innovating firms, in contrast, found patent disclosures an important external source of innovation information. This evidence, which is consistent with the argument that absorptive capacity is necessary to access technological information, suggests that the benefits of patent disclosures go mainly to large firms.

Static market power   One economic argument against a patent system is that to the extent it is effective, it permits the patentholder, for the life of the patent, to maintain a price greater than the marginal cost of production. Thus the patented product is not used as much as it should be, from a social point of view.

Submarine patents   Patents may serve strategic purposes (Cowan and van de Paal, 2000, p. 65) "including to block competitors from applying for a patent, to reduce ... risk of being sued for infringement, and to use in cross-licensing negotiations with other firms".

The patent system itself—the institutions by which patents are applied for and reviewed—is open to strategic abuse.[51] One such abuse is the *submarine patent* (Boldrin and Levine, 2004, pp. 332–333),

> filed, but intentionally delayed by many years through the filing of constant amendments. Because the patent is never granted, it is never made public, and the date at which the patent expires is determined by the time at which the "submarine surfaces." This allows holding a claim to an idea that is currently useless, but might have some use in the future. It keeps everything secret until someone else actually innovates and (usually at some substantial expense) develops the idea into something practical. After a nice business has developed, the submarine surfaces and demands royalties from the unsuspecting innovator. Obviously these activities contribute nothing to social welfare, but do detract from the incentive to innovate—who knows what submarines are lurking nearby?

Restrictive licensing   Strategic abuse of the patent system might include use of licensing agreements to restrict competition, as in the pre-World War II U.S. glass container industry:[52]

> Here is an industry ... where the method of employing patents has resulted in a sort of private N.R.A. This control is employed to adjust and allocate production ... prices are stabilized through production control and ... are further stabilized through the practice of producers to follow the prices of the largest producer. ... Through the refusal to grant licences, persons desiring to enter the industry have not been allowed to do so ... As a result of litigation ... certain producers have been eliminated from the business, or have been purchased wholly or in part, by large interests ... persons with financial means and responsible connections have apparently been excluded from this industry ... Those in control of patents are, as a result of the present state of the law, in a position to issue or refute what amounts to a 'Certificate of convenience and necessity' to those who may desire to enter the industry.

---

[51] Machlup (1958, p. 10); Janis (2002).

[52] Senator Joseph O'Mahoney of the Temporary National Economic Committee is quoted by Polyani (1944, p. 63); Polyani in turn cites Forkosch (1939–1940, pp. 422–423) as his source. On the NRA, see Section 20.3.2.

Etc., etc., and so forth   Other potential abuses could lie in tying the sale of patented and unpatented products (which we discuss below), or successive patenting of incremental improvements, effectively increasing the period of patent protection. Spurious litigation by incumbents alleging patent infringement by entrants, even if ultimately lost, raise the cost of and reduce the profitability of entry.[53]

15.6.2 Patent Effectiveness and Effects

In principle, a patent is a tradeoff of appropriability—limited in time—for disclosure. So the first thing to ask is whether patents are effective in preventing output spillovers, so patent-holders can profit from their innovations. But patents may have other effects, some promoting innovation, some not. A patent, held by a high-tech start-up, may be necessary (but not sufficient) to obtain venture capital financing. Submarine patents, by reducing the income of entrepreneurs who commercialize innovations, may discourage such commercialization. In technology areas where intellectual property rights are fragmented, patents may be sought not so much for the prospect of commecializing them, but to serve as bargaining chips for negotiating cross-licensing arrangements. Such patent thickets may raise the cost of entry for starts-up that have a genuine innovation but little with which to bargain. Further, since essentially all innovation is sequential, building on previous innovation, fragmented intellectual property rights may slow the rate of progress by impeding improvements in existing technology.

 BOX   **Which Came First?**

Bugos (1992) distinguishes five overlapping phases in the evolution of and intellectual-property protection mechanisms employed by firms in the U.S. chicken industry.

In the first phase (Bugos, 1992, p. 129) "breeders purebred new egg-laying breeds, protected their intellectual property by breeding to nationally defined standards, and created industrial units like trade associations and hatcheries to spread the gospel of uniformity".

The second phase saw a shift from eggs to meat as the primary product. 1946 and 1951 nationwide "Chicken of Tomorrow" contests encouraged breeders to develop meat-rich birds, and, as would have been suggested by Hotelling's principle of minimum differentiation, the winners became the leading firms in a breeding oligopoly (Bugos, 1992, p. 139): "few farmers wanted to trust their livelihood to a losing bird".

In the 1950s, leading breeders moved to hybridization and reliance on the laws of genetics to protect their intellectual property. Pairing chickens with different dominant traits resulted in ≫

---

[53] In its November, 2008 Preliminary Report on the pharmaceutical sector (2008a), DG Competition identified manipulations of intellectual property rights to delay the entry of generic substitutes for patented pharmaceuticals, among which (2008b) "nearly 700 cases of reported patent litigation with generic companies, which on average lasted nearly three years. The generic companies ultimately won more than 60% of these cases", and intervention "in national procedures for the approval of generic medicines in a significant number of cases, which on average led to four months of delay for the generic medicine".

≫ uniform offspring, since all chicks inherited the dominant characteristics. If the chicks were bred, recessive characteristics appeared in their offspring (Bugos, 1992, p. 144)—"the pedigrees would genetically self-destruct".

The 1960s and 1970s saw vertical integration among chicken firms, in part to escape dependence on feed producers (who were themselves in the chicken-breeding industry). It also saw the development of brand names via direct advertising to the final consumers. The breeding industry, which supplied broilers, became even more concentrated (Bugos, 1992, p. 161): "By 1989, 90 percent of the market for parent chicks was controlled by three lines on the female side ... and three on the male side ...."

The 1980 Diamond v. Chakrabarty decision (447 U.S. 303 (1980)), which allowed the patenting of a genetically modified bacteria, opened up a new frontier in intellectual property protection for the chicken-breeding industry. It is a frontier they have approached cautiously; patents might threaten the efficacy of the protective mechanisms upon which the industry has successfully relied (Bugos, 1992, p. 167):

> The industrial strategies of the most successful breeders revolved around creating alternative types of protection for their intellectual property. To prevent competitors from copying their "inventions," breeders devised a biological lock through hybridization, and turned the hybridization sequence and the chick multiplication process into trade secrets. Even if their breeding "inventions" were copied, an infringer's ability to profit would be limited by the barrier to entry created through tradenames. Reputations protected each breeder's market shares, and the larger breeders (with the concurrence of the USDA) insisted that reputations be based on expensive reliability testing as much as on research, on instilling genetic uniformity in broiler chicks as much as on harnessing genetic variation.

Protecting intellectual property?

United States   Cohen *et al.* (2000) present the results of a 1994 survey of more than a thousand managers of manufacturing industry R&D laboratories on methods used to protect income flows generated by intellectual assets.[54]

Ways firms protect intellectual property   The survey asked managers to rank the effectiveness of patents and five other strategies as appropriability mechanisms for innovations during the three years preceding the survey. The other five protective mechanisms were the lead time that comes from first innovation, secrecy, possession of complementary manufacturing facilities and know-how, complementary sales and service organizations, and legal protections other than patents. Taking responses from all industries, patents were ranked next-to-last in effectiveness for both product and process innovations (Table 15.1). The three leading protective strategies are taking advantage of lead time, secrecy, and complementary manufacturing facilities and know-how, although the ranking of the three differs between product and process innovations.

Much previous research suggests that patents are not generally important in allowing firms to appropriate the income that flows from intellectual property,[55] but that patents are

---

[54] See also Cohen *et al.* (2002). The later Carnegie-Mellon surveys extend the results of Levin *et al.* (1988).

[55] Jaffe (2000, p. 555) concludes that "patents are not central to appropriating the returns to R&D in most industries".

Table 15.1 Mean percentage of innovations for which appropriability mechanism is considered effective

Product innovations	%	Process innovations	%
Lead time	52.76	Secrecy	50.59
Secrecy	51.00	Complementary manufacturing facilities and know-how	43.00
Complementary manufacturing facilities and know-how	45.61	Lead time	38.43
Complementary sales and service	42.74	Complementary sales and service	30.73
Patents	34.83	Patents	23.30
Other legal mechanisms	20.71	Other legal mechanisms	15.39

Source: Cohen *et al.* (2000, Table 1, Table 2).

Table 15.2 Mean percentage of product innovations for which appropriability mechanism is considered effective, five industry groups

Product innovations	Medical equipment	Drugs	Special purpose machinery, nec	Auto parts	Computers
Lead time	58.06	50.10	59.69	64.35	61.40
Patents	54.70	50.20	48.83	44.35	41.00
Complementary sales and service	52.31	33.37	46.33	44.84	40.20
Secrecy	50.97	53.57	45.08	50.83	44.20
Complementary manufacturing facilities and know-how	49.25	49.39	51.09	53.06	38.00
Other legal mechanisms	29.03	20.82	23.05	15.65	27.20

Note: "nec" indicates "not elsewhere classified".
Source: Cohen *et al.* (2000, Table 1).

effective in some industries, in particular pharmaceuticals.[56] Table 15.2 reports the results of the Cohen *et al.* survey for the five industry groups for which patents were most effect in protecting competitive advantage. Even for these industry groups, at least one other protective mechanism was ranked as being more effective than patents.

Why firms don't patent   Survey results indicate that the most important reasons firms decided not to patent an innovation were the difficulty in demonstrating to the patent office that the innovation was in fact novel. The next most important reasons were the ease of inventing around a patent and the amount of information that had to be disclosed to obtain a patent. That disclosure requirements often discourage firms from filing for patent protection negates one of the main arguments for a system of patent protection, and is consistent with the high ranking of secrecy as a protective device.

Why firms patent, if they do   The survey results also shed light on why firms do patent, when they do. For the sample as a whole, the most important reason (Table 15.3) was to prevent copying, followed closely by strategic attempts to block competing innovation by rivals. Patents are also important assets in interactions with rivals, whether to neutralize patent infringement suits by being able to threaten countersuits or have something to offer in return when a licence is sought for use of another firm's intellectual property.[57]

Table 15.3 Per cent of respondents by reason to patent, 765 product innovations, 674 process innovations

Reasons to patent	Product innovations	Process innovations
Prevent copying	95.8	77.6
Blocking rivals' attempts to patent a related invention	81.8	63.6
Prevent infringement suits	58.8	46.5
Enhance reputation	47.9	34.0
Use in negotiations	47.4	37.0
Licensing revenue	28.3	23.3
Measure internal performance of own technology personnel	5.8	5.0

Source: Cohen *et al.* (2000, Figure 7, Figure 8).

[56] Caves *et al.* (1991) study 30 drugs that lost patent protection in the decade 1976–1987 and find that after patent protection expired, the patented variety suffered only modest reductions in market share, even though generic substitutes sell at substantially lower prices. Marketing efforts aimed at prescribing physicians apparently create a product differentiation advantage that survives well after the introduction of generic substitutes and allows innovators to collect substantial economic profits.

[57] Mowery and Steinmueller (1990, p. 18) suggest that in the U.S. semiconductor industry, patents historically served as bargaining chips that allow a firm to trade licences for access to technology covered by patents held by other firms.

Table 15.4 Standardized patent propensity rates (per cent) for large European and American firms

	Type of Innovation	
	Product	**Process**
EU	44	26
U.S.	52	44

Note: Based on a standardized industrial distribution and weighted by R&D expenditures
Source: Cowen and van de Paal (2000, Table III.3; underlying data 1993 PACE Survey and Cohen *et al.* (2000, 2002).

European Union Cowan and van de Paal (2000, p. 61) report that EU firms patent less than U.S. firms (Table 15.4).[58] Their commentary (2000, p. 67) is hardly a ringing endorsement of patent protection as a public policy aiming to encourage innovation:

[T]he comparison between European and American patent propensity rates in the early 1990s ... indicates that European firms are lagging behind their American competitors in their propensity to patent. Their American competitors also appear to be using patents more aggressively in ways that could be destructive both to the public interest and to the self-interest of the firms. The use of patents to block competitors interferes with the use of information, while patenting to prevent an infringement suit is a waste of the firm's resources if the firm can obtain the same end by publishing the details in trade or scientific journals.

Regarding why firms might find patents useful, Cowan and van de Paal report (no comparable data being available for the EU) estimates for Japan and the United States (Table 15.5) that patent protection impedes imitation (2000, p. 65):

[P]atents do indeed provide protection against imitation, and thus provide incentives to innovate. Patenting increases lag times by roughly 30% ... We should note, though, that even unprotected innovations are not imitated immediately. An imitation time lag between 24 and 41 months is observed. This implies that patents are not the only appropriation method, and thus not the only source of incentives to innovate.

Even the longest imitation lags given in Table 15.5 are substantially less than the legal period of patent protection (now, with some exceptions for pharmaceuticals, 20 years).

Secrecy, lead time But a survey of 5,147 innovative EU firms for 1993 shows that EU firms, like their U.S. counterparts, generally regard secrecy and lead time as being more effective than patents at protecting innovations (Table 15.6). It is generally large EU firms that find patents important. The same exception that appears in the U.S. shows up in the EU as well (2000, p. 63): "small firms that do find patents or other [intellectual property rights] to be a

[58] The patent propensity rate is an estimate of the percentage of innovations that are patented. See Arundel and Kabla (1998) for discussion of alternative definitions and issues of measurement.

Table 15.5 Mean imitation lags in months for the firm's most significant product and process innovations and (in parentheses) per cent increase, patented over unpatented mean imitation lag

Type of Innovation	Japan		U.S.	
	Unpatented	Patented	Unpatented	Patented
Product	24	31 (30)	34	44 (29)
Process	24	41 (71)	41	50 (22)

Source: Cowan and van de Paal (2000, Table III.4).

Table 15.6 Importance of secrecy and lead-time for earning competitive advantages, relative to patents, for innovative EU firms, 1993

	Lead Time	Secrecy
Product	2.01	1.52
Process	2.20	2.00

Source: Cowan and van de Paal (2000, Figures III.10, III.11).

crucial part of their business strategy . . . tend to be in high technology areas such as biotechnology or software where [intellectual property rights] are essential to attracting venture capital".

Tragedy of the anticommons   The last point is confirmed by Haeussler *et al.* (2009), who find that German and French biotechnology firms with patents applications on file at the European Patent Office obtained venture capital financing earlier, all else equal. Against this effect must be set the prospect of the "tragedy of the anticommons", which arises (Heller and Eisenberg, 1998, p. 698) "when multiple owners each have a right to exclude others from a scarce resource and no one has an effective privilege of use". All innovation is in some degree incremental, depending on spillovers from earlier innovations. Just as intellectual property rights that are too weak can discourage innovation because firms will not invest for the profit of other firms, so intellectual property rights that are too strong can discourage innovation because earlier innovators claim too large a share of the income that flows from later innovations.[59]

---

[59] Thus the Wright brothers, whose essential innovation was the first effective mechanism for controlling wing flaps during flight, engaged in years of legal battles with later aviation pioneers, ultimately unsuccessful, making the claim that their patent covered all fixed-wing flying machines. See Shulman (2002).

BOX   Industrial Secrets and the Protection of Intellectual Property

The history of the Farr Alpaca company, for some 60 years the dominant U.S. processor of alpaca and mohair wool into worsted yarn and fabrics, is rich in lessons for students of industrial economics.

In the 1860s, the company moved from Canada to Holyoke, Massachusetts to avoid the protective tariff imposed by the Wool and Woolens Act of 1867.

The textile industry, where technology implies that minimum efficient scale is small relative to market size, is not one where one would expect a firm to maintain a dominant position. The most important factor in Farr Alpaca's success was labour-saving machinery, developed by the company in the 1880s, to finish alpaca fabric used for coat linings. Rather than patent the machinery, Farr Alpaca kept the technology secret (Hutner, 1951, p. 32):

> The newly devised equipment consisted chiefly of various types of heavy presses which gave the cloth a permanent, lustrous, perspiration-proof finish. … The heavier pieces were made to order by a local foundry whose ownership was tied in with the Farr's; the Farr made the smaller parts in its own machine shop. The men who assembled, operated, and repaired the equipment were well paid, thus lessening the hazard that other manufacturers would buy them away; and no one of them had sufficient knowledge of other phases of the fabricating process to be useful to rivals.

Limit pricing was another element in Farr Alpaca's success: it set prices about 10 per cent above cost. Nor was it above strategic entry-deterring behaviour. Early in the history of the company, a foreman jumped ship and opened his own competing alpaca mill. Farr Alpaca responded by buying that year's entire Peruvian alpaca supply, foreclosing the rival from access to an essential ingredient.

The company's decline shows the importance of marketing channels. Not only did the management of Farr Alpaca become set in its ways, but so did the single sales agency that Farr Alpaca relied on to market its fabric to tailors and clothing stores. Although Farr Alpaca kept its prices down, it also maintained insufficient capacity to supply the quantity demanded at those prices, and so rationed the available supply. Impatient clothing producers developed skeleton linings that gave suits a noticeably less attractive appearance, but reduced the need for lining material to one-third or less of its former level. Farr's sales agent, who sat on its Board of Directors, resisted changing operations to react to the rise of skeleton linings, and again resisted reacting to the appearance of rayon linings in the 1920s. When reaction came, it was too late: what had been a prosperous leader of its market segment in 1923 closed its doors in 1939.

Source: Hutner (1951).

15.6.3 The Flow (and Ebb?) of Patent Protection

Novelty

Historical standards for granting a patent required that the innovation covered by the patent be, in some sense, substantial. In the 1882 decision in Atlantic Works v. Brady, the U.S. Supreme Court declared a patent for a dredging boat invalid because the patented object was not sufficiently novel (107 U.S. 192 at 200):

> The design of the patent laws is to reward those who make some substantial discovery or invention, which adds to our knowledge and makes a step in advance in the useful arts. Such

inventors are worthy of all favor. It was never the object of those laws to grant a monopoly for every trifling device, every shadow of a shade of an idea, which would naturally and spontaneously occur to any skilled mechanic or operator in the ordinary progress of manufactures. Such an indiscriminate creation of exclusive privileges tends rather to obstruct than to stimulate invention.

Patentability requirements have drifted far from this standard. As late as 1972, the U.S. Supreme Court ruled[60] that an algorithm for converting decimal numbers to binary numbers, the latter to be used in computer programming, could not be patented. In so doing, it referred (409 U.S. 63 at 67) to early decisions holding that "Phenomena of nature, though just discovered, mental processes, and abstract intellectual concepts are not patentable, as they are the basic tools of scientific and technological work." Under U.S. law, "any new and useful process, machine, manufacture, or composition of matter, or any new and useful improvement thereof" is patentable. But in 1972, for the purposes of U.S. patent law, a mathematical algorithm was not a "process". Twenty-two years later, in its *In re Alappat* decision[61] the Court of Appeals for the Federal Circuit (C.A.F.C.) held that software to smooth waveform data for display on an oscilloscope screen could be patented. The Supreme Court had ruled, said the C.A.F.C. (33 F.3d 1526 at 1543), "that certain mathematical subject matter is not, standing alone, entitled to patent protection". But since Allapat's innovation covered combined software embodying mathematical subject matter with (33 F.3d 1526 at 1541) an "apparatus, made up of a combination of known electronic circuitry elements", it could be patented.

 BOX   Just a Click Away

- September 1999: Amazon.com is granted patent 5,960,411 covering "one-click" placing of internet orders, the essence of the innovation being (Gleick, 2000) "let users choose an item with just one click of the mouse button, and use a shipping address and credit-card number already on file". There is good reason to think that there were many prior references to such internet ordering systems, including, allegedly, a 1993 Doonesbury comic strip.

- October 1999, Amazon.com files suit against Barnes & Noble, Inc.

- December 1999: Amazon.com obtains preliminary injunction against the "Express Lane" feature of Barnes & Noble's web site order entry system.

- Barnes & Noble, apparently able to maintain a sense of perspective, adds a functionless link to its web-based order entry system, admonishing buyers "Please be sure to click this button. If you don't, we won't get your order!"

- March 9, 2000: In an open letter, Amazon.com CEO Jeff Bezos suggests that:

  - "the patent laws should recognize that business method and software patents are fundamentally different than other kinds of patents" and   »

---

[60] In Gottschalk *v.* Benson, 409 U.S. 63 (1972).

[61] 33 F.3d 1526 (1994).

>> – "business method and software patents should have a much shorter lifespan than the current 17 years— ... 3 to 5 years. This isn't like drug companies, which need long patent windows because of clinical testing, or like complicated physical processes, where you might have to tool up and build factories. Especially in the age of the Internet, a good software innovation can catch a lot of wind in 3 or 5 years."

- February 2001: Court of Appeals for the Federal Circuit dissolves injunction,* citing the doubtful validity of the patent given substantial indications of prior references to the subject of the patent

- March 2002: Amazon, Barnes & Noble reach an out-of-court settlement.

*Amazon.com., Inc. v. Barnesandnoble.com., Inc. 239 F.3d 1343 (Fed. Cir. 2001)

Business method patents

In its 1998 *State Street Bank*[62] decision, the Court of Appeals for the Federal Circuit validated the granting of a patent for a data processing system used to manage a mutual fund. The innovation combined software with a machine (elements of which included a central processing unit, a data disc, and arithmetic logic circuits; 149 F.3d at 1371–1372). For the C.A.F.C. (149 F.3d at 1373) "the transformation of data, representing discrete dollar amounts, by a machine through a series of mathematical calculations into a final share price, constitutes a practical application of a mathematical algorithm ... because it produces 'a useful, concrete and tangible result'". State Street Bank & Trust Company's patent was valid.

The C.A.F.C. took advantage of *State Street Bank* to disabuse any who might have held it of the notion that business methods could not be patented. In its opinion, the C.A.F.C. reviewed decisions commonly cited as indicated business methods could not be patented, and found, in each case, that there had been some other, fundamental, reason for denying patentability.[63] After *State Street Bank*, business methods could be patented. And they were. Hall (2003, pp. 3–4) writes that "Under a broad definition of software/business methods, the [U.S. Patent and Trademark Office] is now granting about 10 to 12 thousand patents per year,

---

[62] State Street Bank & Trust Company v. Signature Financial Group, Inc 149 F.3d 1368 (Fed.Cir. 1998).

[63] In Hotel Security Checking Co. v. Lorraine Co. 160 F. 467 (2d Cir. 1908), the Court of Appeals for the Second Circuit denied the patentability of a system designed to prevent theft by waiters and cashiers in hotels and restaurants. One basis for the decision was that the idea was not new (160 F. 467 at 469): "The fundamental principle of the system is as old as the art of bookkeeping, i.e., charging the goods of the employer to the agent who takes them." But before it reaches the question of novelty, the Circuit Court emphasizes that what is sought is a patent on a business method, and that this is not possible. The opinion describes in some detail the physical accoutrements used to implement the system—slips of paper given to each waiter, numbered conformably with columns on a master sheet of paper to keep track of orders by waiter, and so on. In the context of an order entry system, these elements would seem to correspond to the electronic circuitry of *In re Alappat*. But the use of physical components to implement a method was not sufficient to make the system patentable (160 F. 467 at 469, quoting 121 Fed. 747): " 'No mere abstraction, no idea, however brilliant, can be the subject of a patent irrespective of the means designed to give it effect.' It cannot be maintained that the physical means described by Hicks,—the sheet and the slips,—apart from the manner of their use, present any new and useful feature." In Joseph E. Seagram & Sons v. Marzell 180 F.2d 26 (D.C. Cir. 1950), the Circuit Court of Appeals for the District of Columbia affirmed the denial of a patent related to blind taste-testing on grounds that (at 28) "At best, the record appears to show that [Seagram] has developed methods for testing its own product which enable it to gauge with some accuracy the preferences of its customers", and "it seems clear that [Seagram]'s claims do not constitute a 'new and useful art, machine, manufacture, composition of matter, or any new and useful improvements thereof'".

as opposed to fewer than a thousand before 1985." Under the narrow definition of business method patents employed by the Patent and Trademark Office in its 1999 *White Paper*, the number is much less. But the issues raised by business method patents—declining patent quality, the granting of patents for "innovations" that seem obvious, submarine patents, the potential for holdup, an explosion of litigation disputing the validity of dubious patents—arise broadly (for example, in connection with biotechnology patents and software patents), and the larger number seems the more suitable estimate.

Court of Appeals for the Federal Circuit   The evolution of U.S. patent policy to permit business method patents is in some measure an unintended consequence of institutional changes in the U.S. patent system. One of these changes took place in 1982, when the U.S. Congress created C.A.F.C., the Court of Appeals for the Federal Circuit, to hear all appeals in patent cases—lawsuits seeking to enforce or invalidate existing patents, or challenging decisions of the U.S. patent office. Before C.A.F.C. was established, a plaintiff filing a patent-related lawsuit in federal courts had, as a practical matter, some discretion where to file the suit. By consolidating appeals in a single court, Congress sought to eliminate "forum shopping"—hunting for an appeals court thought likely to give a favourable ruling. Congress also hoped that C.A.F.C. would become a centre of expertise on intellectual property within the federal court system. The result, however, was a form of "regulatory capture": C.A.F.C. rulings have strengthened patent rights in a way never thought possible, and without a mandate from Congress to do so.[64]

Patent Office changes   Further, in the early 1990s, the funding of the U.S. Patent and Trademark Office was shifted from the taxpayer through the general budget to fees charged by the Patent Office for processing patent & trademark applications. Although economists are prone to ask what patent policy should be to maximize consumer welfare or net social welfare, if one judges by actions, the Patent and Trademark Office has another take on the matter. The framed motto "Our Patent Mission To Help Our Customers Get Patents" appeared in the office of the Commissioner of Patents and Trademarks (Gleick, 2000), and widespread granting of patents for narrowly defined innovations, many of which were well-known to practitioners in their technology area, followed.

In re Bilski   This particular tide may be turning, or at least eddying about. Following a series of Supreme Court decisions that narrowed some aspects of patent protection,[65] the October 2008 C.A.F.C. *In re Bilski* ruling confirmed the U.S. Patent and Trademark Office's denial of a business method patent for a way to hedge risk in commodities trading. Retreating somewhat

---

[64] What is meant by "regulatory capture" is a seemingly ideological commitment to strengthening property rights in the face of substantial evidence that the proliferation of fragmented property rights slows incremental innovation. This is close to what Kortum and Lerner (1998) call the "friendly court" hypothesis. Their view is that regulatory capture should differentially benefit large U.S. firms, and they reject both the friendly court and regulatory capture hypotheses in favor of improved management of research activities.

[65] See eBay Inc *v.* MercExchange 547 U.S. 388 (2006), making clear that a finding that a patent has been infringed does not automatically entitle the patent-holder to an injunction against the infringer; this weakens the bargaining position of patent trolls; KSR International Co. *v.* Teleflex Inc. *et al.* 550 U.S. 398 (2007), validating rejection of a patent claimed for a combination of two known elements on the ground that the combination was obvious; and Microsoft Corp. *v.* AT&T 550 U.S. 437 (2007), establishing that U.S. software patents cannot be enforced outside the United States.

from the broad reach of *State Street Bank*, the C.A.F.C. found in patent law the requirement for business method patentability that the method either be "tied to a particular machine or apparatus" or "transforms a particular article into a different state or thing" (2007-1130, p. 10). Bilski's method satisfied neither part of this machine-or-transformation test, and was not patentable.[66]

15.6.4 The University-Industrial Complex[67]

In 1980, the Bayh-Dole Act (Patent and Trademark Amendments Act) permitted universities and small businesses to assert ownership of federally-funded innovations developed at their facilities. The goal was to promote commercialization of these innovations by creating property rights in them and (hopefully) making it profitable for private-sector firms to license the right to use them from the patent-holder. It was enacted during the crisis of confidence that led to support for R&D cooperation as a quick fix for real or imagined U.S. "falling behind". The philosophy behind the Bayh-Dole Act failed to take differences in types of research into account (David *et al.*, 1992, p. 80, footnote omitted):

> [P]erverse consequences may result from actions by university administrators or state government policymakers who attempt to "capture" the results of basic research to strengthen university finances or to support regional development. ... the belief that university basic research is a powerful engine of regional development and/or appropriable profit for universities overlooks the critical importance of the complementary investments necessary to realize the returns to the results of university basic research. ... these policies may reduce the economic returns to basic research.

The private sector is cautious about of a shift of university research activity in the direction of applied research. Rosenberg and Nelson discuss the results of interviews (Government-University-Industry-Research Roundtable, 1991) with research managers from large industrial companies (1994, p. 345):

> The industry views ... suggest ... considerable industry skepticism over the ability of academics to contribute directly to industrial innovation, which probably reflects a drawing back from more hopeful and less realistic beliefs held earlier in the 1980s. ... the industry views ... were that the academics should stick with the basic research they are doing, and heed their training functions, and stop thinking of themselves as the source of technology.

There has been a massive increase in patenting by U.S. universities (Henderson *et al.*, 1998, p. 119): "In 1965 just 96 U.S. patents were granted to 28 U.S. universities or related institutions. In 1992 almost 1500 patents were granted to over 150 U.S. universities or related institutions. This 15-fold increase in university patenting occurred over an interval in which total U.S. patenting increased less than 50%, and patents granted to U.S. inventors remained roughly constant." No doubt the contemporaneous promotion of R&D cooperation, which caught university-industry cooperation in its wake, and the general emphasis on property rights in knowledge, along with the Bayh-Dole Act, all contributed to this surge in university patenting (Rafferty, 2008).

---

[66] In June, 2009, the U.S. Supreme Court agreed to hear an appeal of the *Bilski* ruling.

[67] Apologies to Kenney (1986).

"Patent", however, is a variable yardstick. Henderson *et al.* examine patent quality between 1965 and mid 1992 and find (1998, p. 119) "averaged over the whole time period, university patents are both more important and more general than the average patent, but that this difference has been declining over time, so that by the late 1980s we cannot find significant differences between the university patent universe and the random sample of all patents."[68]

There are also indications that the surge in university patents may be levelling off (Leydesdorff and Meyer, 2009), but evidence on this point should be allowed to accumulate. Meanwhile, the Bayh-Dole Act has morphed itself into a policy measure that, along with the goal of promoting the commercialization of university innovation, has the purpose of filling university budget gaps (Nelson, 2006, p. 13):

> Regarding the Bayh-Dole Act itself, the problem is more in the ideology that has surrounded it than the language in the Act itself. There is nothing in the legislation that says that exclusive licensing is usually the best way to effect technology transfer or that a strong if secondary objective is to enable universities to make as much money as they can. But there is widespread belief that the former is true, and without question, universities have taken the Act to be a mandate to make money.

15.6.5 Copyright

United States

In 1998 the U.S. Congress adopted the Sonny Bono Copyright Term Extension Act. This law added 20 years to the existing period of protection:[69] "For works created by identified natural persons, the term now lasts from creation until 70 years after the author's death. ... For anonymous works, pseudonymous works, and works made for hire, the term is 95 years from publication or 120 years from creation, whichever expires first." The extension applied to existing copyrighted works as well as newly copyright works.

The 1998 law continues a series of extensions. The Copyright Act of 1790 granted authors the exclusive right to print, reprint, or publish their work for a period of 14 years and to renew for another 14. In 1831, the term of protection of copyrighted works was extended to 28 years, with the possibility of a 14-year extension. In 1909, copyright protection was extended to all works of authorship, the term of protection being 28 years with a possible renewal of 28. In 1976, the term of protection was made the life of the author plus 50 years. "Works for hire" were protected for 75 years, and "fair use" provisions (governing minor use of copyright material without explicit permission) were clarified. In 1992, copyright renewal became automatic, sharply reducing the entry of works protected by copyright before 1978 into the public domain.

A 1999 District Court decision upheld the constitutionality of the 1998 copyright extension, which had been challenged on three grounds. One of these was that the extension of the period of protection to works already benefiting from copyright was inconsistent with the constitutional grant to Congress, since such an extension could not "promote the progress of

---

[68] Sampat *et al.* (2003) suggest that the Henderson *et al.* results are due to an increase in the length of time it takes for a university to receive a patent in the post-Bayh-Dole period, not a decrease in patent quality.

[69] Eric Eldred *et al. v.* John D. Ashcroft 537 U.S. 186 at 195–196 (2003). See this part of the decision for a review of the history of copyright protection in the United States.

science and useful arts". The Circuit Court of Appeals subsequently found that this preamble did not limit congressional power (239 F.3d 372 at 378). On further appeal, the U.S. Supreme Court rejected arguments that repeated extensions of the period of copyright protection violated both the grant to Congress of power to give copyright protection for a limited time period and constitutional protection of the right to free speech. The Supreme Court majority took the view that it was (537 U.S. 186 at 208) "not at liberty to second-guess congressional determinations and policy judgments of this order, however debatable or arguably unwise they may be", remarking that what the challengers really argued was (537 U.S. 186 at 22) "that Congress pursued very bad policy".

If it receives final court approval, an October 2008 agreement to settle two private copyright infringement lawsuits against Google Inc. promises to transform the practice of U.S. copyright in ways that cannot now be foreseen. To establish Google Book Search, Google scanned the collections of major research libraries. It made digital copies of scanned works available in downloadable form. Works on which copyright had expired were made available in their entirety, along with small portions of works protected by copyright. Google's view was that the limited reproduction of copyright-protected work fell within the fair use provisions of copyright law. The Association of American Publishers and the Authors Guild disagreed, and filed class-action lawsuits resolved by the settlement. Under the agreement, Google will pay $125 million and set up a system to pay copyright-holders for use of their material.[70] As a side effect (Darnton, 2009) "the settlement will give Google control over the digitizing of virtually all books covered by copyright in the United States".

European Union

In adopting the Sonny Bono Copyright Term Extension Act and in confirming its constitutionality, Congress and the Supreme Court, respectively, made reference to harmonizing U.S. policy with that of the European Union. The rationale for the applicable EU policy, laid out in a 1993 Directive,[71] began with reference to the minimum period of copyright protection specified by international agreement,[72] life of the author plus 50 years after his death. This period was, according to the Directive "intended to provide protection for the author and the first two generations of his descendants", but increasing longevity made the minimum period insufficient to accomplish this purpose. The Directive therefore established the EU period of copyright protection as the life of the author plus 70 years after the author's death.[73]

A 2008 initiative by the European Commission[74] proposed to extend period of protection of sound recordings from 50 to 95 years (EC Commission, 2008b). Commission documents

---

[70] It may be that this arrangement will function along the lines of ASCAP and Broadcast Music, Inc.; see Section 20.5.1.

[71] Council Directive 93/98/EEC of 29 October 1993 harmonizing the term of protection of copyright and certain related rights OJ L290 24 November 1993 pp. 9–13. The 1993 Directive was codified by Directive 2006/116/EC (OJ L 372 27 December 2006, pp. 12–18), which in the later words of the Commission "did not entail any substantive changes" (COM(2008) 464 final Brussels, 16 July 2008, p. 6).

[72] The Berne Convention for the Protection of Literary and Artistic Works.

[73] For complete details, see the Directive.

[74] Proposal for a European Parliament and Council Directive amending Directive 2006/116/EC of the European Parliament and of the Council on the term of protection of copyright and related rights COM(2008) 464 final Brussels, 16 July 2008.

supporting the proposal emphasized the disadvantage of artists, *vis-à-vis* performers, in terms of intellectual property protection (EC Commission, 2008b, ¶ 1): "After 50 years, artists lose control over the use of their works and no longer receive this important source of income. Composers on the other hand enjoy this form of copyright protection for 70 years after their death."

Any benefit received by recording artists must be by way of benefits received by recording companies, as the royalties recording artists receive are a percentage of the revenue collected by recording companies. This is acknowledged by the Commission's Staff Report, which in addition to pointing out the differential treatment of recording artists, states that:[75] "The record industry faces significant challenges which undermine its competitiveness: online piracy has lead to significant losses. The ability of the music industry to finance new talent and adapt to dematerialised distribution is severely undermined. In addition, the longer term of protection in the US risks undermining the production of European music."

Helberger *et al.* (2008) point out that any distinction between U.S. and European music markets is dubious, "the worldwide music market" being "dominated by only four multinational companies that can not be characterised as either 'European' or 'American'". They further note potential costs of the proposal, along with a higher cost to consumers, of impediments to the development of new modes of distribution and (2008, pp. 175–176) follow-on artistic creations that do not happen as recorded music is held outside the public domain.

The fate of the proposed extension is, at this writing, undetermined. There is considerable opposition.[76] In February, 2009, the Legal Affairs Committee of the European Parliament approved the proposed directive, a necessary step in its adoption.[77] If the proposed directive is adopted, it will be (like the 1998 U.S. Copyright Term Extension Act), more an example of successful rent seeking than policy to promote creativity.

15.6.6 Reprise: Intellectual Property Rights

By establishing intellectual property rights, society seeks to trade a temporary (for patents and copyright) right to exclude for innovation, disclosure, and diffusion. Yet not much about intellectual property has changed since Marshall wrote (1920, Bk. IV, Ch. XI, fn. 133):[78]

> In many businesses only a small percentage of improvements are patented. They consist of many small steps, which it would not be worth while to patent one at a time. Or their chief point lies in noticing that a certain thing ought to be done; and to patent one way of doing it, is only to set other people to work to find out other ways of doing it against which the patent cannot guard. If one patent is taken out, it is often necessary to "block" it, by patenting other

---

[75] EC Commission (2008a, ¶ 4.6). The Staff Report also sees a consumer benefit in an extension of recording artist protection in that "Consumers may not have access to the widest choice of music available at reasonable prices. The opportunities offered by online digital distribution, allowing the dissemination of local repertoire and catering for niche markets, may not be fully seized by the music industry under the current conditions." It is not clear how a proposal that, if it is to benefit recording artists at all, must support the price at which their product is sold, will deal with the situation of consumers who do not have access to a wide choice of music at reasonable prices.

[76] "EU caves to aging rockers, wants 45-year copyright extension" is one characterization (Anderson, 2008).

[77] See a European Parliament Press Release of 16/02/2009 "The European Parliament is in favour of extending the duration of performers' rights up to 95 years" (<http://www.europarl.europa.eu/news/expert/infopress_page/058-48812-040-02-07-909-20090209IPR48791-09-02-2009-2009-false/default_en.htm>).

[78] This is quoted by Scherer *et al.* (1959, p. 62, fn. 31).

methods of arriving at the same result; the patentee does not expect to use them himself, but he wants to prevent others from using them. All this involves worry and loss of time and money: and the large manufacturer prefers to keep his improvement to himself and get what benefit he can by using it. While if the small manufacturer takes out a patent, he is likely to be harassed by infringements: and even though he may win "with costs" the actions in which he tries to defend himself, he is sure to be ruined by them if they are numerous. It is generally in the public interest that an improvement should be published, even though it is at the same time patented. But if it is patented in England and not in other countries, as is often the case, English manufacturers may not use it, even though they were just on the point of finding it out for themselves before it was patented; while foreign manufacturers learn all about it and can use it freely.

The one clearly positive aspect of patent protection that stands out is that holding a patent makes it easier for biotechnology start-ups to obtain financing. Yet it is precisely in biotechnology that the proliferation of fragmented intellectual property rights seems likely to discourage innovation (Heller and Eisenberg, 1998).[79]

In 1966, Edwin Mansfield wrote that (p. 479) "no serious attempt is being made to abolish the system". This remains true almost half a century later.[80] More's the pity, some might say. The best that economists can find to say about patent protection is remarkably tepid (Machlup, 1958, p. 80):[81]

If one does not know whether a system "as a whole" (in contrast to certain features of it) is good or bad, the safest "policy conclusion" is to "muddle through"— either with it, if one has long lived with it, or without it, if one has lived without it. If we did not have a patent system, it would be irresponsible, on the basis of our present knowledge of its economic consequences, to recommend instituting one. But since we have had a patent system for a long time, it would be irresponsible, on the basis of our present knowledge, to recommend abolishing it.

Hall's (2003, p. 16) assessment of the patent system is similarly lukewarm: [82]

Broad evidence that the patent system encourages innovation always and everywhere is hard to come by. The patent system does encourage publication rather than secrecy; it is probably good at providing incentives for innovations with high development cost that are fairly easily imitated and for which a patent can be clearly defined (e.g., pharmaceuticals). When innovations are incremental and when many different innovations must be combined to make a useful product, it is less obvious that benefits of the patent system outweigh the costs.

---

[79] There is also reason to think that biotechnology is atypical within the set of high-technology industries, so that the experience of biotechnology with intellectual property rights should not be made the basis for a general policy; thus (Mowery and Rosenberg, 1993, p. 54, footnote omitted) "The connection between university research and commercial technology appears to be particularly close in biotechnology, a factor that influences the character of many university-industry research relationships in this field, and may distinguish them from university-industry research collaborations in other fields" and (Rosenberg and Nelson, 1994, p. 343) "Once one sorts through the interviews, biotechnology stands out almost uniquely as an area where corporate managers look to university research as a source of 'inventions.'"

[80] But see Boldrin and Levine (2002, 2004).

[81] This is quoted by David (1993, p. 43).

[82] See also Cowan and van de Paal (200, p. 68): "in fact, a good argument can be made for weakening patents and for making it more difficult to obtain them. This could be achieved by limiting patent width for new technologies in order to reduce the ability of patents to block competitors from using and further developing enabling technologies. In the same line, it may be worth increasing the level of the inventive step to prevent nuisance patents."

Nelson (2006, pp. 12–13) seems to accept patenting by universities in a "since we can't get rid of it, let's minimize the damage" spirit:

> Although the notion that universities can get rich from licensing revenues is, except for a few cases, misguided, dreams die hard. Universities will not give up the right to earn as much as they can from their patenting unless public policy pushes them hard in that direction. In the United States, I see the key as reforming Bayh-Dole ...
>
> My preferred position would be to make it very hard for universities to patent, except in exceptional cases, but my belief is that the road to that reform is now too steep. A second best solution ... would be not to try to eliminate university patenting but to establish a presumption that university research results, patented or not, should as a general rule be made available to all who want to use them at very low transaction costs and reasonable financial costs.

These are slender reeds upon which to base a policy that is central to long-term economic performance.

SUMMARY

Private and social rates of return to innovation are estimated to be large, and greater than rates of return to other types of investments. There is thus a case for government to promote innovation. There are things governments can do to accomplish this goal. They are not high-profile once-and-for-all measures like "promote interfirm cooperation in research, development, and production" or "strengthen intellectual property rights". The most common effect of R&D cooperation may well be to reduce the amount of R&D that takes place, but nonetheless to improve static market performance by ensuring that several firms have access to new products and processes on equal terms. All evidence is that patent protection has at most a limited positive impact on the level of innovation. In part this is because in most sectors firms have other means at their disposal to protect intellectual property, means which they seem to prefer to patents. In other sectors, patents lend themselves to strategic and bargaining uses that have real potential to impede rather than promote innovation.

The policies governments can pursue to promote good technological performance combine infrastructure investment and tough love (Nelson, 1993, p. 515) "First, the education and training systems that ... provide ... firms with the strong skills they [need] to make it on their own. Second, ... provide strong incentives for the firms to quickly start trying to compete on world markets, as contrasted with hunkering down in their protected enclave."

STUDY POINTS

- Rate of return to R&D (Section 15.2)
- R&D subsidies & tax credits (Section 15.3)
- Procurement (Section 15.4)
- R&D cooperation (Section 15.5)
- Intellectual Property Rights (Section 15.6)

FURTHER READING

On the history of the U.S. R&D tax credit, see Hall (1993a, pp. 7–11), and on its administration, Stoffregen (1995). On means of promoting R&D, see Nelson (1982), Martin and Scott (2000). On the spread of university-industry research parks, see Link and Scott (2003), and on university-industry spillovers, Acs *et al.* (1993) and Jaffe *et al.* (1993). For references to the literature on university technology transfer activities, see Jensen *et al.* (2003), Link. and Siegel (2005). For discussions of EU policy toward R&D cooperation, see Jacquemin (1988), Martin (1996b), and Katsoulacos and Ulph (1997).

For discussions of trade secrecy, see Friedman *et al.* (1991), Arundel (2001). On sleeping patents, see Flynn (1998), and for a historical perspective on patent trolls, Magliocca (2007). See Bowrey (1996) on the history of copyright.

APPENDIX I: TAXES AND THE RENTAL COST OF CAPITAL SERVICES

We consider a firm that combines production labour, physical capital, and intangible capital to produce output. As far as provisions of the tax code are concerned, think of "intangible capital" as a stock of firm-specific capabilities that is built up over time from expenditures on research and development. In this section we work out the way marginal tax rates affect a firm's cost of using the services of physical and intangible capital. The analysis is detailed but not, in the end, complex.

Notation is given in Table 15.7. Production workers are hired at the start of the period and paid at the end of the period. Output is sold at the end of the period. Physical and intangible capital are inherited from the past, subject to depreciation, added to by investment flows at the start of the period, and (assuming the firm continues in operation) passed on to the future. For this discussion, "intangible capital" may be thought of as that part of the firm's capabilities created by investments that qualify for an R&D tax credit. Firms will have valuable intangible capabilities that do not qualify for an R&D tax credit.

There are alternative ways to deal with value of capital assets at the end of the period. One is to simply assume that the firm's investments in its tangible and intangible assets are not sunk. Then at the end of the period, if the firm wished, it could sell off its stocks of tangible and intangible capital at what it would cost to purchase the same amounts, new. The opportunity cost to the firm of keeping its capital stocks for the following period is what it would cost to purchase replacement stocks on the markets for physical and intangible capital.

If the resale price of physical capital is $\alpha_K p_2^k$, where $0 \leq \alpha_K \leq 1$ and p_2^k is the purchase price of a new unit of capital at the end of period 1, then a fraction $1 - \alpha_K$ of the firm's investment in physical capital is sunk. If the firm winds up business at the end of period 1, the firm's end of period 1 stock of physical capital should be valued at $(1 - \alpha_K)(1 - \delta_K)p_2^k K_1$ in computing the firm's present discounted value—this is the revenue the firm would get by selling its physical capital at the end of the period. But if the firm continues in business, the firm's end-of-period 1 stock of physical capital should be valued at $(1 - \delta_K)p_2^k k_1$ in computing the firm's present discounted value, since that is what it would cost to replace.

The mere mention of "the market for intangible capital" requires a certain suspension of disbelief, although it should be understood that it is the asset that is created by firm investments that is intangible, not the inputs (services of technical personnel, equipment used for R&D) used to add to the stock of intangible capital. For practical purposes, one expects that a firm's investment in intangible capabilities will be almost entirely sunk, that the resale price of a unit of intangible capital $\alpha_C p_2^C$ will be near zero. If the firm winds up business at the end of period 1, the firm's end of period 1 stock of intangible capital should be valued at $(1 - \alpha_C)(1 - \delta_C)p_2^C C_1$ in computing the firm's present discounted value. If the firm continues

Table 15.7 Notation, rental cost of capital services model

q_1	firm's output, end of period 1
p_1	price for firm's output, end of period 1
L_1	production labour hired at start of period 1
w_1	wage per production worker
δ_K	rate of physical depreciation of capital
$(1 - \delta_K)K_0$	stock of physical capital inherited from the past
δ_C	rate of depreciation of intangible capital
$(1 - \delta_C)C_0$	stock of intangible capital inherited from the past
$I_1 = K_1 - (1 - \delta_K)K_0$	purchases of physical capital at the start of period 1
$c_1 = C_1 - (1 - \delta_C)C_0$	purchases of intangible capital at the start of period 1
p_t^k	purchase price of a unit of physical capital at the start of period t
p_t^c	purchase price of a unit of intangible capital at the start of period t
r	firm's marginal cost of financial capital
t	tax rate
D_0^K	depreciation allowed, for tax purposes, on physical capital inherited from the past
D_0^C	depreciation allowed, for tax purposes, on intangible capital inherited from the past
d_K	rates of depreciation allowed for tax purposes on beginning-of-period investment in tangible capital
d_C	rates of depreciation allowed for tax purposes on beginning-of-period investment in intangible capital
f_K	rate at which tax credit is granted for new investment in physical capital
f_C	rate at which tax credit is granted for new investment in intangible capital

in business, the firm's end of period 1 stock of intangible capital should be valued at $(1 - \delta_C)p_2^c C_1$ in computing the firm's present discounted value, since that is what it would cost to replace.

Even this last argument requires some suspension of disbelief: it takes for granted that a firm could acquire intangible assets at constant cost p_2^c per unit. This is unlikely: more realistically, a firm adds to its stock of intangible capabilities every period by employing research and technical personnel. If it employs more such personnel, it will face rising costs per unit of intangible capital integrated with the stock of intangible capital inherited from the past.

Stare all such difficulties firmly in the face and move on: simply assume that the firm continues in business from the end of period 1. Then at the start of the period, the present discounted value of the firm's cash flow is:

$$PDV = -p_1^k I_1 - p_1^c c_1 + \frac{p_1 q_1 - w_1 L_1 + (1-\delta)p_2^k K_1 + (1-\delta_C)p_2^c C_1 - T}{1+r}. \tag{15.2}$$

T is the end-of-period tax bill:

$$T = t\left(p_1 q_1 - w_1 L_1 - D_0^K - D_0^C - d_K p_1^k I_1 - d_C p_1^c c_1\right) - f_K p_1^k I_1 - f_C p_1^C c_1. \tag{15.3}$$

Tedious rearrangement of terms shows that:

$$PDV = (1-\delta_K)p_1^k K_0 + (1-\delta_C)p_1^c C_0 + T_0 + (1-t)\frac{p_1 q_1 - w_1 L_1 - \rho_1^K p_1^k K_1 - \rho_1^C p_1^c C_1}{1+r}. \tag{15.4}$$

Here:

$$T_0 = \frac{tD_0^K - (1-\delta_K)\left(f_K + td_K\right)p_1^k K_0 + tD_0^C - (1-\delta_C)\left(f_C + td_C\right)p_1^c C_0}{1+r} \tag{15.5}$$

is the present value of tax flows (positive and negative) related to capital inherited from the past. T_0 affects the firm's payoff but not its incentives; it is determined by tax policy and by the firm's past decisions.

The rental costs per unit of tangible and intangible capital are:

$$\rho_1^K = r + \delta_K - \left(f_K + td_K\right) - (1-\delta_K)\frac{p_2^k - p_1^k}{p_1^k} \tag{15.6}$$

and

$$\rho_1^C = r + \delta_C - \left(f_C + td_C\right) - (1-\delta_C)\frac{p_2^c - p_1^c}{p_1^c} \tag{15.7}$$

respectively. See Section 15.3.1 for discussion.

The present value of the firm has two parts. The first three terms, $(1-\delta_K)p_1^k K_0 + (1-\delta_C)p_1^c C_0 + T_0$, are the value of physical capital, the value of intangible capital, and tax flows that are given at the start of the period. The second part, $(1-t)/(1+r^*)$ times $p_1 q_1 - w_1 L_1 - \rho_1^K p_1^k K_1 - \rho_1^C p_1^c C_1$, is the present value of after-tax end-of-period income, with end-of-period capital stocks valued (as discussed above) at replacement cost. In this formulation, increases in f_C or d_C reduce the cost to the firm of investing in R&D assets.

APPENDIX II: DUOPOLY INNOVATION RACES

Duopoly R&D with Stochastic Completion Time and R&D Input Spillovers

Here we outline a duopoly model of firms that compete to develop a cost-reducing (process) innovation. The time of discovery is a random variable that depends on each firm's R&D effort and on R&D effort spillovers. An extension sketches how to modify the model to allow for incomplete appropriability (output spillovers).[83]

There are two firms, 1 and 2. In what follows, when the subscripts i, j are used, it should be understood that i, j may equal 1, 2, and that $i \neq j$.

(a) Before innovation, both firms produce with constant average and marginal cost c_A per unit.

(b) By engaging in research and development, either firm may implement a technology that permits production at unit cost $c_B < c_A$. The size of the cost reduction, $c_A - c_B$, is known. The first firm to

---

[83] For empirical studies of innovation races, see Cockburn and Henderson (1995), Lerner (1997).

implement the technology receives a completely effective patent that prevents the other firm from ever using the lower-cost production technique.

(c) The time it takes for firm i to implement the new technology, τ_i, is a random variable that depends on firm i's research effort and on spillovers of the other firm's research effort as described below.

(d) The cost of carrying out a research project at level h_i is $z(h_i)$ per unit time period; this cost must be paid while the project is active. $z(h_i)$ has positive first and second derivatives (that is, a more intense research effort costs more, and R&D cost rises with size at an increasing rate). Each firm sets the level of its research project at time 0 and continues the research project until one firm implements the new technology.

(e) If firm i's research intensity is h_i and firm j's research intensity is h_j, firm i's effective research intensity is $g_i = h_i + sh_j$, where s is an R&D input spillover parameter and $0 \leq s \leq 1$.

(f) Firm i's expected time to discovery has a negative exponential distribution with hazard or (in this context) discovery rate g_i: $\Pr(\tau_i \leq t) = 1 - e^{-g_i t}$.

(g) In the pre-innovation stage, each firm earns a flow rate of profit, $\pi_N(c_1)$ per time period, that depends on the nature of the oligopoly game that is being played.

(h) In the post-innovation market, the firm that implements the new technology earns profit at the rate $\pi_W(c_A, c_B)$ per time period; the other firm earns profit $\pi_L(c_A, c_B)$ per time period. $\pi_L(c_a, c_B) < \pi_W(c_A, c_B)$.

(i) Objective functions: the probability that neither firm has innovated at time t is $\exp[-(g_1 + g_2)t]$. Firm i's payoff if neither firm has innovated is $\pi_N(c_1) - z(h_i)$. The probability density that firm i is the first to implement the new technology and that this occurs at time t is $g_i \exp[-(g_1 + g_2)t]$. If firm i is the first to implement, its value at the moment of implementation is π_W/r. The probability density that firm j is the first to innovate and that first innovation is at time t is $g_j \exp[-(g_1 + g_2)t]$. If firm j is the first to innovate, firm i's value at the moment of innovation is π_L/r. Firm i's expected value, obtained by multiplying payoffs in alternative states of the world by the corresponding probabilities and adding the resulting terms, and discounting over all future time by the factor $\exp(-rt)$, is:

$$V_i^N = \int_{t=0}^{\infty} e^{-(r+g_1+g_2)t} \left[\pi_N(c_A) - z(h_i) + \frac{g_i \pi_W + g_j \pi_L}{r} \right] dt$$

$$= \frac{\pi_N(c_A) - z(h_i) + \frac{g_i \pi_W + g_j \pi_L}{r}}{r + g_1 + g_2}. \tag{15.8}$$

Substituting $g_i = h_i + sh_j$ and rearranging terms, firm i's objective function is:

$$V_i^N(h_1, h_2) = \frac{\pi_N(c_1) - z(h_i) + \frac{(\pi_W + s\pi_L)h_i + (s\pi_W + \pi_L)h_j}{r}}{r + (1+s)(h_i + h_j)}. \tag{15.9}$$

When firm i increases its own research effort h_i it increases not only the probability that it will discover first, but also (because of input spillovers) the probability that firm j will discover first. Thus the coefficient of h_i/r in the numerator on the right in (15.9) is the sum of π_W and $s\pi_L$.

Discussion: It is a characteristic of the negative exponential distribution with a constant discovery rate that the probability of implementation depends on current effective research intensity. One might think that in some cases, a firm's probability of implementation would depend on its accumulated research efforts, not just its current research effort; for such models, see Fudenberg *et al.* (1983), Doraszelski (2003). By assuming a negative exponential distribution with a constant discovery rate, what is formally a dynamic problem—the maximization of present-discounted value—is reduced to the equivalent of a static optimization problem (non-cooperative maximization of V_i^N by choice of h_i).

The first-order condition to maximize $V_i^N(h_1, h_2)$ with respect to h_i can be rewritten as the equation of an R&D-intensity best-response function. Non-cooperative equilibrium R&D intensities occur at the common point on the best-response functions of the two firms. For discussion of non-cooperative equilibrium comparative statics, see Martin (2002b).

This formulation models a very specific kind of R&D uncertainty; this focus can be justified by the tractability of the model, not because it covers all cases of interest: one might consider uncertainty about the size of the cost reduction, about whether a discovery would be made at all, and, for product innovation, uncertainty about the quality of the new product or of its substitutability for existing varieties.

Incomplete Appropriability

Here we sketch ways the model outlined above can be extended to allow for incomplete appropriability. Suppose the post-innovation outputs of the winning and losing firms are q_W and q_L, respectively. To say more about q_W and q_L would require specifying details of the post-innovation product market, and that is a direction in which we do not need to go. Suppose first that in the post-implementation world, the unit cost of the winning firm falls by $c_A - c_B$, so its unit cost is c_B and the unit cost of the losing firm falls $(1 - \alpha)(c_A - c_B)$, where α is an R&D output appropriability parameter and $0 \leq \alpha \leq 1$. Then the post-innovation unit cost of the losing firm is $c_A - (1 - \alpha)(c_A - c_B) = c_B + (c_A - c_B) - (1 - \alpha)(c_A - c_B) = c_B + \alpha(c_A - c_B)$. The firm that loses the innovation race nonetheless obtains a partial unit cost reduction in the post-innovation world. An alternative formulation would have the winning firm able to license the full cost reduction, $c_A - c_B$, to the losing firm, at a rate $\alpha(c_A - c_B)$ per unit of output. The losing firm's unit cost is once again $c_B + \alpha(c_A - c_B)$. The winning firm's flow rate of profit in the post-innovation market is $(p - c_B)q_W + \alpha(c_A - c_B)q_L$. Either of these specifications can be used to reformulate firms' post-innovation payoffs, in the model of the previous section. This makes it possible to analyse the impact of incomplete appropriability on firms' incentives to invest in R&D. Under reasonable conditions, equilibrium R&D intensity (h) rises as R&D input spillovers (s) fall and as appropriability (α) rises. The effects of input spillovers and appropriability on firm value are, in general, ambiguous. For linear demand and quadratic R&D cost, firm value is maximized with high R&D input spillovers and complete appropriability (see Martin, 2002b).

PROBLEM

Asterisks indicate an advanced problem.

15–1* (R&D cooperation, KMZ-equivalent model) For the model of Problem 14–1, find equilibrium cost reductions for four cooperation regimes:

(a) R&D cartelization: firms behave non-cooperatively in the second stage, each picking output to maximize own profit; in the first stage, firms non-cooperatively select R&D levels to maximize joint profit, anticipating second-stage behaviour.

(b) RJV cartelization: as in (a), with the spillover parameter set equal to one.

(c) Operating entity joint venture: each firm pays half the cost of a single R&D activity. Both firms obtain access to the resulting cost reduction, and firms behave non-cooperatively in the second stage, each picking output to maximize own profit.

(d) Joint R&D and joint production: full cartelization at both stages.

IMPERFECTLY COMPETITIVE INTERNATIONAL MARKETS

Free trade, one of the greatest blessings which a government can confer on a people, is in almost every country unpopular.

Thomas Babington, Lord Macaulay

16.1 Introduction

Questions of trade policy lie at the very roots of modern economics. At the dawn of the industrial age, Mercantilist thought held that the road to national prosperity lay in export promotion and import restriction. The Mercantilist argument was that building up wealth meant accumulating gold and silver, and that export surpluses would cause gold and silver to flow into a country as foreign countries paid with precious metals the bills that they could not pay with what they earned from their own exports.

Adam Smith's view of trade was quite different, and a primary purpose of *The Wealth of Nations* was to expound that view. For Smith, wealth was productive capacity, not the accumulation of precious metals. Smith saw trade as being beneficial to all parties involved, allowing countries to specialize in the production of particular goods and to exchange the surpluses of domestic production over domestic consumption in international markets. Specialization in production would allow overall output to increase; exchange would allow all countries to share in the gains. It is not by accident that it is in his discussion of foreign trade that Smith introduces the notion of the *invisible hand*, guiding individuals who blindly pursue their own self-interest to promote society's interest as well (Smith, 1937, p. 423).

Classical arguments in favour of free trade began with the assumption that product markets are perfectly competitive. New theories of international trade abandon this assumption. They start from the premise that product differentiation and economies of scale make the typical international market imperfectly competitive, and reach the neo-Mercantilist conclusion that there are conditions under which trade restrictions might improve national welfare.

In this chapter we consider the implications of imperfect competition for international market performance and, reciprocally, the implications of international competition for the performance of imperfectly competitive domestic markets. We follow this with a discussion of strategic trade policy, the modern incarnation of the Mercantilist arguments of two centuries ago. Strategic trade arguments notwithstanding, most economists continue to advocate free trade as desirable public policy, and we discuss why this is so. We also examine the determinants of international firm and market structure, including the impact of domestic policy decisions on direct foreign investment flows by firms that set up production operations outside their home market. Finally, we look at the interaction of trade policy and competition policy, first from a strictly national point of view and then from the perspective of international coordination of trade and competition policy.

16.2 Intraindustry Trade

Comparative advantage trade theory explains the exchange of the products of different industries by different countries in international markets. But much trade, especially among developed countries, involves two-way flows of goods that are close substitutes, products of the same industry.

Figure 16.1 shows the value of trilateral trade flows between the EC, Japan, and the U.S. in 1997 for two important industries: motor vehicles and aerospace manufacturing. Japan is a net exporter of motor vehicles to both the U.S. and the EC, and a net importer of aerospace manufactures from both. The U.S. is a net importer of motor vehicles from the EC, and a net exporter of aerospace equipment to the EC. There is substantial *intraindustry trade*—two-way trade flows of products of the same industry—between the three regions for these two industries. Yet if it is comparative advantage alone that drives trade flows, intraindustry trade should not occur. To understand what lies behind the exchange of products of the same industry among industrialized economies, we must look elsewhere than comparative advantage.

One of the central assumptions of classical trade theory is that input markets and output markets are perfectly competitive. Relaxing this assumption generates models of trade that do not depend on relative factor endowments, but on the exercise of market power in the export market.

Two-way or intraindustry trade in substitute products is a major part of trade among industrialized countries.

16.2.1 Quantity-setting Firms

Conditions for interindustry trade

We begin by showing that with two quantity-setting firms the condition for intraindustry trade to take place in an imperfectly competitive market is that the monopoly price-cost margin be greater than transportation cost from one market to the other. Consider a Cournot duopoly model, reinterpreted now by assuming that each of the two firms is located in a different country—firm 1 is based in country 1, firm 2 is based in country 2. We will work

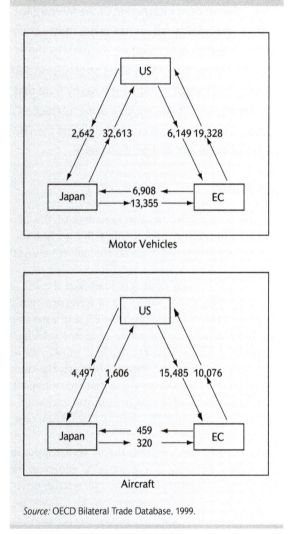

Figure 16.1 Trilateral trade flows, motor vehicle and aircraft industries, EC, Japan, and U.S., 1997 (million dollars)

Motor Vehicles

Aircraft

Source: OECD Bilateral Trade Database, 1999.

with a linear demand, constant marginal and average cost example. With linear demand curves and constant marginal and average cost, output decisions are taken separately for each country, because price in each country depends only on sales in that country, and marginal cost does not change as output changes. This makes it possible to treat the market in each country separately, and we will focus on country 1.[1]

---

[1] This kind of separation is not be possible if there are economies of scale. We consider this case in Section 16.4.5.

Let the equation of the inverse demand curve in country 1 be:

$$p_1 = 100 - (q_{11} + q_{21}),\qquad(16.1)$$

where q_{11} is the quantity sold by firm 1 in country 1, q_{21} is the quantity sold by firm 2 in country 1, and each firm has the same constant marginal and average production cost, 10 per unit.[2] To allow for the extra cost of supplying a foreign market, let there be a transportation cost t for each unit of output sold in the foreign market.

Although the two firms use the same production technology, when firm 2 sells in country 1, it incurs not only production cost c but also transportation cost t for every unit sold. The greater is transportation cost, the smaller the output that firm 2 will find it profitable to sell in country 1, for any output of firm 1. In terms of best-response curves, the greater is transportation cost, the closer is firm 2's best-response curve to the origin (Figure 16.2). Because quantity best-response curves slope downward, the closer is firm 2's best-response curve to the origin, the smaller are firm 2's equilibrium sales and the greater are firm 1's equilibrium sales. Transportation cost insulates the home market from the competition of foreign suppliers.

If transportation cost is sufficiently great, firm 2's best-response curve is below firm 1's best-response curve. This means that firm 1 can sell the monopoly output in market 1

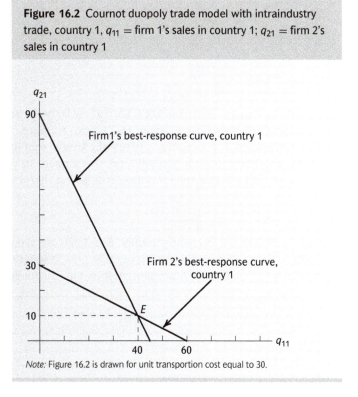

Figure 16.2 Cournot duopoly trade model with intraindustry trade, country 1, q_{11} = firm 1's sales in country 1; q_{21} = firm 2's sales in country 1

Firm1's best-response curve, country 1

Firm 2's best-response curve, country 1

Note: Figure 16.2 is drawn for unit transportion cost equal to 30.

---

[2] For the moment, we ignore the fact that different countries typically use different currencies. The impact of exchange rate fluctuations in imperfectly competitive markets is taken up in Section 16.5.

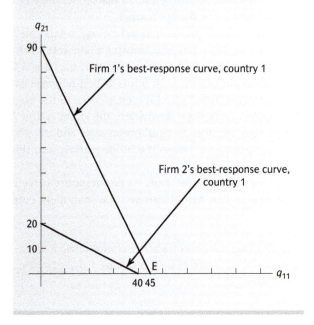

Figure 16.3 No trade equilibrium in country 1, high transportation cost, Cournot duopoly "trade" model, q_{11} = firm 1's sales in country 1; q_{21} = firm 2's sales in country 1

without making it profitable for firm 2 to sell in market 1. Such a case is shown in Figure 16.3, which is drawn for the same parameter values as Figure 16.2 (drawn for transportation cost equal to 50). As shown in Problem 16–1, the condition to rule the kind of equilibrium shown in Figure 16.3—that is, the condition for firm 2 to sell a positive amount in country 1, so that intraindustry trade takes place—is that transportation cost be less than the monopoly price-cost margin:

$$t < \frac{1}{2}(a_1 - c). \tag{16.2}$$

If the foreign firm can profitably sell in country 1 when firm 1 sets the monopoly price, then it will enter the country 1 market, leading to a post-trade price below the monopoly level but high enough to cover production and transportation cost for the foreign firm.

> *Intraindustry trade*: With imperfect competition, it will be profitable for producers of substitute goods to sell in several countries if equilibrium price is greater than marginal production plus transportation cost, even without a comparative advantage in production.

Welfare consequences

In Cournot oligopoly, equilibrium market performance ranges from monopoly to perfect competition as the number of firms rises from one to infinity. One might expect, therefore, that the opening up of previously closed markets to foreign suppliers leaves consumers better off. This is indeed the case: if it is profitable for firm 2 to sell in country 1, then with trade the equilibrium price in country 1 is lower, and consumers' surplus larger, than without trade. Trade leaves consumers better off because the rivalry of foreign suppliers improves market performance in imperfectly competitive markets.

The impact of trade on profit, and the impact of trade on net social welfare—consumers' surplus plus profit—is not so clear-cut. Trade leaves the home country firm worse off in its home market: with trade, it faces competition from the foreign supplier that it would not otherwise face. But on the foreign market it is the new competitor, and it will earn some profit on the foreign market that it would not earn without trade.

The analysis of intraindustry trade arises particularly with respect to trade flows between countries at the same level of development. Consider first, then, a case of trade between identical countries, so that the markets in the two countries are the same size.

If the two markets are the same size, company profits fall with the opening of trade. This should be expected: considering only a single market, the combined profit of both firms in Cournot duopoly is less than monopoly profit. With the opening up of intraindustry trade, each firm earns duopoly profit in two markets instead of monopoly profit in one market. Because Cournot duopoly profit per firm is less than half monopoly profit, the profit earned on the export market is not enough to make up for the profit lost on the home market. This result is reinforced by the cost disadvantage—transportation cost—that a firm has for sales in its export market.

When markets are the same size, then, trade makes consumers better off and firms worse off. For the linear demand, constant marginal cost model, the net effect is positive: intraindustry trade between countries of the same size raises net social welfare in both countries.

If trade is between markets of different sizes, the net welfare effect of trade may be positive or negative.[3] If a small country opens its home market to trade, its domestic firms will face foreign competition, and they will see their profits fall in their home market. If the home market is relatively small, lost profits will also be relatively small. If the foreign market is sufficiently large, the profits earned in the foreign market will more than offset the profits lost at home. If trade leaves home country firms with more profit, it is certainly beneficial overall, since the lower prices that result from trade leave consumers better off. The other side of the coin is that if a large country opens its home market to trade, its domestic firms may lose more profit to firms from small countries than large-country consumers gain in increased consumers surplus, leaving net social welfare in the large country lower with trade than without trade.

16.2.2 Price-setting Firms

Conditions for interindustry trade

For price-setting firms, it is most interesting to consider the case in which products are imperfect substitutes.[4] An example of linear inverse demand equations for country 1 when varieties are differentiated is

---

[3] See Krugman and Venables (1990) for a model of trade between countries of different sizes.

[4] If price-setting firms produce a homogeneous product, the entire market demand will switch from one supplier to another in response to a negligible price difference. This is implausible in general, and particularly so in models of international trade.

$$p_{11} = 100 - \left(q_{11} + \tfrac{1}{2}q_{21}\right)$$
$$p_{21} = 100 - \left(\tfrac{1}{2}q_{11} + q_{21}\right) \qquad (16.3)$$

Let the cost structure be the same as for the discussion of quantity-setting firms: constant average and marginal cost 10 per unit, transportation cost t for each unit sold in the export market.

Price best-response curves slope upward, as shown in Figure 16.4. The greater is transportation cost, the higher the price firm 2 will charge to maximize its own profit, for any price set by firm 1. In terms of Figure 16.4, the greater is t, the higher is firm 2's price best-response curve. Since price best-response curves slope upward, if firm 2's best-response curve is higher, firm 1's equilibrium price will be higher as well: greater transportation cost means greater equilibrium prices for both varieties.

It is generally the case in imperfectly competitive markets that a cost increase is partially passed on to consumers in the form of higher prices and partially absorbed by producers in the form of a reduced profit margin. In the present context, when transportation cost rises, firm 2's price in country 1 rises as well, but by less than the increase in transportation cost. For this example, the equation of firm 2's price best response is:

$$p_{21} = 30 + \frac{1}{2}t + \frac{1}{4}p_{11}. \qquad (16.4)$$

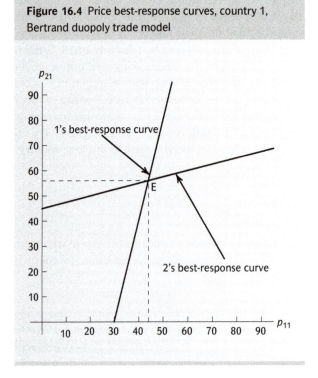

Figure 16.4 Price best-response curves, country 1, Bertrand duopoly trade model

For any price of firm 1 in country 1, firm 2 maximizes its profit by picking a price that passes half of its transportation cost along to consumers in the form of a higher price. Firm 2's profit margin per unit goes down as transportation cost goes up:

$$p_{21} - 10 - t = 20 - \frac{1}{2}t + \frac{1}{4}p_{11}. \tag{16.5}$$

The condition for intraindustry trade to occur—for firm 2 to sell in country 1—is that the equilibrium price with trade be greater than $10 + t$, firm 2's marginal cost of selling in country 1. The condition for p_{21} to be greater than $10 + t$ is that transportation cost t not be too large—$t < 64\frac{2}{7}$ in this example.

In general, the upper limit on transportation cost for trade to take place is larger, the larger is market size and the greater is product differentiation (Problem 16–3). When the goods that are traded are poorer substitutes, each variety faces less competition from the other variety, and can cover higher levels of transportation cost before trade becomes unprofitable. Greater product differentiation promotes intraindustry trade.

Welfare consequences

Intraindustry trade leaves consumers better off when varieties are differentiated and firms set price. Trade results in a lower price for variety 1, and with trade consumers have the possibility of acquiring a new variety. But in contrast to the homogeneous product case, with product differentiation firm profit may rise with intraindustry trade even if countries are the same size. This can occur if the varieties are poor substitutes.

The intuition behind this is clear if products are completely independent in demand: then the opening up of trade effectively means that a new market comes into being in each country. Each firm earns incremental profit in its export market, but does not lose any profit in its home market, because the two products are not demand substitutes. When substitutability is low, there is some loss of profit on the home market because of competition from foreign varieties, but not very much, and a considerable gain in profit in the export market. If varieties are poor substitutes, intraindustry trade benefits firms as well as consumers. If trade benefits both firms and consumers, it is evidently beneficial overall.

We know from our previous discussions of imperfectly competitive price-setting markets that price tends to be near marginal cost when different varieties are close substitutes. If different varieties are close substitutes, the opening up of trade means substantially lower profits for firm 1 on its home market, and a low price-cost margin for sales in its export market. At this point the market size considerations that were present in the homogeneous good, quantity-setting model come into play. If markets are the same size, profit falls after trade opens, and the net effect of trade on national welfare depends on whether the increase in consumers' welfare exceeds domestic firms' lost profit. If markets are of different sizes, intraindustry trade will be profitable for firms based in a small market that gain the chance to sell in a sufficiently large market, and trade will benefit the home country of such firms. But firms based in a large market that gain the chance to sell in a small market may be left worse off by trade.

16.3 Trade and Domestic Market Performance

From the discussion of the Cournot model in Chapter 3, we know that the greater is the number of suppliers in a quantity-setting market, the closer is equilibrium price to marginal cost. It follows that if firms supplying an international market set quantities, domestic firms exercise less market power with than without foreign competition. The same holds for a market in which firms set price, provided there is some product differentiation.

The discussion of collusion and tacit collusion in Chapter 6 suggests that the presence of foreign suppliers should be expected to improve domestic market performance. Since collusive agreements typically are not legally enforceable, all collusion is non-cooperative in the sense that any firm can defect from a collusive strategy if it thinks it is in its interest to do so. In markets where firms differ in their costs, in their rates of time preference, and where there are systematic quality differences, it will be more difficult to reach and maintain collusive agreements. Foreign suppliers are likely to differ from domestic firms in all these dimensions. This makes it less likely that foreign suppliers will adhere to a collusive output path, all else equal.

A large number of empirical studies confirm the prediction that imports temper the exercise of market power by domestic firms. Jacquemin and Sapir (1991) study the impact of trade flows and other factors on industry price-cost margins in France, Germany, Italy, and the UK. Their results for the impact of elements of market structure on margins are consistent with those generally found in the literature: price-cost margins are greater where economies of scale and research and development are greater, and for consumer good industries. Price-cost margins are also higher, the greater are tariffs and when there are high non-tariff barriers to the movement of goods from one EC member state to another.

They find that imports from outside the EC have a significant negative impact on price-cost margins. For example, the average price-cost margin for German industries in their sample was 15.78 per cent (holding all other factors constant). Their results suggest that an increase of 10 percentage points in the share of imports from outside the EC would reduce an industry's price-cost margin by 4.3 percentage points, almost one-third of 15.78. Thus when markets are imperfectly competitive, an important benefit of foreign trade is that it limits the ability of domestic producers to earn economic profit and increases the extent to which the benefits of greater product variety and larger scale of production are passed on to domestic consumers.

In contrast to the results for extra-EC imports, Jacquemin and Sapir find that imports from other EC member states have no statistically significant impact on price-cost margins. An implication, to which we will return in Chapter 17, is that the competitive pressure of foreign suppliers may be necessary to fully realize the benefits of EC market integration.

16.4 Strategic Trade Policy

16.4.1 Subsidies: Quantity-setting Firms

Subsidy by one country

The neo-Mercantilist argument for strategic trade policy takes off from the imperfect nature of competition in international markets. Firms that operate in imperfectly competitive markets may earn economic profits. If so, workers in such markets will be able to bargain for greater-than-competitive wages. If government policy can shift profit from foreign firms and workers to domestic firms and workers, the net effect on social welfare may be positive.

To present this argument in the simplest possible setting, consider a case in which two firms, each based in a different country, are the only suppliers to a third country of a product that is not consumed in their home markets. This setting is very artificial, but because it rules out any negative impact of strategic trade policy on home-country consumer welfare by assumption, it highlights the potential for profit-shifting as a motive for strategic trade policy.

Suppose also that the two firms have the same constant unit cost of supplying the third-country market. This cost includes the expense of production, transportation, tariffs, and anything else. If firms set quantities, then the third-country market is a Cournot duopoly, supplied by two firms with identical marginal cost. Equilibrium outputs in this market are found at the intersection of the best-response curves of the two firms. This is point E_0 in Figure 16.5.[5]

For an oligopolist to maximize profit, it must produce an output that makes its marginal cost equal to marginal revenue along its residual demand curve. If marginal cost falls, a profit-maximizing firm will expand output, so that marginal revenue falls as well. This means that with lower unit cost a firm's quantity best-response curve shifts outward on the best-response-curve diagram. A key insight of the strategic trade policy literature is that an export subsidy has the same effect on firm behaviour as a cost reduction. If country 1 grants a subsidy s_1 on every unit of output exported by its firm to the third-country market, then as far as firm 1 is concerned, its cost of supplying that market falls by s_1 per unit. The direct effect of the subsidy is that firm 1's best-response curve shifts outward. If firm 2 were to

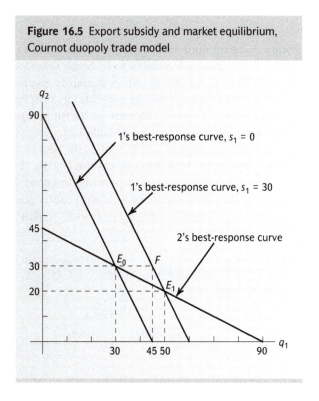

Figure 16.5 Export subsidy and market equilibrium, Cournot duopoly trade model

---

[5] Figure 16.5 is drawn for the inverse demand function $p = 100 - Q$, with marginal cost equal to 10.

maintain its output at the pre-subsidy level, firm 1's sales would go up. In terms of Figure 16.5, the market would move from point E_0 to point F.

But firm 2 will not maintain its output at the pre-subsidy level. When firms in imperfectly competitive markets set quantities and have constant marginal costs, their choice variables are strategic substitutes. The greater is firm 1's output, the lower is firm 2's marginal profitability. The result is that as firm 1's output expands, firm 2 reduces its own output. This indirect, strategic effect of the subsidy implies a further increase in firm 1's output, as the equilibrium moves down firm 2's best-response curve from E_0 to E_1.

Firm 1 profits because of the direct effect of the subsidy, and it profits again because of the strategic effect. The overall result is that firm 1's profit increases by more than the amount of the subsidy (see Problem 16–4), making the net impact of the subsidy on country 1's welfare positive. A strategic trade subsidy increases firm 1's profit and country 1's welfare at the expense of its international rivals.

Profit-shifting export subsidies (I):

When firms produce *strategic substitutes*, the direct (reaction of the subsidized firm) and strategic (reaction of other firms) effects of the subsidy are to increase the profit of the subsidized firm at the expense of rivals.

Duelling subsidies

The strategic export subsidy argument outlined above showed that if firms set quantities one country could benefit by granting an export subsidy to its home firms for sales in foreign markets. But the argument assumed that one and only one country granted such a subsidy. If instead each country in the export subsidy model subsidizes its own firm, the two governments end up trapped in a classic Prisoners' Dilemma, as shown in Figure 16.6. Relative payoffs (from the countries' points of view) are given in Table 16.1.

If neither firm grants a subsidy, equilibrium is at E_0. This is the base case: the net change in social welfare for the (No Subsidy, No Subsidy) combination is (0,0). If country 1 grants a subsidy and country 2 does not, equilibrium is at point E_1 in Figure 16.6; payoffs are $(1/8, -7/16)$. This is the result of the previous discussion: if one country grants a subsidy and the other does not, the subsidizing country improves its net social welfare and the country that does not subsidize is left worse off.

Table 16.1 Payoff matrix, government export-subsidy games, quantity-setting firms

		Firm 2	
		No Subsidy	**Subsidy**
Firm	No Subsidy	(0,0)	$(-7/16, 1/8)$
1	Subsidy	$(1/8, -7/16)$	$(-7/25, -7/25)$

Note: For the parameter values of Figure 16.5. Payoffs are propotional to the values given in the payoff matrix; see Problem 16–7.

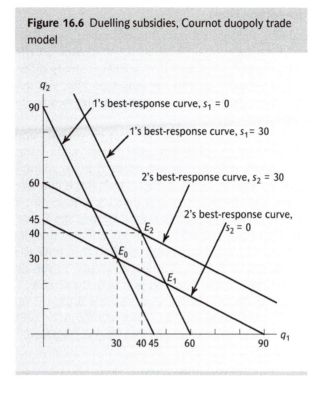

Figure 16.6 Duelling subsidies, Cournot duopoly trade model

Country 2 is not as badly off if it subsidizes as well: equilibrium is then at E_2 in Figure 16.6, where payoffs are $(-7/25, -7/25)$. If country 2's choice is between a welfare change of $-7/25$ and a welfare change of $-7/16$, it will prefer $-7/25$. But it is also clear that both countries would be better off if they could coordinate on the (No Subsidy, No Subsidy) outcome.

 BOX   Adam Smith on Export Subsidies

But it is not the interest of merchants and manufacturers . . . that the home market should be over-stocked with their goods, an event which a bounty upon production might sometimes occasion. A bounty upon exportation, by enabling them to send abroad the surplus part, and to keep up the price of what remains in the home market, effectually prevents this. Of all the expedients of the mercantile system, accordingly, it is the one of which they are the fondest. I have known the different undertakers of some particular works agree privately among themselves to give a bounty out of their own pockets upon the exportation of a certain proportion of the goods which they dealt in. This expedient succeeded so well, that it more than doubled the price of their goods in the home market, notwithstanding a very considerable increase in the produce.

Source: The Wealth of Nations. Edwin Cannan, editor. New York: The Modern Library, 1937, p. 484.

16.4.2 Subsidies: Price-setting Firms

In addition to the condition that rival countries not grant their own subsidies, an essential element of the argument in favour of export subsidies is that the strategic effect of the subsidy reinforce the direct effect—that when the firm that receives a subsidy changes its behaviour, its rival reacts in a way that directly benefits the subsidized firm, and therefore indirectly benefits the country granting the subsidy. This is what happens when firms' choice variables are strategic substitutes.

Matters are different if firms' choice variables are strategic complements, as when firms producing differentiated products set prices with linear demand and constant marginal cost. When firms set prices, if firm 1 receives a subsidy from its home country, it responds by lowering its price, for any price set by firm 2. In Figure 16.7, this is illustrated by the shift of firm 1's price best-response curve to the left moving from the no-subsidy to the subsidy case. Were firm 2 to hold its price constant, equilibrium would move from E_0 to F. But in markets where firms set price and there is some product differentiation, best-response curves slope upward. When firm 1 reduces its price, firm 2 reacts by reducing its price as well: equilibrium moves from E_0 to E_1 in Figure 16.7. Firm 2's strategic reaction to the change in firm 1's behaviour reduces the direct benefit that firm 1 receives from the subsidy.

In view of the strategic relationship between price-setting firms, the optimal policy for country 1 is to levy an export tax, not to grant an export subsidy. An export tax raises firm 1's costs and leads it to raise its price, thereby reducing firm 1's sales. This leaves firm 1 worse off,

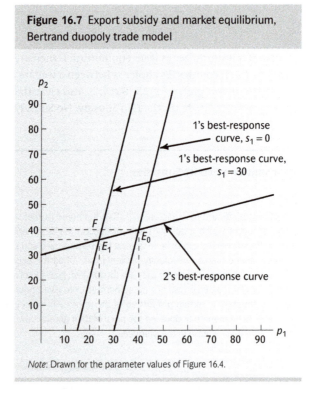

Figure 16.7 Export subsidy and market equilibrium, Bertrand duopoly trade model

Note: Drawn for the parameter values of Figure 16.4.

but country 1 collects the proceeds of the tax. When firm 1 raises its price, firm 2's strategic reaction is to raise its own price. When firm 2 raises its price, this partially neutralizes the reduction in firm 1's sales that is caused by its own price increase. The net result is that country 1 is better off taxing its home firm, even though this leaves firm 1 worse off (see Problem 16-5).

> *Profit-shifting* export subsidies (II): when firms' choice variables are *strategic complements*, the direct (reaction of the subsidized firm) and strategic (reaction of other firms) effects of a subsidy work in opposite directions, with the result that the socially optimal policy is to tax rather than subsidize exports.

16.4.3 The Political Economy of Strategic Trade Policy

Modern governments operate under increasingly severe budget constraints. If a government subsidizes exports, requests for subsidies from different industries will exceed the amount a government can grant. Firms and industry associations can be expected to make the strongest cases they can for subsidies. Government agencies will normally have much less information at their disposal than the groups presenting requests for subsidies. Because these groups pursue their own self-interest, governments will not be able to accept firms' arguments in favour of subsidies at face value. Assuming that the government seeks to maximize social welfare, how is the government to pick and choose which industries it will subsidize and which it will not? If the wrong industries are subsidized, the country could easily end up being worse off than with no subsidies at all.

But "government" is not a homogeneous entity, and it cannot be taken for granted that government will automatically seek to maximize social welfare. Government is the agent of society, and subgoal pursuit is a problem faced by governments as well as firms. Elected representatives will be influenced by campaign contributions as well as by objective assessments of the social benefits that can be expected to flow from export subsidies. Campaign contributions will be motivated by the benefits donors hope to obtain—and donors will include representatives of labour as well as of management. The result may well be that export subsidies are granted to protect jobs, wages, and profits in uncompetitive sectors where firms and workers are highly organized, not to shift profit from foreign to domestic markets.

 BOX   Strategic Trade Policy: Medium-size Commuter Aircraft

Baldwin and Flam (1989) study the impact of strategic trade policy on market performance in the market for 30–40 seat commuter aircraft. The market has three principal suppliers, each located in a different country (Brazil, Canada, Sweden). No one of these firms sells in the home market of the others, and all three compete in the potentially lucrative US market.

Baldwin and Flam present circumstantial evidence suggesting that trade barriers guarantee the Canadian firm privileged access to its home market, and that the Brazilian firm has received direct or indirect export subsidies, at least for its sales in the US market. They use simulation analysis ≫

>> to analyse the consequences of these policies, and their results are broadly consistent with the predictions of the strategic trade policy literature.

Reserving the Canadian market for the Canadian firm appears to increase the Canadian firm's profit and decrease the profits of the two other firms, which is the kind of rent-shifting that lies at the heart of the strategic trade policy literature. The increase in profits of the Canadian firm occur on its home market, at the expense of Canadian consumers, not on foreign markets. Alleged subsidies to the Brazilian firm increase its profit, but by much less than the simulated amount of the subsidy.

The Baldwin and Flam study suggests that strategic rent-shifting can occur in international markets. It does not suggest that such rent-shifting increases the welfare of countries that implement strategic trade policy.

In February 1999, the World Trade Organization found that Brazil and Canada granted illegal export subsidies to their producers of medium-sized commuter aircraft.

Strategic trade policy

Under restrictive conditions—if firms' choice variables are strategic substitutes, if other countries do not grant subsidies of their own—export subsidies can improve domestic welfare by shifting profit from foreign to domestic firms. Otherwise, theory suggests that subsidies will benefit the firms that receive them but not the countries that grant them.

16.4.4 Tariffs and Quotas

Export subsidies are an outward-looking policy. *If* they increase national welfare, it is because of their impact on equilibria in foreign markets. When returns to scale are constant, tariffs and quotas are inward-looking policies: they are undertaken because of their effects on the home market. Any net national benefit from tariffs and quotas comes from the additional economic profit domestic firms are able to earn in their home market because of protection from foreign competition. Tariffs and quotas typically leave domestic consumers worse off.

The issues raised by tariffs and quotas are similar. We discuss quotas here, and leave the discussion of tariffs to Problem 16–6.

Suppose that the inverse demand equation in country 1 is:

$$p_1 = 100 - (q_{11} + q_{21}), \qquad (16.6)$$

that marginal and average cost are constant, 10 per unit, and that the market is a Cournot duopoly. For simplicity, suppose also that there are no transportation costs.

Then Figure 16.8 illustrates the impact of a quota imposed on country 2 sales in country 1. Without a quota, equilibrium is at point E_0, at the intersection of the best-response curves of the two firms. If a quota $\bar{q} = 20$ restricts firm 2's sales to a level below its initial equilibrium output $q_{12}^0 = 30$, equilibrium moves along firm 1's best-response curve from E_0 to E_1, the point that gives firm 1's profit-maximizing output if firm 2's sales are at the quota level.

Moving from E_0 to E_1, firm 1's output rises and total sales fall. Total sales fall because the slope of the best-response curve is less than one: firm 1's additional output is half the reduction in firm 2's output. Since total sales fall, price rises: firm 1 exercises a greater degree of market power. Since firm 1 sells more and at a higher price, its profit definitely goes up. In the short run, a quota is privately profitable for the domestic firms it protects.

However, the price increase leaves consumers worse off. The change in net social welfare combines the profit increase enjoyed by firm 1 and the welfare loss of consumers. For the

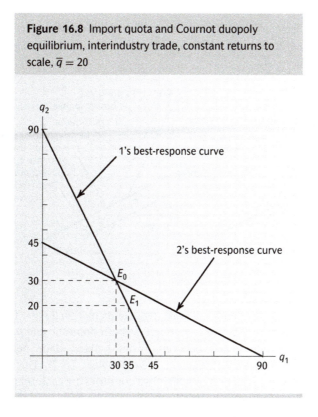

Figure 16.8 Import quota and Cournot duopoly equilibrium, interindustry trade, constant returns to scale, $\bar{q} = 20$

duopoly case (see Problem 16–6)—and more generally, if there are at least as many firms in the home country as there are foreign firms—the net effect of a quota on social welfare is positive. If the number of domestic firms is small relative to the number of foreign firms, a quota allows domestic firms to exercise so much market power that the net welfare effect of the quota is negative.

A difference between tariffs and quotas is that tariffs automatically generate revenue for the government of the importing country. If the country that imposes the quota sells import licences to foreign firms, and for a high enough fee, it can capture all or almost all of the economic profit foreign firms earn in its market.[6]

> *Quotas and tariffs*
>
> Protect domestic producers from foreign competition, increasing their profit and typically leaving consumers worse off.

16.4.5 Import Barriers and Export-Promotion

If marginal cost falls as output rises, then the possibility of taking advantage of economies of scale is an additional incentive to export. By selling in foreign markets, a firm increases

---

[6] For a discussion of an import licensing scheme in New Zealand, see Pickford (1985).

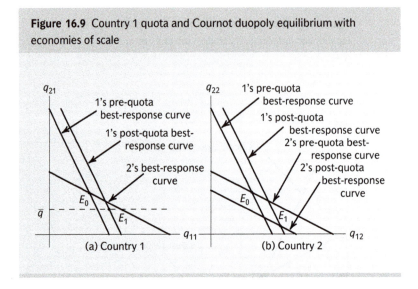

Figure 16.9 Country 1 quota and Cournot duopoly equilibrium with economies of scale

its overall output and, with economies of scale, reduces its marginal cost. This reduction in marginal cost makes it a more effective competitor on both domestic and foreign markets.

Economies of scale create a link between inward-looking trade policy—tariffs and quotas—and strategic trade policy (Krugman, 1984; Problem 16–7). This is illustrated in Figure 16.9, which refers to a situation in which two countries are each home to one firm in a homogeneous-product Cournot industry. Each firm sells in both markets. In Figure 16.9, the best-response curves for each country are drawn supposing that outputs in the other market are at their equilibrium levels.[7]

The initial equilibrium, at E_0 in both diagrams, is without trade barriers. Selling abroad means greater output than in the no-trade case. Higher output levels mean that marginal costs are lower for both firms than would be the case without trade.

Now suppose country 1 imposes a quota that limits firm 2's sales in country 1 to some level $\bar{q}$ that is less than its free-trade sales level—a quota that is small enough to actually restrict firm 2's sales in country 1.

Such a quota has consequences for both markets. Given that quantity best-response curves slope downward, when firm 2's sales fall in country 1, firm 1 expands its output. This output expansion reduces firm 1's marginal cost, causing an outward shift in firm 1's best-response curves *in both markets*. In country 1, equilibrium moves from E_0 to E_1, the intersection of firm 2's quota sales level $\bar{q}$ and firm 1's new best-response curve.

The reduction in firm 1's marginal cost causes an outward shift in its best-response curve for country 2. The increase in firm 2's marginal cost causes an inward shift in its best-response curve in country 2. The new equilibrium in country 2 is at E_1 in Figure 16.9(b): firm 1's equilibrium sales in country 2 rise, and firm 2's equilibrium sales in country 2 fall. In both cases, the changes in output reflect not only direct effects—movements along a fixed best

---

[7] This is an expositional device. In contrast to the constant returns to scale case, when there are increasing returns to scale it is not possible to analyse the two markets separately. See Problem 16–7.

response curve in response to the rival's output changes—but also indirect effects—shifts of the best-response curves.

Empirical studies produce little evidence to suggest that such *internal* economies of scale are common (Chapter 9).[8] There is a dynamic equivalent, however, that may be important for some industries: *learning–by–doing*. Learning-by-doing arises if the cost of current production falls as cumulative production rises. Intuitively, learning-by-doing occurs if experience means that a firm becomes more efficient. Trade barriers that reduce rivals' cumulative outputs will have dynamic strategic effects—favourable to the home firms of the country imposing the barrier, unfavourable to other firms—like the static strategic effects of a quota in the presence of increasing returns to scale.

The analysis of this section is subject to the same general qualifications that apply to other types of strategic trade policy. If firms' outputs are strategic complements rather than strategic substitutes, then a quota forcing a reduction in firm 2's sales on the country 1 market would induce firm 1 to reduce its own sales. All else equal, this output reduction would lead to an increase in firm 1's marginal cost and cause inward shifts in its best-response curves in both markets, making it strategically worse off.

Even if firms' outputs are strategic substitutes, as illustrated in Figure 16.9, a quota imposed by country 2 in reaction to the country 1 quota will create a Prisoners' Dilemma situation that is likely to leave both firms and both countries worse off.

Import barriers and export promotion

If there are internal economies of scale or learning-by-doing, trade barriers that reduce rivals' outputs can benefit the export performance of firms based in the protected market, if outputs are strategic substitutes and if other countries do not retaliate with barriers of their own.

16.5 Exchange Rate Passthrough

We now examine the implications of exchange rate fluctuations for domestic prices when markets are imperfectly competitive. Once again, consider the case of two quantity-setting firms, firm 1 based in country 1 and firm 2 based in country 2. Each firm exports its product to the other country. Returns to scale are constant, which means that we can analyse each country separately.

Suppose that inverse demand curves are linear, with equations

$$p_1 = 100 - (q_{11} + q_{21})$$
$$p_2 = 100 - (q_{12} + q_{22}) \qquad (16.7)$$

To keep the discussion as simple as possible, suppose also that there are no transportation costs, tariffs, or quotas.

The country 1 price p_1 is measured in country 1's currency, which we will call the dollar. Country 2's price p_2 is measured in country 2's currency, which we will call the euro. The exchange rate e gives the number of euros needed to buy a dollar. Higher values of e mean

---

[8] Economies of scale are internal to the firm if they depend on the output level of a specific firm and benefit only that firm. Economies of scale are external to the firm if they depend on industry output and benefit all firms in the industry.

that more euros are needed to buy a dollar, and therefore represent lower values of the euro in terms of dollars.

Firm 1's profit on its sales in country 1 is:

$$\pi_{11} = (p_1 - 10)q_{11} = (100 - 10 - q_{11} - q_{21})q_{11}, \tag{16.8}$$

where firm 1's unit cost is $10. The exchange rate e does not directly affect firm 1's profit on its sales in country 1. The equation of firm 1's best-response function for country 1 is found by maximizing firm 1's profit on its sales in country 1. Since e does not appear in (16.8), e does not affect firm 1's best-response curve for country 1, and changes in e do not shift firm 1's best-response curve for country 1.

Firm 2's unit cost is €10, which is measured in terms of country 2's currency, the euro. Firm 2's profit on its sales in country 1, measured in euros, is:

$$\pi_{21} = (ep_1 - 10)q_{21} = e\left(p_1 - \frac{10}{e}\right)q_{21} = e\left(100 - \frac{10}{e} - q_{11} - q_{21}\right)q_{21}. \tag{16.9}$$

Multiplying the dollar price p_1 by e converts the dollar price into euros. Dividing the euro cost €10 by e converts the euro cost to an equivalent dollar amount. An increase in e, a depreciation of the euro *vis-à-vis* the dollar, has the effect of a reduction in firm 2's unit cost relative to country 1's price p_1—if a dollar will buy more euros, then it takes fewer dollars to buy the euros needed to cover the cost of producing a unit of output in country 2.

The country 1 market is a Cournot duopoly with differences in unit cost. Firm 2's best-response function for country 1 is found by maximizing (16.9). Since e enters directly in (16.9), e affects firm 2's best-response function for country 1, and changes in e shift firm 2's best-response curve for country 1.

From (16.9), as far as the country 1 market is concerned a depreciation of the foreign currency (an increase in e) has the same effect as a reduction in the unit cost of the foreign firm. In Figure 16.10(a), the direct effect of a depreciation of the country 2 currency—an increase in e—is an outward shift in firm 2's best-response curve on the country 1 market. With a euro depreciation, the dollar revenue firm 2 earns on the country 1 market is worth

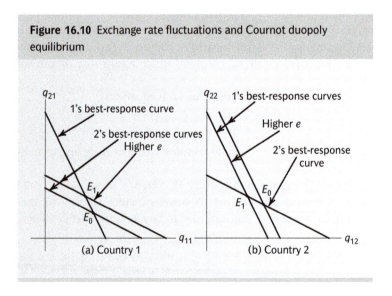

Figure 16.10 Exchange rate fluctuations and Cournot duopoly equilibrium

more in terms of euros, the currency in which it incurs its costs. Firm 2 reacts to this change by a willingness to sell more, whatever the sales of firm 1.

Firm 1's response to this shift is to reduce its own output. In Figure 16.10(a), equilibrium shifts from E_0 to E_1—greater sales by firm 2, lower sales by firm 1—as a result of a euro depreciation.

Exchange rate fluctuations therefore induce changes in country 1 prices. Because competition is imperfect, equilibrium price remains above marginal cost for both firms. And because competition is imperfect, the passthrough of exchange rate changes to changes in domestic price is typically incomplete. If e rises, firm 2 sells more in country 1. Firm 1's strategic response to this increase is to reduce its own sales, meaning that the net increase in country 1 sales is less than the increase in sales by firm 2 and that the fall in country 1 price is proportionally less than the euro depreciation (Problem 16–5).[9] If there is a euro depreciation, the country 2 firm takes part of the implied reduction in its dollar-equivalent cost of supplying country 1 in the form of a higher price-cost margin on its sales in country 1.

A euro depreciation also has an effect on the country 2 market, once again to the detriment of firm 1. An increase in e means that the euro revenue firm 1 earns in country 2 is worth less in terms of dollars. The direct effect of a euro depreciation is to cause an inward shift in firm 1's best-response curve for country 2. Firm 2's strategic response to the shift in firm 1's best-response curve is to expand its own output. In Figure (16.10)(b), equilibrium shifts from E_0 to E_1—greater sales by firm 2, lower sales by firm 1—as a result of a euro depreciation. Once again, equilibrium price in country 2 is above marginal cost for both firms, and the passthrough of exchange rate fluctuations to changes in country 2 price is incomplete: a 10 per cent euro depreciation results in a fall in country 2 price that is less than 10 per cent, because of the output reduction caused by oligopolistic interactions.

Now introduce tariffs into the discussion. A euro depreciation affects the country 1 market equilibrium because it is equivalent to a reduction in the country 2 firm's cost of supplying the country 1 market. If there are tariff barriers around country 1, then a tariff reduction also has the effect of reducing the country 2 firm's cost of supplying country 1. We ought to suspect, therefore, that when markets are imperfectly competitive, tariff reductions and foreign currency depreciations (tariff increases and foreign currency appreciations) will have qualitatively similar effects. This turns out to be the case (Problem 16–9).

A large number of empirical studies confirm the predictions of the exchange rate passthrough literature. For example, in a study of Japanese motor vehicle shipments to the United States, Feenstra finds that tariff changes and exchange rate changes affect U.S. prices in the same general way (1989, p. 43):

> For trucks we have found a pass-through of about 0.6. This means that the increase in the tariff from 4 to 25 percent in August 1980 raised consumer prices by an estimated 13 percent, and lowered Japanese producer prices by about 8 percent. In contrast, for heavy cycles, we found a pass-through of about unity, so the tariff increase in April 1983 and subsequent decreases had little effect on Japanese producer prices. These results have very [different] implications for trade policy. In trucks, the drop in the producer price corresponds to a terms of trade gain ... this is a first step toward establishing a gain for the United States. For heavy cycles, the constant producer prices mean that the tariff led to a conventional deadweight loss.

---

[9] In the international trade literature, this is called pricing-to-market (Krugman, 1987).

> *Exchange rate passthrough*
>
> Oligopolistic interactions and the responses of firms in imperfectly competitive markets to the changes in own-currency value of revenue collected in other currencies means that only part of exchange rate fluctuations are passed on to changes in domestic prices.

16.6 Trade, Market Structure, and Firm Structure

One of the most important lessons of modern industrial economics is that market structure is itself determined by market forces. We have explored the factors that shape domestic firm and market structure in Chapters 9 and 10; here we examine the determinants of firm and market structure when markets are international.

One aspect of this subject concerns how firms choose to supply foreign markets, if they find it profitable to do so at all: by export, by licensing partners in local markets, by joint ventures, or by engaging in direct foreign investment and setting up their own production facilities in foreign markets. We have seen that the opening up of trade exposes firms to greater competition in their home market but gives them the opportunity to earn additional profit in foreign markets, and that the impact of trade on profits and on national welfare is in general ambiguous. However, if the markets in different countries are of comparable size and product differentiation is not too great, profit is likely to fall, and welfare to rise, with the opening up of trade.

If the fall in profit that flows from the internationalization of markets is sufficiently great, some firms will go out of business. If a firm's gross profit is not sufficient to cover its fixed cost, then in the long run it must shut down. Such closures may take the form of bankruptcy; they may take the form of mergers that combine a larger number of parent firms into a smaller number of survivor firms. But they are unavoidable. Increasing competition improves market performance but also increases seller concentration, albeit in larger (world) markets (Problem 16–8). This *concentration effect* of trade is even greater if marginal cost falls as output rises.

Not only can internationalization cause some firms to shut down, but such closures are actually necessary if the full benefits of trade are to be realized. If production is concentrated in the hands of fewer firms, there is a social saving equal to the fixed costs of the firms that go out of business. In the long run, these fixed assets will be transferred to productive uses in other industries. But in the short run, the threat and the reality of bankruptcy will generate political pressure for subsidies and protection that limit the gains from trade.

> *Concentration effect*
>
> In intraindustry trade: lower price-cost margins with intraindustry trade raise the possibility that the equilibrium number of firms will fall because of free trade, economizing on fixed costs.

16.6.1 Mode of Supply to a Foreign Market

There are a range of options open to a firm that operates in international markets. Ranked loosely from least direct to most direct involvement, possible strategies with respect to a foreign market include:

- not supplying the market;
- export;
- licensing a foreign firm to produce the product in a foreign market;
- establishing a joint venture with a local partner;
- purchasing an existing plant in a foreign market;
- setting up a new plant in a foreign market (greenfield investment).

This list is not exhaustive. Two foreign firms might form a joint venture to enter a third market; two foreign firms might set up a joint venture to produce an intermediate good (a car platform, for example) in a third market, but each sell their own final product in the third market and elsewhere.

Each method for entering a foreign market has its own implications for cost and revenue. On the cost side, export means the firm must bear transportation cost and exposes it to the risk of tariffs and other trade barriers. Opening up an operation in the foreign country means an extra investment in fixed and sunk costs. On the revenue side, establishing a foreign plant makes a stronger commitment to supply the foreign market than exports, since shutting down a foreign plant would entail the loss of sunk costs. The equilibrium choice of investment strategy can also be influenced by policy measures. Tariffs, quotas, or voluntary export restraints (VERs) make export sales relatively less profitable, direct foreign investment relatively more profitable, and may alter the method foreign suppliers choose to supply the domestic market.

Mutual forbearance

While the first option might surprise, it might be an equilibrium—a mutual forbearance equilibrium—in a repeated game. Firms could non-cooperatively agree to stay out of each other's home markets, ensuring each firm monopoly profit in a single market.

Less restrictively, but in the same spirit, firms might settle into a strategic pattern in which each firm acts as a Stackelberg leader in its home market, and as a Stackelberg follower in other markets. There is some reason to think that this behaviour described the European car industry in the early years of the Common Market, although the arrival of Japanese producers seems to have disrupted established relationships.

Exporting

Exporting has received most of our attention, and the tradeoffs implied by a decision to export have already been touched upon. If there are plant-specific economies of scale, these can be fully realized only by concentrating production in a single domestic plant and exporting to foreign markets. Much of learning-by-doing is probably plant-specific as well. Exporting, however, means the firm must pay transportation cost, which makes it less competitive on the foreign market. It also leaves the firm open to the threat of protectionist measures—tariffs or quotas—that shield the export market. Export is the most profitable choice for the firm if cost reductions from economies of scale and learning-by-doing outweigh transportation cost and the risk or reality of trade barriers.

Licensing/joint venture

The mainstream approach to modelling international operations is an eclectic one, due to Hymer (1976) and Dunning (1980, 1988). This eclectic approach fits very well with the new industrial economics of international trade, since it begins with the premise that foreign direct investment would not occur in perfectly competitive markets.

The argument is that a foreign supplier will inevitably operate at a cost disadvantage with respect to domestic suppliers, if only because of its lack of familiarity with local market conditions. It follows that a firm establishing an operation in a foreign market must possess a special advantage—based on product differentiation, operating efficiency, R&D competence—that compensates for its disadvantages in the foreign market.

Licensing a foreign firm or establishing a joint venture with a foreign partner are ways of dealing with informational problems. But they open the door to a variety of contracting problems, of the kind discussed in Chapter 12.

If the entering firm really does have an advantage, then at the moment it sets up a foreign arrangement, it is likely to have a choice among several local partners. Competition between the local partners will ensure that the balance of bargaining power lies with the licensing firm, that is to say, that it will be able to strike a bargain that allows it to appropriate most of the profit generated by exploiting its strategic assets in the foreign market.

Once a partner is selected and the project gets underway, the licensing firm will make a variety of sunk investments as part of its contribution to the licensing arrangement or joint venture. These sunk investments lock it into a bilateral arrangement with the foreign partner. As the project develops, the balance of bargaining power will shift from the licensing firm to the foreign partner. The information advantage that the local partner brings to the arrangement means that the licensing firm will not be able to easily evaluate the reports it receives from the foreign partner about the way operations are developing. This exposes the licensing firm to the possibility of holdup by its foreign partner. If a dispute about the interpretation of the licensing contract should arise, it would most likely be adjudicated in the export market, where the foreign partner would have a home court advantage.

Licensing or forming a joint venture can be optimal strategies if transportation cost and/or trade barriers are sufficiently high and if the value of the foreign partner's information is so great that it outweighs the risk of future profit losses due to opportunistic behaviour.

Direct foreign investment

Setting up a wholly owned plant in the foreign market means the domestic firm engages in direct foreign investment and transforms itself from a national firm that sells on world markets into a multinational firm. A firm that sets up a wholly owned plant in a foreign market avoids not only transportation costs but also any quotas or tariffs that have been erected around the target market. It benefits from some economies of scale, since production in a foreign plant means that corporate overhead costs are spread over a larger corporate output. But it incurs the additional sunk cost of setting up a foreign plant.

Direct foreign investment has strategic advantages in the overseas market. In Figure 16.11, E_0 shows the Cournot duopoly equilibrium in country 2 if firm 1 (based in country 1) chooses the export route for supplying country 2. Its marginal cost, $c + t + \tau$, includes unit transportation cost t and a tariff τ per unit of output sold in country 2. If firm 1 sets up a plant in country 2 instead of exporting, its marginal cost falls from $c + t + \tau$ to c per unit. With this reduction in unit cost, firm 1's best-response curve on the country 2 market shifts out from the origin. Since best-response curves slope downward when products are demand substitutes and firms set quantities, equilibrium shifts from E_0 to E_1, moving down along firm 2's best-response curve. The strategic impact of firm 1's direct foreign investment is an output

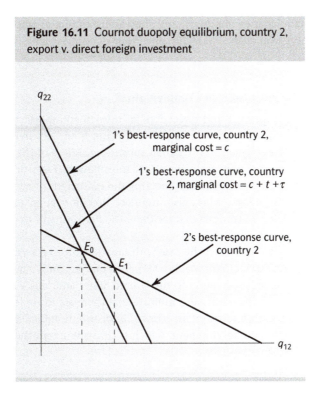

Figure 16.11 Cournot duopoly equilibrium, country 2, export v. direct foreign investment

reduction by firm 2 that improves firm 1's situation on the country 2 market. This strategic effect is greater, the greater is transportation cost and the higher is the tariff rate. This creates the possibility of a long-run effect of trade barriers that may counteract their short-run protective effect.

16.6.2 Tariff-jumping DFI

We have seen that the impact of a quota or a tariff, taking market structure as given, is to protect the home firms of the country imposing the barrier from foreign competition. But in the long run, market structure is not given, and trade barriers may induce changes in market structure that work against the interests of domestic firms. Tariffs and quotas increase the profitability of direct foreign investment relative to exporting. If tariffs are high enough or quotas sufficiently restrictive, foreign firms may find that tariff-jumping direct foreign investment is the most profitable way of selling on the protected market. Such direct foreign investment makes the market more competitive. This is likely to benefit consumers in the target market, but it will leave the original domestic firms with lower profits.

Tariff- and quota-jumping direct foreign investment has taken place in the world car industry. Restrictions on imports into European markets increased the incentives of Japanese firms to set up plants in the EC.[10] The presence of the plants increases rivalry in the host country markets. They also increase pressure on native firms to adapt and

---

[10] Voluntary export restrictions had the same effect in the U.S.

adopt high-productivity Japanese methods, and they alter traditional labour-management relations. These changes would have taken place without import restrictions, but at a slower pace.

16.6.3 Exports vs. DFI: Substitutes or Complements?

From a static viewpoint, exporting and direct foreign investment appear to be alternative strategies: a firm will choose either one or the other, but not both. In a dynamic sense, the two approaches may be complements rather than substitutes. Many of the costs associated with direct foreign investment stem from imperfect information. Exporting can be a way to get information about a market before undertaking direct foreign investment (Veugelers, 1991). Exporting manufactured goods may also stimulate direct foreign investment in servicing, distribution, and finance operations that facilitate the marketing of the exported goods in the foreign market.

This seems particularly to have been the case with Japanese direct foreign investment in both the United States and Europe. Yamawaki (1991), for example, finds a mutually reinforcing relationship between Japanese exports to the United States and Japanese direct foreign investment in distribution.[11] His results also indicate that there are lower levels of Japanese exports and greater Japanese direct foreign investment in distribution for U.S. industries that have high levels of research and development, which is consistent with the "special advantage" theory of direct foreign investment.

> *Direct foreign investment*
>
> DFI is encouraged by high transport costs, tariffs, and other trade barriers, and by agency problems that make licensing of joint ventures risky. DFI normally improves market performance, leaving local consumers better off and reducing the profit of domestic firms.

16.6.4 Hysteresis

"Hysteresis" describes situations in which short-run phenomena have long-run effects, effects that persist even if the short-run phenomena reverse themselves.[12] In the present context, short-run exchange rate fluctuations may alter the entry decision of foreign suppliers, leading to changes in market structure and therefore in market performance that persist even if the exchange rate fluctuations are themselves only temporary.

If a firm decides to set up a plant in an overseas market, it commits itself to paying the fixed and sunk costs that go with setting up that plant. Some of these costs will be incurred in the home market—in particular, information processing costs associated with making decisions about the new plant. But many of the material costs will arise in the foreign market, with the result that the amount of fixed cost, measured in the currency of the investing firm, changes with exchange rate fluctuations.

In terms of the previous example, if the euro-dollar exchange rate e rises, the dollar is worth more in terms of the euro, reducing the dollar cost to a U.S.-based firm of setting up

---

[11] See also Wilkins (1990).

[12] Following Dixit (1989). Ansic (1995) offers experimental support for the hysteresis hypothesis.

a plant in Europe. A higher e also reduces the dollar value of the profit that is earned in the European market. The net impact of an increase in the value of the dollar on the foreign direct investment decision may be positive or negative.

If the euro depreciates enough, direct foreign investment will become the most profitable choice for U.S. firms.[13] If direct foreign investment occurs, the U.S. firm will make a sunk investment in the European market. Once that sunk investment has been made, the U.S. firm would not immediately withdraw from the market if the value of the dollar should fall relative to the euro—if e should decline. The U.S. firm would withdraw from the European market if revenue earned there could not cover variable costs incurred there.[14] Revenue in the European market would be entirely, and variable costs almost entirely, denominated in euros, and to that extent would be little influenced by exchange rate fluctuations. The change in market structure, induced by exchange-rate fluctuations, will last much longer than the exchange-rate fluctuations that caused it.

16.7 Trade Policy and Competition Policy

Rivalry between domestic and foreign firms inevitably occurs in somebody's home market, raising the question of public policy toward such rivalry and more generally of the overlap between trade policy and competition policy.

A recurring theme of antitrust policy and competition policy, in pursuit of promoting good market performance, is hostility toward business strategies that raise entry costs. The rationale for this hostility is that potential competition tempers the exercise of market power and, for the EU, that lower entry costs promote market integration as well. The United States and EU member states are also parties to international agreements by which they commit themselves to a regime of free trade. Yet the evidence suggests that when trade policy and competition policy overlap, protectionist instincts emerge that lead governments to circumvent this commitment to free trade and, in so doing, to adopt policies that not only distort trade on world markets but also worsen domestic market performance.

16.7.1 Export Cartels

In most countries, competition policy forbids collusion. When consumers and producers are both from the same economy, collusion affects their interests in opposite ways, and the usual policy position is to resolve this conflict in favour of consumers.

From the point of view of national welfare, the conflict between producer and consumer welfare evaporates when the producers are located in the domestic market and the consumers are located in a foreign market. Perhaps for this reason, competition policy is often not hostile to collusion when it targets foreign markets. Here we analyse the welfare consequences of export cartels and examine how policy toward export cartels has been implemented.

---

[13] In general terms, this would occur when the exchange rate e has risen so much that it is profitable for U.S. firms to invest abroad, and that further increases in e are unlikely; see Dixit and Pindyck (1994).

[14] Such withdrawals do occur. Volkswagen, which set up production in the U.S. market in 1974, withdrew in 1989, citing among other factors high costs (Womack *et al.*, 1990, p. 214). When it returned to the U.S., opening a factory in Chattanooga, Tennessee in 2009, one motive was to (Rauwald, 2009) "lower its exposure to currency fluctuations".

Theory

An export cartel allows firms to eliminate competition among themselves, and this elimination of competition tends to reduce their combined sales on foreign markets. An export cartel may also allow firms to share the fixed costs of supplying a foreign market, increasing efficiency and therefore tending to increase sales on foreign markets. The net impact of an export cartel on the level of exports is therefore ambiguous.

If exports are reduced, price on the foreign market will rise. The amount of the increase will depend on the reactions of foreign firms to a reduction in exports. If the price increase is large enough, exporters' profits may rise, tending to increase the welfare of the exporting country. However, overt collusion on export markets may also facilitate tacit collusion on the home market. This will tend to reduce the welfare of the exporting country. The net effect of an export cartel on national welfare is therefore also ambiguous.

Market power

Domestic suppliers only, no home-market effects   An export cartel is socially beneficial in the context of the first model we used to discuss strategic export subsidies. Suppose two identical domestic firms are the only suppliers to a foreign market of a product that is not consumed in their home market. If they compete as quantity-setting Cournot duopolists, in equilibrium they each earn duopoly profit. If they are allowed to collude and maximize joint profit, then together they earn monopoly profit. Monopoly profit cannot be less than duopoly profit, and will in general be greater. Collusion on the export market will leave the two firms better off. Since the product is not consumed in their home market, there is no negative impact on home-market consumers. The export cartel thus leaves the home country of the two firms unambiguously better off.

International oligopoly, no home-market effects   Leaving all other elements of the model the same, suppose now that there is a third firm that supplies the product, identical to the first two but based in the foreign market.[15] The result for this case, illustrated in Figure 16.12, differs from the previous one because of the way the equilibrium output of the third firm changes with formation of the export cartel.

If the two domestic firms form a cartel, they export less for any output level of the firm or firms outside the cartel than they would if they acted independently. This is shown in Figure 16.12, where the "domestic firm" best-response curve shows output per domestic firm when the two domestic firms produce identical output levels. Limiting consideration to the case in which the domestic firms product the same amounts does not change the final result (see Problem 16–11), since they produce identical output levels in equilibrium, and it permits us to draw the best-response curves on a two-dimensional graph. Formation of an export cartel means that the two firms produce less than they would with independent (non-cooperative) output decisions; the best-response curve of domestic firms on the export market shifts inward.

When firms set quantities and products are demand substitutes, firms' choice variables are strategic substitutes: the reduction in output by colluding firms increases the marginal

---

[15] It is not essential to the analysis that follows that the third firm be based in the export market. It could be based in the same market as the other two; it could be based in a third market. What is essential is that the third firm not join the export cartel, but acts independently.

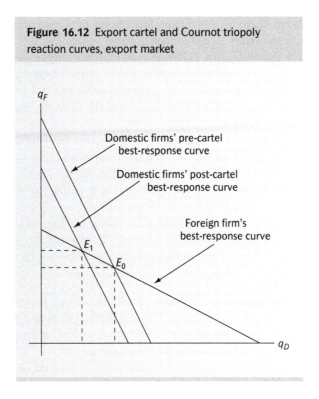

Figure 16.12 Export cartel and Cournot triopoly reaction curves, export market

profitability of the foreign firm, and it expands output. Equilibrium shifts from E_0 to E_1, moving up along the foreign firm best-response curve. Because domestic firms form a cartel, the firm that is outside the cartel takes a larger share of the market.

Unless domestic firms have a very large share of the export market, the reaction of foreign firms will typically mean that cartel members earn a lower profit after forming the cartel. When firms' choice variables are strategic substitutes, the presence of rivals outside the export cartel reduces, and may eliminate, any incremental profit generated by the cartel.

The presence of suppliers outside the cartel has the opposite effect if firms' choice variables are strategic complements, as when products are differentiated and firms set prices rather than quantities. In such markets, price best response curves slope upward. With an export cartel, the colluding firms charge a higher price in response to any price charged by the foreign firm, and the foreign firm responds to this change in behaviour by raising its own price. In such markets, the formation of export cartels will generally be profitable.

Domestic consumption, duelling export cartels (and duelling jurisdictions) Now suppose the product is consumed in both countries, that the two markets are the same size, and that there are two firms based in each country. If firms based in each country form an export cartel, the national markets change from four-firm oligopolies to duopolies. Firms' profits go up, and consumer surplus falls. If demand is linear, marginal cost constant, and markets the same size, then the overall welfare effect for each country is negative, even though the export cartels leave firms better off.

If one country is larger than the other, then firms based in the small market may earn enough profit in the large market to counterbalance the welfare loss of consumers in the small market, leaving the small country better off even with duelling export cartels. If firms from the large country earn only a little extra profit in the small country, they could be left worse off with duelling export cartels. If duelling cartels leave firms from the large country worse off, the large country as a whole is certainly worse off, since the export cartels leave consumers in both countries worse off.

If a country allows export cartels, it exempts its own firms from its own competition laws. A country cannot exempt its own firms from the competition laws of other countries. This raises the possibility that firms might be prosecuted in foreign courts for conduct that takes place legally in their home market but has illegal anticompetitive effects on foreign markets.[16]

One country may also change its own competition law in reaction to a legal export cartel formed by firms from another country. For example, the United Kingdom changed its antimonopoly law to allow its sulphur producers to combine so they could bargain more effectively with an export cartel of U.S. firms.

Domestic consumption, non-cooperative collusion   That competition policy allows domestic firms to overtly collude with respect to sales on foreign markets does not mean that export cartels have no implications for domestic market performance.[17] Explicit collusion on foreign sales may facilitate tacit collusion on the domestic market.

The essential element of non-cooperative collusion is the trading off of the future profit that is lost once rivals realize that some firm has defected against the short-run profit that results from defecting. With this tradeoff in mind, what are the implications of the existence of a legal export cartel for the sustainability of tacit collusion on the domestic market? If firms form an export cartel, it is because they expect the cartel to raise their individual profits. This means that if the export cartel ends, the profit of individual firms goes down. It follows that the threat to break up a legal export cartel if tacit *domestic* collusion collapses can be used as part of the punishment strategy that makes single firms decide, in their own self-interest, to restrict output and raise price on the domestic market. The existence of export cartels makes it more likely that firms will be able to reach collusive outcomes (without colluding in a legal sense) on domestic markets.

If formation of an export cartel allows member firms to sustain non-cooperative or tacit collusion on their home market, they will earn greater profits, but the welfare of domestic consumers will be reduced. In such cases, an essential element in the rationale for allowing export cartels, that they do not reduce the welfare of domestic consumers, fails.

Efficiency   An export cartel restricts sales on the foreign market, hoping to raise price. If there are increasing returns to scale, this output reduction means an increase in average cost. All else equal, this will translate into higher prices for domestic consumers, and reduced competitivity on foreign markets. Once again, the premise behind allowing export cartels— that there is no harm to domestic consumers—fails.

---

[16] This happened in an early *Woodpulp* decision, A. Ahlström Oy and others *v.* E.C. Commission [1988] 4 CMLR 901 at 934, where producers' actions as part of an export cartel that was legal under U.S. law were prosecuted as a concerted action in violation of EU competition policy.

[17] See also Auquier and Caves (1979).

If there are constant returns to scale, formation of an export cartel does not affect the cost of producing for the domestic market. If there are decreasing returns to scale, then a reduction in output reduces unit cost, implying a cost saving on production for the domestic market.

In the same way, if learning-by-doing is important, then domestic interests are served by policies that increase output on foreign markets, not by policies that restrict such output. If an export cartel succeeds in restricting output and raising price on foreign markets, it will reduce the rate at which it accumulates knowledge and worsen technological performance at home and abroad.

Practice

EC The EC Treaty gives the European Community the responsibility and the authority to police trade among the Member States. As a matter of principle, therefore, the Article 101 prohibition of agreements and concerted practices that distort trade *within the Common Market* does not reach pure export cartels.

But EC competition policy is sceptical toward the possibility that firms could cooperate intimately with respect to export markets without having that cooperation also distort competition in the Common Market. This attitude is consistent with the economics of tacit collusion.

A leading Commission decision, *CSV*,[18] involved a joint sales agency and export cartel of Dutch fertilizer producers. CSV was a wholly owned subsidiary of two firms. One of these was the largest nitrogen-based fertilizer producer in the EC; the other was the leading world manufacturer of urea, an important input in the production of fertilizers. CSV allocated market shares within the Netherlands and outside the EC; it provided its parent firms with regular demand predictions for those markets. The parent firms provided CSV with detailed information about their inventories and their production plan. The parent firms' sales in the Netherlands and outside the EC, with minor exceptions, were made only through CSV. Representatives of the parent firms received regular reports comparing actual and predicted sales for the various markets.

CSV's activities were carried out under the supervision of a steering committee made up of representatives of both parent firms; the steering committee met monthly with CSV management.

For the European Commission, it was inevitable that these exchanges of information would affect the Common Market (§70):

> [D]ecisions concerning the quantity or prices of products sold in one Member State can have repercussions not only in that Member State but in others too. Despite the parties' assertions it seems quite predictable that, faced with an unstable market, they should use their information exchange scheme to improve the coordination of their sales policies on other EEC markets.

The essential notion of non-cooperative collusion, that the parent firms would hold off from hard competition in the Common Market to protect the profits they expected to inherit from the joint sales agency, also appeared in the Commission's decision (§68):

---

[18] Commission Decision of 20 July 1978 OJ No L 242/15 4 September 1978. The full name of the joint sales agency was Centraal Stikstof Verkoopkantoor BV.

[The parent firms] must inevitably refrain from competing with one another on markets not included in their pooling arrangements in order to safeguard the joint sales policy they pursue through CSV.

The Commission concluded that CSV was the vehicle for concerted practices by the parent firms, that the concerted practices restricted trade within the common market, and that the arrangements had an appreciable effect on trade within the common market. The concerted practices were therefore inconsistent with the common market and in violation of the EC Treaty.

As a general rule, export cartels formed by EC firms are likely to be disapproved by the European Commission unless the market shares of the firms involved makes the likelihood of distortion of competition seem minimal.

U.S.

The Webb-Pomerene Act   The United States has long had a mercantilist approach to cooperation by U.S. firms on export markets. There is little evidence that this approach accomplishes its stated goals or improves either export or domestic market performance.

The 1918 Webb-Pomerene Act allows U.S. firms to collude with respect to export markets. Firms that exercise this option are obliged to register with the Federal Trade Commission. The law provides that cartel actions are permitted on the condition that they do not lessen competition on the U.S. market. Further, an export cartel cannot restrict the export trade of a U.S. firm that is not a member, and it cannot cooperate with foreign firms to restrict competition on world markets.

The Congress that passed the Webb-Pomerene Act was not (at least, not openly) motivated by the idea that the Act would make the U.S. better off by allowing U.S. firms to more effectively exercise market power in foreign markets. The stated rationale was defensive, to allow U.S. firms to combine and bargain more effectively with large foreign buyers.

There was concern over the relative bargaining power of U.S. and foreign firms because of cases, well known at the time, in which a product's price was lower in the foreign market than in the U.S. market. For example, copper mined in the U.S. and sold both in the U.S. and Germany had a lower price on the German market.

But a lower price need not mean that powerful buyers on foreign markers bargained for a lower price. It could just as well mean that the foreign market was more competitive than the U.S. market, with the result that U.S. firms charged a lower price in the German market because their most profitable price on the German market was lower than their most profitable price on the U.S. market (Fournier, 1932, p. 19).

There is evidence in the legislative record that Congress intended the Webb-Pomerene Act to apply to joint selling agencies, which would generate the aforementioned increase in bargaining power and which might also result in cost savings and efficiency gains. But the 1924 "Silver Letter" of the Federal Trade Commission, so-called because it was issued in response to an inquiry from a group of silver producers, held that the Webb-Pomerene Act also applied to associations that fixed export prices and allocated export sales, without any combination of selling activities. Since that time, many Webb-Pomerene associations have operated as pure price-fixing groups, without any combination of exporting activity. This would seem to eliminate possible efficiency gains rooted in combination and rationalization of exporting operations.

Webb-Pomerene associations have been regularly studied, no doubt because the registration requirement permits identification of such cartels and facilitates the collection of data. They seem never to have accounted for a large part of U.S. trade: less than 3 per cent of U.S. merchandise trade in 1924, rising to 13.8 per cent in 1929 (Fournier, 1932). The increase was apparently related to the FTC's 1924 "Silver Letter," but it did not persist. In the first 50 years of the Act, Webb-Pomerene-related exports were 2.5 per cent of U.S. exports (Dick, 1992, p. 97).

Larson (1970) examines 47 Webb-Pomerene export associations that operated over the period 1958–1962. Six of the 47 associations ran joint sales agencies, and thus had at least the potential to generate operating efficiencies. All of the associations with joint sales agencies were in concentrated industries, suggesting that their operation had more to do with the exercise of market power than with increasing bargaining power. Nine associations were price-fixing associations that also allocated export business. Three others only fixed prices. The Webb-Pomerene associations included firms that were large in an absolute sense and were among the leading firms both in the U.S. and the world.

Dick (1992) examines the impact of 16 Webb-Pomerene cartels on market performance. He concludes that six of the 16 were efficiency-generating, resulting in lower prices and expanded exports. Efficiency-enhancing cartels tended to occur in unconcentrated U.S. industries and were made up of small firms that had a small share of world markets. These cartels often provided marketing and distribution services for members.

Two of the Webb-Pomerene cartels in the Dick sample (carbon black and crude sulphur) resulted in higher prices and reduced export volumes. Both were in concentrated industries, for which U.S. firms were leading world suppliers.

On balance, the empirical evidence suggests that Webb-Pomerene cartels are not formed very often, that those which are formed have little effect on export markets, and that those effects are what would be predicted based on domestic market structure. Webb-Pomerene cartels formed by large firms in concentrated industries facilitate the exercise of market power. Webb-Pomerene cartels formed by small firms in unconcentrated industries, and which involve the combination of export operations, generate efficiency gains.

An interpretation consistent with both theory and empirical evidence is that Webb-Pomerene cartels are not formed very frequently because they do not facilitate collusion on export markets very much, since large firms in concentrated industries are likely to be able to tacitly collude in any event; and that they do not allow small firms in unconcentrated industries to generate much in the way of incremental efficiencies, since the force of competition in unconcentrated markets compels firms to attain reachable efficiencies in any event, or go out of business.

One explanation for the formation of Webb-Pomerene cartels that appear to have no effect on export markets is that their purpose is to facilitate tacit or overt collusion with respect to the domestic market. We have seen that an important effect of collusion is to relax the force of competition and make it more likely that less than completely efficient firms will survive. Amacher *et al.* (1978) report that Webb-Pomerene cartels tend to form in declining industries, and this is consistent with the view that such cartels help less efficient firms to survive.

The Foreign Trade Act and the Export Trading Act   The Webb-Pomerene Act has been largely ineffective in promoting export trade because it is motivated by a theory that is incorrect for most U.S. industries. There are few if any U.S. industries for which export performance is poor because small U.S. firms suffer from a weak bargaining position *vis-à-vis* foreign buyers. In 1982, the U.S. Congress supplemented the Webb-Pomerene Act with two laws based on this same mistaken mercantilist view of the economics of international markets. There is little reason to think that these laws will be effective in promoting U.S. export performance.

The *Foreign Trade Act* requires that actions have a "direct, substantial, and reasonably fore-seeable" effect on U.S. domestic commerce or on U.S. import/export trade before the Sherman Act can be applied. Conduct that would otherwise violate the Sherman Act does not do so if it affects only foreign markets. The *Export Trading Act* allows the Secretary of Commerce to issue a Certificate of Review to a trading entity that protects it from criminal liability and treble damages under state and federal antitrust laws. The Secretary of Commerce must consult with the Department of Justice before issuing such a certificate.

In its first nine years, 127 Certificates of Review were issued under the Export Trading Act, which at a minimum suggests a slow start. The fundamental problem, however, is that the Foreign Trade Act and the Export Trading Act, like the Webb-Pomerene Act, are based on a mistaken theory. All this legislation views vigorous competition policy and tough domestic competition as factors that hold back the performance of U.S. firms on export markets, thus justifying the relaxation of antitrust policy toward business actions aimed at foreign markets. All evidence suggests the contrary, that tough domestic competition improves efficiency and performance on export markets. The risks of allowing cooperation are that if by small firms it will reduce their efficiency and competitiveness, and that if by large firms it will make it easier for them to tacitly collude for the domestic market.

Export cartels

Like other types of strategic trade policy, these may improve national welfare under relatively restrictive conditions. Export cartels may also enhance the likelihood of (tacit or overt) collusion on domestic markets.

16.7.2 Voluntary Export Restraints

Governments that wish to defend a commitment to free trade often find themselves in the situation of wishing also to cushion, over the short- or perhaps not so short run, the competition from foreign suppliers that comes with free trade. There is a long history of resort, in such circumstances, to informal understandings, reached with the tacit or overt participation of foreign governments, under which foreign suppliers agree to limit their exports. Such *Voluntary Export Restraints* have been used in a variety of industries—particularly textiles and clothing, but also cars, machine tools, steel, video cassette recorders, and others.[19]

Innovative Japanese methods of organizing production gave Japanese firms productivity advantages that made them formidable rivals on world markets in the car industry in the 1980s. As it happens, these productivity advantages were developed behind the protection of a variety of trade barriers, including tariffs (Table 16.2) and currency controls. These formal trade barriers were dismantled as Japan assumed its place among leading industrial nations.

The emergence of Japanese car manufacturers on world markets resulted in the imposition of protective barriers—formal and informal—around Japan's export markets. Some of these barriers are described in Table 16.3.

---

[19] See Greenaway and Hindley (1985), Kostecki (1987), and Wolf (1991).

Table 16.2 Japanese tariffs (per cent) on imported cars

	Small Cars	Large Cars
1955	40.0	35.0
1965	40.0	35.0
1967	40.0	28.0
1968	36.0	28.0
1969	36.0	17.5
1970	20.0	17.5
1971	10.0	10.0
1972	6.4	6.4
1978	0.0	0.0

Source: U.S. General Accounting Office, *U.S.–Japan Trade, Issues and Problems.* September 1979, pp. 42 and 44, reproduced in Hadley (1984, p. 326).

Table 16.3 Restrictions on Japanese imports, by country, 1992

Country	Trade barrier	Japanese share, 1992 (%)
France	Limited historically to 3%	4.1
Germany	No restrictions	14.0
Italy	3,000 cars as direct imports	2.7
Netherlands	No restrictions	27.0
Spain	No imports	3.7
Sweden	No restrictions	29.7
Switzerland	No restrictions	30.0
United Kingdom	Imports limited to 11%	12.3
United States	Imports limited to 1.7 million	31.4

Source: "Motor vehicles" in EC Commission *Panorama of EU Industry 1994.* Brussels-Luxembourg 1994, pp. 11–15.

The restrictions often took the form of "voluntary" limits agreed to by Japanese firms under pressure that came directly from the governments of export markets and indirectly from foreign firms and labour unions.[20]

The European Union took the view that the country-by-country limits to Japanese sales in individual EC member states shown in Table 16.3 were in conflict with the 1992 Single Market programme (see Section 17.3.1). The EC therefore negotiated a far-from-transparent accord under which Japanese exports to the EC as a whole would be limited over the period 1993–1999. Restraints were justified on the ground that they would allow EC producers to prepare themselves for effective competition in a fully open Single Market; part of the understanding was that the EC car market would be fully open to Japanese suppliers from the year 2000 onward.

The level of Japanese sales in the EC was initially set at 1.2 million cars a year. The agreement also provided that the ceiling on sales would be reevaluated regularly in the light of market conditions. Such re-evaluations have in fact taken place, and pressure from EC producers is generally to reduce the ceiling.

The overall ceiling on Japanese sales was allocated across EC member states. In general, the effect of this allocation was to permit greater Japanese sales in members states that had previously had very low limits, and to reduce sales somewhat in other member states.

One difficult point in the implementation of the agreement has been the treatment of vehicles produced by Japanese firms at plants located in the EC. Japanese car manufacturers take the view that such vehicles are not covered by the agreement, while native EC car manufacturers have argued that the limits apply to all cars produced by Japanese firms, regardless of the location of production.

Another difficult point in the implementation of the agreement has been the shipment of imported Japanese vehicles from one EC member state to another. On the one hand, it is the essence of a single market that such shipments should be possible. On the other hand, cross-border shipments defeat the purpose of an agreement allocating permitted sales across member states.

Quality upgrading

Voluntary export restraints typically take the form of an agreed number of units that may be sold in the protected market. When products are differentiated in terms of quality, as is almost always the case, quantity limits create an incentive for foreign suppliers to shift their product range to the high-profit, and this usually means high-quality, end of the market.

de Melo and Messerlin (1988) estimate quality indexes for Japanese cars sold in France in the early 1980s, a period when VERs limited the number of Japanese vehicles sold on the French market. They find that the quality index rose 29 per cent between 1981 and 1983, and a further 6 per cent between 1983 and 1985. Over the same periods, the value of Japanese cars sold in France rose 31 per cent and 6 per cent respectively. Under the constraint of VERs, Japanese firms limited the number of Japanese vehicles sold on the French car market, but they also concentrated those sales in the most profitable segment of the market.

---

[20] The very strict limit on sales of Japanese cars in Italy originated in a 1952 reciprocal agreement that was sought by Japan, which wished to limit the sale of small Italian cars in Japan (de Melo and Messerlin, 1988, p. 1529). For further discussion of Japanese VERs, see El-Agraa (1995).

Trade diversion

If the world were bilateral—one exporting country, one importing country—then VERs would benefit firms in the protected market, as exporting rivals restrict output and raise price in the importing market. Of course, the rivals benefit as well: from their point of view, the government of the importing country is establishing and enforcing a collusive agreement for them, an agreement that would normally be considered to violate competition policy if carried out by private firms on their own initiative.

In a multilateral world, however, some of the benefit of VERs goes to firms based in third countries. For example, Smith (1990) presents simulation results suggesting that Japanese VERs for the French car market led to a larger share of the French market for German producers. In the same way, Dinopoulos and Kreinin (1988) present evidence that one consequence of Japanese VERs for the U.S. car market was higher prices for European vehicles sold in the U.S.

It seems, therefore, that VERs often act to shift sales from foreign firms that are covered by the VER to foreign firms that are not covered by the VER, not to increase the sales of domestic firms. Such trade diversions make VERs less effective as a protective device. They also reduce the consumer welfare loss caused by VERs.

Welfare consequences

de Melo and Messerlin (1988) estimate that French VERs for motor vehicles resulted in a welfare loss for France of approximately 320 million FF, while preserving at most 324 jobs in the French car industry.

Takacs and Winters (1991) analyse the impact of British VERs on footwear imports from Korea and Taiwan in the late 1970s and 1980s. They estimate that the VERs in place in 1979 caused an annual loss of consumers' surplus of £79 million and increased UK industry profit by £22 million, for an annual welfare loss of £57 million. Against this loss, they estimate that the VERs may have preserved jobs for as many as 1,064 workers and avoided labour market adjustment costs of £9.6 million.

Smith and Venables (1991) estimate the consequences of various changes in EC car industry VERs. Their calculations suggest that removal of the French VER described in Table 16.3 would have given French consumers an increase in consumers' surplus equivalent to about 6 per cent of their spending on motor vehicles. At the same time, if the French VER had been removed, European car producers would have suffered lost profits almost half of the gain in consumers' surplus. The net welfare effect of removing the VER would have been positive.

Smith and Venables also estimate that if all EC VERs were removed, the result would be a net welfare gain of about 3 per cent of the value of EC motor vehicle sales. They estimate that if country-by-country VERs were replaced by an EC VER that leaving the overall level of Japanese sales in the EC unchanged,[21] the result would be to increase Japanese sales and improve market performance in member states that previously had strict limits on imports, but to reduce Japanese sales in EC members states that had been relatively open to imports. An EC VER benefits Japanese firms, which are able to reallocate sales across EC member states to their own greater profit.

---

[21] At least approximately, this is the policy that has been adopted.

In the U.S., a VER limited sales of Japanese cars to 1.68 million vehicles per year beginning April 1981. This was increased to 1.85 million cars per year from April 1984 and to 2.3 million cars per year from 1985. The VER was continued by MITI (the Ministry of International Trade and Industry) at least through 1987–1988. Feenstra (1988) estimates that by 1984 price increases due to the quota were over $1,000 per vehicle. He also estimates incremental profits to retailers and producers of Japanese cars at $2 billion per year in 1983 and 1984, with an additional loss of consumers' surplus of around $300 million per year.

Dinopoulos and Kreinin (1988, p. 490) estimate that each U.S. job saved in 1981 and 1982 because of the VER cost the U.S. over $180,000 in lost welfare, at a time when the average annual wage in the car industry was around $35,000.

VERs and the WTO Agreements

The ground rules of international trade are laid out in the World Trade Organization Agreements. The WTO Agreements, reached in 1994 and effective from 1 January 1995, were the product of the seven-year long Uruguay Round of multilateral trade negotiations. They established the World Trade Organization to guide international trade flows and reaffirmed the commitment of WTO member states to free trade. As part of that commitment, member states agreed to phase out the use of VERs over a five-year period.[22] As we will see, the WTO Agreements permit policy measures that allow a member state to neutralize its commitment to free trade.

Voluntary export restraints

Informal trade barriers, solicited by governments committed to free trade and inducing foreign suppliers to restrict sales and raise price in ways that would be considered illegal collusion if carried out entirely by private agents.

16.7.3 Dumping

Dumping is traditionally said to occur if a foreign firm sells in its export markets at a price that is below its home market price, taking account of transportation cost and other differences in the cost (for example, tariffs or marketing and sales efforts) of serving the two markets. An increasingly common alternative definition treats dumping as the practice of selling in a foreign market at a price below some measure of the unit cost of production, whether or not prices are different in the home and export markets.

It is often claimed that dumping should be a matter of policy concern because it is unfair. Very often the argument stops at that point. It is not made clear why dumping is unfair, or to whom. Usually, it is simply taken for granted that if conduct were fair (if dumping did not occur), welfare and market performance would be improved. None of these points survive careful analysis.

The unfairness argument often seems to be based on an incorrect model of international markets. Policymakers who express concern about dumping seem to have a vision of international trade in which their home markets are competitive, with domestic firms pricing at

---

[22] VERs were to be eliminated within four years from the entry into effect of the WTO Agreements (that is, by 1 January 1999), with the possibility of maintaining one VER through 31 December 1999. The EU and Japan motor vehicle VER took advantage of this possibility (Hindley and Messerlin, 1996, p. 56).

marginal and average cost and earning only normal ("fair") profits, while foreign markets are imperfectly competitive, supplied by foreign firms that have protected positions of market power from which they can sally forth with impunity, engaging in a variety of ("unfair") strategic schemes. It is difficult to make a rational case for concern with dumping if instead one begins with the more realistic premise that home and domestic markets are both imperfectly competitive.

Dumping as price discrimination: reciprocal dumping

The first definition of dumping focuses on price discrimination—the selling of identical goods at different net prices in different markets. Dumping in the sense of price discrimination occurs if a firm exports its product for a lower net price, after subtracting transportation and other (such as tariff) incremental costs of serving the export market, than the price in its home market.

Dumping in this sense is the natural consequence of profit-maximizing behaviour in imperfectly competitive markets (Brander and Krugman, 1983). At a fundamental level, it has in common with the partial passthrough of exchange-rate changes the fact that firms with market power pass part of cost increases or higher costs on to consumers in the form of higher prices, but also absorb part of such increases or differences in the form of lower profit margins.

To see this, consider the case of two national markets, each with a single domestic producer that sells in both markets. Suppose that the two firms sell slightly differentiated varieties of the same product; this makes it possible to talk about the prices of specific goods in the same national market, as is common in the antidumping literature.

For simplicity, let the structure of demand be the same in both markets, with inverse demand equations in country 1

$$p_{11} = 100 - \frac{3}{4}q_{21} - q_{11} \tag{16.10}$$

for firm 1 and

$$p_{21} = 100 - \frac{3}{4}q_{11} - q_{21} \tag{16.11}$$

for firm 2.

Let firms have the same technology: constant marginal production cost 10 per unit of output and transportation cost t per unit to ship a unit of output from one country to the other.

Figure 16.13 illustrates firm 2's price and sales decision for country 1 if it maximizes profit as a Cournot quantity-setting oligopolist. For any level of sales of firm 1 on market 1 (q_{11}), firm 2's residual marginal revenue curve is:

$$MR_{21} = 100 - \frac{3}{4}q_{11} - 2q_{21}. \tag{16.12}$$

Taking firm 1's sales on market 1 as given, the sales level that maximizes firm 2's profit from country 1 is the output q_{21} that makes marginal revenue from (16.12) equal to firm 2's marginal cost, $10 + t$:

$$100 - \frac{3}{4}q_{11} - 2q_{21} = 10 + t. \tag{16.13}$$

If we solve (16.13) for q_{21}, we obtain the equation of firm 2's best response function,

$$q_{21} = \frac{1}{2}\left(90 - \frac{3}{4}q_{11} - t\right), \tag{16.14}$$

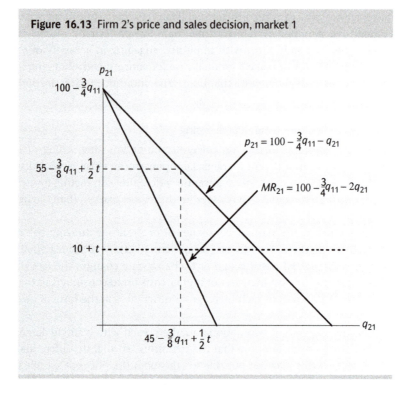

Figure 16.13 Firm 2's price and sales decision, market 1

The corresponding price is:

$$p_{21} = 10 + \frac{1}{2}(90 - \frac{3}{4}q_{11} + t). \tag{16.15}$$

Only half of unit transportation cost is passed on to the price of variety 2 in market 1. Just as the passthrough of exchange fluctuations to export prices is incomplete in imperfectly competitive markets, so the passthrough of transportation and other export costs to export prices is typically incomplete. Because marginal revenue is less than price, and because a profit-maximizing firm sells where marginal revenue equals marginal cost, it will pass only a portion of unit cost differences into price differences.

Equilibrium prices in country 1 are (Problem 16–13):

$$p_{11} = 42\frac{8}{11} + \frac{12}{55}t \qquad p_{21} = 42\frac{8}{11} + \frac{23}{55}t. \tag{16.16}$$

From (16.16), firm 2's net price in country 1, after subtracting unit transportation cost, is:

$$p_{21} - t = 42\frac{8}{11} - \frac{32}{55}t. \tag{16.17}$$

As long as trade actually occurs, prices are above marginal production cost and both firms earn economic profits: in this example, p_{11} and $p_{21} - t$ are both greater than 10.

Because the countries are identical, in equilibrium $p_{22} = p_{11}$; then the difference between firm 2's price in country 2 and firm 2's net price in country 1 is:

$$p_{22} - (p_{21} - t) = 42\frac{8}{11} + \frac{12}{55}t - \left(42\frac{8}{11} - \frac{32}{55}t\right) = \frac{4}{5}t \geq 0. \tag{16.18}$$

It follows that unless transportation cost is zero, when firm 2 independently maximizes its own profit, it is guilty of dumping.

Because we have used an example where the two national markets are identical, the same result holds for firm 1 and its price in country 2. As long as there are some differences in the unit cost of supplying imperfectly competitive export markets, dumping in the sense of net price discrimination is the normal outcome of independent, profit-maximizing behaviour in a market system.

Dumping as predation

The second definition of dumping focuses on predation. Few if any international markets appear to have structures that would make predation a feasible business strategy. In addition, few antidumping cases involve a dominant firm or group of firms: antidumping penalties are typically imposed on groups of small firms (often, located in less-developed countries). It is not plausible that such firms would either undertake or succeed in predatory schemes.[23]

There have been no generally accepted episodes of predatory dumping in international markets, and it seems unlikely that antidumping policy can be convincingly justified as a tool to combat international predation.

Dumping

Dumping as predation in international markets seems unlikely to occur. Dumping as international price discrimination is a normal consequence of independent profit-maximizing behaviour in imperfectly competitive markets.

Antidumping policy: theory

It is the General Agreement on Tariffs and Trade (GATT) that lays down rules for international trade in goods. In 1995, following the conclusion of the Uruguay Round of multilateral trade negotiations, the GATT became part of the World Trade Organization Agreements, which cover trade in goods, services, and intellectual property, and also establish the World Trade Organization as the permanent forum for the management of international trade flows.

The GATT commits the members of the World Trade Organization to free trade. We have seen that as part of the Uruguay Round, WTO members agreed to phase out the use of voluntary export restraints as a protective device. But the GATT allows protective measures if dumping occurs and causes or threatens material injury to domestic industries.[24]

Antidumping duties An antidumping duty has the same effect as any other tariff. In the dumping example, if country 1 imposes an antidumping duty d on sales by firm 2, the resulting changes in equilibrium prices are less than the amount of the antidumping duty:

$$\Delta p_{11} = \frac{12}{55}d < d \qquad \Delta(p_{21} - t) = \frac{23}{55}d < d \qquad (16.19)$$

(see Problem 16–14).

---

[23] In the U.S., the Antidumping Duty Act of 1916 controls dumping that is an attempt to monopolize. Before a finding of predatory dumping can be made under this law, it is necessary to show an intent to monopolize. Following the general development of US policy toward predation, it is also necessary to pass the recoupment test—to show that the predator firm(s) had the reasonable expectation of profitably raising price after injuring domestic firms. This law has been used extremely little, and no violation of the law has ever been found.

[24] The GATT also allows protective measures (countervailing duties) to neutralize subsidies to foreign suppliers.

An antidumping duty is essentially an artificial increase in firm 2's cost of supplying market 1. When firm 2's cost of supplying market 1 goes up, firm 2 reduces output somewhat, moving back and up along its marginal revenue curve until marginal revenue equals the now-higher marginal cost $(10 + t + d)$. Because of this movement up the marginal revenue curve, only part of the antidumping duty is passed along to consumers in the form of a higher p_{21}.

With an antidumping duty, firm 2 reduces its sales in country 1. This tends to increase p_{11} and p_{21}. Firm 1 reacts to firm 2's output reduction by expanding output (quantities are strategic substitutes, quantity best response curves are downward sloping) but the increase in firm 1's output is not so great that it reverses the upward increase in p_{11}.

Since firm 2's price increases by less than the amount of the antidumping duty, if country 1's government wished to impose a large enough duty to make firm 2's net price the same in the two markets (to make $p_{21} - t = p_{22}$), it would need to impose an antidumping duty that is greater than the price difference.

Undertakings A foreign firm can avoid an antidumping duty if it charges the same net price in home and foreign markets. As our discussion of reciprocal dumping shows, profit maximization usually involves setting a lower net price in export markets, so setting the same net price in both markets will involve some sacrifice of profit. It will, however, avoid the payment of an antidumping duty to the government imposing protective measures. An undertaking to equalize net prices in this way is one of the avenues by which an EC antidumping procedure may be concluded.[25]

If the foreign firm undertakes to eliminate any difference in its net prices, it will generally change its prices in both markets, raising the net price in its export market (in our example, raising p_{21} by $\frac{2}{5}t$) but also lowering the price in its home market (reducing p_{22} by $\frac{2}{5}t$).

The increase in p_{21} makes firm 1 better off in country 1. The reduction in p_{22} makes firm 1 worse off in country 2. This means that the net benefit to firm 1 of an antidumping undertaking is less than the extra profit it earns in country 1.

With linear demand, constant marginal cost, and countries of the same size, an antidumping undertaking leaves each firm's total output unchanged (Problem 16–15). The antidumping undertaking causes a reallocation of sales, so that each firm sells more in its home market and less in its export market, but each firm produces the same total output that it would have produced without an antidumping undertaking.

Tacit collusion If tacit collusion is to work, a firm that is tempted to defect from its part of an industry strategy that restricts overall output and allows greater economic profit to all firms must believe that such defection would result in such severe future punishment that defection is not profitable. Antidumping legislation gives collusive domestic firms a credible way to have their government punish defection by foreign firms from a collusive output pattern.

In one example of such official punishment, Hexner (1943, pp. 213–214) reports that in 1938 a publicly owned South African steel firm, a member of the International Steel Cartel,

---

[25] More than half of EU antidumping procedures between 1980 and 1987 ended in undertakings. Since that time, the use of undertakings has declined and the use of duties has increased (Hindley and Messerlin, 1996, p. 40).

complained to its government that U.S. steel firms were dumping in South Africa. Antidumping duties were imposed for several months, then withdrawn.

Messerlin (1990) studies the systematic use of EU antidumping regulation (administered by DG Trade of the European Commission) by chemical industry firms that have themselves been fined for violating EU competition law (administered by DG Competition of the European Commission).[26] His case study evidence indicates that the opening of an antidumping investigation was sufficient to stabilize prices that had been going down, and that when the investigation was ended by an undertaking under which East European firms would end dumping, prices increased substantially. The estimated profits of EC firms due to successful collusion were substantially higher than the fines eventually paid by those same firms for colluding in violation on EC competition law.

The use of antidumping policy to enforce tacit collusion suggests that foreign firms that make undertakings to end antidumping investigations are likely to act in a way that is consistent with tacit collusion, restricting output because of the threat of punishment from government antidumping authorities.

EC antidumping policy: application

Under the World Trade Organization Agreements, a country may impose antidumping measures if dumping occurs and if dumping causes or threatens material injury to domestic industries. As it is administered, EC antidumping procedures are biased both in favor of finding that dumping has occurred and in favor of finding that it has injured EC firms.[27]

Occurrence of dumping The conclusion that dumping has taken place depends on a comparison of the price of the foreign good when it is sold in the EC with its price or its cost of production (the so-called "normal value") in its home market.

To determine whether or not dumping has occurred over a given time period, antidumping authorities calculate the average of the prices at which the foreign good was sold in the EU during that period. If some sales took place above the normal value, those high prices are thrown out in calculating the average and the normal price is substituted for them. A rationale put forward for this procedure is that (Hindley and Messerlin, 1996, p. 62) "a high price should not be allowed to conceal dumped sales".

The result is that "the" price of foreign goods used by EC antidumping authorities to determine if the good has been sold below the normal price is an average of sales taking place below the normal price and other sales that are assumed (counterfactually) to have taken place at the normal price. It is a simple property of arithmetic that this average will always be below the normal price if even a single sale has taken place below the normal price.

When the determination whether dumping has occurred is made based on a comparison of prices and the cost of production, the methodology that is used to construct the cost figure is central to the outcome. In estimating cost of production, EC authorities have allocated

---

[26] The EC chemical cases are reviewed by Hindley and Messerlin (1996, pp. 36–39).

[27] See Council Regulation (E.C.) No. 384/96 of 22 December 1995 1996 OJ L56/1. The same biases appear in US antidumping procedures; see Clarida (1996) (for a concise discussion of US antidumping policy, see Baldwin, 1998). The aspects of antidumping procedures that lead to these biases are consistent with the WTO Agreements. (The fault, dear Brutus, is not in the stars, but in the WTO Agreements.)

fixed costs in ways that appear to inflate the resulting cost figure. For example, in a decision involving the alleged dumping of Japanese semiconductor chips, the Commission allocated the R&D costs of Japanese firms to the period covered by the Commission's investigation, even though the revenues generated by those R&D expenses would be collected over the entire product life-cycle of the chips in question (Tharakan, 1997).

The procedures that are used to construct cost-of-production and normal value figures result in estimates of dumping margins that seem indefensible.[28] In an antidumping decision involving Japanese semiconductors, the Commission's figure for the difference between estimated production costs and the average price of the Japanese chips on the EC market was 206.2 per cent (Tharakan, 1997, p. 11). In one chemical industry case, dumping margins (Messerlin, 1990, p. 478) "on imports from Czechoslovakia, Romania, East Germany and Hungary were, respectively, 53–68 per cent, 58-74 per cent, 26-37 per cent and 25-45 per cent".

The Commission has begun to suppress reporting its estimated dumping margin in published decisions. Nicolaides and van Wijngaarden (1993, p. 42) suggest that the dumping margin is not reported because "its revelation would be embarrassing".

 BOX   Case study: EC Antidumping Action: Cotton Fabrics

The European Commission's persistent efforts to impose antidumping penalties on unbleached cotton fabric imported from China, Egypt, India, Indonesia, Pakistan, and Turkey, over the opposition of a majority of EC member states, illustrate the ease with which WTO-consistent antidumping procedures can be used for protectionist purposes, and demonstrate that antidumping policy not only harms consumers at the expense of favoured business interests, but may also harm segments of the business community.

The argument that fabric producers from the less-developed countries in question have dumped their products in the EC is that they have held their prices constant, even though their costs (as measured by the Commission) have gone up. The evidence that EC weaving firms have been injured by dumping is that their share of the EC market has gone down. This is true, but because total sales in the EC market went down, not because the sales of the non-EC firms (which were limited by quotas) went up.

It would seem difficult to establish that many small weaving firms, selling a largely standardized product, either entered on a predatory scheme against EC firms or were engaged in international price discrimination.

The dispute over whether or not to impose antidumping duties has pitted member states (particularly France) that are home to declining textile sectors against member states (particularly Britain and Germany) that are home to clothing manufacturing firms, for which cotton fabric is a necessary input.

The European Commission rejected an antidumping complaint in 1995, but imposed temporary duties in 1996. In a closely divided vote, EC foreign ministers rejected a proposal to extend the temporary antidumping duties for five years. Despite this decision, the European Commission ⟫

---

[28] For further discussion, see Hindley (1988).

>> began another antidumping procedure less than two months later. EC textile importers unsuccessfully challenged this action before the European Court of Justice as an abuse of power by the Commission.

In March 1998, the Commission again imposed provisional antidumping duties on unbleached cotton imports from the six countries, although an advisory committee of member state representatives voted 9–5 against imposing the duties.

In the run-up to a decision on whether to extend the temporary duties, EC weavers argued for protection against dumped imports, and clothing manufacturers and retailers argued that higher costs for imports would mean higher prices for consumers and could cost up to 200,000 lost jobs.

In October 1998, EC foreign ministers once again rejected a proposal to impose antidumping duties for five years.

Existence of injury or the threat of injury Imposition of an EC antidumping duty requires not only the finding that dumping has occurred but also a finding that the dumping has injured or threatens to injure the competing EC industry. A decision whether such injury has occurred or not is to be based on the volume of imports and their impact on the EC industry. If it should develop that imports of like products from several different countries are the subject of antidumping proceedings, the injury determination may be based on impact of combined imports from all such countries.

If it has been found that products have been dumped, it might be thought that the occurrence of injury would follow automatically (Vermulst and Waer, 1996, p. 281): "every sale of imported products on the domestic market is by definition a potentially lost sale for the domestic industry and hence a cause of injury".

For the purpose of EC antidumping procedures, an injury finding seems to require a showing that a group of EC firms are suffering economic distress, and that foreign firms selling similar products in the EC can be found to have dumped according to official definitions. There does not appear to be a need to show that the economic circumstances of the EC firms would be better if the dumping had not taken place.

For example, in a series of cases involving the EC chemical industry, the growing market share of foreign suppliers was taken to be evidence that dumping was causing injury to EC firms. An expanding market share of fringe foreign suppliers is exactly what would be expected if such firms reacted in an independent way to formation of a cartel by a dominant group of EC firms (Messerlin, 1990, pp. 480–481). The EC chemical firms were in fact found to have formed a cartel. Thus a finding of harm from dumping was based on the reaction that would be expected from independently behaving profit-maximizing firms to a coordinated exercise of market power by EC firms.

Intermediate goods

Antidumping procedures are often opened against firms that produce intermediate goods. Antidumping penalties benefit EC firms that compete against foreign suppliers. But antidumping penalties harm EC firms that purchase the protected goods and use them as inputs to produce other goods that are then sold to final consumer demand. This raises the possibility that antidumping policy, far from merely (!) protecting EC firms at the expense of EC consumers, may in fact protect a subset of EC firms at the expense of other EC firms *and* EC consumers.

Antidumping measures

Policy tools that allow a government that is publicly committed to free trade to engage in selective protection that benefits some domestic firms to the injury of domestic consumers and, in many cases, to the injury of other domestic firms as well.

16.7.4 What Is to Be Done?

The negative impact of protectionist policies on market performance and national welfare could be controlled by administering such policies as part of national competition policy and applying the guidelines about the determinants of market performance that have developed in the enforcement of competition policy to international markets.

Such an approach would require that firms seeking protection from international rivalry demonstrate that market structure (a) suggested that foreign firms were able to exercise market power and that (b) domestic firms in the import-competing industry could not. Export cartels involving the creation of joint-sales agencies would be allowed for small firms, not for large firms with market power. Domestic industries would not be able to invoke antidumping procedures against small foreign rivals based in several different countries.

Trade flows will continue to require adjustments in national market structures: some industries will decline, others will expand. In industrialized countries, industry segments that produce standardized, labour-intensive varieties will decline, industry segments that produce high-quality, differentiated, and capital-intensive varieties will expand. Rather than indirectly deliver adjustment aid to firms in declining sectors by means of export protection, it would be better to allow overt aid for industrial readjustment, subject to rules of the kind that have developed in administering EC state aid policy (Section 17.4) and the EC's own Structural Funds. In general, adjustment aid would be limited in time and conditional on the implementation of a programme of structural adjustment that would allow the industry receiving assistance to reposition itself so that it could eventually compete on international markets without public assistance.

SUMMARY

The new trade theory predicts that intraindustry trade flows will occur in imperfectly competitive industries, particularly if scale economies and product differentiation are important. It also predicts that foreign competition will improve domestic market performance.

These hypotheses have been subject to extensive empirical tests. The predictions of the theory of trade in imperfectly competitive markets generally receive strong support. Imperfect competition emerges as a central factor in the explanation of trade flows among developed countries, and trade flows among developed countries limit the exercise of market power by domestic firms.

The imperfectly competitive nature of international markets raises the possibility that a country can improve its own welfare through policies that allow its firms to earn greater monopoly profits in foreign markets. The conditions that must be satisfied to realize this result are stringent, and are unlikely to be realized in practice. If foreign countries respond to strategic trade policies by adopting their own similar policies, the overall effect is to leave all trading parties worse off.

Strategic interactions in imperfectly competitive markets result in price and output changes that partially neutralize the effects of exchange rate movements. Exchange rate fluctuations are therefore only partially passed on to changes in domestic prices.

A variety of strategies are open to firms that supply international markets. Export exposes such firms to the risk that foreign governments will raise protective trade barriers. Licensing a foreign partner leaves the international firm open to the possibility of holdup once it has committed sunk investments to the local operation.

Tariffs and quotas give domestic producers short-run protection from foreign competition; they typically make consumers in the protected market worse off. Over the long run, tariffs and quotas may induce trade barrier-jumping foreign direct investment, eliminating their short-run protective effect.

The protectionist impulse is deeply rooted. There is a broad consensus that free trade will maximize welfare in the long run, and for this reason most governments take the high road of public commitment to free trade. But free trade also requires costly structural adjustments in the short run, and resistance to such adjustments generates short-run political pressure to circumvent the commitment to free trade in ways that are superficially plausible but do not survive close examination.

Export cartels are defended on the ground that they increase the bargaining power of domestic firms against powerful foreign rivals. More often, it appears, they allow powerful domestic firms to exercise domestic market power.

Voluntary export restraints (set to disappear from the world stage under the WTO Agreements) are an opaque trade barrier and are, in effect, government-sponsored and policed cartels.

There is no convincing evidence that dumping in the sense of international predation has ever occurred. Dumping in the sense of international price discrimination seems likely to occur, but only in situations where domestic and foreign firms exercise some market power and where import competition improves market performance to the benefit of purchasing industries and final consumers. This improvement in market performance is one of the arguments in favour of a free-trade policy. In this context, anti-dumping policy is invoked by firms in declining and non-competitive sectors to limit foreign competition, punish foreign rivals that compete too vigorously, and delay inevitable structural adjustments.

STUDY POINTS

- Intraindustry trade (Section 16.2)
- Trade and domestic market performance (Section 16.3)
- Export subsidies (Section 16.4.1)
- Tariffs and quotas (Section 16.4.4)
- Import protection and export promotion (Section 16.4.5)
- Partial exchange rate passthrough in imperfectly competitive markets (Section 16.5)
- Concentration effect of intraindustry trade (Section 16.6)
- Tariff-jumping direct foreign investment (Section 16.6.2)
- Hysteresis (Section 16.6.4)
- Export cartels and tacit collusion on home market (Section 16.7.1)
- Competition policy toward export cartels (Section 16.7.1)
- Voluntary export restraints, quality upgrading (Section 16.7.2)
- Dumping and antidumping policy (Section 16.7.3)

FURTHER READING

On Adam Smith and mercantilism, see Coats (1975). For studies indicating that foreign competition limits the exercise of domestic market power, see Esposito and Esposito (1971), Pagoulatos and Sorensen (1976), Caves (1980b), Neumann *et al.* (1985), Clark *et al.* (1990), Salinger (1990), Feinberg and Shaanan (1994), and Katics and Petersen (1994). Studies confirming models of exchange rate passthrough include Knetter (1989, 1993); Marston (1990); Yang (1997); Lee (1997). See Veugelers (1995) for a discussion of alternative strategies for supplying a foreign market.

PROBLEMS

16–1 Let there be two countries, each home to one widget producer. The subscript 1 denotes both country 1 and its widget company; the subscript 2 denotes both country 2 and its widget company. Let the inverse demand equations for the two countries be:

$$\begin{aligned} p_1 &= 100 - (q_{11} + q_{21}) \\ p_2 &= 100 - (q_{12} + q_{22}) \end{aligned}, \tag{16.20}$$

where p_1 is the price in country 1, p_2 is the price in country 2, and q_{ij} is the quantity of widgets sold by firm i in country j, for $i, j = 1, 2$.

Suppose also that widgets are produced at a constant marginal cost 10 per unit, and that there is a transportation cost t per unit to ship a widget from one country to another:

(a) write out the payoff functions of the two firms;

(b) show that the amounts the firms sell in one country are independent of the amounts they sell in the other country;

(c) find the equations of the best response functions for country 1;

(d) solve the equations of the best response functions for equilibrium outputs in country 1;

(e) show that inequality (16.2) is the restriction on transportation cost that must hold if firm 2 is to sell in country 1;

(f) what is equilibrium price in country 1? Compare the equilibrium price with each firm's marginal cost of supplying country 1. (This part of the exercise relates to the analysis of dumping.)

16–2 Analyse the Cournot duopoly trade model for general inverse demand curves,

$$\begin{aligned} p_1 &= p_1(q_{11} + q_{21}) \\ p_2 &= p_2(q_{12} + q_{22}) \end{aligned}. \tag{16.21}$$

16–3 (a) Answer Problem 16–1 if firms set prices rather than quantities. Suppose that products are differentiated, with demand curves in country i given by equations:

$$\begin{aligned} p_{1i} &= 100 - (q_{1i} + \tfrac{1}{2}q_{2i}) \\ p_{2i} &= 100 - (\tfrac{1}{2}q_{1i} + q_{2i}) \end{aligned}, \tag{16.22}$$

where the first subscript denotes the firm and the second, $i = 1, 2$, denotes the country, $0 \leq \theta < 1$, with average and marginal cost 10 and transportation cost t per unit as in Problem 16–1.

(b) From Problem 3–10, a representative consumer utility function that produces the demand curves (16.22) is:

$$U = m + 100(q_{1i} + q_{2i}) - \frac{1}{2}\left[q_{1i}^2 + 2\left(\frac{1}{2}\right)q_{1i}q_{2i} + q_{2i}^2\right], \tag{16.23}$$

where m represents consumption on other goods. Analyse the welfare effects of trade.

16–4 Firm 1, based in country 1, and firm 2, based in country 2, sell quantities q_1 and q_2, respectively, in country 3. The demand equation of country 3 is:

$$p = a - (q_1 + q_2),\qquad(16.24)$$

and sales in country 3 have no impact on the country 1 and country 2 markets. The marginal and average cost of production and transportation, c, is constant and the same for both firms.

(a) Find equilibrium outputs and profits in country 3 if there are no export subsidies.

(b) Find equilibrium outputs and profits in country 3 if country 1 grants its firm a subsidy s_1 per unit sold in country 3. What subsidy is best for country 1?

(c) Find equilibrium outputs and profits in country 3 if country 1 grants its firm a subsidy s_1 per unit sold and country 2 grants its firm a subsidy s_2 per unit sold in country 3. What are the equilibrium subsidies if the two countries set subsidy levels non-cooperatively (that is, if each country sets the best possible subsidy level for itself, taking the subsidy level of the other country as given)?

16–5 Answer question 16–4 if products are differentiated, with inverse demand equations:

$$\begin{aligned}p_1 &= a - b(q_1 + \theta q_2)\\p_2 &= a - b(\theta q_1 + q_2)\end{aligned},\qquad(16.25)$$

with $0 \le \theta < 1$, and firms set prices rather than quantities.

16–6 Return to Problem 16–4. Initially, let transportation cost t equal 0.

(a) Analyse the impact of a quota $\bar{q}$ that restricts firm 2's sales in country 1 below the Cournot equilibrium level on outputs, prices, profits, and net social welfare in country 1.

(b) Return to the model without a quota and with $t > 0$, but now interpret t as a tariff collected by country 1 on each unit of output sold by firm 2 in country 1. What is the impact of the tariff on country 1's net social welfare?

16–7 Let there be two countries with identical demand curves, each home to one widget producer. The subscript 1 denotes both country 1 and its widget company; similarly for the subscript 2. Let the inverse demand equations in the two countries be:

$$\begin{aligned}p_1 &= a - (q_{11} + q_{21})\\p_2 &= a - (q_{12} + q_{22})\end{aligned},\qquad(16.26a)$$

where p_1 is the price in country 1, p_2 is the price in country 2, and q_{ij} is the quantity of widgets sold by firm i in country j, for $i, j = 1, 2$. The parameter a is the price-axis intercept of the inverse demand curves, which are the same in both countries. The slope of the inverse demand curves is -1.

Let the cost function be:

$$c(q_{i1} + q_{i2}) = \alpha(q_{i1} + q_{i2}) - \frac{1}{2}\beta(q_{i1} + q_{i2})^2,\qquad(16.27)$$

where α and β are both positive and β is sufficiently small that marginal cost remains positive over the relevant output range. Assume there are no transportation costs or tariffs.

(a) Write out the payoff functions of the two firms.

(b) Find the first-order conditions to maximize the payoffs and solve them for equilibrium outputs.

(c) Substitute equilibrium outputs for country 2 in the equations of the first-order conditions for country 1 outputs, and interpret the resulting expressions as equilibrium best-response functions for country 1.

(d) Suppose now that country 1 imposes a quota that restricts the country 2 firm's sales in country 1 to a level $\bar{q}$ that is below the equilibrium level from (b). Find the new equilibrium outputs; describe the new equilibrium in terms of movements in the equilibrium best-response functions.

16–8 (Concentration effect of trade) Suppose there are two identical countries, each with demand equation:

$$p = a - bQ, \tag{16.28}$$

(where Q is total sales in the country) and that firms in each country operate with the cost function:

$$c(q) = cq + F, \tag{16.29a}$$

where c is constant marginal cost, q is firm output, and F is fixed and sunk cost. Assume that the firms are Cournot oligopolists.

(a) What is the long-run equilibrium number of firms in each country if trade between the two countries is not possible?

(b) Suppose trade opens up between the two countries (and for simplicity, assume there are no transportation costs or tariffs). What is the profit of each firm, after trade, if the number of firms in each country is the long-run equilibrium number of firms from (a)?

(c) What is the long-run equilibrium number of firms (in both countries) after trade opens up?

(d) What is the long-run number of firms if the two countries form a single market?

16–9 (Exchange rate passthrough, quantity-setting firms) Let markets for the same product in two different countries have the inverse demand curves (16.7).

Let firm 1 be based in country 1 and firm 2 in country 2. Call the constant unit cost of firm 1 c_1 dollars and the constant unit cost of firm 2 c_2 euros. Let the exchange rate e be the number of euros required to buy a dollar on world currency markets. Assume firms compete by selecting outputs, and each firm exports to the other market if it is profitable to do so.

(a) Find the equations of the quantity best-response functions of each firm for each country.

(b) Find equilibrium outputs in each country and discuss the way they are affected by changes in e.

(c) Find equilibrium price in each country and discuss how they are affected by changes in e.

(d) Compare the impact of exchange rate fluctuations with changes in:

    (i) a specific tariff t per unit paid by the country 2 firm on each unit of output sold in country 1;

    (ii) an ad valorem tariff τ, a fraction of the country 1 price paid by the country 2 firm on each unit of output sold in country 1.

Note: it is sufficient to write out the expression for firm 2's payoff in country 1 with a specific and alternatively an ad valorem tariff.

16–10 (Exchange rate passthrough, price-setting firms) Suppose that products are differentiated, with inverse demand equations:

$$\begin{aligned} p_{11} &= a_1 - b_1(q_{11} + \theta_1 q_{21}) \\ p_{21} &= a_1 - b_1(\theta_1 q_{11} + q_{21}) \end{aligned} \tag{16.30}$$

in country 1 and

$$\begin{aligned} p_{12} &= a_2 - b_2(q_{12} + \theta_2 q_{22}) \\ p_{22} &= a_2 - b_2(\theta_2 q_{12} + q_{22}) \end{aligned} \tag{16.31}$$

in country 2. Assume firms compete by selecting prices, and each firm exports to the other market if it is profitable to do so. Let other aspects of the model be as in Problem 16–4.

(a) Find the equations of the price best-response functions of each firm for each country.

(b) Find equilibrium prices in each country and discuss the way they are affected by changes in e.

16–11 Analyse the impact of an export cartel on national welfare:

(a) if two domestic firms are the only suppliers in a third market of a good which is not consumed on their home market;

(b) if there is a third firm supplying the product, based in the export market, that competes as a quantity-setting firm with the two domestic firms;

(c) if the product is consumed in both countries, if there are two firms based in each country, and if firms in each country are allowed to form an export cartel;

(d) if formation of an export cartel allows domestic firms to tacitly collude on the home market.

16–12 (VERs and direct foreign investment; see Flam, 1994).

There are three markets, each with a linear inverse demand equation for automobiles:

$$p_i = a - Q_i, i = 1, 2, 3 \tag{16.32}$$

for a homogeneous product.

Countries 1 and 2 form a customs union, which has aggregate inverse demand curve for automobiles:

$$p_U = a - \frac{1}{2}Q_U. \tag{16.33}$$

Countries 1 and 3 are each home to one car manufacturer, which we will call firm 1 and firm 3 respectively.

Only firm 3 sells in country 3; firm 3's cost function for its operations in country 3 is:

$$C_{33}(x_3) = F_3 + c_3 x_3. \tag{16.34}$$

The equation of firm 1's cost function for its operations in the custom union is:

$$C_1(x_1) = F_1 + c_1 x_1. \tag{16.35}$$

The country 3 firm has lower marginal cost in country 3:

$$c_3 < c_1. \tag{16.36}$$

If firm 3 opens a plant in the customs union, its cost function at that plant has equation:

$$C_{3U}(x_{3U}) = F_3 + c_1 x_{3U} \tag{16.37}$$

If firm 3 opens a plant in the customs union, it must pay an extra set of fixed costs. Its marginal cost is the same as firm 1: marginal cost is country specific. This is an assumption that simplifies the analysis of market equilibrium if there is foreign direct investment.

(a) Find Cournot equilibrium profits if there is free trade and firm 3 exports from country 3 to the customs union; find equilibrium consumers' surplus and net social welfare in the customs union.

(b) Suppose firm 3 is persuaded or constrained to limit its exports to a level v that is below its free trade equilibrium export level. Find Cournot equilibrium profits under this voluntary export restraint. Also find equilibrium consumers' surplus and net social welfare in the customs union.

(c) Find Cournot equilibrium profits, consumers' surplus and net social welfare in the customs union if firm 3 sets up a plant in country 1. What is the condition that must be satisfied for direct foreign investment to be the most profitable choice for firm 3? How is this condition affected by v? How is this condition affected by F_3?

16–13 (Reciprocal dumping) Consider two firms, firm 1 based in country 1 and firm 2 based in country 2. Markets in the two countries are identical. The two firms produce differentiated varieties of the same product. Inverse demand equations are

$$p_{11} = a - q_{11} - \theta q_{21} \tag{16.38}$$

$$p_{21} = a - \theta q_{11} - q_{21} \tag{16.39}$$

in country 1 (p_{21} is the price of variety 2 in country 1, and so forth) and

$$p_{12} = a - q_{12} - \theta q_{22} \tag{16.40}$$

$$p_{22} = a - \theta q_{12} - q_{22} \tag{16.41}$$

in country 2. The parameter θ lies between 0 and 1 and measures the degree of substitutability between the two varieties.

The cost of production is c per unit. Transportation cost to ship from one country to another is t per unit.

Calculate equilibrium prices and quantities in both markets. For the exported varieties, calculate price net of transportation cost (i.e., calculate $p_{21} - t$ and $p_{12} - t$). Compare export prices net of transportation cost with the price of the same variety in its home market.

16–14 (Antidumping duties) For the model of Problem 16–13, if country 1 imposes an antidumping dumping d on firm 2's sales in country 1, what is the impact on equilibrium prices in country 1? How great an antidumping duty would country 1 need to impose to make $p_{22} = p_{21} - t$?

16–15 (Antidumping undertaking) For the model of Problem 16–13, what is firm 2's profit-maximizing price if it agrees to charge the same price (net of transportation cost) in both countries? (Assume firm 1 continues to act as a Cournot firm in both markets.)

16–16 Answer Problems 16–14 and 16–15 if firms' choice variables are prices rather than quantities.

MARKET INTEGRATION IN THE EUROPEAN UNION

Consumption is the sole end and purpose of production; and the interest of the producer ought to be attended to, only so far as it may be necessary for promoting that of the consumer.

Adam Smith (1937, p. 625)

17.1 Introduction

The ongoing process of EC market integration makes the study of the organization of European industry a fascinating exercise. Here we begin by using basic models to seek insights into the consequences to be expected when markets, particularly imperfectly competitive markets, merge. We then look at market integration in practice, including the impact of the 1986 Single European Act and the 2002 adoption of the euro as a circulating currency by the eurozone member states on market performance and market structure. We conclude with a discussion of a unique and important part of EC competition policy, the control of member state aid to business.

17.2 Market Integration in Theory

17.2.1 Market Integration and Market Performance

Perfect competition

Identical costs, no taxes, no export costs The simplest possible case, perfect competition, serves as a starting point. Consider two countries, homes to identical markets for a homogeneous product, with demand curves shown in Figure 17.1. In each country the market is perfectly competitive (in particular, firms are price-takers), and production costs are the same in both countries (constant marginal cost 10 per unit of output). Assume also that there are no taxes and no transportation or distribution costs if a firm located in one country sells to a consumer located in the other country.

Under these conditions, what are the consequences for market performance if all barriers to trade between the two countries are eliminated? Prices are the same in both countries, and equal to marginal cost, before and after market integration. The model makes no predictions

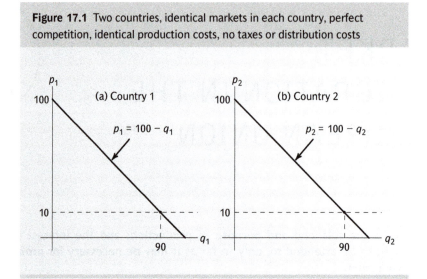

Figure 17.1 Two countries, identical markets in each country, perfect competition, identical production costs, no taxes or distribution costs

about trade flows: in the context of this model, no conclusions can be drawn about market integration by examining data about shipments between countries.

Taxes, no export costs   How does the outcome change if there is a per unit tax t_1 in country 1 and t_2 in country 2, with, for specificity, $t_1 < t_2$?

The pre-integration long-run equilibrium outputs are shown in Figure 17.2. In each country, the long-run perfectly competitive equilibrium price equals marginal production cost

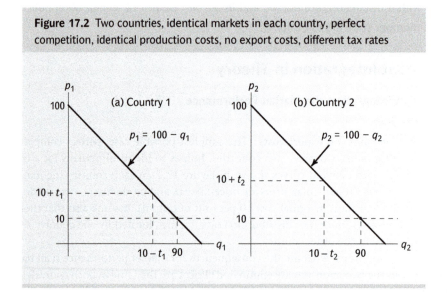

Figure 17.2 Two countries, identical markets in each country, perfect competition, identical production costs, no export costs, different tax rates

plus the per unit tax. Output in each country is less with the tax it would be without a tax, and output is smaller in the country that has the higher tax rate.

If all barriers to trade are removed, one consequence of taxes is that firms must maintain records that treat sales in the two countries separately—a tax t_1 per unit sold must be paid to the government of country 1, a tax t_2 per unit sold must be paid to the government of country 2.

There is no incentive for supply-side arbitrage (as, indeed, is the case without taxes). Firms earn a normal rate of return on investment, net of taxes, on sales in either country, so firms have no incentive to seek (or avoid) sales in one country or the other.

There may be an incentive for demand-side arbitrage. Consumers in the low-tax country have no incentive to buy in the high-tax country. Consumers in the high-tax country have an incentive to buy in the low-tax country if the high-tax country does not control its borders and collect the difference in taxes when returning residents bring in items purchased in the low-tax country. If the high-tax country does use such controls, then (leaving aside the possibility of smuggling), consumers in the high-tax country have no incentive to buy in the low-tax country.

Prices net of taxes are the same in both countries, and equal to marginal cost, before and after market integration. If the high-tax country prevents tax avoidance by collecting the difference in tax rates on imported goods, the model makes no prediction about trade flows. If the high-tax country does not prevent tax avoidance by collecting the difference in tax rates on imported goods, firms in the low-tax country supply all consumers in both markets. The total quantity demanded in both countries will go up (to twice the amount demanded in the low-tax country before integration). Consumers in country 2 will be better off, country 2 tax collections will fall to zero, and suppliers located in country 2 will go out of business.[1]

Export costs Distribution costs tend to insulate national markets. Suppose that in addition to taxes there is an export (transportation or distribution) cost d per unit incurred by a firm from one country if it sells in the other country or by a consumer that purchases outside his/her home country. A firm located in country 2 can supply a customer in country 2 at a cost $10 + t_2$ per unit. The cost to a country 1 firm of supplying a customer in country 2 is $10 + t_2 + d$. No country 1 firm would sell in country 2 for less than that amount; to accept a lower price would mean economic losses. No country 2 consumer would pay more than $10 + t_2$, since that is the price at which country 2 firms offer the product. Firms will sell only in their own market.

If a country 2 consumer buys in country 1, the cost of a unit of output is $10 + t_1 + d$, with the distribution cost d incurred by the consumer in going from one country to the other. If $10 + t_1 + d > 10 + t_2$, consumers from the high-tax country 2 will buy in their home country. Prices net of taxes are the same, 10, in both countries. If $10 + t_1 + d < 10 + t_2$, that is, if $d < t_2 - t_1$, and county 2 does not collect the difference in taxes at the border, consumers from the high-tax country will buy in the low-tax country.[2] All sales will occur in the low-tax country. Firms in the high-tax country will go out of business.

---

[1] Since that there has been an economic union, these firms might in principle move to country 1 and continue operations from a new location. Since the industry is perfectly competitive and they are earning only a normal rate of return on their investment, they would be just as well off investing in some other perfectly competive industry.

[2] Consumer movements of this kind are common across the borders of countries where there are substantial differences in tax rates for particular products, as, for example, alcoholic beverages.

Resumé With perfectly competitive markets, we should observe that prices net of taxes are the same in national submarkets after integration. However, these are markets where performance is optimal before and after formation of an economic union. Perfect competition yields the best possible market performance, so it is not surprising that if markets are perfectly competitive, market integration brings no change in market performance. For perfectly competitive markets, market integration need not lead to important trade flows between national markets. When the perfectly competitive model does yield a prediction about the direction of trade flows, the kind of prediction—all consumers from a high-tax country going to a low-tax country to buy—strikes us as implausible. So it is, because not many real-world industries are perfectly competitive.

17.2.2 Imperfect Competition

Bertrand competition

Now let us examine another extreme case: suppose that before market integration, each country is supplied by a single price-setting firm. Once again, let the product be homogeneous.

Before integration, price is the same in both countries: the monopoly price (45, for the example of Figure 17.1). If a firm based in one country incurs no transportation or distribution costs when it supplies consumers in the other country, then price is the same in both countries after integration: the post-integration price is 10, marginal cost. Further, the model makes no prediction about trade flows.

Thus, the fact that price is the same in both countries tells us nothing about the degree of market integration, since price is the same in both countries before and after integration. The sign that market integration has affected market performance is not that price is the same in both countries after integration, but that price is lower after integration than it was before.

Keeping all other aspects of the model unchanged, suppose now that a firm in one country incurs a distribution charge d if it supplies a customer located in the other market. Each firm acts as a price-setting and profit-maximizing oligopolist, which means that the post-integration market price is slightly less than $10 + d$ in each country. Each firm will set a price just below the level that would make it profitable for the other firm to enter its market. Once again, price is the same in both countries both before and after integration. Once again, the sign of market integration is that price is lower, market performance is better, after integration. With distribution costs, the model does yield a prediction about trade flows: they will not occur.

Cournot competition

Now turn to the case of quantity-setting oligopoly. Suppose that there are two countries, $i = 1, 2$, with markets for a homogeneous product, the equation of the inverse demand curve in country i being:

$$p_i = 100 - Q_i. \tag{17.1}$$

Suppose further that before market integration, n_1 firms supply market 1 and n_2 firms supply market 2. All firms operate with the same cost function,

$$c(q) = 10q, \tag{17.2}$$

and there are no taxes or distribution costs.

If the preintegration markets are Cournot oligopolies, we can apply equations (3.42)–(3.44) to write out expressions for Cournot equilibrium output per firm, total output, and price in the two countries. These are:

$$q_{1i} = \frac{90}{n_i + 1} \qquad Q_i = \frac{n_i}{n_i + 1} 90 \qquad p_i = 10 + \frac{90}{n_i + 1}, \tag{17.3}$$

respectively, for $i = 1, 2$.

If the two countries form a single market, the equation of the aggregate inverse demand curve is:[3]

$$p = 100 - \frac{1}{2}Q. \tag{17.4}$$

Cournot equilibrium output per firm and price in the single market are:

$$q_{sm} = \frac{180}{n_1 + n_2 + 1} \qquad p_{sm} = 10 + \frac{90}{n_1 + n_2 + 1}, \tag{17.5}$$

respectively, where the subscript "sm" denotes "single market."

From (17.3) and (17.5), price falls in each country after integration:

$$p_i - p_{sm} = 90 \frac{n_j}{(n_1 + n_2 + 1)(n_i + 1)} > 0, \tag{17.6}$$

for $i, j = 1, 2$ and $i \neq j$. The reduction in price in each country is proportional to the number of firms in the other country: if there are more firms in country 1 than in country 2, then when the two firms form a single market, price falls more in country 2 than it does in country 1.

The change in output per firm after integration is:

$$q_{sm} - q_i = \frac{180}{n_1 + n_2 + 1} - \frac{90}{n_i + 1} = \frac{90[n_i - (n_j - 1)]}{(n_1 + n_2 + 1)(n_i + 1)}, \tag{17.7}$$

again for $i, j = 1, 2$ and $i \neq j$. If the number of firms is the same in both countries, then output per firm rises in both countries after formation of a single market. In this case, firms in each country produce half of total output. If there is one less firm in country 1 than in country 2, $n_1 = n_2 - 1$, output per country 1 firm does not change with formation of a single market. If $n_1 > n_2 - 1$, then before integration, each firm in country 1 was producing a relatively low output, and after integration, equilibrium output per country 1 firm increases. Corresponding conditions apply to the change in per-firm output of country 2 firms.

After integration, the quantity demanded in each country is:

$$Q_i = 100 - p = 90 \frac{n_1 + n_2}{n_1 + n_2 + 1}. \tag{17.8}$$

The combined post-integration output of country i firms is:

$$n_i q_{sm} = \frac{180 n_i}{n_1 + n_2 + 1}. \tag{17.9}$$

The difference between the quantity produced by country i firms and the quantity demanded by country i consumers in the post-integration market is:

$$n_i q_{sm} - Q_i = 90 \frac{n_i - n_j}{n_1 + n_2 + 1}. \tag{17.10}$$

---

[3] With a common market and a homogeneous product, there is one price, p. The quantities demanded in each country are $Q_1 = 100 - p$ and $Q_2 = 100 - p$, respectively. The total quantity demanded in the common market is $Q = Q_1 + Q_2 = 200 - 2p$, a demand equation that has inverse demand equation (17.4).

Holding the number of firms in each country fixed, in the post-integration market, firms in the country with more firms produce more than they are able to sell to consumers of their own country at the Cournot equilibrium price. There are therefore net exports from the country with more firms to the country with fewer firms.

A Cournot model of market integration with linear inverse demand thus yields the predictions that if markets of equal size integrate, then holding the number of firms constant, consumers will be better off, and if the number of firms in each country is different, there will net exports from the country with more firms to the country with less firms.

The consequences of market integration for market performance are of this same general type if markets are not too different in size and the nature of consumer demand in the integrating countries is roughly the same. Otherwise, it is possible for price to rise in some countries that join an integrated market.[4]

Suppose now that country 1 collects a tax t_1 on every unit sold by a country 1 firm, while country 2 collects a tax t_2 on every unit sold by a country 2 firm. The post-integration market is a Cournot oligopoly in which firms have constant but different average and marginal cost. We considered this kind of market for the duopoly case in Section 3.2.4. There we saw that higher-cost firms have smaller equilibrium sales and price-cost margins than lower-cost firms. In the present case if the number of firms is the same in each country, (and leaving the derivation of the results to Problem 17–3), equilibrium prices in the post-integration market, net of taxes, are:

$$p - t_1 = 10 + \frac{90 - t_1}{2n + 1} \qquad p - t_2 = 10 + \frac{90 - t_2}{2n + 1}. \qquad (17.11)$$

When there are regional tax differences in a single market, prices net of taxes will be different in different regions. When the number of firms is the same or approximately the same in different regions, prices after taxes are lower in the high-tax region: in an imperfectly competitive market, firms absorb part of a higher cost in the form of a lower price-cost margin, and pass only a portion of the tax on to final consumers in the form of a lower after-tax price.

Market integration, price, and market performance

With imperfectly competitive markets, there is no reason to think that market integration will lead to identical prices, or identical net prices after allowing for unit tax and transportation cost, in different regional submarkets of an economic union. To determine the impact of market integration, it is necessary to analyse the way market performance is affected by the removal of barriers to trade. When countries with similar markets and market structures integrate, price in all regions should fall after integration. This may not be the case if regions are very different in size, if regional markets were supplied by quite different numbers of firms before integration, or if demand patterns are quite different in different regional submarkets.

---

[4] Suppose a single market is formed by two countries, a large country where demand is price inelastic and a small country where demand is price elastic. Before integration, price will be high relative to marginal cost in the large country, where demand is not very sensitive to price, and price will be low relative to marginal cost in the small country, where demand is very sensitive to price. The larger the country where demand is inelastic, the more will demand in the single market resemble demand in the large country, and the more likely that price will rise in the small country after integration. See also Problem 17–2.

17.2.3 Market Integration and Market Structure

To this point, our discussion of the impact of market integration on market performance has taken supply-side market structure—the number of firms—as given. For type I, exogenous-sunk-cost industries, however, market integration will lead to a reduction in the number of firms. For such industries, there is a concentration effect of market integration, just as there is a concentration effect of international trade (Problem 16–8). For type II, endogenous-sunk-cost industries, the number of firms is unchanged as market size expands, but the endogenous quality of goods increases.

Exogenous sunk cost

Suppose there are two identical markets, each with inverse demand equation of the form (17.1). Suppose also that all firms operate with the cost function:

$$c(q) = 900 + 10q. \tag{17.12}$$

From equations (3.42)–(3.44), Cournot equilibrium profit per firm in each market, when markets are separate, is:

$$\pi = \left(\frac{90}{n+1}\right)^2 - 900. \tag{17.13}$$

It follows that before integration, the equilibrium market structure in each market is duopoly: with two firms supplying each market, economic profit per firm is zero, meaning each firm earns only a normal rate of return on investment and there is no incentive for entry or exit.

The Cournot duopoly price in each market is:

$$p = 10 + \frac{90}{3} = 40. \tag{17.14}$$

In equilibrium, each firm produces 30 units of output, and average cost is also 40,

$$\frac{900 + 10(30)}{30} = 40. \tag{17.15}$$

If the two countries form a single market, the equation of the post-integration inverse demand curve is (17.4). Equilibrium profit per firm with n firms is:

$$\pi = 2\left(\frac{90}{n+1}\right)^2 - 900. \tag{17.16}$$

Equilibrium profit per firm is zero if:

$$n = \frac{90\sqrt{2}}{\sqrt{900}} - 1 = 3.2426. \tag{17.17}$$

Taking into account that the number of firms must be an integer, the equilibrium number of firms in the integrated market is three. If three firms supply the market, all will earn a rate of return on investment that is slightly greater than normal, but if a fourth firm were to come into the market, all would make losses.

Market integration leaves consumers better off: the post-integration price is lower than the pre-integration price:

$$p = 10 + \frac{90}{3+1} = 32.5. \tag{17.18}$$

Equilibrium triopoly output per firm in the integrated market is $180/4 = 45$. Average cost is less than in the pre-integration market:

$$\frac{900 + 10(45)}{45} = 30. \tag{17.19}$$

A reduction in the number of firms is essential to obtain the full benefit of market integration. With fewer firms, each surviving firm produces more, fixed cost per firm is spread over a larger number of units of output, and average cost falls.

In practice, and with specific reference to the impact of market integration on EC market structure, the supply-side concentration effect of market integration will be most important in sectors where there are potential economies of large scale that extend to output levels sufficient to supply a market of European size. Consolidation on the supply side of such industries will reduce costs, by allowing some firms to reach an output level not available in any one member state market. If the production technology does not offer such economies of scale, or in markets where there is product differentiation based on distinctive national preferences, market integration is likely to have less of an effect in increasing supply-side seller concentration.

Endogenous sunk cost[5]

The impact of market integration on market structure is rather different if horizontal product differentiation is combined with quality differences—vertical product differentiation—that depend on firms' investments in quality. This can be modelled by generalizing the linear horizontal product differentiation model of Section 3.3.3 to allow each of n differentiated varieties to have its own reservation price. We interpret the reservation price as a measure of quality: the higher the maximum amount consumers are willing to pay for a variety, the greater its quality.

If there are N consumers, if the product differentiation parameter is $\frac{1}{2}$, and the reservation price of variety i is ρ_i, a linear inverse demand equation for such a model is:

$$p_i = \rho_i - \frac{1}{N}\left(\rho_i q_i + \frac{1}{2}\sqrt{\rho_i}\sum_{j\neq i}^{n}\sqrt{\rho_j}q_j\right), \tag{17.20}$$

where there are $i = 1, 2, \ldots, n$ varieties.

For simplicity, suppose there are no variable costs, and that all fixed costs are related to quality. Let the fixed cost of a variety of quality ρ—one may think of this as expenditures on research and development—be ρ^3.

Consider a market in which competition takes place in two stages. In the second stage, each firm produces one variety and firms compete in quantities (Cournot oligopoly), with the reservation prices of varieties being given. In the first stage, firms enter and each firm invests ρ^3 to determine the quality of its variety. Payoffs are the difference between second-stage profit and first-stage investment in quality. There are no entry costs other than the cost of quality, and firms enter until profit per firm is zero. Then one can show (Problem 17–4) that the equilibrium number of firms is 7, and that the symmetric equilibrium quality level is:

$$\rho = \frac{\sqrt{N}}{20}.$$

Remarkably, the number of firms is unrelated to the number of consumers in the market. This is an example of Sutton's lower bound on concentration in endogenous sunk cost industries. But quality rises with the number of consumers. If $N = 4{,}000{,}000$, $\rho = 100$. If two identical countries with $N = 4{,}000{,}000$ consumers each form a common market, the equilibrium number of firms remains 7, but quality ρ rises to $\sqrt{2}(100) = 141.4$. With

---

[5] See Martin (2009).

endogenous sunk cost industries, market integration improves market performance by increasing quality, not by inducing some exit.

17.3 Market Integration in Practice

The Single European Act of 1986 set the goal of removing public barriers to intra-EC trade and harmonizing standards and regulatory structures, all to be accomplished by the end of 1992. Removing barriers to trade across national borders was expected to simultaneously increase rivalry and boost economic growth while promoting economic integration.

The 1992 Maastricht Treaty set the stage for monetary integration. The eurozone came into existence on January 1, 1999, when 11 member states fixed the exchange rates of their currencies; euro currency and coins were introduced on January 1, 2002.[6] For countries in the eurozone, currency unification eliminated the risks associated with exchange rate fluctuations and the transaction costs of conversion from one currency to another. For these reasons, adoption of the euro was expected to facilitate intra-EU trade and further promote economic integration, particularly financial services and distribution in sectors previously segmented along member state lines.

Within the eurozone, adoption of a single currency should increase price transparency, with ambiguous implications for market performance. Greater price transparency for consumers should erode price differences across member states, at least for goods and services that are traded among member states. Greater transparency for producers should facilitate tacit collusion, a tendency that would be reenforced if seller concentration increases.

Market integration in general, and therefore market integration in the eurozone, raises two other red flags for competition policy. First, market integration is the erosion of barriers between hitherto segmented markets. If market segmentation is profitable, it is profitable for manufacturers to pursue strategies that maintain market segmentation, and distribution practices may be set up to accomplish this goal. Second, the integration of exogenous sunk cost industries improves market performance by triggering the exit of less efficient firms. Such firms will turn to their home state governments in search of state aid. Full realization of the microeconomic benefits of introduction of the eurozone requires competition policy vigilance against strategic market segmentation and against state aid that would have the effect of frustrating efficiency-enhancing adjustments in market structure.

17.3.1 Price Dispersion

Establishment of a single market in a legal sense does not mean that the European Union has become a single market in an economic sense. Indeed, for most consumer goods and many producer goods, transportation costs imply that even when all artificial barriers to the movements of goods and services are removed, the EC will contain distinct geographic markets. Many, perhaps most, of these markets will be imperfectly competitive. As we have seen, there is no reason in theory to expect one price to reign in imperfectly competitive and incompletely integrated markets. Yet the extent of price dispersion in EU markets remains a widely followed indicator of the progress of market integration.

Engel and Rogers (2004) examine EU price dispersion over the period 1990–2003. Their time period thus precedes Single European Act and includes the early years of the euro. Their

---

[6] Greece joined the eurozone in 2001, and was followed by Slovenia (2007), Cyprus and Malta (2008), and Slovakia (2009).

sample includes prices of traded and non-traded goods, measured at a very disaggregated level, for cities inside and outside the eurozone. They find a significant reduction in price dispersion. They also find that most of the reduction came before introduction of the euro. The narrowing of price dispersion was similar for traded and non-traded goods, suggesting that integration of input markets as well as of product markets was at work. The failure to find an incremental impact of the creation of the euro on price dispersion may indicate that earlier measures substantially increased integration before the euro came on the scene (Engel and Rogers, 2004, p. 353).

Financial markets

The European Commission expected introduction of the euro to promote financial market integration. This expectation has been realized. Lane (2006) reviews studies of EU financial-market integration and concludes that integration of bond markets was rapid and effective (2006, pp. 52–53):

> The most immediate step toward financial unification was the swift integration of the euro-area bond market after the introduction of the single currency: yield differentials across member countries fell sharply and the volume of private bond issues grew rapidly. Moreover, the level of competition among financial intermediaries for underwriting and trading activities increased markedly, leading to a reduction in transactions costs, improved market access for higher-risk issuers, and greater financial innovation ...

At the same time, some segments of EU financial markets were home to what appeared to be strategic efforts to limit market integration, with retail banking largely fragmented along member-state lines (Caprioli *et al.*, 2007).

Cars

Goldberg and Verboven (2001) analyse price dispersion in wholesale car prices for five member states (Belgium, France, Germany, Italy, and the United Kingdom) over the period 1980–1993. On average, prices were highest in the UK and Italy, and lowest in Belgium, with a difference in prices on the order of 20 per cent. A good part of this difference was due to differences in consumer substitution patterns in the different member states. In particular, the combination of a strong preference of Italian consumers for Italian cars and Fiat's dominant market position supported differentially high price-cost margins in Italy (2001, p. 842):

> [O]ur estimates suggest that when the price of a domestic car goes up, consumers are more likely to switch to another domestic car. But while in other countries the substitute car may belong to a different firm, in Italy it is very likely produced by the same firm, namely Fiat. It is this combination of home bias and a near monopoly position of the domestic firm that seems to generate market power in Italy.

Cost differences also contributed to persistent price differences across member states. Exchange rate fluctuations generated transient price differences, (2001, p. 845) "as large as 35–40% in individual years". As Goldberg and Verboven note, introduction of the euro would eliminate car price differences due to exchange rate fluctuations, not price differences due to differences in cost of domestic inputs or to differences in country-specific demand patterns. In later work (Goldberg and Verboven, 2004, p. 40), they confirm this expectation ("[W]e estimated the reduction of cross-country price differences in EMU-countries to be in the range of 1–2%. This is to be contrasted with the quite high international price differentials before the start of the EMU, amounting to an average of 25% among EMU-members . . . ") and highlight the exceptional distribution regime permitted the EU car industry (Section 24.3.6) as a factor contributing to persistent price differences in different member states.

17.3.2 Market Structure

To the extent that segmented markets in individual member states did not permit full realization of economies of scale, integration of exogenous-sunk-cost industries will improve market performance by concentrating production in the hands of a smaller number of larger, and therefore lower cost, producers.

The early years of the European Community (1959 through 1968) saw a phased elimination of tariffs on movements of goods between member states. Sleuwaegen and Yamawaki (1988) examine the impact of this elimination of tariffs on changes in market concentration between 1963 and 1978 for 47 three-digit NACE industries for five member states: Belgium, Italy, France, West Germany, and the Netherlands. They find that seller concentration increased in four of the five member states following tariff reductions; the exception was the Netherlands. This is exactly the kind of seller concentration effect of market integration that is expected in imperfectly competitive exogenous-sunk-cost markets.

Using a sample of 100 NACE three-digit manufacturing industries for 1987, Lyons *et al.* (2001) examine integration and concentration for France, Germany, Italy, and the United Kingdom. They extend Schmalensee's (1992) "type I, type II" terminology and classify each industry into one of four groups. All type II industries have endogenous sunk costs. Type IIA industries are those in which firms make important investments in advertising. Type IIR industries are those in which firms make important investments in research and development. Type IIAR industries are those in which firms make important investments in advertising and in research and development.[7] Industries in which firms lack significant investment in either advertising or research and development are type I industries.

Lyons *et al.* analyse inter-EU trade flows to produce a classification of each industry, for each member state, as having a national or an EU geographic market. In doing so, they recognize that trade flows are an imperfect indicator of market integration (2001, p. 5):

> [W]e should be aware of several reservations to using actual trade to measure integration. For example, potential trade may be a sufficient threat for effective international competition even though actual trade flows are small; moreover, given standard industrial classifications, trade may be in vertically related products, and so not directly competitive; and even if imports are in horizontally related products, they might be controlled by firms already producing in the importing country, and so might not be competitive.

But in practice, they conclude (2001, p. 5) "while these caveats should be borne in mind, it remains true that the actual intensity of intraregional trade is a strong indicator of regional integration in production. Although the threat of arbitrage may be enough to achieve regional competition without regional trade in some narrowly defined markets, this

---

[7] The threshold advertising-sales ratio and R&D-sales ratio above which advertising and R&D investment were considered "important" were around 1 per cent; for details, see Lyons *et al.* (2001), Appendix A.

Table 17.1 Industries more consistent with EU than national markets (%)

	Germany	Italy	UK	France
Type 1	85	50	46	5
Type 2A	81	44	25	0
Type 2R	100	88	88	0
Type 2AR	100	78	67	22
Overall	90	62	56	4

Source: Lyons *et al.* (2001).

is unlikely to apply to more aggregated 3-digit industries, for which actual trade will be a reasonable rank indicator of integration."

The resulting measure of the extent of industry-level integration, by member state, is described in Table 17.1, and summarized by Lyons *et al.* as follows (2001, p. 13, p. 16, footnote omitted):

> It reveals a fairly striking pattern, with German structure mapping more closely to EU market size for all except very low trade industries, and the French structure having a much closer association with its own national market size in all but a few industries. Trade intensity of just 9% is sufficient to place a German industry in an EU market, while French industries remained nationally determined at up to 65% trade.
>
> The United Kingdom and Italy display more similar, intermediate patterns, with strong differences across industry types, and trade thresholds of 31% and 25% respectively. Around half of all type 1 industries operated at the EU level, but, consistent with national advertising media, fewer type 2A industries did so. In contrast, nearly all industries in which R&D was a major competitive weapon had a structure more consistent with EU than national size. This is clearly consistent with the international applicability of much R&D activity.

For market concentration, the results support Sutton's analysis of endogenous sunk cost industries (Lyons *et al.*, 2001, p. 17):

> A very clear pattern emerges, with each of the theoretical predictions set out in Section I receiving clear support. The limiting level of concentration, as market size becomes very large, increases from type [I] to type [IIA] to type [IIR] to type [IIAR] industries. ... This supports the view that, within the class of endogenous fixed-cost industries, the scope for overhead expenditures to promote vertical differentiation is higher with R&D than with advertising, and that the two effects are cumulative. The escalation of competitive R&D spending in EU markets is stronger than that experienced in advertising, and the combined effect is to make concentration insensitive to market size.

Further, there is a relation between the nature of sunk costs and market integration. Exogenous sunk cost industries were more likely to operate in national markets. Endogenous investments in research and development were associated with integration, endogenous investments in advertising were associated with markets that are segmented along national lines (Lyons *et al.*, 2001, p. 19).

17.3.3 Intra-EU Trade

An empirical literature that comes more out of international than industrial economics examines the impact of the euro on intra-EU trade flows.[8] The results of this literature, although carried out using industry classifications at too aggregated a level to constitute meaningful industries in an economic sense, parallel those of the price dispersion literature.

Berger and Nitsch (2005) point out that formation of the eurozone was part of an integration process that can be traced back to 1948 and the Marshall Plan. They use a data set for the years 1948–2003 to test for an impact of the euro on trade flows among 11 EU member states. Controlling for the time trend in integration over this period, there is no independent significant effect of creation of the eurozone.[9]

17.3.4 Market Performance

Market power

In addition to looking at the impact of a reduction of trade barriers on seller concentration in the early EU, Sleuwaegen and Yamawaki (1988) examine the determinants of changes in member state price-cost margins. For France, West Germany, and Italy, increases in EC-wide seller concentration have a positive effect on price-cost margins, suggesting that in 1978 firms in these countries were already, to some extent, operating in an EC-wide market. Seller concentration at the EC level had an impact on price-cost margins because the geographic scope of the relevant market, in many industries, was larger than any one member state.

Bottasso and Sembenelli (2001) use data on a sample of 745 Italian firms over the period 1982–1988 to analyse the impact of the Single Market Programme on firm and market performance. For firms operating in industries where the removal of non-tariff barriers to trade could be expected to make a significant increase in competition possible, they find that estimated price-cost margins (the Lerner index of market power) range from 15.8 per cent to 19 per cent for the years 1982–1987 and from 6.6 per cent to 10.7 per cent for the years 1988–1993, a reduction that signals improved market performance. They also find an increase in productivity growth for the same firms in the years 1985–1987, which is (p. 184) "consistent with the idea of sensitive firms anticipating an ... increase in competitive pressure by reducing inefficiencies".

Wilhelmsson (2006) examines the impact of Sweden's 1995 entry into the European Union on market power using a sample of 530 firms operating in nine three-digit NACE food and beverage industries. He classifies the firms as operating in four-digit industries that either were or were not protected by noteworthy tariff and nontariff trade barriers before 1995. If EU membership has an effect on market performance, it ought to be in sectors formerly protected from international competition. This is what Wilhelmsson finds: price-cost margins in protected sectors fall relative to price-cost margins in other sectors after entry into the EU. Further, the price-cost margins of foreign-owned firms operating in Sweden fell

---

[8] See Baldwin *et al.* (2005) for a literature review.

[9] Bun and Klaassen (2007) report similar results.

after 1995, suggesting that greater competition reduced the ability of such firms to exercise market power in Swedish markets.

Productivity

Greater rivalry in imperfectly competitive markets can be expected to encourage firms to operate more efficiently. There is evidence (Section 9.4) that the entry process acts as a selection mechanism, sorting efficient entrants into markets and sorting inefficient entrants out. In the market integration context, the selection process allows the most-efficient domestic firms to expand in hitherto protected markets of trading partners, causes the least-efficient domestic firms to exit in the face of competition from the most-efficient firms based in other countries, and leaves a residual category of firms of intermediate efficiency operating only in their (more competitive) domestic markets. This selection process should work to increase productivity.

Suggestive evidence is provided by Del Gatto *et al.* (2006), who model trade flows among 11 EU member states in the year 2000, and use their estimates to simulate the productivity impact of two counterfactual scenarios. Their results suggest the importance of the selection effect (2006, p. 29):

> [A]n increase of trade barriers to prohibitive levels would have caused an average productivity loss of roughly 13 per cent, associated with a 16 per cent average increase in both prices and markups as well as a fall of 23 per cent in average profits. On the other hand, a 5 per cent reduction in trade costs, would have raised average productivity by roughly 2 per cent, leading to a 2 per cent average decreases in both prices and markups as well as a 5 per cent increase in average profits.

17.3.5 Resumé

Market integration is a process. In the EU, the process has had and continues to have the beneficial effects on market performance expected to flow from lower entry costs and increased rivalry: less market power in previously protected tradable goods sectors and greater productivity as resources are reallocated to more effective uses. These beneficial effects result from the ongoing process of market integration, more than from any one milestone (the Single Market Programme, European Monetary Union) along the way.

The strains created by resource reallocation greater political pressure for individual member states to adopt policies that would short-circuit the gains from market integration. It is to the consideration of EU policies to insulate against such short circuits that we now turn.

17.4 State Aid in the EU and EU State Aid Policy

The evidence that we have on the actual impact of EC market integration on EC market performance is that market integration is accomplishing its avowed purpose of increasing competitive pressure on firms, inducing greater efficiency gains than would otherwise take place, delivering better market performance for consumers, and making EC firms more competitive on world markets. As we have emphasized, for market integration to have its full effect in exogenous sunk cost industries, supply-side market structure will need to become more concentrated, as surviving firms take advantage of economies of large scale and as other firms go out of business. The danger is the member state governments will resist this kind of structural reorganization (Peck, 1989, pp. 290–291, footnotes omitted):

> The history of industrial policy shows that European national governments have not passively accepted the closing of firms, but rather have devised state aids to rescue some of the losers. Indeed, Europe has a tradition of rescuing national firms in trouble. ... it is state aids of various sorts that explain why Europe has 12 manufacturers of industrial boilers or 16 manufacturers of electric locomotives compared with 2 firms in each industry in the United States.

By the same token, for market integration to have its full effect in endogenous sunk cost industries, firms must upgrade the quality of their products. Particularly for industries in which endogenous sunk costs are for investment in research and development, state aid may facilitate the integration process. EC competition policy includes provisions that attempt to control member state aid to business, with the dual purposes of guarding against protectionist aid while permitting aid that promotes integration or other EU goals.[10]

17.4.1 The Extent of State Aid

Table 17.2 reports the levels of aid by EU member states in the 21st century. In 2007, state aid amounted to about one-half of one per cent of gross domestic product, for EU15 and EU27. There is a modest downward trend in total aid for the 15 members states that made up the EU at the end of 1994, with a less pronounced decline when aid by the 12 member states that joined in and after 2005 is taken into account. To place the figures in Table 17.2 in perspective, the 2009 allocations for the EU's Structural Funds and Cohesion Fund (programmes that deliver EU aid targeting many of the same aims as member state aid) were €39.1 billion and €9.3 billion, respectively (EC Commission, 2009a). The budget allocation for the EU's Common Agricultural Policy is about €53 billion per year, some 40 per cent of the EU budget.[11] Member state aid to manufacturing is thus of the same order of magnitude, although somewhat larger, than each of two of the EU's major programmes.

These figures are dwarfed by the extraordinary amounts of state aid to financial institutions in the wake of the Great Recession of 2008–2010. As of 8 April 2009, such aid included some €400 billion in rescue and restructuring aid to individual financial institutions, €300 billion in recapitalization schemes, as well as massive deposit guarantee measures that will translate into as yet undetermined aid amounts. Aid will flow to non-financial sectors of the economy under the December 2008 *Temporary Framework for state aid measures* (EC Commission, 2009c).[12]

---

[10] The United States has state aid—tax competition by local and regional governments to promote economic development, for example—but U.S. federal antitrust policy does not include provisions to vet state aid that may distort competition. In Parker *v.* Brown 317 US 341 (1943), setting out the *state action doctrine*, the U.S. Supreme Court held that Congress had not intended the Sherman Act to apply to state governments. It may be that the commerce clause of the U.S. constitution gives the federal government the authority to extend the reach of the antitrust laws to include state aid control (317 US 341 at 350), but this remains an open question.

[11] <http://ec.europa.eu/agriculture/faq/cost/index_en.htm>, accessed 24 July 2009.

[12] See the EC Commission's Spring 2009b update of the *State Aid Scoreboard*.

Table 17.2 Total state aid, million 2007 euros

	EUR 15	EU27
2000	60626.6	66287.2
2001	63903.7	68797.2
2002	64504.5	71556.7
2003	54932.3	67431.4
2004	59154.5	66957.7
2005	57950.1	64081.6
2006	59611.5	65990.3
2007	57693.5	64816.0

Source: European Commission web site.

17.4.2 Types of Aid

State aid may be classified as regional, available to firms operating in certain areas, sectoral, available to firms operating in certain industries, or horizontal, available to firms without regard to their location or sector of activity.

Horizontal aid

A market system may underinvest in innovation, relative to the socially desirable level; state aid in a variety of forms to promote innovation may address this shortfall. There are also a variety of barriers to mobility, including financial market imperfections, that affect the ability of small firms to grow from the fringe of an industry to its core of established firms. Direct subsidies to firms, indirect subsidies by way of support for venture capital markets or (for example) industrial parks may reduce transaction costs in the process of entry and growth.

These and other types of horizontal aid carry with them the danger that what is put forward as aid to correct a market failure will in fact deliver operating aid, aid that covers normal and routine expenses, to recipient firms. It is operating aid that short-circuits the supply-side concentration effect of market integration, and prevents market integration from yielding its full potential benefits.

In an integrating market, if one member state subsidizes its firms and others do not, the subsidized firms benefit and firms based in other member states are hurt. If several member states each subsidize their own firms, the result can be an outcome in which subsidies neutralize each other, so that funds are transferred from the rest of society to firms, leaving recipient firms better off but without giving any one firm a competitive advantage over its rivals.[13]

---

[13] The same effect arises with export subsidies; see Figure 16.5 and the accompanying text.

Table 17.3 Average annual horizontal EU state aid, 2002–2004 and 2005–2007, million 2007 euros; EU 27

	2002–2004	2005–2007
Regional aid	10006.1	9508.5
Environment	8735.7	12429.3
Research, development, and innovation	6031.2	6747.9
SME	6024.8	5012.1
Energy	1756.1	1093.5
Employment	1629.1	2868.3
Training	933.4	748.3
Commerce, export, and internationalization aid	912.5	627.6
Culture and heritage conservation	829.2	1291.7
Other	255.3	182.2
Natural disasters	145.5	6.3
Risk capital	93.3	330.0
Social support to individual consumers	0.7	1.6
Total Horizontal	37352.9	40847.3

Source: EC Commission web site.

Table 17.3 gives a breakdown of regional and horizontal state aid. The three major types of horizontal aid are aid in support of the environment, aid to promote research and development, and aid to small- and medium-sized firms.

Regional aid

In the *First Report on Competition Policy*, the Commission highlighted the themes that have animated policy debates about regional aid ever since (EC Commission, 1972, pp. 116–117):

> National initiatives for regional development are becoming more and more costly. Part of the aid granted at present only achieves reciprocal neutralization with unjustified profits for the benefiting enterprises as the only counterpart. In fact, this process of outbidding cannot appreciably affect the aggregate flow of investments, which, at the Community level, can be mobilized for the purpose of regional investment.

The rate of aid and the means employed no longer correspond to the relative seriousness of the situation in the various regions when assessed at Community level. The choice of the location of investments tends to be made at the expense of the less-favored regions and against the distribution of activities required by the common interest.

If regional aid attracts investment from outside to inside the EC, the net gain to the region and the net gain to the EC are the same. If regional aid attracts investment from elsewhere in the EC, the net benefit of the aid to the EC is the incremental development in the aided region, minus the reduction in development that would have taken place in other EC regions if the aid had not been granted. Aid may have positive effects on the aided region, yet have negligible or negative effects on the EC as a whole.

Sectoral aid

Some sectors of the EC economy are in secular decline and carry large amounts of excess capacity. Adjustment to equilibrium market structures in these sectors requires a substantial reduction in the number of firms, often accompanied by a reorientation of production toward specialized market segments. State aid to retrain workers that have been made redundant, or to facilitate restructuring, may be justified on social grounds, but there is a sense in which adapting business operations to changing market conditions is part of normal business operations, so that aid to sectors in secular decline has an unavoidable element of operating aid.

Economic efficiency requires that resources be transferred out of declining industries and into sectors where they can find productive use. There is always the danger that subsidies granted with the intention of easing the transfer of resources out of a declining sector will instead be used to delay inevitable and socially desirable adjustment.

To realize the greatest gains from market integration, it should be the most efficient firms that stay in the market, while less efficient firms exit. Subsidies can distort the selection function of the market by allowing less efficient subsidized firms to survive while more efficient but unsubsidized firms exit. Such outcomes reduce overall gains from formation of a single market.

Table 17.4 gives a breakdown of EU sectoral state aid. The EU, like the United States, rejects use of markets as a resource allocation mechanism in agriculture. The ongoing state aid to agriculture cannot be rationalized on the grounds given above. Coal, on the other hand, is a declining sector, and aid to that sector a legacy that dates to the European Coal and Steel Community. Historically, manufacturing received more state aid than any other sector, and Table 17.4 shows that manufacturing's share of aid has been reduced.[14]

Effectiveness

Glowicka (2006) studies cases of rescue and restructuring state aid during the years 1995–2003. Such aid might facilitate quality upgrading, or might seek to prevent the elimination of less-efficient firms that is part and parcel of the integration process. In either case, the minimum one might ask of an aid package, for it to be considered effective, is that the

---

[14] Manufacturing firms may receive regional or horizontal aid, as may firms in other sectors.

Table 17.4 Average annual sectoral EU state aid, 2002–2004 and 2005–2007, million 2007 euros; EU 27

	2002–2004	2005–2007
Agriculture	10539.9	11918.2
Coal	7753.2	3785.5
Financial services	4994.6	2526.9
Manufacturing	4369.0	1606.0
Transport	2175.7	2474.7
Other services	539.6	463.8
Other	468.0	979.1
Fisheries	455.6	361.1
Total sectoral	31295.6	21115.3

Source: EC Commission web site.

recipient firm remain in the market. Glowicka's results (Table 17.5) suggest that almost one-third of aid packages in her sample fail this elementary test, with the highest failure rates among aid recipients occurring in mining, construction, and manufacturing.

17.4.3 The Application of State Aid Policy

Like the other elements of EC competition policy, state aid control is based on the EC Treaty. The key provisions are in Article 107, which includes a basic prohibition of state aid that distorts competition and affects trade (Article 107(1)), with some mandatory exceptions (Article 107(2)), and discretionary exceptions that may be granted by the Commission (Article 107(3)).

The provision for discretionary exceptions to the Article 107(1) prohibition makes it possible for the Commission to permit various types of aid, including regional aid (107(3)(a) and (c)), aid to combat unemployment (107(a)), aid to advance important EC goals (107(b)), aid to specific economic activities (107(c)), aid to deal with serious economic disturbances (107(b)), and other aid, with authorization of the Council. Aid granted under all these categories may, directly or indirectly, be aid to business, and so affect both market performance and the process of market integration.

Table 17.5 Rescue and recovery aid cases and eventual bankruptcies, 1995–2003

Industry	State Aid Cases	Eventual Bankruptcies
Services	4	1
Finance	9	0
Transport	11	1
Electricity and Water	1	0
Trade	2	0
Construction	10	6
Manufacturing	36	12
Mining	2	2
Total	75	22

Source: Glowicka (2006).

 BOX   Article 107

1. Save as otherwise provided in this Treaty, any aid granted by a Member State or through State resources in any form whatsoever which distorts or threatens to distort competition by favouring certain undertakings or the production of certain goods shall, in so far as it affects trade between Member States, be incompatible with the common market.

2. The following shall be compatible with the common market:

   a. aid having a social character, granted to individual consumers, provided that such aid is granted without discrimination related to the origin of the products concerned;

   b. aid to make good the damage caused by natural disasters or exceptional occurrences;

   c. aid granted to the economy of certain areas of the Federal Republic of Germany affected by the division of Germany, in so far as such aid is required in order to compensate for the economic disadvantages caused by that division.

3. The following may be considered to be compatible with the common market:

   a. aid to promote the economic development of areas where the standard of living is abnormally low or where there is serious underemployment;

   b. aid to promote the execution of an important project of common European interest or to remedy a serious disturbance in the economy of a Member State;   »

>> c. aid to facilitate the development of certain economic activities or of certain economic areas, where such aid does not adversely affect trading conditions to an extent contrary to the common interest ... ;

d. aid to promote culture and heritage conservation where such aid does not affect trading conditions and competition in the Community to an extent that is contrary to the common interest;

e. such other categories of aid as may be specified by decision of the Council acting by a qualified majority on a proposal from the Commission.

Administrative framework and reform

In a June 2005 speech, EC Competition Commissioner Neelie Kroes laid out a State Aid Action Plan to simplify enforcement procedures, harmonize the standards applied to different types of aid, and highlight the analysis of the effects of state aid for compatibility with the common market (2005, p. 5):

[S]tate aid should only be used:

– when it is an appropriate instrument for meeting a well defined objective of common interest (like cohesion, public services, economic growth, or employment);

– when it creates the right incentives and is proportionate to the problem;

– and when it distorts competition to the least possible extent so that on balance it can be authorised by the Commission.

Assessing the compatibility of state aid is fundamentally about balancing the negative effects of aid on competition with its positive effects in terms of common interest.

In 2006, as part of the State Aid Action Plan, the Commission adopted a *de minimis* regulation[15] establishing that as much as €200,000 of state financial support over a three-year period would not be considered state aid and did not, therefore, have to be notified by the member state to the Commission. The rationale behind the regulation is that (Lowe, 2006b, p. 73) "De minimis aid is considered as falling outside the scope of the State aid rules, because of a presumption that it neither affects trade between Member States nor distorts competition."

In 2008, the Commission consolidated and extended a number of existing regulations in a General block exemption Regulation (GBER)[16] specifying broad categories of aid that are considered compatible without notification even if in amounts that do not fall below the *de minimis* thresholds (Ungerer, 2009, p. 6):

The common denominator of these new generation guidelines/frameworks is the use of acceptable aid intensities as proxies for a standard assessment of cases in the fields concerned, with the full detailed assessment under the refined economic approach reserved for those projects that do not fulfil the conditions of the standard assessment as defined in the guidelines.

---

[15] Commission Regulation (EC) No 1998/2006 of 15 December 2006 on the application of Articles 87 and 88 of the Treaty to *de minimis* aid OJ L 379/5 28 December 2006.

[16] Commission Regulation (EC) No 800/2008 of 6 August 2008 declaring certain categories of aid compatible with the common market in application of Articles 87 and 88 of the Treaty (General block exemption Regulation).

BOX   Boch/Noviboch

The European Commission learned that a Belgian public enterprise had invested 475 million Belgian francs (Bfr) in a local firm that manufactured ceramic sanitary ware. In April and June 1982, the Commission contacted the Belgian government to point out that the EC Treaty required prior notification before state aid payments could be made. The Belgian government did not respond to these contacts.

The Commission issued a decision finding that the investment was a state aid affecting trade between the member states and distortive of competition (OJ L 91, p. 33 9 April 1983):

> The purpose of the aid is to permit the maintenance of production capacity and this is likely to strike a particularly grave blow at conditions of competition since free market conditions would normally require the closure of the firm in question so that, in a situation in which the industry is faced with over-capacity, more efficient competitors could expand.

The Commission did not permit the aid under any of the Article 107(3) exemptions and required that it be withdrawn.

Shortly thereafter, the Commission learned that the Belgian public sector had invested 83 million Bfr in the same company. The Commission contacted the Belgian government a number of times, eventually receiving a reply that the decision to grant the aid had been taken in 1981 and was not new. The Commission found that the aid would affect trade among the member states, was incompatible with the common market, did not qualify for exemption, and should be withdrawn.

The Commission then learned that the Belgian government had invested 295.3 million Bfr in the same firm. The Belgian government confirmed the investment, but took the view that it was not state aid, being comparable to an investment decision of a private stockholder. The Commission pointed out that the firm had a series of substantial losses, so that a private investor would not have made the kind of investment undertaken by the Belgian government.

The Belgian government reported to the Commission that the aid had not been paid and that regional authorities had decided "to wind up the firm". The Commission determined that 104 million Bfr had been paid to the firm, rescue aid which permitted the firm to continue operations until its sanitary ware division was taken over by a new firm set up on behalf of the regional authorities. The Commission found the aid to be incompatible with the common market and ordered the Belgian government to recover the aid, insofar as possible given that the firm had been liquidated.

In 1985, Belgian regional authorities arranged for the original firm, Boch, to be closed. They endowed a new firm, Noviboch, with a capital investment of 400 million Belgian francs. Noviboch acquired the assets of the old firm, but not its debts.

Once again the Commission reminded the Belgian government of its treaty obligations to notify aid in advance, and the Belgian government replied that the decision to invest in the new company was not state aid. The Commission again found that the investment was state aid and that it distorted competition in the common market. Finally, however, the Commission was willing to grant an exemption for the aid (OJ L 228, 15 August 1987, p. 41):

> As to the exception in Article [107](3)(c) for aid to facilitate the development of certain economic activities or certain economic areas, Noviboch produces and markets quality ceramic sanitary ware on a fairly modest scale ... its output is currently 20 to 30% lower than that of its predecessor Boch ...   ≫

> ❯❯ ... Noviboch's operations are profitable ...
> The restructuring stemming from the winding-up of Boch has therefore contributed to the reorgani-
> zation of a Community industry suffering from surplus production capacity ...
>
> The Boch/Noviboch decisions illustrate the tenacity with which member state governments have
> sought to deliver operating aid to domestic firms, and the equal tenacity with which the Commission
> has sought to enforce the terms of the EC Treaty, terms that have been agreed to by all member
> states. At different times, members states have tried to deliver aid to private and public or formerly
> public firms in a wide range of markets: steel, shipbuilding, coal, banking, passenger airlines, and
> many others. Often the Commission has managed to block or reduce the aid; often it has not.
>
> See Commission Decisions Boch I, Boch II, Boch III, and Noviboch. Belgium's track record in state
> aid cases is not qualitatively different from that of other member states.

Proposed aid that is not *de minimis* and not covered by the GBER must be notified to the Commission for consideration of a possible Article 107(3) exemption. Only the Commission can grant such an exemption. Although the track record is improving, there is a well-established practice of member states honouring their obligation to notify the Commission of aid proposals more in the breach than the observance (see the accompanying box). In 2006, for example, 1,005 states aid cases (not including those covered by a block exemption) were examined by the Commission. Eighty-four of these, 8.4 per cent, were not notified as required by the Treaty (EC Commission, 2007, p. 6).[17]

The crux of state aid reform is the "refined economic approach" applied to state aid proposals that come before the Commission. What is envisaged is an economic evaluation of the costs and benefits of state aid. In contrast to applications of economic analysis in other areas of competition policy, some of the benefits that may flow from state aid are inherently non-economic[18] (Lowe, 2006b, p. 67, footnote omitted):

State aid may be an appropriate response to a market failure, provided its benefits outweigh its negative impact on competition and trade.

To do this balancing—traditionally dubbed the "balancing test"—it is necessary to identify—and as far as possible to measure—the positive and negative aspects of the aid. In the fields of mergers and antitrust, the negative and positive effects are assessed essentially on the basis of the benchmark of the consumer welfare standard. It is, however, not possible to transpose this consumer welfare standard directly to the world of State aid, not least because State aid can be justified on the basis of non-economic grounds such as social or regional cohesion which consumer welfare does not measure. To that extent, the correct welfare standard for State aid policy—expressed in economic terms—appears to be the social welfare of the European Union, which is equivalent to the notion of common interest found in Article 107(3) of the Treaty.

---

[17] If aid is granted without an exemption, the Commission emphasized in a 2009 Notice (Commission notice on the enforcement of state aid law by national courts OJ C85/1 9 April 2009), parties (such as firms injured by a distortion of competition) can take legal action in national courts to force recovery of illegal aid and, potentially, seek damages.

[18] These issues are touched upon in Section 2.3.3.

SUMMARY

Market integration may lead to increased trade flows between formerly independent markets. It need not lead to identical net prices in different regions, if markets are imperfectly competitive, if regional demand characteristics differ, and if the legal single market contains several geographic submarkets in an economic sense.

Market integration should lead to improved market performance: reduced price-cost margins, greater consumers' surplus, greater efficiency, more extensive exploitation of economies of scale, and more rapid technological progress.

The rivalry- and performance-enhancing effects of market integration will reduce the long-run equilibrium number of firms in many industries. Member state governments will seek to improve the chances that their native firms survive the structural readjustment process. It is by the application of state aid control that the Commission seeks to ensure that more efficient firms survive, delivering the maximum benefit from market integration.

At the end of Chapter 16 we noted a latent protectionist reflex that can lead governments to pursue short-term goals down paths that leave their own countries and their trading partners worse off in the long run. That same protectionist reflex is sometimes seen in EU member states. Part of the Commission's responsibility, in administering state aid policy, is to permit aid that serves the common interest while applying the prohibition of the Treaty to aid would be a retreat into protectionism (Kroes, 2009). In the early days of the Great Recession of 2008–2010, state aid policy proved equal to the task, making the first general use of the Article 107(3)(b) exemption for aid to deal with a "serious disturbance of the economy of a Member State" (Ungerer, 2009). In bad times as well as good, state aid control is an essential element of the process of EC market integration.

STUDY POINTS

- Market integration and market performance (Section 17.2.1, Section 17.3.1)
- Market integration and market structure (Section 17.2.3, Section 17.3.2)
- State aid and state aid control (Section 17.4)

FURTHER READING

For a discussion of the competition and competition policy implications of the euro, see Pons and Lücking (1999). For discussions of integration and the location of production within the EU, see Brülhart (2001), Midelfart-Knarvik *et al.* (2002), Tingvall (2004), and Aiginger and Davies (2004).

Martin and Valbonesi (2006) survey state aid to business. For analyses of the welfare implications of competing state aid in an integrating market, see Collie (2000), Martin and Valbonesi (2008).

PROBLEMS

Asterisks indicate advanced problems.

17–1 Evaluate the consequences of market integration using the model of Section (17.2.2), that is, two countries $i = 1,2$ each with an inverse demand curve with equation (17.1):

$$p_i = 100 - Q_i,$$

n_1 firms in market 1 and n_2 firms in market 2, and all firms operating with the cost function (17.2),

$$c(q) = 10q,$$

if country i collects a per-unit tax t_i on each unit sold within its territory.

17–2 Suppose n_1 Cournot oligopolists supply the market in country 1, where the equation of the inverse demand curve is:

$$p_1 = 100 - Q_1,$$

while n_2 different Cournot oligopolists supply the market in country 2, where the equation of the inverse demand curve is:

$$p_2 = 100 - \frac{1}{2}Q_2.$$

Compare equilibrium prices and outputs before and after market integration, holding the number of firms fixed.

17–3* Market integration, Cournot oligopoly, tax differences.) Verify (17.11).

17–4* Consider a general version of the model of Section 17.2.3. Let the inverse demand equation of variety i be:

$$p_i = \rho_i - \frac{1}{N}\left(\theta\sqrt{\rho_i}\sum_{j\neq i}^{n}\sqrt{\rho_j}q_j + \rho_i q_i\right). \tag{17.21}$$

Let marginal cost per unit of output be constant and proportional to quality, $c\rho_i$. Let the cost of developing a variety of quality i be $\varepsilon\rho^\beta$, where ε is the cost of developing a variety of quality 1. Each firm produces one variety. In the second of two stages, firms compete as Cournot oligopolists, with the quality of each variety given. In the first stage, firms enter and make investments to determine the quality of their varieties. Payoffs are the second-stage profit minus the first-stage cost of quality, and entry occurs until economic profit is zero.

Verify the results of Section 17.2.3.

U.S. ANTITRUST: BACKGROUND

18

... **nothing is said now that has not been said before.**

Terence, *The Eunuch*

18.1 Introduction

In 1865, at the end of its Civil War, the United States was politically united but economically divided into semi-autonomous regional economies. For the most part, businesses operated in local or regional geographic markets. Twenty-five years later, the U.S. was an integrated continent-wide economy. Many industries were supplied primarily by single large firms, organized in an unfamiliar legal form, the trust, or by groups of legally independent firms that coordinated actions as a cartel.

Over the course of the nineteenth century the United States' area nearly doubled, and its population more than tripled (Table 18.1). That population was much younger than is now the case. The impact of the waves of immigration that have given the United States its unique "melting pot" character is evident in the nearly 15 per cent share of the foreign-born among 1890 U.S. residents. Underlying all of those changes were the successive stages in the development of a national transportation infrastructure. The more than five-fold growth in the size of the U.S. railroad network between 1860 and 1890 is evidence of this development.

The passage of the first national U.S. antitrust law, the Sherman Act of 1890, can be understood only against the backdrop of the nineteenth-century transformation of the U.S. economy. In this chapter, we describe this transformation and the political reaction it evoked. We discuss the movements that combined to lead to adoption of the Sherman Act, its early implementation, and the passage of two companion laws, the Clayton Act and the Federal Trade Commission (FTC) Act, in 1914. For nearly 50 years, these three laws were the major elements of U.S. antitrust policy, and they remain its basis. Understanding the debates leading up to their passage is essential to understanding later controversies about their application. It is the purpose of this chapter to present the main elements of those debates.

Table 18.1 Selected U.S. descriptive statistics, 1840–2000

	Area (million sq. miles)	Population (millions)	Median age	Foreign born (%)	Railroad mileage
1840	1.79	17.1			2,818
1850				9.7	
1860	3.02	31.5	19.4	13.2	30,626
1890	3.02	62.9	22.0	14.8	166,703
2000	3.72	281.4	35.3	11.1	

Source: Bureau of the Census publications.

18.2 Roads, Canals, and Regional Railroads

18.2.1 Roads

At the dawn of the nineteenth century, the 16 United States did little more than perch on the eastern rim of the continent. Connections by land were as much theory as fact (Taylor and Neu, 1956, p. 15):

> In 1815, a great network of [humble rural] roads covered the settled portion of the country. ... they were hardly more than broad paths through the forest. In wet places they presented a line of ruts with frequent mud holes, and where dry, a powdered surface of deep dust. The largest stones and stumps were removed only so far as was absolutely necessary to permit passage. ... In the most swampy places where mud rendered passage impossible, logs were laid side by side across the road to form what were known as corduroy roads. Across the rivers a few wooden bridges had been built, but for the most part fords or ferries were the only recourse.

This primitive transportation infrastructure created a niche for businessmen who specialized in the distribution of goods between widely separated geographic markets. Traders—merchant capitalists—based in the coastal commercial centers acted as intermediaries between eastern manufacturers and distant customers. Those distant customers were themselves merchants, based in the hinterland, who in their turn acted as intermediaries between coastal merchants and final consumers. It was these frontier merchants who greased the wheels of commerce, not only arranging the shipment of goods in both directions but also providing credit and other banking services (Madison, 1986, p. 87). Semi-autonomous regional economies were kept mostly separate by high transportation costs (Schmidt, 1939; Meyer, 1983). "Trade flows" between the regional economies were the work of regional merchants.

18.2.2 Canals

There were three great waves of canal building in the first half of the nineteenth century, 1815–1834, 1834–1844, and 1844–1860 (Cranmer, 1960; Segal, 1961). The first wave included the building of the Erie Canal, begun on 4 July 1817 and completed, linking Lake Erie and New York City, on 26 October 1825. Canals became the core of the transportation network because they brought down interregional transportation costs.

The nineteenth-century United States is sometimes depicted as a golden age without extensive government involvement in the economy. But canal construction received substantial government support. Public investment covered 59 and 58.5 per cent of total canal investment in the first and third waves, 67.5 per cent in second (Cranmer, 1960, Table 3). The U.S. Army Engineers were also involved in canal construction.

Canals were viewed as what we would now call "public goods". They were expected to bring external benefits to the community as a whole, benefits that would justify their construction even if they were not profitable on a stand-alone, commercial basis (Bernard and Totten, 1823, quoted by Hill, 1957, p. 32):

> Of all the means which human ingenuity has devised for facilitating communications between different parts of a country, canals occupy, at the present day, the highest rank, and when well planned and judiciously located, they not only become sources of individual wealth; but they diffuse prosperity over extensive regions, and result in economy and advancement to the nation at large.

Such arguments were especially important in what then passed for the West, the area north of the Ohio River. Public investment in the West accounted for over 30 per cent of canal building in the second wave (compared with less than 10 per cent in the first and third wave), because it was seen as a way to promote economic development on the frontier.

Not all canal projects, alas, lived up to these high expectations. Some expectations were unrealistic. Some canals were poorly managed. Some fell prey to economic downturns.[1] The death-knell of the canal era was the arrival of a superior means of transportation, the railroad.

18.2.3 Regional Railroads

American railroad construction began in earnest in May 1830, when 13 miles of Baltimore and Ohio Railroad track came on line.[2] By 1840, a collection of regional railroad networks had been put in place. Although this network gave the appearance of providing a foundation for what might become an integrated national railroad system, that appearance was more illusion than reality. Parochial local economic interests saw the arrival of a regional railroad network as the key to their own economic prosperity (Schmidt, 1939, pp. 811–812): "The Atlantic seaboard cities—New York, Boston, Philadelphia, and Baltimore—became engaged in a desperate competition to reach the Middle West by the construction of east and west railroads." As they did so, each city worked to limit the access of the others to the network it sought to develop. Different railroads employed different track gauges. This meant that freight and passengers had to be physically transferred when passing between incompatible

---

[1] In Indiana, the Mammoth Internal Improvements Act of 1836 had the state borrow, by sale of bonds, $10 million to finance three canal projects. The financial panic of 1839 led the state to default on the bonds. This insolvency imbued Indiana with an enduring tendency toward fiscal conservatism. See Madison (1986, Chapter 5) and Wallis (2003). For references to other state defaults related to canal and railroad financing, see Goodrich (1960, pp. 273–275).

[2] The first general-purpose railroad in the world operated in England from 1825. There were tramways at U.S. mining operations from 1826 (Taylor, 1951, pp. 74–80).

lines. City governments sometimes paid local railroads to adopt a gauge that was incompatible with a connecting line, thus creating local warehousing and transshipment jobs (Taylor and Neu, 1956, p. 52).

18.3 A National Railroad System

The Civil War brought with it advances in railroad technology and the pressure of national interest strong enough to overcome regional obstructionism. By 1860, substantial Midwestern land had been cultivated. It became profitable for eastern merchants to ship U.S. grains from the Midwest to the East Coast, and to supply manufactured goods to the Midwest and beyond. Eastern merchants thus began to support westward railroad expansion. The first transcontinental railroad was completed (at Promontory, Utah) on 10 May 1869.

Westward railroad expansion received active state and federal government support. This support included extensive grants of land along railroad rights-of-way. Goodrich (1960, Chapter 5) refers to "An Era of National Subsidy" beginning with the Illinois Central Act of 1850 (a federal grant of land to support construction of a railroad system from Mobile,

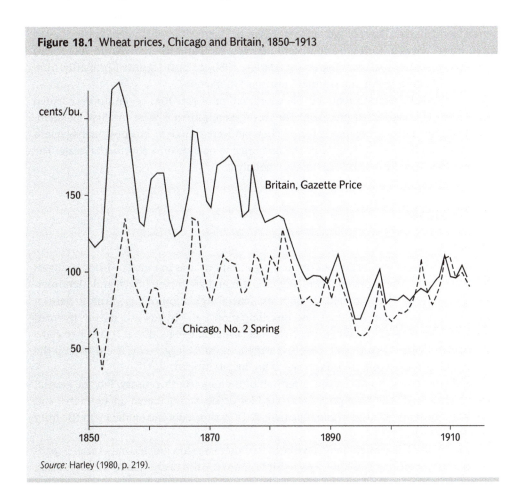

Figure 18.1 Wheat prices, Chicago and Britain, 1850–1913

Source: Harley (1980, p. 219).

Alabama to northern Illinois) and ending with an 1872 grant of land by the state of Michigan to the Chicago and Northwestern Railroad. State and federal governments funded between 25 and 30 per cent of the cost of railroad construction before the Civil War, with a much smaller but still substantial contribution in the postwar period (Goodrich, 1960, pp. 270–271). The support was justified, as support for the development of canals had been, by the argument that railroad development would bring extensive external benefits that would benefit the country as a whole, over and above any profit taken by railroad entrepreneurs.

Agricultural settlement was not merely permitted by development of a true national railroad network. It was actively encouraged by railroads: railroads running through empty prairie would carry little freight and earn little profit. To promote the traffic they would carry at a profit, railroads offered land along their rights-of-way to settlers at low prices and on easy credit terms (Farmer, 1924).

By the end of the nineteenth century, the regional autonomy of a century before had been replaced by a pattern of regional specialization (Meyer, 1983, 1989). Transportation infrastructure—primarily railroads, but including river or coastal water transport in some areas—assumed a central role.

As a result of the transportation revolution, U.S. grain markets were integrated into what became a world market. One consequence is shown in Figure 18.1, which depicts the convergence of wheat prices in Chicago and Britain between 1850 and the start World War I. This convergence, a sign of market integration, (Harley, 1980, p. 219) "resulted primarily from sharp declines in both ocean and overland transportation costs".

Efficient railroad operation required the coordination of activities on an unprecedented scale and with unprecedented precision. For this reason, railroads were the first hierarchically and administratively organized firms. They pioneered modern business management techniques (Chandler, 1965). They were the first firms to operate on a continental scale. The railroad industry was the first U.S. national oligopoly.

18.4 Backlash

18.4.1 Farm

The Grange, the first of several farmers' protest organizations, was founded in 1867. Grangers complained of falling farm prices, monopoly railroads and grain merchants, and high interest rates (Buck, 1913). They agitated for state and federal regulation of large firms in general and railroads in particular. Regional rate discrimination by railroads was deeply resented (Farmer, 1924, pp. 423–424): "When the Nebraska farmer understood that it cost two cents more on a hundred pounds to ship corn from the farm to Chicago than it did to ship the same corn from Chicago to New York, twice as far, he felt injured."

Nominal farm prices did fall in the latter half of the nineteenth century. But the general price level fell as well. Real farm prices, corrected for deflation, fluctuated up and down and were roughly constant over the whole time period. They showed some tendency to rise from 1890 onward (Higgs, 1970).

One cause of farm discontent may have been that there was too much competition in agriculture, not that there was too little competition in other parts of the economy. The steady expansion of cultivated land on the Western border kept agricultural prices near marginal cost (Atack and Passell, 1994, p. 424), which after all is what one expects in a competitive market. Further, the continual opening up of new land to the west meant that the value of cultivated land did not rise in the way that the first waves of settlers might have hoped (Marshall, 1920, p. 429).

Mayhew (1972; see also 1990) argues that late nineteenth-century U.S. farmers were aggrieved simply by the fact that they were caught up in a market system. Rather than being a self-sufficient, independent, Jeffersonian tiller of the soil, the farmer was obliged to borrow money to purchase land and other inputs on credit and then had to sell crops to repay the debts. Nostalgia for real or imagined "good old days" was a factor in rural discontent.

18.4.2 Labour

National U.S. labour unions developed along with national markets and national businesses, but the process was a halting one. The Knights of Labor were founded in 1869, just two years after the Grange. Its membership rose from 9,287 in 1879 to 729,677 in 1886. But its membership fell just as rapidly, to 74,635 in 1893, following the failure of strikes, conflicts with unions organized along craft lines, and public anxiety over its strong reformist positions.

Once again, it was the railroad industry that led the way. The first *enduring* national unions were the railroad brotherhoods, founded between 1863 and 1883.[3] It was the railroad brotherhoods that served as the model for the labour unions of the early twentieth century (Chandler, 1965, pp. 129–132).

Labour unrest was an important factor in the U.S. political climate of the late nineteenth century. The Great Railroad Strike of July 1877 was the first nationwide strike. It was triggered by a collusive agreement of major Eastern railroads to reduce wages by 10 per cent (Kolko, 1965). The strike resulted in widespread civil disorder and was the occasion for the first use of federal troops to deal with labour unrest. A perceived association of organized labour with anarchists and socialists evoked quite as much concern, in some circles, as did the rise of national firms.

18.4.3 Small Business

For many products, the first beneficiaries of the transportation revolution were wholesalers who were able to expand their scale of operation and perform their historical distribution functions on a larger stage. Particularly for consumer goods, such wholesalers were often later displaced by retail chains that built upon their direct contact with the final consumer and integrated backward into wholesaling and manufacturing.

Where the realization of economies of scale permitted, markets that had traditionally been supplied by many small producers followed the railroads and became oligopolies, dominated by a few large firms. What McFadden (1978, p. 471) writes of the late nineteenth-century U.S. barbed wire industry was characteristic of many industries:

> The constantly spreading railroad system broke down the protection of distance and created one vast market, instead of isolated regional or local markets. Small processors soon found that

---

[3] The Locomotive Engineers were founded in 1863, the Railroad Conductors in 1868, the Locomotive Firemen and Engineers in 1873, and the Railroad Trainmen in 1883 (Faulkner, 1962, p. 287).

their local markets no longer operated relatively free from competition, as the giants from the East and Midwest could, with the advent of railroads, reach into markets nearly anywhere in the continental United States.

In some sectors (for example, distilling, flour, iron and steel), the efficiency advantages of large scale were based on economies of continuous production (Chandler, 1977; James, 1983). Continuous production techniques encouraged manufacturers to integrate backward, to assure sources of supply, and forward, into wholesale and retail distribution, to ensure access to final consumer demand. In such sectors, national manufacturers displaced national wholesalers and retailers.

Railroad price discrimination in favour of large firms was also a source of competitive advantage, for the favoured firms. The rise of the Standard Oil Company, was widely (and correctly, as we see in Section 21.2.1) perceived as resulting from the discriminatorily low rail rates it received for shipping oil and refined oil products. Railroads, which themselves operated in oligopoly markets, were thus seen as the foundation of industrial monopolies.

Like the farmer and the worker, regional producers turned to the political system for relief from the competition of national rivals. In the meatpacking industry, for example, the refrigerated railroad car made it possible to ship dressed beef long distances at low cost (McCurdy, 1978, p. 643): "By combining refrigeration with mass-processing techniques and a strategic location amidst the Chicago stockyards, the 'Big Four' packers were able to ship dressed beef thousands of miles and still undersell local butchers by a substantial margin."

Local butchers understandably took exception to this development. Their trade group, the Butcher's Protective Association, proposed model state legislation that would have (McCurdy, 1978, p. 644) "[prohibited] the sale of dressed beef, mutton, or pork unless it had been inspected by state officials twenty-four hours before slaughter". The effect of this legislation would have been to keep the industrial meatpackers out of state markets (other than the state of Illinois, happy home to the city of Chicago).

Laws patterned after the Butcher's Protective Association template were adopted in Minnesota, Indiana, and Colorado. In due course, Minnesota and Indiana defended their laws before the U.S. Supreme Court. Attorneys for the meatpackers argued that if the legislation were allowed to stand, any state could exclude from its own territory any and all products of other states. The Court found[4] the state legislation to be in conflict with the national government's authority over interstate commerce,[5] and from that decision onward, industrial meatpackers were able to ply their trade where they found it profitable to do so.

In the same way, (McCurdy, 1978) when I. M. Singer & Company set up its own sewing machines sales network, states imposed peddler's license requirements on its salesmen. Such laws were struck down by the Supreme Court. The court decisions striking down protective legislation laid a legal foundation for the national U.S. market that was just as essential as the national transportation system.[6]

---

[4] Minnesota *v.* Barber 136 U.S. 313 (1890).

[5] U.S. Constitution, Article 8, Section 1, Clause 3: "Congress has the power 'To regulate Commerce ... among the several States'."

[6] These decisions correspond to the EU's *Cassis de Dijon* decision (REWE-Zentral AG. *v.* Bundesmonopolverwaltung für Branntwein [1979] ER 662; [1979] 3 CMLR 494).

18.5 Public Debate

At least from the mid 1880s onward, the debate about public policy toward business was rarely far from centre stage in the popular press. Table 18.2 reports the number of articles on trusts in periodicals, mainly in U.S. popular and professional publications, listed in a U.S. Library of Congress (1907) bibliography. It includes 30 pages of selected references to periodical publications on trusts from 1902–1907, as well as an extensive bibliography of books on the subject. Topics included monopolies and trusts,[7] cartels and pools,[8] the impact of railroads on all of the above, stockbrokers, and financial speculators (particularly in relation to the formation of trusts), patent protection (a patent being a legal form of monopoly), banks, public utilities, tariffs ("the Mother of Trusts"), and the possibility and/or advisability of government regulation of business.

Table 18.2 Number of articles on trusts in periodicals, 1871–1901

Year	Articles	Year	Articles
1871	1	1891	2
1873	1	1892	1
1874	1	1893	4
1883	1	1894	6
1884	1	1895	6
1885	2	1896	7
1886	1	1897	13
1887	8	1898	19
1888	12	1899	80
1889	18	1900	115
1890	7	1901	72

Source: U.S. Library of Congress, 1907.

---

[7] The trust was a particular legal form of business organization first employed by John D. Rockefeller and Standard Oil. The trust was soon superseded by the corporation as a way of organizing business activity.

[8] Members of a pool would divide sales (shipments, in the case of a railroad pool) or the income from sales. See, generally, Stevens (1913).

18.5.1 Competition Here, Combination There

Economists were prominently represented in the wide-ranging public discussion that took place before passage of the Sherman Antitrust Act in 1890. Sacrificing much detail, we can single out two opposing positions defended by economists One view, that of John Bates Clark, later president of the American Economic Association, who played a pivotal role in discussions of antitrust policy over the following quarter-century, was that competition could continue to be relied upon as an effective resource allocation mechanism in one type of industry, but not in a second, where merger or collusion so reduced the number of independent decision makers as to render competition ineffective (1887, pp. 60–61):

> The industrial world would seem to be dividing into two portions, in one of which, embracing the most important of all forms of production, namely, that of agriculture, the principle of individual competition continues, and produces results so beneficial to society as to justify the enthusiasm of the early economists for competition as a regulator of values and a divider of the fruits of industry. In the other economic division, embracing transportation and a majority of manufactures, the principle of combination is asserting itself . . .

For industries in this second group, Clark thought that some form of public control of business behaviour was needed (1887, p. 60).

18.5.2 Potential Competition

Another view was that no government action was needed, in any sector of the economy. The threat of potential competition would be enough to guarantee good market performance (Gunton 1888, p. 402):

> Capital always shrinks at the sight of losses, and it will run almost any risk for probable profits. Knowing this as no others do, the monopolists, so called, see very clearly that if they put their prices so high that the margin of profit is abnormal, capital will at once leave other industries and rush into theirs.

Clark and Gunton use the term "competition" in different senses. For Clark, in 1887, competition is rivalry among active firms. When firms combine, either by merger or collusion, competition is reduced, because the number of active rivals falls. For Gunton, competition includes the impact of the threat of future rivalry on the conduct of current producers. In Gunton's view, the presence of an active rival is not needed to make current producers refrain from exercising monopoly power: the fear of future rivalry is enough.

 BOX   Potential Competition and Market Performance in Pennsylvania Banking

A major difficulty in analysing the impact of *potential* competition on market performance is that it is potential. Incumbents, in the trenches of the marketplace, are aware of potential entrants in the way an outside observer (such as an economist) cannot be. Further, potential entry, like beauty, is in the eye of the beholder. It is the *threat* of entry, one might even say the perceived threat of entry, that is thought to improve market performance. If an incumbent regards entry as a possibility ⟫

⟫ even though, in some omniscient sense it is not, the incumbent may alter its behaviour. And if entry is objectively possible but an incumbent incorrectly fails to recognize that fact, we would not expect to observe an impact on the incumbent's conduct or on market performance.

Hannan (1979) analyses a market in which the identity of potential entrants was objectively identifiable by incumbents *and* outside observers. Banking regulations in the state of Pennsylvania in 1970 limited branch banking—the expansion of an existing bank by opening a new outlet—to its home country or contiguous counties. Thus, an operating bank would know that it faced potential entry only from existing banks based in immediately neighbouring counties. Further, large banks—those with more than $300 million in deposits—were more than thirty times as likely to enter a new market than were smaller banks. With a high level of confidence, an outside observer could identify large banks with home offices in counties neighbouring a regional market as the most likely potential entrants, and also have confidence that incumbents would view those same banks as the most likely potential entrants.

Controlling for a number of other market characteristics, Hannan examines the impact of market concentration and the number of potential entrants on one index of market performance, the interest rate offered by banks on passbook savings accounts. As suggested by most oligopoly models, the savings account interest rate was lower, the more concentrated the regional market. But the saving account interest rate was higher, the greater the number of potential entrants. In these markets, actual competition (lower concentration) and potential competition (a larger number of potential entrants) both improved market performance, on average.

Source: Hannan (1979).

18.6 The Sherman Act

Several states passed antitrust laws.[9] These proved largely ineffective,[10] and the focus of the debate, passed to the federal level. An initial step was a resolution offered by Senator John Sherman of Ohio and adopted by the Senate on 10 July 1888. The resolution directed the Senate's Committee of Finance to prepare proposed legislation (Kintner, 1978, Volume 1, pp. 54–55; emphasis added):

> to set aside, control, restrain, or prohibit all arrangements, contracts, agreements, trusts, or combinations between persons or corporations, made with a view, or which tend *to prevent free and full competition* in the production, manufacture, or sale of articles of domestic growth or production, or of the sale of articles imported into the United States, or which ... are designed or tend to foster monopoly or *to artificially advance the cost to the consumer* of necessary articles of human life, with such penalties and provisions ... as will tend *to preserve freedom of trade and production*, the natural competition of increasing production, the lowering of prices by such competition ...

---

[9] Seager and Gulick (1929, pp. 341–342) list 14 states and territories with antitrust provisions in their constitutions, 13 with antitrust laws.

[10] But see Pratt's (1980) discussion of the Texas antitrust law and its impact on the oil industry in that state, and Troesken (2000), who tests the hypothesis that Trusts sought passage of a Federal antitrust law as a way of finessing populist state laws.

Senate debate about what became the Sherman Antitrust Act[11] took place on seven days between 27 February and 8 April 1890.[12] There was one day (1 May 1890) of debate in the House and there were meetings of a House-Senate conference committee to iron out differences in the versions passed by the two parts of Congress. The final version of the bill was passed on 20 June 1890, and signed into law by Republican President Harrison on 2 July 1890.

The main substantive provisions of the Sherman Antitrust Act are Section 1, dealing with agreements in restraint of trade, and Section 2, dealing with monopolization. In current form, these are:

> **Section 1**: Every contract, combination in the form of trust or otherwise, or conspiracy, in restraint of trade or commerce among the several States, or with foreign nations, is declared to be illegal. Every person who shall make any contract or engage in any combination or conspiracy hereby declared to be illegal shall be deemed guilty of a felony, and, on conviction thereof, shall be punished by fine not exceeding $10,000,000 if a corporation, or, if any other person, $350,000, or by imprisonment not exceeding three years, or by both said punishments, in the discretion of the court.
>
> **Section 2**: Every person who shall monopolize, or attempt to monopolize, or combine or conspire with any other person or persons, to monopolize any part of the trade or commerce among the several States, or with foreign nations, shall be deemed guilty of a felony, and, on conviction thereof, shall be punished by fine not exceeding $10,000,000 if a corporation, or, if any other person, $350,000, or by imprisonment not exceeding three years, or by both said punishments, in the discretion of the court.

18.6.1 Senate Debates

A review of the Senate debate about the Sherman Act reveals a wide range of not-always-consistent opinions.

Reaffirm the common law

One view expressed during Senate debate was that the Sherman Act would simply put in writing the legal rules governing restraint of trade established by the common law of England and the United States.[13] The common law is the set of legal rules built up over time by the accumulation of judicial precedent, much as a stalagmite is built up by the accumulation of mineral deposits. If it really were the case that the law would do nothing other than write down the existing common law rule, one might well ask, as did Senator Kenna (21 Cong. Rec. 3151), why it was worth the trouble to enact the law. Senator Hoar's response was that while the common law applied to individual states and the commerce within them, "we

---

[11] The authorship of the Sherman Act is ambiguous. John D. Clark (1931, p. 43) writes "the law so slowly attained distinction that no one was anxious to claim authorship until so long after its enactment that participants in the legislation had forgotten what had occurred". Sherman was the author of one of several proposed antitrust laws. He was not a member of the Senate Judiciary Committee, which prepared the law that was eventually adopted. There is reason to think that Senator George F. Edmunds of Vermont was the principal author. See Edmunds (1911, pp. 801–802).

[12] Kintner (1978, p. 17, fn. 86, vol. 1). By contrast, the McKinley Tariff of 1890, signed into law on 1 October, enjoyed Senate debate, from 21 July onward (Stanwood, volume II, 1903, p. 262) "to the exclusion of almost everything else for a period of more than seven weeks". See fn. 16.

[13] English and U.S. common law diverged with the success of the American Revolution.

find the United States without any common law. The great thing that this bill does ... is to extend the common-law principles, which protected fair competition in trade in old times in England, to international and interstate commerce in the United States."[14]

The question just what was the common law rule governing restraint of trade is more complicated than might be expected, and one we take up in Section 20.2.1.

Trusts raise prices

Another view was that trusts were formed to raise prices (Sen. Turpie, 21 Cong. Rec. 138):

> a trust ... is a union or combination ... dealing in or producing a certain commodity, of the total amount of which belong to them a common stock is made with the intention of holding and selling the same at an enhanced price, by suppressing or limiting the supply and by other devices, so that the price of such trust commodity shall depend merely upon the agreement made about it by those in the combination, without reference to the cost of its production, the quantity of the article held for consumption, or the demand therefor among buyers.

Trusts prevent competition

One of Senator Sherman's concerns, in contrast, was that a trust could selectively lower prices in one area, to throttle competition, while holding prices up elsewhere (21 Cong. Rec. 2457):

> The sole object of such a combination [a trust] is to make competition impossible. It can control the market, raise or lower prices, as will best promote its selfish interests, reduce prices in a particular locality and break down competition and advance prices at will where competition does not exist. Its governing motive is to increase the profits of the parties composing it.

Savings from efficiency are not passed on to consumers in the form of lower prices

Senator Sherman also objected to trusts, even if they had efficiency advantages, because the benefits of such efficiency were kept for the trusts, not the public (21 Cong. Rec. 2460):

> It is sometimes said of these combinations that they reduce prices to the consumer by better methods of production, but all experience shows that this saving of cost goes to the pockets of the producer.

These remarks suggest concern with the income distribution effects of market power.

The law would not prohibit monopoly earned by competition on the merits

An exchange between two Senators brought forth the view that Section 2 of the Sherman Act would not touch a firm that gained a monopoly position by competing on the merits:[15]

> (Sen. Kenna, 21 Cong. Rec. 3151) Is it intended ... that if an individual engaged in trade ... , by the propriety of his conduct generally, shall pursue his calling in such a way as to monopolize a trade, his action shall be a crime under this proposed act? ...

---

[14] Seager and Gulick (1929, p. 372) write that "The debates in the Senate were unimportant except for two points". This is one of them: "In the opinion of many students the lack of what might be called 'a common law of the United States' constitutes one of the most substantial justifications for the enactment of the Sherman Act."

[15] This is the other point coming out of the Senate debates that Seager and Gulick (1929, p. 372) regard as important.

Suppose a citizen of Kentucky is dealing in shorthorn cattle and by virtue of his superior skill in that particular product it turns out that he is the only one in the United States to whom an order comes from Mexico for cattle of that stock for a considerable period, so that he is conceded to have a monopoly of that trade with Mexico; is it intended by the committee that the bill shall make that man a culprit?

(Sen. Edmunds, 21 Cong. Rec. 3151–2) It does not do anything of the kind, because in the case stated the gentleman has not any monopoly at all. He has not bought off his adversaries. He has not got the possession of all the horned cattle in the United States. He has not done anything but compete with his adversaries in trade, if he had any, to furnish the commodity for the lowest price.

High tariffs are the mother of trusts

The view was expressed that foreign competition would be one way to promote good market performance (Sen. Vest, 21 Cong. Rec. 2466–7):[16]

If the high protective tariff were removed the foreign competition would furnish, if not an absolute, certainly a most beneficial remedy to remove this evil.

This argument seems consistent with the importance attached to potential competition in public debate about the trusts.

Multiple damages will promote private enforcement

Multiple damages for successful private plaintiffs were defended as necessary to encourage small rivals to turn to the courts for relief (Sen. Sherman, 21 Cong. Rec. 2569):

No, sir, under these circumstances it is important to citizens that they should have some remedy in a court of general jurisdiction in the United States to sue for and recover the damages they have suffered. I think myself the rule of damages is too small. It provides double the damages and reasonable attorneys' fees. Very few actions will probably be brought, but the cases that will be brought will be by men of spirit, who will contest against these combinations . . .

In its final form, the Sherman Act provided for treble damages for private antitrust suits.

Combination is inevitable

Senator Stewart, who thought that the urge to combine was innate, was sceptical about the proposed legislation (21 Cong. Rec. 2564):

this whole subject is surrounded by difficulties of the gravest character. Men must unite their efforts to have any civilization at all. An individual by himself can be but a savage. Combination, co-operation, is the foundation of all civilized society. When you permit that at all, the question is where you are to stop and say there shall be no more combination.

---

[16] The 51st Congress, which passed the Sherman Act, also passed the highly protectionist McKinley Tariff of 1890. As far as congressional intent for the Sherman Act, the protectionist nature of the McKinley Tariff Act makes it difficult to ascribe to the 51st Congress an untrammeled desire to promote either the maximization of consumer welfare or the maximization of net social welfare. See Taussig (1931, Chapter 5).

Small business should be protected

Some Senators conceived of competition in the sense of structure, and wanted the law to protect small businessmen (Sen. George, 21 Cong. Rec. 2598):

It is a sad thought to the philanthropist that the present system of production and of exchange is having that tendency which is sure at some not very distant day to crush out all small men, all small capitalists, all small enterprises. This is being done now. We find everywhere over our land the wrecks of small, independent enterprises, thrown in our pathway. So now the American Congress and the American people are brought face to face with this sad, this great problem: Is production, is trade, to be taken away from the great mass of the people and concentrated in the hands of a few men who, I am obliged to add, by the policies pursued by our Government, have been enabled to aggregate to themselves large, enormous fortunes?

A law against large business will also apply to organized labour and small business

Others warned that the Sherman Act would be applied to labour unions and to associations of small businesses, as well as (or instead of) the trusts (Sen. Stewart, 21 Cong. Rec. 2565):

If you say there shall be no combination the tendency of which shall put up prices, how far would that reach? It would reach to nearly every transaction in life and would be particularly oppressive upon the struggling masses who are making combinations to resist accumulated wealth. Accumulated wealth has the power to prosecute, and if the laborers combine in any form to protect themselves there will be means found of prosecuting them.

If small traders combine together to meet some great trust so as to enable them to carry on their business, the power will be in the hands of the great trust ... This scheme seems to me to put in the hands of accumulated capital the power to have all associations that can possibly be rivals prosecuted ...

During the debate, Senator Sherman asserted that the law would not apply to labour unions. As the Supreme Court later interpreted the law, he was incorrect (Kersch, 2006).

Failure to deal with trusts will lead to political unrest

Senator Sherman argued that the economic power of trusts was comparable to that of a king, and therefore inconsistent with democratic government (21 Cong. Rec. 2457):

If the concentered powers of this combination are intrusted to a single man, it is a kingly prerogative, inconsistent with our form of government, and should be subject to the strong resistance of the State and national authorities. If anything is wrong this is wrong. If we will not endure a king as a political power we should not endure a king over the production, transportation, and sale of any of the necessaries of life. If we would not submit to an emperor we should not submit to an autocrat of trade, with power to prevent competition and to fix the price of any commodity.

Similarly, Sen. Vest argued that if the government did not control the trusts, the result could be political unrest (21 Cong. Rec. 2463):[17]

[17] Galambos (1968) argues that passage of the Sherman Act was a factor in calming the political unrest of the time.

I appreciate fully the significance of the remark of the Senator from Ohio [Senator Sherman] when he says that unless relief [from trusts] is given, to use the language of Mr. Jefferson, "worse will ensue."

Resumé

Writing much after the passage of the Sherman Act, Richard Hofstadter wrote ([1965] 1979, pp. 199–200):

[T]he goals of antitrust were of three kinds. The first were economic; the classical model of competition confirmed the belief that the maximum of economic efficiency would be produced by competition, and at least some members of Congress must have been under the spell of this intellectually elegant model, insofar as they were able to formulate their economic intentions in abstract terms. The second class of goals was political; the antitrust principle was intended to block private accumulations of power and protect democratic government. The third was social and moral; the competitive process was believed to be a kind of disciplinary machinery for the development of character, and the competitiveness of the people—the fundamental stimulus to national morale—was believed to need protection.

It is certainly correct that one class of goals of the Sherman Act was economic. But despite the frequency with which Hofstadter's remark is quoted, there is no evidence in the Congressional debates that these economic goals were conceived of in terms of the intellectually elegant model of perfect competition, which at that time did not exist.[18] Hofstadter himself writes ([1965] 1979, p. 200) "The Sherman Act was framed and debated in the pre-expert era, when economists as a professional group were not directly consulted by the legislators." Thorelli (1955, p. 567, emphasis added) suggests that the failure to consult economists was deliberate: "in accordance with contemporary legislative custom, *rooted in traditional American distrust of experts*, Congress considered one antimonopoly bill after another without ever asking for the advice of" professional political economists.

Although the word "competition" does not appear in the Sherman Act, the Congress that passed the Sherman Act sought to promote competition. Congress sought to promote competition in the sense of independent decision-making. It did this with Section 1 of the Sherman Act, which raises the cost (expected fines and possible criminal punishment) of collusion. Congress sought to promote competition in the sense of rivalry. With Section 2 of the Sherman Act, some members of Congress certainly wished to promote rivalry by maintaining opportunities for actual and potential rivals. Section 2 aimed to prohibit particular types of single-firm conduct that were thought to restrict actual or potential competition by firms that would otherwise be efficient enough to meet the test of the marketplace. But also, with Section 2 some members of Congress wished to promote rivalry by facilitating the survival of independent rivals, whether or not those rivals were efficient enough to survive on their own. This approach conceives of competition in the sense of market structure, not firm conduct or market performance.

There is clear support in the Senate for the political, social, and moral purposes that Hofstadter identifies. In short (Letwin, 1956, p. 222):

---

[18] Posner (1987, p. 210) comments that "... no one in 1890 understood the economic concept of efficiency; it hadn't been developed yet".

the Sherman Act reflects not only the uncertainty present in every general law because its authors cannot foresee the particular cases that will arise, but also the ambiguity that colors many democratic laws because the authors cannot completely resolve the divergent opinions and cross purposes that call it forth.

Much of the long development of the legal interpretation of the Sherman Act (and later companion antitrust laws) involved courts coming to grips with the reality that not all the multiple goals of the antitrust laws were mutually consistent, and sorting out which goals would survive and which would not.

18.6.2 Much Ado About Nothing?

Nothing much happened in the immediate aftermath of the passage of the Sherman Act. The U.S. Department of Justice brought six antitrust actions under the administration that signed the Sherman Act into law, seven in the four years of the following Cleveland administration, and three in the four years of the following McKinley administration (see Figure 18.2[19]). Despite the lure of treble damages, private antitrust suits did not materialize.[20]

Weak enforcement

The slow start of Sherman Antitrust Act enforcement was partly due to a lack of resources (Letwin, 1965, p. 103):[21] "In 1890 the Department of Justice occupied the upper stories of a bank building, employed eighty persons, of whom eighteen were lawyers, and had an increasingly heavy load of routine work."

---

[19] For the years 1890–1997, Figure 18.2 is based on the count of U.S. Department of Justice antitrust actions reported by Gallo *et al.* (2000). They treat multiple antitrust actions stemming from a single course of conduct as a single antitrust action (as does the count presented here for the years 1998–2006). See Gallo *et al.* (2000, pp. 76–81) for further discussion.

[20] Appendix I to U.S. Congress (1966) lists ten private antitrust actions that produced reported decisions between 1892 (the first) and 1900. There were other cases that did not lead to reported decisions (Posner, 1966, p. 371). On the whole, the early private cases for which decisions are available are not inspiring. Some arise from disputes among members of trusts. Some mirror the ambiguity of early public cases, appealing to *E.C. Knight* (see immediately below) to justify a conclusion that there was no Sherman Act violation, or later to *Addyston Pipe and Steel* (Section 20.2.1) to justify a conclusion that there was. One private case was dismissed because it challenged a state-imposed monopoly (of alcoholic beverages, in South Carolina), and state action is not within the reach of the Sherman Act. Two cases were private actions that followed *Addyston Pipe & Steel*. One case was dismissed by the appeals court on the ground that the basis for the damages that had been awarded at trial was speculative, and explicitly avoiding any finding on the merits of the antitrust claim (which was made by an ex-member of a cartel against his former colleagues). The cases are Bishop *v.* American Preservers Co. 51 F. 272 (1892), 105 F. 845 (1900); Dueber Watch Case Mfg. Co. *v.* E. Howard Watch and Clock Co. *et al.* 55 F. 851 (1893), 66 F. 637 (1895); Lowenstein *v.* Evans 69 F. 908 (1895); Prescott and Arizona Central R.R. Co. *v.* Atchison, Topeka and Sante Fe R.R. Co. 73 F. 438 (1896); Block *et al.* v. Standard Distilling and Distributing Co. 95 F. 978 (1899); Lowry *v.* Tile, Mantel and Grate Assoc. *et al.* 98 F. 817 (1899), 106 F. 38 (1900), 115 F. 2 (1902), 193 U.S. 38 (1904); City of Atlanta *v.* Chattanooga Foundry and Pipe Co. 101 F. 900 (1900), 127 F. 23 (1903), 203 U.S. 390 (1906); Gibbs *v.* McNeeley *et al.* 102 F. 594 (1900), 107 F. 210 (1901), 118 F. 120 (1902); Hartman Central Coal & Coke Co. *et al.* v. Hartman 111 F. 96 (1901); and Manion *v.* Chattanooga Foundry and Pipe Co. 101 F. 900 (1900).

[21] Dewey (1959, p. 213) writes that U.S. *v.* Greenhut 50 Fed 469 (D.Mass, 1892) was initially thrown out of court because of a typing error in the indictment. In a letter to the Attorney General, the federal attorney with responsibility for the case wrote (Dewey, 1959, p. 213, fn. 2) "The amount of work which we have to do in this office, with the really insufficient clerical force renders us at times liable to some slip of this kind ... "

Figure 18.2 U.S. Department of Justice antitrust cases, by presidential term

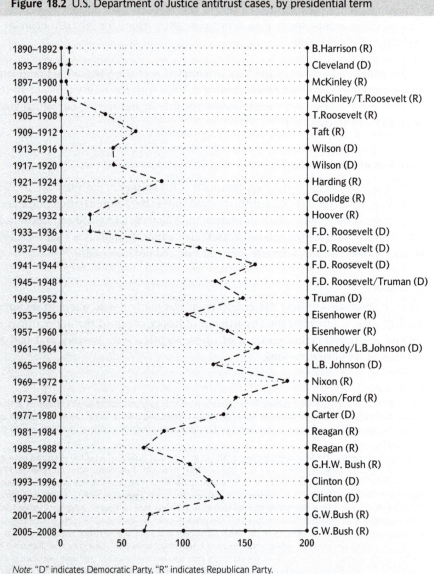

Note: "D" indicates Democratic Party, "R" indicates Republican Party.
Source for underlying data: Gallo *et al*. (2000, Table II), 1890–1997; own tabulations from CCH Trade Cases, 1998–2006. The count for 2005–2006 is doubled to obtain the projected count for 2005–2008.

In part, the slow start was due to poorly structured incentives. Before 1896, U.S. District Attorneys received the majority of their income in the form of fees based on the number of cases pursued. This meant they had little reason to take up time-consuming and resource-intensive antitrust cases—to do so would reduce their expected income. It was only in fiscal year 1904 that funding was authorized for what became the Antitrust Division of the U.S. Department of Justice (Bringhurst, 1978, p. 118, p. 123).

Figure 18.3 "A forceful series of cartoons by F. Opper in the New York *Journal*, that had much influence, pictured President McKinley as the child of the trusts, and Mark Hanna as 'Nursie.' After Roosevelt was nominated for Vice-President he was introduced into the cartoons as a playmate of McKinley" (Sullivan, 1927, p. 374)

"YES, WILLIE, HERE IS A NICE LITTLE BOY NURSIE AND I HAVE FOUND TO PLAY WITH YOU. TREAT HIM KINDLY, AS HE IS VERY TIMID AND RETIRING."

Further, the first Attorney General of the Cleveland administration was sceptical about the possible effectiveness of the Sherman Act.[22] The next President, William McKinley, was popularly perceived as being under the influence of his adviser Senator Mark Hanna, who in turn was thought to work hand in glove with "The Trusts" (Figure 18.3). The record does not obviously contradict this impression.[23]

Restrictive interpretation

In part the slow start of the Sherman Act was due to restrictive judicial interpretation. The first antitrust case to reach the Supreme Court was the 1895 *Sugar Trust* or *E.C. Knight* case.[24] The issue was the acquisition by a Philadelphia-based trust with about 65 per cent of U.S. sugar-refining capacity of four smaller Pennsylvania companies with a combined share of about 33 per cent of U.S. refining capacity.[25] A merger forming a firm with a 98 per cent market share might seem to conflict with the Sherman Act Section 2 prohibition of monopolization. But the U.S. Supreme Court was unwilling to find a violation of Section 2 of the Sherman Act. The logic of the decision was that what was monopolized by the merger was manufacturing activity, and this occurred within a single state, while the commerce clause of the U.S. Constitution gives Congress the power to regulate *interstate* commerce. For the Supreme Court, the monopolization of manufacturing activity was not monopolization of interstate commerce, against which the Sherman Act was aimed.[26] On this reading of the law, the Sherman Act applied to the interstate distribution of manufactured goods but not to manufacturing, at least, not to manufacturing that took place within a single state. This interpretation was reversed in a 1904 decision,[27] but until that reversal took place, contemporaries regarded Section 2 of the Sherman Act as a dead letter (Goodnow, 1897, pp. 237–245; Seager and Gulick, 1929, p. 377). In the 626-page published proceedings of an 1899 conference on trusts, the Sherman Act is mentioned no more than five or six times, mostly in passing. It is a main subject of only two contributions. One of these (Yellott, 1900), argues that the *Sugar Trust* decision had rendered the Sherman Act ineffective. The other (Tuttle, 1900) notes that the Sherman Act had been more vigorously applied to organized labour than to business.

The First Sherman Act Case

As cartels go, if the Nashville Coal Exchange was distinctive in any way, it was for being typical. It shared many of the characteristics of the cartels that we encountered in Chapter 6. ⯈⯈

---

[22] He later came to feel that the rationale for the Sherman Act was completely mistaken (Letwin, 1965, p. 120).

[23] Seager (1911, p. 584). Johnson (1959, p. 571) writes of "the acquiescent attitude of the McKinley administration" toward business.

[24] U.S. *v.* E.C. Knight Co. 156 U.S. 1 (1895).

[25] For discussion of the events leading up to this acquisition, see Section 7.3.2.

[26] Taft (1914, pp. 83–84) points out that the government did not argue that the acquisitions were part of a scheme to monopolize interstate commerce, "a fact that, it would seem, might have been easy to establish". He suggests that the outcome would have been different if the government's case had been presented in this way.

[27] Northern Securities Co. *v.* U.S. 193 U.S. 197 (1904). See Section 20.2.1.

⟩⟩ It was formed during a business downturn. Much empirical evidence suggests, although there are theoretical arguments both for and against the proposition, that cartels are "children of hard times".

Its members were Kentucky coal miners and Nashville wholesale coal dealers, bound together by mutual exclusive-dealing arrangements for traffic in domestic coal to the Nashville market. An earlier (horizontal) coal dealer cartel had failed. The vertical arrangement had more success. Coal dealers in essence policed a mine-owner's cartel and were rewarded with lower prices than those offered to wholesalers that were not members of the Exchange; this raised rivals' costs (Section 7.4) and discouraged entry at the wholesale level. Similar dynamics were at work in the U.S. oil refining and sugar refining industries at about the same time. As Siegfried and Mahony (1990, fn. 46) point out, Levy (1927) discusses such a scheme for the supply of coal to London in the early decades of the nineteenth century. Despite U.S. judicial scepticism (Chapter 24), restrictive vertical contracts have often been a bulwark of the successful exercise of market power.

The Exchange fixed prices, by two-thirds vote, at a monthly meeting. Members who did not adhere to the cartel prices were subject to increasing fines for two offences, expulsion for a third. Such fines reduce the profit to be gained by cheating on the cartel; expulsion would carry with it loss of the funds held by the Exchange. One mine withdrew from the Exchange after it was found to have violated the agreement. A few mines supplying the Nashville market operated outside the cartel. They operated near capacity. The Exchange thus acted as a dominant collusive supplier with a competitive fringe, exercising such control over prices as it was able, taking fringe supply into account (Section 7.2.1).

Siegfried and Mahony (1990) estimate that the cartel was profitable. The same mines supplied Memphis and Nashville at "virtually identical" delivery cost; prices in Nashville were more than 20 per cent higher than those in Memphis. Nashville wholesalers paid mine owners 5 cents per bushel of coal, reported 9 cents expenses per bushel, and resold for 16 cents a bushel, leaving an accounting profit rate of 12.5 per cent on sales.

It is through the diligence of John Ruhm, U.S. Attorney for Nashville, Tennessee, that records of the Nashville Coal Exchange's activities come down to posterity. The defences put forward by the Exchange were harbingers of things to come. Although the mines were located in one state and the wholesaler dealers in another, the Exchange argued that its activities did not involve interstate commerce. The sale of coal at the mines to the dealers took place entirely within Kentucky, and if those transactions were to be subject to legal examination, it should be by Kentucky courts. Similarly, the commercial activities of the wholesale dealers took place entirely within Tennessee, and fell under the supervision, if of anyone, of Tennessee courts. The Circuit Court for the Middle District of Tennessee was not convinced by this argument (but see our discussion of the Supreme Court's later *E.C. Knight* decision). Judge Key declined to consider the constitutionality of the Sherman Act, on the ground that such a weighty question deserved to be heard by a higher court. After reviewing the nature of the agreement, he concluded that (46 F. 432 at 436) "It seems to me that the purposes and intentions of the association could hardly have been more successfully framed to fall within the provisions of the [Sherman Act]." He found the Exchange in violation of Sections 1 and 2 of the Sherman Act, and enjoined its continued operation.

The Exchange did not appeal the Circuit Court decision. Details of the impact of the decision on market performance are lacking. The coal industry, burdened by high sunk costs and declining ⟩⟩

> ⟫ demand, was later no stranger to antitrust (Section 20.2.1) or unhappy regulation (Fisher and James, 1955).
>
> *Sources:* Siegfried and Mahony (1990); see also U.S. v. Jellico Mountain Coal & Coke Co. *et al.* 46 F. 432 (1891), Letwin (1965, pp. 106–107).

18.7 The Progressive Movement, the Clayton Act and the FTC Act

18.7.1 Continued Debate

Public debate on the issues that had led to passage of the Sherman Act accelerated in the late 1890s (see Table 18.2), under the influence of the apparent impotence of the Sherman Act. The entire range of opinions that had been present in the earlier debate—advocating government ownership of all means of production, government ownership of public utility industries, antitrust-type policies, reliance on potential competition—continued to be represented (Cooley and Cooley, 1897, p. 81).

Publicity

The idea of publicity as a way of dealing with trusts and with speculative stock-market abuses made its appearance.[28] Publicity was expected to combat corrupt financial practices, and also to alert actual or potential competitors to profit opportunities, so preventing such opportunities from arising in the first place (Jenks, 1900, pp. 222–224). Publicity was endorsed by Theodore Roosevelt while he was Governor of New York state.[29] As President, Roosevelt took essentially the same position in a December 1901 speech before Congress (Griffith, 1919/1971, pp. 168–169). In 1903, the Roosevelt administration established the Bureau of Corporations, which had the responsibility of gathering and publicizing information about industrial practices.

Theodore Roosevelt

President Roosevelt, as it turned out, had a personality quite different from that depicted in Figure 18.3. He reinvigorated enforcement of the Sherman Act (Figure 18.2) and had a popular image as a trustbuster. His actual position on trusts, however, was more complex. He accepted large business as a natural consequence of industrial development. He did not want to smash big business. He wanted the federal government to establish guidelines for business behavior and punish firms that transgressed those guidelines.[30]

---

[28] This discussion follows Martin (1998a).

[29] See his speech of January 1900 to the New York state legislature, portions of which are quoted by Thorelli (1955, p. 415).

[30] See his December 1906 speech to Congress, quoted by Griffith (1919/1971, p. 463). As Finley Peter Dunne's fictional bartender, Mr. Dooley, described Roosevelt's approach (quoted in Sullivan, 1940, p. 411): "'Th' trusts,' says he, 'are heejous monsthers built up be th' inlightened intherprise iv th' men that have done so much to advance progress in our beloved counthry,' he says. 'On wan hand I wud stamp thim undher fut; on th' other hand not so fast.'"

Figure 18.4 "Bad Trusts", cartoon by Clifford Berryman, c. 1907

In 1908, the Roosevelt Administration supported a bill that would have amended the Sherman Act to give the President substantial discretion in decisions to prosecute "bad trusts" while allowing "good trusts" to go about their business (Figure 18.4[31]). Uncertainty about the standards that would be applied to place firms in one category or the other aroused enough opposition in the business community so that the bill did not become law.[32]

---

[31] Contemporary readers would have seen in the cartoon an allusion to a widely publicized November 1902 episode in which Roosevelt, on a bear hunt in Mississippi, refused (Sullivan, 1940, p. 445, fn. 2) "to shoot a small bear that had been brought into camp for him to kill", popular enthusiasm about the event leading to the marketing of the "Teddy Bear".

[32] For accounts of this episode, see Johnson (1961) or Weinstein (1968, Chapter 3).

18.7.2 The Progressive Movement

Strengthening the antitrust laws became a major theme of the Progressive Movement.[33] The Progressive Movement was the early twentieth-century successor to the Populist movement of the late nineteenth century. It reached a high-water mark with the 1912 presidential campaign. The candidates in this election were the progressive ex-president Theodore Roosevelt (Bull Moose party), the progressive New Jersey governor Woodrow Wilson (Democrat), incumbent president William Howard Taft (Republican) and Eugene V. Debs (Socialist).

The Progressive Movement accepted that the development of methods of mass production and distribution meant the day of small business was done in many sectors of the economy. It did not object to size as such, and proposed reliance on regulation to ensure good performance. Although the positions of Roosevelt, Wilson, and Taft on public policy toward business differed in detail, they were broadly similar, and all similar to the positions Roosevelt had held as President.

Thus Roosevelt wrote (1913, p. 616, italics in original)[34] "[N]othing of importance is gained by breaking up a huge inter-State and international industrial organization *which has not offended otherwise than by its size*, into a number of small concerns without any attempt to regulate the way in which those concerns as a whole shall do business." This is very much like a position taken by Taft in a 1907 speech (Burton and Campbell, 2001, p. 208): "There must ... be an element of duress in the conduct of its business toward the customers in the trade and its competitors before a mere aggregation of plants becomes an unlawful monopoly." And Wilson wrote cryptically (1913, p. 180) "I am for big business, and I am against the trusts."

18.7.3 The Clayton Act and the FTC Act

Woodrow Wilson won the 1912 election.[35] In 1914 President Wilson signed into law the Clayton Act and the Federal Trade Commission Act, companion pieces of legislation that constitute, with the Sherman Act, the basic antitrust laws of the United States.

Economists' input

Economists made no contribution to the writing of the Sherman Act. They were relatively unenthusiastic about it during its early years of lackluster enforcement. In contrast, they were directly involved in preparing the Clayton Act and the FTC Act.

In 1887, John Bates Clark thought that some form of government regulation was needed for markets where efficient operation dictated large firm size, but he was not prepared to commit himself about the form such regulation should take. By the end of the nineteenth century, he had come to the position that the positive role of government should take the form of ensuring the opportunity for potential competition to become real competition, if

---

[33] Other themes, not without interest or importance but outside our topic, included workplace safety, consumer protection, child labour laws, compulsory education for children, and civil rights.

[34] Roosevelt rejected regulation by means of antitrust law on the ground that attempts to administer such a policy through the courts would not work (Roosevelt, 1913, pp. 618–619). He also rejected the insinuation that a call for regulation was a socialist approach to economic management (Roosevelt, 1913, p. 613).

[35] Wilson and Roosevelt together took 69.2 per cent of the popular vote. Roosevelt's 27.4 per cent exceeded Taft's 23.2 per cent. Debs received 6 per cent of the popular vote. The remainder went to splinter candidates. Wilson received 435 votes in the electoral college, with 88 going to Roosevelt and 8 to Taft.

real competition would be profitable. Absent government protection of potential competition, there were simply too many ways a trust could scuttle attempts to enter its market. With government protection of potential competition, the only way a trust could block individual attempts at entry would be to hold prices down, making entry unprofitable in general. In this way, benefits (if any) of trust efficiency would be passed on to the final consumer in the form of low prices.[36]

Clark (1900a, p. 408) argued against price discrimination, predatory pricing, and contracts between large manufacturers and distributors that restricted the access of rivals to wholesale or retail outlets. Prohibiting such practices, he felt, would protect the ability of efficient rivals to compete, thus ensuring good market performance.

In 1911, John Bates Clark and Jeremiah Jenks were members of a four-person committee that drafted preliminary versions of the Clayton Act and the FTC Act.[37] The provisions of the Clayton Act closely followed the approach Clark had advocated for more than a decade.[38]

FTC Act

The Clayton Act and the FTC Act sought to perfect the antitrust policy first implemented in the Sherman Act. The FTC Act created the Federal Trade Commission, an independent government agency, to continue the information-gathering and -disseminating activities of the Bureau of Corporations. In addition to its publicity-related duties, the five-member Federal Trade Commission was charged with enforcing the antitrust laws. It had a mandate to enforce the very general prohibition of Section 5 of the FTC Act:

> Unfair methods of competition in or affecting commerce, and unfair or deceptive acts or practices in or affecting commerce, are hereby declared unlawful.

As to just what constitutes an unfair method of competition, a Senate committee report wrote that[39] "It is believed that the term 'unfair competition' has a legal significance which can be enforced by the commission and the courts, and that it is no more difficult to determine what is unfair competition than it is to determine what is a reasonable rate or what is an unjust discrimination."

It is probably correct to write that it is no more difficult to determine what is unfair competition than it is to determine what is a reasonable railroad rate or an unjust price discrimination. The fullness of time has made clear, however, that determining the reasonableness of a price or the justice of a price discrimination is far from straightforward. The same holds for determining whether a particular type of competition is or is not fair, in the sense of the

---

[36] John Bates Clark (1897; 1902, p. 14; 1900a, b, 1904). See also Dorfman (1949, Volume 3, p. 203; 1971, pp. 10–13).

[37] Kolko (1963, pp. 258–259), Weinstein (1968, p. 88), Sklar (1988, pp. 288–290); Fiorito and Henry (2005). The committee was set up by National Civic Federation, a public interest group based in Chicago.

[38] For details on the legislative process, see David Dale Martin (1959, Chapter 2), Kintner (1978, Volume II, pp. 989–1023, Volume V, pp. 3701–3708), Scherer (1990), Winerman (2003).

[39] *Federal Trade Commission, Report to Accompany H.R. 15613*, by Mr. Newlands, U.S. Committee on Interstate Commerce, 63d Cong., 2d sess., S. Rept. 597, quoted by David Dale Martin (1959, p. 55). See Rublee (1926) for background on the choice of this formulation, Stevens (1914) for a contemporary analysis of what constituted unfair competition.

antitrust laws. The Supreme Court has ruled[40] that actions that violate the Sherman Act also violate the FTC Act Section 5 prohibition of unfair methods of competition.

The Clayton Act

Where the FTC Act is general, the Clayton Act[41] is specific. It identifies practices that are to be considered illegal under the antitrust laws, clarifies nuances of congressional intent that seem to have been misunderstood by courts, and relies on public and private enforcement mechanisms to accomplish the desired effects. The various clauses of the Clayton Act provide that:[42]

- **Section 2(a)**: price discrimination is unlawful . . . ;
- **Section 3**: tying, exclusive dealing, and requirements contracts are unlawful;
- **Section 4(a)**: plaintiffs in private antitrust suits, if successful, may recover three times the amount of the damages suffered, as well as the cost of bringing the suit (including a reasonable legal fee);
- **Section 5(a):** a plaintiff in a private suit may use a finding in a public case as evidence in a private antitrust suit (but not a consent decree or the fact that a case has been settled);
- **Section 6**: antitrust laws do not apply to organized labour;
- **Section 7**: mergers carried out by manipulations of financial shares are illegal "where in any line of commerce or in any activity affecting commerce in any section of the country, the effect of such acquisition may be substantially to lessen competition, or to tend to create a monopoly".

The prohibitions of the specific practices named in Section 2(a) and Section (3) are subject to a number of qualifications. In particular, the Section 2(a) prohibition of price discrimination applies "where the effect of such discrimination may be substantially to lessen competition or tend to create a monopoly in any line of commerce, or to injure, destroy, or prevent competition with any person who either grants or knowingly receives the benefit of such discrimination, or with customers of either of them", and similarly for Section 3.

Section 4(a) allows for treble damages in private antitrust cases under the Clayton Act, as under the Sherman Act, to encourage private enforcement. Section 5(a) also encourages private antitrust cases. It provides that if the government obtains a conviction for an antitrust violation under the Clayton Act, a private antitrust plaintiff may rely on that finding in its own suit to establish that a violation of the antitrust laws has occurred.[43] One effect of this provision is to encourage firms that are defendants in a government antitrust case to agree to a consent decree, since consent decrees cannot be relied upon by plaintiffs in private antitrust suits.

---

[40] FTC *v.* Cement Institute, 333 U.S. 633 (1948).

[41] Young (1915a, p. 305) wrote that "the Clayton act, with its twenty-six sections and its heterogeneous subject-matter, is a particularly formless and unorganized piece of legislation".

[42] The price-discrimination provision, Section 2, was amended by the Robinson-Patman Act of 1936. Section 7 of the Clayton Act was amended in 1950 to cover mergers carried out by means of acquisition of physical capital.

[43] To recover treble damages, a private plaintiff would need to establish that it had been injured by the antitrust violation. It would also need to establish the amount by which it had been injured.

Section 6 reverses a number of court decisions that had applied the Sherman Act to labour unions.

Section 7 was little discussed in congressional debate. When it was, it was usually described as a "holding company" provision.[44] Contemporary commentators thought that this provision simply duplicated that interpretation that had been given to the Sherman Act, and expected it to be little used (Stevens, 1915; Young, 1915b).

It was understood at the time that the law did not attack mergers in general, but rather mergers carried out by means of this one particular technique:[45]

> It is no answer ... to say that the corporation might sell all of its assets to another corporation, or that a corporation might go out of business and its properties might be acquired by another corporation. When that is done, it means an increase of capital stock. It means that there is given to the world knowledge of the fact that the property and the business are thus controlled; whereas, under the method of stock ownership, there has been exercised in this country for years a secret control, and frequently monopoly is almost complete worked out through it.

This approach is very much consistent with the views of John Bates Clark, as well as those of Theodore Roosevelt, Wilson, and Taft. Wilson and Taft had both called specifically for the banning of holding companies in messages to Congress. All of them accepted the rise of large business as inevitable. They did not seek to generally block the creation of large businesses, by merger or otherwise. What they wished to insist upon was that large businesses not be able to block the way for a potential competitor who thought it profitable to become an actual competitor. The objections to holding companies were that they allowed one firm to acquire control of another while paying less than 100 per cent of the controlled firm's value and that they led to exploitation of minority stockholders (Klebaner, 1964, p. 183).

SUMMARY

The Sherman Act was passed in response to waves of political and social discontent that swept the United States at the end of the nineteenth century. The Sherman Act and its later companion laws were passed to accomplish a variety of goals, not all consistent. Some of those goals were purely economic—to maintain actual competition, to maintain opportunities for potential competition. Some goals were political—concentrations of economic power were thought to threaten the workings of a democratic society. Some goals were protectionist, of small business (ostensibly for virtues of its own) and of special interest groups. Any claim to discern a single or even an overriding original goal for antitrust simply tries to fit too broad a foot into the glass slipper.

---

[44] A holding company would acquire control of other firms by purchasing shares of those companies (Bonbright and Means, 1932, pp. 7–10). Often it would pay for these shares with shares of its own stock. In contrast, with a trust (Bonbright and Means, 1932, p. 25) "Controlling stock interests in two or more companies are turned over to a group of trustees, who become the legal owners of these stocks, and who issue trust certificates to the original shareholders entitling these shareholders to dividends declared by the trustees out of common funds. ... In effect, though not in legal form, such a trust is a holding company; but the board of trustees takes the place of the board of directors, and the trust certificates take the place of the capital stock of the holding company."

[45] Senator Reed, 51 Congressional Record, p. 14457. These remarks are quoted by Martin (1959, p. 54), and this part of the Senate debate is cited by the Supreme Court in *Brown Shoe*, 370 U.S. 294 at 313, fn. 23.

Chief Justice Charles Evans Hughes wrote of the Sherman Act that:[46]

> As a charter of freedom, the Act has a generality and adaptability comparable to that found to be desirable in constitutional provisions. It does not go into detailed definitions ...

As is usually the case with broadly drawn laws, the antitrust laws are susceptible to redefinition as the economy evolves and the circumstances to which they are applied changes. The very generality of the antitrust laws ensures their evolution and ongoing debate about their purposes.

STUDY POINTS

- Transportation revolution: roads (Section 18.2.1), canals (Section 18.2.2), railroads (Sections 18.2.3, 18.3)
- Public support for canal construction (Section 18.2.2), public support for railroad construction (Section 18.3)
- The winter of our discontent: agriculture (Section 18.4.1), labour (Section 18.4.2), small business (Section 18.4.3)
- Debates about economic transformation (Sections 18.5, 18.7.1)
- Sherman Act: congressional intent (Section 18.6)
- Sherman Act: early implementation (Section 18.6.2)
- Economists' input: Sherman Act (Section 18.6.1), Clayton Act (Section 18.7.3)
- Publicity (Section 18.7.1)
- Federal Trade Commission Act (Section 18.7.3)
- Clayton Act: Sections 2(a), (3) and views of John Bates Clark (Section 18.7.3)
- Original Clayton Act Section 7: congressional intent (Section 18.7.3)

FURTHER READING

I have drawn on Martin (2007b) for some of the material in this chapter.

For discussions of the economics of and policy toward cartels and monopoly before Adam Smith, see Piotrowski (1933) and de Roover (1951).

On the canal era, see Goodrich (1961). Bertstein (2005) gives an accessible treatment of the building of the Erie Canal. On land-grants along railroad rights-of-way, see Henry (1945), Gates (1954), and Rae (1955). Baskin (1988, pp. 208–210) discusses government support for canals and railroads. On U.S. market integration in the post-Civil War period, and subsequent regional specialization patterns, see Meyer (1987), Kim (1995). On the meatpackers and the railroads, see Kujovich (1970), Yeager (1981), and Libecap (1992). On the Knights of Labor, see Grob (1954, 1958) and Kirkland (1961, Chapter 18). Levenstein (1995) discusses the rise of national manufacturers in the nineteenth-century U.S. salt, bromine, and bleach industries.

To get a feel for the times that led up to passage of the Sherman Act, the Clayton Act, and the FTC Act, see Mark Twain and Charles Dudley Warner, *The Gilded Age* (1873), Frank Norris, *The Octopus*, 1901, and *The Pit*, 1903, and Upton Sinclair, *The Jungle*, 1906. See Limbaugh (1953) for a populist perspective on the historical background of U.S. antitrust.

---

[46] Appalachian Coals, Inc. *v.* U.S. 288 U.S. 344 (1933) at 359–360.

Like Gunton (1888), Chadwick (1859) conceived of competition as including potential competition. So did Van Hise (1912) and Machlup (1942). Durand (1914a, b, c) and Liefmann (1915) took positions that had much in common with those of John Bates Clark and Gunton, respectively. Stigler (1968a) is a useful discussion of potential competition (despite the incorrect statement on p. 19 that "The leading exponent of the importance of potential competition in protecting the community from exploitation by trusts was J. B. Clark"). Baumol *et al.* (1982) explore the implications of unrestricted potential competition for market performance; see Section 3.3.2.[47]

For a contemporary review of the late nineteenth-century trust literature, see Bullock (1901). Gordon (1963), Klebaner (1964), Scherer (1990), Williams (1990), and Morgan (1993) contain references to much of this literature; see also Perelman (1994). Many of the periodicals in which these articles appeared can be accessed digitally at Cornell University's Making of America library (<http://cdl.library.cornell.edu/moa/>).

On the views of late nineteenth-century American economists on trusts, see Gordon (1963). For discussions of the views of Clark, Hadley, and Ely, see Morgan (1993, 1994). On Jenks, see Brown (2004). See Peterson (1957) and Morgan (1993) for discussions of economists' concepts of competition around the time of the passage of the Sherman Act. On the common law, see Hughes (1996).

The literature analysing congressional intent for the Sherman Act is large and contentious. For a concise overview, see Farrell and Katz (2006, Section II). See Kintner (1978, Volume 1) for an annotated transcript of the Senate debates on the Sherman Act, and pages 7–35 for commentary. Thorelli (1955) and Letwin (1956, 1965, Chapter 3) are invaluable. Bork (1966, 1978, Chapter 2) is a brilliant example of argumentation, but ultimately unconvincing. See also Lande (1982) and Flynn (1988). Sullivan (1991) and Scherer (1993) are useful collections. Scherer (1994, Chapter 3) offers a concise discussion of the U.S. adoption of antitrust policy and of the diffusion of the antitrust idea to other countries.

For early arguments advocating a publicity policy, see Adams (1894, 1902) and Ripley (1905, p. xxix). For a contemporary critique, see Yarros (1902); we discuss negative evidence from the U.S. early in the Great Depression in Section 20.3.2. See also Klebaner (1964).

On the National Civic Federation, see Domhoff (1971, pp. 163–168) and Salvato (2001, pp. 4–9). On the Progressive Movement and trusts, see Hofstadter (1955, Chapter VI). On the Progressive Movement generally, see Goldman (1953), or more concisely Schlesinger (1957, Part I), and for a cautionary note, Leonard (2006).

APPENDIX: NUTS AND BOLTS

The executive branch of the U.S. government is headed by the President, who normally reaches office as the result of an election that is held every four years.[48] One member of the President's Cabinet is the

---

[47] Anderson *et al.* (1989) make a Whig history of economic thought argument: "The history of economics has in the main ceased to be a full-time occupation. One powerful rationale for this decline is that economics has become a hard science. It is a plausible characteristic of scientific enterprise that, subject to transaction costs, all old knowledge is embodied in current knowledge. This hypothesis, which we shall call the efficient market model of scientific research, tells us that there is as little to be gained scientifically from reading old texts as there is from prowling old bookstores for undervalued rarities." The regularity with which the importance of potential competition for the nature of equilibrium market performance has been (re)discovered seems a telling counterexample to the efficient market model of economic research.

[48] Abnormally, a president may reach office if the previous president resigns, is removed from office, becomes incapacitated, or dies. The details of the rules by which the outcome of the presidential election is determined—the Electoral College—and the procedures to be followed if no candidate for the presidency obtains a majority in the Electoral College—are too arcane to bear discussion.

Attorney General of the United States. The Attorney General heads the U.S. Department of Justice. One part of the Department of Justice is the Antitrust Division (<http://www.usdoj.gov/atr/index.html>), one of the two federal government units charged with enforcing the antitrust laws.

The other federal antitrust enforcement agency is the Federal Trade Commission (<http://www.ftc.gov/>). The Federal Trade Commission is an independent agency within the federal government. There are five Commissioners, appointed for seven-year terms by the President, subject to confirmation by the U.S. Senate.

The legislative branch of the U.S. government, the U.S. Congress, is bicameral, composed of the Senate and the House of Representatives. Each of the 50 states elects two senators, who serve six-year terms. Roughly one-third of these terms expire every two years. Senators whose terms have ended and who wish to continue in office must run for re-election. There are 435 members of the U.S. House of Representatives, distributed among the states according to population. All Representatives are elected every two years to serve two-year terms.

Legislation—including antitrust legislation—must be passed by both houses of Congress and signed by the President to become law.

Leaving aside special courts, the U.S. judicial system includes 94 District Courts, 12 Circuit Courts of Appeals, one Court of Appeals for the Federal Circuit (CAFC), and the Supreme Court of the United States (<http://www.uscourts.gov/>). The CAFC hears appeals in matters regarding international trade, intellectual property rights, and other assigned topics. Federal judges are nominated by the President. Nominees must be confirmed by the U.S. Senate before taking up a position on the federal bench.

The U.S. judicial system is hierarchical. Trials take place in district court, appeals from district court go to the appropriate circuit court, and appeals from a circuit court go to the Supreme Court. The Antitrust Expediting Act, the first version of which was passed in 1903, permits appeal direct from District Court to the Supreme Court, if this is requested by the Department of Justice and the District Court judge certifies the case as being one of national importance.

Examples of citations of U.S. court decisions are "Addyston Pipe and Steel v. U.S. 175 U.S. 211 (1899)" and "U.S. v. Aluminum Company of America, 148 F.2d 416 (2d Cir. 1945)".

These citations are read as follows. The *Addyston Pipe and Steel* decision was for a case that was an appeal by Addyston Pipe and Steel Company against a lower-court decision in favour of the United States government. The Supreme Court decision is printed in volume 175 of U.S. Reports, beginning on page 211. The year of the decision was 1899. The *Alcoa* decision was for a case that was an appeal by the United States government against a lower court decision in favour of the Aluminum Company of America. The Second Circuit Court of Appeals decision is printed in the Federal Reporter, second series, beginning on page 416. The year of the decision was 1945.

There are various court reporters. The same decision may be reported in more than one series. The most common abbreviations for citations of U.S. decisions are given in Table 18.3. Court reporters may be consulted in law and other libraries. Decisions may often be accessed in digital form (as, for example, using LexisNexis™).

Private antitrust actions and public actions taken by the Department of Justice normally begin in one of the 94 District Courts. Public antitrust actions taken by the Federal Trade Commission begin when the Director of the Federal Trade Commission's Bureau of Competition investigates a possible violation of the antitrust laws.

If the Bureau of Competition concludes that there has been a violation, it may first seek a *consent agreement* with the firms involved. The cynical explanation of a consent agreement is that the firms involved don't admit that they did anything wrong, and promise never to do it again.

Table 18.3 Selected Court Reporter abbreviations

Federal/Supreme Court Cases

U.S.	United States Reports
L.Ed., L.Ed.2d	Lawyer's Edition
S.Ct.	Supreme Court Reporter

Federal/U.S. Courts of Appeals

F.	Federal Reporter
F.2d	Federal Reporter, Second Series
F.3d	Federal Reporter, Third Series

Federal/District Court

F. Supp.	Federal Supplement

If the firms do not accept a consent agreement on terms that are satisfactory to the FTC, the Bureau of Competition issues an *administrative complaint*, which is followed by a trial-like proceeding before an *Administrative Law Judge*. If the ALJ finds a violation, he or she issues a decision and specifies remedies, which may include fines and injunctions.

The decision of an ALJ may be appealed to the full Federal Trade Commission. This step in the process is not a mere formality: the Commission does on occasion reverse ALJ decisions. A decision by the FTC may be appealed to any of the Federal appeals courts, and thence to the Supreme Court.

The FTC and the Department of Justice may both prosecute civil violations of the antitrust laws. Only the Department of Justice may pursue criminal charges. There is a highly successful leniency programme that offers the prospect of reduced fines if a colluding firm turns itself (and its fellows) in (U.S. Department of Justice, 1993, 1994). We discuss such programmes in Chapter 20.

Current penalties for violation of Section 1 of the Sherman Act include fines up to the larger of $10,000,000 or double the amount of the monopoly overcharge. Individuals may be fined up to the larger of $350,000 or 5 per cent of the monopoly overcharge and, for criminal violations, sentenced to up to three years in jail.

Competition kills competition.

Proudhon

19.1 Introduction

The post-World War II process of European integration began with the 1951 Treaty of Paris (or ECSC Treaty). With this treaty, six countries[1] that had been at war a short six years earlier pledged to integrate their markets for two essential products and form the European Coal and Steel Community (ECSC). The ECSC was the prototype for the European Economic Community (EEC), established in 1957 by the Treaty of Rome (or EEC Treaty). With the EEC Treaty, the six founding member states extended the project of economic integration to all economic sectors. Both treaties contained provisions establishing a European competition policy, which of necessity is thus some 60 years younger than U.S. antitrust policy.

But these countries had gone through the same kinds of changes that prompted the United States to adopt the Sherman Act. European countries industrialized at different times, and in different circumstances. Their economies had different structures. Despite these differences, when they responded to the kinds of changes that led the U.S. to go down the antitrust road, they arrived at policies toward business behaviour that had common characteristics.

By and large, European nations came reluctantly to the idea of competition policy. As they moved away from their mercantilist[2] heritage, for them *laissez faire* meant freedom from government-imposed restraints on competition. It did not mean government rules to control restraints imposed by some private parties on the opportunities of other private parties to compete. Some European countries adopted laws with wording that resembles the wording of parts of U.S. antitrust law, but when they were applied, judicial interpretation softened their sting.

---

[1] Belgium, France, (West) Germany, Italy, Luxembourg, and the Netherlands.

[2] Bowman (1951, pp. 1–2): "Two basic factors conditioned mercantilist thought: the attitude that each class should behave in a manner 'suitable' to its 'rank and station,' and the emphasis on the wealth of the state as a goal. National wealth consisted in whatever made the state strong, and in that alone. A strong state was one that had the upper hand in the economic rivalry among nations; hence the emphasis on a favorable balance of trade, making other states dependent and tributary."

The European protagonists of World War I experienced government management of their economies. They fell back on this experience as Europe slid into the Great Depression. When they did so, they mostly spurned the *prohibition* approach of U.S. antitrust—making specific types of conduct illegal—and turned instead to an *abuse control* policy that permitted private restraints on competition but subjected them to publicity and to *ex post* monitoring by public officials. "Bad restraints"—those found to be contrary to the public interest—were prohibited after the fact. "Good restraints"—all the others—were permitted.

Despite conscious rejection of the prohibition approach by most European nations, the ECSC adopted, and passed on to the EEC and the European Union, a competition policy that included significant elements of a prohibition policy. How and why this came about is what we try to understand in this chapter. We begin with a survey of pre-EC national European approaches to business behaviour, particularly collusion. We then examine the rise of the abuse control approach, and post-war German competition policy. The competition policy of the EEC, and its connections to ECSC competition policy and post-war German competition policy, is our final topic.

19.2 Historical National Approaches

19.2.1 UK

Free trade

Combinations in restraint of trade were far from unknown in England, but for most of the nineteenth century the ability of cartels to exercise market power was limited by the export orientation of the British economy and the competition of foreign suppliers permitted by England's free trade policy. The common law was hostile to business practices thought to unjustly raise prices,[3] and forbade agreements that would prevent someone from supporting himself. The only exceptions were (Cooke, 1953, p. 2) "the patent rights granted by the Crown to inventors or to companies and the recognition that the man who bought the goodwill of a business was entitled to some reasonable protection against the competition of the seller".

It was the latter line of decisions, regarding restrictions ancillary to the sale of a business, that had an impact on early applications of Section 1 of the Sherman Act. But while U.S. debates about the heritage of the English common law on restraints of trade were underway, the common law in England took a different direction.

Hands off

The end of the nineteenth century saw the rise of competition for what had been English export markets by firms in later-industrializing countries. It also saw the long depression that

---

[3] From the thirteenth century, forestalling, regrating, and engrossing were crimes. Forestalling was the act of intercepting merchants on the way to authorized fairs at market towns and buying their supplies with the aim of selling them at a higher price. Regrating was buying necessary food items and reselling them within four miles of the market. Engrossing was buying necessary food items with the intention of reselling them; actual resale was not required (Herbruck, 1929). The laws making forestalling, regrating, and engrossing crimes were criticized by Adam Smith ([1776] 1937, pp. 499–501). Some such laws were repealed in 1772, the remainder in 1844.

began in 1873. Refining their legal treatment of cartels, English courts held that freedom to trade included the right to make contracts in the reasonable self-interest of the parties to the contract. The *Mogul Steamship* decision[4] (Section 7.3.2) was a fundamental step in this development. *Mogul Steamship* involved allegations of collusion by firms in a southeast Asian shipping cartel to drive a rival from the market for shipping tea from China. Early decisions in the case were appealed to the English House of Lords, which made its decision in 1889. In an opinion that formed part of the majority, Lord Justice Bowen expressed the views that:

- it was doubtful that cartels could be successful in a country that practised free trade, unless granted a legal monopoly;
- it was not clear that cartels were always harmful to the public;
- the common law rule was that agreements in restraint of trade were not criminal, but they could not be enforced in courts of law; and that
- it was not the place of courts to condemn "peaceable and honest combinations of capital for the purposes of trade competition"; if this were to become public policy, it would require legislation, to replace the common law rule.

After *Mogul Steamship*, English courts would neither condemn nor enforce cartel agreements. Firms were free to make cartel agreements, if they wished. Firms were free to break cartel agreements, if they wished. A defecting cartel member could not be sued by its fellows for breach of contract.[5]

Retreat from the market mechanism

Like the governments of other World War I belligerent nations, the British government used trade associations to manage its wartime economy. Business learned to appreciate the advantages of cooperation, and in the postwar period, trade associations organized formal and informal collusive schemes (Foreman-Peck, 1994, p. 404): "restrictive practices were judged legal if they were intended to forward the trade and no other wrong was committed. No wider public interest was acknowledged. Cartels and related organisations therefore had a free hand." As the *Mogul Steamship* logic was extended in later decisions, it became clear that enterprises could, without penalty of law, agree to employ any and all means short of physical violence to exclude competitors.[6]

Wartime cooperation also taught British business how to lobby government. With the world sliding into inter-war depression, business successfully lobbied for protective tariffs, trade preferences with Commonwealth nations, and the abandonment of free trade (Eichengreen, 1994, pp. 294–295). As the Great Depression dragged on, Britain turned away from use of markets as a resource allocation mechanism (Jewkes, 1958, p. 1):

---

[4] Mogul Steamship Co. v. McGregor, Gow & Co. *et. al.* (1884/1885) 54 L.J.Q.B. 540; (1887/1888) 57 L.J.K.B. 541; (1889) 23 Q.B.D. 598 (C.A.); [1892] A.C. 25.

[5] Cohen (1909, pp. 144–145) and Macdonnell (1909, p. 163) write that *Mogul Steamship* established that conference members did not, by their agreement, enter into a criminal conspiracy, but did not settle the question of the legality of the agreement itself.

[6] In Crofter Hand Woven Harris Tweed Co., Ltd. *v.* Veitch and Another (1942) 1 All E.R. 142, an association of unionized mills on the Isle of Lewis secured, with the assistance of millworkers' unions, the agreement of the dockers' union (not itself involved in the business of Harris Tweed), to refuse to transport yarn from the mainland to competing nonunion mills located on other islands. The competing mills were thus excluded from the market. See Friedmann (1942), Lewis (1943), and Cooke (1953).

Between the two world wars belief in Britain in the merits of competition had almost entirely disappeared. This was largely attributable to the prolonged period of depression suffered by a number of basic British industries, notably coal mining, iron and steel, ship building, and textiles. In these industries it came to be generally assumed that long period decline could best be met by organized control over output and prices.

19.2.2 Germany

Children of bad times

Prussia industrialized in the 1850s and 1860s, and unified Germany by 1870. Although cartels had a long history in German-speaking areas of Europe, the modern era of German cartels followed close upon unification, with the Great Depression of 1873. For this reason, German cartels were often described as "children of bad times", although they were by no means present only during economic downturns.

Bavarian Bricklayers and *Saxon Woodpulp*

The German civil code prohibited contracts *contra bonos mores*—contrary to good morals— and this rule applied to cartel contracts as to other types of contracts. German law treated contracts to collude in the same way that it treated all other contracts, as enforceable in courts of law. An 1888 decision[7] of the Bavarian Supreme Court settled that what later came to be called *crisis cartels* were not contrary to good morals, as far as the German civil code was concerned. The case involved a cartel of Bavarian brickmakers, formed to combat the effects of an economic downturn. Cartel members agreed to restrict output and to set minimum prices at levels to be determined by the cartel.

Each member agreed to pay a fine if it should break the agreement. One of the cartel members broke the agreement. The cartel sued him to compel payment of the fine. The defector defended himself on the ground that the contract was against good morals and therefore invalid. The German court found otherwise, holding that (Wolff, 1935, p. 328):[8] "it was not *contra bonos mores* for business men belonging to a branch of industry which is suffering from a depression to get together and enter into agreements regulating the ways and means of operating their industry with a view to promoting recovery. *On the contrary such course of action would seem to be incumbent upon prudent business men.*"

A similar set of facts arose in the 1897 German Supreme Court *Saxon Woodpulp* decision.[9] In 1893, a group of woodpulp producers in Saxony set up a joint sales agency. Their stated purpose was to eliminate destructive competition among themselves and obtain a fair price for their product. They agreed to sell only through the joint sales agency, and to pay a fine if they should break the agreement. In 1894 and 1895 one cartel member broke the agreement. This cartel too sued its defector to compel payment of the fine. He put forward the same defence that had been tried in *Bavarian Bricklayers*: the contract was against good morals and therefore null and void. The resulting opinion found positive social benefits in collusion:[10]

---

[7] Oberstes Landesgericht, Bavaria, April 7, 1888, Entsch. des Ob. L. G. 12, 67.

[8] Footnotes omitted, emphasis added by Wolff.

[9] Entscheidung des Reichsgerichts in Civilsachen vol xxxviii, pp. 156–158.

[10] Translation of Seager and Gulick, 1929, pp. 552–553, footnote omitted. For the German text, see Röper (1950, p. 240).

When the prices of the products of an industry fall to an unreasonably low level, and the successful operation of the industry is thereby endangered or made impossible, the resulting crisis is detrimental not only to the individuals affected but to society at large. Therefore, it is to the interest of society that prices in any given industry should not remain long at a level that is below the cost of production. ... it cannot be simply and generally contrary to the public welfare that producers interested in a given branch of industry should unite in order to prevent or to moderate price-cutting and the consequent general decline in the prices of their products. ... when prices are for a long time so low that financial ruin threatens the producers, their combination appears to be not merely a legitimate means of self-preservation, but also a measure serving the interests of society.

The German version of *laissez faire* thus emphasized freedom of contract over freedom of trade. Where English courts would allow firms to make and break cartel agreements at will, German courts treated a cartel contract like any other contract, subject to enforcement by the legal system.

To the modern economist, what the reasoning in the *Bavarian Bricklayers* and *Saxon Wood-pulp* decisions misses is the resource allocation effect of the price system. In a market economy, prices below cost are a signal to shift resources out of an industry, just as prices above cost are a signal to move resources into an industry. The argument that it is socially beneficial for firms to get together for the purpose of weathering a cyclical downturn is superficially appealing. But a price that is above marginal cost causes income transfers from consumers to producers and a deadweight welfare loss during a recession as much as in other stages of the business cycle. Further, a public policy that permits the formation of crisis cartels will permit the formation of cartels in industries that are in long-run decline. The effect of such cartels is to drag out the inevitable exit of resources from a declining market.

Cartel Ordinance

Post-World War I hyperinflation in Germany led many industry associations to fix common selling terms in a way that shifted the burden of currency depreciation to buyers (Pribram, 1935, p. 255).[11] There was a popular backlash against this collusion on selling terms. The result was adoption of the first specific German cartel law, the Cartel Ordinance of 2 November 1923. Many of the selling-terms cartels dissolved after the September 1924 Dawes Plan stabilized the German currency. But the Cartel Ordinance remained, and with it the nominal possibility of government supervision of cartels.

The 1923 Ordinance was an abuse control measure: the most it permitted courts to do was declare that a cartel agreement was null and void (Böhm, 1954, p. 161). If, after such a declaration, firms adhered to the agreement anyway, no legal remedies were available (Voight, 1962, pp. 76–78).

State involvement in industry increased throughout the early twentieth century. Beginning in 1910, the German government effectively administered a cartel for the potash industry.[12] What had in 1919 been intended by a short-lived socialist government as the first step

---

[11] Every coin has two sides: it is also true that fiddling with terms of sale (credit terms, quantity discounts) is a favorite way for a cartel member to cheat, not too ostentatiously, on a collusive agreement. By policing selling terms, a cartel could eliminate this particular source of cartel instability.

[12] In 1909, the German Potash Cartel contract ended, and was not renewed because three firms were dissatisfied with their quotas. These three firms signed contracts to supply American firms with potash (used to produce glass,

toward nationalization of the coal industry led instead to a system of mandatory regional coal cartels under the authority of a government minister. Government authority over cartels increased toward the end of the Weimar Republic. This process continued from 1933 under the Nazi government, which made cartels an element of its command-and-control apparatus for the economy.

Ordoliberalism

Although German law was hostile to freedom of trade, Germany was home to the Ordoliberal School, which viewed a competitive market economy as a bulwark of political freedom. The Ordoliberal School began at the University of Freiburg during the interwar period. It continued to develop under Nazi rule, and had an important influence on German and EC competition policy in the post-war period. The Ordoliberal philosophy was shaped by experience with the effects of private economic power exercised by cartels under the Weimar Republic and with the effects of public power, economic and otherwise, under national socialism.

Competition policy was central to the Ordoliberal vision of a free society. Like Henry Simons in *A Positive Program for Laissez Faire*,[13] Ordoliberals saw government's role as one of maintaining conditions under which market prices, freely arrived at, would allocate resources. Ordoliberals felt that government involvement in the marketplace would lead to rent seeking (Böhm, 1954, p. 150):

> The experience of the First World War and of the years 1936 to 1948 showed that in a system of economic control carried out with the help of [industry] associations, competition and attempts to establish monopolies take on a somewhat different character. Competition takes place no longer in the market, but in the ante-chambers of government departments, and attempts at monopoly are also made partly via these ante-chambers and partly through the concentration of enterprises . . .

For Ordoliberals, the most important purpose of competition policy was to maintain individual freedom. They expected economic efficiency to result from maintaining individual freedom (Möschel, 1989, p. 142):

> [C]ompetition policy is primarily oriented to the goal of securing individual freedom of action, from which the goal of economic efficiency is merely derived.

In the Ordoliberal view, the role of government was, and was only, to maintain property rights, to prohibit contracts inconsistent with the role of free decisions in markets as a resource allocation mechanism, and to enforce all other private contracts freely arrived at. The Ordoliberal School's position was that this limited government role should be part of the national constitution.

---

soap, and fertilizer) at prices 45 per cent below those that had been set by the cartel. The contracts specified that the purchasers would pay any taxes imposed after the contracts went into effect. With the Potash Law of 1910, the German government imposed specifically targeted export taxes that raised the prices paid by the American firms above the former cartel level. The reestablished cartel assumed responsibility for the export contracts. The 1910 law also established government control of potash prices (Newman, 1948).

[13] The similarity of Ordoliberalism and Simons' work is noted by Oliver (1960, p. 118).

19.2.3 France

Competition policy manqué

France has a long history of laws that might have become the basis for a vigorous competition policy. Some of these laws date from the time of the French Revolution. A law of March 1791 aimed to eliminate the privileges enjoyed by guilds under the *ancien régime*. It guaranteed that "Any person shall be free to carry on such business, or to exercise such profession, art or trade as he considers desirable ..." This law was intended to stop government-imposed restraints on competition; it did not target private behaviour that restricted competition (Wolff, 1935, p. 333).

A July 1793 law provided penalties including confiscation and death for combinations that acted *to alter price from the level that would have occurred under free competition*. In 1810, the provisions of this law, with less severe penalties (fines, imprisonment of one month to a year, or police supervision), were incorporated in Articles 419 and 420 the French penal code.[14,15]

With such wording, much depends on the reading given to the phrase "the price that would have occurred under free competition". French courts read a distinction between bad trusts, to which the prohibitions of the law applied, and good trusts, to which they did not, into the law (Paxton, 1992, p. 154): "In French political economy, 'good' trusts were defensive coalitions against ruinous competition, intended to stabilize the market and to avoid overproduction. ... 'Bad' trusts ... were offensive coalitions, with a double goal of speculation and driving out competitors."

Cartels became more common during World War I (see the accompanying box on the calcium carbide cartel), in part because the French war government (like war governments everywhere) found it convenient to administer the war economy through existing industry trade groups.[16] These often were, or became, cartels.

 BOX   **The French Calcium Carbide Cartel**

In 1904, seven patent-holders set up a consortium with exclusive rights to sell calcium carbide* in France; each was allocated a share of the market. Patent protection ended in 1909, and the consortium faced the prospect of entry. They obtained tariff protection and negotiated an international cartel agreement under the terms of which France and the French empire were reserved for them and they agreed not to supply markets elsewhere in the world. In 1910 the consortium was able to raise its price from 250 to 290 francs per tonne, and maintain it at the higher level.   »

---

[14] See Walker (1905, pp. 27–28), Deák (1936, pp. 413–414) for English translations of the 1810 Article, Deák (1934, p. 348, fn. 23), Hirsch (1975, p. 49) for the French text. See Castel (1956, p. 99, fn. 9) for an English translation of the Article after 1927 amendments, Hirsch (1975, p. 57) for the French text.

[15] A June 1791 law (the *Loi Chapelier*) prohibited "members of the same branch of business from associating for the purpose of regulating their supposed 'common interest'". By its wording, this law would seem to apply to cartels; in application, it was used against organized labour.

[16] See Stigler (1954, p. 11): "[O]nce a government intervenes in economic life, it finds industries dominated by a few firms much easier to direct, for both administrative and political reasons." Edwards' (1952) discussion of government wartime management of an economy and market performance is in the context of U.S. experience, but the effects he identifies seem likely to generalize to other cases.

> In 1913, the Rochette brothers built a new calcium carbide plant. Its capacity, 10,000 tonnes per year, was 20 per cent of previous French capacity (40,000 tonnes per year). Rochette offered a price 25 to 30 francs per tonne below that of the cartel, and it offered to sell all over Europe. It thus threatened both the French and the international cartel.
>
> Rochette refused invitations to join the cartel. In February 1914, the cartel cut its price to 210 francs per tonne. Rochette joined the cartel, and was awarded a quota of 8,000 tonnes per year.
>
> World War I use of calcium carbide to weld shell casings increased demand from 40,000 tonnes per year in 1913 to 69,000 tonnes per year in 1917. By 1918, price had risen to 500 francs per tonne. On the black market, which served the undersupplied civilian market, prices were higher. Along with the resentment generated by price increases and shortages, the pre-war interactions of French firms with German colleagues in the international cartel lent themselves to treasonous interpretations. In 1915, there began an investigation seeking to apply Article 419 of the Penal Code to the calcium carbide consortium. The calcium carbide producers were eventually acquitted of all charges. They were acquitted of treason on the ground that the acts complained of had taken place before the war. They were acquitted of collusion under Article 419 on the ground that they had formed a good trust (ensuring that French demand was satisfied by French producers), not a bad trust.
>
> * An industrial chemical used to produce acetylene, which in turn is used for lighting, welding, and in the organic chemical industry. For discussion of early development of the industry, see Wallace (1937, pp. 513–516).
>
> *Source:* Based on Paxton (1992).

In December 1926, Articles 419 and 420 of the penal code were amended to make clear that the act of colluding was not, in and of itself, illegal. Only combinations of firms that sought monopoly profits were forbidden. But more than anything else, this was a public relations gesture to soothe public discontent with cartels. The amendments were not really intended to block the formation of cartels (Venturini, 1971, p. 43).

Cartels proliferated in France during the inter-war period, particularly after the Great Depression hit France in 1931. From June, 1940, the Vichy government occupied itself with managing a severely damaged economy. In doing so it relied heavily on industry trade associations.

Planning

Two important aspects of the French economy find their origin in the immediate post-war period. The first was an enduring affinity for government economic planning.[17] The four-year Monnet[18] Plan, developed from 1945 and implemented from 1947, drew on plans prepared by the Vichy government for the postwar period. The Monnet Plan gave priority to investment in capital goods over consumption goods.

---

[17] In the words of Kuisel (1981, p. 133): "Although the French found it difficult to produce goods and services during the war, they excelled at paperwork." See Sheahan (1963, Chapter 10), Estrin and Peter (1983).

[18] Jean Monnet was actively involved in arranging U.S. support for Britain's war effort before the United States entered World War II, was part of the French government in exile, organized French planning for post-war reconstruction, and laid the foundation for European unification.

French plans were indicative rather than mandatory. The government set targets and then persuaded and cajoled rather than ordered business to go along.[19] But planning, a policy of government guidance of economic development, reflected a lack of confidence in the use of markets as a resource allocation mechanism (Fridenson, 1997, p. 226):

> In 1950 the French government finally decided not to send to parliament an antitrust bill which Jean Monnet and his Planning Commission had drafted. A majority of French politicians wanted to keep as much interfirm cooperation as possible in times of hardening international competition.

Nationalization

The immediate post-war period also saw a wave of nationalizations. These nationalizations were in no way the result of a national consensus in favour of bringing the means of production into the hands of the state. Rather, individual nationalizations were responses to specific circumstances.[20]

19.2.4 Elsewhere in Europe

Thorelli (1959b, p. 19) identified a range of European government policies toward business during the inter-war period, and classified countries as follows:

- indifference or scattered regulation: Britain, France, Sweden, Finland, and most East European countries;
- compulsory cartelization: Germany, Italy, the Low Countries; to some extent Norway;
- publicity: Denmark, Norway; and
- prohibitory legislation: none.

In the run-up to World War II, *no* European countries followed the prohibition approach of United States' antitrust policy.

If Europe went to war sceptical about the efficacy of setting rules for market competition, it emerged from war sceptical about the market mechanism, period. In the words of a contemporary British observer (Taylor, 1945, p. 576):

> [A]ll over Europe the Right has ceased to exist as an organised political force ... In no liberated country is there any sizeable party which stands for capitalism: private enterprise, private profit, private property in land on a big scale, these are causes which have no vocal defenders. ... unless there is a counter-revolution, it looks as though nationalisation of industry and state control of foreign trade will be universal in Europe very soon. Nobody in Europe believes in the American way of life—that is, in private enterprise; or rather those who believe in it are a defeated party—a party which seems to have no more future ...

---

[19] In the early post-war years, persuasion was reenforced by government control of access to scarce foreign exchange (i.e., dollars).

[20] The car company Renault was nationalized because it was thought to have collaborated with occupation forces. Coal mines were nationalized following a 1944 strike, in response to worsening work conditions and the need to secure supplies of an essential fuel. Leading banks were nationalized to coordinate the supply of credit for reconstruction efforts. Electric power and gas were nationalized after power interruptions in 1944–1946 and because of their importance for reconstruction.

19.2.5 Abuse Control and Post-war German Competition Policy

Abuse control

During the inter-war period, abuse control became the mainstream European approach to cartel control (Please, 1954, pp. 36–37; Thorelli, 1959a, b). At its 1930 meeting, the Inter-parliamentary Union, the international organization of parliaments, adopted a resolution stating that cartels were natural economic institutions that could not be effectively prohibited. Instead, governments should require cartels to register and take action against a cartel if, but only if, it engaged in abusive conduct.[21] It was this approach to cartel control that, as we shall see (Section 20.3.2), seemed so attractive to U.S. business circles in the 1920s, and it is exactly the policy that was adopted by many European countries.

"As-if"

The Ordoliberal School incorporated elements of the abuse control approach into its ideas about public policy toward business. Recognizing that competition might of necessity be imperfect in some markets, Leonhard Miksch (1949) put forward the "as-if" approach to abuse of market power. If a market was imperfectly competitive, or if a firm had a legal monopoly (as, for example, due to patent protection), the Ordo suggestion was that (Gerber, 1994, p. 52) "competition law was to provide a standard of conduct for the firms involved. ... It required that economically powerful firms act *as if* they were subject to competition—i.e., as if they did not have monopoly power."

Ordoliberal/abuse control compromise

Post-World War II German economic policies were substantially different from those of the 1930s. But prevailing views on public policy toward business in September 1951 were far from supportive of a prohibition approach to cartels (Böhm, 1954, p. 156):

> German public opinion can be summarized as follows: business men have given up the pro-gramme of Adam Smith, for which they never cared greatly, and the workers have renounced the programme of Karl Marx to which they used to be passionately attached, and they are both in process of agreeing on a mercantilist policy which prevailed before the birth of economic science, an economic policy which today ... would be far more faulty and unreasonable than it was in the seventeenth and eighteenth centuries.

Against this background, the Ordoliberal School stood out as a defender of the market system. It was active in efforts to write a German competition law. A 1949 proposal by a committee that included Franz Böhm among its members proposed a competition law that would have prohibited cartels, controlled mergers, and established an independent government enforcement agency (Möschel, 1989, pp. 149–150). The legislative process was a long tug-of-war between disciples of the Ordo School and champions of an abuse policy (Brusse and Griffiths, 1997a, p. 177). The result, the Law against Limitations on Competition (*Gesetz gegen Wettbewerbsbeschränkungen*, GWB) was adopted in July 1957. Like the Treaties of Rome, it was effective from 1 January 1958. It was a compromise that combined Ordoliberal and abuse control themes (Möschel, 1989, p. 150; see also Marberg, 1964, p. 91):

> It contains in Section 1 a general proscription of horizontal arrangements in restraint of trade, but this proscription is significantly watered down by the exemptions in Sections 2–8. The most

---

[21] Interparliamentary Union (1931, p. 33). For discussion, see Boserup and Schlichtkrull (1962).

important exemptions concern export cartels, specialisation cartels and forms of cooperation between small and medium-size firms.

As regards single-firm exercise of market power, the link to the inter-war European approach is evident (Buxbaum, 2006, p. 7): "while U.S. law prohibits firms from deliberately attaining (or attempting to attain) monopolistic power, the GWB condemns only the abusive use of market-dominant power."

19.3 The European Coal and Steel Community

Like post-war Germany, the European Union adopted a competition policy that combines elements of the prohibition approach and elements of the abuse control approach.

Europe started down this road with the European Coal and Steel Community (ECSC), the immediate predecessor of the European Economic Community and, therefore, of the European Union. The ECSC existed from July 1952 to July 2002, and the rules it laid down for European coal and steel were in force throughout that period. Much of the distinct institutional role of the ECSC came to an end in July 1967, however, when the ECSC, Euratom,[22] and the EEC were merged and the European Commission, the executive organ of Euratom and the EEC, assumed the role of the ECSC's executive branch, the High Authority.

19.3.1 The Schuman Plan

The European Coal and Steel Community was proposed by the Schuman Plan, named for French Foreign Minister Robert Schuman. The Schuman Plan was developed by Jean Monnet, the manager of postwar French economic planning, in mid-April 1950. Monnet solicited Schuman's support, and three weeks later Schuman announced the Plan to the world. Nine months of negotiations followed, and on 18 April 1951 the Treaty of Paris was signed by representatives of the original six member states (the Benelux countries, France, Germany, and Italy). The Treaty established the ECSC and created a supranational High Authority to manage the integrated coal and steel markets of the six member states. The competition policy provisions of the European Coal and Steel Community are fundamental predecessors of those of the European Union. They embodied a prohibition approach that on the surface was substantially different from the mainstream European approach.

Prohibition

Article 60 of the ECSC Treaty banned unfair competitive practices, using as an example "purely local price reductions tending towards the acquisition of a monopoly position". It also banned price discrimination within the common market, particularly when the discrimination was made on the basis of nationality, and required that prices be published.

One reason to prohibit price discrimination may have been to protect French steel producers from too-severe competition by German rivals (Haas, 1958, p. 245). The requirement that prices be published seems to have been with the idea of providing consumers with information that would allow them to make the best choice of supplier (Spierenburg and Poidevin, 1994, p. 101). Unfortunately, making price information available to consumers

---

[22] Euratom, the European Atomic Energy Community, was established at the same time as the European Economic Community, by one of two treaties signed in Rome on 25 March 1957.

makes it available to rival producers as well. Economists expect this to make it easier for firms to coordinate prices (Section 20.3.1), and so it did in the ECSC steel market.

Article 65(1) prohibited agreements among firms that would distort competition within the common market. This prohibition was without effective precedent in Europe.

Article 66(1) required prior authorization of mergers—interfirm acquisitions of control, or concentrations—by the High Authority, the executive branch of the ECSC. The High Authority's merger control powers were at that time without precedent anywhere in the world.

Discretionary exceptions

But the influence of the abuse control approach is seen in Articles 65(2) and 66(7). Article 65(2) gave the High Authority the right to permit certain types of agreements that were prohibited by Paragraph 1, if specified conditions were met. The kinds of agreements that could be permitted were agreements to specialize in production and agreements for joint buying and selling. The conditions that had to be met were essentially that the agreement would improve market performance, that the agreement be necessary to improve market performance, and that the agreement would not give the firms involved power over price or interfere with competition from firms not party to the agreement.

Private and public enterprise

Article 83, in its entirety, read "The establishment of the Community does not in any way prejudice the regime of ownership of the enterprises subject to the provisions of the present Treaty." Essentially the same language appears in Article 295 of the Treaty establishing the European Community. Thus, nothing in the ECSC Treaty ruled out public ownership of ECSC coal and steel firms. But the provisions of the ECSC Treaty, including the competition policy provisions, applied to public as well as to private enterprise. Article 66(7) gave the High Authority the right to consult with a national government if a private or public enterprise used a dominant position in ways contrary to the purposes of the Treaty. After such consultation, if need remained, the High Authority was to take measures to prevent such use of a dominant position.

State aid control

Article 4, Paragraph (c) of the ECSC Treaty prohibited subsidies by a member state to its firms. Such subsidies were prohibited on the ground that they would distort competition between firms that did and firms that did not receive them. However, Article 67(2) gave the High Authority the power to authorize state aid to compensate for the effects of a member state's other policies that harmed the member state's own coal or steel firms. These provisions anticipate the state aid control measures of the European Community. In essence they extend the abuse control approach to member state distortions of market competition.

Origins

This combination of the prohibition and abuse control approaches was arrived at through a complex interaction of French strategic interests, changing Allied intentions regarding the post-war structure of West German industry, and German pursuit of a restored place among the community of nations. This interaction had a ripple effect on post-war German competition law, which in turn had its own direct effect on EC competition policy.

The Schuman Plan embraced the strategy of pursuing European integration by way of market integration, because the will to pursue political integration directly was lacking. Coal, iron and steel were chosen because they had high symbolic value. These sectors of the economy were essential to the waging of war. Unifying them would, in the eyes of the European public, go far toward cementing the peace.

Deconcentration   The pursuit of lofty political goals does not preclude the simultaneous pursuit of more prosaic objectives. Coal and steel had advantages on this level as well. Immediately after the war, deconcentration of German industry—breaking up large firms in general and the vertically integrated coal and steel firms of the Ruhr region of Germany in particular—was a goal of the occupation forces.[23] One reason for the deconcentration drive was the perception that German heavy industry had played a role in leading Germany, and the world, into war.[24]

The initial U.S. plan to put in place a less vertically integrated and a less horizontally concentrated supply-side market structure in the Ruhr suited French interests. Breaking the link between Ruhr coal and steel operations would guarantee France access to the German coal it needed to fuel its steel plants. Breaking up Ruhr steel firms would make it easier for French steel firms to sell finished steel products in Germany (Haas, 1958, p. 242; Lynch, 1984).

The American connection   The first reaction of many American observers to the Schuman Plan was that the Coal and Steel Community would simply be a cover for the revival of pre-war cartels. To placate such concerns, Monnet turned to Robert Bowie, an American with antitrust expertise who was at that time attached to the office of the American High Commissioner for Germany. Bowie wrote the first draft of the two competition law articles of the Treaty of Paris, Articles 65 and 66, based on the American experience concerning restrictive commercial practices, cartels, and monopoly (Bowie, 1989, p. 82). As Monnet wrote in his memoirs ([1976, p. 413] 1978, p. 353) "For Europe, they were a fundamental innovation; the extensive anti-trust legislation now applied by the European Community essentially derives from those few lines in the Schuman Treaty."

The French connection   But the extensive competition policy of the European Community does not derive *only* from the United States' antitrust tradition. Bowie's drafts were rewritten in French by Maurice Lagrange (Bowie, 1981, 1989; Lagrange, 1980; Diebold, 1988). Bowie says (1981, p. 6) "Lagrange ... put them into French treaty language." In retrospect, it seems clear that more than mere translation was involved. As we have seen, ECSC competition policy included abuse control aspects unknown to the Sherman Act.

German acquiescence   These two competition law articles responded to U.S. concerns that the ECSC would be a shield for cartels. Under intense U.S. pressure, Germany accepted their inclusion in the ECSC Treaty. Placing the provisions in the Treaty at least guaranteed to Germany that German business would not be the only target of competition policy. The

---

[23] This attitude changed, at least as far as the United States was concerned, in the run-up to the Korean War.

[24] In Section 22.2.2, see remarks by Senator Kefauver to this effect during debate before passage of the Celler-Kefauver Act of 1950. See also Adams (1961, p. 543).

competition policy provisions of the ECSC Treaty, whatever they turned out to be in practice, would apply to coal and steel firms in all six of the ECSC member states.

Resumé   Thus the ECSC applied a basic prohibition approach to business behaviour that distorted competition and/or impeded the process of market integration. But elements of the indigenous European abuse control approach remained. Agreements that distorted competition and state aid to business were in principle prohibited, but could be allowed by the High Authority under some circumstances. The prohibition approach showed up in the general rules against anticompetitive actions by firms or states; the abuse control approach showed up in discretionary exceptions to the general rules.

19.3.2 Epilogue

There were good political reasons for settling on coal and steel as the leading edge of European economic integration. But the technologies of both sectors imply that firms operating in these industries must make substantial sunk investments. To the extent that market integration induces more efficient operation, some firms must shift resources to other sectors for the full benefit of integration to be realized. But it is precisely when firms have made sunk investments that it is difficult for them to shift resources to other sectors. Thus the stage was set for a drawn-out adjustment process as market integration went forward.

To this general consideration must be added the rise of steel producers in other parts of the world and the displacement of coal by oil as the world's primary energy source. The upshot of these factors was that the ECSC coal and steel sectors faced a series of crises that placed the ECSC itself under substantial pressure. With effect from 1 July 1967, the institutions of the three communities—the ECSC, Euratom, and the European Economic Community—were merged. By this time, the main line of development of European competition policy was the competition policy provisions of the 1957 EEC Treaty, to which we now turn.

19.4 EC Competition Policy

19.4.1 The Spaak Report

In June 1955, a conference of foreign ministers of the ECSC member states established an inter-governmental committee to outline a framework for the extension of economic integration from coal and steel to all sectors of the economy. The inter-governmental committee worked under the chairmanship of Paul-Henri Spaak, foreign minister of Belgium. The report of the Comité Intergouvernemental, known formally as the *Rapport des Chefs de Délégation aux Ministres des Affairs Etrangères* and informally as the *Spaak Report*, was delivered on April 21, 1956. It became the blueprint for the EEC Treaty signed in Rome on March 25, 1957.

The Spaak Report said that (Comité Intergouvernemental, 1956, p. 45):

> [T]he treaty should contain general provisions ensuring that monopoly positions or abusive practices do not lead to frustration of the common market. In this connection steps should be taken to prevent
>
> – any distribution of markets by agreement among enterprises, since this would be tantamount to setting up cartels;

- agreements to restrict production or limit technical progress, since such agreements would
  run counter to efforts to bring about greater productivity;
- monopoly or partial domination of the market for a product by a single enterprise, since
  this would do away with one of the essential advantages of a large market, namely that of
  reconciling the use of mass production methods and the maintenance of competition.

The implicit model

The section of the Spaak Report that discusses price discrimination offers insight into the
conception of market processes entertained by the founders of the European Economic Community. Price discrimination could substitute privately erected barriers to trade in place of
the public barriers that would be dismantled by government action (Comité Intergouvernemental, 1956, p. 43):

> A common market would not automatically lead to the most rational distribution of activity
> if producers retained the option of supplying users on different terms, especially according to
> their nationality or country of residence.

But the authors of the Spaak Report thought that increased competition would come with
market integration. Increased competition, they expected, would eliminate firms' ability to
engage in price discrimination (Comité Intergouvernemental, 1956, p. pp. 43–44):[25]

> These problems . . . tend . . . gradually to disappear on a true common market. A supplier cannot
> permanently demand prices above his usual rates if users have the possibility of applying to
> a competitor. Nor can dumping be maintained for any length of time, if the buyer on the
> supplier's home market can buy the firm's products on other markets on which it quotes lower
> prices. In other words, a supplier can undertake dumping on other markets to the extent to
> which it is protected on the home market. Simultaneous and reciprocal abolition of obstacles
> to trade will of itself gradually help to dispose of this problem.

The argument of the Spaak Report, that increased competition will eliminate price discrimination, is correct for price-taking firms (Chapter 8). But if markets that were imperfectly competitive before integration remain imperfectly competitive after integration, then
integration, in and of itself, will not eliminate the possibility of price discrimination across
national markets.

19.4.2 EC Treaty

Article 101

The Spaak Report recommendations are reflected in the provisions of the EC Treaty. Provisions aiming to block collective monopoly practices appear in Article 101[26] of the EC Treaty.
Article 101(1) prohibits agreements that affect trade between the member states and have the
object or effect of preventing, restricting, or distorting competition, on the ground that they
are incompatible with the common market. Article 101(3) allows exceptions to the Article

---

[25] Dumping, which we discuss in the context of imperfectly competitive international markets in Section 16.7.3,
takes place if a firm sells at a lower price on a foreign market than it does on its home market.

[26] The paragraphs of the EC Treaty were renumbered by the 1957 Treaty of Amsterdam and the 2009 Treaty of
Lisbon.

101(1) prohibition for agreements that improve production or distribution, or promote technical or economic progress, provided among other conditions that a fair share of the benefits generated by the agreement goes to consumers.

The Article 101(1) prohibition was reenforced by Article 3 of the EC Treaty, as amended by the 1992 Maastricht Treaty (Treaty on European Union). Article 3 included the provision that "... the activities of the Community shall include ... (g) a system ensuring that competition in the internal market is not distorted ..." But at its 21–22 June 2007 meeting in Brussels, the European Council agreed, on the initiative of France, to remove references to "free and undistorted competition" as a goal of the European Union from the Treaty. The June proposals are an effort to jump start the ratification of proposed Treaty revisions that began life as a proposed constitution for European Union. A protocol to the Council initiatives reaffirms the role of competition policy, but (at this writing) the full implications of the French initiative remain to be seen.

Article 102

Roots

Under the EC Treaty, it is not illegal to have a dominant market position. Article 102 prohibits the abuse—by one or more firms—of a dominant market position. This provision is a combination of features of the ECSC Treaty and the draft German competition law (Focsaneanu, 1977). Thus the impact of U.S. antitrust on the competition policy provisions of the ECSC Treaty turned into an indirect influence on EC competition policy. The abuse control approach of the ECSC Treaty and the German Law Against Limitations on Competition both also influenced EC competition policy. The Ordoliberal School influenced the provisions of EC competition law through its impact on the Law Against Limitations on Competition. The Ordoliberal School also influenced the first applications of EC competition law because many of the early administrators of competition policy at the EC Commission subscribed to Ordoliberal principles. EC competition policy thus has indirect roots in U.S. antitrust policy[27] (by way of ECSC competition policy and German antitrust), direct and indirect roots in the abuse control approach, and (at least) indirect roots in the Ordoliberal School (see Figure 19.1).

Akman (2007) reports the results of an examination of long-sealed preparatory documents leading to the Treaty of Rome. She describes a realization during the negotiations that integration and the adaptation of EC firms to a larger internal market could bring greater efficiency, more rapid growth, and a stronger ability to compete on world markets. One internal memo among the preparatory documents made a distinction between exclusion of

---

[27] On the impact of U.S. antitrust on German antitrust, see among others Bridge (1954), Schwartz (1957), and Berghahn (1986, pp. 155–181). There is a literature that would minimize the impact of U.S. antitrust on EC competition policy (Gerber, 1998; Giocoli, 2007). This literature does great service in emphasizing the links of EC competition policy to indigenous European approaches to the regulation of business behaviour. But the direct link between U.S. antitrust and the competition policy provisions of the ECSC Treaty, and the direct impact of the latter on the competition policy provisions of the EC Treaty establish a substantial impact of U.S. antitrust on EC competition policy. Nor does the existence of that impact take anything away from the distinctive nature of EC competition policy.

Figure 19.1 Roots of European Community competition policy

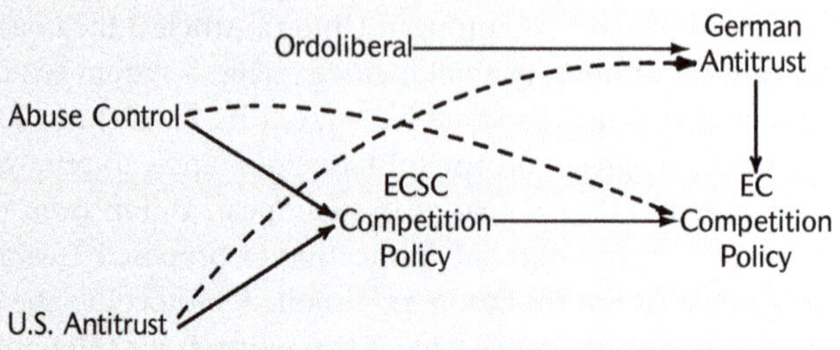

competitors by unfair competition, which the Treaty might prohibit, and exclusion of competitors as a result of strengthened competition, which should not be prohibited.[28]

Penalties

The European Commission may fine firms that violate Article 101 or 102 up to 10 per cent of their annual turnover. The Commission may also order that offending behaviour be ended.

Merger control

Articles 101 and 102 of the EC Treaty deal with business conduct. Although there were some applications of Article 102 to mergers involving dominant firms, it is the 1989 Merger Control Regulation[29] that is the primary competition policy measure dealing with market structure. It gives the European Commission authority over mergers and related types of business combinations that meet specified size and multinationality conditions. Under the merger control regulation, the Commission may block a proposed merger entirely, or permit a merger to go forward on terms different from those originally proposed.

Other provisions

Articles 106, 107, and 108 of the EC Treaty set rules for actions of the member states toward the business sector. Article 106 says that EC competition policy applies to public enterprises and to private enterprises that are given specific missions by a member state. Article 107(1) prohibits member state aid to business, if the aid distorts or threatens to distort competition. Article 107(3) allows exceptions to the Article 107(1) prohibition for aid that promotes regional and other specified types of development.

---

[28] This may be compared with remarks in U.S. Senate debate before passage of the Sherman Act about competition on the merits that might lead a market to have a single supplier and to John Bates Clark's views before passage of the Clayton Act and the FTC Act.

[29] Regulation (EEC) No 4064/89 OJ L 395 30.12.89, p. 1, amended by Regulation (EC) No 1310/97, OJ L 180, 9.7.1997 and succeeded by Council Regulation (EC) No 139/2004 OJ L 24/1, 29.01.2004.

Articles 101(3) and 107(3) transfer the ECSC approach of grafting an element of abuse control onto what is otherwise a prohibition-based competition policy to the EEC.

Goals

In 1963, EC Competition Commissioner Hans von der Groeben identified three purposes of EC competition policy:

- to prevent firms or member states from erecting barriers to trade to replace those dismantled by the EC;
- to promote integration; and
- "to safeguard an economic and social order based on freedom" for businessmen, consumers, and workers.

von der Groeben viewed the three goals—competition, integration, and freedom—as being mutually consistent, and the Commission has consistently defended the ability of competition policy to serve multiple purposes (Lowe, 2006, p. 1):

> Competition is not an end in itself, but an instrument designed to achieve a certain public interest objective, consumer welfare. At the same time, competition policy can contribute to other objectives: in the EU context, for example, it can work towards the success of the strategy for growth and jobs, and form part of the public debate about the role of state intervention and regulation in industry. Only competition ... allows the emergence of firms capable of succeeding in global markets.

While improving consumer welfare has always been a fundamental goal of EC competition policy, it is also the responsibility of the European Community to safeguard the process of market integration. But market integration implies shifts in resources across national boundaries as a way of reaching the allocation of economic activity in the common market that is most productive for the Community as a whole. The net effect of these shifts is positive overall, but in any one member state, some firms and some sectors of the economy will prosper with market integration, while other firms and sectors will suffer. Those who suffer will react by doing what they can to delay market integration, and they will lobby their governments to do the same (Ehlermann, 1992, p. 259). Another aim of EC competition policy, therefore, is to control distortionary practices (private or government) that are a reaction to the integration process itself. EC competition policy seeks to maximize consumer welfare *and* to promote market integration, and views the pursuit of the two goals as mutually reenforcing.

SUMMARY

Individual European nations, responding to nineteenth century economic changes and twentieth century economic disturbances, developed their own distinctive approaches to competition policy. These approaches shared an affinity for an abuse control policy that permitted firms to collude and sought to restrain joint behaviour if it harmed economic performance.

There is little reason to think that the abuse control approach functioned as its advocates described, but it was not for that reason that the European Coal and Steel Community, and later the European Economic Community, adopted a prohibition-based competition policy. The prohibition approach guaranteed, in the eyes of the public, that market integration would go forward on a level playing field. The founding fathers of the European Union aimed to use market integration as the bellwether of integration on all fronts. They adopted a prohibition approach to interfirm agreements, abuse of a dominant position, and state aid because they thought it necessary in order for market integration to work.

At the same time, EU competition policy permits exceptions to the general prohibitions of actions that are classified as being "incompatible with the common market." If specified conditions are met, some interfirm cooperation may be permitted, even though it distorts competition. Similarly, some state aid may be permitted, even though it distorts competition. Much of the distinctive character of EU competition policy lies in Commission and Court decisions permitting (or not) such "abuse control" exceptions.

STUDY POINTS

- European national approaches to business policy (Section 19.2)
- The Ordoliberal School (Section 19.2.2, Section 19.2.5)
- Abuse control (Section 19.2.5 and following)
- ECSC (Section 19.3), ECSC competition policy (Section 19.3.1)
- The Spaak Report (Section 19.4.1)
- European Community Treaty: goals; Articles 101, 102; Merger Control Regulation; state aid control (Section 19.4.2)

FURTHER READING

I have drawn on Martin (2007b) for some of the material in this chapter.

Many late 19th-century U.S. economists studied in Germany, and German and European cartels were a frequent topic of research papers in U.S. journals at the end of the 19th and beginning of the 20th centuries. Walker (1905) is one example.

On early British cartels, see Ashton (1920) and Levy ([1927] 1968). On the impact of the 19th-century free trade policy on cartels, see Allen (1954). On the shift in English competition policy from the old common law approach, see White (1937). On cartels in Germany, see Maschke (1969) and Barnikel (1972). See Venturini (1971, Chapter 1) for a discussion of French competition policy before the end of World War II, and Jeanneney (1954) for a contemporary view of post-war French nationalizations. For an evaluation of the cartel control approach between the wars, see Kronstein and Leighton (1946). On the Interparliamentary Union, see Interparliamentary Union and the United States Group (1985) and its web site, at URL <http://www.ipu.org/english/home.htm>.

For concise summaries of the provisions of national competition law just before the Great Depression, see Lammers (1927). For discussions of English, French, and German competition policy in the 1920s, with comparisons to U.S. antitrust, see Koch (1930) and Wolff (1935); see also Robinson (1941). On post-war competition policy in Europe at the national level, see Chamberlin (1954), Thorelli (1959a, b), Boserup and Schlichtkrull (1962), Edwards (1964), Berghahn (1986), De Jong (1990), and Brusse and Griffiths (1997a). On U.S. influence, see Mercer (1997). Lucas (1935) discusses the British turn away from competition between the wars, and Lucas (1937, Chapter IX) discusses British trade associations in the same period.

For the facts of the *Saxon Woodpulp* case, see Böhm ([1948] 1960), and see Voight (1962) for a useful discussion of Germany's experience with cartels. On German cartels during the World War II see Nathan (1944, Chapter 3), Newman (1948), and Voight (1962). On German business and the descent of Germany into the abyss, see Turner (1985) and Hayes (1987); on post-war efforts to deconcentrate German industry, see Warner (1996).

On the Ordoliberal School, see Böhm (1954), Oliver (1960), and Grossekettler (1989), Möschel (1989), as well as Friedrich (1955), Zweig (1980), Gerber (1994), Möschel (2001) (with comments by Gerber (2001) and Kamecke (2001)), Djelic (1998, pp. 107–111), Sullivan and Fikentscher (1998), Hildebrand (2002, pp. 86–89, pp. 158–162), and Buxbaum (2006). See also the December 1996 issue (on Franz Böhm) of the *European Journal of Law and Economics*.

See Willis (1978) for a concise overview of early post-World War II European integration. On the origins of the Schuman Plan, see Schuman (1953), Gerbet (1956), and Monnet (1976, pp. 349–360), and on the ECSC, EC Commission (1977b), Gillingham (1991), Spierenburg and Poidevin (1994), and Martin (2004b); I have drawn on the latter for some of the discussion here. On the long and generally successful efforts of the Ruhr coal industry to avoid the vagaries of untrammelled competition, see Stockder (1932) and Smith (1970). Heusdens and de Horn (1980) and Bodoff (1984) discuss crisis cartels in the ECSC steel industry.

On the Spaak Report, see Küsters (1989). Riesenfeld (1960) and Scherer (1994, Chapter 3) discuss national competition policies in European countries and the EEC in comparative perspective. See Schröter (1996) and Harding and Joshua (2003) for overviews of European cartel policy, past and present.

Appendix: Nuts and Bolts

The institutions of the European Union include the European Parliament and the Council of the European Union. The 732 members of the European Parliament are elected by popular vote. The Council of the European Union is made up of ministers of member state governments. The identity of the individuals who make up the Council of the European Union varies according to subject matter. Member State ministers of agriculture meet as the Council with respect to agricultural matters, Member State labor ministers meet as the Council with respect to labor matters, and so on. The Parliament and the Council have joint power to adopt legislation.

With the July 2002 expiration of the European Coal and Steel Community Treaty, there are two European Communities, the European Economic Community and Euratom. Under the 1992 Treaty of European Union (the Maastricht Treaty), the European Communities are one of three pillars of the European Union. The other two pillars are the Common Foreign and Security Policy and Police and Judicial Cooperation in Criminal Matters. The provisions of European Union competition policy are part of (or, in the case of the Merger Control Regulation, established under the provisions of) the Treaty on the Functioning of the European Union (TFEU, formerly the EC Treaty).

The executive branch of the European Union is the European Commission, made up of one Commissioner from each Member State, one of whom serves as President. Each commissioner heads a Directorate General with responsibility for a particular policy area, such as the environment or health and consumer protection. It is the Directorate General for Competition that is responsible for the administration of EU competition policy. Competition policy decisions of the European Commission can be appealed to the General Court (formerly the Court of First Instance), an appeals court established in 1988, and thence to the Court of Justice of the European Union (formerly the European Court of Justice).[30] In addition to these bodies, political leadership is provided to the European Union by the European Council (not to be

---

[30] For a discussion of the CJEU, and comparison with the U.S. Supreme Court, see Lagrange (1966–1967).

confused with the Council of the European Union).[31] It is made up of the heads of state or government of the Member States, and meets twice yearly.

Although there have been substantial modifications at the level of detail, broadly speaking the institutional structure of the European Union is an elaboration of the framework set out for the six-member European Economic Community in the 1957 Treaty of Rome. With the accession of 10 new Member States on May 1, 2004, there were 25 Member States of the European Union; the addition of Bulgaria and Romania on January 1, 2007 brings the total to 27. There is a consensus that the infrastructure of the European Union requires fundamental revisions, but the path to realizing those revisions has been a rocky one. Representatives of the EU member states signed a treaty proposing a constitution for the European Union in October, 2004. For the constitution to enter into effect required ratification in each of the 25 member states. In May and June, 2005, popular votes in France and the Netherlands rejected the proposed constitution. In December, 2007, the member states agreed on the Lisbon Treaty, which, after ratification by each member state, came into effect on December 1, 2009. Among the institutional changes provided for by the Lisbon Treaty are the creation of the posts of President of the European Council, to serve for a period of two and one-half years, and of the High Representative for the Union in Foreign Affairs and Security Policy, who also serves as a Vice-President of the European Commission.

Another element of the Lisbon Treaty reflects tension over the role of a market economy in the European Union. The proposed constitution included (in Article I-3) "free and undistorted competition" as one of the objectives of the European Union. On the initiative of France, the Treaty on European Union as amended by the Lisbon Treaty makes no such reference. Instead, a protocol to the TEU notes that the internal market includes undistorted competition and commits the European Union to take action accordingly. The practical implications of this change remain to be seen.

On a more mundane level, the Lisbon Treaty renumbers the competition policy provisions of the TFEU. Article 81 of the EC Treaty, which prohibits anti-competitive agreements, is now Article 101. Article 82 of the EC Treaty, which prohibits abuse of a dominant position, is now Article 102. Articles 87 and 88 of the EC Treaty, which provide for EU control of member state aid to business that distorts competition and affects trade within the EU, are now Articles 107 and 108.

Measures taken before the entry into force of the Lisbon Treaty reformed the infrastructure of competition policy enforcement.[32] Article 101(3) of the TFEU allows exemptions, under some circumstances, to the Article 101(1) prohibition of agreements that distort trade among the member states. From 1962, the Commission's original approach to administering what is now Article 101(3), embodied in Regulation 17,[33] required that interfirm agreements be notified to the Commission in advance, and reserved the right to grant an exemption to the Commission. There was much to recommend this centralized enforcement approach when prohibition-based competition policy was being introduced to a Community of six member states, member states that were much more at home with the abuse-control approach. The centralized approach was less workable in a Union of twenty-five member states, and less necessary as member state competition policies were revised for consistency with the articles of the EC Treaty. As of May 1, 2004, Regulation 17 is repealed and the system it established replaced by a system under which firms may implement an agreement that appears to qualify for an Article 101(3) exemption under a variety

---

[31] Nor should it be confused with the Council of Europe, an intergovernmental organization that is not part of the European Union. The Council of Europe was established in 1949 with the particular vocation of promoting human rights.

[32] For a review of the reforms, see Bloom (2005).

[33] Council Regulation No. 17/62 OJ 13/204 21 September 1962, variously amended.

of guidelines issued by the Commission.[34] The Competition Directorate General and the competition authorities of the member states, working together as the European Competition Network, cooperate in enforcing of EU competition policy.

Decisions of the European Commission are typically cited in the form "*IFTRA glass containers* Commission Decision of 15 May 1974 OJ L 160/1 17 June 1974." IFTRA (International Fair Trade Practice Rules Administration) was a glassmakers' trade association, and the object of the decision. The Commission decision was taken on May 15, 1974 and officially reported in the Official Journal L (legislation), number 160, page 1, on June 17, 1974. There is also an Official Journal C, in which Commission Notices and other information statements appear. The same decision, reported in the *Common Market Law Review*, might also be cited as IFTRA [1974] 2 CMLR D50.

Subject to the whims of the gremlins of the internet, more recent Commission decisions can be downloaded from the Commission's web site (http://ec.europa.eu/competition/index_en.html).

Judgments of the General Court and of the Court of Justice appear in the *European Court Reports* (ECR). A typical citation is "*Sugar Cartel*—Suiker Unie and others *v.* EC Commission, Joined Cases 40–48/73, 50/73, 54–56/73, 111/73, 113–114/73 Judgment of 16 December 1975 [1975] ECR 1663," indicating that the text of the decision is to be found beginning on page 1663 of the 1975 volume of the *European Court Reports*. The text of court decisions are also available, in principle, via the internet (http://curia.europa.eu/jcms/jcms/j_6/).

---

[34] Council Regulation (EC) No. 1/2003 of 16 December 2002 on the implementation of the rules on competition laid down in Articles 81 and 82 of the Treaty OJ L 1/1 4.1.2003. See Gauer *et al.* (2004).

COLLUSION AND COOPERATION: PUBLIC POLICY

People of the same trade seldom meet together, even for merriment and diversion, but the conversation ends in a conspiracy against the public, or in some contrivance to raise prices. It is impossible indeed to prevent such meetings, by any law which either could be executed, or would be consistent with liberty and justice. But though the law cannot hinder people of the same trade from sometimes assembling together, it ought to do nothing to facilitate such assemblies; much less to render them necessary.

Adam Smith ([1776] 1937, p. 128)

20.1 Introduction

In its 1998 Cartel Recommendation, the OECD defines a *hard core cartel* as (1998, p. 3) "an anticompetitive agreement, anticompetitive concerted practice, or anticompetitive arrangement by competitors to fix prices, make rigged bids (collusive tenders), establish output restrictions or quotas, or share or divide markets by allocating customers, suppliers, territories, or lines of commerce". Hard core cartels are widely viewed as having no redeeming social virtue. At best, if successful they enable oligopolists to reach or approach the monopoly outcome, leading to income transfers from consumers to producers, output restriction, and deadweight welfare loss. At worst, they shield firms from the chill winds of competition, permitting less-efficient firms to survive and at the same time reducing the incentive for firms to invest in productivity-enhancing research and development. In the latter case, consumers pay higher prices while firms fritter away what would have been economic profits in inefficiently high costs.

The OECD is at pains to distinguish hard core collusion from other types of interfirm cooperation, in particular (1998, p. 3) "agreements, concerted practices, or arrangements that ... are reasonably related to the lawful realisation of cost-reducing or output-enhancing efficiencies". But any interfirm agreement that has the primary purpose of realizing "cost-reducing or output-enhancing efficiencies" will have some impact on other aspects of the market behaviour of the parties to the agreement. It may be, for example, that the main reason two oil companies form a joint venture to exploit an oil-field is to spread risk. If risk-spreading cannot be obtained in any other way, then the joint venture is essential to attaining the desired reduction in risk borne by either firm. But in the process of managing the joint venture and as each firm quite naturally takes the situation of the subsidiary into account in planning its own actions, each parent firm will inevitably acquire information about the operations of the other. The existence of the joint venture, essential to spread risk, is also the vehicle for to the reciprocal transmission of information. The information exchange will facilitate tacit collusion. But it will be possible for the sophisticated colluder to package almost any arrangement that has that has the facilitation of tacit collusion as its *raison d'être* as an efficiency-enhancing contract.

The Gordian knot of antitrust and competition policy has been where to draw the line between hard core collusion and cooperation that, on balance, improves market performance even though on some subsidiary level it softens incentives to compete. Our topic in this chapter is the way U.S. antitrust and EU competition policy have tried to cut that knot.

20.2 Hard Core Collusion

20.2.1 Sherman Act Section 1

In the run-up to passage of the Sherman Act, railroads were widely perceived as having tried to collude, with at least intermittent success. Railroads' customers thought the consequences of this collusion to be unfair and to distort competition among competing firms that purchased transportation services from railroads.

Restraint of trade

Section 1 of the Sherman Act makes illegal "Every contract, combination in the form of trust or otherwise, or conspiracy, in restraint of trade or commerce among the several States, or with foreign nations". It fell to the courts to interpret the term "restraint of trade" for the purposes of the Sherman Act. What kinds of contracts, combinations, and conspiracies *restrain* trade? Those that are explicitly collusive, in the way of the railroad cartels of the 1880s? What about combinations that are not explicitly collusive, but involve a mixture of conduct, some that worsens and some that improves market performance?

To anticipate the long (and continuing) dance around the Section 1 Maypole, early Section 1 decisions settled that agreements to fix price, and agreements that could *only* have the intent or effect of fixing price, are prohibited under the Sherman Act. The line involving contracts and combinations that do not fall in this "naked collusion" category has been drawn in different places at different times and in different circumstances. Some decisions have placed most weight on the fact that an agreement affects price, and condemned the agreement for that reason, even if it might have non-price effects. In other decisions, courts have been willing to consider the net impact of price and non-price consequences of an agreement on market performance.

Addyston Pipe and Steel[1]

The basis of judicial interpretation of Section 1 of the Sherman Act is due to then-Judge William Howard Taft. He wrote the Circuit Court of Appeals decision in a case involving a

---

[1] U.S. *v.* Addyston Pipe & Steel Co. *et al.* 85 F. 271 (1898); Addyston Pipe & Steel Co. *et al. v.* U.S. 175 U.S. 211 (1899).

pool of six manufacturers of cast iron pipe, the Associated Pipe Works. Cast iron pipe was sold primarily to cities and public utilities, which solicited bids from producers for components to be used in piping water and gas. The pool began in December 1893, during a business depression. Member firms, located in the South and Midwest United States, colluded to charge the highest prices they could without making it profitable for Eastern firms to enter their geographic market.

Reserved cities   In its operating region (that is, outside the Northeast), the pool classified regions into two types. Some cities were *reserved* for specific firms. When contracts were opened for bidding in those areas, the designated firm would submit a bid and inform its fellows of the amount of its bid. They would submit higher bids, so that there would be an appearance of competition. The contract would be awarded to the firm for which the city was reserved, which had submitted the low bid.

Pay territory   Areas that were not reserved were referred to as *pay territory*.[2] When a contract came up for bid in pay territory, a board of representatives of the six firms would determine the amount that was to be the low bid. This having been decided, cartel members would bid in their own internal auction for the right to get the contract. The bids in this internal auction were amounts the firm pledged to pay *to the cartel*, if it should receive the right to win the contract. The winner of the internal auction—the firm offering the highest payment to the pool—would submit a bid at the price decided by the board. Enough other firms would submit higher bids to create an appearance of competition. The payments made by winners of the internal auctions to the pool were periodically divided among all members.[3]

From a resource allocation point of view, there is one thing that can be said in favour of a scheme of this kind. Presumably, the internal auction mechanism resulted in jobs going to the firm that was able to do the work at lowest cost. It is this firm that would be able to offer the largest payment to the cartel.

Miscalculation   Early in 1896, despite the importance of transportation cost in this industry, a Philadelphia firm that was not part of the pool submitted the low bid on a contract put out for bid by the city of Atlanta, Georgia. The cartel had misjudged the price at which it would become profitable for an outside supplier to enter their market. Atlanta rejected all bids on the ground that they were too high. The episode triggered a U.S. government antitrust suit against the pool and its members.

---

[2] Another term might have been chosen if the members of the pool had anticipated their eventual legal problems.

[3] There is nothing new under the sun: on 1 May 2002, the U.S. Department of Justice accepted guilty pleas from two individuals who conspired between August 1996 and January 2001 to rig bids at sheriffs' auctions of property seized for resale to satisfy debts. The mechanical aspects of the conspiracy were essentially the same as those at issue in *Addyston Pipe and Steel* (2005-1 CCH Trade Cases ¶ 74,820): "the individuals carried out the conspiracy by designating one member of the group to bid the lowest price possible to obtain the property at public auction. After the public auction, the conspirators would hold a private auction among themselves where they bid against each other on the foreclosed property at prices higher than the price paid by the designated winning bidder at the public auction. The highest bidder at the private auction would win the property, be assigned the right to purchase the property by the public auction winner, and make commission payoffs to the other conspirators to compensate them for not bidding at the public auction." McMillan (1991) describes broadly similar schemes in the Japanese construction industry.

Collusion at common law (Taft)   The government charged the firms with violations of Sections 1 (restraint of trade) and 2 (conspiracy to monopolize) of the Sherman Act. In 1897, the trial court relied on the Supreme Court's 1895 decision in the *Sugar Trust* case, which seemed to remove manufacturing from the purview of the Sherman Act, and found against the government. The government appealed against this decision to the Sixth Circuit Court of Appeals.

At the Circuit Court of Appeals, the firms defended themselves with the argument that:

(a) the Sherman Act codified the common law on restraint of trade;

(b) under the common law only contracts or combinations that put unreasonable restrictions in place were illegal; and

(c) "the object of their association was not to raise prices beyond what was reasonable, but only to prevent ruinous competition between defendants which would have carried prices far below a reasonable point … "

Ancillary restraints   The view that the effect of the Sherman Act was to codify the existing common law rule had been put forward in Senate debate passage of the Sherman Act. But the common law on restraint of trade was a qualified standard of reasonableness: restraints of trade accepted by the common law if they were incidental or *ancillary* to an otherwise legitimate contract, and no more restrictive than necessary to allow the legitimate contract to be carried out.

It is, for example, a legitimate contract for one baker to sell an established business to another.[4] If as part of such a contract the seller agrees not to open a new bakery in the same area, and for a limited time period, that part of the contract restrains trade. It is an agreement that one baker will not compete with another. But in the context of the agreement to sell the bakery, such a restriction is necessary if the seller is to obtain a price that reflects the value of the business being sold. Without such an agreement, the buyer would discount the value of the business to allow for the possibility that the seller, with established reputation and goodwill, would open up a new bakery in the same area before the buyer could establish his own reputation. The seller of the bakery agrees to limits on his future right to compete in order to get the best possible price for the business that he sells.

The common law view was that as long as the agreement not to compete was limited in geographic scope and duration, and as long as it was necessary for the main contract to be carried out, it was reasonable. It was reasonable even though it was a restriction on competition and limited the ability of seller to support himself.

There was, of course, scope for judgment in the application of this common law rule. It had to be decided if an agreement in restraint of trade was or was not ancillary to a legitimate contract. It had to be decided if it was no broader than necessary to allow that legitimate contract to be carried out.

Judge Taft made an extensive review of the development of the common law toward restraints of trade, and summarized it by writing (85 Fed 271 at 281–283):

---

[4] The example is based on the facts of Mitchel *v*. Reynolds 1 Peere Wms. 181 (1711), discussed by Thorelli (1955, pp. 17–19), Letwin (1965, pp. 42–43) (among many others).

[I]t would certainly seem to follow ... that no conventional restraint of trade can be enforced unless ... it is merely ancillary to the main purpose of a lawful contract, and necessary to protect the covenantee in the enjoyment of the legitimate fruits of the contract ...

... But where the sole object of both parties in making the contract as expressed therein is merely to restrain competition, and enhance or maintain prices, it would seem that there was nothing to justify or excuse the restraint, that it would necessarily have a tendency to monopoly, and therefore would be void ...

 BOX   Collusive Bidding at the Hands of the Common Law

In 1892 the city of Portland, Oregon solicited bids for the construction of a system of waterworks. Lee Hoffman and John McMullen agreed that McMullen would submit a bid that was $49,000 higher than that of Hoffman, so that Hoffman would get the contract from the city, and further that they would then equally divide the cost and profit of the business. Hoffman died, and his widow refused to divide the profit from the job ($140,000), "upon the ground that the bids made by them tended ... to lessen competition, and operated as a fraud under the city, and could not be enforced ... "

McMullen sued to enforce the agreement to divide the profit from the job, and prevailed in lower court. Although the events and the lawsuit occurred after passage of the Sherman Act, that law was not invoked: when the matter reached the Ninth Circuit Court of Appeals, the question was whether or not the contract could be enforced.

For the appeals court, the contract was plainly collusive (83 F. 372 at 375): "they were to pool their bids, and so arrange matters that the highest bid, as between themselves, should, if possible, be accepted, and they would divide the proceeds of the contract." The legal rule was plain (83 F. 372 at 376): "A contract to prevent competition and bidding for public work is contrary to public policy, and cannot be enforced."

Contract law did not object to partnerships (83 F. 372 at 376–377):*

> An honest co-operation between two or more persons to accomplish an object which neither could gain if acting alone in his individual capacity is not within the rule, although, in a certain sense and to a limited degree, such co-operation might have a tendency to lessen competition.

The appeals court recognized that Hoffman was using the law to its own advantage ("the objection that a contract was immoral or illegal as between [Hoffman] and [McMullen] sounds at all times very ill in the mouth of [Hoffman]"), but held that "[t]he refusal of courts to enforce such contracts is always founded in general principles of public policy ... " By means of their contract, Hoffman and McMullen had perpetrated a fraud on the city of Portland:

> In consideration of sharing in the profits, McMullen did not put in an honest bid. He put in a bid much higher than he would otherwise have done but for the agreement. His object, evidently, was to deceive the committee,—to convey the idea that he was a rival bidder, when in fact he was not. Such conduct certainly tended to destroy competition, and to preclude the advantages which inevitably resulted from it.

The appeals court reversed the lower court decision and refused to compel the division of profits specified in the collusive agreement.

*Kolasky and Dick (2003, fn. 4) cite this as an anticipation of the rule of reason

Source: Hoffman v. McMullen 83 F. 372 (1897).

Thus, the common law rule was not to assess whether or not a restraint was reasonable, and to permit reasonable restraints. The common law rule was that restraints on trade were enforceable if they were incidental to some otherwise lawful contract, and no more severe than needed to accomplish the purpose of that contract. Otherwise, they were not enforceable.

The cast iron pipe pool was not ancillary to an otherwise lawful contract. For the Circuit Court, it followed that (85 F. 271 at 291) "the association of the defendants, however reasonable the prices they fixed, however great the competition they had to encounter, and however great the necessity for curbing themselves by joint agreement from committing financial suicide by ill-advised competition, was void at common law, because in restraint of trade, and tending to a monopoly".

Sea of doubt   In their arguments, the attorneys for Addyston Pipe & Steel and its colleagues drew the attention of the court to a number of decisions in which a court appeared to have made its own evaluation of the reasonableness of a restrictive contract. Taft discussed those precedents, found each to be wanting, and dismissed the whole idea of judicial evaluation of the reasonableness of a contractual restraint as inappropriately vague (85 F. 271 at 283–284, emphasis added):

> It is true that there are some cases in which the courts, mistaking, as we conceive, the proper limits of the relaxation of the rules for determining the unreasonableness of restraints of trade, have *set sail on a sea of doubt*, and have assumed the power to say, in respect to contracts which have no other purpose ... than the mutual restraint of the parties, how much restraint of competition is in the public interest, and how much is not.
>
>   The manifest danger in the administration of justice according to so shifting, vague, and indeterminate a standard would seem to be a strong reason against adopting it.

On this view, a legal rule that requires courts to balance out the pluses and minuses of any particular contract in restraint of trade and decide if the contract did or did not violate Section 1 of the Sherman Act would leave businesses with no clear indication what the law expected of them.

On appeal: *per se*   The Circuit Court of Appeals found that the pipe manufacturers had violated the Sherman Act. It directed the lower court to issue an injunction requiring that the pool be dissolved. The pipe manufacturers appealed this decision to the U.S. Supreme Court. The Supreme Court endorsed Judge Taft's Circuit Court of Appeals opinion, writing (175 U.S. 237–238, emphasis added):

> It has been earnestly pressed upon us that the prices at which the cast-iron pipe was sold ... were reasonable. ... We do not think the issue an important one, because ... *we do not think that at common law there is any question of reasonableness open to the courts with reference to such a contract.*

The rule originating in *Addyston Pipe and Steel* is that agreements to fix price are illegal *per se*, in and of themselves. What must be proven to show that there has been a violation of the Sherman Act Section 1 prohibition of contracts, combinations, and conspiracies in restraint of trade is that there has been an agreement to directly or indirectly fix price. It need not be shown that the firms making the agreement were successful in fixing price, or even that they might have been—the absence of market power does not excuse an otherwise *per se* illegal offence. It need not be shown that the prices agreed upon were in some sense unreasonable. Proof of the existence of an agreement to fix price is sufficient to establish a violation of Section 1.

The *per se* rule reduces the administrative burden placed on the legal system. If agreements to fix prices at reasonable levels were permitted and agreements to set prices at unreasonable levels forbidden, courts would be placed in the role of regulatory agencies, continually evaluating whether or not prices were reasonable in light of changing market conditions. Further, the *per se* rule reduces enforcement cost by avoiding the need for an extensive analysis of agreements (to fix price, reduce output, divide markets) that experience teaches are virtually certain to worsen market performance. It also makes clear what the legal standard is: no firm with competent legal advice can claim that it thought its agreement to fix price was legal because it believed that the price fixed was a reasonable one.

Aftermath　As already noted, the remedy imposed in the *Addyston Pipe and Steel* case was the dissolution of the pipe pool. In addition, some years after the decision in the federal case, and as the result of a private antitrust suit, one of the cities that had been a victim of the pool recovered a modest amount in damages, $1,500. This was trebled and, with an additional award of $2,500 in legal fees, resulted in a payment of $7,000.[5]

The aftermath of the *Addyston Pipe and Steel* decision illustrates the implications of antitrust policy toward market conduct for market structure.[6] Between the time of Judge Taft's Circuit Court of Appeals decision and its confirmation by the Supreme Court, the firms that had made up the Associated Pipe Works, together with other firms located in the Northeast, merged to form the United States Cast Iron Pipe and Foundry Company. The post-merger combination, being a single firm, could set prices as it wished, without violating Section 1 of the Sherman Act.

The post-merger firm had a 75 per cent share of U.S. production.[7] If such a merger had taken place a few years later, it might have been challenged as monopolization in violation of Section 2 of the Sherman Act. If it had taken place 55 years later, it would very likely have been challenged as a violation of the amended Section 7 of the Clayton Act. As it was, the merger went forward, and had mixed consequences for market performance. The U.S. Cast Iron Pipe and Foundry Company was large enough to standardize pipe specifications, an efficiency advantage. It established a research and development operation. But it was sufficiently large that it was under no particular competitive pressure to operate at peak efficiency. It was only some 25 years after its formation that it began to close inefficient and out-of-the-way plants. After a period of losses, it returned to profitability by the late 1920s, by which time its share of U.S. output had fallen to under 50 per cent.

Northern Securities

The Supreme Court's 1895 *Sugar Trust* or *E.C. Knight* decision removed manufacturing from the coverage of the Sherman Act. The basis for the decision was that manufacturing took place within state lines, while the Commerce Clause of the U.S. Constitution limits

---

[5] City of Atlanta *v.* Chattanooga Foundry and Pipe Works 127 Fed 23 (1903), 203 U.S. 390 (1906). See the discussion of Thorelli (1955, pp. 489–490).

[6] The discussion that follows is based on Whitney (1958, Chapter 10).

[7] The geographic market very likely was regional rather than national.

Congressional authority to the regulation of interstate commerce. It was not until 1904 and the *Northern Securities* decision[8] that the Supreme Court moved beyond the interpretation it had given to the Sherman Act in *E.C. Knight*.

The *Northern Securities* case was filed when the Theodore Roosevelt administration was not quite six months old. The decision to file the case was taken with the personal involvement of the President as part of his effort to reanimate the Sherman Act.[9]

Community of interest The Northern Securities Company was set up to create what J. Pierpont Morgan called a "community of interest" between the Hill-Morgan and Harriman railroad groups.[10] Formally, Northern Securities was a holding company that owned the Great Northern and the Northern Pacific railroad companies. The government attacked the acquisition of the two railroads by Northern Securities as a violation of both Section 1 (combination in restraint of trade) and of Section 2 (monopolization). From an economic point of view, the Section 2 charge appears somewhat artificial. Northern Securities was not a firm that had monopolized by purchasing two competing railroad lines. It had been created by the two railroad lines as part of their peace treaty with the Harriman interests.

Defence Northern Securities mounted a three-pronged defence. First, it argued that it was not a railway company, it was simply an investment company that happened to own stock in a couple of railroad companies. Second, it relied on the *Sugar Trust* decision to argue that the Sherman Act did not apply to activities taking place within a single state—and that its own activities, the buying and selling of shares of stock, took place in New Jersey. Third, it argued that since the two railroads had not competed in that past, the fact that they had been purchased by the same holding company was not a restraint of trade.

 BOX *The Players*

(A) James J. Hill and J. Pierpont Morgan, whose interests controlled two nominally independent railway lines, the Great Northern and the Northern Pacific (running between Seattle, Washington and Duluth and St. Paul, Minnesota);

(B) Edward H. Harriman, whose interests controlled the Union Pacific Railroad (Sacramento, California to Omaha, Nebraska and Kansas City, Missouri) and the Southern Pacific Railroad (San Francisco, California to New Orleans, Louisiana).   ⟫

---

[8] Northern Securities Co. *v.* U.S. 193 U.S. 197 (1904).

[9] Roosevelt wrote Charles Washburn that *Northern Securities* provided an opportunity to secure a reversal of the *E.C. Knight* decision, something that Roosevelt regarded as essential because "The Knight case practically denied the Federal Government power over corporations, because it whittled to nothing the meaning of 'commerce between the States.' It had to be upset or we could not get any efficient control by the National Government" (Washburn, 1928, p. 114; see also Washburn, 1916, pp. 67–68).

[10] There were other purposes as well. Northern Securities, with a capitalization greater than that of its two properties (the Great Northern and the Northern Pacific) would be largely immune from a takeover attempt of the kind Harriman had mounted on Northern Pacific (Letwin, 1965, pp. 194–195).

Figure 20.1 "Three railroad systems roughly parallel, with the middle one a bone of contention between the other two ... "

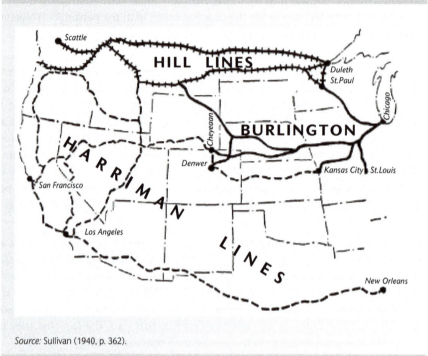

Source: Sullivan (1940, p. 362).

>> *The Object of Their Affections*

(C) The Chicago, Burlington & Quincy Railroad ("the Burlington", with connections to both the Harriman and Hill-Morgan railroads and with access to Chicago, Illinois).

Sequence of Events

(1) 1893: Northern Pacific goes into bankruptcy, reorganized under control of Morgan and Deutsche Bank.

(2) London Agreement of 1896: Hill and allies purchase 10 per cent of Northern Pacific stock, giving Hill-Morgan interests effective control.

(3) Spring 1900: Harriman and allies buy about 10 per cent of stock in the Burlington, decide they cannot obtain control, sell out.

(4) April 1901: Great Northern and Northern Pacific purchase control of the Burlington, gaining control of access to Chicago (for itself and for Union Pacific)] and control of track parallel to that of Union Pacific through Colorado, Nebraska, and Kansas.

(5) Harriman asks Hill and Morgan to sell him part-interest in the Burlington; they decline.

» (6) April–May 1901: Harriman and allies quietly buy stock in Northern Pacific on the open market.

(7) May 1901: Hill and Morgan realize what's up, buy some outstanding stock in Northern Pacific themselves.

(7a) 6 May 1901: financial panic: speculators have signed contracts to sell the two different groups more shares of stock in Northern Pacific than exist, bid price up.

(8) When the dust settles:

a. Harriman and allies have a majority of common and preferred stock together;

b. Hill and Morgan have a majority of common stock;

c. the Board of Directors, which is controlled by Hill and Morgan, has the right to retire preferred stock on 1 January of each year through 1917, for $100 a share.

(9) November 1901: Facing the prospect of a nasty legal battle, the groups kiss and make up. Harriman becomes a member of the Board of Directors of Northern Pacific, they agree that the Burlington will not extend its operations west from Denver without Harriman's consent, and ownership of Northern Pacific *and* the Great Northern is transferred to the Northern Securities Company, a holding company established in New Jersey for this purpose.

Sources: Garner (1904), Meyer (1906), Sullivan (1940, pp. 360–370); Thorelli (1955, pp. 421–425, 470–475, 560–563); Dewey (1959, pp. 214–215); Letwin (1965, Chapter 6), Prager (1992).

Letwin suggests that attorneys for the government might have admitted that the two railroads had not competed in the past, but that this was not inherent in the nature of things (1965, p. 223): "The Government's best tactic, and certainly the position that would best have cleared the air, would have been to insist that the geography of the two lines inevitably made them capable of competing with each other." Combining ownership of the two lines in a single holding company eliminated each as a potential competitor of the other. With the clarity of hindsight, this seems correct. In view of the fact that the Sherman Act was not yet 15 years old when the *Northern Securities* case was tried, it is perhaps not surprising that the Government missed this approach.

Principle of competition   Writing for a narrow majority of the Supreme Court, Justice Harlan reviewed previous decisions under the Sherman Act and read between its lines reliance on competition as a resource allocation mechanism as the purpose of the law (193 U.S. 197 at 337; emphasis added):

Whether the free operation of the normal laws of competition is a wise and wholesome rule for trade and commerce is an economic question which this court need not consider or determine. Undoubtedly, there are those who think that the general business interests and prosperity of the country will be best promoted if the rule of competition is not applied. But there are others who believe that such a rule is more necessary in these days of enormous wealth than it ever was in any former period in our history. Be all this as it may, *Congress has*, in effect, *recognized the rule of free competition* by declaring illegal every combination or conspiracy in restraint of interstate and international commerce.

The Supreme Court affirmed the ruling of the lower court,[11] which had condemned Northern Securities as an unlawful combination.

After this decision, the *principle of competition* assumed a key position in the application of many elements of U.S. antitrust (Letwin, 1965, p. 227): "Harlan's opinion served for years as the great synthesis of all previous interpretations of the statute. The rule, as it now stood, was that 'restraint of trade' meant any *direct* interference with *competition*."

Contracts in restraint of trade vs. conspiracies in restraint of trade   In his dissenting opinion in the 1904 *Northern Securities* case, Justice Holmes, author of an 1881 treatise on the common law, made a distinction between the common law treatment of *contracts in restraint of trade* and the common law treatment of *conspiracies in restraint of trade*. Contracts in restraint of trade were restrictions on competition between the parties to the contract. In Holmes' view, the common law did not object to such contracts unless the limitation of competition was so broad that it led to monopoly. Conspiracies in restraint of trade, in contrast, were agreements between firms in a business to prevent competition from some third party (193 U.S. 197 at 404): "they were regarded as contrary to public policy because they monopolized or attempted to monopolize some portion of the trade of commerce or the realm." As Holmes read the common law, it did not object to combinations (partnerships and mergers) that did not interfere with the ability of those outside the combination to compete.[12]

An economic rationale for permitting contracts in restraint of trade as defined by Holmes would rely on the force of potential competition to obtain good market performance.[13] If firms wish to merge, let them. If they are more efficient after the merger, well and good. If they are less efficient, or exercise market power over some short-run time period, entry will occur and market performance improve—provided there is no strategic behaviour to keep efficient competitors out of the market. This is essentially the position taken by John Bates Clark, and the policy later embodied in the 1914 Clayton Act. Whether or not one thinks such a policy will promote good market performance will depend critically on what one thinks about the ability of antitrust or competition policy authorities and the judiciary to effectively administer a rule against strategic anticompetitive behaviour.[14]

Chicago Board of Trade[15]

Addyston Pipe and Steel lays down a hard line against so-called *naked collusion*—agreements with the purpose or effect of fixing price and/or dividing markets. But Section 1 of the

---

[11] U.S. *v.* Northern Securities Co. *et al.* 120 F. 721 (1903).

[12] At least one author of the Sherman Act seems to have expected that it would be interpreted in this way. According to Washburn (1928, p. 99), thirteen months after passage of the Sherman Act, Senator Hoar wrote to members of a pool (i.e., cartel) that had sought his advice that "it seems to me that a contract, although in partial restraint of trade, which is reasonable and reasonably limited in point of time, which has for its object merely the saving the parties from a destructive competition with each other, is not prohibited by the [Sherman Act]" and "I think the contract above proposed is reasonable, and would be so held by the courts of the United States". Washburn's discussion is noted by Adelman (1956).

[13] This is not to say that this economic rationale is the one upon which the common law position was based.

[14] On this point it may be well to recall the words of Theodore Roosevelt (1913, pp. 618–619): "the effort to administer a law merely by lawsuits and court decisions is bound to end in signal failure, and to put a premium upon legal sharp practice. Such an effort does not adequately punish the guilty, and yet works great harm to the innocent."

[15] Board of Trade of the City of Chicago *v.* US 246 U.S. 231 (1918).

Sherman Act does not prohibit all agreements between firms; it prohibits only agreements that are in restraint of trade or commerce. If an agreement does not seek or obtain immediate control of price, when, as far as antitrust is concerned, does it restrain trade? The 1918 *Chicago Board of Trade* decision established that the answer to this question must be made on a case-by-case basis.

The Chicago Board of Trade was the leading grain market in the world. Regular trading sessions were held from 9:30 am to 1:15 pm, followed by a short session (1:15 pm to 2:00 pm) for trading of futures contracts. The Board of Trade's "Call Rule" obliged members who wished to trade futures contracts between the end of one trading day and the opening of the next to use the most recent closing price. This rule was challenged by the U.S. government as a restraint of trade and therefore a *per se* violation of Section 1 of the Sherman Act. The government's position was accepted by the District Court. The Chicago Board of Trade appealed to the Supreme Court, for which Justice Brandeis wrote (246 U.S. 231 at 244, emphasis added):

> [T]he legality of an agreement or regulation cannot be determined by so simple a test, as whether it restrains competition. Every agreement concerning trade, every regulation of trade, restrains. To bind, to restrain, is of their very essence. *The true test of legality is whether the restraint imposed is such as merely regulates and perhaps thereby promotes competition or whether it is such as may suppress or even destroy competition.* To determine that question the court must ordinarily consider the facts peculiar to the business to which the restraint is applied; its condition before and after the restraint was imposed; the nature of the restraint and its effect, actual or probably. The history of the restraint, the evil believed to exist, the reason for adopting the particular remedy, the purpose or end sought to be attained, are all relevant facts.

As reviewed by Brandeis, the Call Rule promoted good market performance in the trading of futures contracts by limiting the ability of the relatively small number of warehouses in Chicago to make trades at low prices between the close of business one day and the opening of business the next (246 U.S. 231 at 239):[16] "It brought buyers and sellers into more direct relations; because on the Call they gathered together for a free and open interchange of bids and offers."

The Supreme Court reversed the lower Court and permitted the Call Rule. Brandeis' list of factors to be considered—"the facts peculiar to the business to which the restraint is applied; its condition before and after the restraint was imposed; the nature of the restraint and its effect, actual or probably"—amorphous and expansive though it is, is often cited as the classic statement of the *rule of reason*, which originated in the 1911 *Standard Oil* decision, interpreting Section 2 of the Sherman Act, and which we discuss in Section 21.2.1.

Trenton Potteries

The *per se* illegality rule for naked collusion was confirmed in the 1927 *Trenton Potteries* decision.[17] The case involved a trade association, the Sanitary Potters' Association, which on

---

[16] This point may now be viewed in light of the experimental evidence suggesting that trades on organized markets like the Chicago Board of Trade tend to converge quickly to the competitive equilibrium.

[17] U.S. *v.* Trenton Potteries 273 U.S. 392 (1927).

behalf of its members administered an elaborate programme for the exchange of price information and promoted adherence to uniform prices. The members of the trade association operated in several different states. They controlled some 82 per cent of the U.S. market for their product. In a District Court jury trial, the firms requested that the trial judge instruct the jury as follows about the antitrust law (300 F. 550 at 553):

> The essence of the [Sherman] law is injury to the public; it is not every restraint of competition and not every restraint of trade that works an injury to the public; it is only an undue and unreasonable restraint of trade that has such an effect and is deemed to be unlawful.

The judge declined, and the jury returned a guilty verdict. Trenton Potteries and its fellow defendants appealed this outcome to the Second Circuit Court of Appeals. The jury's guilty verdict, they argued, had been based on a faulty explanation of the law, and so the result should be overturned. The Circuit Court accepted this view, and ordered the case back to District Court for a new trial. Before that could happen, the U.S. government appealed the circuit court decision to the U.S. Supreme Court.

Principle of competition   The Supreme Court gave short shrift to the argument that the jury should have been instructed to consider the reasonableness of the prices set by the pottery cartel. In so doing, it reenforced the principle of competition (273 U.S. 392 at 386–397, emphasis added):

> it does not follow that agreements to fix or maintain prices are reasonable restraints and therefore permitted by the statute, merely because the prices themselves are reasonable. ... Whether this type of restraint is reasonable or not must be judged in part at least in the light of its effect on competition, for whatever difference of opinion there may be among economists as to the social and economic desirability of an unrestrained competitive system, *it cannot be doubted that the Sherman Law and the judicial decisions interpreting it are based upon the assumption that the public interest is best protected from the evils of monopoly and price control by the maintenance of competition.*

On a practical level, the Court noted that a policy of evaluating the reasonableness of price restraints would tie courts up in a thicket of industry regulation, giving them (273 U.S. 392 at 398) "the burden of ascertaining from day to day whether it has become unreasonable through the mere variation of economic conditions". The Supreme Court reversed the circuit court ruling and reinstated the result of the District Court trial. The place of the *per se* rule against naked collusion seemed secure.

Appalachian Coals[18]

However, briefly, a 1933 Supreme Court decision placed this security in doubt. The post-World War I U.S. bituminous coal industry suffered from fundamentally irreparable ills. During the war, coal capacity had expanded to 700 million tonnes per year. This investment in new capacity was both literally and economically sunk. Peacetime demand was less than 500 million tonnes per year. Increasing substitution of oil and natural gas for coal reduced

---

[18] Appalachian Coals, Inc. *v.* US 288 U.S. 344 (1933). The District Court decision is U.S. *v.* Appalachian Coals, Inc. *et al.* 1 F. Supp. 339 (1932).

demand for coal, as did more efficient methods for using coal. The upshot of these changes was to make coal a declining industry. The Great Depression pushed it over the brink.

Joint sales agencies   Governors of coal-producing states organized conferences to find strategies that would allow the bituminous coal industry to survive. One proposal was the organization of joint sales agencies. The first such joint sales agency was Appalachian Coals, Inc., formed by 137 bituminous coal producers located in Virginia, West Virginia, Kentucky, and Tennessee. Before it could begin operations, its formation was challenged by the U.S. government as a violation of Sections 1 and 2 of the Sherman Act.

Estimates of the market share the joint sales agency would have, if it were to go into effect, varied. One figure was 54 per cent of the Appalachian and immediately surrounding regions. There was no doubt that the joint sales agency, if in operation, would affect the price of bituminous coal, even though it might not be able to control it.

District Court   The case came before the U.S. courts during the depths of the Great Depression. The coal producers defended the joint sales agency as a reasonable response to the situation of their industry. The District Court judges accepted that this was the intention behind the plan (1 F. Supp. 339 at 341):

> [I]t is but due to defendants to say that the evidence in the case clearly shows that they have been acting fairly and openly, in an attempt to organize the coal industry and to relieve the deplorable conditions resulting from overexpansion, destructive competition, wasteful trade practices, and the inroads of competing industries.

Cooperation vs. merger   The coal producers also contrasted the antitrust treatment of cooperative arrangements made by legally independent firms with the antitrust treatment of large firms. Cooperative arrangements with direct actual or intended effect on price were forbidden by the *per se* rule. A large firm would of necessity set its own prices, and as long as such a firm refrained from the use of tactics regarded by the law as monopolization, it would escape antitrust condemnation.

It is clear from the District Court opinion that its author had much sympathy for the coal companies. It gives every impression that the District Court would have given a verdict permitting the joint sales agency, if its members had thought it within their power to do so. They did not (1 F. Supp. 339 at 349):

> The argument of defendants goes, not to the reasonableness of the agreement as measured by the statute, but to the reasonableness of the statute itself. We sympathize with the plight of those engaged in the coal industry, whether as operators or as miners; but we have no option but to declare the law as we find it. We cannot repeal acts of Congress nor can we overrule decisions of the Supreme Court interpreting them.

Supreme Court: Charter of Freedom   So the coal companies lost in District Court, and it was this outcome that they appealed to the U.S. Supreme Court. The Supreme Court majority[19] made clear it would not consider itself as being painted into a *per se* corner (288 U.S. 344 at 359–360, emphasis added):

---

[19] Justice McReynolds dissented but offered no written opinion.

As a charter of freedom, the Act has a generality and adaptability comparable to that found to be desirable in constitutional provisions. ... *The restrictions the Act imposes are not mechanical or artificial. Its general phrases* ... set up the essential standard of reasonableness. They call for vigilance in the detection and frustration of all efforts unduly to restrain the free course of interstate commerce, but they *do not seek to establish a mere delusive liberty either by making impossible the normal and fair expansion of that commerce or the adoption of reasonable measures to protect it from injurious and destructive practices and to promote competition upon a sound basis.*

The majority referred back to Justice Brandeis' *Chicago Board of Trade* statement of factors to be considered in evaluating whether an agreement restrained or merely regulated trade, and examined, in its opinion (288 U.S. 344 at 361) "the economic conditions peculiar to the coal industry, the practices which have obtained, the nature of defendant's plan of making sales, the reasons which led to its adoption, and the probable consequences of the carrying out of that plan in relation to market prices and other matters affecting the public interest in interstate commerce in bituminous coal". In what was in everything but name a reversal of the positions taken in earlier decisions, the Court accepted the argument that antitrust should not make a distinction between actions of legally formed single firms and actions made by agreement of independent suppliers (288 U.S. 344 at 376):

[T]here is no ground for holding defendants' plan illegal merely because they have not integrated their properties and have chosen to maintain their independent plants, seeking not to limit but rather to facilitate production. We know of no public policy, and none is suggested by the terms of the Sherman Act, that, in order to comply with the law, those engaged in industry should be driven to unify their properties and businesses, in order to correct abuses which may be corrected by less drastic measures.

Aftermath   In March, 1933 the Supreme Court reversed the decision of the District Court. Appalachian Coals, Inc. began operation shortly thereafter. It became involved in the National Recovery Administration, which existed for almost two years from June 1932.[20] Later it was caught up in the 1937 Bituminous Coal Act, an ill-fated attempt to stabilize the industry through government-mandated price-fixing that ended in 1943.

Even leaving aside the long-run shift from coal to oil and natural gas as energy sources, what the Supreme Court decision failed to confront was that with 700 million tonnes of annual capacity in place to meet annual demand amounting to not quite 500 million tonnes of output, the bituminous coal industry was in structural disequilibrium. No amount of private or public price-fixing could alter the fact of excess coal capacity. In order for the most efficient 500 million tonnes of annual capacity to be able to earn a normal rate of return on investment, the least efficient 200 million tonnes of annual capacity had to shut down.

In principle, the profit-maximizing managers of a single firm will consolidate production and close down the least productive mines.[21] A cartel is more likely to negotiate market-sharing agreements that allocate output largely without taking productivity into account, prolonging inevitable adjustments and imposing inefficiently high production costs on society in the process.

---

[20] See Section 20.3.2.

[21] However, the lacklustre performance of the U.S. Cast Iron Pipe and Foundry Company, formed by merger of firms involved in *Addyston Pipe and Steel*, is a cautionary tale.

None of this is to say that if a region faces severe economic readjustment costs, a case can not or should not be made for regional development assistance. From an economic point of view, delivering such assistance through the back door, via cartelization, is likely to be more expensive and less effective than explicit targeted transitional aid programmes.

Socony Vacuum[22]

The *per se* comet returned to its orbit with the 1940 *Socony Vacuum* decision. The case arose in the U.S. oil refining and distribution market. Oil refining is another product market where the technology involves the use of highly specific sunk assets, and where fixed costs are a large fraction of total costs.

Prorationing In October 1930 the discovery of the East Texas oil field expanded the supply of U.S. oil by 20 per cent overnight, and the U.S. oil market descended into chaos. Oklahoma and Texas, the states most immediately concerned, introduced *prorationing* schemes to limit output. Ostensibly, these programmes were motivated by a desire to conserve a scarce non-renewable resource, crude oil. The effect of such programs to raise the price of oil may have been an ancillary result. Or *vice versa*. Be that as it may, oil fields in Oklahoma and Texas were the source of so-called "hot oil"—produced over prorationing limits and shipped across state lines as quickly as possible, where it found its way to the supply side of the market. Sometimes hot oil was refined into "hot gasoline", entering the supply chain closer to final consumer demand.

The refiner-retailer nexus Major, vertically integrated oil companies marketed brand-name petrol to the growing market for car fuel. Much of the petrol was distributed through independent retail petrol stations, under long-term contracts. The long-term contracts tied the price paid by the owner of the independent retail outlet to the spot market price for petrol.

Buyback programmes Major oil companies operating in the U.S. Midwest cooperated to set up buying programmes under which they would take excess supplies of petrol off the hands of independent refiners. These programmes were carried out with the encouragement of Texas lawmakers and, while the National Recovery Administration was in force, of the federal government. The oil majors continued the buyback programmes after the National Recovery Administration was declared unconstitutional.[23]

District Court A District Court jury trial found that the major oil companies had violated Section 1 of the Sherman Act. The government's economic theory was that by raising the spot market price of petrol, the majors had raised the amount paid by the owners of independent retail petrol stations.

Johnsen (1991) points out that spot market price ought to have been affected by the total quantity of refined petrol put on the market, but that moving it around from independent refiners to majors should not have had any effect. Refined petrol purchased by the majors and stored for future sale would increase future supplies, depressing the price of petrol for future delivery and leading independent wholesale and retail distributors to shift their own

---

[22] U.S. *v.* Socony-Vacuum Oil Co. 310 U.S. 150 (1940). Socony, Standard Oil Company of New York, is one of the ancestors of Mobil Oil Corporation and therefore of ExxonMobil Corporation.

[23] On the National Recovery Administration, see Section 20.3.2.

purchases into the future. Such shifts of demand by independents from the present to the future would neutralize the impact of increased present purchases by major oil companies.[24]

Cartel stability   Johnsen explains the buyback programmes in terms of cartel stability. By allowing independent oil refiners to purchase and refine more crude oil, then buying it back at relatively high prices, the major oil companies effectively made side payments to the independents and purchased their loyalty for a (tacit or overt) scheme to restrict crude oil output. The cost of the buyback programme to the majors was the extra profit diverted to the independent refiners. The benefit was the extra profits the majors received from the overall output restriction scheme and the avoidance of the costs that would have been associated with an explicit programme to monitor independents' output levels.

Supreme Court: principle of competition   The oil majors appealed the District Court outcome to the Seventh Circuit Court of Appeals, which ordered a new trial. The government appealed that order to the Supreme Court, which thus had a chance to revisit the status of price-fixing agreements under Section 1 of the Sherman Act.

At the Supreme Court, the oil majors invoked *Chicago Board of Trade* and *Appalachian Coals*. The oil majors were, as they presented it, simply acting to avoid the dread consequences of unhealthy competition in a vital sector of the economy. All factors relevant to the situation should be considered to evaluate whether the buyback programme promoted trade or restrained it.

Writing for the majority of a divided Court, Justice Douglas distinguished the facts in *Socony-Vacuum* from the facts in the cases cited by the oil majors. The buyback programmes had the immediate purpose, and effect, of fixing price; the price effects of the other programmes had been temporary (overnight, for *Chicago Board of Trade*), limited, and indirect. But in Douglas' view, it was the principle of competition that won out (310 U.S. 150 at 221):

> Any combination which tampers with price structures is engaged in an unlawful activity. Even though the members of the price-fixing group were in no position to control the market, to the extent that they raised, lowered, or stabilized prices they would be directly interfering with the free play of market forces. The Act places all such schemes beyond the pale ...

The Supreme Court reversed the Circuit Court decision and confirmed the outcome of the District Court jury trial.

Epilogue and prologue

What explains the back-and-forth motion from *Trenton Potteries* to *Appalachian Coals* to *Socony Vacuum*? The traditional explanation is that *Appalachian Coals* is an aberration, best viewed in the context of its time but not informative of antitrust policy except in times of economic distress as severe as that of the depths of the Great Depression.[25] Yet *Appalachian Coals* makes an appearance from time to time. Thus, in the 1979 *Broadcast Music* decision, which we take up in Section 20.5.1, *Appalachian Coals* is among the decisions cited by the

---

[24] Johnsen credits Aaron Director with an earlier version of this analysis.

[25] "The Soopreme Court follows the iliction returns", Finley Peter Dunne made Mr. Dooley say, and *Appalachian Coals* suggests that the Supreme Court follows the unemployment rate as well.

Supreme Court as it rejected an antitrust challenge to joint licences for copyrighted music (441 U.S. 1 at 14):[26]

> The Sherman Act has always been discriminatingly applied in the light of economic realities. There are situations in which competitors have been permitted to form joint selling agencies or other pooled activities, subject to strict limitations under the antitrust laws to guarantee against abuse of the collective power thus created.

From the end of the twentieth century, U.S. antitrust has set sail on Judge Taft's *sea of doubt*, restricting the scope of the principle of competition and expanding the scope of explicit evaluation of the impact of business conduct on market performance. On this voyage, it can be expected that citations to *Appalachian Coals* will appear in decisions involving the permissible scope of interfirm cooperation.

20.2.2 Article 101(1)

As we have seen in Section 19.4.2, Article 101(1) of the EC Treaty prohibits "all agreements between undertakings, decisions by associations of undertakings, and concerted practices which may affect trade between Member States and which have as their object or effect the prevention, restriction or distortion of competition within the common market" on the ground that they are incompatible with the common market. Vital practical questions include what sort of evidence must be produced to establish the existence of an agreement, decision, or concerted practice, and what the difference is, if any, between an agreement and a concerted practice.

Quinine Cartel

The facts of the *Quinine Cartel* case are given in the accompanying box. The Commission's investigation led it to conclude that the cartel practices were all agreements within the meaning of Article 101, and that they all had as their object or effect the restriction of competition on the Common Market.[27] For the first time, the Commission levied the fines for violating Article 101(1) of the Treaty. Nedchem and Boehringer appealed the Commission's decision

---

 BOX The Quinine Cartel

This is a wonderful tale of cartel dynamics, greed, and duplicity.

Quinine, a drug, is derived from the bark of a tree that grows in tropical regions. Quinine and its derivatives have a variety of medical uses, most importantly the treatment of malaria. Synthetic substitutes to treat malaria now exist, but these were developed after the events described here.

There is a long history of collusion among producers of quinine. Dutch and German firms formed a quinine cartel in 1892. A worldwide cartel, with secretariat located in Amsterdam, was established in 1913. It included all quinine producers in the world, with the exception of a publicly ≫

---

[26] The Supreme Court quotes a brief submitted by the U.S. Department of Justice.

[27] *Quinine Cartel* Commission Decision of 16 July 1969 JO L 192 05/08/1969 pp. 5–22 4 CMLR D41–D76.

⟫ owned Indonesian firm. This firm had a very large capacity, but was kept isolated first under Dutch management and later by a cartel policy not to purchase quinine from Indonesia.

In 1928, U.S. antitrust authorities investigated the cartel. The investigation was settled by a consent decree. There is no evidence that the consent decree affected the operation of the cartel, although it did make the Dutch member of the cartel, Nedchem,* alert to the fact that it would be a good idea not to attract the attention of U.S. antitrust authorities.

Nedchem and the leading German firm, Boehringer, negotiated an Export Agreement and a Gentlemen's Agreement in July 1959. In early 1960, these agreements were extended to include the other German producer and the British and French producers. One of the British firms was a wholly owned subsidiary of the U.S. firm Rexall Drug and Chemical Company.**

The Export Agreement established export quotas for the cartel members, reserved some regions to particular firms, and fixed prices and contract terms to be used by all cartel members. The Export Agreement expressly indicated that its terms were not to apply in the EEC, the United Kingdom, or the United States.

The Gentlemen's Agreement, which was written down but not signed, was that the terms of the Export Agreement would apply to all sales by cartel members in all markets, including the EEC, the United Kingdom, and the United States. The Dutch, German, and French markets were reserved for those countries' domestic suppliers.

In 1961, the cartel organized a system of cooperative buying of the bark from which quinine was processed, to collusively exercise monopsony power and hold down the cost of their essential input.

Parallel to these agreements, the cartel responded to plans by the U.S. government to sell supplies equal to a year and one-half or two years normal world sales from its quinine stockpile. After much wrangling and negotiation, it was agreed that cartel members would not compete to buy the U.S. stockpile: this would only drive up the price.

Nedchem purchased 84 per cent of the stockpile at a relatively low price. The agreement, which cartel members referred to as "the Convention", specified the terms on which Nedchem would redistribute supplies from the American stockpile.

The Treaty of Rome, and with it its competition policy provisions, went into effect on 1 January 1959. On 13 March 1963, the EEC issued Regulation 17, which required that agreements caught or thought likely to be caught by Article 101(1) be notified to the European Commission.

The cartel sought legal advice, and was told for its trouble that even if the Export Agreement were presented as applying only outside the EEC, it might very well be held to violate Article 101(1). Cartel members discussed three options:

- don't report anything;
- abandon the Convention (with disastrous consequences for cartel operations);
- report the bark pool and the export agreement to the Commission, not the gentlemen's agreement.

The cartel settled on the first option. It did not report even the Export Agreement, for fear of attracting the Commission's attention to the other agreements.

In November 1962, Nedchem announced its intention to unilaterally end the Convention. In communications within the cartel, it referred to British and German proposals to change the terms of the bark pool, which in Nedchem's view was a violation of the Gentlemen's Agreement and brought down the Export Agreement and the Convention as well.   ⟫

> ≫ At this point Nedchem, which had acted on behalf of the cartel, had control of the bulk of the U.S. stockpile (which it used to enforce a lower price in the United Kingdom). Nedchem's erstwhile fellow cartel members had little leverage with which to retaliate—they could hardly go to their respective governments and complain the Nedchem was not living up to the terms of an illegal agreement.
>
> But the lure of economic profit was great, and the cartel managed to renegotiate its agreements. (One British firm left the market.) Increased military activity in Vietnam meant increased demand for quinine, and the cartel was able to raise the price of quinine by 500 per cent over the next two years.
>
> In an 15 August 1966 letter to the the German competition authority, the Bundeskartellamt, the leading German member of the quinine cartel, Boehringer, stated that the Export Agreement had been ended at the start of 1965. In March 1967, the U.S. Senate Subcommittee on Antitrust published a 43-page report with extensive quotations from internal cartel documents. The European Commission Competition Directorate contacted the firms involved beginning July, 1967.
>
> *Nederlandse Combinate voor Chemische Industrie.
>
> **Our knowledge of the inner workings of the cartel is thanks to documents produced from the U.S. parent firm's files in response to a congressional subpoena.
>
> *Sources:* Blair (1967); Commission and European Court decisions (citations in the text).

to the European Court of Justice. The resulting decisions[28] gave the Court the opportunity to speak to the treatment of naked collusion under Article 101(1).

The firms appealed the Commission's decision on a number of grounds. Substantively, they argued among other things that the Gentlemen's Agreement was not an agreement for purposes of Article 101, and that in any case it ended in October 1962. The Court considered cartel members' actions in price fixing, reserving home markets for domestic producers, fixing quotas for sales outside reserved markets, and limiting the production of synthetic substitutes, and rejected their appeals ([1970] ECR 769 at 804–805). It reduced the fines imposed by the Commission somewhat, but upheld the principles of the Commission decision.

Dyestuffs[29]

The synthetic dye industry has its origin in chemical processes developed in England but first applied with commercial success in Germany at the end of the nineteenth century. The German industry was cartelized, and was linked in a complex network of alliances with other European firms and with American producers.

In a 1969 decision,[30] the Commission assessed fines against ten dyestuff producers, on the ground that they had engaged in a concerted practice in violation of Article 101(1). The behaviour complained of was a series of essentially identical price increases for aniline dyes in January 1964, January 1965, and October 1967. The firms involved appealed the Commission's decision to the European Court of Justice, arguing that the simultaneous price increases

---

[28] ACF Chemiefarma NV *v.* Commission Case 41-69 Judgment of the Court of 15 July 1970 [1970] ECR 661; Boehringer Mannheim GmbH *v.* Commission Case 45-69 Judgment of the Court of 15 July 1970 [1970] ECR 769.

[29] Imperial Chemical Industries Ltd. *v.* Commission (Cases 48, 49, 51-57/69) [1972] ECR 619; [1972] CMLR 557.

[30] *Dyestuffs* Commission Decision of 24 July 1969 JO L 195 07/08/1969 pp. 11–17.

were the result of independent but parallel decisions of firms in an oligopoly market. For the first time, the Court was able to elaborate on the difference between an agreement and a concerted practice ([1972] ECR 619 at 655):

> Article [101] draws a distinction between the concept of 'concerted practices' and that of 'agreements between undertakings' or of 'decisions by associations of undertakings'; the object is to bring within the prohibition of that article a form of coordination between undertakings which, without having reached the stage where an agreement properly so-called has been concluded, knowingly substitutes practical cooperation between them for the risks of competition.

The Court continued and indicated the kinds of evidence that would be needed to demonstrate the existence of a concerted practice:[31]

> Although parallel behavior may not by itself be identified with a concerted practice, it may however amount to strong evidence of such a practice if it leads to conditions of competition which do not correspond to the normal conditions of the market, having regard to the nature of the products, the size and number of the undertakings, and the volume of the said market. . . .
>
> Therefore the question whether there was a concerted action in this case can only be correctly determined if the evidence upon which the contested decision is based is considered, not in isolation, but as a whole, account being taken of the specific features of the market in the products in question.

Of necessity, this approach makes a role for economic analysis in the application of EU competition policy. It is only through economic analysis that one can take account of the specific features of a market and decide whether or not the conditions of competition in a market are normal.

Among the market characteristics identified by the Court were that the ten largest firms supplied about 80 per cent of the EC market and each firm produced more than 1,000 varieties of dye. Since the price of dye was a small part of the cost of the final product, the price elasticity of demand was low. The EC was composed of five national submarkets, each an oligopoly with a well-established price leader, and there were persistent differences in price levels across submarkets.

These are structural characteristics. The Court also looked at the suppliers' conduct. After the first of the three price increases, they had announced price increases in advance, effectively communicating their intentions to other suppliers ([1972] ECR 619 at 658–659).

Implicit model　Regarding performance, the Court's opinion sheds light on the way it viewed market processes ([1972] ECR 619 at 660):

> The function of price competition is to keep prices down to the lowest possible level and to encourage the movement of goods between the Member States, thereby permitting the most efficient possible distribution of activities in the matter of productivity and the capacity of undertakings to adapt themselves to change.

This is not a bad description of the function of price competition in a perfectly competitive market. In an imperfectly competitive market, it will often be the case that price

---

[31] There is clearly a family resemblance between the approach taken here by the ECJ and Justice Brandeis' guidelines in *Chicago Board of Trade*.

competition keeps prices at the highest level that will not cause a supplier to lose business to rivals. Cooperation, of course, may allow imperfect competitors to obtain even higher prices. This, as the Court saw it, was forbidden by Article 101(1) ([1972] ECR 619 at 660–661):

> Although every producer is free to change his prices, taking into account in so doing the present or foreseeable conduct of his competitors, nevertheless it is contrary to the rules on competition contained in the Treaty for a producer to cooperate with his competitors ... in order to determine a coordinated course of action relating to a price increase and to ensure its success by the prior elimination of all uncertainty as to each other's conduct regarding the essential elements of that action, such as the amount, subject-matter, date and place of the increases.

The Court found that the conduct of the firms involved was a concerted practice, that it had affected trade between the member states, and upheld the fines levied by the Commission.

20.2.3 Leniency programmes

Deterrence

U.S. antitrust policy and EU competition policy are deterrence-based. The theory of deterrence-based antitrust and competition policy is that if the probability of detection and conviction is high enough, and if the fines paid upon conviction large enough, profit-maximizing firms will decide that it is not in their own self-interest to break the law.

 BOX   Lysine (Amino Acids) Cartel

Lysine is an amino acid used as a supplement for animal feedstocks. It is a standardized commodity, the production of which requires a substantial sunk investment in fixed assets. It is used to stimulate an animal's growth.

Modern commercial use of lysine arose with the development of new production techniques in Japan in the 1950s. Until 1991 the world market was controlled by a cartel of two Japanese firms (Ajinomoto and Kyowa) and one Korean firm (Miwon, later Sewon and later still Daesang). The Asian firms imported dextrose from U.S. wet corn millers, among which Archer Daniels Midland (ADM), one of the world's leading agro-industrial food processors. Their lysine sales, including their sales in the United States, made handsome profits.

In 1989 Archer Daniels Midland announced that it would enter the lysine industry. It did so in 1991, with a state-of-the-art plant that doubled world lysine capacity. Thus began a series of events that reflected (216 F.3d 645 at 650) "an inexplicable lack of business ethics and an atmosphere of general lawlessness that infected the very heart of one of America's leading corporate citizens". ADM's entry triggered a price war. Kyowa arranged a June 1992 meeting with ADM and Ajinomoto. The firms agreed to raise the price of lysine. They discussed setting sales quotas, but could not reach agreement (216 F. 3d 645 at 652):

> Still, the cartel considered a price agreement without allocating sales volume to be an imperfect scheme because each company would have an incentive to cheat on the price to get more ≫

⟫ sales, so long as its competitors continued to sell at the agreed price. With cheating, the price ultimately would drop, and the agreement would falter. An effort had to be made to get the parties to agree to a volume agreement, and to that end, [ADM executive and later informant Mark] Whitacre invited Ajinomoto officials to visit ADM's Decatur lysine facility to prove that it could produce the volume ADM claimed.

The Asian firms allowed their sales personnel a substantial degree of autonomy. ADM, in contrast, maintained centralized control of its sales agents (OJ L 152/34):

During the meeting, ADM alluded to the importance of a company controlling its sales force in order to maintain high prices, and explained that its sales people have the general tendency to be very competitive and that, unless the producers had very firm control of their sales people, there would be a price-cutting problem.

Follow-up meetings were required to obtain agreement on output limits (OJ L 152/35):*

On 14 May 1993, Ajinomoto and ADM met in Tokyo in order to continue the discussion commenced in Decatur. … They again discussed the mechanism needed to obtain and police a sales volume agreement. ADM stated that the way for them to communicate is through a trade association. ADM explained by way of example that ADM reported its citric acid sales every month to a trade association, and every year, Swiss accountants audited those figures.

Ultimately, it was settled that Ajinomoto would monitor monthly sales figures of the cartel members.

The cartel ended in June 1995, when FBI agents, acting on information obtained with the assistance of Mark Whitacre, whistleblower, one-time President of ADM's Bioproducts Division, embezzler, and victim of the "Nigeria scam", raided the U.S. offices of ADM, Ajinomoto, and Sewon. Subsequent U.S. antitrust proceedings led to the fines shown in column four of Table 20.1 (as well as personal fines and three-year jail terms for two senior ADM executives).

When the European Commission published its first leniency notice in July 1996, it was contacted by Ajinomoto with an offer of cooperation in return for a hoped-for reduction in fines. This contact took place after the Commission learned of U.S. antitrust actions toward the cartel but before the Commission prepared its statement of objections to the cartel. Ajinomoto, Sewon, and Kyowa cooperated with the Commission in varying degrees. Their fines were reduced by 50 per cent, 50 per cent, and 30 per cent, respectively. ADM received a 10 per cent reduction in firms for cooperation after the Commission made its statement of objections.

*ADM was eventually fined nearly 40 million euros in connection with the citric acid cartel. See the Court of First Instance decision of 27 September 2006 in case T-59/02.

Although antitrust and competition policy fines generate revenue, their purpose is not to raise revenue, but to render certain kinds of behaviour unprofitable.

To make a deterrence-based policy effective, enforcement agencies must have large enough budgets to detect a sufficiently large fraction of offenders. The legal system should be structured to minimize the possibility of type I errors (finding that firms have made independent decisions when they have colluded) and type II errors (finding that firms have colluded when they have made independent decisions).[32] Monetary fines should be large

---

[32] On type I and type II errors in legal systems, see Polinsky and Shavell (1989). There will be a tradeoff between the one and the other type of error.

Table 20.1 1995 sales (in million euros) of amino acid conspirators

Firm	1995 Amino Acid Sales		Fines	
	Worldwide	EEA	US	EU
Archer Daniels Midland	202	41	70	47.3
Ajinomoto	239	75	10	28.3
Kyowa	73	16	10	13.2
Daesang	67	15	1.25	8.9
Cheil	52	17		12.2

Note: U.S. fines in million dollars, EU fines in million euros.
Source: Commission Decision 2001/418/EC OJ L 152/14.

enough so that if a firm is caught and convicted, collusion ends up having been unprofitable, and business executives who lead their companies into conspiracies should (in the interest of deterrence) themselves face the possibility of imprisonment.

Leniency

Cartel policy *leniency programmes* aim to facilitate conviction of violators, thus deterring violations. A *leniency policy* offers a reduced fine to a firm that defects and turns "state's evidence", bringing documentation of illegal behaviour to the enforcement agency. Under its 1993 Corporate Leniency Policy (an earlier programme dates to 1978), the U.S. Department of Justice will waive criminal prosecution for the first firm to provide information about illegal activity (subject to a number of other conditions). DOJ's 1994 Individual Leniency Policy holds out the possibility of a waiver of criminal prosecution for individuals who bring the Department news of a hitherto unsuspected violation.

Leniency programmes have proven to be a powerful tool for uncovering direct evidence of collusion.[33] The European Commission first issued a Leniency Notice in 1996, with successor Notices in 2002 and 2006.[34] The policies set out in the first notice contributed to the prosecution of 16 cartel cases, with fines assessed of €2,240 million and reductions in fines of nearly €1,240 million (Arbault and Pieró, 2002, p. 16). One of these was the *Amino Acid* case described in the accompanying box. The 2002 Notice sharpened incentives to come forward by increasing the assurance that a first whistle-blower would receive immunity from fines, and making reductions in fines for later whistle-blowers strictly related to the incremental value of the information they bring forward. The 2006 Notice added a discretionary "marker

---

[33] In 2004, media reports that construction companies maintained two sets of accounts, one public and one reflecting the reality of collusive activity, resulting in 486 applications for leniency from the Dutch Competition Authority, from which documentation emerged that the Dutch construction sector was riddled with cartels. See Bergeijk (2008).

[34] OJ C 45 19 February 2002, p. 3; OJ C 298 8 December 2006, p. 17.

system" to the leniency programme, allowing the Commission to accept an application for leniency on the basis of limited information, while giving the firm time to bring the information it offers up to the required level.

Desirable characteristics

Several guidelines for a successful leniency programme emerge from the U.S. and EU experiences.[35] First, it should be clear what benefits the programme offers, and the benefits should not be at the discretion of the enforcement agency. The certainly of reduced penalties is a bigger lure than the possibility of reduced penalties.[36]

Second, the greatest reductions—as much as complete leniency—should go to the first party to seek leniency. There should be a significant difference between the reward the first applicant gets and what is offered to late-comers. Structuring leniency rewards in this way maximizes the incentive to bolt the cartel and be "first through the gate".

Third, it should be possible to take advantage of a leniency programme even if the enforcement agency has started an investigation—the knowledge that punishment is an active possibility makes the possibility of avoiding that punishment even more attractive.

Fourth, applications for leniency should be received confidentially and processed in order of receipt.

Coordination

Coordination of the leniency programmes of different jurisdictions remains an issue. Prosecution of a cartel in one jurisdiction may alert enforcement agencies elsewhere and lead to subsequent prosecution in other jurisdictions. This was a factor in the *Amino Acid* case. But then a firm that turns "state's evidence" in return for leniency in one jurisdiction may expose itself to the possibility of prosecution in courts where it has not qualified for leniency. Such exposure reduces the net reward from turning a cartel in to any one competition authority. Particularly for international cartels, the need to coordinate the benefits to be expected from leniency programmes is one element in the case for having some form of international competition policy.

20.3 Facilitating Practices

The *Addyston Pipe and Steel* rule is that agreements to fix price are illegal *per se*. The question then arises just where one draws the line between agreement and independent (non-cooperative) decision-making. To require that an agreement be reduced to writing before a

---

[35] See Directors General of European Competition Authorities (2001), Organization for Economic Co-operation and Development (2003a, pp. 22–23).

[36] In January, 2003, the U.S. Department of Justice granted conditional leniency to the parcel tanker shipping company Stolt-Nielsen, S.A.; information provided by Stolt-Nielsen contributed to convictions of co-conspirator shipping companies and executives. In April, 2003 the Department of Justice suspended the grant of leniency on the ground that Stolt-Nielsen had failed to halt its anticompetitive activities when it learned of them (although Stolt-Nielsen had stopped anticompetitive conduct at the time of the leniency agreement), and charged Stolt-Nielsen, S.A. with antitrust violations. A November 2007 District Court decision obliged the Department of Justice to make good on the leniency agreement (U.S. *v.* Stolt-Nielsen S.A. *et al.* 2007 U.S. Dist. LEXIS 88011 29 November 2007, U.S. *v.* Stolt-Nielsen S.A. *et al.* 2007 U.S. Dist. LEXIS 88628 29 November 2007).

per se violation could be found would render the Section 1 prohibition ineffective. Here we discuss some types of conduct that enhance the stability of tacit or overt collusion. Courts have been willing to accept some of these practices, and not others, as factors demonstrating the existence of an agreement and therefore justifying invocation of the *per se* rule.

20.3.1 Basing-Point Pricing

When markets have a spatial dimension, price may depend on a customer's location. Or not: with uniform pricing—the same price to all consumers—location has no influence. With f.o.b. or *free-on-board* pricing, the supplier sets a price to deliver the product to a location (vessel) specified by the consumer. With f.o.b. mill pricing, the supplier sets a price at the mill gate, the same for all consumers. The consumer is responsible for transportation expense from that location.

The basing-point pricing system is (Marengo, 1955, p. 509):

> a method of pricing which regardless of variations in detail permits only delivered pricing, and makes the price to a buyer the lowest combination of basing point price and outbound rail freight charges, regardless of the actual location of the seller and regardless of the form of transportation actually used.

Basing-point pricing has been used in industries where the product is standardized, of low value in relation to weight or volume, where transportation cost is a large part of the total cost of getting the product to the consumer, and where demand is subject to cyclical fluctuations. Cement, oil, plywood, and steel are examples.

As a method for facilitating tacit collusion, the basing point system has three desirable characteristics (Stegemann, 1968), control, venting, and punishment. By "control" is meant that the tacit collusion price is transparently obvious, and deviations quickly revealed. "Venting" refers to the fact that by absorbing freight, mills with excess capacity due to a regional cyclical downturn can find a temporary outlet in the natural market of an adjacent mill. And if a mill engages in sporadic price cutting, it can be punished by making its location a *punitive base point*, at a price below its marginal cost.

 BOX   Basing-Point Pricing: Mechanics

Under a *single basing-point pricing system*, the price a consumer pays for delivery from any location is the price at the basing point plus the cost of transportation from the basing point, no matter what the location of the plant from which delivery is actually made.

Under a *multiple basing-point system*, the delivered price to any location is the base price plus transportation cost from the basing point that offers the lowest delivered price, whatever the location of the plant from which delivery is actually made.

Figure 20.2* shows a stylized version of a market with three firms, one located at basing point *I*, one located at basing point *II*, and one located at *III*. The plant at *III* is not a basing point. mc_1, mc_2, and mc_3 are marginal production costs at locations *I*, *II*, and *III*, respectively. ≫

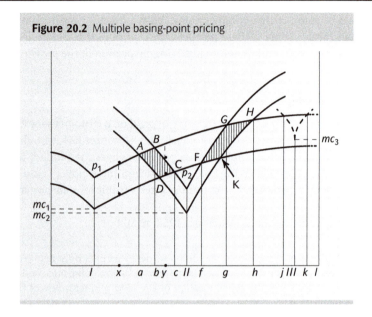

Figure 20.2 Multiple basing-point pricing

» The lower curves rising from location *I* show the marginal cost of delivery—production cost plus transportation cost—from location *I*, and similarly for the lower curves rising from location *II* and location *III*.

p_1 is the price to a consumer located at *I*, and the upper curves rising from *I* show the delivered price from plant *I* to consumers at various distances. In the same way, the upper curves rising from *II* show the delivered price from plant *II* to consumers at various distances.

Over the interval from *I* to *a*, the lowest delivered price is from *I* and this price is below *II*'s marginal cost of delivery. Thus, it would not be profitable for the plant located at *II* to make sales to consumers located between *I* and *a*. Between *a* and *b*, the delivered price from *I* is lower than the delivered price from *II*; it is the delivered price from *I* that is the basing-point price.

Between *b* and *c*, the delivered price from *II* is lower than the delivered price from *I*; it is the delivered price from *II* that is the basing-point price. Firm *I* will make a profit on any sales it makes between *b* and *c*: the delivered price from *II* to these locations is greater than *I*'s marginal cost. But for sales in this region, *I* does not charge the full cost of the delivery service it provides: it engages in *freight absorption*.

Firm *I*'s *net price*—the price paid by the consumer minus the cost of transportation services actually provided—for sales between *a* and *b* is p_1. Firm *I*'s net price for a sale at location *y* is less than p_1, since the cost of the transportation service from *I* to *y* is more than the cost of shipping from *II* to *y*. Thus by using basing-point pricing, firm *I* engages in *price discrimination*: it receives a different net price for sales of an identical product to consumers at different locations.

Between *a* and *c*, the basing-point price is greater than marginal delivery cost for both firms, so both firms would find it profitable to sell to consumers located in this interval. »

>> Between c and f, the delivered price from II is lower than the delivered price from I; it is the delivered price from II that is the basing-point price. This price is less than the marginal cost of delivery from I, so the plant located at I would not find it profitable to make sales to consumers located between c and f. By similar arguments, both firms would find it profitable to sell to consumers located between f and h, and only the plant located at I would find it profitable to sell to consumers located to the right of h. The firm located at II absorbs freight on sales at locations between g and h.

In the neighbourhood of III, the lowest delivered price is from I. It is therefore the delivered price from I that is the basing-point price for sales from III. If the plant at III makes a sale to a customer also located at III, the delivered price is the price at I's mill gate, plus the cost of shipment from I to III. The firm located at III charges for delivery service that is not provided; the customer pays *phantom freight*.

*Figure 20.2 is based on Figure 15.2 of Phlips (1993)

Control

Basing-point systems in the United States usually priced as if their products were shipped by rail. In the U.S. cement industry in the first half of the twentieth century, an industry trade association prepared and distributed a booklet of standardized rail rates, for use in price-setting. In the European Coal and Steel Community, rail and other means of transport used to ship coal and steel were obliged to publish their rates. Suppliers could easily learn from customers the delivered prices quoted by their rivals, and by subtracting transportation cost, work out the rivals' basing-point price. By working out the basing-point price of its immediate neighbours, a firm would know what delivered price it should quote to a customer at any location. If a firm were discovered to have charged a lower price to make a particular sale, it could not convincingly claim that it had misunderstood what the basing-point price ought to have been.

Industries using the basing-point system discouraged the use of trucks because the use of trucks would have introduced uncertainty about the delivered price to a given location. For the same reason, firms would typically refuse to sell to a customer at the mill gate and allow the customer to transport the product. That is, suppliers will not quote an f.o.b. mill price.

Venting

The industries that used basing-point pricing were (and are) subject to cyclical demand fluctuations. Often (cement, plywood, steel) they supply the construction sector, which is itself subject to severe cyclical fluctuations, and transmits its own cyclical fluctuations upstream to its supplying industries.

Cyclical demand fluctuations strain collusive schemes based on geographic market division. A firm assigned to supply a region that happens to suffer a cyclical downturn in demand will be tempted to poach a few orders in the territory of some rival. This will tend to destabilize the cartel. Intermittent freight absorption is a way for oligopolists to accommodate cyclical variations in demand.[37]

---

[37] Stigler (1949b). Hughes and Barbezat (1996) emphasize demand fluctuations as a factor in use of basing-point pricing by a legal German steel cartel between 1926 and 1939.

Freight absorption leads to inefficient *cross-hauling*, when a plant ships to customers that could be served at lower cost by other plants. Cross-hauling is incompatible with joint-profit maximization. A monopolist, or a cartel mimicking a monopolist, would not engage in cross-hauling, since holding sales constant and eliminating cross-hauling would increase profit. Thus basing-point pricing is a system of *imperfect* collusion[38]—the industry falls short of monopoly profit, but as a consequence maintains oligopoly coordination.

Punishment

Stable tacit or overt collusion requires that there be a credible way to punish defectors. The basing-point system provided a natural punishment strategy. The tactic was to make the offending plant an involuntary or *punitive basing point*, at a price below average cost. Punishing firms would lose money on the sales they made near the target plant. But they would have profit coming in from sales in other areas. The target plant would lose money on all its sales. In the U.S. cement industry (333 U.S. 633 at 714):[39]

> In one instance, where a producer had made a low public bid, a punitive base point price was put on its plant and cement was reduced 10 cents per barrel; further reductions quickly followed until the base price at which this recalcitrant had to sell its cement dropped to 75 cents per barrel, scarcely one-half of its former base price of $1.45. Within six weeks after the base price hit 75 cents capitulation occurred and the recalcitrant joined a portland cement association. Cement in that locality then bounced back to $1.15, later to $1.35, and finally to $1.75.

Basing-point pricing and market performance

Basing-point pricing facilitated tacit or overt collusion, by making it relatively easy for firms to determine what their price should be. Basing-point pricing did not, however, eliminate all need for communication (Machlup, 1949, pp. 20–21). Firms communicated when the system was put in place and when mistakes were made. Small firms needed assistance in working out pricing details. This makes plausible the interpretation of basing-point pricing as a characteristic of collusion rather than of tacit collusion.

Under basing-point systems, prices quoted by producers at different locations to the same customer were identical, sometimes to six decimal places. Prices also exhibited considerable rigidity over time. Price stability for important intermediate goods facilitated tacit collusion among consuming firms, by allowing them to estimate rivals' costs with a high degree of accuracy (Commons, 1924, pp. 508–509).

U.S.: cement[40]

Early U.S. cement production was concentrated in Pennsylvania's Lehigh Valley, where it enjoyed access to superior raw materials. At first, the Lehigh Valley was the single basing point for the entire United States. As technological advances raised the quality of cement that could be obtained from different ores, cement mills were built in other places, and a multiple basing-point system developed.

---

[38] Loescher (1959, p. v) credits Lynn C. Paulson with this term.

[39] Loescher (1959, p. 127) reports that state of South Dakota opened a cement plant in Rapid City in 1925. Rapid City was made a punitive base point in 1926, driving the mill net price down to 60 or 70 cents per barrel.

[40] This account is based on Loescher (1959).

The cement industry's reason to find a way to collude was rooted in its cost structure. In an unusually candid letter to the chairman of the National Recovery Administration code authority for the cement industry, the president of a cement company wrote (John Treanor, 17 May 1923, quoted in Loescher, 1959, pp. 85–86):

> Do you think any of the arguments for the basing-point system, which we have thus far advanced, will arouse anything but derision in and out of the government? I have read them all recently. They amount to this however: that we price this way in order to discourage monopolistic practices and to preserve free competition, etc. This is sheer bunk and hypocrisy. The truth is of course—and there can be no serious, respectable discussion of our case unless this is acknowledged—that ours is an industry that cannot stand free competition, that must systematically restrain competition or be ruined. We sell in a buyer's market all the time. The capital cost, as distinguished from the out-of-pocket cost, of producing cement is extraordinarily large. In free competition this capital cost is whittled away and this means loss and ruin.

Basing-point pricing met the cement industry's needs (Loescher, 1959, pp. 141–142):

> The beauty of the basing-point system for the cement industry was that it entailed virtually no *overt* collusion, once the rules of the game had been well established. True, the circulation of common rate books (as well as certain subsidiary features) involved continuing overt collusion. But the plan to adhere to a delivered pricing formula could be easily and almost automatically followed once trucking was controlled and direct sales to large contractors were curtailed.

The Federal Trade Commission challenged use of basing-point pricing in several industries from the 1920s onward, arguing that the system was an unfair method of competition and also led to price discrimination, in violation of Section 2 of the Clayton Act. These challenges were at first unsuccessful. Litigation was delayed by the depression-era National Industrial Recovery Act and World War II. In a 1948 ruling, the Supreme Court supported the FTC's view that use of basing-point pricing could be attributed to agreement and was therefore a violation of the antitrust laws.[41]

ECSC: steel

Article 4 of the ECSC Treaty made discrimination in "prices, delivery terms and transportation rates" incompatible with the common market in coal and steel, and therefore prohibited. This prohibition is repeated in Article 60(1). Article 60(2)(a) provided that for the purposes of accomplishing the prohibition of price discrimination, "the price lists and conditions of sale applied by undertakings within the common market must be made public ... " This provision essentially required coal and steel firms in the Community to maintain a basing point pricing system (Stegemann, 1968; Phlips, 1983, Chapter 1).

Publication The expected effect of the requirement that prices be published was to bring ECSC markets closer to the classroom model of perfect competition by improving the quality of information on the demand sides of the markets (Spierenburg and Poidevin, 1994, p. 101, writing of the rules for steel):

---

[41] FTC v. Cement Institute, 333 U.S. 633 (1948). See also Corn Products Refining Co. *et al.* v. FTC 324 U.S. 726 (1945), and FTC v. A. E. Staley Manufacturing Co. *et al.* 324 U.S. 746 (1945), which condemned single basing-point pricing systems.

Under Article 60, producers were obliged to publish their prices. Accordingly, the High Authority drafted rather elaborate rules to cover not only basis prices but also conditions of sale, delivery dates, standard surcharges for special qualities and discounts for quantity and loyalty. It explained clearly that steel producers 'must ensure that users are able to ascertain the quality and calculate precisely the cost of the products they are considering buying, and also to compare offers from various suppliers'.

It is difficult to promote complete and perfect information on the demand side of a market without at the same time promoting complete and perfect information on the supply side of the market. A more-nearly perfect flow of information on the supply side of a market may well improve market performance if the market approximates the other conditions that define the classroom market of perfect competition, among which "many small firms". Economists now understand that price transparency on the supply side of a market supplied by a few relatively large firms facilitates tacit collusion. This was the effect of the publication requirement embodied in the ECSC Treaty.

Monnet margin   The ECSC High Authority came to realize that the requirement that prices be published and that published prices be adhered to did not result in good market performance. In January 1954 it introduced the so-called "Monnet margin" and issued regulations permitting an average deviation of plus or minus 2.5 per cent of transaction from published prices. France and Italy challenged this measure before the European Court of Justice, which annulled the High Authority action.[42]

The grounds for the Court's decision were strictly legal: under the ECSC Treaty, price publication was an obligatory tool to prevent price discrimination. The High Authority's attempt to finesse the publication requirement of the Treaty was therefore invalid. That the economic effect of the price publication requirement moved the ECSC away from rather than toward the "economic expansion, the development of employment and the improvement of the standard of living" highlighted in Article 2 of the ECSC Treaty simply did not come into consideration.

Redefinition   After the 1967 merger of the three Communities, the European Commission assumed the aspect of the High Authority for matters relating to coal and steel. The Commission dealt with the problem of ECSC Treaty requirements by redefining terms. Price discrimination continued to be a violation of the ECSC Treaty, but a difference between published prices and transactions prices would not, in and of itself, constitute price discrimination.[43] One might question whether this approach was consistent with the letter of the ECSC Treaty (or with the ECJ decision neutralizing the Monnet margin). It was, however, a move from a legalistic interpretation of the pricing provisions of the ECSC to an economic interpretation that was better adapted to the nature of the markets to which the pricing provisions were applied.

---

[42] ECSC, Cour de Justice, *Recueil de la Jurisprudence de la Cour*, Volume I, pp. 7–121; reprinted in English translation in Valentine (1965, Volume II, pp. 18–45).

[43] EC Commission (1972, p. 87). See also the discussion and decisions referenced in the *Second Report on Competition Policy* (1973, pp. 21–22).

20.3.2 Trade Association Activities and Publicity

Trade associations

United States

Open competition In the United States, the 1920s saw a concerted effort to roll back the reach of antitrust. Some support for this effort was motivated by what we would now call rent seeking, but that is only a partial explanation.

Some advocates of changes in the antitrust laws drew on their experience with the government-managed economy of World War I, when firms and government had worked together in pursuit of a common goal (Watkins, 1935, p. 119):

> [The war] provided, as it were, a licensed training school in trade cooperation. It taught business men of every kind and variety of antecedents the forms and advantages of concerted action.

Some support for restricting antitrust policy can be traced to the ideals of the progressive movement, which had found expression in the 1912 presidential election. It is not such a great leap from Theodore Roosevelt's belief that government should work with good trusts and shackle bad trusts to the view cooperation among independent firms need not be, in and of itself, a bad thing for market performance.

Among the idealists, one may count Chicago lawyer Arthur Jerome Eddy, a disciple of the "When I use a word it means just what I choose it to mean, neither more nor less" approach to vocabulary. In 1913 Eddy published the influential book *The New Competition*. For Eddy, "competition" meant "cooperation". He advocated that firms supplying a market organize a trade association to exchange information about costs, about work being done, about business that would become available, and about bids submitted with a view to obtaining business. The result, he said (using the example of a hypothetical carpenters' association; Eddy, 1913, p. 101)

> would be stability of prices at normal levels. Competing in the open with full knowledge of all the conditions influencing others, no man would make a ruinously low price or an arbitrarily high one. The competition would be real, keen and healthful. Prices would vary, but they would not vary widely; men needing work would bid to get it; others with plenty of work would not try; in dull times prices would approach cost, but the educational value of the association would tend to deter ruinous bidding; open criticism of work inefficiently done would expose the tricky bidder.

American Column & Lumber The 1921 *American Column & Lumber* decision[44] dealt with just such an "Open Competition" plan. The plan was administered by the American Hardwood Manufacturers' Association, the members of which accounted for about one-third of U.S. hardwood production. Members were obliged to make frequent and detailed reports covering all aspects of their activity—prices and quantities for individual transactions, identities of customers, stocks in inventory (257 U.S. 377 at 289). Despite the argument that the Open

---

[44] American Column & Lumber Company *et al. v.* U.S. 257 U.S. 377 (1921). But see two 1925 decisions (Maple Flooring Manufacturers Assn. *et al. v.* U.S. 268 U.S. 563 (1925) and Cement Manufacturers Protective Association *et al. v.* U.S. 268 U.S. 588 (1925) (*Old Cement*)) where elaborate information dissemination schemes were permitted because, the Court felt, the government had not proven the existence of agreement among the firms involved.

Competition Plan made no provision for agreement on prices, the Supreme Court had no difficulty in concluding that such an agreement existed (257 U.S. 377 at 410):

> Genuine competitors do not make daily, weekly and monthly reports of the minutest details of their business to their rivals, as the defendants did; they do not contract, as was done here, to submit their books to the discretionary audit and their stocks to the discretionary inspection of their rivals for the purpose of successfully competing with them; and they do not submit the details of their business to the analysis of an expert, jointly employed, and obtain from him a "harmonized" estimate of the market as it is and as, in his specially and confidentially informed judgment, it promises to be. This is not the conduct of competitors but is ... clearly that of men united in an agreement, express or implied ...

Sugar Institute   The 1936 *Sugar Institute* decision[45] condemned a trade association program that required firms to make transactions at announced prices, ruling out (297 U.S. 553 at 585) "the deviations which open and fair competition might require or justify". It was not the collection of announced prices by the Sugar Institute that was seen as a restraint of trade, but the agreement not to deviate from those prices.

Tag Manufacturers   The 1949 *Tag Manufacturers* decision[46] declined to find an unfair method of competition in a trade association price reporting programme where members were free to deviate from announced prices, and the trial record suggested that they did so reasonably often. Another factor in *Tag Manufacturers* was that the prices collected by the trade association were available to consumers, at least in principle, as well as to producers.

Thus, the antitrust questions for trade association price reporting and information circulation programs seem to be (a) whether or not they result in a price agreement among members and (b) whether the programme makes prices more transparent only on the supply side of the market.[47]

Open competition continued   In the immediate aftermath of the *American Column and Lumber* decision, there was an active campaign to reverse its strict approach. One proposal was that public policy toward business should divide industries into three groups (Hamilton, 1932, pp. 11–12). Two groups were essentially those identified by John Bates Clark before passage of the 1914 Clayton Act, those in which competition, with some regulation of business practices, could be relied upon to get good market performance, and monopolistic industries, for which regulation, despite its flaws, seemed called for. The third group was industries for which "there is at least a possibility of contriving ... a control from within. The province of the government may be reduced to a minimum and the industry made self-regulatory. A beginning is to be found in the trade associations and in chambers of commerce". For this third group of industries, the proposal to rely on industrial self-government was intended to limit the antitrust prohibition of agreements in restraint of trade.

---

[45] Sugar Institute, Inc. *et al.* *v.* U.S. 297 U.S. 553 (1936).

[46] Tag Manufacturers Institute *et al.* *v.* FTC 174 F.2d 452 (1949).

[47] See also *Container Corporation of America* (U.S. *v.* Container Corporation of America *et al.* 393 U.S. 333 (1969)) and *U.S. Gypsum* (U.S. *v.* U.S. Gypsum Co. *et al.* 438 U.S. 422 (1978)).

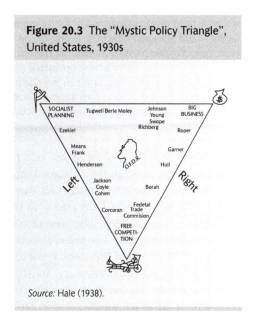

Figure 20.3 The "Mystic Policy Triangle", United States, 1930s

Source: Hale (1938).

Economists opposed these proposals (which were particularly offered by lawyers) (Fetter, 1932a, p. 15):

"Big Business" would replace competition with a plutocratic oligarchy of industries privileged to determine whatever they wish to make the public pay, and socialism—and the plan just proposed is a form of guild socialism—would replace competition with a regime of management and price fixing by public officials.

They defended the antitrust laws (1932a, p. 15):

Happily the choice of a third ideal and policy is open to us, that of publicly regulated and moralized competition; indeed that is the choice the nation made long ago and embodied in the Anti-Trust statutes. Regulated competition is the only conservative policy among the three seriously under discussion.

One hundred and twenty-seven economists signed a statement (Fetter, 1932b) arguing that the spread of monopoly control of prices had a pivotal role in the Great Depression. They called for more, rather than less, enforcement of the antitrust laws, as a way of curing the economy.

It was indeed a matter of curing the economy: as Franklin D. Roosevelt took office in March, 1933, the U.S. unemployment rate was just under 25 per cent. The policy debate that began early in the Roosevelt administration was between three groups, united in their belief that something needed to be done, divided in their beliefs about what that something was (Figure 20.3)(Hawley, 1966, p. 35):[48]

---

[48] Note the charming horse-and-buggy at the bottom of the triangle in Figure 20.3.

At one corner was the vision of a business commonwealth, of a rational, cartelized business order in which the industrialists would plan and direct the economy, profits would be insured, and the government would take care of recalcitrant "chiselers". At the second was the concept of a cooperative, collectivist democracy, a system under which organized economic groups would join to plan their activities, rationalize their behavior, and achieve the good life for all. At the third corner was the competitive ideal, the old vision of an atomistic economy in which basic decisions were made in an impersonal market and the pursuit of self-interest produced the greatest social good.

NRA   Out of this three-way struggle came the United States' one genuine flirtation with corporatism, the National Recovery Administration (NRA), signed into law on 16 June 1933 and remaining on the books for two years. The NRA began as an attempt to take the United States out of depression by increasing wages faster than prices, so that real income would increase. The theory was that where real income led, aggregate demand would follow, that an increase in aggregate demand would stimulate investment spending and trigger a virtuous circle leading to prosperity. In the words of President Roosevelt when he signed the NRA's enabling legislation, the National Industrial Recovery Act (NIRA), "The aim of this whole effort is to restore our rich domestic market by raising its vast consuming capacity. If we now inflate prices as fast and as far as we increase wages, the whole project will be set at naught. We cannot hope for the full effect of this plan unless, in these first critical months, and even at the expense of full initial profits, we defer price increases as long as possible."

To this end, the NIRA contained provisions intended to improve wage rates, working conditions, and the legal position of organized labour. As a *quid pro quo* for these provisions, which were bitterly resented in business circles, the NIRA authorized trade associations to formulate codes of fair competition, subject to Presidential approval. Codes, once approved, were exempted from the antitrust laws. Code violations were declared to be an unfair method of competition within the meaning of Section 5 of the Federal Trade Commission Act. Thus, code violations could be prosecuted by the FTC. The NIRA contained statements to the effect that code provisions should not promote monopoly, but business had obtained, albeit on a provisional basis, the relaxation of antitrust constraints on trade association activities.

The NRA enjoyed widespread initial support; its Blue Eagle symbol sprouted in store windows across the country. But business interests dominated the writing of the codes, which assumed the price-fixing character that might all too easily have been expected (Schlesinger, 1959, p. 125). There were more than 700 codes at the beginning of 1935, and 568 of them had some sort of minimum-price requirement. In January 1935, 420 codes prohibited selling below cost. Four hundred and sixteen of the codes included open price provisions.

The impact of the NRA varied from industry to industry, but the general assessment is that the codes restricted competition, provisions in the enabling legislation not to the contrary. Pennock (1997) suggests that in the rubber tyre industry, where the code did not provide for price controls, it was small firms that sought protection from price competition, and that larger, more efficient firms were able to resist those efforts. Alexander (1997b) similarly argues that more numerous small firms were able to dominate the code-writing process in many industries, that more efficient larger firms in many industries failed to adhere to the codes, and that the NRA failed to enforce compliance. But Alexander (1994) finds that tacit collusion appears to have become sustainable at much lower levels of seller concentration while the NRA was in effect.[49] Baker (1989) produces evidence suggesting that the U.S. steel industry used trigger-strategy-like price wars to enforce tacit collusion before the arrival of the NRA, and that the NRA made these unnecessary.

The nature of the oligopoly problem has not changed much since 1776, when Adam Smith, as noted at the beginning of this chapter, wrote that ([1776] 1937, p. 128) "though the law cannot hinder people of the same trade from sometimes assembling together, it ought to do nothing to facilitate such assemblies; much less to render them necessary". The NRA rendered it necessary for people of the same trade to assemble together, and so greatly facilitated tacit and overt collusion.

The NRA's popularity evaporated as it became clear that it would be dominated by the "industrial self-government" corner of the policy triangle. The Roosevelt administration began procedures to extend the life of the NRA beyond its initial two-year run, but in 1935 the Supreme Court declared the NIRA to be an unconstitutional delegation of legislative authority to groups in the private sector. The United States' fling with industrial self-government came to an end. The second Roosevelt administration resumed vigorous enforcement of the antitrust laws (Figure 18.2; Miscamble, 1982).

European Union

Hard-core collusion: *FEG/TU*   A trade association may provide the institutional framework for a straightforward agreement to restrict competition. Such schemes run afoul of Article 101(1), provided they affect trade among the member states. One example is found in the Commission's *FEG/TU* decision.[50] FEG was an association of Dutch wholesale distributors of electrotechnical equipment (cables pugs, switches, sockets) used in construction. FEG members supplied 96 per cent of the Dutch market for electrotechnical equipment. TU was the largest single member of FEG.

FEG administered informal exclusive dealing arrangements between manufacturers, its members, and the construction firms that were the main direct customers for the products distributed by FEG members. Dutch and foreign manufacturers for the most part agreed to distribute only through FEG members; construction firms for the most part agreed to obtain supplies only through FEG members. This informal agreement was the successor of a formal agreement that had been in place from 1928 to 1959.

Given the large share of the market covered by FEG members, the exclusive dealing arrangements made it difficult for firms based outside the Netherlands to make significant sales in the Netherlands. Combined with the fact that one requirement for FEG membership was annual sales revenue in the Netherlands of 5 million Dutch gilders for three years in a row, the effect of the exclusive dealing arrangements was to create an artificial barrier to entry around the Dutch wholesale market for electrotechnical equipment.[51]

FEG subgroups, organized along product lines, held regular meetings at which members exchanged information about price lists, discounts, and prices actually paid by customers.

---

[49] Controlling for differences in plant size, the importance of product differentiation, and the time it took for an industry to adopt an NRA code, Alexander finds (1994, p. 249) a discrete upward jump in industry profitability at a critical four-firm seller concentration ratio of 60 per cent in 1933, of 38 per cent in 1937.

[50] OJ L 39 14 February 2000, p. 1. FEG is an acronym for Nederlandse Federatieve Vereniging voor de Groothandel op Elektrotechnisch Gebied; TU is an acronym for Technische Unie. See Ferdinandusse (2000).

[51] See similarly the discussion of Japanese public works bidding practices in Section 6.4.2.

Some of the product subgroups took active measures to keep supplies out of the hands of price-cutting wholesalers based in the EC but outside the Netherlands. The result was that the wholesale price level for the products in question in the Netherlands were higher than elsewhere in the EC.

In its decision under Article 101, the European Commission decision concluded that FEG and TU had violated Article 101, ordered them to end the restrictive behaviour, and fined FEG €4.4 million and TU €2.15 million.

Information exchange: *IFTRA*   At least as early as 1955, German, Belgian and Dutch producers of some types of glass bottles subscribed to the International Fair Trade Practice Rules Administration (IFTRA) "fair trade" rules.[52] French and Italian producers, and producers of other types of bottles, later became involved in the programme.

The IFTRA rules defined price competition—systematic matching or undercutting of a competitor's prices—as unfair. They described the publication of price lists as normal practice, and deviations from published price lists as another unfair practice. A firm that signed the IFTRA rules agreed to pay damages (30 per cent of the value of affected sales) to other IFTRA members if it competed "unfairly".

The minutes of meetings of representatives of the IFTRA firms revealed plans to match prices, member state by member state, with those of the local leader (OJ L 160/1 ¶ 11):

> The producer who dominates the market ("natural price leader") determines freely his prices on that market and informs the other producers. The latter fix their export prices for his country on the basis of such information since they will never be able to sell at a price higher than that of the producer who dominates the market, and cannot hope to win the market by charging lower prices since the national producer will follow suit, resulting in a general drop in selling prices. Since wages and other costs are increasing continually, all producers are compelled to make successive increases. The producer who first raises his prices is the price leader if he is followed by the others.

Material collected by the Commission during the course of its investigation indicated that such price matching had in fact taken place.

The glass producers actively exchanged price information—the firms in one country collected information about prices in their market and distributed it to firms in other countries. This kind of exchange was necessary if firms in other member states were to align their prices on those of local leaders. To facilitate price coordination, suppliers also adopted a delivered-price system that was not unlike a basing-point system: "The free delivered price is the price of the goods plus average transport costs."

In its 1974 decision,[53] the Commission had no difficulty discerning the genuine purpose of the fair trade programme (OJ L 160/1 ¶ 34):

> The mere labelling of an agreement between undertakings as "fair trading rules" does not suffice to remove the agreement from the ambit of Article [101] (1) of the EEC Treaty. In the present

---

[52] "Fair trade", in this context, should not be confused with either the laws permitting retail price maintenance adopted by many U.S. states in the 1930s or with a campaign beginning in the late twentieth century to promote international trade between less developed and developed countries on terms that proponents describe as equitable.

[53] *IFTRA glass containers* OJ L 160/1 17 June 1974, pp. 1–17. See also the decision involving fair trade rules for the aluminium industry, *IFTRA aluminium* OJ L 228 29/08/1975, pp. 3–16.

case, the agreement in question contains several clauses, which, although presented as intended to prevent unfair trading, in fact give the parties the opportunity to take joint action against normal methods of competition. Consequently, these clauses have as their real and principal object the restriction of competition between the parties to the detriment of users of glass containers.

The objective of the IFTRA rules was to prevent price competition. The resulting market transparency was entirely one-sided (OJ L 160/1 ¶ 57):

> The exchange of price information benefits only parties to the IFTRA agreement. Consumers, in particular, have knowledge only of the prices charged by the producers who supply them. Neither producers outside the agreement, nor retailers, nor end users have any access to the documents exchanged under the agreement.

The Commission concluded that the adherence to the IFTRA fair trade rules distorted competition in the common market. The other condition for application of Article 101(1), an effect on trade between the member states, was met. Given the entirely anticompetitive nature of the agreement, an exemption under Article 101(3)[54] was out of the question, and the Commission ordered the firms involved to stop the distortionary behaviour.

Publicity

The role of supply-side ambiguity about rivals' conduct in promoting better market performance is illustrated by an application of publicity-oriented competition policy in Denmark.

In the late eighteenth and early nineteenth centuries, publicity was put forward in the United States as a public policy to promote good market performance. A publicity policy was practised in many European nations in the early and mid twentieth century. The publicity approach was gradually abandoned in Europe, but survived in the Danish Competition Act of 1990 (since amended), which provided that:

> The purpose of this Act is to promote competition and, thus, strengthen the efficiency of production and distribution of goods, services, etc., through the largest possible transparency of competitive conditions and through measures against restraints on the freedom of trade and other harmful aspects of anti-competitive practices.

In 1993, the Danish Competition Council suspected that collusion was taking place in the market for ready-mixed concrete,[55] a product that is heavy in relation to value and which is normally shipped no more than 20 to 30 kilometres from the plant.[56] At this time, there were 115 production sites in Denmark. The largest firm had a national market share in 1987 of 37 per cent; the second largest firm had a national market share of 11 per cent. Since geographic markets were local, many local markets were very close to being served by a single supplier.

---

[54] See Section 19.4.2.

[55] (Portland) cement is a processed mixture of limestone and trace elements that becomes adhesive when mixed with water. Concrete, widely used in construction, combines cement, sand and gravel in proportions that vary depending on the intended use.

[56] This discussion is based on Albæk et al. (1997).

Implementing a transparency policy against the suspected anticompetitive practices, the Danish Competition Council began to collect price data—transaction prices, taken from invoices—and publish them on a quarterly basis. Prices rose 15 to 20 per cent in the first year after publication of the transaction prices, and the variability in prices over time fell.

During this period, there was no particular boom in the construction industry, the major user of ready-mix concrete. Thus it does not seem possible to explain the price increase in terms of demand factors. Average concrete prices increased more, in percentage terms, than the price of cement, a major ingredient of concrete. The most likely explanation for the price increase is that by publishing actual transaction prices, the Danish Competition Council reduced incentives for firms to secretly cut prices. With published transaction prices, price cuts would quickly be revealed, inviting retaliation. The Danish Competition Council made it easier for the ready-mix concrete industry to avoid price competition.

In a perfectly competitive market, no transparency policy is needed. In an imperfectly competitive market, the effects of a transparency policy are perverse: it makes non-cooperative collusion easier, because it makes it easier for firms to detect rivals' output expansion.

Price transparency and market performance:

In imperfectly competitive markets, business or government policies that make it easier for firms to detect sporadic price cuts make such price cuts less profitable and so facilitate tacit collusion.

20.3.3 Price Guarantees

Price guarantees convey information to consumers. One example of a price guarantee is a *price-matching* policy: a seller pledges to meet the lower price of a competitor. In a long-term contract, this might take the form of a *meet-or-release* clause: if the supplier does not meet the lower price of a competitor, the customer is no longer bound by the contract, and may take advantage of the lower price that is offered elsewhere. More extreme than price-matching is the *beat-or-pay* policy: the seller pledges to pay a lump sum to the consumer if the seller does not offer a lower price than that of a competitor.[57]

Won't be undersold/won't be undercut

Price-matching guarantees are commitments by a supplier to its customers about the relation between the supplier's price and the prices offered by its competitors. Although the commitment is to the demand side of the market, the information embodied in the commitment is inevitably transmitted to other firms on the supply side of the market as well. When a firm informs consumers that it will not allow itself to be undersold, it also informs rivals that it will not allow them to undersell it. If one firm cuts price, it will expect rivals that have announced a price-matching guarantee to match the price cut, or to offer an even lower price. But this reduces the expected profitability of price-cutting. Price-matching guarantees increase the stability of tacit collusion.

---

[57] Baye and Kovenock (1994) use as an example the advertisement of a Texas car dealer which they paraphrase as "Billy Bob will pay you $1,000 if he doesn't sell you a 1989 pickup for less than any other dealer".

Price discrimination

In a market with imperfectly informed consumers, setting a high price and making a price-matching guarantee is a way for a firm to engage in price discrimination. With imperfect information, some consumers, more naive or less informed than others, will pay a high posted price, believing it is the best they can get. More sophisticated consumers, or those with more information, will be aware of lower prices, if there are any. But sales to informed consumers need not be lost. A lower price elsewhere can be matched and the sale made, at a somewhat lower profit margin than sales to poorly informed buyers. Hence price-matching guarantees encourage setting a higher own price, as well as discouraging rivals from reducing their prices.[58]

Most-favoured-customer

With a *most-favoured-customer* clause, a seller pledges that if it offers a lower price to any customer, it will extend the same price reduction, retroactively, to all other customers. This is a commitment by a supplier to its customers about the relation between the prices it offers them. Such a commitment may well be valued by customers, particularly when the product is an intermediate good that is used as an input for a product that is sold to, or closer to, the final consumer. A most-favoured-customer clause ensures each purchaser that it will not be placed at a competitive disadvantage with respect to some other purchaser who buys at a lower price and for that reason alone has lower costs. At the same time, a most-favoured-customer clause is a commitment to other sellers that the firm will not engage in selective price cutting. By pledging that a price cut made to any customer will be made to all customers, a firm raises its own cost of price cutting. If there is imperfect information on the demand side of the market, price-matching policies, which tend to push prices up, and most-favoured-customer clauses, which discourage selective price reductions, support the collective exercise of market power.[59]

Policy treatment

But the antitrust laws do not prohibit the exercise of market power. What Section 1 of the Sherman Act prohibits is *agreements* that restrain trade. While the price policies we have described support market power, their use is not necessarily connected with agreement (in contrast, for example, to what seems in practice to have been the case with the basing-point system).

Advance announcement of price changes and most-favoured-customer pricing were issues in the 1984 *Ethyl* case.[60] The Federal Trade Commission challenged use of these practices

---

[58] Hviid and Shaffer (1999) point out that the price-increasing effect is weakened if much effort is required on the part of consumers to document a lower-price offer and redeem the price-matching or price-beating pledge.

[59] Phillips and Hall (1960) discuss the *Salk Vaccine* case (U.S. v. Eli Lilly & Co. 1959 U.S. Dist. LEXIS 4048). The U.S. government put forward a conscious parallelism theory of conspiracy by five pharmaceutical producers in the market for polio vaccine. One element of the companies' successful defense was that they employed "most favoured nation" pricing clauses, and this was an explanation for parallel price movements that did not involve conspiracy.

[60] E.I. du Pont de Nemours & Co. v. FTC 729 F.2d 128 (1984). Grether and Plott (1984) report on experiments motivated by the *Ethyl* case. Results suggest that facilitating practices support the exercise of market power in laboratory markets.

during the late 1970s in the highly concentrated[61] antiknock fuel additive market. The FTC argued that the challenged price policies were unfair methods of competition and violations of Section 5 of the FTC Act. The companies appealed an initial negative decision by the FTC to the federal courts. The firms defended themselves on the ground that to the extent that market performance was not competitive, this was inherent in the structure of the industry, not due to the offending market practices. The majority of the Circuit Court of Appeals accepted this view, writing that (729 F.2d 128 at 142):

> [E]ven if the Commission has authority under § 5 to forbid legitimate, non-collusive business practices which substantially lessen competition, there has not been a sufficient showing of lessening of competition in the instant case to permit the exercise of that power.

The upshot of the *Ethyl* decision is that use of facilitating practice that are expected to increase the stability of tacit or overt collusion will not violate U.S. antitrust policy in markets where non-competitive performance might be expected anyway. As with trade association activity, agreement is seen to be an essential element of the antitrust prohibition of contracts, combinations, and conspiracies in restraint of trade. And this leads us once again to consideration of the oligopoly problem.

20.4 Tacit Collusion and the Oligopoly Problem

The oligopoly problem has proven to be a tough nut for antitrust and competition policy to crack. For U.S. antitrust policy, the issue has been one of determining the standards according to which courts will decide whether firms have or have not agreed on a line of conduct that is in restraint of trade. For EU competition policy the issue has been to determine whether the standards for concluding that firms have engaged in a concerted practice are materially less stringent than those applied to determine that firms have reached an agreement.

20.4.1 U.S.: Conscious Parallelism

Interstate Circuit

The issue of proof of agreement arose in a 1939 antitrust decision, *Interstate Circuit*,[62] concerning a vertical agreement to restrain trade in the market for the distribution and exhibition of motion pictures. In this long-ago time before television, DVD, and Blu-ray, the channels by which the recorded entertainment arts reached the viewing public differed from those with which we are familiar. The initial release of a film for exhibition would be to first-run theatres, at a relatively high admission price. The same film would later be re-released for exhibition in second-run theatres, at a lower admission price. Sometimes a lower price per film on second run was obtained by showing second-run films as part of a double bill, so that one admission price carried with it the right to see two films. Second-run showings competed, with a time lag, with first-run showings.

---

[61] Based on figures reported by Hay (1989), the Herfindahl index in the relevant time period was 0.3, implying an equivalent number of 3.3 equally sized firms. There were four firms on the supply side of the market, with market shares of 38.4, 33.5, 16.2, and 11.8 per cent.

[62] Interstate Circuit *et al. v.* U.S. 306 U.S. 208 (1939).

Interstate Circuit, Inc. and Texas Consolidated Theatres, Inc. had near-monopoly positions in the exhibition of first-run movies in their regional markets, major cities in Texas and New Mexico. This gave them bargaining power with respect to film distributors.

Although the two chains of movie theaters were legally independent, they were managed by the same individual, a Mr. R. J. O'Donnell. In 1934, Mr. O'Donnell sent identical copies of a letter to the managers of eight firms involved in the distribution of motion pictures. In the letter, he set out terms intended to have film distributors restrict the ability of second-run theatres to compete with Interstate Circuit's first-run theatres (306 U.S. 208 at 216):

> Interstate Circuit, Inc., will not agree to purchase produce to be exhibited in its 'A' theatres at a price of 40 cents or more for night admission, unless distributors agree that in selling their product to subsequent runs, that this 'A' product will never be exhibited at any time or in any theatre at a smaller admission price than 25 cents for adults in the evening.
>
> In addition to this price restriction, we also request that on 'A' pictures which are exhibited at a night admission price of 40 cents or more—they shall never be exhibited in conjunction with another feature picture under the so-called policy of double-features.

If firm distributors did not agree to these terms, Interstate Circuit would not show their films, keeping those films out of first-run theatres in cities where it held a leading position. The effect of the terms was to raise the price of admission to second-run films, making them less competitive with first-run films.

Film distributors agreed to the terms for four of the six cities served by Interstate Circuit and some of the cities served by Texas Consolidated Theatres. These agreements were reached at meetings that included representatives of all the firm distributors.

In deciding the appeal by Interstate Circuit and its colleagues against the lower-court decision that they had conspired in restraint of trade, the Supreme Court acknowledged that where collusion is illegal, whether or not collusion has taken place is something that will often have to be inferred from indirect evidence (306 U.S. 208 at 221):[63]

> As is usual in cases of alleged unlawful agreements to restrain commerce, the Government is without the aid of direct testimony that the distributors entered into any agreement with each other to impose the restrictions upon subsequent-run exhibitors. In order to establish agreement it is compelled to rely on inferences drawn from the course of conduct of the alleged conspirators.

For the Supreme Court, the trial court inference that agreement had taken place was valid, based on (306 U.S. 208 at 222):

- the fact that each distributor received a copy of the letter containing the addresses of all distributors;
- the joint negotiation of the terms agreed to; and the fact that
- "Each [distributor] was aware that all were in active competition and that without substantially unanimous action with respect to the restrictions for any given territory there was risk of a substantial loss of the business and good will of the subsequent-run and independent exhibitors, but that with it there was the prospect of increased profits".

---

[63] Of course, the conduct at issue in *Interstate Circuit* was prosecuted long before the advent of leniency programmes designed to elicit direct testimony about collusion.

The Supreme Court therefore affirmed the District Court decision that the restrictions contained in the distribution contracts should not be enforced.

The Supreme Court would have found a violation of the Sherman Act based on similar courses of conduct by the distributors, even if the other evidence had not documented the existence of an agreement (306 U.S. 208 at 226, emphasis added):

> While the District Court's finding of an agreement of the distributors among themselves is supported by the evidence, we think that in the circumstances of this case such agreement for the imposition of the restrictions upon subsequent-run exhibitors was not a prerequisite to an unlawful conspiracy. *It was enough that, knowing that concerted action was contemplated and invited, the distributors gave their adherence to the scheme and participated in it.*

This is the doctrine of *conscious parallelism*, which holds that actions taken on the understanding that rivals will take similar actions are sufficient to show conspiracy in restraint of trade in violation of Section 1 of the Sherman Act, even without other evidence of an agreement.

American Tobacco II

Conscious parallelism played a role in the second *American Tobacco* decision.[64] Here three firms, American Tobacco Co., Liggett & Myers Tobacco Co., and R. J. Reynolds Tobacco Co., were convicted of conspiracy in restraint of trade in violation of Section 1 of the Sherman Act and conspiracy to monopolize in violation of Section 2 of the Sherman Act. The companies appealed the Section 2 conviction to the Supreme Court. Here we examine the parts of the Supreme Court decision that referred to the lower court's conclusion that the firms had conspired.[65] The trial judge's instructions to the jury included (328 U.S. 781 at 785–786, italics added by the Supreme Court):

> *An essential element* of the illegal monopoly or monopolization charged in this case *is the existence of a combination or conspiracy to acquire and maintain the power to exclude competitors to a substantial extent.*
>
> Thus you will see that *an indispensable ingredient of each of the offenses charged . . . is a combination or conspiracy.*

The evidence of agreement presented at the trial court largely served to demonstrate parallel behaviour by the tobacco firms. Some of this behaviour involved bidding at auctions for tobacco leaves, an essential ingredient for the production of cigarettes.[66] Some evidence was of simultaneous upward price changes (328 U.S. 781 at 805):

---

[64] American Tobacco *et al. v.* U.S. 328 U.S. 781 (1946). The first *American Tobacco* decision, U.S. *v.* American Tobacco Co. 221 U.S. 106 (1911), a companion decision to the 1911 *Standard Oil* decision under Section 2 of the Sherman Act, broke up the Tobacco Trust. Three of the survivor companies were parties to *American Tobacco II.*

[65] It was also part of the Supreme Court's decision, important for the application of Section 2 of the Sherman Act, that actual exclusion of competitors is not required to find a monopolization or conspiracy to monopolize violation.

[66] Hamilton (1994, p. 37, emphasis in original) makes the case that there was no distinct (tacit or overt) collusion to hold down the price of tobacco leaf: "whatever market power the tobacco companies had in the cigarette and leaf tobacco markets was *unified*: setting the cigarette price was sufficient to curtail both cigarette production and leaf purchases."

On June 23, 1931, Reynolds, without previous notification or warning to the trade or public, raised the list price of Camel cigarettes, constituting its leading cigarette brand, from $ 6.40 to $ 6.85 a thousand. The same day, American increased the list price for Lucky Strike cigarettes, its leading brand, and Liggett the price for Chesterfield cigarettes, its leading brand, to the identical price of $ 6.85 a thousand ...

Some of the evidence was of simultaneous downward price changes, after so-called "10-cent brand" cigarettes, made with lower-quality tobacco, began to cut into the leaders' market shares (328 U.S. 781 at 806):

In response to this threat of competition from the manufacturers of the 10 cent brands, the petitioners, in January, 1933, cut the list price of their three leading brands from $ 6.85 to $ 6 a thousand. In February, they cut again to $ 5.50 a thousand.

For the Supreme Court, this evidence of parallel behaviour was a sufficient basis for the jury to conclude that the tobacco firms had acted pursuant to an agreement (328 U.S. 781 at 809–810, emphasis added):

No formal agreement is necessary to constitute an unlawful conspiracy. *Often crimes are a matter of inference deduced from the acts of the person accused* and done in pursuance of a criminal purpose. Where the conspiracy is proved, as here, from the evidence of the action taken in concert by the parties to it, it is all the more convincing proof of an intent to exercise the power of exclusion acquired through that conspiracy. *The essential combination or conspiracy in violation of the Sherman Act may be found in a course of dealing or other circumstances as well as in an exchange of words.*

Theatre Enterprises

But the 1954 *Theatre Enterprises* decision called a halt to conscious parallelism in U.S. antitrust. Just as *Interstate Circuit* took us back to a land without television or DVDs, so *Theatre Enterprises* takes us back to a time before out-of-town shopping centres dotted the American landscape, a time when city centres were hubs of economic and social activity. This social activity included the viewing of films. Theatre Enterprises, Inc., a firm that may now appear to have been ahead of its time, managed a movie theatre (the Crest) in suburban Baltimore. It sought to obtain first-run movie releases from nine major film producers and distributors. They all refused, on the ground that the commercial success of their films depended on the films first being shown in downtown movie theatres.

Theatre Enterprises filed a private antitrust suit against the distributors, seeking treble damages and an injunction requiring the distributors to supply the Crest with first-run films. As evidence of agreement, it put forward the parallel refusals by film distributors to give it first-run films. The jury in the trial court did not believe there had been a conspiracy, and found against Theatre Enterprises. Theatre Enterprises appealed first to the Fourth Circuit Court of Appeals. Failing to obtain satisfaction there, it appealed to the U.S. Supreme Court. The Supreme Court also sided with the film distributors (346 U.S. 537 at 540–541):

The crucial question is whether [the distributors'] conduct toward [Theatre Enterprises] stemmed from independent decision or from an agreement, tacit or express. To be sure, business behavior is admissible circumstantial evidence from which the fact finder may infer agreement. ... But this Court has never held that proof of parallel business behavior conclusively establishes agreement or, phrased differently, that such behavior itself constitutes a Sherman Act offense. Circumstantial evidence of consciously parallel behavior may have made heavy inroads into the traditional judicial attitude toward conspiracy; but "conscious parallelism" has not yet read conspiracy out of the Sherman Act entirely.

The rule of *Theatre Enterprises* is that parallel behaviour may contribute to a conclusion that firms have agreed on a restrictive course of conduct, but parallel behaviour alone is not sufficient to support such a conclusion.

20.4.2 EU: *Woodpulp*

In its *Woodpulp* decision,[67] the European Court of Justice moved away from accepting parallel conduct as sufficient evidence of a concerted practice.

Wood pulp is an input in the production of paper. During the period involved in this case, the European Community was supplied with wood pulp by firms located in North America and Northern Europe. The European Commission relied on several factors to justify its conclusion that the firms involved in the case had engaged in a concerted practice in violation of Article 101(1). Some U.S. producers were members of an export cartel.[68] Some firms were members of a trade association, based in Switzerland; the trade association hosted regular meetings at which firms exchanged information about prices and formulated price policies. The Commission also relied on evidence of parallel behaviour: the prices set by different firms changed by more or less the same amount at more or less the same time, even though the firms involved were based in many different countries and kept their accounts in many different currencies.

The Advocate General's arguments when the case was appealed, later accepted by the European Court of Justice, rejected the parallel pricing approach ([1993] 4 CMLR 407 at 470):

Each company is entitled to align itself independently on the conduct of its competitors, if knowledge of such conduct is obtained solely by monitoring the market[,]

and ([1993] 4 CMLR 407 at 478):

In any event, if there is a plausible explanation for the conduct found to exist which is consistent with an independent choice by the undertakings concerned, concertation remains unproven.

The European Court of Justice found that while parallel price movements might have been the result of collusion, they might also have been the result of a combination of a high degree of price transparency—prices widely known and news of price changes circulating rapidly—and the oligopoly structure of the market. For the ECJ, evidence of parallel pricing in combination with other factors might justify a finding of concertation, but in this instance the other evidence assembled by the Commission was not sufficient.

---

[67] *Woodpulp*—A. Ahlstrom OY and others *v*. E.C. Commission [1988] 4 CMLR 901; [1993] 4 CMLR 407 (see also the Commission decision, *Woodpulp* OJ L 85/1 26 March 1985, pp. 1–52).

[68] The U.S. 1918 Webb-Pomerene Act makes it legal as far as U.S. law is concerned for U.S. firms to collude with respect to export markets. The United States cannot exempt its firms from the laws of other jurisdictions.

20.4.3 The Oligopoly Problem

In both the U.S. and the EU, genuinely independent business decisions are not condemned by laws that ban collusion, even if the independent decisions lead to market outcomes that are indistinguishable from those of collusion. This is the heart of the problem that oligopoly presents for the enforcement of competition law: if the number of firms is small, independent action can lead to results that closely approximate those of collusion. But competition law in free-market economies does not condemn the results of independent decisions independently arrived at.

There is also the fundamental issue of remedy. Economists conceive of firms as seeking to maximize their value. Managers may well have a legal responsibility to do so. Society can set out rules to which business behaviour must adhere; in the present context, society can insist that firms make decisions independently. But a legal standard that would require firms to do something other than maximize value would be incompatible with a system that aims to rely on the value-maximizing decisions of firms (and the utility-maximizing decisions of consumers) as a resource-allocation mechanism. If each firm is independently maximizing its own value, it is not clear what remedy for tacit collusion could be imposed short of detailed regulation of business conduct. If regulation were costless and able to achieve its stated goals with a minimum of fuss and bother, resorting to regulation when markets fail would not be an issue. But regulation is subject to failure, as are markets, and detailed regulation is not an option that economists have tended to view as a happy one.

A clear implication of the oligopoly problem for competition policy is that if there are practical difficulties in influencing business conduct in oligopoly markets, competition authorities should take great care in administering policy toward market structure. A proposed merger that would lead to market structures conducive to tacit collusion should be vetted, keeping in mind the oligopoly problem that might arise in the post-merger market.

20.5 Cooperation

20.5.1 United States

Topco[69] *and Rothery Storage*[70]

The contrasting outcomes of a 1972 Supreme Court decision and a 1986 Circuit Court of Appeals decision illustrate the retreat of U.S. antitrust from the *per se* rule. With this retreat, U.S. antitrust set sail on Judge Taft's sea of doubt, presuming to say (85 F. 271 at 284) "how much restraint of competition is in the public interest, and how much is not".

Topco Topco Associates, Inc. was a joint purchasing agency owned and operated by 25 grocery chains located in 33 U.S. states. Individual Topco members were small, with an average regional market share of about 6 per cent. At the national level, the combined sales of Topco members were larger than all but three national grocery chains.[71]

---

[69] U.S. *v.* Topco Associates, Inc. 405 U.S. 596 (1972).

[70] Rothery Storage & Van Co. *v.* Atlas Van Lines, Inc. 792 F.2d 210 (1986).

[71] Whereas Topco operated in the wholesale grocery market, its members operated in the retail grocery market. For Topco members, the geographic market was certainly not national.

Topco arranged for the delivery of more than a thousand private-label brand food products to its members. Topco members distributed these products in exclusive territories that were agreed upon at the time a chain joined the association. The U.S. Department of Justice challenged the use of exclusive territories as a scheme for geographic market division and, therefore, a *per se* violation of Section 1 of the Sherman Act. Topco defended itself, successfully in District Court, with the argument that exclusive territories were essential for its members to compete with their larger rivals (405 U.S. 596 at 604–605):

> Private label merchandising is a way of economic life in the food retailing industry, and exclusivity is the essence of a private label program; without exclusivity, a private label would not be private. Each national and large regional chain has its own exclusive private label products in addition to the nationally advertised brands which all chains sell. Each such chain relies upon the exclusivity of its own private label line to differentiate its private label products from those of its competitors and to attract and retain the repeat business and loyalty of consumers. Smaller retail grocery stores and chains are unable to compete effectively with the national and large regional chains without also offering their own exclusive private label products.

The District Court applied the rule of reason, and found that Topco's use of exclusive territories did not violate of Section 1: instead, it promoted competition between Topco members and national chains (319 F. Supp. 1031 at 1042–1043).

The Department of Justice appealed the District Court decision to the Supreme Court, which shied away from trading off the benefits from more competition in one part of the economy against the losses from less competition in another (405 U.S. 596 at 609–610, emphasis added):

> *Our inability to weigh,* in any meaningful sense, *destruction of competition in one sector of the economy against promotion of competition in another sector* is one important reason we have formulated *per se* rules.

It confirmed the principle of competition as a central tenet of antitrust policy (405 U.S. 596 at 610, emphasis added):

> the freedom guaranteed each and every business, no matter how small, is the freedom to compete—to assert with vigor, imagination, devotion, and ingenuity whatever economic muscle it can muster. Implicit in *such freedom* is the notion that it *cannot be foreclosed with respect to one sector of the economy because certain private citizens or groups believe that such foreclosure might promote greater competition in a more important sector of the economy.*

The Supreme Court returned the case to District Court (which issued an injunction against the use of exclusive territories) for reconsideration under the *per se* rule. But it did so over the dissent of Chief Justice Burger, who would have treated Topco's use of exclusive territories as a lawful ancillary restraint (405 U.S. 596 at 613):

> This case does not involve restraints on interbrand competition or an allocation of markets by an association with monopoly or near-monopoly control ... Rather, we have here an agreement among several small grocery chains to join in a cooperative endeavor that, in my view, has an unquestionably lawful principal purpose; in pursuit of that purpose they have mutually

agreed to certain minimal ancillary restraints that are fully reasonable in view of the principal purpose and that have never before today been held by this Court to be *per se* violations of the Sherman Act.

Rothery Storage   Fourteen years later, Chief Justice Burger's view prevailed in a Circuit Court opinion where the antitrust violation that was alleged was a group boycott.[72] Following the deregulation of U.S. trucking in the early 1980s, Atlas Van Lines found itself exposed to legal liability for actions of its independent local moving agents, even with regard to contracts they had entered into on their own behalf. It therefore instituted a policy of dealing only with local moving companies that operated exclusively as part of the Atlas network. Ten local moving companies, among which Rothery Storage & Van Co., filed a private antitrust suit against Atlas, claiming that its policy was a group boycott (on the part of Atlas and its affiliated local agents) in violation of Section 1 of the Sherman Act. The District Court dismissed the local agents' case on several grounds, one being that a rule of reason analysis would exonerate Atlas' policy.

Rothery and its colleagues appealed to the Circuit Court for the District of Columbia, where Judge Bork took a different tack. He contrasted the Supreme Court's use of the *per se* rule in cases like *Topco* with the ancillary restraints doctrine from *Addyston Pipe & Steel* (792 F.2d 210 at 229):[73]

> At one time ... the Supreme Court stated in *Topco* and *Sealy* that the rule for all horizontal restraints was one of per se illegality. The difficulty was that such a rule could not be enforced consistently because it would have meant the outlawing of very normal agreements ... that obviously contributed to economic efficiency. The alternative formulation was that of Judge Taft in *Addyston Pipe & Steel*: a naked horizontal restraint, one that does not accompany a contract integration, can have no purpose other than restricting output and raising prices, and so is illegal per se; an ancillary horizontal restraint, one that is part of an integration of the economic activities of the parties and appears capable of enhancing the group's efficiency, is to be judged according to its purpose and effect.

Since he regarded Atlas' policy as ancillary to its legitimate contracts with its agents, and taking into account Atlas' market share, about 6 per cent, Bork concluded that there was no Section 1 violation and affirmed the judgment of the District Court.

Broadcast Music, Inc.[74]

ASCAP (the American Society of Composers, Authors and Publishers) and Broadcast Music, Inc. are non-profit clearinghouses for the licensing of copyrighted music. A copyright (Section 15.6) gives the holder the exclusive right to perform or grant others the right to perform the copyrighted musical composition for profit.

ASCAP was founded in 1914, BMI in 1939. They exist because it would be extremely costly for an individual composer to negotiate and police copyright licences with the very large number of performers and firms (entertainment establishments, movie and television

---

[72] For references to the antitrust treatment of boycotts and concerted refusals to deal, see Klor's Inc. *v.* Broadway-Hale Stores, Inc., *et al.* 359 U.S. 207 (1959).

[73] *Sealy*, U.S. *v.* Sealy, Inc. 388 U.S. 350 (1967), involved retail price maintenance and exclusive territories.

[74] Broadcast Music, Inc., *et al. v.* CBS, Inc., *et al.* 441 U.S. 1 (1979).

production companies and exhibitors) that are the purchasers of the right to perform a composition.

ASCAP and BMI both grant blanket licences for their portfolios: they license the right to use any piece of music handled by their group and distribute royalties to the copyright holders. After antitrust litigation from the 1940s, it was settled that:

(a) a copyright holder does not assign an exclusive licence to ASCAP—the copyright holder may license the protected music directly to a user, and

(b) ASCAP is obliged to offer licences on a per-programme basis (fee related to the number of programmes that use ASCAP compositions) as well as a blanket or flat fee basis.

Similar arrangements were available from BMI. In practice, however, it was the blanket licence that was used (400 F. Supp. 737 at 743).

CBS (the Columbia Broadcasting System, Inc.) filed a private antitrust suit against ASCAP and BMI, alleging among other things that the use of blanket licences was price fixing and a *per se* violation of Section 1 of the Sherman Act. The District Court declined to apply the *per se* rule. After trial, the District Court ruled that because it was possible to negotiate licences directly with the copyright holder, use of the blanket licence did not amount to price fixing under the antitrust laws. CBS appealed this outcome, and the Second Circuit Court of Appeals accepted CBS' arguments, holding both that the use of blanket licences was price fixing and that such price fixing was a *per se* violation of Section 1. ASCAP and BMI in turn appealed this outcome to the U.S. Supreme Court.

In its ruling, the Supreme Court drew on earlier decisions laying out the scope of the *per se* rule (441 U.S. 1 at 7–8, footnotes and citations omitted):

> [T]he Court has held that certain agreements or practices are so "plainly anticompetitive", ... and so often "lack ... any redeeming virtue", ... that they are conclusively presumed illegal without further examination under the rule of reason generally applied in Sherman Act cases. This *per se* rule is a valid and useful tool of antitrust policy and enforcement. And agreements among competitors to fix prices on their individual goods or services are among those concerted activities that the Court has held to be within the *per se* category. But easy labels do not always supply ready answers.

For the majority of the Supreme Court, the issue was (441 U.S. 1 at 19–20, footnote and citations omitted): "whether the practice facially appears to be one that would always or almost always tend to restrict competition and decrease output, and in what portion of the market, or instead one designed to 'increase economic efficiency and render markets more, rather than less, competitive'".

In the view of the majority of the Court, the product market involved in the case existed only because of copyright protection, and the use of blanket licenses was a device to make that protection effective. The Supreme Court held that use of the *per se* rule was inappropriate, and sent the case back to the Circuit Court of Appeals for a rule of reason analysis of the impact of blanket licences on market performance. In a final decision,[75] the Circuit Court of Appeals reviewed the arguments made initially in District Court, concluded that direct

---

[75] CBS, Inc. *v.* ASCAP *et al.* 620 F.2d 930 (1980).

licensing of copyrighted material from the composer was a feasible alternative to blanket licences, and that, therefore, the use of blanket licences did not restrain trade.

Overlap

In 1958, MIT and the eight Ivy League universities formed what they called "the Overlap group" to coordinate their financial aid processes. The coordination involved the exchange of information and an annual "Ivy Overlap" meeting to "neutralize" competition in the area of financial aid so that[76] "a student may choose among Ivy Group institutions for non-financial reasons".

Hoxby (2000) reports that an important purpose of the information exchange was to confirm the report by an applicant's parents of the amount of aid received by siblings attending some other Overlap university. She notes dryly that (2000, p. 11): "Discussions rarely revealed that parents had underreported their payments to other colleges".

Neutralization of financial aid did *not* mean that an applicant received identical offers of financial aid from different Overlap group schools. Since the different Overlap schools had different strengths and weaknesses, each school would offer a level of financial aid calculated to make itself as attractive, overall, as the other Overlap universities.

Consent agreement   In 1991, the U.S. Department of Justice filed an antitrust suit against the schools making up the Overlap group, alleging that its activities were price fixing and a *per se* violation of Section 1 of the Sherman Act. The eight Ivy League universities signed a consent agreement, admitting no wrongdoing but agreeing to end their Overlap activities. MIT, made of sterner stuff, insisted on its day (ten days, as it turned out) in District Court.

District Court   The District Court declined to apply the *per se* rule, instead engaging in an abbreviated rule of reason analysis. It considered but rejected MIT's efficiency defense, that the Overlap group improved the workings of the financial aid process (805 F. Supp. 288 at 306):

> The Ivy Overlap Group believes that only by eliminating competition is it able to ensure that scarce financial resources are allocated in a manner which it deems to be most advantageous. In so doing, the Ivy Overlap Group was simply imposing its view of the costs and benefits of competition on the marketplace for an education at the elite institutions of higher education.

The District Court relied on the *principle of competition* (805 F. Supp. 288 at 304, citation omitted):

> The Sherman Act presumes that any tampering with the free forces of the market is detrimental. Consequently, any agreement that interferes with the setting of price in the free market "is illegal on its face" . . . MIT may argue that competition was not harmed because the Ivy Overlap process did not raise price, but as far as the Sherman Act is concerned, when competition is eliminated, competition is harmed.

The District Court found in favour of the Department of Justice, and issued an injunction directing MIT not to coordinate its financial aid process with other universities.

---

[76] The quotation is from *The Manual of the Council of Ivy League Presidents*, as reproduced in the District Court decision, U.S. *v.* Brown University *et al.* 805 F. Supp. 288 (1992), at 293, fn. 2.

Circuit Court of Appeals and afterward   MIT appealed this decision to the Third Circuit Court of Appeals. The Circuit Court of Appeals took the view[77] that MIT's arguments deserved to be considered in full, both because of the alleged efficiency benefits and also because a unique characteristic of the higher education "product", that the students who consume the product provided by a university also contribute to making that product what it is (5 F.3d 658 at 677): "MIT alleges that Overlap enhances competition by broadening the socio-economic sphere of its potential student body. Thus, rather than suppress competition, Overlap may in fact merely regulate competition in order to enhance it, while also deriving certain social benefits."

The Circuit Court of Appeals sent the case back to District Court for a full-fledged rule of reason analysis. Before that could take place, the U.S. Department of Justice withdrew its antitrust complaint against MIT and issued guidelines indicating conditions under which not-for-profit universities could coordinate financial aid without subjecting themselves to antitrust complaints.[78]

Collaboration Guidelines

Agreements among competitors that are not *per se* illegal are evaluated under the rule of reason. In 2000 the Federal Trade Commission and the U.S. Department of Justice issued *Antitrust Guidelines for Collaborations Among Competitors* to outline the standards that would be applied to evaluate the reasonableness of proposed collaborations. The Guidelines cover a range of behaviour involving contractual integration that falls short of actual merger, such as (p. 2) research and development, production, marketing, distribution, sales, purchasing, and information sharing and trade association activities.

Under the Guidelines, hard core anticompetitive agreements (p. 8)—"agreements among competitors to fix prices or output, rig bids, or share or divide markets by allocating customers, suppliers, territories, or lines of commerce"—are illegal *per se*.

If, however (p. 8), an arrangement that is typically illegal *per se* is ancillary to an efficiency-enhancing integration, the arrangement may be treated under the rule of reason (p. 8): "In an efficiency-enhancing integration, participants collaborate to perform . . . one or more business functions, such as production, distribution, marketing, purchasing or R&D, and thereby benefit, or potentially benefit, consumers by expanding output, reducing price, or enhancing quality, service, or innovation." If an initial inquiry causes the enforcement agencies to apply the rule of reason, then (p. 10) "analysis begins with an examination of the nature of the relevant agreement, since the nature of the agreement determines the types of anti-competitive harms that may be of concern. . . . the Agencies ask about the business purpose of the agreement and examine whether the agreement, if already in operation, has caused anticompetitive harm".

The family relation of this approach to Justice Brandeis' opinion in *Chicago Board of Trade* is evident.

In evaluating the impact of an agreement on market performance, the enforcement agencies measure market shares and seller concentration in the markets involved. Collaborations

---

[77] U.S. *v.* Brown University *et al.* 5 F. 3d 658 (1993).

[78] See MIT press release on the Overlap Group settlement, MIT News Office, 22 December 1993 (<http://www-tech.mit.edu/Bulletins/ovrlp-pr.html>).

that are not *per se* illegal will not ordinarily face an antitrust challenge if the firms' combined market shares fall in the safety zone of 20 per cent or less (p. 26).

The agencies also examine whether or not an agreement is likely to facilitate collusion (p. 15). Sharing of aggregate, historical information is less likely to lead to a finding that a collaboration is unreasonable. Sharing of current information about prices and outputs is more likely to lead to such a finding (pp. 15–16).

20.5.2 European Union

From its beginnings, EU competition policy embodied positions similar to those set out in the U.S. *Cooperation Guidelines*. While Article 101(1) prohibits agreements, decisions of associations, and concerted practices that distort trade between the member states, Article 101(3) lays out conditions under which this prohibition is waived. The language of the Article is that a distortionary but permitted agreement must contribute "to improving the production or distribution of goods or to promoting technical or economic progress, while allowing consumers a fair share of the resulting benefit". In the vocabulary of economics, this amounts to "increases net social welfare (the sum of consumer surplus and producer surplus), with at least some of the increase being in consumer surplus".

Clima Chappée

Commission decisions taken under the old (Regulation 17) regime, when interfirm agreements had to be notified in advance to the Commission to benefit from Article 101(3), illustrate the application of the exemption.

A 1969 Commission decision, *Clima Chappée*, involved a specialization agreement by two firms, one French (Clima Chappée) and one German (Buderus'sche Eisenwerke). Clima Chappée produced primarily air conditioning equipment suitable for homes and offices. Buderus'sche Eisenwerke produced central heating systems, but had begun preparations to produce air conditioning equipment aimed at a different segment of the market from that served by Clima Chappée. Under the terms of the agreement, each firm would specialize in production and would distribute in the other country only through its contractual partner. Both firms would be free to sell in other EC member states.

On the one hand, this can be described as a specialization agreement. On the other hand, it can be described as an agreement not to compete. The contract eliminates each firm as a potential entrant in the product market supplied by the other. Since each firm was associated with a larger industrial group, each had the resources to undertake production of a full range of products. Thus the agreement suppressed actual and potential competition between the two firms. But the agreement would allow the firms to avoid duplicate (presumably, wasteful, although the Commission does not say that) investment in product development and to produce more nearly at capacity, realizing run-length and scale economies. At the same time, there would continue to be effective competition from the many competing firms in the EU market for air conditioning and heating equipment. The Commission granted the agreement an exemption under Article 101(3).[79]

---

[79] In contrast, in its *Van Katwijk* decision (Commission Decision of 28 October 1970 [1970] 4 CMLR D43), the the Commission declined to apply Article 101(3) to a market sharing agreement unaccompanied by real prospects for improving performance.

Safco

Safco[80] involved a joint export sales agency formed by seven small French producers of canned vegetables and aimed primarily at the German market. The agreement limited competition among the firms; as part of the agreement, Safco members committed themselves not to operate independently on export markets. But they had not done so to any significant extent before setting up the joint sales agency. The agreement did not restrict competition among the firms on their home, French, market. The combined market share of the firms was small: 6 per cent of the French market, between 1 and 8 per cent of the German market. They faced continuing competition in both France and Germany. Taking into account that the joint sales agency permitted competition (on the Germany market) that might not otherwise have been possible, the Commission issued Safco "negative clearance", a statement that on the information available to the Commission there appeared to be no violation of Article 101(1).[81,82]

Guidelines, etc.

The Commission issues Guidelines, Notices, and Block Exemptions to give specific and general indications of the standards used to implement Articles 101(1) and (3). We discuss two of these here.[83] The *de minimis* notice[84] characterizes agreements that affect trade among the member states but to so little an extent that the Commission considers that the agreement does not restrict competition. The basic rule (which is subject to qualifications that are explained in the Notice) is that agreements among actual or potential competitors where the combined market share of parties to the agreement is less than 10 per cent on any relevant market are *de minimis*, with the threshold market share value rising to 15 per cent if parties to the agreement are not actual or potential competitors.

Guidelines issued in 2001 clarify the application of Article 101 to horizontal cooperation agreements,[85] and guidelines issued in 2004 discuss Article 101(1) and deal specifically with Article 101(3).[86] The 2001 guidelines point to low market shares of cooperating firms, low market concentration, and ample competition remaining outside the cooperation as factors

---

[80] *Safco* Commission Decision of 16 December 1971 JO L 13/44 17 January 1972, 1972 CMLR D83.

[81] In *NCH* (Commission Decision of 23 December 1971 OJ L 22/16 26 January 1972), the Commission declined to grant an Article 101(3) exemption for a joint sales agency that served (the Commission concluded) mainly to eliminate competition among German cement firms on their 14 per cent combined share of sales in the Dutch cement market.

[82] The 1968 *Socemas* decision (JO L 201/4 12 August 1968, 1968 CMLR D28), which permitted a joint purchasing agency of French grocery stores, corresponds to *Safco*, with cooperation on the input rather than the output side of the market. The issues in *Socemas* are similar to those in *Topco*.

[83] Some of the specific guidelines are discussed elsewhere in the text; the full panoply is available at the DG Competition web site.

[84] Commission Notice on agreements of minor importance which do not appreciably restrict competition under Article [101](1) OJ C 368/13 22 December 2001. See also the discussion in Section 17.4.3 of the *de minimis* state aid regulation.

[85] Guidelines on the applicability of Article 101 of the EC Treaty to horizontal cooperation agreements OJ C 3/2 6 January 2001. These are supplemented by the later Guidelines on the applicability of Article [101](3) of the Treaty OJ C 101/97 27 April 2004.

[86] Guidelines on the applicability of Article [101](3) of the Treaty OJ C 101/97 27 April 2004.

making a restrictive effect less likely. The guidelines suggest that cooperations resulting in a high level of common costs may make it easier for firms to coordinate their market conduct, thus raising competition policy concerns. The guidelines also emphasize that for a cooperation that restricts competition to go forward, it must generate economic benefits, benefits that go beyond mere increased profit for the cooperating firms. Further, cooperation must be essential to realize those economic benefits if it is to quality for the Article 101(3) exemption.

Like the U.S. Cooperation Guidelines, the Commission's approach to applying Article 101(3) places great weight on the market shares of parties to a cooperative arrangement and on concentration levels in the affected market. These approaches make the way the relevant product and geographic market are defined, the way market shares are calculated, and the way market concentration is measured, of central importance. We take up this topic in the context of merger policy, the arena in which its importance to antitrust and competition policy was first apparent.

SUMMARY

Public policy can affect the stability of jointly exercised market power. But as a device to promote good market performance, a publicity policy is counterproductive. Publicity shines the light of day on the low price of the cheater as well as on the high price of the colluder. The result is to discourage low prices and increase the stability of tacit or overt collusion.

If firms agree to fix price or restrict output on a U.S. market, they have committed a *per se* violation of Section 1 of the Sherman Act. If agreements, decisions of associations, or concerted practices distort competition and affect trade among the EU member states, they violate Article 101(1).

Since it is known that collusion is illegal, miscreants will hide evidence of their misdeeds, insofar as possible. While such evidence may nonetheless survive and come to light, particularly because of leniency programmes, enforcement agencies and courts will often need to infer whether or not agreement has taken place.

The oligopoly problem facing antitrust and competition policy is that in small-numbers oligopoly, the kind of market performance that results from explicit collusion may also result from the independent decisions by firms that recognize their mutual interdependence. Courts, consequently, wrestle with question of the nature of the evidence that will be considered sufficient to conclude that an agreement has taken place.

Facilitating practices can stabilize tacit or overt collusion. Facilitating practices that are the result of agreement among independent firms will be condemned under Section 1 of the Sherman Act. Facilitating practices that are the result of genuinely independent decisions will not.

Cooperation will generally restrict competition, on some level, and very often will affect price. Not all cooperation, however, is naked collusion, restricting competition with the object or effect of increasing the economic profit of those in on the cooperation while worsening market performance. Outside the category of naked collusion, cooperation may on balance improve market performance. EU competition authorities have always had, and U.S. antitrust authorities have moved toward, a judgemental approach to cooperation that restricts competition and also enhances efficiency. The two sides of the Atlantic share, generally, a common view of the kinds of market characteristics that are likely to bring out the best, from a social point of view, in such cooperations: small market shares, low seller concentration, and more competition from outside parties, all else equal, favour efficiency consequences over restrictive consequences of a cooperation.

STUDY POINTS

- The *per se* rule (Section 20.2.1)
- *Northern Securities* (Section 20.2.1)
- Common law treatment of restraint of trade (Section 20.2.1)
- Article 101(1) (Section 20.2.2)
- Leniency programmes (Section 20.2.3)
- Basing-point pricing (Section 20.3.1)
- Trade association activities, the NRA (Section 20.3.2)
- Price transparency and market performance in imperfectly competitive markets (Section 20.3.2)
- Price guarantees (Section 20.3.3)
- Tacit collusion and the oligopoly problem (Section 20.4)
- Conscious parallelism (Section 20.4.1)
- Socially beneficial cooperation (Section 20.5)

FURTHER READING

For discussions of the common law treatment of restraint of trade, see among others Jones (1926, 1927), Jaffe and Tobriner (1932), Thorelli (1955, Chapter 1), and Letwin (1965, Chapter 2). Peppin (1940) disputes Taft's reading of the common law. For statements of the facts of *Addyston Pipe and Steel*, see among others U.S. *v.* Addyston Pipe and Steel 85 Fed 271 (1898), Addyston Pipe and Steel *v.* U.S. 175 US 211 (1899), Edward B. Whitney (1905), Simon N. Whitney (1958, Volume II, Chapter 10), Phillips (1962, Chapter V). On *Chicago Board of Trade*, see Bork (1965, pp. 815–820), Bickel (1984, pp. 177–180). Phillips (1959) reviews the development of the *per se* rule and makes an early plea in favour of the rule of reason.

Fisher and James (1955) offer a detailed account of the Bituminous Coal Act. For the British approach to problems of the coal industry, see Macgregor (1934), Kirby (1973).

On the basing-point system, see Fetter ([1931] 1971), Machlup (1949), Stigler (1949b), Stocking and Watkins (1951, Chapter 7), McGee (1954), Loescher (1959), Carlton (1983), and Phlips (1983, 1993). Commons (1924) discusses the U.S. steel industry's adoption of the Pittsburgh Plus system. Stegemann (1968) discusses basing-point pricing under the ECSC Treaty. For pseudo-competitive explanations of basing-point pricing and comments thereon, see Haddock (1982), Benson *et al.* (1990), Gilligan (1992), and Hughes and Barbezat (1996), as well as Thisse and Vives (1988, 1992). Soper *et al.* (1991) consider the impact of basing-point pricing on firms' location decisions.

Stocking and Watkins (1947, Chapter 11) discuss the history of collusion in the world chemical industries, including (pp. 505–511) dyestuffs. Schröter (1992) discusses the world dyestuffs cartel during the inter-war period.

Levy (1927) is one 1920s argument in favour of trade association activity. On the trade association movement and efforts to limit the role of antitrust, see Stocking and Watkins (1951, Chapter 8), Hawley (1974), Himmelberg (1976), and Barber (1985), and on trade associations generally, Yamazaki and Miyamoto (1988). Gressley's (1964) essay on Thurman Arnold and Wells' (2004) essay on Montague touch on aspects of antitrust before, during, and after the trade association movement. For case studies of a specific trade association and its impact on market performance, see Genesove and Mullin (1999, 2001).

On the National Recovery Administration Act, see among others Lyon *et al.* (1935), Whitney (1935), Schlesinger (1959, Chapters 6–10), Hawley (1966), Barber (1996, Chapters 2–4), Bittlingmayer (1995), Alexander (1997b), Alexander and Libecap (2000), and Taylor (2002).

On price guarantees as a facilitating practice, see Hay (1982, 1989), Salop (1986), Cooper (1986), Holt and Scheffman (1987), Png and Hirshleifer (1987), and Edlin (1997). On the antitrust treatment of facilitating practices, see Hay (2000).

On collusion in the quinine industry, see Blair (1967). On ADM and the lysine cartel, see among others Connor (2000), Eichenwald (2000), Lieber (2000), and de Roos (2006), as well as papers making up a Symposium on the subject in the February 2001 issue of the *Review of Industrial Organization*. On the European Commission's 1996 Leniency Notice, see Peña Castellot (2001) and on the 2002 Notice, Arbault and Peiró (2002).

Neven *et al.* (1998) review EU competition policy toward interfirm agreements.

MONOPOLIZATION AND DOMINANCE

Upon what meat doth this our Caesar feed, that he is grown so great?

Julius Caesar, Act I, scene ii

21.1 Introduction

In this chapter we examine U.S. antitrust policy toward monopolization and EC competition policy toward abuse of dominance. For both, a central issue has been to draw a line for business behaviour that permits dominant firms to compete on the merits but not to deny other firms the opportunity to compete on the merits. Confronting this issue has given U.S. antitrust its fundamental guideline, the rule of reason, and an approach to the treatment of predatory pricing, the Areeda-Turner rule, that avoids application of the rule of reason. For the EC, a long-standing question has been the extent to which competition policy can and should condemn the exercise of market power by firms that have obtained it by competition on the merits. A more recent question is the interaction of an economic approach to dominant-firm behaviour and the promotion of market integration.

21.2 Sherman Act Section 2

21.2.1 Monopolization and the Rule of Reason

Standard Oil *v.* U.S.

In the late nineteenth century, a variety of products were produced from oil, but its economic importance was as a source of fuel for lamps (Gibson, 1886), for the U.S. and even more for export markets.[1] The Standard Oil Company of Ohio, an oil refinery located in Cleveland, was established by the Rockefeller brothers in 1870. Within two years, it controlled most of the oil refineries in Cleveland, and thereafter extended its control to 80 per

---

[1] According to Chandler (1977, p. 322) "in 1880 Europe still took 70 per cent of all the illuminating oil processed in the United States".

cent of the U.S. refining industry.[2] It came to dominate the petroleum industry by means of a strategic alliance with the railroad lines that connected oil-producing regions in Western Pennsylvania with the Atlantic coast, the location of U.S. population centres and gateway to world export markets. This alliance allowed "the Standard" to exploit railroad rate differentials to raise rival refiners' costs and induce them to sell out on favourable terms.

Vertical symbiotic collusion   Figure 21.1 shows the heart of the 1870 U.S. crude oil market. Oil was extracted in the Oil Regions of Western Pennsylvania. For the most part, it was refined in Cleveland, Pittsburgh, and Philadelphia. Crude oil moved from the producing to the refining regions, and thence to the East Coast, on three railroad lines—the Erie Railroad and the New York Central Railroad (connecting Cleveland to New York) and the Pennsylvania Railroad (connecting Pittsburgh and Philadelphia). For the railroads, with high fixed and low marginal cost, the temptation to lower rates and increase volume was always present. But succumbing to this temptation brought its own punishment, rate wars and economic

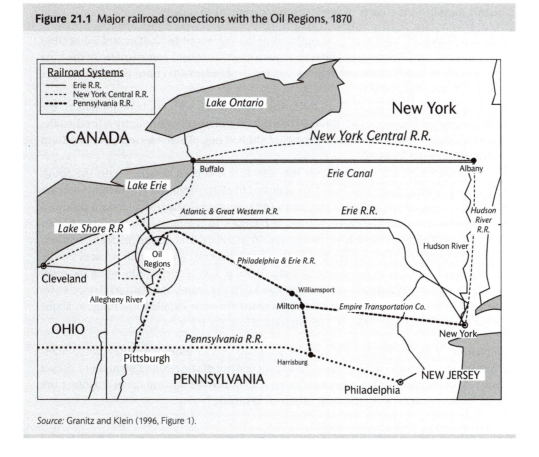

Figure 21.1 Major railroad connections with the Oil Regions, 1870

Source: Granitz and Klein (1996, Figure 1).

---

[2] Standard's position was never based on control of crude oil. Its maximum share of crude oil extraction, reached in 1898, was 33 per cent (Bringhurst, 1979, p. 109).

losses. Collusion seemed like a desirable alternative, but collusive agreements, while not illegal, were unstable and not enforceable in courts of law.

At the start of 1872, and at the instigation of the three railroads, four large oil refiners established the South Improvement Company. One of the refiners was located in Cleveland, one in Pittsburgh, one in Philadelphia, and one in New York City. The Cleveland refiner was Standard Oil.[3] The plan was that the four refineries, working through the South Improvement Company, would police a collusive market-sharing scheme for the railroad companies. The refiners would allocate their shipments across railroads to keep the railroads' shares of traffic at agreed levels. In return, the railroads would give the South Improvement refiners discriminatorily low railroad rates and make a payment—a drawback—to the South Improvement Company for every barrel of oil shipped by independent refiners.

The Oil War of 1872   The South Improvement Company scheme was discovered before it could be put into effect. This discovery triggered a massive protest, the Oil War of 1872, and an embargo by crude oil producers of deliveries to the refineries of the South Improvement Company parent firms. The Oil War of 1872 came to an end when the Pennsylvania legislature annulled the charter of the South Improvement Company.

Rise of "The Standard"   But before the outbreak of the Oil War of 1872, Standard Oil of Ohio used the prospect of differential rail rates to acquire most Cleveland-area refiners. By the time the South Improvement Company scheme collapsed, Standard Oil controlled about 25 per cent of U.S. refinery capacity.

On 1 April 1872 (April Fools' Day), following negotiations with crude oil producers, the railroad companies announced what was to be a public and nondiscriminatory rate schedule, open to all refiners. Within two weeks, Standard Oil had negotiated a secret lower rate from the New York Central Railroad.

Standard Oil proceeded to implement the plan that had been designed with the South Improvement Company in mind. It secretly acquired the Pittsburgh and Philadelphia refiners that had been designated parents of the South Improvement Company. Standard balanced out its shipments among the three railroad companies to maintain the stability of their cartel. This enabled the railroads to raise rates, to Standard and to independent refiners. But Standard benefited from rail rebates on its own shipments, and from drawbacks on the shipments of its competitors (Granitz and Klein, 1996, p. 20): "For example, while the open rate in 1878 for crude shipments to New York was $1.70 per barrel, Standard paid only $1.06 per barrel." In addition, railroads provided Standard Oil with detailed information about rivals' oil shipments (Nash, 1957, p. 185; Thorelli, 1955, pp. 92–93).

Raising rivals' costs   By raising the costs of Standard's rivals more than they raised Standard's costs, the railroads enabled Standard to gain control of the refining segment of the oil industry. Standard's control of refining allowed it to police the railroad cartel, enabling the railroads to differentially raise the costs of Standard's rivals.[4]

---

[3] Standard and the New York refiner that had a share in the South Improvement Company merged on 1 January 1872.

[4] The American Sugar Refining Company was later involved in the same sort of scheme, policing railroad collusion in the shipping of sugar shipments in return for secret rebates on its own railroad rates. During its 1898–1900 price war with Arbuckle Brothers and the New York Sugar Refining Company, ASRC received railroad rebates not only on the sugar it shipped, but also on the sugar its competitors shipped (Eichner, 1969, pp. 195–204, p. 220).

This symbiotic relationship was perceived, by many, although not entirely understood, at the time. Hostility toward railroad rebates, which were seen as falsifying competition among firms that used railroad services, was a major factor in the 1887 creation of the Interstate Commerce Commission and the 1903 passage of the Elkins Anti-Rebate Act, which prohibited railroads from granting rebates or deviating from their published rates.

Trusts   The trust form of business organization involved the consignment of shares of stock in legally independent companies to trustees, in exchange for shares of stock in the trust. The trustees then managed the combined operations of the companies. The trust form of organization was invented by Standard Oil, which established itself as a trust in 1879 in Ohio and reconstituted itself with headquarters in New York City in 1882. Thirty-three state antitrust suits were filed against Standard Oil between 1890 and 1911, all unsuccessful (Bringhurst, 1979, p. 102). A Federal antitrust case began in April 1909, just one month after President Taft took office. The St. Louis circuit court decision, in November 1909, was in favour of the government. Standard Oil appealed that decision to the Supreme Court, which heard arguments in the case in March 1910 and January 1911, and issued a decision, again in favour of the government, in May 1911.

The Rule of Reason   The case gave the Court an opportunity to lay out its interpretation of Section 2 of the Sherman Act. As the Supreme Court saw it, what the Congress that passed the Sherman Act had sought to avoid was the consequences—among which, higher prices—of unreasonable restraints on competition (221 U.S. 1 at 58, emphasis added):

> [T]he dread of enhancement of prices and of other wrongs which it was thought would flow from the undue limitation on competitive conditions caused by contracts or other acts of individuals or corporations, led, as a matter of public policy, to the prohibition or treating as illegal all contracts or acts which were *unreasonably restrictive of competitive conditions* ...

How does one decide if a particular restraint is unreasonable? By looking at the nature of the contract, the circumstances surrounding it, and the intent with which it had been entered into, inferring (221 U.S. 1 at 58)

> either from the nature or character of the contract or act or where the surrounding circumstances were such as to justify the conclusion that they had not been entered into ... with the legitimate purpose of ... developing trade, but on the contrary were of such a character as to ... limit the right of individuals, thus restraining the free flow of commerce and tending to bring about the evils, such as enhancement of prices, which were considered to be against public policy.

Contracts made to promote trade are reasonable; contracts made to restrain trade are unreasonable and (221 U.S. 1 at 62; emphasis added) "the criteria to be resorted to in any given case for the purpose of ascertaining whether violations of [Section 2] have been committed is the *rule of reason* ... "

Normal methods of industrial development   Applying the rule of reason to the facts of the Standard Oil case, the Court concluded that Standard's purpose had been to maintain a dominant position in the oil industry (221 U.S. 1 at 75) "not as a result of normal methods of industrial development" and found Standard Oil in violation of Section 2 of the Sherman Act.

Thus the *Standard Oil* decision was the vehicle by which the rule of reason was introduced to U.S. antitrust.[5] Whether the growth of a firm with market power was or was not "a result of normal methods of industrial development" became a critical question in deciding whether or not it had monopolized in the sense of Section 2.

Remedy Standard Oil was broken up into 33 "survivor companies", which by and large were the components out of which the trust had been made in the first place. Thus were born Standard Oil of New Jersey, Standard Oil of California, and so on. But ownership of the survivor companies remained with the owners of the Standard Oil trust, and control rested largely with John D. Rockefeller, Sr. and the Rockefeller family.[6]

Further, the Trust had organized its components on a regional basis. Most of the survivor companies dominated their regional markets, and the post-divestiture market showed a pattern of *mutual forbearance* (Comanor and Scherer, 1995, p. 266), each survivor company tending to stay out of others' geographic markets. Generations were required before the passage of time, inheritance, and divorce fractured ownership of the survivor companies so much that independent oligopolistic behaviour appeared in the U.S. oil market.

A chilly reception Before and after the Standard Oil decision, the rule of reason was subject to the criticism that it was unacceptably vague. A 1913 Senate Committee report wrote that:[7]

> It is inconceivable that in a country governed by a written Constitution and statute law the courts can be permitted to test each restraint of trade by the economic standard which the individual members of the court may happen to approve.

Congressional hostility toward the rule of reason was a major factor behind the 1914 passage of the Clayton Act, with its enumeration of specific practices held to violate the law "where [their] effect ... may be substantially to lessen competition or tend to create a monopoly". In application, however, it remained with courts to decide whether or not, in any specific instance, the effect of the practices identified in the Clayton Act was to lessen competition or tend to create a monopoly, and in making such decisions, courts largely applied the rule of reason.

U.S. *v.* United States Steel Corporation

United States Steel was formed in 1901, two years after the *Addyston Pipe and Steel* decision made clear that Section 1 of the Sherman Act outlawed overt collusion. Its leading components were the number one and number two firms in the steel industry, Carnegie Steel and Federal Steel. Federal Steel was part of the J. P. Morgan financial and industrial empire.

---

[5] The rule of reason was reaffirmed in a companion decision, *American Tobacco*, handed down two weeks after *Standard Oil*. See U.S. *v.* American Tobacco Co. 221 U.S. 106 (1911), at 178–181.

[6] Berle and Means ([1932] 1991, pp. 76–77) describe a 1929 proxy fight between John D. Rockefeller, Sr., who owned 14.9 per cent of the voting stock in the Standard Oil Company of Indiana, and the management of the company. Berle and Means quote the Wall Street Journal to the effect that the proxy fight "marked the first time Rockefeller domination in a large Standard Oil unit 'had really been in question'". Rockefeller won the proxy battle.

[7] Senate Committee on Interstate Commerce, Control of Corporations, Persons and Firms Engaged in Interstate Commerce, Senate Report No. 1326, 62d Congress, 3d Session (1913), pp. 10–11.

Carnegie Steel and Federal Steel were both vertically integrated backward into extraction of coal and of iron ore.

Hard driving   Carnegie Steel owed its market position to Andrew Carnegie's fiercely rivalrous business approach. Carnegie's policy was to adopt cutting-edge technology and to run his plants at full capacity, obtaining the maximum possible economies of throughput and the ability to undersell any and all rivals.

Tit-for-tat vertical integration   In 1900, major fabricators of steel products—wire, nails tubes, as well as tin plate—began to integrate backward into steel production. As a result, they cut back on orders from Carnegie Steel. Carnegie responded by threatening to integrate forward into fabrication, raising the prospect of substantial excess capacity in the U.S. steel industry (Chandler, 1990, p. 131).

Consolidation   To head off the prospect of steel industry price wars, J. P. Morgan organized the consolidation that led to the formation of the United States Steel Corporation. First he bought Carnegie Steel and combined it with Federal Steel. Then other steel firms were brought into the operation. U.S. Steel combined the assets of more than 180 previously independent operating companies. The deal was done hurriedly, and without the careful evaluation of assets usually undertaken by J.P. Morgan & Co. when it arranged a merger. U.S. Steel's assets, therefore, were tremendously overvalued (Chandler, 1990, p. 132): "the capitalization of the United States Steel Corporation was $1,439.0 million, whereas the value of the securities and cash of the companies coming into the firm was only $881.2 million."

At its formation, United States Steel was the largest U.S. corporation; its component firms supplied almost two-thirds of U.S. steel ingot. It was not an operating company (McCraw and Reinhardt, 1989, pp. 595–596):

> Unlike most successful mergers, U.S. Steel under [its Chairman, Judge Elbert H.] Gary did little to rationalize production facilities, innovate product lines, or consolidate management structure. Through U.S. Steel's Pittsburgh-plus system, the firm facilitated price coordination with smaller competitors, but saddled itself with a locational inertia that minimized its ability to exploit new opportunities in growing geographical markets. ... it persisted in the form of a loose holding company, long keeping intact about 200 subsidiaries ... Many of these subsidiaries had overlapping markets and duplicate sales forces.

Gary dinners   Much to the chagrin of the U.S. Steel executives who had come from Carnegie Steel (many of whom eventually took up employment elsewhere), Gary gave up Carnegie's full-capacity production, low-cost, low price policy in favour of a policy of high and stable prices (Chandler, 1990, p. 135):[8]

---

[8] Burns (1936, p. 78, fn. 5) quotes one steelmaker's doggerel tribute to the impact of the Gary dinners:

> "The melancholy days have gone
> We're feeling light and airy,
> We're not a-cussing anyone
> But just a-blessing Gary."

Less lyrically, Yamawaki (1985, p. 432) reports a statistically significant positive impact of the Gary dinners on steel prices.

When the competitors began to reduce prices to maintain share and profit, Gary instituted his famous dinners of 1907 and 1908 to urge them to support the prices that he had done so much to stabilize. On some products they did; on some they did not. United States Steel continued to lose market share. . . . Finally in February 1909, Gary gave in . . .

With United States Steel operating at full capacity once again the independents were chastened. They held a testimonial dinner for Gary in October 1909 to urge him to return to his earlier policies.

Antitrust suit   The "Gary dinners" took place between 1907 and 1911 and provided a forum at which steel producers could exchange information, manifest and maintain a community spirit, and proclaim the best of intentions. The last dinner took place in the year the *Standard Oil* decision was handed down. This was also the year the U.S. government filed an antitrust suit against U.S. Steel. The government charged that the merger creating U.S. Steel was monopolization in restraint of trade in violation of Section 2 of the Sherman Act, and the government asked that U.S. Steel be dissolved.

The District Court that first heard the case ruled in favour of U.S. Steel, in 1915. It produced four opinions to explain that result.[9] One of those, written by Judge Woolley, laid out the position that was later endorsed by a closely divided Supreme Court.[10] This position was the U.S. Steel could not have committed the offense of monopolization, because it was not, at the time of its formation, a monopoly.[11] That U.S. Steel did *not* have a monopoly position was shown by the fact that it had had to combine with other steel companies to "fix and maintain prices" (223 F. 55 165–166).

Mere size not an offence   The majority of the Supreme Court followed the District Court, and declined to find U.S. Steel in violation of the Sherman Act (251 U.S. 417 at 451, emphasis added):

> The corporation is undoubtedly of impressive size, and it takes an effort of resolution not to be affected by it or to exaggerate its influence. But we must adhere to the law, and *the law does not make mere size an offense*, or the existence of unexerted power an offense. It, we repeat, requires overt acts, and trusts to its prohibition of them and its power to repress or punish them. It does not compel competition, nor require all that is possible.

Opinions at both the District Court and the Supreme Court suggest that U.S. Steel's conduct after its formation (including the Gary dinners) might have been found to be a conspiracy in restraint of trade in violation of Section 1 of the Sherman Act.

Aftermath   U.S. Steel's market share had declined to about 50 per cent at the time of the Supreme Court decision. In 1927, after Judge Gary's death, his successors undertook to reorganize U.S. Steel along rational lines. By this time, competitors had consolidated their own market positions. U.S. Steel's market share continued to decline, falling to something like 25 per cent of the market 50 years after the Supreme Court decision.

---

[9] U.S. *v.* United States Steel Corporation 223 F. 55 (1915).

[10] Four Justices supported the District Court decision, three would have reversed it, and two did not participate.

[11] Mullin *et al.*'s (1995) examination of the impact of events in the antitrust case against U.S. Steel suggests that U.S. Steel was believed by the stock market to exercise some degree of monopoly control over the steel market.

U.S. v. Aluminum Company of America

There is some discussion of the early U.S. aluminum market, in which the Aluminum Company of America was the only domestic supplier of primary aluminum, in Section 7.2.2. The U.S. government charged Alcoa with monopolization in violation of Section 2 of the Sherman Act in 1937. The 1941 District Court decision[12] favoured Alcoa. The government appealed the District Court decision. Exceptionally, as a sufficient number of justices recused themselves from the case that a quorum of six justices was lacking, the government's appeal was heard by a three-judge panel of the Second Circuit Court of Appeals.

Market share   Drawing on the interpretation of Section 2 from *Standard Oil* and later decisions, to prevail the government had to show two things. First, it was obliged to show that Alcoa had a monopoly position within the meaning of the Sherman Act. The assessment of Alcoa's market position was complicated by the fact that primary aluminum, a durable good, faced competition from a fringe of recyclers whose raw material was scrap aluminum, the supply of which at any time depended on Alcoa's past production. Depending on how one treated imported and recycled aluminum, estimates of Alcoa's market share were 33 per cent, 64 per cent, or 90 per cent of the market. The first figure was certainly too low. The last figure, which was the one accepted by the Court, may have been too high. The second figure, 64 per cent, would most likely have been sufficient to support a finding of monopolization, if the remaining element of the proof was satisfied.[13] Judge Hand concluded that fringe supply from suppliers of recycled secondary aluminum did not prevent Alcoa from exercising market power.

Intent to exclude   Second, the government was obliged to show Alcoa had obtained or maintained its position of monopoly power by behaviour that amounted to restraint of trade in violation of Section 1, or not as a result of normal industrial development, or by behaviour showing "an intent and purpose to exclude others".

Judge Hand, writing for the court in a 1945 decision,[14] found the necessary element of intent to exclude in Alcoa's expansion of capacity (148 F.2d 416, at 431):

> It was not inevitable that it should always anticipate increases in demand for ingot and be prepared to supply them. Nothing compelled it to keep doubling and redoubling its capacity before others entered the field. It insists that it never excluded competitors; but we can think of no more effective exclusion than progressively to embrace each new opportunity as it opened, and to face every newcomer with new capacity already geared into a great organization ... Only in case we interpret "exclusion" as limited to manœuvres not honestly industrial, but actuated solely by a desire to prevent competition, can such a course be deemed ... not "exclusionary".

The Circuit Court of Appeals concluded that Alcoa had monopolized in violation of Section 2 of the Sherman Act, although its overall rate of return on investment, about 10 per cent, (148 F.2d 416, at 427) "could hardly be considered extortionate".

---

[12] U.S. *v.* Aluminum Co. of America *et al.* 44 F. Supp. 97 (1941).

[13] On the issue of the calculation of Alcoa's market share, see Fisher (1974), Suslow (1986), and Grant (1999).

[14] U.S. *v.* Aluminum Co. of America *et al.* 148 F.2d 416 (2d Cir. 1945). Judge Hand's opinion was endorsed by the Supreme Court in the second *American Tobacco* case, American Tobacco *et al. v.* U.S. 328 U.S. 781 (1946).

Non-economic goals of antitrust   Parts of Judge Hand's opinion rested on non-economic goals of the Sherman Act (148 F.2d. 416 at 428–9):

> We have been speaking only of the economic reasons which forbid monopoly; but, as we have already implied, there are others, based upon the belief that great industrial consolidations are inherently undesirable, regardless of their economic results. . . . among the purposes of Congress in 1890 was a desire to put an end to great aggregations of capital because of the helplessness of the individual before them. . . . That Congress is still of the same mind appears in the Surplus Property Act of 1944 . . . and the Small Business Mobilization Act . . . . Not only does § 2(d) of the first declare it to be one aim of that statute to "preserve the competitive position of small business concerns," but § 18 is given over to directions designed to "preserve and strengthen" their position.

Kentucky shorthorn cattle[15]   At the same time, parts of the decision acknowledged the intent of Congress not to punish a monopoly obtained by competition on the merits (148 F.2d. 416 at 430, emphasis added):

> A market may . . . be so limited that it is impossible to produce at all and meet the cost of production, except by a plant large enough to supply the whole demand. . . . A single producer may be the survivor out of a group of active competitors, merely by virtue of his superior skill, foresight and industry. In such cases a strong case can be made that, although, the result may expose the public to the evils of monopoly, the [Sherman] Act does not mean to condemn the resultant of those very forces which it is its prime object to foster . . . *The successful competitor, having been urged to compete, must not be turned upon when he wins.*

Assessment   Taking the Circuit Court's finding that Alcoa earned only a normal rate of return at face value, many economists feel that in balancing out the contradictory mandates handed him by Congress, Judge Hand gave too much weight to non-economic goals and not enough to the right of the fair competitor to enjoy the fruits of success.

In a careful study published before Judge Hand delivered his opinion, Wallace (1937, p. 111) finds that Alcoa *did* exercise monopoly power in primary aluminum: "However it may have appeared at the time, hindsight does not demonstrate that the investment and price policy of the American company after 1908 was such as to leave no room for new firms."[16]

The remedy in the *Alcoa* case was, like the nature of the Court that heard it, unusual. As part of the mobilization of the U.S. economy for the conduct of World War II, the government financed the construction of several aluminum plants. The Surplus Property Act of 1944, mentioned by Judge Hand in his opinion, provided that after the war, these plants should be disposed of (148 F.2d. 416 at 446) "without fostering monopoly or restraint of trade". Given the prospect that postwar developments would eliminate Alcoa's monopoly position, Judge Hand did not pursue government dissolution proposals.

---

[15] See Section 18.6.1.

[16] Swan's (1980) estimates imply that Alcoa's Lerner index for primary aluminum was 0.45 (Section 7.2.2). Swan suggests that Alcoa's very high economic profits in primary aluminum were diluted, in computing its overall rate of return (10 per cent on investment) by the low rates of return on its fabricating activities. This possibility is mentioned in the Circuit Court of Appeals decision (148 F.2d. 416 at 430).

As to why, if entry into the production of primary aluminum might have been profitable, it did not occur, see Chapter 9.

U.S. *v.* United Shoe Machinery Corp.

In 1953 the United Shoe Machinery Corporation (USMC) was the leading U.S. supplier of machines for the manufacture of shoes. It supplied between 75 and 85 per cent of the market made up by the 1,460 U.S. shoe manufacturers then in operation.[17]

Leases, tying, penalties   Shoe manufacture was a complicated business, involving some 18 distinct production processes. United was the only shoe machinery manufacturer to offer a full line of machines that could be used for all of them. It offered its major machines only for lease, not for sale. There were no separate charges for repair services, a practice that sharply limited the development of a market for the supply of repair services. The leases were for a period of ten years, and provided for a financial charge if a machine was returned before the lease was up. This charge was reduced if a returned machine was exchanged for another USMC machine. The leases also required that USMC machines be used to full capacity, if there were work to be done, a requirement that reduced the benefit of using a competing machine. It was the impact of these leases on competition in the market for shoe machinery that was at issue in the 1953 case.[18]

Monopolization under Section 2   In his District Court opinion,[19] Judge Wyzanski noted three main readings of Sherman Act Section 2 (110 F. Supp. 295 at 342). The pre-*Alcoa was that* "An enterprise has monopolized in violation of § 2 of the Sherman Act if it has acquired or maintained a power to exclude others as a result of using an unreasonable 'restraint of trade' in violation of § 1 of the Sherman Act". Under *Griffith*,[20] "an enterprise has monopolized in violation of § 2 if it (a) has the power to exclude competition, and (b) has exercised it, or has the purpose to exercise it . . . ". The *Alcoa* standard was that "one who has acquired an overwhelming share of the market 'monopolizes' whenever he does business . . . , apparently even if there is no showing that his business involves any exclusionary practice. . . . [unless] it owes its monopoly solely to superior skill . . . "

Exclusion   The essential element of the first two standards is exclusion. While acknowledging that USMC's success result was in part due to its "superior products and services", Judge Wyzanski found that USMC's leases were exclusionary (110 F. Supp. 295 at 297, emphasis added):[21]

---

[17] USMC had an antitrust past: in 1918, the Supreme Court ruled that the mergers that formed USMC were not a violation of Section 2 of the Sherman Act (U.S. *v.* United Shoe Machinery Corp. 247 U.S. 37 (1918)). Louis Brandeis, later Supreme Court Justice, served variously as an incorporator, attorney, and director for USMC's predecessor trust from 1899 through January 1907. Brandeis' experience with USMC's use of tying contracts led to his successful support for the prohibition of tying in Section 3 of the Clayton Act (Kintner, 1978, p. 994).

[18] The impact of the leases on the market for shoes was procompetitive (Kintner, 1978, p. 1018, fn. 271): "The lease program permitted small companies to enter the shoe manufacturing industry with very little capital, and thereby fostered competition in that industry."

[19] U.S. *v.* United Shoe Machinery Corp. 110 F. Supp. 295 (1953). See among others Keyes (1954), Kaysen (1956), and Director (1957).

[20] *Griffith* (U.S. *v.* Griffith 334 U.S. 100 (1948); see also U.S. *v.* Griffith Amusement Co. *et al.* 94 F. Supp. 747 (1950)) involved joint negotiations for exhibition rights by four movie theater chains in Oklahoma, Texas, and New Mexico.

[21] A portion of this section of the decision is quoted by Keyes (1954, p. 288). Later scholarship suggests other possible motives for USMC's lease-only policy. Masten and Snyder (1993) argue that leases were a substitute for warranties as a way of guaranteeing a quality product and quality maintenance to the user. Waldman (1997) points

In the leases have been provisions such as the 10-year rental term, the full capacity clause, and the deferred payment charges, which, as written and applied, *have adversely affected actual or potential competition* in the shoe machinery market. The methods followed by United in supplying in one bundle machinery and repair services in return for one, unsegregated, set of charges, and the methods used by United in establishing economically discriminatory rates of profit on different machine types, have had additional *adverse effects on competition*. Though these practices and methods have not been predatory, immoral, nor, on their face, discriminatory as between different customers, they have operated as *barriers to competition*.

Judge Wyzanski found that either the *Griffith* or the stricter *Alcoa* standard led to the conclusion that USMC had violated Section 2 of the Sherman Act.

Remedy   In many antitrust cases it is less than obvious how to fashion an appropriate remedy, but not in this instance. Since the essence of the offence lay in the use of specific marketing practices, the Court ordered that those practices be changed—leases shortened, "full capacity" clause eliminated, repair services charged for separately, and machines offered for sale.[22]

21.2.2 Antitrust Treatment of Predation

The premise of a market economy is that more efficient firms will exclude less efficient firms. The Section 2 prohibition of monopolization seeks to prevent the exclusion of as efficient or more efficient firms by leading firms' strategic behaviour. The fundamental challenge is to find a policy that permits competition on the merits while prohibiting conduct that aims to exclude as or more efficient rivals.[23]

The Areeda-Turner rule

Short-run profit maximization   The influential contribution of Areeda and Turner (1975) focuses on the implications of short-run profit-maximizing behaviour for pricing (1975, p. 703): "We would normally expect a profit-maximizing firm, within the limits of data and convenience, to attempt to maximize profit or minimize losses in the short run ... " A firm that maximizes short-run profit would never set a price below marginal cost. For this reason, Areeda and Turner would have Section 2 of the Sherman Act condemn as predatory only prices set below marginal cost. They then acknowledge that it will often be difficult to measure marginal cost, and suggest the use of average variable cost as a practical proxy. This is

---

out that by declining to sell its machines, USMC avoided having to compete with a second-hand market in its own used machines (in contrast with Alcoa, which competed with its own recycled product). In this perspective, a lease-only policy appears as an enabling device that permitted USMC to fully exploit its market power.

[22] In the aftermath of the decision in the Federal antitrust case, USMC defended itself against a number of private antitrust suits, one of which required it to pay $6.1 million in damages (Hanover Shoe, Inc. *v.* United Shoe Machinery 392 US 481 (1968)). The U.S. shoe industry declined, and with it the shoe machinery industry. USMC attempted to diversify, sometimes unwisely (Vanderwicken, 1972). In 1969, in a follow-up to the federal antitrust case, the government required USMC to sell parts of its shoe machinery operations. USMC merged with Emhart Corporation in 1976, and the company formed by this merger in turn merged with Black & Decker Corporation in 1989.

[23] See Figure 7.4 and the associated text.

the *Areeda-Turner predatory pricing rule*: a price below reasonably anticipated average variable cost should be deemed predatory for Sherman Act Section 2 purposes,[24] otherwise not.

The usual assumption in the theory of the firm is that businesses act to maximize value, the expected present-discounted value of profit over all future time, not short-run profit. In some markets, the way to maximize value may be to maximize profit, short-run period by short-run period. In other markets, value maximization may require deviations from short-run profit maximization.[25]

Principle of competition   The fundamental principle that underlies the Areeda-Turner rule is consistent with the views of John Bates Clark in the run-up to passage of the Clayton Act: leave competition on the merits as the only tool open to the dominant incumbent, and if a dominant firm is able to maintain its market position, so be it. It is also consistent with the principle of competition: despite Areeda and Turner's allusion to the resource allocation effects of marginal cost pricing as a justification for their proposed rule, it does not in application involve an explicit welfare analysis, but instead implies reliance on competition as a means of obtaining good market performance.

Scepticism toward equilibrium predation   Areeda and Turner were more cautious toward the possibility of predatory pricing than mainstream economists now think appropriate.[26] They acknowledge the possibility of demonstration effects—an occasional episode of predation in the "Kill an admiral from time to time to encourage the others" spirit, to generate a reputation that will deter entry in the target or other markets (Areeda and Turner, 1975, p. 699). But they do not find it likely enough to depart from their preferred average variable cost pricing rule.

Rule-of-reason alternative   Areeda and Turner's work evoked a wide range of commentary. At the other extreme from their average variable cost rule is Scherer (1976, p. 890), who confronts the fact that below-cost pricing may sometimes improve, sometimes worsen market performance:

> [L]ong-term economic welfare is maximized in some cases when the monopolist's price exceeds its marginal cost and in other cases when marginal cost is undercut. Key variables ... include the relative cost positions of the monopolist and fringe firms, the scale of entry required to

---

[24] They would apply the same standard in Robinson-Patman Act price discrimination cases (Areeda and Turner, 1975, p. 726). The Supreme Court has followed this advice (Section 23.2.3).

[25] Thus the value-maximizing strategy for a firm that exploits a depletable mineral deposit will generally be to set a price above the short-run profit-maximizing level, to take account of higher future costs that result from current extraction. The value-maximizing strategy for a firm in an industry where learning-by-doing is important (semiconductors are an example) is to set a price below the short-run profit-maximizing level, to get the lower future costs that result from higher current production. Other examples, mentioned by Areeda and Turner (1975, p. 704, fn. 21), are "keeping price down to reasonable levels during periods of high demand in order to preserve consumer goodwill" and (1975, p. 714) "selective price reductions to marginal cost to new customers or in new geographical areas".

[26] Areeda and Turner write (1975, pp. 697–698) "Treatment of predatory pricing in the cases and the literature ... has commonly suffered from two interrelated defects: failure to delineate clearly and correctly what practices should constitute the offense, and exaggerated fears that large firms may be inclined to engage in it." Contrast this with Posner (2001, p. 214, footnote omitted): "And recent scholarship has brought to light a nontrivial number of cases of predatory pricing." See also Bolton *et al.* (2000).

secure minimum costs, whether fringe firms are driven out or merely suppressed, whether the monopolist expands its output to replace the output of excluded rivals or restricts supply again when the rivals withdraw, and whether any long-run compensatory expansion by the monopolist entails investment in scale economy-embodying new plant. I do not know how these variables can be assessed properly without a thorough examination of the factual circumstances accompanying the monopolist's alleged predatory behaviour, how the monopolist's officials perceived the probable effects of its behaviour (*i.e.*, intent), and the structural consequences actually flowing from the behaviour.

Scherer calls for a fully fledged rule-of-reason analysis of allegedly predatory behaviour. The Areeda-Turner rule, at heart, substitutes a rule of thumb for the rule of reason.

Matsushita

Matsushita[27] combined private antitrust actions begun by National Union Electric Corporation (NUE) in 1970, the year it stopped producing television sets, and by Zenith Radio Corporation in 1974. The core claim was that ten Japanese television manufacturers, their subsidiaries and two U.S. distributors of Japanese television sets (Sears, Roebuck & Co. and Motorola, Inc.) had conspired to engage in predatory pricing on the U.S. market.

The plaintiffs' theory of the case was that Japanese firms had engaged in a two-decade-long conspiracy to hold up prices in Japan and use the resulting economic profits to finance a predatory campaign on the U.S. market (513 F. Supp. 1100 at 1120). The District Court found the main elements of this theory unconvincing. Although the Japanese firms were supposed to have been holding price up in their domestic market, Japanese prices fell over the relevant time period. Japanese firms charged different customers different prices, but there was no obvious pattern to those differences, no clear case that prices were below costs, and, in view of the essential element of conspiracy in the complaint, no demonstration that the price differences were anything other than the individual decisions of the different Japanese producers. The District Court ruled that the American firms had not presented enough evidence to justify taking the matter to trial, and granted summary judgment in favour of the Japanese firms. The U.S. firms went to the Third Circuit Court of Appeals, which found that the U.S. firms were entitled to a trial. Before that trial could take place, the Japanese firms appealed the Circuit Court decision to the Supreme Court, which thus (in 1985) found itself faced with the question whether there should or should not be a trial on the merits at the District Court level.

Areeda-Turner Setting out the standard of proof that the U.S. firms had to meet, the Supreme Court endorsed the Areeda-Turner approach (475 U.S. 574 at 584):

> Throughout this opinion, we refer to the asserted conspiracy as one to price "predatorily". This term has been used chiefly in cases in which a single firm, having a dominant share of the relevant market, cuts its prices in order to force competitors out of the market, or perhaps to deter potential entrants from coming in. ... In such cases, "predatory pricing" means pricing below some appropriate measure of cost.

---

[27] Matsushita Electrical Industrial Co., Ltd, *et al. v.* Zenith Radio Corp. *et al.* 475 U.S. 574 (1986). See Schwartzman (1993). This action involved not only antitrust law but also antidumping law, which we took up in Chapter 16.

In order to succeed in a Section 1 complaint, the Court wrote, the U.S. firms needed to show that the Japanese firms had conspired to set price "below some appropriate measure of cost" in order to induce the U.S. firms to leave the market.

Scepticism toward equilibrium predation U.S. courts have generally been sceptical toward allegations of predatory pricing, and so was the Supreme Court in this instance. A predatory scheme would have required the Japanese firms to sustain serious losses for many years, in the hope that they would be able to raise prices and recoup their losses after driving American firms out of business. In the apparent absence of costs of entry into the business of manufacturing of consumer electronics equipment, it seemed unlikely that the Japanese firms would have thought recoupment a realistic possibility.

Since a hypothetical collusive predation agreement would not be legally binding, it would involve cartel stability problems. During the predatory period, individual Japanese firms would find it privately profitable to defect to a higher, non-predatory, price. During the hoped-for recoupment period, individual Japanese firms would find it privately profitable to defect to a lower price.[28]

The Court's approach highlighted the role of economic analysis (475 U.S. 574 at 587): "if the factual context renders respondents' claim implausible—if the claim is one that simply makes no economic sense—respondents must come forward with more persuasive evidence to support their claim than would otherwise be necessary." In view of the improbability of the goal imputed to the alleged conspiracy, and without direct evidence that conspiracy had occurred, the Supreme Court reversed the Circuit Court's reversal of the District Court. The District Court's decision to grant summary judgment in favour of the Japanese TV producers became the final word.

Brooke Group[29]

Black-and-whites In 1980, U.S. cigarette manufacturers began to be seriously affected by persistent declining demand for their product. Breaking ranks with industry practice, Liggett & Myers (part of Brooke Group) introduced a line of generic cigarettes, called "black and whites" because they were marketed in plain white packages with black lettering. Liggett sold its black and whites at a price about 30 per cent below the price of branded cigarettes. Black and whites were an immediate success; they accounted for 4 per cent of total cigarette sales by 1984. Twenty per cent of Liggett's sales were to former customers of Brown & Williamson, which introduced its own generics in 1983.

Price war Brown & Williamson sold its generics at a lower price than Liggett's, and Brown & Williamson offered more attractive volume discounts to distributors. One result was a wholesale price war between Liggett and Brown & Williamson, with Brown & Williamson maintaining a lower wholesale price than Liggett.

---

[28] As the Supreme Court also noted, if in a hypothetical recoupment period, the Japanese firms conspired to hold price above competitive levels, they would by so doing violate Section 1 of the Sherman Act and expose themselves to prosecution by U.S. antitrust authorities.

[29] Brooke Group Ltd. *v.* Brown & Williamson Tobacco Corporation 509 U.S. 209 (1993). See Burnett (1999) for discussion.

Antitrust suit   Another result was a private antitrust lawsuit filed by Liggett against Brown & Williamson, alleging that Brown & Williamson's volume discounts were price discrimination that would injure competition and therefore in violation of section 2(a) of the Clayton Act.

Slow the growth of generics   In District Court, Liggett argued that Brown & Williamson had formulated a deliberate plan to kill growth of the generic part of the cigarette market in order to protect its profit in branded cigarettes. The District Court opinion found that Liggett's (748 F. Supp. 344 at 354)

> theory is buttressed by numerous B & W documents written by top executives. These documents, indicating B & W's anticompetitive intent, are more voluminous and detailed than any other reported case. This evidence not only indicates B & W wanted to injure Liggett, it also details an extensive plan to slow the growth of the generic cigarette segment.

According to Liggett, the first element of Brown & Williamson's plan was to offer wholesalers a close substitute for the Liggett generic cigarettes at a discriminatorily low price. As with fighting brands employed in the late nineteenth century, wholesalers would substitute Brown & Williamson generics for Liggett generics, while minimizing the impact on Brown & Williamson branded cigarettes. This would starve capital-strapped Liggett of the profit it would otherwise have earned on generics, without further expanding the generic segment.

Brown & Williamson's expectation, Liggett argued, was that it would immediately recoup the foregone profit on generics with the profit it earned in the branded segment. At a later stage, having acquired control of the generic segment, Brown & Williamson would raise the price of generics toward the price of branded cigarettes, making generics less attractive and further protecting its profit in the branded segment.

The District Court jury found in favour of Liggett and awarded it damages of $46.6 million, trebled to $148.8 million.

The Sugar Trust engaged in predation to starve a rival of financial capital; Bell Telephone behaved in a similar way. Thus, this kind of scheme is not unheard of. But the District Court judge was not convinced that Brown & Williamson would be ever be able to raise the price of generic cigarettes toward the price of branded cigarettes. He regarded this as an essential element of proof of a predatory price discrimination violation of Section 2(a) of the Clayton Act (as amended by the Robinson-Patman Act), and set the jury verdict aside.

Recoupment *in generics*   Liggett appealed the judge's decision to the Fourth Circuit Court of Appeals, which affirmed the decision of the District Court. Liggett appealed the decision of the Circuit Court to the Supreme Court, which held that in order to prevail, Liggett had to (509 U.S. 209 at 223–224): show "that the prices complained of are below an appropriate measure of the rival's costs", and "that the competitor had a reasonable prospect, or, under §2 of the Sherman Act, a dangerous probability, of recouping its investment in below-cost prices".

The Supreme Court felt that summary judgment was justified because Liggett could not show that Brown & Williamson had a realistic possibility of recoupment *in the market for generic cigarettes* (509 U.S. 209 at 2332):

No inference of recoupment is sustainable on this record, because no evidence suggests that Brown & Williamson—whatever its intent in introducing black and whites may have been was likely to obtain the power to raise the prices for generic cigarettes above a competitive level.

Recoupment in another market segment not sufficient   Liggett's theory, however, was that Brown & Williamson's payoff from predation in the generic segment would come by protecting its earnings in the branded segment, and that this goal could be accomplished by denying Liggett cash flow from sale of generic cigarettes. One view of the Supreme Court decision, therefore, is that it added to the two stated requirements for a predation offense (price below cost and realistic possibility of recoupment) a third, that predation and recoupment occur in the same market.

Predatory bidding

With its 2007 *Weyerhaeuser* decision,[30] the U.S. Supreme Court confirmed its sceptical approach to strategic anticompetitive behaviour. In contrast to *Brooke Group*, where the predation claim alleged strategic lowering of the price of the final product to starve a rival of financial capital, the direct antitrust issue in *Weyerhaeuser* was the strategic exercise of monopsony power, the alleged increase in the price of an essential input to raise rivals' costs.

Monopsony predation   The usual complaint about monopoly power is that a firm will find it profitable to restrict output and *raise* price above marginal cost, reducing consumer surplus and creating a deadweight welfare loss. The complaint against predatory product-market pricing is that the firm with the power to control an output price in one market will *lower* price temporarily, to reduce rivals' profitability, and later raise price in the target or some other market. In the first instance, the direct consequence of the exercise of product-market power is to reduce the welfare of consumers. In the second instance, the direct consequence of the exercise of product-market power is to reduce the profitability of rivals, to make them lose money and induce them to leave the market. The eventual reduction in the welfare of consumers is a consequence of the reduction in rival profitability.

In a symmetric way, the usual complaint about monopsony power is that a firm will find it profitable to reduce input purchases and *lower* the input price below what would be the equilibrium level if input purchasers acted as price takers in the input market (see Figure 5.8(a) and the associated text). The complaint against predatory bidding is that a firm with the power to control an input price will *raise* the input price temporarily, to reduce the profitability of rivals who also use the input, and later either lower the input price or raise the output price (or both). In the first instance, the direct consequence of the exercise of input-market power is to reduce the profit of input suppliers (or their welfare, if the input in question is labour). In the second instance, the direct consequence of the exercise of input-market power is to reduce the profitability of rivals and induce them to leave the market. The eventual reduction in the welfare of suppliers (input market) or consumers (output market) is a consequence of the reduction in rival profitability.

In 1980 Weyerhaeuser Company acquired a hardwood sawmill in the U.S. Pacific Northwest. In this market, sawmills purchase timber (principally red alder sawlogs) from logging

---

[30] Weyerhaeuser Co. *v.* Ross-Simmons Hardwood Lumber Co., Inc. 127 S.Ct. 1069 (2007). See also Confederated Tribes of Siletz Indians of Oregon *et al. v.* Weyerhaeuser Company 411 F. 3d 1030 (2005).

operations, process them, and supply finished lumber to producers of flooring, furniture, and cabinets. Weyerhaeuser expanded its operations; by 2005 it operated six sawmills in the region, and purchased about 65 per cent of the Pacific Northwest supply of alder sawlogs (411 F.3d 1030 at 1034).

Ross-Simmons Hardwood Lumber Company also operated a sawmill in the Pacific Northwest, and had done so since 1962. Its profit fell from 1998, when sawlog prices began to rise and the price of finished lumber began to fall. Ross-Simmons went out of business in 2001, and filed a private antitrust suit against Weyerhaeuser, claiming injury by business conduct that was attempted monopolization and a violation of Section 2 of the Sherman Act. Ross-Simmons' economic theory was that it had been driven out of business because Weyerhaeuser had (411 F. 3d 1030 at 1034) "driv[en] up sawlog prices and restrict[ed] access to sawlogs through: (1) predatory overbidding (i.e., paying a higher price for sawlogs than necessary); (2) overbuying (i.e., buying more sawlogs than it needed); (3) entering restrictive or exclusive agreements with sawlog suppliers; and (4) making misrepresentations to state officials in order to obtain sawlogs from state forests".

Weyerhaeuser, which had engaged in substantial investment in new technology, attributed Ross-Simmons' losses to poor management. Ross-Simmons pointed to Weyerhaeuser's own declining profits as evidence of predatory bidding.

Instructions to the jury   During the course of the District Court trial, Weyerhaeuser argued that the type of standard set out by the Supreme Court in *Brooke Group* for predatory selling should also hold for predatory buying. Allowing for the fact that the predation was supposed to have taken on an input market, what would be required to show that such predatory bidding would violate Section 2 would be that the strategically inflated input price had pushed the unit cost of the final product above the price of the final product *and* that the predatory bidder could reasonably have expected to recoup profits lost during the predatory campaign. In Weyerhaeuser's view, Ross-Simmons had not met these requirements, and it asked that the case be dismissed. The District Court judge instead sent the case to the jury with instructions that (127 S.Ct. 1069 at 1073) "Ross-Simmons could prove that Weyerhaeuser's bidding practices were anticompetitive acts if the jury concluded that Weyerhaeuser 'purchased more logs than it needed, or paid a higher price for logs than necessary, in order to prevent [Ross-Simmons] from obtaining the logs they needed at a fair price'." The jury returned a verdict in favour of Ross-Simmons, and found the monetary value of its damages to be $26.25 million, which would have been trebled to $78.77 million. Weyerhaeuser unsuccessfully appealed this outcome to the Ninth Circuit Court of Appeals. It then appealed to the Supreme Court, which accepted Weyerhaeuser's argument that the *Brooke Group* rules, appropriately modified, should apply in predatory bidding.

Scepticism toward equilibrium predation   Writing for a unanimous Supreme Court, Justice Thomas followed *Brooke Group* by quoting *Matsushita*'s doubtful (from an economic point of view) proposition that "predatory pricing schemes are rarely tried, and even more rarely successful".

Yet one of the Supreme Court's own decisions accepts that dominant firms have strategically manipulated input prices to reduce the profitability of fringe firms. This appears in the second *American Tobacco* case, where the Court notes that the Tobacco majors purchased tobacco leaves that they did not use with the goal of driving up the price of an essential input for what we might now call generic cigarettes (328 U.S. 781 at 803–804).

Justice Thomas took the view (127 S.Ct. 1069 at 1077) that as Weyerhaeuser purchased more sawlog input, this would naturally increase Weyerhaeuser's output, so reducing the price of the final product and benefiting the ultimate consumer. *American Tobacco II* suggests that there is no necessary one-to-one relationship between input and output. One may in any case suspect that a *higher* price for an essential input, sawlogs, would not in and of itself tend to bring *down* the price of the finished product.[31] As it had in *Brooke Group*, the Supreme Court held that an essential element to prove a predatory bidding Section 2 violation was (127 S.Ct. 1069 at 1078) "higher bidding that leads to below-cost pricing in the relevant output market", as high predatory bidding pushes unit cost above price in the output market. Further, the Court held that a second necessary element to prove predatory pricing that violates Section 2 was to show that the predator would have (127 S.Ct. 1069 at 1078) "a dangerous probability of recouping the losses incurred in bidding up input prices through the exercise of monopsony power", and that Ross-Simmons had not met this requirement.

Linkline

Price squeeze With its 2009 *Linkline* decision, the U.S. Supreme Court extended the logic of *Brooke Group* and *Trinko* (see below) to a recurring issue in the antitrust treatment of monopolization,[32] the *vertical price squeeze*, said to occur (555 U.S. ____ 1) "when a vertically integrated firm sells inputs at wholesale and also sells finished goods or services at retail. If that firm has [market] power in the wholesale market, it can simultaneously raise the wholesale price of inputs and cut the retail price of the finished good [with] the effect of 'squeezing' the profit margins of any competitors in the retail market". Here AT&T, Inc. provided a transmission services to four DSL (digital subscriber line) internet service providers (ISPs), (among which, Linkline Communications, Inc.), with which it also competed at retail. The ISPs complained that AT&T engaged in a price squeeze that amounted to monopolization in violation of Section 2 of the Sherman. AT&T sought dismissal in District Court on the ground that following *Trinko*, it had no duty to deal with the ISPs at all, so could not have violated U.S. antitrust law if it's prices did not permit them a normal rate of return on investment. The District Court did not accept this argument, the Ninth Circuit Court of Appeals declined to reverse the District Court, and AT&T turned to the Supreme Court.

A predation test In footnote 2 of its opinion, the Supreme Court refers to "the market for digital subscriber line (DSL) service" and indicates that AT&T controls most of the infrastructure need to connect retail customers in the geographic market (California) to the telephone network. From *Trinko*, as AT&T argued, there was no basis for an antitrust challenge to AT&T's

---

[31] This is noted by the Circuit Court of Appeals, quoting an earlier decision (411 F.3d 1030 at 1037, fn. 14): "Consumers don't benefit from higher raw material prices, or by logs rotting in the lumber yard". The Circuit Court did not base its decision on Ross-Simmons' overbuying or other allegations, since it found that ((411 F. 3d 1030 at 1041) "the evidence of predatory overbidding sufficiently supports the finding that Weyerhaeuser engaged in anticompetitive conduct".

[32] See Adams and Dirlam (1964) for an argument that control of the relationahip between prices of vertically related goods and services is essential to the exercise of horizontal market power, and among antitrust precedents, *Alcoa*. *Alcoa*'s import is minimized by the Supreme Court in fn. 3 of its opinion; Justice Breyer, in his concurring opinion, seems to give *Alcoa* more attention.

wholesale prices. To demonstrate that AT&T's *retail* prices offended the antitrust, the ISPs need to satisfy the requirements laid out in *Brooke Group*, that AT&T's retail prices were below its (appropriately measured) cost[33] and that AT&T could reasonably expect to recoup the profits lost while it was settling below-cost prices. At bottom (555 U.S. ____ 12)

> [The ISPs'] price-squeeze claim, looking to the relation between retail and wholesale prices, is thus nothing more than an amalgamation of a meritless claim at the retail level and a meritless claim at the wholesale level. If there is no duty to deal at the wholesale level and no predatory pricing at the retail level, then a firm is certainly not required to price both of these services in a manner that preserves its rivals' profit margins.

Quoting *Trinko* (540 U.S. at 408), the Court also sounds the theme of administratability 555 U.S. ____ 12: "We have repeatedly emphasized the importance of clear rules in antitrust law. Courts are ill suited 'to act as central planners, identifying the proper price, quantity, and other terms of dealing'."

Price and market performance   The issues for market performance can be sketched out, at a level suited to a legal system in which courts do not act as central planners. For discussion purposes, take it that AT&T is the monopoly supplier of a wholesale service that is essential to deliver a standardized product to the final consumer. Suppose that this monopoly position was obtained by competition on the merits. Let c_w^{ATT} and c_r^{ATT} denote AT&T's constant unit wholesale and retail cost, respectively, while c_r^L denotes the constant unit cost of the one ISP that may (if it is profitable to do so) provide retail service.

If AT&T engages in a price squeeze, it offers the wholesale service at a price p_w and sets a retail price p_r^{ps} that do not permit the ISP to earn a normal rate of return,[34]

$$p_r^{ps} < p_w^{ps} + c_r^L. \tag{21.1}$$

The Supreme Court's legal analysis of vertically related prices treats wholesale and retail prices separately. It is evident from (21.1) that from an economic point of view what matters for exclusion at the retail level is the difference between the retail and the wholesale price; there is a vertical price squeeze if:

$$p_r^{ps} - p_w^{ps} < c_r^L. \tag{21.2}$$

If one views the margin $p_r^{ps} - p_w^{ps}$ as the price of retail distribution service, then a wholesale, retail price combination such that:

$$p_r^{ps} - p_w^{ps} < c_r^{ATT} \tag{21.3}$$

would satisfy the first part of the *Brooke Group* test for predatory pricing *in the retail market*.

---

[33] As regards the first element of the predation test, the Court quotes from *Brooke Group* (509 U.S. at 223) "As a general rule, the exclusionary effect of prices above a relevant measure of cost either reflects the lower cost structure of the alleged predator, and so represents competition on the merits ...". The distinction between a vertical squeeze and a predatory price is that a price squeeze allows a vertically integrated firm to raise the cost of its targets, even if the targets have lower cost than the competitor in the market in which they compete.

[34] For comparison purposes, if the product is homogeneous the optimal retail price is the minimum marginal cost of supplying the retail market, $p_r^{op} = c_w^{ATT} + \min\left(c_r^L, c_r^{ATT}\right)$. If AT&T supplies the downstream market as a monopolist, the retail price is the full-integration monopoly price for marginal cost $c_w^{ATT} + c_r^{ATT}$, $p_r^m\left(c_w^{ATT} + c_r^{ATT}\right)$.

Transfer price test   One proposed rule for the antitrust treatment of vertically related prices is the transfer price test, which would find a monopolization if (555 U.S. ___ 14) "the upstream monopolist could not have made a profit by selling at its retail rates if it purchased inputs at its own wholesale rates". The Supreme Court rejects the transfer price test with analysis to its impact on retail market performance (555 U.S. ___ 14):

> Whether or not that test is administrable, it lacks any grounding in our antitrust jurisprudence. An upstream monopolist with no duty to deal is free to charge whatever wholesale price it would like; antitrust law does not forbid lawfully obtained monopolies from charging monopoly prices.

Under a transfer price rule, a vertically integrated firm would be free, under the antitrust laws, to set a combination of wholesale and retail prices that leaves less efficient downstream firms without a normal rate of return on investment. The equilibrium retail price under a transfer price rule depends on details of retail market oligopoly interaction; some considerations are set out in the accompanying box.

Principle of competition   Without more structure, however—without information about retail market competition that a court might not have and in case that a court system in search of a manageable rule would not wish to consider—the consumer welfare impact of a transfer price rule is ambiguous. The policy question becomes what limits, if any, to place on the exercise of legally obtained monopoly power in one market when the impact of the exercise of that market power on market performance is ambiguous. The principle of competition would come down on the side of presuming that retail-market rivalry would benefit consumers. Such a rule would give maximum force to potential competition, permitting a vertically integrated firm to underprice less-efficient retail market rivals.

 BOX   **Transfer Price Rule**

Firm A produces a wholesale (WS) service at unit cost c_A^{WS} and a retail (RTL) service at unit cost c_A^{RTL}. Firm B produces the retail service at unit cost c_B^{RTL}. One unit of wholesale service must be supplied for every unit of retail service delivered to a final consumer.

There are three groups of potential consumers all with reservation price ρ: N_A who buy one unit from A, if they buy at all, N_B who buy one unit from B, if they buy at all, and N_S "shoppers" who buy one unit from whichever supplier offers the lowest price, if they buy at all. If the two firms offer the same retail price, half the shoppers in N_S buy from each firm. In this market, ρ is the monopoly price.

A's profit if it does not sell to B is:

$$\pi_A^{VI} = \left[\rho - \left(c_A^{WS} + c_A^{RTL}\right)\right](N_A + N_S). \tag{21.4}$$

A's profit if it engages in dual distribution (dd) and sells to B at price $p_{WS} = \rho - c_B^{RTL}$ is:

$$\pi_A^{dd} = \left[\rho - \left(c_A^{WS} + c_A^{RTL}\right)\right]\left(N_A + \frac{1}{2}N_S\right) + \left(p_{WS} - c_A^{WS}\right)\left(N_B + \frac{1}{2}N_S\right), \tag{21.5}$$

>> and with some manipulation, this can be rewritten as:

$$\pi_A^{dd} = \pi_A^{VI} + \left[\rho - \left(c_B^{WS} + c_A^{RTL} \right) \right] N_B + \frac{1}{2} \left(c_A^{RTL} - c_B^{RTL} \right) N_S \qquad (21.6)$$

If $c_B^{RTL} < c_A^{RTL}$, (21.6) shows that A maximizes profit using dual distribution. Then B earns a normal rate of return on investment, and all consumers are supplied at the monopoly price. Dual distribution improves market performance in that $\frac{1}{2}N_S$ consumers who would have been supplied at unit retail cost c_A^{RTL} under single distribution are supplied at the lower unit cost c_B^{RTL}.

If $c_B^{RTL} > c_A^{RTL}$, A earns more profit with dual distribution if A's profit on sales to buyers with a preference for B exceeds the profit lost on sales to shoppers who would have purchased from A but instead buy from B:

$$\left(\rho - c_A^{WS} - c_B^{RTL} \right) N_B > \frac{1}{2} \left(c_B^{RTL} - c_A^{RTL} \right) N_S. \qquad (21.7)$$

Under the transfer price rule, if A sells to B, it must be at a wholesale price that would allow A to at least break even if it acquired the wholesale service at that price, $p_{RTL}^{tp} \geq p_{WS}^{tp} + c_A^{RTL}$. As the profit-maximizing retail price remains $p_{RTL}^{tp} = \rho$, the constraint on the wholesale price implied by the transfer price rule is $p_{WS}^{tp} \leq \rho - c_A^{RTL}$.

A's profit if it vertically integrates is π_A^{VI}. If $c_B^{RTL} < c_A^{RTL}$, A's profit if it supplies B at price $p_{WS}^{tp} = \rho - c_A^{RTL}$ is:

$$\pi_A^{tp} = \left[\rho - \left(c_A^{WS} + c_A^{RTL} \right) \right] \left(N_A + \frac{1}{2}N_S \right) + \left(p_{WS}^{tp} - c_A^{WS} \right) \left(N_B + \frac{1}{2}N_S \right)$$

$$= \left[\rho - \left(c_A^{WS} + c_A^{RTL} \right) \right] \left(N_A + N_S + N_B \right). \qquad (21.8)$$

If B is the low-cost retail firm, A earns more with dual distribution than if it vertically integrates. B earns an efficiency rent $\left(c_A^{RTL} - c_B^{RTL} \right) \left(N_B + \frac{1}{2}N_S \right)$. All consumers are supplied, at the reservation price. The change in A's dual-distribution profit under a transfer pricing rule,

$$\pi_A^{tp} - \pi_A^{dd} = - \left(c_A^{RTL} - c_B^{RTL} \right) \left(N_B + \frac{1}{2}N_S \right) < 0, \qquad (21.9)$$

is the amount of B's efficiency rent.

If B is the high-cost retail firm ($c_B^{RTL} > c_A^{RTL}$), A could earn a profit at any wholesale price that would allow B to break even. The transfer price rule does not constrain A's wholesale pricing. A's profit-maximizing distribution strategy depends on whether condition (21.7) is or is not satisfied.

If B is the low-cost retail firm, the transfer price rule allows B to earn more than a normal rate of return. All consumers who buy pay the reservation price in any case; this is a consequence of the assumptions that A is a monopoly supplier of the wholesale service and that there is one non-integrated retail firm. If there are several non-integrated retail distributors, it may not be possible for a monopoly upstream firm to charge the monopoly retail price (see Section 12.3.1), and in such circumstances the presence of non-integrated retail firms benefits consumers.

Principle of monopoly   After *Linkline*, the rule of U.S. antitrust is different: the Supreme Court invokes from *Trinko* (540 U.S. at 407) what might be called the *principle of monopoly*: "The mere possession of monopoly power, and the concomitant charging of monopoly prices, is not only not unlawful; it is an important element of the free-market system."

The logic behind such a position is that the existence of economic profit will attract resources into a market, in this case into the wholesale market, so eventually improving market performance at both the wholesale and retail levels. The application of the principle of monopoly in the example we have discussed leaves it open to a lawful wholesale monopoly to exclude equally or more-efficient non-integrated firms from the retail market, with an ambiguous impact on retail market performance.

Postscript: market definition   It also raises the question of market definition. The discussion here has followed the Supreme Court decision in writing of the "market for digital subscriber line service" and in referring to AT&T's "monopoly profit". It is not clear that either usage is appropriate. The Supreme Court decision touches on this point when it cites the Federal Communications Commission to the effect that "DSL now faces robust competition from cable companies and wireless and satellite services". To draw market boundaries would require analysing product differentiation in the market for internet access; if in the eyes of consumers DSL and other means of providing access to the internet are good substitutes, then rivalry from other modes of internet access would limit the extent to which a single supplier of wholesale DSL service could raise its retail price, with or without a price squeeze on nonintegrated retail DSL firms. In *Linkline*, the Supreme Court did not send the case back to District Court with instructions to consider the matter of product market definition. Instead, it took the opportunity to settle the matter at the level of principle, which it did by invoking the principle of monopoly.

Refusal to deal

Not all strategies that aim to profit by exclusion of an equally efficient competitor take the form of a price below reasonably anticipated average variable cost. Two U.S. Supreme Court decisions, with different outcomes, involved dominant firms that sought to exclude a competitor by the simple expedient of refusing to conduct business with it.

Aspen Skiing   The 1985 *Aspen Skiing* decision arose out of a private lawsuit by Aspen Highlands Skiing Corp., a firm managing a ski resort located on one of four developed mountains in Aspen, Colorado, against the Aspen Skiing Company, which managed facilities located on the remaining three developed mountains. For 26 years, going back to a time before Aspen Skiing acquired control of three of the four mountains, the ski resorts had offered clients a multi-day ski-lift ticket that could be used at any of the four mountains. Revenues from sales of the four-area ticket were divided in proportion to estimated usage at the different locations.

As of the 1978–1979 season, Aspen Skiing withdrew from the four-area package arrangement. It offered a multi-day, three-area ticket, valid at its own resorts. It mounted advertising campaigns that gave the impression that its resorts were on the only developed mountains in the Aspen area. It refused to honour vouchers, redeemable for cash, that were part of a multi-day ticket package developed by Aspen Highlands, and it refused to sell lift tickets to Aspen Highlands, even at the full retail price.

In 1979, Aspen Highlands filed a private antitrust suit against Aspen Skiing, alleging monopolization of the Aspen market for downhill skiing services in violation of Section 2 of the Sherman Act. The District Court judge instructed the jury that proof of monopolization in violation of Section 2 required showing (472 U.S. 585 at 595–596) "(1) the possession of monopoly power in a relevant market, and (2) the willful acquisition, maintenance, or use of that power by anticompetitive or exclusionary means or for anticompetitive or exclusionary purposes". Regarding the second point, the judge told the jury (472 U.S. 585 at 597):

[I]f there were legitimate business reasons for the refusal, then the defendant, even if he is found to possess monopoly power in a relevant market, has not violated the law. We are concerned with conduct which unnecessarily excludes or handicaps competitors. This is conduct which does not benefit consumers by making a better product or service available—or in other ways— and instead has the effect of impairing competition.

The jury found Aspen Skiing guilty of monopolization in violation of Section 2 of the Sherman Act, with Aspen Highlands' damages set at $2.5 million. Aspen Skiing asked the trial judge to set aside the jury verdict, arguing among other things that (472 U.S. 585 at 598) it had no duty under the antitrust laws to cooperate with a competitor. The judge instead awarded Aspen Highlands treble damages, $7.5 million, plus attorney's fees. Aspen Skiing appealed this result to the Tenth Circuit Court of Appeals, which affirmed the District Court decision. Aspen Skiing then appealed from the Circuit Court to the U.S. Supreme Court.

The Supreme Court reviewed previous opinions in which it had made clear that, indeed, even a monopolist was not in general obliged to cooperate with a rival. But then it wrote that the right to refuse to deal with another firm was not absolute (472 U.S. 585 at 601): "The high value that we have placed on the right to refuse to deal with other firms does not mean that the right is unqualified".

For the Supreme Court, Aspen Skiing enjoyed the right not to deal with the operator of a competing resort so long as that refusal was not[35] "a purposeful means of monopolizing interstate commerce". But the District Court instructions to the jury had made this clear, and the Supreme Court's own review of the record did not incline it to set the jury's findings aside. The four-area pass was a well-established, profitable product. Aspen Skiing gave it up at the cost of lost short-run profit, and refused to sell lift passes to Aspen Highlands. Evidence in the record showed that consumers preferred a four-area ticket to a three-area ticket. Aspen Highlands' share of area business fell after Aspen Skiing killed the four-area ticket. Aspen Skiing was unable to offer any efficiency rationale for its decision. For the Supreme Court (472 U.S. 585 at 610) "the record in this case comfortably supports an inference that the monopolist made a deliberate effort to discourage its customers from doing business with its smaller rival", and it affirmed the lower court decisions.

Trinko[36]   The U.S. Telecommunications Act of 1996 permitted *local exchange companies*— incumbent suppliers of local telephone service—to enter the highly profitable market for long-distance telephone service if they faced competition in their local market. In return, local exchange companies were obliged to connect competitors to the telecommunications network, which they controlled.

In February, 2000, the law firm of Curtis V. Trinko filed a class action suit on behalf of telephone service customers (of which it was one), against Verizon Communications, Inc. The basis of Trinko's suit was that Verizon, the local exchange company for New York, had (540 U.S. 398 at 404) "filled rivals' orders on a discriminatory basis as part of an anticompetitive scheme to discourage customers from becoming or remaining customers of competitive [local exchange companies], thus impeding the competitive [local exchange companies'] ability to enter and compete in the market for local telephone service".

---

[35] Quoting United States *v.* Colgate & Co. 250 U.S. 300 (1919) at 307.

[36] Verizon Communications, Inc. *v.* Law Offices of Curtis V. Trinko, LLP 540 U.S. 398 (2004).

The District Court dismissed Trinko's claim without a trial, citing among other authorities *Aspen Skiing* to the effect that even a monopolist did not have a general duty to cooperate with its competitors. Telephone users might have been harmed by reduced competition in the supply of local telephone services, but if the antitrust laws did not oblige Verizon to cooperate with competitor local exchange companies, Trinko could not succeed in a monopolization class-action suit or recover treble damages.

Trinko appealed the District Court dismissal to the Second Circuit Court of Appeals, which ordered the case back to District Court for trial. Verizon then appealed the Circuit Court opinion to the Supreme Court. The Supreme Court took the same view as had the District Court. Its opinion illuminated its views on both the workings of a market system and on the role of antitrust in maintaining such a system. First, it wrote that to find monopolization requires not only a showing of monopoly power but also (540 U.S. 398 at 407)[37] "the willful acquisition or maintenance of that power as distinguished from growth or development as a consequence of a superior product, business acumen, or historic accident".

Principle of monopoly   Although innovation was not obviously an issue in *Trinko*, the Court emphasized the role of economic profit in encouraging innovation (540 U.S. 398 at 407):

> The mere possession of monopoly power, and the concomitant charging of monopoly prices, is not only not unlawful; it is an important element of the free-market system. The opportunity to charge monopoly prices—at least for a short period—is what attracts "business acumen" in the first place; it induces risk taking that produces innovation and economic growth. To safeguard the incentive to innovate, the possession of monopoly power will not be found unlawful unless it is accompanied by an element of anticompetitive conduct.

As we have seen in Section 14.3.2, there is at least as much evidence to suggest that the possession of monopoly power retards innovation as encourages it.

Courts' inability to evaluate market performance   The Court also expressed scepticism about the ability of the legal system to police agreements among competitors to share assets (540 U.S. 398 at 407–408):[38]

> Enforced sharing also requires antitrust courts to act as central planners, identifying the proper price, quantity, and other terms of dealing—a role for which they are ill-suited. Moreover, compelling negotiation between competitors may facilitate the supreme evil of antitrust: collusion.

Yet for the treatment of interfirm agreements under Section 1, U.S. courts increasingly discard the principle of competition in favour of an explicit analysis of the impact of challenged agreements on market performance. Such an approach requires courts to assess what price, quantity, and other terms of dealing will be if an agreement is allowed to go forward. And as a matter of economics, it is straightforward that a mutually profitable interfirm agreement

---

[37] Citing U.S. *v.* Grinnell Corp. 384 U.S. 563 (1966) at 570–571.

[38] Of course, the premise behind the *Antitrust Guidelines for Collaborations Among Competitors* (Section 20.5.1) is that the legal system can police some types of cooperation among competitors.

will facilitate tacit collusion, all else equal.[39] Yet there is a common element to the position that courts are competent to undertake an explicit analysis of interfirm agreements that fall under the purview of Section 1 and the position that courts are not competent to undertake an explicit welfare analysis of sharing agreements that fall under the purview of Section 2. In both, courts defer to incumbents' views.

The Court distinguished the facts in *Trinko* from those in *Aspen Skiing*—among other things, *Aspen Skiing* involved disruption of an ongoing, mutually profitable cooperation, while *Trinko* disputed the consequences of failing to put a cooperative arrangement into effect—and reversed the Circuit Court of Appeals.

Loyalty Rebates (I)

As the facts of *Mogul Steamship* demonstrate, the appropriate public policy treatment of bundled loyalty rebates—which make the retroactive refund received by a buyer conditional on total purchases of a range of goods—is a question that predates passage of the Sherman Act. How U.S. antitrust will answer that question is, at this writing, not yet clear.

LePage's[40]   3M, the Minnesota Mining and Manufacturing Company, developed Scotch brand transparent adhesive tape in the 1920s. Seventy years later, its market share, over 90 per cent of the U.S. market, was more than enough to establish a monopoly for antitrust purposes. In the U.S. market, it faced negligible competition from foreign suppliers. But from about 1980 onward, LePage's, Inc. became a significant supplier of private label transparent tape and "second brand" transparent tape to the office stores and mass merchandisers that developed into an important feature of the U.S. retail landscape. In 1992, LePage's supplied 88 per cent of private label transparent tape sold in the United States. Although private label sales were a small part of the overall market for transparent tape, 3M responded to LePage's presence, entering the private label market and introducing its own second brand tape (Highland).

3M also introduced bundled rebate programmes. The first such programme was selective, and offered rebates to major LePage's customers. The second programme was general. Both linked rebates to customer-specific purchase growth rates and made the rebate received for purchases of any product depend on purchases of all products (324 F.3d 141 at 154).

LePage's, despite maintaining a two-thirds share of U.S. private label sales, had large operating losses in the late 1990s. It filed a private antitrust suit against 3M, claiming restraint of trade in violation of Section 1 of the Sherman Act, monopolization and attempted monopolization in violation of Section 2 of the Sherman Act, and exclusive dealing in violation of Section 3 of the Clayton Act. In District Court, a jury gave LePage's no satisfaction on its Sherman Act Section 1 and Clayton Act Section 3 claims, but found in its favour as far as monopolization was concerned, awarding damages which (after trebling and some modification by the District Court), amounted to $68.5 million. 3M appealed this outcome to the Third Circuit Court of Appeals, which affirmed the District Court judgment.[41] 3M appealed

---

[39] This is because the prospect that the profitable cooperation will come to an end if tacit collusion collapses is an incentive not to defect from tacit collusion.

[40] LePage's Inc. *v*. 3M 324 F.3d 141 (2003). For a critical view of the decision, see Rubinfeld (2005).

[41] An initial ruling by a panel of the Circuit Court reversed the District Court outcome, but LePage's prevailed after the entire Circuit Court agreed to rehear the appeal.

to the U.S. Supreme Court, which declined to take up the case. Among the views considered by the Supreme Court was an *Amicus Curiae* brief from the U.S. government,[42] urging that the Court not accept the appeal (p. 18) "to allow the case law and economic analysis" on bundled rebates "to develop further".

The Circuit Court decision thus became the final word. In that decision, after an extensive review of monopolization decisions (324 F.3d 141 at 147–152), the Circuit Court focused on exclusion as the essential element of a monopolization offence (324 F.3d 141 at 155):

> The principal anticompetitive effect of bundled rebates as offered by 3M is that when offered by a monopolist they may foreclose portions of the market to a potential competitor who does not manufacture an equally diverse group of products and who therefore cannot make a comparable offer.

3M's defence, throughout, was to rely on the Sherman Act treatment of predatory pricing. No evidence demonstrated that 3M had priced below cost; hence the most that it was guilty of was tough but fair competition, and that does not violate the antitrust laws (324 F.3d 141 at 147).

The Appeals Court focus on exclusion and 3M's protest that it had not been shown to be pricing below cost are, fundamentally, at cross purposes. In its decision, the Appeals Court points to a variety of nonprice behaviour by firms with market power that U.S. courts have found to constitute monopolization—among which, fraudulent patent procurement, denial of access to essential goods, and systematic interference with a rival's retail marketing displays. 3M analogized its bundled loyalty programme to discount pricing, and argued that the loyalty programme should be acceptable if not predatory in Areeda-Turner rule sense. The Appeals Court refused to accept the analogy, and having made this decision, ruled that the jury had been within its rights to look for exclusion in the non-price aspects of 3M's marketing strategy.

PeaceHealth[43]   In view of the Supreme Court's decision not to hear 3M's appeal, we do not know where it would have placed bundled loyalty rebates in the received framework of monopolization law. But a 2007 decision by the 9th Circuit Court of Appeals suggests the lines an eventual Supreme Court decision may take.

PeaceHealth operated three hospitals in Lane Country, Oregon. It had a 75 per cent market share in primary and secondary acute care hospital services,[44] and in the provision of such services it faced competition from the only other hospital in the county, a hospital that merged with another hospital and changed its name to Cascade Health Solutions. PeaceHealth's market share in the provision of tertiary acute care,[45] which Cascade Health Solutions did not provide, exceeded 90 per cent.

PeaceHealth bundled its supply of primary, secondary, and tertiary acute care to insurers, and accepted lower reimbursement rates (the fraction of the hospital's regular rate that the

---

[42] Brief for the United States as Amicus Curiae, 3M v LePage's Inc, No 02-1865 (S.Ct. filed 28 May 2004).

[43] Cascade Health Solutions (fka McKenzie-Williamette Hospital) v. PeaceHealth, *et al.*, No. 05-35627, 2007 WL 2473229 (9th Cir. Sept. 4, 2007).

[44] "Common medical services like setting a broken bone and performing a tonsillectomy" (slip op. at 11199).

[45] "[M]ore complex services like invasive cardiovascular surgery and intensive neonatal care" (slip op. at 11200).

insurer is obliged to pay) from some insurers who agreed to make PeaceHealth their unique preferred provider of medical services to the insurers' clients.[46]

Cascade Health Solutions filed a private antitrust suit against PeaceHealth, alleging among other things monopolization and attempted monopolization violations of the Sherman Act.[47] The basis of the monopolization claims was the bundled discounts PeaceHealth offered insurers.[48] District Court instructions to the jury followed the lines of *LePage's*, the jurors being told that (slip op. at 11213) "Bundled price discounts may be anti-competitive if they are offered by a monopolist and substantially foreclose portions of the market to a competitor who does not provide an equally diverse group of services and who therefore cannot make a comparable offer."

The jury found for Cascade Health Solutions on its attempted monopolization claim, and awarded it $5.4 million, which was trebled to $15.2 million. PeaceHealth appealed this outcome to the 9th Circuit Court of Appeals, which recognized the possibility that bundled discounts could exclude an equally or more efficient rival that did not supply all components of the bundle, but took exception to the fact that the *LePage* rule would permit a less-efficient rival to prevail as well. The Circuit Court rejected the *LePage* approach and opted instead for a "discount allocation" rule (slip op. at 11225–11226):

> Under this standard, the full amount of the discounts given by the defendant on the bundle are allocated to the competitive product or products. If the resulting price of the competitive product or products is below the defendant's incremental cost to produce them, the trier of fact may find that the bundled discount is exclusionary for the purpose of § 2.

Discount allocation rule   The discount allocation rule is the kind of cost-based approach applied in *Brooke Group*, but makes allowance for the multiproduct aspect of alleged predation-by-bundling. If a discounting bundler's price on a single component, net of all discounts, is above the bundler's cost of producing the marginal unit of the component, only less-efficient rivals would be injured. This approach is consistent with the overarching purpose of the antitrust laws, to promote consumer welfare.

The Circuit Court returned the matter to District Court for a new trial, to be informed by the discount allocation rule. At the writing, the final outcome remains to be determined.

21.3 Abuse of a Dominant Position

Article 102 of the EC Treaty prohibits abuse of a dominant position. The Article lists as examples of abuse the setting of unfair prices, limiting production "to the prejudice of consumers", price discrimination in sales to other firms when that discrimination puts some firms at a competitive disadvantage, and the use of restrictive clauses in contracts.

---

[46] A patient is generally free to obtain medical services from any provider, but rates from preferred providers are lower. An insurer may, but need not, have more than one preferred provider.

[47] Cascade Health Solutions also claimed it had been injured by tying and exclusive dealing antitrust violations, as well as by violations of some Oregon laws.

[48] In one instance, PeaceHealth offered to accept an 85 per cent reimbursement rate for primary, secondary, and tertiary services if it were the unique preferred provider, but asked for a 90 per cent reimbursement rate if Cascade Health Solutions were also a preferred provider (slip op. at 11202–11203).

BOX   **Article 102 of the EC Treaty**

Any abuse by one or more undertakings of a dominant position within the common market or in a substantial part of it shall be prohibited as incompatible with the common market insofar as it may affect trade between Member States.

Such abuse may, in particular, consist in:

(a) directly or indirectly imposing unfair purchase or selling prices or other unfair trading conditions;

(b) limiting production, markets or technical development to the prejudice of consumers;

(c) applying dissimilar conditions to equivalent transactions with other trading parties, thereby placing them at a competitive disadvantage;

(d) making the conclusion of contracts subject to acceptance by the other parties of supplementary obligations which, by their nature or according to commercial usage, have no connection with the subject of such contracts.

Article 102 pursues economic goals and seeks to promote integration in the common market. The classification "setting unfair prices" as an abuse may condemn the exercise of market power. This depends, of course, on how one defines unfair prices. "Limiting production" must harm consumers, in the sense that it reduces consumers' surplus. Limiting production is also an exercise of market power. Thus, Article 102 may condemn the *use* of market power by a dominant firm, in addition to the acquisition or maintenance of such power by socially disapproved of techniques. This contrasts with U.S. antitrust, the philosophy of which is to prohibit strategic entry deterrence by dominant firms and otherwise rely on market forces to limit the exercise of market power. The difference between the two approaches is controversial.

Price discrimination by a dominant firm is an abuse in the sense of Article 102 if it places other firms at a competitive disadvantage. Price discrimination between firms that purchase inputs from a dominant firm will place customer firms that pay higher prices at a competitive disadvantage *vis-à-vis* customer firms that pay lower prices. The prohibition of abusive price discrimination directly targets dominant firm pricing that interferes with the competitive process. Since it prohibits the systematic charging of different prices to firms in different member states, it also aims to guard the process of market integration. Promoting the competitive process will generally promote consumer welfare, but that is an indirect result, not, on the wording of the Article, the immediate purpose of the prohibition.

The kinds of restrictive contracts that have been targeted under Article 102 are those that have the effect of raising entry costs, particularly the cost of entry across national borders. Prohibiting such restrictions improves market performance and promotes market integration.

As we will see in Chapter 22, Article 102 has also been applied to mergers that create or reenforce a dominant position. We look at the Article 102 treatment of price discrimination in Chapter 23 and of vertical restraints by dominant firms in Section 24. Here we examine the

Article 102 treatment of loyalty rebates, predatory pricing, refusal to deal, and exclusionary behaviour by public monopolies.

21.3.1 Loyalty Rebates (II)

Hoffmann-La Roche

In its 1976 *Hoffmann-La Roche* decision,[49] the Commission condemned the leading world manufacturer of bulk vitamins for abuse of a dominant position in the markets for 7 vitamins (A, B_2, B_3, B_6, C, E, and H). It ordered Hoffman-La Roche to end the use of contracts that provided for bundled loyalty rebates, and fined it slightly more than 1 million deutschemarks (about 428,000 1976 U.S. dollars). Hoffmann-La Roche appealed the Commission decision to the European Court of Justice (ECJ). The 1979 ECJ decision afforded the Court an opportunity to (a) define the concept of dominant position, (b) indicate the kind of evidence that could be adduced to support a conclusion that a firm enjoyed a dominant position, (c) characterize the concept of abuse of a dominant position, and (d) rule whether or not the loyalty rebate contracts condemned by the Commission were such an abuse.

Relevant market   First, the Court wrote that whether or not a firm has a dominant position is a question that can be answered only in the context of the relevant product and geographic market ([1979] ECR 514). The requirement that the degree of dominance be assessed in a market context brings economics to center stage, since market definition must draw upon the tools of economic analysis. In this instance, the geographic market was the European Community as a whole. As one vitamin could not substitute for another, each vitamin was treated as a distinct product market.[50]

Definition of dominance   Second, the Court wrote that Article 102 serves the Community goal of instituting (1979 ECR 520) "a system ensuring that competition in the Common Market is not distorted", and with that purpose in mind, a dominant position is[51] "a position of economic strength enjoyed by an undertaking which enables it to prevent effective competition being maintained on the relevant market by affording it the power to behave to an appreciable extent independently of its competitors, its customers, and ultimately of the consumers".

Not even a monopolist is completely independent of the demand side of its market. A monopolist's profit-maximizing price depends on the price elasticity of demand, which measures the response of demand to price changes. Nor is a firm that is dominant in a market with a fringe of small suppliers, or that faces the possibility of entry, completely independent of actual or potential competitors. From an economic point of view, the constraints on a dominant firm's actions are summarized by the price elasticity of demand of its *residual* demand function, which summarizes consumer and competitor behaviour (la Cour and Møllgaard, 2002). For a firm to have a dominant position in the sense of Article 102, it must have market power with respect to this residual demand function (EC Commission, 2005, ¶ 24). A firm is dominant if the price elasticity of demand of its residual demand function

---

[49] Hoffmann-La Roche & Co. AG *v.* EC Commission [1979] ECR 461. See also Commission Decision of 9 June 1976 OJ L 223 16 August 1976; EC Commission (1977, pp. 88–89; 1980, pp. 27–30).

[50] Hoffman-La Roche made some arguments to the contrary for vitamins C and E, but without success.

[51] Essentially the same characterization appears a year earlier in the *United Brands* decision ([1978] ECR 207 at 277), which we take up in Section 23.3.2.

is small enough so that the firm finds it profitable to raise price above marginal cost to an appreciable extent.

Having a dominant position does not mean the complete absence of competition. It means a firm can largely control or manipulate such competition as exists in its market (¶ 39). But if competition controlled the leading firm, rather than the other way around, the leading firm could not be said to be dominant (¶ 71): "the fact that an undertaking is compelled by the pressure of its competitors' price reductions to lower its own prices is in general incompatible with that independent conduct which is the hallmark of a dominant position."

Evidence of dominance

Multimarket operation (not)   One of the factors considered by the Commission in support of its conclusion that Hoffman-La Roche enjoyed a dominant position in each of the vitamin markets was the fact that it produced a far wider range of vitamins than any of its competitors. The ECJ rejected this approach: since there is little demand-side or supply-side substitutability among vitamins, the Court found the idea of advantages from multiproduct operation unconvincing.

Potential competition, market share and relative market share   However, it accepted the other factors considered by the Commission. One of these was a lack of potential competition, due to the large sunk investment required to enter the industry. Another was that Hoffman-La Roche's market shares were large and typically much larger than those of its nearest rivals ([1978] ECR 525).[52] For example, shares in the vitamin A market were 47 per cent (Roche), 27 per cent, 18 per cent, 7 per cent, 1 per cent.[53] In contrast to the market for vitamin A and the other vitamins, Hoffman-La Roche's share of the market for vitamin B_3 was 34.9 per cent in 1973, 51 per cent in 1974, and there was a Japanese competitor with 30 per cent of the market in 1973. The Court rejected the Commission's finding that Hoffman-La Roche had a dominant position in the market for vitamin B_3.

Abuse   In general, wrote the Court ([1979] ECR 541), "abuse is an objective concept relating to the behaviour of an undertaking in a dominant position which is such as to influence the structure of a market where, as a result of the very presence of the undertaking in question, the degree of competition is weakened and which, through recourse to methods different from those which condition normal competition in products or services ... , has the effect of hindering the maintenance of the degree or competition still existing in the market or the growth of that competition."

Dominance $\neq$ abuse   Thus, abuse arises from firm conduct. Simply having a dominant position is not, in and of itself, an abuse. Abusive conduct takes place in markets where the position of the dominant firm means competition is already weakened. Abusive conduct is different from normal methods of competition,[54] and further weakens or impedes the

---

[52] Similarly, in *American Tobacco II*, the U.S. Supreme Court wrote that (328 U.S. 781 at 796) "The marked dominance enjoyed [American, Liggett and Reynolds], in roughly equal proportions, is emphasized by the fact that the smallest of them at all times showed over twice the production of the largest outsider."

[53] The Herfindahl index was thus $H = 0.3312$, and the inverse of the Herfindahl index, giving the equivalent number of equally sized firms, $1/H = 3.02$.

[54] Recall from *Standard Oil* (221 U.S. 1 at 75): in U.S. antitrust, monopolization is conduct that is "not ... normal methods of industrial development".

growth of competition. Abuse is an objective concept: whether or not conduct is abusive depends on its impact on competition, not the purpose or intent with which it was adopted.

Exclusionary contracts   Keeping these general guidelines in mind, Hoffmann-La Roche's abuse of its dominant positions lay in its use of contracts that contained explicit *exclusive dealing* clauses or *fidelity rebate* provisions that were exclusive in effect if not in form, giving "the purchaser an incentive to obtain ... exclusively from the [firm] in a dominant position".[55] The exclusive dealing clauses specified that the purchaser of bulk vitamins would take all its requirements from Hoffmann-La Roche. The fidelity rebates were not based on the size of individual orders, or on total orders of particular vitamins—they were not quantity discounts. They were retroactive refunds calculated according to targets that were tailored to individual customers and based on the customer's total purchases of all vitamins from Hoffmann-La Roche. For the ECJ, these kinds of contracts were abusive because they are ([1978] ECR 540) "designed to deprive the purchaser of or restrict his possible choices of sources of supply and to deny other producers access to the market" and because they would result in price discrimination (purchasers with different purchase histories would pay different amounts, net of the fidelity rebate, for identical quantities purchased).

Contracts of this kind may increase efficiency. A contractual requirement or incentive for a client to patronize only one supplier allows that supplier to more accurately predict demand. This may allow it to organize production schedules in a way that reduces cost. If the market is sufficiently competitive, some or all of this cost saving might be passed along to purchasers in the form of lower prices.

On the other hand, a fidelity rebate based on a wide range of products raises rivals' costs and is an (Korah, 1978, p. 796) "artificial barrier to entry ... against other suppliers". If a competitor markets only a single vitamin, to match or undercut Hoffmann-La Roche's effective price, the competitor would need not only to sell at a lower price than Hoffmann-La Roche on that particular vitamin, but sufficiently lower to make up for the rebate a purchaser would lose, this rebate being based on purchases of a wide range of vitamins.[56] Alternatively, the competitor would need to make the sunk investment required to produce the whole range of vitamins offered by Hoffmann-La Roche, so that it too could offer bundled fidelity rebates. By linking distinct product markets, loyalty rebates raise rivals' cost and worsen market performance.

Many of Hoffmann-La Roche's contracts included a *meet-or-release* clause. This provided that if a client informed Hoffmann-La Roche of a lower price from some other vitamin producer, Hoffmann-La Roche would have an opportunity to match the lower price. If it choose not to do so, the client could purchase from the other supplier without losing the right to its accumulated fidelity rebate. The Court recognized that this type of contract weakened the binding effect of fidelity rebates, but still found it to be an abuse of a dominant position ([1978] ECR 546).[57] The ECJ upheld the bulk of the fine imposed by the Commission and also the Commission's order that Hoffmann-La Roche put an end to the restrictive contracts.

---

[55] Korah (1978, p. 796) writes: "Loyalty discounts are an attenuated form of requirements contracts. Customers may not be required to buy all their requirements from the same supplier, but offered a discount if they promise to do so, or if they do so in practice. Even a small discount may have considerable foreclosing effects."

[56] See the box in Section 7.5.1 for an example.

[57] See Section 20.3.3 as well as the discussion of *Northern Pacific* in Section 12.3.3, both indicating means by which price guarantees can stabilize tacit collusion.

Michelin I & II

Michelin I The European Court of Justice's 1983 *Michelin I*[58] decision involved a customized rebate scheme employed by the Dutch subsidiary of the Michelin group, a leading world and European tyre supplier. In the Commission decision,[59] which Michelin appealed to the ECJ, the Commission defined the market as that for new replacement tyres for heavy vehicles in the Netherlands. Michelin's share of this market, over the period 1975 to 1980, varied between 57 and 65 per cent, while its competitors had shares of 4 to 8 per cent. Despite Michelin's objections, the ECJ accepted this market definition.

Dominance Among the factors relied upon by the Commission to establish that Michelin enjoyed a dominant position in the Netherlands were ([1983] ECR 3461, ¶55) "the lead which the Michelin group has over its competitors in the matters of investment and research and the special extent of its range of products . . . " Michelin protested (¶57) that it was being "penalized for the quality of its products and services". But these factors, the ECJ wrote, had been relied upon by the Commission to bolster its conclusion that Michelin *had* a dominant position. If there was punishment, it was for *abusing* a dominant position, not for *having* a dominant position.

Special responsibility Here the Court established the *special responsibility* of firms with a dominant position (¶57): "A finding that an undertaking has a dominant position is not in itself a recrimination but simply means that, irrespective of the reasons for which it has such a dominant position, the undertaking concerned has a special responsibility not to allow its conduct to impair genuine undistorted competition on the common market."

Abuse Michelin set individual annual sales targets for its dealers, in a way that was either well understood by dealers (according to Michelin) or not at all transparent (according to the Commission). Each dealer's targets were set at the start of a year after discussions with a Michelin sales representative, and adjusted based on the previous year's sales. The resulting targets were not put in writing.

Use of such a discount system by a dominant firm was an abuse, according the Commission. For Michelin, (¶ 79) "The purpose of the disputed discount system was to reward the purchase of increasing quantities of goods", but the Court was convinced by the Commission's arguments. In what Gyselen (2006, p. 308) calls "the key passage" of the judgment, that Court writes (¶81) that "any system under which discounts are granted according to the quantities sold during a relatively long reference period has the inherent effect, at the end of that period, of increasing pressure on the buyer to reach the purchase figure needed to obtain the discount or to avoid suffering the expected loss for the entire period". The Court set aside other aspects of the Commission's decision, and reduced the fine imposed on Michelin from 1,833,184 to 808,758 Dutch guilders (270,442 1983 U.S. dollars), but upheld the central finding that it is an abuse for a dominant firm to employ a rebate scheme that is not transparent and makes rebates depend on sales over a long period of time.

[58] *Michelin I*, Nederlandsche Banden Industrie Michelin *v* Commission of the European Communities. Case 322/81, Court of Justice of the European Communities, November 09, 1983, [1983] ECR 3461, [1985] 1 CMLR 282.

[59] Michelin OJ L 353 9/12/1981 p. 33.

Michelin II   Twenty years later, the Michelin group was once again before the European courts. In 1995 the Michelin group was the leading European tire supplier, with a market share of 31.4 per cent.[60] It had a "commanding" share of the French market, and the Commission had no difficulty concluding that it had a dominant position on that market. From at least 1980 onward, Michelin employed a variety of fidelity rebate schemes for its French dealers in new replacement and in retreaded truck tyres, which the Commission considered distinct product markets.

Loyalty-inducing effect   The details of the rebate programmes changed from time to time, but a common feature was that the rebate rate applied to all purchases for a calendar year, depended on total annual purchases, and was not paid until the end of the following February. A result was that a dealer could not know the unit cost for any purchase during a calendar year, net of rebate, until well into the following year. For the Commission, in line with the "key passage" of *Michelin I*, the uncertainty implied by the structure of the quantity rebate system had a loyalty-inducing effect that was an abuse of a dominant position (OJ L 143/36 31.5.2002). This loyalty-inducing effect was made stronger, in the Commission's view, by the fact that dealers often sold tyres at prices below their gross cost, realizing a profit only when the cumulative rebate was received.

Taking into account the duration of the abuse and the fact that *Michelin I* involved a similar rebate scheme, the Commission fined Michelin € 19.76 million. Michelin appealed the Commission decision to the Court of First Instance.

Exclusionary purpose   In its opinion,[61] the CFI wrote (¶ 100) that a dominant firm's quantity rebate system would not be an abuse if the amount of the rebate corresponded to the economies of scale permitted by increased sales. But Michelin had provided no specific information about cost savings that flowed from the quantity rebate scheme. Michelin pointed to the language of *Hoffmann-La Roche* that conduct must have the effect of weakening competition to be considered abusive, and asked that the Commission decision be overturned because the Commission had not carried out an analysis of the effects of the rebate programme. For the CFI, however, it was enough for the Commission to show that the *purpose* of a dominant firm's conduct was to weaken competition to qualify the conduct as abusive (¶ 239, ¶ 241). The Commission had established (¶ 244) that the purpose of the rebate programme was to tie dealers to Michelin and so make it more difficult for competitors to enter the market, and no study of actual effects was needed. The Court rejected Michelin's appeal and upheld the Commission's decision.

Travel agent loyalty program(me)s: U.S. antitrust vs. EU competition policy

Before the rise of the internet, passenger airlines depended on travel agents to market their product to the flying public. In the 1990s, therefore, passenger airlines competed as sellers to the flying public in a complex and highly regulated network of city-pair markets and also as buyers in the market for the services of travel agents.

---

[60] Its next largest competitor had 17.1 per cent of the market. There were at least 25 tyre suppliers to the European market. The Herfindahl index was about 0.16574, the value for a market supplied by about six equally sized firms (computed from market share figures given on page 4 of the Commission decision, OJ L 143/4 31 May 2002).

[61] Michelin *v.* Commission T-203/01 30 Sepember 2003 (Michelin II).

Travel agent commission override schemes

In this second market, from at least 1992 British Airways paid commissions to travel agents with a variety of "travel agent commission override" (TACO) schemes that differed in detail but had two features in common:

(a) agents received a base commission (in some plans, 7 per cent) on all BA ticket sales and an additional payment if sales revenue increased by a minimum amount over the previous period (typically, the previous year);

(b) once the threshold to receive the additional commission was reached, the increment applied to all tickets sold ("back to dollar one", in the U.S. context), not just to sales above the threshold.[62]

Virgin Atlantic Airways competed with British Airways on the high-volume transatlantic routes between London (Heathrow and Gatwick) and North America. In July 1993, Virgin complained to the European Commission that the TACO schemes (and other BA conduct) were violations of Articles 101 and 102 of the EC Treaty. At about the same time, Virgin filed a private U.S. antitrust suit against British Airways, seeking treble damages for alleged violations of Sections 1 and 2 of the Sherman Act. BA's loyalty commissions to travel agents were a central part of the economic theory behind Virgin's actions.

EU In the subsequent 1999 decision,[63] the Commission took the relevant product markets to be those for passenger air transport in and out of the United Kingdom and for air travel agency services in the United Kingdom. BA's share of the passenger air transport market could be measured in a variety of ways—landing and take-off slots, passengers, sales revenue—but all produced the same picture: BA had the largest share of the market (around 40 per cent by revenue), a share that was a large multiple of its competitors' market shares. Regulations governing the allocation of landing slots at UK airports and the right to connect to U.S. airports made it impossible for other airlines to duplicate BA's menu of flight offerings.

Abuse: loyalty, price discrimination For the Commission, BA's share of the air passenger market justified the conclusion that BA had a dominant position in the market for air travel agency services. This being the case, BA's use of loyalty commission schemes was an abuse of that dominant position, for two reasons. First, it was akin to an exclusive dealing contract, and the *Hoffmann-La Roche* and *Michelin I* decisions established that a dominant firm (¶ 101) "cannot give discounts or incentives to encourage loyalty, that is for avoiding purchases from a competitor ..." Second, loyalty rebate schemes result in price discrimination (¶ 109): "Two travel agents handling the same number of BA tickets and providing exactly the same level of service to BA will receive a different commission rate, that is a different price for their air travel agency services if their sales of BA tickets were different in the previous year." The Commission directed BA to abandon the use of loyalty rebates and fined it € 6.8 million.

---

[62] European Commission (2005, ¶ 153): "The fact that exceeding the threshold will not only reduce the price for all purchases above the threshold, but also for all previous purchases during the reference period, will create a so-called 'suction' effect. The price of the units of the last transaction before the threshold is exceeded will effectively be seriously lower and is possibly even negative because this transaction triggers the rebate for all the purchases below the threshold in the reference period. The higher the amount that constitutes the threshold and the higher the rebate percentage, the stronger the suction effect will be near the threshold."

[63] *Virgin/BA* Commission Decision of 14 July 1999 OJ L 30 04.02.00 pp. 1–24.

📌 BOX   Price Discrimination by Means of a Retroactive Loyalty Rebate

A supplier offers a rebate of 2.5 per cent on *all* purchases once purchases exceed 1 million units. The price before the rebate is 100 ecu*.

Payment for 950,000 units purchased from firm selling with a retroactive loyalty rebate	$950,000 \times 100 = 95,000,000.$
Payment for 1,000,000 units purchased from firm selling with a retroactive loyalty rebate	$1,000,000 \times 97.5 = 97,500,000.$
Incremental payment for final 50,000 units	$97,500,000 - 95,000,000 = 2,500,000.$
Effective price per unit, final 50,000 units	$\dfrac{2,500,000}{50,000} = 50.$

_____

*ecu = example currency units.

Source: EC Commission (2005, p. 46).

Exclusionary effect   BA appealed against the Commission's decision to the Court of First Instance. One of the grounds for appeal was that the Commission had failed to demonstrate that BA's rebate scheme was exclusionary. The CFI holding on this point was, first, that there was no need for the Commission to show actual exclusionary effect:[64] "It is sufficient in that respect to demonstrate that the abusive conduct of the undertaking in a dominant position tends to restrict competition, or, in other words, that the conduct is capable of having, or likely to have, such an effect."

At the same time, as far as the CFI was concerned, the Commission had in fact established that BA's rebate programme was exclusionary (¶ 295): "Since, at the time of the conduct complained of, travel agents established in the United Kingdom carried out 85% of all air ticket sales in the territory of the United Kingdom, BA's abusive conduct on the United Kingdom market for air travel agency services cannot fail to have had the effect of excluding competing airlines (to their detriment) from the United Kingdom air transport markets ... " The CFI also took the view that a firm with a dominant position committed abuse if it sought to exclude competitors, even if it failed to do so (¶ 297): "[W]here an undertaking in a dominant position actually puts into operation a practice generating the effect of ousting its competitors, the fact that the hoped-for result is not achieved is not sufficient to prevent a finding of abuse of a dominant position within the meaning of Article [102] EC."

_____

[64] British Airways *v.* Commission Case T-219/99, 17 December 2003, [2003] ECR II-5917, ¶ 293.

On appeal BA appealed the Court of First Instance decision to the European Court of Justice, without success. According to the ECJ's ruling, dominant firm rebate schemes are not abusive *per se*: quantity discounts that reflect economies stemming from the volume of purchases do not violate Article 102. But from *Hoffmann-La Roche*, a pure fidelity rebate scheme employed by a dominant firm is an abuse. For rebate programmes that are neither pure quantity discounts nor pure fidelity rebates, the rule of *Michelin I* is that:[65]

- it first has to be determined whether those discounts or bonuses can produce an exclusionary effect ...
- secondly, [whether they are capable] of making it more difficult or impossible for its co-contractors to choose between various sources of supply or commercial partners.
- It then needs to be examined whether there is an objective economic justification for the discounts and bonuses granted.

The ECJ confirmed the CFI's finding that BA's rebate scheme was exclusionary, emphasizing the progressive nature of the rebate scheme and the fact that BA's much larger market share made it effectively impossible for competitors to offer comparable benefits.[66]

U.S. In U.S. District Court, Virgin's private antitrust case survived an initial motion by BA that the complaint be dismissed without trial[67] only to succumb to a second such motion four years later.[68]

In its decision on the motion to dismiss the case, the U.S. court took the relevant markets to be those that Virgin had asserted in its complaint (69 F. Supp. 2d 571 at 573): " 'Heathrow airport', ..., 'Gatwick airport', ... and scheduled airline passenger services between both city pairs and airport pairs ... " The U.S. court's views on this market, its characteristics, and BA's share in that market, were all broadly similar to the views stated in the EU decisions.

Incentive contracts Virgin came into U.S. court with complaints of monopolization in violation of Section 2 of the Sherman Act and agreement in restraint of trade in violation of Section 1 of the Sherman Act. Regarding the monopolization complaint, the U.S. court did not see incentive contracts in the same light as had the Commission (69 F. Supp. 2d 571 at 575):

> The incentive agreements are not exclusive dealing agreements by their terms, and do not require anyone to buy or sell any British Airways tickets, but merely provide larger commissions or discounts if the targets are met.

Actual flight and passenger data Virgin produced expert witness testimony to the effect that the loyalty commissions would have a predatory effect, but the court rejected a theory-based approach (69 F. Supp. 2d 571 at 580):[69] "[the] opinion should be based on actual flight

---

[65] British Airways *v.* Commission Case C-95/04 P 15 March 2007, ¶ 68, ¶ 69; not set off as a bullet list in the original.

[66] British Airways *v.* Commission Case C-95/04 P 15 March 2007, ¶ 74, ¶ 75.

[67] Virgin Atlantic *v.* British Airways plc 872 F. Supp. 52 (1995).

[68] Virgin Atlantic *v.* British Airways plc 69 F. Supp. 2d 571 (1999).

[69] In the U.S. forum, Virgin seems to have made an argument that passenger fares on incremental flights, scheduled as a result of passenger shifting that took place because of the loyalty rebates, were made at a price below (some

and passenger data for the years in question, rather than theory-grounded assumptions and average figures. In addition, because Virgin claims injury on five particular routes, its case should be supported by data specific to those five routes".

Rule of reason and restraint of trade allegations   Virgin also complained that the loyalty commissions were contracts in restraint of trade in violation of Section 1 of the Sherman Act. As loyalty commissions are not illegal *per se*, the district court applied the rule of reason (69 F. Supp. 2d 571 at 582, citations omitted and bullets added):[70]

> Under the rule of reason, whether the restraints in the incentive agreements are reasonable depends on their actual effects on the market and their pro-competitive justification. ... "Establishing a violation of the rule of reason involves three steps."
>
> - First, the "plaintiff bears the initial burden of showing that the challenged action has had an actual adverse effect on competition as a whole in the relevant market ... "
> - If the plaintiff carries its burden, the burden shifts to the defendant to establish the pro-competitive redeeming virtue of the action.
> - Should the defendant carry this burden, the plaintiff must then show that the same pro-competitive effect could be achieved through an alternative means that is less restrictive of competition. ...
>
> Ultimately, the goal is to determine whether restrictions in an agreement among competitors potentially harm consumers.

The District Court concluded that Virgin had failed to show that the loyalty commissions had an adverse affect on competition in the relevant market, and therefore dismissed Virgin's case without trial on the merits.

On appeal   Virgin appealed the District Court's decision to the Second Circuit Court of Appeals. In its decision,[71] the appeals court upheld the District Court. Along the way, it pointed out (257 F.3d 256 at 263) that to show a violation of Section 1 required among other things demonstration of a conscious agreement[72] "to a common scheme designed to achieve an unlawful objective". Virgin made no claim that BA had done anything other than act alone, so for this reason as well its Section 1 claim had to fail.

Comparison   Monopolization under Section 2 of the Sherman Act and abuse of a dominant position under Article 102 of the EC Treaty are *not* the same thing with different names. In particular, systematic price discrimination by a dominant firm is abuse of that dominant position; under U.S. antitrust (as we see in Chapter 23), predatory price discrimination is likely to run afoul of Section 2, while this is much less likely for price discrimination that is

---

measure of) unit cost. Perhaps this approach was an attempt to fit the economic theory into the requirements of the Areeda-Turner rule. An alternative economic characterization might have been: (a) that the loyalty rebates raised rivals' costs by requiring commission payments that would generate travel agent income as much from rival ticket sales on a narrow segment of the market as potential income from sales of a broader bundle of BA tickets; (b) that this raising of rivals' costs in the market for travel agent services was an enabling factor that permitted BA to hold fares above cost on the contested transatlantic routes.

[70] The Court quotes K.M.B. Warehouse Distribs., Inc. *v.* Walker Mfg. Co., 61 F.3d 123 at 127 (2d Cir. 1995).

[71] Virgin Atlantic *v.* British Airways plc 257 F.3d 256 (2001).

[72] Quoting Monsanto Co. *v.* Spray-Rite Service Corp. 465 U.S. 752 (1984) at 768.

not predatory. Commentators have described the U.S. antitrust rule-of-reason treatment of loyalty rebates as "deferential" (Gyselen, 2006, p. 288), and written of the EU approach that it tends (Waelbroeck, 2005, p. 151) "to simply presume systematic anticompetitive effects in the case of any rebate scheme of a 'dominant company' and to underestimate their pro-competitive effects". There is an element of truth in both views, with EU competition policy leaning in one direction, U.S. antitrust in the other (Waelbroeck, 2005, p. 150, footnote omitted):

> Imposing too strict a test on dominant companies as to their rebate schemes can indeed have the effect of chilling price competition, protecting possibly inefficient competitors and raising prices to consumers. However, if it is too difficult to demonstrate that the rebate system of a dominant undertaking is abusive, even an efficient competitor could be forced out of business (and the market be monopolized) before such proof is made.

21.3.2 Exercise of Market Power

Given the now widespread recognition that resource and information constraints make continuous supervision of oligopoly market performance impractical, it is natural to think that for most markets, competition policy toward single-firm conduct should devote itself to preventing dominant firms from engaging in strategic entry- and expansion-deterring behaviour, and otherwise rely on actual and potential competition to get the best possible real-world market performance. Exceptions may be made for natural monopolies,[73] but (in this view), regulation should be the exception, not the rule. Much Article 102 enforcement is in this spirit, and increasingly so.

But Article 102's first two examples of abuse of a dominant position ("unfair purchase or selling prices", "limiting production") describe the exercise of market power, not strategic anticompetitive behaviour. There is reason to think that at its inception, it was the exercise of market power that was the prime target of Article 102. Thus Korah (1978, p. 771, footnote omitted) writes that the English term " 'abuse' hardly does justice to the double concept of *exploitation abusive*—abusive exploitation—in the French text [of the EC Treaty]. In French, 'exploitation' refers to the reaping of monopoly profits rather than to the consolidation or extension of dominance".[74] Thus, Article 102 classifies the exercise of market power, along with strategic behaviour designed to acquire or maintain market power, as an abuse.

British Leyland

In the early 1980s, the publicly owned firm British Leyland plc was the second-largest British car manufacturer, and the seventh-largest, ranked by sales revenue, in Europe. UK regulations required (with unimportant exceptions), that in order for a vehicle to be registered for use on the roads, the vehicle had to have what was called a type-approval certificate, indicating that the vehicle satisfied various safety and other standards.

---

[73] Here many economists will feel, with Simons (1936, p. 74) "that our situation with respect to these industries will always be unhappy, at best; and I have no genuine enthusiasm for public ownership". But this is a question that goes beyond mere economics.

[74] She also writes that while the Dutch text of the Treaty follows the English version, the other official texts have the same implication as the French version.

British Leyland sold left-hand-drive vehicles in continental Europe at a lower price than it sold right-hand-drive versions of the same vehicles within the United Kingdom. This created an opportunity for consumer arbitrage. Individuals could purchase a vehicle on the continent, ship it to the UK, and even (although there was no legal requirement to do so) pay to have the vehicle converted to right-hand-side drive, all at a lower cost than purchase of the corresponding right-hand-side model in the UK.

British Leyland's dealers complained about the inroads competition from the continent made in their profit. British Leyland responded by taking steps to raise barriers to consumer arbitrage. There were, in principle, ways for an importer to obtain the necessary documentation without the cooperation of the manufacturer, but these cost so much that they were not realistic alternatives. First, British Leyland lied to importers about the availability of a national (generic) type approval for the models in question. Then it allowed the national type approval to expire. It also refused to provide importers of left-hand-drive vehicles with information they could use to obtain certificate approvals on their own, although they had a legal right to be provided with the information.

Following inquiries in Parliament about its practices, British Leyland modified its approach. Historically, it had provided certificate information at a price of £25, on request, for right-hand-drive or left-hand-drive vehicles. Rather than simply refusing to provide information for left-hand-drive vehicles, it began to do so, at a price to dealers of £150. The price for certificate information for individuals importing right-hand-drive vehicles remained £25.

A Commission Decision taken in July 1984[75] concluded that as a result of British regulations, British Leyland had a dominant position in "the supply of information relating to national type-approval certification needed by an importer seeking to license a BL vehicle for use on the roads in Great Britain", and that it had abused this dominant position by three types of conduct. The first was allowing the generic national type approval for left-hand-drive vehicles to lapse. The second was its initial refusal to supply information that individuals could use to register their vehicles. The third, of greatest interest for the concept of abuse of a dominant position under Article 102, was the high fee it set for information about left-hand-drive vehicles.

For the Commission, a comparison of the fee set for left-hand-drive vehicles with that set for right-hand side vehicles showed that the former was "both excessive and discriminatory". The Commission fined British Leyland just over £200,000 and ordered it to stop charging different fees for the same service to importers of left-hand-side and right-hand-side vehicles.

British Leyland appealed this decision to the European Court of Justice. In its opinion confirming the Commission decision, the European Court of Justice wrote that[76] "[A]n undertaking abuses its dominant position where it has an administrative monopoly and charges for its services fees which are disproportionate to the economic value of the service provided".

How one assesses the economic value of a product or service is critical for the third element of abuse identified in this decision. Is the economic value of a product what consumers will pay? Is it average or average variable or marginal cost of production? Is it a non-cooperative equilibrium price?

---

[75] *British Leyland* Commission Decision OJ L 207/11, 2 August 1984. See also British Leyland *v.* Commission [1986] ECR 3263.

[76] The Court refers to an earlier statement in General Motors Continental *v.* Commission [1975] ECR 1367.

The Commission has been reluctant to get into the business of price control. In a discussion of the relation between competition policy and inflation, the Commission wrote that (1976, p. 13):

> [M]easures to halt the abuse of dominant positions cannot be converted into systematic monitoring of prices. In proceedings against abuse consisting of charging excessively high prices, it is difficult to tell whether in any given case an abusive price has been set for there is no objective way of establishing exactly what price covers costs plus a reasonable margin.

This statement acknowledges the difficulty of deciding whether or not a particular price is excessive—the situation is seldom as clear-cut as a firm that charges one class of customers six times the price as another for services that are produced at the same cost. But the Commission's statement makes clear that charging an excessive price—the exercise of market power—is, in and of itself, an abuse of a dominant position.

This marks a genuine difference between Article 102 of the EC Treaty and Section 2 of the Sherman Act. As noted by the U.S. Supreme Court in its *United States Steel* opinion (251 U.S. 417 at 451), the Sherman Act does not compel competition. More recently, *Trinko* shows that U.S. antitrust is more willing to rely on market forces to erode positions of market power than is EU competition policy.

21.3.3 Predation

AKZO

EU competition policy takes strategic aspects of predation into account, and considers evidence of intent in interpreting Areeda-Turner-like comparisons of price and unit cost. This appears from the 1985 Commission *AKZO* decision[77] and the subsequent 1991 European Court of Justice decision.[78]

Engineering and Chemical Supplies Ltd, henceforth ECS, produced benzoyl peroxide, a particular type of organic peroxide, for use as a bleaching agent for flour in the United Kingdom and Ireland. It competed in this market with AKZO Chemie, a subdivision of a much larger Dutch chemical firm, and with a third firm that had a small part of the market. According to the Commission decision, in 1982 the three firms had market shares of 52 per cent (AKZO), 35 per cent (ECS), and 13 per cent (Diaflex).[79]

Benzoyl-peroxide has applications not only as a bleaching agent for flour but in the production of plastics. It was the continental Europe plastics industry that was the main interest of AKZO and its parent group.

In 1979, ECS began to offer benzoyl peroxide to plastics producers on the continent. This attracted AKZO's attention. There was a meeting between AKZO and ECS officials. ECS alleged, and AKZO denied, that AKZO threatened to cut prices in the flour additives market, below cost if need be, unless ECS pulled out of the plastics market (OJ L 374/7). The Commission, and later the European Court of Justice, found sufficient corroborating material to accept ECS's account of the meeting.

---

[77] *AKZO* Commission Decision of 14 December 1985 O J L 374/1, 31 December 1985.

[78] AKZO Chemie BV *v.* Commission [1991] ECR I-3359, (1993) 5 CMLR 215. For a critique, see Phlips and Moras (1993).

[79] Thus the Herfindahl index was $H = 0.4098$ and the inverse-Herfindahl numbers equivalent, $1/H = 2.4402$.

Nature of the abuse   In its decision, the Commission defined the relevant market as (OJ L 374/17) "the organic peroxides sector in the EEC as a whole". It reviewed AKZO's share of the market (stable at around 50 per cent), the shares of rivals, AKZO's technological advantages, the high cost of entering the market, and concluded that AKZO had a dominant position. For the Commission, AKZO engaged in predation in the flour additives market to preserve its dominant position in the organic peroxide market.[80] AKZO abused this dominant position by:

(1) offering unreasonably low prices to ECS customers;

(2) while charging up to 60 per cent higher prices to its own established customers;

(3) adding flour additives to its line so it could offer them in a package with benzoyl peroxide to ECS customers;

(4) maintaining UK flour additive prices at an artificially low level for a "prolonged period";

(5) obtaining details of offers from major customers and underbidding those offers on condition of an exclusive supply arrangement.

From an economic point of view, this appears to be (like the Sugar Trust, Bell Telephone, and Brown & Williamson), predation with the purpose of denying a smaller rival the financial capital to expand and/or to convince it of the error of its ways.

Predation: strategic and discriminatory aspects   Before the Commission, AKZO urged the Commission to apply the Areeda-Turner rule (OJ L 374/19), according to which its prices were not predatory. For the Commission, EU competition policy required taking broader considerations into account (OJ L374/20, emphasis added):

> The standard proposed by AKZO based on a static and short-term conception of "efficiency" takes no account of *the broad objectives of EEC competition rules [the requirement that the Community pursue the institution of a system of effective competition]* and particularly the need to guard against the impairment of an effective structure of competition in the common market. It also *fails to take account of the longer-term strategic considerations* which may underlie sustained price cutting and which are particularly apparent in the present case. Further *it ignores the fundamental importance of the element of discrimination* in seeming to permit a dominant manufacturer to recover its full costs from its regular customers while tempting a rival's customers at lower prices.

On appeal   The Commission directed AKZO to end its abusive practices and fined it almost 25 million Dutch guilders. AKZO appealed this decision, without success, to the European Court of Justice. Four aspects of the Court's ruling seem particularly worthy of note.

Large market share   First, the Court indicated that for EC competition policy (¶ 60) "very large shares are in themselves, and save in exceptional circumstances, evidence of the existence of a dominant position ...", and that a 50 per cent market share qualifies as "very large".

---

[80] EC Commission (2005, ¶ 101, fn. 66). This may be contrasted with *Brooke Group*, in which the U.S. Supreme Court did not consider the possibility that predation in the market for generic cigarettes might be made profitable by the recoupment that would be possible in the market for branded cigarettes.

Intent Second, the Court included intent as a factor in application of Article 82 ([1991] ECR I-3359 at I-3455, emphasis added):

> Prices below average variable costs ... by means of which a dominant undertaking seeks to eliminate a competitor must be regarded as abusive. ...
>
> Moreover, prices below average total costs ...but above average variable costs, must be regarded as abusive *if they are determined as part of a plan for eliminating a competitor*. Such prices can drive from the market undertakings which are perhaps as efficient as the dominant undertaking but which, because of their smaller financial resources, are incapable of withstanding the competition waged against them.

Despite the Commission's disavowal of Areeda-Turner-like tests, that is precisely the kind of test the ECJ discusses in this part of its decision. Further, there is tension between the *Hoffmann-La Roche* statement that abuse is an objective concept and the use of intent in *AKZO* as a factor qualifying prices above average variable cost as an abuse.

Cost accounting Third, one section of the decision is a useful antidote to the apparent exactitude of Areeda-Turner-like comparisons of price and unit cost. Accounting cost and economic cost are different, so application of the Areeda-Turner rule requires adjustment of accounting data. In paragraphs 83 through 97 of its decision, the Court sorts out disputes between AKZO and the Commission over the measurement of AKZO's average total and average variable cost, including whether the cost of labour should be treated as fixed or variable. Far from being a relatively straightforward modification of accounting data in the direction of the relevant economic concepts, the analysis involved detailed consideration of input-output relationships in the industry. In the end, the Court came down on the side of treating labour as a fixed cost. But the whole exercise suggests that there are substantial margins for interpretation both in judging intent *and* in comparing price to the economically relevant measure of unit cost.

Competition on the merits Fourth, AKZO appealed (without success) against that part of the Commission decision requiring it to offer the same price to customers for whose business it was in competition with ECS and to customers for whose business it was not in competition with ECS ([1991] ECR I-3359 at I-3474):

> AKZO maintains that this measure is unfair. If ECS approaches its customers, it is faced with a choice: either to align its prices and extend to all its customers of comparable size the prices that it has had to concede in order to retain the customer, which would be very expensive, or to lose the customer.

This is precisely the approach that John Bates Clark advocated for American trusts almost 90 years earlier: deny the trust the possibility of discriminating, and let it compete on the merits. If it maintains its position on the basis of efficiency, bully for it.

Compagnie Maritime Belge

The Commission decision in *Compagnie Maritime Belge* condemned exclusionary conduct by a liner shipping conference serving routes between West Africa and Europe. The Conference had a market share of 90 per cent in 1987 (OJ L 34 1993, ¶ 57), which enabled the Commission to conclude that the conference had a position of collective dominance.[81] Conference practice was to designate "fighting ships" that would offer exceptionally low rates in competition with independent vessels (OJ L 34 1993, ¶ 30, ¶ 73). All members of the conference shared in the resulting reduced profit. The Commission was willing to condemn the use of fighting ships even if the low rates were not predatory in the sense of being below some appropriate measure of unit cost:[82]

> [S]ubsidization of the cost of fighting rates by the conference's normal rates charged on its other sailings is in itself ... abusive, anti-competitive conduct which might have the effect of eliminating from the market an undertaking which is perhaps as efficient as the dominant conference but which, because of its lesser financial capacity, is unable to resist the competition practised in a concerted and abusive manner by a powerful group of shipowners operating together in a shipping conference.

The Commission's decision was upheld by the Court of First Instance[83] and the European Court of Justice.[84] Thus, EU competition policy treats selective exclusionary conduct by a dominant firm or group of firms as abusive (Elhauge, 2006, p. 206): "the cases suggest the European doctrine might ultimately be interpreted to mean that any above-cost price cut made by a monopolist in reaction to entry is illegal if intended to drive out an entrant, and that such an intent can be established not just by subjective evidence but by objective proof that the resulting price failed to maximize the monopolist's short-run profits."

Tetra Pak II

Tetra Pak II involved allegations of tying and predation against the leading European producer of cartons for liquid foods and machines for filling such cartons. The cartons were used mainly as containers for milk, fruit juice, and other liquid foods, with milk overwhelmingly the most important. In the mid-1980s, Tetra Pak International SA had a 90 to 95 per cent share of the EC market for aseptic (sterile) liquid cartons and machines to fill such cartons ("the aseptic sector"; liquids so packaged have a long shelf life), with but one real competitor. Its share of the market for non-aseptic cartons and machines to pack such cartons ("the non-aseptic sector") was 50 to 55 per cent; a second firm (Elopak) had a 27 per cent share of the markets for non-septic cartons and machines. There were substantial barriers to entry into the aseptic sector, rooted in the complexity of the technology, intellectual property rights, and Tetra Pak's distribution practices.

These practices varied from member state to member state—in some, it would only lease its machines, in others it would sell or lease them. In all countries except Spain, Tetra Pak reserved for itself the right to maintain packaging machines. It required that Tetra Pak cartons be used on Tetra Pak machines. It required monthly reports from its Italian customers, and

---

[81] Before the Court of First Instance, the Advocate General described the shipping conference's position as "superdominant". See O'Donoghue and Padilla (2006, Section 3.5).

[82] OJ L 34 1993, ¶ 82. The Conference argued that its members did not lose money on fighting ships. The Commission wrote that there was evidence to the contrary in the minutes of Conference meetings.

[83] Compagnie maritime belge transports SA *et al. v.* Commission [1996] ECR II-1201.

[84] Compagnie maritime belge transports SA *et al. v.* Commission Joined cases C-395/96 P and C-396/96 P 16 March 2000 [2000] ECR I-1365.

had the right to make inspections there without advance notice. Leases ranged from three to nine years, and provided for penalties (the amount of the penalty being decided by Tetra Pak, up to an agreed maximum) in the event the terms of the lease were violated.[85,86]

In 1983 Elopak Italia complained to the Commission that Tetra Pak was abusing its dominant position by predatory pricing of cartons, of machines to fill the cartons, as well as restrictive contracts in the supply of machines. The Commission agreed, finding abuse in the restrictive contractual provisions, the tying of machines and cartons, and predatory pricing in the non-aseptic sector. Taking the view that the abusive practices had been in place for at least 15 years and that Tetra Pak must have known that the practices were abusive, it fined Tetra Pak 75 million ecus (63.4 million 1991 U.S. dollars).[87]

Tetra Pak appealed the Commission decision to the Court of First Instance, which found that in some cases Tetra Pak had priced below average variable cost, in others between average variable and average cost with the intent to eliminate a competitor, and confirmed the Commission's decision.[88]

Intent   Tetra Pak thereupon appealed the Court of First Instance decision to the European Court of Justice. The ECJ[89] ratified the CFI's use of the rule from *AKZO*, in particular the role of intent (¶ 41): "First, prices below average variable costs must always be considered abusive. ... Secondly, prices below average total costs but above average variable costs are only to be considered abusive if an intention to eliminate can be shown." The ECJ also rejected Tetra Pak's argument that the Commission should have been required to show that recoupment was plausible ([1996] ECR I-5951 ¶ 44): "Furthermore, it would not be appropriate, in the circumstances of the present case, to require in addition proof that Tetra Pak had a realistic chance of recouping its losses. It must be possible to penalize predatory pricing whenever there is a risk that competitors will be eliminated."[90]

21.3.4 Refusal to Deal

Commercial Solvents,[91] an early European Court of Justice decision, classified refusal to deal by a dominant producer of an essential input as abusive under Article 102. The U.S. firm Commercial Solvents Corporation had an effective monopoly in the production of nitropropane and aminobutanol, essential ingredients for the manufacture of ethambutol, a drug used to treat tuberculosis. It supplied EC producers of ethambutol through its Italian subsidiary, ICI. One of ICI's clients was the Italian firm Zoja. In 1970, Commercial Solvents decided to

---

[85] Numerous other restrictive clauses, for machines and cartons, are detailed in the Commission decision, Commission Decision of 24 July 1991 relating to a proceeding pursuant to Article 86 of the EEC Treaty (IV/31043 - Tetra Pak II).

[86] The similarity of Tetra Pak's marketing practices to those of the United Shoe Machinery Corporation is evident.

[87] The ecu (European currency unit) was a unit of account, defined as a bundle of currencies of EC member states, employed before introduction of the euro.

[88] Tetra Pak International SA *v.* Commission Case T-83/91 6 October 1994 [1994] ECR II-755.

[89] Tetra Pak International SA *v.* Commission Case C-333/94 P 14 November 1996 [1996] ECR I-5951 (*Tetra Pak II*).

[90] In addition, the ECJ confirmed that tying of cartons and filling machines was an abuse of a dominant position, in view of the facts that other firms were legally and technically able to manufacture cartons for use with Tetra Pak machines and that Tetra Pak had been unable to provide any objective justification for the tie ([1996] ECR I-5951 ¶¶ 34–38).

[91] ICI and Commercial Solvents *v.* Commission Cases 6/73 and 7/73 [1974] ECR 223, [1974] 1 CMLR 309.

become a manufacturer of ethambutol, and as existing contracts expired, it stopped supplying its former customers with nitropropane and aminobutanol. Zoja was one of the firms cut off from supplies of the essential inputs, and it complained to the European Commission. In a 1972 decision,[92] the Commission condemned the refusal to supply as an abuse of a dominant position, ordered Commercial Solvents to supply Zoja, and fined Commercial Solvents 125 million Italian lire.

Commercial Solvents appealed to the European Court of Justice, which confirmed the substance of the Commission's decision, writing that (¶ 25):[93]

> an undertaking ... in a dominant position as regards the production of raw material and therefore able to control the supply to manufacturers of derivatives, cannot, just because it decides to start manufacturing these derivatives (in competition with its former customers) act in such a way as to eliminate their competition ... [If it does, it] is abusing its dominant position within the meaning of Article [102].

21.3.5 Public Monopolies

EC competition policy does not aim to limit the ability of dominant firms to compete on the merits, but it does insist that rivalry be based on efficiency, not on strategic anticompetitive behaviour (European Commission, 1999, p. 38). To this end, the European Commission has applied Article 102 to firms that have a dominant position as a result of member state legislation.

The *FAG* (Flughafen Frankfurt/Main AG.) decision[94] involved the market for the provision of ground-handling services—loading and unloading baggage and cargo, cleaning aircraft cabins, refulling, and the like—at the Frankfurt airport. Under German law, FAG had a legal monopoly managing the Frankfurt airport, hence, for purposes of Article 102, a dominant position. With limited exceptions, FAG reserved the right to perform ground-handling services for itself.

In its decision, the Commission distinguished two markets: that for airport facilities proper, in which FAG had a legal monopoly, and that for the provision of ramp-handling services, in which it did not. In the Commission's view, FAG's refusal to allow other airlines or third parties physical access to the airport ramp was an abuse of FAG's dominant position as airport operator, and the Commission ordered FAG to allow independent firms to supply ground-handling services.[95]

In like manner, until the law was changed in December 1975, the Italian state agency AAMS (Amministrazione Autonoma dei Monopoli di Stato) enjoyed among other privileges a monopoly over the manufacture, importation, and wholesale distribution of cigarettes in

---

[92] *Commercial Solvents* Commission Decision of 14 December 1972 (Case IV/26.911 – Zoja/C.S.C. – ICI) OJ L 299/51–58 31 December 1972.

[93] The ECJ reduced Commercial Solvents' fine to 62.5 million Italian lire, just under $100,000 March 1974 U.S. dollars.

[94] OJ L 72 11 March 1998.

[95] See also *Aéroports de Paris* (ADP, OJ 1998 L 230) decision, in which the Commission found that the firm operating two Paris airports had abused its dominant position by charging discriminatory fees to airlines that provided their own ground-handling services. The subsequent European Court of Justice decision is Aéroports de Paris *v.* Commission Case C-82/01 P (24 October 2002) [2002] ECR I-9297.

Italy. After the law was changed, it became legally possible for other firms to enter whole-sale distribution, but cigarette manufacturers based elsewhere in the Community continued to employ AAMS' network of warehouses. AAMS offered cigarette manufacturers contracts that favoured the distribution of its own cigarettes, limiting the introduction of new brands and the quantities sold. AAMS similarly exercised its obligation to supervise independent cigarette retailers in ways that favoured AAMS' own cigarettes. The Commission concluded that AAMS' actions limiting access of non-Italian cigarette manufacturers to the Italian market were an abuse of its dominant position in the wholesale distribution of cigarettes. It ordered AAMS to end the abuses, and fined AAMS the equivalent of 6.6 million 1998 U.S. dollars.

21.3.6 Article 102: Things to Come?

In a 2005 Report, the Economic Advisory Group on Competition Policy urges a "more eco-nomic approach" to Article 102.[96] The Report stands against a background of commentary that in application, Article 102 has too much worked to protect competitors rather than competition (Fletcher, 2005), and argues that business practices should be treated accord-ing to their effects rather than their legal or contractual form. A more economic approach (EAGCP, p. 2, p. 3) "requires a careful examination of how competition works in each par-ticular market in order to evaluate how specific company strategies affect consumer welfare" and "implies that the assessment of each specific case ... will be based on the assessment of the anti-competitive effects generated by business behaviour". It would oblige enforcers to keep their eyes on the main goal, consumer welfare, with protection of competition a means to the end of promoting consumer but not an end in itself (EAGCP, pp. 8–9).[97]

This will require a rule of reason analysis that will rely on market forces, insofar as possible, to generate good market performance (EAGCP, 2005, p. 3). The tradeoffs raised by the rise of a more economic approach to EC competition policy overlap substantially with those associated with the evolution of the *per se* rule and the rule of reason in U.S. antitrust. But (Lowe, 2006, p. 69, discussing state aid policy):

> [R]efining the economics underlying ... policy does not mean that per se rules disappear entirely to be replaced by pure case-by-case analysis and never-ending economic assessment. As we have found in antitrust and mergers, and as we are already demonstrating in the implemen-tation measures discussed in more detail below, it is perfectly possible to combine clear rules with economic analysis—the safe harbor of the risk capital guidelines, for instance, are ample proof of that.

---

[96] Such an approach would be consistent with a renewed emphasis on the economic foundations of EU compe-tition policy generally. See Section 22.3. The Report contains detailed discussions of policy approaches to specific dominant firm business practices; our focus is on the general principles set out in Chapter I.

[97] Attention to market structure may, however, come in through the back door (EAGCP, 2005, pp. 11–12): "In assessing the implications of alternative policies for the future, one difficulty is that their effects on future market outcomes are difficult to predict. Trying to foresee the different possibilities is sometimes quite hopeless, especially if one takes into account that the genius of competitive markets lies precisely in developing possibilities that no one has thought about before. Given this difficulty, it is sometimes necessary to forego an explicit computation of consumer welfare in future markets and to rely on a proxy instead. Such a proxy may usefully refer to aspects of market structure."

In the same vein, Friederszick *et al.* write that (2006, p. 51, also discussing state aid policy)

[A]n economic approach does not mean a full economic assessment in all cases. The obvious solution—like in all other areas of competition policy, such as mergers and antitrust—has to be a sensible combination of safe harbour thresholds and prohibition thresholds and a more complete economic assessment for those cases (limited in number) which fall between these two thresholds.

The question is not, therefore, a choice between a *per se*/form-based approach and a rule-of-reason/effects-based approach, but rather what types of dominant firm conduct will be evaluated under the former type of standard and what types under the latter.

21.4 Microsoft

Just as the Standard Oil Company's conduct set the twentieth-century course of antitrust treatment of monopolization, so Microsoft's conduct frames the issues for the twenty-first-century antitrust and competition policy treatment of strategic behaviour by dominant firms. Although much was made of the fact that Microsoft operates in high-technology markets, the central element of its travails (outlined in the accompanying boxes) in U.S. and EU courts was much more the traditional concern exclusionary dominant-firm conduct. The U.S. and EU proceedings involved different product markets, similar marketing strategies, and had very different outcomes.

21.4.1 U.S.

The market

A comparison of Figures 21.2 and 21.3 serves to illustrate the theory behind the antitrust suits filed against Microsoft in 1998. Microsoft was by far the leading supplier of the world market for operating systems for Intel-compatible personal computers; the District Court Findings of Fact found its share of this market to be 95 per cent. The Court excluded other operating systems for Intel-compatible personal computers from the market, on the ground that a user with an Intel-compatible personal computer would face substantial switching costs in moving to another operating system (¶ 20). But the Findings of Fact note (¶ 35) that if Intel-compatible PCs and Apple PCs were treated as being in the same market, Microsoft's share of that market would have been 80 per cent.

PC users also have no use for an operating system without complementary applications—software packages that can be made, by the operating system, to run on a PC and perform some function a user finds of interest.[98] The more software packages are available to be used with an operating system, the more attractive PC users will find the operating system. The operating system producer can take steps to make its operating system more attractive to software writers (Durham, 2006, p. 555, emphasis added): "To facilitate the writing

---

[98] Users also have no use for an operating system without a PC, or *vice versa*. But personal computers are a commodity—differing in configuration, but available from many suppliers. For this reason, the personal computer-Microsoft operating system link was not the target of strategic behaviour (although it was a vehicle of strategic behaviour by Microsoft against Netscape Navigator and Java).

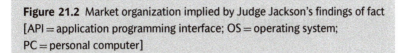

Figure 21.2 Market organization implied by Judge Jackson's findings of fact [API = application programming interface; OS = operating system; PC = personal computer]

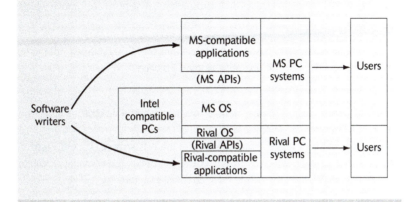

Figure 21.3 Market organization feared by Microsoft

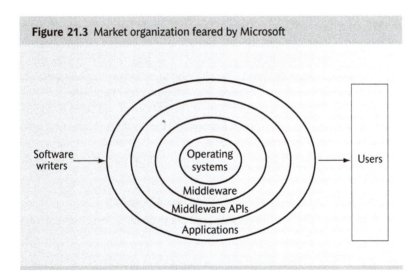

of applications, an operating system developer will create *Application Programming Interfaces* (APIs) that allow programs to call on the features of the operating system to perform various tasks." Judge Jackson's Findings of Fact (¶ 77) indicate that Windows 98 exposed (documented for use by software writers) nearly 10,000 APIs.

BOX   Microsoft Antitrust Timeline

June 1990: FTC initiates investigation of possible collusion between IBM and Microsoft. As the investigation develops, FTC attention focuses on Microsoft marketing practices, among which are:

- preannouncement of products;
- use of licenses specifying payments based on the total number of CPUs shipped, not the number of such CPUs shipped with Microsoft operating systems installed;
- unreasonably long licensing agreements.

February 1990: FTC decides (by a 2–2 vote) to take no action against Microsoft.

August 1993: Justice Department initiates investigation of Microsoft.

August 1995: U.S. District Court Judge Thomas Jackson of the Washington, D.C. U.S. District Court approves a consent decree under which Microsoft agrees not to link the licensing of Windows to other products. Paragraph IV.E.(i) of the consent decree specifies in part:

> Microsoft shall not enter into any License Agreement in which the terms of that agreement are expressly or implied conditioned upon … the licensing of any other Covered Product, operating System Software product or other product (provided, however, that this provision in and of itself shall not be construed to prohibit Microsoft from developing integrated products) . . .

20 October 1997: Department of Justice seeks to fine Microsoft $1 million per day on the ground that Microsoft required PC manufacturers to install and distribute its Internet Explorer as a condition of licensing the Windows operating system, in violation of the August 1995 consent decree.

12 December 1997 Judge Jackson declines to fine Microsoft $1 million per day, issues an injunction requiring Microsoft not to bundle Internet Explorer with Microsoft's operating systems.

18 December 1997: The Department of Justice argues that Microsoft had failed to comply with the court order requiring it to unbundle Internet Explorer and the Windows 95 operating system, by offering unworkable versions of the operating system.

18 May 1998: 20 states and the US government filed new antitrust suits against Microsoft Corp. Complaints include:

- bundling (integrating) Internet Explorer and Windows operating system;
- pressuring OEMs (original equipment manufacturers) not to promote, install, or make available Netscape Navigator.

5 November 1999: Findings of Fact: Microsoft has a monopoly in the market for IBM-compatible PC operating systems, as demonstrated by

- its market share;
- the large amount of software designed to work with Windows operating systems;
- the fact that Microsoft's customers lack viable alternatives.

3 April 2000: Conclusions of Law: Microsoft has monopolized the relevant market, as demonstrated by its record of exclusionary behaviour.

8 June 2000: Judge Jackson orders Microsoft split into two firms, one specializing in operating systems, the other in other products. ≫

> **25 February 2001**: Circuit Court of Appeals begins hearing Microsoft's appeal against the breakup order.
>
> **28 June 2001**: Circuit Court of Appeals:
>
> - upholds finding that Microsoft committed monopolization in violation of US antitrust law;
> - sets aside order that Microsoft be broken up;
> - sends question whether "Microsoft violated § 1 of the Sherman Act by unlawfully tying its browser to its operating system" back to District Court to be considered anew under the rule of reason, since the case offers "the first up-close look at the technological integration of added functionality into software that serves as a platform for third-party applications".
>
> **24 August 2001**: Appeals Court orders new trial (under a new judge) at District Court to settle remaining issues.
>
> **1 November 2001**: Microsoft and the US Department of Justice announce a settlement, the terms of which include (among others):
>
> - Microsoft relaxes contractual restrictions that limited the ability of PC manufacturers to display icons of non-Microsoft products on the PC screen;
> - Microsoft must disclose information about its operating systems that will make it easier for independent software producers to write products to work with those operating systems;
> - Microsoft must disclose information that will allow rival servers to work with PCs driven by Microsoft operating systems;
> - Microsoft will use standard contracts for the 20 largest computer producers;
> - a committee of three computer experts will monitor compliances with the agreement;
> - by the forging of this settlement, the question of the status of bundling operating system and application software under Section 1 remains undecided.

Thus, Figure 21.2 shows the combination of Microsoft operating systems and Microsoft-compatible software, the latter written to take advantage of functions buried within the operating system and accessed via APIs exposed by the operating system and available for the convenience of the software writer, to make Microsoft-software-PC systems that provide services to final consumers. Other Intel-compatible operating systems combine with software and Intel-compatible PCs to make rival PC systems that also offer services to final consumers. Critically, *software written to take advantage of Microsoft operating system functions exposed by Microsoft APIs is incompatible with rival operating systems, and can be made compatible with such systems only with costly modifications ("porting")*. This leads to what Judge Jackson in the Findings of Fact (¶ 30) calls "an intractable 'chicken-and-egg' problem", something that economists call an indirect network externality:[99]

Users do not want to invest in an operating system until it is clear that the system will support generations of applications that will meet their needs, and developers do not want to invest in

---

[99] There is a two-sided market aspect to this market, with producers of operating systems competing to provide platforms upon which the writers and users of software packages interact.

writing or quickly porting applications for an operating system until it is clear that there will be a sizeable and stable market for it.

In the District Court's view, the chicken-and-egg problem created an "applications barrier to entry" that insulated Microsoft from competition in the Intel-compatible PC operating systems market. The applications barrier to entry was one of three factors Judge Jackson relied on to support the conclusion that Microsoft had monopoly power. The other two (Findings of Fact, ¶ 34) were Microsoft's market share and the fact that there was no commercially viable alternative supplier on the market.

Microsoft's conduct

The course of conduct that involved Microsoft with U.S. antitrust authorities was driven by the rise of the Internet and Microsoft's recognition that the market structure depicted in Figure 21.2 is not inherent in the nature of things. It is true that network externalities can lead to an equilibrium market structure with one supplier very much larger than others, and this leaves consumers better off because each consumer finds the product more valuable, the larger the total number of consumers who use the same variety of the product. But the network externalities that underlie Figure 21.2 depend on the incompatibility of APIs across operating systems. The rise of the Internet raised the spectre of a change in technological regime that would make this incompatibility—and with it the basis of Microsoft's dominant position—go away.

The generic challenge was posed by middleware,[100] "[s]oftware that sits between two or more types of software and translates information between them". Middleware (Figure 21.3), written to work with many operating systems, would expose a standardized set of APIs for software writers, who would no longer need to concern themselves with the identity of the operating system whirring away underneath.

Netscape   The wisps on Microsoft's horizon that might have developed into viable middleware were the Netscape Communications Corporation's Navigator web browser and Sun Microsystems' Java programming language. Netscape Navigator was an immediate success after its introduction in December 1994. It exposed a small number of APIs,[101] and was compatible with more than 15 operating systems. The implications were recognized by Microsoft Chairman Bill Gates in an internal Microsoft memo of May 26, 1995, "The Internet Tidal Wave", that became Government Exhibit 20 in District Court (p. 4):[102]

> A new competitor "born" on the Internet is Netscape. Their browser is dominant, with 70% usage share, allowing them to determine which network extensions will catch on. They are pursuing a multi-platform strategy where they move the key API into the client to commoditize the underlying operating system. They have attracted a number of public network operators

---

[100] Durham (2006, p. 554), quoting the definition of the Microsoft Press Computer Dictionary.

[101] The Findings of Fact (¶ 77) indicate that Navigator and Java together exposed less than a thousand APIs.

[102] This paragraph of the memo is widely quoted. The immediately following paragraph, which describes the possible development of an inexpensive device, designed specifically for Web browsing, that would be not use a Microsoft operating system, is equally instructive: "One scary possibility being discussed by Internet fans is whether they should get together and create something far less expensive than a PC which is powerful enough for Web browsing." The operating system for such a less expensive Web browsing device could have become the middleware Microsoft feared—scary.

to use their platform to offer information and directory services. We have to match and beat their offerings including working with MCI, newspapers, and other who are considering their products.

Microsoft undertook a programme to exclude Netscape Navigator from the main and lowest-cost channels by which it might reach users[103] in favour of its own browser, Internet Explorer. Microsoft integrated its browser with its operating systems.[104] In so doing, it explained that the operating system and the browser were (had become) a single product. Yet in 1997, Microsoft concluded an agreement with Apple Computer, Inc., under the terms of which Internet Explorer became the default browser for Apple's Macintosh computer (Findings of Fact, ¶ 351). Internet Explorer for Macintosh plainly was not one product with the Windows family of operating systems. But by ensuring the presence of Internet Explorer on Apple computers, Microsoft made it less attractive for software writers thinking about the Apple market to consider writing programs that would draw on APIs exposed by Netscape Navigator.

Java   Sun Microsystems' Java was intended to develop into fully-fledged middleware (Findings of Fact, ¶ 74): "The inventors of Java at Sun Microsystems intended the technology to enable applications written in the Java language to run on a variety of platforms with minimal porting. . . . The more an application written in Java relies on APIs exposed by the Java class libraries, the less work its developer will need to do to port the application to different operating systems." Java worked out an arrangement with Netscape under which the programs needed for Java to function on a PC were installed along with Navigator. Thus Navigator became the principal vehicle by which Java reached users, and to the extent that Microsoft raised the cost to Navigator of reaching the end user, it did so for Java as well.

But Microsoft specifically targeted Java by setting out to[105] "kill cross-platform Java by growing the polluted Java market". Polluted Java, which Microsoft promoted to software developers, was designed to work with Microsoft operating systems. The strategy of getting a version of Java that is not compatible across platforms out in the market shores up the applications barrier to entry of Figure 21.2, and prevents the commoditization of the operating system market depicted in Figure 21.3.

 BOX   Strategic Behaviour in Pen Computing

The late 1980s saw a first generation of efforts to develop pen computing systems driven by handwriting-recognition software. Although IBM and Apple had their own pen computing projects, one of the most promising was the Silicon Valley start-up GO Corporation's PenPoint system. ≫

---

[103] These channels were original equipment manufacturers, independent software providers, Internet access providers, and Internet hardware providers. See Sections V. F and G of the Findings of Fact.

[104] This either did or did not violate the 1995 consent decree, depending on one's point of view.

[105] This is the "strategic objective" addressed in an internal Microsoft memo introduced as Government Exhibit 259 in District Court.

> ❯❯ PenPoint attracted Microsoft's attention not only because it had a head-start on Microsoft's own Pen Windows, but also because it included an independent—that is, not Windows—operating system.

On 28 June 1990, according to evidence in a 2004 class-action lawsuit, Microsoft Chairman Bill Gales wrote Intel Chairman Andrew S. Grove to discourage Intel investment in GO Corporation (Markoff, 2004): "I guess I've made it very clear that we view an Intel investment in Go as an anti-Microsoft move, both because Go competes with our systems software and because we think it will weaken the 386 PC standard."

The Pen Windows project was organized in early 1990, and its goal was (Edstrom and Eller, 1998, p. 120):

> Kill Go Corp. .... Squashing the competition was not a written policy, but something woven into the ethos of Microsoft. Everyone knew that the company's bread and butter came from DOS, and, eventually, they would realize it would come from Windows. The abiding rule was to kill anyone trying to take that revenue away. The number one mission of Microsoft was to not let anyone else poach on its core asset—the operating systems business. And GO was looking like a serious threat.

At a post-mortem meeting of sorts a few years later, the person in charge of Pen Windows lamented that it had been a disaster (Edstrom and Eller, 1998, p. 144): "[W]e haven't sold a whole lot of copies." His interlocutor replied (Edstrom and Eller, 1998, p. 144):

> This wasn't a thing about making money. ... We were preventing GO from running away with the market. That was our job. ...
> From my view, Pen Windows was a winner. We shut down GO. They spent $75 million pumping up this market, we spent four million shooting them down. They're toast. That company is dead. They won't sell their **** anymore. We did our job.

Sources: Edstrom and Eller (1998); Markoff (2004).

The outcome in District Court

Section 2 To show that a firm had monopolized in violation of Section 2 of the Sherman Act, wrote Judge Jackson, required first a finding that the firm had market power in the relevant market and second a finding that the firm had used anticompetitive means to obtain or maintain that position (Conclusions of Law, I. A). Microsoft's market share and the applications barrier to entry meant it had monopoly power. Microsoft's conduct ("Microsoft strove over a period of approximately four years to prevent middleware technologies from fostering the development of enough full-featured, cross-platform applications to erode the applications barrier") was anticompetitive within the meaning of the Sherman Act. Judge Jackson found that Microsoft's conduct would not have been profit-maximizing, absent its expected impact on rivals, and for that reason was predatory, as far as antitrust law was concerned. Microsoft had monopolized in violation of Section 2.

The other Section 2 charge against Microsoft was that it had attempted to monopolize the browser market, proof of which required showing (Conclusions of Law, I. B):[106]

---

[106] Not set off as a list in the original. The Court quotes Spectrum Sports, Inc. *v.* McQuillan, 506 U.S. 447, 456 (1993).

(1) "that the defendant has engaged in predatory or anticompetitive conduct with

(2) a specific intent to monopolize", and

(3) that there is a "dangerous probability" that the defendant will succeed in achieving monopoly power.

The Court had already concluded that Microsoft had engaged in predatory behaviour. Evidence of intent to monopolize lay in the inevitable consequences of that behaviour:

> ... Microsoft's strategy for protecting the applications barrier became one of expanding Internet Explorer's share of browser usage—and simultaneously depressing Navigator's share—to an extent sufficient to demonstrate to developers that Navigator would never emerge as the standard software employed to browse the Web.

Judge Jackson found that Internet Explorer's rising market share (above 50 per cent at the time of the decision) confirmed the conclusion that there was a dangerous probability that Microsoft would succeed in monopolizing the browser market. Microsoft had therefore attempted to monopolize in violation of Section 2.

Section 1   Tying is a *per se* violation of Section 1 if four conditions are met:[107]

(1) two separate "products" are involved;

(2) the defendant affords its customers no choice but to take the tied product in order to obtain the tying product;

(3) the arrangement affects a substantial volume of interstate commerce; and

(4) the defendant has "market power" in the tying product market.

As regards the first requirement, the Court rejected the argument that product design trumped consumer demand as far as market definition was concerned:[108]

> [P]roduct and market definitions [are] to be ascertained by reference to evidence of consumers' perception of the nature of the products and the markets for them ... . the commercial reality is that consumers today perceive operating systems and browsers as separate "products," for which there is separate demand. .... notwithstanding the fact that the software code supplying their discrete functionalities can be commingled in virtually infinite combinations ... .

On the second point, Microsoft protested that it had not forced anyone to take anything. Internet Explorer was not, in the strict sense, purchased at all, it was simply there along with the rest of the Windows 98 operating system. Judge Jackson rejected this argument. It was not using a tying arrangement to charge a higher price that infringed the law; the focus of the law was exclusion: "[T]he purpose of the Supreme Court's 'forcing' inquiry is to expose those product bundles that raise the cost or difficulty of doing business for would-be competitors to prohibitively high levels, thereby depriving consumers of the opportunity to

---

[107] Conclusions of Law, II. A; not set off as a list in the original. This is the rule of *Eastman Kodak* and *Jefferson Parish Hospital*, which we discuss in Chapter 24.

[108] The Conclusions of Law consider this point at some length, as Judge Jackson declines to follow indications given in a prior related decision by the D.C. Circuit Court of Appeals, U.S. *v.* Microsoft, 147 F.3d 935 (D.C. Cir. 1998) (*Microsoft II*).

evaluate a competing product on its relative merits." The third and fourth requirements for a tying violation being satisfied in a straightforward way, Microsoft had tied two products in violation of Section 1.

Microsoft concluded exclusive dealing contracts with the gatekeepers of various distribution channels through which Netscape Navigator might most easily have reached users. The government viewed these contracts as a violation of Section 1. As Judge Jackson read the guiding precedents "unless the evidence demonstrates that Microsoft's agreements excluded Netscape altogether from access to roughly forty percent of the browser market, the Court should decline to find such agreements in violation of § 1". The evidence did not show exclusion to this extent, so Microsoft's exclusive dealing contracts did not violate Section 1.

Proposed remedy

The District Court's Final Judgment ordered that Microsoft be divided into two firms, one in the market for operating systems and the other in the market for applications.[109] Judge Jackson gave four reasons for favouring breakup as a remedy. Three of these focused on Microsoft's character (or lack thereof):[110]

- First ... Microsoft does not yet concede that any of its business practices violated the Sherman Act.

- Second, there is credible evidence in the record to suggest that Microsoft, convinced of its innocence, continues to do business as it has in the past, and may yet do to other markets what it has already done in the PC operating system and browser markets.

- Third, Microsoft has proved untrustworthy in the past. In earlier proceedings in which a preliminary injunction was entered, Microsoft's purported compliance with that injunction while it was on appeal was illusory and its explanation disingenuous.

Two distinct parts can be distinguished in the fourth reason: competent authorities on the winning side of the case proposed breakup as a remedy, and the Court was convinced that breakup would improve market performance:[111]

- Plaintiffs won the case, and for that reason alone have some entitlement to a remedy of their choice. Moreover, plaintiffs' proposed final judgment is the collective work product of senior antitrust law enforcement officials of the United States Department of Justice and the Attorneys General of 19 states, in conjunction with multiple consultants. These officials are by reason of office obliged and expected to consider—and to act in—the public interest; Microsoft is not.

- The proposed final judgment is represented to the Court as incorporating provisions employed successfully in the past, and it appears to the Court to address all the principal

---

[109] There were also conduct elements to the District Court's remedy; see U.S. District Court for the District of Columbia, *Final Judgment*.

[110] U.S. District Court for the District of Columbia, *Memorandum and Order*, 7 June 2000; downloaded from URL <http://www.usdoj.gov/atr/cases/f219700/219731.htm>, pp. 3–4; not set off as bullet points in the original.

[111] U.S. District Court for the District of Columbia, *Memorandum and Order*, 7 June 2000; downloaded from URL <http://www.usdoj.gov/atr/cases/f219700/219731.htm>, p. 5; footnote omitted; not set off as bullet points in the original.

objectives of relief in such cases, namely, to terminate the unlawful conduct, to prevent its repetition in the future, and to revive competition in the relevant markets.

Because it thought that such hearings would do little to clarify the issue, and over Microsoft's objection, the District Court ordered its remedy without holding additional hearings at which both sides could offer expert testimony on the form a remedy might take. But it stayed implementation of the breakup order to allow Microsoft to appeal.

Microsoft III[112]

Just over a year after the District Court's Final Judgment, the Court of Appeals for the District of Columbia issued its ruling on Microsoft's appeal. It upheld one of the two Section 2 findings of the District Court, that Microsoft's campaigns to exclude Netscape Navigator and fracture Java aimed to maintain its monopoly position in the market for operating systems for Intel-compatible personal computers. It reversed the District Court's finding that Microsoft had attempted to monopolize the internet browser market in violation of Section 2.

One of the elements of an attempted monopolization violation is a dangerous probability of success. The District Court had largely relied on the finding that Microsoft had committed a monopolization violation as demonstrating that it had a dangerous probability of monopolizing the internet browser market. As the Circuit Court read the law, what the government needed to do (and had not) to make its attempted monopolization case was carry out a full-fledged analysis, defining a relevant market and exploring the nature of barriers to entry into that market, distinct and independent of the analysis that had been carried out for the monopolization charge.

There remained Microsoft's appeal against the finding that it had tied the marketing of its operating system and its internet browser in violation of Section 1 of the Sherman Act. Judge Jackson had determined that the conditions required to find a *per se* tying violation were satisfied. Microsoft argued that there were efficiency advantages to integrating the two products. The Circuit Court took the view that a *per se* approach should be taken only where long experience showed that the practice in question unambiguously worsened market performance, and sent the issue back to District Court to be decided under the rule of reason (253 F. 3d 34 at 90–91).

Settlement and remedy

But the rule of reason status of tying in high-technology industries was never examined by the District Court. The U.S. government announced a settlement of the Microsoft case on 1 November 2001. The Bush II Administration took a restricted view of what it had to work with (James, 2001, p. 60):

> Given what was left in the case—essentially a series of heavy-handed contracting practices with computer manufacturers and software developers, unlawful when undertaken to protect the operating system monopoly—a conduct remedy seemed all that could be secured, let alone justified.

---

[112] U.S. *v.* Microsoft 253 F.3d 34 (2001) (*Microsoft III*). *Microsoft II*, U.S. *v.* Microsoft 147 F.3d 935 (D.C. Cir. 1998) was an appeal by Microsoft against a District Court order that it not tie its operating system and its web browser. *Microsoft I*, U.S. *v.* Microsoft 56 F.3d 1448 (1995), was an appeal on the way to the August 1995.

The status of tying in high-technology industries was "not left in the case" only because of the decision to settle. The conduct remedy addressed the specific practices behind the monopolization violation. Under the terms of the settlement,[113] Microsoft was obliged to:

- license its operating systems on uniform terms and at uniform prices for the 20 largest original equipment manufacturers;

- give original equipment manufacturers and users the ability to hide Microsoft software (such as browsers), in favour of rival software;

- disclose application programming interfaces and communication protocols that its own software used to interact with Microsoft operating systems; and

- license any of its intellectual property required to make the terms of the Final Judgment effective on reasonable and nondiscriminatory terms.

The Final Judgment also provided for creation of a three-member Technical Committee to monitor Microsoft's compliance.

The terms of the settlement were widely regarded as a slap on Microsoft's wrist. Even so, at the end of January 2008 (just more than six years after the terms of the settlement were embodied in the District Court's Final Judgment), the Court found it necessary to extend monitoring of Microsoft's compliance for an additional two years, with Judge Kollar-Kotelly commenting that[114] "Although the technical documentation project is complex and novel, it is clear, at least to the Court, that Microsoft is culpable for this inexcusable delay". By this time, however, the focus of public policy toward Microsoft had moved across the Atlantic.

Where the U.S. case went wrong

On one level, of course, the Microsoft case went wrong at the end, because those charged with enforcing a deterrence-based antitrust policy settled it in a cavalier manner.[115] By settling the most visible antitrust case in a generation with a slap on the wrist, the government sent a clear signal that the odds of a tough penalty, if an antitrust violation is detected and successfully prosecuted, were not high.

At a deeper level, however, the case went wrong because both sides drew back from confronting the distinguishing characteristics of information-technology industries (Economides, 2001, pp. 18–19):

> Early in the trial, Microsoft argued that the concept of market definition for antitrust purposes was inappropriate for the dynamic setting of software markets. This position was not very well articulated, and hardly appropriate for a District Court Judge who was very unlikely to subscribe to a major revision to traditional application of antitrust law. Later in the trial, Microsoft argued through its economic witness that platforms rather than operating systems were the appropriate

---

[113] U.S. District Court for the District of Columbia, Final Judgment, 12 November 2002; downloaded from URL <http://www.usdoj.gov/atr/cases/f200400/200457.htm>.

[114] *PC World*, "Judge extends Microsoft antitrust supervision", 31 January 2008, downloaded from URL <http://www.pcworld.com/article/id,142004-page,1/article.html>.

[115] Throughout U.S. legal proceedings, Microsoft insisted that it was technically impossible to separate the Windows operating system and Internet Explorer. In June 2009, Microsoft announced it would market a version of the Windows operating system in the European Union that did not include Internet Explorer. Microsoft Deputy General Counsel Dave Heiner explained (emphasis added): "But we're committed to launching Windows 7 on time in Europe, so we need to address the legal realities in Europe, *including the risk of large fines*."

domain for antitrust analysis, stressing the fact that functions embedded in platforms are used by ISVs to cut their costs of writing applications. However, a full and coherent view of a dynamic market definition was never presented.

In retrospect,[116] one could make a cogent argument that Microsoft and other producers of operating systems operated in a two-sided market (see footnote 99). In such a market, for a firm to charge a zero or negative price to users on one side of the market—as Microsoft did in providing development tools to software writers—*might* be devoid of strategic anticompetitive purpose (Section 3.8). Whether this was the case in *Microsoft* is a question courts did not confront.

Similarly, according to the Circuit Court of Appeals in *Microsoft III* (p. 83), the government argued that network externalities might create barriers to entry into the browser market, but the District Court did not adopt that approach in its Findings of Fact. Network effects are mentioned in the Findings of Fact in connection with barriers to entry into the operating system (¶ 39), largely to support the existence of an applications barrier to entry. The existence of barriers to entry is a condition for a firm to have market power.[117] The welfare implications of a barrier to entry rooted in network externalities are substantially different from the welfare implications of conventional barriers to entry. What this difference might mean for antitrust policy, if anything, is another issue that was never joined.[118]

Aron and Wildman (1999) argue that the government opted to fit its case into the received framework of predation violations, precluding consideration of the kind of strategic bundling issue that contemporary economic analysis highlights as being at least as likely to worsen market performance. The District Court followed the government down this road. As a result, even if an appropriate penalty had been applied to Microsoft for its violation of Section 2 of the Sherman Act, a case that could have provided an ideal forum for considering the issues raised by the application of antitrust to information-technology industries missed the opportunity to do so.

21.4.2 EU

The Commission Decision

Markets   The EU proceedings against Microsoft involved many of the actors from the U.S. case, but performing roles in a different play. With its decision[119] of 24 March 2004, the European Commission found that Microsoft had abused a dominant position, in violation of Article 102 of the EC Treaty, by its refusal to supply Sun Microsystems with information

---

[116] Although many of the building blocks of models of two-sided markets existed in the economics literature on network externalities, those models themselves had yet to be developed at the time of the District Court proceedings.

[117] For legal precedents, see the Findings of Fact, I.A.1 and *Microsoft III*, II.A. For the economic argument, see Section 2.3.5.

[118] It is not obvious that considering this point would have comforted Microsoft's defence. That there are consumer-benefiting network externalities in the market for operating systems does not imply that the lead operating system and various types of software used in connection with the lead operating system should be produced by the same firm. Further, one way to view the Section 2 monopoly maintenance complaint, the charge sustained in *Microsoft III*, is that Microsoft undertook a campaign to strategically maintain network economies to the detriment of consumers.

[119] *Microsoft* Commission Decision of 24 March 2004 Case COMP/C-3/37/792.

required by a work group server[120] to interact with personal computers driven by the Windows family of operating systems and by its bundling of Windows Media Player and Windows operating systems.

The Commission Notice on Market Definition[121] requires that in drawing market boundaries, the Commission evaluate the extent to which consumers regard products as substitutes and the extent to which suppliers of different products could switch production from one variety to another[122] "in the short term without incurring significant additional costs or risks in response to small and permanent changes in relative prices".[123] Based on market surveys carried out on its behalf, on information submitted by interested third parties, and information submitted by Microsoft,[124] the Commission distinguished three product markets relevant to the decision (¶ 323):

 BOX   Microsoft Competition Policy Timeline

10 December 1998: Sun Microsystems complains to European Commission that Microsoft has a dominant position in the market for personal computer operating systems, and that it has abused that position by witholding information needed to make Sun work group server operating stations interact effectively with Microsoft's Windows PC operating systems.

1 August 2000: Commission sends a Statement of Objections to Microsoft, focusing on the possibility that Microsoft has abused its dominant position by witholding interoperability information.

30 August 2001: A second Statement of Objections, continuing concern about Microsoft supply of interoperability information and adding the possibility of abusive tying of Microsoft's Media Player to the Windows operating system, supplants the first.

(**8 March 2002**: Sun Microsystems files private U.S. antitrust suit against Microsoft.)

(**18 December 2003**: Real Networks files private U.S. antitrust suit against Microsoft.)

24 March 2004: Commission Decision holds that Microsoft has abused its dominant position in the market for PC operating systems by refusing to provide interoperability information to competitors in the work group server operating system market and by tying Windows Media Player with Windows.

(**2 April 2004**: Microsoft pays Sun Microsystems $1.6 billion to settle private U.S. lawsuit.)

(**11 October 2005**: Microsoft pays RealNetworks $751 million to settle private U.S. lawsuit.)

22 December 2005: Commission threatens Microsoft with daily fines of up to €2 million retroactive to 15 December 2005 for failure to provide documentation on interoperability.

---

[120] In its decision, (paragraph 53) the Commission explains that "'work group server services' ... are the basic infrastructure services ... used by office workers in their day-to-day work, namely sharing files stored on servers, sharing printers, and ... how users ... access these services and other services of the network", while 'work group server operating systems' are operating systems designed and marketed to deliver these services collectively to relatively small numbers of client PCs linked together in small to medium-sized networks".

[121] Commission notice on the definition of relevant market for the purposes of Community competition law (OJ C 372, 9.12.1997).

[122] Commission decision, ¶ 322, quoting the Commission Notice on Market Definition.

[123] This is the SSNIP (Small Significant Non-transitory Increase in Price) test. See Section 22.3.3 for discussion of the Commisson Notice.

[124] See ¶¶ 7–11 of the Commission decision.

> **12 July 2006**: Commission imposes penalty payment of €280.5 million on Microsoft for continued non-compliance with March 2004 Decision.
>
> **1 March 2007**: Commission warns Microsoft of further penalties over unreasonable pricing of interoperability information.
>
> **17 September 2007**: Court of First Instance upholds Commission decision.
>
> **27 February 2008**: Commission fines Microsoft € 899 million for failure to comply with the decision of 24 March 2004.

- the market for client personal computer operating systems;
- the market for work group server operating systems;
- the market for streaming media players.

For all three product markets,[125] the geographic market was worldwide.

Microsoft's market position For EC competition policy, a firm with a dominant position is able[126] "to prevent effective competition being maintained on the relevant market by affording it the power to behave to an appreciable extent independently of its competitors, its customers, and ultimately of the consumers". Microsoft admitted that it had a dominant position in the market for personal computer operating systems. The Commission documented this by noting Microsoft's extraordinarily large market share (Table 21.1), indicating the absence of effective actual competition, as well as barriers to entry, among which the applications barrier to entry, indicating the absence of effective potential competition.

The Commission cited Microsoft Chairman Bill Gates' own testimony that Microsoft had long recognized the existence of network effects:[127]

> Early on, [Microsoft] recognized that [, as] more products became available and more information could be exchanged, more consumers would be attracted to the platform, which would in turn attract more investment in product development for the platform. Economists call this a 'network effect', but at the time we called it the 'positive feedback loop'.

Not only did Microsoft recognize the existence of network effects, but it understood the strategic role of applications program interfaces to maintain indirect network effects and block effective competition. The Commission quoted an internal Microsoft memo to the effect that:[128,129]

---

[125] Once again following the Commission Notice on the Market Definition, "the area in which the undertakings concerned are involved in the supply and demand of products or services, in which the conditions of competition are sufficiently homogeneous and which can be distinguished from neighbouring areas because the conditions of competition are appreciably different in those areas".

[126] *Hoffmann-La Roche; United Brands.*

[127] ¶ 451 of the Commission decision, quoting the Direct Testimony of Bill Gates, Civil Action No. 98-1233 (CKK), at paragraph 25.

[128] Commisison decision, paragraph 463, quoting a 1997 memo to Bill Gates written by Microsoft's C++ general manager, Aaron Contorer.

[129] In the same 1997 memo, Mr. Contorer wrote that "In economics there is a well-understood concept called switching costs—how much it costs for a trading partner to change partners. Our philosophy on switching costs is very clear: we want low switching costs for customers who want to start using our platform, and we want to

Table 21.1 Personal computer operating system market shares (per cent)

Operating system	2000		2001		2002	
	Units	**Revenues**	**Units**	**Revenues**	**Units**	**Revenues**
Windows	92.1	92.8	93.2	95.4	93.8	96,1
Apple (Mac OS)	3.9	3.3	3.1	2.4	2.9	2.2
Linux	1.7	0.5	2.3	0.4	2.8	0.4
Others	2.4	3.3	1.3	1.8	0.5	1.4
Total	100.0	100.0	100.0	100.0	100.0	100.0

Source: Commission Decision Case COMP/C-3/37/792, Para. 434, based on IDC, Worldwide Client and Server Operating Environments Forecast, 2002–2007.

The Windows API is so broad, so deep, and so functional that most [Independent Software Vendors] would be crazy not to use it. And it is so deeply embedded in the source code of many Windows apps that there is a huge switching cost to using a different operating system instead. [...]

It is this switching cost that has given customers the patience to stick with Windows through all our mistakes, our buggy drivers, our high [total cost of operation], our lack of a sexy vision at times, and many other difficulties. [...] Customers constantly evaluate other desktop platforms, [but] it would be so much work to move over that they hope we just improve Windows rather than force them to move.

In short, without this exclusive franchise called the Windows API, we would have been dead a long time ago.

Microsoft protested that traditional antitrust notions of dominance were inappropriate for information technology industries, where an apparently dominant firm might be swept away at any moment by a technological revolution. The Commission's response was succinct:[130] "Such an argument is invalid. Even if it were to be the case that a dominant position might be limited in time, this does not in itself constitute a limitation to the present market strength of the dominant company." The Commission concluded that Microsoft had a dominant position in the world market for PC operating systems.

Depending on the source of the estimates, Microsoft's share of the market for work group server operating systems was at least 50 per cent; most measures placed it at between 60 and 75 per cent. Direct and indirect network externalities were a source of barriers to entry. Further (¶ 524):

---

provide so much unique value that there are in effect high costs of deciding to move to a different platform" (<http://edge-op.org/iowa/www.iowaconsumercase.org/010807/PLEX_5906.pdf>, downloaded 5 April 2008).

[130] ¶ 469 of the Commission Decision, emphasis in the original. In fn. 588, the Commission noted the similar response of the U.S. Circuit Court of Appeals for the District of Columbia to the same argument in *Microsoft III*, 253 F.3d 34 at 57.

Microsoft's behaviour ... of withholding interoperability information also builds an additional (artificial) barrier to entry in the market. ... there is a strong need for client PC operating systems and work group server operating systems to interoperate. Therefore, if a work group server operating system vendor encounters obstacles to interoperability, these will act [as] a barrier to entry in the market.

The Commission concluded that Microsoft also had a dominant position in the world market for work group server systems.

Abuse

Refusal to supply interoperability information   Microsoft's refusal to provide interoperability information to server providers was a deliberate exclusionary refusal to deal, much like that at issue in *Commercial Solvents* (Lawsky, 2007):

> It used to be that Microsoft did not build servers, but gave outside server producers the information they needed to connect with Windows. Microsoft eventually entered the server market. After that, rivals complained that when Microsoft offered new versions of its operating system, it stopped providing information they needed to interconnect. Microsoft's market share jumped and big competitors quit ...

Article 102 is explicit that "limiting technical development to the prejudice of consumers" is an abuse of a dominant position. In the view of the Commission, the effect of Microsoft's refusal to provide Sun Microsystems with interoperability information was precisely to limit technical development to the prejudice of consumers. Microsoft made it more difficult for Sun to develop work group server operating system technology that some consumers might have preferred to Microsoft's products. Sun might, of course, have developed substitute varieties that consumers, by and large, did not prefer to Microsoft's products. Microsoft's refusal to provide interoperability information meant that consumers were denied the opportunity to manifest their preferences, and that Sun was denied the opportunity to test its ingenuity in the marketplace.

Microsoft's refusal to provide competitors with interoperability information worked to the detriment of consumers not only because it denied consumers the option to select the products that would have been developed by those competitors, but also (¶ 725) because Microsoft itself, insulated from product-market competition, would have a reduced incentive to innovate.

Microsoft sought to explain its refusal to supply interoperability information the protection of its intellectual property rights:[131],[132]

> The objective justification for Microsoft's refusal to disclose its intellectual property rights is self-evident: those rights are meant to protect the outcome of billions of dollars of R&D investments in software features, functions and technologies. This is the essence of intellectual property right protection. Disclosure would negate that protection and eliminate future incentives to invest in the creation of more intellectual property.

---

[131] ¶ 709, footnote omitted.

[132] Microsoft made the "no leverage of market power" argument, that it had no incentive to foreclose competitors, since it could not earn additional economic profit by doing so. The Commission considered and rejected this argument at ¶¶ 764–768.

For the Commission, this argument was not compelling:[133,134]

> The central function of intellectual property rights is to protect the moral rights in a right-holder's work and ensure a reward for the creative effort. But it is also an essential objective of intellectual property law that creativity should be stimulated for the general public good. A refusal by an undertaking to grant a licence may, under exceptional circumstances, be contrary to the general public good by constituting an abuse of a dominant position with harmful effects on innovation and on consumers.

The Commission concluded that Microsoft had a dominant position, which it had abused, and that its conduct had no objective justification.

Tying Windows Media Player and Windows Operating Systems   For tying to abuse a dominant position in violation of Article 102 required that four conditions be met (¶ 794, not set off as a list in the original):

(i)   the tying and tied goods are two separate products;

(ii) the undertaking concerned is dominant in the tying product market;

(iii) the undertaking concerned does not give customers a choice to obtain the tying product without the tied product; and

(iv) tying forecloses competition.

It was relatively straightforward for the Commission to conclude that conditions (ii) and (iii) were satisfied. The Commission had already concluded that Microsoft had a dominant position in the market for personal computer operating systems. Condition (iii) was satisfied by the nature of the licences Microsoft granted to original equipment manufacturers who wished to install Windows on their products: as a condition of licensing Windows, original equipment manufacturers were obliged to ship PCs with Windows Media Player installed.

Microsoft argued that the first condition—two separate products—was not satisfied, since Windows Media Player and Windows were one integrated product. The Commission's analysis was to examine demand-side and supply-side substitutability. There was good evidence that consumers regarded streaming media players and personal computer operating systems as distinct products. There were firms that produced streaming media players, substitutes for Windows Media Player, that were not part of a personal computer operating system. Microsoft produced a version of Windows Media Player to run on Apple's Mac operating systems. Microsoft itself described Windows Media Player as a stand-alone program.[135] The Commission rejected Microsoft's argument and concluded that condition (i) was satisfied.

Regarding condition (iv), the Commission first cited the European Court of Justice in *Hoffmann-La Roche* to the effect that (¶ 835) "it constitutes an abuse when an undertaking in a dominant position directly or indirectly ties its customer by a supply obligation since this

---

[133] On intellectual property rights see Chapters 15 and 25.

[134] In U.S. District Court, Microsoft put forward the defence that its exclusionary contracts were justified by the copyright it held over its software. Judge Jackson dismissed this argument with the observation that (Conclusions of Law, p. 12, emphasis in original) "the *validity* of Microsoft's copyrights has never been in doubt; the issue is what, precisely, they protect".

[135] See fn. 930 of the Commission Decision.

deprives the customer of the ability to choose freely his sources of supply and denies other producers access to the market". The Commission found that this was precisely the effect of tying Windows Media Player to Windows (¶ 842):

> [T]ying [Windows Media Player] with the dominant Windows makes [Windows Media Player] the platform of choice for complementary content and applications which in turn risks fore-closing competition in the market for media players. This has spillover effects on competition in related products such as media encoding and management software (often server-side), but also in client PC operating systems for which media players compatible with quality content are an important application. Microsoft's tying practice creates a serious risk of foreclosing com-petition and stifling innovation.

The economic argument that is made here is the same as that made by Judge Jackson in the U.S. antitrust case: tying preserves a situation in which software writers have no incentive to use application programming interfaces exposed by non-Windows software, so preserving the applications barrier to entry and the network effects that are the source of Microsoft's dominance, to the detriment of consumers.

All four requirements for tying to constitute an abuse in the sense of Article 102 were satisfied, so Microsoft's tying was an abuse of a dominant position.

Remedies The Commission ordered Microsoft to make interoperability information avail-able at reasonable cost and on a non-discriminatory basis, and it ordered Microsoft to offer a version of the Windows operating system that did not include Windows Media Player. In addition, the Commission fined Microsoft € 497.2 million. The Commission arrived at this figure beginning with a base fine of €165.7 million, based on the seriousness of Microsoft's abuses. The fine was doubled to deter future violations by Microsoft.[136] Finally, the fine was increased by an additional 50 per cent, to allow for the duration of the offenses.

Aftermath Microsoft dragged its feet complying with the Commission's order, which it appealed to the Court of First Instance. The Commission imposed additional fines for non-compliance. On 20 April 2007, EU Competition Commissioner Neelie Kroes raised the pos-sibility that the Commission might break up Microsoft:

> Question: What has the Commission learned about remedies in refusal to supply cases from its experiences in the Microsoft case?
> Reply: First of all, I would like to stress that this is a highly exceptional circumstance—in fifty years of EU antitrust policy, we have never before encountered a company that has refused to comply with a Commission Decision. ... there could be a situation in which a dominant company has repeatedly abused its dominant position. Or where it has consistently failed to comply with a behavioural remedy despite repeated enforcement action. From this it could be reasonable to draw the conclusion that behavioural remedies are ineffective and that a structural remedy is warranted.

---

[136] The magnitude of the fine would also tend to deter violations by other firms, quite the opposite of the settle-ment of the U.S. case.

On 17 September 2007, the Court of First Instance upheld all substantive elements of the Commission's decision.[137] One aspect of the Commission's decision was annulled. The Commission decision envisaged establishment of an independent monitor, to be paid for by Microsoft, to keep track of Microsoft's compliance. Microsoft argued, and the Court of First Instance agreed, that in this part of its decision the Commission had exceeded its authority. On all other points—the nature of the abuses, the remedies, the fine—the Court of First Instance upheld the Commission. A month later, on 22 October 2007, Microsoft announced that it would not appeal the Court of First Instance decision to the European Court of Justice. In February 2008, the Commission fined Microsoft an additional € 899 million for non-compliance with the Commission's March 2004 decision.

The extent to which Microsoft will comply with the Commission's decision remains to be seen. Even if it does, its history ensures its future contact with antitrust and competition policy. In 2004, Novell, Inc., which purchased the word-processing software program Word-Perfect in 1994 and sold in it 1996, filed a private antitrust suit against Microsoft, claiming that Microsoft withheld interoperability information needed to make WordPerfect run with Windows operating systems. In January, 2008, the U.S. Supreme Court rejected Microsoft's appeals and indicated that Novell's suit could go forward. In the same month, following complaints by the Norwegian web browser company Opera Software and the European Committee for Interoperable Systems (ECIS), the European Commission opened investigation into the possibility that Microsoft had abused its dominant position in operating systems to falsify competition with Microsoft Office and by tying Internet Explorer to Windows.

SUMMARY

Predatory behaviour by the Standard Oil Company was a main motivation for passage of the Sherman Act. Standard Oil was broken up in the first landmark Sherman Act Section 2 decision, a decision that graced U.S. antitrust with the rule of reason. In application, this rule has been applied with at times excessive indulgence (*U.S. Steel*), at times with excessive severity (*Alcoa*). Subsequent decisions have found a monopolization violation of Section 2 where a firm has monopoly power and has acquired it by anticompetitive conduct. To show attempted monopolization in violation of Section 2 requires, in addition to demonstrating anticompetitive conduct, showing an intent to monopolize and a dangerous probability of success. U.S. courts are willing to characterize prices as predatory if they are below some measure of unit cost and if there is evidence of an ability to recoup profit lost due to predation in the same market in which the alleged predation took place. Strategic implications of pricing policies, and the possibility that recoupment might take place in a related market, are treated with scepticism. Loyalty rebates are viewed through a lens that is colored by the treatment of predatory pricing.

Article 102 of the EC Treaty condemns abuses of a dominant position, including loyalty rebates, excessive prices, predation, refusal to deal, and extension of public monopoly beyond its intended reach. EC competition policy has been willing to conclude that firms are dominant, in the sense of having the discretion to engage in strategic anticompetitive conduct, at lower market shares than U.S. antitrust has been willing to concede that firms have market power. EC competition policy has been willing, to an extent greater than U.S. antitrust, to condemn conduct as abusive where economic analysis suggests

---

[137] Microsoft *v.* Commission of the European Communities Case T-201/04 Judgment of the Court of First Instance 17 September 2007 (*Microsoft*).

that this must be the case. The application of Article 102 thus serves to improve market performance, although it seems fair to say that the underlying goal of Article 102 is to safeguard the process of EC market integration.

STUDY POINTS

- Monopolization:
  - Rule of reason (Section 21.2.1)
  - *Standard Oil*, *U.S. Steel* (Section 21.2.1)
  - Conduct *Alcoa*, *United Shoe Machinery* (Section 21.2.1)
  - Areeda-Turner rule, *Matsushita*, *Brooke Group*, recoupment, predatory bidding (Section 21.2.2)
  - Refusal to deal (21.2.2)
  - Loyalty rebates (Section 21.2.2)
- Article 102
  - Loyalty rebates (Section 21.3.1)
  - Excessive price (Section 21.3.2)
  - Predation (Section 21.3.3)
  - Refusal to deal (Section 21.3.4)
  - Public monopolies (Section 21.3.5)
- Comparing antitrust and competition policy
  - Travel Agent Loyalty Program(me)s (Section 21.3.1)
  - Microsoft (Section 21.4)

DISCUSSION TOPICS

(a) *Berkey Photo* (603 F.2d 263 (1979)), *Calcomp* (613 F. 2d 727 (1979)), and *Eastman Kodak* (504 U.S. 451 (1992)) are instructive private U.S. monopolization actions.

(b) In addition to *Commercial Solvents* ([1974] ECR 223, [1974] 1 CMLR 309), *Télémarketing* ([1985] ECR 3261), *Tiercé Ladbroke* ([1997] ECR p. II-923), and *Bronner* ([1998] ECR I-7791) illustrate EC competition policy treatment of refusals to deal.

(c) As background to the treatment of refusals to deal in U.S. antitrust, see the essential facilities decisions *Terminal Railroad* (U.S. *v*. Terminal Railroad Association 224 U.S. 383 (1912)), *Associated Press* (Associated Press *et al*. *v*. U.S. 326 U.S. 1 (1945)), and *Otter Tail* (Otter Tail Power Co. *v*. U.S. 410 U.S. 366 (1973)).

FURTHER READING

On the history of the Standard Oil Company, see among many others Gibson (1886), Montague (1902, 1903), Tarbell (1925), Hildy and Hildy (1955), Chandler (1977, pp. 321–326; 1990, pp. 92–104), Bringhurst (1979), and Pratt (1980). The discussion of Section 21.2.1 mainly follows Granitz and Klein (1996); see also Sullivan (1940, pp. 281–297), Nevins (1940, Volume I, pp. 321–327, 358–359), Robinson (1941, Chapter IX), Helfman (1950), or Maybee (1974, Part IV). Reksulak *et al*. (2004) analyse the remedy in Standard Oil (concluding that the remedy was ineffective, and that this was anticipated by contemporary financial markets). Raymond (1911) provides a contemporary view of the *Standard Oil* and *American Tobacco* decisions. On the *Standard Oil* remedy, see Johnson (1976); on the gradual emergence of rivalry among the survivor companies, see Dixon (1967).

On the formation of the United States Steel Corporation, see among others Meade (1901), Parsons and Ray (1975), McCraw and Reinhardt (1989), Chandler (1990, pp. 127–138), and Chernow (1990, pp. 82–86). On the aluminum industry, see among others Wallace (1937), Perry (1980), and Smith (1988). For background material on 3M, see Huck (1955).

For comments on or alternatives to the Areeda-Turner rule, see Williamson (1977b), Baumol (1979, 1996), and Joskow and Klevorick (1979). The appendices to Leibeler (1986) survey U.S. antitrust predation decisions from 1975 through early 1986.

Beckenkamp and Maier-Rigaud (2006) report experimental evidence consistent with the view that loyalty rebate schemes have exclusionary effects.

Gal (2004, p. 377) lists Article 102 decisions in which the exercise of market power was held to be an abuse. On applications of Article 102 generally, see DG Competition (2005), O'Donoghue and Padilla (2006). See García Gallego and Geogantzis (1999) for a summary of the facts and critique of *Tetra Pak II*.

On the U.S. Microsoft antitrust cases, see among many others Gilbert and Katz (2001), Whinston (2001), and Bresnahan (2002). For contributions and references to the large literature on possible remedies in the U.S. Microsoft case, see the Spring 2001 special issue of the *George Mason Law Review*, Bresnahan (2001a, b), and Shelanski and Sidak (2001).

MERGER POLICY

How dreadful it is when the right judge judges wrong.

Sophocles

22.1 Introduction

At its origins, U.S. antitrust adopted a minimalist approach to the control of market structure. It prohibited strategic entry-deterring behaviour—in general with the Section 2 Sherman Act prohibition of monopolization and the Section 5 FTC Act prohibition of unfair methods of competition, and specifically as regards practices prohibited by the Clayton Act "where the effect may be substantially to lessen competition". But as long as these restrictions on conduct were adhered to, U.S. antitrust was prepared to live with whatever market structure resulted from rivalry in the marketplace. European Community competition policy similarly began without any explicit merger control authority.

Here we review the process by which antitrust and competition policy moved from passive to active control of merger activity. We examine some of the milestones in the development of merger control policy, a case in which the two jurisdictions reached different conclusions about the same merger, and factors affecting the effectiveness of merger remedies.

22.2 United States

22.2.1 The Original Clayton Act Section 7

The original Section 7 of the Clayton Act embodied a passive approach to merger control. This "holding company" provision made mergers *carried out by manipulations of financial shares* illegal "where in any line of commerce or in any activity affecting commerce in any section of the country, the effect of such acquisition may be substantially to lessen competition, or to tend to create a monopoly".

The applicability of the original Section 7 to stock but not asset mergers is sometimes (for example, Kefauver, 1948) described as "the assets loophole", a kind of inexplicable oversight on the part of the 1914 Congress that passed the Clayton Act. This is a misreading of congressional intent. Section 7 was *not* intended as a general merger control provision: its purpose was to block covert acquisitions of control, to avoid situations in which firms that appeared to be independent in fact served a common master.[1] Fundamentally, it was an application of the publicity approach to the control of market structure.

22.2.2 Celler-Kefauver

Rise of support for structural merger control

Backlash against the NRA   The Great Depression saw an active business campaign to roll back the reach of the antitrust law, a campaign that enjoyed fleeting success with the National Industrial Recovery Act, the National Recovery Administration and the rash of government-sponsored and trade-association administered cartels that accompanied it.

Experience with the actual workings of corporatism allayed its charms. One consequence of the NRA was to shift economists' views on antitrust policy away from the conduct-oriented approach of John Bates Clark and toward direct control of market structure. Henry Simons of the University of Chicago would have allowed the Federal Trade Commission to regulate market structure (1936, p. 71):

> Operating companies must be limited in size, under special limitations prescribed for particular industries by the Federal Trade Commission, in accordance with the policy of preserving real competition.

His motives were as much political as economic: he thought that failure to maintain a competitive structure would lead to loss of political freedom (Simons, 1936, p. 68):

> I believe that we must choose between freer competition and increasing political control and that, for real policy, the choice lies simply between a competitive system and authoritarian collectivism.

Simons was quite willing to accept higher production costs if that was needed to maintain competitive market structures (1936, p. 71):

> If there are cases where real production economies require units too large for effective competition among them, some sacrifices ought to be made in both directions; indeed, one finds here a reason for proposing the generally objectionable expedient of an administrative authority with some discretionary power.

Temporary National Economic Committee   Support for control of market structure grew with the activities of the Temporary National Economic Committee (TNEC), an intergovernmental committee that operated for almost three years, from June 1938 to April, 1941. Its mandate was to conduct (Roosevelt, 1938) "a thorough study of the concentration of economic power in American industry and the effect of that concentration upon the decline of competition".[2] It held extensive hearings into the details of market behaviour in major

---

[1] See Brown Shoe Co., Inc. *v.* U.S. 370 U.S. 294 (1962) at 313–314.

[2] President Roosevelt's message to Congress calling for establishment of the TNEC alludes to political ("the liberty of a democracy is not safe if the people tolerate the growth of private power to a point where it becomes stronger than their democratic state itself") and economic consequences of increasing supplier concentration (increasing inequality in the distribution of income, rigid prices). The converging political currents that led to the TNEC

U.S. industries, and published monographs that remain a rich source of information about the structure of the U.S. markets as the economy came out of the Great Depression. It also recommended (TNEC, 1941, p. 38) amending Section 7 of the Clayton Act to cover asset acquisitions.

Merger boomlet   With the advent of world war, attention turned from antitrust and regulatory policy to more pressing matters. But support grew for control of market structure.[3] In 1950 Congress passed and the President signed the Celler-Kefauver Act, amending Section 7 of the Clayton Act to so it covered asset acquisitions and mergers lessening competition anywhere in the economy, not just competition between the firms involved in the merger.[4]

The 1950 amendments to Section 7 of the Clayton Act were in part a reaction to the perceived role of big business in the rise of fascism in pre-World War II Germany and in the rise of militarism in pre-World War II Japan.[5] The amendments were also a reaction to a perceived postwar U.S. merger movement, one that was seen as threatening the viability of the U.S. as a market economy (FTC, 1948):

> No great stretch of the imagination is required to foresee that if nothing is done to check the growth in concentration, either the giant corporations will ultimately take over the country, or the government will be impelled to step in and impose some form of direct regulation.

No merger wave materialized; Markham (1955, p. 179) called it "a ripple".[6] But Congressional debate reflected a clear concern for the political implications of concentration of economic power, that (Senator Kefauver, 96 Congressional Record 16452, 1950; see also Kefauver, 1948) "we are rapidly reaching [the] point in this country . . . where the public steps in to take over when concentration and monopoly gain too much power. The taking over by the public always follows one or two methods and has one or two political results. It either results in a Fascist state or the nationalization of industries and thereafter a Socialist or Communist state." Bok (1960, pp. 236–237) writes "To anyone used to the preoccupation of professors and administrators with the economic consequences of monopoly power, the curious aspect of the debates is the paucity of remarks having to do with the effects of concentration on prices, innovation, distribution, and efficiency. To be sure, there were allusions to the need for preserving competition. But competition appeared to possess a strong socio-political connotation which centered on the virtues of the small entrepreneur to an extent seldom duplicated in economic literature."

---

included elements of the three sides that disputed control of early New Deal economic policy (Section 20.3.2). Roosevelt's own attitude was ambivalent (Raymond Mobley, quoted by Hawley, 1966, p. 417): "[T]he TNEC was the 'final expression of Roosevelt's personal indecision, an inquiry that would relieve the President from the nagging of his subordinates, put off the adoption of a definite program, and free his mind for consideration of other matters'."

[3] Edward Levi, later Dean of the University of Chicago law school, President of the University of Chicago, and Attorney General of the United States, suggested (1947, pp. 182–183) that courts might turn to the Federal Trade Commission to fashion effective structural remedies in monopolization cases. Stigler (1955, p. 182) suggested rules that would permit mergers leading to market shares of 5 to 10 per cent, prohibit mergers leading to market shares of 20 per cent or more, and leave mergers between these levels to the attention of enforcement agencies.

[4] For the wording of the amendment, see *Brown Shoe*, 370 U.S. 294 at 311, fn. 18.

[5] On the former, see Adams (1961, p. 543) "some students contend that the rise of Hitler in Germany was facilitated by the pervasive cartelization of the German economy—by the absence of competitive freedom in German business and the lack of democratic freedom in German government." On the latter, see Bisson (1954).

[6] For discussion of this aspect of the run-up to passage of the Celler-Kefauver Act, see Bok (1960, pp. 231–233).

Prompted by such noneconomic concerns, Congress enacted legislation that aimed to halt mergers before they reached a level that would bring existing antitrust rules into play:[7]

> The bill is intended to permit intervention in ... [a process of mergers] when the effect of an acquisition may be a significant reduction in the vigor of competition, even though this effect may not be so far-reaching as to amount to a combination in restraint of trade, create a monopoly, or constitute an attempt to monopolize.

The amendment of Section 7 of the Clayton Act meant a shift from reliance on maintaining freedom of entry as a way of ensuring efficient market structure to direct government control of changes in market structure. This shift brought with it an enhanced role for economic analysis in the application of antitrust policy. The amended Section 7 required enforcement agencies to assess whether a proposed merger might lessen competition. Such an assessment requires an analytical framework that permits drawing conclusions about future consequences of a proposed merger. The analytical framework that was adopted was that of industrial economics (370 U.S. 294 at 322, fn. 38):

> Statistics reflecting the shares of the market controlled by the industry leaders and the parties to the merger are, of course, the primary index of market power; but only a further examination of the particular market—its structure, history and probably future—can provide the appropriate setting for judging the probable anticompetitive effect of the merger.

22.2.3 Caselaw: there and back again

Brown Shoe[8]

Brown Shoe Co. was a manufacturer and distributor of shoes. It was the fourth largest U.S. shoe manufacturer. At the retail level, it sold shoes through wholly owned shoe stores, through franchised shoe stores, and through independent shoe stores. Brown Shoe made a series of acquisitions of retail outlets in the early 1950s.

G. R. Kinney Co. was primarily a shoe retailer; its 350 retail outlets were the largest chain of U.S. shoe stores not owned by a leading manufacturer. Kinney was the twelfth largest U.S. shoe manufacturer, with a market share of one-half of one per cent.

The Brown Shoe-Kinney merger, which took place (over FTC objection) in 1956, was thus a horizontal merger at the manufacturing level, a horizontal merger at the retail level, and a vertical merger, principally of Brown's manufacturing and Kinney's retail operations. The District Court that heard the Department of Justice challenge to the merger found that the horizontal merger at the manufacturing level did not offend the Clayton Act, but condemned both the horizontal merger of retail activities and the vertical merger. It ordered that the merger be undone, and Brown Shoe appealed this decision to the Supreme Court.

The vertical dimension
Market definition   To assess the likely impact of the merger on market performance, the Court had to define relevant product and geographic markets. In what Baker and Blumenthal

---

[7] House Report No. 1191, 81st Cong., 1st Sess. 8 (1949). This is quoted by Bok (1960, p. 237).

[8] Brown Shoe Co., Inc. *v.* U.S. 370 U.S. 294 (1962).

(1983, p. 324) call "the Rosetta Stone of market definition", the Court wrote (370 U.S. 294 at 325; footnotes omitted; emphasis added):

> The outer boundaries of a product market are determined by the reasonable interchangeability of use or the cross-elasticity of demand between the product itself and substitutes for it. However, within this broad market, well-defined submarkets may exist which, in themselves, constitute product markets for antitrust purposes. ... The boundaries of such a submarket may be determined by examining such practical indicia as *industry or public recognition* of the submarket as a separate economic entity, the product's *peculiar characteristics and uses, unique production facilities, distinct customers, distinct prices, sensitivity to price changes, and specialized vendors.*

The District Court treated men's, women's, and children's shoes as distinct relevant product markets, and the Supreme Court accepted these definitions (370 U.S. 294 at 326): "These product lines are recognized by the public; each line is manufactured in separate plants; each has characteristics peculiar to itself rendering it generally noncompetitive with the others; and each is, of course, directed toward a distinct class of customers."

For analysis of the vertical merger, the District and the Supreme Courts took the relevant geographic market to be the United States: manufacturers approached distribution "on a nationwide basis".

Foreclosure   For the Supreme Court, manufacturer-distributor mergers could lessen competition through foreclosure (370 U.S. 294 at 323–324; references and footnotes omitted):

> The primary vice of a vertical merger or other arrangement tying a customer to a supplier is that, by foreclosing the competitors of either party from a segment of the market otherwise open to them, the arrangement may act as a "clog on competition," ... which "deprive[s] ... rivals of a fair opportunity to compete."

Noting Congressional intent to prevent (370 U.S. 294 at 333) "the formation of further oligopolies with their attendant adverse effects upon local control of industry and small business", the Supreme Court endorsed the District Court's condemnation of the vertical aspects of the merger. It wrote (370 U.S. 294 at 334):

> We reach this conclusion because the trend toward vertical integration in the shoe industry, when combined with Brown's avowed policy of forcing its own shoes upon its retail subsidiaries, may foreclose competition from a substantial share of the markets for men's, women's, and children's shoes, without producing any countervailing competitive, economic, or social advantages.

The horizontal dimension

Market definition   The Supreme Court also condemned the retail aspects of the merger. It used the same product market classifications to assess the retail merger that it had used to assess the vertical aspect of the merger. It accepted the District Court's view that an appropriate geographic market definition for retailing, by its nature a local activity, was (370 U.S. 294 at 339) "those cities with a population exceeding 10,000 and their environs in which both Brown and Kinney retailed shoes through their own outlets. Such markets are large enough to include the downtown shops and suburban shopping centers in areas contiguous to the city, which are the important competitive factors, and yet are small enough to exclude stores beyond the immediate environs of the city, which are of little competitive significance."

Market shares   The Supreme Court first discussed the combined market shares of the two firms involved in the merger:[9] statistics noted were (among others) that "during 1955 in 32 separate cities ... the combined share of Brown and Kinney sales of women's shoes ... exceeded 20%. In 31 cities ... the combined share of children's shoes sales exceeded 20% ... In 118 separate cities the combined shares of the market of Brown and Kinney in the sale of one of the relevant lines of commerce exceeded 5%. In 47 cities, their share exceeded 5% in all three lines."

A 5 per cent market share would not now be thought likely to substantially worsen market performance. Probably at the time of the Brown Shoe decision, the Supreme Court did not think it likely that a merger resulting in a 5 per cent market share would substantially worsen market performance. The Supreme Court noted that later mergers might follow this one, leading step-by-step to the kind of oligopoly that Congress wished to block in its incipiency.

Efficiency   The Court's evaluation of economic consequences of the vertical aspects of the merger (pages 328–334 of the decision) is confined to the effect the merger would have on market performance because of foreclosure and the impact of foreclosure on the competitive opportunities of rivals. That is a legitimate subject of analysis. What is absent from the discussion is a treatment of the efficiency gains that might arise from the vertical merger.

But there is a discussion of efficiency gains in the evaluation of the impact of the horizontal aspects of the merger on competition (370 U.S. 294 at 344):

> The retail outlets of integrated companies, by eliminating wholesalers and by increasing the volume of purchases from the manufacturing division of the enterprise, can market their own brands at prices below those of competing independent retailers. Of course, some of the results of large integrated or chain operations are beneficial to consumers. Their expansion is not rendered unlawful by the mere fact that small independent stores may be adversely affected. It is competition, not competitors, which the Act protects. But we cannot fail to recognize Congress' desire to promote competition through the protection of viable, small, locally owned businesses. Congress appreciated that occasional higher costs and prices might result from the maintenance of fragmented industries and markets. It resolved these competing considerations in favor of decentralization.

It may well be that the Supreme Court correctly read the will of Congress in this matter. But the condemnation of a merger that would lead to relatively small post-merger market shares because it might produce a more efficient post-merger firm seems contrary to the vision of antitrust as a policy that seeks to obtain good market performance by promoting opportunities for equally efficient rivals to compete.

Philadelphia National Bank (PNB)

The *Philadelphia National Bank*[10] decision took place a year after *Brown Shoe*. The issue was a proposed merger between the second (PNB) and third (Girard Trust Corn Exchange Bank)

---

[9] 370 U.S. 294 at 342–343; footnotes omitted. The Court recognized that the market share of the post-merger firm might differ from the sum of the market shares of the two pre-merger firms (370 U.S. 294 at 343, fn. 70).

[10] U.S. *v.* Philadelphia National Bank & Trust 374 U.S. 321 (1963).

largest Philadelphia-area banks. The post-merger bank would have been the largest bank in the area, with 36 per cent of area bank assets. The two largest post-merger banks would have had 59 per cent of area-bank assets.

District Court[11]

Market definition The District Court defined the product market as commercial banking and the geographic market as the four-country area containing Philadelphia. This was the government's preferred geographic market, which the District Court accepted for the sake of argument. The District Court favoured a much larger geographic market, possibly as large as the Northeast United States.

Rule of reason For the District Court, the Clayton Act question was (201 F. Supp. 348 at 365) "whether, after considering all of the relevant factors, there is a reasonable probability of a significant reduction in the vigor of competition". To answer this question (which it did in the negative), it went through a wide-ranging rule-of-reason inquiry into the impact of the merger on concentration, entry conditions, and market performance. The District Court concluded that the merger would not offend the Clayton Act. Believing, as it did, that in any event the proposed merger was not subject to the provisions of the Clayton Act, and that the merger could not be a restraint of trade in violation of Section 1 of the Sherman Act if it did not violate the less strict Clayton Act, it dismissed the Department of Justice's complaint. The DOJ's appeal brought the matter before the U.S. Supreme Court.

On appeal

Incipiency The Supreme Court emphasized that Congress intended the amended Section 7 to reach incipient lessenings of competition. It recognized that this necessarily involved an assessment of the future impact of a merger, but also that the business community needed clear rules. So, it wrote (374 U.S. 321 at 362) "we must be alert to the danger of subverting congressional intent by permitting a too-broad economic investigation".

Market share The Supreme Court then directed lower courts to look specifically at market shares in evaluating the likely future impact of a merger on market performance, effectively short-circuiting the kind of broad rule-of-reason inquiry for which *Brown Shoe* had called and in which the District Court had engaged (374 U.S. 321 at 363, emphasis added):

> *[I]ntense congressional concern with the trend toward concentration warrants dispensing, in certain cases, with elaborate proof of market structure, market behavior, or probable anticompetitive effects.* Specifically, we think that a merger which produces a firm controlling an undue percentage share of the relevant market, and results in a significant increase in the concentration of firms in

---

[11] U.S. banks are regulated by the Federal Reserve Board, which approved the merger (while agreeing that it would substantially lessen competition). One issue was whether this regulation removed banks from the coverage of the antitrust laws. The District Court that first heard the case took the view that the Clayton Act did *not* apply to bank mergers (201 F. Supp. 348 at 360). But the District Court went ahead on the assumption that the Clayton Act as amended by the Celler-Kefauver Act did apply to the proposed merger. On appeal, the Supreme Court found that bank regulation did not remove banks from the coverage of the antitrust laws (374 U.S. 321 at 355).

that market, is so inherently likely to lessen competition substantially that it must be enjoined in the absence of evidence clearly showing that the merger is not likely to have such anticompetitive effects.

The italicized sentence is a shift from *Brown Shoe*'s indication that market share statistics are but one factor to be considered in evaluating the probable effect of a merger. It makes market structure the primary factor to be considered in deciding the fate of a proposed merger.

Von's Grocery[12]

Where the focus on market share could lead was brought into focus by the 1960 acquisition of Shopping Bag Food Stores by Von's Grocery Company, both Los Angeles-area chains of grocery stores. The Department of Justice sought to block the merger, but this request was denied by the District Court, which found no likelihood that the merger would substantially injure competition. The Department of Justice appealed to the Supreme Court.

Among the facts considered by the Supreme Court were that the two chains were the third and sixth, ranked by sales, in the Los Angeles-area retail grocery market, that their combined market share in 1960 was 7.5 per cent, and that the number of single-location retail grocery stores in the Los Angeles area had fallen from 5,365 in 1950 to 3,818 in 1961, with a further decline to 3,590 in 1963.

Keep small firms in business   The Court's reading of Congressional intent was frankly protectionist (384 U.S. 270 at 275):[13]

> Like the Sherman Act in 1890 and the Clayton Act in 1914, the basic purpose of the 1950 Celler-Kefauver Act was to prevent economic concentration in the American economy by keeping a large number of small competitors in business.

For the *Von's Grocery* majority (384 U.S. 270 at 276),

> Congress sought to preserve competition among many small businesses by arresting a trend toward concentration in its incipiency before that trend developed to the point that a market was left in the grip of a few big companies. Thus, where concentration is gaining momentum in a market, we must be alert to carry out Congress' intent to protect competition against ever-increasing concentration through mergers.

Here the majority conceives of competition in the sense of market structure.

---

[12] U.S. *v.* Von's Grocery Co. 384 U.S. 270 (1966).

[13] As our discussions of congressional intent behind the Sherman Act and the Clayton Act should make clear, what the Court writes here is incorrect. But what it writes about the Celler-Kefauver amendments is correct (Bok, 1960, pp. 247–248, footnote omitted, enphasis added): "Underlying the legislative deliberations was the conviction that small business and the dispersion of economic power are salutary and should be encouraged by the new section 7. This premise clearly suggests reliance upon a structural theory of competition which stresses the advantages of large numbers of small-sized firms. Such theories have been qualified or attacked increasingly by observers who have emphasized the moderating role of potential competition, countervailing power, and a congeries of political and social forces, which brings the behavior of big business more closely into line with the results which would be anticipated under competitive conditions. *But however persuasive these arguments may be in analyzing economic performance in concentrated industries, they simply fail to take account of a wider range of interests that to Congress seemed critically important.*"

Protect competition, not competitors In his dissenting opinion, Justice Stewart would have none of this. *Brown Shoe*, he thought, made two things clear (384 U.S. 270 at 282):

> First, the standards of § 7 require that every corporate acquisition be judged in the light of the contemporary economic context of its industry. Second, the purpose of § 7 is to protect competition, not to protect competitors ... Today the Court turns its back on these two basic principles ...

Assessment *Von's Grocery* is often criticized on the ground that a firm with a 7.5 per cent market share could not exercise market power, and so a merger creating such a firm could not worsen market performance. This is no doubt correct, but in the context of the 1950 amendment to Section 7 of the Clayton Act, beside the point. The amended Section 7 directs enforcement agencies and the courts to halt merger-based concentration trends *in their incipiency*, before the point at which market performance is worsened. The force of Justice Stewart's critique was that the majority's count of the decline in the number of single-unit stores was at best a superficial market analysis, and missed the fact that the decline in the number of single-unit stores was due to the rise of supermarket chains, not to a series of mergers. This too is no doubt correct. Giving the impression of exasperation, he wrote that (384 U.S. 270 at 301) "The sole consistency that I can find is that in litigation under § 7, the Government always wins."

General Dynamics[14]

Beginning with its 1974 *General Dynamics* decision, the Supreme Court began a retreat from the mechanical consideration of market shares emphasized by *Philadelphia National Bank* and *Von's Grocery*.

In 1959 a deep-shaft coal-mining company operating throughout the midwest United States (Material Service Corporation) acquired control of firms operating strip and open-pit coal mines in Illinois and Kentucky (Freeman Coal Mining Corporation and United Electric Coal Companies). Material Service Corporation was then itself taken over by General Dynamics Corporation.

The government challenged the 1959 acquisition as a violation of Section 7 of the Clayton Act, alleging that it would substantially lessen competition in the market for coal in one or both of two alternative proposed geographic markets, Illinois or the Eastern Interior Coal Province (Central and Southern Illinois, Southwestern Indiana, and Western Kentucky, and some nearby areas). The District Court found for General Dynamics, and the government appealed directly to the Supreme Court.

In District Court, the government relied mainly on statistics showing a decline in the number of coal mining firms, an increase in seller concentration, and an increased market share for the merged firm. In its decision, the Supreme Court went out of its way to note that the government's statistics were comparable to those underlying *Von's Grocery*, and added (415 U.S. 486 at 496):

> In prior decisions involving horizontal mergers between competitors, this Court has found prima facie violations of § 7 of the Clayton Act from aggregate statistics of the sort relied on by the United States in this case.

---

[14] U.S. *v.* General Dynamics 415 U.S. 486 (1974).

But the District Court had relied on other factors, and the Supreme Court found that it was proper to do so. First, it appeared that the increase in seller concentration in coal mining reflected a decline in demand for coal, as consumers substituted away from coal and toward oil, natural gas, and nuclear energy as primary energy sources. Second, coal was largely sold to public utilities under long-term contracts. Market share figures, being based on past sales, were a poor indicator of a firm's future ability to compete for long-term contracts. The acquired companies were relatively poor in uncommitted reserves, hence their acquisition could not be expected to substantially lessen competition in the relevant markets.

The upshot of the *General Dynamics* decision is that market share and seller concentration statistics are the beginning of an antimerger case under Section 7 of the Clayton Act, not the end of it. Later decisions, and government Merger Guidelines (to which we turn shortly) confirm this approach.

Brunswick *v.* Pueblo Bowl-o-mat

This decision in a private antitrust suit seeking treble damages under Section 7 of the Clayton Act is noteworthy for introduction of the rule that a private plaintiff must show *antitrust injury* before it can recover damages.

The conglomerate Brunswick Corporation was a leading manufacturer of bowling equipment. Bowling underwent a boom in the United States in the 1950s, and Brunswick sold quite a lot of equipment, some of it on credit, to bowling alleys. When bowling became less popular in the 1960s, many of Brunswick's customers defaulted and left it with the choice between selling used bowling alley equipment in a depressed market or getting into the business of operating bowling alleys.

To operate bowling alleys would entail an accounting loss, but the loss would be less than that implied by the other choice. Brunswick closed down about one-quarter of the defaulting alleys, but kept 168 of them in operation. As a result, by 1968 it operated the largest chain of bowling alleys in the United States, although it had only a 2 per cent share of the national market.

Pueblo Bowl-o-mat, Inc. and other local bowling companies filed a private antitrust suit, claiming that the takeover of the bowling alleys was a violation of Section 7 of the Clayton Act, and that they had been injured by this violation, because their profits would have been greater if Brunswick had allowed the defaulting alleys to go out of business. They sought to recover treble damages.

In District Court, a jury gave a verdict for the private plaintiffs. Brunswick appealed and the Third Circuit Court of Appeals ordered a new trial, on the ground that there had been improper instructions to the jury. Both sides appealed to the Supreme Court.

Antitrust injury   For the Supreme Court in 1977, Congress had not intended to permit any firm injured by a merger to recover damages, only firms that suffered damages from a merger that injured competition (429 U.S. 477 at 487):

> Every merger of two existing entities into one, whether lawful or unlawful, has the potential for producing economic readjustments that adversely affect some persons. But Congress has not condemned mergers on that account; it has condemned them only when they may produce anticompetitive effects.

But the acquisitions in question had not injured competition; fundamentally, the private plaintiffs' complaint was (429 U.S. 477 at 487):

> that by acquiring the failing centers [Brunswick] preserved competition, thereby depriving respondents of the benefits of increased concentration. The damages respondents obtained are designed to provide them with the profits they would have realized had competition been reduced. The antitrust laws, however, were enacted for "the protection of competition, not competitors," ... It is inimical to the purposes of these laws to award damages for the type of injury claimed here.

The concept of *antitrust injury* goes far to reading protectionism out of private antimerger complaints.

22.2.4 Merger Guidelines

The U.S. Department of Justice issued its first set of merger guidelines in 1968; successive guidelines were issued in 1982, 1984, 1992, and 1997.[15] The 1997 Guidelines modified one section of the 1992 Guidelines, both of which were issued jointly by the Department of Justice and the Federal Trade Commission.

The guidelines are not binding. The 1968 Guidelines state that "these guidelines are announced solely as a statement of current Department policy, subject to change at any time without prior notice, for whatever assistance such statement may be in enabling interested persons to anticipate in a general way Department enforcement action under Section 7 [of the Clayton Act]". Despite this lack of commitment on the part of the issuing agencies, the merger guidelines are influential signals of the aims of public enforcers of the antitrust law.[16]

1968 Guidelines

Horizontal mergers The 1968 Merger Guidelines, a mere 17 pages in length, reflect the mainstream industrial economics paradigm of the day—the structure-conduct-performance framework—and the Supreme Court's early interpretations of the Clayton Act. They emphasize market structure as a determinant of market and of firm performance. They emphasize as well that focusing on a small number of high-profile statistics means a clear policy for the business community.

Market definition The 1968 Guidelines highlight interchangeability of use as the standard for product market definition. As for geographic market definition, the 1968 Guidelines look first at where firms sell (p. 4) "The total sales of a product or service in any commercially significant section of the country (even as small as a single community), or aggregate of such sections, will ordinarily constitute a geographic market if firms engaged in selling the product make significant sales of the product make significant sales of the product to purchasers in

---

[15] The Federal Trade Commission earlier issued industry-specific guidelines regarding mergers in the dairy products (1965), cement and food distribution (1967), and grocery and textile mill products (1968) industries. See Keyes (1967) for discusson.

[16] There are guidelines on the licensing of intellectual property, statements on antitrust enforcement policy in health care, on international operations, and on collaboration among competitors. Competition authorities outside the U.S. have issued their own guidelines.

Table 22.1 Horizontal merger investigation thresholds, 1968 Merger Guidelines

CR4 ≥ 75%		CR4 < 75%	
Acquiring Firm	Acquired Firm	Acquiring Firm	Acquired Firm
4%	4% or more	5%	5% or more
10%	2% or more	10%	4% or more
15% or more	1% or more	15%	3% or more
		20%	2% or more
		25% or more	1% or more

CR4 = four-firm seller concentration ratio.

the section or sections." But they also indicate that a properly defined geographic market should include locations of suppliers not facing entry barriers into a region.

Concentration   The 1968 Merger Guidelines classified markets with a four-firm seller concentration ratio of 75 per cent or more as highly concentrated. Justice Department policy was to investigate horizontal mergers in highly concentrated industries involving firms with market share combinations given in the first two columns of Table 22.1. For less-concentrated industries, horizontal merger investigation thresholds were as indicated in the third and fourth columns of Table 22.1. The two sets of 1968 merger investigation thresholds are shown by the dashed lines in Figure 22.1.[17]

The 1968 Guidelines indicated that the Department of Justice would apply stricter standards in markets showing a trend of increasing concentration. They also left open the possibility of challenging horizontal mergers that did not meet the quantitative standards of Table 22.1, if qualitative characteristics of the merger suggested it would fall within "the purposes of [Clayton Act] Section 7". The Guidelines also indicated that a horizontal merger otherwise subject to challenge could be allowed to go forward if the merger involved a failing firm, facing "the clear probability of business failure".

Vertical mergers
Foreclosure   Under the 1968 Merger Guidelines, the Department of Justice focused on vertical mergers that tended "significantly to raise barriers to entry ... or to disadvantage non-integrated or partly integrated firms in either market in ways unrelated to economic efficiency". Foreclosure of rivals following a vertical merger could raise the cost to suppliers of reaching customers, raise the cost of customers to reaching suppliers, or require firms

---

[17] For a similar figure, see Tollison (1983, Figure 1).

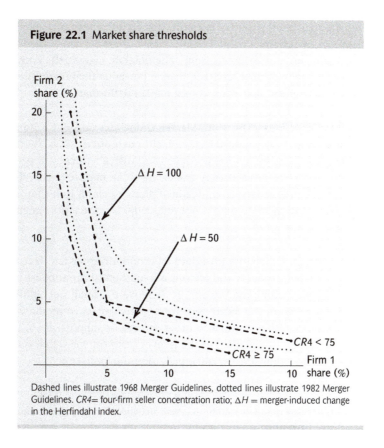

Figure 22.1 Market share thresholds

Dashed lines illustrate 1968 Merger Guidelines, dotted lines illustrate 1982 Merger Guidelines. *CR4*= four-firm seller concentration ratio; ΔH = merger-induced change in the Herfindahl index.

otherwise capable of operating efficiently at one vertical level with the costly option of expanding to the other vertical level if they wished to stay in business.

Efficiency   The 1968 Guidelines recognized the possibility that a vertical merger would carry with it efficiency advantages, but took a dim view of their likely importance (pp. 9–10):

> While it is true that in some instances vertical integration may raise barriers to entry or disadvantage existing competitors only as the result of the achievement of significant economies of production or distribution ... integration accomplished by a large vertical merger will usually raise entry barriers or disadvantage competitors to an extent not accounted for by, and wholly disproportionate to, such economies as may result from the merger.

The 1968 Merger Guidelines indicate that the Department of Justice will look at the market shares of the firms proposing to merger, as well as at entry conditions in the purchasing firm's market. The Guidelines discuss the kinds of conditions that may lead a particular vertical merger to be challenged, and admit a failing firm exception for vertical mergers.

Conglomerate mergers   The 1968 guidelines classify all mergers that are neither horizontal nor vertical as conglomerate. Conglomerate mergers involve firms that operate in markets that are not directly related. The 1968 Guidelines announce concern with conglomerate mergers that eliminate significant potential entrants, that facilitate reciprocal buying, or otherwise have anticompetitive effects.

As an example of anticompetitive effects from conglomerate merger, the knowledge that new entry is possible may temper the exercise of market power by incumbent firms. Mergers that eliminate a potential entrant may thus worsen market performance.

1982 and 1984 Merger Guidelines   The 1982 Merger Guidelines laid out a framework for market definition that is generally regarded as useful, although not in application as distinct a break with previous practice as sometimes portrayed and with a tendency to systematically understate the market shares of firms already exercising some market power. Reactions to the 1982 Guidelines as a whole ranged from qualified praise to alarm that they embodied a distinct ideological bent, and in so doing did not reflect the law the enforcement of which they purported to guide.

SSNIP test   The 1982 Merger Guidelines introduce an economic approach to antitrust market definition by asking what products and regions a hypothetical monopolist would need to control to be able to profitably raise price.[18] If there were a small but significant non-transitory increase in price (thus, the SSNIP test) for a particular set of products and areas, would a significant number of buyers turn to other sources or supply? If so, those other suppliers should be included in the market. At the level of first principles, that is the way the SSNIP test is applied (Geroski and Griffith, 2003, p. 4, footnote omitted):

- we start with the narrowest group of products and geographical area that is reasonable;
- we then suppose that these products sold in that area are wholly monopolized, and ask what would happen if that (hypothetical) monopolist were to raise its prices by [5]% [for a year];
- if that price rise is not profitable, then we add the closest substitute product (or geographical area) to the (hypothetically) monopolized bundle, and repeat the procedure;
- the procedure stops when we find a collection of products sold in a particular area which, if monopolized, would sustain a price rise of [5]% by that monopolist [for a year].

There are *ad hoc* elements to this approach—why a 5 per cent increase? Why sustainable for a year? But it has the merit of focusing attention on what is the central issue for merger control (Areeda, 1983a, pp. 308–309): will the post-merger firm be able to exercise market power, either in its own right, or by way of tacit or overt collusion with firms outside the merger?

In application, data deficiencies, time and resource constraints force compromises with first principles (Geroski and Griffith, 2003, pp. 5–6):[19]

[O]ne of the challenges of applying the SSNIP test is its hypothetical nature and gathering the information needed to put it in to practice. It is almost always the case that one cannot directly observe a SSNIP test in operation. ... In practice the sort of information that is used includes

---

[18] Scherer (2009) attributes the idea to Adelman (1959b).

[19] Along the same lines, see Baker and Blumenthal (1983, p. p. 322, fn.53), Ordover and Willig (1983, p. 541), Carlton (2007, p. 17). Areeda (1987, p. 981) succinctly writes "the data bearing on market definition is usually incomplete and is often obscured by experts functioning as advocates ... "

estimates of the parameters of a demand system (in particular the own and cross price elastic-ities), information on product characteristics and consumer preferences (gathered either from industry sources or consumer surveys), information on past price movements and information on product technologies and costs. As a consequence, calculating the outcome of applying the SSNIP test almost always involves making indirect inferences, and the answers which emerge almost always contain some degree of imprecision.

The 1982 Guidelines indicate that in applying the SSNIP test to product market definition, the Department of Justice will look at evidence of buyers' perceptions, similarities in product design and use, the extent to which prices move in the same way, and whether or not sellers regard products as substitutes. In applying the SSNIP test to geographic market definition, it will look at actual shifts of buyers from suppliers in one region to suppliers in another, the extent to which prices move in the same way, transportation and distribution costs, and the extent of excess capacity in different regions.

Cellophane fallacy   The 1982 Merger Guidelines specify (emphasis added) that "[t]he Depart-ment will include in the provisional market those products that the merging firm's cus-tomers view as good substitutes *at prevailing prices"*, and so fall prey to the *Cellophane fallacy* (see the accompanying box). Unlike the U.S. Supreme Court in 1956, which in some sense encountered the Cellophane fallacy in a dark alley, the 1982 Department of Justice Merger Guidelines embraced it with open arms. It distinguished between antitrust policy toward monopolization and merger control (Baxter, 1983a, p. 623, fn.35): "under § 2 of the Sher-man Act ... it is necessary to determine whether a firm is presently exercising market power in order to determine whether corrective action is necessary to reduce that power. ... hori-zontal merger analysis under § 7 of the Clayton Act is concerned with the probability that a merger will decrease competition in the future." Areeda (1987, p. 976, footnote omitted) comments that the SSNIP test applied to existing prices[20] "would broaden the market too far and thus understate a merger's significance whenever the existing price level was already supracompetitive. The Department justified this approach on the ground that section 7 was designed to catch only those mergers that newly create a danger of oligopoly pricing and not to catch those mergers that reinforce preexisting anticompetitive pricing. The Department's position on this is wrong, will not be fully accepted by courts, and thus is not viable."

 BOX   The *Cellophane* Fallacy

A 1947 federal government antitrust suit charged the DuPont Company with "monopolizing, attempting to monopolize and combining and conspiring to monopolize" the U.S. market for cello-phane and related products, sales of which its share was about 75 per cent, in violation of Section 2 of the Sherman Act. "Each of the section 2 offenses ... involves two elements: monopoly (as a goal or as a result), and purpose and intent, which is principally derived from conduct" (Turner, 1956, p. 304). Allegations of conduct that might, if proven, have been taken to show purpose and intent to monopolize were made, but played little role in the District or Supreme Court decisions that »

---

[20] See similarly Ordover and Willig (1983, pp. 542–543).

>> exonerated DuPont. In making its case, the government pointed to DuPont's 75 per cent share of cellophane sales. DuPont responded that the market was flexible wrapping materials, of which cellophane accounted for no more than 20 per cent, and that a 75 per cent of 20 per cent of a market was not a position of market power.

In *DuPont Cellophane*, as often in antitrust cases, the outcome hinged on market definition (Rowe, 1987, p. 992):

> Once market shares and concentration counts became dispositive of monopolization and merger cases, the manipulation of markets and the massaging of numbers debased antitrust law into farce. Since a firm's telltale market-share percentage was inverse to the size of the chosen market, the search for the relevant market became the focus of each case. Aided by eager economists, astute lawyers maneuvered to make the market look smaller or bigger, in order to bloat or to shrink the defendant's market share.

There were indeed a wide variety of flexible wrapping materials, among which (118 F. Supp. 41 at 72) "aluminum foil, glassine, Pliofilm, polyethylene, cellulose acetate, waxed paper, sulphite, vegetable parchment, … kraft paper". For the Supreme Court (351 U.S. 377 at 395) "In considering what is the relevant market for determining the control of price and competition, no more definite rule can be declared than that commodities reasonably interchangeable by consumers for the same purposes make up that 'part of the trade or commerce,' monopolization of which may be illegal."

In applying this standard, the District Court Judge considered a range of evidence, including a visit to the 1952 Annual Packaging Show at Atlantic City, New Jersey, where he observed displays of firms dealing in flexible wrapping materials. He concluded that cellophane, "functionally interchangeable with other flexible packaging materials and sold at same time to same customers for same purpose at competitive prices", was part and parcel of the market for flexible wrapping materials, a market that DuPont did not monopolize.

In confirming this outcome, the Supreme Court wrote (351 U.S. 377 at 396–397, emphasis added):

> In determining the market under the Sherman Act, it is the use or uses to which the commodity is put that control. The selling price between commodities with similar uses and different characteristics may vary, so that the cheaper product can drive out the more expensive. Or, the superior quality of higher priced articles may make dominant the more desirable. Cellophane costs more than many competing products and less than a few. *But whatever the price*, there are various flexible wrapping materials that are bought by manufacturers for packaging their goods in their own plants or are sold to converters who shape and print them for use in the packaging of the commodities to be wrapped.

It is here that the Court commits what has become known as the *Cellophane fallacy*: the extent to which consumers find one variety of a product interchangeable in use *depends on* the prices charged. Cellophane, by all accounts, dominated other flexible wrapping materials, in terms of quality, for most uses. If priced at competitive levels, it seems likely that most users for most uses would have opted for cellophane. Thus (Areeda, 1983) "a high present demand elasticity does not necessarily connote the absence of market power but may only mean that any power possessed by the firm has already been exercised". But the issue was never joined, because the District and Supreme Courts assessed substitutability at reigning market prices. The (Schaerr, 1985, p. 677) "analytic error" that inflates market size while shrinking measured market share "is a failure to count the market power a firm has already exercised (in raising its price above the competitive level), and instead counting only the market power the firm has not yet used".

Incipiency (not) The Merger Guidelines ignored a key feature of Section 7, that it targets merger-based concentration trends in their incipiency (Areeda, 1983a, p. 310):[21] "[A] a key horizontal merger issue that is only inferentially treated in the Guidelines is whether we should prevent a merger that does not itself impair competition but that would do so if replicated by similarly situated firms in that market."

More broadly, Sullivan (1983, pp. 832–833) notes that the U.S. antitrust laws are laws, not regulations subject to revision by administrative agencies. Harris and Jorde point out that fluctuations in the consistency with which laws are applied goes against one of the stated goals of Guidelines, to made clear what conduct is acceptable and what not (1983, p. 490, fn. 61):

> The Guidelines are a statement of policy of the Justice Department of the current Administration. They are also a clear break with the logical evolution of antitrust law that was occurring before this Administration took office. ... This dramatic shift in antitrust policy invites later administrations to promulgate enforcement policies radically different from those of their immediate predecessors, resulting in antitrust policies that may be stable only until the next presidential election. Business decisions that are significant enough to have potential antitrust effects, however, are made for the long run, and cannot be undone every four years.

In sum, (Pitofsky, 1990, p. 1808) "market definition was a more coherent exercise during the 1980s ..., and that can be attributed in part to the orderly, intellectual approach of the Guidelines". But the exercise was tarnished by its ideological bent (Pitofsky, 1990, pp. 1808–1809, footnote omitted):[22]

> Most of the advocates of revised approaches to relevant market definitions that result in diminished market shares also believe that antitrust enforcement has interfered unduly with legitimate business conduct, and that long-run market forces cure occasional market imperfections more effectively than government or private lawsuits. By modifying relevant market analysis so as to diminish the appearance of market power, these advocates seek to achieve a result that many of them have described candidly as their goal—the removal of antitrust enforcement as an impediment to all business transactions except outright cartels, mergers leading directly to monopoly power, and some unusual types of predatory conduct.

Horizontal mergers: concentration Like the 1968 Merger Guidelines, the 1982 Merger Guidelines state seller concentration and market share thresholds that will trigger examination of a horizontal merger. Unlike the 1968 Guidelines, the 1982 Guidelines express thresholds in terms of the Herfindahl index, not the four-firm seller concentration ratio.

Recall from Section 3.2.4 that the Herfindahl index is the sum of squares of market shares of all firms supplying a market: for n firms,

$$H = s_1^2 + s_2^2 + \ldots + s_n^2. \tag{22.1}$$

If market shares are measured in percentage terms, the maximum possible market share is 100 per cent, and the maximum possible value of the H-index is $(100)^2 = 10,000$.

---

[21] See similarly Schwartz (1983, pp. 600–601).

[22] See also Harris and Jorde (1983), Schwartz (1983).

The 1982 Guidelines classify markets as:[23]

- unconcentrated: $H < 1000$;
- moderately concentrated: $1000 \leq H \leq 1800$;
- highly concentrated: $H > 1800$.

The 1982 Guidelines indicate that the Department of Justice is unlikely to challenge mergers in unconcentrated industries. It will consider challenging mergers in highly concentrated industries that increase the value of the H-index by between 50 and 100 points, and is likely to challenge mergers in moderately concentrated or highly concentrated industries that raise the value of the H-index by 100 points or more.

To interpret these standards, note from the definition of the Herfindahl index, (22.1), firms 1 and 2 merge, with the shares of all other firms unchanged, the increase in the H-index is:

$$\Delta H = (s_1 + s_2)^2 - s_1^2 - s_2^2 = 2s_1 s_2. \tag{22.2}$$

Any combination of market shares of merging firms that satisfy:

$$2s_1 s_2 = 100 \tag{22.3}$$

will increase a market's Herfindahl index by 100 points. Market share pairs satisfying (22.3) are shown by the outermost dotted line in Figure 22.1. Market shares producing an increase of 50 points in the H-index are shown by the innermost dotted line in Figure 22.1.

Comparing the dashed and dotted lines in Figure 22.1, the 1982 Merger Guidelines embody a modest relaxation of the structural standards laid out in the 1968 Guidelines. Under the 1982 Merger Guidelines, the Department of Justice would not challenge some mergers that might have been challenged under the 1968 Guidelines.

Non-horizontal mergers The 1982 Merger Guidelines combine discussion of vertical and conglomerate mergers under the single category of non-horizontal mergers, about which they take a benign view (p. 29):

> By definition, non-horizontal mergers involve firms that do not operate in the same market. It necessarily follows that such mergers produce no immediate change in the level of concentration in any relevant market ... Although non-horizontal mergers are less likely than horizontal mergers to create competitive problems, they are not invariably innocuous.

According to the 1982 Guidelines, a non-horizontal merger might cause competitive problems if it reduces actual or perceived potential entry; vertical mergers might cause competitive problems if they raise barriers to entry. This might happen, according to the Guidelines,

- if a merger led to such a high degree of vertical integration that entrants into one market would also have to enter the other;

---

[23] The inverse of the H-index (when market shares are measured in fractional terms rather than per cent) is a numbers equivalent, giving the number of equally sized suppliers that would produce a given value of the H-index. A market with an H-index less than 1000 is as concentrated, in this numbers equivalent sense, to a market with 10 or more equally sized suppliers. A market with an H-index between 1000 and 1800 is as concentrated as a market with between 5.6 and 10 equally sized suppliers. A market with an H-index greater than 1800 is as concentrated as a market with fewer than 5.6 equally sized suppliers.

- if simultaneous entry is significantly more difficult and less likely than entry at one level alone;

- and if other aspects of market structure are conducive to non-competitive performance, so that an increase in the difficulty of entry is likely to worsen market performance.

The 1982 Guidelines also acknowledge the possibility that vertical integration may facilitate collusion, because retail prices are generally easier to monitor than upstream prices (facilitating detection of defection from a collusive pricing pattern) or if a vertical merger eliminates a price-cutting downstream buyer.

Efficiency: 1982, 1992, and 1997

1982   Like the 1968 Merger Guidelines, the 1982 Guidelines allow for a failing firm exception to the general rules. They are cautious on the weight to be given to efficiencies in evaluating prospective mergers (pp. 42–43; footnote omitted):

> In the overwhelming majority of cases, the Guidelines will allow firms to achieve available efficiencies through mergers without interference from the Department. Except in extraordinary cases, the Department will not consider a claim of specific efficiencies as a mitigating factor for a merger that would otherwise be challenged. Plausible efficiencies are far easier to allege than to prove. Moreover, even if the existence of efficiencies were clear, their magnitudes would be extremely difficult to determine.

1984   The 1984 Guidelines take a different view of the role of efficiency in merger evaluation (pp. 35–36):

> Some mergers that the Department otherwise might challenge may be reasonably necessary to achieve significant net efficiencies. If the parties to the merger establish by clear and convincing evidence that a merger will achieve such efficiencies, the Department will consider those efficiencies in deciding whether to challenge the merger.

The final sentence quoted above is inconsistent with Supreme Court decisions and was dropped from the 1992 Merger Guidelines (issued jointly by the Department of Justice and the Federal Trade Commission). As amended in 1997, those Guidelines focus (p. 30) on *merger-specific efficiencies:* "those efficiencies likely to be accomplished with the proposed merger and unlikely to be accomplished in the absence of either the proposed merger or another means having comparable anticompetitive effects."

 BOX   **Merger-specific Efficiencies Under the U.S. Merger Guidelines**

Nucor Corp.'s [2002] acquisition of substantially all of the assets of Birmingham Steel Corp. raised competitive concerns because the firms owned two of the three mills producing certain types of steel bar in the western United States. The Department [of Justice] concluded ... that the third western mill and other domestic mills would substantially constrain any post-merger price increases and that the merger likely would generate significant efficiencies. ... the acquisition would allow the merged firm to close some distribution facilities and to supply some customers from a closer mill at a lower delivered cost. ... the acquisition would [also] provide a Nucor mill with a lower cost »

>> input supply from Birmingham, although some of the savings might have been obtainable through a contractual arrangement. Even though some of the latter efficiencies may not have been merger specific, the Department concluded that plausible merger-specific reductions in variable costs were significant relative to the worst case scenario of anticompetitive effects from the acquisition, and the Department [did not challenge the merger].

Source: U.S. Department of Justice and FTC *Commentary on the Horizontal Merger Guidelines.* March 2006, p. 50.

1997   The 1997 Merger Guidelines see efficiencies (p. 31) "as difficult to verify and quantify, in part because much of the information relating to efficiencies is uniquely in possession of the merging firms. Moreover, efficiencies projected reasonably and in good faith by the merging firms may not be realized". The Guidelines indicate that the enforcement agencies will look at *cognizable* merger-specific efficiencies: those that can be verified and generate cost savings net of the cost of carrying out the merger. If such efficiencies are present, the agencies will evaluate whether or not they are large enough "to reverse the merger's potential to harm consumers in the relevant market, e.g., by preventing price increases in that market".

22.2.5 Harm to Competition—Damage to Market Performance[24]

Market definition, the calculation of market shares and market concentration levels, and their comparison with the Guidelines thresholds are not ends in themselves.[25] They are grist to the mill that is the central question for merger policy: if the merger goes forward, will market performance worsen?[26]

The U.S. Horizontal Merger Guidelines[27] envisage the possibility that a merger could worsen market performance by facilitating tacit or overt collusion—a reduction in the number of firms could make it easier to reach a common understanding about prices and outputs, and/or make it easier to detect deviations from such an understanding, once reached. A merger may have unilateral effects that worsen market performance—even if firms behave in a completely non-cooperative and non-strategic way in the post-merger market, a merger may move the market to a non-cooperative equilibrium in which market performance is worse than in the pre-merger market.[28] The enforcement agencies take entry conditions into account in evaluating the likely impact of a merger on market performance.

---

[24] For extensive discussion and examples, see the U.S. Department of Justice and FTC *Commentary* (2006).

[25] The Guidelines are only guidelines: Tollison (1983, p. 214) reports that more than 20 per cent of mergers challenged under the 1968 Guidelines fell beneath its market structure thresholds.

[26] See, in this regard, Ordover and Willig (1983, p. 536): "From the perspective of pure theoretical economics, the concern of antitrust analysts with matters of market definition has always seemed misplaced. Arguments for and against a merger that turned upon distinctions between broad and narrow market definitions have always seemed theologic rather than economic. The focus on market definition has seemed to be an inadequate substitute for, and a diversion from, sound direct assessment of a merger's effects."

[27] Issued jointly by the U.S. Department of Justice in 1992 and revised in 1997.

[28] This is the result of a reduction in the number of firms in the basic Cournot and Bertrand with product differentiation models.

22.3 European Union

Control of collusion and of firms with dominant market positions dates to 1957 and the founding of the EC, but explicit merger control was a late addition to European Community competition policy. The founding fathers of what has become the European Union were explicitly concerned with preventing collusion and price discrimination along national lines. They may well have had more sympathy for the idea of promoting EC firms to compete in world markets than for a policy to maintain market structures that were as unconcentrated as possible, within the constraints of efficient operation. It was only in 1989, 32 years into the process of EC market integration and after European Court of Justice decisions approving applications of Articles 101 and 102 to mergers that the European Commission's Directorate General for Competition was able persuade member states to adopt a Merger Control Regulation.

22.3.1 Before the MCR

Merger control under Article 102: *Continental Can*[29]

The first such decision arose out of the 1970 purchase of the Dutch firm TDV by Continental Can Company, Inc., an American-based producer of cans, packaging materials, and machines to make such items. Continental owned a controlling interest in the German firm SLW, the largest Continental producer of light metal containers. In December 1971 the Commission issued a decision that by dint of its ownership of SLW, Continental (a) enjoyed dominant positions in the European markets for light containers for canned meat products, light containers for canned seafood, and metal closures for the food packing industry, other than crown corks, and (b) that the purchase of TDV was an abuse of those dominant positions. The Commission ordered Continental to divest itself of TDV, and Continental appealed that order to the European Court of Justice.

Jurisdiction   Leaving aside procedural points, the Court's response to two of the bases of Continental's appeal are of interest. The Court rejected Continental's argument that the European Community did not have jurisdiction over firms based outside its territory. As one might have expected, the Court simply noted that the takeover of TDV "influences market conditions within the Community" and therefore came under Community law.

Creation of dominance ≠ abuse of dominance?   More substantively, Continental argued that although the takeover of TDV might have *created* a dominant position, creation of a dominant position and abuse of a dominant position are not the same thing. What Article 102 prohibits is abuse of a dominant position; hence (in Continental's view), the Commission had exceeded its authority by ordering that the merger be undone.

---

[29] Europemballage Corporation and Continental Can Company Inc. *v* Commission (Case 6-72) [1973] ECR 215 (*Continental Can*).

In its discussion of the second objection, the Court made the following points ([1973] ECR 244–5):

- Article 102 is one part of the section of the EC Treaty that seeks to promote undistorted competition in the Common Market;

- if competition is eliminated, the policy goal of undistorted competition is frustrated;

- Article 101, which applies to agreements among firms, and Article 102, which applies to actions of single firms, seek the same goals on different levels;

- thus, actions which are forbidden under Article 101 to cooperating firms are not permitted to single firms under Article 102.

EC competition law thus avoided setting up the contrary incentives established by U.S. antitrust in the immediate aftermath of the 1895 *E.C. Knight* and 1899 *Addyston Pipe and Steel* decisions, which (until the 1904 *Northern Securities* decision) created a safe harbour for firms to accomplish by merger what they were forbidden to do by collusion.

Market definition   The ECJ gave the Commission a victory in principle: it is an abuse of a dominant position, within the meaning of Article 102, to *create* or strengthen a dominant position by merger. But the ECJ set a high standard for the application of Article 102 to mergers. To block the merger, the Commission had to show that it would eliminate competition to such an extent that ([1973] ECR 246) "remaining competitors could no longer provide a sufficient counterweight" to the dominant firm. Such an assessment could only be made in the context of sensibly defined product and geographic markets. The Commission's product market definitions were unrealistically narrow: "light containers for canned meat products" and "light containers for canned seafood" might both be regarded as parts of a larger market for food containers. It was not clear that Continental could be considered as having a dominant position in such a larger market. Since the Commission had not met the required legal standard, the Court set aside the Commission's order blocking the merger.

Merger control under Article 101: *Philip Morris*[30]

In 1981, Philip Morris, Inc. agreed to acquire a controlling interest in one of its major European competitors, Rothman's Tobacco. Three of Philip Morris's competitors complained to the Commission that this acquisition of control violated Articles 101 and 102. In the light of subsequent Commission objections, Philip Morris revised the terms of the acquisition, which the Commission then approved. Two of Philip Morris's competitors appealed this approval to the European Court of Justice.

The ECJ affirmed the Commission decision. More importantly, however, the Court held that a merger resulting from agreement[31] could violate Article 101 if it affected trade among the member states and had the object or effect of distorting competition within the common market.

---

[30] British American Tobacco Ltd. *v.* Commission and R.J. Reynolds Inc. *v.* Commission, joined cases 142/84 and 156/84 [1987] ECR 4487 (*Philip Morris*).

[31] This would seem to exclude hostile takeovers.

22.3.2 The Merger Control Regulation

A long campaign

The European Commission sought merger control powers as early as its *Third Report on Competition Policy* (1974, pp. 28–29, emphasis in original):

> [T]he process of industrial concentration is on the increase. The causes lie largely in the desire and need of Community firms to adapt constantly to the new scale of their markets and to improve their competitiveness on the world market. Many mergers, as a result of the structure of the markets in which they occur, in no way lessen competition but, on the contrary, can increase it. However, the Commission cannot overlook that the EEC Treaty ... requires it to preserve the unity of the common market, to ensure that the market remains open and ensure effective competition. *Excessive* concentration is likely to obstruct these aims.

In this passage the Commission recognizes that market structure is determined by economic forces, that the process of market integration would result in increased seller concentration, and highlights its responsibility to maintain undistorted competition. The Commission's particular concern was for mergers that would create dominant positions, for the impact such positions would have on market performance and for the strategic entry-deterring behaviour they would make possible (1974, p. 32):

> The effects of mergers are particularly serious because the merger brings about an irreversible alteration of the structure of the market. Once a dominant position is attained, then substantial competition from the remaining firms on the market is not as a rule to be expected ... Furthermore, dominant firms are often in a position to prevent new competitors from entering the market.

Commission arguments in favor of merger control appear regularly in later *Reports*, but did not receive support of the member states. Two factors changed this. First, after *Continental Can* and *Philip Morris*, it was clear that the Commission had some merger control power under the EC Treaty. By accepting a merger control regulation, the member states could at least put their own imprint on Community control of market structure.

Business community support

Second, as market integration went forward, European businesses were obliged to seek the approval of national competition authorities from cross-border mergers. A "one-stop shop" in Brussels that could vet such mergers for the Community as a whole would be much easier to deal with. Market integration itself thus created support in the business community for EC-level merger control.

MCR

After the *Philip Morris* ruling that agreements to merge were covered by Article 101, and in view of the Regulation 17 notification procedure then in place, businesses began to notify proposed mergers to the Commission. The Single European Act, which had effect from 1 July 1987, aimed to jump-start the integration process. It created the prospect of an upswing in cross-border mergers and a flood of notifications for which the Article 101 notification process was ill-suited. Prompted by these disparate influences, political support coalesced and in 1989 the Council adopted the Merger Control Regulation.[32]

Community dimension   The broad outlines of the current regulation were present in 1989. The Merger Control Regulation makes a distinction between mergers that have and mergers that do not have "a Community dimension", as defined by criteria related to the sizes of the parties to a proposed merger and the extent to which their operations are diversified across member states. Mergers that have a Community dimension are vetted by the Commission; mergers that do not have a Community dimension are treated at the member state level.[33]

Timing   The Merger Control Regulation specifies a timetable intended to ensure prompt decisions. The Commission has a basic period (Phase I) of 25 working days to reach an initial decision on a notified merger. The basic period may be extended in some cases. The decision may be to declare the merger compatible, to refer the merger to a member state, or to open a proceeding, a more detailed examination of the proposed merger to evaluate compatibility. The basic period for a proceeding (Phase 2) is 90 working days. During either Phase 1 or Phase 2, the firms involved in the merger may propose modifications with a view to eliminating concerns about the compatibility of the merger with the common market.

Dominance $\longrightarrow$ significant impediment of competition   The substantive paragraph of the 1989 and 1997 MCRs emphasized impact on dominance as determining whether or not a proposed merger was compatible with the common market:

> A concentration which creates or strengthens a dominant position as a result of which effective competition would be significantly impeded in the common market or in a substantial part of it shall be declared incompatible with the common market.

The impact of the merger on effective competition appears as a qualifying factor. The 2004 revision of the Merger Control Regulation reversed this emphasis, giving priority to the impact of a proposed merger on effective competition. "Creation or strengthening a dominant position" now appears as an example illustrating one way a merger might significantly impede effective competition on the common market:

> A concentration which would significantly impede effective competition, in the common market or in a substantial part of it, in particular as a result of the creation or strengthening of a dominant position, shall be declared incompatible with the common market.

The reversal followed a debate, which we discuss below, about coverage of the Merger Control Regulation.

---

[32] Council Regulation (EEC) No 4064/89 OJ L 395/1 30.12.89, amended by Council Regulation (EC) No 1310/97, OJ L 180, 9.7.1997 and succeeded by Council Regulation (EC) No 139/2004 of 20 January 2004 OJ L 24, 29.01.2004, pp. 1–22.

[33] If a proposed merger does not have a Community dimension but would be examined by the competition authorities of three or more member states, the firms involved may request that the merger be vetted by the Commission. The Commission may assume responsibility for such mergers, if there is no objection by member state Authorities. For details, see Commission Notice on Case Referral in respect of concentrations, OJ C 56/2 5 March 2005.

22.3.3 Market Definition

Whether or not a concentration will impede effective competition can be assessed only in the context of a relevant product and geographic market. The process of market definition thus assumes a central role in EC merger control.

Identify competitive constraints

A 1997 Commission Notice[34] outlines competition policy market definition practice (1997b, p. 1):

> The main purpose of market definition is to identify ... the competitive constraints that the undertakings involved face. The objective of defining a market in both its product and geographic dimension is to identify those actual competitors of the undertakings involved that are capable of constraining their behavior and of preventing them from behaving independently of an effective competitive pressure.

SSNIP test

In principle, the Commission emphasizes the demand side when it defines markets (1997b, ¶ 7): "A relevant product market comprises all those products and/or services which are regarded as interchangeable or substitutable by the consumer" and (¶ 13) "Basically, the exercise of market definition consists in identifying the effective alternative sources of supply for customers of the undertakings involved, both in terms of products/services and geographic location of suppliers". The primary theoretical test that the Commission applies is the SSNIP test, emphasizing customer response (1997b, ¶ 17): "The question to be answered is whether the parties' customers would switch to readily available substitutes or to suppliers located elsewhere in response to an hypothetical small (in the range 5%–10%), permanent relative price increase in the products and areas being considered." The Commission also takes supply-side substitutability into account. Potential competition, on the other hand, is considered in evaluating entry conditions, after a relevant market has been defined.

 The Commission Notice on market definition suggests applying the SSNIP test "as a thought experiment". It may sometimes be possible to carry out apply the SSNIP test explicitly, using econometric analyses of demand to reach conclusions about the consequences of a small permanent price increase. Often the time and data requirements of such methods mean that they cannot be used by the Commission, subject as it is to the relatively strict time limits specified in the Merger Control Regulation. The Commission then looks at practical information about the nature of demand for a class of products (1997b, ¶¶ 37–42): historical substitution patterns, the views of customers and competitors, evidence of costs of switching from one brand or supplier to another, and whether there are distinctive national preferences or national (for example, tax or environmental) policies.

Avoid the *Cellophane* fallacy

The Commission is alert to the *Cellophane* fallacy (¶ 19):

> Generally, and in particular for the analysis of merger cases, the price to take into account will be the prevailing market price. This may not be the case where the prevailing price has been

---

[34] Commission notice on the definition of relevant market for the purposes of Community competition law (OJ C 372, 9.12.1997).

determined in the absence of sufficient competition. In particular for the investigation of abuses of dominant positions, the fact that the prevailing price might already have been substantially increased will be taken into account.

22.3.4 *de Havilland*

The French firm Aerospatiale and the Italian firm Alenia were the parent firms of the French company Avions de Transport Régional (ATR), a producer of regional turbo-prop aircraft. The two firms proposed to acquire de Havilland,[35] a Canadian division of Boeing and also a producer of regional turbo-prop aircraft. The Commission's 1991 *Aerospatiale-Alenia/de Havilland*[36] decision was the first in which it blocked a proposed merger.

Market definition

To assess the impact of the merger, the Commission needed to define the product and geographic market.[37] The nature of the geographic market (worldwide, excluding China and Eastern Europe) was not controversial. The Commission defined three distinct product markets: turbo-prop aircraft with 20 to 39 seats, 40 to 59 seats, and 60 or more seats. Thirty-seat and 60-seat commuter aircraft were viewed differently by consumers, were used on different kinds of routes, and sold for significantly different prices.[38] The Commission excluded jet aircraft from the market on the grounds that they were more expensive and used on different kinds of routes. It excluded smaller turbo-prop aircraft as being subject to different certification procedures and often not specifically designed to carry passengers.

The firms involved in the merger argued that there were only two markets, turbo-prop aircraft with 20–50 seats and with 51–70 seats. The Commission rejected this proposed definition, noting that it would place one 48-seat plane in a different market from three 50-seat planes, although competitors and customers regarded these planes as competing one with another.

The Commission's market share estimates for the European Community for the three product markets and overall are shown in Table 22.2. The direct impact of the merger on single-firm exercise of market power would have been in the 40 to 59 seat market, in which the merger would have created a firm with a market share of 72 per cent. The merger would have had indirect effects on the other two markets: it would have eliminated ATR as a potential entrant into the 20-to-39 seat submarket, and it would have eliminated de Havilland as a potential entrant into the 60 to 70 seat submarket.[39]

---

[35] de Havilland began life as a subsidiary of British de Havilland Aircraft (<http://epe.lac-bac.gc.ca/100/205/301/ic/cdc/canadair/default.htm>). Its connection with the de Havilland Comet (<http://www.geocities.com/CapeCanaveral/Lab/8803/comet.htm>) is therefore only indirect.

[36] Commission Decision 91/619/EEC of 2 October 1991 OJ L 334/42 5.12.91.

[37] The Commission also had to establish that the proposed merger had a community dimension, but this was not in dispute.

[38] The Commission also considered supply-side substitutability, the possibility that a producer of a turbo-prop aircraft of one size class could diversify into production of a turbo-prop aircraft of a different size. It viewed such diversification as possible, but only after a long transition period.

[39] The Commission also wrote (¶ 32) that "It appears that, in the sector concerned, having a complete range of products would give ATR/de Havilland a significant advantage in itself. From the demand side, airlines derive cost

Table 22.2 EEC market share estimates, turbo-prop commuter aircraft

20 to 39 seats		40 to 59 seats		60 to 70 seats		20 to 70 seats	
Embraer	41	ATR	51	ATR	74	ATR	49
Saab	31	DHC	21	BAe	26	DHC	16
DHC	21	Fokker	22			Fokker	12
BAe	6	Saab	7			BAe	8
Dornier	1	Casa	7			Embraer	6
						Saab	5
						Casa	3
						Dornier	1

Note: ATR = Avions de Transport Régional; DHC = de Havilland; BAe = British Aerospace
Source: OJ No L 334/48–9.

Effect

The Commission's decision included a firm-by-firm analysis of the likely competitive strength of rival firms in the post-merger market. It concluded that there would be effective competition only in the 20–39 seat submarket. The Commission also discussed entry conditions. Entry would require two to three years marketing research to understand market needs and another four years to bring an aircraft to market, both involving substantial fixed and sunk costs, so that entry was not a realistic possibility.

The companies suggested that they would save 5 million ECU per year by rationalizing procurement, marketing, and product support. The Commission pointed out that this was 1/2 of 1 per cent of the combined annual turnover of ATR and de Havilland, and that the reorganizations might to a large extent be undertaken by de Havilland alone, or by de Havilland and a partner in an alternative merger.

The Commission concluded that the merger, if allowed to go forward, would establish a dominant position in the 40-to-59-seat and 60-and-over-seat submarkets, and that this dominant position was not likely to be eroded by entry. It therefore declared the merger to be incompatible with the common market, and forbade it.

---

advantages from buying different types from the same seller." Without more, however, that a post-merger firm gains a competitive advantage by offering customers a product that reduces the customers' costs improves market performance.

22.3.5 Joint Dominance

Toward the end of the twentieth century, the Commission applied the Merger Control Regulation to mergers which, in its view, would create market structures compatible with oligopolistic joint dominance. As we have seen in discussion of the *Woodpulp* decision, the Commission has had limited success applying Article 101 to markets with structures that allow firms in oligopoly to jointly but non-collusively exercise market power: the European Court of Justice has held that parallel behaviour alone does not violate EC competition policy. Use of the concept of joint dominance in merger policy can be seen as a logical line of development of competition policy to attempt to prevent the emergence of market structures that would allow firms to non-cooperatively exercise market power. The Court of First Instance reversed several of these decisions, leading the Commission to tighten its procedures and increase the sophistication of its economic analysis.

Gencor/Lonrho

Market definition   The *Gencor/Lonrho* case illustrates the issues involved in the concept of joint dominance. Here the product market was platinum and the geographic market was the world, with various submarkets. The firms directly involved were Gencor, a South African firm controlling the leading South African platinum mining company, and Lonrho, a UK firm controlling two large South African platinum mines. These two firms proposed to merge. A third firm, Amplats (Anglo American Platinum Corporation), was not involved in the merger, but would have become the second largest supplier in the market if the merger had gone forward.

Effects   The European Commission's theory of the case was that if the merger were permitted, Gencor/Lonrho and Amplats together would have a combined world market share of 60–70 per cent, a share that would grow to 80 per cent after Russian supplies were depleted.

As the European Commission (1999b, p. 66) interpreted the rulings of the European Court of Justice, to justify a finding of collective dominance the Commission needed to show that a merger would eliminate competition between the post-merger firm and some other firm or firms, allowing them to jointly act as a dominant firm, even though the behaviour by which such joint dominance would be made effective would not amount to collusion or a concerted practice under Article 101.

Market characteristics that might lead to a finding of joint dominance are high market concentration as well as (EC Commission, 1999b, p. 67) "homogeneous products, transport, high entry barriers, mature technology, static or falling demand, links between suppliers, absence of countervailing buyer power, etc". The Commission concluded that the Gencor/Lonrho merger would create a position of joint dominance, and blocked it. The Court of First Instance upheld the Commission.

Airtours/First Choice[40]

Market structure   The Commission's next joint dominance case involved the markets for short-haul (less than three hour travel time) package holiday tours from and travel agency services in the United Kingdom and Ireland. As the Commission saw it, the supply side

---

[40] *Airtours/First Choice* Commission Decision of 22 September 1999 (Case IV/M.1524); Airtours plc *v.* EC Commission Case T-342/99 (2002).

structure of these markets was a core of four oligopolistic suppliers[41]—Airtours, First Choice, Thomson, and Thomas Cook—and fringes of much smaller travel agencies and tour operators. Firms in the oligopolistic core were vertically integrated, operating charter airlines and setting capacity—in the form of available tour bookings—about 12 to 18 months in advance of vacation travel. Fringe tour operators booked seats on charter airlines, mostly operated by core firms, and marketed them through travel agencies, again mostly operated by core firms.

Effects In the Commission's view, a takeover of First Choice by Airtours would increase oligopolistic interdependence among the reduced number of core firms and marginalize fringe firms, who would be faced with the necessity of purchasing essential inputs— transportation services—from their larger competitors. Increased concentration among leading firms would make it easier for them to restrict capacity, without tacit or overt collusion: the takeover would facilitate joint dominance.[42] The Commission therefore condemned the takeover as incompatible with the common market, on the ground that it would create a position of collective dominance in the UK market for short-haul foreign package holidays. In its decision, the Commission was explicit that collective dominance is not simply another term for tacit collusion—it refers to *unilateral effects* of a merger, a structural change that moves firms in an imperfectly competitive market from an equilibrium in which they non-cooperatively exercise less market power to an equilibrium in which they non-cooperatively exercise more market power (¶ 54, footnote omitted):[43]

> Furthermore ... it is not a necessary condition of collective dominance for the oligopolists always to behave as if there were one or more explicit agreements (e.g. to fix prices or capacity, or share the market) between them. It is sufficient that the merger makes it rational for the oligopolists, in adapting themselves to market conditions, to act, individually, in ways which will substantially reduce competition between them, and as a result of which they may act, to an appreciable extent, independently of competitors, customers and consumers.

On appeal The emphasis here should be on "to act, individually". Airtours appealed the Commission's decision, most importantly on the ground that the Commission had not offered sufficient proof to conclude that the merger would create a position of collective dominance. In dealing with the appeal, the Court of First Instance declined to follow the Commission's conception of collective dominance as including individual firm choices that increase the joint exercise of market power. Instead, it wrote, collective dominance involved adoption of a common policy (¶ 61):

---

[41] The Commission estimated the shares of the four vertically-integrated firms in the short-haul package holiday market at 21 per cent (Airtours), 11 per cent (First Choice), 27 per cent (Thomson), and 20 per cent (Thomas Cook).

[42] In its decision, the Commission suggests a relatively complex model that is reminiscent of the Kreps and Scheinkman (1983) model of oligopolistic capacity decisions followed by price competition. Kreps and Scheinkman show that such a two-stage model has the same equilibrium outcome as the Cournot model. Problem 22–1 asks you to show that in a model of a Cournot oligopoly core with a price-taking fringe, a decrease in the number of core firms from four to three increases the equilibrium price.

[43] Mergers in markets where firms' choice variables are strategic complements (Bulow *et al.*, 1985) will have unilateral effects in this sense. For discussion in the context of EC merger control, see Motta (2000), Kühn (2002a), Ivaldi *et al.* (2003b).

A collective dominant position significantly impeding effective competition in the common market or a substantial part of it may thus arise as the result of a concentration where, in view of the actual characteristics of the relevant market and of the alteration in its structure that the transaction would entail, the latter would make each member of the dominant oligopoly, as it becomes aware of common interests, consider it possible, economically rational, and hence preferable, to adopt on a lasting basis a common policy on the market with the aim of selling at above competitive prices ...

To support a finding of collective dominance, wrote the Court of First Instance (¶ 62), it was necessary to show that the market was sufficiently transparent to allow core oligopolists to monitor each others' conduct, that reactions to competitive behaviour could come quickly enough to make tacit coordination sustainable, and that entry or consumer reaction would not make tacit coordination unprofitable. This conceives of collective dominance as a manifestation of tacit collusion.

Considered in light of these requirements, the Court found the Commission's decision wanting. Contrary to Commission conclusions, there was evidence that the demand for short-haul package tours was both growing and volatile, characteristics that might destabilize oligopoly coordination. The Commission had not provided enough evidence that the market was transparent, had not demonstrated that there were effective retaliatory mechanisms, and had underestimated both the ability of fringe firms to expand and the possibility of entry. For the Court of First Instance, the Commission had not proven its case, and it annulled the Commission's decision.

22.3.6 *Schneider/Legrand*[44]

The Commission's October 2001 *Schneider/Legrand* decision concerned the takeover by Schneider Electric, the French parent firm of a group of companies producing a wide variety of electrical equipment, of Legrand, a French firm specializing in low-voltage electrical equipment. During the Phase 2 procedure, the companies argued that Europe was the appropriate geographic market. The Commission disagreed, and defined each member state as a distinct geographic market, surrounded by entry barriers, with important national product differences, supply and demand decisions, and prices. The Commission prohibited the merger, which had already been carried out, on the ground that it would create or reenforce a dominant position in the relevant product markets.

On appeal

Schneider appealed the Commission decision to the Court of First Instance. One basis of the appeal was that the Commission had designated national geographic markets, but its analysis of the impact of the merger on competition rested heavily on evidence of effects in Europe as a whole. If the geographic markets are national, argued Schneider, then it is the impact of the merger in each geographic market that should be analysed. A procedural objection was that one of the grounds for the Commission's decision (that the merger would strengthen Schneider's dominant position in the French market for panel boards) had not been made

---

[44] *Schneider/Legrand* Commission Decision of 10 October 2001 (Case COMP/M.2283) OJ L 101/1 6 April 2004; Schneider Electric SA *v.* EC Commission, Case T-310/01 (2002); Schneider Electric SA *v.* European Commission, Case T-351/03 (2007).

clear in the Commission's statement of objections to the merger. As a result, Schneider had not been able to make counterarguments or propose modifications to the merger to address that issue.

The Court of First Instance accepted Schneider/Legrand's views, writing in scathing if judicially restrained language that (¶ 404) "The Court considers the errors, omissions and inconsistencies which it has found in the Commission's analysis of the impact of the merger to be of undoubted gravity." The Court nonetheless gave the Commission a small measure of consolation. It accepted that the merger would strengthen or create a dominant position in French markets, and cleared the way for the Commission to reanalyse the impact of the merger on this geographic market, admonishing it to act in such a way the Schneider/Legrand could defend itself properly and offer appropriate remedies, if it were inclined to do so. The Commission carried a reinvestigation through Phase 2, and this process ended in December 2002, when Schneider sold Legrand.[45]

22.3.7 *Tetra Laval/Sidel*[46]

Market definition

The third Commission reversal in its *annus horribilis* of 2002 involved a merger with horizontal and vertical aspects between Tetra Laval, the world leader in carton packaging and producer of liquid food processing equipment and the French firm Sidel, also a producer of packaging equipment and the world leader in equipment for stretch blow molding plastic bottles. Tetra Laval presented the merger as affecting the market for PET (polythylene terephthalate) transparent plastic bottles, commonly used for mineral water and soft drinks. The Commission defined a broad product market for liquid-food packaging and a market for stretch blow molding (SBM) machines. Within the market for liquid food packaging, there were markets for PET plastic bottles, and two types of cartons, aseptic (sterile) and non-aseptic cartons.

Effects

Analysing the impact of the merger, the Commission concluded that (¶ 260) "the operation should be seen primarily as the merger between the dominant company in carton packaging equipment and the leading company in PET packaging equipment, two closely neighboring markets, with significant repercussions in the liquid-food packaging sector". Tetra offered various commitments to alleviate the Commission's concerns, but the Commission condemned the merger.

---

[45] In October, 2003, Schneider filed a claim for damages against the Commission, under the little used Article 340 of the EC Treaty, which provides the possibility of recovery of damages caused by the EC. In July 2007, the Court of First Instance awarded Schneider damages, although less than the € 1.7 billion sought. The award of damages was based on the procedural irregularities of the merger evaluation, not the substance of the Commission's economic analysis. This would have been the first award of damages against the Commission for a merger decision. However, the Commission appealed the Court of First Instance outcome to the European Court of Justice, which overturned the award in July, 2009. The successor of Airtours, MyTravel Group plc, sought damages after the Commission's prohibition of its proposed merger was overturned, but this bid was denied by the Court of First Instance in September, 2008.

[46] *Tetra Laval/Sidel* Commission Decision of 30 October 2001 (Case No COMP/M. 2416) OJ L 43/13 13.2.2004; Tetra Laval BV *v.* Commission Case T-5/02 (2002).

On appeal

Tetra appealed to the Court of First Instance, which saw a fundamental weakness in the Commission's argument. Accepting the product markets as defined by the Commission, the merger was primarily vertical. Sidel's machines, used to make plastic bottles, were an input into production of plastic bottles. It was the bottles that were substitutes, in some measure, for the carton containers that were Tetra's strong suit. As the Court of First Instance saw it, horizontal links were not sufficiently present to justify the conclusion that the merger would strengthen a dominant position, particularly after Tetra's offer to divest itself of its own SBM division (a commitment rejected by the Commission).

This left vertical relationships as the basis for the conclusion that the merger would create or strengthen a dominant position. But Sidel, while the world leader in SBM machines, did not have a dominant position in that market, and the divestitures offered by Tetra would reduce vertical effects. The Commission also relied on conglomerate effects to block the merger: after the merger, Tetra could engage in predatory pricing, price wars, or use loyalty rebates. But the Court pointed out that such conduct, were it to occur, would be based on Tetra's existing dominant position in liquid food cartons, and could in any event be punished by the Commission under Article 102. For the Court, the Commission had to make the case that it was plausible for such behaviour to occur, given its illegality and the likelihood that it would be detected and punished, and this the Commission had not done. The Court of First Instance annulled the Commission's decision.[47]

22.3.8 Institutional Reform and the More Economic Approach to Merger Control

The European Commission contemplated revision of the Merger Control Regulation as early as June 2000 (Monti, 2003, p. 364), and issued a Green Paper on Merger Reform (EC Commission, 2001) the following year. The reform process was accelerated by the three Court of First Instance annulments in 2002, annulments on grounds that seemed clearly to call for reenforced economic input to and rigour in the merger review process. In 2003, to address these issues, DG Competition appointed a Chief Economist, to head a group of industrial economists, and instituted a process of internal review of merger decisions by an independent panel.

The reform process stimulated a debate about the coverage of the MCR. The wording of the MCR expressly prohibited mergers that would create or strengthen a single-firm dominant position. By interpretation, it was applied to mergers that would create or strengthen a joint dominant position. The debate was whether the MCR could be applied to mergers with unilateral effects—mergers that did not create or strengthen a single-firm dominant position, did not alter market conditions to facilitate tacit collusion, but nonetheless worsened market performance.

Some EU member states argued that the MCR should be amended to make clear that it applied to unilateral effects and also, in the interest of international harmonization, that the "significant lessening of competition" standard of U.S. merger control should be adopted. Other member states, and the Commission, argued that it was sufficient to apply the received wording of the MCR, by interpretation, to mergers with unilateral effects. The compromise

---

[47] The European Court of Justice upheld the CFI decision against an appeal by the Commission (Commission v. Tetra Laval BV Case C-13/03 (2005)).

outcome gave the EC the *significant impediment of effective competition* (SIEC) test embodied in the 2004 MCR. The policy treatment of a proposed merger now hinges on the impact of the merger on effective competition. As EC Competition Commissioner Mario Monti wrote (2002), "Preserving competition is not, however, an end in itself. The ultimate policy goal is the protection of consumer welfare."[48]

Horizontal Merger Guidelines

Non-coordinated effects According to the Commission's 2004 *Horizontal Merger Guidelines*, there are two main ways a horizontal merger can fail the SIEC test, either by increasing the market power of individual firms (non-coordinated effects) or by facilitating tacit collusion (coordinated effects). A merger is more likely to increase the market power of individual firms if firms have large market shares and seller concentration is high. The Guidelines indicate that the Commission is unlikely to find a significant impediment to effective competition if the market Herfindahl index is less than 1,000. If the Herfindahl index is between 1,000 and 2,000, the Commission is unlikely to find a significant impediment to effective competition if the merger increases the Herfindahl index by less than 250, and if the Herfindahl index is more than 2,000, if the increase in the Herfindahl index is less than 150.[49] Other factors the Commission takes into account in analysing the impact of a horizontal merger on market performance are substitutability between the merging firms' products, consumer switching costs, rivals' potential to expand output, and possibilities for the post-merger firm to strategically impede rival expansion.

Coordinated effects In line with the economic analysis of tacit collusion, the Commission will consider that the coordinated effects of a merger impede effective competition if the merger makes it easier for firms to coordinate conduct, easier to detect deviations, or easier to punish deviations. The reaction of outsiders to tacit coordination is also taken into account.

Potential competition Ease of entry mitigates against finding against a SIEC—if entry could be "likely, timely and sufficient to deter" anticompetitive effects. The Commission therefore takes the impact of potential competition on market performance into account, provided it is realistic to suppose that potential competition could become actual competition if entry were profitable.

Efficiency The same is true of merger-specific efficiencies that can be verified and would benefit consumers. Finally, the Commission would permit an otherwise troublesome merger involving a failing firm, if the firm and its assets would in any case exit the market and if there were no less anticompetitive feasible merger.

---

[48] Article 2(1)(b) of the Merger Control Regulation, which refers to "the interests of the intermediate and ultimate consumers", makes clear that for EC competition policy, "consumer welfare" means "the welfare of consumers", not "the welfare of consumers plus the welfare of the owners of firms". Recall, from Section 2.3.3, that a consumer welfare standard does not disregard the welfare of the owners of firms: it simply measures their welfare as consumers, not as receivers of dividend income.

[49] These thresholds are somewhat less stringent than those of the U.S. Guidelines; see Section 22.2.4.

Non-horizontal Merger Guidelines

The Commission's *2008 Non-Horizontal Merger Guidelines* follow the Horizontal Guidelines in identifying non-coordinated and coordinated effects as possible sources of significant impediments to effective competition from vertical and conglomerate mergers. Taking the general view that non-horizontal mergers are less likely than horizontal mergers to worsen market performance and have greater potential to generate efficiencies, the Commission indicates it is not likely to be concerned with non-horizontal mergers where post-merger market shares in the relevant markets are below 30 per cent, and the post-merger Herfindahl indices below 2000.

With respect to non-coordinated effects, the Guidelines see the vice of vertical mergers, if there be one, in foreclosure (¶ 29), "where actual or potential rivals' access to supplies or markets is hampered or eliminated as a result of the merger, thereby reducing these companies' ability and/or incentive to compete". For conglomerate mergers, while recognizing that (¶ 93) "[t]ying and bundling as such are common practices that often have no anti-competitive consequences", the Guidelines nonetheless consider that a conglomerate merger may sometimes make it possible and profitable "to leverage a strong market position from one market to another by means of tying or bundling or other exclusionary practices". Non-horizontal mergers may have coordinated effects that raise competition policy concerns if they facilitate tacit collusion.

22.4 Transatlantic Disagreement

"Monopolization" and "abuse of a dominant position" are not the same thing, and facts that overlap substantially are not identical. The Sherman Act Section 2 prohibition of monopolization and the EC Treaty Article 102 prohibition of abuse of a dominant position can therefore yield different results when applied to substantially the same conduct. The conflict can be stark when a proposed merger is approved by antitrust authorities in one jurisdiction and rejected by competition authorities in another, as with the proposed and ultimately blocked *General Electric-Honeywell*[50] merger.[51]

22.4.1 Antitrust

General Electric is a conglomerate with (of particular interest in the present context) a division that produces aircraft engines. It proposed to take over Honeywell International, also highly diversified and a supplier of the aerospace industry. The U.S. Department of Justice was concerned with some of the horizontal aspects of the merger. These were resolved (U.S. DOJ press release, 2 May 2001) when the companies agreed to divest Honeywell's helicopter engine business and to authorize an independent firm to service certain Honeywell engines and power units.

---

[50] *GE/Honeywell* Commission decision of 3 July 2001 OJ L 48/1 18.2.2004; Honeywell International Inc. *v.* EC Commission Case T-209/01 (2005); General Electric Company *v.* EC Commission Case T-210/01 (2005).

[51] See also a near-disagreement, *Boeing/McDonnell Douglas* Commission Decision of 30 July 1997 (Case No IV/M.877) OJ L 336/16 8.12.1997, and an instance of opposite decisions at the level of enforcement agencies, the *Oracle/PeopleSoft* merger, unsuccessfully challenged by the U.S. Department of Justice (U.S. *v.* Oracle Corp. 331 F. Supp. 2d 1098 (2004)) but cleared by the European Commission (*Oracle/PeopleSoft* Commission decision of 26 October 2004 (Case No COMP/M. 3216)).

22.4.2 Competition Policy

The European Commission regarded General Electric as dominant in the markets for jet engines for large commercial aircraft and jet engines for large regional aircraft. The Commission's analysis of the consequences of the merger also involved General Electric's activities in two other markets. Through its GE Capital division, it arranged airline financing for the purchase of aircraft. Through its GE Capital Aviation Services division (GECAS), it leased aircraft, and "[w]ith around 10 % of the total purchases of aircraft, [was] the largest purchaser of new aircraft, ahead of any individual airline". General Electric was thus a significant customer for aircraft manufactured by firms to which it sold engines and aerospace equipment.

Honeywell was a leading producer of avionics and non-avionics products, jet engines for large regional aircraft, jet engines for corporate jets, and jet engine starters. Avionics equipment is used for navigation, communication, and control. Non-avionics equipment handles other essential aircraft functions, such as control of power systems and landing gear. A GE/Honeywell merger would thus combine complementary products—jet engines, avionics and non-avionics are all inputs to the manufacture of jet aircraft—and would therefore have been a conglomerate merger. It would have been a vertical merger, Honeywell's jet engine starters being an input into the manufacture of GE's (and rival) jet engines. It would also have been a horizontal merger, of GE and Honeywell regional jet aircraft operations and of GE and Honeywell small marine gas turbine products.

The Commission found that the horizontal, vertical, and conglomerate aspects of the merger all ran afoul of the 1997 Merger Control Regulation. It concluded that the horizontal combination of the two firms' large regional jet aircraft engine operations would create a monopoly. The merger would also create a dominant position in small marine gas turbines. The vertical merger would allow GE/Honeywell to raise rivals' cost of engine starters, reenforcing GE's dominant position in jet engine markets. The conglomerate merger would allow GE Capital to boost Honeywell's positions in avonics and non-avionics from leading to dominant. It would also make it possible to bundle jet engines, avionics, and non-avionics products and so reenforce GE's dominant position in large commercial jet aircraft engines.

Article 102/MCR

Although they abandoned their proposed merger, GE and Honeywell appealed the Commission's decision to the Court of First Instance as a matter of principle. One ground of the appeal was that the Merger Control Regulation laid out a two-part test—Would the merger create or strengthen a dominant position? Would the merger significantly impede effective competition?—and the Commission decision addressed only the first part.

Special responsibility   Although merger control was a recent addition to EC competition policy, the operative provision of the 1997 Merger Control Regulation hinged on dominance, and applications of Article 102 had given the European courts ample opportunity to speak to the issues of dominance and abuse of dominance. "Abuse of a dominant position" and a "significant impediment to effective competition" are not the same thing, but the Court of First Instance applied two principles from Article 102 jurisprudence to the Merger Control Regulation "by analogy" (¶ 549; see also ¶¶85, 86).[52] First, "a finding that an undertaking

---

[52] There is at least one essential difference between applications of Article 102 and applications of the Merger Control Regulation. Applications of Article 102 are backward looking: is conduct that has occurred abusive?

is in a dominant position is not in itself a finding of fault". Second, "irrespective of the reasons for which it holds such a dominant position, the undertaking concerned has a special responsibility not to allow its conduct to impair genuine undistorted competition on the common market . . . "

In view of the special responsibility that EC competition policy assigns to dominant firms, the Court of First Instance states what approaches a *per se* rule against merger by dominant firms (¶ 87): "It follows . . . that the strengthening or creation of a dominant position, within the meaning of Article 2(3) of Regulation No 4064/89, may amount, in particular cases, to proof of a significant impediment to effective competition."

Dominance

If strengthening or creating a dominant position by merger is sometimes sufficient, in and of itself, to show a significant impediment to competition, that lends importance to the standards for establishing that there is a dominant position. Citing *Hoffmann-La Roche*, the Court of First Instance wrote (¶ 115) that "although the importance of market shares may vary from one market to another, very large shares are in themselves, and save in exceptional circumstances, evidence of the existence of a dominant position", and from *AKZO*, "that was so in the case of a 50% market share". [53] Again from *Hoffmann-La Roche*, however, (¶ 116) "the fact that an undertaking is compelled by the pressure of its competitors' price reductions to lower its own prices is in general incompatible with that independent conduct which is the hallmark of a dominant position".

On Appeal

Those parts of the Commission decision that condemned the merger for its vertical and conglomerate aspects were subject to heavy criticism. In its review, the Court of First Instance accepted the Commission's contention that GE had a dominant position in the market for large commercial aircraft jet engines. But it concluded that the Commission had not proven that vertical raising of rivals' costs, leverage from GE's financial division, or bundling of jet engines and avionics/non-avionics products would create or strengthen dominant positions. It accepted that horizontal aspects of the merger would reenforce a dominant position in regional commercial jet aircraft engines and create dominant positions in corporate aircraft jet engines and small marine gas turbines. Relying on mainstream economic analyses of the horizontal effects of the merger, the Court of First Instance upheld the Commission decision.

22.5 Merger Remedies

The EC's Merger Control Regulation requires that mergers with a Community dimension be notified in advance to the Commission, and merger control procedures provide the possibility for merging parties to alter the terms of their combination to alleviate Commission concerns about anticompetitive effects. Merging parties may agree to sell some of their assets to a third party, or to divest assets and establish a new competitor, to obtain Commission approval. Similar notification and negotiation practices have been part of U.S. antitrust since

---

Applications of the Merger Control Regulation are forward-looking: to prohibit a merger, the Commission must demonstrate that there would be a significant impediment to competition if the merger were allowed (¶ 295).

[53] See similarly the EC Commission's 2004 Horizontal Merger Guidelines, ¶ 17.

passage of the Hart-Scott-Rodino Antitrust Improvements Act of 1976, which requires parties to a merger meeting specified size requirements to provide the Federal Trade Commission and the U.S. Department of Justice with 30 days advance notice (15 days for all-cash transactions) of their intent to merge.[54]

Antitrust and competition policy establish penalties for collusion, monopolization, and abuse of a dominant position to establish incentives that lead firms, in their own self-interest, not to engage in conduct thought to worsen market performance. With merger control, on the other hand, the goal is to permit such rearrangements of assets as firms think privately desirable, without worsening market performance. How well divestitures establish viable competitors is therefore central to the effectiveness of merger control policy.

22.5.1 FTC Study

A 1999 Federal Trade Commission study retrospectively examines the functioning of 35 divestitures carried out in the early 1990s as conditions for merger approval. Three-quarters of the divestitures succeeded in some measure. Buyers of divested assets, whether small or large, established in other markets or new firms, generally lacked adequate information to negotiate terms of acquisition conducive to success. The FTC Report writes (p. 23) "Because the mistakes are so pervasive in the experiences of both successful and unsuccessful buyers, staff is persuaded that mistakes by buyers are inherent in the acquisition process, particularly where buyers have no previous experience in the market. In general, it is not possible to anticipate fully how a firm will operate in advance of the acquisition because the nature of a business is too complex." The FTC Report also observes that before divestiture merging firms tend to seek buyers for to-be-divested assets who will be weak competitors, and after divestiture sometimes engage in strategic behaviour to hamstring the buyer's commercial success.

To promote successful divestiture, the FTC Report suggests appointment of an auditor trustee to monitor the divestiture process. To create incentives for the merging parties to make divestiture work, divestiture orders might include "crown jewel" provisions—further divestiture of vital assets if the initial divestiture stumbles. Buyers should have adequate information before acquisition of the divested assets, and the divestiture agreement should ensure that a buyer receives all necessary technological information.

22.5.2 DG Competition Study

In 2005, DG Competition issued a study of the effectiveness of 96 remedies agreed to in 40 decisions over the five-year period 1996–2000. For 79 per cent of the divestiture remedies studied, it appeared that the divestiture was of insufficient size, inappropriate vertical or geographic structure, was assigned an unsuitable mix of products, or received inadequate

---

[54] Among the early U.S. decisions under the amended Section 7 of the Clayton Act, the legal formalities of the Brown Shoe-Kinney merger were completed while the antitrust action against the merger went forward, but the companies agreed to separate the operations of the two firms until the antitrust case produced a result. The *Von's Grocery* merger was consummated while the government challenge was underway; the final decision blocking the merger came some six years after it had been carried out. The Hart-Scott-Rodino Act makes it possible for U.S. enforcement agencies to collect information needed to evaluate whether or not a merger should be challenged, and avoids situations in which a successful challenge requires a merger to be undone long after it has been carried out (on the latter, see Elzinga, 1969).

intellectual property rights. The study suggests that to obtain an effective remedy, it is not sufficient to focus on the competitive problems created by the merger and focus on divesting a combination of assets that will eliminate those problems. Care must be taken to ensure it is a commercially viable combination of assets that is carved out of the merging firms.

SUMMARY

In both the United States and the European Community, early and limited merger control was under laws that aimed to control collusion, monopolization, or abuse of a dominant position and happened to catch some mergers. The first U.S. approach to merger control, which dates to 1914, was essentially a publicity measure. It sought to promote a complete flow of information and was otherwise content to rely on market forces to determine market structure. The U.S. came late, and the EC after some time, to proactive merger control. Early U.S. applications of that approach were faithful to congressional intent and applied a structuralist approach that reflected the economic knowledge of its day. A series of U.S. merger guidelines have had the merit of highlighting maintenance of good market performance as the fundamental goal of merger control policy, with structure and likely conduct as factors that affect performance but are not goals in themselves. Application of these merger guidelines has sometimes been marked by a willingness to accept efficiency claims for mergers that are not, in general, justified by the evidence.

EC merger control has evolved in response to the insistence of European courts on a high level of economic input. EC horizontal merger guidelines have much in common with their U.S. counterparts. EC guidelines for control of non-horizontal mergers are consistent with the economic analysis of strategic anticompetitive behaviour in imperfect competitive markets, admitting the possibility that such mergers may permit vertical foreclosure or the leveraging of economic power from one market to another with results that worsen market performance.

STUDY POINTS

- U.S. Merger Policy
  - Clayton Act (Original, Section 22.2.1; Celler-Kefauver amendment, Section 22.2.2)
  - Decisions (Section 22.2.3)
    - *Brown Shoe*
    - *Philadelphia National Bank*
    - *Von's Grocery*
    - *General Dynamics*
  - Antitrust injury (Section 22.2.3)
  - Merger Guidelines; market definition; *Cellophane* fallacy (pp. 789–790)
- EC Merger Policy
  - Before the MCR (Section 22.3.1)
  - Merger Control Regulation (Section 22.3.2)
  - Market definition (Section 22.3.3)
  - *de Havilland* (Section 22.3.4)

- Joint dominance (Section 22.3.5)

- *Schneider/Legrand* (Section 22.3.6)

- *Tetra Laval/Sidel* (Section 22.3.7)

- More economic approach (Section 22.3.8)

• *GE/Honeywell* (Section 22.4)

• Merger remedies (Section 22.5)

FURTHER READING

For the background of the Celler-Kefauver Act, see Martin (1959), Bok (1960), Fisher and Lande (1983, Section I. A). On market definition for antitrust and competition policy, see Fingleton *et al.* (1999, Section 4.2), Werden (2003), Baker (2007), and Scherer (2009). On U.S. Guidelines generally, see White (1987), Willig (1991), U.S. Department of Justice and FTC *Commentary* (2006). On the Hart-Scott-Rodino Act, see Eckbo and Wier (1985), the FTC's 1999 *Study of the Commission's Divestiture Process*, and the Symposium in the Spring, 1997 *Antitrust Law Journal*. On EU merger remedies, in addition to EC Commission (2005a), see Motta *et al.* (2007).

On the development of EU merger policy, see Neven *et al.* (1993), Bulmer (1994), and Büthe and Swank (2005). On the 2004 revision, see Kühn (2002b), Lyons (2004), Monti (2004), Röller and Strohm (2006), Röller and de la Mano, (2006), and on the role of economists at DG Competition, Röller (2005).

PROBLEM

21–1 (Cournot oligopoly core, price-taking fringe) Let the market inverse demand equation be:

$$Q = \alpha - \beta p, \tag{22.4}$$

with $\alpha, \beta > 0$.

There is a fringe of small price-taking firms, with (for simplicity) a linear fringe supply curve, with fringe firms shutting down for low prices:

$$q_f = \begin{cases} -d + ep & p \geq \frac{d}{e} \\ 0 & p < \frac{d}{e} \end{cases} \tag{22.5}$$

(with $d, e > 0$).

Find the equation of the residual demand curve. Find Cournot equilibrium outputs and price if there are n firms in the oligopoly core, all with constant marginal cost c per unit.

How does price change if the number of firms in the core changes from four to three?

PUBLIC POLICY TOWARD PRICE DISCRIMINATION

> The peculiar power of the trust ... consists in this ability to make discriminating prices to its own customers; and this power resides entirely in its own hands. It can sell its products in one place more cheaply than it sells them elsewhere. Where a competitor has secured a local trade, it can ruin him by flooding his market with goods sold below the cost of producing them. ... If the low prices had to be universal, the powerful corporation would ruin itself as rapidly as it would its rival.
>
> Clark (1894, p. 26)

23.1 Introduction

The welfare effects of price discrimination are ambiguous. Yet U.S. antitrust policy and EU competition policy have been fundamentally hostile toward price discrimination. The U.S. approach reflects two fundamentally incompatible concerns, a hostility toward *predatory* price discrimination that goes back to the beginning of antitrust and a protectionist reaction to the spread of chain stores that can be traced to the Great Depression of the 1930s. The EU competition policy concern with price discrimination is rooted in a desire to avoid the segmentation of the common market along the lines of national boundaries.

23.2 U.S. Antitrust

23.2.1 Predatory Price Discrimination

The original Section 2(a) of the Clayton Act banned price discrimination that was likely to substantially lessen competition (emphasis added):

> ... it shall be unlawful for any person engaged in commerce, in the course of such commerce, either directly or indirectly to discriminate in price between different purchasers of commodities ... *where the effect* of such discrimination *may be to substantially lessen competition* or tend to create a monopoly in any line of commerce ...

This language was designed to combat practices like the discriminatorily low railroad rates received by the Standard Oil Company. The prohibition of price discrimination aimed to combat strategic exclusion of firms that would have been cost-efficient except for the discriminatorily low price received by a rival. The emphasis on protecting the ability of equally efficient firms to compete was confirmed by the wording of the original Section 2(a), which permitted price differences "between purchasers of commodities on account of differences in the grade, quality, or quantity of the commodity sold".

23.2.2 Protecting Small Grocers

Section 2(a) of the Clayton Act was amended by the Robinson-Patman Act of 1936. The first draft of the amending legislation was written by a lawyer of the United States Wholesale Grocers' Association (Kintner, 1978, p. 2895). It was frankly protectionist (Rowe, 1962, p. 3):[1]

> The Robinson-Patman Act of 1936 was the product of organized political efforts to preserve the traditional marketing system of independent merchants against the encroachment of mass distributors and chains, whose low-price appeal to consumers was enhanced during the general business crisis of the 1930s.

The amended Section 2(a) of the Clayton Act limited the scope of the quantity-discount justification for price differences. It now includes a provision that removes the quantity-discount justification for sales above limits set by the Federal Trade Commission:

> ... the Federal Trade Commission may, after due investigation and hearing to all interested parties, fix and establish quantity limits, and revise the same as it finds necessary, as to particular commodities or classes of commodities, where it finds that available purchasers in greater quantities are so few as to render differentials on account thereof unjustly discriminatory or promotive of monopoly in any line of commerce; and the foregoing shall then not be construed to permit differentials based on differences in quantities greater than those so fixed and established ...

By providing protection for firms that are not able to compete on the merits, in the absence of strategic behaviour by rivals, the amended Section 2(a) of the Clayton Act does not seek to promote good market performance. It is therefore, in its origin, at cross purposes with the main lines of U.S. antitrust policy. But the condition that it applies only "where the effect ... may be to substantially lessen competition" has facilitated an evolutionary judicial interpretation of the Robinson-Patman amendments that has tended to harmonize it with the other antitrust laws (Section 23.2.3).

23.2.3 Interpretation and Reinterpretation

Morton Salt

In September 1940, the Federal Trade Commission began an investigation of the terms upon which the Morton Salt Company sold its salt (see Table 23.1). The Federal Trade Commission

---

[1] See also the 1960 Supreme Court decision in *Anheuser Busch* (363 U.S. 536 at 543–544): "The legislative history of § 2 (a) is ... plain. The section, when originally enacted as part of the Clayton Act in 1914, was born of a desire by Congress to curb the use by financially powerful corporations of localized price-cutting tactics which had gravely impaired the competitive position of other sellers. It is, of course, quite true—and too well known to require extensive exposition—that the 1936 Robinson-Patman amendments to the Clayton Act were motivated principally by congressional concern over the impact upon secondary-line competition of the burgeoning of mammoth purchasers, notably chain stores."

Table 23.1 Morton Salt quantity discount schedule

Quantity	Per Case
Less than carload purchases	$1.60
Carload purchases	1.50
5,000-case purchases in any consecutive 12 months	1.40
50,000-case purchases in any consecutive 12 months	1.35

challenged Morton Salt's price schedule on the ground that it was price discrimination that would distort competition between large chain stores, able to purchase at the lowest per-case price, and other wholesale and retail distributors. It issued an order directing Morton to eliminate its quantity discounts in April 1945.

Quantity discounts   Morton Salt successfully defended itself in the Circuit Court of Appeals, on the ground that the same price schedule was applied to all buyers, and that the lower-per unit price to large-quantity buyers reflected differences in costs.[2] The FTC appealed the Circuit Court decision to the Supreme Court.

First, the Supreme Court gave its reading of the purpose of the amended Section 2 of the Clayton Act (334 U.S. 37 at 43):

> The legislative history of the Robinson-Patman Act shows that Congress considered it to be an evil that a large buyer could secure a competitive advantage over a small buyer solely because of the former's quantity purchasing power; and the Act was passed to deprive a large buyer of such advantages except to the extent that a lower price could be justified by reason of a seller's diminished costs due to quantity production, delivery or sale, or by reason of the seller's good faith effort to meet the equally low price of a competitor.

It was Morton Salt's responsibility to show that the price differences fell within the exceptions (lower cost or matching the equally low price of a competitor).

Competitive opportunities of certain merchants   For the FTC to find a violation, it did not have to show that competition had been harmed, only that there might be a substantial lessening of competition. For the Supreme Court, it was clear that Morton Salt's price schedule harmed specific competitors, and it seemed to equate this injury to competitors with injury to competition (334 U.S. 34 at 46–47, emphasis added):[3]

---

[2] Morton Salt *v.* FTC 162 F.2d 949 (1947).

[3] Even more explicitly, in a discussion of price differences for carload and less-than-carload shipments, the Court failed to make a distinction between injury to competition and injury to competitors (334 U.S. 34 at 48): "However

... we have said that "the statute does not require that the discriminations must in fact have harmed competition, but only that there is a reasonable possibility that they 'may' have such an effect." ... Here the Commission found what would appear to be obvious, that *the competitive opportunities of certain merchants were injured* when they had to pay respondent substantially more for their goods than their competitors had to pay.

Standard Oil Co. of Indiana

The Standard Oil Company of Indiana pumped oil from fields in Kansas, Oklahoma, Texas and Wyoming, refined it in Indiana, and distributed refined products in 14 Midwest States. Between 1936 and 1940, Standard Oil sold refined petrol to four large "jobber" customers at tank-car prices, 1.5 cents per gallon less than prices to retail petrol stations, who purchased in smaller (tank-wagon) lots.

The FTC challenged the price difference as price discrimination in violation of the amended Section 2(a) of the Clayton Act, and ordered Standard Oil to eliminate the price differences. Standard Oil appealed this decision to the Seventh Circuit Court of Appeals. The appeals court agreed with Standard Oil of Indiana that the lower prices had been made to meet a competitor's price (173 F.2d 210 at 213). But the Circuit Court took the view of the FTC that even if Standard Oil offered lower prices in good faith to meet competition, that did not prevent the lower prices from violating the Clayton Act if the lower price injured competition by retail dealers. The Circuit Court found that competition had been injured (173 F.2d 210 at 216):

> The discrimination in price in favor of the parties in this case, which [Standard Oil of Indiana] had a right to make as against its competitors, was then used by [Standard Oil of Indiana's] customers to work havoc among competitors on the retail level. [Standard Oil of Indiana] had given a club to its wholesalers which they passed on to their retailers to bludgeon their competitors. This is what the Commission is trying to stop, and it is towards the elimination of this evil that the cease and desist order is directed.

If Standard Oil of Indiana were in fact offering lower prices to meet a legitimate offer of a rival, then the effect of the FTC order would have been to cause Standard Oil's wholesale customers to buy from the rival. The wholesalers would have obtained their supplies at the same price, and the consequences for the retail market (whatever those consequences were) would have been unchanged. The effect of the order would have been to switch the business from Standard Oil of Indiana to one of its refiner rivals, not at the retail level.

"Meeting competition" defence   Standard Oil of Indiana appealed the Circuit Court decision to the Supreme Court. The majority of the Supreme Court found the "meeting competition in good faith" defence adequate (340 U.S. 231 at 246):[4] "under the Robinson-Patman Act, it is a complete defense to a charge of price discrimination for the seller to show that its

---

relevant the separate carload argument might be to the question of justifying a differential by cost savings, it has no relevancy in determining whether the differential works an injury to a competitor."

[4] In the nether regions on the border between the Sherman Act and the amended Section 2(a) of the Clayton Act there is a line of decisions exploring the limits of the "meeting competition in good faith" defence. See U.S. v. U.S. Gypsum Co. *et al.* 438 U.S. 422 (1978), where sellers defended regular communications about prices (quite possibly a violation of the Sherman Act prohibition against collusion) on the ground that such communication was necessary to be sure price cutting would be permitted under the Robinson-Patman amendments.

price differential has been made in good faith to meet a lawful and equally low price of a competitor".

Principle of competition   The Court also took the opportunity to reread the Robinson-Patman Act as being consistent with the other antitrust laws and with the principle of competition (340 U.S. 231 at 248–249, footnote omitted)[5]

> The heart of our national economic policy long has been faith in the value of competition. In the Sherman and Clayton Acts, as well as in the Robinson-Patman Act, "Congress was dealing with competition, which it sought to protect, and monopoly, which it sought to prevent." ... We need not now reconcile, in its entirety, the economic theory which underlies the Robinson-Patman Act with that of the Sherman and Clayton Acts. It is enough to say that Congress did not seek by the Robinson-Patman Act either to abolish competition or so radically to curtail it that a seller would have no substantial right of self-defense against a price raid by a competitor.

The Supreme Court sent the case back to the FTC with instructions to evaluate whether or not the lower prices were actually made in good faith to meet lawful lower prices of competitors.[6]

Borden

The Borden Company sold condensed milk under its own brand name at one price and sold private brands at a lower price. The FTC condemned this practice as price discrimination in violation of the Clayton Act.

John Bates Clark (1902, pp. 34–35) identified price discrimination as one of the strategic tools available to a dominant firm.[7] This is the use of price discrimination targeted by the original Section 2(a) of the Clayton Act, not Section 2(a) as amended by the Robinson-Patman Act. Clark predicted that it would be difficult to effectively implement a law prohibiting such discrimination, and experience has shown that his prediction was correct.

Borden appealed to the Fifth Circuit Court of Appeals on the argument that selling a physically identical product under different brand names meant the different brands were not "of like grade and quality" as far as the Robinson-Patman Act was concerned. The Circuit Court agreed with Borden, and the FTC appealed the Circuit Court's decision to the Supreme Court.

Physically identical goods   The majority of the Supreme Court agreed with the FTC (383 US 637 at 643–644): "We doubt that Congress intended to foreclose these inquiries in situations where a single seller markets the identical product under several different brands, whether his own, his customers' or both. Such transactions are too laden with potential discrimination and adverse competitive effect to be excluded from the reach of § 2 (a) ... " Thus, the Supreme

---

[5] The Court quotes Staley Manufacturing Co. *v.* FTC 135 F.2d 453 (1943) at 455.

[6] In due course the FTC found that Standard Oil had in any case engaged in price discrimination in violation of the Clayton Act. Standard appealed this FTC decision to the Circuit Court of Appeals, which reversed the FTC. The FTC in its turn appealed the Circuit Court decision to the Supreme Court. The Supreme Court affirmed the Circuit Court of Appeals. See FTC *v.* Standard Oil Co. 355 US 396 (1958).

[7] His specific concern was predatory price discrimination; see the heading of this chapter, and Section 18.7.3.

Court found that physically identical goods marketed under different labels were goods "of like grade and quality" for purposes of the Clayton Act.

Injury to competition   One requirement for proving that Section 2(a) of the Clayton Act has been violated is to show that different prices have been charged for goods of like grade and quality. There are two other requirements. If there are such price differences, it must be shown that they are not merely a reflection of cost differences. If there are price differences and they are not a reflection of cost differences, it must also be shown that there is a reasonable probability that the price differences will injure competition. The Supreme Court sent the case back to the Circuit Court of Appeals to examine these two other requirements.[8]

Price differences might injure competition between Borden and other sellers of condensed milk. This would be primary-line injury to competition. Price differences might injure competition among stores that purchase condensed milk from Borden and other producers. This would be secondary-line injury to competition.

From an economic point of view, the Circuit Court's discussion of primary-line injury is mixed. It made a distinction between injury to competition and injury to competitors (381 F.2d 175 at 178): "injury to a particular seller is to be distinguished from injury to the vigor of competition since here it is the latter to which the statute refers."

Earlier in its decision, the Circuit Court had concluded that Borden was not involved in predatory behaviour (381 F.2d 175 at 177):

> Borden is not in any sense guilty of predatory behavior similar to that which may accompany territorial price wars. Borden did not subsidize below-cost or unrealistically low prices on its private label milk with profits received from sales of the Borden brand.

But the Court then discusses alleged injury to competitors (381 F.2d 175 at 178):

> Seven Midwestern canners, competitors of Borden, testified in support of the complaint with respect to competitive injury to the primary line. . . . The competitors complained that portions of their sales had been lost to Borden during the period in question. The record discloses that sales constituting about 7% of their production, or roughly 240,000 cases, had been diverted to Borden. In essence, this business was attracted to Borden because it was selling private label milk cheaper than were these competitors.

The Court eventually decided that the competitors had not been injured: they had lost some sales to Borden, but they had gained some sales elsewhere. But from an economic point of view, once it decided that Borden was not engaged in predatory behaviour, there was really no reason to evaluate whether primary-line competitors had been injured. Low prices that are not predatory may injure competitors, but they improve market performance.

Cost differences   The Circuit Court was not convinced that there had been a secondary-line injury to competition. In addition, it took the view that the price difference between Borden branded and Borden generic condensed milk was reasonably related to the cost of advertising, incurred over many years, that created the premium brand image of the branded

---

[8] Borden Co. *v*. FTC 381 F.2d 175 (1967).

variety. The Circuit Court concluded that Borden had not violated Section 2(a) of the Clayton Act, and accordingly reversed the Federal Trade Commission decision.

Utah Pie[9]

The Utah Pie Company was a Salt Lake City-based producer of frozen dessert pies with a regional market share of 66.5 per cent in 1958, 34.3 per cent in 1959, 45.5 per cent in 1960, and 45.3 per cent in 1961. The size of the market grew more than four-fold over this period. Utah Pie filed a private antitrust suit against Continental Baking Company and other firms based outside Salt Lake City. It alleged that they had violated Sections 1 and 2 of the Sherman Act (conspiracy in restraint of trade and monopolization) and engaged in price discrimination in violation of Section 2(a) of the Clayton Act as amended by the Robinson-Patman Act. Utah Pie further claimed it had been injured by these violations, and sought to recover three times the amount of the damages.

In District Court, a jury found that there was no violation of the Sherman Act but that there had been price discrimination that injured competition, a violation of the Clayton Act. Continental Baking and its colleagues appealed this decision to the Tenth Circuit Court of Appeals, which concluded that there had been no injury to competition. Utah Pie in its turn appealed to the Supreme Court, which found itself faced with the question "What constitutes injury to competition for purposes of the Clayton Act?"

Injury to competition   The majority opinion makes a detailed review of prices and prices differences in the relevant geographic market. Utah Pie had a natural advantage in the Salt Lake area because its plant was located in the Salt Lake City. The other suppliers, based in other places, sold frozen dessert pies in the Salt Lake City area at lower prices than they charged closer to their own plants. Some of the rival suppliers lost money on sales in the Salt Lake City area, which the majority of the Supreme Court thought might be evidence of predatory behaviour. They wrote that (386 U.S. 686 at 702):

> we disagree with [the Circuit Court's] apparent view that there is no reasonably possible injury to competition as long as the volume of sales in a particular market is expanding and at least some of the competitors in the market continue to operate at a profit.

The majority sent the case back to the Circuit Court of Appeals to consider other arguments made by Continental Baking Company that the jury's ruling should be set aside.

Protecting competitors, not competition   Justices Stewart and Harlan dissented, asking rhetorically if the actions of Continental *et al.* had an anticompetitive effect (386 US 685 at 705, emphasis added):

> The Court's own description of the Salt Lake City frozen pie market from 1958 through 1961, shows that the answer to that question must be no. In 1958 Utah Pie had a quasi-monopolistic 66.5% of the market. In 1961—after the alleged predations of the respondents—Utah Pie still had a commanding 45.3%, Pet had 29.4%, and the remainder of the market was divided almost equally between Continental, Carnation, and other, small local bakers. ... the 1961 situation has to be considered more competitive than that of 1958. Thus, if we assume that the price

---

[9] Utah Pie Co. *v.* Continental Baking Co. 386 U.S. 685 (1967).

discrimination proven against the respondents had any effect on competition, that effect must have been beneficent.

   ... the Court has fallen into the error of reading the Robinson-Patman Act as protecting competitors, instead of competition ...

Aftermath   When it reconsidered the issues, the Circuit Court of Appeals made a detailed review of the basis for the jury decision in the original trial.[10] From this review, it appeared that Utah Pie had itself been a vigorous price competitor. Further, while sales of one of the frozen pie brands of Utah Pie had declined, sales of another of its brands had increased. The Circuit Court ordered a new trial on Utah Pie's claims for damages. It also permitted Continental Baking and the other companies involved to have trials on their counterclaims that it was Utah Pie that violated Section 2(a) of the Clayton Act. A negotiated settlement followed the Circuit Court ruling, and the new District Court trial never took place (Elzinga and Hogarty, 1978, fn. 7).

Retrospective   *Brooke Group* (Section 21.2.2) was a private antitrust suit by Liggett & Myers alleging predatory price discrimination in violation of Section 2(a) of the Clayton Act. In its *Brooke Group* opinion, the Supreme Court emphasized the consistency of the Robinson-Patman Act with other antitrust laws (509 U.S. 220, "By its terms, the Robinson-Patman Act condemns price discrimination only to the extent that it threatens to injure competition") and retrospectively limited the import of *Utah Pie* (509 U.S. 221):

> As the law has been explored since *Utah Pie*, it has become evident that primary-line competitive injury under the Robinson-Patman Act is of the same general character as the injury inflicted by predatory pricing schemes actionable under § 2 of the Sherman Act. ... the essence of the claim under either statute is the same: A business rival has priced its products in an unfair manner with an object to eliminate or retard competition and thereby gain and exercise control over prices in the relevant market.

Payne *v.* Chrysler

As we have pointed out, and as the Supreme Court notes in *Brooke Group*, the Clayton Act Section 2(a) prohibition of price discrimination applies "where the effect may be to substantially lessen competition". It is Section 4(a) of the Clayton Act that provides for private enforcement, "... any person who shall be injured in his business or property by reason of anything forbidden in the antitrust laws may sue therefor ... and shall recover threefold the damages by him sustained, and the cost of suit, including a reasonable attorney's fee".

Antitrust violations without damages   The requirement to show a violation of Section 2(a) is that there *may be* a substantial lessening of competition. The requirement to recover treble damages is that there *be* injury to the party seeking damages, and that that injury be the result of conduct forbidden by the antitrust laws. Thus it is not sufficient to show a violation of Section 2(a) of the Clayton Act to show entitlement to treble damages (Areeda, 1976). To receive treble damages, one must prove that injury has occurred and establish the amount of the injury.

---

[10] Continental Baking Co. *v.* Utah Pie Corp. 396 F.2d 161 (1968).

The 1981 Payne *v.* Chrysler[11] decision arose out of a private antitrust suit by a defunct car dealer. The dealer, Payne, claimed that Chrysler Motors Corporation's dealer rebate programme was discriminatory and might lessen competition, so being a violation of Section 2(a) of the Clayton Act. Payne also claimed damages, in an amount based on estimated lost sales to other dealers that had received greater rebates.

Payne prevailed in an initial jury trial, but this outcome was set aside by the Fifth Circuit Court of Appeals[12] on the ground that Payne had failed to provide sufficient evidence that Chrysler had violated the Robinson-Patman Act. Payne appealed this outcome to the Supreme Court. In its decision, the Court emphasized the need to prove a violation of the Robinson-Patman Act, to prove actual injury resulting from the violation, and to credibly establish the amount of the injury. It sent the case back to the Circuit Court, which after further consideration[13] found that Payne's evidence was insufficient to meet any of the requirements set out by the Supreme Court.

Volvo Trucks[14]

Reeder-Simco GMC, Inc. was an authorized dealer in Volvo heavy-duty trucks, located in Arkansas. The product was made to order: a customer would invite bids from the authorized dealers of different manufacturers for vehicles to be built to the customer's specifications. When preparing its bid, a dealer would solicit from the manufacturer a discount off the wholesale price. The size of the discount would often vary depending on the identity of the final consumer. Only if a dealer received the contract would the manufacturer produce the vehicles.

Volvo dealers were assigned to a geographic area. A dealer could bid outside its home area if it wished. It was unusual for one Volvo dealer to bid against another, but if this happened, Volvo's stated policy was to give the same discount to both dealers. In 1997, Volvo decided to consolidate its distribution network. Reeder learned that Volvo was giving other dealers larger discounts than it received and suspected it was targeted for elimination. Reeder filed suit against Volvo, alleging that Reeder had been injured by price discrimination in violation of the Robinson-Patman Act and seeking treble damages.

A jury in District Court decided in favour of Reeder, and awarded it $1.3 million, which would eventually have been trebled. Volvo appealed the District Court outcome to the Eighth Circuit Court of Appeals which, although divided, upheld the District Court outcome. Volvo appealed again to the U.S. Supreme Court.

Reeder had presented evidence that Volvo sometimes offered other dealers larger discounts than it offered to Reeder, but the evidence did not pertain to cases in which Reeder and another dealer were competing for the same specific order. The Supreme Court held that without Volvo price discrimination on bids for the same piece of business, there was no secondary line injury to competition. Without injury to competition, there was no violation of the Robinson-Patman Act.

---

[11] Payne *v.* Chrysler Motors Corp. 451 U.S. 557 (1981).

[12] Chrysler Credit Corp. *v.* J. Truitt Payne 607 F.2d 1133 (1979).

[13] Chrysler Credit Corp. *v.* J. Truett Payne Company, Inc. et al. 670 F.2d 575 (1982).

[14] Volvo Trucks North America, Inc. *v.* Reeder-Simco GMC, Inc. 546 U.S. 164 (2006), 126 S. Ct. 860 (2006).

23.3 EU Competition Policy

The prohibition of price discrimination that "may substantially lessen competition" entered U.S. antitrust as part of the second generation of antitrust legislation, almost 25 years after adoption of the Sherman Act. For the European Union, the prohibition of discrimination has been a fundamental aspect of policy from the beginning, and extends beyond competition policy (Waelbroeck, 1996).

Article 101(1)(d) prohibits *agreements* that "apply dissimilar conditions to equivalent transactions with other trading parties, thereby placing them at a competitive disadvantage". Thus a single firm does not run foul of Article 101 if its discrimination places some trading partners at a competitive disadvantage. If such a single firm is dominant, however, such discrimination violates Article 102.

For the Articles to apply, the discrimination must place some trading partners in equivalent transactions "at a competitive disadvantage".[15] The concern is therefore with what in U.S. antitrust is called "secondary line" injury to competition. In the EU context, the concern to maintain the legitimacy of the integration process is as important and perhaps more important than the impact of price discrimination on either competition or market performance. It is one thing if firms in Member State F systematically lose market share to firms in Member State G because the firms in Member State G are more efficient, all else equal. It is another thing if firms in member state F systematically lose market share to firms in Member State G because the firms in Member State G systematically receive lower prices on an essential input from suppliers that discriminate on the basis of nationality.

23.3.1 Article 101

Distillers[16]

Different shares in different national markets On 1 January 1973, Denmark, Ireland, and the UK became member states, and the European Community expanded from six to nine members. Businesses in these countries became subject to EC competition rules. One such company was The Distillers Company Limited, the world's largest producer of scotch whisky. Its share of the UK whisky market was between 40 and 50 per cent. Its share of the UK gin market was around 70 per cent. It had major shares of markets for other distilled spirits.

Market conditions in the UK and on the Continent differed, and Distillers' marketing practices differed accordingly. Distilled spirits in the UK were sold to concentrated retail distributors. The five largest retailers took some 40 per cent of scotch sales. The three largest of these were brewing companies that owned chains of licensed retail outlets. There was intense wholesale price competition for sales to retailers.

In each continental country, scotch, gin, and like beverages faced competition from "local favourites" that typically had large bases of loyal consumers. Through its continental subsidiaries, Distillers relied on sole distributors to promote its products against local competitors.

---

[15] The articles also require that actions "may affect trade between the Member States" for the respective prohibitions to apply.

[16] *Distillers* Commission Decision of 20 December 1977 OJ L 50/16 22 February 1978.

Dual price structure   Before the UK joined the European Community, Distillers simply prohibited exports from the UK to the continent. It eliminated this restriction and notified the Commission (as required at that time) of its distribution arrangements. At the same time, Distillers set up a dual price structure for UK wholesalers—if they purchased for export, their price was £5.20 per case greater than if purchased for sale in the UK Distillers justified this surcharge on the ground that continental distributors had higher selling costs than UK. distributors. It did not notify the Commission about the dual price structure. A Glasgow whisky dealer complained to the European Commission that Distillers cut off its suppliers after whisky it purchased at the UK price found its way to the export market.

The contracts between Distillers and its UK wholesale distributors were agreements between undertakings in the sense of Article 101(1), and the Commission viewed the dual price structure as an indirect export ban. The Commission viewed the dual price structure as designed to restrict and distort competition on the common market, and would have denied an exemption in any case. It directed Distillers to end the dual price structure.[17]

Profit maximization   It appears that the Commission expected that Distillers would eliminate the export surcharge and that lower-cost spirits would flow from the UK to continental markets, lowering prices there (Baden Fuller, 1979). For Distillers, the UK was a large but low-margin market. Rather than accept lower profits on the continent, Distillers stopped distributing its major scotch brands in the UK (Waelbroeck, 1984).[18]

The Commission may have come to understand that if a market is imperfectly competitive, it is difficult to oblige firms to behave as if it is perfectly competitive. Distillers later received an exemption from the Commission for a dual-price system that applied to just one of its brands (Johnnie Walker Red Label).

23.3.2 Article 102: *United Brands*

The *United Brands* decision[19] is an early application of Article 102. In the early 1970s the United Brands Company (UBC) was the leading banana producer in the world and in particular in the European Community, where it had a market share of about 40 per cent. It was vertically integrated from banana plantations in equatorial regions to ocean shipping to distribution networks in final markets, where its contracts with banana ripeners and distributors included a variety of vertical restraints. Ripeners could not resell green bananas, keeping them out of competition with UBC or with other importers. UBC cut off supplies to a Danish distributor that dealt in bananas from more than one supplier. The effect of these vertical restraints was to divide the EEC into national submarkets.

Market definition

Product market definition was critical to the outcome of the *United Brands* decision. The European Commission defined bananas as the relevant product market, on the ground that bananas have distinctive characteristics that distinguish the demand for bananas from the

---

[17] The European Court of Justice later upheld the Commission's decision, on the ground that Distillers had failed to notify the Commission of the dual price structure; see Distillers Company *v.* Commission (Case 30/78) [1980] ECR 2229.

[18] See Figure 8.5 and the associated text.

[19] United Brands Company and United Brands Continental BV *v.* EC Commission [1978] ECR 207.

demands for other kinds of fruit. As part of its defense, United Brands argued that the relevant product market was fresh fruit. Using this larger definition, UBC's market share would have been too small to justify a finding that it had a dominant position. The European Court of Justice (ECJ) rejected UBC's arguments and accepted bananas as the relevant product market.

Dominance

The ECJ reiterated the definition of dominance that it had given in *Hoffmann-La Roche* ([1978] ECR 207 at 277):

> The dominant position referred to in [Article 102] refers to a position of economic strength enjoyed by an undertaking which enables it to prevent effective competition being maintained on the relevant market by giving it the power to behave to an appreciable extent independently of its competitors, customers, and ultimately of its consumers.

The Commission argued, based mainly on UBC's market share and vertically integrated operations, that UBC had a dominant position, and the European Court agreed with the Commission.

Price discrimination = abuse of a dominant position

UBC charged distributors located in different member states substantially different prices, although the costs of supplying the different markets were similar. For the European Commission, these price differences were themselves an abuse of a dominant position. UBC's reaction was that ([1978] ECR 207 at 249):

> It is important to understand what is really involved in the Commission's argument that [United Brands] have committed an abuse in this respect. What it amounts to is that it is the duty of an undertaking in a dominant position to create a single market out of the existing national markets and that if it fails to act accordingly it is guilty of an abuse.

Essentially, United Brands argued that it was simply acting as a profit-maximizing firm in distinct regional markets. The European Court of Justice agreed that it was not the responsibility of United Brands to establish a single market ([1978] ECR 207 at 298). But it also wrote that the interplay of supply and demand should take place at each vertical level in the distribution chain: at a lower level between United Brands and distributors, at a higher level between distributors and final consumers. As a dominant firm, UBC committed an abuse if it imposed terms that gave it, rather than distributors, most of the available profit.[20]

---

[20] The European Commission also found that United Brands had abused its dominant position by charging unfair prices. The Commission compared UBC's highest and lowest prices in different national markets, and argued that UBC's prices in the high-price areas must be unfair, if UBC could profitably supply other areas at lower prices. The Court ruled that the Commission should have made a direct investigation of UBC's costs and reached a conclusion about unfairness by comparing costs and prices. The Commission had not done this, and the Court set aside the Commission's conclusion that UBC had abused its dominant position by setting unfair prices. It reduced somewhat the fine imposed by the Commission (to slightly more than 3 million Dutch builders or almost 1.4 million 1978 U.S. dollars), but confirmed the Commission's finding that United Brands had abused its dominant position in violation of Article 102.

Assessment

Despite the protests of the European Commission and of the Court, it is difficult to escape the conclusion that there is an element of truth in UBC's argument. *United Brands* implies that a firm with a dominant position in EC markets runs the risk of violating Article 102 if it fully exploits differences in regional demand characteristics. The underlying rationale may be that to sustain a system of different profit-maximizing prices in national submarkets, a dominant firm will have to put in place formal or informal restrictions that block the flow of goods across national boundaries: otherwise, consumer arbitrage will eventually erode national price differences. Such barriers to cross-border trade, however, undo the process of economic integration that is the core of the European Community. Indeed, the European Court of Justice found that UBC had abused its dominant position by its use of marketing practices that had the effect of dividing the EC into national submarkets.[21]

SUMMARY

Although the welfare consequences of price discrimination are ambiguous, antitrust and competition policy have consistently regarded it with suspicion. The best gloss one can put on this is that the traditional U.S. approach is based on the principle of competition, while EU policy pursues the non-economic goal of market integration. The dark side of these policies—certainly for the U.S. Robinson-Patman Act—is an element of protectionism that is antithetical to a market economy.

STUDY POINTS

- Original Section 7 (Section 23.2.1)
- Robinson-Patman Act (Section 23.2.2)
- Interpretation (Section 23.2.3)
  - quantity discounts
  - good faith defense
  - quality variations
  - predatory price discrimination
  - private damage recovery
- Article 101: *Distillers* (Section 23.3.1)
- Article 102: *United Brands* (Section 23.3.2)

---

[21] In its 2006 *GlaxoSmithKline* decision (Case T-168/01 27 September 2006, under appeal at this writing) the Court of First Instance considered a Commission decision (*Glaxo Wellcome* Commission Decision of 8 May 2001 OJ L 302/1 17 November 2001) that condemned as a violation of Article 101(1) of the EC Treaty a pharmaceutical company's agreement with its Spanish wholesale distributors that provided for one set of prices for products distributed in Spain and another (higher) set of prices for the same products distributed outside Spain. In paragraph 179 of its decision, the Court of First Instance wrote (emphasis added) "[GlaxoSmithKline] GSK is correct to maintain that the finding of a difference in price is not sufficient to support the conclusion that there is discrimination. *It is possible that GSK applies different prices because different markets exist and not so that different markets will exist.*" GlaxoSmithKline thus prevailed in an Article 101 matter on a point of principle that is identical with that faced by United Brands in the context of (what is now) Article 102. (The Court of First Instance rejected GlaxoSmithKline's appeal of this aspect of the Commission's decision on other grounds; see paragraph 190 of the CFI decision.)

FURTHER READING

See Tonning (1956) for a discussion of the passing of first-degree price discrimination on the American frontier. On the Robinson-Patman Act, see Standard Oil Co. *v.* FTC 340 U.S. 231 at 248, fn. 14, Rowe (1962), U.S. Department of Justice (1977), Kintner (1978, Volume 4), and Bean (1996, Chapter One). Bowman (1967) and Elzinga and Hogarty (1978) discuss *Utah Pie*.

Waelbroeck (1996) discusses the treatment of discrimination under what are now Articles 101 and 102. For discussions of the treatment of discrimination under what is now Article 102, see Siragusa (1979) and Bishop (1981).

VERTICAL RESTRAINTS　24

Respect for the law, for example, looked at as a restriction on one's degree of freedom, seems bad. When one recalls that the law is, after all, the protection of other individuals' degree of freedom, the situation changes its form.

Arrow, *The Limits of Organization* (1974, pp. 27–28)

24.1 Introduction

Within the universe of interfirm contracts, manufacturer-distributor contracts link firms in markets that are, in varying degrees, imperfectly competitive. Such contracts frequently go beyond prices and quantities, limiting some choices of one or both parties as conditions of what is often a long-term relationship. Contracts with such clauses commit both parties, but most prominently the distributor, to carry out or to avoid certain types of future conduct. They limit the range of decisions that may be taken by one or both parties, and to this extent constrain certain types of rivalry. For this reason, they have traditionally been looked upon with suspicion by antitrust (informed, at its roots, by the *principle of competition*) and competition policy (alert to possible distortions of trade within the common market). But it is worth keeping in mind that vertical contracts are themselves the product of competition, no doubt imperfect, in the market for distribution services.

The evolution of the treatment of vertical restraints under U.S. antitrust law has been a major factor in the demotion of the principle of competition and the rise of the explicit economic analysis of impact on market performance as an determinant of the antitrust status of business conduct. Economic analysis plays as great a role in EC competition policy, conditioned as it is by its role of in safeguarding the process of market integration.

24.2 Antitrust Policy Toward Vertical Contracts

24.2.1 Resale Price Maintenance (I)

Background on RPM in the Pharmaceutical Industry

In the early years of U.S. antitrust, many of the characteristics of the retail pharmacy market favoured effective collusion. There was little variation in the size of the typical pharmacy: the kinds of price policies that would benefit one pharmacist would benefit most pharmacists. The cost of the professional training required to become a pharmacist meant that entry was costly; high profit would not attract immediate entry. Pharmacists thought of themselves as professionals rather than as businessmen, an outlook that encouraged mutual solidarity. Further, as the contact person with a final consumer who generally had little expertise in the often vitally important (or believed to be so) product that was being purchased, the pharmacist had considerable bargaining power *vis-à-vis* manufacturers.

Tripartite Plan   The pharmacists' trade association, the National Association of Retail Druggists (NARD), was founded in 1898. In 1900, NARD engineered the adoption of what it called the *Tripartite Plan* by three professional associations: itself, the National Wholesale Druggists' Association, and the Proprietary Association of America. The latter was the trade association of manufacturers of patent medicines—which are not patented,[1] but nostrums, heavily dependent on advertising by the manufacturer and marketing by pharmacists for commercial success.

The Tripartite Plan sought to enforce a system of maintained resale prices on patent medicines.[2] It was devised by retailers and enforced by manufacturers through resale price maintenance contracts with wholesale and retail distributors. Recalcitrant manufacturers were persuaded to participate by distributor boycotts.

A 1906 Circuit Court of Appeals decision[3] found the Tripartite Plan to be in violation of the Sherman Act. In language that anticipated much later ambiguity in antitrust policy toward resale price maintenance, the Court wrote that a producer could adopt whatever price policy it pleased, (149 F. 21 at 27) "by independent and individual action". But when producers, wholesalers, and retailers *combined* to implement a resale price maintenance policy, they violated Section 1 of the Sherman Act.

NARD turned to an alternative approach. In 1903 or 1904, it induced the Dr. Miles Medical Company,[4] to adopt a contract and serial number plan, under which its contracts obliged retailers to maintain resale prices on products that bore serial numbers, so that out-of-contract sales could be traced and supplies to the offending retailer cut off (Murchison, 1919, p. 99). At the 1904 NARD convention, 12 of the largest patent medicine producers adopted the contract and serial numbering plan.

Dr. Miles

In its 1911 *Dr. Miles Medical* decision,[5] the Supreme Court confronted the logic of the free rider argument and rejected it as a justification for resale price maintenance.

Dr. Miles Medical Company produced patent medicines, which it distributed through wholesale and retail pharmacies under resale price maintenance contracts. The contracts also provided that authorized wholesale dealers could sell only to authorized retail dealers, and that authorized retail dealers could not resell to unauthorized wholesale or retail distributors.

---

[1] The Merriam-Webster online dictionary defines a patent medicine as "a packaged nonprescription drug which is protected by a trademark and whose contents are incompletely disclosed". See Young (1960).

[2] Palamountain (1955, p. 94). Murchison (1919, pp. 98–99) describes a resale price maintenance plan originated by the Western Association of Wholesale Druggists in 1881, and operated in cooperation with the Proprietary Association of America until 1898 and the formation of the NARD.

[3] Jayne *v.* Loder 149 F. 21 (1906).

[4] Established in 1884 in Elkhart, Indiana; renamed Miles Laboratories, Inc. in 1935, and taken over by Bayer AG in 1978.

[5] 220 U.S. 373 (1911).

John D. Parks & Sons Company was a wholesale drug distributor. It operated (among other places) in Cincinnati, Ohio, where it had sought and been denied a contract as an authorized Dr. Miles wholesale distributor. It nonetheless managed to obtain supplies of Dr. Miles' products, from authorized dealers who violated the terms of their contracts, and it sold the products at cut-rate prices. Dr. Miles sought an injunction to prevent this conduct on the part of John D. Parks & Sons. When the case reached the Supreme Court, it ruled that the contracts used by Dr. Miles Medical were a restraint of trade in violation of the Sherman Act, and therefore could not be enforced.

Free riding   The statement of the case summarized the part of Dr. Miles' argument that is most of interest from the point of view of public policy toward vertical restraints (220 U.S. 374–375):

> The bill alleged that most of [Dr. Miles'] sales were made through retail druggists and that the demand for its remedies largely depended upon their good will ... and their ability to realize a fair profit; that certain retail establishments ... had inaugurated a "cut-rate" or "cut-price" system which had caused "much confusion, trouble and damage" to the complainant's business and "injuriously affected the reputation" and "depleted the sales" of its remedies; that this injury resulted "from the fact that the majority of retail druggists as a rule cannot, or believe that they cannot realize sufficient profits" by the sale of the medicines "at the cut-prices announced by the cut-rate and department stores," and therefore are "unwilling to, and do not keep" the medicines "in stock" or "if kept in stock, do not urge or favor sales thereof ... "

This is the *free-riding* argument: if some distributors accept a low retail margin and sell at low retail prices, other distributors will not find it profitable to sell at high retail prices, and Dr. Miles will not be able to obtain the high level of point-of-sales services it seeks. Unless it fixed resale prices, Dr. Miles could not distribute with a high level of sales efforts through a network of independent distributors.

Not an ancillary restraint   The majority opinion found that the vertical price restraints involved in *Dr. Miles Medical* were different from the sort of ancillary restraint that were valid under the common law (220 U.S. 373 at 407): "The present case is not analogous to that of a sale of good will, or of an interest in a business, or of the grant of a right to use a process of manufacture."

Principle of competition   For the Supreme Court, the restrictions in Dr. Miles' distribution contracts injured the public because they restricted the right of dealers to compete (220 U.S. 373 at 407–408, emphasis added):[6]

> The bill asserts the importance of a standard retail price and alleges generally that confusion and damage have resulted from sales at less than the prices fixed. But the advantage of established retail prices primarily concerns the dealers. The enlarged profits which would result from

---

[6] Bork (1978, p. 33) quotes from "If there be an advantage" through the end of the paragraph. He then describes the court as having (Bork, 1978, p. 33) "equated horizontal cartel behavior with vertical pricing fixing". He characterizes the decision as (Bork, 1978, p. 32) "one decisive misstep that has controlled a whole body of law". Bork's interpretation glosses over the industry context, from which it is clear that Dr. Miles' resale price maintenance programme was in fact an element of a retailer-inspired collusive scheme (Areeda, 1984, p. 20). Bork does not comment on the part of the decision in which the Supreme Court considers and rejects the free-riding argument.

adherence to the established rates would go to them and not to the complainant. It is through the inability of the favored dealers to realize these profits, on account of the described competition, that the complainant works out its alleged injury. *If there be an advantage of a manufacturer in the maintenance of fixed retail prices, the question remains whether it is one which he is entitled to secure by agreements restricting the freedom of trade on the part of dealers who own what they sell. As to this, the complainant can fare no better with its plan of identical contracts than could the dealers themselves if they formed a combination and endeavored to establish the same restrictions, and thus to achieve the same result, by agreement with each other. If the immediate advantage they would thus obtain would not be sufficient to sustain such a direct agreement, the asserted ulterior benefit to the complainant cannot be regarded as sufficient to support its system.*

and (220 U.S. 373 at 409):

[Dr. Miles] having sold its product at prices satisfactory to itself, the public is entitled to whatever advantage may be derived from competition in the subsequent traffic.

The premise of the *principle of competition* is that the best market performance obtainable in the real world is the result of non-cooperative rivalry among independent competitors, whether those competitors operate in the market for a product market or in the market for distribution services. Restrictions on rivalry may be privately profitable, either for the wholesale and retail competitors themselves, and/or for an upstream manufacturer. As seen in 1911, private profitability alone did not make restrictions on competition reasonable in the sense of either the common law or antitrust policy. The standard established in *Dr. Miles Medical*, a standard that lasted almost a century, was that resale price maintenance is illegal *per se* under the antitrust laws.

Policy Circle

Fair Trade   Public policy toward resale price maintenance has varied from one extreme to the other, and back again. Following the 1931 lead of California, many states passed so-called *fair trade laws*, authorizing resale price maintenance. These fair trade laws sometimes included *nonsigner clauses*. A nonsigner clause allowed the majority of manufacturers in a trade to impose resale prices on all dealers in the state, including dealers in goods of manufacturers who did not favour resale price maintenance.

On one level, fair trade laws may have been part of a general search for a policy remedy for depression-era massive unemployment. One might argue[7] that with fair trade laws manufacturers would set prices at a level that would keep retailers and manufacturers in business, thus maintaining jobs in both production and distribution. On another level, fair trade laws were clearly a response to pressure from retail trade associations, which wished to slow the growth of chain stores.

Miller-Tydings and McGuire Acts   State fair trade laws did not apply to interstate commerce, which is the province of the Federal government. In 1937, however, Congress passed the Miller-Tydings Act, making resale price maintenance legal under the Sherman Act in states where it was legal under state law. The Miller-Tydings Act ceded to state legislators the discretion to reverse the *per se* illegality of resale price maintenance. In 1951 the Supreme Court

---

[7] Not necessarily one economist.

ruled[8] that the Miller-Tydings Act did not authorize nonsigner clauses. With the McGuire Act of 1952, Congress explicitly authorized nonsigner clauses.[9] From 1952, resale price maintenance was therefore legal under Federal law where it was legal under state law.

Repeal Support for fair trade laws waned from the 1960s onward (along with the rise of mass-marketers and their employees, who themselves became a political force to be reckoned with). Many states repealed their fair trade laws. In 1975, with the Consumer Goods Pricing Act, Congress repealed both the Miller-Tydings Act and the McGuire Act, thus restoring the 1911 *per se* illegality rule of *Dr. Miles Medical*.

24.2.2 Non-price Vertical Restraints

White Motor Cleveland-based White Motor Company, a truck manufacturer, maintained price, territory, and customer restraints in its distribution system.[10] Resale prices of some of its products were fixed. Distributors agreed to not to sell to others for resale. They agreed to limit sales to customers located within their assigned territory. If a dealer did sell to a customer located outside the dealer's territory, the dealer agreed to make a payment to the dealer within whose territory the customer was located. Dealers agreed not to sell to the U.S. or any state government, such customers being supplied directly by White Motor Company.

In 1958, the Federal government challenged White's distribution system as a restraint of trade in violation of Section 1 of the Sherman Act. In its 1961 decision, the District Court applied the *per se* rule against resale price maintenance to the vertical price fixing elements of White's distribution system.

White defended its territorial restrictions with the logic of the free riding argument (194 F. Supp. 562 at 577):

> White's position is that, in order to market its trucks effectively in competition with the trucks of its competitors, it enters into contracts whereby its distributors agree to maintain sales rooms with stocks adequate to sell and service White Trucks in their assigned territories, to properly display signs, and maintain adequate supplies of parts, and that the "territorial limitations do, in fact, not unreasonably or substantially restrict competition or trade and commerce but have both the purpose and effect of promoting the business and increasing the sales of White trucks in competition with The White Motor Company's powerful competitors."

The District Court made a distinction between two types of territorial restraints (194 F. Supp. 562 at 578):

- a manufacturer bound itself not to supply other dealers located in an authorized dealer's exclusive and territory; and

- authorized dealers bound themselves not to sell outside their designated territory.

The first type of territorial system, which would now be recognized as a device to combat the holdup problem, had been treated as ancillary to a legitimate contact between a

---

[8] Schwegmann Brothers et al. *v.* Calvert Distillers Corp. 341 U.S. 384 (1951).

[9] See "Statement by the President [Harry S. Truman] upon signing the 'fair-trade laws' bill", 14 July 1952, <http://trumanlibrary.org/publicpapers/index.php?pid=23648&st=&st1=>

[10] White Motor Co. *v.* U.S. 372 US 253 (1963). See also U.S. *v.* White Motor Co. 194 F. Supp. 562 (1961).

manufacturer and its authorized distributor, and permissible under the Sherman Act. For the District Court, the second type of exclusive territory was akin to the territorial market division that had been at issue in *Addyston Pipe and Steel*, and therefore violated Section 1 of the Sherman Act. The District Court granted summary judgment against White Motor Company, and White Motor appealed the parts of the decision that applied to nonprice vertical restraints to the Supreme Court.

A divided Supreme Court sent the case back to District Court for retrial. For the majority, Justice Douglas wrote that summary judgment with respect to the price-fixing aspects of White's distribution scheme was in order. The Supreme Court had written that the *per se* rule applied to[11] "agreements or practices which because of their pernicious effect on competition and lack of any redeeming virtue are conclusively presumed to be unreasonable and therefore illegal without elaborate inquiry as to the precise harm they have caused or the business excuse for their use", but also that for restraints that did not fall into this category, *Chicago Board of Trade* required consideration of "the facts peculiar to the business to which the restraint is applied" before appropriate treatment could be determined. The majority of the Court felt it was not in a position to consider the facts appropriate to the business at hand, and returned the case to District Court to amplify the record (372 U.S. 253 at 261):[12]

> This is the first case involving a territorial restriction in a vertical arrangement; and we know too little of the actual impact of both that restriction and the one respecting customers to reach a conclusion on the bare bones of the documentary evidence before us.

The *White Motor* case was settled in lower court, when White agreed to eliminate the contested restrictions from its distribution contracts.[13] The desired amplification of the record never took place.

Schwinn   It was the 1967 *Schwinn*[14] case that gave the Supreme Court its next opportunity to consider the treatment of vertical restraints under the antitrust laws. Schwinn had seen its market share fall from 22.5 per cent in 1951, at which time it had been the market leader, to 12.8 per cent ten years later: the market had grown, but Schwinn's sales had not grown with it. Since before the decline in its market share, Schwinn had used a highly structured distribution system. Each of 22 wholesale distributors was assigned a territory, and authorized to sell only to franchised retail dealers in that territory. Franchised retailers were to sell only from authorized locations. Shipments of bicycles were often direct from Schwinn to retailers, on the basis of orders placed through wholesalers. In some cases Schwinn retained ownership of the bicycles until they reached the final consumer, with the distributors acting as Schwinn's agents. In other cases, the distributors took legal ownership of bicycles before sale to the final consumer.

District Court: independent decisions by independent firms   In 1958, the government challenged this distribution system as a restraint of trade in violation of Section 1 of the Sher-

---

[11] Northern Pacific Railroad Co. *v.* U.S. 356 U.S. 1 (1958) at 5.

[12] In a concurring opinion, Justice Brennan presents a useful analysis of differences between territorial and customer restraints. For Justices Clark and Black and Chief Justice Warren, the record was more than sufficient to justify summary judgment against White Motor Company.

[13] White Motor Co. *v.* U.S. CCH 1964 Trade Cases ¶ 71,195.

[14] U.S. *v.* Arnold, Schwinn & Co. 388 U.S. 365 (1966).

man Act. In its 1965 decision, the District Court declined to find a restraint of trade where Schwinn retained ownership of bicycles, but found territorial restrictions to be illegal *per se* where Schwinn sold bicycles to its distributors.[15] The District Court's rationale went to the antitrust view of competition as a process favouring independent decisions by independent firms (237 F. Supp. 323 at 342):

> [W]hen a distributor fills orders from warehouse stock that he has purchased, where he can set the price, and where there may be a differential in shipping costs or promptness or quality of service, he is acting as an owner and not as an agent or salesman for Schwinn. Where the ultimate risk and loss is borne by the distributor, as where he has purchased and taken title to the Schwinn products, he is truly an entrepreneur ...

The government appealed to the Supreme Court, with the argument that Schwinn's distribution system was an agreement between Schwinn and its distributors and, under the rule of reason, a violation of Section 1 of the Sherman Act.

On appeal: principle of competition   The Supreme Court accepted that Schwinn's motives were to achieve commercial success (388 U.S. 365 at 374): "the reasons which induced [Schwinn] to adopt the challenged distribution program were to enable it and the small, independent merchants that made up its chain of distribution to compete more effectively in the marketplace." The court majority viewed the issue through the lens of the principle of competition. Seen in this way, the question was not Schwinn's motive, but the impact of its marketing strategy on competition (388 U.S. 365 at 375): "Our inquiry is whether, assuming nonpredatory motives and business purposes and the incentive of profit and volume considerations, the effect upon competition in the marketplace is substantially adverse."

The Supreme Court majority agreed that the economic natures of the territorial and customer restrictions on wholesalers were the same, and directed the District Court to refashion its ruling so that neither wholesale nor retail distributors were subject to customer or territory restrictions on bicycles they had purchased. The Court noted that there was vigorous interbrand competition (388 U.S. 365 at 381–382), and was unwilling to follow the government's call to prohibit vertical restraints on distribution—on intrabrand competition—when Schwinn retained ownership of bicycles.

Assessment   From a modern perspective, the combined system of agency distribution plus sales and territorial restrictions appears as a system designed to cope with the holdup problem. Schwinn sought to give its distributors confidence that they would earn a normal rate of return on investment at the wholesale price set by Schwinn.

In partial dissent, Justices Stewart and Harlan protested the majority's *per se* approach to restraints imposed by manufacturers on franchisees who had purchased the product for resale. Justice Stewart foresaw[16] that one consequence of such a *per se* prohibition could be to induce manufacturers to vertically integrate, absorbing the wholesale and/or retail function. This happened in the aftermath of the *Schwinn* decision (Crown and Coleman, 1996).

The *Schwinn* decision was heavily criticized. The essential element of the criticism was that, whatever the effect of the restrictions was, it was the same whether the bicycles were

---

[15] U.S. *v.* Arnold, Schwinn & Co. *et al.* 237 F. Supp. 323 (1965).

[16] The majority also recognized this possibility (388 U.S. 380).

sold to the dealers or marketed by the dealers as agents. What should be evaluated, in this view, was the impact of the restrictions on market performance, not on competition (intra-brand or interbrand). The reaction to *Schwinn* was one step on the path that subordinates the principle of competition to an explicit evaluation of the impact of business practices on consumer welfare.

GTE Sylvania   A decade later, Continental T.V. Inc. *v.* GTE Sylvania[17] gave the Court the opportunity to revisit the antitrust treatment of nonprice restraints. In the early 1960s, Sylvania, the national market share of which had fallen to a negligible 1 or 2 per cent, eliminated its wholesalers and began direct sales to franchised retail dealers. Franchisees neither enjoyed nor were limited to exclusive territories, but they were obliged to sell only from locations authorized by Sylvania. Such a *location clause* may be seen as a way to deal with the holdup problem.

San Francisco-based Continental T.V., a franchised dealer, unsuccessfully sought Sylvania's permission to open a store in Sacramento. Continental nonetheless set up a retail outlet in Sacramento. Following this and other disputes, Sylvania cancelled Continental's position as a franchisee. Continental filed a private antitrust suit against Sylvania, alleging that the territorial restrictions used by Sylvania were a *per se* violation of Section 1 of the Sherman Act. The District Court judge gave the jury instructions that were informed by *Schwinn's per se* approach to restrictions applied after ownership had shifted from the manufacturer to the distributor, and the jury found Sylvania to be in violation of the Sherman Act.

Sylvania appealed this outcome to the Circuit Court of Appeals. The Circuit Court made a distinction between the customer and territory restrictions at issue in *Schwinn* and the location clause of *Continental T.V.*, indicated that a rule of reason should have been applied by the jury, and reversed the outcome in District Court. Continental T.V. appealed this reversal to the Supreme Court.

Interbrand competition the primary concern of antitrust law   The majority of a divided Supreme Court made explicit use of economic analysis, reached back before its decision in *Schwinn*, and built upon the comment in *White Motor* that more needed to be known about the actual impact of non-price vertical restraints before their place on the *per se*-rule of reason spectrum could be determined. The Court did not disturb the *per se* illegality of vertical price restraints, but wrote of non-price restraints that (433 U.S. 36 at 51–52) "The market impact of vertical restrictions is complex because of their potential for a simultaneous reduction of intrabrand competition and stimulation of interbrand competition." Five years after expressing scepticism in *Topco* about courts' ability to balance out the positive and negative impacts of restrictions on competition on market performance (Section 20.5.1), the Supreme Court gave antitrust priority to interbrand competition over intrabrand competition (433 U.S. 36 at 52, fn. 19, emphasis added):

> *Interbrand competition* is the competition among the manufacturers of the same generic product—television sets in this case—and *is the primary concern of antitrust law.*

Justice White: independent decisions by independent firms   Justice White agreed with the majority's decision to sustain the ruling of the Circuit Court of Appeals and direct the use

---

[17] 433 U.S. 36 (1977).

of a rule of reason standard in trial court. But he wrote (433 U.S. 36 at 59) "I cannot agree that the result requires the overruling of [*Schwinn*]. In my view this case is distinguishable from *Schwinn* because there is less potential for restraint of intrabrand competition and more potential for stimulating interbrand competition." He also highlighted the view of antitrust as a device for promoting competitive rivalry (433 U.S. 36 at 66–67):

> I have, moreover, substantial misgivings about the approach the majority takes to overruling *Schwinn*. The reason for the distinction in *Schwinn* between sale and nonsale transactions was not, as the majority would have it, "the Court's effort to accommodate the perceived intrabrand harm and interbrand benefit of vertical restrictions," ... ; the reason was rather ... the notion in many of our cases involving vertical restraints that independent businessmen should have the freedom to dispose of the goods they own as they see fit.

Justice White's view is correct: the Schwinn rule was in line with the principle of competition. What is now clear is that the series of vertical restraint cases was critical in moving antitrust to the position that if there is a conflict between reliance on competition to obtain good market performance and an explicit evaluation of the impact of a business practice on consumer welfare, welfare evaluation trumps reliance on competition.[18]

Justices Brennan and Marshall would have maintained *Schwinn*'s *per se* rule, and so dissented from the majority opinion.

24.2.3 Exclusive Dealing, Requirements, and Tying Contracts

Section 3 of the 1914 Clayton Act provides that:

> It shall be unlawful ... to lease or make a sale or contract for sale ... fix a price ... on the condition, agreement, or understanding that the lessee or purchaser thereof shall not use or deal in the goods ... of a competitor or competitors of the lessor or seller, where the effect of such lease, sale, or contract for sale or such condition, agreement, or understanding may be to substantially lessen competition or tend to create a monopoly in any line of commerce.

Tying, bundling, and exclusive dealing contracts may run afoul of this prohibition, just as they may be contracts in restraint of trade in violation of Section 1 of the Sherman Act.

Standard Fashion[19]

Standard Fashion Company manufactured dress patterns, and had a national market share of about 40 per cent. Magrane-Houston Company was a Boston retail dry goods (clothing and fabric) store. The two firms signed a contract according to which Standard Fashion would make Magrane-Houston one of its retail outlets and Magrane-Houston agreed not to sell dress patterns of other manufacturers.

Effect on market performance   The question before the Supreme Court was whether or not this exclusive dealing contract violated the Clayton Act Section 3 prohibition of contracts with effect that "may be to substantially lesson competition or tend to create a monopoly".

---

[18] Yet it is by no means clear that courts are able to evaluate the impact of a business practice on market performance; see Justice Breyer in dissent in *Leegin* (127 S. Ct. 2705 (2007) at 2730): "How easily can courts identify instances in which the benefits are likely to outweigh potential harms? My own answer is, not very easily."

[19] Standard Fashion Co. *v*. Magrane-Houston Co. 258 U.S. 346 (1922).

For the Supreme Court, the Congress that passed the Clayton Act sought to prohibit the same sorts of restraints of trade that were the target of the Sherman Act, and sought to reach them "in their incipiency". But an actual impact on competition was required (258 U.S. 346 at 356–357; emphasis added):

> Section 3 condemns sales or agreements where the effect of such sale or contract of sale "may" be to substantially lessen competition or tend to create monopoly. . . . But we do not think that the purpose in using the word "may" was to prohibit the mere possibility of the consequences described. *It was intended to prevent such agreements as would* under the circumstances disclosed *probably lessen competition, or create an actual tendency to monopoly.*

Relying on the findings of the Circuit Court of Appeals, the Supreme Court found that exclusive dealing contracts employed by the leading manufacturer in the industry, a firm with a market share of 40 per cent, could reasonably be thought to carry the risk of substantially lessening competition. Such contracts would mean monopoly in many small towns, and encourage mergers in large towns, increasing the leading firm's market share even in larger markets (258 U.S. 346 at 357). The Supreme Court agreed with the lower court that the exclusive dealing contract violated Section (3) of the Clayton Act.

Assessment   Implicit in the logic of the decision is the possibility that an exclusive dealing contract employed by a small firm would not violate the Clayton Act. The likely effect of an exclusive dealing contract on competition will depend on the market position of the manufacturer involved.

The Court did not consider ways in which an exclusive dealing contract might promote competition. The bargain sealed in the exclusive dealing contract required Magrane-Houston to keep a minimum supply of dress patterns on its premises and to promote their sales. The contract also obliged Standard Fashion to repurchase unsold patterns at the end of each season, an obligation that had the effect of reducing Magrane-Houston's risk if Standard Fashion should happen to put out a line of unfashionable patterns. Standard Fashion might reasonably suppose that if Magrane-Houston retailed several different brands of dress patterns, it would divide its sales efforts among all those brands; an exclusive dealing contract would avoid this.

The Court's decision is consistent with the position that the competition-promoting effects of an exclusive dealing contract dominate when it is used by a manufacturer with a small market share, while the entry-restricting effects dominate when an exclusive dealing contract is used by a manufacturer with a large market share. But the issue of the tradeoff between competition-enhancing and competition-restricting effects of an exclusive dealing contract is not explicitly addressed in the decision.

Standard Stations

Yet another *Standard Oil* decision[20] involved Socal (later Chevron and later still ChevronTexaco) and its petrol distributing subsidiary, Standard Stations. Socal was the largest supplier of petrol in what was called the Western Area—Arizona, California, Idaho, Nevada, Oregon, Utah and Washington. In 1946, its market share was 23 per cent, 6.8 percentage points of

---

[20] Standard Oil of California and Standard Stations, Inc. *v.* U.S. 337 U.S. 293 (1949).

which was retail sales through Socal-owned service stations, 6.7 percentage points of which sold under exclusive dealer contracts with independent service stations, and the rest direct sales to industrial customers. Socal's major competitors, with a combined market share of 42.5 per cent, also employed exclusive dealer contracts with independent service stations.

Some of the contracts required independent service stations to take all their requirements of petrol from Socal. Others required in addition that the service station operator also take all requirements of related products, such as tyres, inner tubes, and batteries, from Socal. Tying and exclusive dealing were thus both at issue.

The District Court had said that because of Socal's market share, the contracts resulted in a substantial lessening of competition, a finding stronger than the Clayton Act requirement that the effect "may be to substantially lessen competition" (337 U.S. 293 at 298). The District Court therefore declined to take into account possible pro-competitive effects of the kinds of contracts at issue.

Tying contracts ≠ requirements contracts The Supreme Court made a distinction between tying contracts and requirements contracts. Of tying contracts, it wrote (337 U.S. 293 at 305) that "Tying agreements serve hardly any purpose beyond the suppression of competition."[21] The Court was willing to consider the procompetitive aspects of requirements contracts. It noted (337 U.S. 293 at 306–307) that requirements contracts assured the buyer of a secure supply and allowed the seller to reduce costly sales efforts. In addition, requirements contracts might be used by a new firm to enter a market. But if all firms in the market used requirements contacts, the effect might be to block entry, contrary to the principle of competition (337 U.S. 293 at 309):

> If, indeed, this were a result of the system, it would seem unimportant that a short-run by-product of stability may have been greater efficiency and lower costs, for it is the theory of the antitrust laws that the long-run advantage of the community depends upon the removal of restraints upon competition.

If this decision were made today, it seems likely that an explicit evaluation of the impact of the requirements contracts on consumer welfare would be made, balancing out welfare gains (if any) due to greater efficiency and lower costs against welfare losses (if any) due to higher entry costs.

The Supreme Court also noted that if major refiners were prohibited from using requirements contracts, they might simply integrate forward and distribute petrol at the retail level through their own wholly owned service stations. That issue, the Court felt, was not within its mandate in applying the laws that had been passed by Congress.

Balancing out the procompetitive and restrictive effects of requirements contracts, the Court found the net effect to be to restrict competition (337 U.S. 293 at 314):

> [T]he qualifying clause of § 3 is satisfied by proof that competition has been foreclosed in a substantial share of the line of commerce affected. ... observance by a dealer of his requirements contract with Standard does effectively foreclose whatever opportunity there might be for competing suppliers to attract his patronage ... Standard's use of the contracts creates just

---

[21] We have seen (Section 12.3.3) that tying may also be a vehicle for price discrimination.

such a potential clog on competition as it was the purpose of § 3 to remove wherever, were it to become actual, it would impede a substantial amount of competitive activity.

Eastman Kodak[22]

Kodak sold photocopiers and related equipment. It also supplied service and parts for these machines. In the early 1980s, an industry of independent service organizations (ISOs) developed, competing with Kodak in servicing and supplying parts for Kodak equipment. In 1985 and 1986 Kodak adopted a policy of requiring that its equipment be repaired only with authorized parts and took steps to deny ISOs access to such parts.

Eighteen ISOs filed a private antitrust suit against Kodak, alleging that its actions tied Kodak copiers and postsales service and restrained competition in the services and parts "aftermarkets", in violation of Sections 1 and 2 of the Sherman Act. Kodak made a preliminary claim that it could not have committed the alleged violations since it did not have a position of market power in the market for photocopying equipment. The District Court accepted this argument and granted summary judgment in Kodak's favour. The ISOs appealed to the Ninth Circuit Court of Appeals, which reversed the District Court and indicated that the ISOs were entitled to a trial on the merits. Kodak in its turn appealed the Circuit Court's decision to the Supreme Court.

The Supreme Court summarized Kodak's reasoning (504 U.S. 451 at 470, footnotes omitted):

> "If Kodak raised its parts or service prices above competitive levels, potential customers would simply stop buying Kodak equipment. . . . " . . . Kodak argues that the Court should accept, as a matter of law, this "basic economic reality," . . . that competition in the equipment market necessarily prevents market power in the aftermarkets.

The majority opinion took note that the threat of lost sales need not deter even a monopolist from raising price: the essence of the exercise of market power is that a firm with market power trades off a higher price against lower sales, and settles at the profit-maximizing point beyond which further increases in price would induce so much greater reductions in sales that profit would fall (504 U.S. 451 at 470). The majority examined the reaction of Kodak's customers to actual increases in service prices, and found that equipment sales had not fallen (504 U.S. 451 at 472). The court also noted that switching costs might effectively lock some consumers in to Kodak equipment, giving Kodak leeway to raise aftermarket prices (504 U.S. 451 at 476). For these reasons, it affirmed the Circuit Court of Appeals, Kodak was denied summary judgment, and the case returned to District Court for trial.[23]

Jefferson Parish Hospital[24]

East Jefferson Hospital (of Metairie, Louisiana) had an exclusive dealing contract with Roux & Associates, under which Roux would supply all anesthesiology services needed by the

---

[22] Eastman Kodak Company *v.* Image Technical Services Inc., *et al.* 504 U.S. 451 (1992).

[23] In District Court (Image Technical Services, Inc. *v.* Eastman Kodak Co. 125 F.3d 1195 (9th Cir. 1997)) a jury awarded damages of nearly $24 million (before trebling) to ten plaintiffs. The amount of damages was altered somewhat by the Circuit Court of Appeals, and the Supreme Court declined to hear a further appeal by Kodak.

[24] Jefferson Parish Hospital Dist. No. 2 *v.* Hyde 466 U.S. 2 (1984).

hospital and the hospital would use the services only of anesthesiologists associated with Roux.

Pursuant to this contract, a certified anesthesiologist not employed by Roux, Edwin G. Hyde, was rejected for admission to the hospital staff. Hyde filed a private antitrust suit, claiming that the exclusive dealing contract tied hospital services and anesthesiology services in restraint of trade and in violation of Section 1 of the Sherman Act.

The District Court took the view that tying cases involving professional activities should be evaluated under the rule of reason (466 U.S. 2 at 5), "that the anticompetitive consequences of the Roux contract were minimal and outweighed by benefits in the form of improved patient care", and ruled against Hyde. Hyde appealed to the Fifth Circuit Court of Appeals, which reversed the District Court on the ground that tying contracts were illegal *per se*. The hospital district then appealed the circuit court decision to the Supreme Court.

Supreme Court majority reviewed earlier tying cases and highlighted restriction on consumer choice as the effect of a tie that makes it a restraint of trade in violation of the antitrust laws (466 U.S. 2 at 12):

> Our cases have concluded that the essential characteristic of an invalid tying arrangement lies in the seller's exploitation of its control over the tying product to force the buyer into the purchase of a tied product that the buyer either did not want at all, or might have preferred to purchase elsewhere on different terms. When such "forcing" is present, competition on the merits in the market for the tied item is restrained and the Sherman Act is violated.

Consumer welfare   The antitrust laws object to such forcing because it reduces the welfare of consumers (466 U.S. 2 at 15):

> And from the standpoint of the consumer—whose interests the statute was especially intended to serve—the freedom to select the best bargain in the second market is impaired by his need to purchase the tying product, and perhaps by an inability to evaluate the true cost of either product when they are available only as a package.

Conditional *per se* rule   The majority applied a conditional *per se* rule to the tying contract (466 U.S. 2 at 15): first decide if there is "substantial potential" for an impact on competition. Then decide if anticompetitive forcing is a likely consequence of the tie. If both conditions are met, condemn the tying contract as a *per se* violation of the antitrust laws.

For the Court majority, Hyde had not shown that the hospital's tying contract was likely to have a substantial impact on competition: 70 per cent of area residents used other hospitals. The majority reversed the circuit court decision, leaving the district court's dismissal of Hyde's case as the final word.

Justice O'Connor: three-part rule of reason   A conditional *per se* rule looks an awful lot like a rule of reason. In her concurring opinion, Justice O'Connor argued that the *per se* treatment of tying contracts should be abolished (466 U.S. 2 at 35):

> The time has ... come to abandon the "per se" label and refocus the inquiry on the adverse economic effects, and the potential economic benefits, that the tie may have. The law of tie-ins will thus be brought into accord with the law applicable to all other allegedly anticompetitive economic arrangements, except those few horizontal or quasi-horizontal restraints that can be said to have no economic justification whatsoever.

She proposed a three-part rule of reason test for tying contracts: necessary conditions for a tying contract to violate the antitrust laws would be (466 U.S. 2 at 37–39):

- that the seller have market power in the tying-product market;
- that there be a substantial threat that tying will enable the seller to acquire market power in the tied-product market; and
- that there be a "coherent economic basis for treating the tying and tied products as distinct".

If these conditions are not met, Justice O'Connor would permit a tying contract. If they are met, she would apply a rule of reason treatment, weighing the economic benefits of the tying arrangement against its economic harms (466 U.S. 2 at 41–42). Thus, seven years after *GTE Sylvania*, Justice O'Connor was again willing to have antitrust leave behind the principle of competition in favour of explicit welfare evaluation by the courts.

24.2.4 Resale Price Maintenance (II)

Maximum Resale Price Maintenance

Kiefer-Stewart Although not as numerous as decisions involving minimum resale price maintenance, a line of U.S. Supreme Court decisions, informed by the principle of competition, held agreements to fix maximum resale prices to be a *per se* violation of the Sherman Act. One of these was *Kiefer-Stewart*,[25] a private antitrust suit by an Indiana alcohol distributor against a maximum resale price programme of Seagram & Sons. A District Court jury returned a verdict and damages in favour of Kiefer-Stewart, but the Seventh Circuit Court of Appeals overturned the District Court outcome on the ground that fixing maximum prices, which did not prevent the distributor from cutting price, was not a restraint of trade:[26] "Competition ... does not rest upon the ability to charge a higher price than a competitor but upon the ability to meet the price or undersell that fixed by a competitor."

In ruling on Kiefer-Stewart's appeal, the Supreme Court came down on the side of the District Court (340 U.S. 211 at 213, citation omitted):

> The Court of Appeals erred in holding that an agreement among competitors to fix maximum resale prices of their products does not violate the Sherman Act. For such agreements, no less than those to fix minimum prices, cripple the freedom of traders and thereby restrain their ability to sell in accordance with their own judgment. We reaffirm what we said in *United States* v. *Socony-Vacuum Oil Co.* ... : "Under the Sherman Act a combination formed for the purpose and with the effect of raising, depressing, fixing, pegging, or stabilizing the price of a commodity in interstate or foreign commerce is illegal *per se*."

Albrecht Albrecht *v.* Herald was a private antitrust suit by a newspaper delivery person in St. Louis, Missouri against the maximum resale price policy of the Globe-Democrat morning newspaper. A District Court jury returned a verdict in favour of the newspaper delivery person, and the Judge set the jury verdict aside. Albrecht appealed, and the Eighth Circuit

---

[25] Kiefer-Stewart Co. *v.* Joseph E. Seagram & Sons, Inc. 340 U.S. 211 (1951).

[26] Kiefer-Stewart Co. *v.* Joseph E. Seagram & Sons, Inc. 182 F.2d 228 (1950), at 235. The Circuit Court also doubted that there had been satisfactory proof that the maximum resale price arrangement was the fruit of an agreement, a necessary condition for a violation of Section 1 of the Sherman Act.

Court of Appeals affirmed the District Court outcome,[27] relying precisely, if not by name, on the argument that in this instance, maximum resale price maintenance improved market performance by preventing double marginalization (367 F.2d 517 at 522):

> Globe-Democrat's activity here did not hinder, but fostered and actually created competition to the benefit of the public. To have condoned plaintiff's overcharging would have been a signal to all carriers, each monopolistic in his own right, to mulct the public for all the traffic would bear.

On further appeal, the Supreme Court would have none of this (390 U.S. 145 at 152):[28]

> Maximum and minimum price fixing may have different consequences in many situations. But schemes to fix maximum prices, by substituting the perhaps erroneous judgment of a seller for the forces of the competitive market, may severely intrude upon the ability of buyers to compete and survive in that market. Competition, even in a single product, is not cast in a single mold.

The remark that (emphasis added) "Competition, *even in a single product*, is not cast in a single mold" suggests that the majority regarded intrabrand competition as a determinant of market performance.

Khan   The Supreme Court overruled *Albrecht* in State Oil v. Kahn.[29] Khan's petrol station was supplied by State Oil Company under a contract that specified a maximum 3.25 cent per gallon margin between the price paid by Khan to State Oil and Khan's retail price. Khan was free to reduce the retail price, and doing so would reduce its distribution margin below 3.25 cents per gallon. Khan was also free to raise the retail price; if it did so, the excess over the specified 3.25 cents per gallon margin would go to State Oil.

Khan failed to make payments on his lease, as a result of which a state court appointed a receiver to run Khan's station. The receiver was not bound by the maximum retail margin to which Khan had agreed. The receiver lowered the price of regular petrol, raised the price of premium petrol, and ended up with an average distribution margin greater than 3.25 cents per gallon. Khan filed a private antitrust suit alleging that it had been injured by a maximum price-fixing contract that prevented it from adjusting distribution margins on different grades of petrol as the receiver had done. The District Court took the view that the *per se* rule did not apply, that Khan had not shown harm to competition, and gave summary judgment for State Oil. The Seventh Circuit Court of Appeals reversed the District Court,[30] and State Oil appealed that decision to the Supreme Court.

At the Supreme Court, Justice O'Connor reviewed the antitrust treatment of price and non-price vertical restraints, including the transition from *Schwinn* to *GTE Sylvania*, in light

---

[27] Albrecht v. Herald Co., 367 F.2d 517 (1966). See also Justice Stewart's dissenting opinion, 390 U.S. 145 at 169.

[28] Albrecht v. Herald Co., 390 U.S. 145 (1968). The majority observed that maximum resale prices might allow dealers an insufficient profit margin to provide services desired by consumers. This is in some sense the inverse of the free-rider argument for minimum resale price maintenance, that without minimum resale prices, dealers will not have a sufficient margin to provide services the manufacturer finds profitable. The majority also remarks that maximum resale prices may, as a practical matter, become minimum resale prices, by implication effecting a collusive scheme.

[29] State Oil Co. v. Khan 522 U.S. 3 (1997).

[30] The Circuit Court was overtly sceptical of the *Albrecht* rule, Khan v. State Oil 93 F.3d 1358 (1996) at 1362–1364, but felt bound by it until the Supreme Court said otherwise.

of the Court's (522 U.S. 3 at 15) "general view that the primary purpose of the antitrust laws is to protect interbrand competition" and prior position that[31] "Low prices benefit consumers regardless of how those prices are set, and so long as they are above predatory levels, they do not threaten competition."[32] Taking into account as well Congressional intent that courts give content to the antitrust laws in a common-law manner (522 U.S. 3 at 15), the Court transferred maximum resale price maintenance from the set of agreements illegal *per se* under Section 1 of the Sherman Act to the set of agreements to be considered under the rule of reason, and returned the case to lower courts for proceedings under the rule of reason.[33]

Leegin[34]

Leegin Creative Leather Products, Inc. produced luxury leather goods. It sold them throughout the United States, mainly through small, upscale retail outlets. One of these was PSKS, Inc., which along with Leegin's Brighton line of products sold the products of about 75 other manufacturers from its single retail outlet in Texas. Leegin offered incentives to stores that agreed to maintain suggested retail prices. PSKS was one of these stores. Its involvement in the incentive programme ended after a Leegin employee found the store to be unattractive. But PSKS' sales of the Brighton line increased, until Leegin discovered that PSKS had marked down the entire Brighton line by 20 per cent. Leegin asked PSKS to end discount sales and PSKS refused, from which time Leegin refused to sell to PSKS.

PSKS filed a private antitrust suit against Leegin, alleging among other things that Leegin's incentive and resale price maintenance programme was an agreement in restraint of trade and, under *Dr. Miles*, a *per se* violation of Section 1 of the Sherman Act. Leegin had expert witnesses prepared to testify on it's behalf to certify the procompetitive effects of its marketing policy, but the District Court relied on *Dr. Miles' per se* rule and did not permit them to testify. A jury awarded PSKS $1.2 million in damages, which after trebling and legal fees turned into nearly $4 million. On appeal, the Fifth Circuit Court of Appeals relied on *Dr. Miles* and affirmed the District Court outcome. Leegin appeal to the Supreme Court, where the question was whether or not *Dr. Miles' per se* rule should be overturned.

Per se/rule of reason The majority in *Leegin* first contrasted the *per se* rule and the rule of reason. The rule of reason is (127 S. Ct. 2712) "the accepted standard for testing whether a practice restrains trade in violation of § 1", and in application amounts to[35] "an inquiry into market power and market structure designed to assess [a restraint's] actual effect". The

---

[31] Here Justice O'Connor quotes *ARCO*, Atlantic Richfield Co. *v.* USA Petroleum Co. 495 U.S. 328 (1990), at 340.

[32] Justice O'Connor later noted some commentary suggesting that *Albrecht's per se* prohibition of maximum resale price maintenance had induced manufacturers to integrate forward into distribution, to the detriment of independent distributors. Such a remark confuses competition in the sense of market structure with competition in the sense of market performance. She also mentions the concern of *Albrecht* that maximum resale price maintenance could turn into minimum resale price maintenance (that the time of *Khan*, illegal per se under *Dr. Miles*), and suggests that such cases could be dealt with under the rule of reason.

[33] On return to the Seventh Circuit Court of Appeals, Khan gave up the maximum resale price maintenance argument and instead argued that the maximum resale price in the contract was effectively a minimum resale price, hence *per se* illegal. The Appeals Court did not accept this reasoning, and directed the District Court to close the case by ruling against Khan (Khan *v.* State Oil 143 F.3d 362 (1998)).

[34] Leegin *v.* PSKS, Inc. 127 S. Ct. 2705 (2007).

[35] 127 S. Ct. 2705 at 2712–2713, quoting Copperweld Corp. *v.* Independence Tube Corp., 467 U.S. 752 (1984) at 768.

per se rule, in contrast (127 S. Ct. 2712, citations omitted), which "can give clear guidance for certain conduct", classifies as illegal practices "that would always or almost always tend to restrict competition and decrease output", that are "manifestly anticompetitive", and "lack … any redeeming virtue".

***Dr. Miles* misread**   The majority wrote that the *Dr. Miles* Court had "failed to discuss in detail the business reasons that would motivate a manufacturer situated in 1911 to make use of vertical price restraints", [36] and regarded vertical contracts between a manufacturer and distributors "as analogous to a horizontal combination among competing distributors". [37]

***Dr. Miles* reversed**   Reviewing the antitrust treatment of non-price vertical restraints and the economics literature on resale price maintenance, the majority concluded that resale price maintenance is more likely to present antitrust concerns if adopted by a few suppliers or at the behest of retailers, and less likely to be a concern if adopted by many suppliers or to combat incentives for free-riding. But since its impact on market performance would vary from case to case, it should be judged under the rule of reason. *Dr. Miles* was overruled.[38]

24.2.5 Primary Concern of Antitrust Law

As noted above, writing for the majority in *GTE Sylvania*, Justice Powell in a pregnant foot-note remarked that[39] "*Interbrand competition … is the primary concern of antitrust law.*" There is scarce precedent for this view in prior antitrust. The *principle of competition*, in application, did not distinguish between competition in product markets as a way of getting good market performance in product markets and competition in markets for distribution services as a way of getting good market performance in markets for distribution services. Antitrust decisions from Judge Taft's 1898 "sea of doubt" in *Addyston Pipe & Steel* to the Supreme Court's 1972 opinion in *Topco* held back from permitting restrictions on competition in one arena on the theory that doing so would boost competition in another.

But since it falls to the Supreme Court to interpret the antitrust laws in a common-law way, the weight of precedent is less in antitrust than for other areas of the law. The justification given in footnote 19 for making interbrand competition the primary concern of antitrust is:

> The degree of intrabrand competition is wholly independent of the level of interbrand competition confronting the manufacturer. Thus, there may be fierce intrabrand competition among the distributors of a product produced by a monopolist and no intrabrand competition among

---

[36] As we have seen in Section 24.2.1, the 1911 Court understood the free rider argument for resale price maintenance, but rejected it as a justification for resale price maintenance.

[37] It seems clear that the 1911 Court understood that the resale price maintenance programme in *Dr. Miles* was the vehicle for "horizontal combination among competing distributors" (see the discussion of John D. Park & Sons Company *v*. Samuel B. Hartman, 153 F. 24 (1907) at 220 US 399–400), not merely "analogous to" such combination. The majority in *Leegin* discusses the Dr. Miles retail cartel, at 2717, but not with reference to the *Dr. Miles* decision.

[38] When the case returned to District Court, PSKS alleged that its complaint was justified under the rule of reason. In April 2009, this complaint was dismissed on the ground that PSKS had not properly defined a relevant market, making it impossible to carry out a rule of reason test.

[39] The Supreme Court reaffirms the priority of interbrand competition in Business Electronics Corp. *v*. Sharp Electronics Corp. 485 U.S. 717 (1988) at 726, *Khan* (522 U.S. 3 at 15), and *Reeder-Simco*, 546 U.S. 164 (2006), 126 S. Ct. 860 (2006) at 872.

the distributors of a product produced by a firm in a highly competitive industry. But when interbrand competition exists, as it does among television manufacturers, it provides a significant check on the exploitation of intrabrand market power because of the ability of consumers to substitute a different brand of the same product.

This view is difficult to reconcile with modern economic analysis, which shows that vertical restraints employed to combat the *holdup problem* are a facilitating device to permit the exercise of market power. The economic perspective is that intrabrand competition and interbrand competition interact to determine equilibrium market performance, that restrictions on competition among distributors may be necessary for a manufacturer to exercise market power. Thus, while it is correct that interbrand competition checks the exercise of intrabrand market power, the reverse also correct: when intrabrand competition exists, it provides a significant check on the exploitation of interbrand market power.

In Cascade Health Solutions *v.* PeaceHealth *et al.* No. 05-35627, slip op. at 11191 (9th Cir. 4 September 2007) the 9th Circuit Court of Appeals cites the Supreme Court's emphasis on interbrand competition in *Reeder-Simco* (Section 23.2.3) as an indication of the Supreme Court's guidance that (p. 11219) "the antitrust laws' prohibitions focus on protecting the competitive process and not on the success or failure of individual competitors". But the identification of interbrand competition with the competitive process will not do: intrabrand competition is as much part of the competitive process as is interbrand competition.

Depending on the reason vertical restraints are imposed, restrictions on intrabrand competition may have less, as much, or more impact on market performance than interbrand competition. As the Supreme Court interprets the application of the antitrust laws to vertical contracts, and with its willingness to (Kahn 522 U.S. 3 at 21) "[reconsider] its decisions construing the Sherman Act when the theoretical underpinnings of those decisions are called into serious question", it would do well to turn from giving *per se* priority to inter- over intrabrand competition to having deciders of fact make a rule of reason evaluation of their relative importance in specific cases.

24.3 Competition Policy Toward Vertical Contracts

A fundamental purpose of EC competition policy is to promote market integration. The Commission has, therefore, consistently opposed vertical restraints that have the effect of splitting the Single Market along national boundaries. National resale price maintenance systems do not come under the authority of EC competition law, since they do not affect trade between the member states. But the Commission has held that existence of a legal national resale price maintenance system cannot be used to block shipments of a manufacturer's product from one member state to another.

24.3.1 *Consten & Grundig*[40]

On 1, April 1957, less than a week after the signing of the EEC Treaty but nine months before it took effect, the German consumer electronics company Grundig and the French firm Consten finalized an agreement making Consten the exclusive wholesale distributor of Grundig products in France. Under the terms of the agreement, Consten was to refrain

---

[40] *Consten and Grundig v. Commission* Joined cases 56/64 and 58/64 of 13 July 1966 [1966] ECR 299.

from selling competing consumer electronic products, would make specified sales efforts, maintain an inventory of spare parts, operate a repair shop and provide post-sales service. Grundig agreed that it would not supply its products to other French distributors and that it would require the same of its distributors outside France. Grundig also permitted Consten to register the Grundig trademark "Gint" (Grundig International) in France.

Some Grundig distributors nonetheless supplied Grundig products to the French firm UNEF, which undercut Consten's prices to French retailers. Consten began legal action against UNEF in France, claiming unfair competition and trademark infringement. Meanwhile, under the Regulation 17 procedure then in force, Consten and Grundig notified their distribution agreement to the European Commission. The French court stayed its proceedings to allow the Commission to assess the status of the agreement under EC competition law. The European Commission concluded that the exclusive dealing arrangement violated Article 101. It directed Grundig not to use contracts that interfered with the ability of retailers located anywhere in the EC to acquire supplies from wholesale distributors located anywhere in the EU.

Article 101 applies to vertical as well as horizontal agreements

Consten and Grundig appealed the Commission's decision to the European Court of Justice. One issue was whether Article 101 applied only to horizontal agreements or to vertical agreements as well. The Court wrote that vertical contracts agreements might distort competition between the parties to the contract and third parties, possibly at the expense of consumers, so falling under Article 101 ([1966] ECR 299 at 339). The Court further noted that Article 101 applied to agreements, including vertical agreements, that had the effect of dividing the common market along national boundaries ([1966] ECR 299 at 340).

Trade between member states

Another issue was the Commission's interpretation of the requirement that a prohibited agreement have an effect on trade between member states. Consten, Grundig, and the German government argued that the Commission needed to show that trade would have been greater without the exclusive distributorship agreement. Their view was had that it been incorrect to find that the exclusive distributor contact restricted competition: in fact, the contract promoted competition between Grundig brands and the brands produced by other manufacturers.

No trading-off of competition at one level against competition at another level

The Court rejected the idea of trading off restraints on one type of competition against promotion of another type of competition ([1966] ECR 299 at 342):

> The principle of freedom of competition concerns the various stages and manifestations of competition. Although competition between producers is generally more noticeable than that between distributors of products of the same make, it does not thereby follow that an agreement tending to restrict the latter kind of competition should escape the prohibition of Article [101](1) merely because it might increase the former.

No blocking parallel imports

Finally, the Court found that the Commission had been correct to find that the exclusive distribution contract distorted competition in the Common Market, since its purpose was to isolate France from the rest of the EEC ([1966] ECR 299 at 343), and that the contract therefore violated Article 101(1).

Although the Court confirmed the main elements of the Commission's decision, it reversed the Commission's decision to the extent that it was too broad. The essential offence against EC competition policy was not that Grundig agreed to supply only Consten in the specified territory, but that Grundig acted to block *parallel imports* from distributors in other member states into Consten's territory. Vertical contracts that attempt to impose impermeable barriers around a distributor's territory violate Article 101(1).

24.3.2 *Metro I*[41]

A selective distribution system was at issue in this decision involving Metro, a low-service, low-price distributor that supplied some wholesalers, some retailers, and some final consumers in Germany and other member states, and SABA, a German producer of consumer electronic devices (radios, televisions, tape recorders). SABA imposed requirements on its authorized wholesale and retail dealers. The resulting system:

- limited the number of authorized wholesale and retail dealers, required them to sell only to other authorized dealers (or, in the case of retailers, to final consumers);
- required dealers not to sell outside the EC or to import from outside the EC; and
- required dealers to keep minimum amounts of stock in inventory and to meet specified minimum sales levels.

Dealers could set their own prices and were free to sell throughout the Common Market.

SABA notified the European Commission of its selective distribution system. The Commission required modifications of some features of the system, and gave negative clearance (a statement that on the basis of the information before the Commission, the system did not appear to be a violation of Article 101(1)) to others. The Commission found that the rest of SABA's distribution system restricted competition in the common market—dealers who did not meet the requirements could not distribute SABA products—but this restriction was no more than needed to obtain the efficiency benefits expected to result from selective distribution. Since there was intense competition in the common market for consumer electronics, the Commission expected these benefits to be passed along to consumers, and granted SABA's selective distribution system an exemption under Article 101(3).

Metro sought to become an authorized SABA dealer. SABA said it would admit Metro to its distribution network provided Metro met the conditions it required of wholesale distributors. Metro declined to meet these conditions, and instead asked the European Court of Justice to annul the Commission decision permitting SABA's selective distribution system.

Competition between distribution systems

In its decision, the Court wrote that in the Common Market consumer electronics sector (¶ 20, emphasis added):

> [T]he structure of the market does not preclude the existence of a variety of channels of distribution adapted to the peculiar characteristics of the various producers and the requirements of the various consumers.

---

[41] Metro SB Großmärkte GmbH & Co KG *v*. Commission Case 27/76 judgment of 25 October 1977 [1977] ECR 1875 (*Metro I*).

... the Commission was justified in recognizing that selective distribution systems constituted, together with others, an aspect of competition which accords with Article [101](1) ...

Essentially, the Court found that the Commission was right in relying on rivalry among
distribution systems to obtain good performance in the market for distribution services, just
as it relies on rivalry among producers to obtain good product market performance. The
Court also emphasized that to be consistent with EC competition policy, a selective distribution system had to be based on objective selection standards that were not applied in a
discriminatory way.[42]

24.3.3 *Dutch Books*[43]

The Dutch book trade association VBBB and the Belgian book trade association VBVB each
administered a national resale price maintenance programme. From 1949, they made the
agreements reciprocal, covering the sale of Dutch-language books in both countries. This
reciprocal agreement:

(a) provided for retail sale at prices specified by the publisher;

(b) prohibited the sale of books published by publishers not recognized by one of the
national associations;

(c) prohibited the distribution of books through booksellers not recognized by one of the
national associations; and

(d) provided for penalties if the agreement was violated.

The Commission condemned the agreement as affecting and distorting trade in the common market. The two associations appealed the Commission's decision to the European
Court of Justice, and argued that the Commission had failed to take account of the special
nature of the book market.[44] Among these special characteristics were that:

- each book is a market in itself;
- the price elasticity of demand is low (the Commission disputed this);

---

[42] The Commission later extended its exemption of SABA's selective distribution system (83/672/EEC: Commission Decision of 21 December 1983 concerning a proceeding under Article [101] of the EEC Treaty (IV/29.598—
SABA's EEC distribution system) OJ L 376/41 31 December 1983). Metro challenged the extension, on the ground
that so many consumer electronics manufacturers had adopted selective distribution systems that an exemption
could no longer be justified. In its Metro II decision (Metro SB Großmärkte GmbH & Co KG v. Commission Case
75/84 judgment of 22 October 1986 [1986] ECR 3021), the European Court of Justice again sided with the Commission.

[43] Vereniging ter Bevordering van het Vlaamse Boekwezen (VBVB), Antwerp, and Vereniging tot Bevordering van
de Belangen des Boekhandels (VBBB) v. EC Joined Cases 43/82 and 63/82 [1984] ECR 19.

[44] They also made two non-economic arguments. The first was that an effect of the resale price maintenance
scheme was to ensure the profitability of the book trade, hence to promote the freedom of expression to which
EC member states were committed under the European Convention for the Protection of Human Rights. The
second was that an effect of the resale price maintenance scheme was to prevent loss-leading (selling a popular
product at a low or below-cost price to draw customers into the store), which on some interpretations violates
the Paris Convention on intellectual property rights. Regarding the first point, the Court said that there was no
direct connection between the resale price maintenance scheme and freedom of expression. As for the second, it
noted that if the booksellers were victims of unfair competition, they could pursue remedies under national and
EC competition policy.

- non-price competition, including variety of supply, speed of completing orders, and provision of information and advice, is more important than price competition; and
- resale price maintenance does not limit competition among publishers.

The first "special characteristic" takes a grain of truth and pushes it too far: different titles are imperfect substitutes one for another, but it is the rare title that has no substitutes whatsoever. Even if the price elasticity of demand were low, that would not distinguish the book trade from other markets that are subject to competition policy. Indeed, it might suggest a need for special vigilance toward the book trade on the part of competition authorities, since (all else equal), a low price elasticity of demand would suggest the potential for a high degree of market power.

The argument that for books, non-price competition is more important than price competition, brushes up against the free-rider argument. Some consumers might prefer a high level of sales service, others might prefer low service and low prices. It is not obvious why (as in *Metro I*) one could not rely on competition between different types of distribution channels to sort out the impact of heterogeneous consumer preferences on distribution market structure and performance.

The last point, that resale price maintenance does not limit competition among publishers, is inconsistent with the idea that vertical restraints may be used to mitigate the holdup problem and permit manufacturers (here, publishers) to exercise market power.

For the Court, the resale price maintenance system restricted competition in retail distribution between the member states, and this was sufficient to violate Article [101](1). The trade associations also asked for an exemption under Article [101](3), on the ground that resale price maintenance allowed better market performance (p. 68):

> the existence of a fixed price allows that publisher, as a result of the profit realized on his successful titles, which meet with a ready sale and a rapid turnover, to accept the responsibility and the risk of publishing more difficult and less profitable works. Distributors in their turn are in a position to maintain more extensive stocks and to serve their customers better by helping in this way to disseminate a greater number of varied works.

The Commission did not grant an exemption. It took the view that there had been no proof that this sort of cross-subsidization was necessary to enable distribution of less popular books, which might be distributed under alternative distribution structures that were prevented from developing by the resale price maintenance policy.

24.3.4 *British Books*[45]

The Publishers Association included as its members between 70 and 80 per cent of United Kingdom publishers. It operated the 1957 Net Book Agreement, covering sales in the United Kingdom and Ireland. Under the Net Book Agreement, a so-called "net book" could not be sold to the final consumer for less than the price fixed by the publisher (Section 12.3.4).

The Net Book Agreement was challenged from time to time under United Kingdom competition policy. In a typical ruling, in 1962, the Restrictive Practices Court ([1992] 2 ECR 1995 at 2005):

---

[45] Publishers Association *v.* Commission (Case T-66/89) [1992] 2 ECR 1995 (*British books*).

held with regard to the agreement between the members of the [Publishers Association] that (i) the abolition of the [Net Book Agreement] would deprive the public of special benefits or advantages because it would entail the raising of prices, the reduction of stock-holding book shops and a decline in the number and variety of published titles, (ii) the public would not suffer any appreciable harm from the maintenance of the [Net Book Agreement] as compared with the disadvantages which would arise from its abolition, and (iii) the [Net Book Agreement] was, accordingly, not contrary to the public interest.

After the United Kingdom joined the EEC, the Commission began its own investigation, which led to a 1988 decision[46] that the Net Book Agreement violated Article [101](1) of the EC Treaty and directing that it be ended. The Publishers Association appealed this decision to the Court of First Instance. The Publishers Association pleaded that the Net Book Agreement did not violate Article 101(1), and that if the Court did not accept this view, then the NBA should be granted an exemption under Article 101(3).

The Publishers Association argued that the Net Book Agreement, as applied to books imported into the UK or Ireland, did not affect trade between member states: it was only after such books had been imported that a decision was taken to put them on the market as net books. As the Net Book Agreement did not go into effect until after the arrival of the books in the Irish/UK markets, the Net Book Agreement had no effect on interstate trade.[47] For the Court of First Instance, the fact that more than half of the books sold in Ireland were imports from the UK was sufficient to establish an effect on interstate trade. The Court confirmed the Commission's view that the Net Book Agreement violated Article 101(1).

The Commission based its denial of an Article 101(3) exemption on (a) the collective nature of the Net Book Agreement, which eliminated price competition in trade between the UK and Ireland, and (b) the failure of the Publishers Association to show that such benefits as flowed from a resale price maintenance scheme could not also result if each individual book publisher managed its own resale price maintenance programme.

The Publishers Association replied that a collective resale price maintenance programme was indispensable ([1992] 2 ECR 1995 at 2032–2038):

- as a practical matter, individual publishers could not deal with all individual booksellers;

- booksellers would find it difficult to keep track of potentially different conditions of sale imposed by different publishers;

- with a collection of publisher-specific resale price maintenance schemes, no one individual bookseller could be certain that other booksellers would not be given better terms;

- only the Publishers Association could monitor and enforce standard conditions.

The Court rejected the first argument on the ground that, if true, it was not enough to justify a scheme that distorted competition in the common market. For the second point, the Commission responded that 12 publishers accounted for two-thirds of sales and of exports, suggesting that the number of publishers would not in practice be unmanageably large.

---

[46] Decision 89/44/EEC of 12 December 1988 1989 OJ No L 22.

[47] This argument is akin to the logic of the U.S. Supreme Court in *E.C. Knight*; see Section 18.6.2

The third point is remarkable because it anticipates one of the economic arguments that vertical restraints support the exercise of market power by allowing manufacturers to deal with the holdup problem: since vertical restraints give each individual distributor confidence that rivals will not get better terms, vertical restraints make it rational for an individual distributor to pay a higher wholesale price than would otherwise be the case.

The Commission did not make the economic argument that the defence put forward by the Publishers Association was in fact an admission that the Net Book Agreement worsened market performance. Instead, it argued that the Publishers Association had not shown that booksellers would have any less confidence in the ability of individual manufacturers to enforce individual resale price maintenance schemes than in the ability of the Publishers Association to enforce a collective resale price maintenance scheme.

The Commission rejected the final point (and the Court accepted the Commission's view) on the ground that enforcement of any system of standard sales conditions would depend in the first instance on complaints from booksellers, and this would be the same under collective or individual resale price maintenance. The Court rejected the Publishers Association's appeal and confirmed the Commission's decision.

24.3.5 Regulations and Guidelines

The 1999 vertical restraints regulation[48] adopts an economic effects approach to the treatment of vertical restraints. Minimum resale price maintenance is prohibited. So are airtight exclusive territories: if a dealer receives a request from a customer located outside the dealer's designated territory, the manufacturer must allow the dealer to fill the request. Other types of vertical restraints are permitted under a block exemption if the manufacturer's market share is less than 30 per cent. If a manufacturer's market share exceeds 30 per cent an exemption under Article 101(3) is possible, taking into account the same general elements of market structure—seller concentration, entry conditions, among others—that come into play for a horizontal cooperative agreement.[49,50]

24.3.6 Motor Vehicles

The motor vehicle sector has long benefited from exceptional treatment under EC competition policy. A specific regulation[51] permits car manufacturers to assign dealers to exclusive territories or to use a selective distribution system (to require various quality standards, such as showroom size and post-sales service facilities), but not both (as had been possible under the prior regulation). This policy is said to be justified "because motor vehicles are consumer durables which at both regular and irregular intervals require expert maintenance and repair, not always in the same place". Importantly, the regulation also requires that car

---

[48] OJ L 336 29 December 1999; see also the *Green Paper on Vertical Restraints* (1997a) and Neven *et al.* (1998).

[49] See the *Guidelines on Vertical Restraints* (2000c) for examples.

[50] The 1999 vertical restraints regulation is set to expire in May 2010. In July 2009, the Commission called for comments on proposed revisions in the regulation and in the Vertical Restraints Guidelines. The proposals would essentially continue the provisions of the 1999 regulation, adding a 30 per cent threshold for the buyer in a vertical contract for the block exemption to apply (an adaptation to the rise of large distributors since 1999) and adding provisions to deal with vertical restrictions on internet sales.

[51] Regulation 1400/2002 OJ L 203 1 August 2002. For discussion, see Tsoraklidis (2002), Clark (2002), Brenkers and Verboven (2006).

manufacturers allow a dealer to sell to customers or customers' designated representatives whether or not the customer is resident in the dealer's designated sales area.

Consumer groups have challenged the idea that consumers benefit from the special car distribution regulation. It is seen as contributing to large and persistent car price differences among member states. Further, it appears that car manufacturers have not honoured the part of the regulation that requires them to allow dealers to supply customers resident outside the dealer's home territory. In 1995, the European Commission fined Volkswagen AG €102 million on the ground that VW discouraged its authorized dealers in Italy from supplying cars to customers from parts of Northern Europe. From 1993 to 1995, exchange rate movements made it attractive for customers in Germany and elsewhere to consider buying cars in Italy. VW structured its dealer programmes so that such sales did not count toward satisfying dealer quotas and did not help the dealer meet requirements for some bonus schemes. VW threatened to end the contracts of some Italian dealers if they sold to customers from outside their territories, and 12 dealerships were in fact cancelled. In July 2000, upon appeal by VW, the Court of First Instance allowed €90 million of the fine to stand.

In April 1999, the Commission suggested that DaimlerChrysler had sought to keep some of its dealers from selling outside their territories. In September 1999, VW was the subject of a second investigation by the Commission for restricting dealers in ways inconsistent with the car distribution regulation. In September 2000, the Commission fined General Motors' Dutch subsidiary €43 million for seeking to block sales by Dutch dealers to EC residents from outside the Netherlands (Krause-Heiber, 2001).

In July 2009, the Commission proposed that after a three-year transition period, the general rules that apply to all vertical contracts would apply to new motor vehicle distribution. Sector-specific rules may apply to the car repair and the distribution of spare parts.

SUMMARY

Development of the rule of reason treatment of non-price vertical restraints played an important role in the movement of U.S. antitrust from the principle of competition to a consumer welfare standard. In application, U.S. antitrust gives weight to interbrand competition, and maintains a scepticism toward strategic consequences of interfirm contracts, that go beyond what the economics literature suggests is warranted.

Under Article 101(1), EC competition policy prohibits airtight exclusive territories—vertical contracts may not reestablish the barriers to trade that the common market has dismantled. A manufacturer may agree to supply only one distributor in a territory, but must permit parallel imports from distributors in other territories. Special rules apply to car distribution; the impact of those rules on market performance, and on market integration, has not been felicitous. Selective distribution systems will not run afoul of Article 101(1), provided they are applied in a nondiscriminatory fashion.

STUDY POINTS

- Antitrust treatment
  - fair trade laws (Section 24.2.1)
  - price (Section 24.2.1, Section 24.2.4), non-price (Section 24.2.2) restraints
  - primary concern of antitrust law (Section 24.2.5)

- Clayton Act Section 3 (Section 24.2.3)
- Article 101
  - Parallel imports (Section 24.3.1)
  - Selective distribution (Section 24.3.2)
  - Regulations and Guidelines (Section 24.3.5)
  - Motor vehicle distribution (Section 24.3.6)

DISCUSSION TOPICS

In the early 1920s, there was a series of decisions hinging on the right (or lack of it) for a firm to select its own clients. The first of these decisions appeared to open a breach in the *Dr. Miles per se* rule against resale price maintenance. Later decisions seemed to shore up *Dr. Miles*. But the whole set of decisions is marked by subtle distinctions drawn to justify different findings from similar sets of facts. See *Colgate*,[52] *A. Schrader's Son*,[53] *Frey & Son*,[54] and *Beech-Nut*.[55] A more recent decision is U.S. *v.* Parke, Davis, & Co. 362 U.S. 29 (1960). But the 1984 *Monsanto* decision is a reminder that *Colgate* lives.

FURTHER READING

Merrell *et al.* (1936) discuss pharmaceutical-industry efforts to maintain prices between *Dr. Miles* and the advent of the National Recovery Administration (pp. 8–11), under the NRA, and after the NRA. They also survey early antitrust decisions on resale price maintenance (pp. 299–339). For a survey of such decisions by the U.S. Supreme Court, see *Parke, Davis & Co.*, 362 U.S. 29 (1960), at 38–43. See Grether (1939) for a discussion of fair trade laws, McCraw (1996) for a review of the antitrust treatment of resale price maintenance, Peritz (2007) for background on the patent medicine industry and a legal perspective on *Dr. Miles*, and White (1989) for a review of the development of the treatment of vertical restraints at the hands of U.S. antitrust.

For discussions of *Consten & Grundig*, see Ebb (1967), Steindorff and Hopt (1966–1967). For an account of an encounter between EC competition policy and resale price maintenance in the German-Austrian book trade, see Nehl and Nuijten (2002).

---

[52] U.S. *v.* Colgate & Co., 250 U.S. 300 (1919).

[53] United States *v.* A. Schrader's Son, Inc. 252 U.S. 85 (1920).

[54] Frey & Son *v.* Cudahy Packing Co., 256 U.S. 208 (1921).

[55] FTC *v.* Beech-Nut Packing Co., 257 U.S. 441 (1922).

ANTITRUST, COMPETITION POLICY, AND INTELLECTUAL PROPERTY

No man can serve two masters.

Matthew 6:24

25.1 Introduction

We have seen that product-market rivalry promotes static efficiency and productivity growth. It is not surprising, therefore, that antitrust and competition policy, which seek to maintain opportunities for equally efficient firms to compete seem, on balance, to promote technological advance. In promoting good static market performance, therefore, antitrust and competition policy promote good dynamic market performance as well. Intellectual property rules also seek to promote good dynamic market performance. At the level of goals, therefore, there is no conflict between policies in the two areas.

But there is tension between the means by which the two policies pursue those goals. Antitrust and competition policy aim to maintain opportunities for firms to submit themselves to the test of the marketplace. Intellectual property aims to create incentives to invest in innovation by giving the successful innovator a temporary right to exclude rivals. At the level of means, there can be conflict between antitrust policy and intellectual property rights (Flynn, 1998, fn. 56)

> In situations concerning the acquisition, use, or non-use of patent and other intellectual property rights, the difficulty in drawing a line between permissible and prohibited conduct under the antitrust laws is one of balancing two public interest goals: first, securing disclosure of new ideas by granting exclusive rights in those ideas for a stated period of time; and second, preventing the misuse of these rights to displace the competitive process in ways not necessary to secure disclosure.

Here we consider the antitrust and competition policy treatments of uses of the patent grant to maximize profit that go beyond the "right to exclude": holdup in connection with standard-setting organizations, refusals to license technology, patent pools and cross-licensing, and the tying of patented and non-patented goods.

25.2 Antitrust and (or versus?) Intellectual Property

25.2.1 Standard-Setting Organizations (SSOs), Patent Trolls, and Holdup[1]

The Institute of Electrical and Electronics Engineers (IEEE) is a worldwide professional association. Through its Standards Association (IEEE-SA), it facilitates adoption of a wide range of technical standards, among which those for computer networking. Its 802.3 Working Group develops standards for Ethernet based local area networks (LANs).

Industry standards

By ensuring compatibility, industry standards solve a coordination problem, can smooth the transition from one technological generation to the next, and promote competition. Therein lies the rub: by standardizing, a firm opens up a larger market for itself, but it also exposes itself to a larger number of rivals.

Holdup

The overlap of standard-setting and intellectual property rights creates the possibility of holdup. If many suppliers make sunk investments to conform to standards that incorporate privately held intellectual property, the fundamental transformation kicks in. The owner of some perhaps small but (post-standard setting) essential bit of intellectual property can profit by changing course and licensing its property at substantial fees, fees that it could never have obtained before users committed to the set of standards.

So were firms associated with IEEE Working Group 802.3 exposed to the possibility of holdup. In 1994, National Semiconductor Corporation offered its ethernet communication technology, for which it was in the process of seeking patent protection, for incorporation in industry standards. It committed that it would license the technology for a one-time fee of $1000. National's technology was made part of the industry ethernet standards.

In 1998, National passed control of its patents to Vertical Networks, Inc., a firm formed by National employees. In 2002, at which point the patents covered 70 per cent of world ethernet equipment, Vertical implemented plans to license its technology on a per-unit basis for far more than the one-time fee committed to by National. In 2003, Vertical passed control of the patents to a company formed by its patent attorney, Negotiated Data Solutions LLC, a company ("patent troll") devoted to licensing its patent portfolio.

Unfair competition

In January, 2008, by a 3–2 vote, the Federal Trade Commission issued a complaint against Negotiated Data Solutions, on the ground that its failure to honor National's licensing commitment was an unfair method of competition in violation of Section 5 of the FTC Act. This failure, according to the complaint, would result in higher prices to consumers, discourage adoption of IEEE ethernet standards, and chill reliance on standard setting organizations generally. In a consent decree to settle the complaint, Negotiated Data Solutions agreed to license the technology on the terms originally agreed to by National Semiconductor Corporation.

---

[1] This section is based on the FTC Complaint and Arnold & Porter LLC (2008).

25.2.2 Licensing (or Not): Intel[2]

In 1996 and 1997, Intel Corporation negotiated with one of its clients, Intergraph Corporation, to obtain a licence for certain Intergraph computer microprocessor patents. In the aftermath of the collapse of the negotiations, Intel changed Intergraph's status as a "strategic customer" and altered (for the worse) the terms on which it supplied Intergraph with information and products Intergraph used to produce workstations. Intergraph filed an antitrust suit against Intel, and in District Court obtained a preliminary injunction directing Intel not to alter its business relationships with Intergraph while the antitrust suit went forward. Intel appealed to the Court of Appeals for the Federal Circuit, which overturned the preliminary injunction.

Among the theories rejected by the Circuit Court was that Intel had used its intellectual property to restrain trade in violation of the antitrust laws (195 F.3d 1346 at 1362): "In response to Intel's argument that its proprietary information and pre-release products are subject to copyright and patents, the district court observed that Intel's intellectual property 'does not confer upon it a privilege or immunity to violate the antitrust laws.' That is of course correct. But it is also correct that the antitrust laws do not negate the patentee's right to exclude others from patent property."

Intel prevailed with the Circuit Court of Appeals. But in a parallel proceeding, in June 1998 the Federal Trade Commission issued a complaint that Intel had engaged in unfair competition in violation of Section 5 of the FTC Act, by seeking[3] "to maintain its dominance by ... denying advance technical information and product samples of microprocessors to Intel customers ('original equipment manufacturers' or 'OEMs') and threatening to withhold product from those OEMs as a means of coercing those customers into licensing their patented innovations to Intel". Some eight months before the Circuit Court Intergraph decision, Intel entered into a consent agreement with the FTC,[4] under the terms of which, without admitting that it had engaged in unfair competition, it agreed not to engage in the complained-of conduct.[5]

25.2.3 Cross-Licensing and Patent Pools

Patent cross-licensing agreements and patent pools involve an exchange of the right to use proprietary technology.[6] Patent cross-licensing typically involves two firms, each granting the other the non-exclusive right to use a broad range of patents. A patent pool is a group of patent-holders who license their patents collectively to each other and to outsiders. Such

---

[2] Intergraph Corp. v. Intel Corp. 195 F.3d 1346 (1999).

[3] Federal Trade Commission, "Analysis of Proposed Consent Order to Aid Public Comment," 17 March 1999, <http://www.ftc.gov/alj/D9288/index.shtm>.

[4] In the Matter of Intel Corporation Docket No. 9288.

[5] What, one might ask, was Intel's incentive to accept the constraints on its behaviour that came with a consent agreement? Had the FTC proceeding gone forward, the FTC might have found Intel in violation of Section 5; (Gwennap, 1999): "This ruling, if upheld in the inevitable appeal, would have opened the door for a horde of follow-on suits, allowing both the FTC and various civil parties, including Intel's competitors and customers, to file suit against Intel for a variety of business practices. With Intel declared a monopolist, these cases would be halfway to victory before they even started."

[6] See U.S. Department of Justice and Federal Trade Commission (2007, Chapter 3).

exchanges are a prerequisite for use of a technology if overlapping ownership prevents any one patent-holder from commercializing a technology.[7]

Reciprocal exchanges of the right to use complementary technologies may also improve product-market performance by resolving a non-cooperative equilibrium outcome that is akin to the double-marginalization outcome that arises in vertically related imperfectly competitive markets.[8] Suppose several upstream firms each license (perhaps, under a software patent) use of a bit of technology that is essential to produce downstream product. If each sets the price of its on know-how non-cooperatively to maximize its own profit, the result is a greater combined cost of all required technology than would maximize the profit of a monopolist jointly selling all the technology (Problem 25–1). It follows that independent input producers could increase their combined profit by forming a patent pool and jointly licensing use of their technology. This increases their profit, leaving them better off. By eliminating multiple marginalization, the pool lowers the equilibrium price of the final product, leaving consumers better off as well.

Against these possible efficiency aspects of reciprocal or joint technology licensing must be set the possibility of joint strategic behaviour that worsens market performance (U.S. Department of Justice and Federal Trade Commission, 2007, pp. 9–10) "price fixing, coordinated output restrictions among competitors, or foreclosure of innovation". [9]

General Electric[10]

General Electric held patents on electric light bulbs. It marketed them under licences that required sellers to adhere to prices and other terms of sale set by General Electric. It granted a licence to Westinghouse Company allowing Westinghouse to manufacture light bulbs, and

---

[7] Gilbert (2004, ¶ 13, footnotes omitted): "Patents 'A' and 'B' are in a blocking relationship if the practice of each patent would infringe the other in the absence of a license. Patents 'A' and 'B' are in a one-way blocking relationship if the practice of 'B' requires a license from 'A,' but 'A' does not infringe 'B.' This typically corresponds to a situation where 'B' improves 'A' in some capacity (or 'A' may cover a research tool or some other process that is necessary to produce a product covered by 'B'). Patents that are one-way or two-way blocking are complementary, in the sense that an increase in the price of one patent (or a reduction in its availability) reduces the value of the other patent. ... patents 'A' and 'B' are substitutes for each other if they cover products or processes that can be made or exploited using either patented technology. Patents 'A' and "B" are independent if they are neither substitutes nor complements."

[8] See Section 12.3.4.

[9] Usselman (1990, 1999) discusses "patent pools" set up by U.S. railroads in the post-Civil War period. They were not patent pools in the usual sense—organizations that provided an institutional structure for the cross-licensing of patents, but rather innovation information pools. Usselman's analysis is that at this time and in this industry, innovation was incremental (1990, p. 204: "Rather, the changes seem to have depended on the steady accumulation and systematic evaluation of craft knowledge gained from practical experience and on the ability to use new materials, especially metals"), so that strong patent rights led to a "tragedy of the anticommons", blocking rather than promoting innovation. By widely diffusing information about what were really cumulative innovations, railroad associations weakened patent rights and allowed innovation to go forward. Atack (1999, p. 101) suggests an alternative explanation: "the creation of railroad patent pools slowed the pace of technical change from both within and without. For outside inventors, the pooling of information among railroads reduced the expected return from invention by lowering the likelihood of novelty and by diminishing the probability of adoption by any subset of railroads. On the inside, collusion stilled the winds of 'creative destruction' that jeopardized the value of existing investment."

[10] U.S. v. General Electric Company 272 US 426 (1926). For discussions, see Telser (1960), Priest (1977).

under the terms of the licence required Westinghouse to sell the light bulbs it produced on terms set by General Electric.[11]

The U.S. government challenged these licences as contracts in restraint of trade in violation of Section 1 of the Sherman Act, alleging that (272 U.S. 476 at 479):

> the system of distribution adopted was merely a device to enable the Electric Company to fix the resale prices of lamps in the hands of purchasers, that the so-called agents were in fact wholesale and retail merchants, and the lamps passed through the ordinary channels of commerce in the ordinary way, and that the restraint was the same and just as unlawful as if the so-called agents were avowed purchasers handling the lamps under resale price agreements.

Chief Justice Taft reviewed the terms of the licence agreements (272 U.S. 476 at 483–485) and found that the agency arrangements were genuine: General Electric retained title to the light bulbs it manufactured until they reached the final consumer. For the Supreme Court, so long as General Electric retained ownership of its light bulbs, its actions were lawful (272 U.S. 476 at 485):

> [U]nder the patent law the patentee is given by statute a monopoly of making, using and selling the patented article. ... As long as he makes no effort to fasten upon ownership of the articles he sells control of the prices at which his purchaser shall sell, it makes no difference how widespread his monopoly. It is only when he adopts a combination with others, by which he steps out of the scope of his patent rights and seeks to control and restrain those to whom he has sold his patented articles in their subsequent disposition of what is theirs, that he comes within the operation of the Anti-Trust Act.

Provided the patentholder acted only to exploit the monopoly granted by the patent, he had broad scope to design licences embodying restrictions that would otherwise have been found to violate the antitrust laws.

Hartford-Empire[12]

In December, 1939, the U.S. Department of Justice filed an antitrust suit against the leading U.S. producers of glassware and of machines to make glassware, along with their trade association, the Glass Container Association of America. The industry leader, Hartford-Empire Co., controlled more than 600 patents on glassmaking machinery. Another 232 patents were controlled by 4 other companies. The antitrust complaint was not that the firms had exercised their legitimate rights under the patents they held, but that they cross-licensed their patents among themselves to restrict competition (323 U.S. 386 at 400):[13]

> The District Court found that invention of glassmaking machinery had been discouraged, that competition in the manufacture and sale or licensing of such machinery had been suppressed, and that the system of restricted licensing had been employed to suppress competition in the manufacture of unpatented glassware and to maintain prices of the manufactured product.

---

[11] For discussion of the provisions of the licences, see Bright and MacLaurin (1943).

[12] Hartford-Empire Co. v. U.S. 323 U.S. 386 (1945).

[13] The District Court also found that the regular "statistical reports" of the trade association were actually a device to implement a system of quotas.

The Supreme Court affirmed the District Court decision, establishing that the legal grant of monopoly embodied in a patent cannot be employed strategically to distort competition without thereby violating the antitrust laws. The Court upheld the parts of the District Court's remedy that required the firms to license their patents for use by any parties willing to pay non-discriminatory licensing fees.

25.2.4 Patents and Tying

Motion Picture Patents Co.[14]

A 1902 patent exploited by the Motion Picture Patents Company (MPP) covered improved components of movie projectors, the use of which permitted (243 U.S. 502 at 505) "feeding a film through the machine with a regular, uniform and accurate movement ..." It sold its movie projectors subject to the restriction that the machine could be used only to project movies produced by companies that it had licensed. The movies licensed for use with the projectors had been covered by Thomas Edison's patent on movie cameras and film; this patent expired in 1914.

After the expiration of the Edison patent, independent film distributors supplied films, not licensed by MPP, for use on MPP projectors. MPP challenged this use as an infringement of its rights as a patentholder. It succeeded neither at the District Court nor at the Circuit Court of Appeals, and turned for a final hearing to the Supreme Court. The Supreme Court viewed the question before it as (243 U.S. 502 at 509) "the extent to which a patentee ... is authorized by our patent laws to prescribe by notice attached to a patented machine the conditions of its use and the supplies which must be used in the operation of it ... "

In formulating its answer to that question, the Supreme Court indicated that patent protection applied to the machinery covered by the patent, but did not extend to materials used with that machinery. In so doing, it considered and rejected the argument that tying for the purpose of price discrimination justified extending the practice of tying a patented product and material used with it (243 U.S. 502 at 516–517):

> It is argued as a merit of this system of sale ... that the public is benefited by the sale of the machine at what is practically its cost and by the fact that the owner of the patent makes its entire profit from the sale of the supplies with which it is operated. This fact ... is the clearest possible condemnation of ... the practice adopted, for it proves that under color of its patent the owner intends to and does derive its profit, not from the invention on which the law gives it a monopoly but from the unpatented supplies with which it is used ..., thus in effect extending the power to the owner of the patent to fix the price to the public of the unpatented supplies as effectively as he may fix the price on the patented machine.

It is legal under the patent laws to exercise monopoly power over the protected item. It is illegal under the antitrust laws to use that legal patent monopoly to obtain or maintain monopoly power over items not protected by the patent.

---

[14] Motion Picture Patents Co. *v.* Universal Film Manufacturing Co. *et al.* 243 U.S. 502 (1917). See Cassady (1959), Spivack (1983).

International Salt[15]

International Salt Co. had patents on two machines that were essential to the profitable production of salt. It leased these machines to users, and the leases required that lessees use only rock salt and salt tablets purchased from International Salt Co. in the machines. The government challenged this practice as a violation of the antitrust laws, and the District Court issued summary judgment in favour of the government. International Salt appealed this summary judgment to the Supreme Court, which wrote (332 U.S. 392 at 395–396]:

> [International Salt's] patents confer a limited monopoly of the invention they reward. From them [it] derives a right to restrain others from making, vending, or using the patented machines. But the patents confer no right to restrain use of, or trade in, unpatented salt.

One argument of International Salt to support its right to a trial in District Court relied on the fact that some of its leases allowed clients to buy salt on the open market, if they could find salt of the same quality at a lower price and International Salt chose not to match the lower price. On this matter, the Supreme Court wrote (332 U.S. 392 at 397):

> [This] provision does, of course, afford a measure of protection to the lessee, but it does not avoid the stifling effect of the agreement on competition. [International Salt] had at all times a priority on the business at equal prices. A competitor would have to undercut [International Salt's] price to have any hope of capturing the market, while [International Salt] could hold that market by merely meeting competition. We do not think this concession relieves the contract of being a restraint of trade ...

This reading of the overlap between antitrust and IP policies is that the legal grant of monopoly power embodied in a patent cannot be used, by tying, to support monopoly power over an unpatented product. Nor can it be used to reduce the opportunities of equally efficient competitors to put their products on the market.

The 1988 Patent Misuse Reform Act, which set aside the presumption that patent protection carried with it monopoly power over the patented item, modified the application of antitrust law to tying of a patented product. Under this law, tying a patented and a non-patented good violates the antitrust laws only if "the patent owner has market power in the relevant market for the patent or patented product on which the license or sale is conditioned". [16] This brings the treatment of tying a patented and a non-patented good within the general framework for the antitrust treatment of tying, as set out in *Jefferson Parish Hospital*.[17]

Kodak (bis)[18]

In connection with our treatment of tying, we discussed the U.S. Supreme Court decision[19] to send a private antitrust suit by 18 Independent Service Organizations (ISOs) against Eastman Kodak Company back to District Court for trial. A jury found that Kodak's tying

---

[15] International Salt Co., Inc. *v.* U.S. 332 U.S. 392 (1947). See Peterman (1979).

[16] For the Ninth Circuit Court of Appeals (Image Technical Services, Inc. *et al. v.* Eastman Kodak Company 125 F.3d 1195 (1997) at 1215, fn. 7), the Patent Misuse Reform Act "merely codified existing law".

[17] See U.S. Department of Justice and Federal Trade Commission (2007, p. 12, fn. 23).

[18] Image Technical Services, Inc. *et al. v.* Eastman Kodak Company 125 F.3d 1195 (1997)

[19] Eastman Kodak Company *v.* Image Technical Services Inc., *et al.* 504 U.S. 451 (1992); see Section 24.2.3.

of service and parts was monopolization in violation of Section 2 of the Sherman Act. On appeal of the District Court outcome to the Ninth Circuit Court, one of Kodak's arguments was that it had acted to protect its patented and copyright intellectual property rights, a valid business justification for its conduct that precluded a finding of monopolization (125 F.3d 1195 at 1212). The Circuit Court decision acknowledged that a valid business justification would excuse conduct that might otherwise amount to monopolization. But, it noted, Kodak's conduct involved tying service and thousands of parts, 65 of which were patented. Kodak's "protection of intellectual property" defence was a pretext, "not a genuine reason for Kodak's conduct". [20],[21] The Appeals Court upheld the outcome of the jury trial.[22]

25.3 Intellectual Property Rights and Article 102

25.3.1 Pharmaceuticals

Parke, Davis

We have seen (Section 24.3) that vertical restraints with the effect of dividing the single market along national boundaries violate Article 101(1). Under some circumstances, a firm that holds a patent may be able to divide markets along national lines without, by so doing, abusing a dominant position in violation of Article 102. Thus, in the early *Parke, Davis* case,[23] the pharmaceutical company Parke, Davis held a valid Dutch patent on an antibiotic. Such products could not at that time be patented in Italy. Probel obtained the product from a firm in Italy, and marketed it in the Netherlands. The European Court of Justice held that Parke, Davis did not abuse a dominant position when it used its patent rights to block sale of the Italian version of the product in the Netherlands: a patent is a legal grant of monopoly and Parke, Davis was simply exercising its legal monopoly rights. The facts that Parke, Davis was not itself (directly or indirectly) the source by which the product was available in Italy, and that patent protection was not available in Italy, were central to the Court's decision.

---

[20] 125 F.3d 1195 at 1220, fn. 12, quoting instructions to the jury.

[21] The rule applied by the Circuit Court was that to show monopolization in violation of Section 2, the ISOs needed to demonstrate that Kodak "(1) possessed monopoly power in the relevant market and (2) willfully acquired or maintained that power" (125 F.3d 1195 at 1203). The second requirement calls for an evaluation of Kodak's intent in tying parts and service, and this aspect of the Circuit Court decision has been criticized (U.S. Department of Justice and Federal Trade Commission, 2007, pp. 6–7). Leaving aside the point that (as noted in the Circuit Court decision at 1208) the Supreme Court has endorsed the place of intent in finding (or not) a Section 2 violation, there are many areas in which legal outcomes depend on an evaluation of intent (Justice Holmes, *Abrams v. United States* 250 U.S. 616 (1919) at 626–627): "[T]he word intent as vaguely used in ordinary legal discussion means no more than knowledge at the time of the act that the consequences said to be intended will ensue. ... A man may have to pay damages, may be sent to prison, at common law might be hanged, if at the time of his act he knew facts from which common experience showed that the consequences would follow, whether he individually could foresee them or not." The evaluation of intent in such circumstances is no less difficult than the evaluation of intent in antitrust cases; it is not obvious that a consideration of intent should be excluded from antitrust and competition policy as a matter of first principles.

[22] For a contrary decision involving comparable facts by the Court of Appeals for the Federal Circuit, see *CSU, L.L.C. et al. v. Xerox Corporation* 203 F.3d 1322 (2000).

[23] *Parke Davis v. Probel* [1968] ECR 55; [1968] CMLR 47.

AstraZeneca

A June 2005 European Commission decision[24] fined the pharmaceutical company AstraZeneca €60 million for abuse of the patent system in violation of Article 102 of the EC Treaty. The abuse consisted of behaviour intended to slow the arrival of generic substitutes for its blockbuster ulcer drug Losec. AstraZeneca provided misleading information to several member state patent offices[25] to obtain extended periods of patent protection. In other cases, it withdrew marketing authorizations for Losec in Denmark, Norway, and Sweden. Under the procedures in force at that time, this prevented marketing generic substitutes in those member states.

Pharma sector practices

In November 2008 DG Competition issued a preliminary report on its inquiry into the pharmaceutical sector, identifying a pattern of behaviour much like that condemned in *AstraZeneca*, namely (EC Commission, 2008c, p. 5, not set off as a list in the original):

- filing for up to 1,300 patents EU-wide in relation to a single medicine (so-called "patent clusters");

- engaging in disputes with generic companies leading to nearly 700 cases of reported patent litigation;

- concluding settlement agreements with generic companies which may delay generic entry; and

- intervening in national procedures for the approval of generic medicines.

In the same place, the Commission recognizes "that patents are key in the pharmaceutical sector, as they allow companies to recoup their often very considerable investments and to be rewarded for their innovative efforts". In the EU (as in the U.S.), fine-tuning the competition policy-intellectual property overlap to ensure public benefit as well is on the policy agenda.

25.3.2 IBM Settlement (1984)

In 1984 IBM made a formal commitment[26] to alter some business practices and so bring to a close a commission investigation under Article 102. The Commission had taken the view that IBM held a dominant position in the common market for its System-370 main-frame computer and was able to control the markets for products compatible with it. The Commission argued that IBM had abused this dominant position by withholding interface information essential for independent producers to supply compatible equipment, which thereby also interfered with development of standard computer networking procedures, by bundling CPUs and main memory; and by bundling CPUs and software.

The essence of these alleged abuses involves issues of product design, and thus goes to the heart of the innovative process. In taking steps to end the Commission proceeding, IBM

---

[24] Commission Decision of 15 June 2005 relating to a proceeding under Article [102] of the EC Treaty and Article 54 of the EEA Agreement (Case COMP/A. 37.507/F3). AstraZeneca has appeal the decision.

[25] Quoting Commission Memo/08/746 of 28th November 2008 "Despite significant efforts, there is no single EU-wide patent and no EU jurisdiction for patent matters. The European Patent Office handles centralised patent applications, but the scope of the patent ultimately granted is national and must be challenged nationally."

[26] An undertaking, in Eurospeak. The settlement is discussed in EC Commission (1985, pp. 77–79).

agreed to unbundle CPUs and main memory and to make interface information available to independent hardware producers and software, network designers. The Commission felt that the agreement would improve market performance (EC Commission, 1985, p. 79):

> The undertaking will have the effect of substantially improving the position of both users and competitors in the markets for System/370 products in the EEC. As a result, competition in the common market can be expected to be strengthened and made more effective. Users will now be given the possibility of a choice between different suppliers at an earlier time. They may also be free to choose from a wider selection of products because other manufacturers will now have the incentive to develop new products in the knowledge that the essential interface information will be made available.

25.3.3 *Hilti*

A 1991 decision[27] of the Court of First Instance helped clarify the limits EU competition policy places on the exercise of patent rights. The product market in the *Hilti* decision—nail guns and associated products, used in building and construction—would not normally be thought of as "high tech", but the issues involved in the decision anticipate those present in much more prominent recent cases.

Hilti AG had its legal home in Liechtenstein, and manufacturing operations there and in other EU member states. It held patents on its nail guns, on nails for its guns, and on cartridge strips by means of which nails could be inserted into its nail guns.[28] Hilti tied the sale of nails and cartridge strips to the sale of its nail guns; it obliged its dealers not to supply cartridge strips to independent nail producers. The European Commission found, and the Court of First Instance agreed, that Hilti's 55 per cent in the supply of nail guns in the Community as a whole gave it a dominant position.

Market definition

Although Hilti argued that nail guns, nails, and cartridge strips were components of a single product, the Court found that nail guns, Hilti-compatible nails, and cartridge strips were three distinct product markets. One bit of supporting evidence for the conclusion that these were separate product markets was that there was a history of independent producers specializing in the production of nails specifically designed for Hilti tools.

Raising rivals' costs

Despite the fact that Hilti held patents on the products it was distributing, the Court found that its marketing practices were abusive in the sense of Article 102, because they had the effect of raising entry costs ([1990] ECR II-1483):

> The strategy employed by Hilti against its competitors and their customers is not a legitimate mode of competition on the part of an undertaking in a dominant position. A selective and discriminatory policy such as that operated by Hilti impairs competition inasmuch as it is liable to deter other undertakings from establishing themselves in the market.

The Court confirmed the € 6 million fine levied by the Commission.

---

[27] Hilti AG *v.* EC Commission Case T-30/89 [1990] ECR II-1439; [1990] 4 CMLR 16.

[28] The details of the patents held varied from product to product and from member state to member state.

This decision shows that when a firm has a dominant position in a market for a differentiated product, EU courts will treat products that are compatible with the product of the dominant firm as distinct products. The IBM settlement and the *Hilti* decision together indicate that intellectual property rights—whether based on product design or on patent rights—will not, under EU competition law, permit a dominant firm to divide the common market or to raise rivals' entry costs.

25.3.4 *Tetra Pak Rausing*

More generally, it is an established principle in EU competition law that conduct permitted for a small firm is an abuse in violation of Article 102 if committed by a dominant firm. Thus the 1991 *Tetra Pak* decision involved the leading EU manufacturer of sterile cartons and machines for filled such cartons.[29] In 1986, Tetra Pak took over another firm, Liquipak, and as a result gained control of an exclusive licence for use of a new technique for filling cartons with sterile milk. At the time Tetra Pak got control of the licence, the new technique was not yet being commercially applied, and the parties in the case disagreed about how much additional work would be needed to make commercial use possible. When Tetra Pak got control of the licence, firms that had been working with Liquipak to bring the new technology to the market stopped work on the project. The Commission investigated Tetra Pak's acquisition of the exclusive licence, and as a result Tetra Pak gave up its exclusive right to use the new technology. Nonetheless, to clarify the area of law concerned, the Commission reached a decision that the acquisition of such an exclusive patent licence by a dominant firm was an abuse of a dominant position under Article 102. Tetra Pak appealed the Commission's decision to the Court of First Instance. Once again, the impact of an exclusive licence on the ability of rivals to compete was central when the Court of First Instance upheld the Commission ([1990] ECR II-357):

> the Commission was right not to put in issue the exclusive license as such, but rather to object specifically under Article [102] to the anti-competitive effect of its being acquired by [Tetra Pak]. . . .
>
> The decisive factor in the finding that acquisition of the exclusive licence constituted an abuse lay . . . in particular . . . on the fact that at the material time the right to use the process protected by the . . . licence was alone capable of giving an undertaking the means of competing effectively with [Tetra Pak].

Under EU competition policy, a dominant firm may exercise its intellectual property rights to earn economic profit, subject to the limitation that it may not specifically make it more difficult for rivals to try to compete such profits away.[30]

---

[29] See Section 21.3.3 and the discussion of *Tetra Pak II*.

[30] The issues raised for competition policy in these intellectual property rights cases have also surfaced in several of the Microsoft Corporation's dealings with the European Commission. Some of these are described in EC Commission (1995, pp. 116–121) (marketing practices that had the effect of raising the cost to users of choosing rival operating systems for personal computers), EC Commission (1998, pp. 116–117) (contract requiring a software developer to use a Microsoft version of UNIX as the basis for its own product development); EC Commission (2000c, p. 162) (contractual restrictions on internet service providers concerning their use of rival internet browsers).

SUMMARY

The records of antitrust and competition policy show that left to their own devices, patentholders will employ their intellectual property rights in privately profitable ways that discourage innovation (holdup), strategically grant or withhold licenses, cross-license to raise the cost of entry, tie patented and non-patented goods. Pharmaceutical companies have track records of manipulating intellectual policy to delay generic competition. Antitrust policy has condemned such behavior when it goes beyond the intended patent grant of the right to exclude. Competition policy has condemned strategic uses of the patent grant that rise to the level of abuse of a dominant position.

STUDY POINTS

- Patents and Antitrust
  - Standard setting organizations, patent trolls, and holdup (Section 25.2.1)
  - Patent licences (Section 25.2.2)
  - Cross-licensing and patent pools (Section 25.2.3)
  - Tying patented and unpatented goods (Section 25.2.4)
- Patents and Article 102 (Section 25.3)

FURTHER READING

On the economics of and policy toward intellectual property, see symposia in the Winter 1991 and Spring 2005 issues of the *Journal of Economic Perspectives*. On intellectual property and antitrust, see the U.S. Department of Justice—FTC *Guidelines* (April 2007).

PROBLEM

25–1[31] (Patent pool; à la Shapiro, 2001, pp. 149–150) Each of n upstream firms owns the intellectual property right to the know-how to produce an essential component of a final good that is assembled from the n components by a perfectly competitive downstream assembly industry.

The inverse demand equation for the final good is:

$$p = a - bQ, \tag{25.1}$$

where Q is the quantity of the final good demanded at price p.

There is a constant assembly cost α for each unit of the final good produced.

Each upstream firm's intellectual property can be made available to downstream firms at zero marginal cost. (Think of the components as pieces of software.)

---

[31] The formal similarity of this price-setting problem to the standard Cournot quantity-setting model will be evident. As Shapiro (2001) notes, this problem is considered by Cournot (1838). See also Sonnenschein (1968).

(a) Find equilibrium royalty rates per unit of final good output (ρ_i for component i) if each component producer non-cooperatively maximizes its own profit. Find non-cooperative equilibrium profit per component producer and the equilibrium price of the final good.

(b) Suppose instead that the component producers form a pool, sell all components as a package at price R, and divide the resulting profit equally among themselves. Find the profit-maximizing value of R, the equilibrium price of the final good, and profit per component producer.

(c) Compare (a) and (b).

ARE ANTITRUST AND COMPETITION POLICY WORTH IT?[1]

26

[Coase] said he had gotten tired of antitrust because when the prices went up the judges said it was monopoly, when the prices went down, they said it was predatory pricing, and when they stayed the same, they said it was tacit collusion [laughter].

Landes, quoted in Kitch (1983, p. 193).

Nature's action is complex: and nothing is gained in the long run by pretending that it is simple ...

Marshall (1893, p. 82).

26.1 Introduction

Supreme Court affirmations of the kind found in *Topco* (405 U.S. 596 at 610) would lead one to think that the place of the antitrust laws in the U.S. legal firmament was secure:

> Antitrust laws in general, and the Sherman Act in particular, are the Magna Carta of free enterprise. They are as important to the preservation of economic freedom and our free-enterprise system as the Bill of Rights is to the protection of our fundamental personal freedoms.

Such security is largely illusory. Every 20 or 25 years since passage of the Sherman Act the position is put forward that antitrust laws are at best nugatory and at worst positively harmful. A curious aspect of these assertions is that although they embody substantially the same objections to antitrust policy, each generation of anti-antitrusters seems to perceive its arguments as being completely original, exhibiting no awareness that others have made much the same arguments before, and that the arguments have been found wanting. In this chapter, we first highlight the common elements of these cyclical attacks on the antitrust principle, review the benefits of competition, and discuss the costs and benefits of

---

[1] I owe the title of this chapter to Geroski (2004).

competition policy. We document the retreat of antitrust enforcement in the United States, the prospects for competition policy in the European Union, and draw implications.

26.2 The 25-year Cycle

26.2.1 Before the Sherman Act

We have seen that in the run-up to passage of the Sherman Act there was a wide-ranging public debate, positions in which included on the one hand arguments for various kinds of regulation of business conduct or structure (Henry Adams, 1887; John Bates Clark) and on the other that no such policy was necessary, since the combination of potential and actual combination along with business pursuit of its own self-interest would result in satisfactory market performance (Gunton, 1888; Giddings, 1887). One of the wide range of opinions offered during Senate debate on the Sherman Act was that all one needed to do to tame the trusts was abolish tariff protection; "The tariff is the mother of trusts".

26.2.2 Before the Clayton and FTC Acts

The same kind of debate took place in the decade and a half following passage of the Sherman Act. The views of John Bates Clark and many others converged on the policy embodied in the Clayton Act. Others defended the view that actual and potential competition was sufficient to guarantee good market performance. Charles Francis Adams wrote that (1897, p. 204) "[t]he production of the world is now so great ... , the means of communication so rapid ... , the accumulation of capital is so great" that trusts could only survive by lowering costs and prices—attempts to raise price above average cost would simply result in entry. Once again, the tariff was the mother of trusts.[2]

26.2.3 Post-World War I

In the immediate aftermath of World War I, the business community looked longingly back on the government-sponsored cooperation of the wartime economy and anxiously antici-pated a post-war downtown as public-sector demand returned to peacetime levels (Slichter, 1937, p. 6). The result (Section 20.3.2) was a business campaign with the (Himmelberg, 1968, p. 3) "immediate and urgent goal of ... an emergency suspension of the antitrust laws so as to facilitate the establishment of price agreements against the postwar deflation that most observers expected. But permanent antitrust revision, legislation drastically widening the legal limits of cartelization, was regarded as the fundamental issue".

One theme sounded by advocates of antitrust reform was that antitrust was outmoded and would handicap the United States on world markets (Sisson, 1919, p. 146):

> [W]e cannot adequately coöperate outside of the United States if we are compelled to indulge in costly and wasteful competition within our own borders. Our existing anti-combination legis-lation, in fact, is not only out-of-date but is a positive menace to our industrial and commercial future.

Competition as wasteful and antitrust as out-of-date are recurring themes in attacks on antitrust.

---

[2] See also pp. 435–451 in Chicago Conference on Trusts ([1900] 1973).

26.2.4 Between the World Wars

Between the wars, U.S. antitrust and the principle of competition were contrasted with the cartel control policy followed elsewhere (particularly Germany, but also England, Canada, and Australia, among others).[3] A frequent complaint was that the antitrust laws were so vague and ambiguous that businessmen could not know what would violate the law and what would not.[4] A common suggested remedy was to give a federal agency (the FTC was often mentioned) the authority to vet business arrangements in advance. "Pre-approved" arrangements would receive partial or complete immunity from prosecution under the antitrust laws (Anderson, 1919; Butler, 1919; Shepherd, 1929). This would be accompanied by a shift in the objective of antitrust policy away from consumer welfare to an *abuse control approach*, maximizing net social welfare (Levy, 1927, p. 601: "the interests of the *public as a whole*"; see similarly Williams, 1928a, p. 418, Domeratzky, 1931, p. 35). This campaign culminated in the short-lived National Industrial Recovery Act (Section 20.3.2), which turned out not to be the road to economic recovery its advocates had expected.

26.2.5 Post-World War II

The post-World War II debate about antitrust repeated the themes that had been sounded after World War I. There were calls for a relaxation of antitrust and a switch to a cartel control policy (Perkins, 1944; Haussmann and Ahern, 1945; Comer, 1946). The prevalence of cartels outside the United States was noted, and the antitrust laws were once again said to be out of date (Lilienthal, 1952, p. 5): "the basic governmental business policies and the everyday enforcement of the antitrust laws are still based largely upon prejudice created by abuses long since corrected, upon an antiquarian's portrait of another America, not the America of the mid-twentieth century ... "

Technical progress made antitrust obsolete (Lilienthal, 1952, p. 68):

> The New Competition can be traced to a number of factors, but the central one is the amazing technical advance in American industry due to scientific research and engineering development. The last decade's achievements of the chemical industry and in electronics are perhaps the most spectacular illustrations of how science and technology have intensified competition, and thereby increased the range of free choice that men now have, as contrasted with thirty to fifty years ago. The same thing applies, however, to many other industries.

26.2.6 The 1980s

Some 30 years later, the argument was once again made that foreign competition had rendered antitrust unnecessary. For Thurow (1980), antitrust was out of date ("The time has come to recognize that the techniques of the 19th century are not applicable in getting ready for the 21st",) and had to be abandoned if U.S. firms were to compete abroad ("[The United States] cannot hope to compete in world markets if Americans are unable to respond to

---

[3] See Sisson (1919), Levy (1927), Williams (1928b), National Industrial Conference Board (1931), and Wolff (1935). It later became clear that the record of cartel control was not so positive as it appeared (Kronstein and Leighton, 1946).

[4] The complaint of uncertainty may simply have been a smokescreen. Levy (1927, p. 600) wrote that "The defect in our Anti-Trust laws is not that they are uncertain in their meaning" but rather that they clearly prevented business cooperation and forced firms into "ruthless and cut-throat competition with each other".

Japanese trading companies with American trading companies"). The tariff was the mother of trusts ("If competitive markets are desired, then reduce the barriers to free trade") and in any case, potential competition would assure good market performance ("[O]ligopolistic companies may be able to extract a small price premium from their customers, but this ability is inherently limited. Customers have alternative uses for their income and potential competitors are almost always waiting in the wings").

26.2.7 Early 21st Century

Crandall and Winston (2003) review six Sherman Act Section 2 monopolization cases spanning 71 years,[5] about which they note (2003, p. 7) "To be sure, these cases are decades old ... " They review case studies of two applications of Section 1 of the Sherman Act,[6] one study of price wars in the U.S. airline industry,[7] and Sproul's (1993) analysis of 25 U.S. price-fixing cases between 1973 and 1984,[8] and conclude "To be sure, there are well known examples where firms have clearly colluded to raise prices, including recent cases involving lysine, citric acid and vitamins. However, researchers have not shown that government prosecution of alleged collusion has systematically led to significant nontransitory declines in consumer prices." As for mergers, which they note (2003, p. 15) "may harm or benefit consumers", they present the result of their own statistical study of the impact of merger enforcement activity on price-cost margins for 20 two-digit SIC industries for the years 1984–1996.[9]

---

[5] The cases are Standard Oil v. U.S. 221 U.S. 1 (1911), U.S. v. American Tobacco Co. 221 U.S. 106 (1911), U.S. v. Aluminum Company of America 148 F. 2d 416 2d Cir. (1945), U.S. v. Paramount Pictures 334 U.S. 131 (1948), U.S. v. United Shoe Machinery Corp. 110 F. Supp. 295 (1953), and U.S. v. AT & T 552 F. Supp. 131 (1982).

[6] These are Newmark's (1988) examination of the U.S. FTC's *Bakers of Washington* case (about which see also Mueller and Parker, 1992) and Carlton *et al.* (1995), Hoxby (2000) on *Overlap*, which involved cooperation by non-profit institutions of higher learning to coordinate financial aid (not to raise tuition). Crandall and Winston cite Newmark as finding (2003, p. 14) "that an antitrust indictment of bakers in Seattle had no effect on the price of bread". Yet (while cautioning that they are cases where government or public utilities are on the demand side of the market) Newmark (1988, pp. 469–470, footnotes omitted) also writes "Producers of asphalt, gymnasium bleachers, rock salt, concrete pipe, and circuit breakers all raised prices through conspiracies. One textbook concludes that the average price-fixing agreement increases price by 10–30 percent. Another text asserts that many conspiracies have increased price by 30–60 percent."

[7] Crandall and Winston (2003, p. 4) cite Morrison and Winston's (1996, p. 107), footnote remark that in their econometric study of U.S. airline price wars from 1978 to 1995 "We also specified a dummy variable that identified the time period (March 1994 to the present) that the U.S. Justice Department's consent decree has been in effect. This decree has prohibited all carriers from announcing the ending dates of their fare promotions. It might be expected that this has lowered the likelihood of a fare war, but we found that thus far it has had a statistically insignificant effect." Airline city-pair markets are for the most part small-numbers oligopolies with highly transparent prices; it is not obvious that one should expect an antitrust provision that targets collusion to have an effect on tacit collusion in such a market. Further, as Morrison and Winston note (1996, pp. 106–107, p. 121) their sample period was one of structural and conduct disequilibrium as the airline industry adapted to deregulation.

[8] Sproul (1993, p. 751, footnote omitted) finds that "(1) Average price rises gradually after an indictment for price fixing. (2) The largest immediate drops in price ... were in the range of 9–10 percent. (3) Prices subsequent to the indictment are negatively correlated with the severity of penalties", that alternative explanations for these results are (1993, p. 753) "the government mainly prosecutes cost-reducing cartels" or "penalties are not severe enough, and more vigorous prosecution is needed", and "The evidence does not give a clear answer" which explanation applies. For critical comments on Sproul's methodology, see Werden (2008, p. 437).

[9] They also lament the absence of government studies of the impact of merger policy on market performance, mention studies of the impact of mergers on stock prices, cite case studies of three mergers that improved market performance, and footnote the 1996 Union Pacific/Southern Pacific merger (2003, fn. 5) "which led to disastrous service disruptions in the southwest that cost shippers billions of dollars".

Their findings are that (2003, p. 18)[10] "a successful merger challenge does have a negative effect on the price-cost margin, but that the effect is not statistically significant. In contrast, an unsuccessful challenge in which a court eventually allows the proposed merger is associated with a decline in price-cost margins, and the effect is statistically significant".

In discussion of Baker (2003), they sound the main themes of earlier anti-antitrust campaigns (2003, p. 22, fn. 10) that Baker "fails to acknowledge that the influx of foreign competition, deregulation, the entry of new firms and the emergence of new technologies has created an extremely competitive environment for contemporary U.S. industry".

26.2.8 Recurring Themes

Antitrust is unnecessary because good market performance can be obtained by removing barriers to international trade. Like many false conclusions, this one is based on a kernel of truth. All evidence is that removing trade barriers improves market performance—for tradeable goods. But even worldwide industries may have an oligopoly equilibrium market structure. Examples in the annals of antitrust are not hard to find (vitamins; woodpulp, cars). Nor can lowering trade barriers be expected to ensure good market performance in nontradeable good sectors, in endogenous-sunk-cost consumer good industries, or in local retail markets. There remains a role for prohibition of collusion, of exclusionary conduct, and merger control in promoting good market performance.

Antitrust is also, apparently, inappropriate for high-technology sectors like cars (1920s), chemicals and electronics (1950s), computers (1980s), software (1990s), and the internet (2000s). Simply running down the list suggests that today's high-technology sector often becomes tomorrow's commodity sector. Nothing about competition policy, which at its core is about maintaining the opportunity to compete, aims to prevent a leading incumbent firm from riding a wave of innovation and maintaining its leading position. Competition policy aims to ensure that leading incumbents do not exclude entrants that, if permitted to compete, might spark the next wave of creative destruction. The fact that maintaining opportunities to compete (that is, giving maximum force to potential competition) promotes good static market performance as well as good dynamic market performance is a merit of competition policy, not a mark against it.

26.3 Costs and Benefits of Competition

26.3.1 Concentration

The lower is seller concentration, the closer is economic profit to zero, the closer is price to unit cost, and the greater is efficiency, all else equal. The larger the share of imports in industry supply (that is, the stronger is foreign competition), the better is market performance, all else equal. Actual and potential competition tend to improve static market performance, within limits set by technology and consumer behavior. Evidence for particular industries suggests that actual competition has a greater impact on static market performance than potential competition.

---

[10] The weight to be attached to these results must be qualified by the use of a two-digit industry classification; even classification at the four-digit SIC level is now viewed with caution.

26.3.2 Entry and Exit

Profit attracts entry, within limits determined by the cost of entry. Losses induce exit, within limits determined by the extent to which costs are sunk. Entry and exit function as a triage mechanism, selecting more efficient firms into markets and selecting less efficient firms out of markets, not as an automatic adjustment mechanism that drives economic profit to zero. There are persistent cost and profit differences between firms in most markets. Entry costs can be raised by incumbents' strategic behaviour.

26.3.3 Innovation

For some industries (Schumpeter Mark I), it is actual competition from new firms that drives innovation and technological progress in a cycle of creative destruction. For others (Schumpeter Mark II), it is market leaders that are the source of technological progress. Some evidence suggests that intermediate levels of market concentration on average stimulate private investment in innovation more than either very low or very high levels of market concentration.

26.3.4 Rivalry

All evidence is that competition is beneficial. But what is meant by this conclusion is that competition in the sense of rivalry is beneficial. Most markets—large manufacturing markets in which minimum efficient scale is large, the equilibrium number of firms small, and potential entry has little impact on market performance, small retail markets in which minimum efficient scale is small, the equilibrium number of firms small and potential entry has great impact on market performance—are imperfectly competitive. The classroom model of perfect competition offers a standard of market performance against which to measure the performance of real-world markets. The extremely limited range of conduct open to firms in a perfectly competitive market—cost-minimization and profit-maximization, taking price as given—does not offer a standard against which to measure the conduct of real-world firms. There is no competition—no rivalry—among the price-taking firms of the perfectly competitive market.

26.3.5 Losses from Competition

Competition is not without its costs. Exit entails the loss of sunk investments. Much of the savings that come from the minority of mergers that actually generate savings are realized by the elimination of duplicate costs, which can mean workers thrown into unemployment and communities or regions with the backbones of their local economies broken. Here one can make a case for transitional state aid. But market economies have made the judgement that the benefits of competition exceed the costs (Judge Holmes, Vegelahn v. Guntner 167 Mass. 92 (1896), at 106, in dissent):

> [I]t has been the law for centuries that a man may set up a business in a country town too small to support more than one, although he expects and intends thereby to ruin some one already there, and succeeds in his intent. In such a case he is not held to act "unlawfully and without justifiable cause," ... The reason, of course, is that the doctrine generally has been accepted that free competition is worth more to society than it costs, and that on this ground the infliction of the damage is privileged.

26.4 Costs and Benefits of Antitrust and Competition Policy

26.4.1 Costs

The direct costs of antitrust and competition policy are the budgets of government enforcement agencies, private sector spending on private legal actions, and private sector spending to defend against private or public legal actions. The cost of judicial resources devoted to competition cases is also a cost of the system. Indirect costs are the opportunity costs of type I errors (efficient conduct abandoned because it is mistakenly found to violate antitrust law) and type II errors (continuing anticompetitive conduct that is mistakenly found not to violate antitrust law).

Crandall and Winston (2003) estimate the direct cost of U.S. federal antitrust enforcement at $146.9 million year 2000 dollars, of which $87.9 million for the Antitrust Division of the U.S. Department of Justice, $59 million for the Federal Trade Commission. Baker's (2003, p. 42) estimate for total direct cost is $150 million per year. *Global Competition Review* (2009) reports that the 2009 budget request for the Antitrust Division was $150.6 million, and that the FTC's 2009 budget (for competition policy and consumer protection activity) was $244 million.[11]

Baker further estimates private sector costs of defending against government actions at $500 million per year, and costs of private sector antitrust actions at something under $400 per year. The direct cost of U.S. antitrust enforcement is then around a billion dollars a year. If, he suggests, indirect costs are substantial but no more than direct costs, the direct and indirect cost of U.S. antitrust enforcement is on the order of $2 billion per year.

DG Competition's 2008 budget was €78.2 million.[12] DG Comp's budget is thus between one-quarter and one-third the combined budgets of the two U.S. enforcement agencies. Excluding (for comparability), those working on state aid matters, DG Comp has a staff one-third the combined staff of the two U.S. agencies.

Neven (2006, p. 749) estimates that economics competition policy consulting firms earned £24 million in 2004,[13] and that this was 15 per cent of total fees for competition policy legal advice, suggesting a total of £160 million or about €228.00. Neven (2006, p. 746) comments that "economic resources at the level of the EU Commission remain meagre, and the asymmetry in resources between the authorities and the businesses they regulate is a cause for significant concern".

26.4.2 Benefits

General evidence that competition policy improves market performance is provided by Warzynski (2001). He compares the ratio of price to marginal cost of 450 U.S. four-digit SIC industries for two periods, 1958–1973 (when U.S. antitrust followed a relatively severe

[11] The Antitrust Division employed 564 attorneys, economists, and paralegals at the start of 2009. The Federal Trade Commission had 1,084 full-time-equivalent employees for competition policy and consumer protection (*Global Competition Review*, 2009).

[12] It had 738 permanent employees, of which 179 working on state aid control (*Global Competition Review*, 2009).

[13] This amount is an underestimate to the extent that it does not include income of economics consulting firms on the continent and an overestimate to the extent that it includes some income of consulting firms located in the UK on work done outside the EU. See Neven (2006, fns. 25, 26).

structuralist approach) and 1974–1994 (when U.S. antitrust, under the influence of the Second Chicago School, took a minimalist approach).[14] He finds the price-cost margin to be noticeably and significantly lower during the period of tough antitrust enforcement.[15]

Anticollusion policy

Estimates of the minimum social welfare gains from anticollusion enforcement are large. Werden's (2008, pp. 436–437) estimate is of the price increases consumers do not have to pay because of the impact of antitrust policy on cartel effectiveness; it does not include deadweight welfare losses consumers would suffer in the absence of antitrust policy:

> The available evidence suggests that cartels prosecuted as felonies in the U.S. typically had substantial price effects—at least 10% on average. During fiscal years 2000–2007, the aggregate annual sales of companies convicted in the U.S. of cartel activity was $18.5 billion within the cartelized markets. Assuming the life span of the cartels was shortened by 1 year and that they increased prices 10%, cartel enforcement saved U.S. consumers an estimated $1.85 billion. Because this estimate omits substantial benefits from cartel enforcement, the full effect likely is substantially greater.

There is a deterrence effect of competition policy. Thus, Geroski (2004) reports that a study of the international vitamin cartel "[c]omparing countries with and without an active competition enforcement regime suggested that prices were notably higher in the latter. The estimates suggest that the absence of the competition regime in the UK might have led to overcharging on the scale of a further $30 [million] per annum".

Leaving aside criminal prosecution, which exists in the United States for hard-core cartels, the deterrence effect of antitrust and competition policy is based on the size of the penalty expected to be incurred. While the penalties paid by members of high-profile cartels like the lysine cartel (Section 20.2.3) are impressive, they may not be enough to make collusion unprofitable in an expected value sense. Connor (2002, p. 38) writes of the U.S. fines to three major cartels that:

> [G]overnment and private antitrust penalties on the lysine, citric acid, and vitamins cartels amounted to between $2,850 million and $3,550 million. Although by historical standards these amounts were great accomplishments for public prosecutors and private plaintiffs, they fall far short of what the Sherman Act intended. These price-fixing penalties amounted to about 47 percent of affected U.S. sales, or somewhere between 179 percent and 194 percent of the cartels' illegal profits. Less than double overcharges will not deter absolutely.

Bryant and Eckard (1991) estimate the average annual probability of detection of a cartel by U.S. authorities, given that the cartel is detected eventually, at between 0.13 and 0.17. Combe *et al.* (2008) estimate the corresponding probability for the EU at 0.129 to 0.133. Cartel leniency programmes may increase the probability of detection, and of conviction should detection occur. But estimated detection probabilities of this magnitude suggest that

---

[14] That is, p/c, which can be easily transformed into the Lerner index of market power, $(p - c)/p$. See Boone *et al.* (2007) for a critique of the use of the price-cost margin as a measure of competition.

[15] For estimates suggesting direct or indirect positive effects of competition policy on performance, but using relatively aggregate data, see Voight (2006), Kee and Hoekman (2007), and McCloughan *et al.* (2008).

either cartel enforcement agencies should be given more resources to seek out cartels, or fines paid by cartels that are detected should be increased.

Other types of antitrust activity[16]

Antitrust includes restrictions on strategic entry-deterring behaviour and merger control. EC competition policy includes as well state aid control. The consensus impression of the literature is that there are net welfare gains from these types of enforcement, but the consensus is impressionistic.

It seems clear, for example, that EC competition policy's intolerant attitude toward restrictions on parallel imports by distributors limits manufacturers' ability to exercise market power. Otherwise, why would manufacturers in some sectors go to such lengths to block parallel imports, despite the prohibition? But the benefits of a policy that maintains freedom of entry may manifest itself in different ways—entry is one, limit pricing is another. It is one thing to estimate the amount of a monopoly overcharge that is not paid because a cartel is broken up. It is something else to tie specific episodes of entry to a policy that penalizes strategic entry costs, and estimate the resulting price reductions, or (if entry does not occur) to estimate the savings to consumers because incumbents set an even lower limit price than they would otherwise have done.

Similarly, merger policy may err by blocking efficient mergers or permitting mergers that worsen market performance. It is sometimes possible to estimate the amounts of price increases that follow a merger and can be said in a reasonably convincing way to have been made possible by the merger.[17] If a merger that has been allowed to go forward in anticipation of cost savings instead generates losses, the value of those losses can be estimated, at least to an order of magnitude.[18] Convincing estimates of losses because efficient mergers are blocked or discouraged are less likely. Without hard numbers, however, the conclusion that is justified is that (Werden, 2008, p. 439):[19]

> The available evidence on the actual effects of substantial horizontal mergers demonstrates that they can result in price increases that inflict significant social harm. This evidence supports the proposition that horizontal merger enforcement, if not overly strict, is likely to yield substantial social benefits.

Overall

Baker (2003) makes a rough back-of-the-envelope calculation, based on case studies, international comparisons of different enforcement regimes, and estimates about anticollusion policy. His bottom line is (2003, p. 44):

> [T]he annual welfare benefits from deterring the exercise of market power through the antitrust laws as they are enforced today could readily exceed 1 percent of GDP, or $100 billion per year.

---

[16] See Werden (2008) for a lucid discussion of these measurement issues.

[17] Early in the period of airline deregulation, enforcement agencies took a relaxed attitude toward mergers on the ground that the industry was contestable (Bailey, 1981, pp. 179–180; Bailey and Panzar, 1981, pp. 128–129). Later studies show that airline fares rise with concentration in city-pair markets (Bailey *et al.*, 1985, p. 165).

[18] See the discussion in Section 11.3.2 of the Union Pacific/Southern Pacific merger.

[19] He continues "This evidence, however, is uninformative as to the correctness of specific enforcement decisions by the USDOJ and FTC."

Benefits from antitrust enforcement of this magnitude dwarf any plausible estimate of the costs of antitrust enforcement.

26.5 Competition Policy in a Market Economy

Rather than revisit the topic of the goals of antitrust, as they have been or should be, here we address the more modest question of the role of competition policy in a market economy, warts and all.

On a technical level, the competition policy prohibition of collusion seeks to promote independent decision-making, with emphasis on product-market decisions—price, output, marketing strategy. As a device to obtain good market performance, this works well in sectors where the equilibrium market structure is workably competitive. In many circumstances it does not work well if the equilibrium market structure is small-numbers oligopoly, because tacit collusion often yields market performance that is indistinguishable from the collusive outcome. The competition policy prohibition of joint decision-making on matters that related to price—"the central nervous system of the economy"—does not extend to cooperation in other areas that demonstrably improves market performance (research and development, central distribution of copyright material, standard-setting).

The competition policy prohibition of exclusionary behaviour aims to maximize the force of potential competition. Workable competition policy has no objection to the large firm; in industries where the technology exhibits economies of scale, the best market performance available without regulation may well be obtained when the market is supplied by a multi-plant incumbent, pricing at the higher average cost of an efficient single-plant rival (Clark, 1907, p. 382). Although courts have labored valiantly to rein it in, the Robinson-Patman Act is inconsistent with workable competition policy in this sense. Nor does workable competition policy object to the firm that leads a high-technology sector by dint of network economies. It does object to strategic maintenance of network economies.

One justification for making merger control part of competition policy is the oligopoly problem. If small-numbers oligopoly produces the results of collusion, without collusion, then good market performance can be promoted by permitting mergers that are privately profitable because they hold out efficiency gains, not merely because they facilitate tacit collusion. Merger control can also be justified because the ability of the legal system to block exclusionary practices will always be imperfect.[20] If leading firms unavoidably have residual exclusionary power, it makes sense to ensure that large firms are not formed only to obtain that power.

The justification for state aid control is to ensure that market processes are not falsified by subsidies that allow less efficient firms to survive while more efficient firms fail. This justification is as valid for the United States, which does not control state aid, as it is for the European Union, which does.

---

[20] See Clark (1902, pp. 34–35), who wrote that a multiproduct firm would be able to engage in predatory price discrimination against a single product firm, or Theodore Roosevelt, who saw some merit in administrative control of business conduct (1913, pp. 618–619): "[T]he effort to administer a law merely by lawsuits and court decisions is bound to end in signal failure, and meanwhile to be attended with delays and uncertainties, and to put a premium upon legal sharp practice."

On a more fundamental level, competition policy is one element in the social compact that ensures the legitimacy of the market economy. To be sure, competition policy is about economics. It has never been only about economics; to believe otherwise is little more than (Dewey, 1986, p. 22) "professional conceit". This role of competition policy is explicit for the European Union, with its vocation of shepherding the continuing process of market integration. It is no less present, although sometimes less visible, for the United States, where the role of economics has been to insist that antitrust aims at equality of opportunity, not equality of result.

FURTHER READING

I have drawn on Martin (2007b) for some of the material in this chapter.

On the post-World War I campaign to shackle the antitrust laws, see the *Annals of the American Academy of Political and Social Science* 147, January 1930 (The Anti-Trust Laws of the United States), Handler (1932), Harriman (1932), Fields (1933), and Himmelberg (1976).

For references to the continuing literature on antitrust and competition policy, see Cucinotta *et al.* (2002), Wright (2007), and Pitofsky (2008).

APPENDIX I: INDUSTRY CLASSIFICATION SCHEMES

Taxonomy is often undervalued as a glorified form of filing ...

Gould (1989, p. 98)

I.1 Introduction

Governments collect, combine and report information about economic activity. They collect not only statistics about unemployment, the rate of inflation, the balance of payments, and other macroeconomic data, but also microeconomic data: output, investment, sales, value added, and the like. Such information is reported by businesses, classified by the government into industry categories, and published in a way that does not reveal information about individual companies.

I.2 U.S.

Historically, the U.S. government classified data about economic activity according to the Standard Industrial Classification or SIC.[1] The foundations of the SIC were laid in the late 1930s, when the aftermath of the Great Depression and foreshadowing of World War II made the availability of accurate and usable information essential (Pearce, 1957):[2]

> Standardization ... was an important objective since various agencies collecting industrial data used their own classifications, and thus a given establishment might be classified in one industry by one agency and in another by a second agency. Such a situation made the comparison of industrial data prepared by different agencies difficult and often misleading.

The principles followed in developing the SIC were (Pearce, 1957):

---

[1] See U.S. Department of Commerce (1987). There are other industrial classification schemes. In preparing input-output tables, the Bureau of Economic Analysis has used an input-output table classification that is based on the SIC. The European Union uses NACE (see below). There is also the ISIC, the International Standard Industrial Classification (on which, see United Nations, 1968). See Nightingale (1978, pp. 36–39) for a discussion of the relationships between standard industrial classifications and markets and industries defined in an economic sense.

[2] An establishment is "a single physical location at which economic activity occurs". One can usually think of an establishment as a single plant or factory.

(1)   The classification should conform to the existing structure of American industry.

(2)   The reporting units to be classified are establishments rather than legal entities or companies.

(3)   Each establishment is to be classified according to its major activity.

(4)   To be recognized as an industry, each group of establishments must have significance from the standpoint of the number of establishments, number of wage earners, volume of business, employment and payroll fluctuations, and other important economic features.

The SIC was revised several times, but by the end of the twentieth century it was no longer satisfactory as an organizational framework for information about the economy. The United States, Canada, and Mexico therefore cooperated to develop a system that would reflect the structure of their economies at the dawn of the twenty-first century: NAICS, the North American Industry Classification System (U.S. Census Bureau, 13 December 2002):

> [NAICS] is the first economic classification system to be constructed based on a single economic concept. Economic units that use like processes to produce goods or services are grouped together. This "production-oriented" system means that statistical agencies in the United States will produce data that can be used for measuring productivity, unit labor costs, and the capital intensity of production; constructing input-output relationships; and estimating employment-output relationships and other such statistics that require inputs and outputs to be used together. . . .
> NAICS responds to increasing and serious criticism about the [Standard Industrial Classification]. It reflects the structure of today's economy in the United States, Canada, and Mexico, including the emergence and growth of the service sector and new and advanced technologies.

The principle of classification based on the means of production is applied not only to manufacturing but also to wholesale and retail distribution (Economic Classification Policy Committee, 1998, p. 5):

> Retailers typically sell merchandise in small quantities using public-oriented methods like mass media advertising, high-traffic locations, and attractive displays. Wholesalers sell goods in large quantities using business-oriented methods like specialized catalogs, customer contacts, and warehouse or office locations.

Like the SIC, the NAICS is hierarchical in nature: two-digit NAICS sectors (Table I.1) are broadly defined. They are subdivided into three-, four-, and five-digit industries. Six-digit NAICS industries correspond roughly to the four-digit SIC industries that were most frequently studied by economists who worked with industry-level data. The hierarchical nature of the NAICS classification is illustrated in Table I.3.

Government industry classification schemes tend to be highly aggregated. They also tend to be defined in terms of factors related to the supply side of markets. This is natural, given that it is businesses, suppliers, that provide the underlying information from which official statistics are prepared. But the proper definition of economic markets involves interactions between consumers and suppliers, and in many cases official industry statistics, even those available at the least aggregated level, combine activities of suppliers that operate in what must by any reasonable standard be considered different economic markets.

Table I.1 Number of employees, NAICS two-digit sector, United States, 2002

NAICS code		Number of employees
21	Mining	487,786
22	Utilities	663,044
23	Construction	7,173,996
31–33	Manufacturing	14,664,385
42	Wholesale trade	5,902,852
44–45	Retail trade	14,623,228
48–49	Transportation and warehousing	3,650,859
51	Information	3,748,730
52	Finance and insurance	6,578,817
53	Real estate and rental and leasing	1,948,648
54	Professional, scientific, and technical services	6,977,999
55	Management of companies and enterprises	2,607,962
56	Administrative, support, waste management, remediation services	8,261,008
61	Educational services	430,164
62	Health care and social assistance	15,143,561
71	Arts, entertainment, and recreation	1,848,885
72	Accommodation and food services	10,120,951
81	Other services (except public administration)	3,351,836

Source: U.S. Census Bureau, 2002 Economic Census.

I.3 EU

For the European Union, it is the NACE (nomenclature générale des activités économiques dans les Communautés Européennes) classification scheme that provides a framework for collection and classification of industry data. By way of illustration, Table I.4 lists descriptive

Table I.2 NAICS vs. SIC: Structure and Nomenclature

	NAICS	SIC	
2-digit	Sector	Division	Letter
3-digit	Subsector	Major Group	2-digit
4-digit	Industry Group	Industry Group	3-digit
5-digit	NAICS Industry	Industry	4-digit
6-digit	National	N/A	N/A

Source: U.S. Bureau of the Census "Development of NAICS".

Table I.3 NAICS industries in the food chain

311	Food Manufacturing
3111	Animal Food Manufacturing
3112	Grain and Oilseed Milling
3113	Sugar and Confectionery Product Manufacturing
3114	Fruit and Vegetable Preserving and Specialty Food Manufacturing
3115	Dairy Product Manufacturing
3116	Animal Slaughtering and Processing
3117	Seafood Product Preparation and Packaging
3118	Bakeries and Tortilla Manufacturing
3119	Other Food Manufacturing
312	Beverage and Tobacco Product Manufacturing
3121	Beverage Manufacturing
3122	Tobacco Manufacturing
33311	Agricultural Implement Manufacturing
4244	Grocery and Related Product Merchant Wholesalers

(Continued)

Table I.3 (Continued)

4245	Farm Product Raw Material Merchant Wholesalers
4551	Grocery Stores
4452	Specialty Food Stores
4453	Beer, Wine, and Liquor Stores
49313	Farm Product Warehousing and Storage
722	Food Services and Drinking Places
7221	Full-Service Restaurants
7222	Limited-Service Eating Places
7223	Special Food Services
7224	Drinking Places (Alcoholic Beverages)
92614	Regulation of Agricultural Marketing and Commodities

information for NACE category 15, manufacture of food products and beverages. NACE category 15 is divided into nine three-digit subcategories, one of which is NACE category 15.5, operation of dairies and cheese making. This in turn is further subdivided into two subcategories. One of these, 15.52 (manufacture of ice cream) is fairly homogeneous and might very well correspond to a market, at the manufacturing level, in an economic sense. The other category, 15.51 (operation of dairies and cheese making) includes products which for most purposes would probably be considered part of distinct economic markets (milk and cheese, for example).

Table I.4 NACE Industry 15.5

Code	Title
15	Manufacture of food products and beverages
15.5	Manufacture of dairy products
15.51	Operation of dairies and cheese making;
includes:	production of fresh liquid milk, pasteurized, sterilized, homogenized and/or ultra heat treated
	production of cream from fresh liquid milk, pasteurized, sterilized, homogenized
	manufacture of dried or concentrated milk whether or not sweetened
	production of butter
	production of yoghurt
	production of cheese and curd
	production of whey
	production of casein or lactose
15.52	Manufacture of ice cream
includes	production of ice cream and other edible ice such as sorbet

Source: EC Commission (1996).

APPENDIX II: JUST THE MATH USED IN THIS BOOK

II

> But the age of chivalry is gone; that of sophisters, economists, and calculators has succeeded, and the glory of Europe is extinguished forever.
>
> *Edmund Burke*

Economists use mathematics a lot. But, despite what may be popular impression, we do not use a lot of mathematics, not, at least, at the level of introductory expositions. Here the mathematics is mostly algebra and the little bit of calculus that applies to the optimization of well behaved functions. The qualification "well-behaved" is not because economists believe that only well-behaved functions are useful in describing reality, or even in building economic models; see Mandelbrot and Hudson (2004) for an accessible discussion of counterexamples. It is because the sometimes important complications that require the use of badly behaved functions are properly the subject of advanced treatments. In this Appendix, I give (without proofs and illustrated with examples from the text) a bare-bones exposition of the mathematical concepts involved in the basic models of profit-maximizing firm behaviour in imperfectly competitive markets.

II.1 Slope

Consider the linear cost equation:

$$C(q) = 1 + 9q. \tag{II.1}$$

For every output level q, the function $C(q)$ gives the total cost of producing q. If the firm produces at all, it incurs a fixed cost equal to 1. Every unit of output the firm produces generates a variable cost equal to 9. Marginal cost is therefore constant, and also equal to 9.

If we graph the cost function, as in Figure II.1, fixed cost shows up as the vertical-axis intercept of the cost line. The slope parameter, 9, of the function $C(q)$ is the coefficient of the linear output term q, and shows the change (in this case, increase) in cost as output increases by one unit. Because this change is the same for all units of output—going from 0 to 1 unit of output and going from 100 to 101 units of output both mean cost increases by 9—the cost function is a straight line.

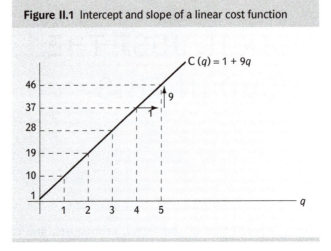

Figure II.1 Intercept and slope of a linear cost function

II.1.1 Of a Smooth Curve

If the graph of an equation is not a straight line, the slope of the graph will be different at different points. When a curve is "smooth" in a mathematical sense that we do not make precise here, we define the slope of the curve at a point to be the slope of a straight line that is tangent to the curve at this point. Since we know how to measure the slope of a straight line (as in Figure II.1), we can measure the slope of a smooth curve at a point by drawing or working out the equation of the corresponding tangent line at that point, and measuring the slope of the tangent line.

For example, Figure II.2 shows the graph of the average cost curve for the cubic cost function:

$$C(q) = 5 + 5q - 5q^2 + 5q^3. \tag{II.2}$$

The average cost curve has a negative slope at point A in Figure II.2: the tangent line is downward sloping, increases in output reduce average cost. The average cost curve has a positive slope at point B in Figure II.2: the tangent line is upward sloping, increases in output increase average cost. Moving from A to D, the slope of the average cost curve is negative, but smaller and smaller in magnitude. At point D, the slope of the average cost curve is zero—the line tangent to the average cost curve at point D is horizontal. Moving from D to B, the slope of the average cost curve is positive, and larger and larger in magnitude.

Point D, where the slope of the average cost curve is zero, shows the minimum value of average cost (and the output level for which average cost is a minimum).

It may be that a curve does not have a well-defined slope at some points. An example is shown in Figure II.3. To the left of point B, the slope of the curve is the slope of the line segment AB. To the right of point B, the slope of the curve is the (steeper, more negative) slope of the line segment BC. When we run into models involving curves of this kind in the book, we will point out the implications.

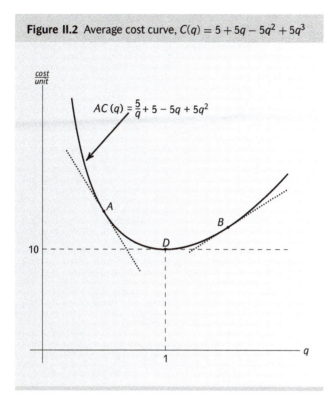

Figure II.2 Average cost curve, $C(q) = 5 + 5q - 5q^2 + 5q^3$

II.2 Minimum and Maximum

The applications of calculus in the book overwhelmingly involve using expressions for the slope of a smooth curve to locate the minimum or maximum value of some expression. Here we show by example how the slope can be used to do this. The next section gives a few rules for finding an equation for the slope of a curve (some kinds of curves) from the equation of the curve.

If a price-taking firm—a firm that faces, or believes it faces, a horizontal demand curve—produces with cost function (II.2), the equation giving its profit at price p and output q is:

$$\pi(q) = pq - C(q)$$
$$= pq - \left(5 + 5q - 5q^2 + 5q^3\right) = -5 + (p - 5)q + 5q^2 - 5q^3. \tag{II.3}$$

Profit curves for such a firm for several different values of p are drawn in Figure II.4. The profit curve for the highest price, $p = 20$, has positive slope to the left of output q_{20}, zero slope at output q_{20}, and negative slope to the right of output q_{20}. The output level q_{20} gives the firm its maximum possible profit if price (which the firm takes as given) is 20. The firm's maximum possible profit for $p = 20$ is 12.08. The profit-maximizing output levels for the other prices are found in the same way.

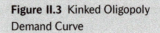

Figure II.3 Kinked Oligopoly Demand Curve

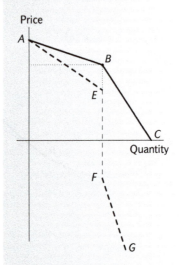

Source: AB, rivals do not match price increases; *BC*, rivals match price decreases; *AEFG*, marginal revenue curve.

As a matter of notation, we write:

$$\frac{d\pi\,(q)}{dq}, \tag{II.4}$$

read pedantically as "the derivative of π with respect to q" and read normally as "dee-π dee-q" for the slope of the profit curve at an output level q, by which we mean the slope of the straight line tangent to the profit curve at output level q.

Other notations for such a derivative are $\pi'\,(q)$ (pi-prime) and $\dot{\pi}\,(q)$ (pi-dot).

For the profit curves drawn in Figure II.4, the maximum profit occurs where the slope of the profit curve is zero,[1]

$$\frac{d\pi\,(q)}{dq} = 0. \tag{II.5}$$

Since profit is the difference between revenue and cost,

$$\pi\,(q) = pq - C\,(q), \tag{II.6}$$

---

[1] In general, a point at which the first derivative of a function is zero identifies a local maximum of the function if the second derivative at that point—the derivative of the first derivative—is negative. A point at which the first derivative of a function is zero identifies a local minimum of the function if the second derivative is positive. In applications, it is important to verify second-order conditions. We will not mention them here unless specific examples require that they be discussed.

Figure II.4 Profit functions of a price-taking firm, alternative price levels, cost function $C(q) = 5 + 5q - 5q^2 + 5q^3$

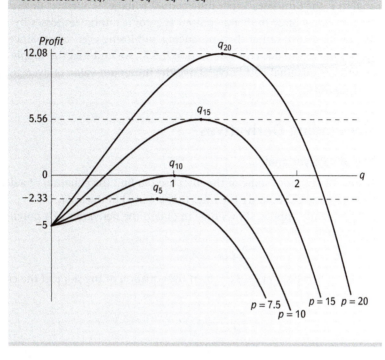

the derivative of profit with respect to output is the difference between the derivative of revenue (pq) with respect to output and the derivative of cost with respect to output, so at the profit-maximizing output level:

$$\frac{d\pi\,(q)}{dq} = \frac{d\,(pq)}{dq} - \frac{dC\,(q)}{dq} = 0 \tag{II.7}$$

or, at the profit-maximizing output level, marginal revenue equals marginal cost:

$$\frac{d\,(pq)}{dq} = \frac{dC\,(q)}{dq}. \tag{II.8}$$

As we will see in the next section, for a firm that takes prices as given, marginal revenue is just price (this is what we would expect from the economics),

$$\frac{d\,(pq)}{dq} = p, \tag{II.9}$$

so a price-taking firm maximizes profit by picking an output level that makes its marginal cost equal to price,

$$p = \frac{dC\,(q)}{dq}. \tag{II.10}$$

Observe in Figure II.4 that for $p = 15$ and $p = 20$, the firm makes positive economic profit. For $p = 10$, the firm earns zero economic profit, which is to say that it earns only a normal rate of return on its investment. For $p = 7.5$, the firm makes an economic loss ("profit" is −2.33), but the loss is smaller than the firm's fixed cost (5). In the short run, at a price of 7.5, it pays the firm to operate and lose 2.33 rather than to shut down and lose 5.

For price equal to 5, the firm loses 5 (per time period) whether it operates or shuts down. For lower prices, the firm's most profitable output is zero: it minimizes losses by shutting down and losing its fixed cost, rather than producing and losing even more. Since 5 is the minimum value of average variable cost (see Section II.3.2), we find that the supply curve of a price-taking firm is its marginal cost curve above the minimum value of average variable cost (the shutdown point).

II.3 Rules for Finding Derivatives

II.3.1 Derivative of a Polynomial

Here I simply state without proof some of the rules used to find the equation of a derivative from the equation of a curve. These are the rules that are used in the book.

The rule most frequently applied shows how to obtain the derivative of a polynomial. If the equation of a curve is:

$$f(x) = Ax^n. \tag{II.11}$$

where A and n are numbers (as, $f(x) = 3x^2$), then the equation of the slope of the curve, the derivative of $f(x)$ at x, is:

$$\frac{df(x)}{dx} = Anx^{n-1}. \tag{II.12}$$

Thus for $f(x) = 3x^2$, $\frac{df(x)}{dx} = f'(x) = 6x$. If a firm sells a quantity q at a given price p, total revenue is:

$$TR = pq = pq^1, \tag{II.13}$$

and marginal revenue is:

$$MR = \frac{dTR}{dq} = \frac{d(pq)}{dq} = p(1)q^{1-1} = p. \tag{II.14}$$

For a price-taking firm, marginal revenue is equal to price.

II.3.2 Derivatives of Products and Quotients

It will sometimes prove useful to be able to find the derivative of a function that is the product of other functions. For example, for a monopolist price is not given but depends on the amount the firm sells, so that total revenue is the product of the equation of the (inverse) demand curve, $p(q)$, and of quantity sold:

$$TR(q) = p(q)q. \tag{II.15}$$

If we consider a function that is the product of two other functions:

$$f(x) = g(x)h(x), \tag{II.16}$$

then the derivative of the product is related to the derivatives of the multiplicands according to the expression:

$$\frac{df(x)}{dx} = g(x)\frac{dh(x)}{dx} + h(x)\frac{dg(x)}{dx}. \tag{II.17}$$

The derivative of the product of two functions is the first function times the derivative of the second plus the second function times the derivative of the first.[2]

Suppose there is a linear inverse demand curve with equation:

$$p(q) = a - bq. \tag{II.18}$$

Then the equation of total revenue for output q is:

$$TR = p(q)q = aq - bq^2. \tag{II.19}$$

We know from the rule for finding the derivative of a polynomial, (II.12), that marginal revenue for this inverse demand equation is:

$$MR = a - 2bq. \tag{II.20}$$

Alternatively, using the rule for finding the derivative of a product of two functions,

$$MR = (a - bq)\frac{dq}{dq} + q\frac{d(a - bq)}{dq}$$

$$= (a - bq)(1) + q(-b) = a - 2bq, \tag{II.21}$$

we obtain the same result.

Generally, applying the product rule to (II.15), we get the expression:

$$MR(q) = \frac{dTR(q)}{dq} = p(q) + q\frac{dp}{dq}, \tag{II.22}$$

which is equation (2.4).

It will also sometimes be useful to be able to find the derivative of a function that is the ratio of two other functions. For example, average cost is the ratio of total cost and output,

$$AC(q) = \frac{C(q)}{q}. \tag{II.23}$$

The derivative of the average cost function gives the slope of the average cost curve (and the slope of the kind of tangent lines shown in Figure II.1).

If we consider a function that is the ratio of two other functions:

$$f(x) = \frac{g(x)}{h(x)}, \tag{II.24}$$

then the derivative of the ratio is related to the derivatives of the numerator and the denominator according to the expression:

$$\frac{df(x)}{dx} = \frac{h(x)\frac{dg(x)}{dx} - g(x)\frac{dh(x)}{dx}}{h(x)^2}. \tag{II.25}$$

(II.24) and (II.25) are valid only if $h(x) \neq 0$. Leaving aside such cases, the general expression for the slope of an average cost equation, (II.23), is:

$$\frac{dAC(q)}{dq} = \frac{q\frac{dC(q)}{dq} - C(q)\frac{dq}{dq}}{q^2} = \frac{q\frac{dC(q)}{dq} - C(q)}{q^2}. \tag{II.26}$$

We have seen in Figure II.1 that the minimum value of average cost occurs where the slope of the average cost curve is zero. Using (II.26), when the slope of the average cost curve is zero,

$$q\frac{dC(q)}{dq} - C(q) = 0 \text{ so that } \frac{dC(q)}{dq} = \frac{C(q)}{q}. \tag{II.27}$$

---

[2] The product rule generalizes in a straightforward way to functions that are the product of three or more other functions.

But $\frac{dC(q)}{dq}$ is marginal cost and $\frac{C(q)}{q}$ is average cost, so the fact that the minimum value of average cost occurs where the slope of the average cost curve is zero implies that the minimum value of average cost occurs where average cost and marginal cost are the same.

In the same way, average variable cost is the ratio of variable cost to output,

$$AVC(q) = \frac{VC(q)}{q}. \tag{II.28}$$

Applying the quotient rule (II.25) to (II.28) and setting the resulting expression for the slope of the average variable cost curve equal to zero shows that the minimum value of average variable cost occurs where average variable cost equals marginal cost.

For the example of Figure II.1, the equation of the average cost curve is:

$$AC(q) = \frac{5 + 5q - 5q^2 + 5q^3}{q} = 5q^{-1} + 5 - 5q + 5q^2. \tag{II.29}$$

Applying the rule for finding the derivative of a polynomial, (II.12), term by term on the right gives an expression for the slope of this particular average cost function,

$$\frac{dAC(q)}{dq} = -5q^{-2} - 5 + 10q = -\frac{5}{q^2} - 5 + 10q. \tag{II.30}$$

II.4 Price Elasticity and Marginal Revenue: Linear Demand

If the inverse demand curve is linear, with equation:

$$p = a - bQ,$$

then the equation of the demand curve is:

$$Q = \frac{a}{b} - \frac{1}{b}p.$$

The slope of the demand curve is:

$$\frac{dQ}{dp} = -\frac{1}{b}.$$

The price elasticity of demand at a point (Q, p) on the demand curve is:

$$\varepsilon_{Qp} = -\frac{p}{Q}\frac{dQ}{dp} = \frac{p}{bQ}.$$

For a linear inverse demand function $p = a - bQ$, total revenue is $pQ = aQ - bQ^2$ and marginal revenue is:

$$MR = \frac{d(pQ)}{dQ} = a - 2bQ.$$

That is, for a linear inverse demand function, price and marginal revenue have the same value for $Q = 0$ (the same price-axis intercept) and the slope of the marginal revenue function is twice as great in absolute value as the slope of the inverse demand function. The graph of the inverse demand curve connects the points $(0,a)$ and $(a/b,0)$ in (Q,p)-space; the graph of the marginal revenue curve connects the points $(0,a)$ and $(a/2b,0)$ in (Q,p)-space. See Figure 2.7.

II.5 The Chain Rule and the Inverse Function Rule

II.5.1 The Chain Rule

It is sometimes useful to be able to find the derivative of a function of a function. If f is a function of g and g is a function of x, then f is indirectly a function of x,

$$f[g(x)], \tag{II.31}$$

and the derivative of f with respect to x is the product of the derivative of f with respect to g and the derivative of g with respect to x:

$$\frac{df[g(x)]}{dx} = \frac{df(g)}{dg}\frac{dg(x)}{dx}. \tag{II.32}$$

II.5.2 The Inverse Function Theorem

We can describe linear demand with an equation expression price as a function of quantity sold,

$$p = a - bQ, \tag{II.33}$$

or with the inverse equation showing quantity demanded as a function of price,

$$Q = \frac{a}{b} - \frac{1}{b}p. \tag{II.34}$$

Equation (II.34) is said to be the inverse of equation (II.33). If we substitute from equation (II.33) for p in the right-hand side of the right-hand side of equation (II.34), we obtain:

$$\frac{a}{b} - \frac{1}{b}p = \frac{a}{b} - \frac{1}{b}(a - bQ) = Q.$$

For well-behaved functions, the inverse function rule is that the derivative of the inverse of a function is the inverse of the function's derivative, that is, for inverse functions:

$$y = f(x) \tag{II.35}$$

and

$$x = g(y), \tag{II.36}$$

and

$$\frac{dx}{dy} = \frac{1}{\frac{dy}{dx}}. \tag{II.37}$$

For example, for the linear inverse demand equation (II.33),

$$\frac{dp}{dQ} = -b.$$

For the linear demand equation (II.34),

$$\frac{dQ}{dp} = -\frac{1}{b} = \frac{1}{\frac{dp}{dQ}}.$$

II.6 Monopoly

II.6.1 Quantity-setting

Write a monopolist's profit function as a function of its output,

$$\pi(Q) = p(Q)Q - C(Q). \tag{II.38}$$

Profit is maximized where the derivative of profit is zero,

$$\frac{d\pi(Q)}{dQ} = p(Q)\frac{dQ}{dQ} + Q\frac{dp(Q)}{dQ} - \frac{dC(Q)}{dQ} \equiv 0. \tag{II.39}$$

(II.39) can be rewritten as the familiar "marginal revenue equal marginal cost" profit-maximization condition,

$$MR(Q) = p(Q) + Q\frac{dp(Q)}{dQ} = \frac{dC(Q)}{dQ} = MC(Q). \tag{II.40}$$

Manipulating (II.39) in one way gives the monopoly expression for the Lerner index:

$$p(Q) - \frac{dC(Q)}{dq} = -Q\frac{dp(Q)}{dq}.$$

$$\frac{p(Q) - \frac{dC(Q)}{dq}}{p(Q)} = -\frac{Q}{p(Q)}\frac{dp(Q)}{dq} = -\frac{1}{\frac{p(Q)}{Q}\frac{dQ(p)}{dp}} = \frac{1}{\varepsilon_{Qp}}. \tag{II.41}$$

Now suppose there is constant marginal and average variable cost,

$$C(Q) = F + cQ. \tag{II.42}$$

The first-order condition for profit maximization, (II.39), becomes:

$$\frac{d\pi(Q)}{dQ} = p(Q) + Q\frac{dp(Q)}{dQ} - c \equiv 0. \tag{II.43}$$

Then if the firm is producing its profit-maximizing output:

$$p(Q) - c = -Q\frac{dp(Q)}{dQ}. \tag{II.44}$$

Hence monopoly profit—the profit function evaluated for monopoly output—is:

$$\pi(Q_m) = [p(Q_m) - c]Q_m - F = -\frac{dp(Q_m)}{dQ}Q_m^2 - F. \tag{II.45}$$

With zero fixed cost and linear inverse demand, monopoly profit is proportional to the square of monopoly output (as in the answer to Problem 2–1).

II.6.2 Price-setting

For the monopoly case, it should not make any difference whether we think of the firm as deciding on monopoly output and letting the inverse demand equation determine the price or as deciding on monopoly price and letting the demand equation determine the amount sold. Monopoly profit is monopoly profit, and the results should be the same. The quantity-setting approach carries with it the nice intuitive explanation that profit is maximized at the output level that makes marginal revenue equal to marginal cost.

The same relationship is implicit, but hidden, if a monopolist is modelled as setting price rather than quantity.

Write monopoly profit as:

$$\hat{\pi}(p) = pQ(p) - C[Q(p)]. \tag{II.46}$$

The demand function $Q(p)$ is the inverse of the inverse demand function $p(Q)$ in (II.38).

$\hat{\pi}(p)$ is maximized for the price that makes the derivative of (II.46) with respect to price equal to zero. Using the product rule and the chain rule, this is:

$$p\frac{dQ(p)}{dp} + Q(p) - C'[Q(p)]\frac{dQ(p)}{dp} \equiv 0. \tag{II.47}$$

Write this as:

$$\left\{ p + Q\left(p\right) \frac{1}{\frac{dQ(p)}{dp}} - C'\left[Q\left(p\right)\right] \right\} \frac{dQ\left(p\right)}{dp} \equiv 0. \tag{II.48}$$

From the inverse function rule, $\frac{1}{\frac{dQ(p)}{dp}} = \frac{dp(Q)}{dQ}$. The slope of the demand curve, $\frac{dQ(p)}{dp}$, is not zero. Hence the expression in braces on the left in (II.48) must be zero, so that:

$$p + Q\frac{dp\left(Q\right)}{dQ} = C'\left(Q\right). \tag{II.49}$$

This is the same "marginal revenue equals marginal cost" condition that characterizes profit-maximization for a quantity-setting monopolist. It is hidden when we model a firm as setting prices rather than quantities, but it is there.

II.7 Systems of Linear Equations

The equations of the best-response functions from the Cournot duopoly with cost differences model of Section 3.2.4 make up a system of two equations in two unknowns, the output levels q_1 and q_2:

$$2q_1 + q_2 = 100 - c_1 \tag{II.50}$$

$$q_1 + 2q_2 = 100 - c_2. \tag{II.51}$$

We will show two ways to solve this system of equations, and mention a third way.

The first way to solve the system of equations is by substitution. Solve (II.50) for q_2:

$$q_2 = 100 - c_1 - 2q_1.$$

Substitute this expression for q_2 into (II.51) to eliminate q_2 and obtain one equation in one unknown, q_1:

$$q_1 + 2\left(100 - c_1 - 2q_1\right) = 100 - c_2.$$

Rearrange terms and solve this equation for q_1:

$$q_1 + 200 - 2c_1 - 4q_1 = 100 - c_2.$$

$$-3q_1 = -100 + 2c_1 - c_2.$$

$$3q_1 = 100 - 2c_1 + c_2.$$

$$q_1 = \frac{1}{3}\left(100 - 2c_1 + c_2\right).$$

This is (3.17).

Substitute this expression for q_1 back into the previous expression for q_2:

$$q_2 = 100 - c_1 - 2\left[\frac{1}{3}\left(100 - 2c_1 + c_2\right)\right].$$

Rearrange terms and solve for q_2:

$$q_2 = 100 - c_1 - \frac{2}{3}\left(100 - 2c_1 + c_2\right)$$

$$q_2 = 100 - c_1 - \frac{2}{3}\left(100\right) + \frac{4}{3}c_1 - \frac{2}{3}c_2$$

$$q_2 = \frac{1}{3}\left(100\right) + \frac{1}{3}c_1 - \frac{2}{3}c_2$$

$$q_2 = \frac{1}{3}(100 + c_1 - 2c_2).$$

This is (3.18).

Small systems of equations—two equations in two unknowns, three equations in three unknowns—can be solved by substitution in a reasonable amount of time.

Alternatively, a cute shortcut that works for examples of this kind is to add (II.50) and (II.51) to obtain:

$$3(q_1 + q_2) = 200 - c_1 - c_2.$$

$$q_1 + q_2 = \frac{1}{3}(200 - c_1 - c_2).$$

Thus we have found total output.

Go back and rewrite (say) (II.50) as:

$$q_1 + (q_1 + q_2) = 100 - c_1.$$

Substitute for total output to obtain:

$$q_1 + \frac{1}{3}(200 - c_1 - c_2) = 100 - c_1.$$

This is now one equation in q_1. q_2 can be found in the same way.

We only mention the natural way to solve systems of linear equations, which is by linear algebra. Writing the system of equations in matrix notation gives:

$$\begin{pmatrix} 2 & 1 \\ 1 & 2 \end{pmatrix} \begin{pmatrix} q_1 \\ q_2 \end{pmatrix} = 100 \begin{pmatrix} 1 \\ 1 \end{pmatrix} - \begin{pmatrix} c_1 \\ c_2 \end{pmatrix}.$$

Solution is immediate by multiplying both sides by the inverse of the coefficient matrix on the left,

$$\begin{pmatrix} 2 & 1 \\ 1 & 2 \end{pmatrix}^{-1} = \frac{1}{3}\begin{pmatrix} 2 & -1 \\ -1 & 2 \end{pmatrix}.$$

But if you understand this, you don't need to read this appendix, and if you don't understand this, it is beyond the role of this appendix to elaborate on the topic.

II.8 The Mechanics of Discounting

The present value of amounts $x_1, x_2, x_3, \ldots$, received at the end of 1, 2, 3, ... periods in the future is:

$$PV = \frac{x_1}{1+r} + \frac{x_2}{(1+r)^2} + \frac{x_3}{(1+r)^3} + \ldots \tag{II.52}$$

If the amount received at the end of each period is the same, say x, the present value is:

$$PV = \left[\frac{1}{1+r} + \frac{1}{(1+r)^2} + \frac{1}{(1+r)^3} + \ldots\right] x. \tag{II.53}$$

To obtain a compact expression for the infinite sum:

$$S = \frac{1}{1+r} + \frac{1}{(1+r)^2} + \frac{1}{(1+r)^3} + \ldots, \tag{II.54}$$

multiply both sides by $\frac{1}{1+r}$ to obtain:

$$\frac{1}{1+r}S = \frac{1}{(1+r)^2} + \frac{1}{(1+r)^3} + \frac{1}{(1+r)^4} + \ldots. \tag{II.55}$$

Then subtract (II.55) from (II.54) to obtain:

$$\left(1 - \frac{1}{1+r}\right)S = \frac{1}{1+r}, \tag{II.56}$$

all terms on the right after the first being eliminated by subtraction. Then,

$$\frac{r}{1+r}S = \frac{1}{1+r}$$

$$S = \frac{1}{r}. \tag{II.57}$$

REFERENCES

Abernethy, Avery M. and Daniel D. Butler "Advertising information: services versus products" *Journal of Retailing* 68(4), Winter 1992, pp. 398–419.

Abernethy, Avery M. and George R. Franke "The information content of advertising: a meta-analysis" *Journal of Advertising* 25(2), Summer 1996, pp. 1–16.

Ackerberg, Daniel A. "Empirically distinguishing informative and prestige effects of advertising" *Rand Journal of Economics* 32(2), Summer 2001, pp. 316–333.

Acs, Zoltan J. and David B. Audretsch "Innovation, market structure, and firm size" *Review of Economics and Statistics* 69(4), November 1987, pp. 567–574.

— "Innovation in large and small firms: an empirical analysis" *American Economic Review* 78(4), September 1988, pp. 678–690.

Acs, Zoltan J., David B. Audretsch, and Maryann P. Feldman "Innovation and R&D spillovers" CEPR Discussion Paper 865, December 1993.

Adams, Charles Francis "The pace of corporate action in our civilization" in Nathaniel Southgate Shaler, editor, *The United States of America*. New York: D. Appleton and Company, 1897, Volume II, pp. 191–213.

Adams, Henry C. "Relation of the state to industrial action" *Publications of the American Economic Association* 1(6), January 1887, pp. 471–549.

— "Publicity and corporate abuses" *Publications of the Michigan Political Science Association* 1, 1894, pp. 109–120.

— "What is publicity?" *North American Review* 175, 1902, pp. 895–904.

Adams, James D. "Endogenous R&D spillovers and industrial research productivity" NBER Working Paper No. W7484, January 2000.

Adams, Walter "Public policy in a free enterprise economy" in Walter Adams, editor, *The Structure of American Industry*. New York: The Macmillan Company, third edition, 1961, pp. 533–563, and in later editions.

Adams, Walter and Joel B. Dirlam "Steel imports and vertical oligopoly power" *American Economic Review* 54(5), September 1964, pp. 626–655.

Adams, William James and Janet L. Yellen "Commodity bundling and the burden of monopoly" *Quarterly Journal of Economics* 90(3), August 1976, pp. 475–498.

Adelman, M. A. "Review: *The Federal Antitrust Policy: Origination of an American Tradition*" *American Economic Review* 46(3), June 1956, pp. 481–487.

— *A & P: A Study in Price-Cost Behavior and Public Policy*. Cambridge, Massachusetts: Harvard University Press, 1959a.

— "Economic aspects of the Bethlehem opinion" *Virginia Law Review* 45(5), June 1959b, pp. 685–696.

— "Comment on the 'H' concentration measure as a numbers equivalent" *Review of Economics and Statistics* 51 February 1969, pp. 99–101.

— "Testimony" pp. 223–248 in *Evidence in Economic Concentration: Part 1, Overall and Conglomerate Aspects*. Hearings before the Subcommittee on Antitrust and Monopoly of the Committee of the Judiciary, United States Senate. Washington, 1964.

Agarwal, Rajshree and Michael Gort "The evolution of markets and entry, exit and survival of firms" *Review of Economics and Statistics* 78(3), August 1996, pp. 489–498.

— "First-mover advantage and the speed of competitive entry, 1887–1986" *Journal of Law and Economics* 44, April 2001, pp. 161–177.

Aghion, Phillippe, Nick Bloom, Richard Blundell, Rachel Griffith, and Peter Howitt "Competition and innovation: an inverted-U relationship" *Quarterly Journal of Economics* 120(2), May 2005, pp. 701–728.

Aguirregabiria, Victor "The dynamics of markups and inventories in retailing firms" *Review of Economic Studies* 66(2), April 1999, pp. 275–308.

Aiginger, Karl and Stephen W. Davies "Industrial specialisation and geographic concentration: two sides of the same coin? Not for the European Union" *Journal of Applied Economics* VII(2), 2004, pp. 231–248.

Aiginger, Karl and Michael Pfaffermayr, Michael "Looking at the cost side of 'monopoly'" *Journal of Industrial Economics* 45(3), September 1997, pp. 245–267.

Aitchison, J. and J. A. C. Brown *The Lognormal Distribution*. Cambridge: Cambridge University Press, 1957.

Akerlof, George A. "The market for 'lemons': quality uncertainty and the market mechanism" *Quarterly Journal of Economics* 89(3), August 1970, pp. 345–364.

Akman, Pinar "Searching for the long-lost soul of Article 82 EC" Center for Competition Policy Working Paper 07-05, March 2007.

Albæk, Svend, Peter Møllgaard, and Per Balzer Overgaard "Government-assisted oligopoly coordination? A *Concrete Case*" *Journal of Industrial Economics* 45(4), December 1997, pp. 429–443.

Alchian, Armen A. and Harold Demsetz "Production, information costs, and economic organization" *American Economic Review* 62, December 1972, pp. 777–795.

Alexander, Barbara "The impact of the National Industrial Recovery Act on cartel formation and maintenance costs" *Review of Economics and Statistics* 76(2), May 1994, pp. 245–254.

— "The rational racketeer: pasta protection in depression-era Chicago" *Journal of Law and Economics* 40, April 1997a, pp. 175–202.

— "Failed cooperation in heterogeneous industries under the National Recovery Administration" *Journal of Economic History* 57(2), June 1997b, pp. 322–344.

Alexander, Barbara J. and Gary D. Libecap "The effect of cost heterogeneity in the success and failure of the New Deal's agricultural and industrial programs" *Explorations in Economic History* 37, 2000, pp. 370–400.

Alford, B. W. E. "Chandlerism, the new orthodoxy of U.S. and European corporate development?" *Journal of European Economic History* 23, 1994, pp. 631–643.

Allen, Bruce T. "Tacit collusion and market sharing: the case of steam turbine generators" *Industrial Organization Review* 4(1), 1976, pp. 48–57.

Allen, G. C. "An eighteenth-century combination in the copper-mining industry" *Economic Journal* 33(129), March 1923, pp. 74–85.

— "Monopoly and competition in the United Kingdom" pp. 88–109 in Chamberlin, Edward H., editor, *Monopoly and Competition and their Regulation*. London: Macmillan Co. Ltd. and New York: St. Martin's Press, 1954.

Allen, R. G. D. "The mathematical foundations of economic theory" *Quarterly Journal of Economics* 63(1), February 1949, pp. 111–127.

— *Mathematical Economics*. London: Macmillan. Second edition, 1966.

Almus, Matthias and Dirk Czarnitzki "The effects of public R&D subsidies on firms' innovation activities: the case of Eastern Germany" *Journal of Business & Economic Statistics* 21(2), April 2003, pp. 226-236.

Amacher, Ryan C., Richard James Sweeney, and Robert D. Tollison "A note on the Webb-Pomerene law and the Webb-cartels" *Antitrust Bulletin* 23(2), 1978, pp. 371–387.

Amir, Rabah "Modelling imperfectly appropriable R&D via spillovers" *International Journal of Industrial Economics* 18(7), October 2000, pp. 1013–1032.

Anderson, B. M. Jr. "Competition and combination" *Annals of the American Academy of Political and Social Science* 82, 1919, pp. 201–214.

Anderson, Erin and David C. Schmittlein "Integration of the sales force: an empirical examination" *Rand Journal of Economics* 15(3), Autumn, 1984, pp. 385–395.

Anderson, Gary M., David M. Levy and Robert D. Tollison "The half-life of dead economists" *Canadian Journal of Economics* 22(1), February 1989, pp. 174–183.

Anderson, Nate "EU caves to aging rockers, wants 45-year copyright extension" 16 July 2008 (<http://arstechnica.com/old/content/2008/07/eu-caves-to-aging-rockers-wants-45-year-copyright-extension.ars>).

Anderson, Simon P. and Régis Renault "Pricing, product diversity, and search costs: a Bertrand-Chamberlin-Diamond model" *Rand Journal of Economics* 30(4), Winter 1999, pp. 719–735.

Andrews, P. W. S. "Industrial analysis in economics" in *Oxford Studies in the Price Mechanism*. T. Wilson and P. W. S. Andrews, editors, Oxford: Clarendon Press, 1951, pp. 139–172.

— "Industrial economics as a specialist subject" *Journal of Industrial Economics* 1(1), November 1952, pp. 72–79.

Angelmar, Reinhard "Market structure and research intensity in high-technological-opportunity industries" *Journal of Industrial Economics* 34(1), September 1985, pp. 69–79.

Anglin, Paul M. "The relationship between models of horizontal and vertical differentiation" *Bulletin of Economic Research* 44(1), January 1992, pp. 1–20.

Ansic, David "Note: a pilot experimental test of trade hysteresis" *Managerial and Decision Economics* 16(1), January–February 1995, pp. 85–91.

Aoki, Masahiko "Managerialism revisited in the light of bargaining-game theory" *International Journal of Industrial Organization* 1(1), March 1983, pp. 1–21.

Arbault, François and Francesco Pieró "The Commission's new notice on immunity and reduction of fines in cartel cases: building on success" *Competition Policy Newsletter* 2002(2), June 2002, pp. 15–22.

Archibald, G. C., B. Curtis Eaton and Richard G. Lipsey "Address models of value theory" in Joseph E. Stiglitz and G. Frank Mathewson, editors, *New Developments in the Analysis of Market Structure*, Cambridge, Massachusetts: MIT Press, 1986, pp. 3–47.

Areeda, Phillip "Antitrust violations without damage remedy" *Harvard Law Review* 89(6), April 1976, pp. 1127–1139.

— "Justice's Merger Guidelines: the general theory" *California Law Review* 71(2), March 1983a, pp. 303–310.

— "The economics of horizontal restraints: market definition and horizontal restraints" *Antitrust Law Journal* 52(3), September 1983, pp. 553ff.

— "The state of the law" *Regulation* January/February 1984, pp. 19–22.

— "Monopolizaton, mergers, and markets: a century past and the future" *California Law Review* 75(3), May 1987, pp. 959–981.

Areeda, Philip and Donald F. Turner "Predatory pricing and related practices under Section 2 of the Sherman Act" *Harvard Law Review* 88(4), February 1975, pp. 697–733.

Arnold & Porter LLP "Federal Trade Commission applies new liability theory to standard setting conduct" 12 February 2008. (Downloaded 19

February 2008 from <http://www.lexology.com/library/detail.aspx? g=45d99836-dbe1-45c7-b084-08d225ff3f85>.)

Aron, Debra J. and Steven S. Wildman "Economic theories of tying and foreclosure applied—and not applied—in *Microsoft*" *Antitrust*, Fall, 1999, pp. 48–52.

Arrow, Kenneth J. "Toward a theory of price adjustment" in Moses Abramovitz *et al. The Allocation of Economic Resources: Essays in Honor of Bernard Francis Haley*. Stanford: Stanford University Press, 1959, pp. 41–51.

— "Economic welfare and the allocation of resources for invention" in *The Rate and Direction of Inventive Activity: Economic and Social Factors*. Princeton: NBER, Princeton University Press, 1962, pp. 609–625.

— "The organization of economic activity: issues pertinent to the choice of market versus non-market allocation" in *The Analysis of Public Expenditure: the PBB System*. Volume I. U.S. Joint Economic Committee, 91st Congress, 1st Session, U.S. GPO, Washington, D. C. 1969, pp. 59–73.

— *The Limits of Organization*. New York: W. W. Norton & Company, Inc., 1974.

— "Vertical integration and communication" *Bell Journal of Economics* 6(1), Spring, 1975, pp. 173–183.

— "Innovation in large and small firms" pp. 15–28 in Joshua Ronen, editor *Entrepreneurship*. Lexington, Massachusetts and Toronto: D.C. Heath and Company, 1983.

Arthur, W. Brian "Competing technologies, increasing returns, and lock-in by historical events" *Economic Journal* 99, 1989, pp. 116–131.

Arundel, Anthony and Isabelle Kabla "What percentage of innovations are patented? empirical estimates for European firms" *Research Policy* 27(2), June 1998, pp. 127–141.

Ashton, T. S. "Early price associations in the British iron industry" *Economic Journal* 30(199), September 1920, pp. 331–339.

— "The records of a pin manufactory, 1814–21" *Economica* November 1925, pp. 281–292.

Asplund, Marcus "What fraction of a capital investment is sunk costs?" *Journal of Industrial Economics* 48(3), September 2000, pp. 287–304.

Asplund, Marcus and Volker Nocke "Firm turnover in imperfectly competitive markets" *Review of Economic Studies* 73(2), April 2006, pp. 295–327.

d'Aspremont, Claude, Jean Jaskold Gabszewicz, and Jacques–François Thisse "On Hotelling's 'Stability in Competition'" *Econometrica* 47(5), September 1979, pp. 1145–1150.

d'Aspremont, Claude and Alexis Jacquemin "Cooperative and noncooperative R&D in duopoly with spillovers" *American Economic Review* 78(5), December 1988, pp. 1133–1137.

Associated Press "Ex-secretary found guilty of stealing Coke secrets" 2 February 2007.

Atack, Jeremy "Comment" in Naomi Lamoreaux, Daniel M. G. Raff, and Peter Temin, editors *Learning by Doing in Markets, Firms, and Countries*. Chicago: University of Chicago Press, 1999, pp. 91–101.

Atack, Jeremy, and Fred Bateman, "Manufacturing concentration—percentage of value added accounted for by the largest companies: 1947–1992" Table Dd875-878 in Susan B. Carter, Scott Sigmund Gartner, Michael R. Haines, Alan L. Olmstead, Richard Sutch, Gavin Wright, editors, *Historical Statistics of the United States, Earliest Times to the Present: Millennial Edition*. New York : Cambridge University Press, 2006.

Atack, Jeremy and Peter Passell *A New Economic View of American History*. New York: W. W. Norton & Company, Inc., 1994.

Audretsch, David B. "New-firm survival and the technological regime" *Review of Economics and Statistics* 73(3), August 1991, pp. 441–450.

— *Innovation and Industry Evolution*. Cambridge, Massachusetts: MIT Press, 1995.

Auquier, Antoine A. and Richard E. Caves "Monopolistic export industries, trade, taxes, and optimal competition policy" *Economic Journal* 89, 1979, pp. 559–581.

Auspitz, Rudolf and Richard Lieben *Untersuchen über die Theorie des Preises*. Leipzig: Verlag von Duncker & Humblot, 1889.

Ausubel, Lawrence M. "The failure of competition in the credit card market" *American Economic Review* 81(1), March 1991, pp. 50–81.

Ausubel, Lawrence M. and Raymond J. Deneckere "One is almost enough for monopoly" *Rand Journal of Economics* 18(2), Summer 1987, pp. 255–274.

Azzam, Azzeddine M., David Rosenbaum, and Ananda Weliwita "Is there more than one critical concentration ratio? An empirical test for the Portland cement industry" *Applied Economics* 28(6), June 1996, pp. 673–678.

Babbage, Charles *On the Economy of Machinery and Manufactures*. Fourth Edition Enlarged (1835). New York: Reprints of Economic Classics, Augustus M. Kelley, Bookseller, 1963.

Bagwell, Kyle and Garey Ramey "Advertising and limit pricing" *Rand Journal of Economics* 19(1), Spring 1988, pp. 59–71.

Bailey, Elizabeth E. "Contestability and the design of regulatory and antitrust policy" *American Economic Review* 71(2), May 1981, pp. 179–183.

Bailey, Elizabeth E., David R. Graham and Daniel P. Kaplan *Deregulating the Airlines*. Cambridge, Massachusetts: MIT Press, 1985.

Bailey, Elizabeth E. and John C. Panzar "The contestability of airline markets during the transition to deregulation" *Law and Contemporary Problems* 44 Winter 1981, pp. 125–145.

Baily, Martin Neil and Alok K. Chakrabarti "Innovation and productivity in U.S. industry" *Brookings Papers on Economic Activity* 1985, pp. 609–639.

Baily, Martin Neil and Hans Gersbach "Efficiency in manufacturing and the need for global competition" *Brookings Papers on Economic Activity Microeconomics* 1995, pp. 307–347.

Bain, Joe S. *The Economics of the Pacific Coast Petroleum Industry*. Part I: Market Structure. Berkeley and Los Angeles: University of California Press, 1944.

— "Price and production policies" in Howard S. Ellis, editor, *A Survey of Contemporary Economics*. Philadelphia: The Blakiston Company, 1949a, pp. 129–173.

— "A note on pricing in monopoly and oligopoly" *American Economic Review* 39(1), March 1949b, pp. 448–469.

— "Relation of profit rate to industry concentration: American manufacturing, 1936–1940" *Quarterly Journal of Economics* 65(3), August 1951, pp. 293–324.

— "Conditions of entry and the emergence of monopoly" pp. 215–241 in Edward H. Chamberlin, editor, *Monopoly and Competition and Their Regulation*. London: Macmillan Co. Ltd. and New York: St. Martin's Press, 1954.

— *Barriers to New Competition*. Cambridge, Massachusetts: Harvard University Press, 1956.

— *Industrial Organization*. New York and London: John Wiley & Sons, Inc., 1959.

— "Survival-ability as a test of efficiency" *American Economic Review* 59(2), May 1969, pp. 99–104.

Baird, Douglas G. "In Coase's footsteps" *University of Chicago Law Review* 70, Winter 2003, pp. 23–37.

Baker, Donald I. and William Blumenthal "The 1982 Guidelines and preexisting law" *California Law Review* 71(2), March 1983, pp. 311–347.

Baker, George P., Robert Gibbons, and Kevin J. Murphy "Relational contracts and the theory of the firm" *Quarterly Journal of Economics* 117(1), February 2002, pp. 39–84

Baker, Jonathan B. "Identifying cartel pricing under uncertainty: the U.S. steel industry, 1933–1939" *Journal of Law and Economics* 32(2, Pt. 2), October 1989, pp. S47–S76.

— "The case for antitrust enforcement" *Journal of Economic Perspectives* 17(4), Autumn 2003, pp. 27–50.

— "Market definition: an analytical overview" *Antitrust Law Journal* 74, 2007, pp. 79 ff.

Baker, Jonathan B. and Timothy F. Bresnahan "Estimating the residual demand curve facing a single firm" *International Journal of Industrial Organization* 6(3), September 1988, pp. 283–300.

Baker, Wayne E. and Robert R. Faulkner "The social organization of conspiracy: illegal networks in the heavy electrical equipment industry" *American Sociological Review* 58(6), December 1993, pp. 837–860.

Bakker, Gerben "The decline and fall of the European film industry: sunk costs, market size and market structure, 1890–1927" *Economic History Review* 58(2), 2005, pp. 310–351.

Bakos, Yannis and Erik Brynjolfsson "Bundling information goods: pricing, profits, and efficiency" *Management Science* 45(12), December 1999, pp. 1613–1630.

— "Bundling and competition on the internet" *Marketing Science* 19(1), Winter 2000, pp. 63–82.

Baldwin, John R. and Paul K. Gorecki "Concentration and mobility statistics in Canada's manufacturing sector" *Journal of Industrial Economics* 42(1), March 1994, pp. 93–103.

Baldwin, Richard and Harry Flam "Strategic trade policies in the market for 30–40 seat commuter aircraft" *Weltwirtschaftliches Archiv* 125, 1989, pp. 484–500.

Baldwin, Robert E. "Imposing multilateral discipline on administered protection" in Anne O. Krueger, editor. *The WTO as an International Organization*. Chicago: University of Chicago Press, 1998, pp. 297–327.

Baldwin, William L. and Gerald L. Childs "The fast second and rivalry in research and development" *Southern Economic Journal* 36(1), July 1969, pp. 18–24.

Baldwin, William L. and John T. Scott *Market Structure and Technological Change*. London: Harwood Academic Publishers, 1987.

Banerjee, Ajeyo and E. Woodrow Eckard "Are mega-mergers anticompetitive? Evidence from the first great merger wave" *Rand Journal of Economics* 29(4), Winter 1998, pp. 803–827.

Barber, William J. *From New Era to New Deal*. Cambridge: Cambridge University Press, 1985.

— *Designs within Disorder*. Cambridge: Cambridge University Press, 1996.

Barjot, Dominique, editor. *International Cartels Revisited, 1880–1980*. Proceedings of the Caen Preconference. Caen: Editions-Diffusion du Lys, 1994.

Barnikel, Hans-Heinrich "Kartelle in Deutschland. Entwicklung, theoretische Ansätze und rechtliche Regelungen" in Hans-Heinrich Barnikel, editor, *Theorie und Praxis der Kartelle*. Darmstadt: Wissenschaftliche Buchgesellschaft, 1972.

Barron, John M. and John R. Umbeck "The effects of different contractual arrangements: the case of retail gasoline markets" *Journal of Law and Economics* 27(2), 1984, pp. 313–328.

Barton, David M. and Roger Sherman "The price and profit effects of horizontal merger" *Journal of Industrial Economics* 33(2), December 1984, pp. 165–177.

Barzel, Yoram "Optimal timing of innovations" *Review of Economics and Statistics* 50(3), August 1968, pp. 348–355.

Baskin, Jonathan Barron "Corporate liquidity in games of monopoly power" *Review of Economics and Statistics* 69(2), May 1987, pp. 312–319.

— "The development of corporate financial markets in Britain and the United States, 1600–1914: overcoming asymmetric information" *Business History Review* 62(2), Summer, 1988, pp. 199–237.

Bateman, Fred and Thomas Weiss "Market structure before the age of big business: concentration and profit in early Southern manufacturing" *Business History Review* 49(3), Autumn 1975, pp. 312–336.

Baumol, William J. "On the theory of oligopoly" *Economica* 25, August 1958, pp. 187–198.

— *Business Behavior, Value and Growth*. New York: Harcourt, Brace & World, Inc. First edition, 1959; revised edition, 1967.

— "Quasi-permanence of price reductions: a policy for prevention of predatory pricing" *Yale Law Journal* 89(1), November 1979, pp. 1–26.

— "Contestable markets: an uprising in the theory of industry structure" *American Economic Review* 72(1), March 1982, pp. 1–15.

— "Horizontal collusion and innovation" *Economic Journal* 102(410), January 1992, pp.129–137.

— "Predation and the logic of the average variable cost test" *Journal of Law and Economics* 39(1), April 1996, pp. 49–72.

Baumol, William J., John C. Panzar, and Robert D. Willig *Contestable Markets and the Theory of Industry Structure*. New York: Harcourt Brace Jovanovich, Inc. 1982.

— "Contestable markets: an uprising in the theory of industry structure: reply" *American Economic Review* 73(3), June 1983, pp. 491–496.

Baxter, William F. "Responding to the reaction: the draftman's view" *California Law Review* 71(2), March 1983a, pp. 618–631.

— "Reflections upon Professor Williamson's comments" *St. Louis University Law Journal* 27(2), April 1983, pp. 315–320.

Baye, Michael R. and Dan Kovenock "How to sell a pickup truck 'beat or pay' advertisements as facilitating devices" *International Journal of Industrial Organization* 12(1), 1994, pp. 21–33.

Beath, John, Yannis Katsoulacos, and David Ulph "R&D rivalry vs. R&D cooperation under uncertainty" *Recherches Economiques de Louvain* 54(4), 1988, pp. 373–384.

Becht, Marco, Patrick Bolton, and Ailsa Röell "Corporate governance and control" ECGI Working Paper Series in Finance Working Paper No. 02/2002, updated August 2005.

Becht, Marco and Colin Mayer "Introduction" in Fabrizio Barca and Marco Becht, editors *The Control of Corporate Europe*. Oxford: Oxford University Press, 2001, pp. 1–45.

Beckmann, Martin J. "Bertrand-Edgeworth duopoly revisited" in R. Henn, editor, *Operations Research*.

Verfahren III, pp. 55–68. Hain: Meisenheim am Glan, 1965.

Beesley, M. E., and R. T. Hamilton, "Small firms' feedbed role and the concept of turbulance" *Journal of Industrial Economics* 33, December 1984, pp. 217–232.

Belcher, Wallace E. "Industrial pooling agreements" *Quarterly Journal of Economics* 19(1), November 1904, pp. 111–123.

Benham, Lee "The effect of advertising on the price of eyeglasses" *Journal of Law and Economics* 15(2), October 1972, pp. 337–352.

Benson, Bruce L., Melvin L. Greenhut, and George Norman "On the basing-point system" *American Economic Review* 80(3), June 1990, pp. 584–588.

Berck, Peter, Jennifer Brown, Jeffrey M. Perloff, and Sofia Berto Villas-Boas "Sales: tests of theories on causality and timing" *International Journal of Industrial Organization* 26(6), 2008, pp. 1257–1273.

Berczi, Andrew "Chamberlin's experimental markets revisited" *American Journal of Economics and Sociology* 38(2), April 1979, pp. 197–206.

Bergeijk, Peter A. G. van "On the allegedly invisible Dutch construction sector cartel" *Journal of Competition Law and Economics* 4(1), March 2008, pp. 115–128.

Berghahn, Volker R. *The Americanisation of West German Industry 1945–1973*. Leamington Spa and New York: Berg, 1986.

Berle, Adolf A. *The Twentieth Century Capitalist Revolution*. New York: MacMillan, 1954.

Berle, Adolf A. and Gardiner C. Means *The Modern Corporation and Private Property*. First edition Harcourt, Brace & World, 1932. New Brunswick, New Jersey, 1991.

Bernard, Simon and Joseph G. Totten "Report on a Proposed Canal Through the Mining District of New Jersey" *Reports of the Board of Internal Improvements* II, pp. 1–27, November 5, 1823.

Berndt, Ernst R. *The Practice of Econometrics*. Reading, Massachusetts and elsewhere: Addison-Wesley Publishing Company, 1991.

Bernheim, B. Douglas and Michael D. Whinston "Multimarket contact and collusive behavior" *Rand Journal of Economics* 21(1), Spring 1990, pp. 1–26.

Bertrand, Joseph "Review" *Journal des Savants* 68 1883, pp. 499–508; reprinted in English translation by James W. Friedman in Daugherty (1988) and by Margaret Chevaillier in an Appendix to Magnan de Bornier (1992).

Bertrand, Marianne and Sendhil Mullainathan "Enjoying the quiet life? Corporate governance and managerial preferences" *Journal of Political Economy* 111(5), October 2003, pp. 1043–1075.

Bertstein, Peter L. *Wedding of the Waters*. New York and London: W. W. Norton & Co., 2005.

Betancourt, Roger P. and Margaret Malanoski "An estimable model of supermarket behavior: prices, distribution services and some effects of competition" *Empirica* 26, 1999, pp. 55–73.

Bickel, Alexander M. "The judiciary and responsible government 1910–21, Part One" Volume IX, *Oliver Wendell Holmes Devise History of the Supreme Court of the United States*. New York: Macmillan Publishing Company, 1984, pp. 3–718.

Bidault, Francis, Charles Despres, and Christina Butler "The drivers of cooperation between buyers and suppliers for product innovation" *Research Policy* 26(7-8), April 1998, pp. 719–732.

Bikhchandani, Sushil, David Hirshleifer and Ivo Welch "Learning from the behavior of others: conformity, fads, and informational cascades" *Journal of Economic Perspectives* 12(3), Summer 1998, pp. 151–170.

Binger, Brian R., Elizabeth Hoffman, Gary D. Libecap, and Keith M. Shacat "An experimetric study of the Cournot model" Discussion Paper 92-13, University of Arizona, January 1992.

Bisson, T. A. *Zaibatsu Dissolution in Japan*. Berkeley and Los Angeles: University of California Press, 1954.

Bittlingmayer, George "Output and stock prices when antitrust is suspended: the effects of the NIRA" in Fred S. McChesney and William F. Shughart II, editors, *The Causes and Consequences of Antitrust: The Public-Choice Perspective*. Chicago: University of Chicago Press, 1995, pp. 287–318.

Black, Bernard S. "The first international merger wave (and the fifth and last U.S. wave)" *University of Miami Law Review* 54, July 2000, pp. 799–818.

Black, Fischer "Noise" *Journal of Finance* 41(3), July 1986, pp. 529–543.

Blair, John M. *The Quinine "Convention" of 1959–62: A Case Study of an International Cartel*. U.S. Senate, 90th Congress, 1st Session, Hearings before the Subcommittee on Antitrust and Monopoly of the Judiciary, Prices of Quinine & Quinidine, Pt. 2, March 1967. Reprinted in Helmut Arndt *Recht, Macht und Wirtschaft*. Berlin: Duncker & Humblot, 1968.

— *Economic Concentration*. New York: Harcourt Brace Jovanovich, Inc., 1972.

Blanchflower, David G., Andrew J. Oswald, and Peter Sanfey "Wages, profits, and rent-sharing" *Quarterly Journal of Economics* 111(1), February 1996, pp. 227–251.

Blass, Asher A. and Dennis W. Carlton "The choice of organizational form in gasoline retailing and the cost of laws that limit that choice" *Journal of Law and Economics* 44(2), October 2001, pp. 511–524.

Bloom, Margaret "The great reformer: Mario Monti's legacy in Article 81 and cartel policy" *Competition Policy International* 1(1), Spring 2005, pp. 55–78.

Bloom, Nick, Rachel Griffith, and John Van Reenen "Do R&D tax credits work? Evidence from a panel of countries 1979–1997" *Journal of Public Economics* 85(1), July 2002, pp. 1–31.

Blundell, Richard, Rachel Griffith, and John Van Reenen "Market share, market value and innovation in a panel of British manufacturing firms" *Review of Economic Studies* 66(3), July 1999, pp. 529–554.

Bodoff, Joan "Competition polices of the US and the EEC: an overview" *European Competition Law Review* 5(1), 1984, pp. 51–81.

Boeri, Tito "Does firm size matter?" *Giornale degli Economisti e Annali di Economia* 48(9-10), 1989, pp. 477–495.

Böhm, Franz "Das Reichsgericht und die Kartelle" *ORDO* I (1948), pp. 197–213, reprinted in Franz Böhm *Reden und Schriften*. Karlsruhe: Verlag C. F. Müller, 1960, pp. 69–81.

— "Monopoly and competition in Western Germany" pp. 141–167 in Edward H. Chamberlin, editor, *Monopoly and Competition and their Regulation*. London: Macmillan Co. Ltd. and New York: St. Martin's Press, 1954.

Bok, Derek C. "Section 7 of the Clayton Act and the merging of law and economics" *Harvard Law Review* 74(2), December 1960, pp. 226–355.

Boldrin, Michaele and David Levine "The case against intellectual property" *American Economic Review* 92(2), March 2002, pp. 209–212.

— "The case against intellectual monopoly" *International Economic Review* 45(2), May 2004, pp. 327–350.

Bolton, Patrick, Joseph F. Brodley, and Michael H. Riordan "Predatory pricing: strategic theory and legal policy" *Georgetown Law Journal* 88, 2000, pp. 2239–2330.

Bonanno, Giacomo and Dario Brandolini "Introduction" in Giacomo Bonanno and Dario Brandolini, editors, *Industrial Structure in the New Industrial Economics*. Oxford: Clarendon Press, 1990, pp. 1–21.

Bonbright, James C. and Gardiner C. Means *The Holding Company*. New York and London: McGraw-Hill Book Company, Inc., 1932.

Boone, Jan, Jan C. van Ours, and Henry van der Wiel "How (not) to measure competition" CEPR Discussion Paper 6275, May 2007.

Borenstein, Severin "Price discrimination in free-entry markets" *Rand Journal of Economics* 16(3), Autumn 1985, pp. 380–397.

Borenstein, Severin "Selling costs and switching costs: explaining retail gasoline margins" *Rand Journal of Economics* 22(3), Autumn, 1991, pp. 354–369.

Borenstein, Severin and Andrea Shepard "Dynamic pricing in retail gasoline markets" *Rand Journal of Economics* 27(3), Autumn 1996, pp. 429–451.

Bork, Robert H. "Vertical integration and the Sherman Act; the legal history of an economic misconception" *University of Chicago Law Review* 22, 1954, pp. 157–201.

— "The rule of reason and the per se concept: price fixing and market division" *Yale Law Journal* 74(5), April 1965, pp. 775–847.

— "Legislative intent and the policy of the Sherman Act" *Journal of Law and Economics* 9, October 1966, pp. 7–48, reprinted in Thomas E. Sullivan (1991).

— *The Antitrust Paradox: A Policy at War With Itself.* New York: Basic Books, 1978.

Bork, Robert H. and Ward S. Bowman, Jr. "The crisis in antitrust" *Columbia Law Review* 65(3), March 1965, pp. 363–376.

Boserup, William and Uffe Schlichtkrull "Alternative approaches to the control of competition" pp. 59–113 in John Perry Miller, editor *Competition Cartels and Their Regulation.* Amsterdam: North-Holland Publishing Company, 1962.

Bottasso, Anna and Alessandro Sembenelli "Market power, productivity and the EU Single Market program: evidence from a panel of Italian firms" *European Economic Review* 45, 2001, pp. 167–186.

Boulding, Kenneth E. *Economic Analysis: I, Microeconomics,* 4th edition. New York: Harpers, 1966.

Bound, John, Clint Cummins, Zvi Griliches, Bronwyn H. Hall, and Adam Jaffe "Who does R&D and who patents" pp. 21–54 in Zvi Griliches, editor *R&D, Patents, and Productivity.* Chicago and London: University of Chicago Press, 1984.

Bowie, Robert R. Interview, 15 June 1981. Transcript on file at the Fondation Jean Monnet pour l'Europe, Lausanne.

— "Réflexions sur Jean Monnet" in *Témoignages à la mémoire de Jean Monnet.* Lausanne: Fondation Jean Monnet pour l'Europe, 1989, pp. 81–88.

Bowley, A. L. *The Mathematical Groundwork of Economics.* Oxford: Oxford University Press, 1924.

Bowman, Mary Jean "The consumer in the history of economic doctrine," *American Economic Review* 41(2), May 1951, pp. 1–18.

Bowman, Ward S. Jr. "Tying arrangements and the leverage problem" *Yale Law Journal* 67(1), November 1957, pp. 19–36.

Bowrey, Kathy "Who's writing copyright's history?" *European Intellectual Property Review* 18(6), 1996, pp. 322–329.

Boyer, Marcel and Alexis Jacquemin "Organizational choices for efficiency and market power" *Economics Letters* 18(1), 1985, pp. 79–82.

Bradburd, Ralph M. "Price-cost margins in producer good industries and 'the importance of being unimportant'" *Review of Economics and Statistics* 64(3), August 1982, pp. 405–412.

Bradburd, Ralph M. and Richard E. Caves "A closer look at the effect of market growth on industries' profits" *Review of Economics and Statistics* 64(4), November 1982, pp. 635–645.

Bradburd, Ralph M. and A. Mead Over, Jr. "Organizational costs, 'sticky equilibria,' and critical levels of concentration" *Review of Economics and Statistics* 64(1), February 1982, pp. 50–58.

Brander, James A. and Paul R. Krugman "A reciprocal dumping model of international trade" *Journal of International Economics* 1983, pp. 313–321.

Brander, James A. and Tracy R. Lewis "Oligopoly and financial structure: the limited liability effect" *American Economic Review* 76(5), December 1986, pp. 956–970.

Brander, James A. and Barbara J. Spencer "Tacit collusion, free entry and welfare" *Journal of Industrial Economics* 33(3), March 1985, pp. 277–294.

Breit, William, and Roger Ransom *The Academic Scribblers: American Economists in Collision.* New York: Holt, Rinehart and Winston, 1971.

Breen, Denis A. "The Union Pacific/Southern Pacific Rail merger: a retrospective on merger benefits" *Review of Network Economics* 3(3), September 2004, pp. 283–322.

Brenkers, Randy and Frank Verboven "Liberalizing a distribution system: the European car market" *Journal of the European Economic Association* 4(1), March 2006, pp. 216–251.

Bresnahan, Timothy F. "Departures from marginal-cost pricing in the American automobile industry" *Journal of Econometrics* 17, 1981, pp. 201–227.

— "Sutton's *Sunk Costs and Market Structure: Price Competition, Advertising, and the Evolution of Concentration*" *Rand Journal of Economics* 23(1), Spring 1992, pp. 137–152.

— "A remedy that falls short of restoring competition" *Antitrust* Autumn 2001a, pp. 67–71.

— "The right remedy" Stanford Institute for Economic Policy Research Discussion Paper No. 00-49, August 2001b.

— "The economics of the Microsoft case" John M. Olin Program in Law and Economics Working Paper 232, March 2002.

Bresnahan, Timothy F. and Manuel Trajtenberg "General purpose technologies 'engines of growth'" *Journal of Econometrics* 65(1), January 1995, pp. 83–108.

Brevoort, Kenneth and Howard P. Marvel "Successful monopolization through predation: the National Cash Register Company" *Research in Law and Economics* 21, 2004, pp. 85–125.

Bridge, F. H. S. "The antecedents of the proposed German law against restraints of competition" *International and Comparative Law Quarterly* 3(2), April 1954, pp. 348–351.

Briggs, Hugh "The effects of concentration and cartels on nineteenth-century railroad rates" pp. 194–212 in Leonard W. Weiss, editor, *Concentration and Price.* Cambridge, Massachusetts: MIT Press, 1989.

Bright, Arthur A. Jr. and W. Rupert MacLaurin "Economic factors influencing the development and introduction of the fluorescent lamp" *Journal of Political Economy* 51(5), October 1943, pp. 429–450.

Bringhurst, Bruce *Antitrust and the Oil Monopoly*. Westport, Connecticut and London, England: Greenwood Press, 1979.

Broadberry, Stephen and Nicolas Crafts "British economic policy and industrial performance in the early postwar period" *Business History* 38(4), 1996, pp. 65–91.

— "Competition and innovation in 1950s Britain" *Business History* 43(1), January 2001, pp. 97–118.

Brod, Andrew C. and Albert N. Link "Trends in cooperative research activity: has the National Cooperative Research Act been successful?" pp. 105–119 in Maryann P. Feldman and Albert N. Link, editors, *Innovation Policy in the Knowledge-Based Economy*. Boston: Kluwer Academic Publishers, 2001.

Brooks, Harvey "Research universities and the social contract for science" in Lewis M. Branscomb, editor, *Empowering Technology*. Cambridge, Massachusetts: MIT Press, 1993, pp. 202–234.

Brooks, John *The Go-Go Years*. New York: Weybright and Talley, 1973.

Brosens, Koenraad *A Contextual Study of Brussels Tapestry, 1670–1770*. Brussels: Paleis der Academiën, 2004.

Brown, James R., Rajiv P. Dant, Charles A. Ingene, and Patrick J. Kaufman "Supply chain management and the evolution of the 'Big Middle'" *Journal of Retailing* 81(2), 2005, pp. 97–105.

Brown, John Howard "Jeremiah Jenks: a pioneer of industrial organization?" *Journal of the History of Economic Thought* 26(1), March 2004, pp. 69–89.

Brozen, Yale "Bain's concentration and rates of return revisited" *Journal of Law and Economics* 14, 1971a, pp. 351–369.

— "Concentration and structural and market disequilibria" *Antitrust Bulletin* 16, 1971b, pp. 241–248.

Brülhart, Marius "Evolving geographical concentration of European manufacturing industries" *Review of World Economics* 137(2), June 2001, pp. 215–243.

Brusse, Wendy Asbeek and Richard T. Griffiths "The management of markets: business, governments and cartels in post-war Europe" pp. 162–188 in Ulf Olsson, editor, *Business and European Integration since 1800*. Göteborg, 1997a.

— "The incidence of manufacturing cartels in post-war Europe" in Carlo Morelli, editor, *Cartels and Market Management in the Post-War World*, London School of Economics Business History Unit Occasional Paper 1997 No. 1, 1997b.

Bryant, Peter G. and E. Woodrow Eckard "Price fixing: the probability of getting caught " *Review of Economics and Statistics* 73(3), August 1991, pp. 531–536.

Buchanan, James M. "Rent seeking and profit seeking" in James M. Buchanan, Robert D. Tollison, and Gordon Tullock, editors, *Toward a Theory of the Rent-Seeking Society*. College Station: Texas A&M University Press, 1980, pp. 3–15.

Buck, Solon Justus *The Granger Movement*. Lincoln, Nebraska: University of Nebraska Press, 1913.

Buigues, Pierre and Alexis Jacquemin "Strategies of firms and structural environments in the large internal market" *Journal of Common Market Studies* 28, 1989, pp. 53–67.

Bullock, Charles J. "Trust literature: a survey and criticism" *Quarterly Journal of Economics* 15(2), February 1901, pp. 167–217.

Bulmer, Simon "Institutions and policy change in the European Communities: the case of merger control" *Public Administration* 72, Autumn 1994, pp. 423–444.

Bulow, Jeremy, John Geanakoplos and Paul D. Klemperer "Multimarket oligopoly: strategic substitutes and complements" *Journal of Political Economy* 93(3), 1985, pp. 488–511.

Burdett, Kenneth and Kenneth L. Judd "Equilibrium price dispersion" *Econometrica* 51(4), July 1983, pp. 955–970.

Burnett, William B. "Predation by a non-dominant firm: Liggett Group, Inc. *vs.* Brown & Williamson Tobacco Corporation" in John E. Kwoka, Jr. and Lawrence J. White, editors, *The Antitrust Revolution: Economics, Competition, and Policy*, 3rd edition. Oxford: Oxford University Press, 1999.

Burns, Arthur Robert *The Decline of Competition*. New York and London: McGraw-Hill Book Company, Inc., 1936.

— "The organization of industry and the theory of prices" *Journal of Political Economy* 45(5), October 1937, pp. 662–680.

Burns, Malcolm R. "Outside intervention in monopolistic price warfare: the case of the 'Plug War' and the Union Tobacco Company" *Business History Review* 56(1), Spring 1982, pp. 33–53.

— "Economies of scale in tobacco manufacture, 1897–1910," *Journal of Economic History* 43(2), June 1983, pp. 461–474.

— "Predatory pricing and the acquisition cost of competitors" *Journal of Political Economy* 94(2), April 1986, pp. 266–296.

— "New evidence on predatory price cutting" *Managerial and Decision Economics* 10(4), December 1989, pp. 327–330.

Burstein, M. L. "The economics of tie-in sales" *Review of Economics and Statistics* 42(1), February 1960, pp. 68–73.

Burton, David H. and A. E. Campbell *The Collected Works of William Howard Taft. Volume I Four Aspects of Civic Duty & Present Day Problems*. Athens, Ohio: Ohio University Press, 2001.

Buson, Isabel "An empirical evaluation of the effects of R&D subsidies" *Economics of Innovation and New Technology* 9(2), 2000, pp. 111–148.

Busse, Meghan "Firm financial condition and airline price wars" *Rand Journal of Economics* 33(2), Summer 2002, pp. 298–318.

Büthe, Tim and Gabriel T. Swank "The politics of antitrust and merger review in the European Union: institutional change and decisions from Messina to 2004" 1 December 2005.

Butler, Rush C. "The Sherman anti-trust law and readjustment" *Annals of the American Academy of Political and Social Science* 82, 1919, pp. 215–230.

Butters, Gerard R. "A survey of advertising and market structure" *American Economic Review* 66(2), May, 1976, pp. 392–397.

Butters, J. Keith, John Lintner and William L. Cary *Effects of Taxation Corporate Mergers*. Boston: Graduate School of Business Administration, Harvard University, 1951.

Buxbaum, Hannah L. "German legal culture and the globalization of competition law: a historical perspective on the expansion of private antitrust enforcement, " *Issues in Legal Scholarship*, Richard Buxbaum and German Reintegration (2006): Article 10. <http://www.bepress.com/ils/iss9/art10>.

Cabellero, Ricardo J. and Adam B. Jaffe "How high are the giants' shoulders: an empirical assessment of knowledge spillovers and creative destruction in a model of economic growth" *NBER Macroeconomics Annual* 8, 1993, pp. 15–74.

Cable, John "Market structure, advertising policy and intermarket differences in advertising intensity" in Keith Cowling, editor, *Market Structure and Corporate Behavior: Theory and Empirical Analysis of the Firm*. London: Gray-Mills Publishing Ltd. 1972, pp. 105–124.

Cable, John and Joachim Schwalbach "International comparisons of entry and exit" in Paul Geroski and Joachim Schwalbach, editors, *Entry and Market Contestability*. Oxford, UK and Cambridge, Massachusetts: Blackwell, 1991, pp. 257–281.

Cabral, Luis M. B. "Conjectural variations as a reduced form" *Economics Letters* 49 1995, pp. 397–402.

Cabral, Luís M. B. and José Mata "On the evolution of the firm size distribution: facts and theory" *American Economic Review* 93(4), September 2003, pp. 1075–1090.

Cabral, Luís M. B. and Thomas W. Ross "Are sunk costs a barrier to entry" *Journal of Economics & Management Strategy* 17(1), Spring 2008, pp. 97–112.

Calem, Paul S. and Loretta J. Mester "Consumer behavior and the stickiness of credit-card interest rates" *American Economic Review* 85(5), December 1995, pp. 1327–1336.

Call, Gregory D. and Keeler, Theodore E. "Airline deregulation, fares, and market behavior: some empirical evidence" in Andrew F. Daughety, editor, *Analytical Studies in Transport Economics*, Cambridge: Cambridge University Press, 1985, pp. 221–247.

Camerer, Colin F. and George Loewenstein "Behavioral economics: past, present, future" in Colin F. Camerer, George Loewenstein, and Matthew Rabin, editors. *Advances in Behavioral Economics*. Princeton: Princeton University Press, 2003, pp. 3–51.

Carbajo, Jose, David de Meza, and Daniel J. Seidmann "A strategic motivation for commodity bundling" *Journal of Industrial Economics* 38(3), March 1990, pp. 283–298.

Carlton, Dennis W. "A reexamination of delivered pricing systems" *Journal of Law and Economics* 26(1), April 1983, pp. 51–70.

— "The rigidity of prices" *American Economic Review* 76(4), September 1986, pp. 637–658.

— "Why barriers to entry are barriers to understanding" *American Economic Review* 94(2), May 2004, pp. 466–470.

— "Market definition: use and abuse" EAG Discussion Paper 07-6, April 2007.

Carlton, Dennis W., Gustavo E. Bamberger, and Roy J. Epstein. "Antitrust and higher education: was there a conspiracy to restrict financial aid?" *Rand Journal of Economics* 26(1), Spring 1995, 26, pp. 131–147.

Carlton, Dennis and Jeffrey M. Perloff *Modern Industrial Organization*. New York: HarperCollins College Publishers, 1994.

Carter, Anne P. "Changes in the structure of the American economy, 1947 to 1958 and 1962" *Review of Economics and Statistics* 49(2), May 1967, pp. 209–224.

Carter, Susan B., Scott Sigmund Gartner, Michael R. Haines, Alan L. Olmstead, Richard Sutch, Gavin Wright *Historical Statistics of the United States: Earliest Times to the Present*. New York : Cambridge University Press, 2006.

Casadesus-Masanell, Ramon and Daniel F. Spulber "The fable of Fisher Body, " *Journal of Law and Economics* 43(1), April 2000, pp. 67–104.

Cason, Timothy and Daniel Friedman "Customer search and market power: some laboratory evidence" manuscript, June 1999.

Cassady, Ralph Jr. "The New York department store price war of 1951: a microeconomic analysis" *Journal of Marketing* 22(1), July 1957a, pp. 3–11.

— "Taxicab rate war: counterpart of international conflict" *Journal of Conflict Resolution* 1(4), December 1957b, pp. 364–368.

— "Monopoly in motion picture production and distribution: 1908–1915" *Southern California Law Review* 32(4), Summer 1959, pp. 325–390.

— *Price Warfare in Business Competition*. Occasional Paper No. 11, Bureau of Business and Economic Research, Michigan State University, 1963.

Cassiman, Bruno, Massimo G. Colombo, Paola Garrone and Reinhilde Veugelers "The impact of M&A on the

R&D process An empirical analysis of the role of technological- and market-relatedness" *Research Policy* 34(2), March 2005, pp. 195–220.

Castel, J. G. "France" in Wolfgang Friedman, editor, *Anti-Trust Laws: A Comparative Symposium*. Toronto: The Carswell Company Limited, 1956, pp. 91–137.

Caswell, Julie A. "Aggregate concentration: significance, trends, and causes" in Robert L. Wills, Julie A. Caswell, and John D. Culbertson, editors, *Issues After a Century of Federal Competition Policy*, Lexington MA: Lexington Books, 1987.

Caves, Richard E. "Industrial organization, corporate strategy and structure" *Journal of Economic Literature* 18(1), March 1980a, pp. 64–92.

— *Symposium on International Trade and Industrial Organization. Journal of Industrial Economics* 29(2), December 1980b.

— "Diversification and seller concentration: evidence from changes, 1963–72" *Review of Economics and Statistics* 63(2), May 1981, pp. 289–293.

— "Mergers, takeovers, and economic efficiency: foresight vs. hindsight" *International Journal of Industrial Organization* 7(1), March 1989, pp. 151–174.

— *Industrial Efficiency in Six Nations*. Cambridge, Massachusetts and London, England: MIT Press, 1992.

— "Industrial organization and new findings on the turnover and mobility of firms" *Journal of Economic Literature* 36(4), December 1998, pp. 1947–1982.

— "In praise of the old I.O." *International Journal of Industrial Organization* 25(1), February 2007, pp. 1–12.

Caves, Richard E. and David R. Barton *Efficiency in U.S. Manufacturing Industries*. Cambridge, Massachusetts and London, England: MIT Press, 1990.

Caves, Richard E., Michael Fortunato, and Pankaj Ghemawat "The decline of dominant firms, 1905–1929" *Quarterly Journal of Economics* 99(3), August 1984, pp. 523–546.

Caves, Richard E. and David P. Greene "Brands' quality levels, prices, and advertising outlays: empirical evidence on signals and information costs" *International Journal of Industrial Organization* 14(1), 1996, pp. 29–52.

Caves, Richard E., Michael D. Whinston, and Mark A. Hurwitz "Patent expiration, entry, and competition in the U.S. pharmaceutical industry" *Brookings Papers on Economic Activity* Microeconomics 1991, pp. 1–48.

Cetorelli, Nicola and Philip E. Strahan "Finance as a barrier to entry: bank competition and industry structure in local U.S. markets" NBER Working Paper 10832, October 2004.

Chadwick, Edwin "Results of different principles of legislation and administration in Europe of competition for the field, as compared with competition within the field, of service" *Journal of the Royal Statistical Society* 22, September 1859, pp. 381–420.

Chamberlin, Edward H. *The Theory of Monopolistic Competition*. Cambridge, Massachusetts: Harvard University Press, [1933] eighth edition, 1962.

— "An experimental imperfect market" *Journal of Political Economy* 56(2), April 1948, pp. 95–108.

— "The product as an economic variable" *Quarterly Journal of Economics* 67(1), February 1953, pp. 1–29.

— *Monopoly and Competition and Their Regulation*. London: Macmillan & Co. Ltd and New York: St. Martin's Press, 1954.

— *Towards a More General Theory of Value*. New York: Oxford University Press, 1957.

— "The origin and early development of monopolistic competition theory" *Quarterly Journal of Economics* 75(4), 1961, pp. 515–543.

Chandler, Alfred D. Jr. *The Railroads: The Nation's First Big Business*. New York: Harcourt, Brace & World, Inc. 1965.

— "The large industrial corporation and the making of the modern American economy" pp. 71–101 in Stephen E. Ambrose, editor, *Institutions in Modern America*. Baltimore: Johns Hopkins University Press, 1967.

— *The Visible Hand: The Managerial Revolution in American Business*. Cambridge, Massachusetts: Harvard University Press, 1977.

— "The growth of the transnational industrial firm in the United States and the United Kingdom: a comparative analysis" *Economic History Review* n.s. 33(3), August 1980a, pp. 396–410.

— "The United States: seedbed of managerial capitalism" in Alfred D. Chandler, Jr. and Herman Daems, editors, *Managerial Hierarchies*. Cambridge, Massachusetts and London, England: Harvard University Press, 1980b, pp. 9–40.

— "The M-form: industrial groups, American style" *European Economic Review* 19(1), 1982, pp. 3–23.

— "Comparative business history" pp. 3–26 in D. C. Coleman and Peter Mathias, editors, *Enterprise and History. Essays in Hounour of Charles Wilson*. Cambridge and elsewhere: Cambridge University Press, 1984.

— *Scale and Scope: The Dynamics of Industrial Capitalism*. Cambridge, Massachusetts and London, England: Harvard University Press, 1990.

— "Organizational capabilities and the economic history of the industrial enterprise" *Journal of Economic Perspectives* 6(3), Summer 1992, pp. 79–100.

— "The competitive performance of U.S. industrial enterprises since the Second World War" *Business History Review* 68(1), Spring 1994, pp. 1–72.

Chandler, Alfred D. Jr. and Stephen Salsbury *Pierre S. Du Pont and the Making of the Modern Corporation*. New York: Harper & Row, 1971.

Chevalier, Judith A. "Do LBO supermarkets charge more? An empirical analysis of the effects of LBOs on supermarket pricing" *Journal of Finance* 50(4), September 1995, pp. 1095–1112.

Chicago Conference on Trusts. *Chicago Conference on Trusts*. Chicago: Civic Federation of Chicago, 1900. Reprinted 1973 by Arno Press, Inc.

Chipman, John S. and James C. Moore "The new welfare economics 1939-1974" *International Economic Review* 19(3), October 1978, pp. 547–584.

Chipty, Tasneem "Vertical integration, market foreclosure, and consumer welfare in the cable television industry" *American Economic Review* 91(3), June, 2001, pp. 428–453.

Chirinko, R. S. and S. M. Fazzari "Economic fluctuations, market power, and returns to scale: evidence from firm-level data" *Journal of Applied Econometrics* 9(1), January–March 1994, pp. 47–69.

Christensen, Clayton M. *The Innovator's Dilemma*. Boston, Massachusetts: Harvard Business School Press, 1997.

Church, Roy "The family firm in industrial capitalism: international perspectives on hypotheses and history" *Business History* 35(3), October 1993, pp. 17–43.

Claessens, Stijn, Simeon Djankov, and Larry H. P. Lang "The separation of ownership and control in East Asian corporations" *Journal of Financial Economics* 58(1–2), 2000, pp. 81–112.

Clarida, Richard H. "Dumping: in theory, in policy, and in practice" in Jagdish Bhagwati and Robert E. Hudec, editors, *Fair Trade and Harmonization*. MIT Press, 1996, pp. 357–389.

Clark, Don P., David L. Kaserman, and John W. Mayo "Barriers to trade and the import vulnerability of US manufacturing industries" *Journal of Industrial Economics* 38(4), June 1990, pp. 433–447.

Clark, John "New rules for motor vehicle distribution and servicing" *Competition Policy Newsletter* 2002(3), October 2002, pp. 3–6.

Clark, John Bates "The limits of competition" *Political Science Quarterly* 2(1), March 1887, pp. 45–61.

— "The modern appeal to legal forces in economic life" *Publications of the American Economic Association* 9(5/6), October–December 1894, pp. 9–30.

— "Trusts and the law" *The Independent* 4 March 1897, pp. 1–2.

— "The necessity of suppressing monopolies while retaining trusts" pp. 404–409 in Chicago Conference on Trusts. *Chicago Conference on Trusts*. Chicago: Civic Federation of Chicago, 1900a. Reprinted 1973 by Arno Press, Inc.

— "Trusts" *Political Science Quarterly* 15(2), June 1900b, pp. 181–195.

— *The Control of Trusts*. New York: The Macmillan Company, 1902.

— *The Problem of Monopoly*. New York: Columbia University Press, 1904.

— *Essentials of Economic Theory*. New York, The Macmillan Company, 1907.

Clark, John D. *The Federal Trust Policy*. Baltimore: Johns Hopkins Press, 1931.

Clark, John Maurice *Studies in the Economics of Overhead Costs*. Chicago: University of Chicago Press, 1923.

— "Remarks" in "Report of the dinner meeting in celebration of the fiftieth anniversary of the founding of the American Economic Association" *American Economic Review* 26(1), March 1936, pp. 317–340.

Clark, Kim B. "Competition, technical diversity, and radical innovation in the U.S. auto industry" *Research on Technological Innovation, Management and Policy* 1, 1983, pp. 103–149.

Clarke, Darral G. "Econometric measurement of the duration of the advertising effect on sales" *Journal of Marketing Research* 13(4), November 1976, pp. 345–357.

Clarke, Ian "Retail power, competition and local consumer choice in the UK grocery sector" *European Journal of Marketing* 34(8), 2000, pp. 975–1002.

Clarke, Roger and Stephen W. Davies "Market structure and price-cost margins" *Economica* n.s. 49(195), August 1982, pp. 277–287.

— "Aggregate concentration, market concentration, and diversification" *Economic Journal* 93(369), March 1983, pp. 182–192.

Clarke, Roger, Stephen W. Davies, and Michael Waterson "The profitability–concentration relation: market power or efficiency?" *Journal of Industrial Economics* 32(4), June 1984, pp. 435–450.

Clay, Karen, Ramayya Krishnan, and Eric Wolff "Prices and price dispersion on the web: evidence from the online book industry" *Journal of Industrial Economics* 49(4), December 2001, pp. 521–539.

Coase, R. H. "The nature of the firm," *Economica* New Series IV, 1937, pp. 386–405, reprinted in George J. Stigler and Kenneth E. Boulding, editors, *Readings in Price Theory*. Chicago: Richard D. Irwin, Inc., 1952, pp. 331–351.

— "Durability and monopoly" *Journal of Law and Economics* 15(1), April 1972a, pp. 143–149.

— "Industrial organization: a proposal for research" in Victor R. Fuchs, editor, *Policy Issues and Research Opportunities in Industrial Organization*. New York: NBER, 1972b, pp. 59–73.

— "The nature of the firm: origin" *Journal of Law, Economics, and Organization* 4(1), Spring 1988a, pp. 3–17; reprinted in Oliver E. Williamson and Sidney G. Winter, editors, *The Nature of the Firm: Origins, Evolution, and Development*. New York & Oxford: Oxford University Press, 1993.

— "The nature of the firm: meaning" *Journal of Law, Economics, and Organization* 4(1), Spring 1988b, pp. 19–32; reprinted in Oliver E. Williamson and Sidney G. Winter, editors, *The Nature of the Firm:*

Origins, Evolution, and Development. New York and Oxford: Oxford University Press, 1993.

— "The nature of the firm: influence" *Journal of Law, Economics, and Organization* 4(1), Spring 1988c, pp. 33–47; reprinted in Oliver E. Williamson and Sidney G. Winter, editors, *The Nature of the Firm: Origins, Evolution, and Development*. New York & Oxford: Oxford University Press, 1993.

— "The institutional structure of production" *American Economic Review* 82(4), September 1992, pp. 713–719.

— "Law and economics at Chicago" *Journal of Law and Economics* 36(1), Part 2, April 1993, pp. 239–254.

— "The acquisition of Fisher Body by General Motors," *Journal of Law and Economics* 43(1), April 2000, pp. 15–31.

— "The conduct of economics: the example of Fisher Body and General Motors" *Journal of Economics & Management Strategy* 15(2), Summer 2006, pp. 255–278.

Coats, A. W. "Adam Smith and the Mercantile System" pp. 218–236 in Andrew S. Skinner and Thomas Wilson, editors, *Essays on Adam Smith*. Oxford: Clarendon Press, 1975.

Cockburn, Ian, and Rebecca Henderson "Racing to invest? The dynamics of competition in ethical drug discovery" *Journal of Economics and Management Strategy* 3(3), 1995, pp. 1481–1519.

Cohen, Arthur "The law as to combinations: memorandum" *Journal of the Society of Comparative Legislation* n.s. 10(1), 1909, pp. 144–153.

Cohen, Wesley M. "Empirical studies of innovative activity" Chapter 6 in Paul Stoneman, editor *Handbook of the Economics of Innovation and Technological Change*. Oxford: Blackwell, 1995.

Cohen, Wesley M., Akira Goto, Akiya Nagata, Richard R. Nelson, and John P. Walsh "R&D spillovers, patents and the incentives to innovate in Japan and the United States" *Research Policy* 31(8–9), December 2002, pp. 1349–1367

Cohen, Wesley M., and Steven Klepper "Firm size and the nature of innovation within industries: the case of process and product R&D" *Review of Economics and Statistics* 78(2), May 1996a, pp. 232–243.

— "A reprise of size and R&D" *Economic Journal* 106(437), July 1996b, pp. 925–951.

Cohen, Wesley M. and Richard C. Levin, "Empirical studies of innovation and market structure" in Richard C. Schmalensee and Robert D. Willig, editors *Handbook of Industrial Organization*. Amsterdam: North-Holland, Volume II, 1989.

Cohen, Wesley M., Richard C. Levin, and David C. Mowery "Firm size and R&D intensity: a re-examination" *Journal of Industrial Economics* 35(4), June 1987, pp. 543–565.

Cohen, Wesley M. and Daniel A. Levinthal "Innovation and learning: the two faces of R&D" *Economic Journal* 99(397), September 1989, pp. 569–596.

Cohen, Wesley M., Richard R. Nelson, and John P. Walsh "Protecting their intellectual assets: appropriability conditions and why U.S. manufacturing firms patent (or not)" NBER Working Paper 7552, February 2000.

Colander, David *The Stories Economists Tell*. New York: McGraw-Hill Irwin, 2006.

Coleman, Jules L. "Efficiency, utility, and wealth maximization" *Hofstra Law Review* 8(1), Autumn 1979, pp. 512–551.

— "Efficiency, exchange, and auction: philosophic aspects of the economic approach in law" *California Law Review* 68, 1980, pp. 221–248.

Collie, David R. "State aid in the European Union" *International Journal of Industrial Organization* (18)6, 2000, pp. 867–884.

Collins, Norman R. and Preston, Lee E. "The size structure of the largest industrial firms, 1909–1958" *American Economic Review* 51, December 1961, pp. 986–1011.

Comanor, William S. and John B. Kirkwood. "Resale price maintenance and antitrust policy" *Contemporary Policy Issues* III(3), Part 1, Spring 1985, pp. 9–16.

Comanor, William S. and Harvey Leibenstein "Allocative efficiency, X-efficiency, and the measurement of welfare losses" *Economica* N.S. 36(143), August 1969, pp. 304–309.

Comanor, William S. and F. M. Scherer "Rewriting history: the early Sherman Act monopolization cases" *International Journal of the Economics of Business* 2(2), 1995, pp. 263–289.

Comanor, William S. and Thomas A. Wilson "Advertising market structure and performance" *Review of Economics and Statistics* 49(4), November 1967, pp. 423–440.

— "Advertising and competition: a survey" *Journal of Economic Literature* 17(2), June 1979, pp. 453–476.

Combe, Emmanuel, Constance Monnier, and Renaud Legal "Cartels: the probability of getting caught in the European Union" Bruges European Economic Research Paper No. 12, March 2008.

Comer, George P. "The outlook for effective competition" *American Economic Review* 36(2), May 1946, pp. 154–171.

Comité Intergouvernemental créé par la Conférence de Messine *Rapport des Chefs de Délégation aux Ministres des Affairs Etrangères (Spaak Report)*. Brussels, 21 April 1956. Page references are to the provisional English text.

Commons, John R. "The delivered price practice in the steel market" *American Economic Review* 14(3), September 1924, pp. 505–519.

Conlisk, John, Eitan Gerstner and Joel Sobel "Cyclic pricing by a durable goods monopolist" *Quarterly Journal of Economics* 99(3), August 1984, pp. 489–505.

Connor, John M. "Archer Daniels Midland: Price-Fixer to the World" 4th edition, Purdue University Department of Agricultural Economics Staff Paper 00-11, 2000.

— "International price fixing: resurgence and deterrence" 26 October 2002

— "Price-fixing overcharges: legal and economic evidence" Staff Paper No. 04-17, Department of Agricultural Economics, Purdue University, revised 10 January 2005 downloaded 4 August 2005 (<http://www.agecon.purdue.edu/staff/connor/papers/PRICE%20FIXING_OVERCHARGES_FULL_TEXT_8-20-05.pdf>).

— *Global Price Fixing*. Springer, 2006.

Cook, P. Lesley and Ruth Cohen *Effects of Mergers*. London: George Allen & Unwin Ltd, 1958.

Cooke, C. A. "English law and monopolistic practices" *Journal of Industrial Economics* 2(1), November 1953, pp. 1–31.

Cool, Karel, Lars-Hendrik Röller, and Benoit Leleux "The relative impact of actual and potential rivalry on firm profitability in the pharmaceutical industry" *Strategic Management Journal* 20(1), January 1999, pp. 1–14.

Cooley, T. M. and C. H. Cooley "Transportation" in Nathaniel S. Shaler, editor, *The United States of America*. Volume II, pp. 65–133. New York: D. Appleton and Company, 1897.

Cooper, Arnold C. and D. Schendel "Strategic responses to technological threats" *Business Horizons* 19(1), February 1976, pp. 61–69.

Cooper, Russell W. and John C. Haltiwanger "On the nature of capital adjustment costs" *Review of Economic Studies* 73, 2006, pp. 611–633.

Cooper, Thomas E. "Most favored customer clauses and tacit collusion" *Rand Journal of Economics* 17 (1986), pp. 377–388.

Corley, T. A. B. "Emergence of the theory of industrial organization, 1890–1990" *Business and Economic History* second series 19, 1990, pp. 83–92.

Corts, Kenneth S. "Conduct parameters and the measurement of market power" *Journal of Econometrics* 88, 1999, pp. 227–250.

— "The strategic effects of vertical market structure: common agency and divisionalization in the US motion picture industry" *Journal of Economics and Management Strategy* 10(4), 2001, pp. 509–528.

Cotterill, Ronald W. "Market power in the retail food industry: evidence from Vermont" *Review of Economics and Statistics* 68(3), August 1986, pp. 379–386.

la Cour, Lisbeth Funding and H. Peter Møllgaard "Market domination: tests applied to the Danish cement industry" *European Journal of Law and Economics* 14(2), September 2002, pp. 99–127.

Cournot, Augustin *Researches into the Mathematical Principles of the Theory of Wealth*. Original Paris: L. Hachette, 1838. English translation by Nathaniel T. Bacon. New York: The Macmillan Company, 1897; reprinted 1927 by The Macmillan Company, New York with notes by Irving Fisher; reprinted 1960, 1964, 1971 by Augustus M. Kelley, New York.

Coursey, Don, R. Mark Isaac, and Vernon L. Smith "Natural monopoly and contested markets: some experimental results" *Journal of Law and Economics* 27(1), April 1984a, pp. 91–113.

Coursey, Don, R. Mark Isaac, Margaret Luke, and Vernon L. Smith "Market contestability in the presence of sunk (entry) costs" *Rand Journal of Economics* 15(1), Spring 1984b, pp. 69–84.

Cowan, Robin and Gert van de Paal *Innovation Policy in a Knowledge-Based Economy*. MERIT Study commissioned by the European Commission, DG Enterprise. June 2000.

Cowling, Keith "On the theoretical specification of industrial structure-performance relationships" *European Economic Review* 8(1), June 1976, pp. 1–14.

Cowling, Keith and Dennis C. Mueller "The social costs of monopoly power" *Economic Journal* 88, December 1978, pp. 727–748.

Cowling, Keith and Michael Waterson "Price-cost margins and market structure" *Economica* 43(171), August 1976, pp. 267–274.

Crandall, Robert W. and Clifford Winston "Does antitrust policy improve consumer welfare? Assessing the evidence" *Journal of Economic Perspectives* 17(4), Autumn 2003, pp. 3–26.

Cranmer, H. Jerome "Canal investment, 1815–1860" pp. 547–564 in National Bureau of Economic Research *Trends in the American Economy in the Nineteeth Century*. Princeton: Princeton University Press, 1960.

Crawford, Gregory S. "The discriminatory incentives to bundle in the cable television industry" 19 July 2005. Available at SSRN: <http://ssrn.com/abstract=829286>.

Crawford, Gregory S. and Joseph Cullen "Bundling, product choice, and efficiency: Should cable television networks be offered à la carte?" *Information Economics and Policy* 19, 2007, pp. 379–404.

Crémer, Jacques "Corporate culture and shared knowledge" *Industrial and Corporate Change* 2(3), 1993, pp. 351–386.

Creswell, Julie "When disillusion sets in" New York Times 24 February 2007, internet edition, <http://select.nytimes.com/search/restricted/article?res=F40A12FF3A5A0C778EDDAB0894DF404482>.

Crown, Judith and Glenn Coleman *No Hands: the Rise and Fall of the Schwinn Bicycle Company*. Harry Holt & Co., 1996.

Crum, William Leonard "Rudimentary mathematics for economists and statisticians" *Quarterly Journal of Economics* 52(Supplement), May 1938, pp. 1–164.

Cuaresma, Jesús and Adelina Gschwandtner "Tracing the dynamics of competition: evidence from company profits" *Economic Inquiry* (OnlineEarly Articles) doi:10.1111/j.1465-7295.2007.00062.x2007, 2007.

Cucinotta, Antonio, Roberto Pardolesi, and Roger Van den Bergh, editors, *Post-Chicago Developments in Antitrust Law*. Cheltenham, UK and Northampton, Massachusetts: Edward Elgar, 2002.

Cummings, F. Jay and Wayne E. Ruhter "The Northern Pacific case" *Journal of Law and Economics* 22(2), October 1979, pp. 329–350.

Cusumano, Michael A., Yiorgos Mylonadis, and Richard S. Rosenbloom "Strategic maneuvering and mass-market dynamics: the triumph of VHS over Beta" *Business History Review* 66(1), Spring 1992, pp. 51–94.

Cyert, Richard M. and Charles L. Hedrick "Theory of the firm: past, present, and future; an interpretation" *Journal of Economic Literature* 10(2), June 1972, pp. 398–412.

Cyert, Richard M. and James G. March *A Behavioral Theory of the Firm*. Englewood Cliffs, New Jersey: Prentice-Hall, Inc., 1963.

Czarnitzki, Dirk and Georg Licht "Additionality of public R&D grants in a transition economy: the case of Eastern Germany" *Economics of Transition* 14 (1), March 2006, pp. 101–131.

Dalton, James A. and Louis Esposito "Predatory price cutting and Standard Oil: a re-examination of the trial record" *Research in Law and Economics* 22, 2007, pp. 155–205.

Darnton, Robert "Google & the future of books" *New York Review of Books* 56(2), 12 February 2009, downloaded 24 February 2009 at <http://www.nybooks.com/articles/22281>.

Dasgupta, Partha and Paul A. David "Towards a new economics of science" *Policy Research* 23(5), September 1994, pp. 487–521.

Dasgupta, Partha and Eric Maskin "The simple economics of research portfolios" *Economic Journal* 97, September 1987, pp. 581–595.

Dasgupta, Partha, and Joseph Stiglitz "Industrial structure and the nature of innovative activity" *Economic Journal* 90(358), June 1980, pp. 266–293.

Datta, Deepak K. and V. K. Narayanan "A meta-analytic review of the concentration- performance relationship: aggregating findings in strategic management" *Journal of Management* 15(3), September 1989, pp. 469–483.

Daughety, Andrew F. "Introduction, purpose, and overview" pp. 3–44 in Daughety (1988).

— "Cournot Competition" in *The New Palgrave Dictionary of Economics*, 2nd edition, Steven N.

Durlauf and Lawrence E. Blume, editors, Basingstoke and New York: Palgrave Macmillan, forthcoming, 2007.

— , editor, *Cournot Oligopoly*. Cambridge: Cambridge University Press, 1988.

David, Paul A. "Clio and the economics of QWERTY" *American Economic Review* 75(2), 1985, pp. 332–337.

— "Intellectual property institutions and the panda's thumb: patents, copyrights, and trade secrets in economic theory and history" in Michael B. Wallerstein, Mary Ellen Mogree, and Roberta A. Schoen, editors, *Global Dimensions of Intellectual Property Rights in Science and Technology*. Washington, D.C.: National Academy Press, 1993, pp. 19–61.

David, Paul A., Bronwyn H. Hall, and Andrew A. Toole "Is public R&D a complement or substitute for private R&D? A review of the econometric evidence" *Research Policy* 29(4-5), April 2000, pp. 497–529.

David, Paul A., David Mowery, and W. Edward Steinmueller "Analyzing the economic payoffs from basic research" *Economics of Innovation and New Technology* 2, 1992, pp. 73–90.

Davies, J. H. "The industry and the representative firm" *Economic Journal* 65(260), December 1955, pp. 710–712.

Davies, Stephen W. and Paul A. Geroski "Changes in concentration, turbulance, and the dynamics of market shares" *Review of Economics and Statistics* 79(3), August 1997, pp. 383–391.

Davies, Stephen W. and Bruce Lyons, "Introduction" in Stephen Davies and Bruce Lyons, with Huw Dixon and Paul Geroski *Economics of Industrial Organization*. London and New York: Longman, 1989, pp. 1–25.

— *Industrial Organization in the European Union*. Oxford: Oxford University Press, 1996.

Davis, Douglas D. and Charles A. Holt *Experimental Economics*. Princeton: Princeton University Press, 1993.

— "Consumer search costs and market performance" *Economic Inquiry* 34, January 1996, pp. 133–151.

Deák, Francis "The place of the 'case' in the common and the civil law" *Tulane Law Review* 8, 1934, pp. 337–357.

— "Contracts and combinations in restraint of trade in French law—a comparative study" *Iowa Law Review* 21, 1936, pp. 397–454.

De Bondt, Raymond "Spillovers and innovative activities" *International Journal of Industrial Organization* 15(1), February 1997, pp. 1–28.

De Jong, Hendrik W. "Nederland: Het Kartelparadijs van Europa" *Economisch-Statistische Berichten* 75, 1990, pp. 244–248.

De Liso, Nicola and Giovanni Filatrella "Technological competition: a formal analysis of the 'sailing-ship' effect—or On optimal spending on R&D for an old technology" 9 May 2004.

de Long, J. Bradford "In defense of Henry Simons' standing as a classical liberal" *Cato Journal* 9(3), Winter 1990, pp. 601–618.

de Melo, Jaime and Patrick A. Messerlin "Price, quality and welfare effects of European VERs on Japanese autos" *European Economic Review* 32(7), September 1988, pp. 1527–1546.

Demsetz, Harold "Information and efficiency: another viewpoint" *Journal of Law and Economics* 12(1), April 1969, pp. 1–22.

— "Industry structure, market rivalry, and public policy" *Journal of Law and Economics* 16(1), April 1973, pp. 1–9.

— "Two systems of belief about monopoly" in Harvey J. Goldschmid, H. Michael Mann, and J. Fred Weston, editors, *Industrial Concentration: the New Learning*. Boston: Little, Brown & Company, 1974.

— "The structure of ownership and the theory of the firm" *Journal of Law and Economics* 26, 1983, pp. 375–390.

Demsetz, Harold and Kenneth Lehn "The structure of corporate ownership: causes and consequences" *Journal of Political Economy* 93, 1985, pp. 1155–1177.

de Roos, Nicolas "Examining models of collusion: the market for lysine" *International Journal of Industrial Organization* 24(6), November 2006, pp. 1083–1107.

DeVany, Arthur and W. David Walls "Bose-Einstein Dynamics and Adaptive Contracting in the Motion Picture Industry," *Economic Journal* 106(439), November 1996, pp. 1493–1514.

Dewatripont, Mathias, Victor Ginsburgh, Patrick Legros, Alexis Walckiers, Jean-Pierre Devroey, Marianne Dujardin, Françoise Vandooren, Pierre Dubois, Jérôme Foncel, Marc Ivaldi, and Marie-Dominique Heusse *Study on the Economic and Technical Evolution of the Scientific Publication Markets in Europe*. Brussels: European Commission, 2006. Downloaded 26 September 2007 at <http://ec.europa.eu/research/science-society/pdf/scientific-publication-study_en.pdf>.

Dewatripont, Mathias, Victor Ginsburgh, Patrick Legros, and Alexis Walckiers "Pricing of scientific journals and market power" *Journal of the European Economic Association* 5(2–3), April–May 2007, pp. 400–410.

Dewey, Donald *Monopoly in Economics and Law*. Chicago: Rand McNally & Company, 1959.

— *The Theory of Imperfect Competition*. New York: Columbia University Press, 1969.

— "Antitrust and its alternatives: a compleat guide to the welfare tradeoffs" in Ronald E. Grieson, editor, *Antitrust and Regulation*. Lexington, Massachusetts: Lexington Books, 1986, pp. 1–27.

— "Getting straight on monopoly and rent: a dissent from Wellington and Gallo" *Review of Industrial Organization* 9(2), April 1994, pp. 227–232.

de Wit, Gerrit "Firm size distributions: an overview of steady-state distributions resulting from firm dynamics models" *International Journal of Industrial Organization* 23(5–6), June 2005, pp. 423–450.

Diamond, Peter "A model of price adjustment" *Journal of Economic Theory* 3(2), June 1971, pp. 156–168.

Dick, Andrew R. "Are export cartels efficiency-enhancing or monopoly promoting?: evidence from the Webb-Pomerene experience" *Research in Law and Economics* 1992, pp. 89–127.

Dick, Andrew R. and John R. Lott Jr. "Comment on 'The role of potential competition in industrial organization' by Richard Gilbert, Summer 1989, pp. 107–27" *Journal of Economic Perspectives* 4(2), Spring 1990, pp. 213–215.

Diebold, William "A personal note" in K. Schwabe, editor, *Die Anfänge des Schumanplanes 1950/51. The Beginnings of the Schuman Plan*. Nomos Verlag, Baden-Baden 1988, pp. 23–31.

Dierickx, I., Carmen Matutes, and Damien Neven "Cost differences and survival in declining industries: a case for 'picking winners'?" *European Economic Review* 35(8), December 1991, pp. 1507–1528.

Dimand, Robert W. "Cournot, Bertrand, and Cherriman" *History of Political Economy* 27(3), 1995, pp. 563–578.

Dinopoulos, Elias and Mordechai E. Kreinin "Effects of the U.S.-Japan auto VER on European prices and on U.S. welfare" *Review of Economics and Statistics* 70(3), August 1988, pp. 484–491.

Director, Aaron "Prefatory note" pp. 5–7 in Henry C. Simons *Economic Policy for a Free Society*. Chicago & London: University of Chicago Press, 1948.

— "Review of *United States v. United Shoe Machinery Corporation: An Economic Analysis of an Anti-trust Case*" *University of Chicago Law Review* 24, 1957, pp. 606–611.

— "The parity of the economic market place" *Journal of Law and Economics* 7, October 1964, pp. 1–10.

Director, Aaron and Edward H. Levi "Law and the future: trade regulation" *Northwestern University Law Review* 51, 1956, pp. 281–296.

Directors General of European Competition Authorities *Principles for Leniency Programmes*. Dublin, 3 and 4 September 2001.

Dixit, Avinash "A model of duopoly suggesting a theory of entry barriers" *Bell Journal of Economics* 10(1), Spring 1979, pp. 20–32.

— "Hysteresis, import penetration, and exchange-rate pass-through" *Quarterly Journal of Economics* 104(2), 1989, pp. 205–228.

Dixit, Avinash and Victor Norman, "Advertising and welfare" *Bell Journal of Economics* 9(1), Spring 1978, pp. 1–17.

Dixit, Avinash K. and Robert S. Pindyck *Investment Under Uncertainty*. Princeton: Princeton University Press, 1994.

Dixit, Avinash and Nicholas Stern "Oligopoly and welfare—a unified presentation with applications to trade and development" *European Economic Review* 19(1), 1982, pp. 123–143.

Dixon, D. F. "The growth of competition among the Standard Oil Companies in the United States, 1911–1961" *Business History* 9(1), 1967, pp. 1–29.

Dixon, Huw "The general theory of household and market contingent demand" *The Manchester School*" 55, 1987, pp. 287–304.

Djelic, Marie Laure *Exporting the American Model: the Postwar Transformation of European Business*. Oxford: Oxford University Press, 1998.

Dobson, Paul and Michael Waterson "Retailer power: recent developments and policy implications" *Economic Policy* 14(28), April 1999, pp. 133–164.

Dockner, E. J. "A dynamic theory of conjectural variations" *Journal of Industrial Economics* 40, 1992, pp. 377–395.

Doi, Noriyuki "Aggregate export concentration in Japan" *Journal of Industrial Economics* 39(4), June 1991, pp. 433–438.

Domeratzky, Louis "Cartels and the business crisis" *Foreign Affairs* 10(1), October 1931, pp. 34–53.

Domhoff, G. William *The Higher Circles*. New York: Vintage Books, 1971.

Donaldson, Gordon "Voluntary restructuring: the case of General Mills" *Journal of Financial Economics* 27, 1990, pp. 117–141.

Doraszelski, Ulrich "An R&D race with knowledge accumulation" *Rand Journal of Economics* 34(1), Spring 2003, pp. 20–42.

Dorfman, Joseph *The Economic Mind in American Civilization*. New York: The Viking Press, 1949.

— "John Bates and John Maurice Clark on monopoly and competition" introductory essay in John Bates Clark and John Maurice Clark *The Control of Trusts*. New York: Augustus M. Kelly Reprints of Economic Classics, 1971.

Dorfman, Robert and Peter O. Steiner "Optimal advertising and optimal quality" *American Economic Review* 44(5), pp. 826–836.

Dosi, Giovanni, Franco Malerba, Giovanni B. Ramello and Francesco Silva "Information, appropriability, and the generation of innovative knowledge four decades after Arrow and Nelson: an introduction" *Industrial and Corporate Change* 15(6), 2006, pp. 891–901.

Downs, Anthony *An Economic Theory of Democracy*. New York: Harper & Row, 1957.

Dumez, Hervé and Alain Jeunemaître *Understanding and Regulating the Market at a Time of Globalization. The Case of the Cement Industry*. Basingstoke, U.K.: Macmillan Press Ltd and New York: St. Martin's Press, 2000.

Dunne, Timothy, Shawn D. Klimek, and Mark J. Roberts "Exit from regional manufacturing markets: the role of entrant experience" *International Journal of Industrial Organization* 23(5-6), June 2005, pp. 399–421.

Dunne, Timothy and Mark J. Roberts "Costs, demand, and imperfect competition as determinants of plant-level prices" pp. 13–33 in David B. Audretsch and John J. Siegfried, editors, *Empirical Studies in Industrial Organization. Essays in Honor of Leonard W. Weiss*. Dordrecht and elsewhere: Kluwer Academic Publishers, 1992.

Dunne, Timothy, Mark J. Roberts, and Larry Samuelson "Patterns of firm entry and exit in U.S. manufacturing industries" *Rand Journal of Economics* 19(4), Winter 1988, pp. 495–515.

— "The growth and failure of U. S. manufacturing plants" *Quarterly Journal of Economics* 104(4), November 1989, pp. 671–698.

Durand, E. Dana "The trust problem" *Quarterly Journal of Economics* 28(3), May 1914a, pp. 381–416, and 28(4), August 1914b, pp. 664–700.

— "The trust legislation of 1914" *Quarterly Journal of Economics* 29(1), November 1914c, pp. 72–97.

Durham, Wayne R. "The determination of antitrust liability in United States v. Microsoft: the empirical evidence the Department of Justice used to prove its case" *Journal of Competition Law and Economics* 2(4), December 2006, pp. 549–671.

Dutz, Mark A. "Horizontal mergers in declining industries: theory and evidence" *International Journal of Industrial Organization* 7(1), March 1989, pp. 11–33.

Duysters, Geert and John Hagedoorn, "Convergence and divergence in the international information technology industry" pp. 205–234 in John Hagedoorn, editor, *Technical Change and the World Economy: Convergence and Divergence in Technology Strategies*, Edward Elgar Publishing, Aldershot, 1995.

— "Internationalization of corporate technology through strategic partnering: an empirical investigation" *Research Policy* 25, 1996 1–12.

Easterbrook, Frank H. "Predatory strategies and counterstrategies" *University of Chicago Law Review* 48(2), Spring 1981, pp. 263–337.

Eaton, B. Curtis and Richard G. Lipsey "Exit barriers are entry barriers: the durability of capital as a barrier to entry" *Bell Journal of Economics* 11(2), Autumn 1980, pp. 721–729.

Ebb, Lawrence F. "The Grundig-Consten case revisited: judicial harmonization of national law and treaty law in the Common Market" *University of Pennsylvania Law Review* 115(60), April 1967, pp. 855–889.

EC Commission *First Report on Competition Policy*. Brussels–Luxembourg April 1972.

— *Second Report on Competition Policy*. Brussels–Luxembourg April 1973.

— *Third Report on Competition Policy*. Brussels–Luxembourg April 1974.

— *Twenty-Five Years of the Common Market in Coal: 1953–1978*. Brussels–Luxembourg, 1977b.

— *14th Annual Report on Competition Policy 1984*. Brussels–Luxembourg, 1985.

— *NACE Rev. 1*. Luxembourg: Office for Official Publications of the European Communities, 1996.

— "Measuring seller concentration in European industry" *Monthly Panorama of European Industry*, 1997, pp. 69–84.

— *White Paper on the Modernisation of the Rules Implementing Articles 81 and 82 of the EC Treaty*. Brussels, 28 April 1999a.

— *XXVIIIth Report on Competition Policy 1998*. Brussels–Luxembourg, 1999b.

— *Guidelines on the Assessment of Horizontal Mergers under the Council Regulation on the Control of Concentrations Between Undertakings* (2004/C 31/03) <http://ec.europa.eu/competition/mergers/legislation/notices_on_substance.html#hor_guidelines>.

— , DG Competition *Merger Remedies Study*, Public version. October 2005a.

— , DG Competition "On the application of Article 82 of the Treaty to exclusionary abuses" Discussion Paper, Brussels, December 2005. <http://europa.eu.int/comm/competition/antitrust/others/discpaper2005.pdf>).

— *State Aid Scoreboard Spring 2007 Update* COM(2007) 347 final Brussels 28 June 2007.

— *Impact Assessment on the Legal and Economic Situation of Performers and Record Producers in the European Union*. Commission Staff Working Document SEC(2008) xxxx, Brussels, 23 April 2008a.

– "Commission Proposal on a Directive for Term Extension—Frequently Asked Questions" MEMO/08/508 Brussels, 16 July 2008b (<http://europa.eu/rapid/pressReleasesAction.do?reference=IP/08/1156>).

— , DG Competition "Pharmaceutical Sector Inquiry Preliminary Report" DG Competition Staff Working Paper, 28 November 2008c (<http://ec.europa.eu/competition/sectors/pharmaceuticals/inquiry/index.html>).

— "Antitrust: preliminary report on pharmaceutical sector inquiry highlights cost of pharma companies' delaying tactics" Press release IP/08/1829, Brussels, 28th November 2008d (<http://europa.eu/rapid/pressReleasesAction. do?reference=IP/08/1829>).

— *Guidelines on the Assessment of Non-Horizontal Mergers under the Council Regulation on the Control of Concentrations between Undertakings* OJ C 256/6 18 October 2008e; <http://eur-lex.europa.eu/LexUriServ/LexUriServ.do?uri=CELEX:52008XC1018(03):EN:NOT>.

— *General Budget of the European Union for the Financial Year 2009*. Brussels, January 2009a.

— *State Aid Scoreboard Spring 2009 Update* COM(2009) 164 Brussels 8 April 2009b.

— *Temporary Community Framework for State Aid Measures to Support Access to Finance in the Current Financial and Economic Crisis*. OJ C 83/1 7 April 2009c.

Eckbo, B. Espen and Peggy Wier "Antimerger Policy under the Hart-Scott-Rodino Act: a reexamination of the market power hypothesis" *Journal of Law and Economics* 28(1), April 1985, pp. 119–149.

Economic Advisory Group on Competition Policy (EAGCP) "An economic approach to Article 82" July 2005, downloaded 23 May 2007 at <http://ec.europa.eu/comm/competition/publications/studies/eagcp_july_21_05.pdf>

Economides, Nicholas "The economics of networks" *International Journal of Industrial Organization* 14(6), October 1996, pp. 673–699.

— "The Microsoft antitrust case" *Journal of Industry, Competition and Trade* 1(1), 2001, pp. 7–39.

Economides, Nicholas and Frederick Flyer "Compatibility and market structure for network goods" manuscript, Stern School of Business, New York University, November 1997.

Eddy, Arthur Jerome *The New Competition*. Chicago: A. C. McClurg & Co., 1913.

Edgeworth, F. Y. "The pure theory of monopoly" *Papers relating to political economy*. Volume I. Royal Economic Society, London, 1925, pp. 111–142 (translation of "Teoria pura del monopolio" *Giornale degli Economisti*, July 1897, pp. 13–31; October 1897, pp. 307–320; November 1897, pp. 405–414).

— "Cournot" in Henry Higgs, editor, *Palgrave's Dictionary of Political Economy*. Volume I, pp. 445–447. London: Macmillan and Co., Limited, 1926.

Edlin, Aaron S. "Do guaranteed-low-price policies guarantee high prices, and can antitrust rise to the challenge?" *Harvard Law Review* 111, 1997, pp. 528–575.

Edlin, Aaron and Daniel L. Rubinfeld "The bundling of academic journals" *American Economic Review* 5(2), May 2005, pp. 441–446.

Edmunds, George F. "The Interstate Trust and Commerce Act of 1890" *North American Review* 94(673), December 1911, pp. 801–817.

Edstrom, Jennifer and Marlin Eller *Barbarians Led by Bill Gates*. New York: Henry Holt and Company, 1998.

Edwards, Corwin D. "Antitrust policy during rearmament" *American Economic Review* 42(2), May 1952, pp. 404–417.

— "Conglomerate bigness as a source of power" in Universities-National Bureau Committee for Economic Research *Business Concentration and Price Policy*. Princeton: Princeton University Press, 1955, pp. 331–352.

— *Cartelization in Western Europe*. U.S. Department of State, Bureau of Intelligence and Research, June 1964.

— "Testimony" pp. 36–56 in *Evidence in Economic Concentration: Part 1, Overall and Conglomerate Aspects.* Hearings before the Subcommittee on Antitrust and Monopoly of the Committee of the Judiciary, United States Senate. Washington, 1964.

Edwards, Richard C. "Stages in corporate stability and the risks of corporate failure" *Journal of Economic History* 15(2), June 1975, pp. 428–457.

Ehlermann, Claus-Dieter "The contribution of EC competition policy to the single market" *Common Market Law Review* 29, April 1992, pp. 257–282.

Eichengreen, Barry "The inter-war economy in a European mirror" in Roderick Floud and Donald McCloskey, editors, *The Economic History of Britain Since 1700.* Volume 2: 1860–1939. Cambridge, England and New York: Cambridge University Press, 2nd edition, 1994, pp. 291–319.

Eichenwald, Kurt *The Informant: a True Story.* New York: Broadway Books, 2000.

Eichner, Alfred S. *The Emergence of Oligopoly: Sugar Refining as a Case Study.* Baltimore and London: Johns Hopkins University Press, 1969.

— "Monopoly, the emergence of oligopoly and the case of sugar refining: a reply" *Journal of Law and Economics* 14(2), October 1971, pp. 521–527.

Eis, Carl "The 1919–1930 merger movement in American industry" *Journal of Law and Economics* 12(2), October 1969, pp. 267–296.

Ekelund, Robert B. Jr. "Economic empiricism in the writing of early railway engineers" *Explorations in Economic History* 9(2), Winter 1971–1972, pp. 179–196.

Ekelund, Robert B. Jr. and Robert F. Hébert "E. H. Chamberlin and contemporary industrial organisation theory" *Journal of Economic Studies* 17(2), 1990a, pp. 20–31.

— "Cournot and his contemporaries: is an obituary the only bad review?" *Southern Economic Journal* 57(1), July 1990b, pp. 139–149.

— *Secret Origins of Modern Microeconomics. Dupuit and the Engineers.* Chicago & London: University of Chicago Press, 1999.

Ekelund, Robert B. Jr., Donald R. Street, and Robert D. Tollison "Rent seeking and property rights' assignments as a process: the Mesta Cartel of medieval-mercantile Spain" in *Journal of European Economic History* 26(1), Spring 1997, pp. 9–35.

El-Agraa, Ali "VERs as a prominent feature of Japanese trade policy: their rationale, costs and benefits" *World Economy* 18(2), 1995, pp. 219–235.

Ellickson, Paul B. "Does Sutton apply to supermarkets?" *Rand Journal of Economics* 38(1), Spring 2007, pp. 43–59.

Ellison, Glenn "Theories of cartel stability and the Joint Executive Committee" *Rand Journal of Economics* 25(1), Spring 1994, pp. 37–57.

Elzinga, Kenneth "The antimerger law: pyrrhic victories?" *Journal of Law and Economics* 12(1), April 1969, pp. 43–78.

— "Walter Adams and Chicago" *Review of Industrial Organization* 6(2), 1991, pp. 117–132.

Elzinga, Kenneth G., and David E. Mills "Switching costs in the wholesale distribution of cigarettes" *Southern Economic Journal* 65(2), October 1998, pp. 282–293.

— "Price wars triggered by entry" *International Journal of Industrial Organization* 17(2), February 1999, pp. 179–198.

Elzinga, Kenneth G., and Thomas F. Hogarty "The problem of geographic market delineation in antimerger suits" *Antitrust Bulletin* 18, 1973, pp. 45.

— "Utah Pie and the consequences of Robinson-Patman" *Journal of Law and Economics* 21(2), October 1978, pp. 427–434.

Emerson, Michael, Michel Aujean, Michel Catinat, Philippe Goybet, and Alexis Jacquemin *The Economics of 1992: The E.C. Commission's Assessment of the Economic Effects of Completing the Internal Market.* Oxford: Oxford University Press, 1988.

Encaoua, David and Alexis Jacquemin "Organizational efficiency and monopoly power" *European Economic Review* 19(1), 1982, pp. 25–51.

Engel, Christoph "How much collusion? A meta-analysis of oligopoly experiments" *Journal of Competition Law and Economics* 3(4), 2007, pp. 491–549.

Epstein, Ralph C. *Industrial Profits in the United States.* New York: National Bureau of Economic Research, 1934.

Erickson, Walter B. *Price Fixing Under the Sherman Act: Case Studies in Conspiracy.* Ph.D. dissertation, Michigan State University, 1965.

— "Economics of price fixing" *Antitrust Law and Economics Review* 2(3), Spring 1969, pp. 83–122.

Ericson, Richard and Ariel Pakes "Markov-perfect industry dynamics: a framework for empirical work" *Review of Economic Studies* 62(1), January 1995, pp. 53–82.

— "Empirical implications of alternative models of firm dynamics" *Journal of Economic Theory* 79(1), March 1998, pp. 1–45.

Eriksson, Tor and Johan Moritz Kuhn "Firm spin-offs in Denmark 1981-2000—patterns of entry and exit" *International Journal of Industrial Organization* 24(5), September 2006, pp. 1021–1040.

Esposito, L. and F. F. Esposito "Foreign competition and domestic industry profitability" *Review of Economics and Statistics* 53, November 1971, pp. 343–353.

Estrin, Saul and Peter Holmes *French Planning in Theory and Practice.* London: Geroge Allen & Unwin, 1983.

Evans, David S. "The antitrust economics of two-sided markets" AEI-Brookings Joint Center for Regulatory Studies Related Publication 02–13, September 2002.

Evans, William N. and Ioannis N. Kessides "Localized market power in the US airline industry" *Review of Economics and Statistics* 75(1), February 1993, pp. 66–75.

— "Living by the 'golden rule': multimarket contact in the U.S. airline industry" *Quarterly Journal of Economics* 109(2), May 1994, pp. 341–366.

Faccio, Mara and Larry H. P. Lang "The ultimate ownership of Western European corporations" *Journal of Financial Economics* 65, 2002, pp. 365–395.

Fakhfakh, Fathi and Felix FitzRoy "Basic wages and firm characteristics: rent-sharing in French manufacturing" Ermes Working Paper 02-15, Université Paris II, revised October 2002.

Fama, Eugene F. "Agency problems and the theory of the firm" *Journal of Political Economy* 88(2), April 1980, pp. 288–307.

Farmer, Hallie "The economic background of frontier populism" *Mississippi Valley Historical Review* 10(4), March 1924, pp. 406–427.

Farrell, Joseph and Michael L. Katz "The economics of welfare standards in antitrust" *Competition Policy International* 2(2), November 2006, pp. 3–28.

Farrell, Joseph and Carl Shapiro "Horizontal mergers: an equilibrium analysis" *American Economic Review* 80(1), March 1990, pp. 107–126.

Farris, Paul W. and Mark S. Albion "The impact of advertising on the price of consumer goods" *Journal of Marketing* 44(3), Summer 1980, pp. 17–35.

Feenstra, Robert C. "Quality change under trade restraints in Japanese autos" *Quarterly Journal of Economics* 1988, pp. 101–146.

— "Symmetric pass-through of tariffs and exchange rates under imperfect competition: an empirical test" *Journal of International Economics* 27, August 1989, pp. 25–45.

Feinberg, Robert M. and Joseph Shaanan "The relative price discipline of domestic versus foreign entry" *Review of Industrial Organization* 9(2), April 1994, pp. 211–220.

Feldenkirchen, Wilfried "Big business in Interwar Germany: organizational innovation at Vereinigte Stahlwerke, IG Farben, and Siemens" *Business History Review* 61(3), Autumn 1987, pp. 417–451.

Ferdinandusse, Ernst "The Commission fines FEG, the Dutch association of electrical equipment wholesalers and its biggest member TU" *Competition Policy Newsletter* 2000(1), February 2000, pp. 17–18.

Fetter, Frank A. *The Masquerade of Monopoly*. First edition, New York: Harcourt, Brace & Company, 1931. Reprinted New York: Augustus M. Kelley Publishers, 1971.

— "Discussion," pp. 14–19 in Milton Handler, *The Federal Anti-Trust Laws*. Chicago: Commerce Clearing House, Inc., 1932a.

— "The economists' Committee on Anti-Trust Law Policy" *American Economic Review* 22(3), September 1932b, pp. 465–469.

Feuerstein, Switgard "Collusion in industrial economics—a survey" *Journal of Industry, Competition and Trade* 5(3/4), 2005, pp. 163–198.

Fields, M. J. "The International Mercantile Marine Company—an ill-conceived trust" *Journal of Business* 5(3), July, 1932a, pp. 268–282.

— "The International Mercantile Marine Company—an ill-conceived trust (concluded)" *Journal of Business* 5(4), July, 1932b, pp. 268–282.

— "Stabilizing the anti-trust laws" *Journal of Business* 6(3), July 1933, pp. 191–214.

Filson, Darren, Eric Fruits, Edward Keen, and Thomas Borcherding "Market power and cartel formation: theory and an empirical test" *Journal of Law and Economics* 44, October 2001, pp. 465–480.

Fingleton, John, Frances Ruane, and Vivienne Ryan "Market definition and State Aid control" *European Economy* 3, 1999, pp. 65–88.

Fiorito, Luca and John F. Henry "John Bates Clark on trusts: new light from the Columbia archives" Università degli Studi di Siena, Dipartimento di Economia Politica, Quaderni No. 462, September 2005.

Fisher, Franklin M. "Alcoa revisited: comment" *Journal of Economic Theory* 9, 1974, pp. 357–359.

— "Diagnosing monopoly" *Quarterly Review of Economics and Business* 19(2), Summer 1979, pp. 7–33.

— "The social costs of monopoly and regulation: Posner reconsidered" *Journal of Political Economy* 93(2), April 1985, pp. 410–416.

— "On the misuse of the profit-sales ratio to infer monopoly power" *Rand Journal of Economics*, 18(3), Autumn 1987, pp. 384–96.

— "Comments" *Brookings Papers on Economic Activity: Microeconomics* 1990, pp. 192–194.

Fisher, Franklin M. and John J. McGowan "On the misuse of accounting rates of return to infer monopoly profits" *American Economic Review* 73 March 1983, pp. 82–97.

Fisher, Irving *A Brief Guide to the Infinitesimal Calculus*. New York: Macmillan Press, 1897; reprinted Norwood, Massachusetts: Norwood Press.

— "Cournot and mathematical economics" *Quarterly Journal of Economics* 12(2), 1898, pp. 119–138.

Fisher, Waldo E. and Charles M. James *Minimum Price Fixing in the Bituminous Coal Industry*. Princeton: Princeton University Press, 1955.

Fiss, Owen M. *Troubled Beginnings of the Modern State, 1888–1910. Oliver Wendell Holmes Devise History of the Supreme Court of the United States*, Volume VIII. New York: Macmillan Publishing Company, 1993.

Flam, Harry "EC members fighting about surplus VERS, FDI, and Japanese cars" *Journal of International Economics* 36, 1994, pp. 117–131.

Flynn, John J. "The Reagan administration's antitrust policy, 'original intent' and the legislative history of the Sherman Act" *Antitrust Bulletin* 33(2), Summer 1988, pp. 259–307.

— "Antitrust policy, innovation efficiencies, and the suppression of technology" *Antitrust Law Journal* 66, 1998, pp. 487ff.

Flynn, Laurie J. "After long dispute, two Apples work it out" *New York Times* internet edition, 6 February 2007.

Focsaneanu, L. "La notion d'abus dans le système de l'article 86 du traité instituant la Communauté Économique Européenne" pp. 324–380 in J. A. van Damme, editor, *Regulating the Behavior of Monopolies and Dominant Undertakings in Community Law*. Bruges: De Tempel, 1977.

Fog, Bjarke "How are cartel prices determined?" *Journal of Industrial Economics* 5(1), November 1956, pp. 16–23.

Forchheimer, Karl "Theoretisches zum unvollstandigen Monopole" *Schmoller's Jahrbuch für Gesetzgebung, Verwaltung und Volkswirtschaft*, XXXII 1908, 1–12.

Foreman-Peck, James "Industry and industrial organisation in the inter-war years" in Roderick Floud and Donald McCloskey, editors, *The Economic History of Britain Since 1700*. Volume 2: 1860–1939. Cambridge, England and New York: Cambridge University Press, 2nd edition, 1994, pp. 386–414.

Forkosch, Morris D. "Economics of American patent law, II" *New York University Law Quarterly Review* 17, 1939–1940, pp. 422–423.

Fortune Magazine "The 30,000 managers" 21(2), February 1940, pp. 58–62, 106–111.

Fourastié, Jean *Documents Pour l'Histoire et la Théorie des Prix*. Paris: Colin, 1959.

Fournier, Leslie T. "The purposes and results of the *Webb-Pomerene* law" *American Economic Review* 22, 1932, pp. 18–33.

Fraas, Arthur and Douglas F. Greer "Market structure and price collusion: an empirical analysis" *Journal of Industrial Economics* 26(1), September 1977, pp. 21–44.

Frantz, Roger S. *X-Efficiency: Theory, Evidence and Applications*. Boston and elsewhere: Kluwer Academic Publishers, 1997.

Frasco, Gregg P. "Exclusive dealing and the Pullman Sleeping Car Corporation" *Review of Industrial Organization* 7(2), June 1992, pp. 227–240.

Freeland, Robert F. "Creating holdup through vertical integration: Fisher Body revisited" *Journal of Law and Economics* 43(1), April 2000, pp. 33–66.

— *The Struggle for Control of the Modern Corporation: Organizational Change at General Motors, 1924–1970*. Cambridge: Cambridge University Press, 2005.

Freeman, Donald B. and Frances L. Dungey "A spatial duopoly: competition in the western Canadian fur trade, 1770–1835" *Journal of Historical Geography* 7(3), July 1981, pp. 252–270.

Fridenson, Patrick "France: the relatively slow development of big business in the twentieth century" in Alfred D. Chandler, Jr., Franco Amatori, and Takashi Hikino, editors *Big Business and the Wealth of Nations*. Cambridge: Cambridge University Press, 1997, pp. 207–245.

Friederszick, Hans W., Lars-Hendrik Röller, and Vincent Verouden "European state aid control: an economic framework" 30 September 2006, forthcoming in Paolo Buccirossi, editor, *Handbook of Antitrust Economics*, Cambridge, Massachusetts: MIT Press, 2008.

Friedman, David D. "In defense of the long-haul/short-haul discrimination" *Bell Journal of Economics* 10(2), Autumn, 1979, pp. 706–708.

Friedman, David D., William M. Landes, and Richard A. Posner "Some economics of trade secret law" *Journal of Economic Perspectives* 5(1), Winter 1991, pp. 61–72.

Friedman, James W. "A non-cooperative equilibrium for supergames" *Review of Economic Studies* 38(1), January 1971, pp. 1–12, reprinted in Andrew F. Daughety, editor, *Cournot Oligopoly: Characterization and Applications*. Cambridge: Cambridge University Press, 1988, pp. 142–157.

— "Advertising and oligopolistic equilibrium" *Bell Journal of Economics* 14(2), Autumn 1983, pp. 464–473.

Friedman, Milton "Comment" in in Universities-National Bureau Committee for Economic Research *Business Concentration and Price Policy*, Princeton: Princeton University Press, 1955, pp. 230–238.

— *Capitalism and Freedom*. Chicago and London: University of Chicago Press, 1962, 1982.

Friedman, Walter A. "John H. Patterson and the sales strategy of the National Cash Register Company, 1884 to 1922" *Business History Review* 72(4), Winter 1998, pp. 552–584.

Friedmann, W. "The Harris Tweed case and freedom of trade" *Modern Law Review* 6(1/2), December 1942, pp. 1–21.

Friedrich, Carl J. "The political thought of neo-liberalism" *American Political Science Review* 49(2), June 1955, pp. 509–525.

Frisch, Ragnar "Monopole—polypole—la notion de force dans l'économie" *Nationalokonomisk Tidsskrift* 1933, pp. 241–259; reprinted in English translation in *International Economic Papers* No. 1, London: Macmillan and Company Limited and New York: The Macmillan Company, 1951, pp. 23–35.

Fudenberg, Drew, Richard Gilbert, Joseph Stiglitz and Jean Tirole "Preemption, leapfrogging and competition in patent races" *European Economic Review* 22(1), June 1983, pp. 3–31.

Fudenberg, Drew and Jean Tirole "A 'signal-jamming' theory of predation" *Rand Journal of Economics* 17(3), Autumn 1986, pp. 366–376.

— "Understanding rent dissipation: on the use of game theory in industrial organization" *American Economic Review* 77(2), May 1987, pp. 176–183.

Gabel, David "Competition in a network industry: the telephone industry, 1894–1910" *Journal of Economic History* 54(3), September 1994, pp. 543–572.

Gabel, Richard "The early competitive era in telephone communication, 1893–1920," *Law and Contemporary Problems* 34(2), Spring, 1969, pp. 340–359.

Gadhoum, Yoser, Larry H. P. Laing, and Leslie Young "Who controls US?" *European Financial Management* 11(3), 2005, pp. 339–363.

Galambos, Louis "The agrarian image of the large corporation, 1879–1920: a study in social accommodation" *Journal of Economic History* 28(3), September 1968, pp. 341–362.

Galbraith, John Kenneth *American Capitalism: The Concept of Countervailing Power*. Boston: Houghton Mifflin, 1952.

— "Countervailing Power" *American Economic Review* 44(2), May, 1954, pp. 1–6.

Gallini, Nancy and Larry Karp "Sales and consumer lock-in" *Economica* n.s. 56(223), August 1989, pp. 279–294.

Gallo, Joseph C., Kenneth Dau-Schmidt, Joseph L. Craycraft, and Charles J. Parker "Department of Justice antitrust enforcement, 1955–1997: an empirical study" *Review of Industrial Organization* 17(1), August 2000, pp. 75–133.

Gandal, Neil "Compatibility, standardization, and network effects: some policy implications" *Oxford Review of Economic Policy* 18(1), 2001, pp. 80–91.

García Gallego, Aurora and Nikolaos Geogantzis "Dominance in the Tetra Pak case: an empirical approach" *European Journal of Law and Economics* 7(2), March 1999, pp. 137–160.

Garner, James Wilford "The Northern Securities case" *Annals of the American Academy of Political and Social Science* 24(1), July 1904, pp. 125–147.

Gaskins, Darius W. Jr. "Dynamic limit pricing: optimal limit pricing under threat of entry" *Journal of Economic Theory* 3, September 1971, pp. 306–322.

Gates, Paul W. "The railroad land-grant legend" *Journal of Economic History* 14(2), Spring 1954, pp. 143–146.

Gates, William H. "The Internet Tidal Wave" May 26, 1995; Government Exhibit 20.

Geithman, Frederick E., Howard P. Marvel, and Leonard W. Weiss "Concentration, price and critical concentration ratios" *Review of Economics and Statistics* 63(3), August 1981, pp. 346–353.

Genesove, David and Wallace P. Mullin "Predation and its rate of return: the sugar industry, 1887–1914" MIT Economics Department Working Paper, 1997.

— "Testing static oligopoly models: conduct and cost in the sugar industry, 1890–1914" *Rand Journal of Economics* 29(2), Summer 1998, pp. 355–377.

— "The Sugar Institute learns to organize information exchange" in Naomi Lamoreaux, Daniel M. G. Raff, and Peter Temin, editors, *Learning by Doing in Markets, Firms, and Countries*. Chicago: University of Chicago Press, 1999, pp. 103–138.

— "Rules, communication, and collusion: Narrative evidence from the Sugar Institute case" *American Economic Review* 91(3), June 2001, pp. 379–398.

Georgrantzis, Nikolaos and Gerardo Sabater-Grande "Market transparency and collusion: on the UK Agricultural Tractor Registration Exchange" *European Journal of Law and Economics* 14(2), September 2002, pp. 129–150.

Gerber, David J. "Constitutionalizing the economy: German neo-liberalism, competition law and the 'new' Europe" *American Journal of Comparative Law* 42(1), Winter 1994, pp. 25–84.

— *Law and Competition in Twentieth Century Europe. Protecting Prometheus*. Oxford: Oxford University Press, 1998.

— "Economic constitutionalism and the challenge of globalization: the enemy is gone? Long live the enemy" *Journal of Institutional and Theoretical Economics* 157(1), March 2001, pp. 14–22.

Gerbet, Pierre "La genèse du Plan Schuman" *Revue Française de Science Politique* 6(3), 1956, pp. 525–553.

Geroski, Paul A. "Modeling persistent profitability" pp. 15–34 in Dennis C. Mueller, editor, *The Dynamics of Company Profits: An International Comparison*. Cambridge: Cambridge University Press, 1990.

— *Market Dynamics and Entry*. Oxford: Basil Blackwell, 1991.

— "What do we know about entry?" *International Journal of Industrial Organization* 13(4), 1995, pp. 421–440.

— "Is competition policy worth it?" Speech at the ESRC Centre for Competition Policy, University of East Anglia, 14 September 2004.

— "Understanding the implications of empirical work on corporate growth rates" *Managerial and Decision Economics* 26, 2005, pp. 129–138.

Geroski, Paul and Rachel Griffith "Identifying anti-trust markets" Institute for Fiscal Studies WP03/01, January 2003.

Geroski, Paul A. and Alexis Jacquemin "Dominant firms and their alleged decline" *International Journal of Industrial Organization* 2(1), March 1984, pp. 1–27.

Geroski, Paul A. and Dennis C. Mueller "The persistence of profit in perspective" pp. 187–204 in Dennis C. Mueller, editor, *The Dynamics of Company Profits: An International Comparison*. Cambridge: Cambridge University Press, 1990.

Geroski, Paul and Joachim Schwalbach, editors, *Entry and Market Contestability*. Oxford, UK and Cambridge, Massachusetts: Blackwell, 1991.

Geroski, Paul A. and Saadet Toker "The turnover of market leaders in UK manufacturing industry, 1979–86" *International Journal of Industrial Organization* 14(2), 1996, pp. 141–158.

Gerstner, Eitan, James D. Hess and Duncan M. Holthausen "Price discrimination through a distribution channel: theory and evidence" *American Economic Review* 84(5), December 1994, pp. 1437–1445.

Ghemawat, Pankaj "Competition and business strategy in historical perspective" *Business History Review* 76(1), Spring 2002, pp. 37–74.

Ghemawat, Pankaj and Barry Nalebuff "The devolution of declining industries" *Quarterly Journal of Economics* 105, 1990, pp. 167–168.

Gibbons, Robert *Game Theory for Applied Economists*. Princeton: Princeton University Press, 1992.

— "Four formal(izable) theories of the firm" *Journal of Economic Behavior and Organization* 58(2), October 2005, pp. 200–245.

Gibrat, Robert *Les Inégalités Économiques*. Paris: Librairie du Recueil Sirey, 1931.

Gibson, George R. "A lampful of oil" *Harper's New Monthly Magazine* 72(428), January 1886, pp. 235–257.

Giddings, Franklin H. "The persistence of competition" *Political Science Quarterly* 2(1), March 1887, pp. 62–78.

Gilbert, Richard J. "The role of potential competition in industrial organization" *Journal of Economic Perspectives* 3(3), Summer, 1989, pp. 107–127.

— "Antitrust for patent pools: a century of policy evolution" *Stanford Technology Law Review* 3, 2004.

— "Looking for Mr. Schumpeter: where are we in the competition–innovation debate?" *NBER Innovation Policy & the Economy* 6, 2006, pp. 159–215.

Gilbert, Richard J. and Michael L. Katz "An economist's guide to U.S. *v.* Microsoft" *Journal of Economic Perspectives* 15(2), Spring, 2001, pp. 25–44.

Gilbert, Richard J. and David M. G. Newbery "Preemptive patenting and the persistence of monopoly" *American Economic Review* 72(3), June 1982, pp. 514–526.

Gilfillan, S. Colum *Inventing The Ship*. Chicago: Follett Publishing Company, 1935.

Gilligan, Thomas W. "Imperfect competition and basing-point pricing" *Economic Inquiry* 31, July 1993, pp. 394–409.

Gillingham, John *Coal, Steel, and the Rebirth of Europe 1945–1955*. Cambridge: Cambridge University Press, 1991.

Giocoli, Nicola, "Competition vs. property rights: American antitrust law, the Freiburg School and the early years of European competition policy " May

2007. Available at SSRN: <http://ssrn.com/abstract=987788>.

Giuletti, Monica, Catherine Waddams Price, and Michael Waterson "Consumer choice and competition policy: a study of UK energy markets" *Economic Journal* 115(506), October 2005, pp. 949–968.

Glazer, Amihai "Advertising, information, and prices—a case study" *Economic Inquiry* 19(4), October 1981, pp. 661–671.

Gleick, James "Patently absurd" *New York Times Magazine*, 12 March 2000; available at <http://www.nytimes.com/library/magazine/home/20000312mag-patents.html.>

Global Competition Review *Handbook of Competition Enforcement Agencies 2009*. Downloaded 5 August 2009 from <http://www.globalcompetitionreview.com/handbooks/15/the-handbook-competition-enforcement-agencies-2009/>.

Glover, J. D. *The Attack on Big Business*. Boston: Division of Research, Graduate School of Business Administration, Harvard University, 1954.

Glowicka, Ela "Effectiveness of bailouts in the EU" GESY Discussion Paper No. 176, October 2006.

Goddard, J. A. and J. O. S. Wilson "The persistence of profit: a new empirical interpretation" *International Journal of Industrial Organization* 17(5), July 1999, pp. 663–687.

Goeree, Michelle Sovinsky "Limited information and advertising in the U.S. personal computer industry" *Econometrica* 76(5), September 2008, pp. 1017–1074.

Goldberg, Victor P. "Relational exchange: economics and complex contracts" *American Behavioral Scientist* 23(3), January/February 1980, pp. 337–352.

Goldman, Eric *Rendezvous with Destiny*. New York: Alfred A. Knopf, 1953.

Goldschmid, Harvey J., H. Michael Mann, and J. Fred Weston, editors, *Industrial Concentration: the New Learning*. Boston: Little, Brown & Company, 1974.

Gollop, Frank M., and James L. Monahan "A generalized index of diversification: trends in U.S. manufacturing" *Review of Economics and Statistics* 73(2), May 1991, pp. 318–330.

Gomez, Rosario, Jacob K. Goeree, and Charles A. Holt "Predatory pricing: rare like a unicorn?" undated; downloaded from URL <http://www.hss.caltech.edu/~jkg/predatory.pdf>, 17 October 2006.

González, Xulia, Jordi Jaumandreu, and Consuelo Pazó "Barriers to innovation and subsidy effectiveness" *Rand Journal of Economics* 36(4), Winter 2005, pp. 930–950.

González, Xulia and Consuelo Pazó "Do public subsidies stimulate private R&D spending?" *Research Policy* 37(3), April 2008, pp. 371–389.

Goodnow, Frank J. "Trust combinations at common law" *Political Science Quarterly* 12(2), June 1897, pp. 212–245.

Goodrich, Carter *Government Promotion of American Canals and Railroads 1800–1890*. New York: Columbia University Press, 1960.

— "Conclusion" in Carter Goodrich, editor, *Canals and American Economic Development*. New York and London: Columbia University Press, 1961, pp. 249–255.

Gordon, Robert A. *Business Leadership in the Large Corporation*. Berkeley and Los Angeles, 1945; with a new preface, 1961.

Gordon, Sanford D. "Attitudes towards trusts prior to the Sherman Act" *Southern Economic Journal* 30(2), October 1963, pp. 156–167.

Gort, Michael *Diversification and Integration in American Industry*. Princeton: Princeton University Press, 1962; <http://www.nber.org/books/gort62-1>.

Gort, Michael and Steven Klepper "Time paths in the diffusion of product innovations" *Economic Journal* 92(367), September 1982, pp. 630–653.

Goto, Akira "Business groups in a market economy" *European Economic Review* 19(1), 1982, pp. 53–70.

Gould, J. R. "Price discrimination and vertical control: a note" *Journal of Political Economy* 85 October 1987, pp. 1063–1071.

Gould, Stephen J. *Wonderful Life. The Burgess Shale and the Nature of History*. London: Penguin Books, 1989.

Government-University-Industry-Research Roundtable *Industrial Perspectives on Innovation and Interactions with Universities*. National Academy Press, Washington, D.C., 1991.

Graddy, Kathryn "Testing for imperfect competition at the Fulton Fish Market" *Rand Journal of Economics* 26(1), Spring 1995, pp. 75–92.

— "The Fulton Fish Market" *Journal of Economic Perspectives* 20(2), Spring 2006, pp. 207–220.

Graham, David R., Daniel P. Kaplan, and David S. Sibley "Efficiency and competition in the airline industry" *Bell Journal of Economics* 14 Spring 1983, pp. 118–138.

Graham, Margaret B. W. "Industrial research in the age of big science" *Research on Technological Innovation, Management and Policy* 2, 1985, pp. 47–79.

Granitz, Elizabeth and Benjamin Klein "Monopolization by 'raising rivals' costs': the Standard Oil case" *Journal of Law and Economics* 39, April 1996, pp. 1–47.

Grant, Darren "Recycling and market power: a more general model and re-evaluation of the evidence" *International Journal of Industrial Organization* 17(1), January 1999, pp. 59–80.

Green, Edward J. and Robert H. Porter "Noncooperative collusion under imperfect price information" *Econometrica* 52(1), January 1984, pp. 87–100.

Greenaway, D. and Hindley, B., editors, *What Britain pays for voluntary export restraints*. Thames Essay 43. London: Trade Policy Research Centre, 1985.

Greenleaf, William *Monopoly on Wheels; Henry Ford and the Selden Automobile Patent*. Detroit: Wayne State University Press, 1961.

Greenstein, Shane M. "Did installed base give an incumbent any (measurable) advantages in federal computer procurement?" *Rand Journal of Economics* 24(1), Spring 1993, pp. 19–39.

Greenstein, Shane M. and Garey Ramey "Market structure, innovation and vertical product differentiation" *International Journal of Industrial Organization* 16, 1998, pp. 285–311.

Gressley, Gene M. "Thurman Arnold, antitrust, and the New Deal" *Business History Review* 38(2), Summer 1964, pp. 214–231.

Grether, David M. and Charles R. Plott "The effects of market practices in oligopolistic markets: an experimental examination of the Ethyl case" *Economic Inquiry* 22(4), October 1984, pp. 479–507.

Grether, Ewald T. *Price Control Under Fair Trade Legislation*. New York: Oxford University Press, 1939.

— "Industrial organization: past history and future problems" *American Economic Review* 60(2), May 1970, pp. 83–89.

Griffin, James M. "Previous cartel experience: any lessons for OPEC?" in Lawrence R. Klein and Jamie Marquez, editors, *Economics in Theory and Practice: An Eclectic Approach*. Dordrecht: Kluwer Academic Publishers, 1989, pp. 179–206.

Griffith, William, editor, *The Roosevelt Policy*. New York: The Current Literature Publishing Company, 1919; New York: Kraus Reprint Co., 1971.

Griliches, Zvi "Issues in assessing the contribution of research and development to productivity growth" *Bell Journal of Economics* 10(1), Spring 1979, pp. 92–116.

— "Productivity, R&D, and the data constraint" *American Economic Review* 84(1), March 1984, pp. 1–23.

— "Patents: recent trends and puzzles" *Brookings Papers on Economic Activity: Microeconomics* (1989), 1989, pp. 291–319.

— "The search for R&D spillovers" *Scandinavian Journal of Economics* 94(Supplement), 1992, pp. S29–S47.

Grimm, Curtis M., Clifford Winston and Carol A. Evans "Foreclosure of railroad markets: a test of Chicago leverage theory" *Journal of Law and Economics* 35(2), October 1992, pp. 295–310.

Grob, Gerard N. "Reform unionism: the National Labor Union" *Journal of Economic History* 14(2), Spring 1954, pp. 126–142.

— "The Knights of Labor and the trade unions, 1878–1886" *Journal of Economic History* 18(2), June 1958, pp. 176–192.

von der Groeben, Hans "The role of competition in the Common Market" in American Bar Association *Proceedings Conference on Antitrust and the European Communities* 1963, pp. 14–27.

Grossekettler, Heinz G. "On designing an economic order. The contributions of the Freiburg School" pp. 38–84 in Donald A. Walker, editor, *Perspectives on the History of Economic Thought* Volume II. Aldershot: Edward Elgar Publishing Limited, 1989.

Grossman, Peter Z. *American Express*. New York: Crown Publishers, Inc., 1987.

—, editor, *How Cartels Endure and How They Fail*. Edward Elgar: Cheltenham, UK and Northampton, Massachusetts, 2004.

Grossman, Sanford J. and Oliver D. Hart "Takeover bids, the free-rider problem, and the theory of the corporation" *Bell Journal of Economics* 11(1), Spring 1980, pp. 42–64.

— "The costs and benefits of ownership: a theory of vertical and lateral integration" *Journal of Political Economy* 94(4), 1986, pp. 691–719.

Grout, Paul and Anna Zalewsha "Measuring the rate of return for competition law" *Journal of Competition Law and Economics* 4(1), March 2008, pp. 155–176.

Grünfeld, Leo A. "Multinational production, absorptive capacity, and endogenous R&D spillovers" *Review of International Economics* 14(5), 2006, pp. 922–940.

Gschwandtner, Adelina and Val E. Lambson "The effects of sunk costs on entry and exit: evidence from 36 countries" *Economics Letters* 77, 2002, pp. 109–115.

Gugler, Klaus, Dennis C. Mueller, B. Burcin Yurtoglu and Christine Zulehner "The effects of mergers: an international comparison" *International Journal of Industrial Organization* 21(5), May 2003, pp. 625–653.

Guinnnane, Timothy, Ron Harris, Naomi R. Lamoreaux, and Jean-Laurent Rosenthal "Putting the corporation in its place" *Enterprise and Society* 8(3), September 2007, pp. 687–729.

Gunton, George "The economic and social aspect of trusts" *Political Science Quarterly* 3(3), September 1888, pp. 385–408.

Gupta, Barnali, Fu-Chuan Lai, Debashis Pal, Jyotirmoy Sarkar, and Chia-Ming Yu "Where to locate in a circular city" *International Journal of Industrial Organization* 22(6), June 2004, pp. 759–782.

Gwennap, Linley "Intel Dodges Bullet FTC Consent Decree Avoids Broader Issues, " *Microprocessor Report* 13(4), 29 March 1999 (downloaded 25 February 2009 from <http://www.mdronline.com/mpr_public/editorials/edit13_04.html>).

Haas, Ernst B. *The Uniting of Europe: Political, Economic and Social Forces 1950–1957*. Stanford, California: Stanford University Press, 1958.

Haddock, David D. "Basing-point pricing: competitive vs. collusive theories" *American Economic Review* 72(3), June 1982, pp. 289–306.

Hadley, Arthur Twining "The good and evil of industrial combination" *Atlantic Monthly* 79(473), March 1897, pp. 377–385.

Hadley, Eleanor "Counterpoint on business groupings and government-industry relations in automobiles" in Masahiko Aoki, editor, *The Economic Analysis of the Japanese Firm*. Amsterdam: North-Holland, 1984, pp. 319–327.

Haeussler, Carolin and Dietmar Harhoff, and Elisabeth Mueller "To be financed or not . . . —the role of patents for venture capital financing" Discussion Papers in Business Administration 2009-2, Munich School of Management, University of Munich, 20 January 2009.

Hagedoorn, John "Inter-firm R&D partnerships: an overview of major trends and patterns since 1960" *Research Policy* 31, 2002, pp. 477–492.

Hale, William Harlan "The men behind the president: what they think" *Common Sense* 7(7), July 1938, pp. 16–20.

Hall, Bronwyn H. "The impact of corporate restructuring on industrial research and development" *Brookings Papers on Economic Activity. Microeconomics 1990* (1990), pp. 85–124.

— "R&D Tax Policy during the Eighties: Success or Failure?" *Tax Policy and the Economy* 7, 1993a, pp. 1–36.

— "Industrial research during the 1980s: did the rate of return fall?" *Brookings Papers on Economic Activity Microeconomics* 1993(2), 1993b, pp. 289–330.

— "Corporate restructuring and investment horizons in the United States, 1976–1987" *Business History Review* 68(1), Spring 1994, pp. 110–143.

— "The private and social returns to research and development" pp. 140–183 in Bruce L. R. Smith and Claude E. Barfield, editors, *Technology, R&D, and the Economy*. Washington, D.C.: The Brookings Institution and American Enterprise Institute, 1996.

— "Mergers and R&D revisited" 30 July 1999.

— "Business method patents, innovation, and policy" NBER Working Paper 9717, May 2003.

Hall, Marshall and Leonard Weiss "Firm size and profitability" *Review of Economics and Statistics* 49(3), August 1967, pp. 319–331.

Hall, R. L. and C. J. Hitch "Price theory and business behavior" *Oxford Economic Papers* 2, May 1939, pp. 12–45.

Haltiwanger, John C. and Joseph E. Harrington Jr. "The impact of cyclical demand movements on collusive behavior" *Rand Journal of Economics* 22(1), Spring 1991, pp. 89–106.

Hamilton, James L. "Joint oligopsony–oligopoly in the U.S. leaf tobacco market, 1924–1939" *Review of Industrial Organization* 9(1), February 1994, pp. 25–39.

Hamilton, Walton H. "The anti-trust laws and the social control of business" pp. 4–14 in Milton

Handler, *The Federal Anti-Trust Laws*. Chicago: Commerce Clearing House, Inc., 1932.

Handler, Milton *The Federal Anti-Trust Laws: A Symposium*. Chicago: Commerce Clearing House, Inc., 1932.

Hannah, Leslie "Mergers in British manufacturing industry, 1880–1918" *Oxford Economic Papers* n.s. 26(1), March 1974a, pp. 1–20.

— "Managerial innovation and the rise of the large-scale company in interwar Britain" *Economic History Review* 27(2), May 1974b, pp. 252–270.

— "Visible and invisible hands in Great Britain" pp. 41–76 in Alfred D. Chandler and Herman Daems, editors, *Managerial Hierarchies*. Cambridge, Massachusetts and London, England: Harvard University Press, 1980.

— "Economic ideas and government policy on industrial organization in Britain since 1945" pp. 354–375 in Mary O. Furner and Barry Supple, editors, *The State and Economic Knowledge*. Cambridge and elsewhere: Woodrow Wilson International Center for Scholars and Cambridge University Press, 1990.

— "Scale and scope: towards a European visible hand?" *Business History*, 33(2), 1991, pp. 297–309.

— "The American miracle, 1875–1950, and after: a view in the European mirror" *Business and Economic History* 24(2), Winter 1995, pp. 197–220.

— "Marshall's 'trees' and the global 'forest': were 'giant redwoods' different?" pp. 253–293 in Naomi Lamoreaux, Daniel M. G. Raff, and Peter Temin, editors, *Learning by Doing in Market, Firms and Countries*. Chicago and London: University of Chicago Press, 1999.

— "The 'divorce' of ownership from control from 1900 onwards: re-calibrating imagined global trends" *Business History* 49(4), July 2007, pp. 404–438.

— "Logistics, market size, and giant plants in the early twentieth centry: a global view" *Journal of Economic History* 68(1), March 2008, pp. 47–79.

Hannan, Timothy H. "Limit pricing and the banking industry" *Journal of Money, Credit and Banking* 11(4), November 1979, pp. 438–446.

Hanssen, F. Andrew "The block booking of films reexamined" *Journal of Law and Economics* 43(2), October 2000, pp. 395–426.

Harberger, Arnold C. "Monopoly and resource allocation" *American Economic Review* 44(2), May 1954, pp. 75–87.

Harding, Christopher and Julian Joshua *Regulating Cartels in Europe*. Oxford: Oxford University Press, 2003.

Harley, C. Knick "Transportation, the world wheat trade, and the Kuznets cycle" *Explorations in Economic History* 17(3), July 1980, pp. 218–250.

— "Oligopoly agreement and the timing of American railroad construction" *Journal of Economic History* 42(4), December 1982, pp. 797–823.

Haro, A. S. "Area cartogram of the SMSA population of the United States" *Annals of the Association of American Geographers* 58(3), September 1968, pp. 452–460.

Harriman, Henry I. "The stabilization of business and employment" *American Economic Review* 22(1), March 1932, pp. 63–74.

Harrington, Joseph E. Jr. "Collusion among asymmetric firms: the case of different discount factors" *International Journal of Industrial Organization* 7(2), June 1989, pp. 289–307.

Harris, Robert G. and Thomas M. Jorde "Market definition in the Merger Guidelines: implications for antitrust enforcement" *California Law Review* 71, March 1983, pp. 464–496.

Harrison, Glenn W. "Predatory pricing in a multiple market experiment" *Journal of Economic Behavior and Organization* 9(4), June 1988, pp. 405–417.

Hart, Oliver D. "The market mechanism as an incentive scheme" *Bell Journal of Economics* 14(2), Autumn 1983, pp. 366–382.

— "An economist's perspective on the theory of the firm" *Columbia Law Review* 89 November 1989, pp. 1757–1774.

— *Firms, Contracts, and Financial Structure*. Oxford: Oxford University Press, 1995.

Hart, Oliver D. and John Moore "Property rights and the nature of the firm" *Journal of Political Economy* 98(6), 1990, pp. 1119–1158.

Hart, Oliver and Jean Tirole "Vertical integration and market foreclosure" *Brookings Papers on Economic Activity: Microeconomics* 1990, pp. 205–276.

Hart, P. E. and Eleanor Morgan "Market structure and economic performance in the United Kingdom" *Journal of Industrial Economics* 25(3), March 1977, pp. 177–193.

Hart, P. E. and S. Prais "The analysis of business concentration: a statistical approach" *Journal of the Royal Statistical Society*, Series A, 119, 1956, pp. 150–181.

Hastings, Justine S. "Vertical relationships and competition in retail gasoline markets: empirical evidence from contract changes in Southern California" *American Economic Review* 94(1), March 2004, pp. 317–328.

Hastings, Justine S. and Richard J. Gilbert "Market power, vertical integration and the wholesale price of gasoline" *Journal of Industrial Economics* 53(4), December 2005, pp. 469–482.

Hausman, Jerry A. "Exact consumer's surplus and deadweight loss" *American Economic Review* 71(4), September 1981, pp. 662–676.

Haussmann, Frederick and Daniel J. Ahern "The international control of cartels—past and future" *Thought* 20(76), March 1945, pp. 85–96.

Hawley, Ellis W. *The New Deal and the Problem of Monopoly*. Princeton, New Jersey: Princeton University Press, 1966.

— "Herbert Hoover, the Commerce Secretariat, and the vision of an 'Associative state,' 1921–1928" *Journal of American History* 61(1), June 1974, pp. 116–140.

Hawtrey, R. G. *The Economic Problem*. London: Longmans, Green, 1926.

Hay, Donald A. and Guy S. Liu "The efficiency of firms: what difference does competition make?" *Economic Journal* 107, 1997, pp. 597–617.

Hay, Donald A. and Derek J. Morris *Industrial Economics*. Oxford: Oxford University Press, 1979.

Hay, George A. "Oligopoly, shared monopoly, and antitrust law" *Cornell Law Review* 67(3), March 1982, pp. 439–481.

— "Practices that facilitate cooperation: the *Ethyl* case" in John E. Kwoka, Jr. and Lawrence J. White, editors, *The Antitrust Revolution*. Glenview, Illinois: Scott, Foresman and Company, 1989, pp. 183–207.

— "The meaning of 'agreement' under the Sherman Act: thoughts from the 'facilitating practices' experience" *Review of Industrial Organization* 16(2), March 2000, pp. 113–129.

Hay, George A. and Daniel Kelley "An empirical survey of price fixing conspiracies" *Journal of Law and Economics* 17(1), April 1974, pp. 13–38.

Hayes, Peter "Carl Bosch and Carl Krauch: chemistry and the political economy of Germany, 1925–1945" *Journal of Economic History* 47(2), June 1987, pp. 353–363.

Hazledine, Tim and John J. Siegfried "How did the wealthiest New Zealanders get so rich?" *New Zealand Economic Papers* 31(1), 1997, pp. 35–47.

Helberger, Natali, Nicole Dufft, Stef van Gompel, and Bernt Hugenholtz "Nothing forever: why extending the term of protection for sound recordings is a bad idea" *European Intellectual Property Review* 5, 2008, pp. 174–181.

Helfman, Harold M. "Twenty-nine hectic days: public opinion and the oil war of 1872" *Pennsylvania History* 17(2), April 1950, pp. 121–138.

Heller, Michael A. and Rebecca S. Eisenberg "Can patents deter innovation? The anticommons in biomedical research" *Science* 280(5364), May 1, 1998, pp. 698–701.

Helper, Susan "Strategy and irreversibility in supplier relations: the case of the US automobile industry" *Business History Review* 65(4), Winter 1991, pp. 781–824.

Helper, Susan, John Paul MacDuffie, and Charles Sabel "Pragmatic collaborations: advancing knowledge while controlling opportunism" *Industrial and Corporate Change* 9(3), September 2000, pp. 443–488.

Hendel, Igal and Aviv Nevo "Sales and consumer inventory" *Rand Journal of Economics* 37(3), 2006a, pp. 543–561.

— "Measuring the implications of sales and consumer inventory behavior" *Econometrica* 74(6), November 2006b, pp. 1637–1673.

Henderson, Rebecca and Cockburn, Iain "Scale, scope and spillovers: the determinants of research productivity in drug discovery" *Rand Journal of Economics* 27(1), Spring 1996, pp. 32–59.

Henry, Robert S. "The railroad land grant legend in American history texts" *Mississippi Valley Historical Review* 32(2), September 1945, pp. 171–194.

Herbruck, Wendell "Forestalling, regrating and engrossing" *Michigan Law Review* 27(4), February 1929, pp. 365–388.

Herfindahl, Orris C. *Concentration in the Steel Industry*, unpublished Ph. D. dissertation, Columbia University, 1950.

— *Copper Costs and Prices: 1870–1957*. Baltimore: Johns Hopkins Press for Resources for the Future, Inc., 1959.

Hermalin, Benjamin E. and Michael L. Katz "Corporate diversification and agency" pp. 17–39 in Peter J. Hammond and Gareth D. Myles, editors, *Incentives, Organization, and Public Economics: Papers in Honour of Sir James Mirrlees* Oxford: Oxford University Press, 2004.

Heusdens, J. J. and R. de Horn "Crisis policy in the European steel industry in the light of the ECSC treaty" *Common Market Law Review* 17(1), 1980, pp. 31–74.

Hexner, Ervin *The International Steel Cartel*. Chapel Hill: University of North Carolina Press, 1943.

Hicks, J. R. "Annual survey of economic theory: the theory of monopoly" *Econometrica* 3(1), January 1935, pp. 1–20.

— "The foundations of welfare economics" *Economic Journal* 49(196), December 1939, pp. 696–712.

— "The rehabilitation of consumers' surplus" *Review of Economic Studies* 8(2), February 1941, pp. 108–116.

Higgs, Robert "Railroad rates and the populist uprising" *Agricultural History* 44(3), July 1970, pp. 291–297.

Hilberry, Russell and David Hummels "Trade responses to geographic frictions: a decomposition using micro-data" NBER Working Paper 11339, May 2005.

Hildebrand, Doris *The Role of Economic Analysis in the EC Competition Rules*. The Hague and elsewhere: Kluwer Law International, second edition, 2002.

Hill, Forest G. *Roads, Rails & Waterways. The Army Engineers and Early Transportation*. Norman: University of Oklahoma Press, 1957.

Hilt, Eric "When did ownership separate from control" *Journal of Economic History* 68(3), September 2008, pp. 645–685.

Himmelberg, Robert F. T. "Business, antitrust policy, and the Industrial board of the Department of Commerce, 1919" *Business History Review* 42(1), Spring 1968, pp. 1–23.

— *The Origins of the National Recovery Administration.* New York: Fordham University Press, 1976.

Hindley, Brian "Dumping and the Far East trade of the European Community" *World Economy* 11(4), 1988, pp. 445–463.

Hindley, Brian and Patrick A. Messerlin *Antidumping Industry Policy: Legalized Protectionism in the WTO and What to Do About It.* Washington, DC: AEI Press, 1996.

Hinloopen, Jeroen "More on subsidizing cooperative and noncooperative R&D in duopoly with spillovers" *Journal of Economics* 72(3), 2000, pp. 295–308.

— "R&D efficiency gains due to cooperation" *Journal of Economics* 80(2), 2003, pp. 107–125.

Hirsch, Anita "Cartels et ententes" in Alfred Sauvy *Histoire Économique de la France Entre Les Deux Guerres.* Paris: Fayard, 1975, pp. 49–78.

Hirshleifer, Jack "The private and social value of information and the reward to inventive activity" *American Economic Review* 61(4), September 1971, pp. 561–574.

Hirschman, A. O. *National Power and the Structure of Foreign Trade.* Berkeley and Los Angeles: University of California Press, 1945.

— "The paternity of an index" *American Economic Review* 54(5), September 1964, pp. 761–762.

Hofstadter, Richard *The Age of Reform.* New York: Alfred A. Knopf, 1955.

— "What happened to the antitrust movement?" in *The Paranoid Style in American Politics and Other Essays.* New York: Alfred A. Knopf, 1965, Chicago: University of Chicago Press, Phoenix edition, 1979, reprinted in Thomas E. Sullivan (1991).

Hogan, Stephen D. and Marsha Cope Huie "Bigness, junk and bust-ups: end of the fourth merger wave?" *Antitrust Bulletin* 37(4), Winter 1992, pp. 881–956.

Holahan, William L. and Schuler, Richard E. "The welfare effects of market shapes in the Löschian location model: squares vs. hexagons" *American Economic Review* 71(4), September 1981, pp. 738–746.

Holmes, Thomas J. "The effects of third-degree price discrimination in oligopoly" *American Economic Review* 79(1), March 1989, pp. 244–250.

— "Bar codes lead to frequent deliveries and superstores" *Rand Journal of Economics* 32(4), Winter 2001, pp. 708–725. 46(4), April 2000, pp. 563–585.

Holmström, Bengt and Jean Tirole "The theory of the firm" Chapter 2 in Richard C. Schmalensee and Robert D. Willig, editors, *Handbook of Industrial Organization.* Amsterdam: North-Holland, Volume I, 1989.

Holt, Charles A. "An experimental test of the consistent-conjectures hypothesis" *American Economic Review* 75(3), June 1985, pp. 314–325.

— "Industrial organization: a survey of laboratory research" in John H. Kagel and Alvin E. Roth, editors, *The Handbook of Experimental Economics.* Princeton: Princeton University Press, 1995, pp. 349–443.

— *Webgames and Strategic Behavior: Recipes for Interactive Learning.* Addison-Wesley, forthcoming, 2006.

— "Industrial organization: a survey of laboratory research" in John H. Kagel and Alvin E. Roth, editors, *The Handbook of Experimental Economics.* Princeton: Princeton University Press, 1995, pp. 349–443.

Holt, Charles A. and David T. Scheffman "Facilitating practices: the effects of advance notice and best-price policies" *Rand Journal of Economics* 18, 1987, pp. 187–197.

Holtermann, Sally E. "Market structure and economic performance in U.K. manufacturing industry" *Journal of Industrial Economics* 22(2), December 1973, pp. 119–139.

Homan, Paul T. "Trusts" pp. 111–115 in Edwin R. A. Seligman, editor, *Encyclopedia of the Social Sciences* 15. New York: Macmillan, 1935.

Horowitz, Ira "Copy watches, tailored clothes, and the structure-conduct-performance paradigm" *Review of Industrial Organization* 9(6), December 1994, pp. 731–743.

Horstmann, Ignatius and Glenn MacDonald "Is advertising a signal of product quality? Evidence from the compact disc player market, 1983–1992" *International Journal of Industrial Organization* 21(3), March 2003, pp. 317–345.

Hortaçsu, Ali and Chad Syverson "Cementing relationships: vertical integration, foreclosure, productivity, and prices" *Journal of Political Economy* 115(2), 2007, pp. 250–301.

Hotelling, Harold H. "Stability in competition" *Economic Journal* 39 March 1929, pp. 41–57, reprinted in George J. Stigler and Kenneth E. Boulding, editors, *A. E. A. Readings in Price Theory.* Chicago: Richard D. Irwin, 1952.

— "Edgeworth's taxation paradox and the nature of demand and supply functions" *Journal of Political Economy* 40(5), October 1932, pp. 577–616.

Houghton, R. W. "A note on the early history of consumer's surplus" *Economica* n.s. 25(97), February 1958, pp. 49–57.

Hounshell, David A. *From the American System to Mass Production, 1800–1932.* Baltimore and London: Johns Hopkins University Press, 1984.

Hovenkamp, Herbert *Enterprise and American Law 1836–1937.* Cambridge, Massachusetts and London, England: Harvard University Press, 1991.

Howard, John A. "Collusive behavior" *Journal of Business* 27(3), July 1954, pp. 196–204.

Howe, J. D. and D. G. McFetridge "The determinants of R & D expenditures" *Canadian Journal of Economics* 9(1), February 1976, pp. 57–71.

Howe, M. "A study of trade association price fixing" *Journal of Industrial Economics* 21(3), July 1973, pp. 236–256.

Hoxby, Caroline M. "Benevolent colluders? The effects of antitrust action on college financial aid and tuition" NBER Working Paper 7754, June 2000.

Hubbard, R. Glenn and Darius Palia "A re-examination of the conglomerate merger wave in the 1960s: an internal capital markets view" *Journal of Finance* 54(3), June 1999, pp. 1131–1152.

Huck, Steffen, Hans-Theo Normann, and Jörg Oechssler "Does information about competitors' actions increase or decrease competition in experimental oligopoly markets?" *International Journal of Industrial Organization* 18(1), January 2000, pp. 39–57.

— "Two are few and four are many: number effects in experimental oligopolies" *Journal of Economic Behavior and Organization* 53, 2004, pp. 435–446.

Huck, Virginia *Brand of the Tartan*. New York: Appleton-Century-Crofts, Inc., 1955.

Hudson, Henry "The Southern Railway & Steamship Association" *Quarterly Journal of Economics* 5(1), October 1890a, pp. 70–94.

— "Appendix: Agreement of the Southern Railway & Steamship Association" *Quarterly Journal of Economics* 5(1), October 1890b, pp. 115–130.

Hughes, Graham "Common law systems, " pp. 9–25 in Alan B. Morrison, editor. *Fundamentals of American Law*. Oxford: Oxford University Press, 1996.

Hughes, James W. and Daniel P. Barbezat "Basing-point pricing and the *Stahlwerksverband*: an examination of the 'New Competitive School" *Journal of Economic History* 56(1), March 1996, pp. 215–222.

Humphrey, Don D. "The nature and meaning of rigid prices, 1890–1933" *Journal of Political Economy* 45(5), October 1937, pp. 651–666.

Hutner, Francis Cornwall *The Farr Alpaca Company A Case Study in Business History*. Northampton, Massachusetts: Smith College Studies in History 23, 1951.

Hunter, Louis C. *Studies in the Economic History of the Ohio Valley*. New York City and London: Johnson Reprint Corporation, 1970.

Hviid, Morten and Greg Shaffer "Hassle costs: the Achilles heel of price-matching guarantees" *Journal of Economics & Management Strategy* 8(4), Winter 1999, pp. 489–521.

Hymer, Stephen and Peter Pashigian "Turnover of firms as a measure of market behavior" *Review of Economics and Statistics* 44(1), February 1962, pp. 82–87.

Ijiri, Yuji and Herbert A. Simon *Skew Distributions and the Sizes of Business Firms*. Amsterdam: North-Holland, 1977.

Interparliamentary Union "Resolution on the control of international trusts and cartels" *Compte rendu de la XXVIe Conférence*. Génève: Payot et Cie, 1931, pp. 33–34.

Interparliamentary Union and the United States Group *General Information and History of the Interparliamentary Union and the United States Group, 99th Congress*. Washington, D.C.: Interparliamentary Union, United States Group, United States Congress, 1985.

Ippolito, Pauline M. and Alan D. Mathios "Information, advertising and health choices: a study of the cereal market" *Rand Journal of Economics* 21(3), Autumn 1990, pp. 459–480.

Ireland, Norman J. "Concentration and the growth of market demand" *Journal of Economic Theory* 5(2), October 1972, pp. 303–305.

Irwin, Douglas A., and Peter J. Klenow, "High-tech R&D subsidies estimating the effects of Sematech" *Journal of International Economics* 40, 1996, pp. 323–344.

Isaac, R. Mark and Charles R. Plott "The opportunity for conspiracy in restraint of trade: an experimental study" *Journal of Economic Behavior and Organization* 2(1), March 1981, pp. 1–30.

Isaac, R. Mark, Valerie Ramey and Arlington W. Williams "The effects of market organization on conspiracies in restraint of trade" *Journal of Economic Behavior and Organization* 5(2), June 1984, pp. 191–222.

Isaac, R. Mark and Vernon L. Smith "In search of predatory pricing" *Journal of Political Economy* 93(2), April 1985, pp. 320–345.

Israel, Mark "Tenure dependence in consumer-firm relationships: an empirical analysis of consumer departures from automobile insurance firms" *Rand Journal of Economics* 36(1), Spring 2005, pp. 165–192.

Ivaldi, Marc, Bruno Jullien, Patrick Rey, Paul Seabright, and Jean Tirole *The Economics of Tacit Collusion*. Final Report for DG Competition, European Commission, March 2003. Downloaded 2 August 2006 from <http://idei.fr/doc/wp/2003/tacit_collusion.pdf>.

— *The Economics of Unilateral Effects*. Report for DG Competition, November 2003b. Downloaded 23 October 2004 from <http://ec.europa.eu/comm/ competition/mergers/studies_reports/ the_economics_of_unilateral_effects_en.pdf>.

Jackson, Thomas Penfield, Judge "Findings of Fact" 5 November 1999, downloaded 5 March 2008 from <http://www.usdoj.gov/atr/cases/f3800/ msjudgex.htm>.

— "Conclusions of Law" 5 November 1999, downloaded 24 June 2002 from <http://www.usdoj. gov/atr/cases/f3800/msjudgex.htm>.

Jacquemin, Alexis P. "Size structure and performance of the largest European firms" *Three Banks Review* 102, June 1974, pp. 61–70.

— "Cooperative agreements in R&D and European antitrust policy" *European Economic Review* 32(2/3), 1988, pp. 551–560.

— "Corporate strategy and competition policy in the post-1992 Single Market" in William James Adams, editor *Singular Europe*. Ann Arbor: University of Michigan Press, 1992, pp. 125–144.

Jacquemin, Alexis P. and Michel Cardon de Lichtbuer "Size structure, stability and performance of the largest British and EEC firms" *European Economic Review* 4(4), December 1973, pp. 393–408.

Jacquemin, Alexis, Tsuruhiko Nambu and Isabelle Dewez "A dynamic analysis of export cartels: the Japanese case" *Economic Journal* 91, 1981, pp. 685–696.

Jacquemin, Alexis and Wistano Saez "A comparison of the performance of the largest, European and Japanese firms" *Oxford Economic Papers* 28(2), July 1976, pp. 271–283.

Jacquemin, Alexis and André Sapir "Competition and imports in the European market" in L. Alan Winters and Anthony Venables, editors, *European Integration: Trade and Industry*. Cambridge: Cambridge University Press, 1991, pp. 82–95.

Jacquemin, Alexis and Bernard Spinott "Economic and legal aspects of cooperative research: a European view" *Annual Proceedings of Fordham Corporate Law Institute*, 1986.

Jaffe, Adam B. "Demand and supply influences in R&D intensity and productivity growth" *Review of Economics and Statistics* 70(3), 1988, pp. 431–437.

— "The U.S. patent system in transition: policy innovation and the innovation process" *Research Policy* 29, 2000, pp. 531–557.

Jaffe, Adam, Manuel Trajtenberg, and Rebecca Henderson, "Geographic localization of knowledge spillovers as evidenced by patent citations" *Quarterly Journal of Economics* 108(3), August 1993, pp. 577–598.

Jaffe, Louis L. and Mathew O. Tobriner "The legality of price-fixing agreements" *Harvard Law Review* 45(7), May 1932, pp. 1164–1195.

Jaffe, Louis L. and Tribe, Lawrence H. *Environmental Protection*. Chicago: Bracton Press, 1971.

James, Charles A. "The real Microsoft case" *Antitrust* Autumn 2001, pp. 58–66.

James, John A. "Structural change in American manufacturing, 1850–1890" *Journal of Economic History* 43(2), June 1983, pp. 433–459.

Janis, Mark D. "Patent abolitionism" *Berkeley Technology Law Journal* 17, 2002, pp. 899–952.

Jeanneney, J. M. "Nationalization in France" pp. 471–489 in Edward H. Chamberlin, editor, *Monopoly and Competition and Their Regulation*. London: Macmillan Co. Ltd. and New York: St. Martin's Press, 1954.

Jenks, Jeremiah W. *The Trust Problem*. New York: McClure, Philips, 1900.

Jenny, Frédéric and Andre-Paul Weber "The determinants of concentration trends in the French manufacturing sector" *Journal of Industrial Economics* 26(3), March 1978, pp. 193–207.

— "Aggregate welfare loss due to monopoly power in the French economy: some tentative estimates" *Journal of Industrial Economics* 32(2), December 1983, pp. 113–130.

Jensen, Michael C. "Agency costs of free cash flow, corporate finance, and takeovers" *American Economic Review* 76(2), May, 1986, pp. 323–329.

Jensen, Michael C. and William H. Meckling "Theory of the firm: managerial behavior, agency costs and ownership structure" *Journal of Financial Economics* 3, 1976, pp. 305–360.

Jensen, Richard A., Richard A., Jerry G. Thursby, and Marie C. Thursby "Disclosure and licensing of University inventions: 'The best we can do with the s**t we get to work with'" *International Journal of Industrial Organization* 21(9), November 2003, pp. 1271–1300.

Jeon, Doh-Shin and Domenico Menicucci "Bundling electronic journals and competition among publishers" *Journal of the European Economic Association* 4(5), September 2006, pp. 1038–1083.

Jewkes, John "The size of the factory" *Economic Journal* 62(246), June 1952, pp. 237–252.

Jewkes, John, David Sawers and Richard Stillerman *The Sources of Invention*. New York: W.W. Norton & Company, Inc. Second edition, 1969.

Johnsen, D. Bruce "Property rights to cartel rents: the *Socony-Vacuum* story" *Journal of Law and Economics* 34, April 1991, pp. 177–203.

Johnson, Arthur M. "Theodore Roosevelt and the Bureau of Corporations" *Mississippi Valley Historical Review* 45(4), March 1959, pp. 571–590.

— "Antitrust policy in transition, 1908: ideal and reality" *Mississippi Valley Historical Review* 48(3), December 1961, pp. 415–434.

— "Lessons of the Standard Oil divestiture" pp. 191–214 in Edward J. Mitchell, editor, *Vertical Integration in the Oil Industry*. Washington, D.C.: American Enterprise Institute for Public Policy Research, 1976.

Jones, Eliot *The Trust Problem in the United States*. New York: Macmillan, 1921.

Jones, Franklin D. "Historical development of the law of business competition" *Yale Law Journal* 35(8), June 1926, pp. 905–938; 36(1), November 1926, pp. 42–55; 36(2), December 1926, pp. 207–234; 36(3), January 1927, pp. 351–383.

Jones, S. H. R. "Price associations and competition in the British pin industry, 1814–40" *Economic History Review* n.s. 26(2), 1973, pp. 237–253.

Jones, Charles I. and Williams, John C. "Measuring the social return to R&D" February 1997. Available at SSRN: <http://ssrn.com/abstract=2155 or DOI: 10.2139/ssrn.2155>.

Joseph, M. F. W. "A discontinuous cost curve and the tendency to increasing returns" *Economic Journal* 43(171), September 1933, pp. 390–398.

Joskow, Paul L. "Vertical integration and long-term contracts: the case of coal-burning electric generating plants" *Journal of Law, Economics, & Organization* 1(1), Spring, 1985, pp. 33–80.

— "Contract duration and relationship-specific investments: empirical evidence from coal markets" *American Economic Review* 77(1), March 1987, pp. 168–185.

— "The performance of long-term contracts: further evidence from coal markets" *Rand Journal of Economics* 21(2), Summer, 1990, pp. 251–274.

Joskow, Paul L. and Alvin K. Klevorick "A framework for analyzing predatory pricing policy" *Yale Law Journal* 89(2), December 1979, pp. 213–270.

Jovanovic, Boyan "Selection and evolution of industry" *Econometrica* 50, May 1982, pp. 649–670.

Jovanovic, Boyan and Peter L. Rousseau "General purpose technologies" NBER Working Paper 11093, January 2005.

Kagel, John H. and Alvin E. Roth, editors, *The Handbook of Experimental Economics*. Princeton: Princeton University Press, 1995.

Kaldor, Nicolas "Welfare propositions of economics and interpersonal comparisons of utility" *Economic Journal* 49(195), September 1939, pp. 549–552.

— "The economic aspects of advertising" *Review of Economic Studies* 18(1), 1950–1951, pp. 1–27.

Kalecki, M. "On the Gibrat distribution" *Econometrica* 13(2), April 1945, pp. 161–170.

Kamecke, Ulrich "The proper scope of government viewed from an Ordoliberal perspective: the example of competition policy" *Journal of Institutional and Theoretical Economics* 157(1), March 2001, pp. 23–27.

Kamien, Morton I. and Nancy L. Schwartz "Limit pricing and uncertain entry" *Econometrica* 39(3), May, 1971, pp. 441–454.

— *Market Structure and Innovation*. Cambridge: Cambridge University Press, 1982.

Kamien, Morton I. and Israel Zang "Meet me halfway: research joint ventures and absorptive capacity" *International Journal of Industrial Economics* 18(7), 2000, pp. 995–1012.

Kamien, Morton I., Eitan Muller, and Israel Zang "Research joint ventures and R&D cartels" *American Economic Review* 82(5), December 1992, pp. 1293–1306.

Kandori, Michihiro "Correlated demand shocks and price wars during booms" *Review of Economic Studies* 58(1), January 1991, pp. 171–180.

Katics, Michelle M. and Petersen, Bruce C. "The effect of rising import competition on market power: a panel data study of US manufacturing" *Journal of Industrial Economics* 42(3), September 1994, pp. 277–298.

Katsoulacos, Yannis and David Ulph "Technology policy: a selective review with emphasis on European policy and the role of RJVs" pp. 13–38 in Joanna A. Poyago-Theotoky, editor, *Competition, Cooperation, Research and Development*. Macmillan, 1997.

— "Endogenous spillovers and the performance of research joint ventures" *Journal of Industrial Economics* 46(3), September 1998, pp. 333–358.

Katz, Michael L. "The welfare effects of third-degree price discrimination in intermediate good markets" *American Economic Review* 77(1), March 1987, pp. 154–167.

— "Vertical contractual relations" in Richard C. Schmalensee and Robert D. Willig, editors, *Handbook of Industrial Organization*. Amsterdam: North-Holland, Volume I, 1989.

Katz, Michael L. and Janusz A. Ordover "R&D cooperation and competition" *Brookings Papers on Economic Activity: Microeconomics* 1990, 1990, pp. 137–203.

Kaysen, Carl *United States* v. *United States Shoe Machinery Corporation: An Economic Analysis of an Antitrust Case*. Cambridge, Massachusetts: Harvard University Press, 1956.

Kaysen, Carl and Donald F. Turner *Antitrust Policy: An Economic and Legal Analysis*. Cambridge, Massachusetts, Harvard University Press, 1959.

Kearl, J. R., Clayne L. Pope, Gordon C. Whiting, and Larry T. Wimmer "A confusion of economists?" *American Economic Review* 69(2), May 1979, pp. 28–37.

Keay, Ian "An empty promise: average cost savings and scale economies among Canadian and American manufacturers, 1910–1988" *Southern Economic Journal* 70(2), October 2003, pp. 374–388.

Kee, Hiau Looi and Bernard Hoekman "Imports, entry and competition law as market disciplines" *European Economic Review* 51(4), May 2007, pp. 831–858.

Keeler, Theodore E. "Deregulation and scale economies in the U.S. trucking industry: an econometric extension of the survivor principle" *Journal of Law and Economics* 32(2), October 1989, pp. 229–253.

Kennery, Roy W. and Benjamin Klein "How block booking facilitated self-enforcing contracts" *Journal of Law and Economics* 43(2), October 2000, pp. 427–435.

Kenney, Martin *Biotechnology: The University-Industrial Complex*. New Haven: Yale University Press, 1986.

Kerkvliet, Joe "Efficiency and vertical integration: the case of mine-mouth electric generating plants" *Journal of Industrial Economics* 39(5), September 1991, pp. 467–482.

Kersch, Ken I. "The *Gompers v. Buck's Stove* Saga: a constitutional case study in dialogue, resistance, and the freedom of speech" *Journal of Supreme Court History* 31(1), March 2006, pp. 28–57.

Kessides, Ioannis N. "Entry and market contestability: the evidence from the United States" in Paul Geroski and Joachim Schwalbach, editors, *Entry and Market Contestability*. Oxford, UK and Cambridge, Massachusetts: Blackwell, 1991, pp. 23–48.

Ketcham, Jon, Vernon L. Smith and Arlington W. Williams "A comparison of posted-offer and double-auction pricing institutions" *Review of Economic Studies* 51(4), October 1984, pp. 595–614.

Keyes, Lucile Sheppard "The Shoe Machinery case and the problem of the good trust" *Quarterly Journal of Economics* 68(2), May 1954, pp. 287–304.

— "Guidelines under Section 7 of the Clayton Act" *Antitrust Law & Economics Review* 1(1), July–August 1967, pp. 79–104.

Keynes, John Maynard "The end of laissez-faire" in *The Collected Writings of John Maynard Keynes* Volume 9: Essays in Persuasion. New York: St. Martin's Press, 1972 (reprint of 1926 pamphlet).

Kim, Jin-Hyuk "Corporate lobbying revisited" *Business and Politics* 10(2), Article 3, <http://www.bepress.com/bap/vol10/iss2/art3>, 2008.

Kim, Sukkoo "Expansion of markets and the geographic distribution of economic activities: the trends in U.S. regional manufacturing structure, 1860–1987" *Quarterly Journal of Economics* 110(4), November 1995, pp. 881–908.

Kintner, Earl W. *The Legislative History of the Federal Antitrust Laws and Related Statutes*. New York and London: Chelsea House Publishers, 1978.

— "Introduction" *The Legislative History of the Federal Antitrust Laws and Related Statutes*, Volume 1. New York and London: Chelsea House Publishers, 1978, pp. 7–50.

— "Introduction" *The Legislative History of the Federal Antitrust Laws and Related Statutes*, Volume 2. New York and London: Chelsea House Publishers, 1978, pp. 989–1023.

— "Introduction" *The Legislative History of the Federal Antitrust Laws and Related Statutes*, Volume 4. New York and London: Chelsea House Publishers, 1978, pp. 2893–2908.

— "Introduction" *The Legislative History of the Federal Antitrust Laws and Related Statutes*, Volume 5. New York and London: Chelsea House Publishers, 1978, pp. 3701–3708.

Kirby, M. W. "The control of competition in the British coal-mining industry in the thirties" *Economic History Review* 26(2), 1973, pp. 273–284.

Kirkland, Edward C. *Industry Comes of Age: Business, Labor and Public Policy 1860–1897*. New York: Holt, Rinehart and Winston, 1961.

Kirkwood, John B. "Consumers, economics, and antitrust" *Research in Law and Economics* 21, 2004, pp. 1–62.

Kirman, Alan P. "Whom or what does the representative individual represent?" *Journal of Economic Perspectives* 6(2), Spring, 1992, pp. 117–136.

Kirman, Alan P. and Annick Vignes "Price dispersion: theoretical considerations and empirical evidence from the Marseilles fish market" pp. 160–185 in Kenneth J. Arrow, editor, *Issues in Contemporary Economics: Proceedings of the Ninth World Congress of the International Economic Association*, Athens, Greece. Volume 1: Markets and Welfare. New York: New York University Press, 1991.

Kirman, Alan P. and Nicolaas J. Vriend "Learning to be loyal. A study of the Marseille fish market" pp. 33–56 in Domenico Delli Gatti, Mauro Gallegati, and Alan Kirman, editors, *Interaction and Market Structure Essays on Heterogeneity in Economics*. Berlin: Springer Verlag, 2000.

Kiser, Elizabeth K. (2002). "Predicting household switching behaviour and switching costs at depository institutions" *Review of Industrial Organization* 20(4), June, 2002, pp. 349–365.

Kitch, Edmund W. "The fire of truth: a remembrance of law and economics at Chicago, 1932–1970" *Journal of Law and Economics* 26(1), April 1983, pp. 163–234.

— "Chicago school of law and economics" in Peter Newman, editor, *The New Palgrave Dictionary of Economics and the Law*. London: Macmillan Reference Limited, 1998, Volume 1, pp. 227–233.

Klebaner, Benjamin J. "Potential competition and the American antitrust legislation of 1914" *Business History Review* 38(2), Summer 1964, pp. 163–185.

Klein, Benjamin. "Hold-up problem" in Peter Newman, editor, *The New Palgrave Dictionary of Economics and the Law*, Volume 2, 241–244. New York: Stockton Press, 1998.

Klein, Benjamin, Robert G. Crawford, and Armen A. Alchian "Vertical integration, appropriable rents, and the competitive contracting process" *Journal of Law and Economics* 21(2), October 1978, pp. 297–326.

Klein, Benjamin and Kevin M. Murphy "Vertical restraints as contract enforcement mechanisms" *Journal of Law and Economics* 31 (1988), pp. 265–297.

Kleinknecht, Alfred and Bart Verspagen "Demand and innovation: Schmookler re-examined" *Research Policy* 19(4), 1990, pp. 387–394.

Kleinschmidt, Christian and Thomas Welskopp "Zuviel 'scale' zu wenig 'scope'" *Jahrbuch für Wirtschaftsgeschichte* 1993, pp. 251–297.

Klemperer, Paul "Markets with consumer switching costs" *Quarterly Journal of Economics* 102(2), May 1987, pp. 375–397.

— "Competition when consumers have switching costs: an overview with applications to industrial organization, macroeconomics, and international trade" *Review of Economic Studies* 62(4), October 1995, pp. 515–539.

Klepper, Steven "Entry, exit, growth, and innovation over the product life cycle" *American Economic Review* 86(3), June 1996, pp. 562–583.

— "Industry life cycles" *Industrial and Corporate Change* 6(1), 1997, pp. 145–181.

Klepper, Steven and Elizabeth Graddy "The evolution of new industries and the determinants of market structure" *Rand Journal of Economics* 21(1), Spring, 1990, pp. 27–44.

Klepper, Steven and Kenneth L. Simons "Dominance by birthright: entry of prior radio producers and competitive ramifications in the U.S. television receiver industry" *Strategic Management Journal* 21(10/11), October–November 2000, pp. 997–1016.

— "Innovation and industry shakeouts" *Business and Economic History* 25(1), Autumn 1996, pp. 81–89.

— "Industry shakeouts and technological change" *International Journal of Industrial Organization* 23, 2005, pp. 23–43.

Klette, Tor Jakob "Market power, scale economies and productivity: estimates from a panel of establishment dta" *Journal of Industrial Economics* 47(4), December 1999, pp. 451–476.

Klevorick, Alvin K., Richard C. Levin, Richard R. Nelson, and Sidney G. Winter "On the sources and significance of interindustry differences in technological opportunities" *Research Policy* 24(2), March 1995, pp. 185–205.

Kling, Gerhard "The long-term impact of mergers and the emergence of a merger wave in pre-World War I Germany" *Explorations in Economic History* 43(4), October 2006, pp. 667–688.

Knetter, Michael M. "Price discrimination by U.S. and German exporters" *American Economic Review* 79, March 1989, pp. 198–210.

— "International comparisons of pricing-to-market behavior" *American Economic Review* 83, June 1993, pp. 473–486.

Knieps, Gunter and Ingo Vogelsang "The sustainability concept under alternative behavioral assumptions" *Bell Journal of Economics* 13(1), Spring 1982, pp. 234–241.

Knight, Frank H. *Risk, Uncertainty and Profit*. Boston and New York: Houghton Mifflin Company, 1921.

— " 'What is truth' in economics?" *Journal of Political Economy* 48(1), February 1940, pp. 1–32, reprinted in *On the History and Method of Economics*. Chicago: University of Chicago Press, 1956.

Knittel, Christopher R. "Interstate long distance rates: search costs, switching costs, and market power" *Review of Industrial Organization* 12, 1997, pp. 519–536.

Knittel, Christopher R. and Victor Stango "Price ceilings as focal points for tacit collusion: evidence from credit cards" *American Economic Review* 93(5), December 2003, pp. 1703–1729.

Koch, Fritz E. "Methods of regulating unfair competition in Germany, England, and the United States" *University of Pennsylvania Law Review* 78(6), April 1930, pp. 693–712 and 78(7), May 1930, pp. 854–879.

Kocka, Jürgen "Family and bureaucracy in German industrial management, 1850–1914: Siemens in comparative perspective" *Business History Review* 45, Summer 1971, pp. 133–156.

— "Germany: cooperation and competition" *Business History Review* 64(4), Winter, 1990, pp. 711–716.

Kogut, Bruce and David Parkinson "Adoption of the multidivisional structure: analyzing history from the start" *Industrial and Corporate Change* 7(2), 1998, pp. 249–273.

Kolasky, William J. and Andrew R. Dick "The merger guidelines and the integration of efficiencies into antitrust review of horizontal mergers" *Antitrust Law Journal* 71(1), 2003, pp. 207–251.

Kole, Stacey R. and Kenneth Lehn "Workforce integration and the dissipation of value in mergers: the case of USAir's acquisition of Piedmont Aviation" in Steven N. Kaplan, editor, *Mergers and Productivity*. Chicago and London: University of Chicago Press, 2000, pp. 239–279.

Kolko, Gabriel *The Triumph of Conservatism: A Reinterpretation of American History, 1900–1916*. New York: Free Press of Glencoe, 1963.

— *Railroads and Regulation 1877–916*. Princeton: Princeton University Press, 1965.

Koller, Roland H. II and Leonard W. Weiss "Price levels and seller concentration: the case of Portland cement" pp. 18–40 in Leonard W. Weiss, editor, *Concentration and Price*. Cambridge, Massachusetts: MIT Press, 1989.

Koopmans, Tjalling C. *Three Essays on the State of Economic Science*. New York: McGraw-Hill, 1957.

Kortum, Samuel and Josh Lerner "Stronger protection or technological revolution: what is behind the recent surge in patenting?" *Carnegie-Rochester Conference Series on Public Policy* 48, June 1998, pp. 247–304.

Kostecki, Michel "Export-restraint arrangements and trade liberalization" *World Economy* December 1987, pp. 425–453.

Krattenmaker, Thomas G. and Steven C. Salop "Anticompetitive exclusion: raising rivals' costs to achieve power over price" *Yale Law Journal* 96(2), December 1986, pp. 209–293.

Krause-Heiber, Ulrich "Commission Decision of 20 September 2000 imposing a fine on Opel Nederland and General Motors Nederland for obstruction of exports of new cars from the Netherlands" *Competition Policy Newsletter* 2001(1), February 2001, pp. 35–38.

Kreps, David M. "Corporate culture and economic theory" pp. 90–143 in James E. Alt and Kenneth A. Shepsle, editors, *Perspectives on Positive Political Economy*. Cambridge: Cambridge University Press, 1990.

Kreps, David M. and José Scheinkman "Quantity precommitment and Bertrand competition yield Cournot outcomes" *Bell Journal of Economics* 14(2), Summer 1983, pp. 326–337.

Kreps, David M. and Spence, A. Michael "Modeling the role of history in industrial organization and competition" pp. 340–378 in George I. Feiwel, editor, *Issues in Contemporary Microeconomics and Welfare*. London: Macmillan, 1985.

Kreps, David M. and Robert Wilson "Reputation and imperfect information" *Journal of Economic Theory* 27 August 1982, pp. 253–279.

Kroes, Neelie "Reforming Europe's State Aid regime: an Action Plan for change" Wilmer Cutler Pickering Hale and Dorr/ University of Leiden Joint conference on European State Aid Reform Brussels, 14th June 2005 (<http://ec.europa.eu/competition/speeches/index_theme_6.html>).

— "Avoiding the protectionist trap" address at conference "Nouveau monde, nouveau capitalisme" Paris 8 January 2009 (<http://ec.europa.eu/competition/speeches/index_theme_6.html>).

Kronstein, Heinrich and Gertrude Leighton "Cartel control: a record of failure" *Yale Law Journal* 55(2), February 1946, pp. 297–335.

Krueger, Anne O. "The political economy of the rent-seeking society" *American Economic Review* 64(3), June 1974, pp. 291–303.

Krugman, Paul R. "Import protection as export promotion" in Henryk Kierzkowski, editor, *Monopolistic Competition and International Trade*. Oxford: Clarendon Press, 1984, pp. 180–193.

— "Pricing to market when the exchange rate changes" in Sven W. Arndt and J. David Richardson, editors, *Real Financial Linkages Among Open Economies*. Cambridge, Massachusetts: MIT Press, 1987, pp. 49–70.

Krugman, Paul R. and Anthony J. Venables. "Integration and the competitiveness of peripheral industry" in Christopher Bliss and Jorge Braga de Macedo, editors, *Unity with Diversity in the European Economy: The Community's Southern Frontier*. Cambridge: Cambridge University Press, 1990, pp. 56–75.

Kühn, Kai-Uwe "Fighting collusion by regulating communication between firms" *Economic Policy* 16(32), April 2001, pp. 169–204.

— "Closing Pandora's box? Joint dominance after the Airtours judgment" in Swedish Competition Authority *The Pros and Cons of Merger Control*. Stockholm, 2002a, pp. 39–61.

— "Reforming European merger review: targeting problem areas in policy outcomes" *Journal of Industry, Competition, and Trade* 2(4), 2002b, pp. 311–364.

Kuisel, Richard F. *Capitalism and the State in Modern France*. Cambridge: Cambridge University Press, 1981.

Kujovich, Mary Yeager "The refrigerator car and the growth of the American dressed beef industry" *Business History Review* 44(4), Winter 1970, pp. 460–482.

Küsters, Hanns Jürgen "The origins of the EEC Treaty" pp. 211–238 in Enrico Serra, editor, *The Relaunching of Europe and the Treaties of Rome*. Brussels: Bruylant, 1989.

Kwoka, John E. Jr. "The effect of market share distribution on industry performance" *Review of Economics and Statistics* 61(1), February 1979, pp. 101–109.

— "Advertising and the price and quality of optometric services" *American Economic Review* 74(1), March 1984, pp. 211–216.

— "The Herfindahl index in theory and practice" *Antitrust Bulletin* 30 Winter 1985, pp. 915–947.

Labaton, Stephen "F.C.C. planning rules to open cable market" *New York Times*, internet edition, 9 November 2007.

Lach, Saul "Do R&D subsidies stimulate or displace private R&D? Evidence from Israel" *Journal of Industrial Economics* 50(4), December 2002, pp. 369–390.

— "Immigration and prices" *Journal of Political Economy* 115(4), August 2007, pp. 548–587.

Lafontaine, Francine, editor, *Franchise Contracting and Organization*. Cheltenham, UK: Edward Elgar, 2005.

Lafontaine, Francine and Margaret Slade "Exclusive contracts and vertical restraints: empirical evidence and public policy" September 2005 (also in Paolo Buccirossi, editor, *Handbook of Antitrust Economics*. Cambridge, Massachusetts: MIT Press, 2008, pp. 391–414).

— "Vertical integration and firm boundaries: the evidence" *Journal of Economic Literature* 45(3), September 2007, pp. 629–685.

Lagrange, Maurice "The Court of Justice as a factor in European integration" *American Journal of Comparative Law* 15(4), 1966–1967, pp. 709–725.

— Interview, 23 September 1980. (Transcript on file with the Fondation Jean Monnet Pour l'Europe, Lausanne).

Lal, Rajiv "Price promotions: limiting competitive encroachment" *Marketing Science* 9(3), Summer 1990, pp. 247–262.

Lambson, Val Eugene "Is the concentration-profit correlation partly an artifact of lumpy technology?" *American Economic Review* 77(4), September 1987, pp. 731–733.

Lammers, M. Clemens *Review of Legislation on Cartels and Trusts*. League of Nations, Economic and Financial Section. Geneva, 1927.

Lamoreaux, Naomi R. *The Great Merger Movement in American Business, 1895–1904*. Cambridge and elsewhere: Cambridge University Press, 1985.

Lancaster, Kelvin J. *Variety, Equity, and Efficiency*. New York: Columbia University Press, 1979.

Lande, Robert H. "Wealth transfers as the original and primary concern of antitrust: the efficiency interpretation challenged" *Hastings Law Journal* 34, September 1982, pp. 65–151, reprinted in Thomas E. Sullivan (1991).

Lang, Larry H. P. and René M. Stulz "Tobin's q, corporate diversification and firm performance" *Journal of Political Economy* 102(6), 1994, pp. 1248–1280.

Lange, Oscar "The scope and method of economics" *Review of Economic Studies* 13(1), 1945–1946, pp. 19–32.

Langlois, Richard N. "The vanishing hand: the changing dynamics of industrial capitalism" *Industrial and Corporate Change* 12(2), 2003, pp. 351–385.

La Porta, Rafael, Florencio Lopez-de-Silanes, and Andrei Shleifer "Corporate ownership around the world" *Journal of Finance* 54(2), April 1999, pp. 471–517.

Larner, Robert J. "Ownership and control in the 200 largest nonfinancial corporations, 1929 and 1963" *American Economic Review* 56(4), Part 1, September 1966, pp. 777–787.

Larson, David A. "An economic analysis of the Webb-Pomerene Act" *Journal of Law and Economics* 13(2), October 1970, pp. 461–500.

Latcovich, Simon and Howard Smith "Pricing, sunk costs, and market structure online: evidence from book retailing" *Oxford Review of Economic Policy* 17(2), 2001, pp. 217–234.

Launhardt, W. *Mathematische Begründung der Volkswirtschaftslehre*. Leipzig: B. G. Teubner, 1885.

— *Principles of Mathematical Economics*. Aldershot: Edward Elgar, 1993.

Lawsky, David "EU antitrust power in balance on Microsoft decision" Reuters, 10 September 2007.

Lazear, Edward P. "Retail pricing and clearance sales" *American Economic Review*, LXXVI (1986), 14–32.

Lean, David F., Jonathan D. Ogur, and Robert P. Rogers *Competition and Collusion in Electrical Equipment Markets: An Economic Assessment*. Bureau of Economics Staff Report to the Federal Trade Commission, July 1982.

Lee, Frederic S. and Warren Samuels *The Heterodox Economics of Gardner C. Means: A Collection*. Armonk: ME Sharpe, 1992.

Lee, Jiawoo "The response of exchange rate pass-through to market concentration in a small economy: the evidence from Korea" *Review of Economics and Statistics* 79(1), February 1997, pp. 142–145.

Lee, Tom and Louis L. Wilde "Market structure and innovation: a reformulation" *Quarterly Journal of Economics* 94(2), March 1980, pp. 429–436.

Leech, Dennis "Ownership concentration and control in large US corporations in the 1930s: an analysis of the TNEC sample" *Journal of Industrial Economics* 35(3), March 1987a, pp. 333–342.

— "Corporate ownership and control: a new look at the evidence of Berle and Means" *Oxford Economic Papers* 39(3), September 1987b, pp. 534–551.

Leibeler, Wesley J. "Whither predatory pricing? From Areeda and Turner to Matsushita" *Notre Dame Law Review* 61, 1986, pp. 1052–1097.

Leibenstein, Harvey "Allocative efficiency vs. 'x-efficiency'" *American Economic Review* 56(3), June 1966, pp. 392–415.

Lemelin, André "Relatedness in the patterns of industry diversification" *Review of Economics and Statistics* 64, November 1982, pp. 646–657.

Lenin, V. I. *Imperialism, the Highest Stage of Capitalism*. Petrograd, 1917, reprinted in Volume 22 V.I. Lenin *Collected Works*. Moscow: Progress Publishers, 1964.

Leonard, Robert J. "Reading Cournot, reading Nash: the creation and stabilisation of the Nash equilibrium" *Economic Journal* 104, May 1994, pp. 492–511.

Leonard, Thomas "American Progressivism and the rise of the economist as expert" July 2006.

Lerner, Abba P. "The concept of monopoly and the measurement of monopoly power" *Review of Economic Studies* 1(3), June 1934, pp. 157–175.

Lerner, Abba P. and H. W. Singer "Some notes on duopoly and spatial competition" *Journal of Political Economy* 45(2), April 1937, pp. 145–186.

Lerner, Josh "An empirical exploration of a technology race" *Rand Journal of Economics* 28(2), Summer 1997, pp. 228–247.

— "The government as venture capitalist: the long-run impact of the SBIR Program" *Journal of Business* 72(3), July 1999, pp. 285–318.

Letwin, William L. "Congress and the Sherman Antitrust Law: 1887–1890" *University of Chicago Law Review* 23(2), Winter 1956, pp. 221–258.

— *Law and Economic Policy in America*. Westwood, Connecticut: Greenwood Press, Publishers, 1965.

Levenstein, Margaret "Mass production conquers the pool: firm organization and the nature of competition in the nineteenth century" *Journal of Economic History* 55(3), September 1995, pp. 575–611.

Levenstein, Margaret C. and Valerie Y. Suslow "What determines cartel success?" *Journal of Economic Literature* 44(1), March 2006a, pp. 43–95.

— "Do cartels last? Determinants of duration of contemporary international cartels" July 2004, revised April 2006, downloaded 6 August 2006b from

<http://zeus.econ.umd.edu/cgi-bin/conference/ download.cgi? db_name=IIOC2006&paper_id=342>.

Levi, Edward H. "The antitrust laws and monopoly" *University of Chicago Law Review* 14(2), February 1947, pp. 153–183.

Levin, Richard C., Wesley M. Cohen and David C. Mowery "R&D appropriability, opportunity, and market structure: new evidence on some Schumpeterian hypotheses" *American Economic Review* 75(2), May 1985, pp. 20–24.

Levin, Richard C., A. K. Klevorick, R. R. Nelson, and Sidney G. Winter "Appropriating the returns from industrial R & D" *Brookings Papers on Economic Activity* 1987, pp. 783–820.

Levitan, R. and Martin Shubik "Price duopoly and capacity constraints" *International Economic Review* 13, 1972, pp. 111–122.

Levy, Felix H. "The Sherman Law is outworn. It should be amended" *Virginia Law Review* 13(8), June 1927, pp. 597–610.

Levy, Hermann *Monopolies, Cartels and Trusts in British Industry*. Second English edition, 1927. London: Frank Cass and Company Limited, reprinted, 1968.

Lévy-Leboyer, Maurice "The large corporation in modern France" in Alfred D. Chandler, Jr. and Herman Daems, editors, *Managerial Hierarchies*. Cambridge, Massachusetts and London, England: Harvard University Press, 1980, pp. 117–160.

Lewis, W. Arthur "Monopoly and the law, an economist's reflections on the Crofter case" *Modern Law Review* 6(3), April 1943, pp. 97–111, reprinted in W. Arthur Lewis *Overhead Costs*. New York: Rinehart & Company, Inc., 1949.

— "Competition in retail trade" *Economica* n.s. 12(48), November 1945, pp. 202–234.

Leydesdorff, Loet and Martin Meyer "The decline of university patenting and the end of the Bayh-Dole effect" downloaded 12 February 2009 from <http:// users.fmg.uva.nl/lleydesdorff/Bayh-Dole/Bayh-Dole%20Effect.pdf>.

Libecap, Gary D. "The rise of the Chicago packers and the origins of meat inspection and antitrust" *Economic Inquiry* 30(2), April 1992, pp. 242–262.

Lichtenberg, Frank R. "Industrial dediversification and its consequences for productivity" *Journal of Economic Behavior and Organization* 18(3), August 1992, pp.427–438.

Lichtenberg, Frank R. and Donald Siegel "Productivity and changes in ownership of manufacturing plants" *Brookings Papers on Economic Activity* 1987(3), 1987, pp. 643–673.

Lieber, James B. *Rats in the Grain: The Dirty Tricks and Trials of Archer Daniels Midland, the Supermarket to the World*. Four Walls Eight Windows, 2000.

Lieberman, Marvin B. and David B. Montgomery "First-mover advantages" *Strategic Management Journal* 9, Summer 1988, pp. 41–58.

— "Exit from declining industries: 'shakeout' or 'stakeout'?" *Rand Journal of Economics* 21(4), Winter 1990, pp. 538–554.

— "First-mover (dis)advantages: retrospective and link with the resource-based view" *Strategic Management Journal* 19(12), December 1998, pp. 1111–1125.

Liebowitz, Stanley J. and Stephen E. Margolis "The fable of the keys" *Journal of Law and Economics* 33(1), April 1990, pp. 1–26.

Liefmann, Robert "Monopoly or competition as the basis of government trust policy" *Quarterly Journal of Economics* 29(2), February 1915, pp. 308–325.

— *Kartelle und Trusts und die Weiterbildung der Volkswirtschaftlichen Organisation*. 5. Auflage. Stuttgart: Moritz, 1922.

— *Cartels, Concerns and Trusts*. New York: E. P. Dutton and Company Inc., 1932.

Lilienthal, David E. *Big Business: A New Era*. New York: Harper & Brothers Publishers, 1952.

Limbaugh, Rush H. "Historic origins of anti-trust legislation" *Missouri Law Review* 18(3), June 1953, pp. 215–248.

Lincoln, Abraham *Discoveries and Inventions*. Lecture, 6 April 1858, Bloomington, Illinois; 14 February 1859, Jacksonville, Illinois. (<http://showcase.netins.net/ web/creative/lincoln/speeches/discoveries.htm>; <http://www.thelincolnlog.org/view/1859/2>).

Link, Albert N. and John T. Scott "U.S. science parks: the diffusion of an innovation and its effects on the academic missions of universities" *International Journal of Industrial Organization* 21(9), November 2003, pp. 1323–1356.

Link, Albert N. and Donald S. Siegel "University-based technology initiatives: quantitative and qualitative evidence" *Research Policy* 34, 2005, pp. 253–257.

Lins, Karl and Henri Servaes "International evidence on the value of corporate diversification" *Journal of Finance* 54(6), December 1999, pp. 2215–2239.

Lipsey, R. G. and Kelvin Lancaster "The general theory of the second best" *Review of Economic Studies* 24(1), 1956–1957, pp. 11–32.

Littlechild, S. C. "Misleading calculations of the social costs of monopoly power" *Economic Journal* 91, June 1981, pp. 348–363.

Livermore, Shaw "Concentration of control now as compared with 1890" *Journal of Marketing* 4(4), Part 1, April 1940, pp. 362–369.

Livingston, Arthur "Biographical note" in Vilfredo Pareto *The Mind and Society*. Arthur Livingston, editor. London: Jonathan Cape, 1935, pp. xv–xviii.

Lobato, Ignacio N. and Patrick P. Walsh "Cartel stability and the Joint Executive Committee, 1880–1886" Trinity College Dublin Economics Technical Papers 941, 1994.

Loescher, Samuel M. *Imperfect Competition in the Cement Industry*. Cambridge, Massachusetts: Harvard University Press, 1959.

Lohr, Steve "Still another adversary for Microsoft" *New York Times* 25 May 1998 (downloaded 26 March 2008 from <http://query.nytimes.com/gst/fullpage.html?res=9F01E2DC1638F936A15756C0A96E958260>).

Lopatka, John E. and Paul E. Godek "Another look at Alcoa: raising rivals' costs does not improve the view" *Journal of Law and Economics* 35(2), October 1992, pp. 311–329.

Lösch, A. *Die raumliche Ordnung der Wirtschaft*. Iena: G. Fisher, second edition, 1944.

— *The Economics of Location*. New Haven: Yale University Press, 1954.

Loury, Glenn C. "Market structure and innovation" *Quarterly Journal of Economics* 93(3), August 1979, pp. 395–410.

Lowe, Philip "Preserving and promoting competition: a European response" *Competition Policy Newsletter* 2006(2), Summer 2006, pp. 1–5.

— "Some reflections on the European Commission's state aid policy" *Competition Policy International* 2(2), Autumn 2006b, pp. 57–77.

Lucas, Arthur Fletcher "The British movement for industrial reconstruction and the control of competitive activity" *Quarterly Journal of Economics* 49(2), February 1935, pp. 206–235.

— *Industrial Reconstruction and the Control of Competition*. London and elsewhere: Longmans, Green and Co., 1937.

Lustgarten, Steven R. "The impact of buyer concentration in manufacturing industries" *Review of Economics and Statistics* 57(2), May 1975, pp. 125–132.

Lynch, Frances M. B. "Resolving the paradox of the Monnet Plan: national and international planning in French reconstruction" *Economic History Review* 37, 1984, pp. 229–243.

Lyon, Leverett S., Paul T. Homan, George Terborgh, Lewis L. Lorwin, Charles Dearing, and Leon C. Marshall. *The National Recovery Administration: An Analysis and an Appraisal*. Washington, D.C.: The Brookings Institution, 1935.

Lyons, Bruce "A new measure of minimum efficient plant size in UK manufacturing industry" *Economica* 47(185), February 1980, pp. 19–34.

— "Reform of European merger policy" *Review of International Economics* 12(2), 2004, pp. 246–261.

Lyons, Bruce, Catherine Matraves, and Peter Moffatt "Industrial concentration and market integration in the European Union" *Economica* 68(269), February 2001, pp. 1–26.

Macdonnell, John "The law as to combinations: memorandum" *Journal of the Society of Comparative Legislation* n.s. 10(1), 1909, pp. 153–175.

Macgregor, D. H. "Rationaliation and the coal trade" pp. 161–172 in D. H. Macgregor *Enterprise Purpose & Profit*. Oxford: Clarendon Press, 1934.

Machlup, Fritz "Competition, pliopoly, and profits" *Economica* 9, February 1942, pp. 1–23; May 1942, pp. 153–73.

— *The Basing-Point System*. Philadelphia and Toronto: The Blakiston Company, 1949.

— *An Economic Review of the Patent System*. Subcommittee on Patents, Trademarks & Copyrights of the Senate Committee on the Judiciary, 85th Congress, 2d Session, 1958.

— "Theories of the firm: marginalist, behavioral, managerial" *American Economic Review* 57(1), March 1967, pp. 1–33.

— "Oligopoly and the free society" *Antitrust Law & Economics Review* 1(1), July–August 1967, pp. 11–34.

Machlup, Fritz and Edith Penrose "The patent controversy in the nineteenth century" *Journal of Economic History* 10(1), 1950, pp. 1–29.

Machlup, Fritz and Martha Taber "Bilateral monopoly, successive monopoly, and vertical integration" *Economica* n.s. 27(106), May 1960, pp. 101–119.

MacLeod, Christine *Inventing the Industrial Revolution*. Cambridge and elsewhere: Cambridge University Press, 1996.

Macneil, Ian R. "Contracts: adjustments of long-term economic relations under classical, neoclassical, and relational contract law" *Northwestern University Law Review* 72, 1978, pp. 854–906.

Macrosty, Henry W. *The Trust Movement in British Industry*. London and elsewhere: Longmans, Green, and Co., 1907.

Madison, James H. *The Indiana Way: A State History*. Bloomington and Indianapolis: Indiana University Press, 1986.

Magenheim, Ellen B. and Dennis C. Mueller "Are acquiring-firm shareholders better off after an acquisition?" in John C. Coffee, Louis Lowenstein, and Susan Rose-Ackerman, editors, *Knights, Raiders, and Targets: The Impact of the Hostile Takeover*. Oxford and New York: Oxford University Press, 1988, pp. 171–193.

Magliocca, Gerard N. "Blackberries and barnyards: patent trolls and the perils of innovation" Berkeley Center for Law and Technology paper 29, 2007.

Magnan de Bornier, Jean "The 'Cournot-Bertrand' debate: a historical perspective" *History of Political Economy* 24(3), 1992, pp. 623–656.

Maksimovic, Vojislav "Financial structure and product market competition" pp. 887–920 in Robert Jarrow, Vojislav Maksimovic, and William T. Ziembra, editors, *Handbooks in Operations Research and Management Science: Finance*. Amsterdam: Elsevier Science B.V., 2007.

Malkiel, Burton G. *A Random Walk Down Wall Street*. New York and London: W. W. Norton & Company, 2007.

Mandelbrot, Benoit and Richard L. Hudson *The (Mis)behavior of Markets*. New York: Basic Books, 2004.

Mankiw, N. Gregory and Michael D. Whinston "Free entry and social inefficiency" *Rand Journal of Economics* 17(1), Spring 1986, pp. 48–58.

Mannering, Fred and Clifford Winston "Brand loyalty and the decline of American automobile firms" *Brookings Papers on Economic Activity: Microeconomics*. 1991, pp. 67–114.

Mansfield, Edwin "Size of firm, market structure, and innovation" *Journal of Political Economy* 71(6), December 1963, pp. 556–576.

— "National science policy: issues and problems" *American Economic Review* 56(1/2), March 1966, pp. 476–488.

— "How rapidly does new industrial technology leak out?" *Journal of Industrial Economics* 34(2), December 1985, pp. 217–223.

— "Comments" *Brookings Papers on Economic Activity Microeconomics* 1993(2), 1993, pp. 330–335.

Mansfield, Edwin, John Rapoport, Anthony Romeo, Samuel Wagner, and George Beardsley "Social and private rates of return from industrial innovations" *Quarterly Journal of Economics* 91(2), May 1977, pp. 221–240.

Mansfield, Edwin, Mark Schwartz and Samuel Wagner "Imitation costs and patents: an empirical study" *Economic Journal* 91 December 1981, pp. 907–918.

Marburg, Theodore F. "Government and business in Germany: public policy toward cartels" *Business History Review* 38(1), Spring 1964, pp. 78–102.

Marengo, Louis "The basing point decisions and the steel industry" *American Economic Review* 45(2), May 1955, pp. 509–522.

Mariger, Randall "Predatory price cutting: the Standard Oil of New Jersey case revisited" *Explorations in Economic History* 15(4), October 1978, pp. 341–367.

Marin, Pedro L. and Georges Siotis "Innovation and market structure: an empirical evaluation of the 'bounds approach' in the chemical industry" *Journal of Industrial Economics* 55(1), March 2007, pp. 93–111.

Mariuzzo, Franco and Patrick Paul Walsh "Deterministic demand cycles and economies of scale in cartel price data: the Joint Executive Committee (1880–1886)" Trinity Economic Papers 2006/12.

Markham, Jesse W. "The nature and significance of price leadership" *American Economic Review* 41, December 1951, pp. 891–905.

— *Competition in the Rayon Industry*. Cambridge, Massachusetts: Harvard University Press, 1952.

— "Survey of the evidence and findings on mergers" in Universities-National Bureau Committee for Economic Research *Business Concentration and Price Policy*. Princeton: Princeton University Press, 1955, pp. 141–182.

Markoff, John "Newly released documents shed light on Microsoft tactics" *New York Times*, internet edition, 24 March 2004.

Marriner, Sheila and Francis E. Hyde *The Senior John Samuel Swire 1825–98*. Liverpool: Liverpool University Press, 1967.

Marris, Robin L. *The Economic Theory of 'Managerial' Capitalism*. New York: Basic Books, 1968.

Marshall, Alfred *Economics of Industry*. London: Macmillan and Co. Limited, 1892; fourth edition, 1909.

— "On rent" *Economic Journal* 3(9), March 1893, pp. 74–90.

— *Industry and Trade*. London: Macmillan and Co. Limited, 1919; fourth edition, 1923.

— *Principles of Economics*. London: The Macmillan Press Ltd, eighth edition, 1920; <http://www.econlib.org/library/Marshall/marP.html>.

— "Some aspects of competition" (Presidential Address to the Economic Science and Statistics Section of the British Association, at Leeds, 1890) in A. C. Pigou, editor, *Memorials of Alfred Marshall*. London: MacMillan, 1925, pp. 256–291.

Marshall, Alfred and Mary Paley Marshall *The Economics of Industry*. First edition, 1879. Reprinted Bristol: Thoemmes Press, 1994.

Marston, Richard C. "Pricing to market in Japanese manufacturing" *Journal of International Economics* 29, 1990, pp. 217–236.

Martin, David Dale *Mergers and the Clayton Act*. Berkeley and Los Angeles: University of California Press, 1959.

— "Industrial organization and reorganization" Chapter 13 in Warren J. Samuels, editor, *The Chicago School of Political Economy*. Association for Evolutionary Economics and Division of Research, Graduate School of Business Administration, Michigan State University, 1976.

Martin, Kenney "Schumpeterian innovation and entrepreneurs in capitalism" *Research Policy* 1, February 1986, pp. 21–33.

Martin, Stephen "Vertical relationships and industrial performance" *Quarterly Review of Economics and Business* 23(1), Spring 1983, pp. 6–18.

— "Market power and/or efficiency?" *Review of Economics and Statistics* 70(2), May 1988a, pp. 331–335.

— "The measurement of profitability and the diagnosis of market power" *International Journal of Industrial Organization* 6(3), September 1988b, pp. 301–321.

— "Sunk cost, financial markets, and contestability" *European Economic Review* 33(6), June 1989, pp. 1089–1113.

— "Fringe size and cartel stability" Department of Economics, European University Institute, Working Paper 90/16, November 1990.

— "R&D joint ventures and tacit product market collusion" *European Journal of Political Economy* 11(4), April 1996, pp. 733–741.

— "Public policies toward cooperation in research and development: the European Union, Japan, the United States" in Leonard Waverman, William S. Comanor, and Akira Goto, editors, *Competition Policy in the Global Economy*. London: Routledge, 1996b, pp. 245–288.

— "Competition policy: publicity vs. prohibition & punishment" in Stephen Martin, editor, *Competition Policies in Europe*, Elsevier-North Holland Publishers, 1998a.

— "Competition policy for high technology industries" *Journal of Industry, Competition and Trade* 1(4), 2001, pp. 441–465.

— *Advanced Industrial Economics*. Basil Blackwell, second edition, 2002a.

— "Spillovers, appropriability, and R&D" *Journal of Economics* 75(1), 2002b, pp. 1–32.

— "Sunk cost and entry" *Review of Industrial Organization* 20(4), June 2002c, pp. 291–304.

— "Globalization and the limits of competition" in Manfred Neumann and Jürgen Weigand, editors, *Handbook of Competition*, Edward Elgar, 2004a.

— "Coal and steel: first steps in European market integration" February 2004b. (<http://www.krannert.purdue.edu/faculty/smartin/vita/EI5060D.pdf and ecscfig.pdf>).

— "Competition policy, collusion, and tacit collusion" *International Journal of Industrial Organization*, 24(6), November 2006, pp. 1299–1332.

— "Remembrance of things past: antitrust, ideology, and the development of industrial economics" in Vivek Ghosal and Johan Stennek, editors, *The Political Economy of Antitrust*, 2007.

— "The goals of antitrust and competition policy" pp. 19–84 in Wayne Dale Collins, editor, *Issues in Competition Law and Policy*, 2008a.

— "Mergers: an overview" in Klaus Gugler and B. Burcin Yurtoglu, editors, *The Economics of Corporate Governance and Mergers*. Edward Elgar, 2008b.

— "Microfoundations for the linear demand product differentiation model, with applications to market structure" Purdue University Department of Economics Working Paper 1221, March 2009.

Martin, Stephen and John T. Scott "The nature of innovation market failure and the design of public support for private innovation" *Research Policy* 19(4–5) April 2000, pp. 437–447; reprinted in Albert N. Link, editor, *The Economics of Innovation Policy*, Edward Elgar, 2007.

Martin, Stephen, Hans-Theo Normann, and Christopher Snyder "Vertical foreclosure in experimental markets" *Rand Journal of Economics* 32(3), Autumn 2001, pp. 466–496.

Martin, Stephen and Paola Valbonesi "State aid to business" in Patrizio Bianchi and Sandrine Labory, editors, *International Handbook of Industrial Policy*, 2006, pp. 134–152..

— "Equilibrium state aid in integrating markets" *B.E. Journal of Economic Analysis & Policy* 8(1), Article 33, 2008.

Marvel, Howard P. "Competition and price levels in the retail gasoline market" *Review of Economics and Statistics* 60(2), April 1978, pp. 252–258.

Maschke, Erich "Outline of the history of German cartels from 1873 to 1914" pp. 226–258 in F. Crouzet, W. H. Chaloner and W. M. Stern, editors, *Essays in European Economic History 1789-1914*. New York: St. Martin's Press, 1969.

Mason, Edward S. "Monopoly in law and economics" *Yale Law Journal* 47(1), 1937, pp. 34–49.

— "Price inflexibility" *Review of Economics and Statistics* 20(2), May 1938, pp. 53–64.

— "Price and production policies of large-scale enterprise" *American Economic Review* 29(1), March 1939, pp. 61–74.

— "The current status of the monopoly problem in the United States" *Harvard Law Review* 62(8), June 1949, pp. 1265–1285.

— "Schumpeter on monopoly and the large firm" *Review of Economics and Statistics* 33(2), May 1951, pp. 139–144.

— "The apologetics of 'managerialism'" *Journal of Business* 31(1), June 1958, pp. 1–11.

Masten, Scott E. "The organization of production: evidence from the aerospace industry" *Journal of Law and Economics* 27(2), October 1984, pp. 403–417.

— "Modern evidence on the firm" *American Economic Review* 92(2), May 2002, pp. 428–432.

Masten, Scott E. and Edward A. Snyder *United States versus United Shoe Machinery Corporation: on the merits* *Journal of Law and Economics* 36, April 1993, pp. 33–70.

Matraves, Catherine "Market structure, R&D and advertising in the pharmaceutical industry" *Journal of Industrial Economics* 47(2), June 1999, pp. 169–194.

Matraves, Catherine and Laura Rondi "Product differentiation, industry concentration and market share turbulence" November 2005. Available at SSRN: <http://ssrn.com/abstract=847684>.

Matsusaka, John G. "Takeover motives during the conglomerate merger wave" *Rand Journal of Economics* 24(3), Autumn 1993, pp. 357–379.

Matutes, Carmen and Pierre Regibeau "A selective review of the economics of standardization: entry deterrence, technological progress, and international competition" *European Journal of Political Economy* 12, 1996, pp. 183–209.

Maybee, Rolland Harper *Railroad Competition and the Oil Trade, 1855–1873*. Philadelphia: Porcupine Press, 1974.

Mayhew, Anne "A reappraisal of the causes of farm protest in the United States, 1870–1900" *Journal of Economic History* 32, June 1972, pp. 464–475.

— "The Sherman Act as protective reaction" *Journal of Economic Issues* 24(2), June 1990, pp. 389–396.

McAfee, R. Preston, Hugo M. Mialon, and Michael A. Williams "What is a barrier to entry" *American Economic Review* 94(2), May 2004, pp. 461–465.

McAfee, R. Preston and Michael A. Williams "Horizontal mergers and antitrust policy" *Journal of Industrial Economics* 40(2), June 1992, pp. 181–187.

McCalla, Alex F. "A duopoly model of world wheat pricing" *Journal of Farm Economics* 48(3), Part 1, August 1966, pp. 711–727.

McChesney, Fred S. "Rent from regulation" in Peter Newman, editor, *The New Palgrave Dictionary of Economics and the Law*. London: Macmillan Press Limited, Volume 3, 1998, pp. 310–315.

McCloughan, Patrick "Simulation of concentration development from modified Gibrat growth-entry-exit processes" *Journal of Industrial Economics* 43(4), December 1995, pp. 405–433.

McCloughan, Patrick, Sean Lyons, and William Batt "The effectiveness of competition policy and the price-cost margin: new econometric evidence" Economic and Social Research Institute Working Paper 209, revised 2008.

McCraw, Thomas K. *Prophets of Regulation*. Cambridge, Massachusetts and London, England: The Belknap Press of Harvard University Press, 1984.

— , editor, *The Essential Alfred Chandler*. Boston, Massachusetts: Harvard Business School Press, 1988.

— "Joseph Schumpeter on competition" *Competition Policy International* 4(2), Autumn 2008, pp. 309–334.

McCraw, Thomas K. and Forest Reinhardt "Losing to win: U.S. Steel's pricing, investment decisions, and market share, 1901–1938" *Journal of Economic History* 49(3), September 1989, pp. 593–619.

— "Competition and 'fair trade': history and theory" *Research in Economic History* 16, 1996, pp. 185–239.

McCurdy, Charles W. "American law and the marketing structure of the large corporation, 1875–1890" *Journal of Economic History* 38(3), September 1978, pp. 631–649.

McFadden, Joseph M. "Monopoly in barbed wire: the formation of the American Steel and Wire Company" *Business History Review* 52(4), Winter 1978, pp. 465–489.

McGahan, Anita M. "The emergence of the national brewing oligopoly: competition in the American market, 1933–1958" *Business History Review* 65(2), Summer 1991, pp. 229–284.

McGee, John S. "Cross hauling: a symptom of incomplete collusion under basing-point systems" *Southern Economic Journal* 20(4), April 1954, pp. 369–379.

— "Predatory price cutting: the Standard Oil (N.J.) case" *Journal of Law and Economics* 1, October 1958, pp. 137–169.

McGuckin, Robert H. and Sang V. Nguyen "On productivity and plant ownership change: new evidence from the longitudinal research database" *Rand Journal of Economics* 26(2), Summer 1995, pp. 257–276.

McKie, James W. "The decline of monopoly in the metal container industry" *American Economic Review* 45(2), May 1955, pp. 499–508.

— "Predatory pricing revisited" *Journal of Law and Economics* 23(2), October 1980, pp. 289–330.

McMillan, John "*Dango*: Japan's price-fixing conspiracies" *Economics and Politics* 3(3), November 1991, pp. 201–218.

Means, Gardiner C. *Industrial Prices and their Relative Inflexibility*. Senate Document 13, 74th Congress, 1st Session, January 17, 1935a, reprinted in Frederic S. Lee and Warren Samuels. *The Heterodox Economics of Gardner C. Means: A Collection*. Armonk: ME Sharpe, 1992.

— "Price inflexibility and the requirements of a stabilizing monetary policy" *Journal of the American Statistical Association* 30(190), June 1935b, pp. 4021–413.

— "Notes on inflexible prices" *American Economic Review* 26(1), March 1936, pp. 23–35.

— "Business combinations and agriculture" *Journal of Farm Economics* 20(1), February 1938, pp. 53–57.

— *The Structure of the American Economy*. Washington, D.C.: National Resources Committee, June 1939.

— "The economics of administered prices: introductory explorations for an atomistic economy" pp. 125–128 in Frederic S. Lee and Warren Samuels, editors, *The Heterodox Economics of Gardiner C. Means*. Armonk, NY and London: M.E. Sharpe, Inc., [29 January 1940a] 1992.

— "Big business, administered prices, and the problem of full employment" *Journal of Marketing* 4(4), Part 1, April 1940b, pp. 370–378.

— "Testimony" pp. 8–36 in *Economic Concentration: Part 1 Overall and Conglomerate Aspects*. Hearings Before the Subcommittee on Antitrust and Monopoly of the Committee on the Judiciary. United States Senate. Eighty-eighth Congress, Second Session. Washington, D.C.: USGPO, 1964.

— "Letter [of 20 March 1964] to Jerry Cohen" pp. 171–179 in Frederic S. Lee and Warren Samuels, editors, *The Heterodox Economics of Gardiner C. Means*. Armonk, NY and London: M.E. Sharpe, Inc., 1992.

— "The administered-price thesis reconfirmed" *American Economic Review* 62(3), June 1972, pp. 292–306.

— "Industrial prices, as administered by Dr. Means—a reply" pp. 180–187 in Frederic S. Lee and Warren J. Samuels, editors, *The Heterodox Economics of Gardiner*

C. Means. Armonk, NY and London: M.E. Sharpe, Inc., 1992.

Mela, Carl F., Sunil Gupta, and Donald R. Lehmann "The long-term impact of promotion and advertising on consumer brand choice" *Journal of Marketing Research* 34(2), May 1997, pp. 248–261.

Mercer, Helen "The rhetoric and reality of anti-cartel policies: Britain, Germany and Japan and the effects of US pressure in the 1940's" in Carlo Morelli, editor, "Cartels and Market management in the Post-War World" Business History Unit, London School of Economics, Occasional Paper 1997 No. 1, pp. 40–77.

Merrell, Mark, E. T. Grether, and Summer S. Kittelle "Restriction of retail price cutting with emphasis on the drug industry" Trade Practices Studies Section, Division of Review, Office of National Recovery Administration, Work Materials No. 57, March 1936.

Messerlin, Patrick A. "The EC antidumping regulations: a first economic appraisal, 1980–85" *Weltwirtschaftliches Archiv* 125, 1989, pp. 563–587.

— "Anti-dumping regulations or pro-cartel law? The EC chemical cases" *World Economy* 13, 1990, pp. 465–492.

Meyer, Balthasar Henry "A history of the Northern Securities case" *Bulletin of the University of Wisconsin* Economics and Political Science Series 1(3), July 1906, pp. 215–350.

Meyer, David R. "Emergence of the American manufacturing belt: an interpretation" *Journal of Historical Geography* 9(2), April 1983, pp. 1451–1474.

— "The national integration of regional economies, 1860–1920" Chapter 14 in Robert D. Mitchell and Paul A. Groves, editors, *North America: the Historical Georgraphy of a Changing Continent*. Totowa, New jersey: Rowman & Littlefield, 1987.

— "Midwestern industrialization and the American manufacturing belt in the nineteenth century" *Journal of Economic History* 49(4), December 1989, pp. 921–937.

Midelfart-Knarvik, Karen Helen, Henry G. Overman, Stephen Redding, and Anthony J. Venables "Integration and industrial specialisation in the European Union" *Revue économique* 53(3), May 2002, pp. 469–481.

Miksch, Leonhard "Die Wirtschaftspolitik des Als Ob" *Zeitschrift für die Gesamte Staatswissenschaft* 105, 1949, pp. 310–338.

Milgrom, Paul and John Roberts "Limit pricing and entry under incomplete information" *Econometrica* 50(2), March 1982, pp. 443–466.

— "Economic theories of the firm: past, present, and future" *Canadian Journal of Economics* 21(3), August 1988, pp. 444–458.

Mill, John Stuart "Thornton on labour and its claims" *Fortnightly Review* Part I May, 1869, pp. 505–18; Part II, June, 1869, pp. 680–700; accessed 1 September 2007 at <http://socserv.mcmaster.ca/econ/ugcm/3ll3/mill/thorn.html>.

Mills, Edwin S. and Lav, Michael R. "A model of market areas with free entry" *Journal of Political Economy* 72(3), June 1964, pp. 278–288.

Milyo, Jeffrey and Joel Waldfogel "The effect of price advertising on prices: evidence in the wake of *44 Liquormart*" *American Economic Review* 89(5), December 1999, pp. 1081–1096.

Mirowski, Philip and Robert Van Horn "The contract research organization and the commercialization of scientific research" *Social Studies of Science* 35(4), August 2005, pp. 503–548.

Mirsky, Jeannette and Allan Nevins. *The World of Eli Whitney*. New York: Macmillan, 1952.

Miscamble, Wilson D. "Thurman Arnold goes to Washington: a look at antitrust policy in the later New Deal" *Business History Review* 56(1), Spring 1982, pp. 1–15.

Mitchell, Wesley C. "The problem of measuring profits, a preliminary note" pp. 3–27 in Ralph C. Epstein, *Industrial Profits in the United States*. New York: NBER and Committee on Recent Economic Changes, 1934.

Miwa, Yoshiro and J. Mark Ramseyer "Rethinking relationship-specific investments: subcontracting in the Japanese automobile industry" *Michigan Law Review* 98, August 2000, 2636–2667.

Modigliani, Franco "New developments on the oligopoly front" *Journal of Political Economy* 66(3), June 1958, pp. 215–232.

Moeller, Sara B., Frederik P. Schlingemann, and René M. Stulz "Wealth destruction on a massive scale? A study of acquiring-firm returns in the recent merger wave" *Journal of Finance* 60(2), April 2005, pp. 757–782.

Mohnen, Pierre and Lars-Hendrik Röller "Complementarities in innovation policy" *European Economic Review* 49(6), August 2005, pp. 1431–1450.

Monnet, Jean *Mémoires*. Fayard, 1976; English translation, Garden City: Doubleday & Company, 1978.

Montague, Gilbert H. "The rise and supremacy of the Standard Oil Company" *Quarterly Journal of Economics* 16(2), February 1902, pp. 265–295.

— "The later history of the Standard Oil Company" *Quarterly Journal of Economics* 17(2), February 1903, pp. 293–325.

Monteverde, Kirk and David J. Teece "Appropriable rents and quasi-vertical integration" *Journal of Law and Economics* 25(2), October 1982, pp. 321–328.

Montgomery, Cynthia A. "Corporate diversification" *Journal of Economic Perspectives* 8(3), Summer, 1994, pp. 163–178.

Monti, Mario "By Invitation" *The Economist* 9 November 2002, pp. 71–72.

— "A reformed competition policy: achievements and challenges for the future" speech at the Center for European Reform, Brussels, 28 October 2004.

Montias, J. Michael "The influence of economic factors on style" *De zeventiende eeuw* 6(1), 1990, pp. 49–57.

Moore, Henry L. "The personality of Antoine Augustin Cournot" *Quarterly Journal of Economics* 19(3), May 1905, pp. 370–399.

Morck, Randall, Andrei Shleifer, and Robert W. Vishny "Management ownership and market valuation: an empirical analysis" *Journal of Financial Economics* 20, 1988, pp. 293–315.

Morgan, Mary S. "Competing notions of 'competition' in late nineteenth-century American economics" *History of Political Economy* 25(4), Winter 1993, pp. 563–604.

— "Marketplace morals and American economists: the case of John Bates Clark" in Neil De Marchi and Mary S. Morgan, editors, *Higgling: Transactors and Their Markets in the History of Economics*. Annual supplement to volume 26, *History of Political Economy*. Durham and London, 1994.

Morris, Claire "'Address' models of product differentiation: a survey" Studies in Economics 9713, Department of Economics, University of Kent, December 1997.

Morrison Paul, Catherine J. "Market and cost structure in the U.S. beef packing industry: a plant-level analysis" *American Journal of Agricultural Economics* 83(1), February 2001a, pp. 64–76.

— "Cost economies and market power: the case of the U.S. meat packing industry" *Review of Economics and Statistics* 83(3), August 2001b, pp. 531–540.

Morrison, Steven A. and Clifford Winston "Causes and consequences of airline fare wars" *Brookings Papers on Economic Activity: Microeconomics* 1996, pp. 85–123.

Möschel, Wernhard "Competition policy from an Ordo point of view" in Alan Peacock and Hans Willgerodt, editors, *German Neo-Liberals and the Social Market Economy*. New York: St. Martin's Press, 1989, pp. 142–159.

— "The proper scope of government viewed from an Ordoliberal perspective: the example of competition policy" *Journal of Institutional and Theoretical Economics* 157, March 2001, pp. 3–13.

Moser, Petra "How do patent laws influence innovation? Evidence from nineteenth-century world fairs" *American Economic Review* 95(4), September 2005, pp. 1214–1236.

Motta, Massimo "E.C. merger policy and the *Airtours* case" *European Competition Law Review* 2000, 199–207.

Motta, Massimo, Michele Polo, and Helder Vasconcelos "Merger remedies in the European Union: an overview" *Antitrust Bulletin* 52(3/4), Autumn–Winter 2007, pp. 603–631.

Mowery, David C. "The relationship between intrafirm and contractual forms of industrial research in American manufacturing, 1900–1940" *Explorations in Economic History* 20(4), October 1983a, pp. 351–374.

— "Industrial research and firm size, survival, and growth in American manufacturing, 1921–1946: an assessment" *Journal of Economic History* 43(4), December 1983b, pp. 953–980.

— "The practice of technology policy" in Paul Stoneman, editor, *Handbook of the Economics of Innovation and Technological Change*. Oxford: Blackwell Publishers Ltd., 1995.

— "The boundaries of the U.S. firm in R&D" in Naomi R. Lamoreaux and Daniel M. G. Raff, editors, *Coordination and Information*, pp. 147–176. Chicago and London: University of Chicago Press, 1995b.

— "The changing structure of the US national innovation system: implications for international conflict and cooperation in R&D policy" *Research Policy* 27, 1998, pp. 639–654.

Mowery, David C. and Nathan Rosenberg "The U. S. national innovation system" pp. 29–75 in Richard R. Nelson, editor, *National Innovation Systems: A Comparative Analysis*. New York and Oxford: Oxford University Press, 1993.

Mowery, David C. and W. Edward Steinmueller "Government policy and industry evolution in the U.S. integrated circuit industry: what lessons for newly industrializing economies?" CEPR Publication No. 192, Center for Economic Policy Research, January 1990.

Mueller, Dennis C. "A theory of conglomerate mergers" *Quarterly Journal of Economics* 83(4), November 1969, pp. 643–659.

— "The effects of conglomerate mergers" *Journal of Banking and Finance* 1, 1977a, pp. 315–347.

— "The persistence of profits above the norm" *Economica* 44(176), November 1977b, pp. 369–380.

— *Profits in the Long Run*. Cambridge and elsewhere: Cambridge University Press, 1986.

— , editor, *The Dynamics of Company Profits: An International Comparison*. Cambridge: Cambridge University Press, 1990.

— "The corporation and the economist" *International Journal of Industrial Organization* 10(2), June 1992, pp. 147–170.

— "The finance literature on mergers: a critical survey" pp. 161–205 in M. Waterson, editor, *Competition, Monopoly and Corporate Governance*. UK: Edward Elgar, 2003.

Mueller, Willard F. and Russell C. Parker "The bakers of Washington cartel: twenty-five years later" *Review of Industrial Organization* 7(1), March 1992, pp. 75–82.

Mueller, Williard F. and Richard T. Rogers "The role of advertising in changing concentration of manufacturing industries" *Review of Economics and Statistics* 52(1), February 1980, pp. 89–96.

Mullin, George L., Joseph C. Mullin, and Wallace P. Mullin "The competitive effects of mergers: stock market evidence from the U.S. Steel dissolution suit" *Rand Journal of Economics* 26(2), Summer 1995, pp. 314–330.

Mullin, Joseph C. and Wallace P. Mullin "United States Steel's acquisition of the Great Northern ore properties: vertical foreclosure or efficient contractual governance?" *Journal of Law, Economics and Organization* April 1997, 13(1), pp. 74–100.

Mund, Vernon A. *Monopoly*. Princeton: Princeton University Press, 1933.

Munsey, Cecil "Lydia's medicine 130 years later" *Bottles and Extras* 14(4), Autumn 2003 (downloaded 24 November 2008 from <http://www.fohbc.com/PDF_Files/Pinkham_130YrsLater.pdf>).

Murchison, Claudius T. "Resale price maintenance" *Studies in History, Economics and Public Law* 192(2), 1919.

Mussa, Michael and Sherwin Rosen "Monopoly and product quality" *Journal of Economic Theory* 18 1978, pp. 301–317.

Nader, Ralph *Unsafe at Any Speed*. New York: Grossman, 1965.

Nalebuff, Barry "Bundling, tying, and portfolio effects" DTI Economics Paper No. 1, Part I: Conceptual Issues. February 2003, <http://www.berr.gov.uk/files/file14774.pdf>.

Nash, Gerald D. "Origins of the Interstate Commerce Act of 1887" *Pennsylvania History* 24(3), July 1957, pp. 181–190.

Nash, John F. Jr. *Non-cooperative Games*. Ph.D. dissertation, Princeton University, 1950.

— "Non-cooperative games" *Annals of Mathematics* 54(2), September 1951, pp. 286–295, reprinted in John F. Nash, Jr. *Essays on Game Theory*. Cheltenham, UK and Brookfield, U.S.: Edward Elgar, 1996.

Nathan, Otto *The Nazi Economic System*. Durham: Duke University Press, 1944.

National Industrial Conference Board, Inc. *Rationalization of German Industry*. New York, 1931.

National Science Foundation, Division of Science Resources Statistics *The Methodology Underlying the Measurement of R&D Expenditures: 2000 (data update)*. December 10, 2001.

— *National Patterns of R&D Resources: 2007 Data Update*. NSF 08-318. Arlington, Virginia. Available at <http://www.nsf.gov/statistics/nsf08318/>.

Navin, Thomas R. and Marian V. Sears "A study in merger: formation of the International Mercantile Marine Company" *Business History Review* 28(4), December 1954, pp. 291–328.

— "The rise of a market for industrial securities, 1887–1902" *Business History Review* 29(2), June 1955, pp. 105–138.

Nehl, Hanns Peter and Jan Nuijten "Commission ends competition proceedings regarding German book price fixing agreements following acceptance of an undertaking on cross-border sales" *Competition Policy Newsletter* 2002(2), June 2002, pp. 35–37.

Nelson, Ralph L. *Merger Movements in American Industry*. Princeton: Princeton University Press, 1959.

— "Business cycle factors in the choice between internal and external growth" pp. 52–70 in William W. Alberts and Joel E. Segall, editors, *The Corporate Merger*. Chicago and London: University of Chicago Press, 1966.

Nelson, Richard R. "The economics of invention: a survey of the literature" *Journal of Business* 32(2), April 1959a, pp. 101–127.

— "The simple economics of basic scientific research" *Journal of Political Economy* 67(3), June 1959b, pp. 297–306.

— "Government stimulus of technological progress: lessons from American history" in Richard R. Nelson, editor, *Government and Technical Progress*. New York: Pergamon Press, 1982, pp. 451–481.

— "Institutions supporting technical change in the United States" pp. 312–329 in Giovanni Dosi, Christopher Freeman, Richard Nelson, Gerald Silverberg, and Luc Soete, editors, *Technical Change and Economic Theory*. London: Pinter Publishers Limited, 1988.

— "U.S. technological leadership: Where did it come from and where did it go?" *Research Policy* 19(2), April 1990, pp. 117–132.

— "A retrospective" pp. 505–523 in Richard R. Nelson, editor, *National Innovation Systems: A Comparative Analysis*. New York and Oxford: Oxford University Press, 1993.

—, editor, *National Innovation Systems: A Comparative Analysis*. New York and Oxford: Oxford University Press, 1993b.

— "Reflections on 'The simple economics of basic scientific research': looking back and looking forward" *Industrial and Corporate Change* 15(6), 2006, pp. 903–917.

Nelson, Richard R. and Nathan Rosenberg "Technical innovation and national systems, pp. 3–27 in Richard R. Nelson, editor, *National Innovation Systems: A Comparative Analysis*. New York and Oxford: Oxford University Press, 1993.

Nelson, Richard R. and Sidney G. Winter "In search of useful theory of innovation" *Research Policy* 6(1), January 1977, pp. 36–76.

— *An Evolutionary Theory of Economic Change*. Cambridge, Massachusetts: Belknap Press of Harvard University Press, 1982.

Nerlove, Marc and Kenneth J. Arrow "Optimal advertising policy under dynamic conditions" *Economica*, n.s. 29(114), May 1962, pp. 129–142.

Neufeld, John L. "Price discrimination and the adoption of the electricity demand charge" *Journal of Economic History* 47(3), September 1987, pp. 693–709.

Neumann, Manfred, Ingo Böbel, and Alfred Haid "Domestic concentration, foreign trade and economic performance" *International Journal of Industrial Organization* 3, 1985, pp. 1–19.

Neumann, Manfred and Alfred Haid "Concentration and economic performance: a cross-section analysis of West German industries" pp. 61–84 in Schwalbach, Joachim, editor, *Industry Structure and Performance*. Berlin: Edition Sigma Rainer Bohn Verlag, 1985.

Neven, Damien "'Address' models of differentiation" in George Norman, editor, *Spatial Pricing and Differentiated Markets*. London: Pion Limited, 1986, pp. 5–18.

— "Competition economics and antitrust in Europe" *Economic Policy* 48, October 2006, pp. 743–781.

Neven, Damien, Robin Nuttall, and Paul Seabright *Merger in Daylight*. London: CEPR, 1993.

Neven, Damien, Pénélope Papandropoulos and Paul Seabright *Trawling for Minnows*. London: CEPR, 1998.

Neven, Damien J., Lars-Hendrik Röller, and Zhentang Zhang "Endogenous costs and price-cost margins: an application to the European airline industry" *Journal of Industrial Economics* 54(3), September 2006, pp. 351–368.

Nevins, Allan *John D. Rockefeller*. New York: Charles Scribner's Sons, 1940.

Nevo, Aviv "Mergers with differentiated products: the case of the ready-to-eat cereal industry" *Rand Journal of Economics* 31(3), Autumn 2000, pp. 395–421.

Newman, Philip C. "Key German cartels under the Naxi regime" *Quarterly Journal of Economics* 62(4), August 1948, pp. 576–595.

Newmark, Craig M. "Does horizontal price fixing raise price? A look at the *Bakers of Washington* case" *Journal of Law and Economics* 31(2), October 1988, pp. 469–484.

— "Price-concentration studies: there you go again" 14 February 2004. Available at SSRN: <http://ssrn.com/abstract=503522>.

Ng, Charles K. and Paul Seabright "Competition, privatisation and productive efficiency: evidence from the airline industry" *Economic Journal* 111(473), July 2001, pp. 591–619.

Nichol, Archibald J. *Partial Monopoly and Price Leadership*. Ph.D. dissertation, Faculty of Political Science, Columbia University, 1930.

— "Tragedies in the life of Cournot" *Econometrica* 6(3), June 1938, pp. 193–197.

Nickell, Stephen J. "Competition and corporate performance" *Journal of Political Economy* 104, 1996, pp. 724–745.

Nicolaides, Phedon and Remco van Wijngaarden "Reform of anti-dumping regulations: the case of the EC" *Journal of World Trade* 27(3), June 1993, pp. 31–53.

Nicholas, Tom "Why Schumpeter was right: innovation, market power, and creative destruction in 1920s America" *Journal of Economic History* 63(4), December 2003, pp. 1023–1058.

Nightingale, John "On the definition of 'industry' and 'market'" *Journal of Industrial Economics* 27, 1978, pp. 31–40.

Nocke, Volker and Martin Peitz "A theory of clearance sales" *Economic Journal* 117(522), July 2007, pp. 964–990.

Nocke, Volker, and Lucy White "Do vertical mergers facilitate upstream collusion?" *American Economic Review* 97(4), September 2007, pp. 1321–1339.

Nordhaus, William D. "Comments" *Brookings Papers on Economic Activity: Microeconomics* 1989, 1989, pp. 320–325.

Norris, Frank *The Octopus*. Garden City, N. Y.: Doubleday & Company, Inc., 1901.

— *The Pit*. New York: Doubleday, Page & Co., 1903.

Note "The Industrial Reorganization Act: an antitrust proposal to restructure the American economy" *Columbia Law Review* 73(3), March 1973, pp. 635–676.

O'Brien, Anthony Patrick "Factory size, economies of scale and the Great Merger Wave of 1898–1902" *Journal of Economic History* 48(3), September 1988, pp. 639–649.

Odagiri, Hiroyuki and Akira Goto "The Japanese system of innovation: past, present, and future" in Richard R. Nelson, editor, *National Innovation Systems*. Oxford: Oxford University Press, 1993.

Ohashi, Hiroshi "The role of network effects in the US VCR market, 1978–1986" *Journal of Economics and Management Strategy* 12(4), Winter 2003, pp. 447–494.

Oliver, Henry M. Jr. "German Neoliberalism" *Quarterly Journal of Economics* 74(1), February 1960, pp. 117–149.

O'Neill, Patrick B. "The trend of aggregate concentration in the United States: problems of scope and measurement" *American Journal of Economics and Sociology* 55(2), April 1996, pp. 197–211.

Organization for Economic Co-operation and Development "Recommendation of the Council concerning effective action against hard core cartels" 14 May 1998.

— *Hard Core Cartels. Recent Progress and Challenges Ahead*. Paris, 2003a.

— *Fighting Hard-Core Cartels*. Paris, 2003b.

Ordover, Janusz A. "Comments on Evans & Schmalensee's 'The industrial organization of markets with two-sided platforms'" *Competition Policy International* 3(1), Spring 2007, pp. 181–189.

Ordover, Janusz A. and Robert D. Willig "The 1982 Department of Justice Merger Guidelines: an economic assessment" *California Law Review* 71(2), March 1983, pp. 535–574.

Osborne, Martin J. and Carolyn Pitchik "Equilibrium in Hotelling's model of spatial competition" *Econometrica* 55(4), July 1987, pp. 911–922.

Oster, Sharon "Intraindustry structure and the ease of strategic change" *Review of Economics and Statistics* 64(3), August 1982, pp. 376–383.

Ouchi, William G. "The new joint R&D" *Proceedings of the IEEE* 77(9), September 1989, pp. 1318–1326.

Pagoulatos, Emilio and Robert Sorensen "Foreign trade, concentration and profitability in open economies" *European Economic Review* 8, 1976, pp. 255–267.

Pakes, Ariel "Mueller's *Profits in the Long Run*" *Rand Journal of Economics* 18(2), Summer 1987, pp. 319–332.

Palamountain, Joseph C. Jr. *The Politics of Distribution.* Cambridge, Massachusetts: Harvard University Press, 1955.

Palay, Thomas M. "Comparative institutional economics: the governance of rail freight contracting" *Journal of Legal Studies* 13, June 1984, pp. 265–287.

Palda, Kristian S. *The Measurement of Cumulative Advertising Effects.* Englewood Cliffs, N.J.: Prentice-Hall, 1964.

Palmer, John "Some economic conditions conducive to collusion" *Journal of Economic Issues* 6, September 1972, pp. 29–37.

Parks, Tim *Medici Money: Banking, Metaphysics, and Art in Fifteenth-Century Floren*ce. New York: W. W. Norton & Co., 2005.

Pashigian, B. Peter "Demand uncertainty and sales: a study of fashion and markdown pricing" *American Economic Review* 78(5), December 1988, pp. 936–953.

Pashigian, B. Peter and and Brian Bowen, "Why are products sold on sale? Explanations of pricing regularities" *Quarterly Journal of Economics* 56, 1991, pp. 1015–1038.

Pavitt, Keith "What makes basic research economically useful?" *Research Policy* 20(2), April 1991, pp. 109–119.

Paxton, Robert O. "The calcium carbide case and the decriminalization of industrial ententes in France, 1915–26" pp. 153–180 in Patrick Fridenson, *The French Home Front, 1914–1918.* Providence: Berg, 1992.

Payne, P. L. "The emergence of the large-scale company in Great Britain, 1870–1914" *Economic History Review* 20(3), December 1967, pp. 519–542.

— "Family business in Britain: an historical and analytical survey" in Akio Okochi and Shigeaki Yasuoka, editors, *Family Business in the Era of Industrial Growth: Its Ownership and Management,* pp. 171–206. Tokyo: Tokyo University Press, 1984.

Pearce, Esther "History of the Standard industrial Classification" July 10, 1957 (http://www.census.gov/epcd/www/sichist.htm)

Peck, Merton J. "Joint R&D: the case of Microelectronics and Computer Technology

Corporation" *Research Policy* 15(5), October 1986, pp. 219–231.

— "Industrial organization and the gains from Europe 1992" *Brookings Papers on Economic Activity* 20, 1989, pp. 277–299.

Peña Castellot, Miguel "An overview of the application of the Leniency Notice" *Competition Policy Newsletter* 2001(1), February 2001, pp. 11–15.

Pennock, Pamela "The National Recovery Administration and the rubber tire industry, 1933–1935" *Business History Review* 71, Winter 1997, pp. 543–568.

Penrose, Edith *The Theory of Growth of the Firm.* Oxford: Blackwell 1959.

Peppin, John C. "Price-fixing agreements under the Sherman Anti-Trust Law" *California Law Review*, Part I 28(3), March 1940, pp. 297–351, Part II, 28(6), September 1940, pp. 667–732.

Perelman, Michael "Fixed capital, railroad economics and the critique of the market" *Journal of Economic Perspectives* 8(3), Summer 1994, pp. 189–195.

Peritz, Rudolph J.R. " 'Nervine' and knavery: the life and times of Dr. Miles Medical Company" American Antitrust Institute Working Paper No. 07-07, March 2007, forthcoming in Eleanor Fox and Dan Crane, editors *Antitrust Stories.* Foundation Press, 2007.

Perkins, Milo "Cartels: what shall we do about them" *Harper's* 189(1134), November 1944, pp. 570–578.

Perry, Martin K. "Price discrimination and forward integration" *Bell Journal of Economics* 9(1), Spring 1978, pp. 209–217.

— "Forward integration by Alcoa: 1888–1930" *Journal of Industrial Economics* 29(1), September 1980, pp. 37–53.

Peterman, John L. "The International Salt case" *Journal of Law and Economics* 22(2), October 1979, pp. 351–364.

Peterson, Everett B. and John M. Connor "A comparison of oligopoly welfare loss estimates for U.S. food manufacturing" *American Journal of Agricultural Economics* 77(2), May 1996, pp. 300–308.

Peterson, Shorey "Antitrust and the classic model" *American Economic Review* 47(1), March 1957, pp. 60–78.

Phillips, Almarin "A critique of United States experience with price-fixing agreements and the *per se* rule" *Journal of Industrial Economics* 8(1), October 1959, pp. 13–32.

— *Market Structure, Organization, and Performance; An Essay on Price Fixing and Combinations in Restraint of Trade.* Cambridge, Massachusetts: Harvard University Press, 1962.

Phillips, Almarin and George R. Hall "The Salk Vaccine case: parallelism, conspiracy and other hypotheses" *Virginia Law Review* 46(4), May 1960, pp. 717–728.

Phillips, Almarin and Rodney E. Stevenson "The historical development of industrial organization" *History of Political Economy* 6(3), Autumn 1974, pp. 324–342.

Phlips, Louis *The Economics of Price Discrimination*. Cambridge: Cambridge University Press, 1983.

— "Basing point pricing, competition, and market integration" in Hiroshi Ohta and Jacques-François Thisse, editors, *Does Economic Space Matter? Essays in Honour of Melvin L. Greenhut*. London: The Macmillan Press Ltd., 1993, pp. 303–315.

Phlips, Louis and Ireneo Miguel Moras "The *AKZO* decision: a case of predatory pricing?" *Journal of Industrial Economics* 41(3), September 1993, pp. 315–321.

Pickford, M. "A new test for manufacturing efficiency: an analysis of the results of licence tendering in New Zealand" *International Journal of Industrial Organization* 3(2), June 1985, pp. 153–177.

Pierce, J. Lamar, Christopher S. Boerner and David J. Teece "Dynamic capabilities, competence and the behavioral theory of the firm" Chapter 4 in Mie Augier and James G. March, editors, *The Economics of Choice, Change and Organization: Essays in Memory of Richard M. Cyert*. Cheltenham, UK and Northampton, Massachusetts: Edward Elgar, 2002.

Piga, Claudio and Joanna Poyago-Theotoky "Endogenous R&D spillovers and locational choice" *Regional Science and Urban Economics* 35, 2005, pp. 127–139

Piotrowski, Roman *Cartels and Trusts*. London: George Allen & Unwin, Ltd., 1933; reprinted Philadelphia, Pennsylvania: Porcupine Press, Inc., 1978.

Pitofsky, Robert "New definitions of relevant market and the assault on antitrust" *Columbia Law Review* 90(7), November 1990, pp. 1805–1864.

— *How the Chicago School Overshot the Mark*. Oxford, New York, and elsewhere: Oxford University Press, 2008.

Please, Arthur L. "Some aspects of European monopoly legislation" *Journal of Industrial Economics* 2(1), December 1954, pp. 34–46.

Plott, Charles R. "Industrial organization theory and experimental economics" *Journal of Economic Literature* 20(4), December 1982, pp. 1485–1527.

Png, I. P. L. and D. Hirshleifer "Price discrimination through offers to match price" *Journal of Business* 60(3), July 1987, pp. 365–383.

Podolny, Joel M. and Fiona M. Scott Morton "Social status, entry and predation: the case of British shipping cartels 1879–1929" *Journal of Industrial Economics* 47(1), March 1999, pp. 41–67.

Polinsky, A. Mitchell and Steven Shavell "Legal error, litigation, and the incentive to obey the law" *Journal of Law, Economics and Organization* 5(1), Spring 1989, pp. 99–108.

Pollay, Richard W. "Lydiametrics: applications of econometrics to the history of advertising" *Journal of Advertising History* 1(2), January 1979, pp. 3–18.

— "The languishing of 'Lydiametrics': the ineffectiveness of econometric research on advertising effects" *Journal of Communication* 34, 1984, pp. 8–23.

Polyani, Michael "Patent reform" *Review of Economic Studies* 11(2), Summer 1944, pp. 61–76.

Porter, Michael E. "Consumer behavior, retailer power and market performance in consumer goods industries" *Review of Economics and Statistics* 56(4), November 1974, pp. 419–436.

Porter, Patrick G. "Origins of the American Tobacco Company" *Business History Review* 43(1), Spring 1969, pp.59–76.

Porter, Robert H. "Optimal cartel trigger price strategies" *Journal of Economic Theory* 29, 1983a, pp. 313–338.

— "A study of cartel stability: the Joint Executive Committee, 1880–1886" *Bell Journal of Economics* 14(2), Autumn 1983b, pp. 301–314.

Posner, Richard A. "A statistical study of antitrust enforcement" *Journal of Law and Economics* 13(2), October 1970, pp. 365–419.

— "The social costs of monopoly and regulation" *Journal of Political Economy* 83(4), August 1976a, pp. 807–827.

— *Antitrust Law: An Economic Perspective*. Chicago: The University of Chicago Press, 1976b; second edition, 2001.

— "The Chicago School of antitrust analysis" *University of Pennsylvania Law Review* 127, 1979, pp. 925–948.

— "Legal formalism, legal realism, and the interpretation of statutes and the Constitution" *Case Western Reserve Law Review* 37, 1987, pp. 179–217.

Poundstone, William *Prisoner's Dilemma*. Doubleday, 1992.

Prager, Robin A. "The effects of horizontal mergers on competition: the case of the Northern Securities Company" *Rand Journal of Economics* 23(1), Spring 1992, pp. 123–133.

Pratt, Joseph A. "The petroleum industry in transition: antitrust and the decline of monopoly control in oil" *Journal of Economic History* 40(4), December 1980, pp. 815–837.

Pratten, Clifford F. "The manufacture of pins" *Journal of Economic Literature* 18, March 1980, pp. 93–96.

— "A survey of the economies of scale" Chapter 2 in EC Commission *Research on the "Cost of Non-Europe" Basic Findings* Volume 2. Brussels–Luxembourg: 1988.

Preston, Lee E. *The Industry and Enterprise Structure of the U.S. Economy*. New York: General Learning Press, 1971.

Pribram, Karl *Cartel Problems*. Washington, D.C.: The Brookings Institution, 1935.

Priest, George L. "Cartels and patent license arrangements" *Journal of Law and Economics* 20(2), October 1977, pp. 309–377.

Priest, George L. and Franco Romani "The GE/Honeywell precedent" *Wall Street Journal Europe* 21 June 2001, p. 6.

Radford, R. A. "The economic organization of a P.O.W. Camp" *Economica* n.s. 12(48), November 1945, pp. 189–201.

Rae, John B. "The railroad land-grant legend" *Journal of Economic History* 15(1), March 1955, pp. 112–113.

— "The electric vehicle company: a monopoly that missed" *Business History Review* 29(4), December 1955, pp. 298–311.

Raff, Daniel M. G. "Making cars and making money in the interwar automobile industry: economies of scale and scope and the manufacturing behind the marketing" *Business History Review* 65(4), Winter 1991, pp. 721–753.

Raff, Daniel M. G. and Peter Temin "Sears, Roebuck in the twentieth century: competition, complementarities, and the problem of wasting assets" pp. 219–248 in Naomi Lamoreaux, Daniel M. G. Raff, and Peter Temin, editors, *Learning by Doing in Markets, Firms, and Countries*. Chicago: University of Chicago Press, 1999.

Rafferty, Matthew "The Bayh–Dole Act and university research and development" *Research Policy* 37(1), February 2008, pp. 29–40.

Rajan, Raghuram, Henri Servaes, and Luigi Zingales "The cost of diversity: the diversification discount and inefficient investment" *Journal of Finance* 55(1), February 2000, pp. 35–80.

Raju, S. Jagmohan, V. Srinivasan and Rajiv Lal "The effects of brand loyalty on competitive price promotional strategies" *Management Science* 36(3), March 1990, pp. 276–304.

Ramey, Valerie A. and Matthew D. Shapiro "Displaced capital: a study of aerospace plant closings" *Journal of Political Economy* 109(5), 2001, pp. 958–992.

Rasmussen, Eric B., J. Mark Ramseyer, and John S. Wiley, Jr. "Naked exclusion" *American Economic Review* 81(5), December 1991, pp. 1137–1145.

Rassenti, Stephen J. and Bart J. Wilson "How applicable is the dominant firm model of price leadership?" *Experimental Economics* 7, 2004, pp. 271–288.

Rau, P. Raghavendra and Theo Vermaelen "Glamour, value and the post-acquisition performance of acquiring firms" *Journal of Financial Economics* 49(2), August 1998, pp. 223–253.

Rauwald, Christoph "Volkswagen to raise U.S., Mexico output by 2018" *Wall Street Journal* internet edition, 28 April 2009.

Ravenscraft, David J. "The 1980s merger wave: an industrial organization perspective" pp. 17–37 in Lynne E. Browne and Eric S. Rosengren, editors, *The Merger Boom*. Federal Reserve Bank of Boston, 1988.

Reader, W. J. *Metal Box: A History*. London: Heineman, 1976.

Reder, Melvin W. "Chicago economics: permanence and change" *Journal of Economic Literature* 20(1), March 1982, pp. 1–38.

Rees, Ray D. "Optimum plant size in United Kingdom industries: some survivor estimates" *Economica* n.s. 40(160), November 1973, pp. 394–401.

Reich, Leonard S. *The Making of American Industrial Research: Science and Business at GE and Bell, 1876–1926*. Cambridge: Cambridge University Press, 1985.

Reid, Gavin C. "Comparative statics of the partial monopoly model" *Scottish Journal of Political Economy* 24(2), June 1977, pp. 153–162.

Reiffen, David and Andrew N. Kleit "Terminal Railroad revisited: foreclosure of an essential facility or simple horizontal monopoly?" *Journal of Law and Economics* 33(2), October 1990, pp. 419–438.

Reinganum, Jennifer F. "A dynamic game of R and D: patent protection and competitive behavior" *Econometrica* 50(3), May 1982, pp. 671–688.

— "Uncertain innovation and the persistence of monopoly" *American Economic Review* 73(4), September 1983, pp. 741–748.

Reksulak, Michael, William F. Shughart II, Robert D. Tollison and Atin Basuchoudhary "Titan Agonistes: the wealth effects of the Standard Oil (N.J.) case" *Research in Law and Economics* 21, 2004, pp. 63–83.

Resnik, Alan and Bruce L. Stern "An analysis of information content in television advertising" *Journal of Marketing* 41(1), January 1977, pp. 50–53.

Rey, Patrick and Jean Tirole "A primer on foreclosure" in Mark Armstrong and Robert Porter, editors, *Handbook of Industrial Organization*, vol. 3. New York: North-Holland, 2007.

Reynolds, Stanley S. "Durable-goods monopoly: laboratory market and bargaining experiments" *Rand Journal of Economics* 31(2), Summer, 2000, pp. 375–394

Rhoades, Stephen A. and Joe M. Cleaver "The nature of the concentration-price/cost margin relationship for 352 manufacturing industries: 1967" *Southern Economic Journal* 40(1), July 1973, pp. 90–102.

Ricardo, David *Principles of Political Economy*. Piero Sraffa, editor. Cambridge: Cambridge University Press. First edition 1817. Published for the Royal Economic Society, 1951.

Richardson, G. B. "The organization of industry" *Economic Journal* 82(327), September 1972, pp. 883–896.

Riegel, Robert E. "The Omaha Pool" *Iowa Journal of History and Politics* 22(4), October 1924, pp. 569–582.

— "Western railroad pools" *Mississippi Valley Historical Review* 18(3), December 1931, pp. 364–377.

Riesenfeld, Stefan A. "Protection of competition" pp, 197–342 in Eric Stein and Thomas L. Nicholson, editors, *American Enterprise in the European Common Market: A Legal Profile*, Volume Two. Ann Arbor: University of Michigan Press, 1960.

Ripley, William Z. "Introduction" in William Z. Ripley, editor, *Trusts, Pools, and Corporations*. Boston: Ginn & Company, 1905, pp. ix–xxx.

— *Railway Problems*. Boston: Ginn and Company, 1907.

Robbins, Lionel *An Essay on the Nature and Significance of Economic Science*. London and Basingstoke: Macmillan Press Limited. First edition, 1932, Third edition, 1984.

— "Interpersonal comparisons of utility: a comment" *Economic Journal* 48(192), December 1938, pp. 635–641.

—"Economics and political economy" *American Economic Review* 71(2), May, 1981, pp. 1–10.

Roberts, John *The Modern Firm*. Oxford: Oxford University Press, 2004.

Robertson, Jordan "Apple's Jobs sorry for iPhone price cut" *myway*, downloaded 2 November 2007 from URL <http://apnews.myway.com/article/20070906/D8RG7O7G0.html>.

Robinson, E.A.G. "The problem of management and the size of firms" *Economic Journal* 44(174), June 1934, pp. 242–257.

— *Monopoly*. Cambridge: Cambridge University Press, 1941.

— *The Structure of Competitive Industry*. Cambridge: Cambridge University Press, 1958.

Robinson, Joan *The Economics of Imperfect Competition*, 2nd edition. London: Macmillan, St. Martin's Press, first edition, 1933, second edition, 1969.

— "The industry and the market" *Economic Journal* 66, 1956, pp. 360–361.

Robinson, William T. and Jeongwen Chiang "Are Sutton's predictions robust? Empirical insights into advertising, R&D, and concentration" *Journal of Industrial Economics* 44(4), December 1996, pp. 398–408.

Rochet, Jean-Charles and Jean Tirole "Platform competition in two-sided markets" *Journal of the European Economic Association* 1(4), June 2003, pp. 990–1029.

— "Two-sided markets: a progress report" 29 November 2005.

Roe, Mark J. "Political and legal restraints on ownership and control of public companies" *Journal of Financial Economics* 27(1), September 1990, pp. 7–41.

Rogers, Richard T. "Structural change in U.S. food manufacturing, 1958–1997" *Agribusiness* 17(1), 2001, pp. 3–32.

Roll, Erich *An Early Experiment in Industrial Organisation, Being a History of the Firm of Boulton & Watt, 1775–1805*. London and New York: Longmans Green and Co., 1930.

Röller, Lars-Hendrik "Economic analysis and competition policy enforcement in Europe" in P.A.G. van Bergeijk and E. Kloosterhuis, editors, *Modelling European Mergers: Theory, Competition Policy and Case Studies*. Cheltenham 2005, pp. 13–26.

Röller, Lars-Hendrik and A. Strohm "Ökonomische Analyse des Begriffs „Significant Impediment to Effective Competition"", in Günter Hirsch, Frank Montag, and Franz Jürgen, editors, *Münchner Kommentar zum Wettbewerbsrecht*, 2006 (Downloaded 7 June 2007 from URL <http://ec.europa.eu/dgs/competition/muenchner_kommentar.pdf>)

Röller, Lars-Hendrik and Miguel de la Mano "The impact of the new substantive test in European merger control" European Commission, 22 January 2006.

Röller, Lars-Hendrik, Ralph Siebert, and Mihkel M. Tombak "Why firms form (or do not form) RJVs" *Economic Journal* 117, July 2007, pp. 1122–1144.

Romano, Richard E. "A note on vertical integration: price discrimination and successive monopoly" *Economica* 55, May 1988, pp. 261–268.

Rondi, Laura, Alessandro Sembenelli, and Elena Ragazzi "Determinants of diversification patterns" in Davies, Stephen W. and Bruce Lyons, editors, *Industrial Organization in the European Union*. Oxford: Oxford University Press, 1996, pp. 168–183.

Roosevelt, Theodore *An Autobiography*. New York: Macmillan, 1913; On-line edition, Bartleby.com 1998 (<http://www.bartleby.com/br/55.html>); Elm Grove, Wisconsin: The Hamilton Press, 2 volume edition, undated. Page references are to Hamilton Press edition.

de Roover, Raymond "Monopoly theory prior to Adam Smith" *Quarterly Journal of Economics* 65(4), November 1951, pp. 492–524.

— *The Rise and Decline of the Medici Bank*. Cambridge, Massachusetts: Harvard University Press, 1963.

Röper, Berkhardt "Der wirtschaftliche Hintergrund der Kartell-Legalisierung durch das Reichsgericht 1897" *ORDO* III (1950), pp. 238–250.

Rosenberg, Nathan "Science, invention and economic growth" *Economic Journal* 84(333), March 1974, pp. 90–108.

— "Why do firms do basic research (with their own money)?" *Research Policy* 19(2), 19 April 1990, pp. 165–174.

Rosenberg, Nathan and Richard R. Nelson "American universities and technical advance in industry" *Research Policy* 23(3), May 1994, pp. 323–348.

Rosenbluth, Gideon "Comment" *Journal of Law and Economics* 19(2), August 1976, pp. 389–392.

Rotemberg, Julio J. and Garth Saloner "A supergame-theoretic model of price wars during booms" *American Economic Review* 76(3), June 1986, pp. 390–407.

Roth, Alvin E. "Introduction to experimental economics" in John H. Kagel and Alvin E. Roth, editors, *The Handbook of Experimental Economics*.

Princeton: Princeton University Press, 1995, pp. 3–110.

Rowe, Frederick M. "The market as mirage" *California Law Review* 75(3), May 1987, pp. 991–996.

Rubinfeld, Daniel L. "3M's bundled rebates: an economic perspective" *University of Chicago Law Review* 72, 2005, pp. 243–264.

Rublee, George "The original plan and early history of the Federal Trade Commission" *Proceedings of the Academy of Political Science* 11(4), January 1926, pp. 666–672.

Sakakibara, Mariko and Michael E. Porter "Competing at home to win abroad: evidence from Japanese industry" *Review of Economics and Statistics* 83(2), May 2001, pp. 310–322.

Salamon, L. M. and J. J. Siegfried "Economic power and political influence: the impact of industry structure on public policy" *American Political Science Review* 67, September 1977, pp. 1026–1043.

Salant, Stephen W., S. Switzer, and Robert J. Reynolds "Losses from horizontal merger: the effects of an exogenous change in industry structure on Cournot-Nash equilibrium" *Quarterly Journal of Economics* 98(2), May 1983, pp. 185–199.

Salinger, Michael "The concentration-margins relationship reconsidered" *Brookings Papers on Economic Activity* Microeconomics 1990, pp. 287–321.

— "A graphical analysis of bundling" *Journal of Business* 68(1), January 1995, pp. 85–98.

Salop, Steven C. "Monopolistic competition with outside goods" *Bell Journal of Economics* 10(1), Spring 1979, pp. 141–156.

— "Practices that (credibly) facilitate oligopoly coordination" pp. 265–290 in J. Stiglitz and F. G. Mathewson, editors, *New Developments in the Analysis of Market Structure*. MIT Press, Cambridge, Massachusetts, 1986.

Salop, Steven C. and David T. Scheffman "Cost-raising strategies" *Journal of Industrial Economics* 36(1), September 1987, pp. 19–34.

— "Raising rivals' costs" *American Economic Review* 73(2), May 1993, pp. 267–271.

Salus, Peter H. *A Quarter Century of UNIX*. Reading, Massachusetts: Addison-Wesley Publishing Company, 1994.

Salvato, Richard *National Civic Federation Records, 1894–1949*. Manuscript and Archives Division, Humanities and Social Sciences Library, The New York Public Library, September 2001 (<http://www.nypl.org/research/chss/spe/rbk/faids/ncf.pdf>).

Sampat, Bhaven N., David C. Mowery and Arvids A. Ziedonis "Changes in university patent quality after the Bayh–Dole Act: a re-examination" *International Journal of Industrial Organization* 21(9), November 2003, pp. 1371–1390.

Samuelson, Paul A. "The monopolistic competition revolution" pp. 105–138 in Kuenne, Robert E., editor, *Monopolistic Competition Theory: Studies in Impact*. New York: John Wiley & Sons, 1967.

— "Trimming consumers' surplus down to size" pp. 261–297 in John D. Hey and Donald Winch, editors, *A Century of Economics*. Oxford, UK and Cambridge, Massachusetts: Basil Blackwell, 1990.

Sappington, David E. M. "Incentives in principal-agent relationships" *Journal of Economic Perspectives* 5(2), Spring 1991, pp. 45-66

Saul, S. B. "The American impact upon British industry, 1895–1914" *Business History* 3(1), December 1960, pp. 19–38.

Schaerr, Gene C. "The Cellophane fallacy and the Justice Department's Guidelines for horizontal mergers" *Yale Law Journal* 94(3), January 1985, pp. 670–693.

Schankerman, Mark and Ariel Pakes, "Estimates of the value of patent rights in European Countries during the post-1950 period" *Economic Journal* 96(384), December 1986, pp. 1052–1076.

Scherer, F. M. "Size of firm, oligopoly and research: a comment" *Canadian Journal of Economics and Political Science* 31(2), May 1965a, pp. 256–266.

— "Firm size, market structure, opportunity, and the output of patented inventions" *American Economic Review* 55(5), Part 1, December 1965b, pp. 1097–1125.

— "Market structure and the employment of scientists and engineers" *American Economic Review* 57(3), June 1967a, pp. 524–531.

— "Research and development resource allocation under rivalry" *Quarterly Journal of Economics* 81(3), August 1967b, pp. 359–394.

— *Industrial Market Structure and Economic Performance*. Chicago: Rand McNally, first edition, 1970; second edition, 1980.

— "The determinants of industrial plant sizes in six nations" *Review of Economics and Statistics* 55(2), May 1973, pp. 135–145.

— "Economies of scale and industrial concentration" pp. 15–54 in Harvey J. Goldschmid, H. Michael Mann, and J. Fred Weston, editors, *Industrial Concentration: the New Learning*. Boston: Little, Brown & Company, 1974.

— "Predatory pricing and the Sherman Act: comment" *Harvard Law Review* 89(5), March 1976, pp. 869–890.

— "Demand-pull and technological invention: Schmookler revisited" *Journal of Industrial Economics* 30(3), March 1982a, pp. 225–237.

— "Inter-industry technology flows in the United States" *Research Policy* 11(4), August 1982b, pp. 227–245.

— "The economics of vertical restraints" *Antitrust Law Journal* 52(3), September 1983, pp. 687–618.

— "Using linked patent and R&D data to measure interindustry technology flows" pp. 417–461 in Zvi Griliches, editor, *R&D, Patents, and Productivity*. Chicago and London: University of Chicago Press, 1984.

— "Efficiency, fairness, and the early contributions of economists to the antitrust debate" *Washburn Law Journal* 29, 1990a, pp. 243–255.

— "Sunlight and sunset at the Federal Trade Commission" *Administrative Law Review* 42, Fall 1990b, pp. 461–487, reprinted in F. M. Scherer, editor, *Monopoly and Competition Policy*. Aldershot: Edward Elgar Publishing Limited, 1993a.

— *Monopoly and Competition Policy*. Aldershot, England and Brookfield, Vermont: Edward Elgar, 1993b.

— *Competition Policies for an Integrated World Economy*. Washington, D.C.: Brookings Institution, 1994.

— "Professor Sutton's 'Technology and Market Structure" *Journal of Industrial Economics* 48(2), June 2000, pp. 215–223.

— "An early application of the average cost concept" *Journal of Economic Literature* 39(3), September 2001, pp. 897–901.

— "The merger puzzle" pp. 1–22 in Wolfgang Franz, Hans Jürgen Ramser and Manfred Stadler, editors, *Fusionen*. Tübingen: Mohr Siebeck, 2002.

— "A new retrospective on mergers" *Review of Industrial Organization* 28(4), June 2006, pp. 327–341.

— "On the paternity of a market delineation approach" American Antitrust Institute Working Paper #09-01, January 12, 2009.

Scherer, F. M., Alan Beckenstein, Erich Kaufer, and R. D. Murphy *The Economics of Multi-Plant Operation: An International Comparisons Study*. Cambridge, Massachusetts: Harvard University Press, 1975.

Scherer, F. M. and Dietmar Harhoff "Technology policy for a world of skew-distributed outcomes" *Research Policy* 29(4–5), April 2000, pp. 559–566.

Scherer, F. M., Sigmund E. Herzstein, Jr., *et al. Patents and the Corporation*. Privately published, second edition, 1959.

Scherer, F. M. and David Ross *Industrial Market Structure and Economic Performance*. Third edition, Boston: Houghton Mifflin Company, 1990.

— *Competition Policies for an Integrated World Economy*. Washington, D.C.: Brookings Institution, 1994.

Schlesinger, Arthur M. Jr. *The Crisis of the Old Order*. Boston: Houghton Mifflin Company, 1957.

— *The Coming of the New Deal*. Boston: Houghton Mifflin Company, 1959.

Schmalensee, Richard C. *The Economics of Advertising*. Amsterdam, North-Holland, 1972.

— "Gaussian demand and commodity bundling" *Journal of Business* 57(1), Part 2, January 1984, pp. S211–S230.

— "The new industrial organization and the economic analysis of modern markets" in Werner Hildenbrand, editor, *Advances in Economic Theory*. Cambridge: Cambridge University Press, 1982, pp. 253–284.

— "Industrial organization" in John Eatwell, Murray Milgate, and Peter Newman, editors, *The New Palgrave*. London: Macmillan Press Limited, Volume 2, 1987, pp. 803–808.

— "Industrial economics: an overview" *Economic Journal* 98(392), September 1988, pp. 643–681.

— "Sunk costs and market structure: a review article" *Journal of Industrial Economics* 40(2), June 1992, pp. 125–34.

— "Sunk costs and antitrust barriers to entry" *American Economic Review* 94(2), May 2004, pp. 471–475.

Schmidt, Bernard Louis "Internal commerce and the development of the national economy before 1860" *Journal of Political Economy* 47(6), December 1939, pp. 798–822.

Schmidt, Ingo L. O. and Jan B. Rittaler *A Critical Evaluation of the Chicago School of Antitrust*. Dordrecht and elsewhere: Kluwer Academic Publishers, 1989.

Schmidt, Jan Host, Fabienne Ilzkovitz, Roderick Meiklejohn, and Ulrik Mogensen "Liberalisation of network industries: economic implications and main policy issues" *Economic Economy* 1999, Number 4, pp. 11–55.

Schmidt, Torsten "Auspitz and Lieben, Kurt Sting, and the market leadership models" Undated.

Schmookler, Jacob "Inventors past and present" *Review of Economics and Statistics* 39, August 1957, pp. 321–333.

— "Economic sources of inventive activity" *Journal of Economic History* 22(1), March 1962, pp. 1–20.

— *Invention and Economic Growth*. Cambridge, Massachusetts: Harvard University Press, 1966.

Schneider, Erich "Milestones on the way to the theory of monopolistic competition" pp. 139–144 in Robert E. Kuenne, editor, *Monopolistic Competition Theory: Studies in Impact*. New York: John Wiley & Sons, 1967.

Schoar, Antoinette "Effects of corporate diversification on productivity" *Journal of Finance* 57(6), December 2002, pp. 2379–2403.

Schohl, Frank "Persistence of profits in the long run: a critical extension of some recent findings" *International Journal of Industrial Organization* 8(3), September 1990, pp. 385–404.

Schröter, Harm G. "The International Dyestuffs Cartel, 1927–39, with special reference to the developing areas of Europe and Japan" in Akira Kudō and Terushi Hara, editors, *International Cartels in Business History*. Tokyo: University of Tokyo Press, 1992, pp. 33–52.

— "Cartelization and decartelization in Europe, 1870–1995: rise and decline of an economic institution" *Journal of European Economic History* 25(1), Spring 1996, pp. 129–153.

Schudel, Matt "Accomplished, frustrated inventor dies" *Washington Post* 26 February 2005, p. B1.

Schuman, Robert "Origines et elaborations du 'Plan Schuman'" Cahiers de Bruges 1953, pp. 266–284.

Schumpeter, Joseph A. "The explanation of the business cycle" Economica 21, December 1927, pp. 286–311.

— "Review of Robinson's Economics of Imperfect Competition" Journal of Political Economy April 1934a, pp. 249–257, reprinted in Richard V. Clemence, editor, Essays of J. A. Schumpeter. Cambridge, Massachusetts, 1951, pp. 125–133.

— The Theory of Economic Development. Cambridge, Massachusetts: Harvard University Press, 1934b.

— "The analysis of economic change" Review of Economics and Statistics 17(4), May 1935, pp. 2–10.

— Business Cycles. New York and London: McGraw-Hill Book Company, Inc., 1939.

— "The creative response in economic history" Journal of Economic History 7(2), November 1947, pp. 149–159.

Schwartz, Ivo E. "Antitrust legislation and policy in Germany—a comparative study" University of Pennsylvania Law Review 105(5), March 1957, pp. 617–690.

Schwartz, Louis B. "The new Merger Guidelines: guide to governmental discretion and private counseling or propaganda for revision of the antitrust laws?" California Law Review 71, March 1983, pp. 575–603.

Schwartz, Marius and Robert J. Reynolds "Contestable markets: an uprising in the theory of industry structure: a comment" American Economic Review 73(3), June 1983, pp. 488–490.

Schwartz, Michael and Andrew Fish "Just-in-time inventories in Old Detroit" Business History 40(3), July 1998, pp. 48–71.

Schwartzman, David The Japanese Television Cartel. Ann Arbor: University of Michigan Press, 1993.

Scitovsky, Tibor "Ignorance as a source of oligopoly power" American Economic Review 40(2), May 1950, pp. 48–53.

Scott, John T. "The pure capital-cost barrier to entry" Review of Economics and Statistics 63(3), August 1981, pp. 444–446.

— "Firm versus industry variability in R&D intensity" in Zvi Griliches, editor, R&D, Patents, and Productivity. Chicago: The University of Chicago Press, 1984, pp. 233–252.

— "Historical and economic perspectives of the National Cooperative Research Act" pp. 65–84 in Albert N. Link and Gregory Tassey, editors, Cooperative Research and Development: The Industry-University-Government Relationship. Dordrecht: Kluwer Academic Publishers, 1989a.

— "Purposive diversification as a motive for merger" International Journal of Industrial Organization 7(1), March 1989b, pp. 35–47.

— "Multimarket contact among diversified oligopolists" International Journal of Industrial Organization 9, 1991, pp. 225–238.

— "Multimarket contacts" pp. 1553–1574 in Wayne Dale Collins, editor, Issues in Competition Law and Policy. American Bar Association, Antitrust Section, 2008a.

— "The National Cooperative Research and Production Act" pp. 1297–1317 in Wayne Dale Collins, editor, Issues in Competition Law and Economics. American Bar Association, August 2008b.

— "Competition in research and development: a theory for contradictory predictions" Review of Industrial Organization, March, 2009, pp. 153–171.

Scott, John T. and George Pascoe "Purposive diversification of R&D in manufacturing" Journal of Industrial Economics 36(2), December 1987, pp. 193–205.

Scott Morton, Fiona "Entry and predation: British shipping cartels 1879–1929" Journal of Economics and Management Strategy 6, 1997, pp. 679–724.

— "Barriers to entry, brand advertising, and generic entry in the US pharmaceutical industry" International Journal of Industrial Organization 18(7), October 2000, pp. 1085–1104.

Seabrook, John "The flash of genius" New Yorker, 11 January 1993, pp. 38–52.

Seager, Henry R. "The recent trust decisions" Political Science Quarterly 26(4), December 1911, pp. 581–614.

Seager, Henry R. and Charles A. Gulick, Jr. Trust and Corporation Problems. New York and London: Harper & Brothers Publishers, 1929.

Segal, Harvey H. "Canals and economic development" in Carter Goodrich, editor, Canals and American Economic Development. New York and London: Columbia University Press, 1961, pp. 216–248.

Segal, Ilya R. and Michael D. Whinston "Naked exclusion: comment" American Economic Review 90(1), March 2000, pp. 296–309.

Selten, Reinhard "A simple model of imperfect competition where four are few and six are many" International Journal of Game Theory 2 1973, pp. 141–201, reprinted in Reinhard Selten Models of Strategic Rationality. Dordrecht: Kluwer Academic Publishers, 1988.

— "The chain store paradox" Theory and Decision 9(2), April 1978, pp. 127–159, reprinted in Reinhard Selten Models of Strategic Rationality. Dordrecht: Kluwer Academic Publishers, 1988.

Shaffer, Sherrill "Stable cartels with a Cournot fringe" Southern Economic Journal 61(3), January 1995, pp. 744–754.

Shaked, Avner and John Sutton "Relaxing price competition through product differentiation" Review of Economic Studies 49(1), January 1982, pp. 3–13.

Shapiro, Carl "Navigating the patent thicket: cross licenses, patent pools, and standard setting" *Innovation Policy and the Economy* 1, 2001, pp. 119–150.

Sharp, Margaret "The single market and European policies for advanced technologies" pp. 57–76 in Christopher Freeman, Margaret Sharp and William Walker, editors, *Technology and the Future of Europe: Global Competition and the Environment in the 1990s.* London: Pinter Publishers, 1991.

Sheahan, John *Promotion and Control of Industry in Postwar France.* Cambridge, Massachusetts: Harvard University Press, 1963.

Shelanski, Howard A. and J. Gregory Sidak "Antitrust divestiture in network industries" *University of Chicago Law Review* 68(1), Winter 2001, pp. 1–99.

Shepard, Andrea "Contractual form, retail price, and asset characteristics in gasoline retailing" *Rand Journal of Economics* 24(1), Spring, 1993, pp. 58–77.

Shepherd, William G. "Today's trust buster" *Collier's* 23 February 1929, pp. 8, 9, 44.

Shepherd, William G. "What does the survivor technique show about economies of scale?" *Southern Economic Journal* 34(1), July 1967, pp. 113–122.

— "Structure and behavior in British Industries, with U.S. comparisons" *Journal of Industrial Economics* 21(1), November 1972, pp. 35–54.

— "Causes of increased competition in the U.S. economy, 1939–1980" *Review of Economics and Statistics* 64(4), November 1982, pp. 613–626.

— "Theories of industrial organization" in Harry First, Eleanor M. Fox, and Robert Pitofsky, editors, *Revitalizing Antitrust in its Second Century.* New York, Westport, & London: Quorum Books, 1991, pp. 37–66.

Shleifer, Andrei and Robert W. Vishny "Large shareholders and corporate control" *Journal of Political Economy* 94(3), Part 1, June 1986, pp. 461–488.

— "Takeovers in the '60s and the '80s: evidence and implications" *Strategic Management Journal* 12, Winter 1991, pp. 51–59.

— "A survey of corporate governance" *Journal of Finance* 52(2), June 1997, pp. 737–783.

Showalter Dean M. "Oligopoly and financial structure: comment" *American Economic Review* 85(3), June 1995, pp. 647–653.

— "Strategic debt: evidence in manufacturing" *International Journal of Industrial Organization* 17, 1999, pp. 319–333.

Shubik, Martin "A further comparison of some models of duopoly" *Western Economic Journal* 6(4), September 1968, pp. 260–275.

— "Cournot" in John Eatwell, Murray Milgate, and Peter Newman, editors, *The New Palgrave*, Volume 1, pp. 708–712. London: Macmillan Press Limited, 1987.

Shulman, Seth *Unlocking The Sky: Glenn Hammond Curtiss and the Race to Invent the Airplane.* HarperCollins, 2002.

Siegfried, John J., Rudolph C. Blitz, and David K. Round "The limited role of market power in generating great fortunes in Great Britain, the United States, and Australia" *Journal of Industrial Economics* 43(3), September 1995, pp. 277–286.

Siegfried, John J. and Michelle Mahony "The first Sherman Act case: *Jellico Mountain Coal*, 1891" *Antitrust Bulletin* 35(4), Winter 1990, pp. 801–832.

Siegfried, John J. and Edwin H. Wheeler "Cost efficiency and monopoly: a survey" *Quarterly Review of Economics and Business* 21(1), Spring 1981, pp. 25–46.

Siegfried, Tom *A Beautiful Math.* Washington, D.C.: John Henry Press, 2006.

Sigurdson, Jon *Industry and State Partnership in Japan: the Very Large Scale Integrated (VLSI) Project.* Lund: Swedish Research Policy Institute, University of Lund, 1986.

Silverberg, Eugene "The Viner-Wong envelope theorem" *Journal of Economic Education* 30(1), Winter 1999, pp. 75–79.

Simon, Herbert A. "On a class of skew distribution functions" *Biometrika* 42(3/4), December 1955, pp. 425–440.

— "Theories of decision-making in economics and behavioral science" *American Economic Review* 49(3), June 1959, pp. 253–283.

— "Behavioral economics" in John Eatwell, Murray Milgate, and Peter Newman, editors, *The New Palgrave.* London: Macmillan Press Limited, 1987, Volume 1, pp. 221–225.

Simons, Henry C. *A Positive Program for Laissez Faire*, Public Policy Pamphlet No. 15, Harry D. Gideonse, editor, Chicago: University of Chicago Press, 1934, reprinted in Henry C. Simons *Economic Policy for a Free Society.* Chicago & London: University of Chicago Press, 1948.

— "The requisites of free competition" *American Economic Review* 26(1), March 1936, pp. 68–76.

Sinclair, Upton *The Jungle.* New York: Doubleday, Page and Co., 1906.

Singal, Vijay "Airline mergers and multimarket contact" *Managerial and Decision Economics* 17(6), November-December 1996, pp. 559–574.

Singh, Nirvikar and Xavier Vives "Price and quantity competition in a differentiated duopoly" *Rand Journal of Economics* 15(4), Winter, 1984, pp. 546–554.

Sisson, Francis H. "The world-wide trend toward cooperation" *Annals of the American Academy of Political and Social Science* 82, March 1919, pp. 143–149.

Sklar, Martin J. *The Corporate Reconstruction of American Capitalism, 1890–1916.* Cambridge: Cambridge University Press, 1988.

Slade, Margaret "Product rivalry with multiple strategic weapons: an analysis of price and advertising competition" *Journal of Economics and Management Strategy* 4(3), September 1995, pp. 445–476.

— "Multitask agency and contract choice: an empirical exploration" *International Economic Review* 37(2), May 1996, pp. 465–486.

— "Strategic motives for vertical separation: evidence from retail gasoline markets" *Journal of Law, Economics and Organization* 14(1), 1998, pp. 84–113.

— "Beer and the tie: did divestiture or brewer-owned public houses lead to higher beer prices?" *Economic Journal* 108, May 1998b, pp. 565–602.

— "The leverage theory of tying revisited: evidence from newspaper advertising" *Southern Economic Journal* 65(2), October 1998, pp. 204–222.

— "Competing models of firm profitability" *International Journal of Industrial Organization* 22(3), March 2004, pp. 289–308.

Sleuwaegen, Leo and Hideki Yamawaki "The formation of the European common market and changes in market structure and performance" *European Economic Review* 32, 1988, pp. 1451–1475.

Slichter, Sumner H. "The period 1919–1936 in the United States: its significance for business-cycle theory" *Review of Economics and Statistics* 19(1), Part 1, February 1937, pp. 1–19.

Smiley, Robert "Tender offers, transaction costs, and the theory of the firm" *Review of Economics and Statistics* 58(1), February 1976, pp. 22–32.

Smirlock, M., Thomas W. Gilligan, and W. Marshall "Tobin's *q* and the structure–performance relationship" *American Economic Review* 74(5), December 1984, pp. 1051–1060.

Smith, Adam *An Inquiry Into the Nature and Causes of the Wealth of Nations.* Edwin Cannan, editor, New York: The Modern Library, 1937.

Smith, Alasdair "The market for cars in the enlarged European Community" in Christopher Bliss and Jorge Braga de Macedo *Unity with Diversity in the European Economy: the Community's Southern Frontier.* Cambridge: Cambridge University Press, 1990, pp. 78–103.

Smith, Alasdair and Anthony J. Venables "Counting the cost of voluntary export restraints in the European car market" in Elhanan Helpman and Assaf Razin, editors, *International Trade and Trade Policy.* Cambridge, Massachusetts: MIT Press, 1991, pp. 187–220.

Smith, Clifford N. "Motivation and ownership: history of the ownership of the *Gelsenkirchener Bergwerks-A.G.*" *Business History* 12(1), January 1970, pp. 1–24.

Smith, Richard A. "The incredible electrical conspiracy" *Fortune* 63(5), May 1961, pp. 164–210.

Smith, Vernon L. "An experimental study of competitive market behavior" *Journal of Political Economy* 70(2), April 1962, pp. 111–137.

— "Bidding and auction institutions: experimental results" in Yakov Amihud, editor, *Bidding and Auctioning for Procurement and Allocation.* New York: New York University Press, 1976, pp. 43–64.

— "An empirical study of decentralized institutions of monopoly restraint" in George Horwich and James P. Quirk, editors, *Essays in Contemporary Fields of Economics in Honor of Emanuel T. Weiler.* West Lafayette, Indiana: Purdue University Press, 1981, pp. 83–106.

Smithies, Arthur "Optimum location in spatial competition" *Journal of Political Economy* 49, 1941, pp. 423–439.

Sobel, Joel "The timing of sales" *Review of Economics Studies* 51(3), July 1984, pp. 353–368.

Sonnenschein, Hugo "The dual of duopoly is complementary monopoly: or, two of Cournot's theories are one" *Journal of Political Economy* 76(2), March–April 1968, pp. 316–318.

Soper, Jean B., George Norman, Melvin L. Greenhut, and Bruce L. Benson "Basing point pricing and production concentration" *Economic Journal* 101(406), May, 1991, pp. 539–556.

Sorkin, Andrew Ross "U.S. businesses turning to Europeans for antitrust help" *New York Times* 19 June 2001.

Souty, François "La politique de la concurrence trente ans après Chicago: principaux enseignements" in Jörn Kruse, Kurt Stockmann, and Lothar Vollmer, editors, *Wettbewerbspolitik im Spannungsfeld nationaler und internationaler Kartellrechtsordnungen.* Baden-Baden: Nomos Verlagsgesellschaft, 1997, pp. 85–96.

Spector, David "Bundling, tying, and collusion" *International Journal of Industrial Organization* 25(3), June 2007, pp. 575–581.

Spence, A. Michael "The economics of internal organization: an introduction" *Bell Journal of Economics* 6(1), Spring 1975, pp. 163–172.

— "Entry, capacity, investment and oligopolistic pricing" *Bell Journal of Economics* 8(2), Autumn 1977, pp. 534–544.

— "Notes on advertising, economies of scale, and entry barriers" *Quarterly Journal of Economics* 95(3), November 1980, pp. 493–507.

— "Contestable markets and the theory of industry structure: a review article" *Journal of Economic Literature* 21 September 1983, pp. 981–990.

— "Cost reduction, competition, and industry performance" *Econometrica* 51(1), January 1984, pp. 101–122.

Spencer, Barbara J. and James A. Brander "International R&D rivalry and industrial strategy" *Review of Economic Studies* 50(4), October 1983, pp. 707–722.

Spierenburg, Dirk and Raymond Poidevin *The History of the High Authority of the European Coal and Steel Community*. London: Weidenfeld and Nicolson, 1994.

Spivack, Gordon B. "The Chicago school approach to single firm exercises of monopoly power: a response" *Antitrust Law Journal* 53(3), September 1983, pp. 651–674.

Spraakman, Gary P. "A critique of Milgrom and Roberts' treatment of incentives vs. bureaucratic controls in the British North American fur trade" *Journal of Management Accounting Research* 14, 2002, pp. 135–151.

Sproul, Michael F. "Antitrust and prices" *Journal of Political Economy* 101(4), August 1993, pp. 741–754.

Sraffa, Piero "The laws of returns under competitive conditions" *Economic Journal* 36(144), December 1926, pp. 535–550.

— *Production of Commodities by Means of Commodities; Prelude to a Critique of Economic Theory*. Cambridge: Cambridge University Press, 1960.

Stack, Martin "Local and regional breweries in America's brewing industry, 1965–1920" *Business History Review* 74(3), Autumn 2000, pp. 435–463.

Stackelberg, Heinrich von *Marktform und Gleichgewicht*. Vienna: Julius Springer, 1934.

Stanwood, Edward *American Tariff Controversies in the Nineteenth Century*. Boston: Houghton, 1903.

Steindel, Charles and Kevin J. Stiroh "Productivity: what is it, and why do we care about it" Staff Report Number 122, Federal Reserve Bank of New York, April 2001

Steindorff, Ernst and Klaus Hopt "European Economic Community—The Grundig-Consten case, a landmark decision of the European Court of Justice on Common Market antitrust law" *American Journal of Comparative Law* 15(4), 1966–1967, pp. 811–822.

Steiner, Peter O. *Mergers: Motives, Effects, Policies*. Ann Arbor: University of Michigan Press, 1975.

Steinmueller, W. Edward "International joint ventures in the integrated circuit industry" CEPR Publication No. 104, September 1987.

— "Industry structure and government policies in the U.S. and Japanese integrated-circuit industries" in John B. Shoven, editor, *Government Policy Towards Industry in the United States and Japan*. Cambridge: Cambridge University Press, 1988, pp. 319–354.

Stegeman, Mark "Advertising in competitive markets" *American Economic Review* 81(1), March 1991, pp. 210–223.

Stegemann, Klaus "Three functions of basing-point pricing and Article 60 of the E.C.S.C. Treaty" *Antitrust Bulletin* 13, Summer 1968, pp. 395–432.

Stern, Bruce L., Dean M. Krugman, and Alan Resnik "Magazine advertising: an analysis of information content" *Journal of Advertising Research* 21, April 1981, pp. 39–44.

Stevens, R. B. and B. S. Yamey *The Restrictive Practices Court*. London: Weidenfeld and Nicolson, 1965.

Stevens, William S. "A classification of pools and associations based on American experience" *American Economic Review* 3(3), September 1913, pp. 545–575.

— "Unfair competition" *Political Science Quarterly* 29(2), June 1914, pp. 282–306; 29(3), September 1914, pp. 460–490.

— "The Clayton Act" *American Economic Review* 5(1), March 1915, pp. 38–54.

Stewart, G. Bennett III and David M. Glassman "The motives and methods of corporate restructuring" *Journal of Applied Corporate Finance* 1(1), Spring 1988a, pp. 85–99.

— "The motives and methods of corporate restructuring" *Journal of Applied Corporate Finance* 1(2), Summer 1988b, pp. 79–88.

Stigler, George J. "Production and distribution in the short run" *Journal of Political Economy* 47(3), June 1939, pp. 305–327.

— *Production and Distribution Theories*. New York: Macmillan, 1941.

— "The extent and bases of monopoly" *American Economic Review* 32(2), Supplement, June 1942, pp. 1–22.

— "Monopolistic competition in retrospect" pp. 12–24 in *Five Lectures on Economic Problems* London: Longmans, Green and Co., 1949a, reprinted in George J. Stigler, *The Organization of Industry*. Homewood, Illinois: Richard D. Irwin, Inc., 1968.

— "A theory of delivered price systems" *American Economic Review* 39(6), December 1949b, pp. 1143–1159.

— "Monopoly and oligopoly by merger" American Economic Review 40(2), May 1950, pp. 23–34.

— "The division of labor is limited by the extent of the market" *Journal of Political Economy* 59(3), June 1951, pp. 185–193.

— "The case against big business" *Fortune* May 1952, pp. 123, 158, 162, 164, 167.

— "The economist plays with blocs" *American Economic Review* 44(2), May 1954, pp. 7–14.

— "Mergers and preventive antitrust policy" *University of Pennsylvania Law Review* 104(2), November 1955, pp. 176–184.

— "The statistics of monopoly and merger" *Journal of Political Economy* 64(1), February 1956, pp. 33–40.

— "The economics of information" *Journal of Political Economy* 69(3), June 1961, pp. 213–225; reprinted in George J. Stigler, *The Organization of Industry*. Homewood, Illinois: Richard D. Irwin, Inc., 1968.

— "Perfect competition, historically contemplated" *Journal of Political Economy* 65(1), February 1957, pp. 1–17, reprinted in George J. Stigler, *Essays in the History of Economics*. Chicago and London: University of Chicago Press, 1965.

— "The economies of scale" *Journal of Law and Economics* 1, October 1958, pp. 54–71; reprinted with addendum in George J. Stigler, *The Organization of Industry*. Homewood, Illinois: Richard D. Irwin, Inc., 1968.

— "Administered prices and oligopolistic inflation" *Journal of Business* 35(1), January 1962, pp. 1–13.

— *Capital and Rates of Return in Manufacturing Industries*. Princeton: Princeton University Press, 1963a.

— "United States v. Loew's Inc.: a note on block-booking" *Supreme Court Review* 1963, 1963b, pp. 152–157.

— "A theory of oligopoly" *Journal of Political Economy* 72(1), February 1964, pp. 44–61 reprinted in George J. Stigler *The Organization of Industry*. Homewood, Illinois: Richard D. Irwin, Inc., 1968, pp. 39–63.

— "Imperfections in the capital market" *Journal of Political Economy* 75(3), June 1967, pp. 287–292, reprinted in George J. Stigler, *The Organization of Industry*. Homewood, Illinois: Richard D. Irwin, Inc., 1968.

— "Addendum 3: A note on potential competition" pp. 19–22 in George J. Stigler, *The Organization of Industry*. Homewood, Illinois: Richard D. Irwin, Inc., 1968a.

— "Barriers to entry, economies of scale, and firm size" Chapter 6 in George J. Stigler, *The Organization of Industry*. Homewood, Illinois: Richard D. Irwin, Inc., 1968b.

— "Editor's note" *Journal of Economic Literature* 9(3), September 1971, p. 852.

— "The xistence of x-efficiency" *American Economic Review* 66(1), March 1976, pp. 213–216.

— "Palgrave's Dictionary of Economics" *Journal of Economic Literature* 26(4), December 1988, pp. 1729–1736.

Stigler, George J. and James K. Kindahl *The Behavior of Industrial Prices*. New York: National Bureau of Economic Research, 1970.

— "Industrial prices, as administered by Dr. Means" *American Economic Review* 63(4), September 1973, pp. 717–721.

Stigler, George J. and Robert A. Sherwin "The extent of the market" *Journal of Law and Economics* 28(3), October 1985, pp. 555–585.

Stiglitz, Joseph E. "Imperfect information in the product market" Chapter 13 in Richard C. Schmalensee and Robert D. Willig, editors, *Handbook of Industrial Organization*. Amsterdam: North-Holland, Volume I, 1989.

Sting, Kurt "Die polypolitische Preisbildung. Ein Kapital der Preistheorie" *Jahrbücher für Nationalökonomie* 79(134), 1931, pp. 761–789.

Stockder, Archibald H. *Regulating an Industry*. New York: Columbia University Press, 1932.

Stocking, George W. and Myron W. Watkins *Cartels in Action*. New York: Twentieth Century Fund, 1947.

— *Monopoly and Free Enterprise*. New York: Twentieth Century Fund, 1951.

Stoffregen, Phillip A. "Giving credit where credit is due: a brief history of the administration of the R&D tax credit" *Tax Notes* 1995, pp. 403–416.

Stoneman, Paul "Patenting activity: a re-evaluation of the influence of demand pressures" *Journal of Industrial Economics* 27(4), June 1979, pp. 385–401.

Strickland, Allyn D. and Leonard W. Weiss "Advertising, concentration, and price-cost margins" *Journal of Political Economy* 84(5), October 1976, pp. 1109–1122.

Strieder, Jakob *Studien zur Geschichte kapitalististischer Organisationsformen*. Second edition, München and Leipzig, 1925, reprinted New York: Lenox Hill Pub. & Dis. Co. (Burt Franklin), 1971.

Sullivan, Lawrence A. "The new Merger Guidelines: an afterword" *California Law Review* 71(2), March 1983, pp. 632–648.

Sullivan, Lawrence A. and Wolfgang Fikentscher "On the growth of the antitrust idea" *Berkeley Journal of International Law* 16, 1998, pp. 197–233.

Sullivan, Mark *Our Times Volume II: America Finding Herself*. New York, Charles Scribner's Sons, [1927] 1940.

Sullivan, Thomas E. *The Political Economy of the Sherman Act: The First One Hundred Years*. Oxford: Oxford University Press, 1991.

Sullivan, Timothy G. "A note on market power and returns to stockholders" *Review of Economics and Statistics* 59(1), February 1977, pp. 108–113.

— "The cost of capital and the market power of firms" *Review of Economics and Statistics* 60(2), April 1978, pp. 209–217.

— "The cost of capital and the market poer of firms: reply and correction" *Review of Economics and Statistics* 64(3), August 1982, pp. 523–525.

Supple, Barry "Scale and Scope: Alfred Chandler and the dynamics of industrial capitalism" *Economic History Review* n.s. 44(3), August 1991, pp. 500–514.

Suslow, Valerie Y. "Estimating monopoly behavior with competitive recycling: an application to Alcoa" *Rand Journal of Economics* 17(3), Autumn, 1986, pp. 389–403.

— "Cartel contract duration: empirical evidence from inter-war international cartels" *Industrial and Corporate Change* 14(5), October 2005, pp. 705–744.

Sutton, John "Endogenous sunk costs and market structure" pp. 22–37 in Giacomo Bonanno and Dario Brandolini, editors, *Industrial Structure in the New Industrial Economics*. Oxford: Clarendon Press, 1990.

— *Sunk costs and Market Structure*. Cambridge, Massachusetts: MIT Press, 1991.

— "Technology and market structure" *European Economic Review* 40, 1996, pp. 511–530.

— "Market share dynamics and the 'persistence of leadership' debate" *American Economic Review* 97(1), March 2007a, pp. 222–241.

— Sutton, John "Gibrat's legacy" *Journal of Economic Literature* 35(1), March 1997b, pp. 40–59.

— *Technology and Market Structure*. Cambridge, Massachusetts: MIT Press, 1998.

— "Market structure: theory and evidence" Chapter 35 in Mark Armstrong and Robert Porter, editors, *Handbook of Industrial Organization*, vol. 3. New York: North-Holland, 2007.

Swan, Peter L. "Alcoa: the influence of recycling on monopoly power" *Journal of Political Economy* 88(1), February 1980, pp. 76–99.

Swedish Competition Authority *Fighting Cartels—Why and How?*. Göteborg, 2001. Downloaded 5 August 2006, <http://www.kkv.se/eng/publications/pdf/3rdnordic010412.pdf>.

Swoboda, Frank "Pilots' curbs on regional jets impede competition, study says" *Washington Post* 27 May 1999, p. A21.

Symeonidis, George "Innovation, firm size and market structure" OECD Economics Department Working Papers 161, 1996.

— "The evolution of UK cartel policy and its impact on conduct and structure" in Stephen Martin, editor, *Competition Policies in Europe*. Amsterdam: North-Holland, 1998.

— *The Effects of Competition: Cartel Policy and the Evolution of Strategy and Market Structure in British Industry*. Cambridge, Massachusetts and London, England: MIT Press, 2002.

Taft, William Howard *The Anti-Trust Act and the Supreme Court*. New York and London: Harper & Brothers Publishers, 1914; New York: Kraus Reprint Co., 1970.

Takacs, Wendy E. and L. Alan Winters "Labour adjustment costs and British footwear protection" *Oxford Economic Papers* 43, 1991, pp. 479–501.

Tapon, Francis and Charles Bram Cadsby "The optimal organization of research: evidence from eight case studies of pharmaceutical firms" *Journal of Economic & Behavioral Organization* 31, 1996, pp. 381–399.

Taussig, Frank H. *The Tariff History of the United States*. New York and London: G.P. Putnam's Sons, 1931. New York: Johnson Reprint Corporation, 1966.

Taylor, A. J. P. "The European revolution" *The Listener* 34(880), 22 November 1945, pp. 575–576."

Taylor, George Rogers *The Transportation Revolution 1815–1860*. New York: Holt, Rinehart and Winston, 1951.

Taylor, George Rogers and Irene D. Neu *The American Railroad Network 1861–1890*. Cambridge, Massachusetts: Harvard University Press, 1956.

Taylor, Jason E. "The output effects of government sponsored cartels during the New Deal" *Journal of Industrial Economics* 50(1), March 2002, pp. 1–10.

Teece, David J. "Profiting from technological innovation: Implications for integration, collaboration, licensing and public policy" *Research Policy* 15, 1986, pp. 285–305.

— "Firm organization, industrial structure, and technological innovation" *Journal of Economic Behavior & Organization* 31, 1996, pp. 193–224.

Telser, Lester G. "Why should manufacturers want fair trade?" *Journal of Law and Economics* 3, October 1960, pp. 86–105.

— "Abusive trade practices: an economic analysis" *Law and Contemporary Problems* 30(3), Summer 1965, pp. 488–505.

— "Cutthroat competition and the long purse" *Journal of Law and Economics* 9, October 1966, pp. 259–277.

— "Why should manufacturers want fair trade II" *Journal of Law and Economics* 33(2), October 1990, pp. 409–417.

Temporary National Economic Committee (TNEC), Congress of the United States. Hearings, Part 5-A *Federal Trade Commission Report on Monopolistic Practices in Industries*. Washington, D.C.: U.S. Government Prining Office, 1939.

— *Final Report and Recommendations*. Washington, D.C.: U.S. Government Printing Office, 1941.

Tharakan, P. K. M. "The Japan-EC DRAMs anti-dumping undertaking: was it justified? What purpose did it serve?" *De Economist* 145(1), 1997, pp. 1–28.

Thisse, Jacques F. and Xavier Vives "On the strategic choice of spatial price policy" *American Economic Review* 78, March 1988, pp. 122–137.

— "Basing-point pricing: competition versus collusion" *Journal of Industrial Economics* 40(3), September 1992, pp. 249–260.

Thomadsen, Raphael "The effect of ownership structure on prices in geographically differentiated industries" *Rand Journal of Economics* 36(4), Winter 2005, pp. 908–929.

Thomas, Charles J. and Robert D. Willig "The risk of contagion from multimarket contact" *International Journal of Industrial Organization*, November 2006, pp. 1157–1184.

Thomas, Louis A. "Brand capital and incumbent firm's positions in evolving markets" *Review of Economics and Statistics* 77(3), August 1995, pp. 522–534.

— "Incumbent firms' response to entry: price, advertising, and new product introduction" *International Journal of Industrial Organization* 17(4), May 1999, pp. 527–555.

Thorelli, Hans B. *The Federal Antitrust Policy*. Stockholm: Akademisk Avhandling, 1955.

— "European antitrust policy" *Law School Record* 8(2), 1959, pp. 1–2, 14–19.

— "Antitrust in Europe: national policies after 1945" *University of Chicago Law Review* 26(2), Winter 1959b, pp. 222–236.

Thornton, William Thomas *On Labour, its Wrongful Claims and Rightful Dues, its Actual Present and Possible Future*. London: Macmillan, 2nd edition, 1870.

Thorp, Willard L. "The persistence of the merger movement" *American Economic Review* 21(1), March 1931, pp. 77–89.

Thurow, Lester C. "Let's abolish the antitrust laws" *New York Times* 19 October 1980, Section 3, page 2, column 3.

Tichy, Walter F. *Technology Review of Mainframe Computer Systems and Their Alternatives: a White Paper*. December 19, 2008, downloaded 21 April 2009 from <http://openmainframe.org/research-resources/technology-review-of-mainframe-computer-systems-and-their-al.html>.

Tingvall, Patrik Gustavsson "The dynamics of European industrial structure" *Review of World Economics* 140(4), 2004, pp. 665–687.

Tirole, Jean *The Theory of Industrial Organization*. Cambridge, Massachusetts and London: MIT Press, 1988.

Tollison, Robert D. "Antitrust in the Reagan administration: a report from the belly of the beast" *International Journal of Industrial Organization* 1(2), June 1983, pp. 211–221.

Trajtenberg, Manuel "Government support for commercial R&D: lessons from the Israeli experience" *Innovation Policy and the Economy* 2(1), 2002, pp. 79–134.

Tremblay, Victor J. and Carol Horton Tremblay *The U.S Brewing Industry*. Cambridge, Massachusetts and London: MIT Press, 2005.

Troesken, Werner "Did the Trusts want a Federal antitrust law? An event study of State antitrust enforcement and passage of the Sherman Act" pp. 77–104 in Jac C. Heckelman, John C. Moorhouse, and Robert M. Whaples, editors, *Public Choice Interpretations of American Economic History*. Boston and elsewhere: Kluwer Academic Publishers, 2000.

Troske, Kenneth R. "The dynamic adjustment process of firm entry and exit in manufacturing and finance, insurance, and real estate" *Journal of Law and Economics* 39(2), 1996, pp. 705–735.

Tsoraklidis, Lazaros "Towards a new motor vehicle block exemption—Commission proposal for motor vehicle distribution, adopted on 5 February 2002" *Competition Policy Newsletter* 2002(2), June 2002, pp. 21–34.

Tull, Donald S. "A re-examination of the causes of the decline in sales of Sapolio" *Journal of Business* 28(2), April 1955, pp. 128–137.

Tullock, Gordon "The welfare costs of tariffs, monopolies and theft" *Western Economic Journal* 5, June 1967, pp. 224–232.

Turner, Donald F. "Antitrust policy and the *Cellophane* case" *Harvard Law Review* 70(2), December 1956, pp. 281–318.

Turner, Henry Ashby *German Big Business and the Rise of Hitler*. Oxford: Oxford University Press, 1985.

Tuttle, William H. "The legal status of combinations of labor" pp. 354–366 in Chicago Conference on Trusts. *Chicago Conference on Trusts*. Chicago: Civic Federation of Chicago, 1900. Reprinted 1973 by Arno Press, Inc.

Twain, Mark and Charles Dudley Warner, *The Gilded Age*. Hartford: American Publishing Company, 1873.

Ulen, Thomas S. *Cartels and Regulation: Late Nineteenth Century Railroad Collusion and the Creation of the Interstate Commerce Commission*. Ph.D. dissertation, Department of Economics, Stanford University, 1978.

Ungerer, Herbert "After the State Aid Action Plan: the EU's new State Aid framework" EU State Aid Summit, Brussels, 23–24 June 2009 (<http://ec.europa.eu/competition/speeches/index_theme_6.html>).

U.S. Bureau of the Budget, Office of Statistical Standards *Standard Metropolitan Statistical Areas, 1967*. Washington, D. C.: 1967.

U.S. Census Bureau *Development of NAICS*. <http://www/census.gov/epcd/www/naicsdev.htm> (downloaded 13 December 2002).

U.S. Congress. Senate Committee on the Judiciary. Subcommittee on Antitrust and Monopoly. *Nolo Contendere and Private Antitrust Enforcement*. Appendix I: Table of Cases—Private Antitrust Suits, 1890–1963. Hearings, Eighty-ninth Congress, second session. May 11 and 12, 13, and 15 July, 1966. Washington, D.C.: U.S. Government Printing Office, 1967.

U.S. Department of Commerce, Bureau of the Census. *Standard Industrial Classification Manual, 1987*. Washington, D.C.:U.S. Government Printing Office, 1987.

U.S. Department of Commerce, U.S. Census Bureau *Concentration Ratios in Manufacturing: 1997*. 1997 Economic Census Manufacturing Subject Series EC97M31S-CR. Issued June 2001.

— *Establishment and Firm Size: 2002*. 2002 Economic Census Retail Trade Subject Series EC02-44SS-SZ. Issued November 2005a.

— *Establishment and Firm Size: 2002*. 2002 Economic Census Wholesale Trade Subject Series EC02-42SS-SZ. Issued December 2005b.

— *Concentration Ratios: 2002*. 2002 Economic Census Manufacturing Subject Series EC02-31SR-1. Issued May 2006.

U.S. Department of Justice *Report on the Robinson-Patman Act*. Washington, D.C. U.S. Government Printing Office, 1977.

— *Corporate Leniency Policy*. August 10, 1993. (<http://www.usdoj.gov/atr/public/guidelines/0091.htm>.)

— *Leniency Policy for Individuals*. August 10, 1994. (<http://www.usdoj.gov/atr/public/guidelines/0092.htm>.)

— "Justice Department requires divestitures in merger between General Electric and Honeywell" press release 2 May 2001, downloaded 26 April 2006 from <http://www.usdoj.gov/atr/public/press_releases/2001/8140.htm>.

U.S. Department of Justice and Federal Trade Commission *Horizontal Merger Guidelines* (jointly issued April 2, 1992 and revised April 8, 1997), available at <http://www.usdoj.gov/atr/public/guidelines/hmg.pdf> and <http://www.ftc.gov/bc/docs/horizmer.htm>.

— *Commentary on the Horizontal Merger Guidelines.* March 2006. Downloadable from URL <http://www.usdoj.gov/atr/public/guidelines/215247.htm#42>.

— *Antitrust Enforcement and Intellectual Property Rights: Promoting Innovation and Competition.* April, 2007. <http://www.ftc.gov/reports/innovation/P040101PromotingInnovationandCompetitionrpt0704.pdf>.

U.S. Federal Trade Commission *Report on the Merger Movement: A Summary Report.* 1948.

— , Bureau of Competition *A Study of the Commission's Divestiture Process.* 1999.

U.S. Library of Congress *List of Books Relating to Trusts. With References to Periodicals.* Washington: Government Printing Office, Third edition, 1907.

U.S. Patent and Trademark Office *White Paper on Automated Financial or Management Data Processing Methods (Business Methods).* 1999. Available at <http://www.uspto.gov/web/menu/busmethp/index.html>.

Usselman, Steven W. "Organizing a market for technological innovation: patent pools and patent politics on American railroads, 1860–1900" *Business and Economic History* 19, 1990, pp. 203–211.

— "Patents, engineering professionals, and the pipelines of innovation: the internalization of technical discovdery by nineteenth-century railroads" in Naomi Lamoreaux, Daniel M. G. Raff, and Peter Temin, editors, *Learning by Doing in Markets, Firms, and Countries.* Chicago: University of Chicago Press, 1999, pp. 61–91.

Utton, M. A. "Some features of the early merger movements in British manufacturing history" *Business History* 14(1), January 1972, pp. 51–60.

— "Aggregate versus market concentration: a note" *Economic Journal* 84(393), March 1974, pp. 150–155.

Valentine, D. G. *The Court of Justice of the European Communities.* London: Stevens & Sons and South Hackensack, New Jersey: Fred B. Rothman & Co., 1965.

Van Cayseele, Patrick J. G. "Market structure and innovation: a survey of the last twenty years" *De Economist* 146(3), 1998, pp. 391–417.

Van Cayseele, Patrick and Dave Furth "Two is not too many for monopoly" *Journal of Economics* 74(3), 2001, pp. 231–258.

Vanderwicken, Peter "USM's hard life as an ex-monopoly" *Fortune* October 1971, pp. 124–130.

Van Hise, Charles R. *Concentration and Control.* New York: The Macmillan Company, 1912.

Van Overtveldt, Johan *The Chicago School.* Chicago: Agate Publishing, 2007.

Vance, Ashkee "Rivals say I.B.M. stifles competition to mainframes" *New York Times*, internet edition, 23 March 2009.

Varian, Hal R. "A model of sales" *American Economic Review* 70(4), September 1980, pp. 651–659.

Vatter, Harold G. "The closure of entry in the American automobile industry" *Oxford Economic Papers* n.s. 4(3), October 1952, pp. 213–234.

Venkatesh,R. and Wagner Kamakura "Optimal bundling and pricing under a monopoly: contrasting complements and substitutes from independently valued products" *Journal of Business* 76(2), April 2003, pp. 211–231.

Venturini, Venturino G. *Monopolies and Restrictive Trade Practices in France.* Leyden: Sijthoff, 1971.

Vermeylen, Filip "The commercialization of art: painting and sculpture in sixteenth-century Antwerp" pp. 46–61 in Mayan W. Ainsworth, editor, *Early Netherlandish Painting at the Crossroads.* New York: Metropolitan Museum of Art, 2001.

Vermulst, Edwin and Paul Waer *E.C. Antidumping Law and Practice.* London: Sweet & Maxwell, 1996.

Veugelers, Reinhilde "Locational determinants and ranking of host countries: an empirical assessment" *Kyklos* 44(3), 1991, pp. 363–382.

— "Strategic incentives for multinational operations" *Managerial and Decision Economics* 16(1), January–February 1995, pp. 47–57.

Vickers, John "Concepts of competition" *Oxford Economic Papers* 47(1), January 1995, pp. 1–23.

— "Market power and inefficiency: a contracts perspective" *Oxford Review of Economic Policy* 11, 1996, pp. 11–26.

Vickrey, William S. *Microstatics.* New York: Harcourt, Brace and World, 1964.

— "Spatial competition, monopolistic competition, and optimum product diversity" *International Journal of Industrial Organization* 17(7), October 1999, pp. 953–963.

Villard, Henry H. "Competition, oligopoly, and research" *Journal of Political Economy* 66(6), December 1958, pp. 483–497.

Viner, Jacob "Cost curves and supply curves" *Zeitschrift für Nationalökonomie* 3, 1931, pp. 23–46; reprinted in George J. Stigler and Kenneth E. Boulding, editors, *A. E. A. Readings in Price Theory.* Chicago: Richard D. Irwin, 1952.

— "The intellectual history of laissez faire" *Journal of Law and Economics* 3, October 1960, pp. 45–69.

Vives, Xavier "Cournot and the oligopoly problem" *European Economic Review* 33, 1989, pp. 503–514.

— "Innovation and competitive pressure" *Journal of Industrial Economics* 56(3), September 2008, pp. 419–469.

Vlasic, Bill and Nelson D. Schwartz "Chrysler and Fiat have hopes for happy relationship" *New York Times* internet edition, 5 May 2009.

Voight, Fritz "German experience with cartels and their control during the pre-war and post-war periods" pp. 169–213 in John Perry Miller, editor, *Competition Cartels and Their Regulation*. Amsterdam: North-Holland Publishing Company, 1962.

Voight, Stefan "The economic effects of competition policy—cross-country evidence using four new indicators" ICER Working Paper 20-06, July 2006.

Von Hippel, Eric "Lead users: a source of novel product concepts" *Management Science* 32(7), July 1986, pp. 791–805.

Von Neumann, John and Oskar Morgenstern *Theory of Games and Economic Behavior*. Princeton: Princeton University Press, 1944.

Vonortas, Nicholas S. "Inter-firm cooperation with imperfectly appropriable research" *International Journal of Industrial Organization* 12(3), September 1994, pp. 413–435.

Waelbroeck, Michel "Price discrimination and rebate policies under EU competition law" pp. 147–160 in Barry E. Hawk, editor, *Annual Proceedings of the Fordham Corporate Law Institute* 1995, London: Sweet & Maxwell, Ltd., 1996.

Waldman, Don E. "The inefficiencies of 'unsuccessful' price fixing agreements" *Antitrust Bulletin* 33(1), Spring 1988, pp. 67–93.

Waldman, Michael "Eliminating the market for secondhand goods: an alternative explanation for leasing" *Journal of Law and Economics* 40(1), April 1997, pp. 61–92.

— "Durable goods theory for real world markets" *Journal of Economic Perspectives* 17(1), Winter 2003, pp. 131–154.

Walker, Francis "The law concerning monopolistic combinations in Continental Europe" *Political Science Quarterly* 20(1), March 1905, pp. 13–41.

Wallace, Donald H. *Market Control in the Aluminum Industry*. Cambridge, Massachusetts: Harvard University Press, 1937.

Wallis, John Joseph "The property tax as a coordinating device: financing Indiana's Mammoth Internal Improvement System, 1835–1842" *Explorations in Economic History* 40, 2003, pp. 223–250.

Walras, Léon *Elements of Pure Economics*. William Jaffé translation of *Eléments d'Économie Politique Pure*, 1926. Homewood, Illinois: Richard D. Irwin, 1954; Fairfield, New Jersey: Augustus M. Kelley Publishers, 1977.

Wallsten, Scott J. "The effects of government-industry R&D programs on private R&D: the case of the Small Business Innovation Research program" *Rand Journal of Economics* 31(1), Spring 2000, pp. 82–100.

Walton, Clarence Cyril and Frederick W. Cleveland, Jr. *Corporations On Trial: the Electric Cases*. Belmont, California: Wadsworth Pub. Co., 1964.

Wang, X. Henry and Bill Z. Yang "Fixed and sunk costs revisited" *Journal of Economic Education* 32(2), Spring 2001, pp. 178–185.

Warner, Elizabeth J. and Robert B. Barsky "The timing and magnitude of retail store markdowns: evidence from weekends and holidays" *Quarterly Journal of Economics* 110(2), May, 1995, pp. 321–352.

Warner, Isabel *Steel and Sovereignty. The Deconcentration of the West German Steel Industry, 1949–54*. Mainz: Verlag Philipp von Zabern, 1996.

Warzynski, Frederic "Did antitrust policy lead to lower mark-ups in the US manufacturing industry?" *Economics Letters* 70, 2001, pp. 139–144.

Washburn, Charles G. *Theodore Roosevelt: the Logic of His Career*. Boston: Houghton Mifflin, 1916.

— "The history of a statute" *Boston University Law Review* 8(2), April 1928, pp. 95–116.

Waterson, Michael "The role of consumers in competition and competition policy" *International Journal of Industrial Organization* 21(2), February 2003, pp. 129–150.

Watkins, Myron W. "Trusts since 1910" pp. 115–122 in Edwin R. A. Seligman, editor, *Encyclopedia of the Social Sciences* 15. New York: Macmillan, 1935.

Weiman, David F. and Richard C. Levin "Preying for monopoly? The case of Southern Bell Telephone Company, 1894–1912" *Journal of Political Economy* 102(1), February 1994, pp. 103–126.

Weinstein, James *The Corporate Ideal in the Liberal State: 1900–1918*. Boston: Beacon Press, 1968.

Weisbuch, Gérard, Alan Kirman, and Dorothea Herreiner "Market organisation and trading relationships" *Economic Journal* 110(463), April 2000, pp. 411–436.

Weiss, Leonard W. "An evaluation of mergers in six industries" *Review of Economics and Statistics* 47(2), May 1965, pp. 172–181.

— "Quantitative studies of industrial organization" in M. D. Intriligator, editor, *Frontiers of Quantitative Economics*. Amsterdam: North Holland, 1971a, Chapter 9, pp. 362–403.

— *Case Studies in American Industry*. New York and elsewhere: John Wiley & Sons, second edition, 1971b.

— "The geographic size of markets in manufacturing" *Review of Economics and Statistics* 1972, pp. 245–257.

— "The concentration–profits relationship and antitrust" in Harvey J. Goldschmid, H. Michael Mann, and J. Fred Weston, editors, *Industrial Concentration: the New Learning*. Boston: Little, Brown & Company, 1974.

— "Optimal plant size and the extent of suboptimal capacity" in Robert T. Masson and P. David Qualls, editors, *Essays in Industrial Organization in Honor of Joe S. Bain*. Cambridge, Massachusetts: Ballinger Publishing Company, 1976, pp. 123–141.

— "Stigler, Kindahl, and Means on administered prices" *American Economic Review* 67(4), September 1977, pp. 610–619.

— "The extent and effects of aggregate concentration" *Journal of Law and Economics* 26(2), June 1983, pp. 429–455.

— "Concentration and price—a possible way out of the box" in Joachim Schwalbach, editor, *Industry Structure and Performance*. Berlin: Edition Sigma Rainer Bohn Verlag, 1985.

—, editor, *Concentration and Price*. Cambridge, Massachusetts: MIT Press, 1989.

Weitzman, Martin L. "Consumer's surplus as an exact approximation when prices are appropriately deflated" *Quarterly Journal of Economics* 103(3), August 1988, pp. 543–553.

von Weizsäcker, C. C., "A welfare analysis of barriers of entry" *Bell Journal of Economics* 11(2), Autumn 1980a, pp. 399–420.

— *Barriers to Entry*. Berlin and elsewhere: Springer-Verlag, 1980b.

Wellford, Charissa P. "Antitrust: results from the laboratory" in Charles A. Holt and R. Mark Isaac, editors, *Experiments Investigating Market Power*. Oxford: Elsevier Science, 2002, pp. 1–60.

Wells, Wyatt "Counterpoint to reform: Gilbert H. Montague and the business of regulation" *Business History Review* Autumn 2004 pp. 423–450.

Welsh, C. A. "Patents and competition in the automobile industry" *Law and Competition Problems* 13(2), Spring 1948, pp. 260–277.

Werden, Gregory "The 1982 Merger Guidelines and the ascent of the Hypothetical Monopolist paradigm" *Antitrust Law Journal* 71, 2003, pp. 253–269.

— "Assessing the effects of antitrust enforcement in the United States" *De Economist* 156(4), 2008, pp. 433–451.

Wernerfelt, Birger "A resource-based view of the firm" *Strategic Management Journal* 5(2), April–June 1984, pp. 171–180.

— "The resource-based view of the firm: ten years after" *Strategic Management Journal* 16(3), March 1995, pp. 171–174.

Whaples, Robert "Do economists agree on anything? Yes!" *Economists' Voice* 3(9), Article 1, <http://www.bepress.com/ev/vol3/iss9/art1>.

Whinston, Michael D. "Tying, foreclosure, and exclusion" *American Economic Review* 80(4), September 1990, pp. 837–859.

— "Exclusivity and tying in U.S. *v*. Microsoft: what we know, and don't know" *Journal of Economic Perspectives* 15(2), Spring 2001, pp. 63–80.

White, E. Wyndham "Competition and the law" *Journal of Comparative Legislation and International Law*, 3rd series, 19(1), 1937, pp. 38–51.

White, Horace G. Jr. "A review of monopolistic and imperfect competition theories" *American Economic Review* 26(4), December 1936, pp. 637–649.

White, Lawrence J. "Searching for the critical concentration ratio: an application of the 'switching of regimes' technique" in S. M. Goldfeld and R. E. Quandt, editors, *Studies in Nonlinear Estimation*. Cambridge, Mass: Ballinger, 1976, Chapter 3, pp. 61–75.

— "What has been happening to aggregate concentration in the United States?" *Journal of Industrial Economics* 29(3), March 1981, pp. 223–230.

— "Antitrust and merger policy: a review and critique" *Journal of Economic Perspectives* 1(2), Autumn 1987, pp. 13–22.

— "The revolution in antitrust analysis of vertical relationships: how did we get from there to here?" in Robert Lamer and James Meehan, editors, *Economics and Antitrust Policy*. London: Quorum Books, 1989, pp. 103–121.

— "Trends in aggregate concentration in the United States" *Journal of Economic Perspectives* 16(4), Autumn, 2002, pp. 137–160.

— "Stapes-Office Depot and UPSP: an antitrust tale of two proposed mergers" in Daniel J. Slottje, editor, *Measuring Market Power*. Amsterdam: Elsevier Science, 2002b, pp. 153–174.

— "Horizontal merger antitrust enforcement: some historical perspectives, some current observations" New York University Law and Economics Working Papers 47, 2006.

Whitney, Edward B. "The Addyston Pipe Company" in William Z. Ripley, editor, *Trusts, Pools, and Corporations*. Boston: Ginn & Company, 1905, pp. 86–104.

Whitney, Simon N. "Competition under secret and open prices" *Econometrica* 3(1), January 1935, pp. 40–65.

— *Antitrust Policies: American Experience in Twenty Industries*. New York: The Twentieth Century Fund, 1958.

Wilkins, Mira "Japanese multinationals in the United States: continuity and change, 1879–1990" *Business History Review* 64(4), Winter 1990, pp. 585–629.

Williams, James Harvey "The Sherman Act to-day: shall the small industrial unit survive?" *Atlantic Monthly* 116, March 1928a, pp. 412–424.

— "The Sherman Act to-morrow" *Atlantic Monthly* 116, June 1928b, pp. 845–852.

Williams, Philip L. "The attitudes of the economics professions in Britain and the United States to the trust movement, 1890–1914" pp. 92–108 in John D. Hey and Donald Winch, editors, *A Century of*

Economics. Oxford and Cambridge, Massachusetts: Basil Blackwell, 1990.

Williamson, Oliver E. *Economics of Discretionary Behavior: Managerial Objectives in a Theory of the Firm.* Prentice Hall: Englewood Cliffs, New Jersey, 1964.

— "Wage rates as a barrier to entry: the Pennington case" *Quarterly Journal of Economics* 85 February 1968a, pp. 85–116.

— "Economies as an antitrust defense: the welfare tradeoffs" *American Economic Review* 58(1), March 1968b, pp. 18–36.

— *Corporate Control and Business Behavior: an Inquiry into the Effects of Organization Form on Enterprise Behavior.* Englewood Cliffs, New Jersey: Prentice-Hall, 1970.

— *Markets and Hierarchies: Analysis and Antitrust Implications.* New York: The Free Press, 1975.

— "Economies as an antitrust defense revisited" *University of Pennsylvania Law Review* 125(4), April 1977a, pp. 699–736.

— "Predatory pricing: a strategic and welfare analysis" *Yale Law Journal* 87(2), December 1977b, pp. 284–340.

— "Assessing vertical market restrictions: antitrust ramifications of the transaction cost approach" *University of Pennsylvania Law Review* 127(4), April 1979a, pp. 953–993.

— "Transaction-cost economics: the governance of contractual relations" *Journal of Law and Economics* 22(2), October 1979, pp. 233–261.

— "The modern corporation: origins, evolution, attributes" *Journal of Economic Literature* 19(4), December 1981, pp. 1537–1568.

— "Credible commitments: using hostages to support exchange" *American Economic Review* 73(4), September 1983, pp. 519–540.

— "Organizational innovation: the transaction-cost approach" pp. 101–133 in Joshua Renen, editor, *Entrepreneurship.* Lexington, Massachusetts and Toronto: Lexington Books, 1983b.

— *The Economic Institutions of Capitalism.* New York: The Free Press, 1985.

— "Transaction cost economics and organization theory" *Industrial and Corporate Change* 2(2), 1993, pp. 107–156.

Willig, Robert D. "Consumer's surplus without apology" *American Economic Review* 66(4), September 1976, pp. 589–597.

— "Merger analysis, industrial organization theory, and merger guidelines" *Brookings Papers on Economic Activity Microeconomics*, 1991, pp. 281–332.

Willis, F. Roy "Origins and evolution of the European Communities" *Annals of the American Academy of Political and Social Science* 440, November 1978, pp. 1–12.

Willner, Johan and Leila Ståhl "Where are the welfare losses of imperfect competition large?" *European Journal of Political Economy* 8(3), October 1992, pp. 477–491.

Wilson, Robert W. "The effect of technological environment and product rivalry on R&D effort and licensing of inventions" *Review of Economics and Statistics* 59(2), May 1977, pp. 171–178.

Wilson, Woodrow *The New Freedom.* New York: Doubleday, Page and Co., 1913.

— "Trusts and monopolies" special address to Congress, 20 January 1914, in *The Public Papers of Woodrow Wilson.* Ray S. Baker and William E. Dodd, editors, 4 volumes. New York: Harper Brothers, 1925, 1926, Volume 1, pp. 81–88.

Winerman, Marc "The origins of the FTC: concentration, cooperation, control, and competition" *Antitrust Law Journal* 71, 2003, pp. 1–97.

Winter, Sidney G., "Schumpeterian competition in alternative technological regimes" *Journal of Economic Behavior and Organization* 5, September-December 1984, pp. 287–320.

Wolf, Martin "Why voluntary export restraints: A historical analysis" in Ad Koekkoek and L. B. M. Mennes, editors, *International Trade and Global Development Essays in Honour of Jagdish Bhagwati.* Routledge: London and New York, 1991, pp. 83–104.

Wolff, John "Business monopolies: three European systems in their bearing on American law" *Tulane Law Review* 9(3), April 1935, pp. 325–377.

Wolinsky, Asher "True monopolistic competition as a result of imperfect information" *Quarterly Journal of Economics* 101(3), August 1986, pp. 493–512.

Womack, James P., Daniel T. Jones, and Daniel Roos *The Machine That Changed The World.* New York: Rawson Associates, 1990.

Worcester, Dean A. Jr. "A reconsideration of the theory of rent" *American Economic Review* 36(3), June 1946, pp. 258–277.

— "Why 'dominant firms' decline" *Journal of Political Economy* 65(4), August 1957, pp. 338–346.

Wright, Chris "The National Cooperative Research Act of 1984: a new antitrust regime for joint research and development ventures" *High Technology Law Journal* 1, 1986, pp. 133–193.

Yamawaki, Hidecki "Dominant firm pricing and fringe expansion: the case of the U.S. iron and steel industry, 1907–1930" *Review of Economics and Statistics* 67(3), August 1985, pp. 429–437.

— "Exports and foreign distributional activities: evidence on Japanese firms in the United States" *Review of Economics and Statistics* 73(2), May 1991, pp. 294–300.

Yamazaki, Hiroaki and Matao Miyamoto *Trade Associaitons in Business History.* Tokyo: University of Tokyo Press, 1988.

Yamey, B. S. "Predatory price cutting: notes and comments" *Journal of Law and Economics* 15(1), April 1972, pp. 129–144.

Yang, Jiawen "Exchange rate pass-through in U.S. manufacturing industries" *Review of Economics and Statistics* 79(1), February 1997, pp. 95–104.

Yarros, Victor S. "The trust problem restudied" *American Journal of Sociology* 8(1), July 1902, pp. 58–74.

Yeager, Mary *Competition and Regulation: The Development of Oligopoly in the Meat Packing Industry*. Greenwich, Connecticut: JAI Press, 1981.

Yellen, Janet L. "Testimony" Senate Judiciary Committee, 16 June 1998, downloaded 8 October 2007 from <http://judiciary.senate.gov/oldsite/yellen.htm>.

Yellott, John I. "The trust: an institution pronounced by the United States Supreme Court, in 1895, beyond Congressional control" pp. 427–437 in Chicago Conference on Trusts. *Chicago Conference on Trusts*. Chicago: Civic Federation of Chicago, 1900. Reprinted 1973 by Arno Press, Inc.

Young, Allyn A. "The Sherman Act and the new anti-trust legislation: II" *Journal of Political Economy* 23(4), April 1915a, pp. 305–326.

— "The Sherman Act and the new anti-trust legislation: III" *Journal of Political Economy* 23(5), May 1915b, pp. 417–436.

— "Increasing returns and economic progress" *Economic Journal* 38(152), December 1928, pp. 527–542.

Young, James Harvey "Patent medicines: an early example of competitive marketing" *Journal of Economic History* 20(4), December 1960, pp. 648–656.

Zippel, G. "L'allume de Tolfa e il suo commercio" *Archivio della R. Società Romana di Storia Patria* XXX(I–II), pp. 4–51, XXX(III–IV), pp. 389–462, 1907.

Zweig, Konrad "The origins of the German social market economy" Adam Smith Institute, 1980. (<http://www.adamsmith.org/policy/publications/pdf-files/social-market-economy.pdf>.)

LEGAL DECISIONS INDEX

SUBJECTS INDEX

O

P

Lightning Source UK Ltd.
Milton Keynes UK
UKHW02f0157270418
321616UK00002B/2/P